Alan Greenwood launched *Vintage Guitar* magazine in 1986 and in 1990 created *The Official Vintage Guitar Price Guide* (visit www.VintageGuitar.com to see everything *VG* now offers). His collection includes several vintage guitars, amps, effects, and ukuleles from the '20s to the '80s, as well as newer instruments. He lives in Bismarck, North Dakota.

Gil Hembree began collecting guitars in 1966 while working at Kitt's Music, in Washington, D.C. During his 30-year corporate career in Michigan he played in bands and continued to search for original-owner vintage guitars. In 2000, he became the co-author of *The Official Vintage Guitar Price Guide*. In '07, Hal Leonard released his biography of Ted McCarty: *Gibson Guitars: Ted McCarty's Golden Era: 1948-1966*. He and his wife, Jane, live in Austin, Texas.

The Official Vintage Guitar® magazine Price Guide
By Alan Greenwood and Gil Hembree
ISBN: 978-1-884883-45-3

In loving memory of Jack David Greenwood, 1990-2020

Vintage Guitar, PO Box 7301, Bismarck, ND 58507, publishers of Vintage Guitar® magazine and Vintage Guitar® Online at www.VintageGuitar.com. Vintage Guitar is a registered trademark of Vintage Guitar, Inc.

Cover: 1968 Fender Telecaster Thinline (left). 1972 Fender, Telecaster Thinline courtesy of Willie's American Guitars. 1968 Fender Telecaster Thinline (right) courtesy of Dave Rogers. Photos property of *VG* Archive.
Back: 1966 Gibson ES-335 courtesy of Alan Greenwood. 1964 Gibson, Firebird III courtesy of Dave Rogers. Photos property of VG Archive. Chris Leuzinger: Liz Leuzinger. J.D. Simo: Adam Abrashoff. Jeff Hanna: Bob Delevante. Matt Stubbs: Whitney Pelfrey. Nate Westgor: Willie's American Guitars. Gary Dick: Gary's Classic Guitars.

Cover Design: Doug Yellow Bird/Vintage Guitar, Inc.

Printed in the United States of America

WE BUY USED, VINTAGE & COLLECTIONS

514 Main Street
Historic Downtown Garland Square
Garland, TX 75040
PH: 469-562-8545
EM: info@jimmywallaceguitars.com

Hours:
Tues - Fri: 11am -6pm
Sat: 11am - 6pm

www.jimmywallaceguitars.com

TABLE OF CONTENTS

*Gibson Les Paul Standards from 1962 in
Black and Olympic White. VG Archive.*

Vintage Fender Stratocaster

More Than 300 Vintage Fender Stratocaster Stocks

USING THE GUIDE

UNDERSTANDING THE VALUES

The values presented in *The Official Vintage Guitar Price Guide* are for excellent-condition, all-original instruments. Our definition of excellent condition allows for some wear, but the instrument should be well-maintained, with no significant blemishes, wear, repairs, or damage. All-original means the instrument has the parts and finish it had when it left the factory. Replacement parts and refinishes can greatly affect value, as can the appropriate case (or cover) in excellent condition. In many instances, a "wrong" case will not greatly affect value, but with the top-dollar collectibles, it can.

We use a range of excellent-condition values, as there is seldom agreement on a single price point for vintage and used instruments. A tighter range suggests there is a general consensus, while a wide range means the market isn't in strict agreement. A mint-condition instrument can be worth more than the values listed here, and anything in less-than-excellent condition will have a reduced value.

Repairs affect value differently. Some repair is necessary to keep an instrument in playable condition. The primary concern is the level of expertise displayed in the work and an amateurish repair will lower the value more than one that is obviously professional. A refinished guitar, regardless of the quality of the work, is generally worth 50% or less of the values shown in *The Guide*. A poorly executed neck repair or significant body repair can mean a 50% reduction in a guitar's value. A professional re-fret or minor, nearly invisible body repair will reduce a guitar's value by only 5%.

The values in the *The Guide* are for unfaded finishes. Slight color fade reduces value by only 5%, but heavy fading can reduce value by 25% to 50%.

FINDING THE INFORMATION

The table of contents shows the major sections and each is organized in alphabetical order by brand, then by model. In a few instances, there are separate sections for a company's most popular models, especially when there is a large variety of similar instruments. Examples include Fender's Stratocasters, Telecasters, Precision and Jazz basses, and Gibson's Les Pauls. The outer top corner of each page includes a dictionary-type index that tells the models or brands on that page. This provides a quick way to navigate each section.

The Guide has excellent brand histories and in most cases the guitar section has the most detailed information for each brand. When possible, *The Guide* lists each model's years of availability and any design changes that affect values.

More information on many of the brands covered in *The Guide* is available in the pages of *Vintage Guitar* magazine and on the "Features" section of our website, www.VintageGuitar.com.

The authors of *The Guide* appreciate your help, so if you find any errors or have additional information on certain brands or models, please drop us a line at Alan@VintageGuitar.com.

NEW RETAIL PRICING INFORMATION

The Guide continues to add information on individual luthiers and smaller shops. It's difficult to develop values on used instruments produced by these builders because much of their output is custom work, production is low, and/or they haven't been producing for a period of time sufficient to see their instruments enter the used/resale market. To give you an idea about their instruments, we've developed five grades of retail values for new instruments. These convey only the prices charged by the builder, and are not indicative of the quality of construction. *The Guide* applies this scale to all builders and manufacturers of new instruments.

> **The five retail-price grades are:**
> **Budget - up to $250,**
> **Intermediate - $251 to $1,000,**
> **Professional - $1,001 to $3,000,**
> **Premium - $3,001 to $10,000,**
> **Presentation - more than $10,000.**

The Guide uses the terms "production" and "custom" to differentiate between builders who do true custom work versus those who offer standard production models. "Production" means the company offers specific models, with no variations. "Custom" means they do only custom orders, and "production/custom" indicates they do both. Here's an example:

> **Scarlett Guitars**
> 2016-present. Premium grade, custom solidbody guitars built by luthier Scarlett Flanagin in Mandan, North Dakota. She also builds ukuleles.

This tells who the builder is, the type of instruments they build, where they build them, how long they've been operating under that brand, that they do only custom work, and that they ask between $3,000 and $10,000 for their guitars (premium-grade).We've applied the retail price grades and production and/or custom labels to most new-instrument manufacturers.

A LIFE PURSUIT OF TONE

web: www.jimmywallacepickups.com
phone: 972-740-9925
email: info@jimmywallacepickups.com

EST. 1978

Digf

DALLAS INTERNATIONAL

2023

45TH ANNUAL

GUITAR FESTIVAL

2023

WWW.GUITARSHOW.COM

INTRODUCTION

If this is your first time using *The Official Vintage Guitar Price Guide*, please read "Using The Guide" on page 18. We alternate sections for banjos and mandolins with those for ukuleles and steel guitars; this edition includes banjos and mandolins.

This edition of *The Guide* is the final one for Gil Hembree as co-author, who is stepping aside to dedicate more time to his family and other interests. Because he has played such a pivotal role in helping the book improve and grow, we asked him to share the story of how he became involved, and offer insight to his work on 23 editions of the book.

How did you become involved with *The Guide*?

In January of 2000, I was preparing to retire after a 30-year career with General Motors. I started there as a junior accountant responsible for reconciling bank accounts – using a mechanical adding machine to input thousands of checks for each statement, then verifying the totals. All GM accountants were given massive amounts of work to be completed quickly and accurately, and there was zero tolerance for mistakes. During my time in Detroit, I also played in bands and did my share of buying and selling guitars. My wife, Jane, and I attended vintage-guitar shows and knew many of the dealers. I wondered if *Vintage Guitar* might be able to use my knowledge and connections to help with *The Guide*, so I contacted *VG* editor Ward Meeker, who put me in touch with founder/publisher Alan Greenwood. With the following issue, I became a co-author with Alan.

What do you feel was your greatest accomplishment as co-author?

At GM, I attended meetings of the Rationalization Committee, where engineers and accountants determined selling prices of cars by analyzing costs and features, and comparing them with competitors. I wanted to use similar analysis to establish price ranges of instruments for *The Guide*. So, I accumulated data such as the actual selling price of instruments as reported by a list of dealers, show promoters, and others who make up *The Guide*'s Survey Advisory Board, then selected the best data to produce a rational price range for an instrument. I believe the ranges listed in *The Guide* are valid and can be relied on by users. The thing to remember about *The Guide* is that it's just that – a guidance document that presents a base from which buyers and sellers can work.

What were a few surprises over your 22 years as co-author?

My greatest surprise was how expensive vintage guitars kept getting, year after year. A 1952 Les Paul that sold for $1,300 in the mid '70s was an expensive guitar. Now, that guitar is worth $25,000. Is that expensive? Will it sell for $35,000 in a few years? Who knows? Historically, the thinking was, "Vintage guitars can't get very much more expensive!" But, history has shown there's a good chance they will increase in value. But

that's up to the market – not a price guide – to forecast.

Do you think vintage instruments are a good investment?

An investment is defined as an asset that increases in monetary value. From that perspective, a vintage guitar is a good investment, but it's a *long-term* investment. Market history shows a guitar should be held 10 years or more. Also, a vintage guitar is an illiquid asset, meaning it may not be easy to sell and convert to cash. Often, there is a 20 percent expense if a guitar is consigned or sold at wholesale. Guitar owners often do not think of that. In 1991, the average guitar listed in *The Guide*'s annual 42 Guitar Index carried a value of $3,660. That average value is now $26,265. If you deduct a 20 percent selling expense from $26,265, net proceeds are $21,012 – a gain of $17,352.

In 1993, a 30-year-old sunburst Stratocaster was a $5,300 guitar. Now an excellent-condition '63 sunburst Strat is $34,000. Do you expect any popular major brand models from the '90s, which are now 30 years old, to experience that kind of growth?

It is possible that '90s models from the popular major brands will experience notable appreciation. In '95, a '75 Stratocaster with a natural finish was 20 years old and dealers viewed it as a $500 guitar and thought it would never be anything but, because it had the enlarged headstock, bullet truss rod, three-

THE 42 GUITAR INDEX

FROM FENDER	
1952 blond Precision Bass	1958 natural ES-335
1952 blond Esquire	1958 Super 400CES
1953 blond Telecaster	1959 Les Paul Jr.
1956 sunburst Stratocaster	1959 J-160E
1958 sunburst Jazzmaster	1961 ES-355
1958 blond Telecaster	1961 Les Paul SG
1960 sunburst Stratocaster	1964 sunburst Thunderbird II
1961 sunburst, stack knob, Jazz	Bass
Bass	1965 EB-3 Bass
1962 sunburst, 3-knob, Jazz	1969 sunburst Citation
Bass	
1963 sunburst Telecaster	**FROM MARTIN**
Custom	1931 OM-28
1963 sunburst Esquire Custom	1936 00-28
1964 Lake Placid Blue Jaguar	1935 D-18
1964 sunburst Precision Bass	1944 scalloped-brace 000-28
1966 Candy Apple Red	1944 D-28
Stratocaster	1950 D-28
	1958 000-18
FROM GIBSON	1959 D-18
1952 sunburst ES-5	1959 D-28E
1952 Les Paul Model	1962 D-28
1954 Les Paul Jr.	1967 GT-75
1958 sunburst EB-2 Bass	1968 000-18
1958 Les Paul Custom	1969 N-20
	1969 D-45

bolt neck plate, excessive weight, and questionable quality. But that thinking was so wrong! Now, a '75 Strat is a $4,000 guitar. Anything is possible, and there are all sorts of interesting '90s guitars including limited and anniversary editions, signature models, etc. that could see decent increases, especially if they remain in exceptionally fine or near-mint condition.

Any other thoughts about your years working on The Guide?
It has been a pleasure working with Alan and the core employees who have been at *VG* for decades, including Wanda Huether, editor of *The Guide*, Doug Yellow Bird, Ward Meeker, and James Jiskra, and it has been a pleasure working with them. Jane and I traveled all over the United States, going to

The 42 Guitar Index 1991 - 2023

SURVEY ADVISORY BOARD

The information refined on these pages comes from several sources, including the input of many knowledgeable guitar dealers. Without the help of these individuals, it would be very hard for us to provide the information here and in each issue of *Vintage Guitar* magazine. We deeply appreciate the time and effort they provide.

Brian Goff
Bizarre Guitars

Garrett Tung
Boingosaurus Music

Dave Belzer
Burst Brothers

Walter Carter
Carter Vintage

Daniel Escauriza
Chicago Music Exchange

John Majdalani
Cream City Music

Dave Rogers
Dave's Guitar Shop

David Davidson and Paige Davidson
Davidson's Well Strung Guitars

Drew Berlin
Drew Berlin's Vintage Guitars

Stan Werbin & S.J. "Frog" Forgey
Elderly Instruments

Dewey Bowen
Freedom Guitar

Rick Hogue
Garrett Park Guitars

Gary Dick
Gary's Classic Guitars

Eric Newell
Gruhn Guitars

Richard Johnston
Gryphon Strings

Kennard Machol & Leonard Coulson
Intermountain Guitar & Banjo

Jim Singleton
Jim's Guitars

Kevin Borden
Kebo's BassWorks

Dave Hinson
Killer Vintage

Timm Kummer
Kummer's Vintage Instruments

Buzzy Levine
Lark Street Music

Larry Wexer
Laurence Wexer, Ltd.

Artie Leider
McKenzie River Music

Neal Shelton
Neals Music (California)

Lowell Levinger

Players Vintage Instruments

Howie Statland
Rivington Guitars

Eliot Michael
Rumble Seat Music

Sammy Ash
Sam Ash Music Stores

Eric Schoenberg
Schoenberg Guitars

Richard Gellis
Union Grove Music

Fred Oster
Vintage Instruments

Richard Friedman
We Buy Guitars

Nate Westgor
Willie's American Guitars

Alan Greenwood

Gil Hembree with Bob Shane's (The Kingston Trio) 1958 Martin D-28 used for six gold albums and 800 concerts between 1958 and 1961.

guitar shows to investigate and understand the market. We made a lot of friends.

42 GUITAR INDEX

Since 1991, Vintage Guitar's 42 Guitar Index has tracked the cumulative value of a selection of models from the three largest companies of the "classic era" – 14 each from Fender, Gibson, and Martin. The Index *excludes* the most-valuable instruments for each brand, such as pre-war D-45s, Les Paul Standards (a.k.a. 'burst), early Explorers, first-year Teles and Strats. The value of the 14 Fenders in 1991 was $50,875, the Gibsons $51,100, and the Martins at $51,750.

For this edition, the Index has gone up 25.7% which is the second largest annual increase in the Index's history. The largest increase, 53.9%, was reflected in the 2007 edition (followed, unfortunately, by the largest drop in the Index's history). The average yearly increase in the '90s was 8.6%, and in the 2000s the average was 12.8%. The 2010s (2010-2019) saw the 42 Index fall in seven of the 10 years, with the average being a negative 1.9%.

In 2023 the following sub-indices increased as follows: Fender 19.1%, Gibson 26.7%, and Martin 31.5%. All 42 guitars increased in value. The average 2023 Index price is $26,265. The average Index Price in the first edition (1991) was $3,660, and during the 2008 peak was $23,243. Ten years ago, it was $16,729.

We strive to ensure the Index provides an accurate reflection of the market, but it is intended only as a *guide*. The best way to evaluate your collection's value is to reference each instrument in the following pages. Recent editions listed random instruments that increased in value by 20% or more. Nearly every instrument increased in value in this edition; extraordinary increases were no longer the exception.

MORE INFORMATION

Much of the information in this book comes from *Vintage Guitar* magazine, which is offered in both print and digital formats; you can subscribe at www.VintageGuitar.com or find it on the newsstand. VintageGuitar.com has a vast trove of feature interviews, instrument histories and profile, gear and music reviews, and historical information on the brands and models covered in this book. You'll also find links to *VG* podcasts, VG Spotify playlists, our online archives of back issues, the *VG* YouTube channel, and our free e-mail *VG Overdrive* newsletter. Find us on Facebook, Twitter, YouTube, and Instagram, where we talk guitars and offer prizes. We'd love to have you join us.

UPDATES AND CORRECTIONS

If you spot errors in the information about brands and models, have information on a brand you'd like to see included, or produce instruments for sale and would like to be included in the next edition of The Guide, email Wanda at Library@VintageGuitar.com.

If a model is missing from The Guide, or if you spot something that needs to be clarified, please drop a line to Alan@VintageGuitar.com.

20%, but rather 30% or more. For that reason, we will not provide a sample of guitars increasing by 20%.

*The 42 Index's 1956 Fender Stratocaster
and 1958 Gibson Les Paul Custom.*

ACKNOWLEDGEMENTS

Wanda Huether, as the Editor of *The Guide*, keeps us all on deadline and makes all this possible. Michael Dregni provided values, information, and photos for effects. Doug Yellow Bird continues his fine work on the design and layout of the book. Larry Huether and Ward Meeker helped with editing and proofreading, James Jiskra, Johnny Zapp, and Mike Naughton handled the advertising and directory listings. We thank all of them for their usual fine work.

We use many sources to determine values, but the vintage instrument dealers who give their time and expertise to provide market information play an important role. Many provide info on brands and models, and they are acknowledged on page 26.

Once again, Heritage Auctions (HA.com) graciously gave us access to their photo archives. Thanks to all the readers that submitted photos with a special shout-out to David Stone, Trey Rabinek, Frank Manno, Tom Pfeifer, W. H. Stephens, and Scott Anderson for sending pics of large portions of their collections.

Thank you,
Alan Greenwood, Gil Hembree, and Wanda Huether

GUITARS

GUITARS

Airline Archtop
Tom Pfeifer

1960 Airline Town and Country
Tom Pfeifer

MODEL YEAR	FEATURES	EXC. COND. LOW	HIGH

17th Street Guitars

2004-2009. Founded by Dave Levine and Colin Liebich. Professional grade, production/custom, solidbody guitars built by luthier John Carruthers in Venice, California.

A Fuller Sound

Luthier Warren Fuller began building professional and premium grade, custom nylon and steel-string flat-tops in '98 in Oakland, California.

Abel

Custom aircraft-grade aluminum body, wood neck, guitars built by twins Jim and Jeff Abel in Evanston, Wyoming. They offered the Abel Axe from '94-'96 and 2000-'01, and still do custom orders. They also made the Rogue Aluminator in the late '90s.

Axe

1994-1996. Offset double-cut aluminum body with dozens of holes in the body, wood neck, various colors by annodizing the aluminum body. Abel Axe logo on the headstock.

1994-1996	Non-trem or trem	$700	$900

Abilene

Budget and intermediate grade, production, acoustic and electric guitars imported by Samick.

Abyss

See listing under Pederson Custom Guitars.

Acme

1960s. Imported inexpensive copy electric guitar models for the student market.

Acoustic

Ca. 1965-ca. 1987, 2001-2005, 2008-present. Mainly known for solidstate amps, the Acoustic Control Corp. of Los Angeles, California, did offer guitars and basses from around '69 to late '74. The brand has been revived on a new line of amps.

Black Widow

1969-1970, 1972-1974. Double-cut body, 2 pickups, and protective pad on back. The early version (AC500) had 22 frets, ebonite 'board and later one was 24 frets, rosewood 'board. Acoustic outsourced production, possibly to Japan, but final 200 or so guitars produced by Semie Moseley. The AC700 Black Widow 12-string was also available for '69-'70.

1969-1970		$1,450	$1,875
1972-1974		$1,225	$1,600

Agile

1985-present. Budget grade, production, acoustic and electric guitars imported by Rondo Music of Union, New Jersey. They also offer mandolins.

Aims

Ca. 1972-ca. 1976. Aims (American International Music Sales, Inc.) instruments, distributed by Ran-

MODEL YEAR	FEATURES	EXC. COND. LOW	HIGH

dall Instruments in the mid-'70s, were copies of classic American guitar and bass models. They also offered a line of Aims amps during the same time.

Airline

Ca. 1958-1968, 2004-present. Airline originally was a brand used by Montgomery Ward on acoustic, electric archtop and solidbody guitars and basses, amplifiers, steels, and possibly banjos and mandolins. Instruments manufactured by Kay, Harmony and Valco. In '04, the brand was revived on a line of imported intermediate grade, production, reissues from Eastwood guitars.

Acoustic Res-O-Glas Resonator

1964. Res-o-glas, coverplate with M-shaped holes, asymmetrical peghead.

1964		$725	$950

Amp-In-Case Model

1960s. Double-cut, single pickup, short scale guitar with amplifier built into the case, Airline on grille.

1960s		$615	$800

Archtop Acoustic

1950s-1960s. Various models.

1950s-60s	Higher-end	$290	$375
1950s-60s	Lower-end	$140	$180

Electric Hollowbody

1950s-1960s. Various models.

1950s	Kay B Kessel copy	$850	$1,100
1960s	ES-175 copy	$450	$600
1960s	Harmony H-54 copy	$450	$600
1960s	Harmony H-75 copy	$525	$675
1960s	Harmony H-76 copy	$775	$1,025
1960s	Kay B Kessel Swingmaster copy	$675	$875
1960s	Kay Swingmaster copy	$400	$525
1960s	Kay Tuxedo copy	$675	$875
1960s	National Town & Country copy	$850	$1,100

Electric Res-O-Glas

1960s. Res-o-glas is a form of fiberglass. The bodies and sometimes the necks were made of this material.

1960s	Jack White style	$2,050	$2,650
1960s	JB Hutto style	$2,050	$2,650
1960s	Other styles, 1 pu	$400	$525
1960s	Other styles, 2 pus	$900	$1,175
1960s	Other styles, 3 pus	$925	$2,500

Electric Res-O-Glas Resonator

1960s, 2010-present. Res-o-glas is a form of fiberglass. These models have resonator cones in the body.

1960s		$825	$1,075
2010-2021	Folkstar	$650	$850

Electric Solidbody (Standard)

1950s-1960s. Various models.

1950s-60s	Lower-end	$650	$850

Electric Solidbody (Deluxe)

1950s-1960s. Appointments may include multiple pickups, block inlays, additional logos, more binding.

1950s-60s	Higher-end	$925	$1,200

MODEL YEAR	FEATURES	EXC. COND. LOW	HIGH
Flat-Top Acoustic			
1950s-1960s. Various models.			
1950s-60s	Higher-end, 14"-15"	$325	$425
1950s-60s	Lower-end, 13"	$175	$225

Alamo

1947-1982. Founded by Charles Eilenberg, Milton Fink, and Southern Music, San Antonio, Texas, and distributed by Bruno & Sons. Alamo started out making radios, phonographs, and instrument cases. In '49 they added amplifiers and lap steels. From '60 to '70, the company produced beginner-grade solidbody and hollow-core body electric Spanish guitars. The amps were all-tube until the '70s. Except for a few Valco-made examples, all instruments were built in San Antonio.

MODEL YEAR	FEATURES	EXC. COND. LOW	HIGH
Electric Hollowbody			
1950s-70s	Higher-end	$925	$1,200
1950s-70s	Lower-end	$550	$725
Electric Solidbody			
1950s-70s	Higher-end	$925	$1,200
1950s-70s	Lower-end	$550	$725

Alamo Guitars

1999-2008. The Alamo brand was revived for a line of handcrafted, professional grade, production/custom, guitars by Alamo Music Products, which also offered Robin and Metropolitan brand guitars and Rio Grande pickups.

MODEL YEAR	FEATURES	EXC. COND. LOW	HIGH
Tonemonger			
1999-2005. Ash or African Fakimba offset double cut solidbody, 3 single coils, tremolo.			
1999-2005		$925	$1,200

Alan Carruth

1970-present. Professional and premium grade, production/custom, classical and archtop guitars built by luthier Alan Carruth in Newport, New Hampshire. He started out building dulcimers and added guitars in '74. He also builds violins and harps.

Albanus

Ca. 1954-1977. Luthier Carl Albanus Johnson built around 75 high quality custom archtop guitars in Chicago, Illinois. He died in '77. He also built violins and at least two mandolins.

Alberico, Fabrizio

1998-present. Luthier Fabrizio Alberico builds his premium grade, custom, flat-top and classical guitars in Cheltenham, Ontario.

Alden

2005-present. Budget and intermediate grade, production, acoustic and electric guitars, and basses designed by Alan Entwhistle and imported from China.

Alden (Chicago)

1960s. Chicago's Alden was a department store and mail-order house offering instruments from Chicago builders such as Harmony.

MODEL YEAR	FEATURES	EXC. COND. LOW	HIGH
H-45 Stratotone			
1960s. Alden's version of the H45 Stratotone Mars model, single plain cover pickup.			
1960s		$450	$600

Alembic

1969-present. Premium and presentation grade, production/custom, guitars, baritones, and 12-strings built in Santa Rosa, California. They also build basses. Established in San Francisco by Ron and Susan Wickersham, Alembic started out as a studio working with the Grateful Dead and other bands on a variety of sound gear. By '70 they were building custom basses, later adding guitars and cabinets. By '73, standardized models were being offered.

MODEL YEAR	FEATURES	EXC. COND. LOW	HIGH
California Special			
1988-2009. Double-cut neck-thru solidbody, six-on-a-side tuners, various colors.			
1988-2009		$2,225	$2,900
Distillate			
1979-1991. Various wood options.			
1979-1991		$2,500	$3,250
Little Darling			
2006-present. Exotic woods offered, heart inlay at 12th fret, brass bird tailpiece.			
2006-2021		$4,600	$6,000
Orion			
1990-present. Offset double-cut glued neck solidbody, various colors.			
1990-2016		$2,200	$2,900
Series I			
1972-present. Neck-thru, double-cut solidbody, bookmatched koa, black walnut core, 3 pickups, optional body styles available, natural.			
1970s-2013	12-string	$5,100	$6,600
1970s-2021	6-string	$5,100	$6,600

Alfieri Guitars

1990-present. Luthier Don Alfieri builds his premium and presentation grade, custom/production, acoustic and classical guitars in Long Island, New York.

Alhambra

1930s. The Alhambra brand was most likely used by a music studio (or distributor) on instruments made by others, including Regal-built resonator instruments.

Allen Guitars

1982-present. Premium grade, production resonators, steel-string flat-tops, and mandolins built by Luthier Randy Allen, Colfax, California.

Alleva-Coppolo Basses and Guitars

1995-present. Professional and premium grade, custom/production, solidbody electric guitars and basses built by luthier Jimmy Coppolo in Dallas, Texas for '95-'97, in New York City for '98-2008, and since in Upland, California.

1960s Alamo Fiesta
Imaged by Heritage Auctions, HA.com

1964 Alden Chicago
Tom Pfeifer

GUITARS

1992 Alvarez Dana Scoop
Tom Pfeifer

1976 Alvarez Yairi DY-74
Tom Pfeifer

MODEL		EXC. COND.	
YEAR	FEATURES	LOW	HIGH

Aloha

1935-1960s. Private branded by Aloha Publishing and Musical Instruments Company, Chicago, Illinois. Made by others. There was also the Aloha Manufacturing Company of Honolulu which made musical instruments from around 1911 to the late '20s.

Alosa

1947-1958. Luthier Alois Sandner built these acoustic archtop guitars in Germany.

Alpha

1970s-1980s. One of the brand names of guitars built in the Egmond plant in Holland. Sold by Martin for a while in the 1980s.

Alray

1967. Electrics and acoustics built by the Holman-Woodell guitar factory in Neodesha, Kansas, who also marketed similar models under the Holman brand.

Alternative Guitar and Amplifier Company

Intermediate grade, custom/production, solid-body electric guitars and basses made in Piru, California, by luthiers Mal Stich and Sal Gonzales and imported from Korea, beginning in 2006, under the Alternative Guitar and Amplifier Company, and Mal n' Sal brands.

AlumiSonic

2006-present. Luthier Ray Matter builds his production/custom, professional grade, aluminum/wood hybrid electric guitars in Bohemia and West Islip, New York.

Alvarez

1965-present. Intermediate and professional grade, production, acoustic guitars imported by St. Louis Music. They also offer lap steels, banjos and mandolins. Initially high-quality handmade guitars Yairi made by K. (Kazuo) Yairi were exclusively distributed, followed by lower-priced Alvarez line. In '90 the Westone brand used on electric guitars and basses was replaced with the Alvarez name; these Alvarez electrics were offered until '02. Many Alvarez electric models designed by luthier Dana Sutcliffe; several models designed by Dan Armstrong.

Alvarez Yairi

1966-present. Alvarez Yairi guitars are hand-crafted and imported by St. Louis Music.

Alvarez, Juan

1952-2019. Professional and premium grade, production/custom, classical and flamenco guitars made in Madrid, Spain, originally by luthier Juan Alvarez Gil (died in 2001), then by son Juan Miguel Alvarez.

MODEL		EXC. COND.	
YEAR	FEATURES	LOW	HIGH

American Acoustech

1993-2001. Production steel string flat-tops made by Tom Lockwood (former Guild plant manager) and Dave Stutzman (of Stutzman's Guitar Center) as ESVL Inc. in Rochester, New York.

American Archtop Guitars

1995-present. Premium and presentation grade, custom 6- and 7-string archtops by luthier Dale Unger, in Stroudsburg, Pennsylvania.

American Conservatory (Lyon & Healy)

Late-1800s-early-1900s. Guitars, mandolins and harp guitars built by Chicago's Lyon & Healy and sold mainly through various catalog retailers. Mid-level instruments above the quality of Lyon & Healy's Lakeside brand, and generally under their Washburn brand. Generally of negligible value because repair cost often exceed their market value.

Acoustic

1920s	Spanish 6-string	$525	$675
1920s	Tenor 4-string	$525	$675

G2740 Monster Bass

Early-mid-1900s. Two 6-string neck (one fretless), acoustic flat-top harp guitar, spruce top, birch back and sides with rosewood stain, natural. Their catalog claimed it was "Indispensable to the up-to-date mandolin and guitar club."

1917		$3,200	$4,200

Style G Series Harp Guitar

Early-1900s. Two 6-string necks with standard tuners, 1 neck fretless, rosewood back and sides, spruce top, fancy rope colored wood inlay around soundhole, sides and down the back center seam.

1917	Natural	$3,200	$4,200

American Showster

1986-2004, 2010-2011. Established by Bill Meeker and David Haines, Bayville, New Jersey, building guitars shaped like classic car tailfins or motorcycle gas tanks. The Custom Series was made in the U.S.A., while the Standard Series (introduced in '97) was made in Czechoslovakia. They also made a bass. Bill Meeker started production again around 2010 until his death in late '11.

AS-57 Classic

1987-2004. American-made until 2000, body styled like a '57 Chevy tail fin, basswood body, bolt-on neck, 1 humbucker or 3 single-coils, various colors.

1987-1999	US-made	$4,000	$5,200
2000-2004	Import	$1,400	$1,800

The Biker/Tank

1987-1989. Alder body shaped like motorcycle gas tank, 3 single-coil or 2 humbucker pickups, maple neck, rosewood 'board.

1987-1989		$1,350	$1,750

Ampeg

1949-present. Founded in '49 by Everett Hull as the Ampeg Bassamp Company in New York and

MODEL		EXC. COND.	
YEAR	FEATURES	LOW	HIGH

has built amplifiers throughout its history. In '62 the company added instruments with the introduction of their Baby Bass and from '63 to '65, they carried a line of guitars and basses built by Burns of London and imported from England. In '66 the company introduced its own line of basses. In '67, Ampeg was acquired by Unimusic, Inc. From '69-'71 contracted with Dan Armstrong to produce lucite "see-through" guitars and basses with replaceable slide-in pickup design. In '71 the company merged with Magnavox. Beginning around '72 until '75, Ampeg imported the Stud Series copy guitars from Japan. Ampeg shut down production in the spring of '80. MTI bought the company and started importing amps. In '86 St. Louis Music purchased the company. In '97 Ampeg introduced new and reissue American-made guitar and bass models. They discontinued the guitar line in '01, but offered the Dan Armstrong plexi guitar again starting in '05, adding wood-bodied versions in '08. They also offered a bass. In '05 LOUD Technologies acquired SLM and the Ampeg brand. In '18, the brand was sold to Yamaha.

AMG1
1999-2001. Dan Amstrong guitar features, but with mahogany body with quilted maple top, 2 P-90-style or humbucker-style pickups.

1999-2001	Hums, gold hw	$575	$750
1999-2001	Kent Armstrong pus	$375	$500
1999-2001	P-90s, standard hw	$375	$500

Dan Armstrong Lucite
1969-1971. Clear plexiglas solidbody, with interchangable pickups, Dan Armstrong reports that around 9,000 guitars were produced, introduced in '69, but primary production was in '70-'71, reissued in '98.

1969-1971	Clear	$2,425	$3,150
1969-1971	Smoke	$2,775	$3,600

Dan Armstrong Plexi
1998-2001, 2006-2011. Reissue of Lucite guitar, produced by pickup designer Kent Armstrong (son of Dan Armstrong), offered in smoked (ADAG2) or clear (ADAG1). Latest version is Japanese-made ADA6.

1998-2011	Clear or Smoke	$775	$1,000

Heavy Stud (GE-150/GEH-150)
1973-1975. Import from Japan, single-cut body, weight added for sustain, single-coils or humbuckers (GEH).

1973-1975		$425	$550

Sonic Six (By Burns)
1964-1965. Solidbody, 2 pickups, tremolo, cherry finish, same as the Burns Nu-Sonic guitar.

1964-1965		$450	$600

Stud (GE-100/GET-100)
1973-1975. Import from Japan, double-cut, inexpensive materials, weight added for sustain, GET-100 included tremolo.

1973-1975		$425	$550

Super Stud (GE-500)
1973-1975. Double-cut, weight added for sustain, top-of-the-line in Stud Series.

1973-1975		$425	$550

MODEL		EXC. COND.	
YEAR	FEATURES	LOW	HIGH

Thinline (By Burns)
1963-1964. Semi-hollowbody, 2 f-holes, 2 pickups, double-cut, tremolo, import by Burns of London, same as the Burns TR2 guitar.

1963-1964		$600	$800

Wild Dog (By Burns)
1963-1964. Solidbody, 3 pickups, shorter scale, tremolo, sunburst finish, import by Burns of London, same as the Burns Split Sound.

1963-1964		$625	$825

Wild Dog De Luxe (By Burns)
1963-1964. Solidbody, 3 pickups, bound neck, tremolo, sunburst finish, import by Burns of London, same as the Burns Split Sonic guitar.

1963-1964		$700	$900

Anderberg
2002-present. Professional and premium grade, production/custom, electric guitars and basses built by luthier Michael Anderberg in Jacksonville, Florida.

Andersen Stringed Instruments
1978-present. Luthier Steve Andersen builds premium and presentation grade, production/custom flat-tops and archtops in Seattle, Washington. He also builds mandolins.

Andreas
1995-2004. Luthier Andreas Pichler built his aluminum-necked, solidbody guitars and basses in Dollach, Austria.

Andrew White Guitars
2000-present. Premium and presentation grade, custom, acoustic flat-top guitars built by luthier Andrew White in Morgantown, West Virginia. He also imports a production line of intermediate and professional grade, acoustic guitars from his factory in Korea.

Andy Powers Musical Instrument Co.
1996-2010. Luthier Andy Powers built his premium and presentation grade, custom, archtop, flat-top, and semi-hollow electric guitars in Oceanside, California. He also built ukes and mandolins.

Angelica
Ca. 1967-ca. 1990s. Entry-level guitars and basses imported from Japan.

Acoustic
1967-1972	Various models	$190	$250

Electric Solidbody
1967-1972	Various models	$275	$375

Angus
1976-present. Professional and premium grade, custom-made steel and nylon string flat-tops built by Mark Angus in Laguna Beach, California.

American Showster Biker
Billy White Jr.

Ampeg Super Stud
Imaged by Heritage Auctions, HA.com

GUITARS

Aria Pro II Fullerton
Imaged by Heritage Auctions, HA.com

1980s Aria Pro II TS-600
Tom Pfeifer

MODEL YEAR	FEATURES	EXC. COND. LOW	HIGH

Antares

1980s-1990s. Korean-made budget electric and acoustic guitars imported by Vega Music International of Brea, California.

Acoustic

1980s-90s	Various models	$100	$130

Double Neck 6/4

1990s. Cherry finish double-cut.

1990s		$550	$725

Solidbody

1980s-90s	Various models	$150	$225

Antique Acoustics

1970s-present. Luthier Rudolph Blazer builds production/custom flat-tops, 12 strings, and archtops in Tubingen, Germany.

Antonio Hermosa

Imported budget grade, production, acoustic and acoustic/electric classical guitars from The Music Link, starting in 2006..

Antonio Lorca

Intermediate and professional grade, production, classical guitars made in Valencia, Spain.

Apollo

Ca. 1967-1972. Entry-level guitars imported by St. Louis Music. They also offered basses and effects.

Electric

1967-1972. Japanese imports, various models.

1967-1972		$1,550	$2,000

Applause

1976-present. Budget grade, production, acoustic and acoustic/electric guitars, basses, mandolins and ukes and previously solidbody electrics. Originally Kaman Music's entry-level Ovation-styled brand, it is now owned by Drum Workshop, Inc. The instruments were made in the U.S. until around '82, when production was moved to Korea. On the U.S.-made guitars, the back of the neck was molded Urelite, with a cast aluminum neck combining an I-beam neck reinforcement, fingerboard, and frets in one unit. The Korean models have traditional wood necks.

AA Models

1976-1990s. Acoustic, laminate top, plastic or composition body. Specs and features can vary on AA Models.

1976-1981	US-made	$150	$225
1980s-90s	Import	$85	$110

AE Models

1976-2000s. Acoustic/electric, laminate top, plastic or composition body. Specs and features can vary on AE Models.

1976-1981	US-made	$200	$290
1980-2000s	Import	$110	$160

Applegate

2001-present. Premium grade, production/custom, acoustic and classical guitars built by luthier Brian Applegate in Minneapolis, Minnesota.

MODEL YEAR	FEATURES	EXC. COND. LOW	HIGH

APS Custom

2005-present. Luthier Andy Speake builds his production/custom, professional and premium grade, solidbody guitars in Victoria, British Columbia.

Arbor

1983-ca. 2013. Budget and intermediate grade, production, classical, acoustic, and solid and semi-hollow body electric guitars imported by Musicorp (MBT). They also offered basses.

Acoustic

1980s-2013	Various models	$100	$200

Electric

1980s-2013	Various models	$250	$400

Arch Kraft

1933-1934. Full-size acoustic archtop and flat-top guitars. Budget brand produced by the Kay Musical Instrument Company and sold through various distributors.

Aria Diamond

1960s. Brand name used by Aria in the '60s.

Electric

1960s. Various models and appointments in the '60s.

1960s		$500	$650

Aria/Aria Pro II

1956-present. Budget, intermediate and professional grade, production, electric, acoustic, acoustic/electric, and classical guitars. They also make basses, mandolins, and banjos. Aria was established in Japan in '56 and started production of instruments in '60 using the Arai, Aria, Aria Diamond, and Diamond brands. The brand was renamed Aria Pro II in '75. Aria Pro II was used mainly on electric guitars, with Aria used on others. Over the years, they have produced acoustics, banjos, mandolins, electrics, basses, amplifiers, and effects. Around '87 production of cheaper models moved to Korea, reserving Japanese manufacturing for more expensive models. Around '95 some models were made in U.S., though most contemporary guitars sold in U.S. are Korean. In '01, the Pro II part of the name was dropped altogether.

Early Arias don't have serial numbers or pot codes. Serial numbers began to be used in the mid '70s. At least for Aria guitars made by Matsumoku, the serial number contains the year of manufacture in the first one or two digits (Y##### or YY####). Thus, a guitar from 1979 might begin with 79####. One from 1981 might begin with 1#####. The scheme becomes less sure after 1987. Some Korean- made guitars use a serial number with year and week indicated in the first four digits (YYWW####). Thus 9628#### would be from the 28th week of 1996. However, this is not the case on all guitars, and some have serial numbers which are not date-coded.

MODEL YEAR	FEATURES	EXC. COND. LOW	HIGH

Models have been consolidated by sector unless specifically noted.

Acoustic Solid Wood Top
1960s-present. Steel string models, various appointments, generally mid-level imports.

1960s-2021		$550	$725

Acoustic Veneer Wood Top
1960s-present. Steel string models, various appointments, generally entry-level imports.

1960s-2021		$250	$325

Classical Solid Wood Top
1960s-present. Various models, various appointments, generally mid-level imports.

1960s-2021		$300	$400

Classical Veneer Wood Top
1960s-present. Various models, various appointments, generally entry-level imports.

1960s-2021		$175	$225

Fullerton Series
1995-2000. Various models with different appointments and configurations based on the classic offset double-cut solidbody.

1995-2000		$550	$725

Herb Ellis (PE-175/FA-DLX)
1978-1987 (Model PE-175) and 1988-1993 (Model FA-DLX). Archtop hollowbody, ebony 'board, 2 humbuckers.

1978-1993		$700	$925

Solidbody
1960s-present. Various models, various appointments, generally mid-level imports.

1960s-2021		$650	$850

Titan Artist (TA) Series
1967-2012. Double cut, semi-hollow bodies, 2 pickups, various models.

1967-2012		$650	$850

Aristides
2010-present. Dutch engineer Aristides Poort developed the material (arium) used to build production/custom, premium grade, solidbody electric guitars in the Netherlands. They also build basses.

ARK - New Era Guitars
2006-present. Luthier A. R. Klassen builds his professional and premium grade, production/custom, reproductions of vintage Larson Brothers instruments in Chesterton, Indiana.

Armstrong, Rob
Custom steel- and nylon-string flat-tops, 12 strings, and parlor guitars made in Coventry, U.K. by luthier Rob Armstrong, starting in 1971. He also builds mandolins and basses.

Arpeggio Korina
1995-present. Professional, premium and presentation grade, production/custom, korina wood solidbody guitars built by luthier Ron Kayfield in Pennsylvania.

Art & Lutherie
Budget and intermediate grade, production, steel- and nylon-string acoustic and acoustic/electric guitars. Founded by luthier Robert Godin, who also has the Norman, Godin, Seagull, and Patrick & Simon brands of instruments.

Artesano
Intermediate and professional grade, production, classical guitars built in Valencia, Spain, and distributed by Juan Orozco. Orozco also made higher-end classical Orozco Models 8, 10 and 15.

Artinger Custom Guitars
1997-present. Luthier Matt Artinger builds his professional and premium grade, production/custom, hollow, semi-hollow, and chambered solidbody guitars and basses in Emmaus, Pennsylvania.

Artur Lang
1949-1975. German luthier Artur Lang is best known for his archtops, but did build classicals early on. His was a small shop and much of his output was custom ordered. The instruments were mostly unbranded, but some have L.A. engraved on the headstock.

Asama
1970s-1980s. Some models of this Japanese line of solidbody guitars featured built-in effects. They also offered basses, effects, drum machines and other music products.

Ashborn
1848-1864. James Ashborn, of Wolcottville, Connecticut, operated one of the largest guitar making factories of the mid-1800s. Models were small parlor-sized instruments with ladder bracing and gut strings. Most of these guitars will need repair. Often of more interest as historical artifacts or museum pieces versus guitar collections.

Model 2
1848-1864. Flat-top, plain appointments, no position markers on the neck, identified by Model number.

1855	Fully repaired	$525	$675

Model 5
1848-1864. Flat-top, higher appointments.

1855	Fully repaired	$1,275	$1,650

Asher
1982-present. Luthier Bill Asher builds his professional grade, production/custom, solidbody electric guitars in Venice, California. He also builds lap steels.

Ashland
Intermediate grade, production, acoustic and acoustic/electric guitars made by Korea's Crafter Guitars.

1984 Aria Pro II ZZ Deluxe
Kris Fox

Aristides 080s

Asher T Deluxe

Atomic STD 1

MODEL YEAR	FEATURES	EXC. COND. LOW	HIGH

Astro

1963-1964. The Astro AS-51 was a 1 pickup kit guitar sold by Rickenbacker. German luthier Arthur Strohmer also built archtops bearing this name.

Asturias

Professional and premium grade, production, classical guitars built on Kyushu island, in Japan.

Atkin Guitars

1995-present. Luthier Alister Atkin builds his production/custom steel and nylon string flat-tops in Canterbury, U.K. He also builds mandolins.

Atlas

Archtop guitars, and possibly other types, built in East Germany and by Zero Sette in Italy.

Atomic

2006-present. Production/custom, intermediate and professional grade, solidbody electric guitars and basses built by luthiers Tim Mulqueeny and Harry Howard in Peoria, Arizona.

Audiovox

Ca. 1935-ca. 1950. Paul Tutmarc's Audiovox Manufacturing, of Seattle, Washington, was a pioneer in electric lap steels, basses, guitars and amps. Tutmarc was a talented Hawaiian steel guitarist and ran a music school and is credited with inventing the electric bass guitar in '35, which his company started selling in the late '30s.

Austin

1999-present. Budget and intermediate grade, production, acoustic, acoustic/electric, resonator, and electric guitars, basses, amps, mandolins, ukes and banjos imported by St. Louis Music.

Acoustic Flat-Top

1999-2021	Various models	$125	$175

Solidbody Electric

1999-2021	Various models	$175	$300

Austin Hatchet

Mid-1970s-mid-1980s. Trademark of distributor Targ and Dinner, Chicago, Illinois.

Hatchet

1981. Travel guitar.

1981		$450	$600

Solidbody Electric

1970s-1980s. Various classic designs.

1970s-80s		$375	$500

Avalon

1920s. Instruments built by the Oscar Schmidt Co. and possibly others. Most likely a brand made for a distributor.

Avalon (Ireland)

2002-present. Luthiers Stevie Graham, Mark Lyttle, Ernie McMillan, Balazs Prohaszka and

Robin Thompson build premium and presentation grade, production/custom, steel-string and classical, acoustic and electro-acoustic guitars in Northern Ireland. In '04-'05 their Silver series was imported from South Korea, and '05 the Gold series from Czech Republic.

Avante

1997-2007. Intermediate grade, production, imported sharp cutaway acoustic baritone guitars designed by Joe Veillette and Michael Tobias and offered by MusicYo. Originally higher priced instruments offered by Alvarez, there was the baritone, a 6-string and a bass.

AV-2 Baritone

1997-2007. Baritone guitar tuned B to B, solid spruce cutaway top, mahogany sides and back.

1997-2007		$300	$400

Avanti

1964-late 1960s. Italian-made guitar brand imported by European Crafts, of Los Angeles. Earlier models were plastic covered; later ones had paint finishes.

Electric Solidbody

1960s. Solidbody, 3 single-coils, dot markers.

1960s		$250	$375

Avar

Late-1960s. Import copy models from Japan, not unlike Teisco, for the U.S. student market.

Solidbody Electric

1969		$250	$375

Aztec

1970s. Japanese-made copy guitars imported into Germany by Hopf.

B.C. Rich

Ca. 1966/67-present. Budget, intermediate, and premium grade, production/custom, import and U.S.-made, electric and acoustic guitars. They also offer basses. Founded by Bernardo Chavez Rico in Los Angeles, California. As a boy he worked for his guitar-maker father Bernardo Mason Rico (Valencian Guitar Shop, Casa Rico, Bernardo's Guitar Shop), building first koa ukes and later, guitars, steel guitars and Martin 12-string conversions. He started using the BC Rich name ca. '66-'67 and made about 300 acoustics until '68, when first solidbody electric made using a Fender neck.

Rich's early models were based on Gibson and Fender designs. First production instruments were in '69 with 10 fancy Gibson EB-3 bass and 10 matching Les Paul copies, all carved out of single block of mahogany. Early guitars with Gibson humbuckers, then Guild humbuckers, and, from '74-'86, DiMarzio humbuckers. Around 150 BC Rich Eagles were imported from Japan in '76. Ca. '76 or '77 some bolt-neck guitars with parts made by Wayne Charvel were offered. Acoustic production ended in '82 (acoustics were again offered in '95).

For '83-'86 the BC Rich N.J. Series (N.J. Nagoya, Japan) was built by Masan Tarada. U.S. Production Series (U.S.-assembled Korean kits) in '84. From '86 on, the N.J. Series was made by Cort in Korea. Korean Rave and Platinum series begin around '86. In '87, Rich agrees to let Class Axe of New Jersey market the Korean Rave, Platinum and N.J. Series. Class Axe (with Neal Moser) introduces Virgin in '87 and in '88 Rave and Platinum names are licensed to Class Axe. In '89, Rico licensed the BC Rich name to Class Axe. Both imported and American-made BC Riches are offered during Class Axe management. In 2000, BC Rich became a division of Hanser Music Group.

During '90-'91, Rico begins making his upscale Mason Bernard guitars (approx. 225 made). In '94, Rico resumes making BC Rich guitars in California. He died in 1999.

First 340-360 U.S.-built guitars were numbered sequentially beginning in '72. Beginning in '74, serial numbers change to YYZZZ pattern (year plus consecutive production). As production increased in the late-'70s, the year number began getting ahead of itself. By '80 it was 2 years ahead; by '81 as much as 4 years ahead. No serial number codes on imports.

The American B.C. Rich company was first and foremost a custom shop, therefore surprising variants are possible for the models described below, especially in the early years of the company. Many of the first models were offered as either a Standard (also called Deluxe) model or as an upgrade called the Supreme model.

The Deluxe or Standard model has diamond markers, unbound rosewood fretboard, three-on-a-side tuners, generally solid mahogany body, some rare examples with maple body or other woods, some with runners or stringers of alternate exotic wood.

The Supreme model has specific options including cloud markers, fully bound ebony fretboard and three-on-a-side headstock, various woods including solid koa, maple, highly-figured maple (birdseye, quilted, curly), other exotic woods offered, most models with runners or stringers of alternating exotic wood, also available as single solid wood, mid-1980s with original Kahler tremolo unit option, custom colors and sunburst finishes generally on a custom order basis, certain custom colors are worth more than the values shown, early models circa '75-'82 had a Leo Quan Badass bridge option and those models are highly favored by collectors, early style control knobs had silver metal inserts and full electronics with Varitone and PreAmp and Grover Imperial bullseye tuners, the earliest models had red head mini-switches (later became silver-chrome switches). Technically speaking the Supreme model only applied to the Mockingbird, Eagle, Bich, and Wave.

The prime collector's market for B.C. Rich is the '72-'85 era. The Seagull, Eagle, Mockingbird, Bich, and Wave models are the true vintage models

from that '72-'85 epoch. Pre-1985 BC Rich Standard Finishes were Natural, Gloss White, Black, Competition Red, Medium Blue, Metallic Red, and Cherry. Any other finish would be a Custom Color. Most custom colors started appearing in late 1978. Prior to '78, guitars had two tone transparent burst finishes, natural finishes and occasional one color paint schemes. Custom Color finishes are worth 10% more than standard finish colors.

MODEL YEAR	FEATURES	EXC. COND. LOW	HIGH
Assassin			
1986-1998, 2000-2010. Double-cut body, 2 humbuckers, maple thru-neck dot markers, various colors.			
1986-1989	1st Rico era	$600	$800
1989-1993	Class Axe era	$600	$800
1994-1998	2nd Rico era USA	$525	$700
2000-2010	Includes QX & PX	$250	$325
B-28 Acoustic			
Ca.1967-1982. Acoustic flat-top, hand-built, herringbone trim, pearl R headstock logo.			
1967-1982		$1,675	$2,175
B-30 Acoustic			
Ca.1967-1982. Acoustic flat-top.			
1967-1982		$1,675	$2,175
B-38 Acoustic			
Ca.1967-1982. Acoustic flat-top, herringbone trim.			
1967-1982		$1,675	$2,175
B-41 Acoustic			
1970s. Acoustic flat-top.			
1970s		$1,750	$2,300
B-45 Acoustic			
1970s. Hand-built, D-style acoustic flat-top.			
1970s		$2,100	$2,700
Beast (U.S.A. Custom Shop)			
1999-2015. Exaggerated four point cutaway body, flamed or quilted top.			
1999-2015		$925	$1,200
Bich (U.S.A. Assembly)			
1978-1998. Four-point sleek body, came in Standard top or Supreme with highly figured maple body and active EQ.			
1978-1979	Standard/Deluxe	$2,225	$2,900
1978-1979	Supreme	$2,900	$3,800
1980-1985	Standard/Deluxe	$1,400	$1,800
1980-1985	Supreme	$2,500	$3,250
1986-1988	Standard/Deluxe	$950	$1,250
1986-1988	Supreme	$2,025	$2,650
1989-1993	Class Axe era	$950	$1,250
1994-1998	2nd Rico era USA	$950	$1,250
Bich 10-String			
1977-2015. U.S.-made, doubles on 4 low strings.			
1977-1982	Highly flamed	$4,200	$5,400
1977-1982	Koa	$4,200	$5,400
1977-1982	Opaque finish	$3,700	$4,800
1985	Highly quilted	$3,900	$5,100
2005-2015	Highly quilted	$3,500	$4,600
Black Hole			
1988. Bolt neck, rosewood 'board, integrated pickup design, Floyd Rose.			
1988		$225	$300

B.C. Rich Beast
Imaged by Heritage Auctions, HA.com

1982 B.C. Rich Bich
Erik Van Gansen

GUITARS

1978 B.C. Rich Eagle
Imaged by Heritage Auctions, HA.com

2001 B.C. Rich Exclusive EM I
John

MODEL YEAR	FEATURES	EXC. COND. LOW	HIGH

Body Art Collection
2003-2006. Imports, 'Body Art Collection' headstock logo, different graphics/different models issued each month from January '03 to March '04, 25th Anniversary model available into '06.

2003-2006	Various models	$180	$250

Bronze Series
2001-2007. Made in China. Includes 2 models; Mockingbird and Warlock.

2001-2007		$60	$90

Doubleneck
1980-1988. Doublenecks were sporadically made, specs (and values) may vary.

1980-1988	Bich	$7,400	$9,600
1980-1988	Eagle	$8,300	$11,000
1980-1988	Iron Bird	$6,500	$8,500
1980-1988	Mockingbird	$8,300	$11,000
1980-1988	Seagull	$9,300	$12,000

Eagle
1975-1982, 2000-2004. Made in USA, often called the Eagle model, but also called Eagle Deluxe or Eagle Standard, features include diamond inlays, unbound rosewood fretboard, 3-on-a-side tuners, generally solid mahogany body, some rare examples with maple body or other woods, some with runners or stringers of alternate exotic wood. (See additional notes in the Eagle Supreme listing.)

1975-1982		$2,600	$3,400

Eagle Special (U.S.A.)
1977-1982. A variant of the Eagle with even more switches and electronic options, the extra options are not particularly considered an advantage in the BC Rich collector community, therefore an Eagle Special is worth less than the Standard or Eagle Supreme.

1977-1982		$2,600	$3,400

Eagle Supreme
1975-1982, 2000-2004. Made in USA, Eagle body style with specific options including cloud inlays, fully bound ebony fretboard, 3-on-a-side headstock, various woods including solid koa, maple, highly-figured maple (birdseye, quilted, curly), other exotic woods offered, most with runners or stringers of alternating exotic wood, also available as single solid wood, mid-'80s with original Kahler tremolo unit option, custom colors and sunburst finishes generally on a custom order basis, certain custom colors are worth more than the values shown, early models ca. '75-'82 had a Leo Quan Badass bridge option and those models are highly favored by collectors, early style control knobs with silver metal inserts, full electronics with Varitone and PreAmp and Grover Imperial bullseye tuners, the earliest models had red head mini-switches (later became silver-chrome switches).

1975-1982		$3,400	$4,500
2000-2004		$2,000	$2,600

Eagle Supreme Condor
1983-1987. Less than 50 made, simplified electronics system based on customer's requests, features can include cloud inlays, fully bound ebony fretboard neck, bound 3-on-a-side headstock, bookmatched figured maple top over solid mahogany body with

slight arch, no runners or stringers, basic electronics with master volume, master tone, and pickup switch, also commonly called Condor Supreme.

1983-1987		$1,400	$1,800

Elvira
2001. Elvira (the witch) photo on black Warlock body, came with Casecore coffin case.

2001		$450	$600

Exclusive EM I
1996-2004. Platinum Series, offset double-cut, bound top, 2 humbuckers.

1996-2004		$150	$200

Gunslinger
1987-1999. Inverted headstock, 1 (Gunslinger I) or 2 (Gunslinger II) humbuckers, recessed cutout behind Floyd Rose allows player to pull notes up 2 full steps.

1987-1989	Graphic designs	$725	$950
1987-1989	Standard finish	$675	$900
1989-1993	Class Axe era	$675	$900
1994-1999	2nd Rico era, bolt-on	$575	$750
1994-1999	2nd Rico era, neck-thru	$575	$750

Ironbird
1983-2004. Pointy body and headstock.

1983-1989		$1,025	$1,325
1989-1993	Class Axe era	$925	$1,200
1994-1998	2nd Rico era	$855	$1,125

Kerry King Wartribe 1 Warlock
2004-2015. Tribal Fire finish, 2 pickups.

2004-2015		$150	$200

Mockingbird
1976-present. Made in USA, often called the Mockingbird model, but also called the Mockingbird Standard or Mockingbird Deluxe, features include diamond inlays, unbound rosewood fretboard, 3-on-a-side tuners, generally solid mahogany body, some rare examples with maple body or other woods, some with runners or stringers of alternate exotic wood. In 2016 'Mk' added to name (Mk1, Mk3, Mk5, Mk7, Mk9, Mk11). (See additional notes in the Mockingbird Supreme listing.)

1976		$2,575	$3,400
1977-1978	Short horn	$2,575	$3,400
1979-1983	Long horn	$2,575	$3,400
1984		$2,200	$2,900
1985		$2,100	$2,800
1986-1989	Last of 1st Rico era	$1,500	$1,950
1989-1993	Class Axe era	$1,500	$1,950
1994-1999	2nd Rico era, bolt-on	$1,400	$1,850
2000-2021	Custom Shop (COA)	$2,100	$2,700

Mockingbird Ice Acrylic
2004-2006. See-thru acrylic body.

2004-2006		$275	$375

Mockingbird Legacy
2019-present. Mahogany body, koa or quilted maple top, 2 humbucker pickups, Floyd Rose or STQ hardtail, various colors.

2019-2021		$925	$1,200

MODEL YEAR	FEATURES	EXC. COND. LOW	HIGH

Mockingbird Supreme

1976-1989. Made in USA, Mockingbird body style with specific options including cloud inlays, fully bound ebony fretboard, 3-on-a-side headstock, various woods including solid koa, maple, highly-figured maple (birdseye, quilted, curly), other exotic woods offered, most with runners or stringers of alternating exotic wood, also available as single solid wood, mid-'80s with original Kahler tremolo unit option, custom colors and sunburst finishes generally on a custom order basis, certain custom colors are worth more than the values shown, early models ca. '76-'82 had a Leo Quan Badass bridge option and those models are highly favored by collectors, early style control knobs with silver metal inserts, full electronics with Varitone and PreAmp and Grover Imperial bullseye tuners, the earliest models had red head mini-switches (later became silver-chrome switches).

YEAR	FEATURES	LOW	HIGH
1976-1978	Earlier short horn	$3,400	$4,500
1976-1978	Short horn	$3,400	$4,500
1979-1982	Later long horn	$3,400	$4,500
1983-1985		$2,400	$3,200
1986-1989		$2,200	$2,800
1989-1993	Class Axe era	$2,100	$2,700
1994-1999	2nd Rico era	$2,000	$2,600

Nighthawk

1978-ca.1982. Eagle-shaped body with bolt neck.

YEAR		LOW	HIGH
1978-1982		$750	$1,000

NJ Series/NJC Series

1983-2006. Earlier models made in Japan. Made in Korea '86 forward. All NJ models fall within the same price range. Models include; Assassin, Beast, Bich, Ironbird, Eagle, Mockingbird, Outlaw, ST III, Virgin, Warlock. C for Classic added in '06.

YEAR	FEATURES	LOW	HIGH
1983-1984	Early NJ Japan	$550	$725
1985-1986	Later Japan	$425	$550
1987-2006	Made in Korea	$300	$400

Phoenix

1977-ca.1982. Mockingbird-shaped with bolt neck.

YEAR		LOW	HIGH
1977-1982		$750	$1,000

Platinum Series

1986-2006. Lower-priced import versions including Assassin, Beast, Bich, Ironbird, ST, Warlock.

YEAR		LOW	HIGH
1986-2006		$275	$375

Rave Series

1986-ca. 1990. Korean-made down-market versions of popular models.

YEAR		LOW	HIGH
1986-1990		$225	$325

Seagull

1972-1975. Single-cut solidbody, neck-thru, 2 humbuckers.

YEAR	FEATURES	LOW	HIGH
1972-1973	Earliest, 30 made	$2,950	$3,900
1973-1974		$2,600	$3,400
1975		$2,400	$3,200

Seagull II

1974-1977. Double-cut solidbody, neck-thru, 2 humbuckers. Transitional model in '75 between Seagull and Eagle, Seagull Jr. is used interchangable with Seagull II, the company made several variants during this period which some collectors consider to be Seagull Jr. while others consider to be Seagull II. The II/Jr. design finally was changed and called the Eagle.

YEAR	FEATURES	LOW	HIGH
1974	1st 50, Gibson pus	$2,400	$3,150
1974	Moser, 16 made	$2,400	$3,150
1974	Other from '74	$2,400	$3,150
1976-1977		$2,200	$2,800

Seagull II/Seagull Jr.

1975-1977. Another transitional model starting in '75, the model name Seagull Jr. is used interchangable with Seagull II, the company made several variants during this period which some collectors consider to be Seagull Jr. while others consider to be Seagull II. The design finally was changed and called the Eagle.

YEAR	FEATURES	LOW	HIGH
1975-1977	II and Jr	$2,100	$2,700

Stealth I Series

1983-1989. Includes Standard (maple body, diamond inlays) and Series II (mahogany body, dot inlays), 2 pickups.

YEAR	FEATURES	LOW	HIGH
1983-1989	Series II	$1,575	$2,100
1983-1989	Standard	$1,575	$2,100

ST-III (U.S.A.)

1987-1998. Double-cut solidbody, hum/single/single or 2 humbucker pickups, Kahler tremolo.

YEAR	FEATURES	LOW	HIGH
1987-1989	Bolt-on	$675	$875
1987-1989	Neck-thru	$700	$925
1989-1993	Class Axe era	$675	$875
1994-1998	New Rico era	$675	$875

The Mag

2000. U.S. Handcrafted Series Mockingbird Acoustic Supreme, solid spruce top, quilt maple back and sides, pickup with preamp and EQ optional, dark sunburst.

YEAR		LOW	HIGH
2000		$550	$725

Warlock

1981-present. Made in USA, also called Warlock Standard, 4-point sleek body style with widow headstock. In 2016 'Mk' added to name (Mk1, Mk3, Mk5, Mk7, Mk9, Mk11).

YEAR	FEATURES	LOW	HIGH
1981-1989	Standard	$1,400	$1,800
1990-1999	2nd Rico era, bolt-on	$1,025	$1,325
1990-1999	2nd Rico era, neck-thru	$1,025	$1,325

Warlock Extreme

2019-present. Mahogany body, spalted maple and quilted maple top, 2 humbucker pickups, Floyd Rose, various colors.

YEAR		LOW	HIGH
2019-2021		$1,000	$1,300

Warlock Ice Acrylic

2004-2006. See-thru acrylic body.

YEAR		LOW	HIGH
2004-2006		$275	$375

Wave

1983. U.S.-made, very limited production based upon the Wave bass.

YEAR		LOW	HIGH
1983		$2,200	$2,900

B.C. Rico

1978-1982. B.C. Rich's first Japan-made guitars were labeled B.C. Rico until they were sued for patent infringement on the Rico name. They made around 200 guitars and basses with the Rico headstock logo. After '82, B.C. Rich offered the NJ Series (Import) models.

1977 B.C. Rich Mockingbird Supreme

1986 B.C. Rich ST-III

GUITARS

B3 Phoenix

*Babicz Identity Series
Dreadnought*

MODEL YEAR	FEATURES	EXC. COND. LOW	HIGH

Eagle
1978-1982. All mahogany, rosewood 'board, Dimarzio pickups, mother-of-pearl headstock logo.

| 1978-1982 | | $2,600 | $3,400 |

Mockingbird
1978-1982. All mahogany, rosewood 'board, Dual DiMarzio humbuckers.

| 1978-1982 | | $2,600 | $3,400 |

RW-2A
1978-1982. Acoustic D-style, Brazilian rosewood laminate body, spruce top, herringbone trim, natural finish.

| 1978-1982 | | $650 | $850 |

RW-7
1978-1982. D-style, spruce top, Brazilian rosewood back and sides, abalone markers, natural finish.

| 1978-1982 | | $650 | $850 |

B3 Guitars
2004-present. Premium grade, custom/production, solid, chambered and hollow-body guitars built by luthier Gene Baker in Arroyo Grande, California. He previously made Baker U.S.A. guitars.

Babicz
2004-present. Started by luthier Jeff Babicz and Jeff Carano, who worked together at Steinberger, the company offers intermediate, professional, and premium grade, production/custom, acoustic and acoustic/electric guitars made in Poughkeepsie, New York, and overseas.

Bacon & Day
Established in 1921 by David Day and Paul Bacon, primarily known for fine quality tenor and plectrum banjos in the '20s and '30s. Purchased by Gretsch ca. '40.

Belmont
1950s. Gretsch era, 2 DeArmond pickups, natural.

| 1950s | | $1,300 | $1,700 |

Flat-Top
1930s-1940s. Large B&D headstock logo, fancy or plain appointments.

1930s	Fancy	$2,700	$3,500
1930s	Plain	$1,950	$2,525
1940s	Fancy	$2,225	$2,900
1940s	Plain	$1,775	$2,300

Ramona Archtop
1938-1940. Sunburst.

| 1938-1940 | | $750 | $975 |

Senorita Archtop
1940. Lower-end, sunburst, mahogany back and sides.

| 1940 | | $1,900 | $2,475 |

Silver Bell Style 1 Guitar Banjo (Bacon)
1920s. F-hole flange.

| 1920s | | $3,350 | $4,350 |

Style B Guitar Banjo (Bacon)
1920s. Banjo-resonator body with 6-string guitar neck.

| 1920s | | $1,025 | $1,325 |

MODEL YEAR	FEATURES	EXC. COND. LOW	HIGH

Sultana I
1930s. Large 18 1/4" acoustic archtop, Sultana engraved on tailpiece, block markers, bound top and back, sunburst.

| 1938 | | $3,800 | $4,950 |

Baden
Founded in 2006, by T.J. Baden, a former vice president of sales and marketing at Taylor guitars, initial production based on six models built in Vietnam, intermediate retail-price grade.

Baker U.S.A.
1997-present. Professional and premium grade, production/custom, solidbody electric guitars. Established by master builder Gene Baker after working at the Custom Shops of Gibson and Fender, Baker produced solid- and hollowbody guitars in Santa Maria, California. They also built basses. Baker also produced the Mean Gene brand of guitars from '88-'90. In September '03, the company was liquidated and the Baker U.S.A. name was sold to Ed Roman. Gene Baker currently builds b3 Guitars.

Baldwin
1965-1970. Founded in 1862, in Cincinnati, when reed organ and violin teacher Dwight Hamilton Baldwin opened a music store that eventually became one of the largest piano retailers in the Midwest. By 1965, the Baldwin Piano and Organ company was ready to buy into the guitar market but was outbid by CBS for Fender. Baldwin did procure Burns of London in September '65, and sold the guitars in the U.S. under the Baldwin name. Baldwin purchased Gretsch in '67. English production of Baldwin guitars ends in '70, after which Baldwin concentrates on the Gretsch brand.

Baby Bison (Model 560)
1965-1970. Double-cut solidbody, V headstock, 2 pickups, shorter scale, tremolo, black, red or white finishes.

| 1965-1966 | | $850 | $1,125 |
| 1966-1970 | Model 560 | $775 | $1,025 |

Bison (Model 511)
1965-1970. Double-cut solidbody, scroll headstock, 3 pickups, tremolo, black or white finishes.

| 1965-1966 | | $1,075 | $1,425 |
| 1966-1970 | Model 511 | $1,025 | $1,350 |

Double Six (Model 525)
1965-1970. Offset double-cut solidbody, 12 strings, 3 pickups, green or red sunburst.

| 1965-1966 | | $1,425 | $1,875 |
| 1966-1970 | Model 525 | $1,425 | $1,875 |

G.B. 65
1965-1966. Baldwin's first acoustic/electric, single-cut D-style flat-top, dual bar pickups.

| 1965-1966 | | $650 | $850 |

G.B. 66 De Luxe
1965-1966. Same as Standard with added density control on treble horn, golden sunburst.

| 1965-1966 | | $775 | $1,025 |

MODEL YEAR	FEATURES	EXC. COND. LOW	HIGH

G.B. 66 Standard
1965-1966. Thinline Electric archtop, dual Ultra-Sonic pickups, offset cutaways, red sunburst.

| 1965-1966 | | $650 | $850 |

Jazz Split Sound/Split Sound (Model 503)
1965-1970. Offset double-cut solidbody, scroll head-stock, 3 pickups, tremolo, red sunburst or solid colors.

| 1965-1966 | | $850 | $1,125 |
| 1966-1970 | Model 503 | $775 | $1,025 |

Marvin (Model 524)
1965-1970. Offset double-cut solidbody, scroll headstock, 3 pickups, tremolo, white or brown finish.

| 1965-1966 | | $1,075 | $1,425 |
| 1966-1970 | Model 524 | $1,025 | $1,350 |

Model 706
1967-1970. Double-cut semi-hollowbody, scroll headstock, 2 pickups, 2 f-holes, no vibrato, red or golden sunburst.

| 1967-1970 | | $900 | $1,200 |

Model 706V
1967-1970. Model 706 with vibrato.

| 1967-1970 | | $950 | $1,300 |

Model 712R Electric XII
1967-1970. Double-cut semi-hollow body with regular neck, red or gold sunburst.

| 1967-1970 | | $600 | $800 |

Model 712T Electric XII
1967-1970. Model 712 with thin neck, red or gold sunburst.

| 1967-1970 | | $600 | $800 |

Model 801CP Electric Classical
1968-1970. Grand concert-sized classical with transducer based pickup system, natural pumpkin finish.

| 1968-1970 | | $600 | $800 |

Nu-Sonic
1965-1966. Solidbody electric student model, 6-on-a-side tuners, black or cherry finish.

| 1965-1966 | | $650 | $850 |

Vibraslim (Model 548)
1965-1970. Double-cut semi-hollowbody, 2 pickups, vibrato, 2 f-holes, red or golden sunburst. Notable spec changes with Model 548 in '66.

| 1965-1966 | | $850 | $1,125 |
| 1966-1970 | Model 548 | $775 | $1,025 |

Virginian (Model 550)
1965-1970. Single-cut flat-top, 2 pickups (1 on each side of soundhole), scroll headstock, tremolo, natural.

| 1965-1966 | | $1,075 | $1,400 |
| 1966-1970 | Model 550 | $1,025 | $1,350 |

Ballurio
Luthier Keith Ballurio builds his intermediate, professional, and premium grade, production/custom, solidbody and chambered guitars in Manassas, Virginia, starting in 2000.

Baltimore
2007-2008. Budget grade, production, solidbody electric guitars imported by The Music Link.

Bambu
1970s. Short-lived brand name on a line of guitars built by Japan's Chushin Gakki Co., which also built models for several other manufacturers.

Baranik Guitars
1995-present. Premium grade, production/custom steel-string flat-tops made in Tempe, Arizona by luthier Mike Baranik.

Barclay
1960s. Thinline acoustic/electric archtops, solidbody electric guitars and basses imported from Japan. Generally shorter scale beginner guitars.

Electric Solidbody
1960s. Various models and colors.

| 1960s | | $225 | $300 |

Barcus-Berry
Founded by John Berry and Les Barcus, in 1964, introducing the first piezo crystal transducer. Martin guitar/Barcus-Berry products were offered in the mid-'80s. They also offered a line of amps from around '76 to ca. '80.

Barrington
1988-1991. Imports offered by Barrington Guitar Werks, of Barrington, Illinois. Models included solidbody guitars and basses, archtop electrics, and acoustic flat-tops. Barrington Music Products is still in the music biz, offering LA saxophones and other products.

Acoustic/Electric
1988-1991. Acoustic/electric, flat-top single-cut with typical round soundhole, opaque white.

| 1988-1991 | | $190 | $250 |

Solidbody
1988-ca 1991. Barrington's line of pointy headstock, double-cut solidbodies, black.

| 1988-1991 | | $190 | $250 |

Bartell of California
1964-1969. Founded by Paul Barth (Magnatone) and Ted Peckles. Mosrite-inspired designs.

Double Neck
| 1967 | | $2,300 | $3,000 |

Electric 12
1967. Mosrite-style body.

| 1967 | | $1,300 | $1,700 |

Barth
1950s-1960s. Paul Barth was involved with many guitar companies including National, Rickenbacker, Magnatone and others. He also built instruments under his own brand in California, including guitars, lap steels and amps. Most will have either a Barth logo on plastic plate, or decal.

Mark VIII
1959. Double-cut solidbody, 2 pickups, dot markers, Barth headstock logo.

| 1959 | | $2,500 | $3,300 |

1967 Baldwin Model 706 V
Rivington Guitars

1965 Baldwin Vibrasilm
Imaged by Heritage Auctions, HA.com

Bazzolo Guitarworks

Bedell Wildfire

MODEL YEAR	FEATURES	EXC. COND. LOW	HIGH

Bartolini

1960s. European-made (likely Italian) guitars made for the Bartolini Accordion Company. Similar to Gemelli guitars, so most likely from same manufacturer. Originally plastic covered, they switched to paint finishes by the mid '60s.

Solidbody

1960s		$525	$700

Bashkin Guitars

1998-present. Luthier Michael Bashkin builds his premium grade, custom, steel-string acoustics in Fort Collins, Colorado.

Basone Guitars

1999-present. Luthier Chris Basaraba builds his custom, professional grade, solid and hollowbody electric guitars and basses in Vancouver, British Columbia.

Bauer, George

1894-1911. Luthier George Bauer built guitars, mandolins, and banjos in Philadelphia, Pennsylvania. He also built instruments with Samuel S. Stewart (S.S. Stewart).

Baxendale

1974-present. Luthier Scott Baxendale builds his professional and premium grade, custom, steel-string acoustic and solidbody electric guitars in Athens, Georgia and previously in Colorado, Tennessee and Texas.

Bay State

Ca.1890-ca.1910. Bay State was a trademark for Boston's John C. Haynes & Co., and offered guitars and banjos.

Parlor

1890-1910. Small parlor size, mahogany body with salt & pepper binding.

1890-1910		$775	$1,000

Bazzolo Guitarworks

1983-present. Luthier Thomas Bazzolo began building his premium grade, production/custom, classical and flat-top guitars in Lebanon, Connecticut and since 2008 in Sullivan, Maine.

BC Kingston

1977-present. From 1977 to '96, luthier Brian Kingston built flat-top and semi-hollow acoustic guitars along with a few solidbodies. Presently he builds premium grade, production/custom, archtop jazz and semi-hollow guitars in Prince Edward Island, Canada.

Bear Creek Guitars

Luthier Bill Hardin worked for OMI Dobro and Santa Cruz Guitar before introducing his own line of professional and premium grade, custom-made Weissenborn-style guitars in 1995, made in Kula, Hawaii. He also builds ukes.

Beardsell Guitars

1996-present. Production/custom flat-tops, classical and electric solidbody guitars built by luthier Allan Beardsell in Toronto, Ontario.

Beaulieu

2006-present. Luthier Hugues Beaulieu builds his production/custom, professional and premium grade, flat-top, flamenco and classical guitars in Pont-Rouge, Quebec.

Beauregard

1992-present. Luthier Mario Beauregard builds his premium and presentation grade, production/custom, flat-top, archtop and jazz guitars in Montreal, Quebec.

Bedell Guitars

1964-present. Intermediate and premium grade, production/custom, flat-top guitars built in Spirit Lake, Iowa and imported from China, designed by luthier Tom Bedell, Dan Mills and Sophia Yang. They also offer Great Divide Guitars and in 2010 acquired Breedlove.

Behringer

1989-present. The German professional audio products company added budget, production, solidbody guitars in '03, sold in amp/guitar packages. They also offer effects and amps.

Beltona

1990-present. Production/custom metal body resonator guitars made in New Zealand by Steve Evans and Bill Johnson. Beltona was originally located in England. They also build mandolins and ukes.

Beltone

1920s-1930s. Acoustic and resonator guitars made by others for New York City distributor Perlberg & Halpin. Martin did make a small number of instruments for Beltone, but most were student-grade models most likely made by one of the big Chicago builders. They also made mandolins.

Archtop

1920s-30s		$425	$550

Resonator Copy

1930s. Resonator copy but without a real resonator, rather just an aluminum plate on a wooden top, body mahogany plywood.

1938		$575	$750

Beltone (Import)

1950s-1960s. Japan's Teisco made a variety of brands for others, including the Beltone line of guitars, basses and amps. Carvin sold some of these models in the late 1960s. Italy's Welson guitars also marketed marble and glitter-finished guitars in the U.S. under this brand.

Electric Solidbody

1960s. Japan, 4 pickups.

1960s		$350	$450

MODEL		EXC. COND.	
YEAR	FEATURES	LOW	HIGH

MODEL		EXC. COND.	
YEAR	FEATURES	LOW	HIGH

Benedetto

1968-present. Premium and presentation grade, production/custom archtop and chambered solid-body guitars, built by luthier Robert Benedetto. He has also built a few violins and solidbodies. He was located in East Stroudsburg, Pennsylvania, up to '99; in Riverview, Florida, for '00-'06; and in Savanah, Georgia, since '07. He is especially known for refining the 7-string guitar. From '99 to '06 he licensed the names of his standard models to Fender (see Benedetto FMIC); during that period, Benedetto only made special order instruments. In '06, Howard Paul joined Benedetto as President of the company to begin manufacturing a broader line of more affordable professional instruments.

Benedetto (FMIC)

1999-2006. Premium and presentation, production/custom, acoustic and electric archtops. From '99 to '06, Bob Benedetto had an agreement with Fender (FMIC) to build Benedetto guitars under his guidance and supervision. The guitars were originally built in the FMIC Guild Custom Shop in Nashville, and later in Fender's Corona, California, facility.

Benedict

1988-present. Founded by Roger Benedict. Professional and premium grade, production/custom, solid and semi-hollow body guitars and basses built by luthier Bill Hager in Cedar, Minnesota.

Beneteau

1974-present. Custom, premium grade, classical, baritone and steel string acoustic guitars built first in Ottawa, Ontario, and since 1986 in St. Thomas, Ontario by luthier Marc Beneteau. He also builds ukuleles.

Bennett Music Labs

1998-present. Custom guitars built by luthier Bruce Bennett, who helped design the first Warrior line of instruments with J.D. Lewis. He also built amps and Brown Sound effects and also guitars for J. Backlund Designs.

Bently

Ca.1985-1998. Student and intermediate grade copy style acoustic and electric guitars imported by St. Louis Music Supply. Includes the Series 10 electrics and the Songwriter acoustics (which have a double reversed B crown logo on the headstock). St. Louis Music replaced the Bently line with the Austin brand.

Berkowitz Guitars

1995-present. Luthier David D. Berkowitz builds his premium grade, custom/production, steel string and baritone guitars and basses in Washington, D.C.

Bernie Rico Jr. Guitars

Professional and premium grade, production/custom, solidbody electrics guitars and basses built by luther Bernie Rico, Jr., the son of B.C. Rich founder, in Hesperia, California.

Bertoncini Stringed Instruments

Luthier Dave Bertoncini began building in 1995, premium grade, custom, flat-top guitars, in Olympia, Washington. He has also built solidbody electrics, archtops, mandolins and ukuleles.

Beyond The Trees

1976-present. Luthier Fred Carlson offers a variety of innovative designs for his professional and presentation grade, production/custom 6- and 12-string flat-tops in Santa Cruz, California. He also produces the Sympitar (a 6-string with added sympathetic strings) and the Dreadnautilus (a unique shaped headless acoustic).

Big Lou Guitar

Mid-2010-present. Located in Perris, California, owner Louis Carroll imports his intermediate grade, production, electric guitars from China.

Big Tex Guitars

Production/custom, professional grade, vintage-style replica guitars, started in 2000, built for owner Eric Danheim, by luthiers James Love, Mike Simon and Eddie Dale in Houston and Dripping Springs, Texas and Seattle, Washington.

Bigsby

1947-1965, 2002-present. Pedal steel guitars, hollow-chambered electric Spanish guitars, electric mandolins, doublenecks, replacement necks on acoustic guitars, hand vibratos, all handmade by Paul Arthur Bigsby, machinist and motorcycle enthusiast (designer of '30s Crocker motorcycles), in Downey, California. Initially built for special orders.

Bigsby was a pioneer in developing pedal steels. He designed a hand vibrato for Merle Travis. In '48, his neck-through hollow electrics (with Merle Travis) influenced Leo Fender, and Bigsby employed young Semie Moseley. In '56, he designed the Magnatone Mark series guitars and 1 Hawaiian lap steel. He built guitars up to '63.

He built less than 50 Spanish guitars, 6 mandolins, 70 to 150 pedal steels and 12 or so neck replacements. SN was stamped on the end of fingerboard: MMDDYY. In '65, the company was sold to Gibson president Ted McCarty who moved the tremolo/vibrato work to Kalamazoo. Bigsby died in '68. Fred Gretsch purchased the Bigsby company from Ted McCarty in '99 and sold it to Fender in 2019. A solidbody guitar and a pedal steel based upon the original Paul Bigsby designs were introduced January, 2002. These were modeled on the 1963

Benedetto Benny
Imaged by Heritage Auctions, HA.com

1949 Bigsby
Imaged by Heritage Auctions, HA.com

Bischoff nine-string

Blade Texas Deluxe

MODEL YEAR	FEATURES	EXC. COND. LOW	HIGH

Bigsby catalog but look very similar to ttypical Bigsby solidbodys made in the early '50s. Early Bigsby guitars command high value on the collectible market and values here assumes authentication by an industry expert.

Standard (Japan)
2007-2008. Various models made in Japan.

2007	Model BY-48N	$1,200	$1,600
2007	Model BY-50	$1,200	$1,600
2007	Model BYS-48	$1,200	$1,600

Standard Solidbody (Spanish)
Late-1940s-1950s, 2002. Standard Guitar, solidbody, natural. Reissue offered in '02.

1948		$268,000	$350,000
1949		$260,000	$340,000
1950-1956		$230,000	$300,000
2002	Reissue	$3,500	$4,500

Bil Mitchell Guitars
1979-present. Luthier Bil Mitchell builds his professional and premium grade, production/custom, flat-top and archtop guitars originally in Wall, New Jersey, and since '02 in Riegelsville, Pennsylvania.

Bill Foley Fine Instruments
2012-present. Luthiers Bill Foley, his son Sam, and Brad Lewis build professional and premium grade, custom electric guitars and basses in Columbus, Ohio.

Bilt Guitars
2010-present. Professional grade, production/custom, solidbody and semi-hollowbody electric guitars built in Des Moines, Iowa by luthiers Bill Henss and Tim Thelen.

Birdsong Guitars
2001-present. Luthiers Scott Beckwith and Jamie Hornbuckle build their professional grade, production/custom, solidbody guitars and basses in Wimberley, Texas.

Bischoff Guitars
1975-present. Professional and premium-grade, custom-made flat-tops built by luthier Gordy Bischoff in Eau Claire, Wisconsin.

Bishline
1985-present. Luthier Robert Bishline, of Tulsa, Oklahoma, mainly builds banjos, but did build flat-tops and resonators in the past, and still does occasionally.

Black Jack
1960s. Violin-body hollowbody electric guitars and basses, possibly others. Imported from Japan by unidentified distributor. Manufacturers unknown, but some may be Arai.

MODEL YEAR	FEATURES	EXC. COND. LOW	HIGH

Blackbird
2006-present. Luthier Joe Luttwak builds his professional grade, production/custom, carbon fiber acoustic guitars in San Francisco, California. He also offers a uke.

Blackshear, Tom
1958-present. Premium and presentation grade, production, classical and flamenco guitars made by luthier Tom Blackshear in San Antonio, Texas.

Blade
1987-present. Intermediate and professional grade, production, solidbody guitars and basses from luthier Gary Levinson and his Levinson Music Products Ltd. located in Switzerland.

California Custom
1994-2010. California Standard with maple top and high-end appointments.

1994-2010		$850	$1,100

California Deluxe/Deluxe
1994-1995. Standard with mahogany body and maple top.

1994-1995		$575	$750

California Hybrid
1998-1999. Standard with piezo bridge pickup.

1998-1999		$525	$675

California Standard
1994-2007. Offset double-cut, swamp ash body, bolt neck, 5-way switch.

1994-2007		$375	$500

R3
1988-1993. Offset double-cut maple solidbody, bolt maple neck, 3 single-coils or single/single/humbucker.

1988-1993		$575	$750

R4
1988-1993. R3 with ash body and see-thru color finishes.

1988-1992		$575	$750

Texas Series
2003-present. Includes Standard (3 single-coils) and Deluxe (gold hardware, single/single/hum pickups).

2003-2010	Deluxe	$450	$575
2003-2010	Special	$425	$550
2003-2021	Standard	$425	$550

Blanchard Guitars
1994-present. Luthier Mark Blanchard builds premium grade, custom steel-string and classical guitars originally in Mammoth Lakes, California, and since May '03, in northwest Montana.

Blindworm Guitars
2008-present. Luthiers Andrew J. Scott and Steven Sells build premium and presentation grade, production/custom, acoustic, electric and electric-acoustic guitars, basses, mandolins, banjos and others in Colorado Springs, Colorado.

MODEL		EXC. COND.	
YEAR	FEATURES	LOW	HIGH

Blount

Professional and premium grade, production/custom, acoustic flat-top guitars built by luthier Kenneth H. Blount Jr. in Sebring, Florida. He started in 1985.

Blue Star

1984-present. Luthier Bruce Herron builds his production/custom guitars in Fennville, Michigan. He also builds mandolins, lap steels, dulcimers and ukes.

Bluebird

1920s-1930s. Private brand with Bluebird painted on headstock, built by the Oscar Schmidt Co. and possibly others. Most likely made for distributor.

13" Flat-Top

1930s		$150	$200

Bluebird Guitars

2011-present. Luthiers Rob Bluebird and Gian Maria Camponeschi build premium grade, custom, archtop and solidbody guitars in Rome, Italy. They build production resonator guitars in Bali, Indonesia. They also offer basses and ukuleles.

Blueridge

Early 1980s-present. Intermediate and professional grade, production, solid-top acoustic guitars distributed by Saga. In '00, the product line was redesigned with the input of luthier Greg Rich (Rich and Taylor guitars).

Bluesouth

1991-ca. 2006. Custom electric guitars built by luthier Ronnie Knight in Muscle Shoals, Alabama. He also built basses.

Boaz Elkayam Guitars

Presentation grade, custom steel, nylon, and flamenco guitars made by luthier Boaz Elkayam, starting in 1985, in Chatsworth, California.

Boedigheimer Instruments

2000-present. Luthier Brian Boedigheimer builds his professional and premium grade, production/custom, semi-hollowbody electric guitars in Red Wing, Minnesota.

Bohmann

1878-ca. 1926. Acoustic flat-top guitars, harp guitars, mandolins, banjos, violins made in Chicago Illinois, by Joseph Bohmann (born 1848, in Czechoslovakia). Bohmann's American Musical Industry founded 1878. Guitar body widths are 12", 13", 14", 15". He had 13 grades of guitars by 1900 (Standard, Concert, Grand Concert sizes). Early American use of plywood. Some painted wood finishes. Special amber-oil varnishes. Tuner bushings. Early ovalled fingerboards. Patented tuner plates and bridge design. Steel engraved label inside. Probably suc-

ceeded by son Joseph Frederick Bohmann.

Ca. 1896 12" body faux rosewood, 13", 14" and 15" body faux rosewood birch, 12", 13", 14" and 15" body sunburst maple, 12", 13", 14" and 15" body rosewood. By 1900 Styles 0, 1, 2 and 3 Standard, Concert and Grand Concert maple, Styles 1, 2, 3, 4, 5, 6, 7, 8, 9, 10, 11 and 12 in Standard, Concert, and Grand Concert rosewood.

14 3/4" Flat-Top

Solid spruce top, veneered Brazilian rosewood back and sides, wood marquetry around top and soundhole, natural. Each Bohmann should be valued on a case-by-case basis.

1896-1900	Brazilian	$1,150	$1,500
1896-1900	Other woods	$550	$725

Harp Guitar

1896-1899	All styles	$3,200	$4,200

Bolin

1978-present. Professional and premium grade, production/custom, solidbody guitars and basses built by luthier John Bolin in Boise, Idaho. Bolin is well-known for his custom work. His Cobra guitars are promoted and distributed by Sanderson Sales and Marketing as part of the Icons of America Series.

NS

1996-2011. Slot-headstock, bolt-on neck, single-cut solidbody, Seymour Duncan passive pickups or EMG active, from '96 to the fall of 2001 custom-built serial numbers to 0050 then from the fall of '01 to the present production model build starting with SN 0051.

1996-2001	Custom-built	$2,300	$3,000
2001-2011	Standard production	$850	$1,100

Bolt

1988-1991. Founded by luthier Wayne Bolt and Jim Dala Pallu in Schnecksville, Pennsylvania, Bolt's first work was CNC machined OEM necks and bodies made for Kramer and BC Rich. In '90, they started building solidbody Bolt guitars, many with airbrushed graphics. Only about 100 to 125 were built, around 40 with graphics.

Bond

1984-1985. Andrew Bond made around 1,400 Electraglide guitars in Scotland. Logo says 'Bond Guitars, London'.

ElectraGlide

1984-1985. Black carbon graphite 1-piece body and neck, double-cut, 3 single-coils (2 humbuckers were also supposedly available), digital LED controls that required a separate transformer.

1984-1985	With attachments	$1,400	$1,800

Borges Guitars

2000-present. Luthier Julius Borges builds his premium grade, production/custom, acoustic guitars in Groton, Massachusetts.

Blindworm The Mighty Kraken

Blueridge BG-1500E

Boulder Creek Grand Auditorium

Bourgeois Country Boy

MODEL YEAR	FEATURES	EXC. COND. LOW	HIGH

Boucher

2005-present. Professional and premium grade, acoustic guitars built by luthier Robin Boucher in Quebec.

Boulder Creek Guitars

2007-present. Intermediate and professional grade, production, imported dreadnought, classical, and 12-string guitars, basses and ukes distributed by Morgan Hill Music of Morgan Hill, California.

Bourgeois

1993-1999, 2000-present. Luthier Dana Bourgeois builds his professional and premium grade, production/custom, acoustic and archtop guitars in Lewiston, Maine. Bourgeois co-founded Schoenberg guitars and built Schoenberg models from '86-'90. Bourgeois' 20th Anniversary model was issued in '97. Bourgeois Guitars, per se, went out of business at the end of '99. Patrick Theimer created Pantheon Guitars, which included 7 luthiers (including Bourgeois) working in an old 1840s textile mill in Lewiston, Maine and Bourgeois models continue to be made as part of the Pantheon organization.

A-500
Top-of-the-line acoustic cutaway archtop, natural.

1997		$4,600	$6,000

Blues
1996. D-style, all koa.

1996		$2,900	$3,800

Country Boy
1998-present. Pre-war D-style designed for Ricky Skaggs, Sitka spruce top, mahogany back and sides, Ricky Skaggs label, natural.

1998-2021		$2,700	$3,500

Country Boy Custom
1999-2016. Adirondack spruce top, figured mahogany back and sides.

1999-2016		$2,900	$3,800

Country Boy Deluxe
2003-2015. Country Boy with Adirondack spruce top, rosewood binding.

2003-2015		$2,900	$3,800

D - 20th Anniversary
1997. 20 made, bearclaw spruce top, rosewood back and sides, mother-of-pearl 'board, ornate abalone floral pattern inlay, abalone rosette and border, natural.

1997		$2,900	$3,800

D-150/Style 150/"One-Fifty"
2002-present. Brazilian rosewood, premium Adirondack, abalone rosette. Called Style 150 in '20, then "One-Fifty" in '22.

2002-2021		$5,400	$7,000

DBJC
Jumbo cutaway, Indian rosewood back and sides, redwood top, gloss finish.

2007		$3,200	$4,200

Georgia Dreadnought
2003. Mahogany, Adirondack.

2003		$2,200	$2,900

MODEL YEAR	FEATURES	EXC. COND. LOW	HIGH

JOM
1993-2015. Jumbo Orchestra Model flat-top, 15 5/8". Model includes one with cedar top, mahogany back and sides, and one with spruce top, Brazilian rosewood back and sides.

1993	Brazilian rosewood	$5,400	$7,000
1993	Mahogany	$2,500	$3,300
1993-2015	Indian rosewood	$2,500	$3,300

JOMC/OMC
1995-2015. Jumbo Orchestra cutaway, figured mahogany (OMC) and Indian rosewood (JOMC).

1995-2011	OMC, mahogany	$3,600	$4,700
1995-2015	JOMC200, Indian rw	$3,100	$4,000

JR-A
1990s. Artisan Series, 15 5/8", spruce top, rosewood back and sides.

1990s		$1,275	$1,650

LC4 Archtop Limited Edition
2002. Limited edition of 12, signed and numbered, premium sitka and carved curly maple.

2002		$10,800	$14,000

Martin Simpson
1997-2003. Grand auditorium with unusual cutaway that removes one-half of the upper treble bout, Englemann spruce top, Indian rosewood back and sides, natural.

1997-2003		$2,400	$3,200

OM
1993-1999. Standard size OM, spruce top, rosewood back and sides.

1993-1999		$3,200	$4,200

OM Deluxe Artisan
2002. Indian rosewood, sitka.

2002		$2,100	$2,800

OM Soloist
1990s-present. Full-sized, soft cutaway flat-top, Adirondack spruce top, figured Brick Red Brazilian rosewood back and sides, natural. Named just Soloist in '22.

1990-2021		$5,400	$7,000

Ricky Skaggs Signature
1998. D-style, rosewood sides and back, spruce top.

1998		$2,900	$3,800

Slope D
1993-2021. D-size, 16", spruce top, mahogany back and sides.

1993-2021		$3,600	$4,800

Vintage D
2000-present. Adirondack spruce (Eastern red spruce) top, optional rosewood back and sides. D dropped from name in '22.

2000-2021	Indian rosewood	$2,300	$3,000
2000s	Brazilian rosewood	$5,400	$7,000

Vintage OM
2005. Madagascar rosewood and Italian spruce top.

2005		$3,300	$4,300

Bown Guitars

Luthier Ralph Bown builds custom steel-string, nylon-string, baritone, and harp guitars, starting 1981, in Walmgate, U.K.

MODEL YEAR	FEATURES	EXC. COND. LOW	HIGH

Bozo

1964-present. Bozo (pronounced Bo-zho) Podunavac learned instrument building in his Yugoslavian homeland and arrived in the United States in '59. In '64 he opened his own shop and has built a variety of high-end, handmade, acoustic instruments, many being one-of-a-kind. He has built around 570 guitars over the years. There were several thousand Japanese-made (K. Yairi shop) Bell Western models bearing his name made from '79-'80; most of these were sold in Europe. He currently builds premium and presentation grade, custom guitars in Port Charlotte, Florida.

Acoustic

1970s-1980s. US-made, 6- and 12-string, appointments vary.

1970s-80s	Various models	$2,000	$10,000

Bradford

Mid-1960s. Brand name used by the W.T. Grant Company, one of the old Five & Ten style retail stores similar to F.W. Woolworth and Kresge. Many of these guitars and basses were made in Japan by Guyatone.

Acoustic Flat-Top

1960s		$200	$300

Electric Solidbody

1960s	1 or 2 pickups	$200	$300
1960s	3 pickups	$300	$400
1960s	4 pickups	$350	$450

Bradley

1970s. Budget Japanese copy models imported by Veneman's Music Emporium.

Brawley Basses

Headquartered in Temecula, California, and designed by Keith Brawley, offering solidbody guitars and basses made in Korea.

Brazen

Starting in 2005, owner Steve Tsai, along with luthier Eddie Estrada, offered professional and premium grade, production, electric guitars. Steve also imports a line of intermediate grade guitars from China which are set up in the U.S.

Breedlove

1990-present. Founded by Larry Breedlove and Steve Henderson. Intermediate, professional, premium, and presentation grade, production/custom, steel and nylon string flat-top built in Bend, Oregon and imported. They also build mandolins, basses, lapsteels and ukes. Several available custom options may add to the values listed here. They offered chambered electric guitars starting in 2008 but in January 2010, Breedlove discontinued all electric guitar production. Also in '10, they became part of Two Old Hippies.

Brentwood

1970s. Student models built by Kay for store or jobber.

K-100

1970s. 13" student flat-top, K-100 label inside back, K logo on 'guard.

1970s		$50	$100

Brian May Guitar Company

2006-present. Guitarist Brian May teamed up with Barry Moorhouse and Pete Malandrone to offer versions of his Red Special Guitar. They also offered a bass.

Brian May Special

2006-present. Mahogany solidbody, 3 pickups, various colors

2006-2021		$450	$600

Brian Moore

1992-present. Founded by Patrick Cummings, Brian Moore and Kevin Kalagher in Brewster, New York; they introduced their first guitars in '94. Initially expensive custom shop guitars with carbon-resin bodies with highly figured wood tops; later went to all wood bodies cut on CNC machines. The intermediate and professional grade, production, iGuitar/i2000series was introduced in 2000 and made in Korea, but set up in the U.S. Currently the premium grade, production/custom, Custom Shop Series guitars are handcrafted in La Grange, New York. They also build basses and electric mandolins.

C/DC/MC Series

1994-2011. Various models.

1994-2011		$1,300	$1,700

iGuitar Series

2000-present. Various models.

2000-2021		$750	$1,000

Brian Stone Classical Guitars

Luthier Brian Stone builds his classical guitars in Corvallis, Oregon.

Briggs

1999-present. Luthier Jack Briggs builds his professional and premium grade, production/custom, chambered and solidbody guitars in Raleigh, North Carolina.

Broman

1930s. The Broman brand was most likely used by a music studio (or distributor) on instruments made by others, including Regal-built resonator instruments.

Bronson

Ca. 1934-early 1960s. George Bronson was a steel guitar instructor in the Detroit area and his instruments were made by other companies. They were mainly lap steels (usually sold with a matching amp), but some other types were also offered.

Honolulu Master Hawaiian

1938		$3,600	$4,700

Student Hawaiian (Acoustic)

1930s	13" flat-top	$200	$300

2015 Bourgeois JOM
Imaged by Heritage Auctions, HA.com

1999 Brian Moore C90
Imaged by Heritage Auctions, HA.com

R. E. Bruné 30-S

Burns Brian May Red Special
Imaged by Heritage Auctions, HA.com

Brook Guitars

1993-present. Simon Smidmore and Andy Petherick build their production/custom Brook steel-string, nylon-strings, and archtops in Dartmoor, U.K.

Brown's Guitar Factory

1982-present. Luthier John Brown builds professional and premium grade, production/custom, solidbody guitars, basses and lap steels in Inver Grove Heights, Minnesota.

Bruné, R. E.

1966-present. Luthier Richard Bruné builds his premium and presentation grade, custom, classical and flamenco guitars in Evanston, Illinois. He also offers his professional and premium grade Model 20 and Model 30, which are handmade in Japan.

Bruno and Sons

Distributor Bruno and Sons marketed a variety of brands, including their own. Later became part of Kaman Music.

Harp Guitar

MODEL YEAR	FEATURES	EXC. COND. LOW	HIGH
1924		$2,150	$2,800

Hollowbody Electric

1960s-1970s. Various imported models.

1960s		$150	$300

Parlor Guitar

1880-1920. Various woods used on back and sides.

1880-1920	Birch	$500	$650
1880-1920	Brazilian rosewood	$1,025	$1,325
1880-1920	Mahogany	$525	$700

Buddy Blaze

1985-present. Professional and premium grade, custom/production, solidbody electric guitars built by luthier Buddy Blaze from '85 to '87 in Arlington, Texas, and presently in Kailua Kona, Hawaii. He also designs intermediate grade models which are imported.

Bunker

1961-present. Founder Dave Bunker built custom guitars and basses while performing in Las Vegas in the '60s and developed a number of innovations. Around '92 Bunker began PBC Guitar Technology with John Pearse and Paul Chernay in Coopersburg, Pennsylvania, building instruments under the PBC brand and, from '94-'96, for Ibanez' USA Custom Series. PBC closed in '97 and Bunker moved back to Washington State to start Bunker Guitar Technology and resumed production of several Bunker models. In early 2002, Bunker Guitars became part of Maple Valley Tone Woods of Port Angeles, Washington. Currently Bunker offers intermediate, professional, and premium grade, production/custom, guitars and basses built in Port Angeles. Most early Bunker guitars were pretty much custom-made in low quantities.

Burke

Ca. 1960-ca. 1966. 6- and 12- string electric guitars built by Glen Burke's Tuning Fork Guitar Company in Eugene and Grants Pass, Oregon and mostly sold in kit form. The guitars featured an aluminum neck-thru design with the body portion of the neck shaped being a rectangular box where the body wings are attached. Being kit guitars finishes, pickups, options and build quality will vary.

Burlesk Guitars

1994-present. Professional and premium grade, custom, solidbody electric guitars and basses, built by luthier James Burley in Alberta, Canada.

Burly Guitars

Luthier Jeff Ayers, starting in 2007, builds professional and premium grade, custom, solid and semi-hollowbody guitars, in Land O' Lakes, Wisconsin.

Burns

1960-1970, 1974-1983, 1992-present. Intermediate and professional grade, production, electric guitars built in the U.K. and Asia. They also build basses. Jim Burns began building guitars in the late-'50s and established Burns London Ltd in '60. Baldwin Organ (see Baldwin listing) purchased the company in '65 and offered the instruments until '70. The Burns name was revived in '91 by Barry Gibson as Burns London, with Jim Burns' involvement, offering reproductions of some of the classic Burns models of the '60s. Jim Burns passed away in August '98. In 2020, it was announced new instruments coming in '21.

Baby Bison

1965. Double-cut solidbody, scroll headstock, 2 pickups, shorter scale, tremolo.

1965		$800	$1,050

Bison

1964-1965, 2003-2020. Double-cut solidbody, 3 pickups, tremolo, black or white, scroll-headstock, replaced flat headstock Black Bison. Has been reissued with both types of headstocks.

1961-1962	Black, 4 pus, flat hs	$1,950	$2,550
1962-1965	Black, 3 pus, scroll hs	$1,750	$2,300
1962-1965	White, 3 pus, scroll hs	$1,750	$2,300
2003-2020	Reissue	$525	$700

Brian May Signature - Red Special

2001-2006. Replica of May's original 'Red Special' but with added whammy-bar, red finish. Korean-made.

2001-2006		$750	$1,000

Cobra

2004-2020. Double-cut solid, 2 pickups.

2004-2020		$135	$180

Double Six

1964-1965, 2003-2020. Solidbody 12-string, double-cut, 3 pickups, greenburst. Reissue made in Korea.

1964-1965		$1,650	$2,200
2003-2020		$260	$350

MODEL YEAR	FEATURES	EXC. COND. LOW	HIGH

Flyte

1974-1977. Fighter jet-shaped solidbody, pointed headstock, 2 humbucking pickups, silver, has been reissued.

| 1974-1977 | | $775 | $1,025 |

GB66 Deluxe

1965. Like 66 Standard, but with bar pickups and add Density control.

| 1965 | | $925 | $1,225 |

GB66 Deluxe Standard

1965. Offset double-cut, f-holes, 2 Ultra-Sonic pickups.

| 1965 | | $850 | $1,125 |

Jazz

1962-1965. Offset double-cut solid, shorter scale, 2 pickups.

| 1962-1965 | | $1,075 | $1,400 |

Jazz Split Sound

1962-1965. Offset double-cut solid, 3 pickups, tremolo, red sunburst.

| 1962-1965 | | $1,325 | $1,750 |

Marquee

2000-2020. Offset double-cut solid, 3 pickups, scroll headstock

| 2000-2020 | | $260 | $350 |

Marvin

1964-1965. Hank Marvin, offset double-cut solidbody, scroll headstock, 3 pickups, tremolo, white.

| 1964-1965 | | $1,800 | $2,375 |

Nu-Sonic

1964-1965. Solidbody, 2 pickups, tremolo, white or cherry, has been reissued.

| 1964-1965 | | $925 | $1,225 |

Sonic

1960-1964. Double shallow cut solid, 2 pickups, cherry.

| 1960-1964 | | $775 | $1,025 |

Split Sonic

1962-1964. Solidbody, 3 pickups, bound neck, tremolo, red sunburst.

| 1962-1964 | | $1,100 | $1,450 |

Steer

2000-2020. Semi-hollowbody, sound-hole, 2 pickups, non-cut and single-cut versions.

| 2000-2020 | | $385 | $500 |

TR-2

1963-1964. Semi-hollow, 2 pickups, red sunburst.

| 1963-1964 | | $1,000 | $1,300 |

Vibra Artist

1960-1962. Double-cut, mahogany, 3 pickups, 6 knobs.

| 1960-1962 | | $850 | $1,125 |

Vibraslim

1964-1965. Double-cut, f-holes, 2 pickups, red sunburst.

| 1964-1965 | | $1,000 | $1,300 |

Virginian

1964-1965. Burns of London model, later offered as Baldwin Virginian in '65.

| 1964-1965 | | $1,275 | $1,675 |

Vista Sonic

1962-1964. Offset double-cut solid, 3 pickups, red sunburst.

| 1962-1964 | | $850 | $1,125 |

Burnside

1987-1988. Budget solidbody guitars imported by Guild.

Solidbody Electric/Blade

1987-1988. Solidbody, fat pointy headstock.

| 1987-1988 | | $185 | $250 |

Burns-Weill

1959. Jim Burns and Henry Weill teamed up to produce three solidbody electric and three solidbody bass models under this English brand. Models included the lower end Fenton, a small single-cutaway, 2 pickups and an elongated headstock and the bizarrely styled RP2G. Henry Weill continued to produce a slightly different RP line under the re-named Fenton-Weill brand.

Burny

1980s-1990s. Solidbody electric guitars from Fernandes and built in Japan, Korea or China.

Burrell

1984-2010. Luthier Leo Burrell built his professional grade, production/custom, acoustic, semi-hollow, and solidbody guitars and basses in Huntington, West Virginia. Leo retired in '10.

Burton Guitars

1980-present. Custom classical guitars built by luthier Cynthia Burton in Portland, Oregon.

Buscarino Guitars

1981-present. Luthier John Buscarino builds his premium and presentation grade, custom archtops and steel-string and nylon-string flat-tops in Franklin, North Carolina.

Byers, Gregory

1984-present. Premium grade, custom classical and Flamenco guitars built by luthier Gregory Byers in Willits, California.

Byrd

1998-present. Custom/production, professional and premium grade, V-shaped electric guitars, built by luthiers James Byrd and Joe Riggio, in Seattle and several other cities in the state of Washington.

C. Fox

1997-2002. Luthier Charles Fox built his premium grade, production/custom flat-tops in Healdsburg, California. In '02 he closed C. Fox Guitars and moved to Portland, Oregon to build Charles Fox Guitars.

1965 Burns GB66 Deluxe
Peter Hvidegaard

1963 Burns Sonic
Imaged by Heritage Auctions, HA.com

Carvin Allan Holdsworth
Robbie Keene

Casio DG-20

MODEL		EXC. COND.	
YEAR	FEATURES	LOW	HIGH

C.F. Mountain

1970s-early 1980s. Japanese copy acoustics made by Hayashi Musical Instrument Ltd with headstock logo that looks very much like that of a certain classic American guitar company.

Acoustic

1970s-80s		$75	$100

CA (Composite Acoustics)

1999-2010, 2011-present. Professional grade, production, carbon fiber composite guitars that were built in Lafayette, Louisiana. The company ceased production in February, '10. At the end of '10 CA was acquired by Peavey, which launched the new Meridian, Mississippi-based line in January, '11.

Califone

1966. Six and 12-string guitars and basses made by Murphy Music Industries (maker of the Murph guitars) for Rheem Califone-Roberts which manufactured tape recorders and related gear. Very few made.

Callaham

1989-present. Professional, production/custom, solidbody electric guitars built by luthier Bill Callaham in Winchester, Virginia. They also make tube amp heads.

Camelli

1960s. Line of solidbody electric guitars imported from Italy.

Solidbody Electric

1960s		$600	$800

Cameo

1960s-1970s. Japanese- and Korean-made electric and acoustic guitars. They also offered basses.

Electric

1960s-70s	Various models	$325	$450

Campbell American Guitars

2005-2015. Luthier Dean Campbell built his intermediate and professional grade, production/custom, solidbody guitars originally in Pawtucket, Rhode Island, then in Westwood, Massachusetts. From '02 to '05, he built guitars under the Greene & Campbell brand.

Campellone

1978-present. Luthier Mark Campellone builds his premium grade, custom archtops in Greenville, Rhode Island. He also made electrics and basses in the '70s and '80s, switching to archtops around '90.

Deluxe

1990-present. 16" to 18" archtop, middle of the company product line, blond or sunburst.

1990-2021		$4,400	$5,700

Special

1994-present. 16" to 18" archtop, top of the company product line, carved spruce top, carved flamed maple back, flamed maple sides, blond or sunburst.

1994-2021		$4,800	$6,200

MODEL		EXC. COND.	
YEAR	FEATURES	LOW	HIGH

Standard

2000-present. 16" to 18" archtop, lower of the 3 model lines offered.

2000-2021		$3,300	$4,300

Canvas

2004-2012. Budget and intermediate grade, production, acoustic and electric guitars and basses imported from China by America Sejung Corp. until '11, then in South Korea.

Carbonaro

Luthier Robert Carbonaro began building in 1975, premium grade, production/custom, archtop and flat-top guitars in Santa Fe, New Mexico. Relocated his shop to Mexico in 2016, then Vietnam in '19.

Carl Fischer

1920s. Most likely a brand made for a distributor. Instruments built by the Oscar Schmidt Co. and possibly others.

Carlos

Ca.1976-late 1980s. Imported copies of classic American acoustics distributed by Coast Wholesale Music.

Acoustic Flat-Top

1976-1980s	Various models	$175	$250

Carson Robison

1933-1938. Wards sold guitars endorsed by popular country artist Carson Robison. Built by Gibson, the guitars were the same as models sold under the Kalamazoo brand.

Model K

1933-1938. Flat top, ladder, K #926 same as Kalamzoo KG-11, K #1281/#1115 same as Kalamzoo K-14. Becomes the Recording King (Ward's main brand) Model K in '38.

1933-1935	K#926	$1,300	$1,700
1936-1938	K#1281/1115	$2,000	$2,600

Carvin

1946-present. Intermediate and professional grade, production/custom, acoustic and electric guitars and basses built in San Diego, California. They also offer amps and mandolins. Founded in Los Angeles by Hawaiian guitarist and recording artist Lowell C. Kiesel as the L.C. Kiesel Co. making pickups for guitars. Bakelite Kiesel-brand electric Hawaiian lap steels are introduced in early-'47. Small tube amps introduced ca. '47. By late-'49, the Carvin brand is introduced, combining parts of names of sons Carson and Gavin. Carvin acoustic and electric Spanish archtops are introduced in '54. Instruments are sold by mail-order only. Kiesel brand name revived by Carvin in '15 for use on their guitars.

2,000-4,000 guitars made prior to '70 with no serial number. First serial number appeared in

MODEL		EXC. COND.	
YEAR	FEATURES	LOW	HIGH

'70, stamped on end of fingerboard, beginning with #5000. All are consecutive. Later SN on neck plates.

Approximate SN ranges include:
1970: First serial number #5000 to 10019 ('79).
'80-'83: 10768 to 15919.
'84-'87: 13666 to 25332.
'88-'90: 22731 to 25683.
'91-'94: 25359 to 42547.
'95-'99: 45879 to 81427.
'00-present: 56162 upward.

Acoustic-Electric AC/AE Series

1990s-2021	Various models	$400	$1,700

Solidbody B/C/D Series (Mid-Level)

1990s-2021	Various models	$400	$1,700

Solidbody Carved-Top (Higher-End)

2000s-2021	Various models	$900	$2,000

Casa Montalvo

1987-present. Intermediate and professional grade, production/custom flamenco and classical guitars made in Mexico for George Katechis of Berkeley Musical Instrument Exchange.

Casio

In 1987 Casio introduced a line of digital MIDI guitars imported from Japan, sporting plastic bodies and synthesizer features. They offered them for just a few years.

DG1
1980s. Squared plastic body.

1980s	$75	$110

DG10
1987-1989. Self-contained digital guitar.

1987-1989	$150	$200

DG20
1987-1989. Midi-capable digital guitar.

1987-1989	$225	$300

MG-500 Series MIDI Guitar
1987-1989. Cut-off teardrop (MG-500) or Strat-shaped (MG-510), basswood body, maple neck, rosewood 'board, 3 pickups.

1987-1989	500	$525	$700
1987-1989	510	$450	$600

PG-300
1988-1989. Similar to PG-380, but with less features.

1988-1989	$375	$500

PG-310
1988-1989. Similar to PG-380, but with less features.

1988-1989	$475	$625

PG-380
1988-1989. Guitar synth, double-cut, over 80 built-in sounds, midi controller capable.

1988-1989	$650	$850

Casper Guitar Technologies

Professional grade, production/custom, solidbody electric guitars and basses built by luthier Stephen Casper in Leisure City, Florida, starting in 2009.

Cat's Eyes

1980s. Made by Tokai, Cat's Eyes headstock logo, see Tokai guitar listings.

Champion

Ca. 1894-1897. Chicago's Robert Maurer built this brand of instruments before switching to the Maurer brand name around 1897.

Champlin Guitars

2006-present. Professional and premium grade, custom, flat-top and archtop guitars, and mandolinettos, built by Devin Champlin in Bellingham, Washington.

Chandler

Intermediate and professional grade, production/custom, solidbody electric guitars built by luthiers Paul and Adrian Chandler in Chico, California. They also build basses, lap steels and pickups. Chandler started making pickguards and accessories in the '70s, adding electric guitars, basses, and effects in '84.

555 Model
1992-2000s. Sharp double-cut, 3 mini-humbuckers, TV Yellow.

1992-2000s	$675	$875

Austin Special
1991-1999. Resembles futuristic Danelectro, lipstick pickups, available in 5-string version.

1991-1999	$575	$750

Austin Special Baritone
1994-1999. Nicknamed Elvis, gold metalflake finish, mother-of-toilet-seat binding, tremolo, baritone.

1994-1999	$575	$750

LectraSlide
2000s. Single-cut, Rezo 'guard, 2 pickups.

2000s	$625	$825

Metro
1995-2000. Double-cut slab body, P-90 in neck position and humbucker in the bridge position.

1995-2000	$575	$750

Telepathic
1994-2000. Classic single-cut style, 3 models; Basic, Standard, Deluxe.

1994-2000	Basic	$475	$625
1994-2000	Deluxe 1122 Model	$575	$750
1994-2000	Standard	$525	$700

Chantus

Premium grade, production/custom, classical and flamenco guitars built in Austin, Texas, by luthier William King starting in '84. He also builds ukes.

Chapin

Professional and premium grade, production/custom, semi-hollow, solidbody, and acoustic electric guitars built by luthiers Bill Chapin and Fred Campbell in San Jose, California.

Casper CGT-20 Classic

Chandler 555

Imaged by Heritage Auctions, HA.com

1990 Charvel 750XL Soloist
Imaged by Heritage Auctions, HA.com

EVH Art Series (by Charvel)

MODEL		EXC. COND.	
YEAR	FEATURES	LOW	HIGH

Chapman

1970-present. Made by Emmett Chapman, the Stick features 10 strings and is played by tapping both hands. The Grand Stick features 12 strings.

Stick

1970-present. Touch-tap hybrid electric instrument, 10 or 12 strings.

1970-2021	10- or 12-string	$2,000	$2,650

Char

1985-present. Premium grade, custom, classical and steel string acoustic guitars built in Portland, Oregon by luthier Kerry Char. He also builds harp-guitars and ukuleles.

Charis Acoustic

1996-present. Premium grade, custom/production, steel-string guitars built by luthier Bill Wise in Bay City, Michigan.

Charles Fox Guitars

1968-present. Luthier Charles Fox builds his premium and presentation grade, custom, steel and nylon string guitars in Portland, Oregon. He also produced GRD acoustic and electric guitars for '78-'82 and C. Fox acoustic guitars for '97-'02. He also operates The American School of Lutherie in Portland.

Charles Shifflett Acoustic Guitars

Premium grade, custom, classical, flamenco, resonator, and harp guitars, basses and banjos built by luthier Charles Shifflett, starting 1990, in High River, Alberta.

Charvel

1976 (1980)-present. Intermediate and professional grade, production, solidbody electric guitars. They also build basses. Founded by Wayne Charvel as Charvel Manufacturing in '76, making guitar parts in Asuza, California. Moved to San Dimas in '78. Also in '78 Grover Jackson bought out Charvel. In '79 or early '80 Charvel branded guitars are introduced. U.S.-made to '85, a combination of imports and U.S.-made post-'85. Charvel also manufactured the Jackson brand.

Charvel licensed its trademark to IMC (Hondo) in '85. IMC bought Charvel in '86 and moved the factory to Ontario, California. On October 25, 2002, Fender Musical Instruments Corp. (FMIC) took ownership of Jackson/Charvel Manufacturing Inc.

Pre-Pro (Pre-Production) Charvels began in November 1980 and ran until sometime in 1981. These are known as 'non-plated' indicating pre-production versus a production neck plate. Production serialized neck plates are considered to be San Dimas models which have a Charvel logo, serial number, and a PO Box San Dimas notation on the neck plate. These Serialized Plated Charvels came after Pre-Pros. Late '81 and '82 saw the early serialized

guitars with 21-fret necks; these are more valuable. During '82 the 22-fret neck was introduced. The so-called Soft Strat-, Tele-, Flying V-, and Explorer-style headstocks are associated with the early San Dimas Charvel models. In late '82 the pointy headstock, called the Jackson style, was introduced. In '82 the Superstrat style with a neck plate was introduced. Superstrats with a Kahler tailpiece have a lower value than the Pre-Pro models (with Fender-style trem tailpiece).

Collectors of vintage Charvels look for the vintage Charvel 3-on-a-side logo. This is a defining feature and a cutoff point for valuations. Bogus builders are replicating early Charvels and attempting to sell them as originals so fakes can be a problem for Charvel collectors, so buyer beware.

Other electric guitar manufacturing info:
1986-1989 Japanese-made Models 1 through 8
1989-1991 Japanese-made 550 XL, 650 XL/Custom, 750 XL (XL=neck-thru)
1989-1992 Japanese-made Models 275, 375, 475, 575
1990-1991 Korean-made Charvette models
1992-1994 Korean-made Models 325, 425

Early Charvel serial numbers (provided by former Jackson/Charvel associate Tim Wilson):
The first 500 to 750 guitars had no serial number, just marked "Made In U.S.A." on their neckplates. Five digit serial numbers were then used until November '81 when 4-digit number adopted, starting with #1001.
1981: 1001-1095
1982: 1096-1724
1983: 1725-2938
1984: 2939-4261
1985: 4262-5303
1986: 5304-5491

Pre-Pro

November 1980-1981. Pre-Pros came in different configurations of body styles, pickups, and finishes. There are five basic Pre-Pro formats: the Standard Body, the Bound Body, the Graphic Body, the Flamed Top, and the Matching Headstock. It is possible to have a combination, such as a Bound Body and Matching Headstock. Line items are based on body style and can feature any one of four neck/headstock-styles used: the so-called Tele-headstock, Strat-headstock, Flying V headstock, and Explorer headstock. Finishes included white, black, red, metallic Lake Placid Blue, and special graphics. All original parts adds considerable value and it is often difficult to determine what is original on these models, so expertise is required. An original Fender brass trem tailpiece, for example, adds considerable value. The Pre-Pro models were prone to modification such as added Kahler and Floyd Rose trems. Price ranges are wide because this is a relatively new market without mature pricing.

1980-1981	Bound body	$2,775	$3,600
1980-1981	Flamed top, stained	$3,225	$4,200
1980-1981	Graphic body	$3,700	$4,800
1980-1981	Matching headstock	$4,200	$5,400

MODEL YEAR	FEATURES	EXC. COND. LOW	HIGH
1980-1981	Standard body	$4,600	$6,000

275 Deluxe Dinky
1989-1991. Made in Japan, offset double-cut solidbody, 1 single-coil and 1 humbucker in '89, 2 humbuckers after, tremolo.

1989-1991		$390	$510

325SL
1992-1994. Dot inlays.

1992-1994		$460	$600

325SLX
1992-1994. Surfcaster-like thinline acoustic/electric, dual cutaways, f-hole, on-board chorus, shark inlays, made in Korea.

1992-1994		$460	$600

375 Deluxe
1989-1991. Maple or rosewood 'board, dot inlays, single-single-humbucker.

1989-1991		$690	$900

475 Deluxe/475 Special
1989-1991. Introduced as Special, changed to Deluxe in '90, bound rosewood board, shark tooth inlays, 2 oval stacked humbuckers and 1 bridge humbucker. Was also offered as Deluxe Exotic with figured top and back.

1989-1991		$690	$900

525
1989-1994. Acoustic-electric, single-cut.

1989-1994		$390	$510

550XL
1987-1989. Neck-thru (XL), dot markers, 1 single-coil and 1 bridge humbucker.

1987-1989		$800	$1,050

625-C12
1993-2000. Acoustic-electric cutaway 12-string, spruce top.

1993-2000		$390	$510

625F/625ACEL
1993-1995. Acoustic-electric cutaway, figured maple top.

1993-1995		$450	$575

650XL/Custom
1989-1990. Introduced as neck-thru XL and discontinued as Custom, shark fin markers, 2 stacked oval humbuckers and 1 bridge humbucker, custom version of 550XL.

1989-1990		$850	$1,100

750XL Soloist
1989-1990. Shark fin markers, cutaway body, 2 humbuckers, large Charvel logo.

1989-1990		$925	$1,200

Avenger
1990-1991. Randy Rhoads-style batwing-shaped solidbody, 1 humbucker, 1 single-coil, tremolo, made in Japan.

1990-1991		$475	$625

Charvette
1989-1991. Charvette Series made in Korea, superstrat-style, model number series 100 through 300.

1990-1991		$375	$500

CX Series
1991-1994. Imported solidbodies, body-mounted or pickguard mounted pickups, standard or deluxe tremolo.

1991-1994		$250	$325

EVH Art Series (by Charvel)
2004-2007. Offset double-cut solidbody, 1 humbucker, striped finish.

2004-2007	Black/white	$3,900	$5,100
2004-2007	Black/white on red	$4,100	$5,300
2004-2007	Black/yellow	$3,900	$5,100

Fusion Deluxe
1989-1991. Double-cut solidbody, tremolo, 1 humbucker and 1 single-coil, made in Japan.

1989-1991		$825	$1,075

Fusion Standard/AS FX 1
1993-1996. Double-cut solidbody, tremolo, 1 regular and 2 mini humbuckers, made in Japan, also named AS FX1.

1993-1996		$775	$1,025

Model 1/1A/1C
1986-1988. Offset double-cut solidbody, bolt-on maple neck, dot inlays, 1 humbucker, tremolo, made in Japan. Model 1A has 3 single-coils. Model 1C has 1 humbucker and 2 single-coils.

1986-1988		$775	$1,000

Model 2
1986-1988. As Model 1, but with rosewood 'board.

1986-1988		$775	$1,000

Model 3/3A/3DR/3L
1986-1989. As Model 2, but with 1 humbucker, 2 single coils. Model 3A has 2 humbuckers. Model 3DR has 1 humbucker and 1 single-coil.

1986-1989		$775	$1,000

Model 4/4A
1986-1988. As Model 2, but with 1 regular humbucker and 2 stacked humbuckers (no pickguard), active electronics, dots in '86, shark-fin inlays after. Model 4A has 2 regular humbuckers and dot markers.

1986-1988		$925	$1,200

Model 5/5A
1986-1988. As Model 4A, but neck-thru, with JE1000TG active elctronics. Model 5A is single humbucker and single knob version, limited production, made in Japan.

1986-1988		$925	$1,200

Model 6
1986-1988. As HSS Model 4, but with shark's tooth inlays, standard or various custom finishes.

1986-1988		$1,075	$1,400

Model 7
1988-1989. Single-cut solidbody, bound top, reversed headstock, 2 single-coils, made in Japan.

1988-1989		$1,075	$1,400

Model 88 LTD
1988. Double-cut solidbody, 1 slanted humbucker, shark fin inlay, 1000 built, made in Japan.

1988		$1,075	$1,400

Predator
1989-1991. Offset double-cut, bridge humbucker, single-coil neck, bolt-on.

1989-1991		$575	$750

1987 Charvel Model 1
Imaged by Heritage Auctions, HA.com

1986 Charvel Model 3
Imaged by Heritage Auctions, HA.com

Cimarron Model P

Citron CF1

MODEL YEAR	FEATURES	EXC. COND. LOW	HIGH

San Dimas Serialized Plated
1981-1986, 1995-1997. U.S.-made with San Dimas neck plate, bolt neck, rounded headstock early production, pointy headstock later, reissued in mid-'90s.

1981-1982	Soft headstock	$2,775	$3,600
1982-1986	Pointy headstock	$1,850	$2,400
1995-1997	Soft headstock	$775	$1,025

San Dimas LTD 25th Anniversary
2006. About 100 made, 25th Anniversary logo on neck plate with production number, highly figured top, high-end appointments.

2006		$1,450	$1,900

San Dimas Reissue (FMIC)
2004-present. USA Select series, alder body, bolt neck.

2004-2011	Custom Shop	$1,200	$1,575
2004-2021	Factory model	$875	$1,150

So-Cal Series
2008-2012. Offset double-cut solidbody.

2008-2012	Various options	$950	$1,250

ST Custom
1990-1991. Offset double-cut ash solidbody, 2 single-coils and 1 humbucker, rosewood 'board, tremolo, made in Japan.

1990-1991		$375	$500

ST Deluxe
1990-1991. Same as ST Custom but with maple 'board.

1990-1991		$375	$500

Standard
2002-2003. Typical offset double-cut Charvel body, 2 Seymour Duncan humbucker pickups, various opaque colors.

2002-2003		$375	$500

Star
1980-1981. The Star is considered by early-Charvel collectors to be Charvel's only original design with its unique four-point body.

1980-1981		$2,450	$3,200

Surfcaster
1991-1996. Offset double-cut, f-hole, various pickup options, bound body, tremolo, made in Japan.

1991-1996	1 single, 1 hum	$1,250	$1,625
1991-1996	2 singles, hardtail	$1,250	$1,625
1991-1996	2 singles, vibrato	$1,375	$1,775

Surfcaster 12
1991-1996. Made in Japan, 12-string version of Surfcaster, no tremolo.

1991-1996		$1,325	$1,725

Surfcaster Doubleneck
1992. Very limited production, 6/12 double neck, Charvel logo on both necks, black.

1992		$2,175	$2,825

Surfcaster HT (Model SC1)
1996-2000. Made in Japan. Hard Tail (HT) non-tremolo version of Surfcaster, has single-coil and bridge humbucker.

1996-2000		$1,250	$1,625

MODEL YEAR	FEATURES	EXC. COND. LOW	HIGH

Chiquita
1979-present. Intermediate grade, production guitars made by Erlewine Guitars in Austin, Texas (see that listing). There was also a mini amp available.

Travel Guitar
1979-present. Developed by Mark Erlewine and ZZ Top's Billy Gibbons, 27" overall length solidbody, 1 or 2 pickups, various colors.

1979-2021		$450	$600

Chris George
1966-present. Professional and premium grade, custom, archtop, acoustic, electric and resonator guitars built by luthier Chris George in Tattershall Lincolnshire, U.K.

Christopher Carrington
1988-present. Production/custom, premium grade, classical and flamenco acoustic guitars built by luthier Chris Carrington in Rockwall, Texas.

Chrysalis Guitars
1998-2015. Luthier Tim White built his premium grade, production/custom Chrysalis Guitar System, which included interchangeable components that can be quickly assembled into a full-size electric/acoustic guitar, in New Boston, New Hampshire. White introduced his new brand, Ridgewing, at January 2016 NAMM.

Cimar/Cimar by Ibanez
Early-1980s. Private brand of Hoshino Musical Instruments, Nagoya, Japan, who also branded Ibanez. Headstock with script Cimar logo or Cimar by Ibanez, copy models and Ibanez near-original models such as the star body.

Cimar

1982	Classical	$70	$100
1982	Double-cut solidbody	$225	$300
1982	Star body style	$225	$300

Cimarron
1978-present. Luthiers John Walsh and Clayton Walsh build their professional grade, production/custom, flat-top acoustic guitars in Ridgway, Colorado. Between '94 and '98 they also produced electric guitars.

Cipher
1960s. Solidbody electric guitars and basses imported from Japan by Inter-Mark. Generally strange-shaped bodies.

Electric Solidbody
1960s. For any student-grade import, a guitar with any missing part, such as a missing control knob or trem arm, is worth much less.

1960s		$225	$300

Citron
1995-present. Luthier Harvey Citron builds his professional and premium grade, production/cus-

MODEL YEAR	FEATURES	EXC. COND. LOW	HIGH

tom solidbody guitars and basses in Woodstock, New York. He also builds basses. In '75, Citron and Joe Veillette founded Veillette-Citron, which was known for handcrafted, neck-thru guitars and basses. That company closed in '83.

Clark

1985-present. Custom, professional grade, solid-body electric guitars and basses, built by luthier Ed Clark, first in Amityville, New York ('85-'90), then Medford ('91-'99) and presently Lake Ronkonkoma.

Clifford

Clifford was a brand manufactured by Kansas City, Missouri instrument wholesalers J.W. Jenkins & Sons. First introduced in 1895, the brand also offered mandolins.

Clovis

Mid-1960s. Private brand guitars, most likely made by Kay.

Electric Solidbody
Mid-1960s. Kay slab solidbody, 2 pickups.

1965		$350	$475

CMG Guitars

2012-present. Owner Chris Mitchell imports intermediate grade, acoustic and acoustic-electric guitars from China. He also offers professional grade, production/custom, electric guitars built by luthiers Russell Jones and James Horel in Statesboro, Georgia.

Cole

1890-1919. W.A. Cole, after leaving Fairbanks & Cole, started his own line in 1890. He died in 1909 but the company continued until 1919. He also made mandolins and banjos.

Parlor
1897. Small size, Brazilian rosewood sides and back, spruce top, ebony 'board, slotted headstock, dot markers.

1897		$850	$1,100

Coleman Guitars

1976-1983. Custom made presentation grade instruments made in Homosassa, Florida, by luthier Harry Coleman. No headstock logo, Coleman logo on inside center strip.

Collings

1986-present. Professional, premium, and presentation grade, production/custom, flat-top, archtop and electric guitars built in Austin, Texas. They also build mandolins and ukuleles. Bill Collings started with guitar repair and began custom building guitars around '73. In '80, he relocated his shop from Houston to Austin and started Collings Guitars in '86. In '06 they moved to a new plant in southwest Austin.

01
2005-present. Mother-of-pearl inlays, sitka spruce, mahogany neck, back & sides, ebony 'board and bridge, high gloss lacquer finish.

2005-2021		$2,900	$3,800

01A
2010-2017. As 01 with Adirondack spruce top.

2010-2017		$3,600	$4,700

01G
As 01 with German spruce top.

2009		$3,500	$3,600

01SB
Sitka spruce, mahogany.

2006-2015		$3,500	$4,500

02G
German spruce, sunburst.

1996		$3,700	$4,800

02H
Parlor, 12 frets.

2008		$3,000	$3,900

02SB
Parlor, 12 frets, 12-string.

2016		$3,700	$4,800

001G
German spruce.

2009		$3,500	$4,600

001MH
All mahogany body.

2010		$3,500	$4,500

002H
1999-present. Indian rosewood.

1999-2021		$3,000	$3,900

0041
2001. Premium Brazilian rosewood back and sides, Adirondack spruce top, abalone top purfling.

2001		$7,400	$9,600

0001 ICC
0001 with Indian rosewood back and sides.

2003-2013		$2,900	$3,725

0001 Series
1990s-present. 12-fret 000 size, Sitka spruce top (standard) or other top wood options, including mahogany, Adirondack, Honduran mahogany, etc.

1990s-2021	0001 Sitka	$2,900	$3,725
1990s-2021	0001A Adirondack	$3,600	$4,700
2006-2021	0001Mh Mahogany	$3,500	$4,500
2013-2021	0001 Cutaway	$2,900	$3,725

0002H
1994-present. 15" 000-size, 12-fret, Indian rosewood back and sides, spruce top, slotted headstock. AAA Koa back and sides in '96.

1994-1995	Indian rosewood	$3,000	$3,900
1996	AAA Koa	$3,900	$5,000
2007-2021	Indian rosewood	$3,000	$3,900

0002HAC
2009-present. With cutaway and herringbone trim.

2009-2021		$3,500	$4,500

00041
1999. Indian rosewood sides and back, Sitka spruce top, slotted headstock.

1999		$4,300	$5,600

Collings 01

Collings 0001

Collings CL Deluxe

Collings DS2H

290 Series
2004-present. Solid Honduran mahogany body, East Indian rosewood 'board, 2 P-90 style pickups, '50s style wiring, high gloss lacquer finish.

2004-2021	Custom/Deluxe	$2,000	$3,200

360 Baritone
2020-present. Solid ash body, doghair finish.

2020		$2,800	$3,700

360 LT
2015-present. Solidbody electric, level top (LT), mahogany, ash or alder body, rosewood 'board, high gloss nitro finish.

2015-2021		$2,800	$3,700

AT 16
2006-present. 16" archtop, limited numbers built, fully carved premium figured maple body and neck, carved solid spruce top, f-holes, high-end appointments, high gloss nitro finish.

2006-2021		$13,500	$17,500

AT 17
2008-present. 17" single-cut archtop, limited numbers built, S-holes, Adirondack or European spruce top, premium flamed maple back and sides, and premium appointments, sunburst or blonde. Options include scale length, pickup and bindings.

2008-2021		$12,500	$16,500

Baby Series
1997-present. Various 3/4 size models, Englemann (E) or German (G) spruce top, rosewood back and sides, Ivoroid with herringbone trim, tortoise 'guard, gloss nitro lacquer finish.

1997-2021	Various models	$2,500	$4,100

C10
1986-present. 000-size, mahogany back and sides, spruce top, sunburst or natural.

1986-2021		$3,000	$3,900

C10 Deluxe
1986-present. C10 with Indian rosewood back and sides (mahogany, flamed maple or koa optional), sunburst or natural.

1986-2021	Indian rosewood	$3,600	$4,700
1994-2000s	Flamed maple	$3,500	$4,600
1994-2000s	Koa option	$3,500	$4,600
1994-2000s	Varnish	$3,500	$4,600
1994-2021	Mahogany	$3,500	$4,600

C100
1986-1994, 2019-present. Quadruple 0-size, mahogany back and sides, spruce top, natural, replaced by CJ Jumbo. Reintroduced '19 with Honduran mahogany back, sides and neck.

1986-1994		$3,400	$4,400
2019-2021		$3,400	$4,400

C100 Deluxe
1986-1994, 2019-present. C-100 with rosewood back and sides. Reintroduced in '19 with East Indian rosewood and Honduran mahogany.

1986-1994		$3,400	$4,400

CJ
1995-present. Quadruple 0-size, Sitka spruce top (standard), Indian rosewood back and sides, natural.

Various other wood options available.

1995-2021	Sitka, Indian	$3,100	$4,100

CJ A
2019. Adirondack spruce top, Indian rosewood back and sides.

2019		$3,500	$4,500

CJ Koa ASB
2007. Adirondack spruce top, scalloped bracing ASB, flamed koa sides and back.

2007		$3,800	$4,900

CJ Mh
2020-present. Sitka spruce top (standard), Honduran mahogany back, sides and neck, sunburst. Various other wood options available.

2020-2021	Sitka, mahogany	$3,100	$4,100

CJ-35
2014-present. Sitka spruce top (standard), Honduran mahogany back, sides and neck, tigerstripe 'guard. Various other wood options available.

2014-2021	Sitka, mahogany	$3,100	$4,100

CL Series (City Limits)
2004-present. City Limits Jazz series, fully carved flame maple top, solid Honduran mahogany body, East Indian rosewood 'board, high gloss lacquer finish.

2004-2021		$3,500	$4,500

Clarence White
1989-2000. Adirondack top, Brazilian rosewood back and sides (CW-28), or mahogany (CW-18), herringbone trim.

1989-2000	CW-28, Brazilian	$7,400	$9,600
1993-2000	CW-18, Mahogany	$3,800	$4,900

CW Indian A
2019-present. Collings Winfield (CW), named after the Walnut Valley Festival in Winfield, Kansas, modified version of standard dreadnought, Adirondack spruce top, East Indian rosewood back and sides, ivoroid binding with herringbone purfling.

2019-2021		$3,800	$4,900

D1 Gruhn
1989. Short run for Gruhn Guitars, Nashville, Gruhn script headstock logo, signed by Bill Collings, choice of Indian rosewood or curly maple back and sides, Engelman spruce top.

1989		$3,100	$4,000

D1 Series
1992-present. Dreadnought, Sitka spruce top (standard), mahogany back and sides. Various other wood options available.

1992-2018	D1A, Adirondack	$3,700	$4,700
1992-2018	D1H, Herringbone	$2,800	$3,700
1992-2021	D1, Mahogany	$2,800	$3,700
2010	D1VN, Vintage neck	$3,900	$5,100
2016-2021	D1AT, Adirondack, Torrefied	$4,700	$6,100

D2 Series
1986-present. Dreadnought, Sitka spruce top (standard), Indian rosewood back and sides. Various other wood options available.

1986-1995	D2, Sitka, Indian	$2,900	$3,800

MODEL YEAR	FEATURES	EXC. COND. LOW	HIGH
1986-2021	D2H, Herringbone	$2,900	$3,800
1994	D2HV, Vintage neck	$2,900	$3,800
1994-2005	D2HB, Brazilian	$7,400	$9,600
2004-2010	D2HAV, Varnish	$4,200	$5,475
2004-2021	D2HA, Adirondack	$3,650	$4,800
2008	D2HGV, German spruce	$5,000	$6,500
2017-2021	D2HT, Traditional	$3,900	$5,000

D3 Series

1990-present. Dreadnought, Sitka spruce top (standard), Brazilian or Indian rosewood back and sides. Various other wood options available.

1990-1999	D3, Brazilian	$7,700	$10,000
2000-2021	D3, Indian	$3,200	$4,100
2004-2021	D3A, Adirondack	$4,300	$5,700

D42

2000s. Brazilian rosewood back and sides, fancy.

2000s		$7,700	$10,000

DS1/DS1A

2004-present. D-size, slope shoulders, 12 fret neck, slotted headstock, mahogany back and sides, A is Adirondack upgrade.

2004-2021		$3,650	$4,750

DS2H/DS2HA

1995-present. D-size, 12-fret, slotted headstock, Sitka spruce top, Indian rosewood back and sides, herringbone purfling. A is Adirondack upgrade.

1995-2021		$3,650	$4,750

DS41

1995-2007. Indian rosewood, fancy, abalone top trim, snowflake markers.

1995-2007		$4,200	$5,400

I-30

2017-present. Flamed maple top, f-holes, mahogany neck, 2 P-90 pickups.

2017-2021		$3,600	$4,700

I-35 Deluxe

2007-present. Premium flamed maple top (standard), mahogany body, gloss lacquer finish. Various other wood options available.

2007-2021	Various options	$4,400	$5,700

OM1 Series

1994-present. Orchestra model, Sitka spruce top (standard), mahogany back and sides, natural. Various other wood options available.

1994-2021	OM1, Mahogany	$2,800	$3,700
1994-2021	OM1A, Adirondack	$3,500	$4,600
2000-2016	OM1, Koa	$3,000	$4,000
2000-2016	OM1MH, Mahogany	$2,900	$3,800
2007-2016	OM1A, Cutaway, Adirondack	$3,700	$4,800
2016-2021	OM1T, Traditional	$3,600	$4,700
2018-2021	OM1AT, Adirondack	$5,200	$6,800
2020-2021	OM1JL, Julian Lage	$4,050	$5,250

MODEL YEAR	FEATURES	EXC. COND. LOW	HIGH

OM2 Series

1990-present. Sitka spruce top (standard), Indian rosewood back and sides. Various other wood options available.

1990-2020	OM2, Sitka, Indian	$3,100	$4,100
1990-2021	OM2H, Herringbone	$3,500	$4,500
1998	OM2HAV, Varnish	$7,300	$9,500
2001	OM2H SSB, Brazilian	$7,300	$9,500
2003-2018	OM2HA, Adirondack	$3,900	$5,100
2008	OM2H GSS, German spruce	$3,600	$4,700
2018-2021	OM2HAT, Traditional, Adirondack	$4,900	$6,300

OM3 Series

1986-present. Sitka spruce top (standard), first Brazilian later Indian rosewood back and sides. Various other wood options available.

1986-1996	OM3HC Cutaway, Indian	$3,700	$4,800
1986-1999	OM3B, Brazilian	$7,400	$9,600
1994-2007	OM3HBA, Adirondack, Brazilian	$7,400	$9,600
2000-2021	OM3, Indian	$3,200	$4,200
2003	OM3, Figured maple	$3,200	$4,200
2004-2021	OM3A, Adirondack	$3,700	$4,800
2008-2021	OM3, Mahogany	$3,200	$4,200

OM41BrzGCut

2007. Brazilian rosewood sides and back, German spruce top, rounded cutaway.

2007		$7,700	$10,000

OM42B

Brazilian rosewood back and sides, Adirondack spruce top, fancy rosette and binding.

2000		$8,500	$11,000

OM42G

German spruce top, Indian rosewood back and sides.

1999		$4,200	$5,500

OMC2H

Adirondack top, Brazilian rosewood back and sides, herringbone trim.

2008		$7,300	$9,500

SJ

1986-present. Spruce top, quilted maple back and sides or Indian rosewood (earlier option), later mahogany.

1986-2021	Various options	$3,500	$4,600

SJ41

1996		$3,500	$4,600

SoCo Deluxe

2007-present. Premium figured maple top over semi-hollow mahogany body, rosewood 'board, f-holes, various finish options.

2007-2021		$3,500	$4,600

Winfield

2004-2006. D-style, Adirondack spruce top, Brazilian or Indian rosewood back and sides, later mahogany.

2004	Indian	$3,500	$4,600
2005-2006	Brazilian	$3,500	$4,600
2006	Mahogany	$3,500	$4,600

Collings SJ

Collings SoCo DLX

GUITARS

*Comins 16 Vintage
Burst Concert Model*

*Conrad Acoustical
Slimline 12-String*

Imaged by Heritage Auctions, HA.com

MODEL		EXC. COND.	
YEAR	FEATURES	LOW	HIGH

Columbia
Late 1800s-early 1900s. The Columbia brand name was used on acoustic guitars by New York's James H. Buckbee Co. until c.1987 and afterwards by Galveston's Thomas Goggan and Brothers.

Comins
1992-present. Premium and presentation grade, custom archtops built by luthier Bill Comins in Willow Grove, Pennsylvania. He also builds mandolins and offers a combo amp built in collaboration with George Alessandro.

Commander
Late 1950s-early 1960s. Archtop acoustic guitars made by Harmony for the Alden catalog company.

Concertone
Ca. 1914-1930s. Concertone was a brand made by Chicago's Slingerland and distributed by Montgomery Ward. The brand was also used on other instruments such as ukuleles.

Conklin
1984-present. Intermediate, professional and premium grade, production/custom, 6-, 7-, 8-, and 12-string solid and hollowbody electrics, by luthier Bill Conklin. He also builds basses. Originally located in Lebanon, Missouri, in '88 the company moved to Springfield, Missouri. Conklin instruments are made in the U.S. and overseas.

Conn Guitars
Ca.1968-ca.1978. Student to mid-quality classical and acoustic guitars, some with bolt-on necks, also some electrics. Imported from Japan by band instrument manufacturer and distributor Conn/Continental Music Company, Elkhart, Indiana.

Acoustic

| 1968-1978 | Various models | $175 | $250 |

Classical

| 1968-1978 | Student-level | $125 | $175 |

Electric Solidbody

| 1968-1978 | Various models | $200 | $275 |

Connor, Stephan
1995-present. Luthier Stephan Connor builds his premium grade, custom nylon-string guitars in Waltham, Massachusetts.

Conrad Guitars
Ca. 1968-1978. Mid- to better-quality copies of glued-neck Martin and Gibson acoustics and bolt-neck Gibson and Fender solidbodies. They also offered basses, mandolins and banjos. Imported from Japan by David Wexler and Company, Chicago, Illinois.

Acoustic 12-String

1970s. Dreadnought size.

| 1970s | | $175 | $225 |

MODEL		EXC. COND.	
YEAR	FEATURES	LOW	HIGH

Acoustical Slimline (40080/40085)

1970s. Rosewood 'board, 2 or 3 DeArmond-style pickups, block markers, sunburst.

| 1970s | | $450 | $575 |

Acoustical Slimline 12-String (40100)

1970s. Rosewood 'board, 2 DeArmond-style pickups, dot markers, sunburst.

| 1970s | | $450 | $575 |

Bison (40035/40030/40065/40005)

1970s. 1 thru 4 pickups available, rosewood 'board with dot markers, six-on-side headstock.

| 1970s | | $450 | $575 |

Bumper (40223)

1970s. Clear Lucite solidbody.

| 1970s | | $525 | $700 |

Classical Student (40150)

| 1970s | | $135 | $175 |

De Luxe Folk Guitar

1970s. Resonator acoustic, mahogany back, sides and neck, Japanese import.

| 1970s | | $275 | $350 |

Master Size (40178)

1972-1977. Electric archtop, 2 pickups.

| 1972-1977 | | $400 | $525 |

Resonator Acoustic

1970s. Flat-top with wood, metal resonator and 8 ports, round neck.

| 1970s | | $500 | $650 |

Violin-Shaped 12-String Electric (40176)

1970s. Scroll headstock, 2 pickups, 500/1 control panel, bass side dot markers, sunburst.

| 1970s | | $500 | $650 |

Violin-Shaped Electric (40175)

1970s. Scroll headstock, 2 pickups, 500/1 control panel, bass side dot markers, vibrato, sunburst.

| 1970s | | $500 | $650 |

White Styrene (1280)

1970s. Solid maple body covered with white styrene, 2 pickups, tremolo, bass side dot markers, white.

| 1970s | | $450 | $600 |

Contessa
1960s. Acoustic, semi-hollow archtop, solidbody and bass guitars made in Italy by Zero Sette and imported by Hohner. They also made banjos.

Acoustic

| 1960s | | $100 | $250 |

Electric Solidbody

1967. Various models.

| 1960s | | $250 | $425 |

Contreras
See listing for Manuel Contreras and Manuel Contreras II.

Coral
1967-1969. In '66 MCA bought Danelectro and in '67 introduced the Coral brand of guitars, basses and amps.

MODEL YEAR	FEATURES	EXC. COND. LOW	EXC. COND. HIGH

Bellzouki 7021
1967. 12-string electric, modified teardrop shape with body points on treble and bass bouts, 2 pickups.

1967		$1,400	$1,800

Combo/Vincent Bell Combo
1967-1969. Cutaway acoustic/electric, 1 or 2 pickups.

1967-1969	V1N6, 1 pu	$2,600	$3,400
1967-1969	V2N6, 2 pu	$3,000	$3,900

Firefly
1967-1969. Double-cut, f-holes, 2 pickups, vibrato available (2V) and 12-string (2N12), red or sunburst.

1967-1969	F2N, no vibrato	$875	$1,150
1967-1969	F2V, vibrato	$1,200	$1,600
1968-1969	F2N12, 12-string	$1,200	$1,600

Hornet (2 Pickups)
1967-1969. Solidbody, 2 pickups, vibrato available (2V or 3V), sunburst, black or red.

1967-1969	H2N, black or red	$1,200	$1,600
1967-1969	H2N, sunburst	$1,000	$1,300
1967-1969	H2V, black or red	$1,300	$1,700
1967-1969	H2V, sunburst	$1,050	$1,400

Hornet (3 Pickups)
1967-1969. As above with 3 pickups, with or without vibrato.

1967-1969	H3N, black or red	$1,300	$1,700
1967-1969	H3N, sunburst	$1,150	$1,500
1967-1969	H3V, black or red	$1,375	$1,800
1967-1969	H3V, sunburst	$1,150	$1,500

Long Horn
1967-1969. Deep double-cut hollowbody, 2 lipstick tube pickups, 6-string (2N6) or 12 (2N12), sunburst.

1967-1969	L2N12	$1,425	$1,850
1967-1969	L2N6	$1,300	$1,700

Scorpion
1967-1969. Offset double-cut solidbody, 12-string, 2 or 3 lipstick tube pickups, vibrato available (2V or 3V).

1967-1969	S2N12, black or red	$1,200	$1,550
1967-1969	S2N12, sunburst	$1,000	$1,300
1967-1969	S2V12, black or red	$1,200	$1,550
1967-1969	S2V12, sunburst	$1,200	$1,550
1967-1969	S3N12, black or red	$1,300	$1,700
1967-1969	S3N12, sunburst	$1,200	$1,550
1967-1969	S3V12, black or red	$1,400	$1,850
1967-1969	S3V12, sunburst	$1,200	$1,550

Sitar
1967-1969. Six-string guitar with drone strings and 3 pickups (2 under the 6 strings, 1 under the drones), kind of a USA-shaped body.

1967-1969	3S18, 18-string	$2,300	$3,000
1967-1969	3S19, 19-string	$2,500	$3,300
1967-1969	3S9, 9-string	$2,100	$2,700

Teardrop
1967-1969. Teardrop shaped hollowbody, 2 lipstick tube pickups.

1967-1969	T2N6	$1,950	$2,550

Córdoba
Line of classical guitars handmade in Portugal and imported by Guitar Salon International. By '13, U.S. production was added.

Classical

2000s	Higher-end	$1,700	$2,200
2000s	Mid-level	$450	$600
2000s	Student-level	$300	$375

Cordova
1960s. Classical nylon string guitars imported by David Wexler of Chicago.

Grand Concert Model WC-026
1960s. Highest model offered by Cordova, 1-piece rosewood back, laminated rosewood sides, spruce top, natural.

1960s		$300	$375

Corey James Custom Guitars
2005-present. Luthier Corey James Moilanen builds his professional and premium grade, production/custom solidbody guitars and basses in Howell, Michigan.

Coriani, Paolo
1984-present. Production/custom nylon-string guitars and hurdy-gurdys built by luthier Paolo Coriani in Modeila, Italy.

Cort
1973-present. North Brook, Illinois-based Cort offers budget, intermediate and professional grade, production/custom, acoustic and solidbody, semi-hollow, hollow body electric guitars and basses built in Korea.

Cort was the second significant Korean private-label (Hondo brand was the first) to come out of Korea. Jack Westheimer entered into an agreement with Korea's Cort to do Cort-brand, private-label, and Epiphone-brand guitars.

CP Thornton Guitars
1985-present. Luthier Chuck Thornton builds professional and premium grade, production/custom, semi-hollow and solidbody electric guitars in Sumner, Maine. Up to '96 he also built basses.

Crafter
1986-present. Crafter offers budget and intermediate grade, production, classical, acoustic, acoustic/electric, and electric guitars, basses and mandolins made in Korea. They also offer the Cruzer and Ashland brands of instruments. From '72 to '86 they made Sungeum classical guitars.

Cranium
Introduced 1996, professional grade, production/custom, hollow, semi-hollow, and solidbody electrics built by luthier Wayne O'Connor in Peterborough, Ontario.

Crescent Moon
Professional grade, production/custom, solidbody guitars and basses built by luthier Craig Muller in Baltimore, Maryland, starting 1999.

Cort Classic TC

CP Thornton Improv

GUITARS

CSR Serenata

1966 Custom Kraft Lexington
Rivington Guitars

MODEL YEAR	FEATURES	EXC. COND. LOW	HIGH

Creston

2004-present. Professional grade, custom, solid-body electric guitars and basses built by luthier Creston Lea in Burlington, Vermont.

Crestwood

1970s. Copies of the popular classical guitars, flat-tops, electric solidbodies and basses of the era, imported by La Playa Distributing Company of Detroit.

Acoustic 12-String

1970s		$200	$300

Electric

1970s. Various models include near copies of the 335 (Crestwood model 2043, 2045 and 2047), Les Paul Custom (2020), Strat (2073), Jazzmaster (2078), Tele (2082), and the SG Custom (2084).

1970s		$275	$575

Crimson Guitars

2005-present. Luthiers Benjamin Crowe and Aki Atrill build professional and premium grade, custom, solidbody guitars and basses in Somerset, U.K.

Cromwell

1935-1939. Budget model brand built by Gibson and distributed by mail-order businesses like Grossman, Continental, Richter & Phillips, and Gretsch & Brenner.

Acoustic Archtop

1935-1939. Archtop acoustic, f-holes, pressed mahogany back and sides, carved and bound top, bound back, 'guard and 'board, no truss rod.

1935-1939	Various models	$1,000	$1,300
1935-1939	With '30s era pu	$1,300	$1,700

Acoustic Flat-Top

1935-1939	G-2 (L-00)	$1,775	$2,300

GT-2 Tenor

1935-1939	1474" flat-top	$975	$1,250

GT-4 Tenor

1935-1939	16" archtop	$975	$1,250

Cromwell (Guild)

1963-1964. Guild imported these 2- or 3-pickup offset double cut solidbodies from Hagstrom. These were basically part of Hagstrom's Kent line with laminated bodies and birch necks. About 500 were imported into the U.S.

Solidbody

1963-1964		$1,100	$1,400

Crook Custom Guitars

1997-present. Professional grade, custom, solidbody electric guitars and basses built in Moundsville, West Virginia by luthier Bill Crook.

Crossley

2005-present. Professional grade, production/custom, solidbody and chambered electric guitars built in Melbourne, Victoria, Australia by luthier Peter Crossley.

Crown

1960s. Violin-shaped hollowbody electrics, solid-body electric guitars and basses, possibly others. Imported from Japan.

Acoustic Flat-Top

1960s. 6-string and 12-string.

1960s		$125	$200

Electric Archtop

1960s. Double pointed cutaways, 2 humbucking pickups, laminated top, full-depth body.

1960s		$375	$600

Electric Solidbody/Semi-Hollow

1960s. Student-level Japanese import.

1960s	Copy models	$350	$450
1960s	Standard models	$200	$300
1960s	Violin-shaped body	$350	$450

Crucianelli

Early 1960s. Italian guitars imported into the U.S. by Bennett Brothers of New York and Chicago around '63 to '64. Accordion builder Crucianelli also made Imperial, Elite, PANaramic, and Elli-Sound brand guitars.

Cruzer

Intermediate grade, production, solidbody electric guitars, basses, amps and effects made by Korea's Crafter Guitars.

CSR

1996-present. Father and daughter luthiers Roger and Courtney Kitchens build their premium grade, production/custom, archtop guitars and basses in Byron, Georgia.

Cumpiano

1974-present. Professional and premium grade, custom steel-string and nylon-string guitars, and acoustic basses built by luthier William Cumpiano in Northampton, Massachusetts.

Curbow String Instruments

1994-2007. Premium grade, production/custom, solidbody guitars and basses built by luthier Doug Somervell in Morganton, Georgia. Founded by Greg Curbow who passed away in '05.

Custom

1980s. Line of solidbody guitars and basses introduced in the early '80s by Charles Lawing and Chris Lovell, owners of Strings & Things in Memphis, Tennessee.

Custom Kraft

Late-1950s-1968. A house brand of St. Louis Music Supply, instruments built by Valco and Kay. They also offered basses and amps.

Electric Solidbody

1950s-1960s. U.S.-made or import, entry-level, 1 or 2 pickups.

1950s-60s	Import	$200	$300
1950s-60s	USA, Kay, 2 pu	$575	$750

MODEL YEAR FEATURES	EXC. COND. LOW	HIGH
Sound Saturator		
1960s 12-string	$450	$600
Super Zapp		
1960s	$525	$700
Thin Twin Jimmy Reed (style)		
Late-1950s-early-1960s. Single cut, 2 pickups, 4 knobs and toggle, dot markers.		
1950s-60s US-made	$775	$1,000

D.J. Hodson

1994-2007. Luthier David J.Hodson built his professional and premium grade, production/custom, acoustic guitars in Loughborough, Leicestershire, U.K. He also built ukes. He passed away in '07.

Daddy Mojo String Instruments Inc.

2005-present. Luthiers Lenny Piroth-Robert and Luca Tripaldi build their intermediate and professional grade, production/custom, solidbody electric, resonator and cigar box guitars in Montreal, Quebec.

Dagmar Custom Guitars

Luthier Pete Swanson builds custom, premium and presentation grade, acoustic and electric archtop guitars in Niagara, Ontario, starting in 2008.

D'Agostino

1976-early 1990s. Acoustic and electric solidbody guitars and basses imported by PMS Music, founded in New York City by former Maestro executive Pat D'Agostino, his brother Steven D'Agostino, and Mike Confortti. First dreadnought acoustic guitars imported from Japan in '76. First solidbodies manufactured by the EKO custom shop beginning in '77. In '82 solidbody production moved to Japan. Beginning in '84, D'Agostinos were made in Korea. Overall, about 60% of guitars were Japanese, 40% Korean. They also had basses.

Acoustic Flat-Top
1976-1990. Early production in Japan, by mid-'80s, most production in Korea.

1976-1990	$525	$675

Electric Semi-Hollowbody
1981-early 1990s. Early production in Japan, later versions from Korea.

1981-1990	$175	$775

Electric Solidbody
1977-early 1990s. Early models made in Italy, later versions from Japan and Korea.

1981-1990	$175	$775

Daily Guitars

1976-present. Luthier David Daily builds his premium grade, production/custom classical guitars in Sparks, Nevada.

Daion

1978-1984. Mid- to higher-quality copies imported from Japan. Original designs introduced in the '80s. Only acoustics offered at first; in '81 they added acoustic/electric and solid and semi-hollow electrics. They also had basses.

Acoustic
1978-1985. Various flat-top models.

1978-1985 Higher-end	$600	$1,350
1978-1985 Lower-end	$200	$600

Electric
1978-1985. Various solid and semi-hollow body guitars.

1978-1985 Higher-end	$600	$1,350
1978-1985 Lower-end	$200	$600

Daisy Rock

2001-present. Budget and intermediate grade, production, full-scale and 3/4 scale, solidbody, semi-hollow, acoustic, and acoustic/electric guitars and basses. Founded by Tish Ciravolo as a Division of Schecter Guitars, the Daisy line is focused on female customers.

D'Ambrosio

2001-present. Luthier Otto D'Ambrosio builds his premium grade, custom/production, acoustic and electric archtop guitars in Providence, Rhode Island.

Dan Armstrong

Dan Armstrong started playing jazz in Cleveland in the late-'50s. He moved to New York and also started doing repairs, eventually opening his own store on 48th Street in '65. By the late-'60s he was designing his Lucite guitars for Ampeg (see Ampeg for those listings). He moved to England in '71, where he developed his line of colored stomp boxes. He returned to the States in '75. Armstrong died in '04.

Wood Body
1973-1975. Sliding pickup, wood body, brown.

1973-1975	$1,775	$2,300

Wood Body AMG 100 (reissue)
Various wood body options, BLD (blond, swamp ash), CH (cherry, mahogany) and BK (black, alder).

2008-2009 BK	$375	$500
2008-2009 BLD	$625	$825
2008-2009 CH	$450	$600

Dan Armstrong Guitars

Introduced 2015, professional grade, production/custom, acrylic solidbody electrics based on the original Dan Armstrong models, built in Everett, Washington.

Dan Kellaway

1976-present. Production/custom, premium grade, classical and steel string guitars built by luthier Dan Kellaway in Singleton NSW, Australia. He also builds mandolins and lutes.

Dagmar Custom

2016 Dan Armstrong 50th Anniversary Custom

Imaged by Heritage Auctions, HA.com

GUITARS

1960s Danelectro Convertible
Tom Pfeifer

1967 Danelectro Dane B
Rivington Guitars

Danelectro

1946-1969, 1996-present. Founded in Red Bank, New Jersey, by Nathan I. (Nate or Nat) Daniel, an electronics enthusiast with amplifier experience. In 1933, Daniel built amps for Thor's Bargain Basement in New York. In '34 he was recruited by Epiphone's Herb Sunshine to build earliest Electar amps and pickup-making equipment. From '35 to '42, he operated Daniel Electric Laboratories in Manhattan, supplying Epiphone. He started Danelectro in '46 and made his first amps for Montgomery Ward in '47. Over the years, Danelectro made amplifiers, solidbody, semi-hollow and hollowbody electric guitars and basses, electric sitar, and the Bellzouki under the Danelectro, Silvertone, and Coral brands. In '48, began supplying Silvertone amps for Sears (various coverings), with his own brand (brown leatherette) distributed by Targ and Dinner as Danelectro and S.S. Maxwell. He developed an electronic vibrato in '48 on his Vibravox series amps. In '50 he developed a microphone with volume and tone controls and outboard Echo Box reverb unit. In the fall of '54, Danelectro replaced Harmony as provider of Silvertone solidbody guitars for Sears. Also in '54, the first Danelectro brand guitars appeared with tweed covering, bell headstock, and pickups under the pickguard. The Coke bottle headstock debuts as Silvertone Lightning Bolt in '54, and was used on Danelectros for '56 to '66. The company moved to Red Bank, New Jersey in '57, and in '58 relocated to Neptune, New Jersey. In '59, Harmony and Kay guitars replace all but 3 Danelectros in Sears catalog. In '66, MCA buys the company (Daniel remains with company), but by mid-'69, MCA halts production and closes the doors. Some leftover stock is sold to Dan Armstrong, who had a shop in New York at the time. Armstrong assembled several hundred Danelectro guitars as Dan Armstrong Modified with his own pickup design.

Rights to name acquired by Anthony Marc in late-'80s, who assembled a number of thinline hollowbody guitars, many with Longhorn shape, using Japanese-made bodies and original Danelectro necks and hardware. In '96, the Evets Corporation, of San Clemente, California, introduced a line of effects bearing the Danelectro brand. Amps and guitars, many of which were reissues of the earlier instruments, soon followed. In early 2003, Evets discontinued offering guitar and amps, but revived the guitar and bass line in '05.

MCA-Danelectro made guitars were called the Dane Series. Dane A model numbers start with an A (e.g. A2V), Dane B models start with a B (e.g. B3V), Dane C (e.g. C2N), and Dane D (e.g. D2N). The least expensive series was the A, going up to the most expensive D. All Dane Series instruments came with 1, 2 or 3 pickups and with hand vibrato options. The Dane Series were made from '67 to '69. MCA did carry over the Convertible, Guitarlin 4123, Long Horn Bass-4 and Bass-6 and

Doubleneck 3923. MCA also offered the Bellzouki Double Pickup 7021. Each Dane Series includes an electric 12-string. Danelectro also built the Coral brand instruments (see Coral).

Baritone 6-String Reissue

1999-2003, 2008-present. Danelectro has offered several models with 6-string baritone tuning, often with various reissue-year designations, single- or double-cut, 2 or 3 pickups.

MODEL YEAR	FEATURES	LOW	HIGH
1999-2021	Various models	$450	$575

Bellzouki

1963-1969. 12-string electric. Teardrop-shaped body, 1 pickup, sunburst (7010) for '63-'66. Vincent Bell model (7020) with modified teardrop shape with 2 body points on both treble and bass bouts and 2 pickups for '63-'66. Same body as Coral Electric Sitar for '67-'69.

MODEL YEAR	FEATURES	LOW	HIGH
1963-1969	1 pu, teardrop body	$900	$1,175
1963-1969	2 pu, pointy body	$1,225	$1,600
1967-1969	2 pu, sitar body	$1,950	$2,525

Companion

1959-1960. Hollowbody double-cut, 2 pickups, concentric TV knobs.

MODEL YEAR	FEATURES	LOW	HIGH
1959-1960		$1,625	$2,100

Convertible

1959-1969. Acoustic/electric, double-cut, guitar was sold with or without the removable single pickup.

MODEL YEAR	FEATURES	LOW	HIGH
1959-1969	Acoustic, no pu, natural	$375	$500
1959-1969	Pickup installed, natural	$575	$750
1967-1969	Red, white, blue	$900	$1,175

Convertible Reissue

1999, 2000-2003. The Convertible Pro was offered '00-'03 with upgraded Gotoh tuners and metalflake and pearl finishes.

MODEL YEAR	FEATURES	LOW	HIGH
1999-2003	Blond or green	$300	$400

Dane A Series

1967-1969. 1or 2 pickups, with or without vibrato (V), solid wood slab body, hard lacquer finish with 4 color options, 12-string also offered.

MODEL YEAR	FEATURES	LOW	HIGH
1967-1969	1N12, 12-string	$1,375	$1,775
1967-1969	2N12, 12-string	$1,500	$1,950
1967-1969	N, 1 pickup	$1,000	$1,300
1967-1969	N, 2 pickpus	$1,200	$1,550
1967-1969	V, 1 pu, vibrato	$1,200	$1,550
1967-1969	V, 2 pu, vibrato	$1,275	$1,650

Dane B Series

1967-1969. 2 or 3 pickups, with or without vibrato (V), semi-solid Durabody, 6 or 12 strings.

MODEL YEAR	FEATURES	LOW	HIGH
1967-1969	12-string	$1,250	$1,625
1967-1969	6-string, 2 pu	$1,000	$1,300
1967-1969	6-string, 3 pu	$1,150	$1,500

Dane C Series

1967-1969. 2 or 3 pickups, with or without vibrato (V), semi-solid Durabody with 2-tone Gator finish, 6 or 12 strings.

MODEL YEAR	FEATURES	LOW	HIGH
1967-1969	12-string	$1,775	$2,300
1967-1969	6-string	$1,550	$2,000

Dane D Series

1967-1969. 2 or 3 pickups, with or without vibrato (V), solid wood sculptured thinline body, 'floating

MODEL YEAR	FEATURES	EXC. COND. LOW	HIGH

adjustable pickguard-fingerguide', master volume with 4 switches, 6 or 12 strings.

1967-1969	12-string	$1,475	$1,900
1967-1969	6-string, 2 pu	$1,150	$1,500
1967-1969	6-string, 3 pu	$1,325	$1,725

Danoblaster Series
2000-2003. Offset double-cuts, 3 pickups, built-in effects – distortion on the Hearsay, distortion, chorus, trem and echo on Innuendo. Also in 12-string and baritone.

| 2000-2003 | | $135 | $175 |

DC-3/DDC-3
1999-2003. Shorthorn double-cut, 3 pickups, seal-shaped pickguard, Coke bottle headstock, solid and sparkle finishes.

| 1999-2003 | | $300 | $400 |

DC-12/Electric XII
1999-2003. 12-string version of 59-DC.

| 1999-2003 | | $375 | $500 |

59-DC/'59 Dano (Reissue)
1998-1999, 2007. Shorthorn double-cut, 2 pickups, seal-shaped pickguard, Coke bottle headstock, '07 version called '59 Dano.

| 1998-1999 | | $275 | $360 |

Deluxe Single Pickup
1959-1966. Double-cut, Coke bottle headstock, 1 pickup, 2 knobs.

| 1959-1960 | Walnut or white | $1,250 | $1,625 |
| 1961-1966 | Walnut, white, honey | $1,125 | $1,450 |

Deluxe Double Pickup
1959-1966. As Single above, but with 2 pickups, and added master volume on later models.

| 1959-1960 | Walnut or white | $1,300 | $1,625 |
| 1961-1966 | Walnut, white, honey | $1,225 | $1,600 |

Deluxe Triple Pickup
1959-1966. As Single above, but with 3 pickups, 3 knobs, and added master volume on later models.

| 1959-1960 | Walnut or white | $1,375 | $1,800 |
| 1961-1966 | Walnut, white, honey | $1,300 | $1,675 |

Doubleneck (3923)
1958-1966. A shorthorn double-cut, bass and 6-string necks, 1 pickup on each neck, Coke bottle headstocks, white sunburst.

| 1958-1966 | | $2,300 | $3,000 |

Doubleneck Reissue
1999-2003. Baritone 6-string and standard 6-string double neck, shorthorn body style, or the 6-12 model with a 6-string and 12-string neck. Price includes $75 for a guitar case, but many sales do not seem to include a guitar case because of unusual body size.

| 1999-2003 | | $525 | $675 |

Electric Sitar
1968-1969. Traditional looking, oval-bodied sitar, no drone strings as on the Coral Sitar of the same period.

| 1968-1969 | | $2,300 | $3,000 |

Guitarlin (4123)
1958-1966. The Longhorn guitar, 2 huge cutaways, 31-fret neck, 2 pickups.

| 1958-1960 | | $2,300 | $3,000 |
| 1961-1966 | | $2,150 | $2,800 |

Hand Vibrato Single Pickup (4011)
1958-1966. Short horn double-cut, 1 pickup, batwing headstock, simple design vibrato, black w/ white guard.

| 1958-1966 | | $950 | $1,250 |

Hand Vibrato Double Pickup (4021)
1958-1966. Same as Single Pickup, but with 2 pickups and larger pickguard.

| 1958-1966 | | $1,125 | $1,450 |

Hawk
1967-1969. Offered with 1 or 2 pickups, vibrato (V models) or non-vibrato (N models), 12-string model also offered.

1967-1969	1N, 1 pickup	$1,125	$1,450
1967-1969	1N12, 12-string	$1,375	$1,800
1967-1969	1V, vibrato, 1 pu	$1,200	$1,600
1967-1969	2N, 2 pickups	$1,200	$1,600
1967-1969	2N12, 12-string	$1,600	$2,100
1967-1969	2V, vibrato, 2 pu	$1,350	$1,750

Hodad/Hodad 12-String
1999-2003. Unique double-cut with sharp horns, 6 or 12 strings, sparkle finish.

| 1999-2003 | | $360 | $475 |

Model C
1955. Single-cut, 1or 2 pickups, ginger colored vinyl cover.

| 1955-1958 | | $600 | $800 |

Pro 1
1963-1964. Odd-shaped double-cut electric with squared off corners, 1 pickup.

| 1963-1964 | | $900 | $1,200 |

Pro Reissue
2007. Based on '60s Pro 1, but with 2 pickups.

| 2007 | | $275 | $360 |

Slimline (SL) Series
1967-1969. Offset waist double-cut, 2 or 3 pickups, with or without vibrato, 6 or 12 string.

1967-1969	12-string	$1,325	$1,725
1967-1969	6-string, 2 pu	$1,025	$1,325
1967-1969	6-string, 3 pu	$1,225	$1,600

Standard Single Pickup
1958-1966. Nicknamed the Shorthorn, double-cut, 1 pickup, 2 regular control knobs, kidney-shaped pickguard originally, seal-shaped 'guard by ca. 1960, Coke bottle headstock, in black or bronze.

| 1958-1959 | Kidney guard | $900 | $1,175 |
| 1960-1966 | Seal guard | $900 | $1,175 |

Standard Double Pickup
1958-1966. As Single Pickup above but with 2 pickups and 2 stacked, concentric volume/tone controls, in black, bronze and later blond. The black, seal-shaped pickguard version of this guitar is often referred to as the Jimmy Page model because he used one. Reissued in 1998 as 59-DC.

1958-1959	Kidney guard, black	$975	$1,275
1960-1966	Bronze	$950	$1,225
1960-1966	Jimmy Page, black	$1,375	$1,800
1961-1966	Blond	$1,125	$1,450

1964 Danelectro 3923 Doubleneck

Izzy Miller

1963 Danelectro Standard Double Pickup

Trey Rabinek

GUITARS

1957 Danelectro U2
Imaged by Heritage Auctions, HA.com

1961 D'Angelico New Yorker
Cartwright Thompson

MODEL YEAR	FEATURES	EXC. COND. LOW	HIGH

Standard Triple Pickup
1958. As Single Pickup above but with 3 pickups and 3 stacked, concentric pointer volume/tone controls, in white to bronze sunburst, very rare.

1958		$1,225	$1,600

Tweed Model
1954-1955. First production models, single-cut, bell-shape headstock, 1 or 2 pickups, tweed vinyl cover.

1954-1955	1 pickup	$2,725	$3,525
1954-1955	2 pickups	$2,950	$3,825

U-1
1955-1958. Single-cut, 1 pickup, 2 regular knobs, bell-shape headstock originally, switching to Coke bottle in late '55. The U Series featured Dano's new 'solid center' block construction.

1955	Enamel, bell hdsk	$2,125	$2,775
1956-1957	Enamel, Coke hdsk	$1,925	$2,500
1956-1957	Ivory, Coke hdsk	$1,975	$2,575
1958	Enamel, Coke hdsk	$1,675	$2,175
1958	Ivory, Coke hdsk	$1,950	$2,525

U-1 '56 Reissue
1998-1999. Reissue of '56 U-1, various colors.

1998-1999		$225	$300

U-2
1955-1958. As U-1, but with 2 pickups and 2 stacked concentric volume/tone controls.

1955	Enamel, bell hdsk	$2,325	$3,000
1956-1957	Enamel, Coke hdsk	$2,100	$2,700
1956-1957	Ivory, Coke hdsk	$2,325	$3,000
1958	Enamel, Coke hdsk	$1,950	$2,525
1958	Ivory, Coke hdsk	$2,100	$2,700

U-2 '56 Reissue
1998-2003. Reissue of '56 U-2, various colors.

1998-2003		$250	$325

U-3
1955-1958. As U-2, but with 3 pickups and 3 stacked concentric volume/tone controls.

1958	Enamel, Coke hdsk	$2,125	$2,775

U-3 '56 Reissue
1999-2003. Reissue of '56 U-3, various colors.

1999-2003		$300	$400

D'Angelico
John D'Angelico built his own line of archtop guitars, mandolins and violins from 1932 until his death in 1964. His instruments are some of the most sought-after by collectors. The binding on some D'Angelico guitars can become deteriorated and requires replacing.

D'Angelico (L-5 Snakehead)
1932-1935. D'Angelico's L-5-style with snakehead headstock, his first model, sunburst.

1932-1935		$10,000	$13,000

Excel/Exel (Cutaway)
1947-1964. Cutaway, 17" width, 1- and 3-ply bound f-hole.

1947-1949	Natural, original binding	$33,000	$43,000
1947-1949	Sunburst, original binding	$29,000	$38,000

MODEL YEAR	FEATURES	EXC. COND. LOW	HIGH
1950-1959	Natural, original binding	$33,000	$43,000
1950-1959	Sunburst, original binding	$30,000	$39,000
1960-1964	Natural	$33,000	$43,000
1960-1964	Sunburst	$30,000	$39,000

Excel/Exel (Non-Cutaway)
1936-1949. Non-cut, 17" width, 1- and 3-ply bound f-hole, natural finishes were typically not offered in the '30s, non-cut Excels were generally not offered after '49 in deference to the Excel cutaway.

1936-1939	Sunburst, straight f-hole	$17,000	$22,000
1938-1939	Sunburst, standard f-hole	$17,000	$22,000
1940-1949	Natural	$18,000	$23,000
1940-1949	Sunburst	$14,500	$19,000

New Yorker (Non-Cutaway)
1936-1949. Non-cut, 18" width, 5-ply-bound f-hole, New Yorker non-cut orders were overshadowed by the cut model orders starting in '47.

1936-1939	Sunburst	$22,000	$29,000
1940-1949	Natural	$24,000	$31,000
1940-1949	Sunburst	$21,000	$28,000

New Yorker Deluxe (Cutaway)
1947-1964. Cutaway, 18" width, 5-ply-bound f-hole, New Yorker non-cut orders were overshadowed by the cut model orders starting in '47.

1947-1949	Natural	$46,000	$60,000
1947-1949	Sunburst	$40,000	$52,000
1950-1959	Natural	$46,000	$60,000
1950-1959	Sunburst	$39,000	$51,000
1960-1964	Natural	$41,000	$53,000
1960-1964	Sunburst	$36,000	$47,000

New Yorker Special
1950-1964. Also called Excel New Yorker or Excel Cutaway New Yorker Cutaway, 17" width, New Yorker styling, not to be confused with D'Angelico Special (A and B style).

1950-1959	Natural	$30,000	$39,000
1950-1959	Sunburst	$27,000	$36,000
1960-1964	Natural	$27,000	$36,000
1960-1964	Sunburst	$24,000	$31,000

Special (Cutaway)
1950-1964. Generally Style A and B-type instruments made for musicians on a budget, plain specs with little ornamentation, not to be confused with New Yorker Special.

1950-1959	Sunburst	$10,100	$13,100
1960-1964	Sunburst	$9,200	$12,000

Special (Non-Cutaway)
1950-1964. Non-cut Special, not to be confused with New Yorker Special.

1950-1959	Sunburst	$6,100	$8,000
1960-1964	Sunburst	$5,300	$6,900

Style A
1936-1945. Archtop, 17" width, unbound f-holes, block 'board inlays, multi-pointed headstock, nickel-plated metal parts.

1936-1939	Sunburst	$10,600	$13,800
1940-1945	Sunburst	$9,600	$12,500

MODEL YEAR	FEATURES	EXC. COND. LOW	HIGH
Style A-1			
1936-1945. Unbound f-holes, 17" width, arched headstock, nickel-plated metal parts.			
1936-1939	Sunburst	$10,600	$13,800
1940-1945	Sunburst	$9,600	$12,500
Style B			
1933-1948. Archtop 17" wide, unbound F-holes, block 'board inlays, gold-plated parts.			
1936-1939	Sunburst	$12,000	$15,500
1940-1948	Sunburst	$11,000	$14,500
Style B Special			
1933-1948. D'Angelico described variations from standard features with a 'Special' designation, Vintage dealers may also describe these instruments as 'Special'.			
1936-1939	Sunburst	$12,300	$16,000
1940-1948	Sunburst	$11,500	$15,000

D'Angelico (D'Angelico Guitars of America)

1988-present. Intermediate and professional grade, production/custom, archtop, flat-top, and solidbody guitars made in South Korea and imported by D'Angelico Guitars of America, of Colts Neck, New Jersey. From 1988 to '04, they were premium and presentation grade instruments built in Japan by luthier Hidesato Shino and Vestax. In '12, GTR announced they bought the brand name and are offering premium grade D'Angelicos built in the U.S.

D'Angelico (Lewis)

1994-2011. Luthier Michael Lewis built presentation grade, custom/production, D'Angelico replica guitars in Grass Valley, California, under an agreement with the GHS String Company, which owned the name in the U.S. He also builds guitars and mandolins under the Lewis name.

D'Angelico II

Mid-1990s. Archtops built in the U.S. and distributed by Archtop Enterprises of Merrick, New York. Mainly presentation grade copies of Excel and New Yorker models, but also made lower cost similar models.

MODEL YEAR	FEATURES	EXC. COND. LOW	HIGH
Jazz Classic			
1990s. Electric archtop, cutaway, carved spruce top, figured maple back and sides, single neck pickup, transparent cherry.			
1990s		$2,250	$2,900

Daniel Friederich

1955-2015. Luthier Daniel Friederich built his custom/production, classical guitars in Paris, France.

D'Aquisto

1965-1995. James D'Aquisto apprenticed under D'Angelico until the latter's death, at age 59, in '64. He started making his own brand instruments in '65 and built archtop and flat-top acoustic guitars, solidbody and hollowbody electric guitars. He also designed guitars for Hagstrom and Fender. He died in '95, at age 59.

MODEL YEAR	FEATURES	EXC. COND. LOW	HIGH
Avant Garde			
1987-1994. 18" wide, non-traditional futuristic model, approximately 5 or 6 instruments were reportedly made, because of low production this pricing is for guidance only.			
1990	Blond	$74,000	$96,000
Centura/Centura Deluxe			
1993-1994. 17" wide, non-traditional art deco futuristic archtop, approximately 10 made, the last guitars made by this luthier, due to the low production this pricing is for guidance only.			
1993-1994	Centura	$90,000	$117,000
1993-1994	Deluxe	$98,000	$127,000
Excel (Cutaway)			
1965-1992. Archtop, 17" width, with modern thin-logo started in '81.			
1965-1967	Blond	$33,000	$43,000
1965-1967	Sunburst	$31,000	$41,000
1968-1981	Blond	$33,000	$43,000
1968-1981	Sunburst	$31,000	$41,000
1982-1992	Blond	$35,000	$46,000
1982-1992	Sunburst	$34,000	$44,000
Excel (Flat-Top)			
1970s-1980s. Flat-top, 16", flamed maple back and sides, Sitka spruce top, about 15 made, narrow Excel-style headstock, oval soundhole, D'Aquisto script logo on headstock.			
1970s-80s		$17,500	$23,000
Hollow Electric			
Early model with bar pickup, D'Aquisto headstock, '70s model with humbuckers.			
1960s-80s		$14,700	$19,000
Jazz Special			
1985	1st version	$14,700	$19,000
1988	2nd version	$21,000	$27,000
New Yorker Classic (Archtop)			
1986. Single-cut acoustic archtop with new modern design features such as large S-shaped soundholes.			
1986		$54,000	$70,000
New Yorker Classic (Solidbody)			
1980s. Only 2 were reported to be made, therefore this pricing is for guidance only.			
1980s		$17,300	$22,500
New Yorker Deluxe (Cutaway)			
1965-1992. Most are 18" wide.			
1965-1981	Blond	$41,000	$53,000
1965-1981	Sunburst	$36,000	$47,000
1982-1992	Blond	$43,000	$56,000
1982-1992	Sunburst	$39,000	$51,000
New Yorker Special (7-String)			
1980s. Limited production 7-string, single-cut.			
1980s		$31,000	$41,000
New Yorker Special (Cutaway)			
1966-1992. Most are 17" wide.			
1966-1992	Blond	$27,000	$35,000
1966-1992	Sunburst	$24,000	$31,000
Solo/Solo Deluxe			
1992-1993. 18" wide, non-traditional non-cut art deco model, only 2 reported made, because of low production this pricing is for guidance only.			
1992-1993		$95,000	$125,000

Late-'30s D'Angelico Style B
Andy Nelson

1967 D'Aquisto New Yorker
Imaged by Heritage Auctions, HA.com

GUITARS

2002 D'Aquisto (Aria) New Yorker
Mike Thompson

J. Thomas Davis

MODEL YEAR	FEATURES	EXC. COND. LOW	HIGH

D'Aquisto (Aria)

May 2002-2013. Premium grade, production, D'Aquisto designs licensed to Aria of Japan by D'Aquisto Strings, Inc., Deer Park, New York.

Various Models

2002-2013		$2,500	$3,300

Dauphin

1970s-late 1990s. Classical and flamenco guitars imported from Spain and Japan by distributor George Dauphinais, located in Springfield, Illinois.

Dave King Acoustics

1980-present. Premium grade, custom/production, acoustic and resonator guitars built by luthier Dave King in Berkshire, U.K.

Dave Maize Acoustic Guitars

1991-present. Luthier Dave Maize builds his professional and premium grade, production/custom, flat-tops and basses in Cave Junction, Oregon.

David Rubio

1960s-2000. Luthier David Spink built his guitars, lutes, violins, violas, cellos and harpsichords first in New York, and after '67, in the U.K. While playing in Spain, he acquired the nickname Rubio, after his red beard. He died in '00.

David Thomas McNaught

1989-present. Professional, premium, and presentation grade, custom, solidbody guitars built by luthier David Thomas McNaught and finished by Dave Mansel in Locust, North Carolina. In '97, they added the production/custom DTM line of guitars.

Davis, J. Thomas

1975-present. Premium and presentation grade, custom, steel-string flat-tops, 12-strings, classicals, archtops, Irish citterns and flat-top Irish bouzoukis made by luthier J. Thomas Davis in Columbus, Ohio.

Davoli

See Wandre listing.

DBZ

2008-2012. Solidbody electric guitars from Dean B. Zelinsky, founder of Dean Guitars, and partners Jeff Diamant and Terry Martin. Dean left the partnership February, '12 and established Dean Zelinsky Private Label guitars.

de Jonge, Sergei

1972-present. Premium grade, production/custom classical and steel-string guitars built by luthier Sergei de Jonge originally in Oshawa, Ontario, and since '04 in Chelsea, Quebec.

MODEL YEAR	FEATURES	EXC. COND. LOW	HIGH

De Paule Stringed Instruments

1969-1980, 1993-present. Custom steel-string, nylon-string, archtop, resonator, and Hawaiian guitars built by luthier C. Andrew De Paule in Eugene, Oregon.

Dean

1976-present. Intermediate, professional and premium grade, production/custom, solidbody, hollowbody, acoustic, acoustic/electric, and resonator guitars made in the U.S., Korea, the Czech Republic and China. They also offer basses, banjos, mandolins, and amps. Founded in Evanston, Illinois, by Dean Zelinsky. Original models were upscale versions of Gibson designs with glued necks, fancy tops, DiMarzio pickups and distinctive winged headstocks (V, Z and ML), with production beginning in '77. In '80 the factory was relocated to Chicago. Dean's American manufacturing ends in '86 when all production shifts to Korea. In '91 Zelinsky sold the company to Tropical Music in Miami, Florida. For '93-'94 there was again limited U.S. (California) production of the E'Lite, Cadillac and ML models under the supervision of Zelinsky and Cory Wadley. Korean versions were also produced. In '95, Elliott Rubinson's Armadillo Enterprises, of Clearwater, Florida, bought the Dean brand. In '97 and '98, Dean offered higher-end USA Custom Shop models. In '98, they reintroduced acoustics. From 2000 to '08, Zelinsky was once again involved in the company.

Dating American models: First 2 digits are year of manufacture. Imports have no date codes.

Baby ML

1982-1986, 2000-2014. Downsized version of ML model.

1982-1986	Import	$400	$525
1982-1986	US-made	$575	$750

Baby V

1982-1986, 2000-2014. Downsized version of the V model.

1982-1986	Import	$400	$525
1982-1986	US-made	$575	$750

Baby Z

1982-1986, 2000-2014. Downsized version of the Z model.

1982-1986	Import	$400	$525
1982-1986	US-made	$575	$750

Bel Aire

1983-1984. Solidbody, possibly the first production guitar with humbucker/single/single pickup layout, U.S.-made, an import model was introduced in '87.

1980s	Import	$400	$525
1983-1984	US-made	$575	$750

Budweiser Guitar

Ca.1987. Shaped like Bud logo.

1987		$225	$300

Cadillac (U.S.A.)

1979-1985. Single long treble horn on slab body.

1979-1985		$1,700	$2,250

MODEL YEAR	FEATURES	EXC. COND. LOW	HIGH

Cadillac 1980
2006-2018. Block inlays, 2 humbuckers, gold hardware.

2006-2018		$425	$550

Cadillac Deluxe (U.S.A.)
1993-1994, 1996-1997. Made in U.S., single longhorn shape, various colors.

1993-1997		$1,200	$1,600

Cadillac Reissue (Import)
1992-1994. Single longhorn shape, 2 humbuckers, various colors.

1992-1994		$325	$425

Cadillac Select
2009-2017. Made in Korea, figured maple top, mahogany, pearl block inlays.

2009-2017		$400	$525

Cadillac Standard
1996-1997. Slab body version.

1996-1997		$1,475	$1,925

Del Sol
2008. Import, small double-cut thinline semi-hollow, ES-335 style body, rising sun fretboard markers.

2008		$350	$450

Dime O Flame (ML)
2005-2018. ML-body, Dimebuckers, burning flames finish, Dime logo on headstock.

2005-2018		$400	$525

Eighty-Eight (Import)
1987-1990. Offset double-cut solidbody, import.

1987-1990		$200	$300

E'Lite
1978-1985, 1994-1996. Single-horn shape.

1978-1985		$1,150	$1,500
1994-1996		$1,050	$1,350

E'Lite Deluxe
1980s. Single-horn shape.

1980s		$1,400	$1,800

EVO XM
2004-present. Single-cut slab body, 2 humbuckers.

2004-2021		$135	$175

Golden E'Lite
1980. Single pointy treble cutaway, fork headstock, gold hardware, ebony 'board, sunburst.

1980		$1,400	$1,800

Hollywood Z (Import)
1985-1986. Bolt-neck Japanese copy of Baby Z, Explorer shape.

1985-1986		$175	$250

Jammer (Import)
1987-1989. Offset double-cut body, bolt-on neck, dot markers, six-on-a-side tuners, various colors offered.

1987-1989		$175	$250

Leslie West Standard
2008-2017. Flame maple top, mahogany body, rosewood 'board.

2008-2017		$450	$575

Mach I (Import)
1985-1986. Limited run from Korea, Mach V with six-on-a-side tunes, various colors.

1985-1986		$175	$250

Mach V (Import)
1985-1986. Pointed solidbody, 2 humbucking pickups, maple neck, ebony 'board, locking trem, various colors, limited run from Korea.

1985-1986		$175	$250

Mach VII (U.S.A.)
1985-1986. Mach I styling, made in America, offered in unusual finishes.

1985-1986		$1,200	$1,600

ML (ML Standard/U.S.A.)
1977-1986. There is a flame model and a standard model.

1977-1986	Burst flamed top	$2,400	$3,100
1977-1986	Burst plain top	$2,300	$3,000
1977-1986	Common opaque	$1,850	$2,400

ML (Import)
1983-1990. Korean-made.

1983-1990		$500	$700

Soltero SL
2007-2010. Made in Japan, single-cut solidbody, 2 pickups, flame maple top.

2007-2010		$1,700	$2,200

USA Time Capsule Exotic V
2005-2014. Flying V style, solid mahogany body with exotic spalted and flamed maple top, Dean V neck profile (split V headstock).

2005-2014		$2,300	$3,000

USA Time Capsule Z
2000-2014. Explorer style body, figured maple top.

2000-2014		$2,300	$3,000

V Standard (U.S.A.)
1977-1986. V body, there is a standard and a flame model offered.

1977-1981	Burst flamed top	$2,700	$3,500
1977-1981	Burst plain top	$2,300	$3,000
1977-1981	Common opaque	$2,000	$2,600
1982-1986	Burst flamed top	$2,200	$2,900
1982-1986	Burst plain top	$2,100	$2,700
1982-1986	Common opaque	$1,700	$2,200

Z Standard (U.S.A.)
1977-1986. Long treble cutaway solidbody, 2 humbuckers.

1977-1983	Common finish	$1,600	$2,100
1977-1983	Rare finish	$2,100	$2,700

Z Autograph (Import)
1985-1987. The first Dean import from Korea, offset double-cut, bolt neck, dot markers, offered in several standard colors.

1985-1987		$250	$350

Z Coupe/Z Deluxe
1997-1998. US Custom Shop, mahogany body offered in several standard colors, Z Deluxe with Floyd Rose tremolo.

1997-1998		$1,000	$1,300

Z Korina
1997-1998. US Custom Shop, Z Coupe with korina body, various standard colors.

1997-1998		$1,150	$1,500

Z LTD
1997-1998. US Custom Shop, Z Coupe with bound neck and headstock, offered in several standard colors.

1997-1998		$1,150	$1,500

1981 Dean ML
Imaged by Heritage Auctions, HA.com

1979 Dean Z Standard
Imaged by Heritage Auctions, HA.com

GUITARS

DeArmond M-70
Vic Hines

2000 DeArmond
Starfire Special

MODEL		EXC. COND.	
YEAR	FEATURES	LOW	HIGH

Dean Markley

The string and pickup manufacturer offered a limited line of guitars and basses for a time in the '80s. They were introduced in '84.

Dean Zelinsky Private Label

2012-present. Premium grade, production/custom, hollow, semi-hollow and solidbody electric guitars built in Chicago, Illinois by luthier Dean Zelinsky, founder of Dean Guitars. He also imports a line of intermediate grade guitars from South Korea and Indonesia.

DeArmond Guitars

1999-2004. Solid, semi-hollow and hollow body guitars based on Guild models and imported from Korea by Fender. They also offered basses. The DeArmond brand was originally used on pickups, effects and amps built by Rowe Industries.
Electric
1999-2004. Various import models, some with USA electronic components.

1999-2004	Various models	$275	$750

Dearstone

1993-2017. Luthier Ray Dearstone built his professional and premium grade, custom, archtop and acoustic/electric guitars in Blountville, Tennessee. He also built mandolin family instruments and violins.

Decar

1950s. A private brand sold by Decautur, Illinois music store, Decar headstock logo.
Stratotone H44
1956. Private branded Stratotone with maple neck and fretboard instead of the standard neck/fretboard, 1 pickup and other Harmony H44 Stratotone attributes, bolt-on neck.

1956		$600	$800

DeCava Guitars

1983-present. Professional and premium grade, production/custom, archtop and classical guitars built by luthier Jim DeCava first in Stratford, then Ansonia, Connecticut. He also builds ukes, banjos, and mandolins.

Decca

Mid-1960s. Acoustic, solid and hollow body guitars, basses and amps made in Japan by Teisco and imported by Decca Records, Decca headstock logo, student-level instruments.
Acoustic Flat-Top
1960s. Decca label on the inside back.

1960s		$175	$250

Electric Solidbody
1960s. Teisco-made in Japan, 3 pickups, sunburst.

1960s		$350	$450

MODEL		EXC. COND.	
YEAR	FEATURES	LOW	HIGH

Defil

Based out of Lubin, Poland, Defil made solid and semi-hollowbdy electric guitars at least from the 1970s to the '90s.

DeGennaro

2003-present. Premium grade, custom/production, acoustic, archtop, semi-hollow and solidbody guitars, basses and mandolins built by luthier William DeGennaro in Grand Rapids, Michigan.

Del Oro

1930s-1940s. Flat-top (including cowboy stencil models) and resonator guitars, built by Kay. At least the cowboy stencils were sold by Spiegel.
Small Acoustic

1930s	13" to 14" body	$225	$300

Del Pilar Guitars

1956-1986. Luthier William Del Pilar made his classical guitars in Brooklyn, New York.
Classical
1950s-1980s. Brazilian rosewood back and sides, cedar top, quilt rosette, 9-ply top binding.

1960-1969		$4,600	$6,000

Del Vecchio

1902-present. Casa Del Vecchio builds a variety of Spanish instruments including acoustic and resonator guitars in São Paulo, Brazil.

Delaney Guitars

2004-present. Luthier Mike Delaney builds his professional grade, production/custom, chambered, solidbody, and semi-hollowbody electric guitars and basses in Atlanta, Georgia. Prior to 2008 he built in Florence, Montana.

Delgado

1928-present. Delgado began in Torreon, Coahuila, Mexico, then moved to Juarez in the '30s with a second location in Tijuana. In '48 they moved to California and opened a shop in Los Angeles. Since 2005, Manuel A. Delgado, a third generation luthier, builds his premium and presentation grade, production/custom, classical, flamenco and steel string acoustic guitars in Nashville, Tennessee. He also builds basses, mandolins, ukuleles and banjos.

Delirium Custom Guitars

Luthiers Patrick and Vincent Paul-Victor along with Gael Canonne build their professional and premium grade, production/custom, solidbody electric guitars in Paris and Toulouse, France.

Dell'Arte

1997-present. Production/custom Maccaferri-style guitars from John Kinnard and Alain Cola. In '96, luthier John Kinnard opened a small shop called Finegold Guitars and Mandolins. In '98 he met Alain Cola, a long time jazz guitarist who was selling Mexican-made copies of Selmer/Maccaferri guitars under the Dell'Arte brand. Cola wanted better workmanship for his guitars, and in October '98, Finegold and Dell'Arte merged. As of May '99 all production is in California.

Delta Guitars

2005-2010. Acoustic, acoustic/electric, and solidbody electric guitars from Musician's Wholesale America, Nashville, Tennessee.

Dennis Hill Guitars

Premium and presentation grade, production/custom, classical and flamenco guitars built by luthier Dennis Hill in Panama City, Florida. He has also built dulcimers, mandolins, and violins.

Desmond Guitars

1991-present. Luthier Robert B. Desmond builds his premium grade, production/custom classical guitars in Orlando, Florida.

DeTemple

1995-present. Premium grade, production/custom, solidbody electric guitars and basses built by luthier Michael DeTemple in Sherman Oaks, California.

DeVoe Guitars

1975-present. Luthier Lester DeVoe builds his premium grade, production/custom flamenco and classical guitars in Nipomo, California.

Diamond

Ca. 1963-1964. Line of sparkle finish solidbody guitars made in Italy for the Diamond Accordion company.

Ranger

Ca. 1963-1964. Rangers came with 1, 2, 3, or 4 pickups, sparkle finish.

1960s		$600	$800

Dick, Edward Victor

1975-present. Luthier Edward Dick currently builds his premium grade, custom, classical guitars in Denver, Colorado (he lived in Peterborough and Ottawa, Ontario until '95). He also operates the Colorado School of Lutherie.

Dickerson

1937-1947. Founded by the Dickerson brothers in '37, primarily for electric lap steels and small amps. Instruments were also private branded for Cleveland's Oahu company, and for the Gourley brand. By '47, the company changed ownership and was renamed Magna Electronics (Magnatone).

Dillion

1996-2021. Dillion, of Cary, North Carolina, offers intermediate grade, production, acoustic, acoustic/electric, hollow-body and solidbody guitars, basses and mandolins made in Korea and Vietnam. Stopped making instruments in '21.

Dillon

1975-2006. Professional and premium grade, custom, flat-tops and basses built by luthier John Dillon in Taos, New Mexico, and in Bloomsburg, Pennsylvania ('81-'01).

Dino's Guitars

Custom, professional grade, electric solidbody guitars built by a social co-op company founded by Alessio Casati and Andy Bagnasco, in Albisola, Italy. They also build effects.

DiPinto

1995-present. Intermediate and professional grade, production retro-vibe guitars and basses from luthier Chris DiPinto of Philadelphia, Pennsylvania. Until late '99, all instruments built in the U.S., since then all built in Korea.

Ditson

1835-1937. Started in Boston by music publisher Oliver Ditson, by the end of the 1800s the company was one of the East Coast's largest music businesses, operating in several cities and was also involved in distribution and manufacturing of a variety of instruments, including guitars and ukes. From 1916-1930 Ditson guitars were made by Martin. The majority of Martin production was from '16 to '22 with over 500 units sold in '21. Ditson also established Lyon and Healy in Chicago and the John Church Company in Cincinnati.

Values for Ditson Models 111 and 1-45 would be equivalent to those for Martin models from that era with similar specs.

Concert

1916-1922. Similar in size to Martin size 0. Models include Style 1, Style 2 and Style 3.

1916-1922	Style 1	$5,150	$6,700
1916-1922	Style 2	$6,100	$8,000
1916-1922	Style 3	$6,700	$8,700

Standard

1916-1922. Small body similar to Martin size 3, plain styling. Models include Style 1, Style 2 and Style 3.

1916-1922	Style 1	$3,400	$4,400
1916-1922	Style 2	$4,100	$5,300
1916-1922	Style 3	$5,300	$6,900

D'Leco Guitars

1991-2003. Guitarist Maurice Johnson and luthier James W. Dale built premium grade, production/custom archtops in Oklahoma City, Oklahoma.

DM Darling Guitars

Luthier Denis Merrill, began in 2006, builds professional and premium grade, custom, acoustic, classical, resonator and solidbody guitars in Tacoma, Washington. From 1978 to '06 he built under his own name and Merrill Custom Shop. He also builds mandolin family instruments.

DeTemple Spirit Series Stellacasta

DiPinto Orbital

1976 Dobro Bicentennial

James Seldin

Dobro D-10

Bernunzio Uptown Music

Dobro

1929-1942, ca. 1954-2019. Currently, professional and premium grade, production, wood and metal body resophonic guitars offered by Gibson.

Founded 1929 in Los Angeles by John Dopyera, Rudy Dopyera, Ed Dopyera and Vic Smith (Dobro stands for Dopyera Brothers). Made instruments sold under the Dobro, Regal, Norwood Chimes, Angelus, Rex, Broman, Montgomery Ward, Penetro, Bruno, Alhambra, More Harmony, Orpheum, and Magn-o-tone brands.

Dobro instruments have a single cone facing outward with a spider bridge structure and competed with National products. Generally, model names are numbers referring to list price and therefore materials and workmanship (e.g., a No. 65 cost $65). Because of this, the same model number may apply to various different instruments. However, model numbers are never identified on instruments!

In '30, the company name was changed to Dobro Corporation, Ltd. In '32, Louis Dopyera buys Ted Kleinmeyer's share of National. Louis, Rudy and Ed now hold controlling interest in National, but in '32 John Dopyera left Dobro to pursue idea of metal resophonic violin. In December of '34 Ed Dopyera joins National's board of directors (he's also still on Dobro board), and by March of '35 Dobro and National have merged to become the National Dobro Corporation. Dobro moves into National's larger factory but continues to maintain separate production, sales and distribution until relocation to Chicago is complete. Beginning in early-'36 National Dobro starts relocating its offices to Chicago. L.A. production of Dobros continues until '37, after which some guitars continue to be assembled from parts until '39, when the L.A. operations were closed down.

All resonator production ended in '42. Victor Smith, Al Frost and Louis Dopyera buy the company and change the name to the Valco Manufacturing Company. The Dobro name does not appear when production resumes after World War II.

In mid-'50s - some sources say as early as '54 - Rudy and Ed Dopyera began assembling wood-bodied Dobros from old parts using the name DB Original. In about '59, some 12-fret DB Originals were made for Standel, carrying both DB Original and Standel logos. In around '61, production was moved to Gardena, California, and Louis Dopyera and Valco transferred the Dobro name to Rudy and Ed, who produce the so-called Gardena Dobros. At this time, the modern Dobro logo appeared with a lyre that looks like 2 back-to-back '6s'. Dobro Original debuts ca. '62. In late-'64 the Dobro name was licensed to Ed's son Emil (Ed, Jr.) Dopyera. Ed, Jr. designs a more rounded Dobro (very similar to later Mosrites) and has falling out with Rudy over it.

In '66 Semi Moseley acquires the rights to the Dobro brand, building some in Gardena, and later moving to Bakersfield, California. Moseley introduced Ed, Jr's design plus a thinline double-cutaway Dobro. He also made MoBros during this time period. Moseley Dobros use either Dobro or National cones. In '67 Ed, Sr., Rudy and Gabriella Lazar start the Original Music Instrument Company (OMI) and produce Hound Dog brand Dobros. In '68 Moseley goes bankrupt and in '70 OMI obtains the rights to the Dobro brand and begins production of OMI Dobros. In '75 Gabriella's son and daughter, Ron Lazar and Dee Garland, take over OMI. Rudy Dupyera makes and sells Safari brand resonator mandolins. Ed, Sr. dies in '77 and Rudy in '78. In '84 OMI was sold to Chester and Betty Lizak. Both wood and metal-bodied Dobros produced in Huntington Beach, California. Chester Lizak died in '92. Gibson purchased Dobro in '93 and made Dobros in Nashville, Tennessee.

Dobros generally feature a serial number which, combined with historical information, provides a clue to dating. For prewar L.A. guitars, see approximation chart below adapted from "Gruhn's Guide to Vintage Guitars." No information exists on DB Originals.

Gardena Dobros had D prefix plus 3 digits beginning with 100 and going into the 500s (reportedly under 500 made). No information is available on Moseley Dobros.

OMI Dobros from '70-'79 have either D prefix for wood bodies or B prefix for metal bodies, plus 3 or 4 numbers for ranking, space, then a single digit for year (D XXXX Y or B XXX Y; e.g., D 172 8 would be wood body #172 from '78). For '80-'87 OMI Dobros, start with first number of year (decade) plus 3 or 4 ranking numbers, space, then year and either D for wood or B for metal bodies (8 XXXX YD or 8 XXX YB; e.g., 8 2006 5B would be metal body #2008 from '85). From '88-'92, at least, a letter and number indicate guitar style, plus 3 or 4 digits for ranking, letter for neck style, 2 digits for year, and letter for body style (AX XXXX NYYD or AX XXX NYYB).

L.A. Guitars (approx. number ranges, not actual production totals):

1929-30	900-2999
1930-31	3000-3999
1931-32	BXXX (Cyclops models only)
1932-33	5000-5599
1934-36	5700-7699
1937-42	8000-9999

Angelus

1933-1937. Wood body, round or square neck, 2-tone walnut finish, continues as Model 19 in Regal-made guitars.

MODEL YEAR	FEATURES	EXC. COND. LOW	EXC. COND. HIGH
1933-1937	Round neck	$1,300	$1,700
1933-1937	Square neck	$1,400	$1,800

Artist M-16

1934-1935. German silver alloy body, engraved.

1934-1935	H square neck	$3,800	$4,900
1934-1935	M round neck	$6,000	$7,800

Columbia D-12

1967-1968. Acoustic 12-string, typical Dobro resonator with spider style bridge, made during Dobro-Moseley era.

1967-1968		$850	$1,100

MODEL YEAR	FEATURES	EXC. COND. LOW	HIGH

Cyclops 45
1932-1933. Bound walnut body, 1 screen hole.

| 1932-1933 | Round neck | $2,850 | $3,700 |
| 1932-1933 | Square neck | $3,300 | $4,300 |

D-40 Texarkana
1965-1967. Mosrite-era (identified by C or D prefix), traditional Dobro style cone and coverplate, dot inlays, Dobro logo on headstock, sunburst wood body. Red and blue finishes available.

| 1965-1967 | | $1,100 | $1,400 |

D-40E Texarkana
1965-1967. D-40 electric with single pickup and 2 knobs.

| 1965-1967 | | $1,150 | $1,500 |

D-100 The Californian
1965-1969. Dobro's version of Mosrite (thus nicknamed the "Mobro") thinline double-cut, resonator, 2 small metal ports, 2 pickups, 2 knobs, sunburst.

| 1965-1969 | | $1,600 | $2,100 |

DM-33 California Girl/DM-33H
1996-2006. Chrome-plated bell brass body, biscuit bridge, spider resonator, rosewood 'board. Girl or Hawaiian-scene (H) engraving.

| 1996-2006 | | $1,450 | $1,900 |

Dobjo
Dobro body, banjo neck, 5-string.

| 1989 | | $1,150 | $1,500 |

Dobro/Regal Model 19
Ca.1934-1938. In the 1930s Dobro licensed Chicago's Regal Company to build Dobro-style guitars. The headstocks on these models can have a Dobro logo, Regal logo, or no logo at all. The 19 is a lower-end model, round holes in coverplate, square neck.

| 1934-1938 | | $1,300 | $1,700 |

Dobro/Regal Model 46/47
1935-1942. Dobro/Regal 46, renamed 47 in '39, aluminum body, round neck, 14 frets, slotted headstock, silver finish. Degraded finish was a common problem with the Dobro/Regal 47.

| 1935-1938 | Model 46 | $1,600 | $2,100 |
| 1939-1942 | Model 47 | $2,200 | $2,900 |

Dobro/Regal Model 62/65
1935-1942. Renamed Model 65 in '39, nickel-plated brass body, Spanish dancer etching, round or square neck. Note: Dobro/Regal 65 should not be confused with Dobro Model 65 which discontinued earlier.

| 1935-1942 | Model 62 | $2,600 | $3,400 |
| 1935-1942 | Model 65 | $2,600 | $3,400 |

Dobro/Regal Tenor 27-1/2
1930. Tenor version of Model 27.

| 1930 | | $600 | $800 |

Dobrolektric
1996-2005. Resonator guitar with single-coil neck pickup, single-cut.

| 1996-2005 | | $1,300 | $1,700 |

DS-33/Steel 33
1995-2000. Steel body with light amber sunburst finish, resonator with coverplate, biscuit bridge.

| 1995-2000 | | $1,000 | $1,300 |

DW-90C
2001-2006. Single sharp cutaway, wood body, metal resonator, f-hole upper bass bout.

| 2001-2006 | | $975 | $1,250 |

E3 (C, M, W, B)
Late 1970s-1986. Double-cut solidbodies with necks and bodies of laminated select hardwoods, Cinnamon (C), Maple (M), Walnut (W) or plain Black (B) finish, 2 pickups.

| 1979-1986 | | $1,300 | $1,700 |

F-60/F-60S
1986-2005. Round neck (60, discontinued '00) or square neck (60S), f-holes, brown sunburst.

| 1986-2005 | | $1,300 | $1,700 |

Gardena
1968. Electric Dobro body, 2 knobs, single-coil soap bar pickup.

| 1968 | | $850 | $1,100 |

Hound Dog
2002-2019. Laminated wood, 10 1/2" spider-bridge resonator.

| 2002-2019 | | $425 | $550 |

Hula Blues
1987-1999. Dark brown wood body (earlier models have much lighter finish), painted Hawaiian scenes, round neck.

| 1987-1999 | | $1,200 | $1,600 |

Jerry Douglas
1995-2005. Mahogany body, square neck, limited run of 200 with signature, but also sold without signature.

| 1995-2005 | | $2,100 | $2,800 |

Josh Graves
1995-2005. First 200 made were signed, single bound ample body, spider cone, nickel plated. Includes DW Josh Graves and Uncle Josh Limited models.

| 1995 | Signed | $1,775 | $2,300 |
| 1996-2005 | Unsigned | $1,450 | $1,900 |

Leader 14M/14H
1934-1935. Nickel plated brass body, segmented f-holes.

| 1934-1935 | H square neck | $2,200 | $2,900 |
| 1934-1935 | M round neck | $1,850 | $2,400 |

Model 25
1930-1935. Sunburst wood body, f-holes upper bout, large single metal cone, square neck.

| 1930-1935 | | $1,700 | $2,200 |

Model 27 (OMI)
1976-1994. Wood body, square neck.

| 1976-1994 | | $1,400 | $1,800 |

Model 27 Cyclops
1932-1933.

| 1932-1933 | Round neck | $1,850 | $2,400 |
| 1932-1933 | Square neck | $1,950 | $2,500 |

Model 27 Deluxe
1995-2005. 27 with figured maple top, nicer appointments.

| 1996-2005 | | $1,800 | $2,300 |

Model 27/27G
1933-1937. Regal-made, wooden body.

| 1933-1937 | Round neck | $1,550 | $2,000 |
| 1933-1937 | Square neck | $1,800 | $2,300 |

1986 Dobro E3 C

Imaged by Heritage Auctions, HA.com

2003 Dobro Hound Dog

Tom Pfeifer

1937 Dobro Model 62
Bernunzio Uptown Music

1973 Dobro Model 63
Imaged by Heritage Auctions, HA.com

MODEL YEAR	FEATURES	EXC. COND. LOW	HIGH
Model 32			
1939-1941. Regal-made, wooden body.			
1939-1941		$2,100	$2,700
Model 33 (Duolian)			
1972. Only made in '72, becomes Model 90 in '73.			
1972		$1,075	$1,400
Model 33 H			
1973-1997 (OMI & Gibson). Same as 33 D, but with etched Hawaiian scenes, available as round or square neck.			
1980s-90s	Round neck	$1,550	$2,000
1980s-90s	Square neck	$1,550	$2,000
Model 35 (32)			
1935-1942. Metal body, called Model 32 (not to be confused with wood body 32) for '35-'38.			
1935-1942		$2,200	$2,900
Model 36			
1932-1937. Wood body with resonator, round or square neck.			
1932-1937	Round neck	$1,400	$1,800
1932-1937	Square neck	$1,800	$2,300
Model 36/36S			
1970s-1997, 2002-2005. Chrome-plated brass body, round or square (S) neck, dot markers, engraved rose floral art.			
1970s-2005		$1,600	$2,100
Model 37			
1933-1937. Regal-made wood body, mahogany, bound body and 'board, round or square 12-fret neck.			
1933-1937	Round neck	$1,600	$2,100
1933-1937	Square neck	$1,900	$2,500
Model 37 Tenor			
1933-1937 (Regal). Tenor version of No. 37.			
1933-1937		$1,000	$1,300
Model 45			
1934-1939. Regal-made wood body, round or square neck.			
1934-1939	Round neck	$2,000	$2,600
1934-1939	Square neck	$2,300	$3,000
Model 55/56 Standard			
1929-1934. Model 55 Standard, renamed 56 Standard 1932-1934. Unbound wood body, metal resonator, bound neck, sunburst.			
1929-1934	Round neck	$1,800	$2,300
1929-1934	Square neck	$2,150	$2,800
Model 60			
1933-1936. Similar to Model 66/66B.			
1933-1936	Round neck	$4,000	$5,200
1933-1936	Square neck	$4,900	$6,400
Model 60 Cyclops			
1932-1933. Round neck, 12-fret model, black walnut finish.			
1932-1933		$4,000	$5,200
Model 60/ 60D (OMI)/ 60DS			
1970-1993. Wood body (laminated maple) with Dobro resonator cone, model 60 until '73 when renamed 60 D, and various 60 model features offered, post-'93 was Gibson-owned production.			
1970-1993	Model 60 Series	$1,075	$1,400
Model 63			
1973-1996. Wood body, 8-string, square neck.			
1973-1996		$1,125	$1,450

MODEL YEAR	FEATURES	EXC. COND. LOW	HIGH
Model 64			
1980s-1995. Walnut body, tree-of-life inlay.			
1982		$1,550	$2,000
Model 65/66/66B			
1929-1933. Wood body with sandblasted ornamental design top and back, metal resonator, sunburst. Model 66 B has bound top.			
1929-1931	Model 65	$2,500	$3,300
1932-1933	Model 66	$2,500	$3,300
1932-1933	Model 66B	$2,500	$3,300
Model 66/66 S			
1972-1995. Wood body with sandblasted ornamental design top and back, metal resonator, sunburst, round or square (S) neck.			
1972-1995		$925	$1,200
Model 75/Lily of the Valley			
1972-1997, 2002-2005. Chrome plated bell brass body resonator, round neck, Lily of the Valley engraving.			
1972-1997		$1,850	$2,400
Model 85/86			
1929-1934. Wood body, triple-bound, round or square neck, renamed 86 in '32.			
1929-1934		$2,500	$3,200
Model 90 (Duolian) (OMI)			
1972-1995. Chrome-plated, f-holes, etched Hawaiian scene.			
1972-1995	Various models	$1,300	$1,700
Model 90 (Woodbody)/WB90G/WB90S			
1984-2005. Maple body with upper bout f-holes or sound holes, round neck, metal resonator with spider bridge, sunburst.			
1984-2005		$1,125	$1,450
Model 125 De Luxe			
1929-1934. Black walnut body, round or square neck, Dobro De Luxe engraved, triple-bound top, back and 'board, nickel-plated hardware, natural.			
1929-1934	Round neck	$5,600	$7,300
1929-1934	Square neck	$10,400	$13,500
Professional 15M/15H			
1934-1935. Engraved nickel body, round (M) or square (H) neck, solid peghead.			
1934-1935	H square neck	$2,700	$3,500
1934-1935	M round neck	$2,400	$3,100

Dodge

1996-present. Luthier Rick Dodge builds his intermediate and professional grade, production, solidbody guitars with changeable electronic modules in Tallahassee, Florida. He also builds basses.

Doitsch

1930s. Acoustic guitars made by Harmony most likely for a music store or studio.

Domino

Ca. 1967-1968. Solidbody and hollowbody electric guitars and basses imported from Japan by Maurice Lipsky Music Co. of New York, New York, previously responsible for marketing the Orpheum brand. Models are primarily near-copies of EKO, Vox, and

MODEL YEAR	FEATURES	EXC. COND. LOW	HIGH

Fender designs, plus some originals. Models were made by Arai or Kawai. Earlier models may have been imported, but this is not yet documented.

Electric
1967-1968. Various models including the Baron, Californian, Californian Rebel, Dawson, and Spartan.

1967-1968		$300	$500

Dommenget
1978-1985, 1988-present. Luthier Boris Dommenget (pronounced dommen-jay) builds his premium grade, custom/production, solidbody, flat-top, and archtop guitars in Balje, Germany. From '78 to '85 he was located in Wiesbaden, and from '88-'01 in Hamburg. He and wife Fiona also make pickups.

Don Musser Guitars
Luthier Don Musser, in 1976, began building custom, classical and flat-top guitars in Silver City, New Mexico. He later moved his shop to Cotopaxi, Colorado.

Doolin Guitars
1997-present. Luthier Mike Doolin builds his premium grade, production/custom acoustics featuring his unique double-cut in Portland, Oregon.

Dorado
Ca. 1972-1973. Six- and 12-string acoustic guitars, solidbody electrics and basses. Brand used briefly by Baldwin/Gretsch on line of Japanese imports.

Acoustic Flat-Top/Acoustic Dobro
1972-1973. Includes folk D, jumbo Western, and grand concert styles (with laminated rosewood back and sides), and Dobro-style.

1972-1973	Higher-end	$300	$500
1972-1973	Lower-end	$175	$250
1972-1973	Mid-level	$200	$300

Solidbody Electric
1972-1973. Includes Model 5985, a double-cut with 2 P-90-style pickups.

1972-1973		$300	$500

Douglas Ching
Luthier Douglas J. Ching builds his premium grade, production/custom, classical, acoustic, and harp guitars currently in Chester, Virginia, and previously in Hawaii ('76-'89) and Michigan ('90-'93). He also builds ukes, lutes and violins.

D'Pergo Custom Guitars
2002-present. Professional, premium, and presentation grade, production/custom, solidbody guitars built in Windham, New Hampshire. Every component of the guitars is built by D'Pergo.

Dragge Guitars
1982-2010. Luthier Peter Dragge builds his custom, steel-string and nylon-string guitars in Ojai, California.

MODEL YEAR	FEATURES	EXC. COND. LOW	HIGH

Dragonfly Guitars
1994-present. Professional grade, production/custom, sloped cutaway flat-tops, semi-hollow body electrics, basses and dulcitars built by luthier Dan Richter in Roberts Creek, British Columbia.

Drive
Ca. 2001-ca. 2011. Budget grade, production, import solidbody electric guitars and basses. They also offered solidstate amps.

DTM
See David Thomas McNaught listing.

Dudley Custom Guitars
2005-present. Luthier Peter Dudley builds his custom, premium grade, chambered solidbody electric guitars in Easton, Maryland.

Duelin Guitars
Professional grade, production/custom, 6 ½ string guitars designed by Don Scheib of Simi Valley and built by luthier Mike Lipe in Sun Valley, California.

Duesenberg
1995-present. Professional and premium grade, production/custom, solid and hollow body electric guitars and basses built by luthier Dieter Goelsdorf in Hannover, Germany. Rockinger had a Duesenberg guitar in the 1980s.

Dunwell Guitars
Professional and premium grade, custom, flat-tops built by luthier Alan Dunwell in Nederland, Colorado.

Dupont
Luthier Maurice Dupont builds his classical, archtop, Weissenborn-style and Selmer-style guitars in Cognac, France.

Dwight
See info under Epiphone Dwight guitar.

Dyer
1902-1939. The massive W. J. Dyer & Bro. store in St. Paul, Minnesota, sold a complete line of music related merchandise though they actually built nothing but a few organs. The Larson Brothers of Chicago were commissioned to build harp guitar and harp mandolin pieces for them somewhat following the harp guitar design of Chris Knutsen, until 1912 when the Knutsen patent expired. Although the body design somewhat copied the Knutsen patent the resulting instrument was in a class by itself in comparison. These harp guitars have become the standard by which all others are judged because of their ease of play and the tremendous, beautiful sound they produce. Many modern builders are using the body design and the same structural

1965 Domino Californian
Rivington Guitars

Duesenberg Mike Campbell II

Eastman T146SM

Eastwood Sidejack Pro DLX

ideas evidenced in the Larson originals. They were built in Styles 4 (the plainest), 5, 6, 7 and 8. The ornamentation went from the no binding, dot inlay Style 4 to the full treatment, abalone trimmed, tree-of-life fingerboard of the Style 8. All had mahogany back and sides with ebony fingerboard and bridge. There are also a very few Style 3 models found of late that are smaller than the standard and have a lower bout body point. Other Dyer instruments were built by Knutsen. Dyer also carried Stetson brand instruments made by the Larson Brothers.

MODEL		EXC. COND.	
YEAR	FEATURES	LOW	HIGH
Harp Guitar Style 3			
1902-1920s	Small, short scale	$3,800	$5,000
Harp Guitar Style 4			
1902-1920s	No binding	$3,800	$5,000
Harp Guitar Style 5			
1902-1920s	Bound top	$4,600	$6,000
Harp Guitar Style 6			
1902-1920s	Bound top/bottom	$5,300	$7,000
Harp Guitar Style 7			
1902-1920s	Fancy inlays	$6,000	$8,000
Harp Guitar Style 8			
1902-1920s	Tree-of-life	$9,000	$12,000

Dynacord

1950-present. Dynacord is a German company that makes audio and pro sound amps, as well as other electronic equipment. In 1966-'67 they offered solidbody guitars and basses from the Welson Company of Italy. They also had the Cora guitar and bass which is the center part of a guitar body with a tube frame in a guitar outline. They also offered tape echo machines.

Dynelectron

1960s-late 1970s. This Italian builder offered a variety of guitars and basses, but is best known today for their almost exact copies of Danelectro Longhorns of the mid-'60s.

E L Welker

Luthier Eugene L. Welker began building in 1984, premium and presentation grade, production/custom, leather-wrapped archtop guitars in Claremont, New Hampshire.

E.L. Bashore Guitars

2011-present. Professional grade, custom, steel string and classical acoustic and solidbody electric guitars, basses and banjos built by luthier Eric L. Bashore in Danville, Pennsylvania.

Earthwood

1972-1985. Acoustic designs by Ernie Ball with input from George Fullerton and made in Newport Beach, California. One of the first to offer acoustic basses.

Eastman

1992-present. Intermediate and professional grade, production, archtop and flat-top guitars

and basses, mainly built in China, with some from Germany and Romania. Beijing, China-based Eastman Strings started out building violins and cellos. They added guitars in '02 and mandolins in '04.

Eastwood

1997-present. Mike Robinson's company imports budget and intermediate grade, production, solid and semi-hollowbody guitars, many styled after 1960s models. They also offer basses and mandolins.

Eaton, William

1976-present. Luthier William Eaton builds custom specialty instruments such as vihuelas, harp guitars, and lyres in Phoenix, Arizona. He is also the Director of the Robetto-Venn School of Luthiery.

Echopark Guitars

2010-present. Premium and presentation grade, production/custom, solidbody electric guitars built by luthier Gabriel Currie in Detroit, Michigan, formerly in Los Angeles, California.

Ed Claxton Guitars

1972-present. Premium grade, custom flat-tops made by luthier Ed Claxton, first in Austin, Texas, and currently in Santa Cruz, California.

Eduardo Duran Ferrer

Luthier Eduardo Duran Ferrer, since 1987, builds premium grade, classical guitars in Granada, Spain.

Edward Klein

1998-present. Premium grade, custom, guitars built by luthier Edward Klein in Mississauga, Ontario.

EER Custom

2005-present. Professional and premium grade, custom, soldibody and semi-hollowbody electric guitars built by luthier Ernest E. Roesler in Forks, Washington.

Egmond

1935-1972. Founded by Ulke Egmond, building acoustic, archtop, semi-hollow and solidbody guitars originally in Eindhoven, later in Best Holland. They also made basses. Egmond also produced instruments under the Orpheum (imported into U.S.), Rosetti (England), Miller, Wilson and Lion brands.

Electric			
1960-1972. Solid or semi-hollow bodies.			
1960-1972		$500	$700

Ehlers

1968-2011. Luthier Rob Ehlers built his premium grade, production/custom, flat-top acoustic guitars, originally in Oregon and from '06 to '11, in Veracruz, Mexico. Rob died in November, 2011.

MODEL YEAR	FEATURES	EXC. COND. LOW	HIGH
15 CRC			
Cutaway, Western red cedar top, Indian rosewood back and sides.			
1996		$2,300	$3,000
15 SRC			
Cutaway, European spruce top, Indian rosewood back and sides.			
1998		$2,300	$3,000
16 BTM			
European spruce top, mahogany back and sides, Troubadour peghead, black lacquer finish.			
1998		$2,400	$3,100
16 C			
16" lower bout, cutaway, flamed maple sides and back, European spruce top.			
1990		$2,400	$3,100
16 SK Concert			
16" lower bout, relatively small upper bout, small waist, European spruce top, flamed koa back and sides, diamond markers, natural.			
1993		$2,100	$2,800
16 SM			
European spruce top, mahogany back and sides.			
1999		$2,000	$2,650
16 SSC			
Cutaway, European spruce top, English sycamore back and sides.			
1996		$2,100	$2,800
25 C			
Limited Edition Anniversary Model, European spruce top, Indian rosewood back and sides, abalone top border.			
2001		$3,100	$4,100
GJ (Gypsy Jazz)			
2000s	D-style	$2,100	$2,700

Eichelbaum Guitars

2006-present. Luthier David Eichelbaum builds his premium grade, custom, flat-tops in Santa Barbara, California.

EKO

1959-present. Originally acoustic, acoustic/electric, electric thinline and full-size archtop hollowbody, solidbody electric guitars and basses built by Oliviero Pigini and Company in Recanati, Italy, and imported by LoDuca Brothers, Milwaukee, Radio and Television Equipment Company in Santa Ana, California and others. First acoustic guitars followed by sparkle plastic-covered electrics by '62. Sparkle finishes are gone ca. '66. Pigini dies ca. '67. LoDuca Bros. phases out in early-'70s. By '75 EKO offers some copy guitars and they purchased a custom shop to make other brands by '78. In '85 they ceased production in Italy, continuing the brand for a few years with Asian imports, and continued to distribute other brands. By 2004, the Eko line of guitar was revived with budget and intermediate grade, production, classical, acoustic, acoustic/electric, solidbody, solidbody, and hollowbody guitars made in Asia. They also make basses and amps.

MODEL YEAR	FEATURES	EXC. COND. LOW	HIGH
Barracuda VI			
1966-ca.1978. Double-cut semi-hollow, 2 pickups, 6-string.			
1966-1978		$600	$800
Barracuda XII			
1966-ca.1978. Double-cut semi-hollow, 2 pickups, 12-string.			
1966-1978		$650	$850
Cobra I/II/III/XII			
1966-1978. Double-cut solidbody, 2 knobs. Cobra I has 1 pickup, II 2 pickups and III 3 pickups. 12-string Cobra XII offered '67-'69, has 2 pickups.			
1966-1978	Cobra I	$375	$500
1966-1978	Cobra II	$450	$600
1966-1978	Cobra III	$500	$650
1966-1978	Cobra XII	$500	$650
Commander			
1965. Single-cut archtop electric, 1 pickup, 2 controls, EKO logo on upper bass bout, maple body in 'dura-glos' finish.			
1965		$425	$550
Condor			
1966-ca.1969. Double-cut solidbody with 3 or 4 pickups.			
1966-1969		$550	$725
Dragon			
1967-ca.1969. Single-cut archtop, 2 f-holes, 3 pickups, tremolo.			
1967-1969		$650	$850
Flat-Top Acoustic			
1960s. Various student-level flat-top acoustic models.			
1960s		$275	$350
Florentine			
1964-ca.1969. Double-cut archtop, 2 pickups.			
1964-1969		$575	$750
Kadett/Kadett XII			
1967-ca.1978. Double-cut solidbody with point on lower bass side of body, 3 pickups, tremolo. 12-string Kadett XII offered '68-'69.			
1967-1978	Kadett	$575	$750
1968-1969	Kadett XII	$575	$750
Lancer Stereo			
1967-1969. Lancer VI with stereo output (route output to 2 amplifiers requires EKO stereo cable for stereo application).			
1967-1969		$450	$600
Lancer VI			
1967-ca.1969. Double-cut solidbody, 2 pickups.			
1967-1969		$350	$450
Lancer XII			
1967-1969. Double-cut solidbody electric, 12-string.			
1967-1969		$425	$550
Lark I/II			
1970. Thin hollow cutaway, sunburst. Lark I has 1 pickup and Lark II 2.			
1970	Lark I	$500	$650
1970	Lark II	$500	$650
Model 180			
1960s. Cutaway acoustic archtop.			
1960s		$350	$450

EER Custom E-06 Classic

Ehlers 15" SJC
Nort Graham

EKO Ranger 12
Seth Andrews

1976 Electra Elvin Bishop
Greg Perrine

MODEL		EXC. COND.	
YEAR	FEATURES	LOW	HIGH

Model 285 Modello
1960s. Thinline single-cut, 1 pickup.

| 1962 | | $450 | $600 |

Model 290/2V
1963-1965. Maple body and neck, ebony 'board, dot markers, 2 pickups, tremolo, renamed Barracuda in '66.

| 1963-1965 | | $575 | $750 |

Model 300/375
1962. Copy of Hofner Club-style electric, single-cut, 2 pickups, set-neck.

| 1962 | | $850 | $1,100 |

Model 400 Ekomaster
1960-1962. Jazzmaster-style, 1, 2 or 4 (2+2) pickups, sparkle finish.

| 1960-1962 | 4 pickups | $775 | $1,000 |

Model 500/1 and 500/1V
1961-1965. Plastic covered solidbody, 1 pickup. 500/1 no vibrato, 1V with vibrato.

| 1961-1965 | 500/1 | $650 | $850 |
| 1961-1965 | 500/1V | $725 | $950 |

Model 500/2 and 500/3V
1961-1964. Plastic covered solidbody, plastic sparkle finish. 500/2 no vibrato, 2 pickups. 3V with vibrato, 3 pickups.

| 1961-1965 | 500/2 | $725 | $950 |
| 1961-1965 | 500/3V | $775 | $1,000 |

Model 500/4 and 500/4V
1961-1964. Plastic covered solidbody, 4 pickups. 500/4 no vibrato, 4V with vibrato.

| 1961-1965 | 500/4 | $925 | $1,200 |
| 1961-1965 | 500/4V | $1,000 | $1,300 |

Model 540 (Classical)
1960s. Nylon-string classical guitar.

| 1960s | | $275 | $350 |

Model 700/3V
1961-1964. Map-shape/tulip-shape body, 3 pickups, vibrato, woodgrain plastic finish.

| 1961-1964 | | $1,150 | $1,500 |

Model 700/4V
1961-1967. Map-shape/tulip-shape body, 4 pickups, multiple switches, vibrato.

| 1961-1967 | Red, blue, silver sparkle | $1,300 | $1,700 |
| 1961-1967 | Standard finish | $1,150 | $1,500 |

Ranger 6/12
1967-ca.1982. D-size flat-top acoustic, large 3-point 'guard, dot inlays, EKO Ranger label. Ranger 12 is 12-string.

| 1967-1982 | Ranger 12 | $425 | $550 |
| 1967-1982 | Ranger 6 | $425 | $550 |

Ranger 6/12 Electra
1967. Ranger 6/12 with on-board pickup and 2 controls, 6-string with dot markers, 12-string with block markers.

| 1967 | 12 Electra | $450 | $600 |
| 1967 | 6 Electra | $450 | $600 |

Rocket VI/XII (Rokes)
1967-ca.1969. Rocket-shape design, solidbody, 6-string, says Rokes on the headstock, Rokes were a popular English band that endorsed EKO guitars, mar-

MODEL		EXC. COND.	
YEAR	FEATURES	LOW	HIGH

keted as the Rocket VI in the U.S.; and as the Rokes in Europe, often called the Rok. Rocket XII is 12-string.

| 1967-1969 | Rocket VI | $850 | $1,100 |
| 1967-1969 | Rocket XII | $850 | $1,100 |

El Degas
Early 1970s-early '80s. Japanese-made copies of classic America electrics and acoustics, imported by Buegeleisen & Jacobson of New York, New York.
Solidbody
Copies of classic American models, including the Let's Play model.

| 1970s | | $350 | $450 |

El Maya
1970s-1980s. Also labeled Maya. Solidbody, archtop and semi-hollow guitars built by Japan's Chushin Gakki Co., which also built models for several other manufacturers.

Eleca
2004-present. Student/budget level, production, acoustic and electric guitars, imported by Eleca International. They also offer amps, effects and mandolins.

Electar
See Epiphone listing.

Electra
1970-1984, 2013-present. Imported from Japan by St. Louis Music. Most instruments made by Matsumoku in Japan. The Electra line replaced SLM's Japanese-made Apollo and U.S.-made Custom Kraft lines. First guitar, simply called The Electra, was a copy of the Ampeg Dan Armstrong lucite guitar and issued in '70, followed quickly by a variety of bolt-neck copies of other brands. In '75 the Tree-of-Life guitars debut and the line is expanded. Open-book headstocks changed to wave or fan shape by '78. Some Korean production begins in early-'80s. In the fall of '83, the Electra Brand becomes Electra Phoenix. By beginning of '84, the brand becomes Electra-Westone and by the end of '84 just Westone. In 2013, the brand was revived with guitars built by luthiers Ben Chafin and Mick Donner in Tampa, Florida. Matsumoku-made guitars have serial number in which first 1 or 2 digits represent the year of manufacture. Thus a guitar with a serial number beginning in 0 or 80 would be from 1980.
Concert Professional
Late 1970s. Howard Roberts style, single-cut electric flat-top with oval sound hole, single humbucking pickup, fancy markers.

| 1977 | | $850 | $1,100 |

Custom
1970s. Double-cut solidbody, 2 pickups, Custom logo on truss rod, cherry finish.

| 1970s | | $675 | $900 |

MODEL		EXC. COND.	
YEAR	FEATURES	LOW	HIGH

Elvin Bishop
1976-ca.1980. Double-cut semi-hollow body, tree-of-life inlay.

1976-1980		$800	$1,075

Flying Wedge
1970s. V body, six-on-a-side tuners.

1970s		$600	$800

MPC Outlaw
1977-1980. Symmetric horn body, neck-thru, has separate modules (Modular Powered Circuits) that plug in for different effects. Includes X710 (peace sign burned into natural mahogany top), X720 (gray sunburst), X730 (tobacco sunburst) and X 740 (maple top).

1977-1980		$925	$1,200
1977-1980	MPC plug-in module	$150	$200

MPC X310
1976-1980. MPC model, LP solidbody, 2 humbuckers (bridge w/ exposed zebra bobbins), 4 in-line control knobs plus 2 toggles, gold hardware, black finish.

1976-1980		$850	$1,100

MPC X320
1976-1980. Same as X310, but with transparent cherry red finish over mahogany top.

1976-1980		$850	$1,100

MPC X330
1976-1980. Same as X310, but with cherry sunburst finish on maple top.

1976-1980		$850	$1,100

MPC X340
1976-1980. Same as X310, but with Jacaranda rosewood top.

1976-1980		$850	$1,100

MPC X350
1977-1980. Same as X310, but with tobacco sunburst on a maple top.

1977-1980		$850	$1,100

Phoenix
1980-1984. Classic offset double-cut solidbody, Phoenix logo on headstock.

1980-1984		$375	$500

Rock
1971-1973. Single cut solidbody, becomes the Super Rock in '73.

1971-1973		$500	$650

Super Rock
1973-ca.1978. Renamed from Rock ('71-'73).

1973-1978		$575	$750

X135
1982. Offset double-cut solidbody, 2 humbucker pickups.

1982		$350	$475

X145 60th Anniversary
1982. Classic offset double-cut only made one year, Anniversary plate on back of headstock, single/single/hum pickups.

1982		$350	$475

X150
1975. Offset double-cut, 2 humbucker pickups.

1975		$500	$650

X220 Omega
1976-ca. 1980. Single-cut solidbody, block inlays, Omega logo on truss rod, black with rosewood neck, or natural with figured top and maple neck.

1976-1980		$525	$700

X280/X290 Working Man
1980-1984. Modified double-cut solidbody, 2 exposed-coil humbuckers, dot inlays, natural satin finish (X280) or jet black (X290).

1980-1984		$275	$375

X410
1975. Double-cut thinline acoustic archtop, 2 humbucker pickups, large split triangle markers, open-book style headstock shape.

1975		$850	$1,100

X420
1978. Double-cut thinline acoustic archtop, 2 humbucker pickups, dot markers, wave-shape style headstock.

1978		$550	$725

X935 Endorser
1983-1984. Double-cut solidbody, 2 humbucker pickups, tune-o-matic, dot markers.

1983-1984		$425	$550

X960 Ultima
1981. Hybrid single-cut with additional soft bass bout cutaway, slab solidbody, dot markers, 2 humbucker pickups, wave-shape style headstock.

1981		$500	$650

Electric Gypsy
See listing under Teye.

Electro
1964-1975. The Electro line was manufactured by Electro String Instruments and distributed by Radio-Tel. The Electro logo appeared on the headstock rather than Rickenbacker. Refer to the Rickenbacker section for models.

Electromuse
1940s-1950s. Mainly known for lap steels, Electromuse also offered acoustic and electric hollowbody guitars. They also had tube amps usually sold as a package with a lap steel.

Elferink
1993-present. Production/custom, premium grade, archtop guitars built in the Netherlands by luthier Frans Elferink.

Elijah Jewel
2009-present. Luthier Michael Kerry builds his professional grade, production/custom, acoustic guitars in Mineola, Texas. He also builds mandolins.

Elite
1960s. Guitars made in Italy by the Crucianelli accordion company, which made several other brands.

Elferink

Elijah Jewel

Epiphone AJ-500M Masterbilt
Rivington Guitars

Epiphone B.B. King Lucille

MODEL YEAR	FEATURES	EXC. COND. LOW	HIGH

Elk

Late-1960s. Japanese-made by Elk Gakki Co., Ltd. Many were copies of American designs. They also offered amps and effects.

Elliott Guitars

1966-present. Premium and presentation grade, custom, nylon-string classical and steel-string guitars built by luthier Jeffrey Elliott in Portland, Oregon.

Ellis

2000-present. Luthier Andrew Ellis builds his production/custom, premium grade, steel string acoustic and resophonic guitars in Perth, Western Australia. In 2008 he also added lap steels.

Elli-Sound

1960s. Guitars made in Italy by the Crucianelli accordion company, which made several other brands.

Ellsberry Archtop Guitars

2003-present. Premium and presentation grade, custom/production, acoustic and electric archtops built by luthier James Ellsberry previously in Torrance and Harbor City, California, and presently in Huntington Beach.

Emperador

1966-1992. Guitars and basses imported from Japan by Westheimer Musical Instruments. Early models appear to be made by either Teisco or Kawai; later models were made by Cort.

Acoustic

1960s	Archtop or flat-top	$200	$300

Electric Solidbody

1960s		$250	$350

Empire

1997-present. Professional and premium grade, production/custom, solidbody guitars from Lee Garver's GMW Guitarworks of Glendora, California.

Encore

Mid-1960s-present. Budget grade, production, classical, acoustic, and electric guitars imported from China and Vietnam by John Hornby Skewes & Co. in the U.K. They also offer basses.

Engel Guitars

1990-present. Luthier Robert Engel builds his premium grade, production/custom, hollowbody and solidbody guitars in Stamford, Connecticut.

English Electronics

1960s. Lansing, Michigan, company named after owner, some private branded guitars and amps by Valco (Chicago), many models with large English Electronics vertical logo on headstock.

MODEL YEAR	FEATURES	EXC. COND. LOW	HIGH

Tonemaster

1960s. National Val-Pro 84 with neck pickup and bridge mounted pickup, black.

1960s		$850	$1,100

Epcor

1967. Hollowbody electirc guitars and basses built by Joe Hall's Hallmark Guitars in Bakersfield, CA for manufacturer's rep Ed Preager (the EP in the name). Only about 35 were built.

Epi

1970s. Typical Japanese copy-import, Epi logo on headstock with capital letter split-E logo, inside label says "Norlin," probably for Japanese domestic market.

Acoustic Flat-Top

1970s. D-style, mahogany body.

1970s		$200	$300

Epiphone

Ca. 1873-present. Budget, intermediate, professional and premium grade, production, solidbody, archtop, acoustic, acoustic/electric, resonator, and classical guitars made in the U.S. and overseas. They also offer basses, amps, mandolins, ukes and banjos. Founded in Smyrna, Turkey, by Anastasios Stathopoulos and early instruments had his label. He emigrated to the U.S. in 1903 and changed the name to Stathoupoulo. Anastasios died in '15 and his son, Epaminondas ("Epi") took over. The name changed to House of Stathopoulo in '17 and the company incorporated in '23. In '24 the line of Epiphone Recording banjos debut and in '28 the company name was changed to the Epiphone Banjo Company. In '43 Epi Stathopoulo died and sons Orphie and Frixo took over. Labor trouble shut down the NYC factory in '51 and the company cut a deal with Conn/Continental and relocated to Philadelphia in '52. Frixo died in '57 and Gibson bought the company. Kalamazoo-made Gibson Epiphones debut in '58. In '69 American production ceased and Japanese imports began. Some Taiwanese guitars imported from '79-'81. Limited U.S. production resumed in '82 but sourcing shifted to Korea in '83. In '85 Norlin sold Gibson to Henry Juszkiewicz, Dave Barryman and Gary Zebrowski. In '92 Jim Rosenberg became president of the new Epiphone division.

AJ Masterbilt Series

2004-present. Sloped shoulder D size, solid spruce tops, solid rosewood or mahogany (M) back and sides.

2004-2021	Import	$550	$725

Alleykat

2000-2010. Single cut small body archtop, 1 humbucker and 1 mini-humbucker.

2000-2010		$270	$350

MODEL YEAR	FEATURES	EXC. COND. LOW	HIGH

B.B. King Lucille
1997-2019. Laminated double-cut maple body, 2 humbuckers, Lucille on headstock.

1997-2019		$490	$635

Barcelona CE
1999-2000. Classical, solid spruce top, rosewood back and sides, EQ/preamp.

1999-2000		$290	$375

Barcelone (Classical)
1963-1968. Highest model of Epiphone '60s classical guitars, maple back and sides, gold hardware.

1963-1964		$750	$975
1965-1968		$625	$825

Bard 12-String
1962-1969. Flat-top, mahogany back and sides, natural or sunburst.

1962-1964		$1,475	$1,950
1965		$1,325	$1,750
1966-1969		$1,150	$1,500

Beverly
1931-1936. Flat-top, arched back, tenor or Hawaiian versions.

1931-1936	Hawaiian	$800	$1,050
1931-1936	Tenor	$575	$750

Biscuit
1997-2000, 2002-2010. Wood body resonator, biscuit bridge, round neck.

1997-2010		$290	$375

Blackstone
1931-1950. Acoustic archtop, f-holes, sunburst.

1933-1934	Masterbilt	$1,000	$1,300
1935-1937		$875	$1,125
1938-1939		$750	$975
1940-1941		$700	$900
1948-1950		$575	$750

Blueshawk Deluxe
2015-2018. Single-cut semi-hollowbody, AAA flamed maple top, mahogany back and sides, 2 P-90s, Midnight Sapphire, Wine red or trans black.

2015-2018		$490	$635

Broadway (Acoustic)
1931-1958. Non-cut acoustic archtop.

1931-1938	Sunburst, walnut body	$2,400	$3,100
1939-1942	Sunburst, maple body	$2,400	$3,100
1946-1958	Natural	$2,000	$2,600
1946-1958	Sunburst	$1,825	$2,400

Broadway Regent (Acoustic Cutaway)
1950-1958. Single-cut acoustic archtop, sunburst.

1950-1958		$2,000	$2,600

Broadway (Electric)
1958-1969. Gibson-made electric archtop, single-cut, 2 New York pickups (mini-humbucking pickups by '61), Frequensator tailpiece, block inlays, sunburst or natural finish with cherry optional in '67 only.

1958-1959	Natural	$2,750	$3,600
1958-1959	Sunburst	$2,450	$3,200
1960-1964	Natural	$2,600	$3,400
1960-1964	Sunburst	$2,350	$3,100
1965	Natural	$2,150	$2,800
1965	Sunburst	$2,000	$2,650
1966-1967	Natural, cherry	$2,000	$2,650
1966-1967	Sunburst	$2,000	$2,600
1968-1969	Natural, cherry	$2,000	$2,600
1968-1969	Sunburst	$2,000	$2,600

Broadway Reissue
1997-2019. Full depth acoustic-electric single cut archtop, 2 humbuckers.

1997-2019		$490	$635

Broadway Tenor
1937-1953. Acoustic archtop, sunburst.

1937-1953		$1,250	$1,626

Byron
1949-ca.1955. Acoustic archtop, mahogany back and sides, sunburst.

1949-1955		$425	$550

C Series Classical (Import)
1995-2006. Nylon-string classical guitars, including C-25 (mahogany back & sides), C-40 (cedar top, mahogany), C-70-CE (rosewood).

1998-2005	C-40	$150	$200

Caiola Custom
1963-1970. Introduced as Caiola, renamed Caiola Custom in '66, electric thinbody archtop, 2 mini-humbuckers, multi-bound top and back, block inlays, walnut or sunburst finish (walnut only by '68).

1963-1964		$2,450	$3,200
1965		$2,250	$2,950
1966-1970		$2,000	$2,650

Caiola Standard
1966-1970. Electric thinbody archtop, 2 P-90s, single-bound top and back, dot inlays, sunburst or cherry.

1966-1967		$1,875	$2,450
1968-1970		$1,700	$2,250

Casino (1 Pickup)
1961-1969. Thinline hollowbody, double-cut, 1 P-90 pickup, various colors.

1961-1964		$5,000	$6,650
1965		$4,100	$5,450
1966-1969		$3,800	$5,000

Casino (2 Pickups)
1961-1970. Two pickup (P-90) version, various colors. '61-'63 known as Keith Richards model, '64-'65 known as Beatles model.

1961-1962		$6,700	$8,900
1963-1964		$5,600	$7,450
1965		$5,300	$7,050
1966-1970		$4,700	$6,250

Casino (Japan)
1982-1983. Epiphone built a few of its classic models, including the Casino, in Japan from mid-'82 to mid-'83.

1982-1983		$875	$1,125

Casino J.L. U.S.A. 1965
2003-2006. 1,965 made.

2003-2006		$2,375	$3,075

Casino Reissue
1995-2019. Import, sunburst.

1995-2019		$675	$875

1946 Epiphone Broadway
Bernunzio Uptown Music

2002 Epiphone Casino Reissue
Bernunzio Uptown Music

1964 Epiphone Coronet

Trey Rabinek <treyrabinek@google.com>

1998 Epiphone Del Ray

Rivington Guitars

MODEL YEAR	FEATURES	EXC. COND. LOW	HIGH

Casino Revolution
1999-2005. Limited production 1965 reissue model, with certificate of authenticity, sanded natural.

1999-2005		$2,400	$3,100

50th Anniversary 1961 Casino
2011. Trapeze (TD) or TremTone vibrato (TDV), limited run of 1,961 built.

2011	TDV	$725	$950
2011	Trapeze	$725	$950

Century
1939-1970. Thinline archtop, non-cut, 1 pickup, trapeze tailpiece, walnut finish, sunburst finish available in '58, Royal Burgundy available '61 and only sunburst finish available by '68.

1939-1948	Oblong shape pu	$1,100	$1,400
1949-1958	NY pickup	$900	$1,200
1958-1962	P-90, plate logo	$1,100	$1,450
1963-1964	P-90, no plate logo	$1,100	$1,450
1965-1970	Sunburst, cherry	$975	$1,275

Classic (Classical)
1963-1970.

1963-1964		$450	$600
1965-1970		$400	$525

Collegiate
2004-2005. Les Paul-style body, 1 humbucker, various college graphic decals on body.

2004-2005		$175	$230

Coronet (Electric Archtop)
1939-1949. Electric archtop, laminated mahogany body, 1 pickup, trapeze tailpiece, sunburst, name continued as an electric solidbody in '58.

1939-1949		$875	$1,150

Coronet (Solidbody)
1958-1969. Solidbody electric, 1 New York pickup ('58-'59), 1 P-90 ('59-'69), cherry or black finish, Silver Fox finish available by '63, reintroduced as Coronet USA '90-'94, Korean-made '95-'98.

1958-1959	Cherry, NY pu	$3,900	$5,100
1959	Black (rare), NY pu	$6,650	$8,700
1960-1964	Various colors	$3,550	$4,650
1965	Standard color	$2,500	$3,300
1965-1966	Custom color	$5,000	$6,550
1966-1969	Standard color	$2,250	$2,950

Coronet U.S.A.
1990-1994. Made in Nashville, reverse banana headstock, typical Coronet styled body, single-coil and humbucker.

1990-1994		$850	$1,125

Coronet (Import)
1995-1998. Import version.

1995-1998		$365	$475

Crestwood Custom
1958-1970. Solidbody, 2 New York pickups ('58-'60), 2 mini-humbuckers ('61-'70), symmetrical body and 3+3 tuners ('58-'62), asymmetrical and 1x6 tuners ('63-'70), slab body with no Gibson equivalent model.

1958-1960	Cherry, NY pus	$3,200	$4,250
1959-1960	Sunburst, NY pus	$3,200	$4,250
1961-1962	Cherry, mini-hums	$3,100	$4,000
1961-1962	White, mini-hums	$3,700	$4,800
1963-1964	Cherry, mini-hums	$2,300	$3,000
1963-1964	Custom color	$4,100	$5,400
1965	Cherry	$2,150	$2,800
1965	Custom color	$4,000	$5,250
1966-1967	Cherry	$2,100	$2,700
1966-1967	Custom color	$2,550	$3,350
1968-1970	Cherry, white	$1,850	$2,450

Crestwood Deluxe
1963-1969. Solidbody with 3 mini-humbuckers, block inlay, cherry, white or Pacific Blue finish, 1x6 tuners.

1963-1964	Cherry, mini-hums	$2,550	$3,350
1963-1964	Custom color	$4,100	$5,400
1965	Cherry	$2,300	$3,000
1965	Custom color	$3,800	$5,000
1966-1967	Cherry	$2,050	$2,700
1966-1967	Custom color	$2,650	$3,450
1968-1969	Cherry, white	$2,050	$2,700

De Luxe
1931-1957. Non-cut acoustic archtop, maple back and sides, trapeze tailpiece ('31-'37), frequensator tailpiece ('37-'57), gold-plated hardware, sunburst or natural finish.

1931-1935	Sunburst, 17⅜"	$5,500	$7,200
1935-1944	Sunburst, 16⅜"	$4,875	$6,325
1939-1944	Natural	$4,875	$6,325
1945-1949	Natural	$4,200	$5,400
1945-1949	Sunburst	$3,950	$5,100
1950-1957	Natural	$4,000	$5,200
1950-1957	Sunburst	$3,750	$4,850

De Luxe Regent (Acoustic Archtop)
1948-1952. Acoustic cutaway archtop, high-end appointments, rounded cutaway, natural finish, renamed De Luxe Cutaway in '53.

1948-1952	Natural	$6,700	$8,650
1948-1952	Sunburst	$5,550	$7,200

De Luxe Cutaway/Deluxe Cutaway
1953-1970. Renamed from De Luxe Regent, cataloged Deluxe Cutaway by Gibson in '58, special order by '64 with limited production because acoustic archtops were pretty much replaced by electric archtops. There is also a FT Deluxe Cutaway flat-top (see FT listings).

1953-1957	Natural	$6,675	$8,650
1953-1957	Sunburst	$5,525	$7,175
1958-1959		$6,000	$7,900
1960-1964	Gibson Kalamazoo	$5,500	$7,250
1965-1970	Special order only	$4,700	$6,150

De Luxe Electric (Archtop)
1954-1957. Single-cut electric archtop, 2 pickups, called the Zephyr De Luxe Regent from '48-'54. Produced with a variety of specs, maple or spruce tops, different inlays and pickup combinations.

1954-1957	Natural	$4,000	$5,200
1954-1957	Sunburst	$3,800	$4,900

Del Ray
1995-2000. Offset double-cut body, 2 blade humbuckers, tune-o-matic, flamed maple top.

1995-2000		$365	$475

MODEL YEAR	FEATURES	EXC. COND. LOW	HIGH

Devon

1949-1957. Acoustic archtop, non-cut, mahogany back and sides, sunburst finish, optional natural finish by '54.

| 1950-1957 | Sunburst | $1,625 | $2,100 |
| 1954-1957 | Natural | $1,625 | $2,100 |

Don Everly (SQ-180)

1997-2004. Jumbo acoustic reissue, large double 'guard, black gloss finish.

| 1997-2004 | | $600 | $775 |

Dot (ES-335 Dot)/Dot Archtop

2000-2020. Dot-neck ES-335.

| 2000-2020 | | $440 | $575 |

Dot Studio

2004-2019. Simplified Dot, 2 control knobs, black hardware.

| 2004-2019 | | $325 | $425 |

Dove Limited Edition

2008. Dove Limited Edition logo on label, Dove script logo on truss rod cover, classic dove logo art on 'guard and dove inlay on bridge, cherry or ebony.

| 2008 | | $270 | $350 |

DR Series/Songmaker Series

2004-present. Dreadnought, spruce top, mahogany back and sides, various models including: DR-100 (various colors), DR-200C (single-cut, natural or vintage sunburst), DR-212 (12-string, natural) and DR-500RNS (rosewood, natural satin).

| 2012-2021 | Songmaker DR-212 | $175 | $225 |

Dwight

1963, 1967. Coronet labeled as Dwight and made for Sonny Shields Music of St. Louis, 75 made in '63 and 36 in '67, cherry. National-Supro made Dwight brand lap steels in the '50s.

| 1963 | | $3,600 | $4,700 |
| 1967 | | $2,250 | $3,000 |

EA/ET/ES Series (Japan)

1970-1979. Production of the Epiphone brand was moved to Japan in '70. Models included the EA (electric thinline) and ET (electric solidbody).

1970-1975	EA-250 Riviera	$450	$575
1970-1975	ET-270	$500	$650
1970-1975	ET-275	$500	$650
1972	ES-255 Casino	$540	$700
1975-1979	ET-290 Crestwood	$500	$650

EJ-160E John Lennon

1997-2013. Based on John's Gibson acoustic/electric, sunburst, signature on body.

| 1997-2013 | | $385 | $500 |

EJ-200 Series

1994-2020. Solid spruce top, laminate maple body.

| 1994-2020 | Various models | $350 | $460 |

EJ-300

2004-2006. Solid spruce top, laminate rosewood body.

| 2004-2006 | | $490 | $635 |

El Diablo

1994-1995. Offset double-cut acoustic/electric, onboard piezo and 3-band EQ, composite back and sides, spruce top, cherry sunburst.

| 1994-1995 | | $400 | $525 |

Electar Model M

1935-1939. Epiphone's initial entry into the new electric guitar market of the mid-'30s, 14 3/4" laminate maple archtop, horseshoe pickup, trap door on back for electronics, Electar logo on headstock, oblong pickup replaces horseshoe in late-'37.

| 1935-1936 | 2 control knobs | $1,300 | $1,700 |
| 1937-1939 | 3 control knobs | $1,300 | $1,700 |

Electar Model M Tenor

1937-1939. Electric tenor 4-string with Electar specs.

| 1937-1939 | 3 knobs, natural | $1,200 | $1,550 |

Elitist Series

2003-2019. Made in Japan, higher-grade series, using finer woods and inlays and U.S.-made Gibson pickups.

2003-2004	J-200	$1,480	$1,925
2003-2004	L-00/VS	$1,210	$1,575
2003-2005	'61 SG Standard	$975	$1,265
2003-2005	'65 Texan	$1,475	$1,925
2003-2005	Riviera	$1,675	$2,185
2003-2008	'63 ES-335 Dot	$1,550	$2,010
2003-2008	Byrdland/L5	$2,175	$2,825
2003-2009	Broadway	$1,460	$1,900
2003-2009	LP Custom	$975	$1,265
2003-2009	LP Standard	$975	$1,265
2003-2009	LP Standard '57 Goldtop	$975	$1,265
2003-2009	LP Studio	$800	$1,035
2003-2009	Sheraton	$1,675	$2,185
2003-2019	Casino	$1,480	$1,925
2004-2005	Jim Croce L-00	$975	$1,265
2005	Chet Atkins Country Gent	$1,480	$1,925
2007-2009	LP Plus	$975	$1,265
2012	D Yoakam Trash Casino	$1,480	$1,925

Emperor (Acoustic Archtop)

1935-1954. Acoustic archtop, non-cut, maple back and sides, multi-bound body, gold-plated hardware, sunburst, optional natural finish by '39.

1935-1939	Natural	$7,400	$9,600
1935-1939	Sunburst	$5,200	$6,750
1940-1949	Natural, Sunburst	$6,600	$8,600
1950-1954	Natural	$5,900	$7,700
1950-1954	Sunburst	$5,500	$7,100

Emperor Regent

1948-1953. Acoustic archtop with rounded cutaway, renamed Emperor Cutaway in '53.

| 1948-1953 | Natural | $6,300 | $8,100 |
| 1948-1953 | Sunburst | $5,700 | $7,400 |

Emperor Cutaway

1953-1957. Renamed from Emperor Regent, acoustic archtop, single-cut, maple back and sides, multi-bound body, gold-plated hardware, sunburst or natural.

| 1953-1957 | Natural | $6,600 | $8,600 |
| 1953-1957 | Sunburst | $6,000 | $7,800 |

Emperor Electric

1953-1957. Archtop, single-cut, 3 pickups, multi-bound body, sunburst, called the Zephyr Emperor Regent in '50-'53.

| 1953-1957 | | $3,600 | $4,600 |

Epiphone Songmaker DR-212

1959 Epiphone Emperor

1997 Epiphone Flying V

Johnny Zapp

1958 Epiphone FT45 Cortez

Jim Dikel,

MODEL YEAR	FEATURES	EXC. COND. LOW	HIGH
Emperor (Thinline Electric)			

1958-1969. Single-cut, thinline archtop, 3 New York pickups in '58-'60, 3 mini-humbuckers '61 on, multibound, gold-plated hardware, sunburst or natural finish until '65 when only sunburst was made.

MODEL YEAR	FEATURES	EXC. COND. LOW	HIGH
1958-1959	Natural, 3 NY pus	$9,000	$11,800
1958-1959	Sunburst, 3 NY pus	$7,000	$9,100
1960-1962	Natural	$8,500	$11,200
1960-1962	Sunburst	$7,000	$9,100
1963-1969	Special order	$5,900	$7,750

Emperor/Emperor II

1982-1994. Single-cut archtop jazz guitar, 2 humbuckers, blocks, gold hardware. II added to name in '93, became Joe Pass Emperor II (see that listing) in '95, although his name was on the guitar as early as '91.

1982-1989	Matsumoku, Japan	$825	$1,075
1990-1994		$825	$1,075

Entrada (Classical)

1963-1968. Small classical, 13.25" bout, natural.

1963-1964		$450	$600
1965-1968		$400	$525

ES-175 Premium

2010-2019. Limited Edition, vintage "aged" lacquer finish, various colors.

2010-2019		$675	$900

ES-295

1997-2001, 2003-2016. Epiphone's version of classic Gibson goldtop.

1997-2016		$675	$900

ES-339 PRO/ES-339

2012-present. Maple laminate body, 2 pickups. PRO dropped from name in 2020.

2012-2021		$350	$460

Espana (Classical)

1962-1968. Classical, U.S.-made, maple back and sides, natural, imported in '69 from Japan.

1962-1964		$650	$850
1965-1968		$600	$775

Exellente

1963-1969, 1994-1995. Flat-top, Brazilian rosewood back and sides (Indian rosewood '68-'69), cloud inlays. Name revived on Gibson Montana instrument in '90s.

1963-1964	Brazilian	$7,650	$10,000
1965	Brazilian	$7,150	$9,400
1966-1967	Brazilian	$6,650	$8,700
1968-1969	Indian	$4,100	$5,375

1958 Korina Explorer

1998-2011. Explorer with typical appointments, korina body. This guitar was produced with a variety of specs, ranging from maple tops to spruce tops, different inlay markers were also used, different pickup combinations have been seen, natural or sunburst finish.

1998-2011		$500	$650

1958 Gothic Explorer/Flying V

2002-2012. Flat black finish, V ends in 2010.

2002-2012		$500	$650

Firebird

1995-2000. Two mini-humbuckers, Firebird Red, dot markers.

1995-2000		$500	$650

MODEL YEAR	FEATURES	EXC. COND. LOW	HIGH
Firebird 300			

1986-1988. Korean import, Firebird Red.

1986-1988		$500	$650

Firebird 500

1986-1988. Korean import, Firebird Red.

1986-1988		$500	$650

1963 Firebird VII/Firebird VII

2000-2010. Reverse body, 3 mini-humbuckers, gold hardware, Maestro-style vibrato, block markers, Firebird Red. 1963 dropped from name in '03.

2000-2010		$575	$750

Firebird I Joe Bonamassa

2016. Artist Limited Edition, modeled after his Gibson '63 Firebird I (nicknamed "Treasure"), Tobacco Sunburst or Polymist Gold.

2016		$1,250	$1,625

Firebird Studio

2006-2011. Two humbuckers, with worn cherry finish.

2006-2011		$500	$650

Flamekat

1999-2005. Archtop, double dice position markers, 2 mini-humbuckers, Epiphone Bigsby, flame finish.

1999-2005		$290	$375

Flying V/'67 Flying V

1989-1998, 2003-2005. '67 or '58 specs, alder body, natural.

1989-1998	'67 specs	$490	$635
2003-2005	'58 specs	$490	$635

1958 Korina Flying V

1998-2011, 2016. Typical Flying V configuration, korina body, veneer top. Limited Edition offered in '16 with solid korina, 2 humbucker pickups and gold hardware.

1998-2011	Factory, veneer	$490	$635
2016	Limited Edition	$525	$675

1958 Korina Flying V Joe Bonamassa

2017-2018. Limited Edition, modeled from his first '58 Korina Flying V (nicknamed "Amos"), '50s-style Flying V case, hand-signed COA.

2017-2018		$900	$1,200

Flying V Prophecy

2020-present. AAA figured maple top, Yellow Tiger or Black with aged gloss finish.

2020-2021		$575	$750

FT 30

1941-1949. Acoustic flat-top, brown stain, mahogany back and sides, reintroduced as Gibson-made FT 30 Caballero in '58.

1941-1943		$1,225	$1,600
1944-1949		$1,050	$1,350

FT 30 Caballero

1959-1970. Reintroduced from Epiphone-made FT 30, Gibson-made acoustic flat-top, natural, all mahogany body, dot inlay, tenor available '63-'68.

1959-1961		$1,150	$1,500
1962-1964		$850	$1,125
1965		$750	$1,000
1966-1970		$650	$850

FT 45

1941-1948. Acoustic flat-top, walnut back and sides, cherry neck, rosewood 'board, natural top, reintroduced as Gibson-made FT 45 Cortez in '58.

1941-1943		$1,750	$2,275
1944-1948		$1,375	$1,775

FT 45 Cortez

1958-1969. Reintroduced from Epiphone-made FT 45, Gibson-made acoustic flat-top, 16.5", mahogany back and sides, sunburst or natural top (sunburst only in '59-'62).

1958-1959	Sunburst	$1,650	$2,175
1960-1964	Sunburst, natural	$1,500	$1,975
1965-1966	Sunburst, natural	$1,325	$1,750
1967-1969	Sunburst, natural	$1,025	$1,350

FT 79

1941-1958. Acoustic 16" flat-top, square shoulder dreadnought, walnut back and sides until '49 and laminated maple back and sides '49 on, natural, renamed FT 79 Texan by Gibson in '58.

1941-1943	Walnut	$2,600	$3,400
1944-1949	Walnut	$2,400	$3,100
1949-1958	Maple	$1,900	$2,500

FT 79 Texan

1958-1970, 1993-1995. Renamed from Epiphone FT 79, Gibson-made acoustic flat-top, mahogany back and sides, sunburst or natural top, Gibson Montana made 170 in '93-'95.

1958-1959		$3,250	$4,250
1960-1964		$3,125	$4,100
1965		$3,000	$3,950
1966-1967		$2,800	$3,675
1968-1969		$2,400	$3,150
1970		$2,025	$2,650

Paul McCartney 1964 Texan (U.S.A.)

2005-2006. Reproduction of McCartney's '64 Texan made in Gibson's Montana plant, two runs, one of 40 guitars ('05), second of 250 ('05-'06). First 40 were hand-aged and came with Sir Paul's autograph, display case and certificate; the 250 run were not-hand aged, but have signed labels.

2005-2006		$3,700	$4,900

Paul McCartney 1964 Texan (Japan)

2006-2010. Limited run of 1,964 guitars.

2006-2010		$1,300	$1,700

1964 Texan (Inspired By Series)

2010-2019. Imported production model, acoustic/electric, non-adjustable bridge.

2010-2019		$275	$360

FT 85 Serenader 12-String

1963-1969. 12 strings, mahogany back and sides, dot inlay, natural.

1963-1964		$1,125	$1,475
1965		$925	$1,225
1966-1969		$875	$1,150

FT 90 El Dorado

1963-1970. Dreadnought flat-top acoustic, mahogany back and sides, multi-bound front and back, natural.

1963-1964		$2,500	$3,250
1965		$1,925	$2,550

1966-1967		$1,825	$2,400
1968-1970		$1,725	$2,275

FT 95 Folkster

1966-1969. 14" small body, mahogany back and sides, natural, double white 'guards.

1966-1969		$725	$950

FT 98 Troubadour

1963-1969. 16" square shouldered drednought, maple back and sides, gold-plated hardware, classical width 'board.

1963-1964		$2,100	$2,750
1965		$1,925	$2,500
1966-1969		$1,825	$2,400

FT 110

1941-1958. Acoustic flat-top, natural, renamed the FT 110 Frontier by Gibson in '58.

1941-1943	Square shoulder	$4,100	$5,300
1944-1949	Square shoulder	$3,800	$4,900
1949-1958	Round shoulder	$3,200	$4,100

FT 110 Frontier

1958-1970, 1994. Renamed from FT 110, acoustic flat-top, natural or sunburst, Gibson Montana made 30 in '94. Reintroduced '21, Antique Natural or Frontier Burst.

1958-1959		$5,500	$7,250
1960-1964		$4,900	$6,400
1965		$4,500	$5,900
1966-1970		$4,200	$5,500

FT Deluxe

1939-1941. Acoustic flat-top, 16.5".

1939-1941		$5,900	$7,700

FT Deluxe Cutaway (FT 210)

1954-1957. Acoustic flat-top, cutaway, 16.5". Some labeled FT 210.

1954-1957		$5,900	$7,600

FT Series (Flat-Tops Japan)

1970s. In '70 Epiphone moved production to Japan. Various 6- to 12-string models were made, nearly all with bolt necks and small rectangular blue labels on the inside back, rangeing from the budget FT 120 to the top-of-the-line FT 570 Super Jumbo.

1970s	Various models	$400	$525

G 310

1989-2019. SG-style model with large 'guard and gig bag.

1989-2019		$230	$300

G 400

1989-2013. SG-style, 2 humbuckers, crown inlays.

1989-2013		$325	$425

G 400 Custom

1998-2000, 2003-2011. 3 humbucker version, gold harware, block inlays.

1998-2011		$450	$575

G 400 Deluxe

1999-2007. Flame maple top version of 2 humbucker 400.

1999-2007		$490	$635

G 400 Limited Edition

2001-2002. 400 with Deluxe Maestro lyra vibrola, cherry red.

2001-2002		$490	$635

1958 Epiphone FT 79 Texan
Bernunzio Uptown Music

1955 Epiphone FT Deluxe Cutaway
Craig Brody

To get the most from this book, be sure to read "Using *The Guide*" in the introduction.

1967 Epiphone Howard Roberts Standard

Imaged by Heritage Auctions, HA.com

Epiphone Hummingbird Pro

MODEL YEAR	FEATURES	EXC. COND. LOW	HIGH

G 400 Tony Iommi
2003-2011. SG-style model with cross 'board inlay markers, black finish.

2003-2011		$490	$635

G 1275 Custom Double Neck
1996-2011. SG-style alder body, 6- & 12-string, maple top, mahogany neck, cherry red, set neck. Also offered as bolt-neck Standard for '96-'98.

1996-2011		$640	$835

Genesis
1979-1980. Double-cut solidbody, 2 humbuckers with coil-taps, carved top, red or black, available as Custom, Deluxe, and Standard models, Taiwan import.

1979-1980		$730	$950

Granada (Non-cutaway Thinbody)
1962-1969. Non-cut thinline archtop, 1 f-hole, 1 pickup, trapeze tailpiece, sunburst finish.

1962-1964		$1,200	$1,575
1965-1969		$1,025	$1,325

Granada (Cutaway)
1965-1970. Single-cut version.

1965-1970		$1,400	$1,850

Hollywood Masterbilt Tenor
1931-1936. Tenor version of the Triumph, acoustic archtop 15.4", 19-fret Brazilian rosewood 'board, diagonal diamond markers.

1931-1936		$1,700	$2,200

Howard Roberts Standard
1964-1970. Single-cut acoustic archtop, bound front and back, cherry or sunburst finish, listed in catalog as acoustic but built as electric.

1964-1970		$2,400	$3,150

Howard Roberts Custom
1965-1970. Single-cut archtop, bound front and back, 1 pickup, walnut finish (natural offered '66 only).

1965-1970		$2,650	$3,475

Howard Roberts III
1987-1991. Two pickups, various colors.

1987-1991		$575	$750

Hummingbird/Hummingbird Pro
1994-present. Twin parallelogram inlays, hummingbird 'guard, replaced by Pro, with added electronics, in '13. Pro dropped from name in 2020.

1994-2021		$240	$315

Inspiration Style A Tenor
1928-1929. Banjo resonator style body with round soundhole, A headstock logo, spruce top, walnut back, sides and neck.

1928-1929		$2,100	$2,700

Joe Pass/Joe Pass Emperor II
1995-2019 Single-cut archtop jazz guitar, 2 humbuckers, blocks, gold hardware, natural or sunbusrt, renamed from Emperor II (see that listing) Limited Edition all-gold finish or Wine Red were available early on

1995-2019		$575	$750

Johnny A Signature Custom Outfit
2017-2018. Artist Signature series, Limited Edition, double-cut hollowbody, flamed maple top, 2 pickups, Bigsby tail, Sunset Glow gloss finish.

2017-2018		$900	$1,200

Les Paul 100/LP-100
1993-2019. Affordable single-cut Les Paul, bolt-on neck.

1993-2019		$200	$265

Les Paul '56 Goldtop
1998-2013. Made in China, based on '56 Goldtop specs with 2 P-90s. Black finish was offered starting in '09.

1998-2013	Gold	$575	$750
2009-2013	Black	$575	$750

Les Paul Ace Frehley
2001. Les Paul Custom 3-pickups, Ace's signature on 22nd fret, lightning bolt markers.

2001		$825	$1,100

Les Paul Alabama Farewell Tour
2003. Limited production, 1 pickup single-cut Jr., American flag and Alabama logo graphics and band signatures on body, Certificate of Authenticity.

2003		$600	$775

Les Paul Black Beauty
1997-2019. Classic styling with three gold plated pickups, black finish, block markers.

1997-2019		$575	$750

Les Paul Classic
2003-2005. Classic Les Paul Standard specs, figured maple top, sunburst.

2003-2005		$575	$750

Les Paul Custom
1989-2011. Various colors.

1989-2011		$575	$750

Les Paul Custom Plus (Flame Top)
1998-2010. Flamed maple top version of 2 pickup Custom, gold hardware, sunburst.

1998-2010		$575	$750

Les Paul Custom Silverburst
2007-2008. 2 humbuckers, silverburst finish.

2007-2008		$575	$750

Les Paul Dale Earnhardt
2003. Dale Earnhardt graphics, 1 humbucker.

2003		$575	$750

Les Paul Deluxe
1998-2000. Typical mini-humbucker pickups.

1998-2000		$575	$750

Les Paul ES Limited Edition
1999-2000. Les Paul semi-hollow body with f-holes, carved maple top, gold hardware, cherry sunburst and other color options.

1999-2000	Custom	$625	$825
1999-2000	Standard	$625	$825

Les Paul Gold Top
1994-1998. Goldtop, 2 humbuckers. Listed as Les Paul Standard Goldtop in '94.

1994-1998		$575	$750

Les Paul Joe Perry Boneyard
2004-2006. Boneyard logo on headstock, figured Boneyard finish.

2004-2006		$575	$750

Les Paul Jr. '57 Reissue
2006. '57 Reissue on truss rod cover, logo and script Les Paul Junior stencil on headstock, lower back headstock states 'Epiphone Limited Edition Custom Shop'.

2006		$275	$350

MODEL YEAR	FEATURES	EXC. COND. LOW	HIGH

Les Paul Music Rising

2006-2007. Music Rising (Katrina charity) graphic, LP Studio, 2 humbuckers.

2006-2007		$290	$375

Les Paul Prophecy

2020-present. Modern Collection, mahogany body, AAA flame maple veneer top in Red Tiger or Olive Tiger aged gloss, or plain top in black aged gloss.

2020-2021		$575	$750

Les Paul Sparkle L.E.

2001. Limited Edition LP Standard, silver, purple, red (and others) glitter finish, optional Bigsby.

2001		$575	$750

Les Paul Special

1994-2000, 2020-present. Double-cut, bolt neck. Reintroduced in '20 with P-90 Pro pickups, CTS electronics, TV yellow finish.

1994-2000		$200	$265

Les Paul Special II

1996-2019. Economical Les Paul, 2 pickups, single-cut, various colors.

1996-2016	Guitar and amp	$105	$140
1996-2019	Guitar only	$95	$125

Les Paul Special/TV Special

2006. Copy of single-cut late '50s Les Paul Special with TV finish.

2006		$250	$325

Les Paul Standard

1989-2019. Solid mahogany body, carved maple top, 2 humbuckers.

1989-2019	Various colors	$360	$465

Les Paul Standard Baritone

2004-2005. 27-3/4" long-scale baritone model.

2004-2005		$575	$750

Les Paul Standard Plus FMT

2003-2012. LP Standard figured curly maple sunburst top.

2003-2012		$575	$750

Les Paul Standard Ultra/Ultra II

2005-2012. LP Standard with chambered and contoured body, quilted maple top.

2005-2012	Ultra	$575	$750
2005-2012	Ultra II	$575	$750

Les Paul Studio

1995-present. Epiphone's version of Gibson LP Studio.

1995-2021		$250	$325

Les Paul XII

1998-2000. 12-string solidbody, trapeze tailpiece, flamed maple sunburst, standard configuration.

1998-2000		$500	$650

Slash Les Paul

1997-2000. Slash logo on body.

1997-2000		$700	$925

Slash Les Paul Goldtop

2008-2012. Limited Edition 2,000 made, goldtop finish, Seymour Duncan exposed humbuckers, Slash logo on truss rod cover, includes certificate of authenticity.

2008-2012	With COA	$775	$1,000

Slash Les Paul Standard Plus Top

2008-2012. Figured top, exposed humbuckers, includes certificate of authenticity.

2008-2012	With COA	$850	$1,125

Zakk Wylde Les Paul Custom

2002-2019. Bull's-eye graphic, block markers, split diamond headstock inlay.

2002-2019		$500	$650

Madrid (Classical)

1962-1969. Classical, natural.

1962-1964		$400	$525
1965-1969		$285	$375

MD-30

1993. D-size, round metal resonator, spruce top with dual screens.

1993		$500	$650

Melody Tenor

1931-1937. 23" scale, bound body.

1931-1937	Masterbilt	$1,050	$1,400

Moderne

2000. Copy of '58 Gibson Moderne design, dot markers, Moderne script logo on 'guard, black.

2000		$625	$825

Navarre

1931-1940. Hawaiian flat-top, mahogany back and sides, bound top and back, dot inlay, brown finish.

1931-1937	Masterbilt label	$2,800	$3,600
1938-1940	Standard label	$2,500	$3,250

Nighthawk Standard

1995-2000. Epiphone's version of the Gibson Nighthawk, single-cut, bolt neck, figured top.

1995-2000		$285	$375

Noel Gallagher Union Jack/Super Nova

1997-2005. Limited edition, higher-end ES-335. Union Jack with British flag finish (introduced '99) or Supernova in solid blue.

1997-2005		$980	$1,275

Olympic (Acoustic Archtop)

1931-1949. Mahogany back and sides.

1931-1936	Smaller body	$850	$1,100
1937-1939	Larger body	$725	$950
1940-1949		$700	$900

Olympic Tenor (Acoustic Archtop)

1937-1949. 4-string version of the Olympic.

1937-1949		$675	$875

Olympic Single (Solidbody)

1960-1970. Slab body, the same as the mid-'60s Coronet, Wilshire and Crestwood Series, single-cut '60-'62, asymmetrical double-cut '63-'70, 2 Melody maker single-coil pickups, vibrato optional in '64 and standard by '65.

1960-1962	Single-cut	$1,425	$1,875
1963-1964	Double-cut	$1,275	$1,675
1965-1970		$1,100	$1,450

Olympic Double (Solidbody)

1960-1969. Slab body, the same as the mid-'60s Coronet, Wilshire and Crestwood Series, single-cut '60-'62, asymmetrical-cut '63-'70, 2 Melody Maker single-coils, vibrato optional in '64 and standard by '65.

1960-1963	Single-cut	$2,475	$3,250
1963-1964	Double-cut	$2,200	$2,900
1965-1969	Cherry, sunburst	$1,825	$2,400

2004 Epiphone Zakk Wylde Les Paul Custom

Epiphone Les Paul Standard
Steve Alvito

1965 Epiphone Olympic Special
Carter Vintage Guitars

1990 Epiphone PR-325
Dave Mullikin

MODEL YEAR	FEATURES	EXC. COND. LOW	HIGH
Olympic (3/4 Scale Solidbody)			
1960-1963. 22" scale, sunburst.			
1960-1963		$1,400	$1,850
Olympic Special (Solidbody)			
1962-1970. Short neck with neck body joint at the 16th fret (instead of the 22nd), single Melody Maker-style single-coil bridge pickup, small headstock, double-cut slab body, dot markers, Maestro or Epiphone vibrato optional '64-'65, slab body contour changes in '65 from symmetrical to asymmetrical with slightly longer bass horn, sunburst.			
1962-1964	Symmetrical	$950	$1,250
1965-1970	Asymmetrical	$900	$1,175
PR Series			
1980-2004. Budget acoustics, mainly D size but some smaller, cut and non-cut bodies.			
1980-2004	Various models	$250	$425
Pro 1			
1989-1996. Solidbody, double-cut, 1 single-coil and 1 humbucking pickup, bolt-on neck, various colors.			
1989-1996		$350	$465
Pro 2			
1995-1998. Higher-end Pro I with Steinberger DB bridge, set-neck, 2 humbuckers, various colors.			
1995-1998		$350	$465
Professional			
1962-1967. Double-cut, thinline archtop, 1 pickup, mahogany finish. Values include matching Professional amp.			
1962-1964	With matching amp	$2,850	$3,750
1965	With matching amp	$2,450	$3,200
1966-1967	With matching amp	$2,150	$2,800
Prophecy Extura			
2020-present. Modern Collection, mahogany body, AAA flame maple veneer top, 2 Fishman pickups, various colors with aged gloss finish.			
2020-2021		$575	$750
Recording A			
1928-1931. Asymmetrical body flat-top with exaggerated treble bout cutaway, celluloid headstock veneer, dot inlays. All Recording models were offered in concert or auditorium body sizes.			
1928-1931	Standard 6-string	$1,700	$2,200
1928-1931	Tenor 4-string	$1,200	$1,575
Recording B			
1928-1931. As Recording A but with arched back, bound fingerboard, fancier body binding and zigzagging double slotted-diamond inlays.			
1928-1931		$2,350	$3,050
Recording C			
1928-1931. As Recording B but with arched top.			
1928-1931		$2,450	$3,200
Recording D			
1928-1931. As Recording C, but with large cross-hatched block inlays.			
1928-1931		$3,200	$4,200
Recording E			
1928-1931. As Recording D, but with large floral engraved block inlays.			
1928-1931		$4,100	$5,300

MODEL YEAR	FEATURES	EXC. COND. LOW	HIGH
Ritz			
1940-1949. 15.5" acoustic archtop, large cello f-holes, dot inlays, no headstock ornamentation other than script Epiphone inlay, blond finish.			
1940-1949		$775	$1,000
Riviera			
1962-1970. Double-cut thinline archtop, 2 mini-humbuckers, Royal Tan standard finish changing to sunburst in '65, cherry optional by '66-'70, additional 250 were made in Nashville in '93-'94, a Riviera import was available in '82 and for '94-'06.			
1962-1964	Tan or cherry	$4,300	$5,650
1964	Sunburst	$4,100	$5,375
1965	Sunburst, cherry	$3,700	$4,850
1966-1967	Sparkling Burgundy	$3,600	$4,725
1966-1970	Sunburst, cherry	$3,450	$4,525
1967-1968	Walnut	$3,450	$4,525
Riviera (U.S.A.)			
1993-1994. Made in U.S.A. on back of headstock.			
1993-1994		$1,325	$1,750
Riviera Reissue (Korea)			
1994-2006. Korean-made contemporary reissue, natural.			
1994-2006		$500	$650
Riviera 12-String			
1965-1970. Double-cut, 12 strings, thinline archtop, 2 mini-humbuckers, sunburst or cherry.			
1965-1970		$2,925	$3,800
Riviera 12-String Reissue (Korea)			
1997-2000. Korean-made reissue, natural.			
1997	Humbuckers	$825	$1,075
1998-2000	Mini-hums	$500	$650
Royal			
1931-1935. 15 1/2" acoustic archtop, mahogany back and sides, dot markers, sunburst, bound top, back and neck, Masterbilt headstock logo.			
1931-1935		$1,550	$2,000
S-900			
1986-1989. Neck-thru-body, locking Bender tremolo system, 2 pickups with individual switching and a coil-tap control.			
1986-1989		$350	$465
SC350			
1976-1979. Mahogany solidbody, scroll bass horn, rosewood 'board, dot inlays, bolt neck, 2 humbuckers, made in Japan.			
1976-1979	Mahogany	$625	$810
SC450			
1976-1979. Like SC350, but with maple body, glued neck, and coil tap.			
1976-1979	Maple	$625	$810
SC550			
1976-1979. Like SC450, but with gold hardware, block inlays, neck and body binding, and ebony 'board.			
1976-1979	Maple, gold hdwr	$625	$810
Seville EC-100 (Classical)			
1938-1941, 1961-1969 (Gibson-made). Classical guitar, mahogany back and sides, natural, the '61-'63 version also available with a pickup.			
1961-1964		$450	$600
1965-1969		$385	$500

MODEL YEAR	FEATURES	EXC. COND. LOW	HIGH

Prophecy SG
2020-present. Modern Collection, mahogany body, AAA flame maple veneer top, 2 Fishman pickups, various colors with aged gloss finish.

2020-2021		$575	$750

SG Special
2000-present. SG body, dot markers, 2 open-coil humbuckers, later P-90s.

2000-2016	Guitar and amp	$120	$160
2000-2021	Guitar only	$95	$125

Sheraton
1958-1970. Double-cut thinline archtop, 2 New York pickups '58-'60, 2 mini-humbuckers '61 on, frequensator tailpiece, multi-bound, gold-plated hardware, sunburst or natural finish with cherry optional by '65. Reissued '93-'94.

1958-1960	Natural, NY pus	$10,200	$13,400
1959-1964	Sunburst, mini-hums	$9,200	$12,050
1961-1964	Natural, mini-hums	$10,200	$13,400
1962	Cherry, few made	$9,200	$12,050
1965	Cherry, natural	$6,900	$9,000
1965	Sunburst	$5,450	$7,100
1966-1967	Natural	$6,450	$8,450
1966-1970	Cherry, sunburst	$5,000	$6,600

Sheraton (Japan)
1982-1983. Early reissue, not to be confused with Sheraton II issued later, natural or sunburst.

1982-1983		$1,550	$2,000

Sheraton (Reissue U.S.A.)
1993-1994, 2005. An additional 250 American-made Sheratons were built from '93-'94.

1993-1994		$2,300	$3,000
2005		$2,300	$3,000

Sheraton II/Sheraton II PRO
1986-present. Contemporary reissue, natural or sunburst.

1986-2021		$500	$650

Slasher
2001. Reverse offset double cut solidbody, bolt neck, six-on-a-side tuners, 2 pickups, dot markers.

2001		$350	$465

Sorrento (1 pickup)
1960-1970. Single-cut thinline archtop, 1 pickup in neck position, tune-o-matic bridge, nickel-plated hardware, sunburst, natural or Royal Olive finish, (cherry or sunburst by '68).

1960-1964		$2,100	$2,750
1965		$2,000	$2,625
1966-1970		$1,850	$2,450

Sorrento (2 pickups)
1960-1970. Single-cut thinline archtop, 2 pickups, tune-o-matic bridge, nickel-plated hardware, sunburst, natural or Royal Olive finish, (cherry or sunburst by '68).

1960-1964		$3,175	$4,200
1965		$2,700	$3,500
1966-1970		$2,550	$3,350

Sorrento (Reissue)
1994-2000. Reissue of 2 pickup model, import.

1994		$525	$675
1995-2000		$500	$650

Spartan
1934-1949. Acoustic archtop, 16 3/8", laminated maple body, multi-bound, trapeze tailpiece, sunburst or natural.

1934-1939	Sunburst	$875	$1,125
1940-1949	Sunburst	$775	$1,000
1941-1947	Natural	$875	$1,125

Special/SG Special (U.S.A.)
1979-1983. SG Special body style, dot markers, 2 exposed humbuckers, Special logo on truss rod cover.

1979-1983		$800	$1,050

Spider/The Spider
1997-2000. Wood body resonator, spider bridge, square neck.

1997-2000		$500	$650

Spirit I/Spirit II
1982. U.S.-made electric solidbody, double-cut, flat-top with 1 (I) or 2 (II) humbuckers, Epiphone U.S.A. script logo on headstock, Spirit logo on truss rod cover.

1982		$1,200	$1,600

SST
2007-2011. Acoustic/electric solidbody, either Classic (nylon) or Studio (steel). Chet Atkins model also available.

2007-2011		$290	$375

Tom Delonge Signature ES-333
2008-2019. One humbucker, dot inlays.

2008-2019		$575	$750

Trailer Park Troubadour Airscreamer
2003-2005. Airstream trailer-shaped body, identifying logo on headstock.

2003-2005		$500	$650

Triumph
1931-1957. 15 1/4" '31-'33, 16 3/8" '33-'36, 17 3/8" '36-'57, walnut back and sides until '33, laminated maple back and sides '33, solid maple back and sides '34, natural or sunburst.

1931-1932	Sunburst, laminated walnut	$1,400	$1,850
1933	Sunburst, laminated maple	$1,400	$1,850
1934-1935	Sunburst, solid maple	$1,475	$1,900
1936-1940	Sunburst 17 3/8" body	$1,475	$1,900
1941-1957	Natural	$1,475	$1,900
1941-1957	Sunburst	$1,475	$1,900

Triumph Regent (Cutaway)
1948-1969. Acoustic archtop, single-cut, F-holes, renamed Triumph Cutaway in '53, then Gibson listed this model as just the Triumph from '58-'69.

1948-1952	Regent, natural	$2,250	$2,900
1948-1952	Regent, sunburst	$2,250	$2,900
1953-1957	Cutaway, natural	$2,200	$2,850
1953-1957	Cutaway, sunburst	$1,925	$2,500
1958-1964	Sunburst	$2,150	$2,825
1965	Sunburst	$2,050	$2,675
1966-1969	Sunburst	$1,950	$2,550

1964 Epiphone Professional
Rivington Guitars

1961 Epiphone Triumph Regent
Carter Vintage Guitars

Epiphone Wildkat

1964 Epiphone Wilshire
Imaged by Heritage Auctions, HA.com

MODEL YEAR	FEATURES	EXC. COND. LOW	HIGH

USA Map Guitar
1982-1983. U.S.-made promotional model, solid-body electric, mahogany body shaped like U.S. map, 2 pickups, natural.

1982-1983		$2,750	$3,600

USA Map Guitar Limited Edition
2007	Import	$575	$750

Vee-Wee (Mini Flying V)
2003. Mini Flying V, single bridge pickup, gig bag.

2003		$90	$115

Wildkat
2001-2019. Thinline, single-cut, hollow-body, 2 P-90s, Bigsby tailpiece, various colors.

2001-2019		$350	$465

Wilshire
1959-1970. Double-cut solidbody, 2 pickups, tune-o-matic bridge, cherry.

1959	Symmetrical	$4,300	$5,650
1960-1962	Thinner-style, P-90s	$3,300	$4,325
1962-1963	Symmetrical, mini-hums	$3,300	$4,325
1963-1964	Asymmetrical, mini-hums	$3,000	$4,000
1965-1966	Custom color	$3,300	$4,325
1965-1966	Standard color	$2,600	$3,400
1967-1970		$2,300	$3,000

Wilshire 12-String
1966-1968. Solidbody, 2 pickups, cherry.

1966-1968		$2,300	$3,000

Wilshire II
1984-1985. Solidbody, maple body, neck and 'board, 2 humbuckers, 3-way switch, coil-tap, 1 tone and 1 volume control, various colors.

1984-1985		$500	$650

Windsor (1 Pickup)
1959-1962. Archtop, 1 or 2 pickups, single-cut thinline, sunburst or natural finish.

1959-1960	Natural, NY pu	$2,450	$3,200
1959-1960	Sunburst, NY pu	$2,350	$3,100
1961-1962	Natural, mini-hum	$2,150	$2,800
1961-1962	Sunburst, mini-hum	$2,050	$2,700

Windsor (2 Pickups)
1959-1962. Archtop, 1 or 2 pickups, single-cut thinline, sunburst or natural finish.

1959-1960	Natural, NY pu	$2,925	$3,850
1959-1960	Sunburst, NY pu	$2,800	$3,675
1961-1962	Natural, mini-hum	$2,500	$3,300
1961-1962	Sunburst, mini-hum	$2,400	$3,150

X-1000
1986-1989. Electric solidbody, Korean-made, various colors.

1986-1989		$325	$425

Zenith
1931-1969. Acoustic archtop, bound front and back, f-holes, sunburst.

1931-1933		$975	$1,275
1934-1935	14 3/4" body	$1,125	$1,475
1936-1949	16 3/8" body	$1,125	$1,475
1950-1957	Natural	$1,250	$1,625
1950-1957	Sunburst	$1,125	$1,475
1958-1969		$1,025	$1,350

Zephyr
1939-1957. Non-cut electric archtop, 1 pickup, bound front and back, blond or sunburst (first offered '53), called Zephyr Electric starting in '54.

1939-1940	Natural, metal handrest pu	$1,250	$1,625
1941-1943	Natural, no metal handrest	$1,250	$1,625
1944-1946	Natural, top mounted pu	$1,250	$1,625
1947-1948	17 3/8", metal covered pu	$1,250	$1,625
1949-1957	Natural, NY pu	$1,125	$1,475
1953-1957	Sunburst, NY pu	$1,050	$1,375

Zephyr Regent
1950-1953. Single-cut electric archtop, 1 pickup, natural or sunburst, called Zephyr Cutaway for '54-'57.

1950-1953	Natural	$2,200	$2,750
1950-1953	Sunburst	$1,925	$2,500

Zephyr Cutaway
1954-1957. Cutaway version of Zephyr Electric, called Zephyr Regent for 1950-'53.

1954-1957	Natural	$2,250	$2,900
1954-1957	Sunburst	$2,000	$2,600

Zephyr Electric (Cutaway)
1958-1964. Gibson-made version, thinline archtop, single-cut, 2 pickups, natural or sunburst.

1958-1959	Natural	$2,500	$3,300
1958-1959	Sunburst	$2,100	$2,800
1960-1964	Natural	$2,300	$3,000
1960-1964	Sunburst	$2,050	$2,650

Zephyr De Luxe (Non-cutaway)
1941-1942, 1945-1954. Non-cut electric archtop, 1 or 2 pickups, multi-bound front and back, gold-plated hardware, natural or sunburst.

1941-1942	Natural	$1,925	$2,500
1945-1949	Natural, 1 pu	$2,250	$2,900
1945-1954	Natural, 2 pus	$2,450	$3,200
1950-1954	Sunburst, 2 pus	$2,250	$2,900

Zephyr De Luxe Regent (Cutaway)
1948-1954. Single-cut electric archtop, 1 or 2 pickups until '50, then only 2, gold-plated hardware, sunburst or natural finish. Renamed Deluxe Electric in '54.

1948-1949	Natural, 1 pu	$2,450	$3,200
1948-1949	Natural, 2 pus	$3,100	$4,000
1948-1949	Sunburst, 1 pu	$2,250	$2,900
1948-1949	Sunburst, 2 pus	$2,850	$3,700
1950-1954	Natural, 2 pus	$3,000	$3,900
1950-1954	Sunburst, 2 pus	$2,750	$3,550

Zephyr Emperor Regent
1950-1954. Archtop, single rounded cutaway, multi-bound body, 3 pickups, sunburst or natural finish, renamed Emperor Electric in '54.

1950-1954	Natural	$5,500	$7,100
1950-1954	Sunburst	$4,200	$5,600

Zephyr Tenor
1940-1950. Natural, figured top.

1940-1950		$850	$1,100

Zephyr Blues Deluxe
1999-2005. Based on early Gibson ES-5, 3 P-90 pickups.

1999-2005		$500	$650

MODEL		EXC. COND.	
YEAR	FEATURES	LOW	HIGH

Epoch

Economy level imports made by Gibson and sold through Target stores.

Equator Instruments

2006-present. Production/custom, professional and premium grade, solidbody, hollowbody, acoustic and classical guitars built in Chicago, Illinois by luthier David Coleman.

Erlewine

1979-present. Professional and premium grade, production/custom guitars built by luthier Mark Erlewine in Austin, Texas. Erlewine also produces the Chiquita brand travel guitar.

Esoterik Guitars

Professional grade, production/custom, electric guitars built in San Luis Obispo, California by luthier Ryan Cook. He began with guitars in 2010 and plans to add basses.

ESP

1983-present. Intermediate, professional, and premium grade, production/custom, Japanese-made solidbody guitars and basses. Hisatake Shibuya founded Electronic Sound Products (ESP), a chain of retail stores, in '75. They began to produce replacement parts for electric guitars in '83 and in '85 started to make custom-made guitars. In '87 a factory was opened in Tokyo. In '86 ESP opened a sales office in New York, selling custom guitars and production models. From around '98 to ca. '02 they operated their California-based USA custom shop. In '96, they introduced the Korean-made LTD brand and in '03 introduced the Xtone brand, which was folded into LTD in '10. Hisatake Shibuya also operated 48th Street Custom Guitars during the '90s but he closed that shop in 2003.

20th Anniversary

1995. Solidbody, double-cut, ESP95 inlaid at 12th fret, gold.

1995		$1,150	$1,500

Eclipse Custom (U.S.A.)

1998-2002. U.S. Custom Shop-built, single-cut, mahogany body and maple top, various colors offered.

1998-2002		$775	$1,000

Eclipse Custom/Custom T (Import)

1986-1988, 2003-2010. Single-cut mahogany solidbody, earliest model with bolt dot marker neck, 2nd version with neck-thru and blocks, the Custom T adds locking trem. Current has quilt maple top.

1986-1987	Bolt-on, dots	$850	$1,100
1987-1988	Neck-thru, blocks	$925	$1,200
1987-1988	Neck-thru, Custom T	$900	$1,150

Eclipse Deluxe

1986-1988. Single-cut solidbody, 1 single-coil and 1 humbucker, vibrato, black.

1986-1988		$800	$1,050

Eclipse Series

1995-present. Recent Eclipse models.

1995-2000	Eclipse/Eclipse I	$600	$800
1996-2000	Eclipse Archtop	$600	$800

George Lynch M-1

2000s. Signature series, sunburst tiger finish.

1996-2021		$1,725	$2,250

Horizon (Import)

1986, 1996-2001. Double-cut neck-thru, bound ebony 'board, 1 single-coil and 1 humbucker, buffer preamp, various colors, reintroduced '96-'01with bolt neck, curved rounded point headstock.

1986		$850	$1,100
1996-2001		$700	$900

Horizon Classic (U.S.A.)

1993-1995. U.S.-made, carved mahogany body, set-neck, dot markers, various colors, optional mahogany body with figured maple top also offered.

1993-1995		$1,400	$1,800

Horizon Custom (U.S.A.)

1998-2001. U.S. Custom Shop-made, mahogany body, figured maple top, bolt-on neck, mostly translucent finish in various colors.

1998-2001		$1,400	$1,800

Horizon Deluxe (Import)

1989-1992. Horizon Custom with bolt-on neck, various colors.

1989-1992		$925	$1,200

Hybrid I (Import)

1986 only. Offset double-cut body, bolt maple neck, dots, six-on-a-side tuners, vibrato, various colors.

1986		$450	$600

Hybrid II (Import)

1980s. Offset double-cut, rosewood 'board on maple bolt neck, lipstick neck pickup, humbucker at bridge, Hybrid II headstock logo.

1980s		$525	$675

LTD EC-GTA Guitarsonist

2008. Flame graphic by Matt Touchard, 100 made.

2008		$1,200	$1,600

LTD EC-SIN Sin City

2008. Vegas graphic by Matt Touchard, 100 made.

2008		$1,200	$1,600

LTD Series

1998-present. Various Limited Edition models, range of prices due to wide range of specs.

1998-2021	Various models	$150	$700

Maverick/Maverick Deluxe

1989-1992. Offset double-cut, bolt maple or rosewood cap neck, dot markers, double locking vibrola, six-on-a-side tuners, various colors.

1989-1992		$525	$700

Metal I

1986 only. Offset double-cut, bolt maple neck, rosewood cap, dots, various colors.

1986		$500	$650

Metal II

1986 only. Single horn V body, bolt on maple neck with rosewood cap, dot markers, various colors.

1986		$500	$650

ESP Eclipse I

ESP George Lynch M-1 Tiger

1996 ESP Vintage Plus S
Curtis Hill

Essex (SX) EH3D-CS

MODEL YEAR	FEATURES	EXC. COND. LOW	HIGH

Metal III
1986 only. Reverse offset body, bolt maple neck with maple cap, dot markers, gold hardware, various colors.

1986		$500	$650

M-I Custom
1987-1994. Offset double-cut thru-neck body, offset block markers, various colors.

1987-1994		$775	$1,000

M-I Deluxe
1987-1989. Double-cut solidbody, rosewood 'board, 2 single-coils and 1 humbucker, various colors.

1987-1989		$750	$975

M-II
1989-1994, 1996-2000. Double-cut solidbody, reverse headstock, bolt-on maple or rosewood cap neck, dot markers, various colors.

1989-1994		$750	$975

M-II Custom
1990-1994. Double-cut solidbody, reverse headstock, neck-thru maple neck, rosewood cap, dot markers, various colors.

1990-1994		$750	$975

M-II Deluxe
1990-1994. Double-cut solidbody, reverse headstock, Custom with bolt-on neck, various colors.

1990-1994		$750	$975

Mirage Custom
1986-1990. Double-cut neck-thru solidbody, 2-octave ebony 'board, block markers, 1 humbucker and 2 single-coil pickups, locking trem, various colors.

1986-1990		$800	$1,050

Mirage Standard
1986 only. Single pickup version of Mirage Custom, various colors.

1986		$650	$850

Phoenix
1987 only. Offset, narrow waist solidbody, thru-neck mahogany body, black hardware, dots.

1987		$800	$1,050

Phoenix Contemporary
Late-1990s. 3 pickups vs. 2 on the earlier offering.

1998		$825	$1,075

S-454/S-456
1986-1987. Offset double-cut, bolt maple or rosewood cap neck, dot markers, various colors.

1986-1987		$650	$850

S-500
1991-1993. Double-cut figured ash body, bolt-on neck, six-on-a-side tuners, various colors.

1991-1993		$775	$1,000

SV-II
2009-2012. Part of Standard Series, made in Japan, neck-thru offset v-shaped solidbody, 2 pickups, dot inlays.

2009-2012		$1,700	$2,200

Traditional
1989-1990. Double-cut, 3 pickups, tremolo, various colors.

1989-1990		$800	$1,050

Vintage/Vintage Plus S
1995-1998. Offset double-cut, bolt maple or rose-wood cap neck, dot markers, Floyd Rose or standard vibrato, various colors.

1995	20th Anniv Ed	$1,125	$1,450
1995-1998		$1,000	$1,300

Viper Series
2004-present. Offset double-cut SG style, 2 hum-buckers, various models

2010	300M	$350	$475

Espana
1963-ca. 1973. Primarily acoustic guitars distributed by catalog wholesalers Bugeleisen & Jacobson. Built by Watkins in England.

Classical
1963-1973. Guitars with white spruce fan-braced tops with walnut, mahogany, or rosewood back and sides.

1963-1973		$250	$400

EL (Electric) Series
1963-1973. Various double-cut models, 2 or 3 pickups, tremolo, '63-ca. '68 with nitro finish, ca. '69-'73 poly finish.

1963-1973	EL-30, 2 pickups	$350	$475
1963-1973	EL-31, 3 pickups	$375	$500
1963-1973	EL-32, 12-string	$350	$475
1963-1973	EL-36, 2 pickups	$375	$500

Jumbo Folk
1969-1973. Natural.

1969-1973		$300	$400

Essex (SX)
1985-present. Budget grade, production, electric and acoustic guitars imported by Rondo Music of Union, New Jersey. They also offer basses.

Solidbody Electric
1980s-1990s. Copies of classic designs like the Les Paul and Telecaster.

1980s		$150	$250

Este
1909-1939. Luthier Felix Staerke's Este factory built classical and archtop guitars in Hamburg, Germany. They also built high-end banjos. The plant ceased instrument production in '39 and was destroyed in WW II.

Esteban
2002-present. Budget grade, production, acoustic and classical import guitars sold as packages with classical guitarist Esteban's (Stephen Paul) guitar lesson program, other miscellany and sometimes a small amp.

Steel and Nylon Acoustics

2002-2021	Various models	$40	$190

EtaVonni
2008-2010. Luthier Ben Williams built premium grade, production/custom, carbon fiber and aluminum electric guitars in Kentwood, Michigan.

MODEL YEAR	FEATURES	EXC. COND. LOW	HIGH

Euphonon

1930-1944. A Larson brothers brand, most Euphonons date from 1934-'44. Body sizes range from 13 ½" to the 19" and 21" super jumbos. The larger body 14-fret neck sizes have body woods of Brazilian rosewood, mahogany, or maple. Ornamentation and features are as important to value as rosewood vs. mahogany. Production also included mandolins, and most models were A-style, with teardrop body and flat backs.

Everett Guitars

1977-present. Luthier Kent Everett builds his premium and presentation grade, production/custom, steel-string and classical guitars in Atlanta, Georgia. From '01 to '03, his Laurel Series guitars were built in conjunction with Terada in Japan and set up in Atlanta. He has also built archtops, semi-hollow and solidbody electrics, resonators, and mandolins.

Evergreen Mountain

1971-present. Professional grade, custom, flat-top and tenor guitars, basses and mandolins built by luthier Jerry Nolte in Cove, Oregon. He also built over 100 dulcimers in the '70s.

Everly Guitars

1982-2001. Luthier Robert Steinegger built these premium grade, production/custom flat-tops in Portland, Oregon (also see Steinegger Guitars).

EVH

2007-present. Eddie Van Halen works with FMIC to create a line of professional and premium grade, production, solidbody guitars built in the U.S. and imported from other countries. They also build amps.

Wolfgang Special

2010-present. Made in Japan, offset double-cut solidbody, figured maple top over basswood body, birdseye maple 'board, 2 pickups, tremolo, opaque finish. Some more recent models made in Mexico.

2010-2021		$1,100	$1,450

Excelsior

The Excelsior Company started offering accordions in 1924 and had a large factory in Italy by the late '40s. They started building guitars around '62, which were originally plastic covered, switching to paint finishes in the mid '60s. They also offered classicals, acoustics, archtops and amps. By the early '70s they were out of the guitar business.

The Excelsior brand was also used ca.1885-ca.1890 on guitars and banjos by Boston's John C. Haynes & Co.

Dyno and Malibu

1960s. Offset, double cut, 2 or 3 pickups, vibrato.

1960s	Dyno I	$350	$450
1960s	Dyno II	$375	$475
1960s	Malibu I	$375	$475
1960s	Malibu II	$400	$500

Exlusive

2008-2013. Intermediate grade, production, electric guitars and basses, imported from Asia and finished in Italy by luthier Galeazzo Frudua.

Fairbuilt Guitar Co.

2000-present. Professional and premium grade, custom guitars and mandolins, built by luthier Martin Fair in Loudoun County, Virginia.

Falk

1989-present. Professional and premium grade, production/custom archtop guitars built by luthier Dave Falk, originally in Independence, Missouri, and currently in Amarillo, Texas. He also builds mandolins and dulcimers.

Fano

1995-present. Professional grade, production/custom, solidbody electric guitars and basses built by luthier Dennis Fano in Fleetwood, Pennsylvania.

Farnell

1989-present. Luthier Al Farnell builds his professional grade, production, solidbody guitars and basses in Ontario, California. He also offers his intermediate grade, production, C Series which is imported from China.

Fat Cat Custom Guitars

2004-present. Intermediate to premium grade, production/custom, solidbody and chambered electric guitars and basses built in Carpentersville, Illinois by luthier Scott Bond.

Favilla

1890-1973. Founded by the Favilla family in New York, the company began to import guitars in 1970, but folded in '73. American-made models have the Favilla family crest on the headstock. Import models used a script logo on the headstock.

Acoustic Classical

1960s-1973. Various nylon-string classical models.

1960s-1973		$150	$500

Acoustic Flat-Top

1960s-1973. Various flat-top models, 000 to D sizes, mahogany to spruce.

1960s-1973		$150	$500

Fell

One of the many guitar brands built by Japan's Matsumoku company.

Fender

1946 (1945)-present. Budget, intermediate, professional and premium grade, production/custom, electric, acoustic, acoustic/electric, classical, and resonator guitars built in the U.S. and overseas. They also build amps, basses, mandolins, bouzoukis, banjos, lap steels, ukes, violins, and PA gear. Ca. 1939 Leo Fender opened a radio and record

1968 Excelsior Dyno III
Rivington Guitars

Fat Cat Custom Guitars

2003 Fender Custom Shop
'51 Nocaster
Carter Vintage Guitars

1956 Fender Stratocaster
David Stone

store called Fender Radio Service, where he met Clayton Orr 'Doc' Kauffman, and in '45 they started KF Company to build lap steels and amps. In '46 Kauffman left and Fender started the Fender Electric Instrument Company.

In January '65 CBS purchased the company and renamed it Fender Musical Instruments Corporation. The CBS takeover is synonymous with a perceived decline in quality among musicians and collectors, and Pre-CBS Fenders are more valuable. Fender experienced some quality problems in the late-'60s. Small headstock is enlarged in '65 and the 4-bolt neck is replaced by the 3-bolt in '71. With high value and relative scarcity of Pre-CBS Fenders, even CBS-era instruments are now sought by collectors. Leo Fender was kept on as consultant until '70 and went on to design guitars for Music Man and G&L.

In '82 Fender Japan is established to produce licensed Fender copies for sale in Japan. Also in '82, the Fender Squier brand debuts on Japanese-made instruments for the European market and by '83 they were imported into U.S. In March '85, the company was purchased by an investor group headed by Bill Schultz but the purchase does not include the Fullerton factory. While a new factory was being established at Corona, California, all Fender Contemporary Stratocasters and Telecasters were made either by Fender Japan or in Seoul, Korea. U.S. production resumes in late '85. The Fender Custom Shop, run by Michael Stevens and John Page, opens in '87. The Mexican Fender factory is established in '90. In '95, Fender purchased the Guild guitar company. On January 3, 2002, Fender Musical Instruments Corporation (FMIC) recapitalized a minority portion of common stock, with partners including Roland Corporation U.S. and Weston Presidio, a private equity firm in San Francisco. In 2003, Fred Gretsch Enterprises, Ltd granted Fender the exclusive rights to develop, produce, market and distribute Gretsch guitars worldwide. Around the same time, Fender also acquired the Jackson/Charvel Guitar Company. In October, '04, Fender acquired Tacoma Guitars. On January 1, '08, Fender acquired Kaman Music Corporation and the Hamer, Ovation, and Genz Benz brands. The Groove Tubes brand was purchased by Fender in June, '08.

Dating older Fender guitars is an imprecise art form at best. While serial numbers were used, they were frequently not in sequence, although a lower number will frequently be older than a substantially higher number. Often necks were dated, but only with the date the neck was finished, not when the guitar was assembled. Generally, dating requires triangulating between serial numbers, neck dates, pot dates, construction details and model histories.

From '50 through roughly '65, guitars had more-or-less sequential numbers in either 4 or 5 digits, though some higher numbers may have an initial 0 or - prefix. These can range from 0001 to 99XXX. From '63 into '65, some instruments had serial

numbers beginning with an L prefix plus 5 digits (LXXXXX). Beginning in '65 with the CBS take-over into '76, 6-digit serial numbers were stamped on F neckplates roughly sequentially from 10XXXX to 71XXXX. In '76 the serial number was shifted to the headstock decal. From '76-'77, the serial number began with a bold-face 76 or S6 plus 5 digits (76XXXXX).

From '77 on, serial numbers consisted of a 2-place prefix plus 5 digits (sometimes 6 beginning in '91): '77 (S7, S8), '78 (S7, S8, S9), '79 (S9, E0), '80-'81 (S9, E0, E1), '82 (E1, E2, E3), '84-'85 (E4), '85-'86 (no U.S. production), '87 (E4), '88 (E4, E8), '89 (E8, E9), '90 (E9, N9, N0), '91 (N0), '92 (N2).

Serial numbers on guitars made by Fender Japan consist of either a 2-place prefix plus 5 digits or a single prefix letter plus 6 digits: '82-'84 (JV), '83-'84 (SQ), '84-'87, '85-'86+ (A, B, C), '86-'87 (F), '87-'88+ (G), '88-'89 (H), '89-'90 (I, J), '90-'91 (K), '91-'92 (L), '92-'93 (M).

Factors affecting Fender values: The sale to CBS in '65 is a major point in Fender instrument values as CBS made many changes collectors feel affected quality. The '70s introduced the 3-bolt neck and other design changes that aren't as popular with guitarists. Custom color instruments, especially Strats from the '50s and early-'60s, can be valued much more than the standard sunburst finishes. In '75 Fender dropped the optional custom colors and started issuing the guitars in a variety of standard colors.

Custom colors are worth more than standard colors. For a Stratocaster, Telecaster Custom and Esquire Custom the standard color is sunburst, while the Telecaster and Esquire standard color is blond. The first Precision Bass standard color was blond but changed to sunburst in the late 1950s. The Jazz Bass standard color is sunburst. The Telecaster Thinline standard color is natural. To understand a custom color, you need to know what the standard color is. Some custom colors are rarer than others. Below is a list of the custom colors offered in 1960. They are sorted in ascending order with the most valuable color, Shell Pink, listed last. For example, Fiesta Red is typically worth 12% more than a Black or Blond, though all are in the Common Color category. In the Rare Color group, Foam Green is normally worth 8% more than Shoreline Gold. The two Very Rare colors are often worth 30% more than Shoreline Gold. In our pricing information we will list the standard color, then the relative value of a common custom color, and then the value of a rare custom color. Remember that the amount of fade also affects the price. These prices are for custom colors with slight or no fade, which implies a lighter color, but with custom colors a faded example can also be much darker in color. Blue can fade to dark green. White can fade to deep yellow.

The various Telecaster and Stratocaster models are grouped under those general headings.

Common Color: Black, Blond, Candy Apple Red, Olympic White, Lake Placid Blue,

MODEL YEAR	FEATURES	EXC. COND. LOW	HIGH

Dakota Red, Daphne Blue, Fiesta Red

Rare Color: Shoreline Gold, Inca Silver, Burgundy Mist, Sherwood Green, Sonic Blue, Foam Green

Rare (Very Rare) Color: Surf Green, Shell Pink

1960 - 1962: Black, Blond, Burgundy Mist, Dakota Red, Daphne Blue, Fiesta Red, Foam Green, Inca Silver, Lake Placid Blue, Olympic White, Shell Pink, Sherwood Green, Shoreline Gold, Sonic Blue, Sunburst, Surf Green

1963 - 1964: Black, Blond, Burgundy Mist, Candy Apple Red, Dakota Red, Daphne Blue, Fiesta Red, Foam Green, Inca Silver, Lake Placid Blue, Olympic White, Sherwood Green, Shoreline Gold, Sonic Blue, Sunburst, Surf Green

1965 - 1969: Black, Blond, Blue Ice, Candy Apple Red, Charcoal Frost, Dakota Red, Fiesta Red, Firemist Gold, Firemist Silver, Foam Green, Lake Placid Blue, Ocean Turquoise, Olympic White, Sonic Blue, Sunburst, Teal Green

1970 - 1971: Black, Blond, Candy Apple Red, Firemist Gold, Firemist Silver, Lake Placid Blue, Ocean Turquoise, Olympic White, Sonic Blue, Sunburst

1972: Black, Blond, Candy Apple Red, Lake Placid Blue, Olympic White, Sonic Blue, Sunburst

1973: Black, Blond, Candy Apple Red, Lake Placid Blue, Natural, Olympic White, Sunburst, Walnut

1974 - 1977: Black, Blond, Natural, Olympic White, Sunburst, Walnut

1978 - 1979: Antigua, Black, Blond, Natural, Olympic White, Sunburst, Walnut, Wine

Arrow

1969-1972. See listing for Musiclander.

Avalon

1985-1995. California Series, acoustic import, 6-on-a-side tuners, mahogany neck, back and sides (nato after '93), spruce top, various colors.

1985-1995		$225	$300

Balboa

1983-1987. California Series, acoustic import.

1983-1987		$375	$500

Brawler Baritone (Custom Shop)

2019-2020. Journeyman Relic, masterbuilt by Carlos Lopez.

2019-2020		$6,800	$9,000

Broadcaster

Mid-1950-early-1951. For a short time in early-'51, before being renamed the Telecaster, models had no Broadcaster decal; these are called No-casters by collectors.

1950	Blond	$72,000	$94,000
1951	Clipped decal, "No Caster"	$65,000	$85,000

Broadcaster Leo Fender Custom Shop

1999 only. Leo Fender script logo signature replaces Fender logo on headstock, Custom Shop certificate signed by Phyllis Fender, Fred Gretsch, and William Schultz, includes glass display case and poodle guitar case.

1999		$6,000	$8,000

'50s Relic/'51 NoCaster Custom Shop

1995-2014. Called the '50s Relic NoCaster for '96-'99, and '51 NoCaster in NOS, Relic, or Closet Classic versions 2000-'10, with the Relic Series being the highest offering. From June '95 to June '99 Relic work was done outside of Fender by Vince Cunetto and included a certificate noting model and year built, an instrument without the certificate is worth less than the value shown. Blonde or Honey Blonde finish. Also in '09, the Limited '51 NoCaster Relic was offered with Twisted Tele neck pickup, 50 each in 2-tone sunburst or Dakota Red.

1995-1997	Cunetto built Relic	$2,900	$3,800
1997-1999	Cunetto era Closet Classic	$2,500	$3,300
1997-1999	Cunetto era NOS	$2,500	$3,300
1998-1999	Cunetto era Relic	$2,800	$3,700
2000-2009	Closet Classic	$2,500	$3,300
2000-2014	NOS	$2,500	$3,300
2000-2014	Relic	$2,700	$3,600

'51 NoCaster Limited Edition

2009. Custom Shop Limited Edition, as above but with Twisted Tele neck pickup, 50 each in 2-tone sunburst or Dakota Red.

2009	Relic	$2,700	$3,600

70th Anniversary Broadcaster Limited Edition

2020 only. Production model has ash body, black 'guard, '50s spaghetti logo, blonde lacquer finish. Custom Shop model available with aging Relic, Heavy Relic, NOS Time Capsule and Journeyman Relic.

2020	Custom Shop	$2,900	$3,800
2020	Production	$1,450	$1,900

Bronco

1967-1980. Slab solidbody, 1 pickup, tremolo, red.

1967-1968	Nitro	$1,250	$1,650
1969-1980	Poly	$1,250	$1,650

Buddy Miller Signature

2007-2009. Artist Design series, flat-top, Fishman Ellipse Aura, signature on headstock.

2007-2009		$700	$925

Bullet/Bullet Deluxe

1981-1983. Solidbody, came in 2- and 3-pickup versions (single-coil and humbucker), and single- and double-cut models, various colors. Becomes Squire Bullet in '85.

1981-1983	Various models	$675	$875

Catalina

1983-1995. California Series, acoustic dreadnought, import.

1983-1995		$225	$300

CC-60SCE Concert

2020-present. Single-cut, spruce top, mahogany back and sides, Fishman pickup, black or natural.

2020-2021		$210	$275

1951 Fender Broadcaster
John Amaral

1969 Fender Bronco
Imaged by Heritage Auctions, HA.com

Fender CD-320AS

1967 Fender Coronado II

Tom Pfeifer

MODEL YEAR	FEATURES	EXC. COND. LOW	HIGH

CD (Classic Design) Series
2006-present. Imported, intermediate grade, various models, acoustic or acoustic-electric, steel or nylon string.

| 2006-2021 | Various models | $150 | $350 |

CG (Classical Guitar) Series
1995-2005. Imported, various nylon-string classical acoustic and acoustic/electric models, label on the inside back clearly indicates the model number, back and sides of rosewood, mahogany or other woods.

| 1995-2005 | Various models | $60 | $400 |

Concert
1963-1970. Acoustic flat-top slightly shorter than King/Kingman, spruce body, mahogany back and sides (optional Brazilian or Indian rosewood, zebrawood or vermillion), natural, sunburst optional by '68.

| 1963-1970 | Natural or sunburst | $1,050 | $1,400 |

Concord
1986-1995. Dreadnought flat-top, 6-on-a-side headstock, natural.

| 1986-1995 | | $150 | $200 |

Coronado I
1966-1969. Thinline semi-hollowbody, double-cut, tremolo, 1 pickup, single-bound, dot inlay.

| 1966-1969 | Various colors | $1,600 | $2,075 |

Coronado II
1966-1969 (Antigua finish offered until '70). Thinline semi-hollowbody, double-cut, tremolo optional, 2 pickups, single-bound, block inlay, available in standard finishes but special issues offered in Antigua and 6 different Wildwood finishes (labeled on the pickguard as Wildwood I through Wildwood VI to designate different colors). Wildwood finishes were achieved by injecting dye into growing trees.

1966-1969	Various colors	$1,825	$2,400
1966-1969	Wildwood	$2,525	$3,300
1967-1970	Antigua	$1,825	$2,400

Coronado XII
1966-1969 (Antigua finish offered until '70). Thinline semi-hollowbody, double-cut, 12 strings, 2 pickups, block inlay, standard, Antigua and Wildwood finishes available.

1966-1969	Various colors	$1,825	$2,400
1966-1969	Wildwood	$2,500	$3,300
1967-1970	Antigua	$1,825	$2,400

Custom
1969-1971. Six-string solidbody that used up parts from discontinued Electric XII, asymmetrical-cut, long headstock, 2 split pickups, sunburst. Also marketed as the Maverick.

| 1969-1971 | | $3,600 | $4,800 |

Cyclone
1998-2006. Mexican import, solidbody, contoured offset waist, poplar body, various colors.

| 1998-2006 | Various options | $650 | $850 |

D'Aquisto Elite
1984, 1989-1994, 1994-2002. Part of Fender's Master Series, 16" laminated maple-side archtop, single-cut, glued neck, 1 pickup, gold hardware, made in Japan until '94, in '94 the Fender Custom Shop issued a version that retailed at $6,000, various colors.

| 1984-2002 | | $2,500 | $3,300 |

D'Aquisto Standard
1984 (Serial numbers could range from 1983-1985). Like D'Aquisto Elite, but with 2 pickups.

| 1984 | | $2,500 | $3,300 |

D'Aquisto Ultra
1984, 1994-2000. USA Custom Shop, made under the supervision of James D'Aquisto, solid flamed maple back and sides, spruce top, ebony tailpiece, bridge and 'guard, all hand carved.

| 1994-2000 | | $3,300 | $4,300 |

DG (Dreadnought Guitar) Series
1995-1999, 2002-2014. Made in China, various lower-end acoustic and acoustic/electric models.

| 1995-2014 | Various models | $100 | $350 |

Duo-Sonic/Player Duo-Sonic
1956-1969, 2016-present. Solidbody, 3/4-size, 2 pickups, Desert Sand ('56-'61), sunburst ('61-'63), blue, red or white after, short- and long-scale necks, short-scale necks listed here (see Duo-Sonic II for long-scale), reissued Mexican-made in '94. In 2016 it becomes part of Player Series.

1956-1958	Desert Sand	$2,800	$3,600
1959	Maple neck	$2,800	$3,600
1960	Rosewood 'board	$2,200	$2,900
1961-1963	Desert Sand	$2,200	$2,900
1963	Sunburst (rare)	$2,200	$2,900
1964-1965	Blue, red, sunburst, white	$2,200	$2,900
1966-1969	Blue, red or white	$1,525	$1,975

Duo-Sonic II
1965-1969. Solidbody, 2 pickups, blue, red or white, long-scale neck, though the long-scale neck Duo-Sonic was not known as the Duo-Sonic II until '65, we have lumped all long-scales under the II for the purposes of this Guide.

| 1965-1969 | | $1,600 | $2,100 |

Duo-Sonic Reissue
1994-1997. Made in Mexico, black, red or white.

| 1994-1997 | | $300 | $400 |

Duo-Sonic HS/Player Duo-Sonic HS
2017-present. Player Series, humbucker and single-coil pickups.

| 2017-2021 | | $375 | $500 |

Electric XII
1965-1969. Solidbody, 12 strings, long headstock, 2 split pickups. Custom colors can fade or become darker; for example Lake Placid Blue changes to green. The price ranges below are for instruments that are relatively unfaded. Many older guitars have some color fade and minor fade is factored into these values. Each custom color should be evaluated on a case-by-case basis. Custom color Fenders can be forged and bogus finishes have been a problem. As the value of custom color Fenders has increased, so has the problem of bogus non-original finishes. The prices in the Guide are for factory original finishes in excellent condition. The prices noted do not take into account market factors such as fake instruments, which can have the effect of lowering a guitar's market value unless the guitar's provenance can be validated. Please refer to the Fender Guitar Intro Section for details on Fender color options.

| 1965-1969 | Common color | $6,600 | $8,600 |

MODEL YEAR	FEATURES	EXC. COND. LOW	HIGH
1965-1969	Rare color	$8,300	$10,800
1965-1969	Sunburst	$4,400	$5,700

Electric XII Alternate Reality
2019. Modern updated reissue.

2019		$700	$925

Ensenada Series
2005-2007. Made in Mexico acoustics, solid top, back and sides, A (grand auditorium), D (dreadnought), M (mini jumbo) and V (orchestra) sizes, E suffix denotes on-board electronics.

2005-2007	Acoustic	$450	$600
2005-2007	Acoustic-electric	$525	$700

Esprit Elite
1984. Master Series, made in Japan, double-cut, semi-hollow, carved maple top, 2 humbuckers, 4 controls, bound rosewood 'board, snowflake inlays.

1983-1985		$1,600	$2,100

Esprit Standard
1984. Like Esprit Elite, but with dot inlays, 2 controls.

1983-1985		$1,550	$2,000

Esprit Ultra
1984. Like Esprit Elite, but with bound ebony 'board, split-block inlays, gold hardware.

1984		$1,600	$2,100

Esquire
1950-1970. Ash body, single-cut, 1 pickup, maple neck, black 'guard '50-'54, white 'guard '54 on. Please refer to the Fender Guitar Intro Section for details on Fender color options.

MODEL YEAR	FEATURES	EXC. COND. LOW	HIGH
1950-1951	Blond, black 'guard	$38,000	$49,000
1952-1953	Blond, black 'guard	$33,000	$44,000
1954	Blond, black 'guard	$31,000	$40,000
1954-1955	Blond white 'guard	$26,000	$34,000
1956-1957	Blond	$26,000	$34,000
1958	Blond, backloader	$20,000	$26,000
1958	Blond, toploader	$17,500	$23,000
1959	Blond, maple 'board	$17,500	$23,000
1959	Blond, rosewood 'board	$17,500	$23,000
1960	Blond	$15,000	$19,500
1960	Sunburst	$16,400	$21,300
1961	Blond, slab 'board	$14,000	$18,200
1961	Custom color	$31,000	$40,000
1961	Sunburst, slab	$15,800	$20,500
1962	Blond, curved 'board	$12,800	$16,600
1962	Blond, slab	$14,000	$18,200
1962	Custom color	$31,000	$40,000
1962	Sunburst, curved	$15,400	$19,900
1962	Sunburst, slab	$15,800	$20,500
1963	Blond	$12,800	$16,600
1963	Common color	$22,600	$29,300
1963	Rare color	$29,800	$38,700
1963	Sunburst	$15,400	$19,900
1964	Blond	$12,800	$16,600

MODEL YEAR	FEATURES	EXC. COND. LOW	HIGH
1964	Common color	$21,000	$27,000
1964	Rare color	$27,000	$36,000
1964	Sunburst	$15,400	$19,900
1965	Blond	$10,900	$14,100
1965	Common color	$16,300	$22,000
1965	Rare color	$22,000	$33,000
1965	Sunburst	$11,000	$14,100
1966	Blond	$9,100	$11,800
1966	Common color	$10,300	$15,000
1966	Rare color	$15,000	$18,800
1966	Sunburst	$10,000	$13,000
1967	Blond	$9,100	$11,800
1967	Blond, smuggler cavity	$9,200	$11,900
1967	Common color	$10,300	$15,000
1967	Rare color	$15,000	$18,800
1967	Sunburst	$10,000	$13,000
1968	Blond, nitro	$9,100	$11,800
1968	Common color, nitro	$10,300	$15,000
1968	Rare color, nitro	$15,000	$18,800
1968	Sunburst, nitro	$10,000	$13,000
1969	Blond, poly	$6,500	$8,500
1969	Common color, poly	$11,200	$14,500
1969	Rare color, poly	$14,500	$18,800
1969	Sunburst, poly	$9,100	$11,800
1970	Blond	$5,600	$7,300
1970	Common color	$8,800	$12,000
1970	Rare color	$12,000	$15,800
1970	Sunburst	$5,500	$7,200

Esquire (Japan)
1985-1994. Made in Japan, '54 specs.

1985-1986		$1,050	$1,350
1987-1989	'50s Esquire	$1,050	$1,350
1990-1994	'50s Esquire	$925	$1,200

'50s Esquire (Mexico)
2005-2010. Maple neck, ash body.

2005-2010		$575	$750

'52 Esquire
2012. Custom Shop, price includes Certificate of Authenticity.

2012	NOS	$2,500	$3,300

'53 Esquire
2012. Custom Shop, price includes Certificate of Authenticity.

2012	NOS	$2,500	$3,300

'59 Esquire
2003-2007, 2013-2016. Custom Shop, Relic version lasted to '07, then came back in '13 for limited run.

2003-2013	Closet Classic	$2,500	$3,300
2003-2013	NOS	$2,500	$3,300
2003-2016	Relic	$2,700	$3,600

'60 Esquire
Custom Shop, NOS.

2010		$2,500	$3,300

'70 Esquire
2008. Custom Shop, only 20 made.

2008	Heavy Relic	$2,900	$3,800
2008	Relic	$2,700	$3,600

1968 Fender Coronado XII Wildwood
Tim Kummer

1986 Fender Esquire
SMichael Alonzi

1961 Fender Esquire Custom

Carter Vintage Guitars

1997 Fender Jag-Stang

Imaged by Heritage Auctions, HA.com

MODEL YEAR	FEATURES	EXC. COND. LOW	HIGH

70th Anniversary Esquire
2020 only. Roasted pine body, 1-piece maple neck, 1 pickup, Anniversary neck plate, white blond.

2020		$1,300	$1,700

Custom Esquire '95
1995. Custom Shop, limited run of 12 for Sam Ash Music, stealth pickup under 'guard, bird's-eye maple neck.

1995		$2,500	$3,300

Esquire Custom
1959-1970. Same as Esquire, but with bound alder sunburst body and rosewood 'board.

1959	Sunburst	$26,000	$34,000
1960	Custom color	$39,000	$50,000
1960	Sunburst	$26,000	$34,000
1961	Custom color	$37,000	$48,000
1961	Sunburst	$25,000	$32,000
1962	Custom color	$35,000	$45,000
1962	Sunburst, curve	$22,000	$29,000
1962	Sunburst, slab	$24,000	$31,000
1963	Custom color	$33,000	$43,000
1963	Sunburst	$22,000	$29,000
1964	Custom color	$28,000	$36,000
1964	Sunburst	$19,000	$25,000
1965	Custom color	$24,500	$32,000
1965	Sunburst	$14,500	$19,000
1966	Custom color	$19,500	$25,000
1966-1970	Sunburst	$12,000	$16,000

Esquire Custom (Import)
1983-1994. Made in Japan with all the classic bound Esquire features, sunburst.

1983-1987		$1,150	$1,500
1988-1994		$1,050	$1,350

Esquire Custom GT/Celtic/Scorpion
2003. Made in Korea, single-cut solidbody, 1 humbucker, 1 knob (volume), set-neck, solid colors.

2003		$500	$650

Esquire Z
2001. Custom Shop, black body and headstock, curly maple neck, ebony 'board, 25 made.

2001		$5,100	$6,600

Brad Paisley Esquire
2020-present. Spruce top and back, 2 single-coil pickups, black and silver paisley 'guard, road worn black sparkle finish.

2020-2021		$925	$1,200

Jeff Beck Tribute Esquire (Custom Shop)
2006. Also called Beck Artist Esquire or Tribute Series Jeff Beck Esquire, specs include an extremely lightweight 2-piece offset ash body with Beck's original contours, distressed for an appearance like Beck's original Esquire that was used on many Yardbird records.

2006		$8,000	$10,300

F (Flat-Top) Series
1969-1981. The F-Series were Japanese-made flat-top acoustics, included were Concert- and Dreadnought-size instruments with features running from plain to bound necks and headstocks and fancy inlays, there was also a line of F-Series classical, nylon-string guitars. A label on the inside indicates the model. FC-

20 is a classical with Brazilian rosewood. There was also an Asian (probably Korean) import Standard Series for '82-'90 where the models start with a F.

1969-1981	Dreadnought, laminated	$75	$175
1969-1981	Dreadnought, solid top	$150	$400
1972-1981	Classical (FC)	$150	$400

FA (Fender Alternative) Series
2009-present. Entry-level acoustic series, various Concert, Dreadnought and Auditorium sized models.

2009-2021	FA-115, FA-125	$115	$150
2018-2021	FA-345CE	$285	$375

Flame Elite
1984. Master Series, made in Japan, neck-thru, offset double-cut, solidbody, 2 humbuckers, rosewood 'board, snowflake inlays.

1984-1988		$1,600	$2,100

Flame Standard
1984-1988. Like Flame Elite, but with dot inlays.

1984-1988		$1,550	$2,000

Flame Ultra
1984. Like Flame Elite, but with split block inlays (some with snowflakes), gold hardware.

1984-1988		$1,600	$2,100

FR-48 Resonator
2003-2009. Made in Korea, steel body.

2003-2009		$275	$350

FR-50 Resonator
2000-2015. Spruce top, mahogany back and sides, sunburst, optional square-neck.

2000-2015		$275	$350

FR-50CE Resonator
2000-2015. Same as FR-50 with cutaway and pickups.

2009-2015		$350	$450

FR-55 Hawaiian Resonator
2012-2013. Bell brass nickel-plated body etched with scenes of South Seas.

2012-2013		$375	$475

GA (Grand Auditorium) Series
2001-2009. Various grand auditorium models made in Korea, an oval label on the inside back clearly indicates the model number.

2001-2009		$150	$475

GC (Grand Concert) Series
1997-2009. Various grand concert models, an oval label on the inside back clearly indicates the model number.

1997-2009		$125	$175

GDO (Global Design Orchestra) Series
2004-2008. Various orchestra-sized acoustic models, an oval label on the inside back clearly indicates the model number.

2004-2008		$350	$550

Gemini Series
1983-1990. Korean-made flat-tops, label on inside indicates model. I is classical nylon-string, II, III and IV are dreadnought steel-strings, there is also a 12-string and an IIE acoustic/electric.

1984-1987	Gemini II	$90	$210

The *Vintage Guitar Price Guide* shows low to high values for items in all-original excellent condition, and, where applicable, with original case or cover.

MODEL YEAR	FEATURES	EXC. COND. LOW	HIGH
1984-1988	Gemini I	$85	$165
1987-1988	Gemini III	$140	$240
1987-1990	Gemini IIE	$140	$240
1987-1990	Gemini IV	$140	$240

GN (Grand Nylon) Series
2001-2007. Various grand nylon acoustic models, an oval label on the inside back clearly indicates the model number.

2001-2007		$300	$475

Harmony-Made Series
Late-1960s-1973. Various Harmony-made models, with white stencil Fender logo, mahogany, natural or sunburst.

1960s	D-style model	$250	$900
1970-1973	Stella model	$100	$200

Jag-Stang
1996-1999, 2003-2004. Made in Japan, designed by Curt Cobain, body similar to Jaguar, tremolo, 1 pickup, oversize Strat peghead, Fiesta Red or Sonic Blue. First year has 50th Anniversary label.

1996-2004		$875	$1,150

Jaguar
1962-1975. Reintroduced as Jaguar '62 in '95-'99. Custom colors can fade and often the faded color has very little similarity to the original color. The values below are for an instrument that is relatively unfaded. Each custom color should be evaluated on a case-by-case basis.As the value of custom color Fenders has increased, so has the problem of bogus non-original finishes. The prices in the Guide are for factory original finishes in excellent condition. Please refer to the Fender Guitar Intro Section for details on Fender color options.

1962-1964	Common color	$7,400	$9,700
1962-1964	Rare color	$9,700	$13,000
1962-1964	Sunburst	$5,100	$6,700
1965	Common color	$6,500	$8,600
1965	Rare color	$8,600	$11,500
1965	Sunburst	$4,600	$6,000
1966	Common color	$5,500	$7,200
1966	Rare color	$7,200	$11,200
1966	Sunburst	$4,300	$5,700
1967-1969	Common color	$5,500	$7,200
1967-1969	Rare color	$7,200	$11,200
1967-1969	Sunburst	$4,600	$6,100
1970	Common color	$4,500	$6,000
1970	Rare color	$6,000	$8,300
1970-1975	Sunburst	$3,700	$4,900
1971-1974	Custom color	$4,500	$6,000
1975	Custom color	$4,000	$5,300

Jaguar '62
1986-2012. Reintroduction of Jaguar, Japanese-made until '99, then U.S.-made American Vintage series, basswood body, rosewood 'board, various colors.

1986-1999	Import	$1,125	$1,450
1999-2012	USA	$1,300	$1,700

50th Anniversary Jaguar
2012. USA, modeled after '62, classic 24" scale, new one-degree neck-angle pocket, repositioned tremolo plate, redesigned hot Jaguar single-coils, lacquer finish in Lake Placid Blue, Candy Apple Red, or burgundy.

2012		$1,275	$1,650

American Vintage '62 Jaguar
2000. Export version, Lake Placid Blue, Candy Apple Red, Shell Pink, Burgundy Mist Metallic and Ice Blue Metallic with matching headstocks, a special run for Yamano, Japan. Limited to 50 in each color.

2000		$1,500	$1,950

Blacktop Jaguar HH
2010-2014. Stripped-down electronics with 2 humbuckers, 1 volume, 1 tone, single 3-way switch, maple neck, rosewood 'board, black 'guard, black or silver.

2010-2014		$575	$750

Jaguar Baritone Special HH
2005-2010. Japan, limited edition, Baritone Special logo on matching headstock, 2 humbuckers, no trem, black.

2005-2010		$600	$800

Jaguar Classic Player Special
2009-2019. Classic Player series, classic Jag look, tremolo, 2 single-coils

2009-2019		$625	$800

Jaguar Classic Player Special HH
2009-2019. Classic Player series. 2 humbucker version.

2009-2019		$625	$800

Jaguar FSR Classic '66 Reissue
2008-2010. Fender Special Run, '66 specs, block inlays, black logo, custom colors, limited edition.

2008-2010		$1,125	$1,475

Jaguar FSR Thinline
2012. Limited Edition, semi-hollowbody with f-hole, 2 vintage-style single-coil pickups.

2012		$1,275	$1,650

Jaguar HH/Special Edition Jaguar HH
2005-2014. Japan, 2 Dragster humbuckers, matching headstock, chrome knobs and pickup covers.

2005-2014		$600	$800

Jaguar Limited Edition Classic Series
2002-2003. Crafted in Japan.

2002-2003	Various models	$1,000	$1,300

Johnny Marr Signature Jaguar
2012-present. Artist series, based on Marr's '65 Jaguar, Olympic White or Metallic KO.

2012-2021		$1,200	$1,600

Kurt Cobain Signature Jaguar
2011-present. Artist Series, based on Cobain's '65 Jaguar, 3-color sunburst.

2011-2021		$1,200	$1,600

Modern Player Jaguar
2012-2014. Mahogany body, maple neck, rosewood 'board, 2-color chocolate burst, trans red or trans black.

2012-2014		$325	$425

Pawn Shop Jaguarillo
2012-2013. Alder body, maple neck, rosewood 'board, HSS pickups, various colors.

2012-2013		$575	$750

Player Jaguar
2018-present. Alder body, maple neck, 1 humbucker and 1 single-coil, various colors with gloss finish.

2018-2021		$475	$625

1966 Fender Jaguar
Patrick McHaffie

1966 Fender Jaguar
Rob Zolezzi

1962 Fender Jazzmaster
Kevin Rush

*Fender American
Performer Jazzmaster*

MODEL YEAR	FEATURES	EXC. COND. LOW	HIGH

Jazzmaster
1958-1980. Contoured body, 2 pickups, rosewood 'board, clay dot inlay, reintroduced as Japanese-made Jazzmaster '62 in '94. Custom color Fenders can be forged and bogus finishes have been a problem. As the value of custom color Fenders has increased, so has the problem of bogus non-original finishes. The prices in the Guide are for factory original finishes in excellent condition. Please refer to the Fender Guitar Intro Section for details on Fender color options.

1958	Sunburst	$11,300	$15,000
1958	Sunburst, maple 'board	$11,000	$14,500
1959	Custom color, includes rare	$20,500	$27,000
1959	Sunburst	$10,000	$13,300
1960-1961	Common color	$15,000	$20,000
1960-1961	Rare color	$20,000	$25,000
1960-1961	Sunburst	$9,300	$12,200
1962-1964	Common color	$10,000	$13,300
1962-1964	Rare color	$13,300	$19,700
1962-1964	Sunburst	$6,300	$8,300
1965	Common color	$8,000	$11,000
1965	Rare color	$11,000	$15,000
1965	Sunburst	$5,700	$7,500
1966-1969	Common color	$6,000	$8,000
1966-1969	Rare color	$8,000	$12,000
1966-1969	Sunburst	$5,500	$7,300
1970	Common color	$5,800	$7,600
1970	Rare color	$7,600	$10,000
1970-1980	Sunburst	$3,700	$4,900
1971-1974	Custom color	$5,500	$7,200
1975	Custom color	$4,500	$5,900
1976-1980	Custom color	$4,000	$5,300

Road Worn '60s Jazzmaster
2015-2019. '60s style with aged/worn alder body and maple neck, worn nitro-lacquer finish. Replaced by American Original '60s Jazzmaster.

2015-2019		$600	$775

Jazzmaster '62
1986-2012. Japanese-made reintroduction of Jazzmaster, basswood body, rosewood 'board, from '99 U.S.-made American Vintage series, various colors.

1986-1989	Import	$1,175	$1,525
1990-1998	Import	$1,100	$1,425
1999-2012	USA	$1,300	$1,700

Jazzmaster '65/American Vintage '65
2013-2018. Alder body, maple neck, mid-'60s neck profile, rosewood 'board. Part of American Vintage series in '16.

2013-2018		$1,500	$1,950

Jazzmaster '69
1986-1990s. Made in Japan.

1986-1989		$1,300	$1,700
1990-1999		$1,200	$1,600

American Performer Jazzmaster
Introduced Dec. 2018-present. Made in US, new features include Yosemite single-coil pickups, Grease-bucket tone system, various colors.

2018-2021		$775	$1,025

American Ultra Jazzmaster
2019-present. Alder or ash body, maple neck, rosewood 'board, 2 pickups.

2019-2021		$1,300	$1,700

Blacktop Jazzmaster HS
2010-2014. Stripped-down electronics with a single-coil and a humbucker, 1 volume, 1 tone, single 3-way switch, maple neck, rosewood 'board, black or sunburst.

2010-2014		$575	$750

Classic Player Jazzmaster Special
2008-2019. Alder body, maple neck, rosewood 'board, 2 single-coils, 3-color sunburst or black.

2008-2019		$625	$800

Elvis Costello Jazzmaster
2008-2010. Artist series, walnut stain, '70s neck, vintage style tremolo.

2008-2010		$1,450	$1,900

J Mascis Jazzmaster
2007-2009. Artist series, purple sparkle finish, matching headstock, Adjusto-Matic bridge, reinforced tremolo arm.

2007-2009		$1,275	$1,675

Noventa Jazzmaster
2021. Alder body, maple neck, 3 single-coil pickups, Fiesta Red, Surf Green or Walnut.

2021		$750	$975

Pinup Girl Jazzmaster
1997. Custom Shop Limited Edition, pinup girl art on body, figured maple neck, 3 pickups, certificate of authenticity.

1997		$2,400	$3,100

Select Jazzmaster
2012-2013. Chambered alder body with a carved flame maple top, Fender Select headstock medallion, various finish options.

2012-2013		$1,900	$2,500

Sonic Youth Signature Jazzmaster
2009-2014. Lee Ranaldo and Thurston Moore Signature models based on their modified Jazzmasters which basically removed the standard control layout and replaced it with a 3-way switch.

2009-2014	Lee Ranaldo	$1,400	$1,825
2009-2014	Thurston Moore	$1,400	$1,825

The Ventures Limited Edition Jazzmaster
1996. Japanese-made, ash body, 2 pickups, block inlay, transparent purple/black.

1996		$1,200	$1,600

Troy Van Leeuwen Jazzmaster
2014-present. Alder body, maple neck, Oxblood finish, red tortoiseshell 'guard, matching headstock, various custom colors.

2014-2021		$850	$1,125

White Opal Jazzmaster HH
2016. Special Edition, made in Mexico, white opal body and headstock, pearloid 'guard, 2 humbuckers.

2016		$450	$575

JZM Deluxe
2007-2009. Electracoustic Series, acoustic/electric, Jazzmaster/Jaguar body styling, Fishman and Tele pickups, sunburst or trans amber.

2007-2009		$425	$550

MODEL YEAR	FEATURES	EXC. COND. LOW	HIGH

Katana
1985-1986. Japanese-made wedge-shaped body, 2 humbuckers, set neck, triangle inlays, black.

1985-1986		$850	$1,100

King
1963-1965. Full-size 15 5/8" wide acoustic, natural. Renamed Kingman in '65.

1963-1965	Brazilian rosewood	$2,900	$3,800
1963-1965	Indian, Zebra, Vermillion	$1,500	$1,950

Kingman
1965-1971. Full-size 15 5/8" wide acoustic, slightly smaller by '70, offered in 3 Wildwood colors, referred to as the Wildwood acoustic which is a Kingman with dyed wood. Reissued as import in '06.

1965-1968		$1,425	$1,850
1969-1971		$1,300	$1,675

Kingman Antigua
1968-1971. Kingman in Antigua finish (silver to black sunburst).

1968-1971		$1,600	$2,100

Kingman ASCE
2008-2017. Cutaway acoustic-electric, mahogany back and sides.

2008-2017		$375	$500

Kingman SCE
2008-2017. Cutaway acoustic-electric, mahogany back and sides.

2008-2017		$365	$475

Kingman USA Pro Custom
2013-2014. Custom Shop Pro series, limited run of 50, AA sitka spruce top, maple back/sides/neck, Firemist Gold.

2013-2014		$1,125	$1,475

Kingman USA Select
2012. All solid woods, rosewood 'board, Fishman electronics, 3-color sunburst.

2012		$1,175	$1,525

Kingman USA Select C
2012. Custom Shop limited edition of 150, Engelmann spruce top, mahogany back and sides, vintage C-shaped maple neck, rosewood 'board, Fiesta Red.

2012		$1,200	$1,575

Kingman/Elvis Kingman
2012-2013. Wildwood model as used by Elvis Presley in the '67 film 'Clambake', spruce top, mahogany back and sides, rosewood 'board, natural.

2012-2013		$365	$475

Lead I
1979-1982. Double-cut solidbody with 1 humbucker, maple or rosewood 'board, black or brown.

1979-1982		$700	$900

Lead II
1979-1982. Lead with 2 pickups, black or brown.

1979-1982		$875	$1,150

Lead III
1982. Lead with 2 split-coil humbuckers, 2 3-way switches, various colors.

1982		$875	$1,150

Player Lead II
2020-present. Reintroduced using late-70s and updated model features.

2020-2021		$400	$525

Player Lead III
2020-present. Reintroduced using late-70s and updated model features.

2020-2021		$400	$525

LTD
1969-1975. Archtop electric, single-cut, gold-plated hardware, carved top and back, 1 pickup, multi-bound, bolt-on neck, sunburst.

1969-1975		$3,100	$4,000

Malibu
1965-1971. Flat-top, spruce top, mahogany back and sides, black, mahogany or sunburst. Later version is import.

1965-1971		$750	$975

Malibu (California Series)
1983-1995. Made first in Japan, then Korea in '85.

1983-1995		$225	$300

Malibu SCE
2006-2013. Imported single-cut acoustic/electric, solid spruce top, laminated mahogany back and sides, block inlays.

2006-2013		$235	$310

Marauder
1965 only. The Marauder has 3 pickups, and some have slanted frets, only 8 were made, thus it is very rare. 1st generation has hidden pickups, 2nd has exposed.

1965	1st generation	$11,000	$14,400
1965	2nd generation	$8,100	$10,600

Marauder (Modern Player)
2011-2014. Jazzmaster-type body, 1 Jazzmaster pickup and 1 Triple Bucker, rosewood 'board.

2011-2014		$425	$550

Maverick Dorado (Parallel Universe)
2020. Parallel Universe Vol. II series, alder body, 22-fret maple neck, 2 pickups, Bigsby vibrato, Mystic Pine Green, Ultraburst and Firemist Gold.

2020		$1,600	$2,100

Meteora (Parallel Universe)
November 2018-2019. Parallel Universe Vol. II series, sleek offset body with both Jazzmaster and Telecaster features.

2018-2019		$600	$800

Mod Shop
2016-present. Models designed by customer by choosing options from a menu and built by Fender, 4 models offered – Jazz Bass, Precision Bass, Stratocaster and Telecaster. Values should be determined on case-by-case basis.

2016-2021		$2,000	$2,600

Montara (California Series)
1990-1995. Korean-made single-cut acoustic/electric flat-top, natural, sunburst or black. Maple with flamed sides starting '92.

1990-1995		$475	$625

2011 Fender Blacktop Jazzmaster HS

Imaged by Heritage Auctions, HA.com

1980 Fender Lead II

Tom Pfeifer

1965 Fender Mustang
Robbie Keene

1969 Fender Mustang
Suzie Williams

MODEL YEAR	FEATURES	EXC. COND. LOW	HIGH

Montego I/II
1968-1975. Electric archtop, single-cut, bolt-on neck, 1 pickup (I) or 2 pickups (II), chrome-plated hardware, sunburst.

1968-1975	I	$2,700	$3,600
1968-1975	II	$2,900	$3,800

Musiclander
1969-1972. Also called Swinger and Arrow, solidbody, 1 pickup, arrow-shaped headstock, no model name on peghead, red, white, and blue. Fender used '66-'68 dated necks but final assembly did not begin until '69.

1969-1972		$2,700	$3,500

Musicmaster
1956-1980. Solidbody, 1 pickup, short-scale (3/4) neck, Desert Sand ('56-'61), sunburst ('61-'63), red, white or blue after. Regular-scale necks were optional and are called Musicmaster II from '64 to '69, after '69 II is dropped and Musicmaster continues with regular-scale neck.

1956-1959	Blond	$2,000	$2,600
1960-1964	Blond	$1,600	$2,100
1964-1965	Nitro, red, white, blue	$1,600	$2,100
1966-1968	Nitro, red, white, blue	$1,450	$1,900
1969-1972	Poly, red, white, blue	$1,350	$1,750
1973-1980	Red, white, blue	$1,350	$1,750

Musicmaster II
1964-1969. Solidbody, 1 pickup, long regular-scale neck version of Musicmaster, red, white, or blue.

1964-1965		$1,600	$2,100
1966-1969		$1,350	$1,750

Mustang
1964-1982, 1997-1998, 2016-present. Solidbody, 2 pickups. Reissued as '69 Mustang in 1990s, name changed back to Mustang '97-'98. Dakota Red, Daphne Blue and Olympic White with Competition Red, Blue and Orange finishes with a racing stripe on the front of the body added '69-'73 (with matching headstock for '69-'70).

1964-1965	Red, white or blue	$2,300	$3,000
1966-1969	Red, white or blue	$2,100	$2,700
1969-1970	Competition color	$2,100	$2,700
1970-1979	Contour body, poly	$1,950	$2,550
1978-1980	Antigua	$1,950	$2,550
1980-1982	Various colors	$1,400	$1,850

Vintera '60s Mustang
2019-present. Alder body, '60s C-neck, 2 single-coils, 3-color sunburst, Lake Placid Blue or Seafoam Green.

2019-2021		$600	$775

Mustang '65 Reissue
2006-2016. Made in Japan, Classic Series.

2006-2016		$725	$950

Mustang '69 Reissue
1986-1998, 2005. Japanese-made, blue or white.

1986-1998		$725	$950

Mustang 90/Player Mustang 90
2016-present. Made in Mexico, 2 MP-90 pickups. Named to Player series in '20.

2016-2021		$400	$525

MODEL YEAR	FEATURES	EXC. COND. LOW	HIGH

American Performer Mustang
Introduced Dec. 2018-present. Made in U.S.A., Yosemite single-coil pickups, Greasebucket tone system, various colors.

2018-2021		$775	$1,000

American Special Mustang
2017-2018. FSR model, 2 humbucking pickups, ash body with natural finish or alder Olympic White Pearl.

2017-2018		$775	$1,000

Ben Gibbard Mustang
2021-present. Artist series, chambered ash body, natural poly gloss finish.

2021-2022		$725	$950

Kurt Cobain Mustang
2012-2016. Artist Series, rosewood 'board, Fiesta Red finish.

2012-2016		$725	$950

Mustang Special
2011-2013. Pawn Shop series, 2 humbucker pickups. 3-color sunburst, Candy Apple Red or Lake Placid Blue.

2011-2013		$525	$675

Newporter
1965-1971. Acoustic flat-top, mahogany back and sides. Reissued as import.

1965-1968	Spruce top	$625	$825
1968-1971	Mahogany top	$600	$775

Newporter (California Series)
1983-1995. Made first in Japan, then Korea in '85.

1983-1995		$210	$275

Newporter (Custom Shop USA)/USA Select Newporter
2013-2014. Fishman electronics, 150 offered, certificate of authenticity.

2013-2014		$1,650	$2,150

Newporter Classic
2018-present. Spruce top, matching headstock, natural mahogany back and sides, pau ferro 'board.

2018-2021		$525	$675

Newporter Player
2018-present. California series, solid spruce top, mahogany back and sides, walnut 'board, various colors with gloss poly finish.

2018-2021		$290	$375

Palomino
1968-1971. Acoustic flat-top, spruce top, mahogany back and sides, triple-bound, black or mahogany.

1968-1971		$850	$1,100

Paramount Series Acoustic
2016-present. Various Standard and Deluxe acoustic models introduced at Jan. '16 NAMM.

2016-2021		$550	$725

Pawn Shop Series
2011-2014. All-new designs with diverse Fender components and the philosophy "guitars that never were but should have been".

2011-2014	Various models	$600	$775

Performer
1985-1986. Imported Swinger-like body design, 2 slanted humbuckers.

1985-1986		$1,500	$1,950

MODEL YEAR	FEATURES	EXC. COND. LOW	HIGH

Prodigy
1991-1993. US-made, electric solidbody, double-cut, chrome-plated hardware, 2 single-coil and 1 humbucker pickups, blue or black.

1991-1993		$1,000	$1,300

Redondo
1969-1970. Mid-size flat-top, 14 3/8" wide, replaces Newport spruce top model.

1969-1970		$600	$775

Redondo (California Series)
1983-1995. Made first in Japan, then Korea in '85.

1983-1995		$200	$265

Redondo Player
2018-present. California series, solid Sitka spruce top, mahogany back and sides, walnut 'board, various colors with gloss poly finish.

2018-2021		$290	$375

Robben Ford Signature
1989-1994. Symmetrical double-cut, 2 pickups, glued-in neck, solidbody with tone chambers, multibound, gold-plated hardware, sunburst. After '94 made in Fender Custom Shop.

1989-1994		$1,750	$2,300
1995	Custom Shop	$2,500	$3,300

San Luis Rey (California Series)
1990-1995. Acoustic flat-top, solid spruce top, rosewood back and sides.

1990-1995		$290	$375

San Miguel (California Series)
1990-1992. Acoustic cutaway flat-top, spruce top, mahogany back and sides.

1990-1992		$200	$265

Santa Maria (California Series)
1988-1992. Acoustic flat-top 12-string, spruce top, mahogany back and sides.

1988-1992		$200	$265

Santa Marino (California Series)
1990-1992. Acoustic flat-top, solid spruce top, mahogany back and sides.

1990-1992		$200	$265

Sergio Vallin Signature
2015-2017. New offset double-cut body shape, HSS pickups.

2015-2017		$500	$650

Shenandoah 12-String
1965-1971. Acoustic flat-top, spruce top, mahogany back and sides.

1965-1971	Antigua	$1,425	$1,850
1965-1971	Blond	$1,100	$1,425

Showmaster (Import)
2003-2007. Off-set double-cut solidbody, set neck, various models.

2003	Celtic, 1 bridge hum	$525	$675
2003-2007	HH, 2 hums	$525	$675
2004-2006	3 single coils	$525	$675

Showmaster FMT (Custom Shop)
2000-2007. Bound figured maple top (FMT), 2 single-coil pickups and a bridge position humbucker, maple neck, Custom Shop certificate.

2000-2007		$1,725	$2,250

Sonoran SCE (California Series)
2006-2018. Cutaway flat-top acoustic, 6-on-a-side tuners, spruce top, laminated mahogany back and sides, rosewood 'board, electronics options.

2006-2018		$200	$265

Squier Series
The following are all Squier Series instruments from Fender, listed alphabetically. Fender Japan was established in '82 with Squier production beginning that same year. Production was shifted to Korea in '87 and later allocated to China, India (Squier II '89-'90), Mexico and other countries.

Squier '51
2004-2006. Korean-made, Strat-style body with a Tele-style neck, various colors.

2004-2006		$115	$150

Squier Bullet
1983-1988, 1995-1996, 2000-2011. Strat style, early with Tele headstock, 1980s' models include H-2 ('83-'86, 2 humbuckers), S-3 ('83-'86, 3 single-coils), S-3T ('83-'88, 3 single-coils, vibrato). Name revived in 1995 (3 SC, vib.) and in 2000 on various models with 3 SC or 2 HB pickups.

1983-1984	S-3, T	$500	$650
1983-1986	H-2	$500	$650
1985-1988	S-3, T	$425	$550
2000-2011		$115	$150

Squier Bullet Stratocaster HT HSS
2017-present. Thin poplar body, maple neck, 1 humbucker and 2 single coil pickups, Shell Pink, Brown Sunburst or black.

2017-2021		$115	$150

Squier Duo-Sonic '50s (Classic Vibe Series)
2008-2010. Classic Vibe Series, made in China.

2008-2010		$225	$300

Squier Jaguar HH ST (Contemporary Series)
2021-present. Poplar body, roasted maple neck, Indian Laurel 'board, 2 humbucker pickups, stop tailpiece, Shorline Gold or Sky Burst Metallic.

2021-2022		$300	$400

Squier Jazzmaster (Classic Vibe Series)
2010-present. Includes both '60s ('10-present) and '70s ('10-'20) Jazzmaster, inspired by vintage-era models, various colors with gloss poly finish.

2010-2021	'60s or '70s	$250	$325

Squier Katana
1985-1987. Wedge-shaped body, 1 humbucker, bolt neck, dot inlays.

1985-1987		$725	$950

Squier Mini Stratocaster
2020-present. Poplar body, maple neck, 3 single-coil pickups, various colors. Dual humbucker pickups (HH) available.

2020-2021		$120	$155

Squier Showmaster Series
2002-2005. Made in China, various pickup configs.

2002-2005	Various models	$160	$210

Fender Redondo Player

2005 Fender Squier '51
Fred Schweng

GUITARS

Fender Squier J5 Telecaster

1976 Fender Starcaster

James Seldin

MODEL YEAR	FEATURES	EXC. COND. LOW	HIGH

Squier Stagemaster HH
1999-2002. 2 humbuckers, reverse headstock, 6- or 7-string.

1999-2002		$160	$210

Squier Standard Double Fat Strat
1999-2007. 2 humbucker pickups.

1999-2007		$115	$150

Squier Standard Fat Strat
1996-2006. Hum/single/single pickups. Replaced by the HSS.

1996-2006		$115	$150

Squier Standard Floyd Rose Strat
1992-1996. Floyd Rose tailpiece, black, white or foto flame finish, Fender and Squier headstock logos.

1992-1996		$350	$450

Squier Standard Stratocaster
1982-2019. Standard Series represent the classic designs.

1982-1984	1st logo, JV serial	$1,200	$1,550
1985-1989	2nd logo, SQ serial	$575	$750
1990-1999	Mexico	$350	$450
2000-2019	Indonesia	$150	$200

Squier II Stratocaster
1988-1992. Squier II models were targeted at a lower price point than regular Squier series. Mainly built in Korea but some early ones from India. Line was replaced by other models under regular Squier instruments.

1988-1992		$210	$275

Squier Stratocaster (Affinity Series)
1997-present. Affinity Series, lower priced version, made in China.

1997-2021		$150	$200

Squier Stratocaster (Contemporary Series)
2020-present. Poplar body, roasted maple neck, 2 humbucker pickups, various colors with gloss poly finish. Floyd Rose tremolo available.

2020-2021	HH	$250	$325
2020-2021	HH FR, Floyd Rose	$290	$380

Squier Stratocaster '50s (Classic Vibe Series)
2008-present. China, alder body, maple 'board, white pickguard, 2-tone sunburst, Lake Placid Blue or Oly White.

2008-2021		$250	$325

Squier Stratocaster '60s (Classic Vibe Series)
2008-present. China, as '50s Classic Vibe but with rosewood 'board, tortoise pickguard, 3-tone sunburst or candy apple red.

2008-2021		$250	$325

Squier Stratocaster Pro-Tone
1996-1998. Korean-made, higher-end Squier series with solid ash bodies, one-piece maple necks, alnico single-coils.

1996-1998		$450	$575

Squier Stratocaster Special (Contemporary Series)
2021-present. Poplar body, roasted maple neck, 3 single-coil pickups, painted headstock with chrome

MODEL YEAR	FEATURES	EXC. COND. LOW	HIGH

logo, various colors with gloss poly finish. Hardtail bridge (HT) available.

2021-2022		$290	$380

Squier Tom Delonge Stratocaster
2002-2003. Hardtail, 1 humbucker.

2002-2003		$300	$400

Squier Standard Telecaster
1982-2019. Standard Series represent the classic designs.

1982-1984	1st logo, JV serial	$1,200	$1,550
1985-1989	2nd logo, SQ serial	$575	$750
1990-1999	Mexico	$350	$450
2000-2019	Indonesia	$150	$200

Squier Standard Telecaster Special
2004-2007. Made in Indonesia, 1 humbucker, 1 single-coil.

2004-2007		$150	$200

Squier Telecaster (Affinity Series)
1998-present. Lower priced version, made in China.

1998-2021		$150	$200

Squier Telecaster HH/RH
2020-present. Contemporary series, poplar body, maple neck, 2 dual humbucking (HH) pickups, in '22 changed to RH (rail humbucker, hum), black metallic with pearl white 'guard or pearl white with black 'guard.

2020-2021		$300	$400

Squier Telecaster Custom/Custom II
2003-2012. 2 humbuckers, Custom II has 2 soapbar single-coils. Changed to Vintage Modified series in '12.

2003-2012		$150	$200

Squier J5 (John 5) Telecaster
2009-2020. Artist Series, black with chrome hardware or Frost Gold with gold hardware (introduced '14), matching headstock.

2014-2020		$290	$375

Squier Telecaster Thinline (Classic Vibe Series)
2014-2020. Semi-hollow mahogany body with f-hole.

2004-2020		$225	$300

Squier Venus
1997-1998. Offset double-cut solidbody, 2 pickups, co-designed by Courtney Love, also offered as 12-string.

1997-1998		$450	$590

Squier Vintage Modified Series
2012-2020. Imported, various models, large script Squier logo and small Fender logo on headstock.

2012-2016	Jazzmaster Special	$185	$240
2012-2016	Surf Stratocaster	$190	$250
2012-2016	Telecaster Special	$190	$250
2012-2020	'70s Stratocaster	$190	$250
2012-2020	Stratocaster HSS	$190	$250

Starcaster
1974-1980, 2014-2017. Offset double-cut, thinline semi-hollowbody, arched maple top and back, 2 humbuckers, 5 knobs (2 tone, 2 volume, 1 master volume), originally offered in tobacco sunburst, natural, walnut, black, white or custom blond finish. Model revived in Modern Player Series in '14 without master volume.

MODEL YEAR	FEATURES	EXC. COND. LOW	HIGH

Fender also used the Starcaster name as a brand on a line of budget guitars in the 2000s.

| 1974-1980 | Various colors | $4,600 | $6,000 |
| 2014-2017 | Modern Player | $700 | $900 |

Starcaster by Fender

2000s. Fender used the Starcaster brand on a line of budget versions of the Strat, Tele, and J- and P-Bass. They also offered small solid state amps and guitar packages with nylon- or steel-string acoustic or a Strat/ amp combo. Sold in Costco and other discounters.

2000s	Acoustic	$125	$160
2000s	Electric guitar only	$125	$160
2000s	Guitar with amp & stand	$135	$175

Stratacoustic Series

2000-2019. Thinline acoustic/electric, single-cut, spruce top, fiberglass body, various colors. Stratacoustic discontinued '05, Deluxe begins '07 and Standard added in '09. Both Plus and Premier '14-'17.

| 2000-2019 | | $350 | $500 |

Stratocaster

The following are all variations of the Stratocaster. The first six listings are for the main American-made line. All others are listed alphabetically after that in the following order:

Stratocaster
Standard Stratocaster (includes "Smith Strat")
American Standard Stratocaster
American Series Stratocaster
American Professional Stratocaster
American Professional II Stratocaster
20th Century American Standard Stratocaster
21st Century American Standard Stratocaster
25th Anniversary Stratocaster
30th Anniversary Guitar Center Stratocaster
35th Anniversary Stratocaster
40th Anniversary 1954 Stratocaster Limited Edition
40th Anniversary American Standard Stratocaster
40th Anniversary Stratocaster Diamond Dealer
40th Anniversary Stratocaster ST62 (Japan)
'50s Stratocaster/Classic Series '50s Stratocaster
American Original '50s Stratocaster
Classic Player '50s Stratocaster
Classic Series '50s Stratocaster Lacquer
Road Worn '50s Stratocaster
50th Anniversary 1954 Stratocaster
50th Anniversary American Deluxe Stratocaster
50th Anniversary American Standard Stratocaster
50th Anniversary American Vintage 1957 Stratocaster
50th Anniversary Stratocaster
50th Anniversary Stratocaster Relic
'54 Stratocaster (Custom Shop)
'54 Stratocaster FMT

'55 Stratocaster (Custom Shop)
'55 Dual-Mag Strat Journeyman Relic
'55 Historic 1955 NOS Stratocaster
'55 Rocking Dog Stratocaster
'55 Stratocaster Journeyman Relic
'56 Stratocaster (Custom Shop)
'56 Stratocaster Heavy Relic
'56 Stratocaster Journeyman Closet Classic
American Vintage '56 Stratocaster
American Vintage '56 Stratocaster Limited Edition Roasted Ash
'57 Stratocaster (Custom Shop)
'57 Stratocaster (CS)
'57 Stratocaster (USA)
'57 Special Stratocaster
'57 Vintage Stratocaster (Japan)
American Vintage '57 Commemorative Stratocaster
Time Machine 1957 Stratocaster Relic
Vintage Custom 1957 Stratocaster NOS
Wildwood "10s" 1957 Limited Stratocaster Relic
'58 Stratocaster (Custom Shop)
'58 Stratocaster (Dakota Red)
'58 Limited Edition MIJ Stratocaster
'58 Stratocaster Journeyman Relic
Time Machine 1958 Stratocaster Heavy Relic
'59 Rocking Dog Stratocaster
'59 Stratocaster (Custom Shop)
1959 Stratocaster LTD Journeyman
American Vintage '59 Pine Stratocaster
American Vintage '59 Stratocaster
Time Machine 1959 Stratocaster
Wildwood "10s" 1959 Limited Stratocaster Relic
'60 Stratocaster (Custom Shop)
'60 Stratocaster FMT (Custom Shop)
Custom 1960 Stratocaster
'60s Stratocaster/Classic Series '60s Stratocaster
'60s Stratocaster/Time Machine 1960 Stratocaster
American Original '60s Stratocaster
Classic Player '60s Stratocaster
Classic Series '60s Stratocaster Lacquer
Limited Edition '60s Daybreak Stratocaster
Road Worn '60s Stratocaster
60th Anniversary '54 Stratocaster (Custom Shop)
60th Anniversary American Stratocaster
60th Anniversary American Vintage 1954 Stratocaster
60th Anniversary Commemorative Stratocaster
60th Anniversary Presidential Stratocaster
'61 Stratocaster (Custom Shop)
Wildwood "10s" 1961 Limited Stratocaster
'62 Stratocaster (USA)
'62 Commemorative Stratocaster
'62 Heavy Relic Stratocaster
'62 Stratocaster ST62D/ST54 DEX2
'62 Stratocaster ST62US Reissue
'62 Vintage Stratocaster (Japan)
Dave's Guitar Shop American 1962 Stratocaster

Fender Squire Vintage Modified Surf Stratocaster

Fender Stratacoustic

1954 Fender Stratocaster
Tony Sheedy

1956 Fender Stratocaster (lefty)
HI Guitars

Deluxe Vintage Player '62 Stratocaster
Vintage Custom 1962 Stratocaster
Willcutt Guitars True '62 Stratocaster
'63 Stratocaster (Custom Shop)
'63 Stratocaster Journeyman Relic
'64 Stratocaster (Custom Shop)
Time Machine 1964 Stratocaster Journeyman
    Relic
'65 Stratocaster (Custom Shop)
'65 Stratocaster Journeyman Closet Classic
American Vintage '65 Stratocaster
Time Machine 1965 Stratocaster Journeyman
    Relic
Total Tone '65 Stratocaster Relic
'66 Stratocaster (Custom Shop)
Time Machine 1967 Stratocaster Journeyman
    Relic Aged
Time Machine 1967 Stratocaster Journeyman
    Relic Custom Top
'68 Heavy Relic Stratocaster
'68 Reverse Strat Special (USA)
'68 Stratocaster (Japan)
'69 Stratocaster (Custom Shop)
Wildwood "10s" 1969 Limited Stratocaster
'70s Stratocaster/Classic Series '70s Strato-
    caster
American Vintage '70s Stratocaster
'72 Stratocaster (Japan)
'72 Stratocaster Limited Edition
75th Anniversary Commemorative Strato-
    caster
75th Anniversary Stratocaster
Acoustasonic Stratocaster
Aerodyne Classic Stratocaster
Aerodyne Stratocaster
Albert Hammond Jr. Signature Stratocaster
Aluminum Stratocaster (Custom Shop)
Aluminum Stratocaster American Standard
American Acoustasonic Stratocaster
American Classic Holoflake Stratocaster
American Classic Stratocaster
American Custom Stratocaster (Custom Shop)
American Deluxe Stratocaster
American Deluxe Stratocaster Dealer Event
American Deluxe Stratocaster Designer Series
American Deluxe Stratocaster FMT HSS
American Deluxe Stratocaster HSS Mahogany
American Elite Stratocaster
American Elite Stratocaster Limited Edition
American Longboard Stratocaster HSS
American Performer Stratocaster
American Special Stratocaster
American Standard Stratocaster Limited
    Edition
American Ultra Luxe Stratocaster
American Ultra Stratocaster
Ancho Poblano Stratocaster Journeyman Relic
Ancho Poblano Roasted Stratocaster Relic
Antigua Stratocaster
Artisan Series Stratocaster (Custom Shop)
Big Apple Stratocaster
Big Block Stratocaster
Big Head Stratocaster

Bill Carson Stratocaster
Billy Corgan Stratocaster
Blackie Stratocaster (Custom Shop 1987)
Blackie Stratocaster (Custom Shop)
Black Paisley Stratocaster
Blacktop Stratocaster
Mahogany Blacktop Stratocaster Limited
    Edition
Blue Flower Stratocaster
Bonnie Raitt Stratocaster
Bowling Ball/Marble Stratocaster
Buddy Guy Signature Stratocaster
Buddy Guy Standard Stratocaster
Buddy Holly Tribute Stratocaster
California Stratocaster/California Fat Strato-
    caster
Carroll Shelby Limited Edition Stratocaster
Carved Top Stratocaster HSS (Custom Shop)
Classic Player Stratocaster
Classic Player Stratocaster HH
Collector's Edition Stratocaster ('62 Reissue)
Contemporary Stratocaster (Custom Shop)
Contemporary Stratocaster (Import)
Crash Stratocaster
Custom Classic Stratocaster
Custom Deluxe Stratocaster
Custom Shop Limited Edition Stratocaster
Dave Murray Stratocaster
David Gilmour Signature Stratocaster
Deluxe Lone Star Stratocaster
Deluxe Players Special Edition Stratocaster
Deluxe Players Stratocaster
Deluxe Roadhouse Stratocaster
Deluxe Stratocaster
Deluxe Stratocaster HSS Plus Top IOS
Deluxe Stratocaster Plus
Dick Dale Stratocaster
Elite Stratocaster
EOB (Ed O'Brien) Sustainer Stratocaster
Eric Clapton Crossroads Stratocaster
Eric Clapton Gold Leaf Stratocaster
Eric Clapton Signature Journeyman Relic
    Stratocaster
Eric Clapton Signature Stratocaster (Custom
    Shop)
Eric Clapton Stratocaster
Eric Clapton Stratocaster (Custom Shop)
Eric Johnson 1954 "Virginia" Stratocaster
Eric Johnson Signature Stratocaster Thinline
Eric Johnson Stratocaster
Floyd Rose Classic Relic Stratocaster
Floyd Rose Classic Stratocaster (Strat HSS)
    (Strat HH)
Ford Shelby GT Stratocaster
Foto Flame Stratocaster
Freddy Tavares Aloha Stratocaster
FSR Stratocaster
George Fullerton 50th Anniversary '57 Strat
    Ltd. Ed. Set
George Harrison Rocky Stratocaster
Gold Stratocaster
Gold Elite Stratocaster
Gold Stratocaster (Custom Shop)

The *Vintage Guitar Price Guide* shows low to high values for items in all-original excellent condition, and, where applicable, with original case or cover.

GT11 Stratocaster
H.E.R. Stratocaster
Hank Marvin Stratocaster
Hank Marvin 40th Anniversary Stratocaster
Harley-Davidson 90th Anniversary Stratocaster
Highway One Stratocaster/HSS
HM Strat (USA/Import)
HM Strat Limited Edition
Homer Haynes HLE Stratocaster
Hot Wheels Stratocaster
HRR Stratocaster/Floyd Rose HRR (Japan)
Ike Turner Tribute Stratocaster
Jeff Beck Signature Stratocaster (CS)
Jeff Beck Stratocaster
Jerry Donahue Hellecaster Stratocaster
Jim Root Stratocaster
Jimi Hendrix Limited Edition Stratocaster (Custom Shop)
Jimi Hendrix Monterey Pop Stratocaster
Jimi Hendrix Monterey Stratocaster
Jimi Hendrix Stratocaster
Jimi Hendrix Tribute Stratocaster
Jimi Hendrix Voodoo 29th Anniversary (Guitar Center) Stratocaster
Jimi Hendrix Voodoo Child Signature Stratocaster NOS
Jimi Hendrix Voodoo Child Stratocaster Journeyman Relic
Jimi Hendrix Voodoo Stratocaster
Jimmie Vaughan Tex-Mex Stratocaster
John Jorgenson Hellecaster Stratocaster
John Mayer Limited Edition Black1 Stratocaster
John Mayer Stratocaster
Kenny Wayne Shepherd Stratocaster
Koa Stratocaster
Kon Tiki Stratocaster
Lenny Stratocaster
Limited Roasted Tomatillo Stratocaster Relic
Lincoln Brewster Signature Stratocaster
Lite Ash Stratocaster Special Edition
Lone Star Stratocaster
Mark Kendrick Master Design '65 Stratocaster
Mark Knopfler Stratocaster
Masterbuilt Custom Shop Stratocaster
Matthias Jabs Signature Stratocaster
Michael Landau Signature Relic Stratocaster 1963/1968
Milonga Deluxe Stratocaster
MLB Major League Baseball Stratocaster
Mod Shop Stratocaster
Modern Player Stratocaster HSH/HSS
Moto Limited Edition Stratocaster
Moto Set Stratocaster
Noventa Stratocaster
Orange Krush Limited Edition Stratocaster
Paisley Stratocaster
Parallel Universe Volume II Strat Jazz Deluxe
Parallel Universe Volume II Strat-Tele Hybrid
Playboy 40th Anniversary Stratocaster
Player Series Stratocaster
Post Modern Stratocaster (Custom Shop)

Post Modern Stratocaster Closet Classic (Custom Shop)
Post Modern Stratocaster Journeyman Relic (Custom Shop)
Post Modern Stratocaster NOS (Custom Shop)
Powerhouse/Powerhouse Deluxe Stratocaster
Proud Stratocaster
Rarities Stratocaster
Richie Sambora Stratocaster
Ritchie Blackmore Stratocaster
Ritchie Blackmore Tribute Stratocaster
Roadhouse Stratocaster
Robert Cray Signature Stratocaster
Robert Cray Stratocaster (Mexico)
Robin Trower Signature Stratocaster
Rory Gallagher Tribute Stratocaster
Sandblasted Stratocaster
Select Stratocaster
Set-Neck Stratocaster
Short-Scale (7/8) Stratocaster
So-Cal J.W. Black Stratocaster
So-Cal Speed Shop Stratocaster
Special Edition David Lozeau Art Stratocaster
Special Edition Stratocaster
Special Edition Stratocaster (Matching Headstock)
Special Edition White Opal Stratocaster
Splatter Stratocaster
Standard Roland Ready Stratocaster
Standard Stratocaster (Japan)
Standard Stratocaster (Mexico)
Standard Stratocaster Plus Top
Standard Stratocaster Satin Finish
Stevie Ray Vaughan Signature Stratocaster
Stevie Ray Vaughan Signature Stratocaster (Custom Shop)
Stevie Ray Vaughan Tribute #1 Stratocaster
Strat Plus
Stratocaster Junior
Stratocaster Pro Closet Classic (Custom Shop)
Stratocaster Pro NOS (Custom Shop)
Stratocaster Special
Stratocaster XII
Strat-o-Sonic
Sub Sonic Stratocaster
Super Stratocaster
Supreme Stratocaster
Tanqurey Tonic Stratocaster
Tash Sultana Stratocaster
Texas Special Stratocaster
The Edge Stratocaster
The Strat
Tie-Dye Stratocaster
Tom Delonge Stratocaster
Tom Morello "Soul Power" Stratocaster
Tree of Life Stratocaster
Turquoise Sparkle Stratocaster
U.S. Ultra / Ultra Plus Stratocaster
Ventures Limited Edition Stratocaster
VG Stratocaster
Vintage Hot Rod Stratocaster
Vintera Series Stratocaster
Walnut Elite Stratocaster

1959 Fender Stratocaster
Tracy Farmer

1961 Fender Stratocaster
Marty Fab

GUITARS

1962 Fender Statocaster
Tony Sheedy

1963 Fender Stratocaster
Scott Dailey

Walnut Stratocaster
Western Stratocaster
Whiteguard Stratocaster Limited Edition
Yngwie Malmsteen Signature Stratocaster
(Custom Shop)
Yngwie Malmsteen Stratocaster

Stratocaster

1954-1981. Two-tone sunburst until '58, 3-tone after. Custom color finishes were quite rare in the '50s and early-'60s and are much more valuable than the standard sunburst finish. By the '70s, color finishes were much more common and do not affect the value near as much. In '75 Fender dropped the optional custom colors and started issuing the guitars in a variety of standard colors (sunburst, blond, white, natural, walnut and black).

Custom color Fenders can be forged and bogus finishes have been a problem. As the value of custom color Fenders has increased, so has the problem of bogus non-original finishes. The prices in the Guide are for factory original finishes in excellent condition. One color, Shell Pink, is notable because many vintage authorities wonder if a Shell Pink Strat even exists? An ultra-rare custom color should have strong documented provenance and be verifiable by at least one (preferable two or more) well-known vintage authorities. Please refer to the Fender Guitar Intro Section for details on Fender color options.

Three-bolt neck '72-'81, otherwise 4-bolt. Unless noted, all Stratocasters listed have the Fender tremolo system. Non-tremolo models (aka hardtails) typically sell for less. Many guitarists feel the tremolo block helps produce a fuller range of sound. On average, many more tremolo models were made. One year, '58, seems to be a year where a greater percentage of non-tremolo models were made. Tremolo vs. non-tremolo valuation should be taken on a brand-by-brand basis; for example, a pre-'65 Gibson ES-335 non-tremolo model is worth more than a tremolo equipped model.

From '63-'70, Fender offered both the standard Brazilian rosewood fretboard and an optional maple fretboard. Prices listed here, for those years, are for the rosewood 'board models. Currently, the market considers the maple 'board to be a premium, so guitars with maple, for those years, are worth 10% to 15% more than the values shown.

Renamed Standard Stratocaster for '82-'84 (see following listings), American Standard Stratocaster for '86-2000, the American Series Stratocaster for '00-'07, and the American Standard Stratocaster (again) for '08-'16. Currently called the American Professional Stratocaster.

MODEL YEAR	FEATURES	EXC. COND. LOW	HIGH
1954	Very first '54, rare features	$170,000	$220,000
1954	Early-mid '54, typical features	$105,000	$140,000
1954	Sunburst, later production	$70,000	$95,000
1955	Late-'55, blond, nickel hw	$66,000	$86,000
1955	Sunburst, ash body	$48,000	$63,000
1956	Blond, nickel hw	$55,000	$75,000
1956	Mary Kaye, gold hw	$90,000	$117,000

MODEL YEAR	FEATURES	EXC. COND. LOW	HIGH
1956	Sunburst, alder body	$41,000	$54,000
1956	Sunburst, ash body	$45,000	$59,000
1956	Sunburst, non-trem	$28,000	$37,000
1957	Blond, nickel hw	$50,000	$65,000
1957	Mary Kaye, gold hw	$80,000	$105,000
1957	Sunburst	$41,000	$54,000
1957	Sunburst, non-trem	$28,000	$37,000
1958	Blond, nickel hw	$46,000	$60,000
1958	Mary Kaye, gold hw	$79,000	$103,000
1958	Sunburst 2-tone, maple	$40,000	$52,000
1958	Sunburst 2-tone, non-trem	$27,000	$35,000
1958	Sunburst 3-tone, maple	$37,000	$49,000
1958	Sunburst 3-tone, non-trem	$25,000	$33,000
1959	Blond, nickel hw, maple 'board	$46,000	$60,000
1959	Blond, nickel hw, slab 'board	$45,000	$59,000
1959	Custom color	$66,000	$86,000
1959	Mary Kaye, gold hw, maple	$79,000	$103,000
1959	Mary Kaye, gold hw, slab	$72,000	$94,000
1959	Sunburst 3-tone, maple	$37,000	$49,000
1959	Sunburst, non-trem, slab	$25,000	$33,000
1959	Sunburst, slab, 1-ply 'guard	$31,000	$41,000
1959	Sunburst, slab, 3-ply 'guard	$29,000	$38,000
1960	Common color	$36,000	$47,000
1960	Rare color	$47,000	$68,000
1960	Sunburst	$29,000	$38,000
1961	Common color	$36,000	$47,000
1961	Rare color	$47,000	$68,000
1961	Sunburst	$29,000	$38,000
1962	Common color, early slab	$36,000	$47,000
1962	Common color, late curve	$26,000	$40,000
1962	Rare color, early slab	$47,000	$68,000
1962	Rare color, late curve	$40,000	$60,000
1962	Sunburst, early slab	$29,000	$38,000
1962	Sunburst, late curve	$26,000	$34,500
1963	Common color	$25,000	$39,000
1963	Rare color	$39,000	$59,000
1963	Sunburst	$26,000	$34,500
1964	Common color	$25,000	$39,000

The *Vintage Guitar Price Guide* shows low to high values for items in all-original excellent condition, and, where applicable, with original case or cover.

MODEL YEAR	FEATURES	EXC. COND. LOW	HIGH
1964	Rare color	$39,000	$59,000
1964	Sunburst, spaghetti logo	$23,000	$30,000
1964	Sunburst, transition logo	$21,000	$27,000
1965	Common color	$23,000	$30,000
1965	Rare color	$30,000	$43,000
1965	Sunburst, early-'65 green 'guard	$20,000	$26,000
1965	Sunburst, late-'65 F-plate	$14,500	$19,000
1965	Sunburst, white 'guard	$18,500	$24,000
1966	Common color	$20,000	$27,000
1966	Common color, bound 'board (rare)	$25,000	$33,000
1966	Rare color	$27,000	$37,000
1966	Sunburst, block markers	$21,000	$27,000
1966	Sunburst, dot markers	$14,000	$19,000
1967	Common color	$20,000	$27,000
1967	Rare color	$27,000	$37,000
1967	Sunburst	$14,000	$19,000
1968	Common color, nitro	$20,000	$27,000
1968	Common color, poly	$13,800	$18,000
1968	Common color, poly body, nitro neck	$14,000	$19,000
1968	Rare color, nitro	$27,000	$37,000
1968	Rare color, poly	$12,000	$16,000
1968	Rare color, poly body, nitro neck	$19,000	$28,000
1968	Sunburst, nitro	$14,000	$19,000
1968	Sunburst, poly	$12,000	$16,000
1968	Sunburst, poly body, nitro neck	$13,000	$17,000
1969	Common color	$13,800	$18,000
1969	Rare color	$18,000	$25,000
1969	Sunburst	$12,000	$16,000
1970	Common color, 4-bolt	$11,500	$15,000
1970	Rare color, 4-bolt	$15,000	$20,000
1970	Sunburst, 4-bolt	$10,000	$13,000
1971	Common color, 4-bolt	$11,500	$15,000
1971	Early-mid '71, sunburst, 4-bolt	$10,000	$13,000
1971	Late '71, sunburst, 3-bolt	$4,200	$5,500
1971	Rare color, 4-bolt	$15,000	$20,000
1972	Common color, 3-bolt	$5,800	$7,600
1972	Rare color, 3-bolt	$7,600	$10,000
1972	Sunburst, 3-bolt	$4,200	$5,500
1973	Common color	$5,000	$6,500
1973	Natural	$3,900	$5,100
1973	Rare color	$6,500	$8,500
1973	Sunburst	$3,900	$5,100

MODEL YEAR	FEATURES	EXC. COND. LOW	HIGH
1973	Walnut	$3,800	$5,000
1974	Black, blond, white (white parts)	$4,500	$5,900
1974	Natural (white parts)	$3,500	$4,600
1974	Sunburst (white parts)	$3,900	$5,100
1974	Walnut (white parts)	$3,800	$5,000
1975	Black, blond, white (black parts)	$3,900	$5,100
1975	Black, blond, white (white parts)	$4,500	$5,800
1975	Early-'75, sunburst (white parts)	$3,800	$5,000
1975	Late-'75, sunburst (black parts)	$2,900	$3,800
1975	Natural (black parts)	$3,100	$4,000
1975	Walnut (black parts)	$2,800	$3,700
1976-1977	Various colors	$2,600	$3,400
1978	Various colors	$2,400	$3,200
1979	Antiqua	$2,300	$3,000
1979	Various colors	$2,250	$2,900
1980	Various colors	$2,100	$2,800
1980-1981	International colors	$2,700	$3,600
1981	Various colors	$2,200	$2,900

Standard Stratocaster (includes "Smith Strat")

1981-1984. Replaces the Stratocaster. Renamed the American Standard Stratocaster for '86-'00 (see next listing). Renamed American Series Stratocaster in '00. From '81/'82 to mid-'83, 3 knobs same as regular Strat but with 4-bolt neck. In August '81, Dan Smith was hired by Bill Schultz and Fender produced an alder body, 4-bolt neck, 21-fret, small headstock Standard Stratocaster that has been nicknamed the Smith Strat (made from Dec. '81-'83). Mid-'83 to the end of '84 2 knobs and 'guard mounted input jack. Not to be confused with current Standard Stratocaster, which is made in Mexico.

1981-1983	Various colors	$2,100	$2,800
1983-1984	Sunburst, 2-knob	$1,125	$1,450
1983-1984	Various colors, 2-knob	$1,125	$1,450

American Standard Stratocaster

1986-1999, 2008-2016. Fender's new name for the American-made Strat when reintroducing it after CBS sold the company. The only American-made Strats made in 1985 were the '57 and '62 models. See Stratocaster and Standard Stratocaster for earlier models. Name used again for '08-'16, various pickup options including SSS, HH, HSH, HSS, Fat and HSS plus. Renamed American Series Stratocaster in 2000 and again renamed the American Professional Series Stratocaster in 2017.

1986-1999	Various colors & options	$1,000	$1,300
2008-2016	Various colors & options	$1,000	$1,300

1968 Fender Stratocaster
Daniel Hess

1983 Fender Standard Stratocaster "Smith Strat"
Bill Beals

GUITARS

Fender American Professional II Stratocaster

1994 Fender 40th Ann. 1954 Stratocaster Limited Edition
Craig Brody

MODEL YEAR	FEATURES	EXC. COND. LOW	HIGH

American Series Stratocaster
2000-2007. Ash or alder body, rosewood or maple 'board, dot markers, various pickup options including HSS and HH, 5-way switch, hand polished fret edges. Renamed the American Standard Stratocaster again in '08.

2000-2007	Various colors & options	$1,000	$1,300
2004	50th Anniversary	$1,000	$1,300

American Professional Stratocaster
2017-2020 Model replaces American Standard Series Strat, redesign includes new V-Mod pickups, narrow-tall frets, new 'deep C' neck profile, genuine bone nut, various colors Also available left-hand model Renamed American Professional II in '20

2017-2020	High-end features	$1,100	$1,450
2017-2020	Low-end features	$1,000	$1,300

American Professional II Stratocaster
2020-present. Various pickup options, woods and various colors.

2020-2021	HSS	$975	$1,275
2020-2021	Roasted Pine	$1,025	$1,350
2020-2021	Roasted Pine HSS	$1,050	$1,375
2020-2021	SSS	$950	$1,250

20th Century American Standard Stratocaster
1999. Limited Edition of the last 100 Strats off the line in 1999. COA signed by William Schultz. "20th Century American Standard" headstock stamp and neckplate.

1999		$1,175	$1,525

21st Century American Standard Stratocaster
2000. Limited Edition of the first 100 Strats off the line in 2000. COA signed by William Schultz. "21st Century American Standard" headstock stamp and neckplate.

2000		$1,175	$1,525

25th Anniversary Stratocaster
1979-1980. Limited Edition, 4-bolt neck plate, standard truss rod, has ANNIVERSARY on upper body horn, early-'79 has pearlescent finish which flaked, late-'79-'80 was changed to silver metallic.

1979	Early run, pearlescent	$2,125	$2,750
1979-1980	Silver	$2,550	$3,300

30th Anniversary Guitar Center Stratocaster

1994		$1,150	$1,500

35th Anniversary Stratocaster
1989-1991. Custom Shop, 500 made, figured maple top, Lace Sensor pickups, Eric Clapton preamp circuit.

1989-1991		$2,275	$2,950

40th Anniversary 1954 Stratocaster Limited Edition
1994. Standard production (not Custom Shop), 1,954 made, "40th Anniversary STRATOCASTER 1994" neck plate, serial number series xxxx of 1954, spaghetti logo, tremolo, Kluson tuners, solid maple neck, 2-tone sunburst semi-transparent finish on ash body.

1994		$2,275	$2,950

MODEL YEAR	FEATURES	EXC. COND. LOW	HIGH

40th Anniversary American Standard Stratocaster
1994 only. US-made, American Standard model (not Custom Shop), plain top, appearance similar to a '54 maple-neck Strat, sunburst, 2 neck plates offered "40th Anniversary" and "40th Anniversary and still rockin'".

1994		$1,150	$1,500

40th Anniversary Stratocaster Diamond Dealer
1994 only. Custom Shop model, 150 made, 40th Anniversary headstock inlay, flamed maple top on ash body, '54-'94 inlay at 12th fret, gold etched 'guard, gold hardware, sunburst.

1994		$3,500	$4,600

40th Anniversary Stratocaster ST62 (Japan)
1994 only. Made in Japan, '62 reissue specs.

1994		$1,150	$1,500

'50s Stratocaster/Classic Series '50s Stratocaster
1985-2019. 'Made in Japan' logo until 'Crafted in Japan' logo mid-'97, basswood body, then mid-'99 made in Mexico with poplar or alder body. Foto-Flame finish offered '92-'94.

1985-1996	Made in Japan	$775	$1,000
1997-1999	Crafted in Japan	$700	$915
1999-2019	Mexico	$550	$725

American Original '50s Stratocaster
2018-present. Vintage-style appointments, 3 pickups, alder or ash body (White Blonde only), 2-color sunburst or Aztec Gold.

2018-2021		$1,300	$1,700

Classic Player '50s Stratocaster
2006-2019. U.S.-made components but assembled in Mexico, alder body, maple neck and 'board, vintage-style pickups.

2006-2019		$550	$725
2014	50th Anniversary	$625	$800

Classic Series '50s Stratocaster Lacquer
2014-2019. Candy Apple Red nitro-lacquer finish.

2014-2019		$550	$725

Road Worn '50s Stratocaster
2009-2019. Made in Mexico, maple 'board, '50s specs, aged finish.

2009-2019		$600	$775

50th Anniversary 1954 Stratocaster
2004-2005. Custom Shop, celebrates 50 years of the Strat, 1954 specs and materials, replica form-fit case, certificate, Fender took orders for these up to December 31, 2004.

2004-2005		$4,000	$5,200

50th Anniversary American Deluxe Stratocaster
2004-2005. Deluxe series features, engraved neck plate, tweed case.

2004-2005		$1,475	$1,925

50th Anniversary American Standard Stratocaster
2004. Mexico, engraved neck plate, '54 replica pickups, tweed case.

2004		$625	$825

The Official Vintage Guitar magazine Price Guide 2023   **Fender** 50th Ann. American Vintage '57 Strat – Wildwood "10s" '57 Ltd. Strat Relic   **111**

GUITARS

MODEL YEAR	FEATURES	EXC. COND. LOW	HIGH

50th Anniversary American Vintage 1957 Stratocaster
1996. V serial number, 50th decal back of headstock.

1996		$1,600	$2,100

50th Anniversary Stratocaster
1995-1996. Custom Shop, 2500 made, flame maple top, 3 vintage-style pickups, gold hardware, gold 50th Anniversary (of Fender) coin on back of the headstock, sunburst.

1995-1996		$1,525	$1,975

50th Anniversary Stratocaster Relic
1995-1996. Custom Shop relic model, aged played-in feel, diamond headstock inlay, Shoreline Gold finish.

1995-1996		$3,400	$4,400

'54 Stratocaster (Custom Shop)
1992-1998. Classic reissue, ash body, Custom '50s pickups, gold-plated hardware.

1992-1998		$2,700	$3,600

'54 Stratocaster FMT
1992-1998. Custom Classic reissue, Flame Maple Top, also comes in gold hardware edition.

1992-1998		$2,500	$3,300

'55 Stratocaster (Custom Shop)
2006, 2013. 1st version is Limited Edition of 100 Relics with 2-tone sunburst; 2nd version is Closet Classic. Both include certificate of authenticity.

2006	Relic	$2,700	$3,600
2013	Closet Classic	$2,500	$3,300

'55 Dual-Mag Strat Journeyman Relic
2017-2019. Custom Shop Limited Edition, certificate of authenticity.

2017-2019		$3,100	$4,000

'55 Historic 1955 NOS Stratocaster
2018-2020. Custom Shop NOS, certificate of authenticity.

2018-2020		$2,700	$3,600

'55 Rocking Dog Stratocaster
2007. Custom Shop, commissioned by Garrett Park Guitars, various colors.

2007		$2,900	$3,800

'55 Stratocaster Journeyman Relic
2017. Custom Shop, vintage-correct appointments, certificate of authenticity.

2017		$2,700	$3,600

'56 Stratocaster (Custom Shop)
1996-2016. Most detailed replica (and most expensive to date) of '56 Strat, including electronics and pickups, offered with rosewood or maple 'board, gold hardware is +$100.

1996-1998	Cunetto built Relic	$3,000	$4,000
1997-1998	Cunetto era (staff built)	$2,900	$3,900
1999-2010	Closet Classic	$2,500	$3,300
1999-2010	NOS	$2,500	$3,300
1999-2014	Relic	$2,700	$3,600
2014-2016	Heavy relic	$2,900	$3,800

'56 Stratocaster Heavy Relic
2020. Custom Shop, certificate of authenticity.

2020		$2,900	$3,800

'56 Stratocaster Journeyman Closet Classic
2020. Custom Shop, certificate of authenticity.

2020		$3,000	$3,900

American Vintage '56 Stratocaster
2013-2018. Vintage '56 style, maple 'board, black, Shell Pink or aged white blonde.

2013-2018		$1,425	$1,850

American Vintage '56 Stratocaster Limited Edition Roasted Ash
2017. Roasted ash body, roasted maple neck and 'board, nitro lacquer finish.

2017		$1,750	$2,300

'57 Stratocaster (Custom Shop)
1994-1996. Custom Shop models can be distinguished by the original certificate that comes with the guitar. Replaced by the more authentic, higher-detailed '56 Custom Shop Stratocaster by '99.

1994-1996	Various colors	$2,700	$3,600

'57 Stratocaster (CS)
2007, 2010-2016. Custom Shop models, Relic ('07), Closet Classic ('10-'13), Heavy Relic ('15-'16), NOS Dealer Select program ('13-'16) where models are built for specific dealers.

2007	Relic	$2,700	$3,600
2010-2013	Closet Classic	$2,500	$3,300
2013-2016	NOS	$2,500	$3,300
2015-2016	Heavy relic	$2,900	$3,900

'57 Stratocaster (USA)
1982-2012. U.S.-made at the Fullerton, California plant ('82-'85) and at the Corona, California plant ('85-'12), American Vintage series.

1982-1984	SN: V series	$3,600	$4,700
1986-1989	Common color	$1,700	$2,200
1986-1989	Rare color	$2,000	$2,600
1990-1999		$1,425	$1,850
1990-1999	Rare color	$1,725	$2,250
2000-2012	Various colors	$1,300	$1,700

'57 Special Stratocaster
1992-1993. Custom Shop, limited run of 60, flamed maple top, birdseye maple neck, sunburst.

1992-1993		$2,700	$3,500

'57 Vintage Stratocaster (Japan)
1982-1998. Made in Japan logo, JV serial numbers '82-'84, E serial '84-'87, Crafted in Japan logo by '98, various colors.

1982-1985	MIJ logo	$1,600	$2,100
1998	CIJ logo	$1,075	$1,400

American Vintage '57 Commemorative Stratocaster
2007. Limited production, 1957-2007 Commemorative logo neckplate.

2007-2012		$1,450	$1,900

Time Machine 1957 Stratocaster Relic
2020. Custom Shop Time Machine series, certificate of authenticity.

2020		$2,400	$3,200

Vintage Custom 1957 Stratocaster NOS
2019-present. Custom Shop, maple 'board, aged white blonde with gold hardware.

2019-2021		$2,800	$3,700

Wildwood "10s" 1957 Limited Stratocaster Relic
2014-2015. Custom Shop Dealer Select model for Wildwood Music, '57 specs with 3 single coil or HSS pickups, certificate of authenticity.

2014-2015		$2,700	$3,600

2003 Fender '57 Stratocaster
Rivington Guitars

Fender Vintage Custom 1957 Stratocaster NOS

2006 Fender '60s Stratocaster
Michael Alonzi

1982 Fender '62 Stratocaster
Imaged by Heritage Auctions, HA.com

MODEL YEAR	FEATURES	EXC. COND. LOW	HIGH

'58 Stratocaster (Custom Shop)
1996-1999. Ash body, Fat '50s pickups, chrome or gold hardware (gold is +$100.), Custom Shop models have certificate of authenticity.

1996-1999	Various colors	$2,800	$3,700

'58 Stratocaster (Dakota Red)
1996. Custom Shop, run of 30 made in Dakota Red with matching headstock, maple neck, Texas special pickups, gold hardware.

1996		$2,950	$3,900

'58 Limited Edition MIJ Stratocaster
2013. Made in Japan logo, 252 offered.

2013		$950	$1,225

'58 Stratocaster Journeyman Relic
2016. Custom Shop, vintage-correct appointments, certificate of authenticity.

2016		$2,700	$3,600

Time Machine 1958 Stratocaster Heavy Relic
2020. Custom Shop Time Machine series, certificate of authenticity.

2020		$3,200	$4,200

'59 Rocking Dog Stratocaster
2007. Custom Shop, commissioned by Garrett Park Guitars, based on '59 rosewood 'board Strat, various colors.

2007		$3,000	$3,900

'59 Stratocaster (Custom Shop)
2010-2013. Rosewood 'board, vintage appointments, COA, various colors with Relic or Heavy Relic finish.

2010-2013	Relic	$2,700	$3,600
2013	Heavy Relic	$2,900	$3,800

1959 Stratocaster LTD Journeyman
2019-2020. Custom Shop, limited edition, vintage and modern appointments, COA, various colors with Relic or Heavy Relic lacquer finish.

2019	Relic	$2,900	$3,800
2019-2020	Heavy Relic	$2,900	$3,800

American Vintage '59 Pine Stratocaster
2017. Limited Edition neck plate, pine body built from re-claimed 100-year-old wood, 3 vintage '59 single-coil pickups.

2017		$1,450	$1,875

American Vintage '59 Stratocaster
2013-2018. Maple or slab rosewood 'board.

2012-2018		$1,450	$1,875

Time Machine 1959 Stratocaster
2019-2021. Custom Shop Time Machine series, vintage and modern appointments, COA, various colors with Relic or Heavy Relic lacquer finish.

2019-2020	Relic	$2,500	$3,300
2020-2021	Heavy Relic	$3,200	$4,200

Wildwood "10s" 1959 Limited Stratocaster Relic
2011-2017. Custom Shop, quartersawn maple neck, Brazilian rosewood 'board, 3 pickups, faded 3-color sunburst. Limited Edition neck plate decal, and certificate of authenticity.

2011	Maple 'board	$2,700	$3,600
2011-2017	Brazilian 'board	$5,000	$6,600

'60 Stratocaster (Custom Shop)
1992-1999. 3 Texas Special pickups, various colors, optional gold hardware is +$100, with certificate of authenticity. In 2000 the '60 Stratocaster name was applied to the Time Machine model (see following).

1992-1999		$2,800	$3,700

'60 Stratocaster FMT (Custom Shop)
1997-1999. Flame maple top (FMT).

1997-1999		$2,700	$3,600

Custom 1960 Stratocaster
1994. Short run of 20 custom ordered and specified instruments that have 1960 specs along with other specs such as a pearloid 'guard, matching headstock color, came with certificate of authenticity.

1994		$2,800	$3,700

'60s Stratocaster/Classic Series '60s Stratocaster
1985-2019. 'Made in Japan' logo until 'Crafted in Japan' logo mid-'97, basswood body, then mid-'99 made in Mexico with poplar or alder body. Foto-Flame finish offered '92-'94.

1985-1996	Made in Japan	$775	$1,000
1997-1999	Crafted in Japan	$700	$915
1999-2019	Mexico	$550	$725

'60s Stratocaster/Time Machine 1960 Stratocaster
1996-2020. Custom Shop Relic/Time Machine. For '96-'99 was called the '60s Stratocaster, in 2000 name was changed to Time Machine 1960 Stratocaster. Heavy Relic began late-'15. Optional gold hardware is +$100. Vince Cunetto and company did the aging of the guitars to mid-1999. The price includes the original Certificate of Authenticity, a guitar without the original COA is worth less than the values shown.

1996-1998	Cunetto built Relic	$2,900	$3,800
1997-1999	Cunetto era (staff built)	$2,800	$3,700
1999-2010	Closet Classic	$2,500	$3,300
1999-2010	NOS	$2,500	$3,300
1999-2015	Relic	$2,700	$3,600
2015-2020	Heavy relic	$2,900	$3,800

American Original '60s Stratocaster
2018-present. Vintage-style appointments, 3 pickups, alder body, 3-color sunburst. Candy Apple Red or Olympic White.

2018-2021		$1,400	$1,800

Classic Player '60s Stratocaster
2006-2019. U.S.-made components but assembled in Mexico, alder body, maple neck, rosewood 'board, vintage-style pickups.

2006-2019		$550	$725

Classic Series '60s Stratocaster Lacquer
2014-2019. Made in Mexico, 3-color sunburst nitrolacquer finish.

2014-2019		$550	$725

Limited Edition '60s Daybreak Stratocaster
2019-2020. Traditional series, made in Japan, Olympic White with matching headstock, gold hardware.

2019-2020		$550	$725

The *Vintage Guitar Price Guide* shows low to high values for items in all-original excellent condition, and, where applicable, with original case or cover.

MODEL YEAR	FEATURES	EXC. COND. LOW	HIGH

Road Worn '60s Stratocaster
2009-2020. Rosewood 'board, '60s specs, aged finish. Renamed Vintera Road Worn '60s Strat in '20.

2009-2020		$550	$725

60th Anniversary '54 Stratocaster (Custom Shop)
2014. Heavy relic, certificate of authenticity, 60th guitar case.

2014		$2,700	$3,600

60th Anniversary American Stratocaster
2006-2007. Celebrates Fender's 60th, US-made, 'Sixty Years' decal logo on headstock, engraved 60th Anniversary neck plate, Z-series serial number, coin on back of headstock, sunburst only, paperwork.

2006-2007	American flag logo	$1,200	$1,600

60th Anniversary American Vintage 1954 Stratocaster
2014-2016. 1,954 built, came with reproduction 1954 paperwork and 1954 Anniversary Strat Certificate.

2014-2016		$1,450	$1,900

60th Anniversary Commemorative Stratocaster
2014. Celebrates the Strat's 60th, US-made, 60th Anniversary neckplate, 60th medallion on back of headstock, gold hardware, special case, commemorative book.

2014		$1,000	$1,300

60th Anniversary Presidential Stratocaster
2006. Custom Shop, Diamond (60th) anniversary, limited to 100, bookmatched maple top stained using grapes from Hill Family Winery (California), '1946-2006' logo on neck, 'Limited Edition 60th Anniv. Presidential' neck plate logo, certificate of authenticity.

2006		$5,500	$7,200

'61 Stratocaster (Custom Shop)
2001-2012. Relic, certificate of authenticity.

2001-2012		$2,700	$3,600

Wildwood "10s" 1961 Limited Stratocaster
2010-present. Custom Shop, NOS, relic or heavy relic, quartersawn maple and AA flame maple necks, 3 pickups, "faded" thin nitro finishes in multiple colors.

2010-2016	NOS	$2,500	$3,300
2010-2021	Relic	$2,700	$3,600

'62 Stratocaster (USA)
1982-1984, 1986-2012. Made at Fullerton plant ('82-'84) then at Corona plant ('86-2012), American Vintage series.

1982-1984	SN: V series	$3,600	$4,700
1986-1989	Common color	$1,700	$2,200
1986-1989	Rare color	$2,000	$2,600
1990-1999	Common color	$1,425	$1,850
1990-1999	Rare color	$1,725	$2,250
2000-2012	Common color	$1,300	$1,700

'62 Commemorative Stratocaster
2007. Limited production, part of American Vintage Series, 1957-2007 Commemorative logo neckplate.

2007		$1,425	$1,850

'62 Heavy Relic Stratocaster
2007-2010. Custom Shop Dealer Select series, extreme Relic work.

2007-2010		$2,800	$3,700

'62 Stratocaster ST62D/ST54 DEX2
1996 Made in Japan, '54 maple neck, '62 body

1996		$1,350	$1,750

'62 Stratocaster ST62US Reissue
2008-2012. Crafted in Japan, US-made 'vintage' pickups.

2008-2012		$700	$900

'62 Vintage Stratocaster (Japan)
1982-1984. Made in Japan, JV serial numbers, various colors.

1982-1984		$1,600	$2,100

Dave's Guitar Shop American 1962 Stratocaster
2019-2020. Limited Edition, various colors with nitro lacquer finish.

2019-2020		$1,450	$1,900

Deluxe Vintage Player '62 Stratocaster
2005-2006. Limited Edition, vintage and modern features based upon '62 specs, 3 Samarium Cobalt Noiseless pickups, Deluxe American Standard electronics, Olympic White or Ice Blue Metallic.

2005-2006		$1,400	$1,800

Vintage Custom 1962 Stratocaster
2019-present. Custom Shop Limited Edition, NOS finish, alder body, maple neck and 'board, 3-color sunburst.

2019-2021		$2,700	$3,600

Willcutt Guitars True '62 Stratocaster
2016-2020. Custom Shop, limited run for Bob Willcutt Guitars, 4 models; 'V' neck, '59 'C' neck, '60s 'C' neck and large 'C' neck.

2016-2020		$2,700	$3,600

'63 Stratocaster (Custom Shop)
2015-2018. Time Machine series, Relic in '15-'17, Heavy Relic '18.

2015-2017	Relic	$2,700	$3,600
2018	Heavy Relic	$2,700	$3,600

'63 Stratocaster Journeyman Relic
2015. Custom Shop, vintage-correct appointments, alder body, bird's-eye maple neck, rosewood 'board, 3 single-coil pickups, certificate of authenticity.

2015		$2,900	$3,800

'64 Stratocaster (Custom Shop)
2009-2014. Relic or Closet Classic, certificate of authenticity.

2009-2012	Relic	$2,700	$3,600
2011-2014	Closet Classic	$2,500	$3,300

Time Machine 1964 Stratocaster Journeyman Relic
2018-2020. Custom Shop Time Machine series, vintage-correct appointments, certificate of authenticity.

2018-2020		$2,700	$3,600

'65 Stratocaster (Custom Shop)
1998-1999, 2003-2006, 2010 (no Closet Classic). Custom Shop model, '65 small-headstock specs, rosewood or maple cap 'board, transition logo, offered in NOS, Relic, or Closet Classic versions.

1998-1999	Cunetto era (staff built)	$2,850	$3,800
2003-2006	Closet Classic	$2,500	$3,300
2003-2010	NOS	$2,500	$3,300
2003-2010	Relic	$2,700	$3,600

2003 Fender '62 Stratocaster
Tom Pfeifer

1984 Fender '62 Vintage Stratocaster
Tom Pfeifer

GUITARS

2005 Fender '69 Stratocaster (Custom Shop)

Rivington Guitars

Fender 75th Anniversary Commemorative Stratocaster

MODEL YEAR	FEATURES	EXC. COND. LOW	HIGH

'65 Stratocaster Journeyman Closet Classic
2019-2020. Custom Shop, vintage-correct appointments, certificate of authenticity.

2019-2020		$2,800	$3,700

American Vintage '65 Stratocaster
2013-2017. V serial number, flash coat finish, various colors, some with matching headstock.

2013-2017		$1,300	$1,700

Time Machine 1965 Stratocaster Journeyman Relic
2010. Custom Shop Time Machine series, vintage-correct appointments, certificate of authenticity.

2010		$2,800	$3,700

Total Tone '65 Stratocaster Relic
2013. Custom Shop Limited Edition, alder body, maple neck, reverse wound middle pickup for noise reduction, various colors with Relic nitro lacquer finish.

2013		$2,700	$3,600

'66 Stratocaster (Custom Shop)
2004-2008. Custom Shop model, offered in Closet Classic, NOS or Relic versions.

2004-2008	Closet Classic	$2,500	$3,300
2004-2008	NOS	$2,500	$3,300
2004-2008	Relic	$2,700	$3,600

Time Machine 1967 Stratocaster Journeyman Relic Aged
2020. Custom Shop Time Machine series, vintage-correct appointments.

2020		$2,800	$3,700

Time Machine 1967 Stratocaster Journeyman Relic Custom Top
2020. Custom Shop Time Machine series, vintage-correct appointments.

2020		$2,800	$3,700

'68 Heavy Relic Stratocaster
2007-2010. Custom Shop Dealer Select, extreme relic work.

2007-2010		$2,900	$3,800

'68 Reverse Strat Special (USA)
2001-2002. With special reverse left-hand neck, large headstock (post-CBS style).

2001-2002		$2,900	$3,800

'68 Stratocaster (Japan)
1996-1999, 2013. Part of Collectables Series, '68 specs including large headstock, sunburst, natural or Olympic White.

1996-1999		$1,100	$1,425
2013		$950	$1,250

'69 Stratocaster (Custom Shop)
1997-2012, 2016. Large headstock, U-shaped maple neck with rosewood or maple cap options, '69-style finish, gold hardware is +$100, since 2000, offered in NOS, Relic, or Closet Classic (no CC after '08) versions. Heavy Relic in '16.

1997-1999	Cunetto era (staff built)	$2,900	$3,800
2000-2008	Closet Classic	$2,500	$3,300
2000-2009	NOS	$2,500	$3,300
2000-2012	Relic	$2,700	$3,600
2016	Heavy Relic	$2,900	$3,800

MODEL YEAR	FEATURES	EXC. COND. LOW	HIGH

Wildwood "10s" 1969 Limited Stratocaster
2014. Custom Shop, Relic, Jimi Hendrix specs, certificate of authenticity.

2014		$2,700	$3,600

'70s Stratocaster/Classic Series '70s Stratocaster
1999-2019. Made in Mexico, large headstock, white pickups and knobs, rosewood 'board.

1999-2019		$550	$725

American Vintage '70s Stratocaster
2009-2012. Large '70s headstock, early '70s white pickups and knobs, 3-bolt neck. Hardtail version in '15.

2009-2012		$1,375	$1,775

'72 Stratocaster (Japan)
1985-1996. Basswood body, maple 'board, large headstock, various colors (does not include the Paisley '72).

1985-1996		$1,650	$2,150

'72 Stratocaster Limited Edition
2013. Made in Japan for US domestic sales, 144 made, large headstock, bullet truss rod, 3-bolt maple neck, 21 frets, 3 Alnico pickups.

2013		$725	$950

75th Anniversary Commemorative Stratocaster
2021. US-made, limited edition, inlaid 75th Anniversary ingot back of headstock, gold hardware, 2-color Bourbon Burst gloss finish. Includes custom Inca Silver case with Lake Placid Blue interior.

2021		$1,275	$1,650

75th Anniversary Stratocaster
2021. Made in Mexico, 75th Anniversary neck plate, Diamond Anniversary satin finish with matching painted headstock.

2021		$550	$725

Acoustasonic Stratocaster
2003-2009. Hollowed out alder Strat body with braceless graphite top, 3 in-bridge Fishman piezo pickups, acoustic sound hole.

2003-2009		$675	$875

Aerodyne Classic Stratocaster
2020. Limited run made in Japan, figured maple top, rosewood 'board, 3 pickups, various colors with gloss poly finish.

2020		$700	$925

Aerodyne Stratocaster
2004-2009. Import Strat with Aerodyne body profile, bound body, black.

2004-2009		$750	$975

Albert Hammond Jr. Signature Stratocaster
2018-present. Made in Mexico, styled after his 1985 reissue of a '72 Strat.

2018-2021		$575	$750

Aluminum Stratocaster (Custom Shop)
1994. Custom Shop aluminum bodies, chrome body with black 'guard, black body with chrome 'guard, or green with black lines and red swirls. There are also several Custom Shop one-offs with aluminum bodies.

1993-1994		$2,500	$3,300

The *Vintage Guitar Price Guide* shows low to high values for items in all-original excellent condition, and, where applicable, with original case or cover.

The Official Vintage Guitar magazine Price Guide 2023   **Fender** Aluminum Strat American Stnd. — Artisan Series Strat   **115**

GUITARS

MODEL YEAR	FEATURES	EXC. COND. LOW	HIGH

Aluminum Stratocaster American Standard

1994-1995. Aluminum-bodied American Standard with anodized finish in blue marble, purple marble or red, silver and blue stars and stripes. Some with 40th Anniversary designation. There is also a Custom Shop version.

1994-1995	Various patterns & options	$2,000	$2,600

American Acoustasonic Stratocaster

2019-present. Solid A sitka spruce top, mahogany back and sides, ebony 'board, various colors. Also offered with cocobolo and ziricote top.

2019-2021		$1,300	$1,675
2020-2021	Cocobolo top	$2,125	$2,750

American Classic Holoflake Stratocaster

1992-1993. Custom Shop model, splatter/sparkle finish, pearloid 'guard.

1992-1993		$2,700	$3,600

American Classic Stratocaster

1992-1999. Custom Shop version of American Standard, 3 pickups, tremolo, rosewood 'board, nickel or gold-plated hardware, various colors.

1992-1999	Various options	$2,700	$3,600

American Custom Stratocaster (Custom Shop)

2020-present. Custom Shop American Custom series, various woods and colors.

2020-2021		$3,100	$4,100

American Deluxe Stratocaster

1998-2016. Premium alder or ash body, maple neck, various pickup options including SSS, HSS, HSH, HSS Plus, Fat and Shawbucker, various colors.

1998-2016	Various options	$1,225	$1,600

American Deluxe Stratocaster Dealer Event

2013. Sold at private dealer event at Fender Corona, various premium tonewoods, various colors and finishes.

2013		$1,400	$2,400

American Deluxe Stratocaster Designer Series

2004-2015. Limited production, various upgrades such as flamed maple top, mahogany, etc.

2004-2015		$1,300	$1,700

American Deluxe Stratocaster FMT HSS

2004-2009. Flame maple top version of the HSS.

2004-2009		$1,300	$1,700

American Deluxe Stratocaster HSS Mahogany

2015-2016. Limited Edition 10 for 15 series, 2-piece mahogany body.

2015-2016		$1,175	$1,525

American Elite Stratocaster

2016-2019. Alder body, 3 single-coil pickups or HSS with Shawbucker.

2016-2019		$1,275	$1,650

American Elite Stratocaster Limited Edition

2016. Various color options with matching headstock.

2016		$1,325	$1,725

American Longboard Stratocaster HSS

2015. Part of Fender's limited edition 10 for 15 series, vintage surfboard laminate top design.

2015		$1,000	$1,300

American Performer Stratocaster

2018-present. Made in US, new features include 3 Yosemite single-coil pickups, Greasebucket tone system, various colors.

2018-2021		$775	$1,025

American Special Stratocaster

2010-2018. Limited Edition, '70s headstock with post-CBS black Stratocaster logo, Texas Special pickups (SSS or HSS), satin (early were gloss) finish.

2010-2018		$775	$1,000

American Standard Stratocaster Limited Edition

1990s-2019. American Standard series, various limited edition models.

1995-2000	Matching hdstk	$1,375	$1,775
2001	Standard hdstk	$1,375	$1,775
2009	Matching hdstk, Seafoam/Surf Green	$1,375	$1,775
2014-2017	Channel Bound	$1,000	$1,300
2015	Mystic Black	$1,000	$1,300
2015-2016	Mystic Aztec Gold	$1,000	$1,300
2015-2016	Oiled Ash	$1,000	$1,300
2015-2016	Vintage White	$1,000	$1,300
2017	Rosewood neck	$1,000	$1,300
2019	Pale Moon Quilt	$1,500	$1,950

American Ultra Luxe Stratocaster

2021-present. Pickups options and various colors.

2021-2022	Floyd Rose HHS	$1,450	$1,850
2021-2022	SSS	$1,450	$1,850

American Ultra Stratocaster

2019-present. Various options and colors.

2019-2021		$1,200	$1,600

Ancho Poblano Stratocaster Journeyman Relic

2018-2019. Custom Shop Limited Edition series, alder body, 2-color sunburst or opaque white blonde, with Journeyman Relic nitro lacquer finish.

2018-2019		$2,650	$3,500

Ancho Poblano Roasted Stratocaster Relic

2019-2020. Custom Shop Limited Edition series, roasted alder body with Relic lacquer finish, various colors.

2019-2020		$2,700	$3,600

Antigua Stratocaster

2004. Made in Japan, limited-edition reissue, '70s features and antigua finish.

2004		$800	$1,050

Artisan Series Stratocaster (Custom Shop)

2015-present. Features distinctively figured woods, gold hardware, hand-rubbed oil finishes, certificate of authenticity, various models: Okoume, Claro Walnut, Figured Rosewood, Spalted Maple, Tamo Ash, Thinline Koa.

2015	Okoume	$2,550	$2,950
2016-2021	Spalted Maple	$2,700	$3,600
2020-2021	Maple Burl	$2,800	$3,700

2018 Fender American Elite Stratocaster

Carter Vintage Guitars

Fender Artisan Series Spalted Maple Thinline Stratocaster

GUITARS

2005 Fender Big Block Stratocaster

Tom Pfeifer

1992 Fender Bill Carson Stratocaster

Bob Moreland

MODEL YEAR	FEATURES	EXC. COND. LOW	HIGH

Big Apple Stratocaster
1997-2000. Two humbucking pickups, 5-way switch, rosewood 'board or maple neck, non-tremolo optional.

1997-2000	Various colors	$875	$1,150

Big Block Stratocaster
2005-2006. Pearloid block markers, black with matching headstock, 2 single coils (neck, middle) 1 humbucker (bridge), vintage style tremolo.

2005-2006		$650	$850

Big Head Stratocaster
2020. Custom Shop Limited Edition series.

2020		$2,400	$3,100

Bill Carson Stratocaster
1992. Based on the '57 Strat, birdseye maple neck, Cimarron Red finish, 1 left-handed and 100 right-handed produced, serial numbers MT000-MT100, made in Fender Custom Shop, and initiated by The Music Trader (MT) in Florida.

1992		$2,200	$2,900

Billy Corgan Stratocaster
2008-2012. US-made, 3 DiMarzio pickups, string-thru hardtail bridge.

2008-2012		$1,100	$1,450

Blackie Stratocaster (Custom Shop 1987)
1987. 12 made, includes Certificate of Authenticity.

1987		$2,900	$3,800

Blackie Stratocaster (Custom Shop)
November 2006. Blackie tribute, 185 instruments for U.S. market, 90 made for export, original retail price $24,000.

2006		$13,000	$17,000

Black Paisley Stratocaster
2020. Made in Japan, Limited Edition, run of 300, silver and black paisley-print design on basswood body, rosewood 'board, 3 single-coil pickups.

2020		$650	$850

Blacktop Stratocaster
2011-2015. Alder body, maple neck, rosewood or maple 'board, various pickup options including HH and HSH, various finish options. Floyd Rose version also available.

2011-2015		$575	$750

Mahogany Blacktop Stratocaster Limited Edition
2019. 2 or 3 Alnico humbuckers, mahogany body, black headstock, Oly White, black or crimson red, chrome or gold hardware.

2019		$575	$750

Blue Flower Stratocaster
1984-1997, 2002-2004. Made in Japan, '72 Strat reissue with a '68 Tele Blue Floral finish.

1984-1987	1st issue	$1,400	$1,850
1988-1994	MIJ	$1,400	$1,850
1995-1997	CIJ	$950	$1,250
2002-2004	2nd issue	$825	$1,075

Bonnie Raitt Stratocaster
1995-2001. Alder body, often in blueburst, Bonnie Raitt's signature on headstock.

1995-2001		$2,200	$2,900

Bowling Ball/Marble Stratocaster
1984. Standard Strat with 1 tone and 1 volume

MODEL YEAR	FEATURES	EXC. COND. LOW	HIGH

control, jack on 'guard, called Bowling Ball Strat due to the swirling, colored finish.

1984	All colors	$3,600	$4,700

Buddy Guy Signature Stratocaster
1995-2009. Maple neck, 3 Gold Lace Sensor pickups, ash body, blond or sunburst.

1995-2009		$1,125	$1,500

Buddy Guy Standard Stratocaster
1996-present. Made in Mexico, maple neck, polka-dot finish.

1996-2021		$625	$825

Buddy Holly Tribute Stratocaster
2014. Custom Shop, 50 made, '55 specs, with certificate of authenticity.

2014		$7,200	$9,500

California Stratocaster/California Fat Stratocaster
1997-1999. Made in the U.S., painted in Mexico, 3 single coils, Fat has HSS, various colors.

1997-1999	SSS or HSS	$650	$850

Carroll Shelby Limited Edition Stratocaster
2009. Built for Ford Motor Co. as tribute to Shelby's life, graphic photo montage on front, engraved Shelby Automobiles logo on 'guard, only 100 produced.

2009		$2,100	$2,800

Carved Top Stratocaster HSS (Custom Shop)
1995-1998. Carved figured maple top, HSS (HH offered in '98), certificate of authenticity, various colors.

1995-1998		$2,250	$2,950

Classic Player Stratocaster
2000. Custom Shop, Standard Stratocaster with useful 'player-friendly features' such as noiseless stacked single-coil pickups and factory Sperzel locking tuners, black, gold anodized 'guard.

2000		$1,500	$2,000

Classic Player Stratocaster HH
2015-2016. Alder body, maple neck, bound rosewood 'board, 2 humbuckers, dark Mercedes Blue gloss finish with matching headstock.

2015-2016		$600	$800

Collector's Edition Stratocaster ('62 Reissue)
1997. Pearl inlaid '97 on 12th fret, rosewood 'board, alder body, gold hardware, tortoise 'guard, nitro finish, sunburst, 1997 made.

1997		$1,350	$1,800

Contemporary Stratocaster (Custom Shop)
1989-1998. 7/8 scale body, hum/single/single pickups, various colors.

1989-1998		$1,600	$2,100

Contemporary Stratocaster (Import)
1985-1987. Import model used while the new Fender reorganized, black or natural headstock with silver-white logo, black or white 'guard, 2 humbucker pickups or single-coil and humbucker, 2 knobs and slider switch.

1985-1987		$800	$1,050

MODEL YEAR	FEATURES	EXC. COND. LOW	HIGH

Crash Stratocaster
2005-2007. Master Built Custom Shop, hand painted by John Crash Matos, approximately 50, comes with certificate, the prices shown include the original certificate.

2005-2007		$5,200	$6,800

Custom Classic Stratocaster
2000-2008. Custom Shop version of American Standard Strat.

2000-2008		$2,400	$3,100

Custom Deluxe Stratocaster
2009-2014. Custom Shop, birdseye maple neck, rosewood or maple 'board, certificate. Model also available with flame maple top.

2009-2014		$3,300	$4,300

Custom Shop Limited Edition Stratocaster
1992. Only 100 made, flame maple top, birdseye maple neck, rosewood 'board, gold hardware, trans red finish.

1992		$2,800	$3,600

Dave Murray Stratocaster
2009-present. Alder body, maple neck, rosewood 'board, 3 pickups, 2-color sunburst.

2009-2021		$700	$900

David Gilmour Signature Stratocaster
2008-2019. Custom Shop, NOS or Relic, based on Gilmour's '70 black Stratocaster, certificate of authenticity.

2008-2019		$3,500	$4,500

Deluxe Lone Star Stratocaster
2007-2016. Reissue of Lone Star Strat, made in Mexico, 1 humbucker and 2 single-coils, rosewood 'board.

2007-2016		$400	$525

Deluxe Players Special Edition Stratocaster
2007. Made in Mexico, Special Edition Fender oval sticker on back of headstock along with 60th Anniversary badge.

2007		$425	$550

Deluxe Players Stratocaster
2004-2016. Made in Mexico, 3 noiseless single-coils, push-button switching system.

2004-2016		$475	$625

Deluxe Roadhouse Stratocaster
2008-2021. Deluxe series reissue, Texas Special pickups.

2008-2021		$575	$750

Deluxe Stratocaster
2016-2021. Mexico-made, double-cut, 3 vintage noiseless single-coils or 1 humbucker and 2 single-coils.

2016-2021	SSS or HSS	$575	$750

Deluxe Stratocaster HSS Plus Top With IOS Connectivity
2014-2016. Deluxe series, plugs into iOS devices.

2014-2016		$475	$625

Deluxe Stratocaster Plus
1987-1998. Alder (poplar earlier) with ash veneer front and back, 3 Lace Sensor pickups, Floyd Rose, various colors. Becomes American Deluxe Strat Plus.

1987-1998		$1,200	$1,575

Dick Dale Stratocaster
1994-present. Custom Shop signature model, alder body, reverse headstock, sparkle finish.

1994-2021		$2,700	$3,600

Elite Stratocaster
1983-1984. The Elite Series feature active electronics and noise-cancelling pickups, push buttons instead of 3-way switch, Elite script logo on 4-bolt neck plate, various colors. Also see Gold Elite Stratocaster and Walnut Elite Stratocaster.

1983-1984		$2,100	$2,800

EOB (Ed O'Brien) Sustainer Stratocaster
2017-present. Alder body, maple neck and 'board, 3 pickups (Sustainer in neck position), custom "Flower of Life" neck plate, gloss poly white finish.

2017-2021		$750	$975

Eric Clapton Crossroads Stratocaster
2007. Custom Shop Limited Edition of 100, Crossroads graphic, 50 sold with matching '57 Twin amp autographed by Clapton (and with other goodies) retailed at $30,000. The other 50 sold guitar alone (with less goodies) at $20,000.

2007	Guitar & Twin Amp	$21,000	$28,000
2007	Guitar only	$18,000	$24,000

Eric Clapton Gold Leaf Stratocaster
2004. Custom Shop model, special build for Guitar Center, 50 made, 23k gold leaf finish/covering.

2004		$5,400	$7,100

Eric Clapton Signature Journeyman Relic Stratocaster
2020-present. Custom Shop, Clapton's signature on the headstock, 2-color sunburst or aged white blonde.

2020		$3,700	$4,900

Eric Clapton Signature Stratocaster (Custom Shop)
2019-present. Alder body, maple neck, three Vintage Noiseless pickups, Clapton's signature on headstock, black or Mercedes Blue.

2019-2021		$3,400	$4,500

Eric Clapton Stratocaster
1988-present. U.S.-made, '57 reissue features, had Lace Sensor pickups until '01, when switched to Vintage Noiseless. Black versions have added "Blackie" decal on headstock.

1988-1999	Lace Sensors	$1,450	$1,900
2000	Lace Sensors	$1,200	$1,575
2001-2021	Noiseless	$1,200	$1,575

Eric Clapton Stratocaster (Custom Shop)
2004-2016. Custom Shop model, standard non-active single-coil pickups, black or blue finish.

2004-2016		$2,700	$3,600

Eric Johnson 1954 "Virginia" Stratocaster
2020-present. Stories Collection, limited numbers offered from both Custom Shop (see Masterbuilt listing) and Corona production.

2020-2021	Fender Corona	$1,750	$2,300

Eric Johnson Signature Stratocaster Thinline
2018-2020. Alder body, maple neck and 'board, 3 single-coil pickups, 2-color sunburst or vintage white.

2017-2020		$1,175	$1,525

1984 Fender Bowling Ball/ Marble Stratocaster

Fender Eric Clapton Signature Journeyman Relic Stratocaster

Tyler Willison

GUITARS

*2017 Fender Eric
Johnson Stratocaster*

*Fender George Harrison
Rocky Stratocaster*

MODEL YEAR	FEATURES	EXC. COND. LOW	HIGH

Eric Johnson Stratocaster
2005-present. '57 spec body and 1-piece maple soft-v-neck, or, for '09 to '15, rosewood 'board, special design pickups, vintage tremolo with 4 springs, EJ initials and guitar-player figure engraved neck plate. Also listed as Eric Johnson Stratocaster Maple or Rosewood.

2005-2021	Maple or rosewood	$1,200	$1,550

Floyd Rose Classic Relic Stratocaster
1998. Custom Shop, late '60s large headstock, 1 humbucker and 1 Strat pickup.

1998		$2,700	$3,600

Floyd Rose Classic Stratocaster (Strat HSS) (Strat HH)
1992-2002. Two single-coils, bridge humbucker, Floyd Rose tremolo, becomes Floyd Rose Classic Strat HSS or HH (2 humbuckers) in '98.

1992-2002		$1,200	$1,600

Ford Shelby GT Stratocaster
2007. 200 made, black with silver Shelby GT racing stripe.

2007	200 made	$2,200	$2,900

Foto Flame Stratocaster
1994-1996, 2000. Japanese-made Collectables model, alder and basswood body with Foto Flame (simulated woodgrain) finish on top cap and back of neck.

1994-2000		$700	$925

Freddy Tavares Aloha Stratocaster
1993-1994. Custom Shop, hollow aluminum body with hand engraved Hawaiian scenes, custom inlay on neck, 153 made.

1993-1994		$7,000	$9,200

FSR Stratocaster
2012-2019. Factory Special Run models might be 'dealer exclusive' or open to all dealers as limited run. FSR have a special set of appointments that are not standard to the core lineup.

2012	Antigua Strat	$600	$800
2013	Hot Rod Strat	$475	$625
2013-2017	Classic '60s Strat	$775	$1,000
2015-2016	Amer Std '54 Strat	$950	$1,250
2017-2019	Classic '50s Strat	$600	$775
2018-2019	Traditional '50s Strat	$550	$725

George Fullerton 50th Anniversary '57 Strat Ltd. Ed. Set
2007. Limited Edition, 150 made, '57 Strat with matching relic Pro Junior tweed amp, 2 certificates of authenticity signed by Fullerton, commemorative neck plate.

2007		$3,800	$5,000

George Harrison Rocky Stratocaster
2020-present. Custom Shop Limited Edition, 2-piece alder body, 5A flame maple neck, 3 '60s Strat pickups, finish is designed from Harrison's psychedelic paint job including the "Grimwoods" decal, Sonic Blue with custom Rocky graphics top.

2020-2021		$16,500	$22,000

Gold Stratocaster
1981-1983. Gold metallic finish, gold-plated brass hardware, 4-bolt neck, maple 'board, skunk strip, trem.

1981-1983		$2,100	$2,750

Gold Elite Stratocaster
1983-1984. The Elite series feature active electronics and noise-cancelling pickups, the Gold Elite has gold hardware and pearloid tuner buttons, also see Elite Stratocaster and Walnut Elite Stratocaster.

1983-1984		$2,100	$2,800

Gold Stratocaster (Custom Shop)
1989. Custom Shop, 500 made, gold finish with gold anodized and white 'guards included.

1989		$2,800	$3,600

GT11 Stratocaster
2019-2020. Custom Shop, exclusive models for Sweetwater, relic and heavy relic.

2019-2020	Heavy Relic	$2,950	$3,900
2019-2020	Relic	$2,700	$3,600

H.E.R. Stratocaster
2020-present. Made in Mexico, Artist Signature series, alder body with Chrome Glow finish, matching painted headstock.

2020-2021		$700	$925

Hank Marvin Stratocaster
1995-1996. Custom Shop, Feista Red.

1995-1996		$2,900	$3,800

Hank Marvin 40th Anniversary Stratocaster
1998. Custom Shop logo with '40 Years 1958-1998' marked on back of headstock, Fiesta Red, only 40 made, COA.

1998		$6,200	$8,100

Harley-Davidson 90th Anniversary Stratocaster
1993. Custom Shop, 109 total made, Harley-Davidson and Custom Shop V logo on headstock (Diamond Edition, 40 units), 9 units produced for the Harley-Davidson company without diamond logo, 60 units were not Diamond Edition, chrome-plated engraved metal body, engraved 'guard, COA necessary.

1993		$11,000	$14,000

Highway One Stratocaster/HSS
2002-2014. U.S.-made, alder body, satin lacquer finish, 3 single-coil pickups or HSS version has humbucker/single/single.

2002-2014		$675	$875

HM Strat (USA/Import)
1988-1992 ('88 Japanese-made, '89-'90 U.S.- and Japanese-made, '91-'92 U.S.-made). Heavy Metal Strat, Floyd Rose, regular or pointy headstock, black hardware, H, HH, SH, or SSH pickup options. Later models have choice of SHH or SSH.

1988-1990	Import	$900	$1,200
1989-1992	USA	$1,000	$1,300

HM Strat Limited Edition
2020-2021. '88-'92 HM specs, available in era-correct Day-Glo colors, Frozen Yellow, Flash Pink, Ice Blue and Bright White.

2020-2021		$800	$1,050

Homer Haynes HLE Stratocaster
1988-1989. Custom Shop, limited edition of 500, '59 Strat basics with gold finish, gold anodized guard and gold hardware.

1988-1989		$2,700	$3,600

MODEL YEAR	FEATURES	EXC. COND. LOW	HIGH

Hot Wheels Stratocaster

2003. Custom Shop model commissioned by Hot Wheels, 16 made, orange flames over blue background, large Hot Wheels logo.

2003		$2,200	$2,800

HRR Stratocaster/Floyd Rose HRR (Japan)

1990-1994. Made in Japan, hot-rodded vintage-style Strat, Floyd Rose tremolo system, H/S/S pickups, maple neck, sunburst or colors. Called the Floyd Rose HRR for '92-'94 (with optional Foto Flame finish).

1990-1994		$1,000	$1,300

Ike Turner Tribute Stratocaster

2005. Custom Shop model, 100 made, replica of Ike Turner's Sonic Blue Strat.

2005		$3,200	$4,200

Jeff Beck Signature Stratocaster (CS)

2004-present. Custom Shop, 3 Noiseless dual-coils, Olympic White or Surf Green.

2004-2019		$2,000	$2,650
2020-2021		$3,200	$4,200

Jeff Beck Stratocaster

1991-present. Alder body, originally 3 Lace Sensors (HSS) changing to 3 Noiseless dual-coils in '01, rosewood 'board, Olympic White and Surf Green (Midnight Purple until '02).

1991	1st issue, Lace Sensors	$2,100	$2,750
1992-1993	Lace Sensors	$1,700	$2,200
1994-2000	Lace Sensors	$1,450	$1,900
2001-2009	Noiseless	$1,250	$1,625
2010-2021	Artist Series	$1,250	$1,625

Jerry Donahue Hellecaster Stratocaster

1997. Made in the Fender Japan Custom Shop as one part of the 3-part Hellecasters Series, limited edition, Seymour Duncan pickups, maple, blue with blue sparkle guard.

1997		$900	$1,175

Jim Root Stratocaster

2010-present. Artist series, mahogany body, ebony or maple 'board, 2 active pickups, black hardware, black or white finish.

2010-2021		$1,075	$1,400

Jimi Hendrix Limited Edition Stratocaster (Custom Shop)

2019-2021. Custom Artist series, designed from Hendrix's modified '68 Strat used at Woodstock ('69), aged Olympic White.

2019-2021		$5,100	$6,700

Jimi Hendrix Monterey Pop Stratocaster

1997-1998. Custom Shop, near replica of Monterey Pop Festival sacrifice guitar, red psychedelic-style finish.

1997-1998		$14,500	$19,000

Jimi Hendrix Monterey Stratocaster

2017-2018. Body art like Hendrix's hand-painted original that he destroyed at Monterey Pop Festival, custom neck plate, signature on headstock rear.

2017-2018		$575	$750

Jimi Hendrix Stratocaster

2015-present. Reverse headstock, silhouette and engraved 'Authentic Hendrix' on neckplate.

2015-2021		$600	$800

Jimi Hendrix Tribute Stratocaster

1997-2000. Left-handed guitar strung right-handed, maple cap neck, Olympic White. Fender headstock logo positioned upside down, made for right-handed player to look as if they are playing a left-handed guitar flipped over.

1997-2000		$2,250	$2,950

Jimi Hendrix Voodoo 29th Anniversary (Guitar Center) Stratocaster

1993. Custom Shop made only 35 for Guitar Center, large 'Guitar Center 29th Anniversary' logo on neckplate, right-handed body with reverse left-handed headstock and reversed Fender headstock logo, purple sparkle finish.

1993		$3,000	$3,900

Jimi Hendrix Voodoo Child Signature Stratocaster NOS

2018-present. Custom Shop, Custom Artist series, 2-piece alder body, maple neck and 'board, 3 pickups, Olympic White or black, with NOS nitro lacquer finish.

2018-2021		$3,600	$4,700

Jimi Hendrix Voodoo Child Stratocaster Journeyman Relic

2020-present. Custom Shop, Olympic White or black with aged relic finish.

2020-2021		$3,600	$4,700

Jimi Hendrix Voodoo Stratocaster

1997-2002. Right-handed body with reverse headstock, maple neck, Olympic White, sunburst or black.

1997-2002		$2,250	$2,950

Jimmie Vaughan Tex-Mex Stratocaster

1997-present. Poplar body, maple 'board, signature on headstock, 3 Tex-Mex pickups, various colors.

1997-2021		$550	$725

John Jorgenson Hellecaster Stratocaster

1997. Fender Japan Custom Shop, part of the 3-part Hellecasters Series, limited edtion, Seymour Duncan pickups, gold sparkle 'guard, gold hardware, split single-coils, rosewood 'board.

1997		$1,000	$1,300

John Mayer Limited Edition Black1 Stratocaster

2010. Custom Shop, 83 made, black finish NOS or extreme relic option, JC serial number, Custom Shop/ John Cruz logo on back of headstock includes personal letter from John Mayer.

2010	NOS	$3,000	$4,000

John Mayer Stratocaster

2005-2014. Alder body, special scooped mid-range pickups, vintage tremolo, special design gigbag with pocket for laptop computer.

2005-2014		$1,200	$1,600

Kenny Wayne Shepherd Stratocaster

2009-2016, 2020-present. Artist series, based on Shepherd's '61, rosewood 'board, jumbo frets, Artic White with cross, black with racing stripes or 3-color sunburst. Reintroduced '20, chambered ash body, 3 single-coil pickups, trans Faded Sonic Blue with matching painted headstock.

2009-2016	Import	$625	$825
2020-2021	US-made	$1,350	$1,800

Fender HM Strat Limited Edition

1997 Fender Jerry Donahue Hellecaster Stratocaster

Stoeffu Vogt

GUITARS

2007 Fender Lenny Stratocaster
Imaged by Heritage Auctions, HA.com

2006 Fender Masterbuilt
Stratocaster
David Stone

MODEL YEAR	FEATURES	EXC. COND. LOW	HIGH

Koa Stratocaster
2006-2008. Made in Korea, Special Edition series, sunburst over koa veneer top, plain script Fender logo, serial number on back of headstock with.

2006-2008		$500	$650

Kon Tiki Stratocaster
2003. Custom Shop, limited run of 25, Tiki Green including Tiki 3-color art work on headstock.

2003		$2,700	$3,500

Lenny Stratocaster
Introduced Dec. 12, 2007 by Guitar Center stores, Custom Shop model, 185 guitars made, initial product offering price was 17K.

2007		$10,000	$13,000

Limited Roasted Tomatillo Stratocaster Relic
2019-2020. Custom Shop Limited Edition series, roasted alder body and 4A flame maple neck, various colors with Relic lacquer finish.

2019-2020		$3,100	$4,100

Lincoln Brewster Signature Stratocaster
2019-present. Ash body, 1-piece maple neck, 3 single-coil pickups, gold with lacquer finish.

2019-2021		$1,300	$1,700

Lite Ash Stratocaster Special Edition
2004-2007. Korea, light ash body, birds-eye maple neck.

2004-2007		$475	$625

Lone Star Stratocaster
1996-2001. Alder body, 1 humbucker and 2 single-coil pickups, rosewood 'board or maple neck, various colors.

1996	50th Anniv Badge	$850	$1,125
1997-2001		$850	$1,125

Mark Kendrick Master Design '65 Stratocaster
2004. Custom Shop Limited Edition, run of 65, alder body, maple neck, African rosewood 'board, Lake Placid Blue over Olympic White.

2004		$2,800	$3,800

Mark Knopfler Stratocaster
2003-2013. '57 body with '62 maple neck.

2003-2013		$1,200	$1,600

Masterbuilt Custom Shop Stratocaster
2006-present. Builder Select series, various models and builders, specific identification to builder, must include certificate of authenticity.

2006-2021	Various models	$4,000	$15,000

Matthias Jabs Signature Stratocaster
1998. Made in Japan, 200 offered, Candy Apple Red.

1998		$1,000	$1,300

Michael Landau Signature Relic Stratocaster 1963/1968
2014-present. Custom Shop Artist series, Relic, alder body, rosewood 'board, '63 is worn Fiesta Red over 3-color sunburst, '68 is black or bleached 3-color sunburst.

2014-2021	1963 Relic	$3,000	$4,000
2014-2021	1968 Relic	$3,000	$4,000

MODEL YEAR	FEATURES	EXC. COND. LOW	HIGH

Milonga Deluxe Stratocaster
2005. Special Edition made in Mexico, Vintage Noiseless pickups, rosewood 'board, Olympic White, gold hardware.

2005		$450	$575

MLB Major League Baseball Stratocaster
2014. Official team logos and imagery unique to each, licensed by Major League Baseball Properties.

2014	Various models	$525	$700

Mod Shop Stratocaster
2017-present. Mod Shop allows you to create your own factory-customized electric guitar or bass.

2017-2021		$1,600	$2,600

Modern Player Stratocaster HSH/HSS
2013-2015. Made in China, hum-single-hum or hum-single-single.

2013-2015		$400	$525

Moto Limited Edition Stratocaster
1995. Custom Shop model, pearloid cover in various colors, includes Certificate of Authenticity, not to be confused with white pearloid Moto Strat which is part of a guitar and amp set (as listed below).

1995		$3,000	$4,000

Moto Set Stratocaster
1995-1996. Custom Shop set including guitar, case, amp and amp stand, white pearloid finish.

1995-1996	Red (few made)	$5,100	$6,700
1995-1996	White	$5,100	$6,700

Noventa Stratocaster
2021-present. Alder body, maple neck, Pau Ferro 'board, 2 single-coil pickups, Crimson Red Trans, Daphne Blue or Surf Green.

2021		$675	$875

Orange Krush Limited Edition Stratocaster
1995. Custom Shop, 25 made, based on '57 Strat, orange finish with matching headstock, certificate of authenticity.

1995		$2,700	$3,600

Paisley Stratocaster
1984-1997, 2003-2004, 2008. Japanese-made '72 Strat reissue with a reissue '68 Tele Pink Paisley finish, large headstock until mid-'94, 'Made in Japan' logo used until early-'97, 'Crafted in Japan' after.

1984-1987	1st issue	$1,775	$2,300
1988-1994	MIJ	$1,450	$1,900
1995-1997	MIJ	$1,200	$1,550
2003-2004	CIJ	$800	$1,050
2008	2nd issue, 200 made	$800	$1,050

Parallel Universe Volume II Strat Jazz Deluxe
2019-2021. Limited Edition, alder body, 2 pickups, Mystic Surf Green with nitro lacquer finish.

2019-2021		$1,300	$1,800

Parallel Universe Volume II Strat-Tele Hybrid
2017-2018. Limited Edition, Tele body, Strat neck and headstock, 3 single-coil Strat pickups, 2-color sunburst with gloss nitro lacquer finish.

2017-2018		$1,300	$1,800

MODEL YEAR	FEATURES	EXC. COND. LOW	HIGH

Playboy 40th Anniversary Stratocaster
1994. Custom Shop, 175 made, nude Marilyn Monroe graphic on body.

1994		$17,000	$22,000

Player Series Stratocaster
2017-present. Various models include SSS, HSS, HSH, HSS Plus, Floyd Rose, SSS LH and SSS Plus, various colors and finishes.

2017-2019	SSS, HSS, HSH	$450	$575
2018-2021	Floyd Rose HSS	$500	$650
2018-2021	Plus Top SSS, HSS	$475	$600

Post Modern Stratocaster (Custom Shop)
2015-2019. Offered in Journeyman Relic, NOS, and lush Closet Classic finishes.

2015-2017	NOS	$2,500	$3,300
2016-2019	Journeyman Relic	$2,700	$3,600
2019	Closet Classic	$2,700	$3,600

Post Modern Stratocaster Closet Classic (Custom Shop)
2019-2020. Made exclusive for Sweetwater, certificate.

2019-2020	Aged natural	$2,700	$3,600

Post Modern Stratocaster Journeyman Relic (Custom Shop)
2019-2020. Made exclusive for Sweetwater, alder or ash, certificate.

2019-2020	Alder or ash	$2,700	$3,600

Post Modern Stratocaster NOS (Custom Shop)
2019-2020. Made exclusive for Sweetwater, certificate.

2019-2020	Aged natural	$2,700	$3,600

Powerhouse/Powerhouse Deluxe Stratocaster
1997-2010. Made in Mexico, Standard Strat configuration with pearloid 'guard, various colors.

1997-2010		$450	$575
2005	Powerbridge, TRS stereo	$450	$575

Proud Stratocaster
2003. Custom Shop, 3 made to commemorate United Way and Rock & Roll Hall of Fame project, body painted in detail by Fender's artist.

2003		$3,200	$4,200

Rarities Stratocaster
2019-2020. Rarities Collection series, limited edition, models include; Flame Maple Top, Flame KOA Top, Quilt Maple Top.

2019-2020	Various models	$1,600	$2,100

Richie Sambora Stratocaster
1993-2002. U.S. and Mexico models offered, alder body, Floyd Rose tremolo, maple neck, various colors.

1993-2002	USA	$2,800	$3,700
1994-2002	Mexico	$475	$625
1995-1997	Mexico, swirl color	$600	$775

Ritchie Blackmore Stratocaster
2009-present. Based on Blackmore's '70s large headstock model, scalloped rosewood 'board, Duncan Quarter Pound Flat pickups, Olympic White.

2009-2021		$800	$1,050

Ritchie Blackmore Tribute Stratocaster
2014. Custom Shop, '68 specs, maple neck.

2014		$4,500	$5,900

Roadhouse Stratocaster
1997-2000. U.S.-made, poplar body, tortoise shell 'guard, maple 'board, 3 Texas Special pickups, various colors.

1997-2000		$750	$975

Robert Cray Signature Stratocaster
1991-present. Custom Shop, rosewood 'board, chunky neck, lighter weight, non-trem, alder body, gold-plated hardware, various colors.

1991-2021		$2,700	$3,600

Robert Cray Stratocaster (Mexico)
1996-present. Artist series, chrome hardware.

1996-2021		$600	$775

Robin Trower Signature Stratocaster
2004-present. Custom Shop Custom Artist series, 100 made, large headstock (post '65-era), with '70s logo and 3-bolt neck, bullet truss rod, white.

2004-2021		$2,600	$3,400

Rory Gallagher Tribute Stratocaster
2004-present. Custom Shop, based on Gallagher's '61 model, heavily distressed, price includes the original certificate.

2004-2019		$3,300	$4,300
2020-2021		$3,900	$5,100

Sandblasted Stratocaster
2014-2015, 2019-2020. Limited Edition series, ash body, sandblasted finish. Limited run '19-'20 exclusive for Sweetwater USA.

2014-2015		$775	$1,000
2019-2020	Sweetwater	$775	$1,000

Select Stratocaster
2012-2015. Select Series, figured top, rear-headstock 'Fender Select' medallion, gloss-lacquer finish, various colors.

2012-2015		$1,700	$2,450

Set-Neck Stratocaster
1992-1999. Custom Shop model, mahogany body and figured maple top, 4 pickups, glued-in neck, active electronics, by '96 ash body.

1992-1999		$2,300	$3,000

Short-Scale (7/8) Stratocaster
1989-1995. Similar to Standard Strat, but with 2 control knobs and switch, 24" scale vs. 25" scale, sometimes called a mini-Strat, Japanese import, various colors.

1989-1995		$600	$800

So-Cal J.W. Black Stratocaster
2000-2001. Custom Shop, So-Cal logo art on body, 20 offered.

2000-2001		$1,900	$2,500

So-Cal Speed Shop Stratocaster
2005-2006. Limited Edition for Musician's Friend, red, white, and black So-Cal paint job, basswood body, rosewood 'board, 1 humbucker, So-Cal Speed Shop decal.

2005-2006		$550	$725

2007 Fender Stratocaster Powerhouse Deluxe

Lew Campbell

2001 Fender Richie Sambora Stratocaster

Imaged by Heritage Auctions, HA.com

*2005 Fender Standard
Stratocaster (Mexico)*

Tom Pfeifer

1991 Fender Strat Plus

David Mullins.

MODEL YEAR	FEATURES	EXC. COND. LOW	HIGH

Special Edition David Lozeau Art Stratocaster

2015-2016. Finishes include orange Tree of Life, blue Dragon, yellow Rose Tattoo and red Sacred Heart, etched David Lozeau neck plate.

2015-2016		$475	$625

Special Edition Stratocaster

2004-2009. Import model, Special Edition oval logo on back of headstock, various styles offered, '50s or '60s vintage copy specs, maple 'board, ash or koa body, see-thru or opaque finish.

2004-2009		$475	$625

Special Edition Stratocaster (Matching Headstock)

2016-2017. Made in Mexico, various colors with matching headstock.

2016-2017		$475	$625

Special Edition White Opal Stratocaster

2016. Made in Mexico, white opal body and headstock, pearloid 'guard, 3 humbuckers.

2016		$475	$625

Splatter Stratocaster

2003. Made in Mexico, splatter paint job, various color combinations, with gig bag.

2003		$650	$1,000

Standard Roland Ready Stratocaster

1998-2011. Made in Mexico, built-in Roland pickup system and 3 single-coils.

1998-2011		$400	$525

Standard Stratocaster (Japan)

1985-1989. Interim production in Japan while the new Fender reorganized, standard pickup configuration and tremolo system, 3 knobs with switch, traditional style input jack, traditional shaped headstock, offered in black, red or white.

1985-1989		$875	$1,150

Standard Stratocaster (Mexico)

1990-2018. Made in Mexico, renamed Player Series in '18. Not to be confused with the American-made Standard Stratocaster of '81-'84. Various models and colors, high-end range includes a hard guitar case, while low-end includes only a gig bag.

1990-2018	Various models	$400	$525

Standard Stratocaster Plus Top

2014-2018. Made in Mexico, alder body with flamed maple top. Renamed Player Series Plus Top in '18.

2014-2018		$425	$550

Standard Stratocaster Satin Finish

2003-2006. Basically Mexico-made Standard with satin finish.

2003-2006		$300	$400

Stevie Ray Vaughan Signature Stratocaster

1992-present. U.S.-made, alder body, sunburst, gold hardware, SRV 'guard, lefty tremolo, Brazilian rosewood 'board (pau ferro by '93).

1992	1st year, Brazilian	$3,500	$4,600
1992-2021	Pau Ferro	$1,225	$1,600

Stevie Ray Vaughan Signature

MODEL YEAR	FEATURES	EXC. COND. LOW	HIGH

Stratocaster (Custom Shop)

2019-present. Custom Artist series, 3-color sunburst with NOS or aged relic lacquer finish.

2019-2021	NOS	$3,300	$4,400
2019-2021	Relic	$3,700	$4,900

Stevie Ray Vaughan Tribute #1 Stratocaster

2004. Custom Shop Limited Edition, recreation of SRV's #1 made by Master Builder John Cruz in the Custom Shop, 100 made, $10,000 MSRP, includes flight case stenciled "SRV - Number One," and other goodies.

2004		$22,500	$29,000

Strat Plus

1987-1999. Three Lace Sensor pickups, alder (poplar available earlier) body, tremolo, rosewood 'board or maple neck, various colors. See Deluxe Strat Plus for ash veneer version.

1987-1999	Various colors	$975	$1,275

Stratocaster Junior

2004-2006. Import, short 22.7" scale, Alder body, non-trem hardtail bridge.

2004-2006		$400	$525

Stratocaster Pro Closet Classic (Custom Shop)

2006-2013. Ash body, early '60s neck, rosewood or maple board, solid or sunburst finish.

2006-2013		$2,500	$3,300

Stratocaster Pro NOS (Custom Shop)

2012-2016. Ash body, maple neck, rosewood 'board, solid or 3-tone sunburst.

2012-2016		$2,500	$3,300

Stratocaster Special

1993-1995. Made in Mexico, a humbucker and a single-coil pickup, 1 volume, 1 tone.

1993-1995		$375	$500

Stratocaster XII

1988-1997, 2003-2010. 1st version Japanese-made, alder body, 22-fret rosewood 'board. 2nd version is 21-fret Classic Series model for 2 years then Classic Series.

1988-1997	1st version	$875	$1,150
2003-2010	2nd version	$875	$1,150

Strat-o-Sonic

2003-2006. American Special Series, Stratocaster-style chambered body, includes Strat-o-Sonic Dove I (1 pickup, '03 only), Dove II/DV II (2 black P-90s, '03-'06) and HH (2 humbuckers, '05-'06).

2003	Dove I	$900	$1,175
2003-2006	Dove II/DV II	$900	$1,175
2003-2006	HH	$900	$1,175

Sub Sonic Stratocaster

2000-2001. Baritone model, offered in 2 production models - HH (2 humbuckers, 2000-'01), HSS (hum-single-single, '01) - and in a Custom Shop version of the HSS (2000-'01).

2000-2001		$900	$1,175
2000-2001	Custom Shop, COA	$1,800	$2,300

Super Stratocaster

1997-2003. Deluxe series, made in Mexico, 3 Super Fat single-coils, Super Switching gives 2 extra pickup options, gold tremolo.

1997-2003		$475	$625

MODEL YEAR	FEATURES	EXC. COND. LOW	HIGH

Supreme Stratocaster

2017. Limited Edition, collaboration with Supreme (NY-based fashion brand), all white color with red Supreme logo on front.

| 2017 | | $6,800 | $8,900 |

Tanqurey Tonic Stratocaster

1988. Made for a Tanqurey Tonic liquor ad campaign giveaway in '88, Tanqurey Tonic Green; many were given to winners around the country, ads said that they could also be purchased through Tanqurey, but that apparently didn't happen.

| 1988 | | $1,600 | $2,100 |

Tash Sultana Stratocaster

2020-present. Artist series, all gold hardware, aged white pearl 'guard, trans cherry finish with matching painted headstock.

| 2020-2021 | | $725 | $950 |

Texas Special Stratocaster

1991-1992. Custom Shop, 50 made, state of Texas map stamped on neck plate, Texas Special pickups, maple fretboard, sunburst.

| 1991-1992 | | $2,700 | $3,600 |

The Edge Stratocaster

2016-2020. U2 guitarist The Edge signature on large '70s-style headstock, alder body, 1-piece quartersawn maple neck and 'board, 3 pickups, black.

| 2016-2020 | | $1,400 | $1,900 |

The Strat

1980-1983. Alder body, 4-bolt neck, large STRAT on painted peghead, gold-plated brass hardware, various colors.

| 1980-1983 | | $1,500 | $2,000 |

Tie-Dye Stratocaster

2004-2005. Single-coil neck and humbucker bridge pickups, Band of Gypsies or Hippie Blue tie-dye pattern, poly finish.

| 2004-2005 | | $500 | $700 |

Tom Delonge Stratocaster

2001-2004. 1 humbucker, rosewood back and sides. Also in Squier version.

| 2001-2004 | | $650 | $850 |

Tom Morello "Soul Power" Stratocaster

2020-present. Alder body, rosewood 'board, black with white 'guard. Shipped with "Soul Power" decal for face of guitar.

| 2020-2021 | | $875 | $1,150 |

Tree of Life Stratocaster

1993. Custom Shop, 29 made, tree of life fretboard inlay, 1-piece quilted maple body.

| 1993 | | $5,400 | $7,200 |

Turquoise Sparkle Stratocaster

2001. Custom Shop, limited run of 75 for Mars Music, turquoise sparkle finish.

| 2001 | | $1,600 | $2,100 |

U.S. Ultra / Ultra Plus Stratocaster

1990-1997. Alder body with figured maple veneer on front and back, single Lace Sensor pickups in neck and middle, double Sensor at bridge, ebony 'board, sunburst.

| 1990-1997 | | $1,700 | $2,200 |

MODEL YEAR	FEATURES	EXC. COND. LOW	HIGH

Ventures Limited Edition Stratocaster

1996. Japanese-made tribute model, matches Jazzmaster equivalent, black.

| 1996 | | $1,200 | $1,600 |

VG Stratocaster

2007-2009. American Series, modeling technology using Roland's VG circuitry, 5 guitar tone banks deliver 16 sounds.

| 2007-2009 | | $1,000 | $1,300 |

Vintage Hot Rod Stratocaster

2007-2014. Vintage styling with modern features, '07-'13 named '57 Strat and '62 Strat, in '14 changed to '50s and '60s.

| 2007-2014 | All models | $1,300 | $1,700 |

Vintera Series Stratocaster

2019-present. Modified and non-modified '50s, '60s and '70s Strat models, various options and colors.

2019-2020	'70s	$650	$850
2019-2020	'70s modified	$650	$850
2019-2021	'50s	$650	$850
2019-2021	'50s modified	$650	$850
2019-2021	'60s	$650	$850
2019-2021	'60s modified	$650	$850

Walnut Elite Stratocaster

1983-1984. The Elite Series features active electronics and noise-cancelling pickups, Walnut Elite has a walnut body and neck, gold-plated hardware and pearloid tuner buttons. Also see Elite Stratocaster and Gold Elite Stratocaster.

| 1983-1984 | | $2,100 | $2,800 |

Walnut Stratocaster

1981-1983. American black walnut body and 1-piece neck and 'board.

| 1981-1983 | | $1,900 | $2,500 |

Western Stratocaster

1995. Custom Shop, only 5 made, featured in Fender Custom Shop book from the 1990s.

| 1995 | | $8,500 | $11,000 |

Whiteguard Stratocaster Limited Edition

2018. Limited Edition neck plate, ash body, Tele hardware and white 'guard, 2 single-coil pickups, lacquer finish.

| 2018 | | $1,250 | $1,650 |

Yngwie Malmsteen Signature Stratocaster (Custom Shop)

2020-present. Custom Artist series, 2-piece select alder body, flat sawn maple neck, various colors with nitro lacquer finish.

| 2020-2021 | | $3,900 | $5,200 |

Yngwie Malmsteen Stratocaster

1988-present. U.S.-made, maple neck, scalloped 'board, 3 single-coil pickups, Vintage White.

| 1988-2021 | | $1,175 | $1,525 |

Swinger

1969-1972. See listing for Musiclander.

SX Series

1992-1995. Dreadnought and jumbo acoustics, ply or solid spruce tops with various wood options on back and sides, E models with electronics.

| 1992-1994 | 1200sx | $500 | $650 |
| 1992-1994 | 1300sx | $650 | $850 |

2005 Fender Tie-Dye Stratocaster
Imaged by Heritage Auctions, HA.com

1993 Fender U.S. Ultra Stratocaster
Keith Myers

GUITARS

1952 Fender Telecaster
Trey Rabinek

1956 Fender Telecaster
Frank Manno

MODEL YEAR	FEATURES	EXC. COND. LOW	HIGH
1992-1994	1500sx	$550	$725
1992-1994	1505sx	$600	$800
1992-1995	1000sx	$350	$450
1992-1995	1100sx	$400	$525
1992-1995	1105sxe	$450	$600
1993-1994	1600sxe	$650	$850
1994-1995	600sx	$150	$200
1994-1995	800sx	$175	$250

T-Bucket 300CE
2016-2018. Acoustic/electric, D-size, cutaway.

2016-2018		$210	$275

TC-90/TC-90 Thinline
2004-2007. Made in Korea, 2 single-coil P90s, double-cut, Vintage White or Black Cherry Burst.

2004-2007		$525	$700

Telecaster

The following are all variations of the Telecaster. Broadcaster and Nocaster models are under Broadcaster. The first five listings are for the main American-made line. All others are listed alphabetically after that in the following order:

Telecaster
Standard Telecaster
American Standard Telecaster
American Series Telecaster
American Professional/Professional II Telecaster
30th Anniversary Guitar Center Tree of Life Telecaster
40th Anniversary Telecaster
'50 Custom Telecaster
'50s Telecaster/Classic Series '50s Telecaster
Road Worn '50s Telecaster
50th Anniversary Spanish Guitar Set
50th Anniversary Telecaster
'52 Telecaster/American Vintage '52 Telecaster
American Vintage '52 Telecaster Korina (U.S.A.)
'52 Telecaster (Custom Shop)
'52 LTD Telecaster NOS
'52 Vintage Telecaster (Japan)
'54 Telecaster (Custom Shop)
'58 Telecaster (Custom Shop)
American Vintage '58 Telecaster (U.S.A.)
'60s Telecaster Custom
'60s Telecaster/Classic Series '60s Telecaster
American Original '60s Telecaster
American Original '60s Telecaster Thinline
'60 Telecaster Custom
60th Anniversary American Telecaster
60th Anniversary Telecaster (U.S.A.)
60th Anniversary Telecaster Limited Edition
'61 Telecaster Custom
'62 Telecaster Custom (Import)
'62 Telecaster Custom (U.S.A.)
'62 Mod Squad Custom Telecaster
'62 Telecaster Reissue (Japan)
Junkyard Dog 1962 Telecaster Relic
'63 Telecaster (Custom Shop)
'63 Telecaster Custom Relic LTD

'64 Telecaster Limited Relic
American Vintage '64 Telecaster
'67 Telecaster (Custom Shop)
'68 Telecaster Rosewood
'69 Tele/Telecaster Thinline (Import)
'69 Telecaster Thinline (Custom Shop)
'72 Telecaster Custom/Classic Series '72 Telecaster Custom
'72 Telecaster Deluxe/Classic Series '72 Telecaster Deluxe
'72 Telecaster Thinline American Vintage
'72 Telecaster Thinline/Classic Series Telecaster Thinline
1972 Telecaster Custom Closet Classic
75th Anniversary Commemorative Telecaster
75th Anniversary Telecaster
'90s Telecaster Deluxe
'90s Telecaster Thinline
1998 Collectors Edition Telecaster
Aerodyne Telecaster
Albert Collins Telecaster
Aluminum Telecaster
American Acoustasonic Telecaster
American Classic Holoflake Telecaster
American Classic Telecaster
American Deluxe HH Telecaster
American Deluxe Power Telecaster
American Deluxe Telecaster
American Deluxe/Elite Telecaster Thinline
American Elite Telecaster
American Nashville B-Bender Telecaster
American Performer Telecaster
American Professional II Telecaster Deluxe
American Professional Telecaster Deluxe Shawbucker
American Special Telecaster
American Standard Telecaster Limited Edition
American Standard Telecaster Special Edition
American Ultra Luxe Telecaster
American Ultra Telecaster
Andy Summers Masterbuilt Tribute Telecaster
Antigua Telecaster
Big Block Telecaster
Bigsby Telecaster
Blacktop Telecaster Series
Blue Flower Telecaster
Bowling Ball/Marble Telecaster
Britt Daniel Telecaster Thinline
Brown's Canyon Redwood Telecaster
Buck Owens Limited Edition Telecaster
Cabronita Telecaster (American Standard)
Cabronita Telecaster (Classic Player)
Cabronita Telecaster Thinline
California Fat Telecaster
California Telecaster
Chambered Mahogany Telecaster
Chrissie Hynde Telecaster
Clarence White Telecaster (Custom Shop)
Classic Player Baja Telecaster
Collector's Edition Telecaster
Contemporary Telecaster (Import)
Custom Carved Telecaster HH
Custom Classic Telecaster

Custom Deluxe Telecaster
Custom Telecaster
Danny Gatton Signature Telecaster
Deluxe Nashville Power Telecaster
Deluxe Nashville Telecaster (Mexico)
Deluxe Telecaster (U.S.A.)
Elite Nashville Telecaster
Elite Telecaster
Fat Telecaster
Foto Flame Telecaster
G.E. Smith Telecaster
Graham Coxon Special Run Telecaster
Highway One Telecaster/Texas Telecaster
HMT Telecaster (Import)
J5 Triple Telecaster Deluxe
James Burton Standard Telecaster
James Burton Telecaster
Jason Isbell Custom Telecaster
Jerry Donahue JD Telecaster
Jerry Donahue Telecaster
Jim Adkins JA-90 Telecaster Thinline
Jim Root Telecaster
Jimmy Bryant Tribute Telecaster
Jimmy Page Mirror Telecaster
Jimmy Page Telecaster
Joe Strummer Telecaster
John Jorgenson Telecaster
Jr. Telecaster
La Cabronita Especial Telecaster
Mahogany Offset Telecaster
Masterbuilt Custom Shop Telecaster
Matched Set Telecaster
Merle Haggard Signature Telecaster
Mod Shop Telecaster
Modern Player Telecaster Plus
Moto Limited Edition Telecaster
Muddy Waters Signature Telecaster Custom
Muddy Waters Tribute Telecaster
Nashville Telecaster
NHL Premier Edition Telecaster
Nokie Edwards Telecaster
Noventa Telecaster
Old Pine Telecaster
Paisley Telecaster
Palo Escrito Telecaster
Parallel Universe Jazz-Tele
Parallel Universe Troublemaker Telecaster
Parallel Universe Volume II Tele Mágico
Player Telecaster
Plus Telecaster
Rarities Telecaster
Richie Kotzen Telecaster
Rosewood Telecaster
Rosewood Telecaster (Japan)
Rosewood Telelcaster Limited Edition
Select Telecaster
Select Telecaster Thinline
Set-Neck Telecaster
Snakehead Telecaster
Sparkle Telecaster
Special Edition Custom Telecaster FMT HH
Special Edition Deluxe Ash Telecaster
Special Edition Koa Telecaster

Special Edition White Opal Telecaster
Special Telecaster/Telecaster Special
Standard Telecaster (Japan)
Standard Telecaster (Mexico)
Telecaster (Japanese Domestic)
Telecaster Custom
Telecaster Custom (Japan)
Telecaster Custom FMT HH (Korea)
Telecaster Stratocaster Hybrid (Custom Shop)
Telecaster Thinline
Tele-Sonic
Texas Special Telecaster
Twisted Telecaster Limited Edition
Two-Tone Telecaster Thinline
Vintage Hot Rod Telecaster
Waylon Jennings Tribute Telecaster
Will Ray Signature Jazz-A-Caster
Will Ray Signature Mojo Telecaster

Telecaster

1951-1982. See Standard Telecaster (following listing) for '82-'85, American Standard Telecaster for '88-'00, the American Series Telecaster for '00-'07. and the American Standard Telecaster (again) for '08-'16. Currently called the American Professional Telecaster.

In the late '60s and early '70s Fender began to increase their use of vibrato tailpieces. A vibrato tailpiece for this period is generally worth about 13% less than the values shown. Please refer to the Fender Guitar Intro Section for details on Fender color options. The "rare color" listing have a wide range due to the various colors included in that category.

From '63-'70, Fender offered both the standard Brazilian rosewood fretboard and an optional maple fretboard. Prices listed here, for those years, are for the rosewood 'board models. Currently, the market considers the maple 'board to be a premium, so guitars with maple, for those years, are worth 10% to 15% more than the values shown.

MODEL YEAR	FEATURES	EXC. COND. LOW	HIGH
1951	Blond, black 'guard	$45,000	$59,000
1952	Blond, black 'guard	$42,000	$55,000
1953	Blond, black 'guard	$40,000	$52,000
1954	Blond, black 'guard	$38,000	$50,000
1954	Blond, white 'guard	$28,000	$37,000
1955	Blond, white 'guard	$28,000	$37,000
1956	Blond	$28,000	$37,000
1957	Blond, backloader	$24,000	$32,000
1958	Blond, backloader	$23,000	$30,000
1958	Blond, top loader	$21,000	$27,000
1958	Sunburst, backloader	$24,500	$32,000
1958	Sunburst, top loader	$23,000	$30,000
1959	Blond, maple	$20,700	$27,000
1959	Blond, slab	$20,700	$27,000
1959	Custom color	$47,000	$65,000
1959	Sunburst, maple	$22,200	$29,000
1959	Sunburst, slab	$22,200	$29,000
1960	Blond, slab	$19,000	$25,000
1960	Common color	$30,000	$40,000
1960	Rare color	$40,000	$55,000
1960	Sunburst, slab	$22,000	$28,500

1961 Fender Telecaster
Gordon Kennedy

1963 Fender Telecaster
Kevin Rush

GUITARS

1964 Fender Telecaster

1967 Fender "smuggler"
Telecaster
Lynn Rose

MODEL YEAR	FEATURES	EXC. COND. LOW	HIGH
1961	Blond, slab	$17,000	$23,000
1961	Common color	$24,000	$31,000
1961	Rare color	$31,000	$41,000
1961	Sunburst, slab	$21,000	$27,000
1962	Blond, curve	$14,000	$18,500
1962	Blond, slab	$15,700	$20,600
1962	Common color	$24,000	$31,000
1962	Rare color	$31,000	$41,000
1962	Sunburst, curve	$18,500	$24,100
1962	Sunburst, slab	$20,000	$26,000
1963	Blond	$14,000	$18,500
1963	Common color	$24,000	$31,000
1963	Rare color	$31,000	$41,000
1963	Sunburst	$18,500	$24,100
1963-1964	Mahogany, see-thru cherry	$28,000	$37,000
1964	Blond	$13,000	$17,000
1964	Common color	$21,500	$28,000
1964	Rare color	$28,000	$36,000
1964	Sunburst	$16,500	$21,500
1965	Blond	$11,200	$14,500
1965	Common color	$17,000	$22,000
1965	Early '65, Sunburst	$13,500	$17,500
1965	Late '65, Sunburst	$11,200	$14,500
1965	Rare color	$22,000	$30,000
1966	Blond	$8,600	$11,200
1966	Common color	$10,800	$14,000
1966	Rare color	$14,000	$19,000
1966	Sunburst	$9,600	$12,000
1967	Blond	$8,600	$11,200
1967	Blond, smuggler	$10,800	$14,000
1967	Common color	$10,800	$14,000
1967	Rare color	$14,000	$19,000
1967	Sunburst	$9,600	$12,000
1968	Blond	$7,900	$10,200
1968	Blue Flora	$17,000	$22,000
1968	Common color	$10,400	$13,500
1968	Pink Paisley	$17,000	$22,000
1968	Rare color	$13,500	$18,000
1968	Sunburst	$8,600	$11,000
1969	Blond, poly	$7,000	$9,000
1969	Blue Flora	$16,000	$21,000
1969	Common color, poly	$9,400	$12,300
1969	Pink Paisley	$16,000	$21,000
1969	Rare color, poly	$12,300	$17,400
1969	Sunburst, poly	$7,700	$10,200
1970	Blond, poly	$5,600	$7,400
1970	Common color, poly	$9,200	$12,000
1970	Rare color, poly	$12,000	$16,000
1970	Sunburst, poly	$5,700	$7,500
1971	Blond	$4,000	$5,200
1971	Common color	$7,000	$9,000
1971	Rare color	$9,000	$12,300
1971	Sunburst	$4,000	$5,200
1972	Blond	$3,700	$4,900
1972	Common color	$5,300	$6,900
1972	Natural	$3,300	$4,300
1972	Rare color	$6,900	$9,400
1972	Sunburst	$3,500	$4,500

MODEL YEAR	FEATURES	EXC. COND. LOW	HIGH
1973	Black, white	$3,500	$4,600
1973	Blond	$3,700	$4,900
1973	Natural	$2,700	$3,500
1973	Rare color	$6,300	$8,200
1973	Sunburst	$3,300	$4,300
1973	Walnut	$2,700	$3,500
1974	Blond, black, white	$3,500	$4,600
1974	Natural	$2,700	$3,500
1974	Sunburst	$3,300	$4,300
1974	Walnut	$2,700	$3,500
1975	Blond, black, white	$3,200	$4,200
1975	Natural	$2,700	$3,500
1975	Sunburst	$3,200	$4,200
1975	Walnut	$2,700	$3,500
1976	Blond, black, white	$2,600	$3,400
1976	Natural	$2,600	$3,400
1976	Sunburst	$2,600	$3,400
1976	Walnut	$2,600	$3,400
1977	Black, blond, white	$2,600	$3,400
1977	Natural	$2,600	$3,400
1977	Sunburst	$2,600	$3,400
1977	Walnut	$2,600	$3,400
1978-1979	All colors	$2,400	$3,100
1980-1981	All colors	$2,200	$2,900
1980-1981	International colors	$2,800	$3,600

Standard Telecaster

1982-1984. See Telecaster for '51-'82, and American Standard Telecaster (following listing) for '88-2000. Not to be confused with the current Standard Telecaster, which is made in Mexico.

1982	Blond, sunburst	$2,200	$2,900
1983-1984	Blond, sunburst	$1,125	$1,475

American Standard Telecaster

1988-2000, 2008-2016. Name used when Fender reissued the standard American-made Tele after CBS sold the company. The only American-made Tele available for '86 and '87 was the '52 Telecaster. See Telecaster for '51-'81, and Standard Telecaster for '82-'84. All '94 models have a metal 40th Anniversary pin on the headstock, but should not be confused with the actual 40th Anniversary Telecaster model (see separate listing), all standard colors. Renamed the American Series Telecaster in 2000, then back to American Standard Series Telecaster in '08. Becomes American Professional in '17.

1988-2000		$1,000	$1,300
2008-2016		$1,000	$1,300

American Series Telecaster

2000-2007. See Telecaster for '51-'81, Standard Telecaster for '82-'84, and American Standard for '88-'99. Renamed American Standard again in '08.

2000-2007		$1,000	$1,300

American Professional/Professional II Telecaster

2017-present. Model replaces American Standard Tele, redesign includes 2 V-Mod pickups, narrow-tall frets, new 'deep C' neck profile, various colors. Also available left-hand model. Renamed American Professional II in '20.

2017-2020	Pro	$1,000	$1,300
2020-2021	Pro II	$1,000	$1,300

The *Vintage Guitar Price Guide* shows low to high values for items in all-original excellent condition, and, where applicable, with original case or cover.

The Official Vintage Guitar magazine Price Guide 2023   **Fender** 30th Ann. Guitar Center Tree of Life Tele — 60th Ann. Tele   **127**

GUITARS

MODEL		EXC. COND.	
YEAR	FEATURES	LOW	HIGH

30th Anniversary Guitar Center Tree of Life Telecaster

1994. Limited Edition, produced for 30th anniversary of Guitar Center, engraved neckplate with GC logo, tree-of-life 'board inlay.

| 1994 | | $5,200 | $6,800 |

40th Anniversary Telecaster

1988, 1999. Custom Shop, limited edition run of 300, 2-piece flamed maple top, gold hardware ('88), flamed maple top over ash body, gold hardware ('99).

| 1988 | 1st run, high-end | $5,300 | $7,000 |
| 1999 | 2nd run, plain top | $4,100 | $5,400 |

'50 Custom Telecaster

1997. Custom Shop, limited run of 10, humbucker neck pickup, standard unbound body, highly figured maple neck, blackguard specs.

| 1997 | | $2,500 | $3,300 |

'50s Telecaster/Classic Series '50s Telecaster

1990-2019. Made in Japan (basswood body) until mid '99, then in Mexico with ash body. Foto-Flame finish offered in '94 (see separate listing).

| 1990-1999 | Japan | $775 | $1,000 |
| 1999-2019 | Mexico | $550 | $725 |

Road Worn '50s Telecaster

2009-2019. Maple 'board, '50s specs, aged finish.

| 2009-2019 | | $750 | $975 |

50th Anniversary Spanish Guitar Set

1996. Custom Shop, 50 sets made, Tele Prototype reproduction with similar era copy of woodie amp.

| 1996 | | $5,300 | $7,000 |

50th Anniversary Telecaster

1995-1996. Custom Shop, flame maple top, 2 vintage-style pickups, gold hardware, sunburst, gold 50th Anniversary coin on back of the headstock, 1250 made.

| 1995-1996 | | $1,675 | $2,200 |

'52 Telecaster/American Vintage '52 Telecaster

1982-1984, 1986-2017. Ash body, maple neck or rosewood 'board, blond. Replaced by the American Original '50s Telecaster.

1982-1984		$2,500	$3,400
1986-1999		$1,800	$2,350
1990-1999	Copper (limited)	$1,800	$2,350
2000-2009		$1,500	$2,100
2010-2017		$1,400	$1,800

American Vintage '52 Telecaster Korina (U.S.A.)

2015. Part of Fender's limited edition 10 for 15 series, Korina body, '52 specs.

| 2015 | | $1,700 | $2,200 |

'52 Telecaster (Custom Shop)

2004-2018. Custom Shop Dealer Select model, NOS, Relic and Closet Classic offered, changed to Heavy Relic in '15.

2004-2012	NOS	$2,500	$3,300
2004-2014	Relic	$2,700	$3,600
2010-2011	Closet Classic	$2,500	$3,300
2015-2018	Heavy Relic	$2,900	$3,800

'52 LTD Telecaster NOS

2020. Custom Shop, ash body, maple neck, faded blonde, lacquer finish.

| 2020 | | $2,350 | $3,100 |

'52 Vintage Telecaster (Japan)

1982-1984. Made in Japan, JV serial numbers.

| 1982-1984 | | $1,600 | $2,100 |

'54 Telecaster (Custom Shop)

1997-1998, 2013-2016. Relic, Closet Classic available with more recent model.

| 2013-2016 | Relic | $2,700 | $3,500 |

'58 Telecaster (Custom Shop)

2008. Custom Shop, relic and heavy relic.

2008	Heavy relic	$2,900	$3,900
2008	NOS	$2,500	$3,300
2008	Relic	$2,700	$3,600

American Vintage '58 Telecaster (U.S.A.)

2013-2018. Ash body, white 'guard, Aged White Blonde.

| 2013-2018 | | $1,450 | $1,900 |

'60s Telecaster Custom

1997-1999. Custom Shop, bound alder body, sunburst, black or custom colors, nickel or gold hardware.

| 1997-1999 | | $2,700 | $3,600 |

'60s Telecaster/Classic Series '60s Telecaster

1992-2019. Made in Japan (basswood body) until mid '99, then in Mexico with ash body. Foto-Flame finish offered in '94 (see separate listing). '06 version may have 60th Anniversary Badge on back of headstock.

1992-1996	Made in Japan	$775	$1,025
1997-1999	Crafted in Japan	$675	$875
1999-2019	Mexico	$550	$725

American Original '60s Telecaster

2018-present. '60s specs, rosewood 'board, alder body.

| 2018-2021 | | $1,300 | $1,700 |

American Original '60s Telecaster Thinline

2020-present. '60s specs, ash body, maple neck, aged natural, 3-color sunburst or Surf Green.

| 2020-2021 | | $1,400 | $1,800 |

'60 Telecaster Custom

2003-2004. Custom Shop Time Machine, bound alder body, offered in NOS, Closet Classic and Relic versions and in sunburst, CA Red and Sonic Blue.

2003-2004	Closet Classic	$2,500	$3,300
2003-2004	NOS	$2,500	$3,300
2003-2004	Relic	$2,700	$3,600

60th Anniversary American Telecaster

2006-2007. Special Edition commemorating Fender's 60th year, banner headstock 60th logo, neck plate reads Diamond Anniversary 1946-2006, made in U.S.A., rosewood 'board, sunburst.

| 2006-2007 | | $1,200 | $1,575 |

60th Anniversary Telecaster (U.S.A.)

2011-2012. Celebrating 60 years of the Tele, commemorative chrome neck plate, ash body, blonde thin-skin finish.

| 2011-2012 | | $1,200 | $1,600 |

1972 Fender Telecaster
John Hosford

Fender American Original '60s Telecaster

2006 Fender 60th Anniversary Telecaster Limited Edition

Imaged by Heritage Auctions, HA.com

2012 Fender American Standard Telecaster

Steve Alvito

MODEL YEAR	FEATURES	EXC. COND. LOW	HIGH

60th Anniversary Telecaster Limited Edition
2006. Limited Edition of 1,000, 60 Diamond Anniversary 1946-2006 logo engraved in neck plate, American Flag logo on pickguard, '51 NoCaster pickup layout, 60 wood inlay on the face below bridge, clear nitro finish on natural ash body, silver guitar case with Fender 60 logo on inside lid.

2006		$2,000	$2,650

'61 Telecaster Custom
2010-2012. Custom Shop Dealer Select model, bound body Custom, NOS, Relic or Heavy Relic.

2010-2012	Closet Classic	$2,500	$3,300
2010-2012	NOS	$2,500	$3,300
2010-2012	Relic	$2,700	$3,600

'62 Telecaster Custom (Import)
1985-1999. Made in Japan, bound top and back, rosewood 'board, sunburst or red.

1985-1989		$1,200	$1,650
1990-1999		$1,125	$1,450

'62 Telecaster Custom (U.S.A.)
1999-2012. American Vintage Series, rosewood board.

1999-2012		$1,200	$1,550

'62 Mod Squad Custom Telecaster
2013. Custom Shop, Broadcaster bridge pickup and Duncan neck humbucker.

2013		$2,900	$3,800

'62 Telecaster Reissue (Japan)
1989-1990, 2005-2006. Made by Fender Japan.

1989-1990		$1,300	$1,700
2005-2006		$1,150	$1,500

Junkyard Dog 1962 Telecaster Relic
2014-2015. Custom Shop Dealer Select series, ash body, rosewood neck and 'board, white guard, Vintage Blonde.

2014-2015		$2,700	$3,600

'63 Telecaster (Custom Shop)
1999-2010, 2018-2019. Alder body (or blond on ash), original spec pickups, C-shaped neck, rosewood 'board. Relic offered in '07 and later heavy relic in '18.

1999-2010	Closet Classic	$2,500	$3,300
1999-2010	NOS	$2,500	$3,300
2007	Relic	$2,700	$3,600
2018-2019	Heavy relic	$2,900	$3,900

'63 Telecaster Custom Relic LTD
2006. Custom Shop, Limited Edition.

2006		$2,700	$3,600

'64 Telecaster Limited Relic
2009. Custom Shop, rosewood 'board, thin nitro finish, 50 each of black, aged white, and 3-tone chocolate sunburst.

2009		$2,700	$3,600

American Vintage '64 Telecaster
2013-2018. Ash body, mid-'60s 'C' neck profile, rounded rosewood 'board, 2 vintage single-coil pickups, White Blonde.

2013-2018		$1,450	$1,900

'67 Telecaster (Custom Shop)
2005-2008, 2010-2011. Alder body, rosewood or maple 'board, Relic, NOS or Closet Classic, 2010 and later is rosewood 'board, Relic or NOS.

2005-2008	Closet Classic	$2,500	$3,300

MODEL YEAR	FEATURES	EXC. COND. LOW	HIGH
2005-2011	NOS	$2,500	$3,300
2005-2011	Relic	$2,700	$3,600

'68 Telecaster Rosewood
Custom Shop, rosewood body.

2007	NOS	$2,500	$3,300

'69 Tele/Telecaster Thinline (Import)
1986-2015. Import, Classic Series, 2 Tele pickups.

1986-1996	Made in Japan	$1,000	$1,300
1997-1999	Crafted in Japan	$800	$1,050
2000-2015	Mexico	$625	$825

'69 Telecaster Thinline (Custom Shop)
2005-2006. Semi-hollow mahoganhy body, maple neck with maple 'board.

2005-2006		$2,500	$3,300

'72 Telecaster Custom/Classic Series '72 Telecaster Custom
1986-2019. Import, 1 humbucker and 1 single-coil, 2 humbuckers after '99.

1986-1989	Japan	$1,250	$1,625
1990-1999	Japan	$1,125	$1,450
2000-2019	Mexico	$575	$750

'72 Telecaster Deluxe/Classic Series '72 Telecaster Deluxe
2004-2019. Made in Mexico, alder body, large Deluxe 'guard, 2 humbuckers.

2004-2019		$450	$575

'72 Telecaster Thinline American Vintage
2012-2013. US-made, American Vintage FSR model, f-hole, 2 humbuckers.

2012-2013		$1,300	$1,700

'72 Telecaster Thinline/Classic Series Telecaster Thinline
1986-2019. Import, 2 humbuckers, f-hole.

1986-1999	Japan	$1,050	$1,350
2000-2019	Mexico	$550	$725

1972 Telecaster Custom Closet Classic
2013. Custom Shop, ash body, maple neck and 'board, 2 pickups, black finish.

2013		$2,500	$3,300

75th Anniversary Commemorative Telecaster
2021. US-made, limited edition, inlaid 75th Anniversary ingot back of headstock, gold hardware, 2-color Bourbon Burst gloss finish. Includes custom Inca Silver case with Lake Placid Blue interior.

2021		$1,275	$1,650

75th Anniversary Telecaster
2021. Made in Mexico, 75th Anniversary neck plate, Diamond Anniversary satin finish with matching painted headstock.

2021		$575	$750

'90s Telecaster Deluxe
1995-1998. Import, 1 Tele-style bridge pickup and 2 Strat-style pickups, rosewood 'board, Foto Flame '95-'97 and standard finishes '97-'98.

1995-1997	Foto-Flame	$725	$950
1997-1998	Standard finish	$725	$950

'90s Telecaster Thinline
1998-2001. Bound semi-hollow ash body, f-hole, white or brown shell 'guard, 2 single-coils, sunburst, black, natural, or transparent crimson.

1998-2001		$1,800	$2,350

The ***Vintage Guitar Price Guide*** shows low to high values for items in all-original excellent condition, and, where applicable, with original case or cover.

MODEL YEAR	FEATURES	EXC. COND. LOW	HIGH

1998 Collectors Edition Telecaster
1998. 1,998 made, 1998 logo inlay on 'board, maple, gold hardware.
| 1998 | | $1,275 | $1,650 |

Aerodyne Telecaster
2004-2009. Imported Tele with Aerodyne body profile, bound body, black.
| 2004-2009 | | $700 | $900 |

Albert Collins Telecaster
1990-2018. Custom Shop signature model, bound swamp ash body, humbucker pickup in neck position, natural or silver sparkle.
| 1990-2018 | | $3,000 | $3,900 |

Aluminum Telecaster
1994-1995. Aluminum-bodied American Standard with anodized finish in blue marble, purple marble or red, silver and blue stars and stripes.
| 1994-1995 | Flag option | $2,000 | $2,600 |
| 1994-1995 | Marble patterns | $2,000 | $2,600 |

American Acoustasonic Telecaster
2019-present. Solid A sitka spruce top, mahogany back, sides and neck, various colors.
| 2019-2021 | | $1,300 | $1,675 |

American Classic Holoflake Telecaster
1996-1999. Custom Shop, splatter/sparkle finish, pearloid 'guard.
| 1996-1999 | | $2,700 | $3,600 |

American Classic Telecaster
1996-1999. Custom Shop model, handcrafted version of American Standard, thin lacquer-finished ash body, maple or rosewood 'board, various options and colors, earlier versions had gold hardware and custom-color options.
| 1996-1999 | | $2,700 | $3,600 |

American Deluxe HH Telecaster
2004-2006. Rosewood, maple top, 2 humbucker pickups.
| 2004-2006 | | $1,225 | $1,600 |

American Deluxe Power Telecaster
1999-2001. Made in USA, with Fishman power bridge piezo pickups.
| 1999-2001 | | $1,225 | $1,600 |

American Deluxe Telecaster
1998-2017. Premium ash or alder body with see-thru finishes.
| 1998-2017 | | $1,225 | $1,600 |

American Deluxe/Elite Telecaster Thinline
2015-2019. Single-cut, alder body, f-hole, maple neck, 2 Noiseless pickups, various colors.
| 2015-2019 | | $1,225 | $1,600 |

American Elite Telecaster
2016-2020. Single-cut, alder body, maple neck, rosewood 'board, 2 single-coil pickups, various colors.
| 2016-2020 | | $1,225 | $1,600 |

American Nashville B-Bender Telecaster
1998-2015. US-made, alder body, added Texas Special Strat pickup in middle position, white pearloid 'guard, Parsons-Fender B-string bender, 5-way switch.
| 1998-2015 | | $1,600 | $2,100 |

American Performer Telecaster
Introduced Dec. 2018-present. Made in US, new features include Yosemite single-coil pickups, Greasebucket tone system, various colors.
| 2018-2021 | | $775 | $1,025 |

American Professional II Telecaster Deluxe
2020-present. Alder body, maple neck, 2 humbucking pickups, various colors with gloss finish.
| 2020-2021 | | $1,000 | $1,300 |

American Professional Telecaster Deluxe Shawbucker
2017-2018. With 2 ShawBucker humbucking pickups, various colors.
| 2017-2018 | | $1,100 | $1,450 |

American Special Telecaster
2010-2018. Alder body, gloss finish, Texas Special pickups.
| 2010-2018 | | $775 | $1,000 |

American Standard Telecaster Limited Edition
1990s-2019. American Standard series, various limited edition models.
1995-1997	B-Bender	$1,550	$2,000
2009	Matching hdstk	$1,200	$1,600
2014-2015	Channel Bound	$1,000	$1,300
2015	Rosewood neck	$1,550	$2,000
2015-2016	HH	$1,000	$1,300

American Standard Telecaster Special Edition
2009. Surf Green, Fiesta Red or Daphne Blue with matching headstock.
| 2009 | | $1,250 | $1,650 |

American Ultra Luxe Telecaster
2021-present. 2 Noiseless single-coil or Floyd Rose with 2 humbucker, 2-color sunburst, trans Surf Green or black.
| 2021 | Floyd Rose HH | $1,425 | $1,975 |
| 2021 | SS | $1,450 | $1,850 |

American Ultra Telecaster
2019-present. Alder or ash body, upgrades include 2 Ultra Noiseless Vintage Tele single-coil pickups and 7 new colors with gloss poly finish.
| 2019-2021 | | $1,200 | $1,600 |

Andy Summers Masterbuilt Tribute Telecaster
2009. Custom shop, based on Summer's '61 Tele, heavy relic, 250 made, custom electronics rear-mounted overdrive unit controlled by a third knob, includes DVD, strap and Andy Summer's logo travel guitar case.
| 2009 | | $7,000 | $9,100 |

Antigua Telecaster
2004. Made in Japan, limited edition, 400 made, '70s features and antigua finish.
| 2004 | | $825 | $1,075 |

Big Block Telecaster
2005-2006. Pearloid block markers, black with matching headstock, 3 single-coils with center pickup reverse wound.
| 2005-2006 | | $650 | $850 |

Fender American Ultra Telecaster

Fender Antigua Telecaster

GUITARS

1974 Fender Telecaster Custom
Scott Casey

Fender Deluxe Nashville Telecaster (Mexico)

MODEL YEAR	FEATURES	EXC. COND. LOW	HIGH

Bigsby Telecaster
2003. Made in Mexico, standard Tele specs with original Fender-logo Bigsby tailpiece.

2003		$650	$850

Blacktop Telecaster Series
2012-2015. Includes 2 humbucker HH and hum-single-single Baritone.

2012-2015	Various models	$575	$750

Blue Flower Telecaster
1985-1993, 2003-2004. Import, Blue Flower finish.

1985-1993	1st issue	$800	$1,050
2003-2004	2nd issue	$625	$825

Bowling Ball/Marble Telecaster
1983-1984. Standard Tele, called Bowling Ball Tele due to the swirling color, blue, red or yellow.

1983-1984		$3,600	$4,700

Britt Daniel Telecaster Thinline
2019-present. Ash body, maple neck, 2 single-coil pickups, Amarillo Gold lacquer finish.

2019-2021		$1,300	$1,700

Brown's Canyon Redwood Telecaster
2011. For Fender's 60th anniversary in 2011, they released 12 limited edition U.S.-made Tele-bration Telecasters, including this one with body made from 1890s California redwood.

2011		$1,500	$1,950

Buck Owens Limited Edition Telecaster
1998-1999. Red, white and blue sparkle finish, 250 made, gold hardware, gold 'guard, rosewood 'board.

1998-1999		$1,700	$2,250

Cabronita Telecaster (American Standard)
2011. For Fender's 60th anniversary in 2011, American Standard series, they released 12 limited edition U.S.-made Tele-bration Telecasters, including this one with 2 TV Jones Filter'Trons.

2011		$1,125	$1,450

Cabronita Telecaster (Classic Player)
2014-2015. Mexico version, Classic Player series.

2014-2015		$425	$550

Cabronita Telecaster Thinline
2012-2013. Made in Mexico, ash body, maple neck, 2 Fideli'Tron humbucking pickups, 2-Color Sunburst, Shoreline Gold or White Blonde.

2012-2013		$675	$875

California Fat Telecaster
1997-1998. Alder body, maple fretboard, Tex-Mex humbucker and Tele pickup configuration.

1997-1998		$650	$850

California Telecaster
1997-1998. Alder body, maple fretboard, sunburst, Tex-Mex Strat and Tele pickup configuration.

1997-1998		$650	$850

Chambered Mahogany Telecaster
2006. U.S.-made, chambered mahogany body, Delta Tone System.

2006		$1,075	$1,400

Chrissie Hynde Telecaster
2021-present. Artist series, alder body with Faded Ice Blue Metallic Road Worn finish, chrome mirror 'guard.

2021		$925	$1,200

Clarence White Telecaster (Custom Shop)
1994-2000. Parsons-White B-Bender and Scruggs-style tuners on both E strings, sunburst.

1994-2000		$8,500	$11,200

Classic Player Baja Telecaster
2007-2019. Made in Mexico, Custom Shop designed neck plate logo, thin gloss poly blond finish.

2007-2019		$675	$875

Collector's Edition Telecaster
1998. Mid-1955 specs including white 'guard, offered in sunburst with gold hardware (which was an option in '55), 1,998 made, Collector's Edition neck plate with serial number.

1998		$1,350	$1,800

Contemporary Telecaster (Import)
1985-1987. Japanese-made while the new Fender reorganized, 2 or 3 pickups, vibrato, black chrome hardware, rosewood 'board.

1985-1987		$700	$900

Custom Carved Telecaster HH
2013. Figured maple top, carved back, 2 humbucking pickups.

2013		$1,925	$2,500

Custom Classic Telecaster
2000-2008. Custom Shop, maple or rosewood 'board, certificate of authenticity.

2000-2008		$2,400	$3,100

Custom Deluxe Telecaster
2009-2014. Custom Shop model, ash body, AA birdseye maple neck, rosewood or maple 'board, abalone dot inlays, 2 pickups, certificate, black Bakelite 'guard, Aged White Blonde, Dakota Red or faded 2-color sunburst.

2009-2014		$3,300	$4,300

Custom Telecaster
1972-1981. One humbucking and 1 Tele pickup, standard colors, see Telecaster Custom for 2 Tele pickup/bound body version.

1972		$3,300	$4,300
1973-1974		$3,100	$4,100
1975-1977		$2,700	$3,500
1978-1979		$2,400	$3,100
1980-1981		$2,200	$2,900

Danny Gatton Signature Telecaster
1990-2018. Custom Shop, like '53 Telecaster, maple neck, 2 humbuckers.

1990-1999	Frost Gold	$3,700	$4,900
2000-2018	Various colors	$2,400	$3,200

Deluxe Nashville Power Telecaster
1999-2014. Like Deluxe Nashville, but with piezo transducer in each saddle.

1999-2014		$550	$725

Deluxe Nashville Telecaster (Mexico)
1997-2021. Tex-Mex Strat and Tele pickup configuration, various colors.

1997-2021		$550	$725

Deluxe Telecaster (U.S.A.)
1972-1981. Two humbuckers, various colors. Mexican-made version offered starting in 2004.

1972	Common color	$3,500	$4,500

MODEL YEAR	FEATURES	EXC. COND. LOW	HIGH
1972	Less common color	$4,300	$5,600
1973-1974	Common color	$3,275	$4,250
1973-1974	Less common color	$4,200	$5,400
1975	Common color	$2,700	$3,500
1975	Less common color	$3,600	$4,700
1976-1977	Common color	$2,700	$3,525
1978-1979	Common color	$2,350	$3,050
1980-1981	Common color	$2,200	$2,900

Elite Nashville Telecaster
Custom Shop Limited Edition, ash body, 3 pickups, Antique Cherry Burst.

2016		$1,600	$2,100

Elite Telecaster
1983-1985. Two active humbucker pickups, 3-way switch, 2 volume knobs, 1 presence and filter controls, chrome hardware, various colors.

1983-1985		$2,100	$2,700

Fat Telecaster
1999-2001. Humbucker pickup in neck, Tele bridge pickup.

1999-2001		$650	$850

Foto Flame Telecaster
1994-1996. Import, sunburst or transparent.

1994-1996		$700	$925

G.E. Smith Telecaster
2007-2014. Swamp ash body, vintage style hardware, U-shaped neck, oval and diamond inlays.

2007-2014		$1,200	$1,600

Graham Coxon Special Run Telecaster
2011, 2013-2014. Blond, Tele bridge and humbucker neck pickup, rosewood 'board, limited run in 2011.

2011-2014		$1,125	$1,450

Highway One Telecaster/Texas Telecaster
2003-2011. U.S.-made, alder body, satin lacquer finish, Texas version (introduced in '04) has ash body and Hot Vintage pickups.

2003-2011		$675	$875

HMT Telecaster (Import)
1990-1993. Japanese-made Heavy Metal Tele, available with or without Floyd Rose tremolo, 1 Fender Lace Sensor pickup and 1 DiMarzio bridge humbucker pickup, black.

1990-1993		$900	$1,200

J5 Triple Telecaster Deluxe
2007-2017. John 5 model, made in Mexico, 3 humbuckers, medium jumbo frets.

2007-2017		$725	$950

James Burton Standard Telecaster
1995-2016. Mexico, 2 Texas Special Tele pickups, standard colors (no paisley).

1995-2016		$600	$775

James Burton Telecaster
1990-present. Ash body, 3 Fender Lace pickups, available in black with Gold Paisley, black with Candy Red Paisley, Pearl White, and Frost Red until '05. In '06 in black with red or blue flame-shaped paisley, or Pearl White.

1990-2005	Black & gold paisley, gold hw	$2,300	$3,000
1990-2005	Black & red paisley, black hw	$1,900	$2,500
1990-2010	Frost Red or Pearl White	$1,100	$1,500
1994	Blue Paisley, gold hw	$1,800	$2,400
2006-2021	Paisley flames	$1,100	$1,500

Jason Isbell Custom Telecaster
2021-present. Artist series, double-bound body, aged hardware, Road Worn Chocolate Sunburst with lacquer finish.

2021		$975	$1,275

Jerry Donahue JD Telecaster
1993-1999. Made in Japan, Custom Strat neck pickup and Custom Tele bridge pickup, basswood body, special "V" shaped maple neck.

1993-1999		$1,200	$1,600

Jerry Donahue Telecaster
1992-2001. Custom Shop model designed by Donahue, Tele bridge pickup and Strat neck pickup, birdseye maple neck, top and back, gold hardware, passive circuitry, sunburst, transparent Crimson Red or Sapphire Blue. There was also a Japanese-made JD Telecaster.

1992-2001	Various colors	$2,300	$3,000

Jim Adkins JA-90 Telecaster Thinline
2008-present. Rosewood 'board, vintage-style P-90 soapbars.

2008-2021		$550	$725

Jim Root Telecaster
2007-present. Made in Mexico, black hardware, mahogany body.

2007-2021		$725	$950

Jimmy Bryant Tribute Telecaster
2004-2005. Custom Shop, hand-tooled leather 'guard overlay with JB initials.

2004-2005		$2,700	$3,600

Jimmy Page Mirror Telecaster
2019-present. Ash body with white blonde lacquer finish, rosewood 'board, 2 single-coil pickups, vintage-style tweed case, shipped with 8 round mirrors.

2019-2021		$1,800	$2,350

Jimmy Page Telecaster
2020-present. Ash body with gloss finish over Page's artwork, maple neck with Road Worn nitro finish, rosewood 'board.

2020-2021		$900	$1,175

Joe Strummer Telecaster
2007-2009. Limited edition, heavily relic'd based on Strummer's '66 Tele, Fender offered a limited edition art customization kit as part of the package.

2007	Limited Edition	$975	$1,275
2007-2009	Standard run	$975	$1,275

John Jorgenson Telecaster
1998-2001. Custom Shop, korina body, double-coil stacked pickups, sparkle or black finish.

1998-2001	Sparkle	$2,700	$3,600

Jr. Telecaster
1994, 1997-2000. Custom Shop, transparent blond ash body, 2 P-90-style pickups, set neck, 11 tone chambers, 100 made in '94, reintroduced in '97.

1994		$2,700	$3,600
1997-2000		$2,700	$3,600

2008 Fender G.E. Smith Telecaster

Fender James Burton Telecaster

To get the most from this book, be sure to read "Using *The Guide*" in the introduction.

GUITARS

1986 Fender Paisley Telecaster

Fender Richie Kotzen Telecaster

MODEL YEAR	FEATURES	EXC. COND. LOW	HIGH

La Cabronita Especial Telecaster
2009-2010. Custom Shop relics, 1 or 2 TV Jones pickups. In '09, 10 each with 1 pickup in black or Shoreline Gold and 20 each with 2 pickups in black or Shoreline Gold. In '10, 10 each with 1 pickup in Candy Apple Red or Sonic Blue and 20 each with 2 pickups in Candy Apple Red or Sonic Blue.

2009-2010	Various colors	$3,500	$4,500

Mahogany Offset Telecaster
2020. Made in Japan series, mahogany body and neck, rosewood 'board, 2 pickups, natural finish.

2020		$575	$750

Masterbuilt Custom Shop Telecaster
2006-present. Various models and builders, specific identification to builder, must include certificate of authenticity.

2006-2021	Various models	$3,800	$8,300

Matched Set Telecaster
1994. Matching Tele and Strat Custom Shop models, model name on certificate is "Matched Set Telecaster", 3 sets were built, each set has serial number 1, 2, or 3.

1994		$5,000	$6,500

Merle Haggard Signature Telecaster
2009-2018. Custom Shop, figured maple body and neck, maple 'board, 2-color sunburst.

2009-2018		$3,400	$4,500

Mod Shop Telecaster
2017-present. Mod Shop allows you to create your own factory-customized electric guitar or bass.

2017-2021		$1,600	$2,600

Modern Player Telecaster Plus
2012-2018. Import, pine body, maple neck, HSS pickups, Honey Burst or Trans Charcoal.

2012-2018		$400	$525

Moto Limited Edition Telecaster
1990s. Custom Shop, pearloid cover in various colors. There were also Strat and Jag versions.

1990s		$3,000	$3,900

Muddy Waters Signature Telecaster Custom
2001-2009. Mexico, Fender amp control knobs, Telecaster Custom on headstock, Muddy Waters signature logo on neck plate, Candy Apple Red.

2001-2009		$750	$975

Muddy Waters Tribute Telecaster
2000. Custom Shop, 100 made, Fender amp control knobs, rosewood 'board, relic Candy Apple Red finish, certificate of authenticity.

2000		$3,300	$4,400

Nashville Telecaster
1995. Custom Shop model, 3 pickups.

1995		$2,250	$2,900

NHL Premier Edition Telecaster
1999-2000. Limited edition of 100 guitars with NHL hockey art logo on the top.

1999-2000	All models	$900	$1,300

Nokie Edwards Telecaster
1996. Made in Japan, limited edition, book matched flamed top, multi-lam neck, Seymour Duncan pickups, gold hardware, zero fret, tilted headstock.

1996		$1,550	$2,000

MODEL YEAR	FEATURES	EXC. COND. LOW	HIGH

Noventa Telecaster
2021-present. Alder body, maple neck, maple or pau ferro 'board, single-coil pickup, 2-Color Sunburst, Fiesta Red or Vintage Blonde.

2021		$675	$875

Old Pine Telecaster
2011. For Fender's 60th anniversary in 2011, they released 12 limited edition U.S.-made Tele-bration Telecasters, including this one with 100-year-old pine body, 300 made.

2011		$1,450	$1,900

Paisley Telecaster
1986-1998, 2003-2004, 2008. Import, 'Made in Japan' logo used until '98, 'Crafted in Japan' after, Pink Paisley finish.

1986-1994		$800	$1,050
1995-1998		$750	$975
2003-2004		$625	$825
2008	600 made	$625	$825

Palo Escrito Telecaster
2006-2007. Mexico, Classic series, palo escrito is tonewood from Mexico with unique grain patterns, natural finish.

2006-2007		$750	$975

Parallel Universe Jazz-Tele
June 2018. Parallel Universe series, limited edition, Tele body, 2 Jazzmaster single-coil pickups, 2-Color Sunburst or Surf Green.

2018		$1,300	$1,800

Parallel Universe Troublemaker Telecaster
July 2018. Parallel Universe series, limited edition, mahogany body, maple top, custom Cabronita 'guard, 2 ShawBucker (1T and 2T) humbucking pickups. Bigsby optional.

2018		$1,300	$1,800
2018	with Bigsby	$1,300	$1,800

Parallel Universe Volume II Tele Mágico
2020-2021. Parallel Universe Volume II series, limited edition, ash body, flame maple neck and 'board, Daphane Blue or Surf Green.

2020-2021		$1,400	$1,900

Player Telecaster
2018-present. Alder body, maple neck, 2 SS or HH pickups, various colors with gloss finish.

2018-2021		$450	$575

Plus Telecaster
1994-1997. Lace Sensor pickups, various colors.

1994-1997		$1,925	$2,500

Rarities Telecaster
2019-2020. Rarities Collection series, limited edition, models include; Flame Maple Top, Quilt Maple Top, Red Mahogany Top.

2019-2020		$1,600	$2,100

Richie Kotzen Telecaster
2017-present. Ash body, bound flame maple top, 2 DiMarzio pickups, gold hardware, signature on headstock.

2017-2021		$950	$1,225

Rosewood Telecaster
1969-1972. Rosewood body and neck.

1969-1972		$13,500	$17,700

MODEL YEAR	FEATURES	EXC. COND. LOW	HIGH

Rosewood Telecaster (Japan)

1986-1996. Japanese-made reissue, rosewood body and neck.

1986-1996		$2,100	$2,700

Rosewood Telelcaster Limited Edition

2014. Custom Shop, Limited Edition neck plate, based on George Harrison's rosewood Tele.

2014		$4,100	$5,400

Select Telecaster

2012-2013. Select Series, figured maple top, rear-headstock 'Fender Select' medallion, gloss-lacquer finish, chrome or gold hardware.

2012-2013		$1,900	$2,500

Select Telecaster Thinline

2012-2013. Select Series, rear-headstock 'Fender Select' medallion, chrome or gold hardware, various finish options.

2012-2013		$1,700	$2,450

Set-Neck Telecaster

1990-1996. Glued-in neck, Custom Shop, 2 humbucking pickups, Set-Neck CA (Country Artist) has 1 humbucker and 1 Tele pickup, various colors.

1990-1996		$2,100	$2,700

Snakehead Telecaster

Custom Shop Limited Edition, 45 offered.

2010		$4,500	$6,000

Sparkle Telecaster

1993-1995. Custom Shop model, poplar body, white 'guard, sparkle finish: champagne, gold, silver.

1993-1995		$2,000	$2,600

Special Edition Custom Telecaster FMT HH

2020-present. Mahogany body with carved flame maple top, 2 Seymour Duncan pickups, various colors with matching headstock.

2020-2021		$475	$625

Special Edition Deluxe Ash Telecaster

2009-2016. Mexico, butterscotch finish, ash body, 1-piece maple neck.

2009-2016		$475	$625

Special Edition Koa Telecaster

2006-2008. Made in Korea, standard Tele specs, koa veneer top over basswood body, pearloid 'guard, sunburst.

2006-2008		$475	$625

Special Edition White Opal Telecaster

2016. Made in Mexico, white opal body and headstock, pearloid 'guard.

2016		$475	$625

Special Telecaster/Telecaster Special

2004-2008. Made in Mexico, Special Edition logo with star logo sticker on back of headstock, special features like 6-way bridge and modern tuners.

2004-2008		$475	$625

Standard Telecaster (Japan)

1985-1989. In '85, the only Teles were interim production in Japan while the new Fender reorganized, no serial number, Japan headstock logo in '85, back of neck '86-'89.

1985-1989		$875	$1,150

Standard Telecaster (Mexico)

1990-2018. Guitar production at the Mexico facility started in '90. High end of range includes a hard guitar case, while the low end of the range includes only a gig bag, various colors. Replaced by Player Series.

1990-2018		$400	$525

Telecaster (Japanese Domestic)

1982-1997. Made in Japan for Japanese domestic market (not for export), suffix serial numbers JV5 ('82-'84) and A6 through V6 ('84-'97).

1982-1984	JV serial	$1,200	$1,575
1985-1989		$1,175	$1,525
1990-1997		$825	$1,075

Telecaster Custom

1959-1972. Body bound top and back, rosewood 'board, 2 Tele pickups, see Custom Telecaster for the 1 Tele/1 humbucker version. Please refer to the Fender Guitar Intro Section for details on Fender color options.

1959	Sunburst, maple	$29,000	$39,000
1960	Custom color	$40,000	$55,000
1960	Sunburst	$28,000	$36,000
1961	Custom color	$40,000	$55,000
1961	Sunburst	$26,600	$34,500
1962	Custom color	$36,000	$50,000
1962	Sunburst, curve	$24,000	$31,000
1962	Sunburst, slab	$25,000	$32,000
1963	Custom color	$36,000	$50,000
1963	Sunburst	$24,000	$31,000
1964	Custom color	$28,000	$40,000
1964	Sunburst	$21,000	$28,000
1965	Custom color	$26,000	$37,000
1965	Sunburst	$17,000	$24,000
1966	Custom color	$21,000	$29,000
1966	Sunburst	$13,000	$17,000
1967	Custom color	$21,000	$29,000
1967	Sunburst	$13,000	$17,000
1968	Custom color	$21,000	$29,000
1968	Sunburst	$13,000	$17,000
1969	Custom color	$21,000	$29,000
1969	Sunburst	$13,000	$17,000
1970	Custom color	$11,500	$20,000
1970	Sunburst	$10,000	$13,000
1971	Custom color, 4-bolt	$13,900	$18,000
1971	Sunburst, 3-bolt	$3,500	$4,500
1971	Sunburst, 4-bolt	$9,600	$12,500
1972	Custom color, 3-bolt	$7,300	$9,400
1972	Sunburst, 3-bolt	$3,500	$4,500

Telecaster Custom (Japan)

1985. Made in Japan during the period when Fender suspended all USA manufacturing in '85, Tele Custom specs including bound body.

1985		$1,200	$1,600

Telecaster Custom FMT HH (Korea)

2003-2019. Korean-made, flamed maple top, 2 humbuckers.

2003-2019		$775	$1,000

1969 Fender Rosewood Telecaster

Keith Hardie

Fender Telecaster Custom

1972 Fender Telecaster Thinline

2000 Fender Will Ray Signature Mojo Telecaster

Jimmy James

Telecaster Stratocaster Hybrid (Custom Shop)

2006. Tele body shape, Strat pickup system and wiring, Strat headstock shape, dot markers on rosewood board, reissue tremolo, includes Custom Shop COA that reads "Telecaster Stratocaster Hybrid".

MODEL YEAR	FEATURES	EXC. COND. LOW	HIGH
2006		$2,700	$3,600

Telecaster Thinline

1968-1980. Semi-hollowbody, 1 f-hole, 2 Tele pickups, ash or mahogany body, in late-'71 the tilt neck was added and the 2 Tele pickups were switched to 2 humbuckers. Please refer to the Fender Guitar Intro Section for details on Fender color options.

MODEL YEAR	FEATURES	EXC. COND. LOW	HIGH
1968	Common color	$13,500	$17,500
1968	Natural ash	$8,800	$11,500
1968	Natural mahogany	$8,800	$11,500
1968	Rare color	$17,500	$22,000
1968	Sunburst	$10,000	$13,000
1969	Common color	$11,500	$15,000
1969	Natural ash	$8,900	$11,500
1969	Natural mahogany	$8,900	$11,500
1969	Rare color	$15,000	$19,000
1969	Sunburst	$10,000	$13,000
1970	Common color	$10,400	$13,500
1970	Natural ash	$8,700	$11,300
1970	Natural mahogany	$8,700	$11,300
1970	Rare color	$13,500	$17,500
1970	Sunburst	$10,000	$13,000
1971	Color option, 3-bolt, hums	$7,200	$9,400
1971	Color option, 4-bolt, singles	$10,000	$16,000
1971	Natural ash, 3-bolt	$3,800	$5,000
1971	Natural ash, 3-bolt, hums	$3,800	$5,000
1971	Natural ash, 4-bolt, singles	$4,500	$5,900
1971	Natural mahogany, 3-bolt	$3,800	$5,000
1971	Natural mahogany, 3-bolt, hums	$3,800	$5,000
1971	Natural mahogany, 4-bolt, singles	$4,500	$5,900
1971	Sunburst, 3-bolt, hums	$3,800	$5,000
1971	Sunburst, 4-bolt, singles	$5,200	$6,700
1972	Color option	$7,200	$9,400
1972	Mahogany	$3,800	$5,000
1972	Natural ash	$3,800	$5,000
1972	Sunburst	$3,800	$5,000
1973	Color option	$5,000	$8,500
1973	Mahogany	$3,800	$5,000
1973	Natural ash	$3,800	$5,000
1973	Sunburst	$3,800	$5,000
1974	Color option	$3,900	$5,900
1974	Mahogany	$3,000	$4,000
1974	Natural ash	$3,000	$4,000
1974	Sunburst	$3,600	$4,800
1975	Color option	$3,900	$5,900
1975	Natural ash	$2,900	$3,700
1975	Sunburst	$2,900	$3,700
1976	Color option	$2,600	$3,400
1976	Natural ash	$2,600	$3,400
1976	Sunburst	$2,600	$3,400
1977	Color option	$2,600	$3,400
1977	Natural ash	$2,600	$3,400
1977	Sunburst	$2,600	$3,400
1978	Color option	$2,400	$3,200
1978	Natural ash	$2,400	$3,200
1978	Sunburst	$2,400	$3,200

Tele-Sonic

1998-2000. U.S.A., chambered Telecaster body, 2 DeArmond pickups, dot markers, upper bass bout 3-way toggle switch.

MODEL YEAR	FEATURES	EXC. COND. LOW	HIGH
1998-2000		$1,150	$1,500

Texas Special Telecaster

1991-1992. Custom Shop, 60 made, state of Texas outline on the 'guard, ash body with Texas Orange transparent finish, large profile maple neck, with certificate of authenticity.

MODEL YEAR	FEATURES	EXC. COND. LOW	HIGH
1991-1992		$2,700	$3,600

Twisted Telecaster Limited Edition

2005. Custom Shop, 50 built by Master Builder Yuriy Shishkov, 100 built by the Custom Shop team, top loaded Bigsby.

MODEL YEAR	FEATURES	EXC. COND. LOW	HIGH
2005	Shishkov built	$4,500	$5,900
2005	Team built	$2,500	$3,300

Two-Tone Telecaster Thinline

2019-2020. FSR Limited Edition, alder body, various top color with matching headstock and white back and sides.

MODEL YEAR	FEATURES	EXC. COND. LOW	HIGH
2019-2020		$1,275	$1,650

Vintage Hot Rod Telecaster

2007-2014. Vintage styling with modern features, '07-'13 named '52 Tele and '62 Tele, in '14 changed to '50s, and '60s.

MODEL YEAR	FEATURES	EXC. COND. LOW	HIGH
2007-2014	All models	$1,300	$1,700

Waylon Jennings Tribute Telecaster

1995-2003. Custom Shop, black with white leather rose body inlays.

MODEL YEAR	FEATURES	EXC. COND. LOW	HIGH
1995-2003		$6,600	$8,700

Will Ray Signature Jazz-A-Caster

1997. Made in Fender Japan Custom Shop as one part of the three part Hellecasters Series, limited edition, Strat neck on a Tele body with 2 soap-bar Seymour Duncan Jazzmaster-style pickups, gold leaf finish.

MODEL YEAR	FEATURES	EXC. COND. LOW	HIGH
1997		$1,200	$1,575

Will Ray Signature Mojo Telecaster

1998-2001. Custom Shop, ash body, flamed maple Strat neck, locking tuners, rosewood 'board, skull inlays, double coil pickups, optional Hipshot B bender.

MODEL YEAR	FEATURES	EXC. COND. LOW	HIGH
1998-2001		$2,800	$3,700

Telecoustic Series

2000-2016. Thinline acoustic/electric, single-cut, spruce top, fiberglass body, various colors. Telecoustic discontinued '05, Deluxe begins '07-'09 and Standard added in '09-'16. Both Plus and Premier '14-'16.

MODEL YEAR	FEATURES	EXC. COND. LOW	HIGH
2000-2016		$365	$475

MODEL		EXC. COND.	
YEAR	FEATURES	LOW	HIGH

Toronado/Deluxe/HH/Highway 1/GT HH

1998-2006. American Special series, various models and colors. Deluxe model made in Mexico.

1998-2006		$600	$800

Villager 12-String

1965-1969, 2011-present. Acoustic flat-top, spruce top, mahogany back and sides, 12 strings, natural. Reintroduced in '11 (California Series) with on-board Fishman System, made in China.

1965-1969		$850	$1,100
2011-2021	Reintroduced	$325	$425

Violin - Electric

1958-1976, 2013. Violin-shape, solidbody, sunburst is the standard finish.

1958-1976		$2,200	$2,900
2013		$600	$800

Wildwood

1963-1971. Acoustic flat-top with Wildwood dyed top.

1966-1971	Various (unfaded)	$2,150	$2,800

Fenix

Late 1980s-mid 1990s. Brand name of Korean manufacturer Young Chang, used on a line of original-design and copy acoustic, electric and bass guitars. They also built Squier brand guitars for Fender during that period.

Fenton-Weill

See info under Burns-Weill.

Fernandes

1969-present. Established in Tokyo. Early efforts were classical guitars, but they now offer a variety of intermediate grade, production, imported guitars and basses.

Fina

Production classical and steel-string guitars and acoustic basses built in Huiyang City, Guang Dong, China.

Finck, David

1986-present. Luthier David Finck builds his production/custom, professional and premium grade, acoustic guitars, presently in Valle Crucis, North Carolina. In the past, he has built in Pittsburg, Kansas and Reader, West Virginia.

Fine Resophonic

1988-present. Professional and premium grade, production/custom, wood and metal-bodied resophonic guitars (including reso-electrics) built by luthiers Mike Lewis and Pierre Avocat in Vitry Sur Seine, France. They also build ukes and mandolins.

Firefly

Independent brand, budget models produced in China.

Electric

Various copy models made in China.

2019-2021		$120	$250

First Act

1995-present. Budget and professional grade, production/custom, acoustic, solid and semi-hollow body guitars built in China and in their Custom Shop in Boston. They also make basses, violins, and other instruments.

Firth Pond & Company

1822-1867. An east coast retail distributor that sold Martin and Ashborn private brand instruments. The company operated as Firth and Hall from 1822-1841 (also known as Firth, Hall & Pond) in New York City and Litchfield, Connecticut. Most instruments were small parlor size (11" lower bout) guitars, as was the case for most builders of this era. Sometimes the inside back center seam will be branded Firth & Pond. Brazilian rosewood sides and back instruments fetch considerably more than most of the other tone woods and value can vary considerably based on condition. Guitars from the 1800s are sometimes valued more as antiques than working vintage guitars. In 1867 Firth & Sons sold out to Oliver Ditson Company.

Flammang Guitars

1990-present. Premium grade, custom/production, steel string guitars built by luthier David Flammang in Greene, Iowa and previously in East Hampton and Higganum, Connecticut.

Flaxwood

2004-present. Professional grade, production/custom, solid and semi-hollow body guitars built in Finland, with bodies of natural fiber composites.

Fleishman Instruments

Introduced in 1974, premium and presentation grade, custom flat-tops made by luthier Harry Fleishman in Sebastopol, California. He also offers basses and electric uprights. Fleishman is the director of Luthiers School International.

Fletcher Brock Stringed Instruments

1992-present. Custom flat-tops and archtops made by luthier Fletcher Brock originally in Ketchum, Idaho, and currently in Seattle, Washington. He also builds mandolin family instruments.

Flowers Guitars

1993-present. Premium grade, custom, archtop guitars built by luthier Gary Flowers in Baltimore, Maryland.

Floyd Rose

2004-2006. Floyd Rose, inventor of the Floyd Rose Locking Tremolo, produced a line of intermediate and professional grade, production, solidbody guitars from '04 to '06. They continue to offer bridges and other accessories.

1968 Fender Villager 12-String
Imaged by Heritage Auctions, HA.com

2006 First Act Volkswagen Garagemaster
Billy White Jr.

Frame Works

1960s Framus Missouri
Model 5/60

Imaged by *Heritage Auctions, HA.com*

Foggy Mountain

Intermediate grade, production, steel and nylon string acoustic and acoustic/electric guitars imported from China.

Fontanilla Guitars

1987-present. Luthier Allan Fontanilla builds his premium grade, production/custom, classical guitars in San Francisco, California.

Fouilleul

1978-present. Production/custom, classical guitars made by luthier Jean-Marie Fouilleul in Cuguen, France.

Fox Hollow Guitars

2004-present. Luthier Don Greenough builds his professional and premium grade, custom, acoustic and electric guitars in Eugene, Oregon. He also builds mandolins.

Fox or Rocking F

1983-present. Premium grade, custom, steel string acoustic guitars built in Seattle, Washington by luthier Cat Fox.

Foxxe

1990-1991. Short-lived brand of solidbodies offered by the same company that produced Barrington guitars, Korean-made.

Frame Works

1995-present. Professional grade, production/custom, steel- and nylon-string guitars built by luthier Frank Krocker in Burghausen, Germany. The instruments feature a neck mounted on a guitar-shaped frame. Krocker has also built traditional archtops, flat-tops, and classicals.

Framus

1946-1977, 1996-present. Professional and premium grade, production/custom, guitars made in Markneukirchen, Germany. They also build basses, amps, mandolins and banjos. Frankische Musikindustrie (Framus) founded in Erlangen, Germany by Fred Wilfer, relocated to Bubenreuth in '54, and to Pretzfeld in '67. Begun as an acoustic instrument manufacturer, Framus added electrics in the mid-'50s. Earliest electrics were mostly acoustics with pickups attached. Electric designs begin in early-'60s. Unique feature was a laminated maple neck with many thin plies. By around '64-'65 upscale models featured the organtone, often called a spigot, a spring-loaded volume control that allowed you to simulate a Leslie speaker effect. Better models often had mutes and lots of switches.

In the '60s, Framus instruments were imported into the U.S. by Philadelphia Music Company. Resurgence of interest in ca. '74 with the Jan Akkermann hollowbody followed by original mid-'70s design called the Nashville, the product of an alli-

ance with some American financing.

The brand was revived in '96 by Hans Peter Wilfer, the president of Warwick, with production in Warwick's factory in Germany.

Amateur

Early-1960s to mid-1970s. Model 5/1, small flat-top, early without pickguard, plain, dot markers.

MODEL YEAR	FEATURES	EXC. COND. LOW	HIGH
1960s-70s	Model 5/1	$200	$275

Atilla Zoller AZ-10

Early-1960s-early-1980s. Single-cut archtop, 2 pickups, neck glued-in until the '70s, bolt-on after, sunburst. Model 5/65 (rounded cutaway, made until late '60s) and Model 5/67 (sharp cutaway).

1960s	Model 5/65	$700	$900
1960s-70s	Model 5/67	$700	$900

Atlantic

Ca. 1965-ca. 1970. Model 5/110, single-cut thin body electric archtop, 2 pickups, tremolo optional.

1965-1970	Model 5/110	$600	$800

Atlantic Elec-12

Mid- to late-1960s. Model 5/011 and 5/013, double cut semi-hollow, 2 pickups, 12-string.

1960s	Model 5/011 & /013	$600	$800

Big 18 Doubleneck

Late-1960s. Model 5/200 is a solidbody and Model 5/220 is acoustic.

1960s	Model 5/200 & /220	$775	$1,000

Caravelle

Ca.1965-ca. 1975. Double-cut archtop, tremolo, model 5/117-52 has 2 pickups and 5/117-54 has 3.

1965-1975	Model 5/117	$700	$900

Gaucho

1967 to mid-1970s. Lower grade flat-top, concert size, spruce top, mahogany sides and back, rosewood bridge and 'board, sunburst or natural finish.

1967-70s	Model 5/194	$200	$300

Guitar-Banjo 6/76 Dixi, SL-76

Ca. 1957-early 1970s. Banjo body, guitar neck, silver hardware.

1957-1970s		$525	$700

Hollywood

1960s. Double-cut, 3 pickups, red sunburst.

1960s	Model 5/132	$850	$1,100

Jan Akkerman

1974-1977. Single-cut semi-hollowbody, 2 pickups, gold hardware.

1974-1977		$500	$650

Jumbo

1963 to late-1970s. Models earlier 5/97, later 5/197, jumbo flat-top, mahogany or maple sides and back.

1960s-70s		$525	$675

Jumbo 12-String

Late-1960s to mid-1970s. 12-string version.

1960s-70s	Model 5/297	$525	$675

Missouri (E Framus Missouri)

Ca.1955-ca. 1975. Originally non-cut acoustic archtop until early '60s when single-cut archtop with 1 or 2 pickups added.

1960s	Model 5/60	$575	$750

MODEL YEAR	FEATURES	EXC. COND. LOW	HIGH

New Sound Series
1960s. Double-cut semi-hollowbody, model 5/116-52 has 2 pickups and 5/116-54 has 3.

1960s		$850	$1,100

Sorella Series
Ca.1955 to mid-1970s. Single-cut, Model 5/59 is acoustic archtop (with or without single pickup), 5/59-50 is 1-pickup electric archtop, 5/59-52 is electric 2-pickup.

1955-1975	Model 5/59	$725	$950
1965-1972	Model 5/59-50	$800	$1,050
1965-1972	Model 5/59-52	$800	$1,050

Sorento
Ca.1963-ca. 1970. Thinline archtop, single-cut, 2 pickups, organ effect, f-holes.

1963-1970	Model 5/112-53	$800	$1,050

Sorento 12
Ca.1963-ca. 1970. 12-string version.

1963-1970	Model 5/012	$850	$1,100

Sport
Early 1950s-mid-1970s. Small beginner flat-top, plain appointments, dot markers.

1950s-70s	Model 50/1	$190	$250

Strato de Luxe 12 String
Ca. 1963-ca. 1970. Model 5/067(metal pickguard) and 5/068 (wood grain pickguard and large gold cover plates), 2 pickups, tremolo.

1963-1970	Model 5/068	$800	$1,050

Strato de Luxe Series
Ca.1964-ca. 1970. Various models, 1 or 2 pickups (5/155, 5/167-52, 5/168-52), 3 pickups (5/167-54, 5/168-54), some models have gold hardware.

1964-1970	2 pickups	$675	$875
1964-1970	3 pickups	$725	$925

Strato Super
Early to late-1960s. Offset double-cut, 2 pickups.

1960s	Model 5/155-52	$725	$925

Studio Series
Late-1950s to mid-1970s. Model 5/51 (a.k.a. 030) is non-cut acoustic archtop (some with pickup - 5/51E), 5/108 is electric archtop, 1 pickup.

1960s-70s	Model 5/51	$200	$275
1960s-70s	Model 5/51E	$250	$325

Television Series
Early to late-1960s. Model 5/118-52 2 pickups and 5/118-54 3 pickups, offset double-cut thinline hollowbody.

1960s	Model 5/118-52	$650	$850
1960s	Model 5/118-54	$770	$1,000

Texan Series
Late-1960s to early-1980s. Model 5/196, 5/196E (with pickup) and 5/296 12-string flat-top, mahogany back and sides. 6-string ends in late '70s.

1960s-70s	6-string	$300	$400
1960s-80s	12-string	$300	$400

Western
1960s. Model 5/195, grand concert size, lower grade flat-top, spruce top, maple sides and back.

1960s	Model 5/195	$200	$275

Franklin Guitar Company
1974-present. Premium and presentation grade, custom, flat-top steel string guitars built first in Franklin, Michigan and since 2003 in Rocheport, Missouri by luthier Nick Kukich. He also built in Idaho, Washington and Oregon.

Fraulini
2001-present. Luthier Todd Cambio builds his professional and premium grade, primarily custom, early 20th century style guitars, in Madison, Wisconsin.

FreeNote
Intermediate to professional grade, the innovative FreeNote 12-Tone Ultra Plus provides two frets for every traditional fret placement which provides an unlimited number of playable notes.

Fresher
1973-1985. The Japanese-made Fresher brand models were mainly copies of popular brands and limited numbers were imported into the U.S. They also made basses.

Solidbody Electric
1970s. Import from Japan, various models.

1970s		$200	$500

Fret-King
2008-present. Luthier Trev Wilkinson builds professional and premium grade, production, solidbody and semi-hollow electric guitars and basses in Yorkshire, U.K., and also offers a line imported from Korea.

Fritz Brothers
1988-present. Premium grade, production/custom, acoustic, semi-hollow, and solidbody guitars and basses built by luthier Roger Fritz, originally in Mobile, Alabama, then in Mendocino, California. In 2013 he again relocated to Mobile.

Froggy Bottom Guitars
1974-present. Luthier Michael Millard builds his premium and presentation grade, production/custom flat-tops in Newfane, Vermont (originally in Hinsdale, New York, and until '84 production was in Richmond, New Hampshire).

Frudua Guitar Works
1988-present. Luthier Galeazzo Frudua builds his intermediate to premium grade, production/custom, electric guitars, basses and amps in Imola, Italy.

Fukuoka Musical Instruments
1993-present. Custom steel- and nylon-string flat-tops and archtops built in Japan.

1962 Framus Sorella Model 5/59-50
Rivington Guitars

Fritz Brothers Roy Buchanan Bluesmaster

1993 G&L ASAT Classic
Rivington Guitars

G&L ASAT Classic Bluesboy
Emmitt Omar

MODEL YEAR	FEATURES	EXC. COND. LOW	HIGH

Furch
See listing for Stonebridge.

Furnace Mountain Guitar Works
1995-1999. Instruments built by luthier Martin Fair in New Mexico. He currently builds under the Fairbuilt Guitar Co. brand.

Fury
1962-2017. Founded by Glenn McDougall in Saskatoon, Saskatchewan, Fury offered production, hollow, semi-hollow and solidbody electric guitars and basses. McDougall died in early '17.

Futurama
1957-mid to late 1960s. Futurama was a brand name used by Selmer in the United Kingdom. Early instruments made by the Drevokov Cooperative in Czechoslovakia, models for '63-'64 made by Sweden's Hagstrom company. Some later '60s instruments may have been made in Japan. Beatles fans will recognize the brand name as Beatle George Harrison's first electric.

Futurama I/II/III
1957-1969. Offset double-cut, 2- or 3-pickup versions available, large Futurama logo on headstock with the reverse capital letter F. George Harrison purchased his Futurama in '59; maple neck, 3 pickups, 3 push button levels, 2 knobs, Futurama logo on 'guard. The price shown for the Harrison model assumes an all-original, excellent condition that exactly matches his '59 model.

MODEL YEAR	FEATURES	EXC. COND. LOW	HIGH
1960-1969	III, Harrison, maple	$1,700	$4,800
1960-1969	III, rosewood	$975	$1,275

Fylde Guitars
1973-present. Luthier Roger Bucknall builds his professional and premium grade, production/custom acoustic guitars, basses, mandolins, mandolas, bouzoukis, and citterns in Penrith, Cumbria, UK.

G&L
1980-present. Intermediate and professional grade, production/custom, solidbody and semi-hollowbody electric guitars made in the U.S. and overseas. They also make basses. Founded by Leo Fender and George Fullerton following the severance of ties between Fender's CLF Research and Music Man. Company sold to John MacLaren and BBE Sound, when Leo Fender died in '91. In '98 they added their Custom Creations Department. In '03 G&L introduced the Korean-made G&L Tribute Series. George Fullerton died in July, '09.

ASAT
1986-1998. Called the Broadcaster in '85. Two or 3 single-coil or 2 single-coil/1 humbucker pickup configurations until early-'90s, 2 single-coils after.

MODEL YEAR	FEATURES	EXC. COND. LOW	HIGH
1986		$1,225	$1,600
1987	Leo sig on headstock	$1,225	$1,600
1988-1991	Leo sig on body	$1,225	$1,600
1992-1998	BBE era	$1,150	$1,500

MODEL YEAR	FEATURES	EXC. COND. LOW	HIGH

ASAT 20th Anniversary
2000. Limited Edition run of 50, ash body, tinted birdseye maple neck, 2-tone sunburst.

2000		$1,325	$1,725

ASAT '50
1999. Limited edition of 10.

1999		$1,325	$1,725

ASAT Bluesboy Limited Edition
1999. Limited edition of 20.

1999		$1,200	$1,550

ASAT Bluesboy Semi-Hollow Limited Edition
1999. Limited edition of 12, thin semi-hollow.

1999		$1,200	$1,550

ASAT Classic
1990-present. Two single-coil pickups, individually adjustable bridge saddles, neck-tilt adjustment and tapered string posts.

1990-1991	Leo sig on body	$1,000	$1,300
1992-1997	3-bolt neck	$825	$1,100
1997-2021	4-bolt neck	$825	$1,100

ASAT Classic B-Bender
1997. 12 made with factory-original B-Bender.

1997		$1,100	$1,450

ASAT Classic Bluesboy
2001-present. Humbucker neck pickup, single-coil at bridge.

2001-2021		$1,050	$1,400

ASAT Classic Bluesboy Rustic
2010-2015. Classic Bluesboy with Rustic aging and refinements.

2010-2015		$1,350	$1,800

ASAT Classic Bluesboy Semi-Hollow
1997-present. Chambered Classic with f-hole.

1997-2021		$1,200	$1,600

ASAT Classic Commemorative/Commemorative
1991-1992. Leo Fender signature and birth/death dating, Australian lacewood (6 made) and Cherryburst or Sunburst (1,000 made).

1991-1992	Australian	$7,000	$10,000
1991-1992	Cherryburst	$1,700	$2,200
1991-1992	Sunburst	$1,700	$2,200

ASAT Classic Custom
1996-1997, 2002-2013. Large rectangular neck pickup, single-coil bridge pickup. 2nd version has 4-bolt neck.

1996-1997	1st version	$1,100	$1,450
2002-2013	2nd version	$1,100	$1,450

ASAT Classic Custom Semi-Hollow
2002-2013. Custom with f-hole.

2002-2013		$1,075	$1,400

ASAT Classic S
2007. Limited run of 50, certificate, swamp ash body, 3 single-coil pickups, Nashville pickup configuration.

2007		$1,100	$1,450

ASAT Classic Semi-Hollow
1997-2021. With f-hole.

1997-2021		$1,100	$1,450

The *Vintage Guitar Price Guide* shows low to high values for items in all-original excellent condition, and, where applicable, with original case or cover.

MODEL YEAR	FEATURES	EXC. COND. LOW	HIGH
ASAT Classic Three			
1998. Limited Edition run of 100.			
1998		$1,250	$1,625
ASAT Custom			
1996. No pickguard, 25 to 30 made.			
1996		$1,075	$1,400
ASAT Deluxe			
1997-present. Flamed maple top, bound body, 2 humbuckers.			
1997	3-bolt neck	$1,250	$1,650
1997-2021	4-bolt neck	$1,250	$1,650
ASAT Deluxe Semi-Hollow			
1997-2018. Two humbuckers.			
1997-2018		$1,250	$1,650
ASAT III			
1988-1991, 1996-1998. Single-cut body, 3 single-coil pickups.			
1988-1991	Leo era, 150 made	$1,250	$1,650
1996-1998	Post Leo era	$1,250	$1,650
ASAT JD-5/Jerry Donahue JD-5			
2004-2007. Jerry Donahue model, single-cut, 2 single-coils, special wired 5-way switch.			
2004-2007		$1,350	$1,750
ASAT Junior			
1998-1999. Limited Edition run of 250, single-cut semi-hollowbody, 2 single-coils.			
1998-1999		$1,250	$1,650
ASAT S-3			
1998-2000. Three soap-bar single-coil pickups, limited production.			
1998-2000		$875	$1,150
ASAT Special			
1992-present. Like ASAT, but with 2 larger P-90-type pickups, chrome hardware, various colors.			
1992-1997	3-bolt neck	$1,050	$1,350
1997-2019	4-bolt neck	$1,050	$1,350
ASAT Special Semi-Hollow			
1997-2018. Semi-hollow version of ASAT Special.			
1997-2018		$875	$1,150
ASAT Special Deluxe			
2001-2015. No 'guard version of the Special with figured maple top.			
2001-2015		$1,125	$1,475
ASAT Special Detroit Muscle Series			
2015. Classic automobile colors include; Daytona Yellow, Hugger Orange, Cranberry Red and Marina Blue.			
2015		$1,050	$1,350
ASAT Z-2 Limited Edition			
1999. Limited run of 10, semi-hollow construction, natural ash, tortoise bound, engraved neckplate.			
1999		$1,250	$1,625
ASAT Z-3			
1998-2020. Three offset-style Z-3 high output pickups, sunburst.			
1998-2020		$1,050	$1,350
ASAT Z-3 Semi-Hollow			
1998-2020. F-hole version of Z-3.			
1998-2020		$1,050	$1,350

MODEL YEAR	FEATURES	EXC. COND. LOW	HIGH
Broadcaster			
1985-1986. Solidbody, 2 single-coils with adjustable polepieces act in humbucking mode with selector switch in the center position, black parts and finish, name changed to ASAT in early-'86.			
1985-1986	Kahler	$2,100	$2,800
1985-1986	Signed by Leo	$2,100	$2,800
Cavalier			
1983-1986. Offset double-cut, 2 humbuckers, 700 made, sunburst.			
1983-1986		$1,100	$1,425
Climax			
1992-1996. Offset double-cut, bolt maple neck, six-on-a-side tuners, double locking vibrato, blue.			
1992-1996		$950	$1,250
Climax Plus			
1992-1996. Two humbuckers replace single-coils of the Climax, plus 1 single-coil.			
1992-1996		$950	$1,250
Climax XL			
1992-1996. Two humbuckers only.			
1992-1996		$950	$1,250
Comanche V			
1988-1991. Solidbody, 3 Z-shaped single-coil humbuckers, maple neck in choice of 3 radii, rosewood 'board, vibrato, fine tuners, Leo Fender's signature on the body, sunburst.			
1988-1991		$1,225	$1,600
Comanche VI			
1990-1991. Leo Fender's signature on the body, 6 mini-toggles.			
1990-1991		$1,225	$1,600
Comanche (Reintroduced)			
1998-present. Reissue with either swamp ash or alder body, bolt-on maple neck, 3 Z-coil pickups, standard or premium finish options.			
1998-2021	Premium finish	$1,225	$1,600
1998-2021	Standard finish	$1,100	$1,425
Comanche Deluxe (Reintroduced)			
2018-present. Fullerton Deluxe series, old style double-cut, 3 Z-coil pickups, alder or swamp ash top, various colors with vintage tint satin finish.			
2018-2021		$1,175	$1,525
F-100 (Model I and II)			
1980-1986. Offset double-cut solidbody, 2 humbuckers, natural. Came in a I and II model - only difference is the radius of the 'board.			
1980-1986		$850	$1,100
F-100E (Model I and II)			
1980-1982. Offset double-cut solidbody, 2 humbuckers, active electronics, pre-amp, natural. Came in a I and II model - only difference is the radius of the 'board.			
1980-1982		$850	$1,100
Fallout			
2013-present. SC-2 body style, P-90 and humbucker, swamp ash body on premier and alder on standard finishes, maple neck, maple or rosewood 'board.			
2013-2021		$1,100	$1,450

G&L Comanche

1980 G&L F-100

G&L Fullerton Deluxe Dohney

G&L S-500

MODEL YEAR	FEATURES	EXC. COND. LOW	HIGH
Fullerton Deluxe Dohney			
2018-present. Fullerton Deluxe series, old style, 2 pickups, alder or swamp ash top, various colors with vintage tint satin finish.			
2018-2021		$1,050	$1,350
G-200/G-201			
1981-1982. Mahogany solidbody, maple neck, ebony 'board, 2 humbucking pickups, coil-split switches, natural or sunburst, 209 made.			
1981-1982	Front load	$2,100	$2,700
1981-1982	Rear load	$3,000	$4,000
GBL-LE (Guitars by Leo Limited Edition)			
1999. Limited edition of 25, semi-hollowbody, 3 pickups.			
1999		$1,200	$1,600
George Fullerton Signature			
1995-2007. Double-cut solidbody, sunburst.			
1995-1997	3-bolt neck	$1,250	$1,625
1997-2007	4-bolt neck	$1,250	$1,625
HG-1			
1982-1983. Offset double-cut, 1 humbucker, dot inlays. Very rare as most were made into HG-2s.			
1982-1983	5 made	$1,700	$2,200
HG-2			
1982-1984. 2-humbucker HG, body changes to classic offset double-cut in '84.			
1982-1983	Mustang-body	$1,400	$1,800
1984	Double-cut	$1,400	$1,800
Interceptor			
1983-1991. To '86 an X-shaped solidbody, either 3 single-coils, 2 humbuckers, or 1 humbucker and 2 single-coils, '87-'91 was an offset double-cut solidbody.			
1983-1985	1st X-body, 70 made	$2,700	$3,500
1985-1986	2nd X-body, 12 made	$2,700	$3,500
1987-1991	Double-cut	$1,400	$1,800
Invader			
1984-1991, 1998-2018. Double-cut solidbody, 2 single-coil and 1 humbucker pickups.			
1984-1991	1st version	$1,200	$1,600
1998-2018	2nd version	$1,200	$1,600
Invader Plus			
1998-2018. Two humbuckers and single blade pickup in the middle position.			
1998-2018		$1,150	$1,500
Invader XL			
1998-2018. Fancy top, 2 humbuckers.			
1998-2018		$1,300	$1,700
John Jorgenson Signature ASAT			
1995. About 190 made, Silver Metalflake finish.			
1995		$1,300	$1,700
Legacy			
1992-present. Classic double-cut configuration, USA logo, 3-bolt neck until '97, 4-bolt after, various colors.			
1992-1994	3-bolt, Duncans	$1,000	$1,300
1995-1997	3-bolt, Alnicos	$1,000	$1,300
1996-1997	Swirl finish	$1,150	$1,500
1998-2021	4-bolt, Alnicos	$1,000	$1,300
Legacy Deluxe			
2001-2015. No 'guard, figured maple top.			
2001-2015		$1,050	$1,350

MODEL YEAR	FEATURES	EXC. COND. LOW	HIGH
Legacy HH			
2001-present. Two humbucker pickups.			
2001-2021		$1,000	$1,300
Legacy HSS			
2001-present. One humbucker pickup at bridge position plus 2 single-coil pickups.			
2001-2021		$1,000	$1,300
Legacy Special			
1993-present. Legacy with 3 humbuckers, various colors.			
1992-1997	3-bolt neck	$1,000	$1,300
1998-2021	4-bolt neck	$1,000	$1,300
Limited Edition 25th Anniversary			
2006. G&L Custom Creations, 250 made, combines appearance of '81 F-100 with contours and control layout of ASAT Super, single-cut mahogany body, 2 custom wound MFD humbuckers, custom blend 'root beer' finish.			
2006		$1,125	$1,450
Nighthawk			
1983. Offset double-cut solidbody, 269 made, 3 single-coil pickups, sunburst, name changed to Sky-hawk in '84.			
1983		$875	$1,150
Rampage			
1984-1991. Offset double-cut solidbody, hard rock maple neck, ebony 'board, 1 bridge-position hum-bucker pickup, sunburst. Currently available as Jerry Cantrell Signature Model.			
1984-1991	Common color	$1,150	$1,500
1984-1991	Rare color	$1,700	$2,200
Rampage (Reissue)			
2000. Limited Edition run of 70, supplied with gig bag and not hard case, ivory finish.			
2000		$700	$900
S-500			
1982-present. Double-cut mahogany or ash solid-body, maple neck, ebony or maple 'board, 3 single-coil pickups, vibrato.			
1982-1987		$1,150	$1,500
1988-1991	Mini-toggle, Leo sig on body	$1,050	$1,350
1992-1997	3-bolt neck	$850	$1,100
1997-2021	4-bolt neck	$850	$1,100
S-500 Deluxe			
2001-2015. Deluxe Series features, including no 'guard and flamed maple top, natural.			
2001-2015		$1,050	$1,350
SC-1			
1982-1983. Offset double-cut solidbody, 1 single-coil pickup, tremolo, sunburst, 250 made.			
1981-1982		$875	$1,150
SC-2			
1982-1983, 2010-2018. Offset double-cut solidbody, shallow cutaways change to deeper pointed in '83, 2 MFD soapbar pickups, about 600 made in original run. Reissue maple or rosewood 'board.			
1982-1983		$1,200	$1,550
2010-2018	Reissue	$650	$850

MODEL YEAR	FEATURES	EXC. COND. LOW	HIGH

SC-3
1982-1991. Offset double-cut solidbody, shallow cutaway changes to deeper pointed in '84, 3 single-coil pickups, tremolo.

1982-1987	No 'guard	$1,000	$1,300
1988-1991	With 'guard	$925	$1,200

Skyhawk
1984-1991. Renamed from Nighthawk, offset double-cut, 3 single-coils, signature on headstock '84-'87, then on body '88-'91.

1984-1987	Dual-Fulcrum or saddle lock	$950	$1,250
1984-1987	Kahler	$750	$975
1988-1991	Dual-Fulcrum or saddle lock	$775	$1,000
1988-1991	Kahler	$725	$950

Superhawk
1984-1987. Offset double-cut, maple neck, ebony 'board, G&L or Kahler tremolos, 2 humbuckers, signature on headstock.

1984-1987		$875	$1,150

Tribute Series
2003-present. Import versions of regular models.

2003-2021	Various models	$250	$700

Trinity
2006. Only 25 made, ASAT-style with 3 new style single-coils, designed by Tim Page of Buffalo Brothers, the last G&L to have COA signed by George Fullerton.

2006		$1,700	$2,200

Will Ray Signature
2002-2018. Will Ray signature on headstock, 3 Z-coil pickups, Hipshot B-Bender.

2002-2018		$800	$1,050

G.L. Stiles
1960-1994. Built by Gilbert Lee Stiles primarily in the Miami, Florida area. First solidbody, including pickups and all hardware, built by hand in his garage. Stiles favored scrolls, fancy carving and walnut fingerboards. His later instruments were considerably fancier and more refined. He moved to Hialeah, Florida by '63 and began making acoustic guitars and other instruments. Only his solidbodies had consecutive serial numbers. Stiles, who died in '94, made approximately 1000 solidbodies and 500 acoustics.

Gadotti Guitars
1997-present. Luthier Jeanfranco Biava Gadotti builds his premium grade, custom/production, nylon- and steel-string, carved, chambered solidbodies in Orlando, Florida.

Gadow Guitars
2002-2019. Luthier Ryan Gadow built his professional and premium grade, custom/production, solid and semi-hollow body guitars and basses in Durham, North Carolina.

MODEL YEAR	FEATURES	EXC. COND. LOW	HIGH

Gagnon
Luthier Bill Gagnon began building his premium and presentation grade, production/custom, archtop guitars in Beaverton, Oregon, starting in 1998.

Galanti
Ca.1962-ca.1967. Electric guitars offered by the longtime Italian accordion maker, some built by Zero Sette. They may have also offered acoustics.

Electric
1962-1967. Solidbody or hollowbody.

1962-1967	Fancy features	$600	$1,000
1962-1967	Plain features	$350	$700

Galiano
New Yorkers Antonio Cerrito and Raphael Ciani offered guitars under the Galiano brand during the early part of the last century. They used the brand both on guitars built by them and others, including The Oscar Schmidt Company. They also offered mandolins.

Gallagher
1965-present. Professional and premium grade, production/custom, flat-top guitars built in Wartrace, Tennessee. J. W. Gallagher started building Shelby brand guitars in the Slingerland Drum factory in Shelbyville, Tennessee in '63. In '65 he and his son Don made the first Gallagher guitar, the G-50. Doc Watson began using Gallagher guitars in '68. In '76, Don assumed operation of the business when J. W. semi-retired. J. W. died in '79.

71 Special
1970s-2015. Rosewood back and sides, spruce top, herringbone trim, bound ebony 'board, natural.

1970s-2015		$2,100	$2,700

72 Special
1977-2016. Rosewood back and sides, spruce top, abalone trim, bound ebony 'board, natural.

1977-2016		$3,700	$4,800

A-70 Ragtime Special
1978-2015. Smaller auditorium/00 size, spruce top, mahogany back and sides, G logo, natural.

1978-2015		$1,450	$1,900

Custom 12-String
Introduced in 1965-present. Mahogany, 12-fret neck, natural.

1965		$1,550	$2,000

Doc Watson
1968-present. Spruce top, mahogany back and sides, scalloped bracing, ebony 'board, herringbone trim, natural.

1968-2021		$2,600	$3,400

Doc Watson (Cutaway)
1975-2010. Spruce top, mahogany back and sides, scalloped bracing, ebony 'board, herringbone trim, natural.

1975-2010		$2,700	$3,600

Doc Watson 12-String
1995-2000. Natural.

1995-2000		$2,300	$3,000

1987 G&L SC-3
Carter Vintage Guitars

G&L Tribute ASAT Classic

GUITARS

Gallaher Doc Watson Signature

2017 Gallagher G-70

MODEL YEAR	FEATURES	EXC. COND. LOW	HIGH

Doc Watson Signature
2000-present. Signature inlay 12th fret.

2000-2021		$2,700	$3,600

G-45
1970-2008. Mahogany back and sides, spruce top, ebony 'board, natural.

1970-1979		$1,600	$2,100
1980-2008		$1,350	$1,750

G-50
1960s-2015. Mahogany back and sides, spruce top, ebony 'board, natural.

1960s		$2,400	$3,100
1970-2015		$1,775	$2,300

G-65
1980s-2015. Rosewood back and sides, spruce top, ebony 'board, natural.

1980s-2015		$1,850	$2,400

G-70
1978-present. Rosewood back and sides, herringbone purfling on top and soundhole, mother-of-pearl diamond 'board inlays, bound headstock, natural.

1978-2021		$1,850	$2,400

G-71
1970s. Indian rosewood, gold tuners.

1970s		$2,200	$2,900

Gallagher, Kevin
1996. Kevin Gallagher, luthier, changed name brand to Omega to avoid confusion with J.W. Gallagher. See Omega listing.

Gallotone
1950s-1960s. Low-end foreign brand similar to 1950s Stellas, the Gallotone Champion, a 3/4 size student flat-top, is associated with John Lennon as his early guitar.

Galloup Guitars
1994-present. Luthier Bryan Galloup builds his professional and premium grade, production/custom flat-tops in Big Rapids, Michigan. He also operates the Galloup School of Lutherie and The Guitar Hospital repair and restoration business.

Galveston
Budget and intermediate grade, production, imported acoustic, acoustic/electric, resonator and solidbody guitars. They also offer basses and mandolins.

Gamble & O'Toole
1978-present. Premium grade, custom classical and steel string guitars built by luthier Arnie Gamble in Sacramento, California, with design input and inlay work from his wife Erin O'Toole.

Ganz Guitars
1995-present. Luthier Steve Ganz builds his professional grade, production/custom classical guitars in Bellingham, Washington.

Garcia
Made by luthier Federico Garcia in Spain until late-1960s or very early-'70s when production moved to Japan.

Classical
1960s-1970s. Mid-level, '60s model is solid spruce top with solid mahogany, rosewood or walnut back and sides, '70s model is Spanish pine top with walnut back and sides.

1960s-70s	Various wood	$250	$400
1970s	Spanish pine/ Brazilian	$500	$750

Garrison
2000-2007. Intermediate and professional grade, production, acoustic and acoustic/electric guitars designed by luthier Chris Griffiths using his Active Bracing System (a single integrated glass-fiber bracing system inside a solid wood body). He started Griffiths Guitar Works in 1993 in St. John's, Newfoundland, and introduced Garrison guitars in 2000. In '07, the Garrison facility was acquired by Gibson.

Gary Kramer
2006-present. Intermediate and professional grade, production/custom, solidbody electric guitars built by luthier Gary Kramer in El Segundo, California, and imported. Kramer was one of the founders of the Kramer guitar company in the '70s.

Gauge Guitars
Luthier Aaron Solomon builds custom, professional and premium grade, solidbody and semi-solid electric guitars in New Jersey, starting in 2002.

Gemelli
Early 1960s-ca. 1966. European-made (likely Italian) guitars. Similar to Bartolini guitars, so most likely from same manufacturer. Originally plastic covered, they switched to paint finishes by around '65.

Gemunder
1870s-1910s. New York shop that specialized in reproduction-aged violins, but also made parlor-sized guitars that were similar to Martin guitars of the era. An original label on the inside back identifies August Gemunder and Sons, New York.

Parlor
1870s-1910s. Style 28 appointments, rosewood body, spruce top.

1870-1910s		$1,200	$1,600

George
See listing under Chris George.

German Guitars
2001-present. Luthier Greg German builds his premium grade, custom/production, acoustic archtop guitars in Broomfield, Colorado.

MODEL YEAR	FEATURES	EXC. COND. LOW	HIGH

Giannini

1900-present. Classical, acoustic, and acoustic/electric guitars built in Salto, SP, Brazil near Sao Paolo. They also build violas, cavaquinhos and mandolins. Founded by guitar-builder Tranquillo Giannini, an Italian who traveled to Brazil in 1890 and discovered the exotic woods of Brazil. The company was producing 30,000 instruments a year by '30. They began exporting their acoustic instruments to the U.S. in '63. They added electric guitars in '60, but these weren't imported as much, if at all. Gianninis from this era used much Brazilian Rosewood.

Classical
Early-1970s. Nylon string import, small body.

1970s	Brazilian rosewood	$450	$600
1970s	Pau ferro, mahogany	$175	$375

CraViolia
1972-1974, 2004-present. Kidney bean-shaped rosewood body, acoustic, natural, line included a classical, a steel string, and a 12-string.

1972-1974	$575	$750

CraViolia 12-String
1972-1974, 2004-present. Kidney bean-shaped body, 12 strings.

1972-1974	$575	$750

Gibson

1890s (1902)-present. Intermediate, professional, and premium grade, production/custom, acoustic and electric guitars made in the U.S. They also build basses, mandolins, amps, and banjos. Gibson also offers instruments under the Epiphone, Kramer, Steinberger, Dobro, Tobias, Valley Arts, Garrison, Slingerland (drums), Baldwin (pianos), Trace Elliot, Electar (amps), Maestro, Gibson Labs, Oberheim, and Echoplex brands.

Founded in Kalamazoo, Michigan by Orville Gibson, a musician and luthier who developed instruments with tops, sides and backs carved out of solid pieces of wood. Early instruments included mandolins, archtop guitars and harp guitars. By 1896 Gibson had opened a shop. In 1902 Gibson was bought out by a group of investors who incorporated the business as Gibson Mandolin-Guitar Manufacturing Company, Limited. The company was purchased by Chicago Musical Instrument Company (CMI) in '44. In '57 CMI also purchased the Epiphone guitar company, transferring production from Philadelphia to the Gibson plant in Kalamazoo. Gibson was purchased by Norlin in late-'69 and a new factory was opened in Nashville, Tennessee in '74. The Kalamazoo factory ceased production in '84. In '85, Gibson was sold to a group headed by Henry Juskewiscz. Gibson purchased the Flatiron Company in '87 and built a new factory in '89, moving acoustic instrument production to Bozeman, Montana. In '18 Gibson went into Chapter 11 bankruptcy, emerging later in the year with KKR as new majority owner and James "JC" Curleigh as CEO.

The various models of Firebirds, Flying Vs, Les Pauls, SGs, and Super 400s are grouped together under those general headings. Custom Shop and Historic instruments are listed with their respective main model (for example, the '39 Super 400 Historical Collection model is listed with the Super 400s).

Model specifications can cross model years. For example, it is possible that an early '60 Gibson guitar might have a specification, such as a wider-rounder neck, which is typically a '59 spec. In that case it is possible for the early '60 model to be valued more closely to the late '59 model than to a mid to late '60 model with a thinner-flatter neck profile.

Orville Gibson
1894-1902. Hand-made and carved by Orville Gibson, various models and sizes most with standard printed white rectangle label "O.H. Gibson" with photo of Orville Gibson and lyre-mandolin. Prices are for fully functional original or refurbished examples. It is almost expected that a black Orville Gibson instrument has been refinished, and most of those were done by Gibson.

1894-1902	Basic plain model	$4,500	$55,000
1894-1902	Fancy rare model	$55,000	$70,000
1894-1902	Very rare, historical	$70,000	$95,000

335 S Custom
1980-1981. Solidbody, 335-shaped, mahogany body, unbound rosewood 'board, 2 exposed Dirty Finger humbuckers, coil-tap, TP-6 tailpiece. Also available in natural finish, branded headstock Firebrand version.

1980-1981	$1,350	$1,750

335 S Deluxe
1980-1982. Same as 335 S Custom but with bound ebony 'board, brass nut.

1980-1982	$1,350	$1,750

335 S Limited Run
2011-2013. Maple body and neck, rosewood 'board, nitro-finish sunburst.

2011-2013	$1,175	$1,525

335 S Standard
1980-1981. Same as 335 S Custom except stop tailpiece, no coil-tap. Also available in natural finish, branded headstock Firebrand version.

1980-1981	$1,350	$1,750

Advanced Jumbo
1936-1940. Dreadnought, 16" wide, round shoulders, Brazilian rosewood back and sides, sunburst, reintroduced '90-'97.

1936-1940	$70,000	$90,000

Advanced Jumbo (Reissue)
1990-1999, 2002-2018. Issued as a standard production model, but soon available only as a special order for most of the '90s; currently offered as standard production. Renamed 1936 Advanced Jumbo for 1997-1998. There were also some limited-edition AJs offered during the '90s.

1990-1999	Reissue	$2,100	$2,800
2002-2018	Reintroduced	$2,300	$3,000

Advanced Jumbo 12
2015. 12-fret neck.

2015	$2,400	$3,200

German DB6

1972 Giannini Craviola 12-String
Tom Pfeifer

*Gibson Randy Scruggs
Advanced Jumbo Limited Edition*

*2005 Gibson B.B. King
80th Birthday Lucille*

MODEL YEAR	FEATURES	EXC. COND. LOW	HIGH

Advanced Jumbo 75th Anniversary
2011-2012. 75th Anniversary label, 2nd edition 75 made with on-board electronics.

2011	1st edition	$2,400	$3,200
2012	2nd edition	$2,400	$3,200

1935 Advanced Jumbo
2013. Limited run of 35, Adirondack red spruce top, Indian rosewood back and sides, Vintage Sunburst.

2013		$4,300	$5,600

Advanced Jumbo Koa
2006. Custom Shop, koa back and sides, Adirondack top.

2006		$2,700	$3,500

Advanced Jumbo Luthier's Choice
2000-2008. Custom Shop, various wood options.

2000-2005	Brazilian	$6,700	$8,700
2008	Cocobolo	$3,400	$4,400

Advanced Jumbo Pro
2011-2013. Made for Guitar Center, Baggs pickup, Sitka top, solid rosewood back and sides.

2011-2013		$1,550	$2,000

Advanced Jumbo Red Spruce/AJ Red Spruce
2013. Limited Edition, Adirondack red spruce top, rosewood back and sides.

2013		$2,150	$2,800

Advanced Jumbo Supreme
2007. Custom Shop, Madagascar rosewood back and sides, Adirondack spruce top.

2007		$2,700	$3,500

Iron Mountain Advanced Jumbo
2014. Custom Shop model, limited run of 65, Adirondack red spruce top, Birdseye maple back and sides, Honeyburst finish.

2014		$2,700	$3,500

Randy Scruggs Advanced Jumbo Limited Edition
2010-2018. Sitka spruce top, East Indian rosewood body, king's crown headstock logo on, crown markers, Fishman pickup, vintage sunburst.

2010-2018		$2,700	$3,500

All American I
1995-1997. Solidbody electric with vague double-cut Melody Maker body style, 1 pickup. Renamed the SG-X in '98.

1995-1997		$600	$800

All American II
1996-1997. As American I with 2 pickups.

1996-1997		$650	$850

B.B. King Custom
1980-1988. Lucille on peghead, 2 pickups, multibound, gold-plated parts, Vari-tone, cherry or ebony, renamed B.B. King Lucille in '88.

1980-1988		$2,900	$3,800

B.B. King Lucille
1988-2019. Introduced as B.B. King Custom, renamed B.B. King Lucille. Lucille on peghead, 2 pickups, multi-bound, gold-plated parts, Vari-tone, cherry or ebony. In '07 B.B. King logo and large king's crown on headstock with Lucille logo on truss rod cover.

1988-2019		$2,900	$3,800
2007-2009	King logo	$2,900	$3,800

B.B. King Standard
1980-1985. Like B.B. King Custom, but with stereo electronics and chrome-plated parts, cherry or ebony.

1980-1985		$2,500	$3,300

B.B. King 80th Birthday Lucille
2005. Custom Shop, limited run of 80, 'guard engraved with crown and signature, headstock engraved with artwork from King's birthday tribute album.

2005		$4,700	$6,100

B.B. King Super Lucille
2002-2004. Signed guard, abalone inlays, custom black sparkle finish.

2002-2004		$4,200	$5,400

B-15
1967-1971. Mahogany, spruce top, student model, natural finish.

1967-1971		$850	$1,100

B-20
1971-1972. 14.5" flat-top, mahogany back and sides, dot markers, decal logo, strip in-line tuners with small buttons.

1971-1972		$1,150	$1,500

B-25 3/4 / B-25N 3/4
1962-1968. Short-scale version, flat-top, mahogany body, cherry sunburst (natural finish is the B-25 3/4N).

1962	Wood bridge	$1,250	$1,625
1963-1964	Plastic bridge	$1,075	$1,400
1965		$950	$1,250
1966-1968		$875	$1,150

B-25/B-25N
1962-1977, 2008-2012. Flat-top, mahogany, bound body, upper belly on bridge (lower belly '68 on), cherry sunburst or black (natural finish is B-25N). Reissued in '08.

1962	Wood bridge	$2,150	$2,800
1963-1964	Plastic bridge	$2,150	$2,800
1965		$1,625	$2,125
1966-1968	Above belly bridge	$1,550	$2,000
1968	Black, white 'guard	$3,100	$4,000
1968	Red, white 'guard	$2,625	$3,425
1969	Below belly bridge	$1,250	$1,625
1970-1977		$1,150	$1,500
2008-2012	Reissue, black	$1,425	$1,850

B-25-12/B-25-12N
1962-1977. Flat-top 12-string version, mahogany, bound body, cherry sunburst (natural finish is the B-25-12N).

1962-1964	No tailpiece	$1,775	$2,300
1965	Trapeze tailpiece	$1,400	$1,825
1966-1968	Trapeze tailpiece	$1,325	$1,725
1969	Below belly bridge	$1,125	$1,475
1970-1977		$1,050	$1,375

B-45-12/B-45-12N
1960-1979. Flat-top 12-string, mahogany, round shoulders for '60-'61, square after, sunburst (natural finish is the B-45-12N).

1960	Early specs	$2,800	$3,600
1961-1962	Round shoulder	$2,000	$2,600
1962-1963	Square shoulder	$2,000	$2,600
1964	No tailpiece	$2,000	$2,600
1965	Trapeze tailpiece	$1,400	$1,800
1966-1968		$1,400	$1,800

MODEL YEAR	FEATURES	EXC. COND. LOW	HIGH
1969	Below belly bridge	$1,200	$1,600
1970-1979		$1,125	$1,450

B-45-12 Limited Edition
1991-1992. Limited edition reissue with rosewood back and sides, natural.

1991-1992		$1,125	$1,450

Barney Kessel Custom
1961-1973. Double-cut archtop, 2 humbuckers, gold hardware, cherry sunburst.

1961	PAFs	$7,900	$10,300
1962	Pat #	$5,200	$6,700
1963-1964		$5,200	$6,700
1965		$4,600	$6,000
1966-1969		$4,400	$5,700
1970-1973		$3,400	$4,400

Barney Kessel Regular
1961-1974. Double-cut archtop, 2 humbuckers, nickel hardware, cherry sunburst.

1961	PAFs	$7,600	$9,900
1962	Pat #	$4,800	$6,300
1963-1964		$4,800	$6,300
1965		$4,300	$5,600
1966-1969		$4,200	$5,400
1970-1974		$3,000	$3,950

Blue Ridge
1968-1979, 1989-1990. Flat-top, dreadnought, laminated rosewood back and sides, natural finish, reintroduced for '89-'90.

1968-1969	Brazilian	$1,275	$1,650
1970-1979		$1,275	$1,650

Blue Ridge 12
1970-1978. Flat-top, 12 strings, laminated rosewood back and sides, natural finish.

1970-1978		$1,275	$1,650

Blues King
2012-2013. Acoustic/electric, non-cut, bubinga back and sides, dot inlays.

2012-2013		$1,750	$2,275

Blueshawk
1996-2006. Small single-cut, f-holes, 2 single-coil hum cancelling Blues 90 pickups, 6-way Varitone dial, gold hardware, Bigsby option starts '98.

1996-2006		$1,000	$1,300

B-SJ Blue Ridge
1989. Model name on label is B-SJ, truss rod covers logo is Blue Ridge, SJ appointments but with narrow peghead shape.

1989		$1,500	$1,950

Byrdland
1955-1992. Thinline archtop, single-cut (rounded until late-'60, pointed '60-late-'69, rounded after '69, rounded or pointed '98-present), 2 pickups, now part of the Historic Collection.

1956-1957	Natural, Alnicos	$9,600	$12,500
1956-1957	Sunburst, Alnicos	$9,600	$12,500
1958-1959	Natural, PAFs	$14,300	$18,500
1958-1959	Sunburst, PAFs	$14,300	$18,500
1960-1962	Natural, PAFs	$12,800	$16,700
1960-1962	Sunburst, PAFs	$12,800	$16,700
1963-1964	Natural, pat #	$7,800	$10,200
1963-1964	Sunburst, pat #	$7,800	$10,200

MODEL YEAR	FEATURES	EXC. COND. LOW	HIGH
1965	Natural	$7,000	$9,000
1965	Sunburst	$7,000	$9,000
1966-1969	Natural	$5,800	$7,500
1966-1969	Sunburst	$5,800	$7,500
1970-1992	Various colors	$4,400	$5,700

Byrdland Historic Collection
1993-2018. Custom shop, various colors.

1993-2018		$5,300	$7,000

C-0 Classical
1962-1971. Spruce top, mahogany back and sides, bound top, natural.

1962-1964		$675	$875
1965		$575	$750
1966-1971		$525	$700

C-1 Classical
1957-1971. Spruce top, mahogany back and sides, bound body, natural.

1957-1959		$700	$925
1960-1964		$675	$875
1965		$600	$775
1966-1971		$540	$700

C-1 D Laredo
1963-1971. Natural spruce top, mahogany sides and back, upgrade to standard C-1.

1963-1965		$675	$875

C-1 E Classical Electric
1960-1967. C-1 with ceramic bridge pickup, catalog notes special matched amplifier that filters out fingering noises.

1960-1964		$700	$925
1965		$600	$785
1966-1967		$540	$700

C-1 S Petite Classical
1961-1966. Petite 13 1/4" body, natural spruce top, mahogany back and sides.

1961-1964		$675	$875
1965		$600	$775
1966-1967		$540	$700

C-2 Classical
1960-1971. Maple back and sides, bound body, natural.

1960-1964		$775	$1,000
1965		$700	$900
1966-1971		$625	$825

C-4 Classical
1962-1968. Maple back and sides, natural.

1962-1964		$775	$1,000
1965		$700	$925
1966-1968		$675	$875

C-6 Classical/Richard Pick
1958-1971. Rosewood back and sides, gold hardware, natural.

1958-1959	Brazilian	$1,625	$2,125
1960-1964	Brazilian	$1,500	$1,950
1965	Brazilian	$1,375	$1,800
1966-1969	Brazilian	$1,250	$1,625
1970-1971	Indian	$775	$1,000

C-8 Classical
1962-1969. Rosewood back and sides, natural.

1962-1964		$1,500	$1,950
1965		$1,375	$1,800
1966-1969		$1,250	$1,625

1964 Gibson B-25-12N
Ted Wulfers

1967 Gibson C-O
Imaged by Heritage Auctions, HA.com

To get the most from this book, be sure to read "Using *The Guide*" in the introduction.

GUITARS

1982 Gibson Chet Atkins CE
Geoff Barker

1984 Gibson Corvus II
Imaged by Heritage Auctions, HA.com

MODEL YEAR	FEATURES	EXC. COND. LOW	HIGH

C-100 Classical
1971-1972. Slotted peghead, spruce top, mahogany back and sides, ebony 'board, Gibson Master Model label, non-gloss finish.

| 1971-1972 | | $540 | $700 |

C-200 Classical
1971-1972. C-100 with gloss finish.

| 1971-1972 | | $625 | $825 |

C-300 Classical
1971-1972. Similar to C-100, but with rosewood 'board, wood binding, wider soundhole ring.

| 1971-1972 | | $625 | $825 |

C-400 Classical
1971-1972. Rosewood sides and back, spruce top, high-end appointments, chrome hardware.

| 1971-1972 | | $675 | $875 |

C-500 Classical
1971-1972. C-400 with gold hardware.

| 1971-1972 | | $775 | $1,000 |

CF-100
1950-1958. Flat-top, pointed cutaway, mahogany back and sides, bound body, sunburst finish.

| 1950-1958 | | $5,400 | $7,000 |

CF-100 E
1951-1959, 2009. CF-100 with a single-coil pickup. Also offered in '94 1950 CF-100 E limited edition and in '07 as a Custom Shop model.

| 1950-1959 | | $5,200 | $6,900 |

CF-100 E Reissue
2007. Custom Shop, all maple body, ebony 'board, 24 made.

| 2007 | | $2,150 | $2,800 |

Challenger I
1983-1985. Single-cut Les Paul-shaped solidbody, 1 humbucker, bolt-on maple neck, rosewood 'board, dot markers, silver finish standard.

| 1983-1985 | | $600 | $775 |

Challenger II
1983-1985. 2 humbucker version.

| 1983-1985 | | $625 | $825 |

Challenger III
1984. 3 single-coil version, never cataloged so could be very limited.

| 1984 | | $650 | $850 |

Chet Atkins CE
1981-2005. CE stands for Classical Electric, single-cut, multi-bound body, rosewood 'board until '95, then ebony, standard width nut, gold hardware, various colors.

| 1981-2005 | | $1,400 | $1,825 |

Chet Atkins CEC
1981-2005. Same as CE, but with ebony 'board and 2" classical width nut, black or natural.

| 1981-2005 | | $1,400 | $1,825 |

Chet Atkins Country Gentleman
1986-2005. Thinline archtop, single rounded cutaway, 2 humbuckers, multi-bound, gold hardware, Bigsby. Part of Gibson's Custom line.

| 1986-2005 | | $2,450 | $3,200 |

Chet Atkins SST
1987-2006. Steel string acoustic/electric solidbody, single-cut, bridge transducer pickup, active bass and treble controls, gold hardware.

1987-1993	White	$2,000	$2,600
1987-2006	Black	$2,000	$2,600
1987-2006	Natural	$1,300	$1,700
1993	Red Wine or Antique	$2,000	$2,600
1994	Cherry Sunburst	$2,000	$2,600

Chet Atkins SST Celebrity
1991-1993. Gold hardware, 200 made, black body with unique white 'guard.

| 1991-1993 | | $2,200 | $2,900 |

Chet Atkins SST-12
1990-1994. 12-string model similar to 6-string, mahogany/spruce body, preamp circuit controls single transducer pickup, natural or ebony finish.

| 1990-1994 | | $1,300 | $1,700 |

Chet Atkins Super 4000
1997-2000. Custom Shop, figured curly maple back and sides, orange amber finish, 25 built, COA.

| 1997-2000 | | $19,000 | $25,000 |

Chet Atkins Tennessean
1990-2005. Single rounded cutaway archtop, 2 humbuckers, f-holes, bound body. Part of Gibson's Custom line.

| 1990-2005 | | $1,550 | $2,000 |

Chicago 35
1994-1995. Flat-top dreadnought, round shoulders, mahogany back and sides, prewar script logo.

| 1994-1995 | | $1,125 | $1,450 |

Citation
1969-1971. 17" full-depth body, single-cut archtop, 1 or 2 floating pickups, fancy inlay, natural or sunburst. Only 8 shipped for '69-'71, reissued the first time '79-'83 and as part of the Historic Collection in '93.

| 1969-1971 | | $19,000 | $25,000 |

Citation (1st Reissue)
1979-1983. Reissue of '69-'71 model, natural or sunburst. Reintroduced in '93 as part of Gibson's Historic Collection.

| 1979-1983 | | $19,000 | $25,000 |

Citation (2nd Reissue)
1993-2018. Limited production via Gibson's Historic Collection, natural or sunburst.

| 1994-2018 | | $14,500 | $19,000 |

Citation Vanderbilt Rose
2015. Custom Shop, very few made, Vanderbilt Rose lacquer finish with matching maple 'guard.

| 2015 | | $8,000 | $10,500 |

CJ-165/CJ-165 Modern Classic
2006-2008. Called J-165 in first year of production, classic small body non-cutaway flat-top, solid spruce top, maple or rosewood back and sides.

| 2006-2008 | | $1,575 | $2,050 |

CJ-165 EC Modern Classic
2007-2009. As above, but with single-cut, electronics, maple or rosewood back and sides.

| 2007-2009 | | $1,750 | $2,275 |

MODEL YEAR	FEATURES	EXC. COND. LOW	HIGH

CL-10 Standard
1997-1998. Flat-top, solid spruce top, laminated mahogany back and sides.

1997-1998		$975	$1,275

CL-20 Standard Plus
1997-1998. Flat-top, laminated back and sides, 4-ply binding with tortoiseshell appointments, abalone diamond inlays.

1997-1998		$1,175	$1,525

CL-30 Deluxe
1997-1998. J-50 style dreadnought, solid spruce top, bubinga back and sides, factory electronics.

1997-1998		$1,200	$1,575

CL-35 Deluxe
1998. Single cutaway CL-30.

1998		$1,300	$1,700

CL-40 Artist
1997-1998. Flat-top, gold hardware, rosewood back and sides.

1997-1998		$1,750	$2,275

CL-45 Artist
1997-1998. Single cutaway CL-40.

1997-1998		$1,850	$2,375

CL-50
1997-1999. Custom Shop model, D-style body, high-er-end appointments, offered with Brazilian rosewood.

1997-1999		$3,700	$4,800

Corvus I
1982-1984. Odd-shaped solidbody with offset V-type cut, bolt maple neck, rosewood 'board, 1 humbucker, standard finish was silver gloss, but others available at an additional cost.

1982-1984		$1,050	$1,350

Corvus II
1982-1984. Same as Corvus I, but with 2 humbuckers, 2 volume controls, 1 master tone control.

1982-1984		$1,150	$1,500

Corvus III
1982-1984. Same as Corvus I, but with 3 single-coil pickups, master volume and tone control, 5-way switch.

1982-1984		$1,300	$1,700

Crest Gold
1969-1971. Double-cut thinline archtop, Brazilian rosewood body, 2 pickups, bound top and headstock, bound f-holes, gold-plated parts. The Crest name was also used on a few (3-6) custom guitars based on the L-5CT built in 1959-'61.

1969-1971		$5,800	$7,500

Crest Silver
1969-1972. Silver-plated parts version of Crest.

1969-1972		$5,200	$6,800

CS Series
2002-2017. Custom Shop, scaled down ES-335 body style, plain top or F indicates figured top.

2002-2003	CS-356	$2,400	$3,100
2002-2012	CS-336F	$2,775	$3,600
2002-2014	CS-356F	$3,200	$4,200
2002-2017	CS-336	$2,550	$3,300

MODEL YEAR	FEATURES	EXC. COND. LOW	HIGH

Dave Grohl DG-335
2007-2008. Custom Shop Inspired By series, Trini Lopez Standard specs, Certificate of Authenticity, Pelham Blue or black finish.

2007-2008		$6,700	$8,700

Dove
1962-1996, 1999-2013. Flat-top acoustic, maple back and sides, square shoulders, natural or sunburst.

1962-1964		$5,700	$7,400
1965	Early '65	$5,000	$6,500
1965	Late '65	$3,800	$5,000
1966-1969		$3,200	$4,200
1970-1979	Various colors	$2,400	$3,100
1980-1984	Double X	$2,100	$2,800
1985-1988	Single X	$2,100	$2,800
1989	New specs	$2,100	$2,800
1990-1996	Various colors	$2,100	$2,800
1999-2013	Reissue model	$2,100	$2,800

'60s Dove
1997-2004. Spruce top, maple back and sides, Dove appointments.

1997-2004		$2,700	$3,600

'60s Dove Limited Edition
2014. Sitka spruce top, flame maple back and sides, Indian rosewood 'board, Vintage Cherryburst finish.

2014	50 offered	$2,500	$3,300

Dove Artist
1999-2005. Sitka spruce, Indian rosewood.

1999-2005		$2,100	$2,700

Dove Commemorative
1994-1996. Commemorates Gibson's 100th anniversary, Heritage or Antique Cherry finish, 100 built.

1994-1996		$2,800	$3,600

Dove In Flight Limited Edition
1996-1997. Custom Shop, 250 made, figured maple sides and back, Adirondack top, Certificate of Authenticity, dove inlays on headstock.

1996-1997		$5,000	$6,500

Doves In Flight (Brazilian)
2003. Custom Shop, only 2 made.

2003		$10,000	$13,000

Doves In Flight (Production Model)
1996-present. Gibson Custom model, maple back and sides, doves in flight inlays.

1996-2021		$3,900	$5,100

Dove Elvis Presley Signature
2008-2010. Artist Series, Certificate of Authenticity, black.

2008-2010		$3,000	$4,000

Super Dove
2009-2012. Cutaway, on-board electronics, sold through certain retailers.

2009-2012		$3,000	$4,000

Duane Eddy Signature
2004-2009. Single rounded cut, flamed maple top and back, 2 single-coils and piezo, pearl 'moustache' markers, signature engraved on 'guard, Bigsby, Rockabilly Brown finish.

2004-2009		$4,400	$5,700

Gibson CS-336
Emmitt Omar

Gibson Doves in Flight

GUITARS

1955 Gibson ES-5 Switchmaster
Jim King

1964 Gibson EDS-1275
John Wesley

MODEL YEAR	FEATURES	EXC. COND. LOW	HIGH

EAS Deluxe
1992-1994. Single-cut flat-top acoustic/electric, solid flamed maple top, bound rosewood 'board, trapezoid inlays, 3-band EQ, Vintage Cherry Sunburst.

1992-1994		$1,075	$1,400

EAS Standard/Classic
1992-1995. Like EAS Deluxe, but with spruce top, unbound top, dot inlays, called EAS Classic for '92.

1992-1995		$950	$1,250

EBS(F)-1250 Double Bass
1962-1968. Double-cut SG-type solidbody, double-neck with bass and 6-string, originally introduced as the EBSF-1250 because of a built-in fuzztone, which was later deleted, only 22 made.

1962-1964	Various colors	$20,000	$26,000
1965	Various colors	$15,200	$19,800
1966-1968	Various colors	$14,500	$18,800

EC-10 Standard
1997-1998. Jumbo single-cut, on-board electronics, solid spruce top, maple back and sides.

1997-1998		$950	$1,250

EC-20 Starburst
1997-1998. Jumbo single-cut, on-board electronics, solid spruce top, maple back and sides, renamed J-185 EC in '99.

1997-1998		$1,600	$2,100

EC-30 Blues King Electro (BKE)
1995-1998. Jumbo single-cut, on-board electronics, solid spruce top, maple back and sides, double parallelogram inlays, renamed J-185 EC in '99.

1995-1998		$1,875	$2,450

EDS-1275 Double 12
1958-1967, 1977-1990. Double-cut doubleneck with one 12- and one 6-string, thinline hollowbody until late-'62, SG-style solidbody '62 on.

1958-1961	Custom order	$38,000	$50,000
1962-1964	SG body	$33,000	$43,000
1965	SG body	$25,500	$33,200
1966-1967	SG body	$19,000	$25,000
1977-1979	Various colors	$5,300	$6,900
1977-1979	White	$5,300	$6,900
1980-1989	Various colors	$3,900	$5,100
1990	Various colors	$3,100	$4,100

EDS-1275 Double 12 (Historic Collection)
1991-2018. Custom Shop Historic Collection reissue.

1991-2018	Various colors	$3,100	$4,100

EDS-1275 Double 12 Centennial
1994. Guitar of the Month (May), gold medallion on back of headstock, cherry with gold hardware.

1994		$3,200	$4,200

EDS-1275 Double 12 Jimmy Page VOS Signature
2008. Custom Shop model with Certificate of Authenticity, 250 made.

2008		$8,000	$10,500

EDS-1275 Double Neck Alex Lifeson
2015-2016. Custom Shop model based on Lifeson's '70s Gibson, limited run of 100, first 25 signed and played by Alex, aged Arctic White.

2015-2016		$5,200	$6,800

MODEL YEAR	FEATURES	EXC. COND. LOW	HIGH

EMS-1235 Double Mandolin
1958-1963, 1965-1967. Double-cut, doubleneck with 1 regular 6-string and 1 short 6-string (the mandolin neck), thinline hollowbody until late-1962, SG-style solidbody '62-'68, black, sunburst or white, total of 61 shipped.

1958-1961	Custom order	$25,000	$33,000
1962-1963	SG body	$24,000	$31,000
1965	SG body	$20,000	$26,000
1966-1967	SG body	$19,000	$25,000

ES-5/ES-5N
1949-1955. Single-cut archtop, 3 P-90 pickups, sunburst or natural (5N). Renamed ES-5 Switchmaster in '55.

1949-1955	Natural	$8,300	$10,800
1949-1955	Sunburst	$7,700	$10,000

ES-5 Switchmaster/ES-5N Switchmaster
1956-1962. Renamed from ES-5, single-cut (rounded until late-'60, pointed after) archtop, 3 P-90s until end of '57, humbuckers after, switchmaster control.

1956-1957	Natural, P-90s	$10,100	$13,100
1956-1957	Sunburst, P-90s	$9,300	$12,100
1957-1960	Natural, hums	$17,500	$23,000
1957-1960	Sunburst, hums	$15,500	$20,100
1960-1962	Pointed Florentine cutaway	$12,000	$15,500

ES-5/ES-5 Switchmaster Historic
1995-2006. Custom Shop Historic Collection.

1995-2002	ES-5, sunburst, P-90s	$3,850	$5,000
1995-2002	Switchmaster, Wine Red, hums	$3,850	$5,000
1995-2006	Switchmaster, natural, hums	$3,850	$5,000
1995-2006	Switchmaster, sunburst, hums	$3,850	$5,000

ES-100
1938-1941. Archtop, 1 pickup, bound body, sunburst, renamed ES-125 in '41.

1938-1941		$1,750	$2,300

ES-120 T
1962-1970. Archtop, thinline, 1 f-hole, bound body, 1 pickup, sunburst.

1962-1964		$1,425	$1,850
1965		$1,350	$1,750
1966-1970		$1,300	$1,700

ES-125
1941-1943, 1946-1970. Archtop, non-cut, 1 pickup, sunburst, renamed from ES-100.

1941-1943	Blade pickup	$2,400	$3,200
1947-1949	1st non-adj, P-90s	$2,400	$3,200
1950	1st non-adj, P-90s	$2,200	$2,900
1951-1959	Adj P-90s with poles	$2,200	$2,900
1960-1964		$1,600	$2,100
1965		$1,550	$2,000
1966-1970		$1,375	$1,775

ES-125 C
1966-1970. Wide body archtop, single pointed cutaway, 1 pickup, sunburst.

1965		$1,700	$2,200
1966-1970		$1,700	$2,200

MODEL YEAR	FEATURES	EXC. COND. LOW	HIGH

ES-125 CD
1965-1970. Wide body archtop, single-cut, 2 pickups, sunburst.

1965		$2,400	$3,100
1966-1970		$2,200	$2,900

ES-125 D
1957. Limited production (not mentioned in catalog), 2 pickup version of thick body ES-125, sunburst.

1957		$2,600	$3,400

ES-125 T
1956-1968. Archtop thinline, non-cut, 1 pickup, bound body, sunburst.

1956-1959		$2,250	$2,925
1960-1964		$2,000	$2,600
1965		$1,900	$2,500
1966-1968		$1,700	$2,300

ES-125 T 3/4
1957-1968. Archtop thinline, short-scale, non-cut, 1 pickup, sunburst.

1957-1960		$2,200	$2,900
1961-1964		$2,200	$2,900
1965		$2,200	$2,900
1966-1968		$2,200	$2,900

ES-125 TC
1960-1970. Archtop thinline, single pointed cutaway, bound body, 1 P-90 pickup, sunburst.

1960-1964		$2,200	$2,900
1965		$2,200	$2,900
1966-1970		$2,200	$2,900

ES-125 TD
1957-1963. Archtop thinline, non-cut, 2 pickups, sunburst.

1957-1963		$2,775	$3,600

ES-125 TDC or ES-125 TCD
1960-1971. Archtop thinline, single pointed cutaway, 2 P-90 pickups, sunburst.

1960-1964		$3,425	$4,450
1965	Early '65	$3,225	$4,200
1965	Late '65	$2,875	$3,725
1966-1971		$2,875	$3,725

ES-130
1954-1956. Archtop, non-cut, 1 pickup, bound body, sunburst, renamed ES-135 in '56.

1954-1959		$2,550	$3,300

ES-135
1956-1958. Renamed from ES-130, non-cut archtop, 1 pickup, sunburst, name reused on a thin body in the '90s.

1957-1959		$2,550	$3,300

ES-135 (Thinline)
1991-2003. Single-cut archtop, laminated maple body, 2 humbuckers or 2 P-90s, chrome or gold hardware, sunburst.

1991-2003	Stop tail	$1,600	$2,075
1991-2003	Trapeze	$1,600	$2,075

ES-137 Classic
2002-2015. Thin-body electric single cut, trapezoid inlays, 2 humbuckers, f-holes, gold hardware.

2002-2015		$1,600	$2,075

ES-137 Custom
2002-2011. Like Classic, but with split-diamond inlays and varitone.

2002-2011		$1,600	$2,075

ES-137 P (Premier)
2002-2005. Like Classic, but with exposed humbuckers, chrome hardware and very small trapezoid inlays.

2002-2005		$1,350	$1,750

ES-139
2013-2016. Semi-hollow Les Paul style body, 2 humbuckers, Guitar Center model.

2013-2016		$1,050	$1,400

ES-140 (3/4) or ES-140N (3/4)
1950-1956. Archtop, single-cut, 1 pickup, bound body, short-scale, sunburst or natural option (N).

1950-1956	Natural option	$2,675	$3,475
1950-1956	Sunburst	$2,475	$3,225

ES-140 (3/4) T or ES-140N (3/4) T
1957-1968. Archtop thinline, single-cut, bound body, 1 pickup, short-scale, sunburst or natural option (140N).

1957-1959	Natural option	$2,675	$3,475
1957-1959	Sunburst	$2,475	$3,225
1960-1964	Sunburst	$2,300	$3,000
1965	Sunburst	$2,125	$2,750
1966-1968	Sunburst	$1,925	$2,500

ES-150
1936-1942, 1946-1956. Historically important archtop, non-cut, bound body, Charlie Christian bar pickup from '36-'39, various metal covered pickups starting in '40, sunburst.

1936-1939	Charlie Christian pu	$6,200	$8,200
1940-1942	Metal covered pu	$6,200	$8,200
1946-1949	P-90 pickup	$2,600	$3,400
1950-1956	P-90 pickup	$2,450	$3,200

ES-150 DC
1969-1975. Archtop, double rounded cutaway, 2 humbuckers, multi-bound, cherry, natural or walnut.

1969-1975		$3,250	$4,300

ES-165 Herb Ellis
1991-2011. Single pointed cut hollowbody, 1 humbucker, gold hardware.

1991-2011		$2,050	$2,700

ES-175 or ES-175N
1949-1971. Archtop, single pointed cutaway, 1 pickup (P-90 from '49-early-'57, humbucker early-'57-'71), multi-bound, sunburst or natural option (175N).

1949-1956	Natural, P90	$4,550	$5,900
1949-1956	Sunburst, P-90	$4,550	$5,900
1957-1959	Natural, hum	$6,800	$8,925
1957-1963	Sunburst, PAF	$6,500	$8,600
1964	Sunburst, pat #	$5,400	$7,000
1965	Sunburst, hum	$3,600	$4,700
1966-1969	Sunburst, pat #	$2,900	$3,800
1967-1969	Black	$2,900	$3,800
1970-1971	Various colors	$2,600	$3,375

ES-175 CC
1978-1979. 1 Charlie Christian pickup, sunburst or walnut.

1978-1979		$2,600	$3,375

ES-175 D or ES-175N D
1952-2016. Archtop, single-cut, 2 pickups (P-90s from '53-early-'57, humbuckers early-'57 on), sunburst or natural option (175N D). Humbucker pickups were

1961 Gibson ES-125 TC
Jim King

1952 Gibson ES-150
Frank Manno

1970s Gibson ES-175D
Bernunzio Uptown Music

Gibson ES-235

converted from PAF-stickers to Pat. No.-stickers in '62. Different models were converted at different times. An ES-175 model, made during the transitional time, with PAFs, will fetch more. In some of the electric-archtop models, the transition period may have been later than '62. Cataloged as the ES-175 Reissue in the '90s, Currently as the ES-175 under Gibson Memphis.

MODEL YEAR	FEATURES	EXC. COND. LOW	HIGH
1952-1956	Natural, P-90s	$4,900	$6,400
1952-1956	Sunburst, P-90s	$4,400	$5,700
1957-1963	Natural, PAFs	$11,500	$15,000
1957-1963	Sunburst, PAFs	$10,300	$13,400
1964	Natural, pat #	$5,850	$7,600
1964	Sunburst, pat #	$5,100	$6,650
1965	Natural, pat #	$5,000	$6,500
1965	Sunburst, hums	$4,450	$5,800
1966	Natural, pat #	$4,100	$5,350
1966	Sunburst, hums	$4,200	$5,500
1967-1969	Black	$4,200	$5,500
1967-1969	Various colors	$4,200	$5,500
1970-1979	Various colors	$3,000	$3,900
1980-2016	Various colors	$2,825	$3,675

ES-175 D Tenor
1966. Rare custom ordered tenor version, sunburst.

1966		$3,550	$4,600

ES-175 D-AN
1999-2000. Limited run, P-90s, Antique Natural finish.

1999-2000		$2,850	$3,700

ES-175 SP
2006. Single humbucker version, sunburst.

2006		$2,700	$3,500

ES-175 Steve Howe
2001-2007. Maple laminate body, multi-bound top, sunburst.

2001-2007		$3,000	$3,900

ES-175 T
1976-1980. Archtop thinline, single pointed cutaway, 2 humbuckers, various colors including international colors.

1976-1980		$3,000	$3,900

ES-225 T or ES-225N T
1955-1959. Thinline, single pointed cutaway, 1 P-90 pickup, bound body and neck, sunburst or natural option (225N T).

1955-1959	Natural	$3,800	$4,900
1955-1959	Sunburst	$2,850	$3,700

ES-225 TD or ES-225N TD
1956-1959. Thinline, single-cut, 2 P-90s, bound body and neck, sunburst or natural option (225N TD).

1956-1959	Natural	$5,600	$7,300
1956-1959	Sunburst	$4,200	$5,400

1959 ES-225 Historic
2014-2016. Single-cut TD reissue with 2 P-90s, sunburst.

2014-2016		$2,675	$3,475

ES-235 Gloss
2018-2020. Semi-hollow single-cut, maple neck, rosewood 'board, 2 pickups.

2018-2020		$1,150	$1,500

ES-250 or ES-250N
1939-1940. Archtop, carved top, special Christian pickup, multi-bound, high-end appointments, stairstep headstock

'39 and standard in '40, sunburst or natural option (250N).

MODEL YEAR	FEATURES	EXC. COND. LOW	HIGH
1939	Natural, stairstep hs	$27,300	$35,400
1939	Sunburst, stairstep hs	$17,300	$22,500
1940	Natural, standard hs	$27,300	$35,400
1940	Sunburst, standard hs	$17,300	$22,500

ES-275
2016-2019. Hollowbody archtop, single-cut, 2 humbucker pickups standard or optional P-90s, various colors and finishes, certificate of authenticity.

2016	Gloss, opaque	$2,750	$3,575
2016-2019	Gloss, figured	$3,300	$4,300
2017	Gloss, P-90s	$3,300	$4,300
2018	Custom metallic	$3,300	$4,300
2019	Satin, opaque	$2,650	$3,450

ES-295
1952-1958. Single pointed cutaway archtop, 2 pickups (P-90s from '52-late-'57, humbuckers after), gold finish, gold-plated hardware.

1952-1957	P-90s	$7,200	$9,400
1957-1958	Humbuckers	$15,500	$20,200

ES-295 Historic Collection
1990-2000. Custom Shop, 2 P-90 pickups, Bigsby, Antique Gold finish.

1990-2000		$3,500	$4,500

ES-295 '52 Historic Collection
2013-2015. Custom Shop. Limited VOS Vintage Cherry offered in '15.

2013-2015		$3,500	$4,500
2015	Limited Cherry	$3,500	$4,500

ES-295 Scotty Moore Signature
1999. Custom Shop, 15 produced, 12 with Scotty's actual signature on lower bout, Bullion Gold, trapeze tailpiece.

1999		$7,400	$9,600

ES-300 or ES-300N
1940-1942, 1945-1953. Archtop, non-cut, f-holes, had 4 pickup configurations during its run, sunburst or natural (300N).

1940	Natural, oblong diagonal pu	$3,900	$5,100
1940	Sunburst, oblong diagonal pu	$3,500	$4,500
1941-1942	Natural, 1 pu	$3,900	$5,100
1941-1942	Sunburst, 1 pu	$3,500	$4,500
1945	Black, 1 pu	$3,200	$4,200
1945-1949	Sunburst, 1 pu	$3,200	$4,200
1945-1953	Natural, 1 pu	$3,300	$4,300
1949-1953	Natural, 2 pus	$4,600	$6,000
1949-1953	Sunburst, 2 pus	$3,500	$4,500

ES-320 TD
1971-1974. Thinline archtop, double-cut, 2 single-coil pickups, bound body, cherry, natural, or walnut.

1971-1974		$1,700	$2,200

ES-325 TD
1972-1978. Thinline archtop, double-cut, 2 mini-humbuckers, 1 f-hole, bound body, top mounted control panel, cherry or walnut.

1972-1978		$2,000	$2,600

MODEL YEAR	FEATURES	EXC. COND. LOW	HIGH

ES-330 L

2009-2015. Custom Shop, classic 330 design, 2 dog-ear P-90 pickups, sunburst or black. 2015 model has humbuckers.

2009-2015		$2,600	$3,400

ES-330 T or ES-330N T

1959-1963. Double rounded cutaway, thinline, 1 pickup, bound body and neck, sunburst, cherry or natural option (330N T). In the '60s came with either an original semi-hard case (better than chip board) or a hardshell case. Prices quoted are for hardshell case; approximately $100 should be deducted for the semi-hard case.

1959-1961	Natural	$9,100	$12,000
1959-1963	Cherry	$5,100	$6,800
1959-1963	Sunburst	$5,100	$6,800

ES-330 TD or ES-330N TD

1959-1972. Double rounded cutaway, thinline, 2 pickups, bound body and neck, dot markers early then blocks, sunburst, cherry or natural option (330N TD). In the '60s came with either an original semi-hard case (better than chip board) or a hardshell case. Prices noted for the hardshell case; approximately $100 should be deducted for the semi-hard case.

1959-1961	Natural	$12,500	$16,500
1959-1962	Cherry, dots	$7,500	$10,000
1959-1962	Sunburst, dots	$7,500	$10,000
1963-1964	Cherry, blocks	$6,500	$8,600
1963-1964	Sunburst, blocks	$6,500	$8,600
1965	Cherry, sunburst	$5,600	$7,300
1966-1968	Cherry, sunburst	$4,400	$5,700
1967-1968	Burgundy Metallic	$4,400	$5,700
1968	Walnut option	$4,400	$5,700
1969-1972	Various colors	$4,400	$5,700

ES-330 TDC

1998-2000. Custom Shop model, block markers.

1998-2000		$2,600	$3,400

1959 ES-330 Historic VOS

2012-2019. Gibson Memphis, Historic series, P-90 pickups, trapeze tailpiece, certificate, VOS finish in sunburst, natural or cherry.

2012-2019		$2,600	$3,400

1959 ES-330 Wildwood Spec

2015. Gibson Memphis, Limited Edition, figured top, natural, certificate.

2015		$2,950	$3,850

1964 ES-330 Historic VOS

2015-2019. Historic series, vintage specs, P-90 pickups, trapeze tailpiece, certificate.

2015-2019		$2,600	$3,400

ES-333

2002-2005. Economy ES-335, no 'guard, no headstock inlay, exposed coils, stencil logo, satin finish.

2002-2005		$1,550	$2,000

ES-335 TD or ES-335N TD

1958-1981. The original design ES-335 has dot 'board inlays and a stop tailpiece, sunburst, cherry or natural option (335N). Block inlays replaced dots in mid-'62, in late-'64 the stop tailpiece was replaced with a trapeze tailpiece. Replaced by the ES-335 DOT in '81.

MODEL YEAR	FEATURES	EXC. COND. LOW	HIGH
1958	Natural, bound neck	$92,000	$123,000
1958	Natural, bound neck, Bigsby	$69,000	$92,000
1958	Natural, unbound neck	$92,000	$123,000
1958	Natural, unbound neck, Bigsby	$69,000	$92,000
1958	Sunburst, bound neck	$38,000	$50,000
1958	Sunburst, bound neck, Bigsby	$31,000	$42,000
1958	Sunburst, unbound neck	$38,000	$50,000
1958	Sunburst, unbound neck, Bigsby	$31,000	$42,000
1959	Cherry (early), stop tail	$36,000	$47,800
1959	Natural, bound neck	$102,000	$136,000
1959	Natural, bound neck, Bigsby	$86,000	$115,000
1959	Sunburst, bound neck	$46,000	$61,000
1959	Sunburst, bound neck, Bigsby	$35,000	$46,500
1960	Cherry, factory Bigsby	$27,000	$36,000
1960	Cherry, factory stop tail	$33,000	$44,000
1960	Natural, factory Bigsby	$53,000	$71,000
1960	Natural, factory stop tail	$65,000	$86,000
1960	Sunburst, factory Bigsby	$27,000	$36,000
1960	Sunburst, factory stop tail	$33,000	$44,000
1961	Cherry, factory Bigsby	$24,000	$32,000
1961	Cherry, factory stop tail	$30,000	$40,000
1961	Sunburst, factory Bigsby	$24,000	$32,000
1961	Sunburst, factory stop tail	$30,000	$40,000
1962	Cherry, blocks, PAFs	$22,500	$29,000
1962	Cherry, blocks, pat#	$18,400	$24,500
1962	Cherry, dots, PAFs	$27,500	$36,500
1962	Cherry, vibrola, pat#	$15,300	$20,300
1962	Sunburst, blocks, PAFs	$22,500	$29,000
1962	Sunburst, blocks, pat#	$18,400	$24,500
1962	Sunburst, dots, PAFs	$27,500	$36,500
1962	Sunburst, dots, pat#	$18,400	$24,500

1956 Gibson ES-225 T

1959 Gibson ES-330 T
David Stone

1967 Gibson ES-335-12
Carter Vintage Guitars

1979 Gibson ES-335 Pro
Michael Campbell

MODEL YEAR	FEATURES	EXC. COND. LOW	HIGH
1962	Sunburst, vibrola, pat#	$15,300	$20,300
1963-1964	Cherry, factory Bigsby	$15,500	$20,600
1963-1964	Cherry, factory Maestro	$15,500	$20,600
1963-1964	Cherry, factory stop tail	$18,400	$24,500
1963-1964	Sunburst, factory Bigsby	$15,500	$20,600
1963-1964	Sunburst, factory Maestro	$15,500	$20,600
1963-1964	Sunburst, factory stop tail	$18,400	$24,500
1965	Early '65, wide neck	$12,000	$16,000
1965	Mid '65, narrow neck	$6,900	$9,200
1966	Cherry, sunburst	$6,400	$8,500
1966	Pelham Blue	$13,800	$18,400
1966	Sparkling Burgundy	$8,000	$10,600
1967	Black	$10,000	$13,300
1967	Cherry, sunburst	$6,400	$8,500
1967	Pelham Blue	$13,800	$18,400
1967	Sparkling Burgundy	$8,000	$10,600
1968	Cherry, sunburst	$6,200	$8,300
1968	Pelham Blue	$13,800	$18,400
1968	Sparkling Burgundy	$8,000	$10,700
1969	Cherry, sunburst	$5,400	$7,200
1969	Walnut option	$4,600	$6,200
1970-1976	Cherry, sunburst	$3,800	$5,000
1970-1976	Walnut option	$3,500	$4,600
1977-1979	All colors	$3,200	$4,200
1980-1981	All colors	$2,900	$3,750

ES-335 Dot
1981-1990. Reissue of '60 ES-335 and replaces ES-335 TD. Name changed to ES-335 Reissue. Various color options including highly figured wood.

1981	Black	$3,300	$4,300
1981-1984	Natural	$3,600	$4,700
1981-1990	Cherry, sunburst	$2,950	$3,900
1985-1990	Natural	$2,950	$3,900

ES-335 Dot CMT (Custom Shop)
1983-1985. Custom Shop ES-335 Dot with curly maple top and back, full-length center block, 2 PAF-labeled humbuckers, natural or sunburst.

1983-1985		$3,600	$4,700

ES-335 Reissue/ES-335 '59 Dot Reissue/ES-335
1991-present. Replaced the ES-335 DOT, dot inlays, various color options including highly figured wood. Renamed the 1959 ES-335 Dot Reissue in '98 and currently just ES-335 followed by options - Dot, Block (added in '98), Fat Neck (added in '08), Figured (added in '06), Plain, Satin (added in '06).

1991-2020	Cherry, sunburst, walnut, black	$2,300	$3,000
1991-2021	Natural	$2,300	$3,000
2006-2017	Satin	$1,775	$2,300

ES-335 Dot P-90
2007. Custom Shop limited edition with black dog-ear P-90s, stop tailpiece.

2007		$2,600	$3,400

ES-335-12
1965-1971. 12-string version of the 335.

1965-1968		$3,500	$4,650

ES-335 '59 Dot Historic
1999-2000, 2002-2016. Custom Shop Historic Collection, based upon 1959 ES-335 dot neck, figured maple top on early series, plain on later, nickel hardware.

1999-2016	Figured top	$3,700	$4,800
2002-2016	Plain top	$3,400	$4,400

1959 ES-335 Dot Reissue Limited Edition
2009-2017. Custom Shop, plain laminated maple top/back/sides, rounded '59 neck profile, '57 Classic humbuckers, Certificate of Authenticity, 250 each to be made in Antique Vintage Sunburst or Antique Natural (standard gloss or V.O.S. treatments).

2009-2017		$3,700	$4,900

1959 ES-335 Ultra Heavy Aged/Ultra Light Aged
2021-present. Custom Shop Murphy Lab Collection, ultra heavy aged (Vintage Natural) and ultra light (Ebony or Vintage Natural).

2021-2022	Ultra Heavy Aged	$6,300	$8,200
2021-2022	Ultra Light Aged	$3,900	$5,100

ES-335 '60s Block Inlay
2004-2007. Made in Memphis facility, plain maple top, small block markers.

2004-2007		$2,400	$3,100

50th Anniversary 1960 ES-335
2009-2010. Custom Shop, dot markers, natural.

2009-2010		$3,500	$4,500

1961 ES-335 Heavy Aged/Ultra Light Aged
2021-present. Custom Shop Murphy Lab Collection, heavy or ultra light aged, Sixties Cherry finish.

2021-2022	Heavy Aged	$6,300	$8,200
2021-2022	Ultra Light Aged	$3,900	$5,100

1961 ES-335 Reissue (Custom Shop)
2020-present. Historic series, 3-Ply maple/poplar/maple body, solid mahogany neck, Indian rosewood 'board, 2 Alnico pickups, Sixties Cherry or Vintage Burst.

2020-2021		$3,550	$4,600

50th Anniversary 1963 Block ES-335TD/ES-335TDC
2010-2013. Memphis Custom Shop, block markers, double-ring vintage-style tuners, Antique Vintage Sunburst (TD), Antique Faded Cherry (TDC).

2010-2013	TD, sunburst	$3,500	$4,500
2010-2013	TDC, cherry	$3,500	$4,500

ES-335 '63 Block Historic
1998-2000, 2002-2018. Custom Shop Historic Collection, based upon 1963 ES-335 with small block markers, figured maple top on early series, plain on later, nickel hardware.

1998-2000	1st release, figured top	$3,800	$4,900
2002-2018	2nd release, figured top	$3,800	$4,900
2002-2018	Plain top	$3,500	$4,500

MODEL YEAR FEATURES	EXC. COND. LOW	HIGH

1964 ES-335 Ultra Light Aged
2021-present. Custom Shop Murphy Lab Collection, Sixties Cherry finish.

2021-2022	$3,900	$5,100

ES-335 Alvin Lee
2006-2007. Custom Division Nashville, 50 made, features reflect Alvin Lee's Big Red ES-335 complete with decal art, cherry red, includes certificate of authenticity (if missing value is reduced). There is also an unlimited version without certificate.

2006-2007 With certificate	$4,700	$6,100

ES-335 Andy Summers
2002. Custom Shop, 50 made, script signature on 'guard, early dot neck specs, nitro cherry finish, certificate of authenticity.

2002	$3,500	$4,500

ES-335 Artist
1981. Off-set dot markers, large headstock logo, metal truss rod plate, gold hardware, 3 control knobs with unusual toggles and input specification.

1981	$3,300	$4,300

ES-335 Canadian Custom
2007. Custom Shop Canadian exclusive, run of 50, maple leaf 'Limited Edition' decal on back of headstock, 'Custom Made' engraved plate on guitar front, solid mahogany neck, pearloid block inlays, antique cherry finish with aged binding.

2007	$2,450	$3,200

ES-335 Centennial
1994. Centennial edition, gold medallion in headstock, diamond inlay in tailpiece, cherry.

1994	$3,500	$4,500

ES-335 Chris Cornell
2012-2016. Olive Drab Green or black.

2012-2016	$3,400	$4,400

ES-335 CRR/CRS
1979. Country Rock Regular with standard wiring and CRR logo. Country Rock Stereo with stereo wiring and CRS logo, 300 of each built, 2 pickups, coil-tap.

1979	CRR	$3,200	$4,200
1979	CRS	$3,300	$4,300

ES-335 Diamond Edition
2006. Trini Lopez style diamond f-holes, Bigsby tailpiece option, gold hardware, Pelham Blue, pearl white or black pearl.

2006	$2,600	$3,400

ES-335 Eric Clapton Crossroads '64 Reissue
2005. Reissue of EC's, with certificate of authenticity.

2005	$10,800	$14,000

ES-335 Goldtop
2013-2016. Gibson Memphis, limited-edition, 2 Burstbucker humbuckers, gold finish.

2013-2016	$2,400	$3,100

ES-335 Gothic
1998-1999. Gothic appointments including ebony 'board and black satin finish.

1998-1999	$1,375	$1,775

ES-335 Government Series
2015-2016. Made from guitar bodies, necks and 'boards returned from Federal Government after '11 raid on Gibson, special run of 300 built, each with Certificate of Authenticity.

2015-2016	$2,100	$2,700

ES-335 Jim Beam Limited Edition
1999. Promotional Custom Shop model, approximately 18 made, large Jim Beam notation on body, comes with certificate.

1999	$2,150	$2,800

ES-335 Jimmy Wallace Reissue
Special order by Texas Gibson dealer Jimmy Wallace.

1980	$3,100	$4,000

ES-335 Joe Bonamassa Signature
2012. Custom Shop, based on Joe's '61 335, VOS sunburst.

2012	$3,700	$4,900

ES-335 King of the Blues
2006. Offered through Guitar Center, 150 made, based on B.B.'s Lucille, King of the Blues logo on 'guard.

2006	$2,900	$3,800

ES-335 Larry Carlton
2002-2016. Mr. 335 logo on truss rod cover, block neck like Larry's guitar, vintage (faded) sunburst.

2002-2016	$3,500	$4,500

ES-335 Lee Ritenour
2008. Custom Shop, COA, 50 signed and 100 unsigned, Antique Cherry finish.

2008	$3,500	$4,500

ES-335 Limited Edition (P-90s)
2001. ES-335 style crown inlay on headstock, P-90 pickups.

2001	$2,500	$3,200

ES-335 Nashville
1994. All serial numbers begin with 94, first year Custom Shop run (not the Centennial).

1994	$3,000	$4,000

ES-335 Pro
1979-1981. Two humbucking pickups with exposed coils, bound 'board, cherry or sunburst.

1979-1981	$2,500	$3,200

ES-335 Rich Robinson
2014-2016. Bigsby, small blocks, Cherry VOS finish.

2014-2016	$3,400	$4,400

ES-335 Roy Orbison
2006. About 70 made, RO serial number, black finish.

2006	$3,800	$4,900

ES-335 Rusty Anderson
2013. Figured maple, natural, dot neck specs.

2013	$3,800	$4,900

ES-335 Showcase Edition
1988. Guitar of the Month series, limited production, black gothic-style hardware, EMG pickups, transparent white/beige finish.

1988	$2,700	$3,500

ES-335 Studio
1986-1991, 2013-2020. Bound body, 2 Dirty Finger humbuckers, cherry or ebony. Reissued in '13 by Gibson Memphis using '58 specs but with Vintage Sunburst or ebony finish.

1986-1991		$1,775	$2,350
2013-2020	Memphis	$1,075	$1,425

*2014 Gibson ES-335
Rich Robinson*
Michael Alonzi

1990 Gibson ES-335 Studio
Kurt Davey

GUITARS

1979 Gibson ES-347
Steve Alvito

1962 Gibson ES-350 T
Landy Hardy

MODEL YEAR	FEATURES	EXC. COND. LOW	HIGH

ES-335 Warren Haynes
2013-2015. Custom Shop model.

| 2013-2015 | 500 made | $3,400 | $4,400 |
| 2014 | 1961 Ltd Ed | $3,400 | $4,400 |

ESDT-335
2001-2009. Memphis Custom Shop, flame maple top and back, 2 humbucking pickups, various colors.

| 2001-2009 | | $2,900 | $3,800 |

ES-336
1996-1998. Custom Shop smaller sized ES-335 with smaller headstock, dot markers.

| 1996-1998 | All options | $2,200 | $2,900 |

ES-339
2007-present. Modern series, smaller-sized bound 335 body, 2 humbuckers, block inlays, various colors.

| 2007-2021 | All options | $2,000 | $2,600 |

ES-339 Studio
2013-2018. Stripped-down 339, no binding or pickguard, dot inlays.

| 2013-2018 | | $950 | $1,250 |

ES-339 Traditional Pro
2013. Figured or plain, cherry or vintage sunburst.

| 2013 | | $1,875 | $2,450 |

ES-340 TD
1968-1973. The 335 with a laminated maple neck, master volume and mixer controls, various colors.

| 1968-1973 | Natural, Walnut | $3,200 | $4,200 |

ES-345 TD or ES-345 TDSV
1959-1983. The 335 with Vari-tone, stereo, 2 humbuckers, gold hardware, double parallelogram inlays, stop tailpiece '59-'64 and '82-'83, trapeze tailpiece '65-'82. Cataloged as ES-345 TDSV by '80.

1959	Cherry, Bigsby	$21,400	$27,800
1959	Cherry, stud tail	$27,700	$36,000
1959	Natural, Bigsby	$35,000	$45,800
1959	Natural, stud tail	$54,000	$70,000
1959	Sunburst, Bigsby	$21,400	$27,800
1959	Sunburst, stud tail	$27,700	$36,000
1960	Cherry, Bigsby	$19,000	$24,600
1960	Cherry, stud tail	$25,200	$32,700
1960	Natural, Bigsby	$32,800	$42,500
1960	Natural, stud tail	$50,300	$65,300
1960	Sunburst, Bigsby	$19,000	$24,600
1960	Sunburst, stud tail	$25,200	$32,700
1961	Cherry, Bigsby	$15,200	$19,700
1961	Cherry, stud tail	$20,300	$26,300
1961	Sunburst, Bigsby	$15,200	$19,700
1961	Sunburst, stud tail	$20,300	$26,300
1962	Bigsby, PAF	$15,200	$19,700
1962	Stud tail, PAF	$16,400	$21,300
1963-1964	Bigsby, pat #	$12,300	$16,000
1963-1964	Stud tail, pat #	$14,600	$19,000
1965	Early '65 wide neck	$8,100	$10,500
1965	Mid '65 narrow neck	$5,200	$6,800
1966-1969	Various colors	$4,400	$5,700
1970-1976	Various colors	$3,800	$5,000
1977-1979	Various colors	$3,200	$4,200
1980-1983	Various colors	$2,900	$3,750

ES-345 Historic
1998-1999. Custom Shop Historic Collection, stopbar, Bigsby or Maestro tailpiece, Viceroy Brown, Vintage Sunburst, Faded Cherry or natural.

| 1998-1999 | | $3,600 | $4,700 |

ES-345 Reissue
2002-2010. ES-345 features with 6-position Varitone selector, gold hardware, stop tailpiece, various colors.

| 2002-2010 | | $2,300 | $3,000 |

1959 ES-345 TD
2014-2015. Period-correct '59 specs with VOS aged look, certificate of authenticity, Historic Burst or natural (TDN) finish.

| 2014 | '59 reissue | $3,200 | $4,200 |
| 2015 | VOS | $3,600 | $4,700 |

ES-346 Paul Jackson Jr.
1997-2006. Custom Shop, 335-like with figured or plain maple top, rosewood 'board, double-parallelogram inlays.

| 1997-2006 | | $2,900 | $3,800 |

ES-347 TD or ES-347 S
1978-1985, 1987-1993. 335-style with gold hardware, tune-o-matic bridge, 2 Spotlight double-coil pickups, coil-tap, bound body and neck, S added to name in '87.

| 1978-1985 | TD | $2,600 | $3,400 |
| 1987-1993 | S | $2,600 | $3,400 |

ES-350 or ES-350N
1947-1956. Originally the ES-350 Premier, full body archtop, single-cut, 1 P-90 pickup until end of '48, 2 after, sunburst or natural (350N).

1947-1948	Natural, 1 pu	$7,100	$9,200
1947-1948	Sunburst, 1 pu	$7,000	$9,100
1949-1956	Natural, 2 pu	$7,500	$9,700
1949-1956	Sunburst, 2 pu	$7,500	$9,700

ES-350 Centennial
1994. Guitar of the Month, sunburst, gold hardware, gold medallion on back of headstock, diamond accents, 101 made with serial numbers from 1984-1994. Included a gold signet ring.

| 1994 | | $3,700 | $4,900 |

ES-350 T or ES-350N T
1955-1963, 1977-1981, 1992-1993. Called the ES-350 TD in early-'60s, thinline archtop, single-cut (round '55-'60 and '77-'81, pointed '61-'63), 2 P-90 pickups '55-'56, humbuckers after, gold hardware. Limited runs were done in 1992-1993.

1956	Natural, P-90s	$7,000	$9,150
1956	Sunburst, P-90s	$7,000	$9,150
1957-1959	Natural, PAFs	$11,500	$15,000
1957-1959	Sunburst, PAFs	$11,500	$15,000
1960-1963	Natural, PAFs	$11,200	$14,600
1960-1963	Sunburst, PAFs	$11,200	$14,600
1977-1981	Natural, sunburst	$3,200	$4,200

ES-350 T Historic
1998-2000. Custom Shop Historic Collection reissue.

| 1998-2000 | | $3,500 | $4,500 |

Chuck Berry 1955 ES-350 T
2019. Limited to 55, antique natural with VOS finish.

| 2019 | | $10,900 | $14,100 |

The *Vintage Guitar Price Guide* shows low to high values for items in all-original excellent condition, and, where applicable, with original case or cover.

MODEL YEAR	FEATURES	EXC. COND. LOW	HIGH

ES-355 TD

1958-1970. 335-style with large block inlays, multi-bound body and headstock, 2 humbuckers, the 355 model was standard with a Bigsby, sideways or Maestro vibrato, non-vibrato models were an option. The prices shown assume a vibrato tailpiece, a factory stop tailpiece was considered an advantage and will fetch more. Early examples have factory Bigsby vibratos, early '60s have sideways vibratos, and late '60s have Maestro vibratos, cherry finish was the standard finish.

1958-1959	Cherry, PAFs, Bigsby, vibrato	$29,000	$38,000
1960-1962	Cherry, PAFs, Bigsby, vibrato	$23,000	$30,000
1962	Cherry, PAFs, side-pull, vibrato	$23,000	$30,000
1963-1964	Cherry, pat#, Bigsby, vibrato	$15,300	$20,000
1965	Early '65, wide neck	$11,100	$14,400
1965	Mid '65, narrow neck	$7,400	$9,600
1966-1968	Cherry or sunburst	$7,400	$9,600
1966-1968	Sparkling Burgundy	$11,100	$14,400
1969-1970	Cherry or sunburst	$5,900	$7,700

ES-355 TDSV

1959-1982. Stereo version of ES-355 with Vari-tone switch, a mono version was available but few were made, the 355 model was standard with a Bigsby, sideways or Maestro vibrato, non-vibrato models were an option. The prices shown assume a vibrato tailpiece. A factory stop tailpiece was considered an advantage and will fetch more, early examples have factory Bigsby vibratos, early-'60s have sideways vibratos and late-'60s have Maestro vibratos, cherry finish was standard, walnut became available in '69.

1959	Bigsby	$21,000	$28,000
1959	Factory stop tail	$37,000	$48,000
1960	Bigsby	$20,000	$26,500
1961-1963	Sideways, late PAFs	$20,000	$26,500
1962	Maestro, late PAFs	$20,000	$26,500
1963-1964	Maestro, pat #	$14,100	$18,300
1965	Early '65 wide neck	$10,200	$13,200
1965	Mid '65 narrow neck	$6,800	$8,800
1966	Sparkling Burgundy	$10,200	$13,200
1966-1967	Cherry or sunburst, Maestro	$6,100	$8,000
1968	Various colors, Maestro	$6,100	$8,000
1969	Various colors, Bigsby	$5,450	$7,100
1970-1982	Various colors, Bigsby	$4,900	$6,400

ES-355/ES-355 TD (Custom Shop)

1994, 1997, 2006-2010. Mono, Bigsby or stop tail.

1994-2010		$3,550	$4,650

1959 ES-355 Light Aged/Ultra Light Aged

2021-present. Custom Shop Murphy Lab Collection, light aged (Watermelon Red) and ultra light (Ebony or Vintage Natural).

2021-2022	Light Aged	$5,100	$6,600
2021-2022	Ultra Light Aged	$4,450	$5,800

ES-355 Alex Lifeson

2008-2010. Custom Shop Inspired By series, gold hardware, Alpine White finish.

2008-2010		$4,600	$6,000

ES-355 Centennial

1994. Guitar of the Month, sunburst, gold hardware, gold medallion on back of headstock, diamond accents, 101 made with serial numbers from 1984-1994. Included a gold signet ring.

1994		$3,500	$4,600

ES-355 Curly Maple Limited Edition

2010-2012. Figured flamed maple top, stop tailpiece, natural finish.

2010-2012		$3,775	$4,900

ES-355 Limited Edition (VOS)

2015-2018. Gibson Memphis, Bigsby, gold hardware, various colors with VOS finish.

2015-2018		$4,000	$5,200

ES-355 Summer Jam Series

2011. Custom Shop Summer Jam series, 25 made in Bourbon Burst.

2011		$3,775	$4,900

ES-359

2008-2016. Custom Shop, ES-335/ES-339 style with LP Custom style appointments, minor-figured top and back, sunburst.

2008-2016		$2,200	$2,900

ES-369

1981-1982. A 335-style with 2 exposed humbucker pickups, coil-tap, sunburst.

1981-1982		$2,450	$3,200

ES-390

2014-2018. Memphis model, thinline hollow-body, rosewood 'board, 2 P-90s, Vintage Dark Burst finish.

2014-2018		$2,050	$2,650

ES-446

1999-2003. Single cut semi-hollow, 2 humbuckers, Bigsby, Custom Shop.

1999-2003	Various colors	$2,600	$3,400

ES-775

1990-1993. Single-cut hollowbody, 2 humbuckers, gold hardware, ebony, natural or sunburst.

1990-1993		$2,600	$3,400

ES-Artist

1979-1985. Double-cut thinline, semi-hollowbody, no f-holes, 2 humbuckers, active electronics, gold hardware, ebony, fireburst or sunburst. Moog electronics includes 3 mini-switches for compressor, expander and bright boost.

1979-1985		$3,000	$4,000

EST-150 (Tenor)

1937-1939. Tenor version of ES-150, Charlie Christian pickup, sunburst, renamed ETG-150 in '40.

1937-1939		$3,500	$4,500

1966 Gibson ES-355 TD
Ted Wulfers

2001 Gibson ES-446
Greg Perrine

GUITARS

1983 Gibson Explorer Heritage
Steve Evans

*1984 Gibson Explorer
Designer Series*
Imaged by Heritage Auctions, HA.com

MODEL YEAR	FEATURES	EXC. COND. LOW	HIGH

ETG-150
1940-1942, 1947-1971. Renamed from EST-150, tenor version of ES-150, 1 metal-covered pickup '40-'42, P-90 after, sunburst.

MODEL YEAR	FEATURES	LOW	HIGH
1940-1942		$3,200	$4,200
1947-1959		$1,950	$2,550
1960-1971		$1,550	$2,000

Everly Brothers
1962-1972. Jumbo flat-top, huge double 'guard, star inlays, natural is optional in '63 and becomes the standard color in '68, reintroduced as the J-180 Everly Brothers in '86.

1962-1964	Black	$14,000	$18,000
1963	Natural option	$14,000	$18,000
1965	Early '65, black, large neck	$11,750	$15,250
1965	Late '65, black, small neck	$9,200	$11,900
1966-1967	Black	$8,100	$10,500
1968-1969	Natural	$6,200	$8,050
1970-1972	Natural	$5,200	$6,800

Explorer
1958-1959, 1963. Some '58s shipped in '63, korina body, 2 humbuckers. The Explorer market is a very specialized and very small market, with few genuine examples available and a limited number of high-end buyers. The slightest change to the original specifications can mean a significant drop in value. The narrow price ranges noted are for all original examples that have the original guitar case.

1958-1959		$700,000	$900,000
1963		$300,000	$385,000

Explorer (Mahogany)
1975-1982. Mahogany body, 2 humbuckers, black, white or natural.

1975-1982	Black or white	$3,600	$4,700
1975-1982	Natural	$3,600	$4,700

Explorer I
1981-1982. Replaces Explorer (Mahogany), 2 Dirty Finger humbuckers, stoptail or Kahler vibrato, becomes Explorer 83 in '83.

1981-1982		$1,050	$1,375

Explorer 83 or Explorer (Alder)
1983-1989. Renamed Explorer 83 from Explorer I, changed to Explorer in '84, alder body, 2 humbuckers, maple neck, ebony 'board, dot inlays, triangle knob pattern.

1983-1984		$1,800	$2,350
1985-1989	Custom color, limited run	$1,575	$2,050
1985-1989	Standard finishes	$1,400	$1,825

Explorer II (E/2)
1978-1983. Five-piece maple and walnut laminate body sculptured like V II, ebony 'board with dot inlays, 2 humbuckers, gold-plated hardware, natural finish.

1978-1983	Figured top	$3,150	$4,100
1978-1983	Various colors	$3,000	$3,900

Explorer III
1984-1985. Alder body, 3 P-90 pickups, 2 control knobs, chrome or black hardware ('85 only), optional locking trem.

1984-1985	All options	$1,200	$1,575

Explorer '76/X-plorer/Explorer
1990-2014, 2019-present. Mahogany body and neck, rosewood 'board, dot inlays, 2 humbucking pickups, name changed to X-plorer in 2002 and to Explorer in '09. Reintroduced in '19.

1990-1999	Various colors	$1,200	$1,575
2002-2014	Various colors	$1,200	$1,575

Explorer 90 Double
1989-1990. Mahogany body and neck, 1 single-coil and 1 humbucker, strings-thru-body.

1989-1990		$1,700	$2,225

Explorer Baritone
2011-2013. 28"-scale, 2 exposed humbuckers.

2011-2013		$1,700	$2,225

Explorer Centennial
1994 only. Les Paul Gold finish, 100 year banner inlay at 12th fret, diamonds in headstock and gold-plated knobs, Gibson coin in rear of headstock, only 100 made.

1994		$4,700	$6,100

Explorer CMT/The Explorer
1981-1984. Flamed maple body, bound top, exposed-coil pickups, TP-6 tailpiece.

1981-1984		$3,650	$4,750

Explorer Custom Shop
2003-2012. Custom Shop model with Certificate of Authenticity, Korina body, gold hardware.

2003-2012		$5,400	$7,000

Explorer Designer Series
1983-1985. Custom paint finish.

1983-1985		$1,650	$2,150

Explorer Gothic
1998-2003. Gothic Series with black finish and hardware.

1998-2003		$975	$1,275

Explorer Government Series
2012-2016. Made from guitar bodies, necks and 'boards returned from Federal Government after '11 raid on Gibson, special run of 300 built, each with Certificate of Authenticity.

2013		$1,150	$1,500

Explorer Heritage
1983. Reissue of '58 Explorer, korina body, gold hardware, inked serial number, limited edition.

1983	Black, white, red	$3,800	$5,000
1983	Natural	$5,300	$7,000

Explorer Korina
1982-1984. Korina body and neck, 2 humbucking pickups, gold hardware, standard 8-digit serial (versus the inked serial number on the Heritage Explorer of the same era).

1982-1984		$5,400	$7,000

Explorer 1958 Korina/Split Headstock
1994. Split headstock, 50 made.

1994		$7,800	$10,200

Explorer 50th Anniversary '58 Korina
2007-2008. Custom Shop, natural korina, includes custom colors.

2007-2008		$7,800	$10,200

The Official Vintage Guitar magazine Price Guide 2023   **Gibson** Explorer 50-Year Brimstone Comm. — E. C. 1964 Firebird I   **157**

GUITARS

MODEL YEAR	FEATURES	EXC. COND. LOW	HIGH

Explorer 50-Year Brimstone Commemorative
2008. Guitar of the month Oct. '08, solid mahogany body, AA figured maple top, higher-end appointments, 50th logo on truss rod cover, Brimstone Burst finish.

2008		$2,700	$3,500

Explorer 120
2014. 120th Anniversary inlay at 12th fret, mahogany body, cherry or black.

2014		$1,350	$1,800

Explorer Pro
2002-2005, 2007-2008. Explorer model updated with smaller, lighter weight mahogany body, 2 humbuckers, ebony or natural.

2002-2008		$1,400	$1,850

Allen Collins Tribute Explorer
2003. Custom Shop, limited production, korina body and neck, rosewood 'board, 2 humbucker pickups.

2003		$8,800	$11,500

Dethklok "Thunderhorse" Explorer
2011-2012. Limited Edition of 400, Thunderhorse logo on truss rod cover, silverburst finish.

2011-2012		$2,100	$2,700

Explorer Limited Edition (Korina)
1976. Limited edition korina body replaces standard mahogany body, natural.

1976		$6,300	$8,300

Explorer Limited Edition (Mahogany)
1999. Mahogany with natural finish.

1999		$1,725	$2,250

Explorer Robot
2008-2012. Announced Sept. '08, Robot Tuning System, trapezoid markers, 2 exposed humbuckers, red finish.

2008-2012		$1,050	$1,350

Explorer Split Headstock Collection
2001. Custom Shop model, 25 made, Explorer body with V-split headstock.

2001		$3,300	$4,300

Explorer T/Explorer 2016 T/2017 T
2016-2018. Mahogany body, rosewood 'board, white 'guard, ebony or cherry finish.

2016-2018		$1,200	$1,600

Explorer Voodoo
2002-2004. Juju finish, red and black pickup coils.

2002-2004		$1,275	$1,650

Explorer XPL
1985. Gibson Custom Shop logo on back of headstock, factory Gibson Kahler tremolo, extra cutaway on lower treble bout.

1985		$1,175	$1,525

Holy Explorer
2009-2011. Explorer body 7 routed holes, 1 knob, 2 exposed humbuckers, Limited Run Series certificate of authenticity, 350 made.

2009-2011		$1,125	$1,475

Reverse Explorer
2008. Guitar of the Month Sept. '08, 1,000 made, Antique Walnut finish, includes custom guitar case.

2008		$1,500	$1,950

Sammy Hagar Signature Explorer
2011-2013. Mahogany with Red Rocker finish, ghosted Chickenfoot logo on back.

2011-2013		$1,975	$2,575

Shred X Explorer
2008. Guitar of the Month June '08, 1,000 made, ebony finish, black hardware, 2 EMG 85 pickups, Kahler.

2008		$1,175	$1,525

Tribal Explorer
2009-2011. Black tribal graphics on white body. Limited run of 350.

2009-2011		$1,075	$1,400

X-Plorer/X-Plorer V New Century
2006-2007. Full-body mirror 'guard, mahogany body and neck, 2 humbuckers, mirror truss rod cover.

2006-2007		$1,150	$1,500

Firebird I
1963-1969. Reverse body and 1 humbucker '63-mid-'65, non-reversed body and 2 P-90s mid-'65-'69.

YEAR	FEATURES	LOW	HIGH
1963	Sunburst, reverse, hardtail	$13,600	$17,700
1963	Sunburst, reverse, trem	$8,800	$11,400
1964	Cardinal Red, reverse	$14,100	$18,300
1964	Sunburst, reverse, hardtail	$12,900	$16,700
1964	Sunburst, reverse, trem	$7,200	$9,400
1965	Cardinal Red, reverse	$11,200	$14,600
1965	Custom color, non-reverse	$9,500	$12,400
1965	Sunburst, non-reverse, 2 P-90s	$4,000	$5,200
1965	Sunburst, reverse	$6,100	$8,000
1966	Custom color, non-reverse	$7,000	$9,000
1966	Sunburst, non-reverse	$3,900	$5,100
1967	Custom color, non-reverse	$7,100	$9,200
1967	Sunburst, non-reverse	$3,900	$5,100
1968-1969	Sunburst, non-reverse	$3,900	$5,100

Firebird I (Custom Shop)

1991-1992		$2,550	$3,300

Firebird I 1963 Reissue Historic
2000-2006. Custom Shop Historic Collection, neck-thru, reverse body, Firebird logo on 'guard, various colors including sunburst and Frost Blue.

2000-2006	Various colors	$2,550	$3,300

Eric Clapton 1964 Firebird I
2019. Custom Shop, limited run of 100, mahogany body, mahogany/walnut neck, Indian rosewood 'board, signed backplate, 1 Alnico pickup, Vintage Sunburst, certificate.

2019		$6,400	$8,300

1983 Gibson Explorer Korina
Bo Belaski

1965 Gibson Firebird I
Matt Carleson

GUITARS

1976 Gibson Firebird 76
Imaged by Heritage Auctions, HA.com

1963 Gibson Firebird V
Daniel Hess

Firebird 76

1976-1978. Reverse body, gold hardware, 2 pickups.

MODEL YEAR	FEATURES	EXC. COND. LOW	HIGH
1976	Bicentennial	$3,200	$4,200
1976	Black	$3,000	$3,900
1976	Sunburst, red/white/ blue 'guard logo	$3,200	$4,200
1977-1978	Sunburst	$3,000	$3,900
1977-1978	White	$3,000	$3,900

Firebird I/ Firebird 76

1980-1982. Reintroduced Firebird 76 but renamed Firebird I.

1980-1982		$2,775	$3,600

Firebird II/Firebird 2

1981-1982. Maple body with figured maple top, 2 full size active humbuckers, TP-6 tailpiece.

1981-1982		$3,100	$4,050

Firebird III

1963-1969. Reverse body and 2 humbuckers '63-mid-'65, non-reversed body and 3 P-90s mid-'65-'69, various colors.

1963	Cardinal Red	$13,000	$17,000
1963	Golden Mist	$13,000	$17,000
1963	Polaris White	$12,000	$15,600
1963	Sunburst	$9,700	$12,600
1964	Cardinal Red, reverse	$12,900	$16,700
1964	Golden Mist, reverse	$12,900	$16,700
1964	Pelham Blue	$12,900	$16,700
1964	Polaris White, reverse	$11,000	$14,200
1964	Sunburst, reverse	$9,550	$12,400
1965	Cherry, non-reverse, 3 P-90s	$5,400	$7,000
1965	Cherry, reverse	$9,500	$12,500
1965	Frost Blue, non-reverse	$9,900	$12,900
1965	Frost Blue, reverse	$11,800	$15,300
1965	Golden Mist, reverse	$11,800	$15,300
1965	Inverness Green, non-reverse	$9,900	$12,900
1965	Iverness Green, reverse	$11,800	$15,300
1965	Sunburst, non-reverse, 2 P-90s	$4,600	$6,000
1965	Sunburst, non-reverse, 3 P-90s	$4,800	$6,200
1965	Sunburst, reverse, 2 P-90s	$6,900	$9,000
1965	Sunburst, reverse, mini hums	$7,400	$9,600
1966	Frost Blue	$9,900	$12,900
1966	Pelham Blue	$9,900	$12,900
1966	Polaris White	$9,100	$11,900
1966-1969	Sunburst	$4,700	$6,100
1967	Cherry	$4,850	$6,300
1967	Frost Blue	$10,100	$13,100
1967-1969	Pelham Blue	$10,100	$13,100

Firebird III 1964 Reissue Historic

2000-2013. Custom Shop Historic Collection, Maestro, mini-humbuckers, sunburst or color option.

2000-2013		$3,000	$3,900

Firebird Non-Reverse

2002-2004. Non-reverse body, 2 humbuckers, standard finishes. There was also a limited edition in '02 with swirl finishes.

2002-2004		$1,425	$1,850

Firebird Studio Non-Reverse

2011-2012. Non-reverse body, 3 tapped P-90 pickups, 5-way pickup selector switch, dot markers, Vintage Sunburst or Pelham Blue nitro finish.

2011-2012		$1,200	$1,550

Firebird Studio Tribute/Studio T

2012-2017. Reverse mahogany body, '70s profile maple neck, 2 mini-humbuckers.

2012-2017		$1,200	$1,550

Firebird Studio/Firebird III Studio

2004-2010. Two humbuckers, dot markers, tune-o-matic and bar stoptail, reverse body, dark cherry finish.

2004-2010		$1,200	$1,550

Firebird V

1963-1969. Two humbuckers, reverse body '63-mid-'65, non-reversed body mid-'65-'69.

1963	Sunburst, reverse	$14,700	$19,100
1963-1964	Pelham Blue, reverse	$21,100	$27,400
1964	Cardinal Red, reverse	$19,100	$24,800
1964	Sunburst, reverse	$14,900	$19,300
1965	Cardinal Red, reverse	$17,100	$22,200
1965	Sunburst, non-reverse	$5,800	$7,500
1965	Sunburst, reverse	$10,100	$13,100
1966-1967	Cardinal Red, non-reverse	$11,000	$14,300
1966-1969	Sunburst	$5,700	$7,400

Firebird V/Firebird V Reissue/Firebird V 2010

1986-1987, 1990-2018. Based on Firebird V specs, reverse body, 2 pickups, tune-o-matic bridge, vintage sunburst, classic white or ebony with Cardinal Red optional in '91. Called Reissue for '90-'93, renamed V in '94, then V 2010 in '10.

1986-1987	Sunburst, white, black	$2,550	$3,400
1990	Sunburst, white, black	$2,550	$3,400
1991	Cardinal Red	$2,200	$2,900
1991-1999	Sunburst, white, black	$1,600	$2,100
2000-2018	Sunburst, white, black	$1,425	$1,850

Firebird V-12

1966-1967. Non-reverse Firebird V-style body with standard six-on-a-side headstock and split diamond headstock inlay (like ES-335-12 inlay), dot markers, special twin humbucking pickups (like mini-humbuckers).

1966-1967	Custom color	$10,000	$13,000
1966-1967	Sunburst	$4,600	$6,000

MODEL YEAR	FEATURES	EXC. COND. LOW	HIGH

Firebird V 1963 Aged (Custom Shop)
2016. Reverse body, Vintage Sunburst, aged hardware.

2016		$3,500	$4,600

Firebird V 1963 Johnny Winter
2008. Johnny Winter script logo, certificate of authenticity.

2008		$6,800	$8,800

1963 Firebird V (Maestro Vibrola) Murphy Lab Aged
2021-present. Custom Shop Murphy Lab Collection, heavy aged (Antique Frost Blue), light aged (Cardinal Red) and ultra light (Ember Red or Pelham Blue).

2021-2022	Heavy aged	$5,700	$7,500
2021-2022	Light aged	$5,000	$6,500
2021-2022	Ultra Light aged	$4,200	$5,500

Firebird V 1964 Johnny Winter
2021-present. Mahogany/walnut body, Indian rosewood 'board, 2 Alnico pickups, banjo tuners, Murphy Lab aged Polaris White finish.

2021-2022		$7,000	$9,000

Firebird V 1965 Reissue (Custom Shop)
2000-2013. Reverse body, 2 mini-humbuckers, Maestro tremolo, certificate, sunburst or colors.

2000-2013		$2,800	$3,700

Firebird V 50th Anniversary
2013. Gold hardware, '50th Anniversary 1963-2013' on 'guard, gold finish.

2013		$1,650	$2,150

Firebird V Celebrity Series
1990-1993. Reverse body, gold hardware, 2 humbuckers, various colors.

1990-1993		$2,800	$3,700

Firebird V Guitar Trader Reissue
1982. Guitar Trader commissioned Firebird reissue, only 15 made, sunburst or white.

1982		$3,800	$4,900

Firebird V Limited Edition Zebrawood
2007. Limited edition from Gibson USA, Guitar of the Week #12, 400 made, zebrawood reverse body.

2007		$1,900	$2,500

Firebird V Medallion
1972-1973. Reverse body, 2 humbuckers, Limited Edition medallion mounted on body.

1972-1973		$5,700	$7,500

Firebird VII
1963-1969. Three humbuckers, reverse body '63-mid-'65, non-reversed body mid-'65-'69, sunburst standard.

1963-1964	Sunburst, reverse	$15,500	$20,000
1964	Custom color, reverse	$24,700	$32,000
1965	Custom color, non-reverse	$16,500	$21,500
1965	Custom color, reverse	$20,000	$26,000
1965	Sunburst, non-reverse	$6,500	$8,500
1965	Sunburst, reverse	$11,700	$15,200
1966-1967	Custom color, non-reverse	$13,000	$17,000
1966-1969	Sunburst, non-reverse	$6,100	$7,900
1968	Custom color, non-reverse	$10,500	$14,000

Firebird VII (Reissued)
2002-2007. Designer collection, various production models, reverse and non-reverse, 3 pickups, block markers, vibrola, various color options with matching headstock.

2002-2007	All colors	$1,950	$2,550

Firebird VII 1965 Historic
1998-2013. Custom Shop Historic Collection, 3 mini-humbuckers, Vintage Sunburst or solid colors.

1998-2013		$3,000	$3,900

20th Anniversary 1965 Firebird VII
2014. Custom Shop, '65 specs, gold hardware, Golden Mist finish, certificate of authenticity.

2014		$3,200	$4,200

Firebird VII Centennial
1994 only. Headstock medallion, sunburst.

1994		$4,000	$5,200

Firebird X Limited Edition Robot
2011-2018. 1800 to be made, lightweight swamp ash body, 1-piece maple neck, curly maple 'board, 3 pickups, robot electronics, nitro lacquer finish in Redolution or Bluevolution.

2011-2018		$2,600	$3,375

Elliot Easton "Tikibird" Firebird
2013-2018. Reverse body, mahogany, rosewood 'board, 2 pickups, Tiki graphic on 'guard, signature on headstock back, Gold Mist Poly finish.

2013-2018		$1,750	$2,275

Firebird Custom Acoustic
2004-2018. Sitka spruce top, quilted maple back and sides, ebony 'board, mother-of-pearl headstock logo with MOP and abalone flames inlay, antique natural finish.

2004-2018		$2,250	$3,350

Firebird Zero
2016-2018. S Series, new body design, 2 pickups, poplar body, maple neck, rosewood 'board, various colors.

2016-2018		$345	$445

Flamenco 2
1963-1967. Natural spruce top, 14 3/4", cypress back and sides, slotted headstock, zero fret.

1963-1967		$1,350	$1,750

Flying V
1958-1959, 1962-1963. Only 81 shipped in '58 and 17 in '59, guitars made from leftover parts and sold in '62-'63, natural korina body, string-thru-body design. Original case with oxblood interior adds $2,500.

As with any ultra high-end instrument, each instrument should be evaluated on a case-by-case basis. The Flying V market is a very specialized market, with few untouched examples available, and a limited number of high-end buyers. The price ranges noted are for all-original, excellent condition guitars with the original Flying V case. The slightest change to the original specifications can mean a significant drop in value.

1958-1959		$335,000	$435,000

Gibson 1963 Firebird V Murphy Lab Aged

1959 Gibson Flying V
Kris Blakely

1982 Gibson Flying V Heritage
Steve Evans

2002 Gibson Flying V Voodoo
Imaged by Heritage Auctions, HA.com

MODEL YEAR	FEATURES	EXC. COND. LOW	HIGH

Flying V (Mahogany)
1966-1970, 1975-1981. Mahogany body, around 200 were shipped for '66-'70. Gibson greatly increased production of Flying Vs in '75. See separate listing for the '71 Medallion V version.

1966	Cherry, sunburst	$28,000	$36,300
1967-1970	Cherry, sunburst	$21,200	$27,600
1975-1981	Various colors	$4,500	$5,875
1979	Silverburst	$5,500	$7,200
1980-1981	Silverburst	$5,100	$6,600

Flying V (Mahogany String-through-body)
1982. Mahogany body, string-thru-body design, only 100 made, most in white, some red or black possible.

1982	All colors	$3,200	$4,200

Flying V (Custom Shop)
2004-2008. A few made each year, figured maple top, options include standard point-headstock or split-headstock.

2004-2008	All options	$4,400	$5,700

Flying V Heritage
1981-1982. Limited edition based on '58 specs, korina body, 4 colors available.

1981-1982	Natural	$5,400	$7,000
1981-1982	Various colors	$3,800	$4,950

Flying V I/V '83/Flying V (no pickguard)
1981-1988. Introduced as Flying V I, then renamed Flying V '83 in 1983, called Flying V from '84 on. Alder body, 2 exposed humbuckers, maple neck, ebony 'board, dot inlays, black rings, no 'guard, ebony or ivory finish, designed for lower-end market.

1981-1988		$1,800	$2,350

Flying V Korina
1983. Name changed from Flying V Heritage, korina body, various colors.

1983		$5,400	$7,000

Flying V Reissue/'67/Factor X/Flying V
1990-2014. Mahogany body, called Flying V Reissue first year, then '67 Flying V '91-'02, V Factor X '03-'08, Flying V '09-'14.

1990-2014	Various colors	$1,200	$1,575

Flying V II
1979-1982. Five-piece maple and walnut laminate sculptured body (1980 catalog states top is either walnut or maple), ebony 'board with dot inlays, 2 V-shaped pickups (2 Dirty Fingers humbuckers towards end of run), gold-plated hardware, natural.

1979-1982		$3,000	$3,900
1982	Silverburst	$3,000	$3,900

Flying V 50th Anniversary
2008. Built as replica of '58 square shoulder V, 100 made, natural finish on korina body and neck, rosewood 'board, 8-series serial number, price includes original certificate.

2008		$6,400	$8,300

Flying V '58 Historic
1991-2013. Custom Shop Historic Collection, based on '58 Flying V, gold hardware, natural korina.

1991-1999		$5,800	$7,550
2000-2013		$5,200	$6,700

Flying V 1958 Mahogany
2021-present. Custom Shop Designer series, mahogany with walnut finish.

2021-2022		$3,400	$4,400

Flying V '59 (Custom Shop)

2001	Natural	$4,200	$5,500
2004	Cherry	$4,200	$5,500
2013	Natural	$3,200	$4,200
2020	TV Black Gold	$3,200	$4,200

Flying V 1959 Mahogany
2014-2020. Custom Shop Designer series, mahogany with various colors.

2014-2020		$2,850	$3,700

Flying V '67 Historic
1997-2004. Custom Shop Historic Collection, '67 Flying V specs, korina body, natural or opaque colors.

1997-2004		$2,700	$3,500

Flying V '84 Silverburst
2007. Limited Edition Guitar of the Week.

2007		$1,225	$1,600

Flying V '90 Double
1989-1990. Mahogany body, stud tailpiece, 1 single-coil and 1 double-coil humbucker, Floyd Rose tremolo, ebony, silver or white.

1989-1990		$1,700	$2,225

Flying V '98
1998. Mahogany body, '58 style controls, gold or chrome hardware.

1998		$1,400	$2,225

Flying V 120
2014. Mahogany body and neck, 120th Anniversary inlay at 12th fret, rosewood 'board, 2 BurstBucker pickups, ebony, classic white or Heritage Cherry.

2014		$1,325	$1,725

Flying V 50-Year Commemorative
2008. Guitar of the Month March '08, 1,000 made, AA flamed maple top, higher-end appointments, 50th logo on truss rod cover, Brimstone Burst finish.

2008		$2,150	$2,800

Flying V Brendon Small Snow Falcon
2013. Snow Falcon decal on headstock back, 2 Burstbucker pickups, chrome hardware, Snow Burst finish, limited run.

2013		$1,775	$2,300

Flying V Centennial
1994 only. 100th Anniversary Series, all gold, gold medalion, other special appointments.

1994		$4,700	$6,125

Flying V CMT/The V
1981-1985. Maple body with a curly maple top, 2 pickups, stud tailpiece, natural or sunburst.

1981-1985		$3,650	$4,750

Flying V Custom
2002. Limited Edition, appointments similar to Les Paul Custom, including black finish, only 40 made.

2002		$5,400	$7,000

Flying V Designer Series
1983-1984. Custom paint finish.

1983-1984		$1,650	$2,150

Flying V Faded
2002-2012. Worn cherry finish.

2002-2012		$725	$950

MODEL YEAR	FEATURES	EXC. COND. LOW	HIGH

Flying V Gothic/'98 Gothic
1998-2003. Satin black finish, black hardware, moon and star markers.

1998-2003		$975	$1,275

Flying V Government Series
2012-2016. Made from guitar bodies, necks and 'boards returned from Federal Government after '11 raid on Gibson, special run of 300 built, each with Certificate of Authenticity.

2013		$1,150	$1,500

Flying V Hendrix Hall of Fame
Late-1991-1993. Limited Edition (400 made), numbered, black.

1991-1993		$3,000	$4,000

Flying V Hendrix Psychedelic
2005-2006. Hand-painted 1967 Flying V replica, 300 made, includes certificate, instruments without the certificate are worth less than the amount shown.

2005-2006		$8,000	$10,500

Flying V Kirk Hammett Signature
2012. Custom Shop, '76 specs, aged ebony.

2012		$4,800	$6,400

Flying V Lenny Kravitz
2002. Custom Shop, 125 made.

2002		$3,650	$4,750

Flying V Lonnie Mack
1993-1995. Mahogany body with Lonnie Mack-style Bigsby vibrato, cherry.

1993-1995		$4,150	$5,375

Flying V LTD
2001. Limited Edition logo, certificate of authenticity.

2001		$1,150	$1,500

Flying V Medallion
1971. Mahogany body, stud tailpiece, numbered Limited Edition medallion on bass side of V, 350 made in '71 (3 more were shipped in '73-'74).

1971-1974		$14,400	$18,700

Flying V New Century
2006-2007. Full-body mirror 'guard, mahogany body and neck, 2 humbuckers, Flying V style neck profile, mirror truss rod cover.

2006-2007		$1,150	$1,500

Flying V Primavera
1994. Primavera (light yellow/white mahogany) body, gold-plated hardware.

1994		$2,075	$2,675

Flying V Robot
2008-2011. Robot Tuning System.

2008-2011		$1,050	$1,350

Flying V T
2016-2017. Mahogany body, thicker 1-piece 'board.

2016-2017		$1,200	$1,575

Flying V The Holy V
2009. Guitar of the month for Jan. '09, large triangular cutouts in bouts, split diamond markers, 1 humbucker, 1 control knob.

2009		$1,125	$1,475

Flying V Voodoo
2002-2003. Black finish, red pickups.

2002-2003		$1,275	$1,650

Limited Edition Flying V
2016. Dirty Fingers, faded amber finish, gig bag.

2016		$575	$750

Reverse Flying V
2006-2008. Introduced as part of Guitar of the Week program, reintroduced by popular demand in a '07 limited run, light colored solid mahogany body gives a natural Korina appearance or opaque white or black, V-shaped reverse body, traditional Flying V neck profile.

2006-2007		$1,700	$2,200
2008	Guitar of the Week	$1,500	$1,950

Rudolph Schenker Flying V
1993. Only 103 made, black and white body and headstock, signature on 'guard.

1993		$1,775	$2,300

Shred V
2008. Guitar of the Month, 1000 made, EMG humbuckers, Kahler, black.

2008		$1,175	$1,525

Tribal V
2009-2011. Black tribal graphics on white body. Limited run of 350.

2009-2011		$1,075	$1,400

Zakk Wylde Flying V
2007-2011. Custom Shop, with Floyd Rose and typical bullseye finish.

2007-2011		$4,700	$6,100

F-25 Folksinger
1963-1971. 14-1/2" flat-top, mahogany body, most have double white 'guard, natural.

1963-1964		$1,075	$1,400
1965		$975	$1,275
1966-1971		$925	$1,200

FJN Folk Singer
1963-1967. Jumbo flat-top, square shoulders, natural finish with deep red on back and sides.

1963-1964		$2,100	$2,750
1965		$1,925	$2,500
1966-1967		$1,825	$2,375

Futura
1982-1984. Deep cutout solidbody, 2 humbucker pickups, gold hardware, black, white or purple.

1982-1984		$2,075	$2,675

Historic Korina Futura
1998-1999. Custom Shop Historic Collection, Explorer body with V headstock.

1998-1999		$7,800	$10,100

G-00
2021-present. Generation Collection, parlor-sized, sitka spruce top, walnut back and sides, natural finish.

2021-2022		$650	$850

G-45 (Standard/Studio)
2019-present. Slim body, Fishman pickup, solid sitka spruce top, walnut back and sides, Antique Natural satin finish (standard) or gloss (studio).

2019-2021	Gloss	$825	$1,075
2019-2022	Satin	$675	$875

1999 Gibson Historic Korina Futura
Imaged by Heritage Auctions, HA.com

Gibson G-45 Standard

To get the most from this book, be sure to read "Using **The Guide**" in the introduction.

1977 Gibson Howard Roberts Custom
Bernunzio Uptown Music

1963 Gibson Hummingbird
Craig Brody

MODEL YEAR	FEATURES	EXC. COND. LOW	HIGH

GB Series Guitar Banjos
See listings in Banjo section of the Price Guide.
GGC-700
1981-1982. Slab single-cut body, 2 exposed humbuckers, dots.

1981-1982		$850	$1,100

GK-55 Active
1979-1980. LP body style, 2 exposed Dirty Fingers humbuckers, bolt neck, dot markers.

1979-1980		$825	$1,075

Gospel
1973-1979. Flat-top, square shoulders, laminated maple back and sides, arched back, Dove of Peace headstock inlay, natural.

1973-1979		$1,125	$1,450

Gospel Reissue
1992-1997. Laminated mahogany back and sides, natural or sunburst (walnut added in '94, blue and red in '95), changes to old-style script logo and headstock ornamentation in '94.

1992-1993	Reissue specs	$1,375	$1,800
1994-1997	Old-style specs	$1,375	$1,800

GS-1 Classical
1950-1956. Mahogany back and sides.

1950-1956		$700	$925

GS-2 Classical
1950-1956. Maple back and sides.

1950-1959		$775	$1,000

GS-5 Custom Classic/C-5 Classical
1954-1960. Brazilian rosewood back and sides, renamed C-5 Classical in '57.

1954-1960		$1,625	$2,125

GS-35 Classical/Gut String 35
1939-1942. Spruce top, mahogany back and sides, only 39 made.

1939-1942		$1,900	$2,450

GS-85 Classical/Gut String 85
1939-1942. Brazilian rosewood back and sides.

1939-1942		$3,600	$4,700

GY (Army-Navy)
1918-1921. Slightly arched top and back, low-end budget model, Sheraton Brown.

1918-1921		$800	$1,050

Harley Davidson LTD
1994-1995. Limited Edition, 16" wide body, flat-top, Harley Davidson in script and logo, black, 1500 sold through Harley dealers to celebrate 100th Anniversary of Harley.

1994-1995		$2,150	$2,800

Heritage
1965-1982. Flat-top dreadnought, square shoulders, rosewood back and sides (Brazilian until '67, Indian '68 on), bound top and back, natural finish.

1965-1967	Brazilian	$2,900	$3,800
1968-1982	Indian	$1,425	$1,850

Heritage-12
1968-1971. Flat-top dreadnought, 12 strings, Indian rosewood back and sides, bound top and back, natural finish.

1968-1971		$1,425	$1,850

HG-00 (Hawaiian)
1932-1942. Hawaiian version of L-00, 14 3/4" flat-top, mahogany back and sides, bound top, natural.

1932-1947		$4,500	$5,800

HG-20 (Hawaiian)
1929-1933. Hawaiian, 14 1/2" dreadnought-shaped, maple back and sides, round soundhole and 4 f-holes.

1929-1933		$4,500	$5,800

HG-22 (Hawaiian)
1929-1932. Dreadnought, 14", Hawaiian, round soundhole and 4 f-holes, white paint logo, very small number produced.

1929-1932		$4,800	$6,300

HG-24 (Hawaiian)
1929-1932. 16" Hawaiian, rosewood back and sides, round soundhole plus 4 f-holes, small number produced.

1929-1932		$6,600	$8,600

HG-Century (Hawaiian)
1937-1938. Hawaiian, 14 3/4" L-C Century of Progress, pearloid 'board.

1937-1938		$4,600	$5,900

Howard Roberts Artist
1976-1980. Full body single-cut archtop, soundhole, 1 humbucking pickup, gold hardware, ebony 'board, various colors.

1976-1980		$2,650	$3,450

Howard Roberts Artist Double Pickup
1979-1980. Two pickup version of HR Artist.

1979-1980		$2,850	$3,700

Howard Roberts Custom
1975-1981. Full body single-cut archtop, soundhole, 1 humbucking pickup, chrome hardware, rosewood 'board, various colors.

1975-1981		$2,750	$3,600

Howard Roberts Fusion/Fusion II/Fusion III
1979-2009. Single-cut, semi-hollowbody, 2 humbucking pickups, chrome hardware, ebony 'board (unbound until '78), TP-6 tailpiece, various colors, renamed Howard Roberts Fusion II in late-'88, and Howard Roberts Fusion III in '91.

1979-2009		$2,550	$3,300

HP-415 W
2017-2018. High Performance series, slimmer round shoulder cutaway, sitka spruce top, walnut back and sides.

2017-2018		$1,025	$1,325

Hummingbird
1960-2020. Flat-top acoustic, square shoulders, mahogany back and sides, bound body and neck. Name changes to Hummingbird Standard in '20.

1960	Cherry Sunburst	$6,800	$8,800
1961-1964	Cherry Sunburst	$6,500	$8,500
1963-1965	Natural	$6,800	$8,800
1965	Cherry Sunburst	$4,700	$6,200
1966	Cherry Sunburst	$3,900	$5,100
1966	Natural	$4,100	$5,400
1967-1968	Natural, screwed 'guard	$4,100	$5,400

MODEL YEAR	FEATURES	EXC. COND. LOW	HIGH
1967-1968	Sunburst, screwed 'guard	$3,900	$5,100
1969	Natural, screwed 'guard	$3,400	$4,450
1969	Sunburst, screwed 'guard	$3,400	$4,450
1970-1971	Natural, sunburst	$2,900	$3,800
1972-1979	Double X, block markers	$2,900	$3,800
1980-1985	Double X, block markers	$2,500	$3,200
1985-1988	Single X	$2,000	$2,600
1989	25 1/2" scale	$2,000	$2,600
1990-2020		$2,300	$3,000
1994	100 Years 1894-1994 label	$2,300	$3,000
2015-2020	Custom Shop, ebony	$2,300	$3,000

Hummingbird Standard
2020-present. Modern series, mahogany body with sitka spruce top, Vintage Sunburst or ebony.

| 2020-2021 | | $2,550 | $3,400 |

Hummingbird Historic
2005-2006. Custom Shop Historic Collection, Vintage Honeyburst.

| 2005-2006 | | $2,350 | $3,100 |

50th Anniversary 1960 Hummingbird
2010-2012. Limited Edition, 200 made, 50th Anniversary logo on truss rod cover.

| 2010-2012 | | $3,850 | $5,000 |

Hummingbird 12
2005-2011. Custom Shop, 12-string, Vintage Sunburst.

| 2005-2011 | | $3,200 | $4,200 |

Hummingbird Artist
2007-2011. Plain (no Hummingbird) small 'guard, L.R. Baggs Element, sold through Guitar Center.

| 2007-2011 | | $1,650 | $2,150 |

Hummingbird Custom Koa
2004, 2009-2018. Highly flamed koa back and sides, spruce top, gloss finish.

| 2004-2018 | | $3,850 | $5,000 |

Hummingbird Limited Edition
1993-1994. Only 30 made, quilted maple top and back.

| 1993-1994 | | $2,900 | $3,800 |

Hummingbird Madagascar Honeyburst
2009. Limited run of 20, figured Madagascar rosewood back and sides, factory electronics, certificate of authenticity.

| 2009 | | $2,900 | $3,800 |

Hummingbird Modern Classic
2010-2012. Cherry sunburst or ebony finish, L.R. Baggs Element Active pickup system.

| 2010-2012 | | $2,350 | $3,100 |

Hummingbird Pro
2010-2013. Non-cut, plain (no Hummingbird) small 'guard, L.R. Baggs Element, Guitar Center.

| 2010-2013 | | $1,525 | $1,975 |

Hummingbird Pro EC
2010-2013. Cutaway version, Fishman Prefix Plus-T, Guitar Center.

| 2010-2013 | | $1,600 | $2,100 |

Hummingbird Pro 12-String
2018. Custom Shop Limited Edition, sitka spruce top, mahogany back and sides, Vintage Sunburst or Heritage Cherry Sunburst.

| 2018 | | $1,700 | $2,200 |

Hummingbird Quilt Series

| 2007-2014 | Custom Shop | $2,900 | $3,800 |

Hummingbird Studio
2019-2020. Slim body, on-board electronics, Antique Natural or Walnut Burst.

| 2019-2020 | | $1,450 | $1,900 |

Hummingbird Studio Rosewood
2020-present. Sitka spruce top, rosewood back and sides, Antique Natural or Rosewood Burst.

| 2020-2021 | | $1,900 | $2,500 |

Hummingbird Studio Walnut
2020-present. Sitka spruce top, walnut back and sides, Antique Natural or Walnut Burst.

| 2020-2021 | | $1,450 | $1,900 |

Hummingbird True Vintage
2007-2013. Sitka spruce top, Madagascar rosewood bridge and 'board, special '60s Heritage Cherry or sunburst finish.

| 2007-2013 | | $3,400 | $4,400 |

Invader
1983-1988. Single cutaway solid mahogany body, two humbucker pickups, four knobs with three-way selector switch, stop tailpiece, bolt-on maple neck.

| 1983-1988 | All colors | $800 | $1,050 |

J-15/J-15 Standard
2014-2021. Acoustic-electric dreadnought, slope shoulder, walnut back and sides, Antique Natural.

| 2014-2021 | | $1,300 | $1,675 |

J-25
1983-1985. Flat-top, laminated spruce top, synthetic semi-round back, ebony 'board, natural or sunburst.

| 1983-1985 | | $550 | $725 |

J-29 Rosewood
2014-2016. Sitka spruce top, solid rosewood back and sides.

| 2014-2016 | | $1,300 | $1,700 |

J-30
1985-1993. Dreadnought-size flat-top acoustic, mahogany back and sides, sunburst, Renamed J-30 Montana in '94.

| 1985-1993 | | $1,625 | $2,100 |

J-30 Cutaway
1990-1995. Cutaway version of J-30, transducer pickup.

| 1990-1995 | | $1,675 | $2,150 |

J-30 Montana
1994-1997. Renamed from J-30, dreadnought-size flat-top acoustic, mahogany back and sides, sunburst.

| 1994-1997 | | $1,625 | $2,100 |

J-30 RCA Limited Edition
1991. Limited edition for RCA Nashville, RCA logo on headstock.

| 1991 | | $1,625 | $2,100 |

J-35
2012-2018. Sitka spruce top, mahogany back, sides and neck, rosewood 'board.

| 2012-2018 | | $1,450 | $1,900 |

Gibson Hummingbird Studio Rosewood

2012 Gibson J-35
Bernunzio Uptown Music

1958 Gibson J-45

John Wesley

Gibson J-45 Studio Walnut

MODEL YEAR	FEATURES	EXC. COND. LOW	HIGH

J-40
1971-1982. Dreadnought flat-top, mahogany back and sides, economy satin finish.

1971-1982		$1,200	$1,600

J-45
1942-1982, 1984-present. Dreadnought flat-top, mahogany back and sides, round shoulders until '68 and '84 on, square shoulders '69-'82, sunburst finish (see J-50 for natural version) then natural finish also available in '90s, renamed J-45 Western in '94, renamed Early J-45 in '97 then renamed J-45 Standard in '99. The prices noted are for all-original crack free instruments. A single professionally repaired minor crack that is nearly invisible will reduce the value only slightly. Two or more, or unsightly repaired cracks will devalue an otherwise excellent original acoustic instrument. Repaired cracks should be evaluated on a case-by-case basis.

1942-1945	Banner, Adirondack	$10,800	$14,200
1942-1945	Banner, mahogany	$9,500	$12,500
1945	Banner, sitka	$8,700	$11,600
1946-1948	Script, sitka	$8,700	$11,600
1949	Small 'guard	$8,000	$10,500
1950-1954		$7,000	$9,200
1955-1959	Big 'guard	$6,000	$7,900
1960-1964	Round shoulders	$4,500	$6,000
1965	Early '65, wide nut	$4,000	$5,300
1965	Late '65, slim nut	$3,250	$4,300
1966-1967	Round shoulders	$3,000	$4,000
1968	Black, Cherry	$5,000	$6,550
1968	Blue, Green	$6,500	$8,500
1968-1969	Sunburst, Gibson 'guard	$3,000	$4,000
1969	Square D-shape, late '69	$2,600	$3,400
1970	Square, sunburst	$2,000	$2,650
1971-1975	Deluxe, sunburst	$2,000	$2,600
1976-1979	Sunburst	$2,000	$2,600
1980-1982	Sunburst	$1,900	$2,500
1984-1993	Various Colors	$1,900	$2,500
1994-1997	Western	$1,900	$2,500
1997-1998	Early J-45	$1,900	$2,500
1999-2021	Standard	$1,900	$2,500

J-45 1942 Legend
2006-2014. Early J-45 specs, Adirondack red spruce body, mahogany back/sides/neck, rosewood 'board, Vintage Sunburst finish, certificate of authenticity.

2006-2014		$4,700	$6,100

J-45 1968 Reissue
2004-2007. Limited Edition, special run using '68 specs including Gibson logo 'guard, black or cherry finish.

2004-2007		$1,900	$2,500

J-45 Brad Paisley
2010-2016. Adirondack red spruce top, mahogany back and sides, cherry sunburst.

2010-2016		$3,000	$4,000

J-45 Buddy Holly
1995-1996. Limited Edition, 250 made.

1995-1996		$3,000	$4,000

J-45 Celebrity
1985. Acoustic introduced for Gibson's 90th anniversary, spruce top, rosewood back and sides, ebony 'board, binding on body and 'board, only 90 made.

1985		$1,850	$2,450

J-45 Custom
1999-2020. Custom logo on truss rod, maple, mahogany or rosewood body, abalone trim, fancy headstock inlay.

1999-2020	Various options	$1,800	$3,700

J-45 Custom Vine
1999-2010. Custom Shop, Indian rosewood back and sides, fancy pearl and abalone vine inlay in ebony 'board, pearl Gibson logo and crown, natural gloss finish.

1999-2010		$3,450	$4,350

J-45 Elite Mystic
2014. Figured back, limited edition, rosewood back and sides.

2014		$2,600	$3,400

J-45 Heart of Texas Rosewood
2004. Custom Shop, soundhole label signed by Master Luthier Ren Ferguson, Indian rosewood back and sides, abalone top trim.

2004		$3,900	$5,200

J-45 Historic
2005. Limited edition, 670 made, Historic Collection logo rear headstock, sunburst.

2005		$2,400	$3,100

J-45 John Hiatt
2010-2011. Signature on truss rod cover, 100 offered, Tri Burst top with Tobacco Brown back and sides.

2010-2011		$2,900	$3,800

J-45 Natural Anniversary
2009. Custom Shop Limited Edition, decal on headstock back, 20 made, spruce top, maple neck, zebrawood back and sides, natural finish.

2009		$2,700	$3,600

J-45 Red Spruce Edition
2007. Custom Shop limited edition, only 50 made.

2007		$3,000	$4,000

J-45 Rosewood
1999-2006. Indian rosewood body, spruce top.

1999-2006		$1,875	$2,450

J-45 Studio Rosewood
2020-present. Sitka spruce top, rosewood back and sides, Antique Natural or Rosewood Burst.

2020-2021		$1,425	$1,850

J-45 Studio Sustainable
2019-2020. Sitka spruce top, sustainably harvested North American walnut back and sides, hand-rubbed beeswax finish, Antique Natural.

2019-2020		$1,500	$1,975

J-45 Studio Walnut
2020-present. Sitka spruce top, walnut back and sides, Antique Natural or Walnut Burst.

2020-2021		$1,075	$1,400

J-45 True Vintage/J-45 Vintage
2007-2019. Part of Vintage Series, vintage sunburst finish. True dropped from name in '19.

2007-2019		$2,400	$3,100

MODEL YEAR	FEATURES	EXC. COND. LOW	HIGH

J-45 Walnut Limited Edition
2015. Adirondack, flamed walnut.

2015		$3,000	$4,000

Working Man 45 (J-45)
1998-2005. Soft shoulder J-45 style, gloss finish spruce top, satin finish mahogany back and sides, dot markers, natural.

1998-2005		$1,200	$1,575

J-50
1942, 1945-1981, 1990-1995, 1998-2008 (present). Dreadnought flat-top, mahogany back and sides, round shoulders until '68, square shoulders after, natural finish (see J-45 for sunburst version). Though not labeled J-50, the J-45 Standard is now also available in natural finish.

1945	Banner logo	$10,800	$11,600
1946-1948	Script logo	$8,700	$11,600
1949	Small 'guard	$8,000	$10,500
1950-1954	Small 'guard	$5,900	$7,700
1955	Big 'guard	$5,500	$7,200
1956-1959	Standard fixed bridge	$5,500	$7,200
1960-1964	Round shoulders	$4,500	$6,000
1965	Early '65, wide nut	$4,000	$5,300
1965	Late '65, slim nut	$3,250	$4,300
1966-1969	Round shoulders	$3,000	$4,000
1969	Late '69, square D-shape	$2,600	$3,400
1970-1979	Square shoulders	$2,000	$2,600
1980-2008		$1,900	$2,500

J-55 (Jumbo 55) Limited Edition
1994 only. 16" flat-top, spruce top, mahogany back and sides, 100 made, sunburst.

1994		$1,875	$2,450

J-55 (Reintroduced)
1973-1982. Flat-top, laminated mahogany back and sides, arched back, square shoulders, sunburst. See Jumbo 55 listing for '39-'43 version.

1973-1982		$1,175	$1,525

J-60 Curly Maple
1993 and 1996. Curly maple back and sides, limited edition from Montana shop, natural.

1993,1996		$2,100	$2,750

J-60/J-60 Traditional
1992-1999. Solid spruce top dreadnought, square shoulders, Indian rosewood back and sides, ebony 'board, multiple bindings, natural or sunburst.

1992-1999		$1,600	$2,100

J-100/J-100 Custom
1970-1974, 1985-1997. Flat-top jumbo, multi-bound top and back, black 'guard, dot inlays, mahogany back and sides, '80s version has maple back and sides, dot inlays and tortoise shell 'guard, '90s model has maple back and sides, no 'guard, and J-200 style block inlays.

1970-1974	Mahogany	$1,450	$1,900
1985-1997	Maple	$1,450	$1,900

J-100 Xtra
1991-1997, 1999-2004. Jumbo flat-top, mahogany back and sides, moustache bridge, dot inlays, various colors, J-100 Xtra Cutaway also available, reintroduced in '99 with maple back and sides and single-bound body.

1991-2004		$1,650	$2,200

J-150/SJ-150 Maple
1999-2008. Super jumbo body, solid spruce top, figured maple back and sides (rosewood in '05), MOP crown inlays, moustache bridge with transducer. Renamed SJ-150 in 2006.

1999-2005	J-150	$2,100	$2,800
2006-2008	SJ-150	$2,100	$2,800

J-160E
1954-1979. Flat-top jumbo acoustic, 1 bridge P-90 pickup, tone and volume controls on front, sunburst finish, reintroduced as J-160 in '90.

1954-1964		$6,200	$8,100
1965		$4,500	$5,900
1966-1969		$3,625	$4,800
1970-1979		$2,100	$2,800

J-160E Reissue/Standard/VS
1990-1997, 2003-2008. Reintroduced J-160E with solid spruce top, solid mahogany back and sides.

1990-2008		$2,000	$2,700

J-160E John Lennon Peace
2003-2013. J-160E with tortoise 'guard, natural, signature on truss rod cover.

2003-2013		$2,500	$3,300

J-160E John Lennon Peace Limited Edition
2009. Certificate of authenticity, 750 made.

2009		$2,650	$3,500

J-160E Montana Special
1995 only.

1995		$2,000	$2,650

J-160VS/John Lennon 70th
2010. Commemorative edition for John Lennon's 70th birthday, 500 made, vintage sunburst gloss finish.

2010		$2,500	$3,300

J-165 (Maple)
See CJ-165 listing.

J-180 Billy Jo Armstrong
2011. Certificate of authenticity, 300 made.

2011		$2,750	$3,600

J-180/Everly Brothers/The Everly Brothers
1986-2005. Reissue of the '62-'72 Everly Brothers model, renamed The Everly Brothers ('92-'94), The Everly ('94-'96), then back to J-180, black.

1986-2005		$2,500	$3,200

J-180 Special Edition
1993. Gibson Bozeman, only 36 made, Everly Brother specs, large double white pearloid 'guard.

1993		$2,950	$3,850

J-185/J-185N
1951-1959. Flat-top jumbo, figured maple back and sides, bound body and neck, sunburst (185) or natural (185N).

1951-1959	Natural, sunburst	$14,500	$19,000

J-185 Reissue
1990-1995, 1999-2018. Flat-top jumbo, figured maple back and sides, bound body and neck, natural or sunburst, limited run of 100 between '91-'92.

1990-2018		$2,300	$3,050

1957 Gibson J-50
Skip Crum

1999 Gibson J-150
Ted Wulfers

GUITARS

2007 Gibson J-185 Reissue

1964 Gibson J-200N

Smyth Jones

MODEL YEAR	FEATURES	EXC. COND. LOW	HIGH

J-185-12
2001-2004. 12-string J-185, flamed maple sides and back.

2001-2004		$2,325	$3,050

1951 J-185 Limited Edition
1994-1995. Oct. '94 Centennial model, limited run of 100.

1994-1995		$3,500	$4,600

J-185 Custom Vine
2004-2012. J-185 with abalone and mother-of-pearl vine 'board inlay.

2004-2012		$2,700	$3,500

J-185 EC
1999-2018. Acoustic/electric, rounded cutaway, flamed maple back and sides. Replaced EC-30 Blues King.

1999-2018		$1,950	$2,550

J-185 EC Custom
2005. Limited Edition, 200 made, spruce top, figured maple sides and back, pearl double parallelogram markers, Fishman Prefix Plus on-board electronics.

2005		$1,950	$2,550

J-185 EC Rosewood
2006-2018. Acoustic/electric, rounded cutaway, Indian rosewood back and sides.

2006-2018		$1,950	$2,550

J-185 EC Modern Rosewood
2020-present. Slim body, sitka spruce top, rosewood back and sides, Antique Natural or Rosewood Burst.

2020-2021		$1,950	$2,550

J-185 EC Modern Walnut
2020-present. Slim body, sitka spruce top, walnut back and sides, Antique Natural or Walnut Burst.

2020-2021		$1,675	$2,200

J-185 EC Quilt
2002. Quilted maple top, flamed maple body.

2002		$3,300	$4,300

J-190 EC Super Fusion
2001-2004. Jumbo single cut acoustic/electric, spruce top, curly maple back and sides, neck pickup and Fishman Piezo.

2001-2004		$2,500	$3,300

J-200/SJ-200/J-200N/SJ-200N
1946-present. Labeled SJ-200 until ca.'54. Super Jumbo flat-top, maple back and sides, see Super Jumbo 200 for '38-'42 rosewood back and sides model, called J-200 Artist for a time in the early-'70s, renamed '50s Super Jumbo 200 in '97 and again renamed SJ-200 Reissue in '99. Currently called the SJ-200 Standard. 200N indicates natural option.

1946-1949	Natural, sunburst	$16,000	$21,000
1950-1959	Natural, sunburst	$13,500	$17,700
1960-1964	Natural, sunburst	$11,000	$14,400
1965	Natural, sunburst	$7,200	$9,400
1966-1969	Natural, sunburst	$5,100	$6,600
1970-1979	Natural, sunburst	$3,900	$5,100
1972	Artist (label)	$3,900	$5,100
1980-1989	Natural, sunburst	$3,600	$4,700
1990-1999	Natural, sunburst	$3,600	$4,700
2000-2009	Natural, sunburst	$3,600	$4,700
2010-2021	Natural, sunburst	$3,400	$4,500

MODEL YEAR	FEATURES	EXC. COND. LOW	HIGH

J-200 Celebrity
1985-1987. Acoustic introduced for Gibson's 90th anniversary, spruce top, rosewood back, sides and 'board, binding on body and 'board, sunburst, only 90 made.

1985-1987		$3,500	$4,600

J-200 Custom/SJ-200 Custom
2009-2013. Additional abalone trim, gold hardware, sunburst or natural. Model name also used in 1993 on J-200 with tree-of-life fingerboard inlay.

2009-2013		$3,700	$4,900

J-200 Deluxe Rosewood
1993-1996. Rosewood back and sides, abalone trim, gold hardware, sunburst or natural.

1993-1996		$4,500	$5,900

J-200 E
1986-1987. Built in Nashville, on-board volume control, sunburst.

1986-1987		$3,700	$4,900

J-200 Elvis Presley Signature
2002. 250 made, large block letter Elvis Presley name on 'board, figured maple sides and back, gloss natural spruce top, black and white custom designed 'guard after one of Presley's personal guitars.

2002		$4,900	$6,400

J-200 Jr.
1991-1996, 2002. Smaller 16" body, sunburst, natural, black or cherry.

1991-1996		$2,100	$2,700

J-200 Koa
1994-2013. Figured Hawaiian Koa back and sides, spruce top, natural.

1994-2013		$3,400	$4,500

J-200 M Trophy 75th Anniversary
2012-2013. Limited Edition, 75 made, quilt maple back and sides, rosewood 'board, abalone crown inlays, antique natural or vintage sunburst nitro finish.

2012-2013		$3,500	$4,600

J-200 Montana Gold Flame Maple
1998-2012. SJ-200 design, AAA Sitka spruce top with Eastern curly maple back and sides, ebony 'board, Custom Montana Gold banner peghead logo, antique natural.

1998-2012		$3,400	$4,500

J-200 Montana Western Classic Supreme
2016. Spruce top, rosewood back and sides, maple neck, Sunset Burst finish.

2016		$4,300	$5,600

J-200 Ron Wood/SJ-200 Ron Wood
1997. Based on a '57 SJ-200 with Wood's oversized double 'guard on either side of the sound hole, flame-pattern fretboard inlays, script signature inlay on headstock, natural.

1997		$4,700	$6,200

J-200 Rose
1994-1995. Centennial Series model, based on Emmylou Harris' guitar, black finish, rose 'guard, gold tuners, 100 built.

1994-1995		$5,000	$6,500

MODEL YEAR	FEATURES	EXC. COND. LOW	HIGH

J-200 Rosewood
1991, 1994-1996. Made in Bozeman, rosewood back and sides.

1991-1996		$4,400	$5,800

J-200 Studio
2009-2018. Studio logo on truss rod cover, unbound 'board, plain 'guard.

2009-2018		$2,300	$3,000

J-200 Western Classic Pre-War
1999-2012. Indian rosewood.

1999-2012		$3,500	$4,600

J-200 Western Classic Pre-War 200 Brazilian
2003. Custom Shop, limited run, based on Ray Whitley's '37 J-200, Brazilian rosewood back and sides.

2003		$8,600	$11,300

J-250 Monarch/SJ-250 Monarch
1995-2018. Rosewood back and sides, maple neck, ebony 'board, abalone trim, certificate of authenticity.

1995-2018		$13,000	$17,000

J-250 R
1972-1973, 1976-1978. A J-200 with rosewood back and sides, sunburst, only 20 shipped from Gibson.

1972-1978		$3,900	$5,100

J-1000/SJ-1000
1992-1994. Jumbo cutaway, spruce top, rosewood back and sides, on-board electronics, diamond-shape markers and headstock inlay.

1992-1994		$2,300	$3,000

J-1500
1992. Jumbo cutaway flat-top, higher-end appointments including Nick Lucas-style position markers, sunburst.

1992		$2,400	$3,100

J-2000/J-2000 Custom/J-2000 R
1986, 1992-1999. Cutaway acoustic, rosewood back and sides (a few had Brazilian rosewood or maple bodies), ebony 'board and bridge, Sitka spruce top, multiple bindings, sunburst or natural. Name changed to J-2000 Custom in '93 when it became available only on a custom-order basis.

1986-1999	All models	$3,800	$5,000

Jackson Browne Signature
2011-2016. Based on '30s Jumbo style with increased body depth and upgraded tonewoods, Model 1 without pickup, Model A with pickups, Adirondack red spruce top, English walnut back and sides, nitro lacquer sunburst finish.

2011-2016	Model 1	$4,200	$5,500
2011-2016	Model A	$4,350	$5,650

JG-0
1970-1972. Economy square shouldered jumbo, follows Jubilee model in '70.

1970-1972		$950	$1,225

JG-12
1970. Economy square shouldered jumbo 12-string, follows Jubilee-12 model in '70.

1970		$950	$1,225

Johnny A Signature Series
2004-2013. Thinline semi-hollow, sharp double-cut, flamed maple top, humbuckers, gold hardware, Bigsby, sunburst, includes certificate of authenticity.

2004-2013	Includes rare color option	$2,900	$3,800

Johnny Smith/Johnny Smith Double
1961-1989. Single-cut archtop, 1 or 2 humbucker pickups, gold hardware, multiple binding front and back, natural or sunburst. By '80 cataloged as JS and JSD models.

1961-1964		$11,500	$15,000
1965		$7,500	$11,000
1966-1969		$7,300	$9,500
1970-1989		$7,000	$9,100

Jubilee
1969-1970. Flat-top, laminated mahogany back and sides, single bound body, natural with black back and sides.

1969-1970		$950	$1,225

Jubilee Deluxe
1970-1971. Flat-top, laminated rosewood back and sides, multi-bound body, natural finish.

1970-1971		$950	$1,225

Jubilee-12
1969-1970. Flat-top, 12 strings, laminated mahogany back and sides, multi-bound, natural.

1969-1970		$950	$1,225

Jumbo
1934-1936. Gibson's first Jumbo flat-top, mahogany back and sides, round shoulders, bound top and back, sunburst, becomes the 16" Jumbo 35 in late-'36.

1934	Unbound	$26,000	$34,000
1935-1936	Bound	$20,000	$26,000

Jumbo 35/J-35
1936-1942. Jumbo flat-top, mahogany back and sides, silkscreen logo, sunburst, reintroduced as J-35, square-shouldered dreadnought, in '83.

1936-1938	Sunburst, 3 tone bars	$16,500	$22,000
1939	Natural, 3 tone bars	$16,500	$22,000
1940-1942	Sunburst, 2 tone bars	$13,000	$17,000

Jumbo 55/J-55
1939-1943. Flat-top dreadnought, round shoulders, mahogany back and sides, pearl inlaid logo, sunburst, reintroduced in '73 as J-55.

1939-1940	Stairstep	$18,000	$24,500
1941-1943	Non-stairstep	$18,000	$24,500

Jumbo Centennial Special
1994. Reissue of 1934 Jumbo, natural, 100 made.

1994		$2,700	$3,500

Junior Pro
1987-1989. Single-cut, mahogany body, KB-X tremolo system 1 humbucker pickup, black chrome hardware, various colors.

1987-1989		$600	$775

Gibson Johnny A Signature Series
Imaged by Heritage Auctions, HA.com

1960s Gibson Johnny Smith Double
Freedom Guitars

1980 Gibson Kalamazoo Award

1942 Gibson L-O
David Stone

Kalamazoo Award Model
1978-1981. Single-cut archtop, bound f-holes, multi-bound top and back, 1 mini-humbucker, gold-plated hardware, woodgrain 'guard with bird and branch abalone inlay, highly figured natural or sunburst.

		LOW	HIGH
1978-1981	Natural	$14,000	$18,000
1978-1981	Sunburst	$14,000	$18,000

Keb' Mo' Royale
2016. Limited to 50, aged Adirondack red spruce top, vintage sunburst finish, label signed by artist, includes certificate of authenticity.

2016		$2,600	$3,400

Keb' Mo' Signature Bluesmaster
2010-2015. Limited run of 300, small-bodied flat-top acoustic, Baggs pickup, soundhole-mounted volume control, vintage sunburst or antique natural finish.

2010-2015		$2,300	$3,000

Kiefer Sutherland KS-336
2007. Custom Shop Inspired By Artist series.

2007		$3,400	$4,400

KZ II
1980-1981. Double-cut solidbody, 2 humbuckers, 4 knob and toggle controls, tune-o-matic, dot markers, stencil Gibson logo on headstock, KZ II logo on truss rod cover, walnut stain finish.

1980		$1,000	$1,300

L-0
1926-1933, 1937-1942. Acoustic flat-top, maple back and sides '26-'27, mahogany after. Reissued '37 with spruce top.

1926-1928	135", maple	$4,500	$6,000
1928-1930	135", mahogany	$4,500	$6,000
1931-1933	1475"	$4,750	$6,200
1937-1942	1475", spruce	$4,750	$6,200

L-00
1932-1946. Acoustic flat-top, mahogany back and sides, bound top to '36 and bound top and back '37 on.

1932-1946		$4,750	$6,200

L-00 1937 Legend
2006-2016. Part of the Vintage Series.

2006-2016		$3,300	$4,300

L-00 Standard
2016-present. Small body, sitka spruce top, mahogany back and sides, Vintage Sunburst nitro finish.

2016-2021		$1,950	$2,600

L-00 Studio Walnut
2020-present. Walnut back and sides, Fishman pickup, nitro finish, Antique Natural or Walnut Burst.

2020-2021		$1,075	$1,400

L-00 Studio/Montana Studio
2019-2020. Sitka spruce top, walnut back and sides, Fishman pickup, aged nitro finish.

2019-2020		$1,075	$1,400

L-00 Sustainable
2018-2021. Sitka spruce top, richlite 'board and bridge made from recycled trees pulp, Antique Natural.

2018-2021		$1,475	$1,925

L-00/Blues King
1991-1997, 1999-2019. Reintroduced as L-00, called Blues King L-00 for '94-'97, back as L-00 for '99-'02, called Blues King '03-present.

1991-1997		$1,675	$2,200
2003-2019		$1,675	$2,200

L-1 (Archtop)
1902-1925. Acoustic archtop, single-bound top, back and soundhole, name continued on flat-top model in '26.

1902-1907	125"	$1,825	$2,400
1908-1919	135"	$1,825	$2,400
1920-1925	135", Loar era	$1,825	$2,400

L-1 (Flat-Top)
1926-1937. Acoustic flat-top, maple back and sides '26-'27, mahogany after.

1926-1929	135", 12-fret	$5,400	$7,100
1930-1931	1475", 13-fret	$5,600	$7,300
1932-1937	14-fret	$5,700	$7,500

L-1 1928 Blues Tribute
2014-2018. Adirondack red spruce top, mahogany back and sides, rosewood 'board, faded Vintage Sunburst.

2014-2018		$2,300	$3,000

L-1 Robert Johnson
2007-2016. 1926 specs, Robert Johnson inlay at end of 'board.

2007-2016		$1,725	$2,250

L-1 Special
2016. Adirondack red spruce top, limited edition of 75.

2016		$2,200	$2,900

L-2 (Archtop)
1902-1926. Round soundhole archtop, pearl inlay on peghead, 1902-'07 available in 3 body sizes: 12.5" to 16", '24-'26 13.5" body width.

1902-1907	125"	$1,825	$2,400
1924-1926	135"	$1,825	$2,400

L-2 (Flat-Top)
1929-1935. Acoustic flat-top, rosewood back and sides except for mahogany in '31, triple-bound top and back, limited edition model in '94.

1929-1933	Brazilian	$16,000	$21,300
1931-1932	Mahogany	$13,000	$17,100

L-2 1929 Reissue
1994 only. Spruce top, Indian rosewood back and sides, raised 'guard.

1994		$2,275	$3,000

L-3 (Archtop)
1902-1933. Acoustic archtop, available in 3 sizes: 12.5", 13.5", 16".

1902-1907	125", round hole	$2,300	$3,000
1908-1919	135", round hole	$2,300	$3,000
1920		$2,300	$3,000
1921-1926	Loar era	$2,300	$3,000
1927-1928	135", oval hole	$2,300	$3,000
1929-1933	135", round hole	$2,300	$3,000

L-4
1912-1956. Acoustic archtop, 16" wide.

1912-1919	12-fret, oval hole	$2,650	$3,450
1920		$2,650	$3,450
1921-1924	Loar era	$2,650	$3,450
1925-1927	12-fret, oval hole	$2,650	$3,450
1928-1934	14-fret, round hole	$2,650	$3,450
1935-1946	Fleur-de-lis, f-holes	$3,200	$4,200
1947-1949	Crown, double-parallel	$3,200	$4,200
1950-1956		$3,100	$4,000

MODEL YEAR	FEATURES	EXC. COND. LOW	HIGH

L-4 A or L-4 A EC
2003-2008. 15 3/4" lower bout, mid-size jumbo, rounded cutaway, factory electronics with preamp.

2003-2008		$1,725	$2,250

L-4 C or L-4 CN
1949-1971. Single-cut acoustic archtop, sunburst or natural (CN).

1949-1959	Natural	$5,100	$6,700
1949-1959	Sunburst	$4,700	$6,100
1960-1964	Natural	$4,700	$6,100
1960-1964	Sunburst	$4,000	$5,200
1965	Natural	$3,300	$4,300
1965	Sunburst	$3,000	$3,900
1966-1969	Natural, sunburst	$2,300	$3,000
1970-1971	Natural, sunburst	$1,750	$2,300

L-4 CES/L-4 CES Mahogany
1958, 1969, 1986-2018. Single pointed cutaway archtop, 2 humbuckers, gold parts, natural or sunburst, maple back and sides '58 and '69, mahogany laminate back and sides for '86-'93, became part of Gibson's Historic Collection (Custom Shop) with laminated maple back and sides for '94, renamed L-4 CES Mahogany with solid mahogany back and sides in '04.

1958	Natural, PAFs	$11,500	$15,000
1958	Sunburst, PAFs	$10,300	$13,400
1969	Natural, sunburst	$4,200	$5,500
1986-1993	Laminate mahogany	$2,825	$3,675
1994-2003	Laminate maple	$2,825	$3,675
2004-2018	Solid mahogany	$2,825	$3,675

L-4 Special Tenor/Plectrum
Late-1920s. Limited edition 4-string flat-top.

1929		$2,200	$2,900

L-5 '34 Non-Cutaway Historic
1994. 1934 specs including block pearl inlays, bound snakehead peghead, close grained solid spruce top, figured solid maple sides and back, replica Grover open back tuners, Cremona Brown Sunburst finish.

1994		$4,250	$5,600

L-5 Premier/L-5 P/L-5 PN
1939-1947. Introduced as L-5 Premier (L-5 P) and renamed L-5 C in '48, single rounded cutaway acoustic archtop, sunburst or natural option (PN).

1939-1947	Natural option	$19,000	$25,000
1939-1947	Sunburst	$16,000	$21,000

L-5/L-5N
1924-1958. Acoustic archtop, non-cut, multiple bindings, Lloyd Loar label in '24, 17" body by '35, Master Model label until '27, sunburst with natural option later.

1924	'24 ship date, Loar era	$45,000	$60,000
1925	Early '25, value per specs	$45,000	$60,000
1925	Late '25, value per specs	$30,000	$53,000
1926	'26 ship date, value per specs	$30,000	$53,000
1927	'27 ship date, value per specs	$30,000	$53,000
1928-1932	Value per specs	$20,000	$32,000
1933-1934	Value per specs	$7,000	$12,000
1935-1940	Value per specs	$5,000	$9,800
1939-1940	Natural option, value per specs	$8,000	$11,000
1946-1949	Natural option, value per specs	$7,000	$12,000
1946-1949	Sunburst, value per specs	$6,000	$10,500
1950-1958	Natural, value per specs	$6,000	$9,400
1950-1958	Sunburst, value per specs	$4,500	$7,800

L-5 C/L-5 CN
1948-1982. Renamed from L-5 Premier (L-5 P), single rounded cutaway acoustic archtop, sunburst or natural option (CN)

1948-1949	Natural	$14,000	$19,000
1948-1949	Sunburst	$12,000	$16,000
1950-1959	Natural	$12,000	$16,000
1950-1959	Sunburst	$10,000	$13,000
1960-1964	Natural	$10,000	$13,000
1960-1964	Sunburst	$9,000	$12,000
1965	Natural	$7,700	$10,000
1965	Sunburst	$7,700	$10,000
1966-1969	Natural	$6,400	$8,400
1966-1969	Sunburst	$6,400	$8,400
1970-1982	Natural, sunburst	$4,700	$6,200

L-5 CES/L-5 CESN
1951-2018. Electric version of L-5 C, single round cutaway (pointed mid-'60-'69), archtop, 2 pickups (P-90s '51-'53, Alnico Vs '54-mid-'57, humbuckers after), sunburst or natural (CESN), now part of Gibson's Historic Collection.

1951-1957	Natural, single coils	$17,000	$22,500
1951-1957	Sunburst, single coils	$16,000	$21,400
1958-1959	Natural, PAFs	$22,000	$28,500
1958-1959	Sunburst, PAFs	$20,200	$26,200
1960-1962	Natural, PAFs	$20,200	$26,200
1960-1962	Sunburst, PAFs	$17,300	$22,500
1963-1964	Natural, pat #	$14,500	$19,000
1963-1964	Sunburst, pat #	$12,000	$15,700
1965	Natural, sunburst	$9,200	$12,000
1966-1969	Natural	$7,300	$9,600
1966-1969	Sunburst	$6,000	$8,000
1970-1979	Natural, sunburst	$5,500	$7,100
1980-1984	Kalamazoo made	$5,500	$7,100
1985-1992	Nashville made	$5,500	$7,100

L-5 CES Historic
1994-1997. Custom Shop Historic Collection series, sunburst or natural.

1994	100th Anniv, black	$5,500	$7,100
1994-1996	Natural, highly figured	$5,500	$7,100
1994-1996	Sunburst	$5,500	$7,100
1997	Wine Red	$5,500	$7,100

L-5 CT (George Gobel)
1959-1961. Single-cut, thinline archtop acoustic, some were built with pickups, cherry.

1959-1961		$18,000	$24,000

1917 Gibson L-3
Frank Manno

1938 Gibson L-4
David Stone

1973 Gibson L-6 S

Tom Pfeifer

1967 Gibson L-7 CN

Imaged by Heritage Auctions, HA.com

MODEL YEAR	FEATURES	EXC. COND. LOW	HIGH
L-5 CT Reissue			
1998-2007. Historic Collection, acoustic and electric versions, natural, sunburst, cherry.			
1998-2007		$5,600	$7,300
L-5 S			
1972-1985, 2004-2005. Single-cut solidbody, multi-bound body and neck, gold hardware, 2 pickups (low impedance '72-'74, humbuckers '75 on), offered in natural, cherry sunburst or vintage sunburst. 1 humbucker version issued in '04 from Gibson's Custom, Art & Historic division.			
1972-2005	All options	$4,900	$6,500
L-5 S Ron Wood			
2015. Custom Shop, limited run of 250 with 1st 50 signed by Ron, certificate of authenticity, 2 Burstbucker pickups, ebony gloss finish.			
2015		$4,900	$6,500
L-5 Signature			
2001-2004. Carved spruce top, AAA maple back, tangerineburst or vintage sunburst.			
2001-2004		$5,600	$7,300
L-5 Studio			
1996-2000. Normal L-5 dual pickup features, marble-style 'guard, translucent finish, dot markers.			
1996-2000		$2,500	$3,250
L-5 Wes Montgomery			
1993-2018. Custom Shop, various colors.			
1993-2018		$6,100	$7,900
L-6 S			
1973-1975. Single-cut solidbody, 2 humbucking pickups, 6 position rotary switch, stop tailpiece, cherry or natural. Renamed L-6 S Custom in '75.			
1973-1975	Cherry, natural	$1,700	$2,250
L-6 S Custom			
1975-1980. Renamed from the L-6 S, 2 humbucking pickups, stop tailpiece, cherry or natural.			
1975-1980		$1,700	$2,250
1978-1980	Silverburst option	$1,700	$2,250
L-6 S Deluxe			
1975-1981. Single-cut solidbody, 2 humbucking pickups, no rotary switch, strings-thru-body design, cherry or natural.			
1975-1981		$1,700	$2,250
L-6 S Reissue			
2011-2012. With rotary switch, 2 humbuckers, natural or silverburst.			
2011-2012		$900	$1,200
L-7/L-7N			
1932-1956. Acoustic archtop, bound body and neck, fleur-de-lis peghead inlay, 16" body '32-'34, 17" body X-braced top late-'34, sunburst or natural (N).			
1932-1934	16" body	$3,400	$4,500
1935-1939	17" body, X-braced	$3,400	$4,500
1940-1949	Natural	$3,300	$4,300
1940-1949	Sunburst	$3,000	$3,900
1950-1956	Natural	$3,000	$4,000
1950-1956	Sunburst	$2,900	$3,800
L-7 C/L-7 CN			
1948-1972. Single-cut acoustic archtop, triple-bound top, sunburst or natural (CN). Gibson revived the L-7 C name for a new acoustic archtop in 2002.			
1948-1949	Natural	$4,800	$6,200

MODEL YEAR	FEATURES	EXC. COND. LOW	HIGH
1948-1949	Sunburst	$4,300	$5,600
1950-1959	Natural	$4,300	$5,600
1950-1959	Sunburst	$4,000	$5,200
1960-1964	Natural	$3,800	$5,000
1960-1964	Sunburst	$3,675	$4,775
1965	Natural	$3,600	$4,650
1965	Sunburst	$3,300	$4,300
1966-1972	Natural	$3,400	$4,400
1966-1972	Sunburst	$3,025	$3,925
L-7 Custom Electric			
1936. L-7 with factory Christian-style pickup, limited production, often custom ordered.			
1936		$9,000	$12,000
L-7 E/L-7 CE			
1948-1954. L-7 and L-7 C with "McCarty"assembly of pickguard-mounted pickups (1 or 2), sunburst only.			
1948-1954	L-7 CE, cutaway	$4,850	$6,300
1948-1954	L-7 E, non-cut	$4,000	$5,200
L-7 C (Custom Shop)			
2002-2013. Custom Shop logo, Certificate of Authenticity.			
2002-2013		$4,200	$5,400
L-10			
1923-1939. Acoustic archtop, single-bound body and 'board, black or sunburst (added in '35).			
1923-1934	16", F-holes	$5,000	$6,500
1935-1939	17", X-braced	$5,000	$6,500
L-12			
1930-1955. Acoustic archtop, single-bound body, 'guard, neck and headstock, gold-plated hardware, sunburst.			
1930-1934	16"	$5,400	$7,100
1935-1939	17", X-braced	$5,400	$7,100
1940-1941	Parallel top braced	$5,400	$7,100
1946-1949	Post-war	$3,300	$4,300
1950-1955		$3,100	$4,100
L-12 Premier/L-12 P			
1947-1950. L-12 with rounded cutaway, sunburst.			
1947-1950		$4,600	$6,000
L-20 20th Anniversary Limited Edition			
2009. Custom Shop, 20 made, "20th Anniversary" logo on back of headstock and on label, Certificate of Authenticity.			
2009		$3,100	$4,100
L-20 Special/L-20 K International Special			
1993-1994. Rosewood or mahogany back and sides (koa on the K), ebony 'board, block inlays, gold tuners, multi-bound.			
1993-1994	L-20, mahogany	$2,000	$2,550
1993-1994	L-20, rosewood	$2,000	$2,550
1993-1994	L-20K, koa	$2,000	$2,550
L-30			
1935-1943. Acoustic archtop, single-bound body, black or sunburst.			
1935-1943		$1,450	$1,800
L-37			
1937-1941. 14-3/4" acoustic archtop, flat back, single-bound body and 'guard, sunburst.			
1937-1941		$1,450	$1,900
L-47			
1940-1942. Acoustic archtop.			
1940-1942		$1,550	$2,025

MODEL YEAR	FEATURES	EXC. COND. LOW	HIGH

L-48
1946-1971. 16" acoustic archtop, single-bound body, mahogany sides, sunburst.

1946-1949		$1,575	$2,050
1950-1959		$1,450	$1,900
1960-1964		$1,300	$1,700
1965		$1,100	$1,425
1966-1969		$850	$1,100
1970-1971		$750	$1,000

L-50
1932-1971. 14.75" acoustic archtop, flat or arched back, round soundhole or f-holes, pearl logo pre-war, decal logo post-war, maple sides, sunburst, 16" body late-'34.

1932-1934	1475" body	$2,300	$3,000
1934-1943	16" body	$2,300	$3,000
1946-1949	16", trapezoids	$2,100	$2,700
1950-1959		$1,700	$2,200
1960-1964		$1,600	$2,100
1965		$1,325	$1,725
1966-1969		$1,100	$1,425
1970-1971		$1,000	$1,300

L-75
1932-1939. 14.75" archtop with round soundhole and flat back, size increased to 16" with arched back in '35, small button tuners, dot markers, lower-end style trapeze tailpiece, pearl script logo, sunburst.

1932	1475", dot neck	$3,000	$3,875
1933-1934	1475", pearloid	$3,000	$3,875
1935-1939	16" body	$3,000	$3,875

L-130
1999-2005. 14 7/8" lower bout, small jumbo, solid spruce top, solid bubinga back and sides, rosewood 'board, factory electronics with preamp.

1999-2005		$1,200	$1,575

L-140
1999-2005. Like L-130 but with rosewood back and sides, ebony 'board.

1999-2005		$1,375	$1,775

L-200 Emmylou Harris
2001-2016. Smaller and thinner than standard 200, flamed maple sides and back, gold hardware, crest markers, natural or sunburst.

2001-2016		$2,250	$2,925

L-C Century
1933-1939. Curly maple back and sides, bound body, white pearloid 'board and peghead (all years) and headstock (until '38), sunburst.

1933-1938	Pearloid	$7,000	$9,300
1939		$6,400	$8,300

L-C Century Elvis Costello Limited
2016. Signed custom label, pearloid 'board, Adirondack red spruce top, AAA flamed maple back and sides, 300 made.

2016		$4,600	$6,000

L-C Century Reissue
1994. Pearloid headstock and 'board.

1994		$2,700	$3,500

L-Jr.
1918-1927. Archtop, solid carved spruce top, carved figured birch back, Sheraton Brown or natural finish.

1918-1927		$1,925	$2,500

LC-1 Cascade
2002-2006. LC-Series acoustic/electric, advanced L-00-style, solid quilted maple back and sides.

2002-2006		$1,600	$2,100

LC-2 Sonoma
2002-2006. Released November '02, LC-Series acoustic/electric, advanced L-00-style, solid walnut back and sides.

2002-2006		$1,925	$2,500

LC-3 Caldera
2003-2004. 14 3/4" flat-top, soft cutaway, solid cedar top, solid flamed Koa back and sides, fancy appointments.

2003-2004		$2,000	$2,600

Le Grande
1993-2010. Electric archtop, 17", formerly called Johnny Smith.

1993-2010		$7,500	$9,700

Les Paul
Following are models bearing the Les Paul name. In order to keep certain models grouped together, subheadings have been included for Classic, Custom, Deluxe, Goldtop, Junior, Special, Standard and Studio models. All others are then listed pretty much alphabetically as follows:

'60 Les Paul Corvette
Les Paul 25/50 Anniversary
Les Paul 40th Anniversary (from 1952)
Les Paul (All Maple)
Les Paul Artisan and Artisan/3
Les Paul Artist/L.P. Artist/Les Paul Active

LES PAUL CLASSIC
Following are Les Paul Classic models listed alphabetically.
Les Paul Classic
Les Paul Classic 1960 Mars Music
Les Paul Classic Antique Mahogany
Les Paul Classic Custom
Les Paul Classic H-90
Les Paul Classic Limited Edition
Les Paul Classic Mark III/MIII
Les Paul Classic Plus
Les Paul Classic Premium Plus
Les Paul Classic Premium Plus (Custom Shop)
Les Paul Classic Tom Morgan Limited Edition

LES PAUL CUSTOM
Following are Les Paul Custom models listed alphabetically.
Les Paul Custom
Les Paul Custom 25
Les Paul Custom '54
Les Paul Custom Historic '54
Les Paul Custom Historic '57 Black Beauty
1957 Les Paul Custom (2-Pickup) Ultra Light Aged
1957 Les Paul Custom (3-Pickup) Light Aged
Les Paul Custom Historic '68

1935 Gibson L-30
Tyler Willison

1937 Gibson L-37
Robbie Keene

1953 Gibson Les Paul Model

*2002 Gibson Les Paul
Indian Motorcycle*

1968 Les Paul Custom Reissue (Custom
 Shop)
1968 Les Paul Custom Ultra Light Aged
20th Anniversary Les Paul Custom
25th Anniversary (Guitar Center) Les Paul
 Custom
35th Anniversary Les Paul Custom
120th Anniversary Les Paul Custom
120th Anniversary Les Paul Custom Lite
Les Paul Custom Ace Frehley "Budokan"
Les Paul Custom Ace Frehley Signature
Les Paul Custom Adam Jones 1979
Les Paul Custom F (Custom Shop)
Les Paul Custom Jeff Beck 1954 Oxblood
Les Paul Custom Jimmy Page
Les Paul Custom John Sykes 1978
Les Paul Custom Lite
Les Paul Custom Lite (Show Case Edition)
Les Paul Custom Mick Ronson '68
Les Paul Custom Music Machine
Les Paul Custom Peter Frampton Signature
Les Paul Custom Plus
Les Paul Custom Showcase Edition
Les Paul Custom Silverburst
Les Paul Custom Steve Jones 1974
Les Paul Custom Zakk Wylde Signature

Les Paul Dale Earnhardt
Les Paul Dale Earnhardt Intimidator
Les Paul Dark Fire
Les Paul Dark Knight Quilt Top
Les Paul DC AA
Les Paul DC Classic
Les Paul DC Pro
Les Paul DC Standard (Plus)
Les Paul DC Studio

LES PAUL DELUXE
 Following are Les Paul Deluxe models
 listed alphabetically.
Les Paul Deluxe
Les Paul Deluxe 30th Anniversary
Les Paul Deluxe '69 Reissue
Les Paul Deluxe Hall of Fame
Les Paul Deluxe Limited Edition
Les Paul Deluxe Limited Edition AMS
Les Paul Deluxe Reissue
Les Paul Deluxe #1 Pete Townshend
Les Paul Deluxe #3 Pete Townshend
Les Paul Deluxe #9 Pete Townshend
Les Paul Pro Deluxe
Les Paul Pro Showcase Edition

Les Paul Dusk Tiger
Les Paul ES-Les Paul
Les Paul ES-Les Paul Custom
Les Paul ES-Les Paul Standard
Les Paul ES-Les Paul Studio
Les Paul Florentine Plus
Les Paul Supreme Florentine
Les Paul Futura
Les Paul Goddess

LES PAUL GOLDTOP
 Following are Les Paul Goldtop models
 listed alphabetically.
Les Paul Model
'52 Les Paul Goldtop
'52 Les Paul Tribute
'54 Les Paul Goldtop
'54 Les Paul Wildwood
1954 Les Paul Goldtop Heavy Aged
'55 Les Paul Goldtop Hot-Mod Wraptail
'56 Les Paul Goldtop
1956 Les Paul Goldtop "CME Spec"
1956 Les Paul Goldtop Reissue
1956 Les Paul Goldtop Ultra Light Aged
'57 Les Paul Goldtop
'57 Les Paul Goldtop (R-7 wrap-around)
1957 Les Paul Goldtop Darkback Light Aged
1957 Les Paul Goldtop Reissue
1957 Les Paul Goldtop Ultra Light/Ultra
 Heavy Aged
Les Paul 30th Anniversary
Les Paul 50th Anniversary 1956 Les Paul
 Standard Goldtop
Les Paul 50th Anniversary 1957 Les Paul
 Standard Goldtop
Les Paul Billy F. Gibbons Goldtop
Les Paul Centennial ('56 LP Standard Gold-
 top)
Les Paul Dickey Betts Goldtop
Les Paul Joe Bonamassa Aged Goldtop
Les Paul LP-295 Goldtop
Les Paul Reissue Goldtop
Les Paul Slash Signature Goldtop

Les Paul Government Series II
Les Paul GT
Les Paul HD.6-X Pro Digital
Les Paul Indian Motorcycle
Les Paul Jumbo

LES PAUL JUNIOR
 Following are Les Paul Junior models
 listed alphabetically.
Les Paul Junior
Les Paul Junior 3/4
1957 Les Paul Junior (Single-Cut) Ultra Light
 Aged/Heavy Aged
1957 Les Paul Junior (Single-Cut) VOS
1958 Les Paul Junior (Double-Cut) VOS
'60 Les Paul Junior
1960 Les Paul Junior (Double-Cut) Ultra
 Heavy Aged
Les Paul J / LPJ
Les Paul Junior Billie Joe Armstrong Signa-
 ture
Les Paul Junior DC Hall of Fame
Les Paul Junior Double Cutaway
Les Paul Junior Faded
Les Paul Junior John Lennon LTD
Les Paul Junior Lite
Les Paul Junior Special
Les Paul Junior Special Robot
Les Paul Junior Tenor/Plectrum

Les Paul TV
Les Paul TV 3/4
Les Paul TV Junior

Les Paul Limited Run 2016 Series
Les Paul Lou Pallo Signature
Les Paul Marc Bolan
Les Paul Menace
Les Paul Old Hickory
Les Paul Personal
Les Paul Professional
Les Paul Recording
Les Paul Richard Petty LTD
Les Paul Signature/L.P. Signature
Les Paul Silver Streak
Les Paul SM
Les Paul SmartWood Exotic
Les Paul SmartWood Standard
Les Paul SmartWood Studio

LES PAUL SPECIAL
Following are Les Paul Special models listed alphabetically.
Les Paul Special
Les Paul 55
'60 Les Paul Special
Les Paul Special (Reissue)
Les Paul Special 100/100 Special
Les Paul Special 3/4
Les Paul Special Centennial
Les Paul Special Double Cutaway
Les Paul Special Faded
Les Paul Special New Century
Les Paul Special Robot
Les Paul Special Tenor
Les Paul Special Worn Cherry

LES PAUL STANDARD
Following are Les Paul Standard models, beginning with the original model, then listed alphabetically.
Les Paul Standard (Sunburst)
Les Paul Standard (SG body)
Les Paul Standard (reintroduced)
'50s Les Paul Standard
'58 Les Paul Figured Top
'58 Les Paul Plaintop (VOS)
1958 Les Paul Standard "CME Spec"
1958 Les Paul Standard Light Aged/Heavy Aged
1958 Les Paul Standard Ultra Light Aged
'59 Les Paul Flametop/Reissue/Standard
'59 Les Paul Burst Brothers
'59 Les Paul Korina Reissue
'59 Les Paul Plaintop (VOS)
1959 Les Paul Standard "CME Spec"
1959 Les Paul Standard Heavy Aged
1959 Les Paul Standard Light Aged
1959 Les Paul Standard Reissue
1959 Les Paul Standard Ultra Heavy Aged
1959 Les Paul Standard Ultra Light Aged
True Historic 1959 Les Paul
'60s Les Paul Standard

'60 Les Paul Flametop/Standard '60s
'60 Les Paul Plaintop (VOS)
1960 Les Paul Standard Heavy Aged
1960 Les Paul Standard Light Aged
1960 Les Paul Standard Reissue
1960 Les Paul Standard Ultra Light Aged
True Historic 1960 Les Paul
'82 Les Paul Standard
Les Paul 10th Anniversary Chambered '58 Reissue
Les Paul 40th Anniversary (from 1959)
Les Paul 50th Anniversary (Historic)
Les Paul 50th Anniversary 1959 Les Paul Standard
Les Paul 50th Anniversary 1960 Les Paul Standard
Les Paul 50th Anniversary DaPra
Les Paul 50th Anniversary Korina Tribute
Les Paul 50th Anniversary Les Paul Standard (Sweetwater)
Les Paul 60th Anniversary 1960 Les Paul Standard "CME Spec"
Les Paul 120th Anniversary
Les Paul Axcess Alex Lifeson
Les Paul Axcess Dave Amato
Les Paul Axcess Standard
Les Paul BFG
Les Paul Bird's-Eye Standard
Les Paul Carved Series
Les Paul Catalina
Les Paul Centennial ('59 LP Special)
Les Paul Class 5
Les Paul Cloud 9 Series
Les Paul Collector's Choice Series
Les Paul Dickey Betts Red Top
Les Paul Don Felder Hotel California 1959
Les Paul Duane Allman
Les Paul Duane Allman Hot 'Lanta
Les Paul Elegant
Les Paul Eric Clapton 1960
Les Paul Gary Moore BFG
Les Paul Gary Moore Signature
Les Paul Gary Rossington Signature
Les Paul Guitar Trader Reissue
Les Paul Heritage 80
Les Paul Heritage 80 Award
Les Paul Heritage 80 Elite
Les Paul Heritage 80/Standard 80
Les Paul Hot Rod Magazine '58 Standard
Les Paul Jim Beam (Custom Shop)
Les Paul Jimmy Page "Number Two"
Les Paul Jimmy Page (Custom Authentic)
Les Paul Jimmy Page Signature
Les Paul Jimmy Page Signature (Custom Shop)
Les Paul Jimmy Wallace Reissue
Les Paul Joe Bonamassa Bonabyrd
Les Paul Joe Bonamassa Skinnerburst 1959
Les Paul Joe Bonamassa 'Tomato Soup Burst' Limited Edition
Les Paul Joe Perry 1959
Les Paul Joe Perry Signature
Les Paul KM (Kalamazoo Model)

1976 Gibson Les Paul Deluxe
Ted Wulfers

2019 Gibson Les Paul Traditional

2018 Gibson Classic Player Plus
Dan Lussier

2002 Gibson Les Paul Classic
Ted Dewars

Les Paul Korina
Les Paul Leo's Reissue
Les Paul Limited Edition (3-tone)
Les Paul Modern
Les Paul Music Machine 25th Anniversary
Les Paul Music Machine Brazilian Stinger
Les Paul Music Rising Katrina
Les Paul Neal Schon Signature
Les Paul Peace
Les Paul Reissue Flametop
Les Paul SG '61 Reissue
Les Paul SG Standard Authentic
Les Paul SG Standard Reissue
Les Paul Signature "T"
Les Paul Slash Appetite
Les Paul Slash Appetite For Destruction
Les Paul Slash Signature
Les Paul Slash Signature VOS
Les Paul Slash Snakepit
Les Paul Southern Rock Tribute 1959
Les Paul Spider-Man
Les Paul Spotlight Special
Les Paul Standard 100
Les Paul Standard 2008
Les Paul Standard 2010 Limited
Les Paul Standard Billy Gibbons 'Pearly Gates'
Les Paul Standard F
Les Paul Standard Faded
Les Paul Standard HP
Les Paul Standard Lite
Les Paul Standard Lite Limited Edition
Les Paul Standard Michael Bloomfield 1959
Les Paul Standard Mike McCready 1959
Les Paul Standard Music Zoo 25th Anniversary
Les Paul Standard Paul Kossoff 1959
Les Paul Standard Plus
Les Paul Standard Premium Plus
Les Paul Standard Raw Power
Les Paul Standard Rick Nielsen 1959
Les Paul Standard Robot
Les Paul Standard RSM 1959 / RSM '59 Les Paul Standard
Les Paul Standard Showcase Edition
Les Paul Standard Sparkle
Les Paul Strings and Things Standard
Les Paul Tie Dye (St. Pierre)
Les Paul Tie Dye Custom Shop
Les Paul Traditional Pro/Pro II
Les Paul Traditional/Plus
Les Paul Ultima
Les Paul Ultra-Aged
Les Paul Warren Haynes
Les Paul Zebra Wood

LES PAUL STUDIO
Following are Les Paul Studio models listed alphabetically.
Les Paul Studio
Les Paul Studio 120th Anniversary
Les Paul Studio '50s Tribute
Les Paul Studio '60s Tribute
Les Paul Studio '70s Tribute

MODEL YEAR	FEATURES	EXC. COND. LOW	HIGH
Les Paul Studio Baritone			
Les Paul Studio BFD			
Les Paul Studio Custom			
Les Paul Studio Deluxe '60s			
Les Paul Studio Deluxe II			
Les Paul Studio Faded Vintage Mahogany			
Les Paul Studio Faded/Pro Faded			
Les Paul Studio Gem			
Les Paul Studio Gothic			
Les Paul Studio Gothic Morte			
Les Paul Studio Joe Bonamassa			
Les Paul Studio Limited Edition			
Les Paul Studio Lite			
Les Paul Studio Lite Mark III/M3/M III			
Les Paul Studio MLB Baseball			
Les Paul Studio Platinum			
Les Paul Studio Platinum Plus			
Les Paul Studio Plus			
Les Paul Studio Premium Plus			
Les Paul Studio Raw Power			
Les Paul Studio Robot			
Les Paul Studio Robot Limited Edition			
Les Paul Studio Roland Synthesizer			
Les Paul Studio Shred			
Les Paul Studio Special			
Les Paul Studio Special Limited Edition			
Les Paul Studio Standard			
Les Paul Studio Swamp Ash			
Les Paul Studio USA Anniversary Flood			

Les Paul Supreme
Les Paul Vixen
Les Paul Voodoo/Voodoo Les Paul
Les Paul XR-I / II / III
The Les Paul
The Paul
The Paul Firebrand Deluxe
The Paul II

'60 Les Paul Corvette
1995-1997. Custom Shop Les Paul, distinctive Chevrolet Corvette styling from '60, offered in 6 colors.

1995-1997	$4,700	$6,200

Les Paul 25/50 Anniversary
1978-1979. Split-block inlays, five- or seven- piece maple and walnut neck, gold and silver hardware, 2 humbuckers, coil splitter, TP-6 tailpiece, antique sunburst, natural, wine red, black, and white finishes offered, 8-digit SN followed by 4-digit limited edition number, 1,106 made in '78, 2,305 in '79.

1978-1979	$4,150	$5,400

Les Paul 40th Anniversary (from 1952)
1991-1992. Black finish, 2 soapbar P-100 pickups, gold hardware, stop tailpiece, 40th Anniversary inlay at 12th fret.

1991-1992	$2,650	$3,450

Les Paul (All Maple)
1984. Limited run, all maple body, Super 400-style inlay, gold hardware.

1984	$2,675	$3,475

MODEL YEAR	FEATURES	EXC. COND. LOW	HIGH

Les Paul Artisan and Artisan/3

1976-1982. Carved maple top, 2 or 3 humbuckers, gold hardware, hearts and flowers inlays on 'board and headstock, ebony, sunburst or walnut.

| 1976-1982 | 2 pickups | $5,000 | $6,500 |
| 1976-1982 | 3 pickups | $5,000 | $6,500 |

Les Paul Artist/L.P. Artist/Les Paul Active

1979-1982. Two humbuckers (3 optional), active electronics, gold hardware, 3 mini-switches, multi-bound, Fireburst, ebony or sunburst.

| 1979-1982 | | $2,400 | $3,200 |

LES PAUL CLASSIC

Following are Les Paul Classic models listed alphabetically.

Les Paul Classic

1990-1998, 2000-2008, 2014-present. Early models have 1960 on pickguard, 2 exposed humbuckers, Les Paul Model on peghead until '93, Les Paul Classic afterwards. Limited run of Ebony finish in 2000, 2014 and 2015 have those years in the model name.

| 1990-2008 | Various colors | $1,700 | $2,200 |
| 2014-2021 | Various colors | $1,450 | $1,900 |

Les Paul Classic 1960 Mars Music

2000. All black.

| 2000 | | $1,450 | $1,900 |

Les Paul Classic Antique Mahogany

2007. All mahogany body, exposed humbuckers, Guitar of the Week, limited run of 400 each of cherry (week 27) and sunburst (week 33).

| 2007 | | $1,700 | $2,200 |

Les Paul Classic Custom

2007-2008, 2011-2012. Mahogany body with carved maple top, 2 exposed humbuckers in '07-'08, covered afterwards, various colors.

| 2007-2012 | | $1,800 | $2,325 |

Les Paul Classic H-90

2008. Guitar of the Week, 400 made, gold hardware, H-90 soapbar pickups.

| 2008 | | $1,450 | $1,900 |

Les Paul Classic Limited Edition

2000. Limited Edition logo on back of headstock, Les Paul Classic stencil logo, 3 exposed humbuckers, gold hardware, black finish.

| 2000 | | $1,700 | $2,200 |

Les Paul Classic Mark III/MIII

1991-1993. Les Paul Classic features, no 'guard, exposed-coil humbuckers at neck and bridge and single-coil at middle position, 5-way switch, coil-tap.

| 1991-1993 | | $1,800 | $2,325 |

Les Paul Classic Plus

1991-1996, 1999-2003. Les Paul Classic with fancier maple top, 2 exposed humbucker pickups. Price depends on top figure.

| 1991-2003 | | $1,800 | $2,325 |

Les Paul Classic Premium Plus

1993-1996, 2001-2002. Les Paul Classic with AAA-grade flame maple top, 2 exposed humbucker pickups. Price depends on top figure.

| 1993-2002 | | $2,000 | $2,600 |

Les Paul Classic Premium Plus (Custom Shop)

1994-1998. Custom Shop version, quilted maple top, Custom Shop logo, various colors.

| 1994-1998 | | $2,150 | $2,800 |

Les Paul Classic Tom Morgan Limited Edition

2007. 400 made, custom finish top, black finish back/sides, Classic logo on truss rod cover.

| 2007 | | $1,800 | $2,325 |

LES PAUL CUSTOM

Following are Les Paul Custom models listed alphabetically.

Les Paul Custom

1953-1963 (renamed SG Custom late-1963), 1968-present (production moved to Custom Shop in 2004). Les Paul body shape except for SG body '61-'63, 2 pickups (3 humbuckers mid-'57-'63 and '68-'70, 3 pickups were optional various years after), '75 Price List shows a Les Paul Custom (B) model which is equipped with a Bigsby tailpiece versus a wraparound. By '80 offered as Les Paul Custom/Gold Parts and /Nickel Parts, because gold plating wears more quickly and is therefore less attractive there is no difference in price between an '80s Gold Parts and Nickel Parts instrument.

1953	Very early NSN model	$25,500	$33,000
1954-1957	Single coils	$25,500	$33,000
1954-1957	Single coils, factory Bigsby	$24,500	$32,000
1957-1961	Bigsby	$60,000	$80,000
1957-1961	Stoptail	$65,000	$85,000
1961-1963	White, SG body, Maestro	$21,500	$28,000
1961-1963	White, SG body, side-pull vibrato	$15,000	$19,500
1962-1963	Black option, SG body, factory stop tail	$24,000	$31,000
1962-1963	Black option, SG body, side-pull vibrato	$15,000	$19,500
1962-1963	White, SG body, factory stop tail	$24,000	$31,000
1968	Black, 1-piece body	$17,700	$23,000
1969	Black, 1-piece body	$14,100	$18,300
1969	Black, 3-piece body	$10,000	$13,100
1970-1973	Various colors, 3 pu	$5,600	$7,300
1970-1974	Various colors, 2 pu	$5,600	$7,300
1974	Black, white, 3 pu	$5,600	$7,300
1974	Natural, cherry sunburst	$3,900	$5,100
1975-1976	Maple 'board, 2 pu	$4,150	$5,400
1975-1976	Maple 'board, 3 pu	$4,150	$5,400
1975-1978	Volute, 2 pu	$3,900	$5,100
1975-1978	Volute, 3 pu	$3,900	$5,100
1977	Maple 'board, black, 2 pu	$4,150	$5,400
1977-1978	Maple 'board, blond, 2 pu	$4,150	$5,400

1993 Les Paul Classic Premium Plus
Dave Meyer

1978 Gibson Les Paul Custom
Kevin Okanos

1985 Gibson Les Paul Custom

Luis R Barrios

Gibson 1957 Les Paul Custom (3-Pickup) Light Aged

MODEL YEAR	FEATURES	EXC. COND. LOW	HIGH
1979	2 or 3 pickups	$3,900	$5,100
1979	Silverburst, 2 pu	$5,900	$7,700
1980-1984	Silverburst, 2 pu	$5,400	$7,200
1980-1986	2 or 3 pickups	$3,900	$5,100
1987-1989	Various colors	$3,900	$5,100
1990-1999	Limited Edition color series	$3,100	$4,100
1990-1999	Various colors	$2,900	$3,800
2000-2021	Various colors	$2,900	$3,800

Les Paul Custom 25
2007. Custom Shop Limited Edition run of 100, Les Paul "25" logo on truss rod cover, COA name Custom 25, triple-split block inlays, mahogany body with flame maple top, gold hardware, sunburst.

2007		$3,650	$4,750

Les Paul Custom '54
1972-1973. Reissue of 1954 Custom, black finish, Alnico V and P-90 pickups.

1972-1973		$5,500	$7,200

Les Paul Custom Historic '54
1991-2013. Custom Shop Historic Collection, 1954 appointments and pickup configuration, black, gold hardware.

1991-2013		$4,000	$5,250

Les Paul Custom Historic '57 Black Beauty
1991-2013. Black finish, gold hardware, 2 or 3 humbucker pickups, part of Gibson's Historic Collection.

1991-2012	2 pickups	$3,000	$3,925
1991-2013	3 pickups	$3,000	$3,925
2007	Goldtop, 3 pu	$3,000	$3,925
2007	Murphy aged, 3 pu	$3,000	$3,925

1957 Les Paul Custom (2-Pickup) Ultra Light Aged
2021-present. Custom Shop Murphy Lab Collection, Ebony finish.

2021-2022		$4,900	$6,400

1957 Les Paul Custom (3-Pickup) Light Aged
2021-present. Custom Shop Murphy Lab Collection, with Bigsby vibrato, Ebony finish.

2021-2022		$5,800	$7,500

Les Paul Custom Historic '68
1999-2007. Custom Shop Historic Collection, flamed maple top, 2 pickups.

1999-2007	Flamed maple	$3,000	$3,900
2000	Black	$3,000	$3,900

1968 Les Paul Custom Reissue (Custom Shop)
2020-present. Solid maple top, mahogany back, 2 humbucker pickups, gold hardware, Ebony gloss nitro finish. Limited slightly aged Silverburst in '20.

2020	Aged Silverburst	$5,400	$7,100
2020-2021	Ebony	$3,850	$5,000

1968 Les Paul Custom Ultra Light Aged
2021-present. Custom Shop Murphy Lab Collection, Ebony finish.

2021-2022		$4,200	$5,400

20th Anniversary Les Paul Custom
1974. Regular 2-pickup Custom, with 20th Anniversary inlay at 15th fret, cherry sunburst, natural, black or white.

1974	Black, white	$5,500	$7,200
1974	Cherry Sunburst, natural	$4,200	$5,400

25th Anniversary (Guitar Center) Les Paul Custom
1977-1978. Guitar Center Silver Anniversary, 50 made, 'Les Paul Custom' logo on truss rod cover, special 'Les Paul Custom Made in USA' on back of headstock, silver finish.

1977-1978		$3,650	$4,750

35th Anniversary Les Paul Custom
1989. Gold hardware, 3 pickups, carved, solid mahogany body and neck, 35th Anniversary inlay on headstock, black.

1989		$3,650	$4,750

120th Anniversary Les Paul Custom
2014. Custom Shop, 120th Anniversary neck inlay.

2014		$4,000	$5,200

120th Anniversary Les Paul Custom Lite
2014. Custom Shop, 120th Anniversary neck inlay.

2014		$2,075	$2,700

Les Paul Custom Ace Frehley "Budokan"
2012-2013. Custom Shop, limited edition of 50 hand-aged signed by Frehley, 100 hand-aged unsigned and 150 additional with VOS finish.

2012-2013	All options	$4,200	$5,500

Les Paul Custom Ace Frehley Signature
1997-2001. Ace's signature inlay at 15th fret, 3 humbuckers, sunburst.

1997	Pilot run, CS specs	$7,100	$9,200
1997-2001		$5,300	$6,900

Les Paul Custom Adam Jones 1979
2021-present. Custom Shop Limited Edition, recreates Jones' '79 LP Custom, 1st 79 aged and signed by Jones, Antique Silverburst VOS finish.

2021-2022	Signed	$6,700	$8,800
2021-2022	Unsigned	$4,100	$5,400

Les Paul Custom F (Custom Shop)
2014-2018. Figured maple top, various colors.

2014-2018		$4,100	$5,300

Les Paul Custom Jeff Beck 1954 Oxblood
2009. Custom Shop, limited run of 150, 1st 50 aged, hand-signed and played by Beck, next 100 VOS, mahogany body, carved maple top, rosewood 'board, Burstbucker humbucking pickups, Oxblood VOS finish.

2009		$5,000	$6,500

Les Paul Custom Jimmy Page
2008. Based on Page's '60 LP Custom with 3 pickups, stop tailpiece or Bigsby option, certificate of authenticity, black VOS finish.

2008		$7,300	$9,500

Les Paul Custom John Sykes 1978
2006. Custom Shop Limited Edition, run of 66, recreates Sykes' '78 LP Custom including mods he made, aged Ebony finish.

2006		$4,200	$5,500

Les Paul Custom Lite
1987-1990, 2013-2016. Carved maple top, ebony 'board, pearl block inlays, gold hardware, PAF pickups, bound neck, headstock and body. Reissue in '13

MODEL YEAR	FEATURES	EXC. COND. LOW	HIGH
with new options and colors.			
1987-1990	Floyd Rose, opaque	$2,100	$2,700
1987-1990	Other colors	$2,100	$2,700
1987-1990	Sunburst, mild figure	$2,100	$2,700
2013-2016		$2,100	$2,700

Les Paul Custom Lite (Show Case Edition)
1988. Showcase Edition, only 200 made, gold top.

1988		$2,150	$2,800

Les Paul Custom Mick Ronson '68
2007. Custom Shop, includes certificate and other authentication material.

2007		$3,200	$4,200

Les Paul Custom Music Machine
2003. Custom run for dealer Music Machine with special serial number series, chambered body style for reduced body weight, quilt tops.

2003	Figured Brazilian	$9,000	$11,700
2003	Quilted	$3,100	$4,100

Les Paul Custom Peter Frampton Signature
2008. Limited Edition 3-pickup version of Frampton's LP Custom, PF serial number series, black.

2008		$3,550	$4,600

Les Paul Custom Plus
1991-1998. Regular Custom with figured maple top, sunburst finish or colors.

1991-1998		$3,000	$3,925

Les Paul Custom Showcase Edition
1988. Showcase Edition logo on back of headstock, goldtop, black hardware.

1988		$3,300	$4,300

Les Paul Custom Silverburst
2007-2014. Custom Shop Limited Edition.

2007-2014		$3,400	$4,500

Les Paul Custom Steve Jones 1974
2008. Custom Shop Limited Edition, recreates Jones' '74 LP Custom including pin-up girl stickers, aged white finish.

2008		$4,200	$5,400

Les Paul Custom Zakk Wylde Signature
1999, 2003-2016. Custom shop, black and antique-white bullseye graphic finish. Green Camo option.

1999-2016	Various options	$4,000	$6,500

Les Paul Dale Earnhardt
1999. 333 made, Dale's image and number 3 on front and headstock, signature script on fretboard, several pieces of literature and an original certificate are part of the overall package, a lower serial number may add value.

1999		$2,900	$3,800

Les Paul Dale Earnhardt Intimidator
2000. 333 made, Dale's 'Goodwrench' car on the front of the body, The Intimidator inlay on the fretboard, includes certificate, chrome hardware.

2000		$2,900	$3,800

Les Paul Dark Fire
2009. Limited edition, 1st run of Les Pauls with Robot 2 Chameleon tone Technology designed to produce various classic guitar tones, completely computer

interactive, Burstbucker3 bridge pickup, P-90H neck pickup and 6 Piezo pickups.

2009		$1,850	$2,400

Les Paul Dark Knight Quilt Top
2019. Exclusive limited run made for Guitar Center, trans black satin finish over quilted maple top.

2019		$2,000	$2,600

Les Paul DC AA
2007. Double A flamed top.

2007		$1,675	$2,175

Les Paul DC Classic
1992-1993. Gold finish.

1992-1993		$1,275	$1,675

Les Paul DC Pro
1997-1998, 2006-2007. Custom Shop, body like a '59 Les Paul Junior, carved highly figured maple top, various options. Name revived in '06 but not a Custom Shop model.

1997-1998		$1,775	$2,300
2006-2007		$1,225	$1,600

Les Paul DC Standard (Plus)
1998-1999, 2001-2006. Offset double-cut, highly flamed maple top, translucent lacquer finishes in various colors, reintroduced as Standard Lite in '99 but without Les Paul designation on headstock or truss rod cover.

1998-1999		$1,400	$1,825
2001-2006		$1,450	$1,900

Les Paul DC Studio
1997-1999. DC Series double-cut like late '50s models, carved maple top, 2 humbucker pickups, various colors.

1997-1999		$775	$1,025

LES PAUL DELUXE
Following are Les Paul Deluxe models listed alphabetically.

Les Paul Deluxe
1969-1985. In 1969, the Goldtop Les Paul Standard was renamed the Deluxe. Two mini-humbuckers (regular humbuckers optional in mid-'70s). Mid-'70s sparkle tops are worth more than standard finishes. The market slightly favors the Goldtop finish, but practically speaking condition is more important than finish, such that all finishes fetch about the same amount (with the exception of the sparkle finish). Initially, the Deluxe was offered only as a Goldtop and the first year models are more highly prized than the others. Cherry sunburst was offered in '71, cherry in '71-'75, walnut in '71-'72, brown sunburst in '72-'79, natural in '75, red sparkle in '73-'75 only, blue sparkle in '73-'77, wine red/see-thru red offered '75-'85. In '99, the Deluxe was reissued for its 30th anniversary.

1969	Goldtop	$6,200	$8,200
1970	Goldtop	$5,100	$6,700
1971-1975	Goldtop	$4,500	$6,000
1971-1975	Natural	$3,400	$4,500
1971-1975	Red (solid)	$3,400	$4,500
1971-1975	Sunburst	$3,400	$4,500
1971-1975	Wine	$3,500	$4,500

1997 Gibson Les Paul Ace Frehley Signature

Eric Van Gansen

1973 Gibson Les Paul Deluxe

Rich Goldman

1952 Gibson Les Paul Model
mrosenow2

1957 Gibson Les Paul Model
Robert

MODEL YEAR	FEATURES	LOW	HIGH
1973-1975	Red sparkle, few made	$4,700	$6,200
1973-1977	Blue sparkle, more made	$4,300	$5,600
1976-1979	All other colors	$2,900	$3,800
1976-1979	Goldtop	$3,900	$5,100
1976-1979	Natural	$3,250	$4,250
1976-1979	Sunburst	$3,250	$4,250
1980-1985	Various colors	$2,900	$3,800

Les Paul Deluxe 30th Anniversary
1999. Limited Edition logo on the lower back of the headstock, Deluxe logo on truss rod cover, Wine Red.

1999		$1,450	$1,900

Les Paul Deluxe '69 Reissue
2000-2005. Mini-humbuckers, gold top

2000-2005		$1,600	$2,100

Les Paul Deluxe Hall of Fame
1991. All gold finish.

1991		$1,900	$2,500

Les Paul Deluxe Limited Edition
1999-2002. Limited edition reissue with Les Paul Standard features and Deluxe mini-humbuckers, black.

1999-2002		$1,650	$2,150

Les Paul Deluxe Limited Edition AMS
2014. Limited edition chocolate finish, offered only by American Musical Supply.

2014		$500	$650

Les Paul Deluxe Reissue
2012. Mini-humbuckers, chambered body.

2012		$2,100	$2,750

Les Paul Deluxe #1 Pete Townshend
2006. Limited to 75, red.

2006		$6,200	$8,100

Les Paul Deluxe #3 Pete Townshend
2006. Limited to 75, goldtop.

2006		$6,200	$8,100

Les Paul Deluxe #9 Pete Townshend
2006. Limited to 75, cherry burst.

2006		$6,200	$8,100

Les Paul Pro Deluxe
1978-1982. Chrome hardware, 2 P-90s, various colors. Les Pauls could vary significantly in weight during the '70s and '80s and lighter-weight examples may be worth up to 25% more than these values.

1978-1982		$2,275	$3,000

Les Paul Pro Showcase Edition
1988. Goldtop 1956 specs, Showcase Edition decal, 200 made.

1988		$3,050	$3,950

Les Paul Dusk Tiger
Late-2009-2012. Limited edition, 1000 to be made, features Gibson's Robot Technology, Burstbucker bridge, P-90H neck and 6 Piezo pickups.

2009-2012		$1,850	$2,400

Les Paul ES-Les Paul
2014-2018. Semi-hollow Les Paul body with f-holes, 3-ply maple/basswood/maple top and back, mahogany neck with maple spline, dark rosewood 'board, 2 pickups, light burst or black.

2014-2018		$1,925	$2,500

Les Paul ES-Les Paul Custom
2015. Memphis Shop, limited run, semi-hollow maple/poplar/maple body, f-holes, high gloss Ebony finish.

2015		$3,600	$4,700

Les Paul ES-Les Paul Standard
2016. Memphis Shop, limited run, semi-hollow, figured maple, various colors.

2016		$3,600	$4,700

Les Paul ES-Les Paul Studio
2016. Memphis Shop, limited run, semi-hollow maple body, f-holes, Ginger Burst or Wine Red.

2016		$1,700	$2,200

Les Paul Florentine Plus
1997-2001. Custom Shop model, hollowbody with f-holes, higher-end appointments.

1997-2001		$3,200	$4,200

Les Paul Supreme Florentine
2009-2015. Les Paul Standard with sharp Florentine cutaway, 350 made, Bigsby tailpiece, chambered mahogany body, highly figured maple top and back, Caribbean Blue finish.

2009-2015		$2,900	$3,800

Les Paul Futura
2014-2015. Light weight, unbound, Min-Etune, various bright colors.

2014-2015		$850	$1,125

Les Paul Goddess
2006-2007. Maple carved top, trapezoid inlays, smaller body, 2 humbuckers, 2 controls, tune-a-matic bridge.

2007		$1,200	$1,575

LES PAUL GOLDTOP

Following are Les Paul Goldtop models listed alphabetically.

Les Paul Model
1952-1958. The Goldtop, 2 P-90 pickups until mid-'57, humbuckers after, trapeze tailpiece until late-'53, stud tailpiece/bridge '53-mid-'55, Tune-o-matic bridge '55-'58, renamed Les Paul Standard in '58. All gold option add +10% if the neck retains 90% of the gold paint. All gold option with ugly green wear on the neck is equal to or below the value of a standard paint job. Some instruments had all mahogany bodies which did not have the maple cap. The all-mahogany version, although rarer, has a 10% lower value. A factory installed Bigsby tailpiece will reduce value by 30%. A non-factory installed Bigsby will reduce value up to 50%.

1952	1st made, unbound neck	$22,000	$29,000
1952	5/8" knobs, bound neck	$19,000	$25,000
1953	1/2" knobs, trapeze tailpiece	$19,000	$25,000
1953	Late-'53, 1/2" knobs, stud tailpiece	$33,000	$43,000
1954	Stud tailpiece, wrap-around	$33,000	$43,000

GUITARS

MODEL YEAR	FEATURES	EXC. COND. LOW	HIGH
1955	Early-'55, stud tailpiece, wrap-around	$35,000	$45,000
1955	Late-'55, tune-o-matic tailpiece	$44,000	$57,000
1956	Tune-o-matic tailpiece	$43,000	$56,000
1957	Early-'57, P-90s	$43,000	$56,000
1957	PAFs, black plastic	$127,000	$165,000
1957-1958	PAFs, white plastic	$135,000	$175,000

'52 Les Paul Goldtop
1997-2002. Goldtop finish, 2 P-90s, '52-style trapeze tailpiece/bridge.

1997-2002		$2,025	$2,625
1997-2002	Murphy aged	$2,200	$2,850

'52 Les Paul Tribute
2009. Recreation of '52 Les Paul Goldtop model, 564 made, special serialization, each guitar has 'prototype' impressed on back of headstock, Tribute designation logo on truss rod, includes COA booklet with serialized COA and tribute dates 1915-2009.

2009		$2,400	$3,100

'54 Les Paul Goldtop
1996-2013. Goldtop finish, 2 P-90s, '53-'54 stud tailpiece/bridge.

1996-2013		$2,800	$3,600
2003	Brazilian, COA	$5,900	$7,700

'54 Les Paul Wildwood
2012. Wildwood guitars special run, '54 specs, wrap-around tailpiece, 2 P-90 pickups, plaintop sunburst.

2012		$2,800	$3,600

1954 Les Paul Goldtop Heavy Aged
2021. Custom Shop Murphy Lab Collection, Double Gold finish.

2021		$4,700	$6,100

'55 Les Paul Goldtop Hot-Mod Wraptail
2010. Musician's Friend, based on '55 LP Humbucking Pickup Test Guitar, '55 specs, aged nitrocellulose gold finish, includes COA.

2010		$2,800	$3,600

'56 Les Paul Goldtop
1991-2016. Renamed from Les Paul Reissue Goldtop. Goldtop finish, 2 P-90 pickups, Tune-o-matic, now part of Gibson's Historic Collection, Custom Authentic aging optional from '01, Vintage Original Specs aging optional from '06.

1991-2016		$2,800	$3,600
2003	Brazilian	$6,000	$7,800

1956 Les Paul Goldtop "CME Spec"
2019-2020. Custom Shop special run for Chicago Music Exchange, Double Gold with VOS finish.

2019-2020		$3,500	$4,700

1956 Les Paul Goldtop Reissue
2020-present. Custom Shop, authentic replica parts, Double Gold nitro finish.

2020-2021		$3,200	$4,200

1956 Les Paul Goldtop Ultra Light Aged
2021-present. Custom Shop Murphy Lab Collection, Double Gold finish.

2021-2022		$3,550	$4,600

'57 Les Paul Goldtop
1993-2018. Goldtop finish, 2 humbuckers, now part of Gibson's Historic Collection.

1993-2018		$2,800	$3,600
2003	Brazilian	$6,000	$7,800

'57 Les Paul Goldtop (R-7 wrap-around)
2007. Special run with wrap-around bar tailpiece/ bridge similar to tailpiece on an original '54 Les Paul Goldtop.

2007		$2,800	$3,600

1957 Les Paul Goldtop Darkback Light Aged
2021-present. Custom Shop Murphy Lab Collection, Double Gold finish with dark back.

2021-2022		$4,200	$5,500

1957 Les Paul Goldtop Reissue
2020-present. Custom Shop, authentic replica parts, all Double Gold or Double Gold with dark back.

2020-2021		$3,200	$4,200

1957 Les Paul Goldtop Ultra Light/Ultra Heavy Aged
2021-present. Custom Shop Murphy Lab Collection, ultra light or heavy aged, Double Gold finish.

2021-2022		$3,600	$4,700

Les Paul 30th Anniversary
1982-1984. Features of a 1958 Les Paul Goldtop, 2 humbuckers, 30th Anniversary inlay on 19th fret.

1982-1984		$3,200	$4,200

Les Paul 50th Anniversary 1956 Les Paul Standard Goldtop
2006. Custom Shop, '56 tune-o-matic P-90 specs.

2006		$2,750	$3,575

Les Paul 50th Anniversary 1957 Les Paul Standard Goldtop
2007. Custom Shop, limited run of 150, humbucker pickups, large gold 50th Anniversary headstock logo.

2007		$4,500	$5,800

Les Paul Billy F. Gibbons Goldtop
2014-2018. Custom Shop, mahogany neck with maple spline, rosewood 'board, holly headstock, 2 Duncan Pearly Gates pickups, Goldtop VOS or Goldtop Aged.

2014-2018		$6,100	$7,900

Les Paul Centennial ('56 LP Standard Goldtop)
1994. Guitar of the Month, limited edition of 100, Goldtop mahogany body, gold hardware, gold truss rod plate, gold medallion, engraved light-gold 'guard, with COA.

1994		$3,300	$4,300

Les Paul Dickey Betts Goldtop
2001-2003. Aged gold top.

2001-2003		$6,200	$8,100

Les Paul Joe Bonamassa Aged Goldtop
2008. Inspired By Series, LP Standard aged goldtop with black trim (including black pickup rings), serial number starts with BONAMASSA.

2008		$2,850	$3,700

2006 Gibson '56 Les Paul Goldtop

Johnny Zapp

Gibson Les Paul 50th Anniversary 1957 Les Paul Standard Goldtop

Matt Carleson

1957 Gibson Les Paul Junior
Frank Thoubboron

Gibson Les Paul TV Junior
Bill Miller

MODEL YEAR	FEATURES	EXC. COND. LOW	HIGH

Les Paul LP-295 Goldtop
2008. Guitar of the Month (April, '08), limited run of 1000, Les Paul body style, goldtop, 2 humbuckers, ES-295 appointments such as 'guard and fretboard markers, Bigsby tailpiece option.

2008		$2,400	$3,100

Les Paul Reissue Goldtop
1983-1991. Goldtop finish, 2 P-100 pickups, renamed '56 Les Paul Goldtop in '91.

1983-1991		$2,775	$3,600

Les Paul Slash Signature Goldtop
2008. Limited Edition, 1000 made, LP Standard model, Slash logo truss rod cover, Limited Edition logo back of headstock, certificate of authenticity.

2008		$3,400	$4,400

Les Paul Government Series II
2014-2018. 2 Dirty Fingers pickups, certificate of authenticity, Government Tan finish.

2013-2018		$1,100	$1,425

Les Paul GT
2007. Includes over/under dual truss rods, GT logo on truss rod cover, several specs designed to add durability during heavy professional use.

2007		$1,575	$2,050

Les Paul HD.6-X Pro Digital
2008-2009. Digital sound system, hex pickups.

2008-2009		$2,075	$2,700

Les Paul Indian Motorcycle
2002. 100 made, has Indian script logo on fretboard and chrome cast war bonnet on the body, crimson red and cream white.

2002		$4,100	$5,400

Les Paul Jumbo
1969-1970. Single rounded cutaway, flat-top dreadnought acoustic/electric, 1 pickup, rosewood back and sides, natural.

1969-1970		$3,000	$4,000

LES PAUL JUNIOR
Following are Les Paul Junior models listed alphabetically.

Les Paul Junior
1954-1963, 1986-1992, 2001-2002, 2005-2013. One P-90 pickup, single-cut solidbody '54-mid-'58, double-cut '58-early-'61, SG body '61-'63, renamed SG Jr. in '63, reintroduced as single-cut for '86-'92, reissued as the 1957 Les Paul Jr. Single Cutaway in '98. Headstock repair reduces the value by 40%-50%. Reinstalled tuners reduces the value by 5% to 10%. Replaced tuner buttons reduces the value by 5% to 10%.

1954-1958	Sunburst, single-cut	$8,000	$10,500
1958-1961	Cherry, double-cut	$7,600	$10,000
1961-1963	Cherry, SG body	$4,300	$5,700
1986-1992	Sunburst, single-cut, tune-o-matic	$1,000	$1,300
1998-2013	Sunburst, single-cut, stop tail	$1,000	$1,300

Les Paul Junior 3/4
1956-1961. One P-90 pickup, short-scale, single-cut solidbody '54-mid-'58, double-cut '58-early-'61.

1956-1958	Sunburst, single-cut	$3,800	$5,000
1958-1961	Cherry, double-cut	$3,300	$4,400

1957 Les Paul Junior (Single-Cut) Ultra Light Aged/Heavy Aged
2021-present. Custom Shop Murphy Lab Collection, ultra light or heavy aged, TV Yellow finish on both.

2021-2022	Heavy aged	$4,200	$5,500
2021-2022	Ultra Light aged	$2,900	$3,800

1957 Les Paul Junior (Single-Cut) VOS
1998-2014. Custom Shop, nickel-plated hardware, Vintage Original Spec aging optional from '06.

1998-2014		$2,300	$3,000

1958 Les Paul Junior (Double-Cut) VOS
1998-2013. Custom Shop, nickel plated hardware, Vintage Original Spec aging optional from '06.

1998-2013		$2,300	$3,000

'60 Les Paul Junior
1992-2003. Historic Collection reissue.

1992-2003		$2,100	$2,750

1960 Les Paul Junior (Double-Cut) Ultra Heavy Aged
2021. Custom Shop Murphy Lab Collection, Ebony finish.

2021		$5,200	$6,800

Les Paul J / LPJ
2013-2018. Mahogany body with carved maple top, '50s profile maple neck, rosewood 'board, 2 Modern Classics humbucking pickups, various finishes.

2013-2018		$575	$750

Les Paul Junior Billie Joe Armstrong Signature
2006-2013. 1956 LP Junior specs.

2006-2013		$1,175	$1,525

Les Paul Junior DC Hall of Fame
1990-1992. Part of Hall of Fame Series, limited run of LP Junior Double Cutaway but with P-100 pickup.

1990-1992		$950	$1,225

Les Paul Junior Double Cutaway
1986-1992, 1995-1996. Copy of '50s double-cut Jr., cherry or sunburst, reissued as the 1958 Les Paul Jr. Double Cutaway in '98.

1986-1989		$950	$1,225

Les Paul Junior Faded
2010-2012. Single-cut, faded cherry finish.

2010-2012		$685	$885

Les Paul Junior John Lennon LTD
2008. Custom Shop Inspired By series, 300 made, Charlie Christian neck pickup and P-90 bridge as per Lennon's modified Junior, aged-relic finish, certificate, book and New York t-shirt.

2008		$4,200	$5,500

Les Paul Junior Lite
1999-2002. Double-cut, Tune-o-matic, 2 P-100 pickups, stop tail, mini-trapezoid markers, burnt cherry gloss finish.

1999-2002		$700	$925

MODEL YEAR	FEATURES	EXC. COND. LOW	HIGH

Les Paul Junior Special
1999-2004. LP Jr. single-cut slab body with 2 P-90s (making it a Special) instead of the standard single P-90, double pickup controls, cherry, tinted natural or sunburst.

1999-2004		$775	$1,025

Les Paul Junior Special Robot
2008. P-90s, TV Yellow.

2008		$800	$1,050

Les Paul Junior Tenor/Plectrum
Late-1950s. Four string neck on Junior body, cherry.

1959		$4,700	$6,100

Les Paul TV
1954-1959. Les Paul Jr. with limed mahogany (TV Yellow) finish, single-cut until mid-'59, double-cut after, renamed SG TV (see that listing for more) in late-'59.

1954-1959	Single-cut	$13,000	$17,000
1958-1959	Double-cut	$12,000	$15,500

Les Paul TV 3/4
1954-1957. Limed mahogany (TV Yellow) Les Paul Jr. 3/4, short-scale, single-cut.

1954-1957		$6,000	$8,000

Les Paul TV Junior
2001-2016. Custom Shop, TV Yellow.

2001-2016		$2,100	$2,750

Les Paul Limited Run 2016 Series
Various Les Paul limited edition models released in 2016.

2016-2018	Fort Knox	$3,700	$4,800
2016-2018	Mahogany Limited	$3,700	$4,800
2016-2018	Pete Townshend Deluxe	$3,700	$4,800
2016-2018	Redwood	$3,700	$4,800
2016-2018	Standard Figured Walnut	$3,700	$4,800
2016-2018	Sunken Treasure	$3,700	$4,800

Les Paul Lou Pallo Signature
2010. Maple top, mahogany back and neck, rosewood 'board, 2 pickups, ebony finish.

2010		$1,900	$2,500

Les Paul Marc Bolan
2011. Artist model with certificate of authenticity, limited run of 100 hand aged and 350 VOS, Bolan Chablis finish.

2011		$4,400	$5,800

Les Paul Menace
2006-2007. Carved mahogany body, 2 humbucker pickups.

2006-2007		$600	$800

Les Paul Old Hickory
1998 only. Limited run of 200, tulip poplar body wood from The Hermitage, Custom-style trim.

1998		$4,400	$4,700

Les Paul Personal
1969-1972. Two angled, low impedance pickups, phase switch, gold parts, walnut finish.

1969-1972		$2,400	$3,100

Les Paul Professional
1969-1971, 1977-1979. Single-cut, 2 angled, low impedance pickups, carved top, walnut or white.

1969-1971	Walnut	$2,400	$3,100
1969-1971	White	$2,400	$3,100

Les Paul Recording
1971-1979. Two angled, low impedance pickups, high/low impedance selector switch, walnut '71-'77, white added '75, natural, ebony and sunburst added '78.

1971-1977	Walnut	$2,400	$3,200
1975-1979	White	$3,275	$4,250
1978-1979	Black, Natural, Sunburst	$2,500	$3,300

Les Paul Richard Petty LTD
2003. Richard Petty's image on front and back, 'The King' inlay on fretboard.

2003		$3,100	$4,050

Les Paul Signature/L.P. Signature
1973-1978. Thin semi-hollowbody, double-cut, 2 low impedance pickups, f-holes, various colors. The Price List refers to it as L.P. Signature.

1973-1978		$4,000	$5,200

Les Paul Silver Streak
1982. Custom Shop decal, silver finish.

1982		$3,000	$3,900

Les Paul SM
1980. Solid mahogany, single-cut with coil-tap, Les Paul SM truss rod logo, burgundy or silverburst finish.

1980		$2,150	$2,800

Les Paul SmartWood Exotic
1998-2001. Full-depth Les Paul-style built with eco-friendly woods, Muiracatiara (or Muir) top, mahogany back, Preciosa 'board, pearloid dots.

1998-2001		$1,125	$1,450

Les Paul SmartWood Standard
1996-2002. Smartwood Series, figured maple top, mahogany body, Smartwood on truss rod cover, antique natural.

1996-2002		$1,125	$1,450

Les Paul SmartWood Studio
2002-2006. Muiracatiara (Muir) top and mahogany back, Preciosa (Prec) 'board, Studio appointments including pearl-style dot markers.

2002-2006		$950	$1,225

LES PAUL SPECIAL
Following are Les Paul Special models listed alphabetically.

Les Paul Special
1955-1959. Slab solidbody, 2 pickups (P-90s in '50s, P-100 stacked humbuckers on later version), single-cut until end of '58, double in '59, the '89 reissue is a single-cut, renamed SG Special in late-'59.

1955-1959	TV Yellow	$12,100	$15,700
1959	Cherry	$8,500	$11,000

Les Paul 55
1974, 1976-1981. Single-cut Special reissue, 2 pickups. By '78 the catalog name is Les Paul 55/78.

1974-1981	Sunburst	$2,000	$2,600
1974-1981	TV Yellow (limed)	$2,100	$2,800
1976-1981	Wine	$1,900	$2,500

'60 Les Paul Special
1998-2012. Historic Collection reissue, limited edition, single-cut or double-cut.

1998-2012		$2,400	$3,100
2007	Murphy aged	$2,500	$3,200

1969 Gibson Les Paul Personal
Frank Manno

1969 Gibson Les Paul Professional
Pete Pensec

1959 Gibson Les Paul Special 3/4
Alex Sauceda

1994 Gibson Les Paul Special Centennial
Imaged by Heritage Auctions, HA.com

Les Paul Special (Reissue)

1989-1998, 2002-2006. Briefly introduced as Les Paul Junior II but name changed to Special in the first year, single-cut, 2 P-100 stacked humbuckers, TV Yellow, in '90 there was a run of 300 with LE serial number, renamed Special SL in '98.

Year	Features	Low	High
1989-1998	P-100s	$850	$1,125
2002-2006	Humbuckers	$850	$1,125

Les Paul Special 100/100 Special

2015-2016. Reissue double-cut slab body, 2 P-90s, 'Les Paul 100' birthday signature on headstock.

Year	Low	High
2015-2016	$800	$1,050

Les Paul Special 3/4

1959. Slab solidbody, 2 P-90 pickups, double-cut, short-scale, cherry finish, renamed SG Special 3/4 in late-'59.

Year	Low	High
1959	$5,200	$6,700

Les Paul Special Centennial

1994 only. 100 made, double-cut, cherry, 100 year banner at the 12th fret, diamonds in headstock and in gold-plated knobs, gold-plated Gibson coin in back of headstock.

Year	Low	High
1994	$3,800	$4,900

Les Paul Special Double Cutaway

1976-1979, 1993-1994. Double-cut, 2 P-90s, 1990s version was made in Custom Shop and was reintroduced as the '60 Les Paul Special Historic in '98.

Year	Features	Low	High
1976-1979		$2,400	$3,100
1993-1994	Custom Shop	$1,350	$1,750

Les Paul Special Faded

2005-2012. Double- or single-cut, dot markers, 2 P-90s, Special logo on truss rod cover, faded TV limed mahogany or cherry finish.

Year	Low	High
2005-2012	$700	$925

Les Paul Special New Century

2006-2008. Full-body mirror 'guard, 2 exposed humbuckers, single-cut LP Special body, mirror truss rod cover.

Year	Low	High
2006-2008	$1,150	$1,500

Les Paul Special Robot

2008. Two P-90 pickups, various colors.

Year	Low	High
2008	$850	$1,125

Les Paul Special Tenor

1959. Four-string electric tenor, LP Special body, TV Yellow.

Year	Low	High
1959	$5,000	$6,500

Les Paul Special Worn Cherry

2003-2006. Single-cut, non-bound LP Special with 2 humbuckers.

Year	Low	High
2003-2006	$675	$875

LES PAUL STANDARD

Following are Les Paul Standard models, beginning with the original model, then listed alphabetically.

Les Paul Standard (Sunburst)

1958-1960, special order 1972-1975. Les Paul Sunbursts from '58-'60 should be individually valued based on originality, color and the amount and type of figure in the maple top, changed tuners or a Bigsby removal will drop the value. Approximately 15% came with the Bigsby tailpiece. The noted price ranges are guidance valuations. Each '58-'60 Les Paul Standard should be evaluated on a case-by-case basis. As is always the case, the low and high ranges are for an all original, excellent condition, undamaged guitar. About 70% of the '58-'60 Les Paul Standards have relatively plain maple tops. The majority of '58-'60 Les Paul Standards have moderate or extreme color fade.

Wider fret wire was introduced in early-'59. White bobbins were introduced in early- to mid-'59. Double ring Kluson Deluxe tuners were introduced in late-'60. It has been suggested that all '58-'60 models have 2-piece centerseam tops. This implies that 1-piece tops, 3-piece tops and off-centerseam tops do not exist.

The terminology of the 'Burst includes: arching medullary grain, swirling medullary grain, ribbon-curl, chevrons, Honey-Amber, receding red aniline, pinstripe, bookmatched, double-white bobbins, zebra bobbins, black bobbins, fiddleback maple, sunburst finish, Honeyburst, lemon drop, quarter sawn, blistered figure, width of gradation, flat sawn, Teaburst, Bigsby-shadow, rift sawn, heel size, aged clear lacquer, 3-dimensional figure, intense fine flame, tag-shadow, red pore filler, Eastern maple fleck, medium-thick flame, shrunk tuners, wave and flame, flitch-matched, elbow discoloration, ambered top coat, natural gradation, grain orientation, script oxidation, asymmetrical figure Tangerineburst, Greenburst, and birdseye.

The bobbins used for the pickup winding were either black or white. The market has determined that white bobbin PAFs are the most highly regarded. Generally speaking, in '58 bobbins were black, in '59 the bobbin component transitioned to white and some guitars have 1 white and 1 black bobbin (aka zebra). In '60, there were zebras and double blacks returned.

Rather than listing separate line items for fade and wood, the Guide lists discounts and premiums as follows. The price ranges shown below are for instruments with excellent color, excellent wood, with the original guitar case. The following discounts and premiums should be considered.

An instrument with moderate or total color fade should be discounted about 10%.

One with a factory Bigsby should be discounted about 10%-15%.

Original jumbo frets are preferred over original small frets and are worth +10%.

		Low	High
1958	Highly figured	$340,000	$440,000
1958	Minor figured	$281,000	$366,000
1958	Plain top, no figuring	$205,000	$265,000
1959	Highly figured	$425,000	$555,000
1959	Minor figured	$305,000	$395,000
1959	Plain top, no figuring	$233,000	$302,000
1960	Early '60, fat neck, highly figured	$318,000	$413,000
1960	Early '60, fat neck, minor figured	$261,000	$345,000

MODEL YEAR	FEATURES	EXC. COND. LOW	HIGH
1960	Early '60, fat neck, plain top	$186,000	$242,000
1960	Late '60, flat neck, highly figured	$305,000	$395,000
1960	Late '60, flat neck, minor figured	$233,000	$305,000
1960	Late '60, flat neck, plain top	$174,000	$266,000

Les Paul Standard (SG body)

1961-1963 (SG body those years) Renamed SG Standard in late-'63

MODEL YEAR	FEATURES	EXC. COND. LOW	HIGH
1961-1963	Cherry, side vibrola, PAFs	$17,000	$22,500
1962	Cherry, Bigsby, 1 pat #, 1 PAF	$13,800	$18,100
1962-1963	Cherry, side vibrola, pat #	$12,700	$16,700
1962-1963	Ebony block, SG, PAFs, dlx vibrola	$19,000	$24,900
1962-1963	Ebony block, SG, pat #, dlx vibrola	$15,600	$20,500

Les Paul Standard (reintroduced then renamed)

1968-1969. Comes back as a goldtop with P-90s for '68-'69 (renamed Les Paul Deluxe, '69), available as special order Deluxe '72-'76.

MODEL YEAR	FEATURES	EXC. COND. LOW	HIGH
1968	P-90s, small hdsk, no volute	$18,600	$24,200
1968-1969	P-90s, large hdsk	$14,300	$18,600

Les Paul Standard (reintroduced)

1971-July 2008, 2012-2018. Available as special order Deluxe '72-'76, reintroduced with 2 humbuckers '76-present. The '75 Price List shows a Les Paul Standard (B) model which is equipped with a Bigsby tailpiece versus a wraparound, also shows a Les Paul Standard (B) with palm pedal. Replaced by Les Paul Standard 2008 in August '08. Name revived in '12 on chambered-body version with tapped Burstbucker pickups, available in AAA tops, black, Gold Top or Blue Mist finishes.

MODEL YEAR	FEATURES	EXC. COND. LOW	HIGH
1971	Early special order goldtop, P-90s	$10,300	$13,400
1972-1974	Special order goldtop, P-90s	$7,500	$9,700
1972-1974	Special order sunburst, P-90s	$6,300	$8,200
1974-1975	Special order, hums	$6,300	$8,200
1976	Sunburst, 4-piece pancake body	$4,150	$5,400
1976-1978	Other colors	$3,300	$4,300
1977-1978	Sunburst	$4,050	$5,300
1978-1979	Natural	$3,300	$4,300
1979	Brown Sunburst	$4,050	$5,300
1979	Cherry Sunburst	$4,050	$5,300
1979	Goldtop	$4,050	$5,300
1979	Wine Red	$3,300	$4,300
1980-1984	Other colors	$3,100	$4,050
1980-1984	Sunburst	$3,100	$4,050
1980-1984	White (RRhoads)	$3,100	$4,050
1985-1989	Various colors	$2,950	$3,900
1985-1989	White (RRhoads)	$2,950	$3,900

MODEL YEAR	FEATURES	EXC. COND. LOW	HIGH
1990-1993	Ltd Ed colors with sticker	$2,950	$3,900
1990-1999	White (RRhoads)	$1,950	$2,600
1990-2018	Figured top	$2,150	$2,800
1990-2018	Plain top	$1,750	$2,350
2000-2018	Opaque solid color	$1,850	$2,400

'50s Les Paul Standard

2005-present. Originally an AMS exclusive with AA (later AAA) maple top and various finishes. In '19, Gibson introduced a regular production model with the same name with standard maple top finished in Goldtop, Heritage Cherry Sunburst or Tobacco Burst.

2005-2021	AA & AAA top	$2,150	$2,800

'58 Les Paul Figured Top

1996-2000, 2002-2003, 2009-2012. Custom Shop, less top figure than '59 Reissue, sunburst.

1996-2000		$4,200	$5,400
2002-2012		$4,200	$5,400
2003	Brazilian	$11,300	$14,700

'58 Les Paul Plaintop (VOS)

1994-1999, 2003-2013. Custom Shop model, plain maple top version of '58 Standard reissue, sunburst, VOS model starts in '04. Replaced by the 1958 Les Paul Reissue with a non-chambered body.

1994-1999	Non-VOS	$3,200	$4,200
2003-2013	VOS, non-chambered	$3,200	$4,200
2006-2013	VOS, chambered	$3,200	$4,200

1958 Les Paul Standard "CME Spec"

2019-2020. Custom Shop special run for Chicago Music Exchange, various colors with VOS finish.

2019-2020		$3,600	$4,700

1958 Les Paul Standard Light Aged/ Heavy Aged

2021-present. Custom Shop Murphy Lab Collection, light or heavy aged, Lemon Burst.

2021-2022		$4,400	$5,700

1958 Les Paul Standard Ultra Light Aged

2021-present. Custom Shop Murphy Lab Collection, Bourbon Burst or Washed Cherry Sunburst.

2021-2022		$3,800	$4,900

'59 Les Paul Flametop/Reissue/Standard

1993-2016. Renamed from Les Paul Reissue Flametop, for 2000-'05 called the 1959 Les Paul Reissue, in '06 this model became part of Gibson's Vintage Original Spec series and is called the '59 Les Paul Standard VOS. Flame maple top, 2 humbuckers, thick '59-style neck, sunburst finish, part of Gibson's Historic Collection, the original certificate authenticity adds value, an instrument without the matching certificate has less value. By '98 Gibson guaranteed only AAA Premium grade maple tops would be used.

Collectors of Historic Collection instruments tend to buy and store these instruments, maintaining them in near mint to New Old Stock (NOS) mint condition. In recent years, NOS instruments that are up to five years old, but in like-new mint condition, have been sold at prices that are higher than instruments in excellent condition, which is the usual condition that VG Price Guide values are given. Because of that trend, the prices shown here give consideration to the

1958 Gibson Les Standard
Gary's Classic Guitars

1962 Gibson Les Paul Standard

2009 Gibson '59 Les Paul Burst Brothers

Anthony Perrotta

1994 Gibson '59 Les Paul Flametop

MODEL YEAR	FEATURES	EXC. COND. LOW	HIGH

numerous NOS instruments that have sold. The inclusion of both excellent condition instruments and mint NOS instruments creates a wider than normal price range, but the high-side of the range is very realistic for NOS instruments.

MODEL YEAR	FEATURES	EXC. COND. LOW	HIGH
1993	Custom Shop decal, early '93	$6,500	$8,500
1993	Historic decal, late '93	$5,400	$7,000
1994-1995	Murphy aged	$5,400	$7,000
1994-1999	Aged, figured top	$5,400	$7,000
1996-1999	Figured top	$5,400	$7,000
2000-2016	Aged, figured top	$5,000	$6,500
2000-2016	Figured top	$4,500	$5,900
2003	Brazilian, aged, figured	$12,300	$16,000
2003	Brazilian, highly figured	$11,400	$14,800
2003	Brazilian, low figured	$10,000	$13,000

'59 Les Paul Burst Brothers

2009-2010. Limited edition created with Dave Belzer and Drew Berlin, sold through Guitar Center, wood figure selected to reflect the nature of a '50s LP Standard rather than using only best-quality flame, first run of 34 (serial no. BB 9 001-034) with dark Madagascar rosewood 'board, second run was 37 (serial no. BB 0 001-037).

2009	First run (34)	$7,700	$10,000
2010	Second run (37)	$6,700	$8,700

'59 Les Paul Korina Reissue

2008. Custom Shop Limited Edition, korina body and neck, quilted maple top, rosewood 'board, natural finish.

2008		$5,700	$7,500

'59 Les Paul Plaintop (VOS)

2006-2013. Custom Shop, very little or no-flame.

2006-2013		$3,200	$4,200

1959 Les Paul Standard "CME Spec"

2019-2020. Custom Shop special run for Chicago Music Exchange, various colors with VOS finish.

2019-2020		$6,100	$8,000

1959 Les Paul Standard Heavy Aged

2021-present. Custom Shop Murphy Lab Collection, Green Lemon Fade, Golden Poppy Burst or Slow Iced Tea Fade.

2021-2022		$6,150	$8,000

1959 Les Paul Standard Light Aged

2021-present. Custom Shop Murphy Lab Collection, Cherry Tea Burst, Lemon Burst or Royal Tea Burst.

2021-2022		$5,500	$7,100

1959 Les Paul Standard Reissue

2020-present. Custom Shop, authentic replica parts, Washed Cherry Sunburst, Iced Tea Burst or Dirty Lemon, all colors with VOS finish.

2020-2021		$4,400	$5,700

1959 Les Paul Standard Ultra Heavy Aged

2021-present. Custom Shop Murphy Lab Collection, Kindred Burst or Lemon Burst.

2021-2022		$7,150	$9,300

1959 Les Paul Standard Ultra Light Aged

2021-present. Custom Shop Murphy Lab Collection, Factory Burst, Southern Fade Burst or Sunrise Teaburst.

2021-2022		$4,700	$6,200

True Historic 1959 Les Paul

2015-2018. Figured maple top, Indian rosewood 'board, certificate of authenticity, various vintage finishes including Murphy aged option.

2015-2018		$4,700	$6,200

'60s Les Paul Standard

2005-present. Originally an AMS exclusive with AA (later AAA) maple top and various finishes. In '19, Gibson introduced a regular production model with the same name with standard maple top finished in Ice Tea, Bourbon Burst, or Unburst.

2005-2021	AA & AAA top	$2,150	$2,800

'60 Les Paul Flametop/Standard '60s

1991-present. Renamed from Les Paul Reissue Flametop, flame maple top, 2 humbuckers, thinner neck, sunburst finish, part of Gibson's Historic Collection. In '06 this model became part of Gibson's Vintage Original Spec series and called '60 Les Paul Standard VOS, then in '17 the name changed to Les Paul Standard '60s.

1991-1999	Figured top	$5,400	$7,000
1994-1999	Aged, figured	$5,400	$7,000
2000-2016	Aged, figured	$4,600	$6,000
2000-2021	Figured top	$4,200	$5,500
2003	Brazilian, aged, figured	$12,000	$16,000
2003	Brazilian, figured	$11,500	$15,000

'60 Les Paul Plaintop (VOS)

2006-2010. Plain maple top version of '60 Standard reissue, certificate of authenticity, VOS cherry sunburst.

2006-2010		$3,200	$4,200

1960 Les Paul Standard Heavy Aged

2020-present. Custom Shop Murphy Lab Collection, heavy aged Tangerine Burst.

2020-2022		$6,000	$8,000

1960 Les Paul Standard Light Aged

2020-present. Custom Shop Murphy Lab Collection, light aged Tomato Soup Burst.

2020-2022		$5,500	$7,100

1960 Les Paul Standard Reissue

2020-present. Custom Shop, authentic reproduction, vintage-style appointments, various colors with VOS finish.

2020-2022		$4,400	$5,700

1960 Les Paul Standard Ultra Light Aged

2020-present. Custom Shop Murphy Lab Collection, ultra light aged Orange Lemon Fade Burst or Wide Tomato Burst.

2020-2022		$4,700	$6,100

True Historic 1960 Les Paul

2015-2018. Figured maple top, Indian rosewood 'board, certificate of authenticity, various vintage finishes including Murphy aged option.

2015-2018		$5,000	$6,500

MODEL YEAR	FEATURES	EXC. COND. LOW	HIGH

'82 Les Paul Standard

1982. Standard 82 on truss rod cover, made in Kalamazoo, Made in USA stamp on back of the headstock, generally quilted maple tops.

| 1982 | | $3,050 | $3,950 |

Les Paul 10th Anniversary Chambered '58 Reissue

2014. Custom Shop, chambered mahogany body, carved maple top, '50s neck profile, rosewood 'board.

| 2014 | | $3,200 | $4,200 |

Les Paul 40th Anniversary (from 1959)

1999. Reissue Historic, humbuckers, highly figured top, price includes 40th Anniversary Edition Certificate of Authenticity with matching serial number, a guitar without the certificate is worth less.

| 1999 | | $4,500 | $5,900 |

Les Paul 50th Anniversary (Historic)

2002. From Gibson Custom Art & Historic Division, 50 made, carved figured koa top, figured maple back and sides, 3-piece figured maple neck, abalone cloud inlay markers, pearl split-diamond headstock inlay and pearl Gibson logo, Antique Natural.

| 2002 | | $7,100 | $9,300 |

Les Paul 50th Anniversary 1959 Les Paul Standard

2009-2011. Custom Shop, highly figured top, certificate of authenticity.

| 2009-2011 | | $4,600 | $6,000 |

Les Paul 50th Anniversary 1960 Les Paul Standard

2010-2011. Limited Edition, offered in Heritage Cherry Sunburst, Heritage Dark Burst, Sunset Tea Burst and Cherry Burst.

| 2010-2011 | | $4,600 | $6,000 |

Les Paul 50th Anniversary DaPra

2009. Limited run of 25 made for Vic DaPra of Guitar Gallery, '59 Historic R9.

| 2009 | | $4,900 | $6,400 |

Les Paul 50th Anniversary Korina Tribute

2009. Custom Shop model, 100 made, single-cut Korina natural finish body, 3 pickups, dot markers, V-shaped Futura headstock, Custom logo on truss rod cover, slanted raised Gibson logo on headstock.

| 2009 | | $5,400 | $7,100 |

Les Paul 50th Anniversary Les Paul Standard (Sweetwater)

2009. Custom Shop, limited run of 25 for Sweetwater Music, exclusive custom Ruby 'Burst finish.

| 2009 | | $4,900 | $6,400 |

Les Paul 60th Anniversary 1960 Les Paul Standard "CME Spec"

2020. Custom Shop, special run for Chicago Music Exchange, Orange Lemon Fade or Tomato Soup Burst, with VOS finish.

| 2020 | | $4,400 | $5,700 |

Les Paul 120th Anniversary

2014. Custom Shop, 120th Anniversary neck inlay, heavy quilted top.

| 2014 | | $2,700 | $3,600 |

Les Paul Axcess Alex Lifeson

2011-2018. Custom Shop, push-pull volume pots, nitrocellulose lacquer finish in Royal Crimson or Viceroy Brown Sunburst, first 25 of each color signed by Lifeson with additional production unsigned, certificate of authenticity.

| 2011 | Signed | $4,600 | $6,000 |
| 2011-2018 | Unsigned | $3,300 | $4,300 |

Les Paul Axcess Dave Amato

2016. Custom Shop, figured maple top, mahogany back and neck, single '57 Classic Plus pickup, Floyd Rose tailpiece, TV yellow.

| 2016 | | $4,200 | $5,400 |

Les Paul Axcess Standard

2009-present. Custom Shop, new neck joint carve allows access to high frets, Floyd Rose, slightly thinner body, nitro lacquer Iced Tea Burst or Gun Metal Gray. In '20 DC Rust (unique stain) only.

| 2009-2021 | | $2,300 | $3,000 |

Les Paul BFG

2006-2008, 2018. Burstbucker 3 humbucker at bridge and P-90 at neck, 2 volume and 1 tone knobs, figured maple top over mahogany body. Reissued in '18.

| 2006-2008 | | $1,000 | $1,325 |
| 2018 | | $1,000 | $1,325 |

Les Paul Bird's-Eye Standard

1999. Birdseye top, gold hardware, 2 humbucking pickups, transparent amber.

| 1999 | | $1,900 | $2,500 |

Les Paul Carved Series

2003-2005. Custom Shop Standards with relief-carved tops, one in diamond pattern, one with flame pattern.

| 2003-2005 | | $2,000 | $2,600 |

Les Paul Catalina

1996-1997. Large Custom Shop logo on headstock.

| 1996-1997 | | $2,450 | $3,200 |

Les Paul Centennial ('59 LP Special)

1994. Guitar of the Month, limited edition of 100, slab body Special-style configuration, gold hardware, P-90s, gold medallion, commemorative engraving in 'guard, cherry, with COA.

| 1994 | | $3,125 | $4,050 |

Les Paul Class 5

2001-2017. Custom Shop, various woods, highly flamed or quilt top, or special finish, 1960 profile neck, weight relieved body, Burst Bucker humbucking pickups, several color options.

| 2001-2017 | All models | $3,200 | $6,000 |

Les Paul Cloud 9 Series

2003-2006. Special lightweight Les Paul series run for three dealers, Music Machine, Dave's Guitar Shop, and Wildwood Guitars, '59 Les Paul body specs, CR serial series number, '59 or '60 neck profile options, various colors, other reissue models available.

| 2003-2006 | All models | $3,200 | $4,200 |

Les Paul Collector's Choice Series

2010-2018. Custom Shop models based on Gibson replicas of one-of-a-kind historic guitars.

| 2010-2018 | All models | $4,900 | $6,500 |

Gibson '60s Les Paul Flametop
Tyler Willison

Les Paul 50th Anniversary 1959 Les Paul Standard
Paul Harbinson

GUITARS

2009 Gibson Les Paul
Gary Moore BFG

James Magrini

1992 Gibson Les
Paul Heritage 80

Sam Gabriel

MODEL YEAR	FEATURES	EXC. COND. LOW	HIGH

Les Paul Dickey Betts Red Top
2003. Transparent red, gold hardware.

2003		$4,600	$6,000

Les Paul Don Felder Hotel California 1959
2010. Custom Shop, '59 sunburst specs, 50 Murphy aged and signed by Felder, 100 aged, and 150 in VOS finish.

2010	Aged, signed	$7,400	$9,600
2010	Aged, unsigned	$6,800	$8,800
2010	VOS	$5,700	$7,400

Les Paul Duane Allman
2013. Custom Shop certificate, Murphy Aged or VOS, 150 made of each.

2013	Aged	$8,000	$10,400
2013	VOS	$6,200	$8,100

Les Paul Duane Allman Hot 'Lanta
2003. "DUANE" spelled out in fret wire on back, Custom Shop certificate, 55 made.

2003		$22,000	$29,000

Les Paul Elegant
1994-2004. Custom Shop, highly flamed maple top, abalone crown markers and Custom Shop headstock inlay.

1994-2004		$3,800	$4,900

Les Paul Eric Clapton 1960
2011. Nicknamed the Beano Burst, '60 thinner 'Clapton' neck profile, Custom Bucker pickups, nickel-plated Grover kidney button tuners, lightly figured maple cap, traditional 17-degree angled headstock, total of 500 made; 55 Murphy Aged and signed by Clapton, 95 unsigned Murphy Aged, 350 finished with Gibson's VOS treatment.

2011	Aged, signed	$20,000	$26,000
2011	Aged, unsigned	$8,500	$11,200
2011	VOS	$6,000	$7,900

Les Paul Gary Moore BFG
2009-2012. Plain appointment BFG specs, P-90 neck pickup and Burstbucker 3 bridge pickup.

2009-2012		$1,300	$1,700

Les Paul Gary Moore Signature
2000-2002. Signature Series model, Gary Moore script logo on truss rod cover, flamed maple top.

2000-2002		$2,850	$3,700

Les Paul Gary Rossington Signature
2002. GR serial number, replica of his '59 LP Standard, Custom Shop, aged finish, 250 made, includes display case with backdrop photo of Rossington, price includes certificate with matching serial number.

2002		$8,500	$11,000

Les Paul Guitar Trader Reissue
1982-1983. Special order flametop Les Paul by the Guitar Trader Company, Redbank, New Jersey. Approximately 47 were built, the first 15 guitars ordered received original PAFs, all were double black bobbins (except 1 Zebra and 1 double white), 3 of the guitars were made in the '60-style. The PAF equipped models were based on order date and not build date. The serial number series started with 9 1001 and a second serial number was put in the control cavity based upon the standard Gibson serial number system, which allowed for exact build date identification. Gibson's pickup designer in the early-'80s was Tim Shaw and the pickups used for the

last 32 guitars have been nicknamed Shaw PAFs. After Gibson's short run for Guitar Trader, 10 non-Gibson replica Les Pauls were made. These guitars have a poorly done Gibson logo and other telltale issues.

1982-1983	Actual PAFs installed	$14,000	$18,000
1982-1983	Shaw PAFs, highly flamed	$7,000	$9,000
1982-1983	Shaw PAFs, low flame	$5,300	$7,000

Les Paul Heritage 80
1980-1982. Copy of '59 Les Paul Standard, curly maple top, mahogany body, rosewood 'board, nickel hardware, sunburst. In '80 cataloged as Les Paul Standard-80 without reference to Heritage, the catalog notes that the guitar has Heritage Series truss rod cover.

1980-1982	Figured top	$4,700	$6,100
1980-1982	Plain top	$3,600	$4,700

Les Paul Heritage 80 Award
1982. Ebony 'board, 1-piece mahogany neck, gold-plated hardware, sunburst.

1982	Figured	$5,500	$7,200
1982	Highly figured	$6,800	$8,800

Les Paul Heritage 80 Elite
1980-1982. Copy of '59 Les Paul Standard, quilted maple top, mahogany body and neck, ebony 'board, chrome hardware, sunburst. In '80 cataloged as Les Paul Standard-80 Elite without reference to Heritage, the catalog notes that the guitar has the distinctive Heritage Series truss rod cover.

1980-1982		$5,200	$6,700

Les Paul Heritage 80/Standard 80
1982. Based on '57 Les Paul Standard Goldtop, Heritage Series Standard 80 logo on truss rod cover.

1982		$3,900	$5,100

Les Paul Hot Rod Magazine '58 Standard
2008. Custom Shop, Hot Rod inspired flames over a figured-maple top, Hot Rod truss rod cover.

2008		$3,850	$5,000

Les Paul Jim Beam (Custom Shop)
Ca. 2002-2003. JBLP serial number series, several versions of Jim Beam logo art on top of guitar, award-ribbon-style B Bean logo on headstock, around 75 made.

2002-2003		$1,750	$2,300

Les Paul Jimmy Page "Number Two"
2009-2010. Custom Shop, 1st 25 aged and signed, 100 aged and unsigned, 200 VOS.

2009-2010		$11,400	$14,800

Les Paul Jimmy Page (Custom Authentic)
2004-2006. Custom Shop, includes certificate.

2004-2006		$7,900	$10,300

Les Paul Jimmy Page Signature
1995-1999. Jimmy Page signature on 'guard, mid-grade figured top, push-pull knobs for phasing and coil-tapping, Grover tuners, gold-plated hardware. This is not the '04 Custom Shop Jimmy Page Signature Series Les Paul (see separate listing).

1995	1st year, highly figured	$6,200	$8,100
1995	1st year, low figure	$5,000	$6,500

The Official Vintage Guitar magazine Price Guide 2023   **Gibson** Les Paul Jimmy Page Sig. (CS) — Music Rising Katrina   **187**

GUITARS

MODEL YEAR	FEATURES	EXC. COND. LOW	HIGH
1995	1st year, moderate figure	$5,400	$7,000
1996-1999	Highly figured	$5,000	$6,500
1996-1999	Low figure	$3,400	$4,400
1996-1999	Moderate figure	$4,300	$5,600

Les Paul Jimmy Page Signature (Custom Shop)

2004. January '04 NAMM Show, 175 planned production, the first 25 were personally inspected, played-in, and autographed by Jimmy Page. Initial retail price for first 25 was $25,000, the remaining 150 instruments had an initial retail price of $16,400. Cosmetically aged by Tom Murphy to resemble Page's No. 1 Les Paul in color fade, weight, top flame, slab cut attribution on the edges, neck size and profile.

2004	1st 25 made	$19,000	$25,000
2004	Next 26-150	$14,500	$19,000

Les Paul Jimmy Wallace Reissue

1978-1997. Les Paul Standard '59 reissue with Jimmy Wallace on truss rod cover, special order by dealer Jimmy Wallace, figured maple top, sunburst.

1978-1982	Kalamazoo, low flame	$4,000	$5,200
1978-1983	Kalamazoo, high flame	$4,800	$6,300
1983-1997	Nashville-made	$3,800	$4,900

Les Paul Joe Bonamassa Bonabyrd

2015-2016. Limited Edition, 100 made each signed by Joe, plain maple top, retro Firebird headstock, Indian rosewood 'board, 2 Custom Bucker pickups, Antique Pelham Blue finish.

2015-2016		$5,600	$7,300

Les Paul Joe Bonamassa Skinnerburst 1959

2014. Custom Shop, recreation of '59 Les Paul, 150 Murphy aged (first 50 signed by Joe) and 150 VOS, faded Dirty Lemon finish.

2014	All options	$9,100	$11,800

Les Paul Joe Bonamassa 'Tomato Soup Burst' Limited Edition

2016. Limited run of 150, AAA flamed maple top, mahogany back and neck, rosewood 'board, Tomato Soup Burst finish.

2016		$4,100	$5,300

Les Paul Joe Perry 1959

2013. Custom Shop, recreation of '59 Les Paul, 150 Murphy aged (first 50 signed by Perry) and 150 VOS, faded Tobacco Sunburst finish.

2013		$12,000	$15,500

Les Paul Joe Perry Signature

1997-2001. Unbound slab body with push-pull knobs and Joe Perry signature below bridge, Bone-Yard logo model with typical Les Paul Standard bound body, configuration and appointments.

1997-2001	Bone-Yard option	$1,850	$2,400
1997-2001	Unbound standard	$1,850	$2,400

Les Paul KM (Kalamazoo Model)

1979. Regular Les Paul Standard with 2 exposed humbuckers, KM on headstock, sunburst, approximately 1500 were made in the Kalamazoo plant.

1979		$3,500	$4,600

Les Paul Korina

1999. Custom Shop logo on back of headstock, limited run with figured Korina top.

1999		$3,500	$4,500

Les Paul Leo's Reissue

1980-1985. Special order from Gibson's Nashville facility for Leo's Music, Oakland, California. Identified by serial number with L at the beginning, flamed maple top. About 800 guitars were made, with about 400 being exported to Japan. Kalamazoo-made Leo's have a 2nd serial number in the control cavity, Nashville-made Leo's do not have a 2nd serial number.

1980-1983	Kalamazoo, high flame	$4,850	$6,350
1980-1983	Kalamazoo, low flame	$3,800	$5,000
1983-1985	Nashville-made	$4,400	$5,800

Les Paul Limited Edition (3-tone)

1997. Limited Edition stamped on the back of the headstock, Les Paul Standard configuration with cloud inlay markers, 2-piece 3-tone sunburst finish over non-figured maple top.

1997		$2,300	$3,000

Les Paul Modern

2017-present. Custom Shop, new light-weight features, mahogany body with maple top, back is natural finish, top with faded pelham blue, sparkling burgundy or graphite black.

2017-2021		$2,850	$3,700

Les Paul Music Machine 25th Anniversary

2002. Custom run for dealer Music Machine with special serial number series, 14 flame top and 14 quilt top instruments were produced, Music Machine 25th Anniversary logo on truss rod cover, special cherry sunburst finish.

2002	Flame top	$5,200	$6,700
2002	Quilt top	$4,700	$6,100

Les Paul Music Machine Brazilian Stinger

2003. Custom run for dealer Music Machine with special serial number series, Brazilian rosewood 'board, black stinger paint on back of neck-headstock, '59 or '60 reissue body and neck profile options, highly figured flame or quilt top options, other reissue options available.

2003	'54, '56 or '58, figured flame or quilt	$12,300	$16,000
2003	'54, '56 or '58, goldtop	$9,100	$11,900
2003	'59 or '60, figured flame or quilt	$12,800	$16,700
2003	'59 or '60, plain top	$11,400	$14,700

Les Paul Music Rising Katrina

2005. Built for U2's Music Rising campaign to raise funds to replace instruments lost to hurricane Katrina. Multi-colored Mardi Gras motif, less than 300 made, no two finishes the same. Wood back plate, pickguard, toggle cover, and truss rod cover. Music Rising logo etched into pickguard.

2005		$2,575	$3,350

1995 Gibson Les Paul Jimmy Page Signature

Imaged by Heritage Auctions, HA.com

Gibson Les Paul Modern

*2005 Gibson Les Paul
Neal Schon Signature*

Wayne Stephens

Gibson Les Paul Standard Faded

Ted Mottor

MODEL		EXC. COND.	
YEAR	FEATURES	LOW	HIGH

Les Paul Neal Schon Signature
2005. Custom Shop, 80 made, Floyd Rose tremolo, signature on truss rod cover, COA, black.

2005		$10,200	$13,200

Les Paul Peace
2014-2015. AA top, rosewood 'board, 2 pickups, various color finishes.

2014-2015		$1,750	$2,275

Les Paul Reissue Flametop
1983-1990. Flame maple top, 2 humbuckers, thicker '59-style neck, sunburst finish, renamed '59 Les Paul Flametop in '91.

1983-1990	Highly figured	$5,200	$6,800

Les Paul SG '61 Reissue
1993-2003. Renamed the Les Paul SG '61 Reissue from SG '62 Reissue, early '60s Les Paul Standard SG specs with small guard, trapezoid markers, heritage cherry finish, by 2003 the Les Paul script marking was not on the truss rod cover, renamed to SG '61 Reissue.

1993-2003	Stud tail	$1,800	$2,325

Les Paul SG Standard Authentic
2005. SG '61 specs, small guard, Les Paul truss rod logo, stud tailpiece.

2005		$2,300	$3,000

Les Paul SG Standard Reissue
2000-2004. Reissue of early-'60s specs including Deluxe Maestro vibrato with lyre tailpiece (stop bar tp offered), small 'guard, holly head veneer, standard color faded cherry, available in Classic White or TV Yellow, becomes the SG Standard Reissue by '05.

2000-2004	Maestro	$2,300	$3,000

Les Paul Signature "T"
2014-2018. Chambered solidbody, 2 exposed split-coil humbuckers, "Les Paul" signature on 'guard, Mini-Etune.

2014-2018		$1,925	$2,500

Les Paul Slash Appetite
2010-2012. Figured maple top, Slash artwork headstock logo, 2 Alnico II Pro Slash pickups, Appetite Amber finish.

2010-2012		$5,000	$6,500

Les Paul Slash Appetite For Destruction
2010-2011. Custom Shop, figured maple top, 2 Duncan Slash pickups, butterscotch finish available as VOS or Aged.

2010-2011	VOS	$9,800	$12,800

Les Paul Slash Signature
2008. Slash logo on truss rod, Darkburst, SL serial number series.

2008		$3,400	$4,400

Les Paul Slash Signature VOS
2008-2010. Inspired By series, Slash hat logo on body and signature logo on guitar case, plain maple top with faded VOS finish.

2008-2010		$4,175	$5,425

Les Paul Slash Snakepit
1996-1997. Custom Art Historic, highly figured top, cobra inlay neck, snake and hat on body.

1996-1997		$27,000	$36,000

Les Paul Southern Rock Tribute 1959
2014-2018. Limited Edition, commemorative medallion on switch-cavity cover, first 50 aged and signed by Southern Rock Ambassadors (Dickey Betts, Charlie

Daniels, Gary Rossington, Jimmy Hall), remainder are VOS, reverse burst finish.

2014-2016	Aged	$5,900	$7,700
2014-2018	VOS	$5,000	$6,450

Les Paul Spider-Man
2002. Custom Shop, superhero depicted on the body, red spider logo, gold hardware, Standard appointments. 15 guitars were produced as a Gibson/Columbia TriStar Home Entertainment/Tower Records promotion, while a larger batch was sold at retail.

2002		$3,500	$4,600

Les Paul Spotlight Special
1983-1984. Curly maple and walnut top, 2 humbuckers, gold hardware, multi-bound top, Custom Shop Edition logo, natural or sunburst.

1983-1984	Figured top	$6,700	$8,700

Les Paul Standard 100
2015. Les Paul 100 on headstock (facsimile of his actual signature) honoring his 100th birthday, Les Paul hologram back of headstock, G-Force tuning, various new colors with high gloss finish.

2015		$1,875	$2,450

Les Paul Standard 2008
August 2008-2012. 2008 added to name, chambered mahogany body, new asymmetrical neck profile, locking grovers, plain or AA flamed maple top, Ebony, Gold Top, various sunbursts.

2008-2012	Figured top	$2,400	$3,100
2008-2012	Gold top	$2,100	$2,800
2008-2012	Plain top	$2,050	$2,650

Les Paul Standard 2010 Limited
2010. Robot tuning technology, 2 pickups, scripted "Limited Edition" logo on headstock, Fireball Sunburst finish.

2010		$1,825	$2,375

Les Paul Standard Billy Gibbons 'Pearly Gates'
2009-2011. Aged - 50 made, Aged and signed - 50 made, V.O.S. - 250 made.

2009-2011	Aged	$10,300	$13,300
2009-2011	VOS	$9,700	$12,600

Les Paul Standard F
2010-2017. Custom Shop, also called LPS-F, 5A flame maple top, 2 Burstbucker pickups, various new colors with gloss nitro finish.

2010-2017		$3,000	$3,900

Les Paul Standard Faded
2005-2008. Figured top, exposed humbuckers, faded satin finish.

2005-2008		$2,025	$2,625

Les Paul Standard HP
2016-2018. Solidbody, figured maple top, mahogany back and sides, 2 humbucker pickups, G-Force automatic tuners, various colors with gloss nitro finish.

2016-2018		$2,150	$2,800

Les Paul Standard Lite
1999-2001. DC body-style, renamed from DC Standard in '99, reintroduced as Les Paul Standard DC Plus in 2001, various translucent finishes, available in 2004 under this name also.

1999-2001		$1,350	$1,750

MODEL YEAR	FEATURES	EXC. COND. LOW	HIGH

Les Paul Standard Lite Limited Edition
2014. Thin body LP, Burstbuckers, 3 knobs, coil tap switch, "120th Anniversary" on 12th fret, highly figured flame top or plain top offered.

| 2014 | Plain top | $1,150 | $1,500 |

Les Paul Standard Michael Bloomfield 1959
2009-2011. Custom Shop, limited production of 100 Murphy-aged and 200 VOS, matching certificate of authenticity.

| 2009-2011 | | $7,500 | $9,800 |

Les Paul Standard Mike McCready 1959
2010-2016. Custom Shop, limited to 50 aged and signed, 100 VOS finish.

| 2010-2016 | Aged, signed | $7,500 | $9,800 |
| 2010-2016 | VOS | $6,500 | $8,700 |

Les Paul Standard Music Zoo 25th Anniversary
2019. Custom Shop special run for Music Zoo, styled from '59 LP Standard, figured maple top, mahogany body and neck, Indian rosewood 'board, VOS Orange Drop finish.

| 2019 | | $5,100 | $6,600 |

Les Paul Standard Paul Kossoff 1959
2012-2013. Custom Shop, 100 aged and 250 VOS, green lemon finish, certificate of authenticity.

| 2012-2013 | Aged | $5,800 | $7,500 |
| 2012-2013 | VOS | $5,275 | $6,850 |

Les Paul Standard Plus
1995-2012. Gibson USA model, figured maple top, Vintage Sunburst, Heritage Cherry Sunburst or Honeyburst finish.

| 1995-2012 | | $2,400 | $3,125 |

Les Paul Standard Premium Plus
1999-2007. Premium plus flamed maple top.

| 1999-2007 | | $2,525 | $3,275 |

Les Paul Standard Raw Power
2000-2001, 2006-2007. Natural gloss finish on maple top, appears to have been a Musician's Friend version in '06-'07.

| 2000-2001 | | $1,725 | $2,250 |

Les Paul Standard Rick Nielsen 1959
2016-2017. Custom Shop, first 50 aged and signed, figured maple top, mahogany back and neck, Indian rosewood 'board, aged or vintage gloss finish.

| 2016-2017 | Signed | $7,850 | $10,200 |
| 2016-2017 | Unsigned | $5,900 | $7,600 |

Les Paul Standard Robot
2007. Blueburst finish, robot tuning.

| 2007 | | $1,050 | $1,375 |

Les Paul Standard RSM 1959 / RSM '59 Les Paul Standard
2018 and 2020. Custom Shop special run for Rumble Seat Music, recreation of the original 1959 LP Standard, limited run of 6 each year, highly flamed top, Brazilian rosewood 'board.

| 2018 | | $15,000 | $28,000 |
| 2020 | | $13,500 | $18,000 |

Les Paul Standard Showcase Edition
1988. Showcase Edition logo on back of neck, Guitar of the Month, silverburst.

| 1988 | | $4,000 | $5,300 |

Les Paul Standard Sparkle
2001. Sparkle holoflake top, reflective back, Standard logo on truss rod.

| 2001 | | $2,450 | $3,200 |

Les Paul Strings and Things Standard
1975-1978. Special order flamed maple top Les Paul Standard model, built for Chris Lovell, owner of Strings and Things, a Gibson dealer in Memphis, approximately 28 were built, sunburst. Authentication of a Strings and Things Les Paul is difficult due to no diffinitive attributes, valuation should be on a case-by-case basis.

1975-1978	Figured 2-piece top	$8,100	$10,500
1975-1978	Plain 2-piece top	$6,500	$8,400
1975-1978	Plain 3-piece top	$4,400	$5,700

Les Paul Tie Dye (St. Pierre)
1996-1997. Hand colored by George St. Pierre, just over 100 made.

| 1996-1997 | | $2,500 | $3,300 |

Les Paul Tie Dye Custom Shop
2002. Limited series of one-off colorful finishes, Custom Shop logo.

| 2002 | | $2,500 | $3,300 |

Les Paul Traditional Pro/Pro II
2010-2014. Exposed tapped coil humbuckers, sunbursts, goldtop, ebony or wine red.

| 2010-2014 | Various colors | $1,575 | $2,050 |

Les Paul Traditional/Plus
2008-2019. Traditional on truss rod, '80s styling with weight-relief holes in an unchambered body, standard appointments. Figured maple (Plus) or opaque color top.

2008-2014	Opaque	$1,700	$2,225
2008-2019	Plain sunburst	$1,700	$2,225
2008-2019	Plus, figured maple	$1,900	$2,500

Les Paul Ultima
1996-2007. Custom Shop, flame or quilt sunburst, abalone and mother-of-pearl tree of life, harp, or flame fingerboard inlay, multi abalone bound body.

| 1996-2007 | | $6,000 | $8,000 |

Les Paul Ultra-Aged
2011-2012. Custom Shop, '59 specs, Bigsby optional, aged by Tom Murphy.

| 2011-2012 | | $5,000 | $6,600 |

Les Paul Warren Haynes
2007. Custom Shop, Inspired by Artist series.

| 2007 | | $3,000 | $4,000 |

Les Paul Zebra Wood
2007. Zebrawood top, mahogany back and neck, rosewood 'board, 2 '57 Classic pickups, natural satin zebrawood finish.

| 2007 | | $2,000 | $2,600 |

LES PAUL STUDIO
Following are Les Paul Studio models listed alphabetically.

Les Paul Studio
1983-present. Unbound mahogany body, (early models have alder body), 2 humbuckers, various colors.

1983-2009		$1,200	$1,550
2009-2012	Silverburst	$1,125	$1,475
2010-2019		$1,100	$1,425
2020-2021		$1,000	$1,300

2011 Gibson Les Paul Standard Plus

Rivington Guitars

1998 Gibson Les Paul Ultima

Imaged by Heritage Auctions, HA.com

GUITARS

Gibson Les Paul Studio '60s Tribute

2003 Gibson Les Paul Studio Plus

MODEL YEAR	FEATURES	EXC. COND. LOW	HIGH

Les Paul Studio 120th Anniversary
2014. Figured maple top, 120th Anniversary badge on 12th fret, vintage gloss finish on various colors.

2014		$1,125	$1,475

Les Paul Studio '50s Tribute
2010-2016. '56 LP Goldtop specs, P-90s, '50s neck, Tune-o-matic, stopbar tailpiece, chambered unbound body.

2010-2016		$750	$975

Les Paul Studio '60s Tribute
2011-2016. Similar to '50s Tribute except for '60 slim taper neck.

2011-2016		$750	$975

Les Paul Studio '70s Tribute
2012-2016. Similar to '50s Tribute except for '70s neck profile with volute.

2012-2016		$750	$975

Les Paul Studio Baritone
2004-2012. 28" baritone scale, maple top, mahogany back and neck, 2 pickups, nitro gloss honeyburst finish.

2004-2012		$1,225	$1,600

Les Paul Studio BFD
2007. Studio specs but with BFD electronics.

2007		$700	$900

Les Paul Studio Custom
1981-1985. 2 humbucking pickups, multi-bound top, gold-plated hardware, various colors.

1981-1985		$1,350	$1,750

Les Paul Studio Deluxe '60s
2010-2012. Exposed pickups, Deluxe logo on truss rod cover, sunburst.

2010-2012		$1,050	$1,350

Les Paul Studio Deluxe II
2008-2013. Carved flame maple top, mahogany back, 2 pickups, various colors.

2008-2013		$1,050	$1,350

Les Paul Studio Faded Vintage Mahogany
2007-2010. Vintage mahogany with faded satin.

2007-2010		$750	$975

Les Paul Studio Faded/Pro Faded
2005-2012. Faded sunburst tops. Name changes to Studio Pro Faded in '12, then ends production.

2005-2012		$750	$975

Les Paul Studio Gem
1996-1998. Limited edition with Les Paul Studio features, but using P-90 pickups instead of humbucker pickups, plus trapezoid markers and gold hardware.

1996-1998		$1,050	$1,375

Les Paul Studio Gothic
2000-2001. Orville Gibson image on back of headstock, single Gibson crescent and star neck marker, Gothic Black with black hardware.

2000-2001		$850	$1,125

Les Paul Studio Gothic Morte
2011-2012. All-mahogany body, African Obeche 'board, 2 humbuckers, satin ebony finish.

2011-2012		$850	$1,125

Les Paul Studio Joe Bonamassa
2011-2013. Maple top, mahogany back and neck, 2 Alnico II pickups, goldtop finish.

2011-2013		$1,475	$1,925

Les Paul Studio Limited Edition
1997. P-100 pickups, black.

1997		$850	$1,125

Les Paul Studio Lite
1987-1998. Carved maple top, mahogany back and neck, 2 humbucker pickups, various colors.

1987-1998		$1,050	$1,375

Les Paul Studio Lite Mark III/M3/M III
1991-1994. HSH pickup configuration, trans finishes.

1991-1994		$1,050	$1,375

Les Paul Studio MLB Baseball
2008. Major League Baseball graphics on body, only 30 made, satin finish, dot markers.

2008		$1,475	$1,925

Les Paul Studio Platinum
2004-2006. 2 Humbuckers, no position markers, brushed metal hardware, body, neck and headstock in satin platinum finish, matching platinum hardshell case.

2004-2006		$1,100	$1,425

Les Paul Studio Platinum Plus
2004-2006. Same as Platinum but with trapezoid markers and black hardshell case.

2004-2006		$1,100	$1,425

Les Paul Studio Plus
2002-2007. Two-piece AA flamed unbound top, gold hardware, Desert Burst or see-thru black.

2002-2007		$1,150	$1,500

Les Paul Studio Premium Plus
2006-2008. AAA flamed-maple top.

2006-2008		$1,475	$1,925

Les Paul Studio Raw Power
2009-2012. Unbound maple top, chambered maple body, 2 humbuckers, dots, satin finishes.

2009-2012		$1,100	$1,425

Les Paul Studio Robot
2007-2011. Robot tuning, trapezoid inlays, silverburst, fireburst, wine red, black, red metallic, green metallic.

2007-2011	All colors	$875	$1,150

Les Paul Studio Robot Limited Edition
2012. 'Chameleon' tone circuit.

2012		$900	$1,175

Les Paul Studio Roland Synthesizer
1985. With Roland 700 synth.

1985		$900	$1,175

Les Paul Studio Shred
2012. Unbound body, trapezoid markers, 2 humbuckers. Floyd Rose, high-gloss ebony nitro finish.

2012		$1,100	$1,425

Les Paul Studio Special
2001. Solidbody, single-cut, 2 pickups, various colors.

2001-2020		$1,000	$1,300

Les Paul Studio Special Limited Edition
2019-2020. Limited Edition, nitro finish in Lemon Burst or Desert Burst.

2019-2020		$975	$1,275

Les Paul Studio Standard
1984-1987. Cream top and neck binding, dots.

1984-1987		$1,550	$2,000

The Official Vintage Guitar magazine Price Guide 2023   **Gibson** Les Paul Studio Swamp Ash — Longhorn Double Cutaway   **191**

GUITARS

MODEL YEAR	FEATURES	EXC. COND. LOW	HIGH

Les Paul Studio Swamp Ash
2004-2012. Studio model with swamp ash body.

2004-2012		$1,100	$1,425

Les Paul Studio USA Anniversary Flood
2011. Commemorating the Nashville flood of May, 2010, blue or green swirl.

2011		$1,175	$1,525

Les Paul Supreme
2003-2018. Highly figured AAAA maple top and back on translucent finishes only, custom binding, deluxe pearl markers, chambered mahogany body, globe logo or "Supreme" on headstock, solid colors available by '06.

2003-2018	Various tops & colors	$3,100	$4,000

Les Paul Vixen
2006-2007. Les Paul Special single-cut slab body, dot markers, 2 humbuckers, 2 controls, wrap-around bridge.

2006-2007	Various colors	$950	$1,225

Les Paul Voodoo/Voodoo Les Paul
2004-2005. Single-cut, swamp ash body, 2 exposed humbuckers, black satin finish.

2004-2005		$1,500	$2,000

Les Paul XR-I / II / III
1981-1983. No frills model with Dirty Finger pickups, dot markers, Les Paul stencil logo on headstock, goldburst, silverburst and cherryburst finishes.

1981-1983	All models	$1,200	$1,550

The Les Paul
1976-1979. Figured maple top, 2 humbuckers, gold hardware, rosewood binding, 'guard, 'board, knobs, cover plates, etc., natural or rosewood finishing, natural only by '79.

1976-1979	Natural or rosewood	$10,000	$13,000

The Paul
1978-1982. Offered as The Paul Standard with solid walnut body and The Paul Deluxe with solid mahogany body, 2 exposed humbuckers.

1978-1982	Walnut or mahogany	$1,050	$1,400

The Paul Firebrand Deluxe
1980-1982. Single-cut mahogany solidbody, Gibson branded in headstock, 2 exposed humbuckers, black, Pelham Blue or rough natural finish.

1980-1982	All colors	$1,200	$1,550

The Paul II
1996-1998. Mahogany body, 2 humbucking pickups, rosewood dot neck, renamed The Paul SL in '98.

1996-1998		$725	$925

LG-0
1958-1974. Flat-top acoustic, mahogany, bound body, rosewood bridge '58-'61 and '68-'74, plastic bridge '62-'67, natural.

1958-1961	Rosewood bridge	$1,125	$1,475
1962-1964	Plastic bridge	$950	$1,250
1965	Plastic bridge	$875	$1,125
1966	Plastic bridge	$725	$950
1967-1969	Rosewood bridge	$725	$950
1970-1974		$625	$825

LG-1
1943-1968. Flat-top acoustic, spruce top, mahogany back and sides, bound body, rosewood bridge '43-'61, plastic bridge after, examples seen to '74, sunburst.

1943-1945		$2,475	$3,200
1946-1949		$2,300	$3,000
1950-1959	Rosewood bridge	$2,000	$2,600
1960-1961	Rosewood bridge	$1,900	$2,500
1962-1964	Plastic bridge	$1,700	$2,200
1965		$1,450	$1,900
1966-1968		$1,400	$1,825

LG-2
1942-1962. Flat-top acoustic, spruce top, mahogany back and sides (some with maple '43-'46), banner headstock '42-'46, bound body, X-bracing, sunburst finish, replaced by B-25 in '62.

1942-1945	Banner, mahogany	$4,000	$5,200
1942-1945	Banner, spruce	$5,200	$6,800
1946-1949	Sitka	$4,200	$5,500
1950-1959		$3,800	$5,000
1960-1961	Rosewood bridge	$2,800	$3,700
1962	Adjustable bridge	$2,650	$3,500

LG-2 3/4
1949-1962. Short-scale version of LG-2 flat-top, wood bridge, sunburst.

1949	Rosewood bridge	$2,350	$3,100
1950-1959	Rosewood bridge	$2,200	$2,800
1960-1961	Rosewood bridge	$2,000	$2,600
1962	Adjustable bridge	$2,000	$2,600

LG-2 3/4 Arlo Guthrie
2003, 2005-2018. Vintage replica finish.

2003-2018		$1,625	$2,100

LG-2 American Eagle
2013-2018. Sitka top, mahogany back and sides, L.R. Baggs.

2013-2018		$1,350	$1,750

LG-2 Banner
2013. All mahogany, only 50 made.

2013		$1,850	$2,400

LG-2 H
1945-1955. Flat-top, Hawaiian, natural or sunburst.

1944-1945		$4,000	$5,200
1946-1949		$3,150	$4,150
1950-1955		$2,775	$3,650

LG-3
1942-1964. Flat-top acoustic, spruce top, mahogany back and sides, bound body, natural finish, replaced by B-25 N.

1942-1945	Banner	$4,900	$6,400
1946-1949		$4,600	$6,000
1950-1959		$3,600	$4,700
1960-1961	Last wood bridge	$3,075	$4,025
1962-1964	Plastic bridge	$2,850	$3,750

Longhorn Double Cutaway
2008. Guitar of the Month for July '08, AA figured maple top, 2 active pickups, piezo pickup, sunburst or transparent finishes.

2008		$1,600	$2,075

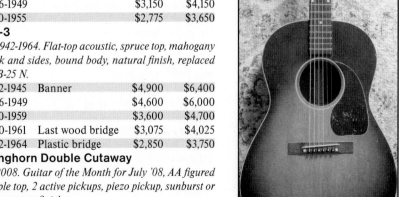

1958 Gibson LG-0
Ted Wulfers

1946 Gibson LG-2
David Stone

1976 Gibson Marauder

Tom Pfeifer

1967 Gibson Melody Maker D

Tim McClutchy

MODEL YEAR	FEATURES	EXC. COND. LOW	HIGH

M III Series
1991-1996, 2013-2018. Double-cut solidbody with extra long bass horn, six-on-a-side tuners on a reverse pointy headstock, dot markers, reverse Gibson decal logo. Reissued in '13 with natural finish on 'board and choice of Cosmic Cobalt, Electric Lime, Vibrant Red, or Orange Glow.

Year	Features	Low	High
1991-1992	Deluxe	$1,500	$1,950
1991-1996	Standard	$1,500	$1,950
2013-2018	Reissue	$1,050	$1,350

M IV Series
1993-1995. M III with Steinberger vibrato.

Year	Features	Low	High
1993-1995	S Deluxe	$1,450	$1,900
1993-1995	S Standard	$1,275	$1,650

Mach II
1990-1991. Renamed from U-2, offset double-cut, 2 single coils and 1 humbucking pickup.

Year	Features	Low	High
1990-1991		$950	$1,250

Map Guitar
1983, 1985. Body cutout like lower 48, 2 humbuckers, limited run promotion, '83 version in natural mahogany or red, white and blue, '85 version red, white and blue stars and stripes on a white background. This model can often be found in better than excellent condition because the instrument is as much a show piece as it is a player guitar, and the price range reflects that.

Year	Features	Low	High
1983	Natural	$3,300	$4,300
1983	Red, white & blue	$3,550	$4,600

Marauder
1975-1980. Single-cut solidbody, pointed headstock, 2 pickups, bolt-on neck, various colors.

Year	Features	Low	High
1975-1980		$1,150	$1,500

Marauder Custom
1976-1977. Marauder with 3-way selector switch, bound 'board, block markers, bolt-on neck, Marauder logo on truss rod cover, sunburst.

Year	Features	Low	High
1976-1977		$1,650	$2,175

Melody Maker
1959-1971, 1986-1993. Slab solidbody, 1 pickup, single-cut until '61, double '61-'66, SG body '66-'71, reintroduced as single-cut in '86-'93. A single-cut Les Paul Melody Maker was offered from '03-'06.

Year	Features	Low	High
1959-1961	Sunburst, single-cut	$1,700	$2,250
1962-1964	Sunburst, cherry, double-cut	$1,500	$2,000
1965-1966	Cherry, double cut	$1,375	$1,800
1966-1971	Various colors, SG body	$1,700	$2,200
1986-1993	Reintroduced as single-cut	$825	$1,075

Melody Maker 3/4
1959-1963. Short-scale version.

Year	Features	Low	High
1959-1963		$1,625	$2,100

Melody Maker D
1960-1970. Two pickup version of Melody Maker, reintroduced as Melody Maker Double in '77.

Year	Features	Low	High
1960-1961	Sunburst, single-cut	$2,600	$3,400
1961-1964	Sunburst, cherry, double-cut	$2,350	$3,000
1965-1966	Sunburst, cherry, double-cut	$1,950	$2,500
1966-1970	Various colors, SG body	$2,000	$2,650

Melody Maker Double
1977-1983. Reintroduction of Melody Maker D, double-cut solidbody, 2 pickups, cherry or sunburst.

Year	Features	Low	High
1977-1983	Bolt-on	$1,000	$1,300
1977-1983	Set-neck	$1,200	$1,575

Melody Maker III
1967-1971. SG-style double-cut solidbody, 3 pickups, various colors.

Year	Features	Low	High
1967-1971		$2,100	$2,750

Melody Maker 12
1967-1971. SG-style solidbody, 12 strings, 2 pickups, red, white or Pelham Blue.

Year	Features	Low	High
1967-1971		$1,900	$2,475

Melody Maker Faded
2003. Les Paul Jr. styling, single-cut, 1 P-90 style pickup, Nashville tune-o-matic bridge, black satin finish.

Year	Features	Low	High
2003		$475	$625

Les Paul Melody Maker
2003-2008. Slab single-cut solidbody, one P-90, tune-o-matic bridge, dot markers, 2 knobs. Revised in '07 with 1 single-coil (2 also offered), wrap around tailpiece, 1 knob, pickguard mounted jack.

Year	Features	Low	High
2003-2006	1 pickup	$525	$675
2007-2008	1 pickup, revised specs	$525	$675
2007-2008	2 pickup option	$525	$675

Les Paul Melody Maker 120th Anniversary
2014. Custom Shop, 120th Anniversary neck inlay, maple top, mahogany back, Charcoal, TV Yellow, Wine Red or Manhattan Midnight, all with satin finish.

Year	Features	Low	High
2014		$825	$1,075

Melody Maker Joan Jett Signature
2008-2012. Double-cut, worn-white (til '11), 1 Burstbucker 3. Blackheart version in black with red dots starts '10.

Year	Features	Low	High
2008-2012		$1,100	$1,450

Midnight Special
1974-1975. L-6S body style, maple 'board, dot markers, 2 humbucker pickups, custom colors.

Year	Features	Low	High
1974-1975		$1,550	$2,000

Midtown Custom
2012-2014. 335-style semi-hollow, 2 humbuckers, block markers.

Year	Features	Low	High
2012-2014		$1,600	$2,100

Midtown Kalamazoo
2013-2015. Limited run of 600, maple top, mahogany back and sides, 2 pickups, 165-style tailpiece, Vintage Sunburst.

Year	Features	Low	High
2013-2015		$1,350	$1,800

Midtown Standard P-90
2011-2014. Like Midtown Custom but with P-90s.

Year	Features	Low	High
2011-2014		$1,450	$1,900

MK-35
1975-1978. Mark Series flat-top acoustic, mahogany back and sides, black-bound body, natural or sunburst, 5226 made.

Year	Features	Low	High
1975-1978		$750	$975

MODEL		EXC. COND.	
YEAR	FEATURES	LOW	HIGH

MK-53
1975-1978. Mark Series flat-top acoustic, maple back and sides, multi-bound body, natural or sunburst, 1424 made.

| 1975-1978 | | $850 | $1,125 |

MK-72
1975-1978. Mark Series flat-top acoustic, rosewood back and sides, black-bound body, chrome tuners, natural or sunburst, 1229 made.

| 1975-1978 | | $925 | $1,200 |

MK-81
1975-1978. Mark Series flat-top acoustic, rosewood back and sides, multi-bound body, gold tuners, high-end appointments, natural or sunburst, 431 made.

| 1975-1978 | | $1,175 | $1,525 |

Moderne
2012. Limited run, mahogany body and neck, dual '57 Classic humbuckers, trans amber or ebony finish.

| 2012 | | $1,575 | $2,075 |

Moderne Heritage
1981-1983. Limited edition, korina body, 2 humbucking pickups, gold hardware, natural, black or white.

| 1981-1983 | Black or white | $6,000 | $8,000 |
| 1981-1983 | Natural | $7,500 | $10,000 |

Nick Lucas / Gibson Special
1926-1941. Though they were shipped into '41, the last year of production was '37. Mahogany 13 ½" L-1 body ('26-'29), 14 ¾" L-00 body ('30-'41), parallel bracing '26-'27, X-braced '28-'41, 12 frets early (13 and 14 later), banjo tuners early (guitar style later), black (rare) or sunburst finish. Reintroduced in '91.

| 1926-1941 | Various specs | $9,000 | $48,000 |

Nick Lucas Reissue Limited Edition
1991-1992. 100 made, label signed by Ren Ferguson.

| 1991-1992 | | $2,300 | $3,000 |

Nick Lucas Tenor
1928-1938. 14 3/4", 12-fret, early models have mahogany, later maple, The Gibson headstock logo.

| 1928-1930 | Mahogany | $7,000 | $9,000 |
| 1931-1938 | Maple | $7,000 | $9,000 |

Nick Lucas Elite
1999-2002. Ebony 'board, abalone inlay and inlays.

| 1999-2002 | | $3,300 | $4,400 |
| 2001 | Elite Custom | $3,300 | $4,400 |

Nick Lucas Grande
2015-2016. Limited Edition of 50, sitka spruce top, English walnut back and sides, COA, Honeyburst finish.

| 2015-2016 | | $3,000 | $3,900 |

Nick Lucas Koa Elite
2015. Limited to 50, Adirondack and koa, COA.

| 2015 | | $3,000 | $3,900 |

Nick Lucas Supreme
2015. Limited to 40, Adirondack red spruce top, AAA flame koa back and sides, abalone trim, certificate of authenticity, Honeyburst finish.

| 2015 | | $3,300 | $4,400 |

Nighthawk 2009 Limited
2009. Limited series, AAA figured maple top, mahogany body, Translucent Amber finish.

| 2009 | | $1,300 | $1,700 |

Nighthawk Custom
1993-1998. Flame maple top, ebony 'board, gold hardware, fireburst, single/double/mini pickups.

| 1993-1998 | | $1,300 | $1,675 |

Nighthawk Special
1993-1998. Single-cut solidbody, figured maple top, double-coil and mini-pickup or with additional single-coil options, dot marker inlay, cherry, ebony or sunburst.

| 1993-1998 | | $1,050 | $1,350 |

Nighthawk Standard
1993-1998. Single-cut solidbody, figured maple top, 2 or 3 pickups, double-parallelogram inlay, amber, fireburst or sunburst.

| 1993-1998 | | $1,200 | $1,550 |

Nighthawk Standard 2010 Limited
2010-2012. Limited Run series, AAA quilted maple top, chambered poplar body, 3 pickups, Memphis Mojo, St. Louis Sauce or Chicago Blue finishes.

| 2010-2012 | | $1,300 | $1,700 |

Nighthawk Studio
2011-2012. AAA quilted maple top, dots.

| 2011-2012 | | $700 | $900 |

Nouveau NV6T-M
1986-1987. Hybrid USA/Japan, a line of Gibson flat-tops with imported parts assembled and finished in the U.S., acoustic dreadnought, bound maple body, natural.

| 1986-1987 | | $475 | $625 |

NR-336F
2012. Custom Shop, 25 made, double-cut, non-reverse (NR) Firebird headstock, flamed maple top, rosewood 'board, antique sunburst top, cherry back.

| 2012 | | $2,700 | $3,500 |

OP-25
1991-1992. Acoustic-electric, limited production run, synthetic back.

| 1991-1992 | | $750 | $975 |

Original Jumbo (Custom Shop)
2003. 16" jumbo body, Adirondack top, mahogany sides and back, butterbean tuner buttons, deep sunburst finish on complete body, Custom Art Historic.

| 2003 | | $2,550 | $3,350 |

Pat Martino Custom/Signature
1999-2006. Sharp single-cut thinline, f-holes, 2 humbuckers, flamed cherry sunburst maple top, small snakehead style headstock, Pat Martino logo on truss rod cover.

| 1999-2006 | | $2,800 | $3,700 |

PG-00
1932-1937. Plectrum neck, flat-top.

| 1932-1937 | | $1,925 | $2,500 |

PG-1
1928-1938. Plectrum neck, flat-top.

| 1929 | | $1,875 | $2,450 |

PG-175
1950. Acoustic/electric with ES-175 bobdy and 4-string plectrum neck, bow-tie markers, sunburst.

| 1950 | | $3,500 | $4,600 |

1982 Gibson Moderne Heritage
Steve Evans

1936 Gibson Nick Lucas
M. Mattingly

To get the most from this book, be sure to read "Using *The Guide*" in the introduction.

GUITARS

2001 Gibson SG '61 Reissue

Bernunzio Uptown Music

1971 Gibson SG-200

Imaged by Heritage Auctions, HA.com

MODEL YEAR	FEATURES	EXC. COND. LOW	HIGH

Q-100
1985-1986. Offset double-cut solidbody, Kahler trem, 6-on-a-side tuners, 1 humbucker, black hardware.

1985-1986		$925	$1,200

Q-200/Q2000
1985-1986. Like Q-100, but with 1 single and 1 hum, black or chrome hardware. Name changed to 2000 late '85.

1985-1986		$1,050	$1,400

Q-300/Q3000
1985-1986. Like Q-100, but with 3 single-coils, black or chrome hardware. Name changed to 3000 late '85.

1985-1986		$1,150	$1,500

Q-3000 Custom Shop
1985. Limited Custom production, 3 single-coil pickups.

1985		$1,600	$2,100

Q-4000/Q400
Late-1985-1987. Limited custom production, like Q-100, but with 2 singles and 1 hum, black hardware, Name changed to 400 late '85. Ferrari Red or Pink Panther finish as 4000, ebony as 400.

1985-1987		$1,600	$2,100

RD Artist CMT
1981. Figured top.

1981		$3,000	$3,900

RD Artist/77
1980. The 77 model has a 25.5" scale versus 24.75".

1980		$2,150	$2,850

RD Artist/79
1978-1982. Double-cut solidbody, 2 humbuckers, TP-6 tailpiece, active electronics, ebony 'board, block inlays, gold-plated parts, various colors, called just RD (no Artist) in '81 and '82.

1978-1982		$2,250	$3,000

RD Custom
1977-1979. Double-cut solidbody, 2 humbuckers, stop tailpiece, active electronics, dot inlays, maple 'board, chrome parts, natural or walnut.

1977-1979		$2,200	$2,900

RD Standard
1977-1979. Double-cut solidbody, 2 humbuckers, stop tailpiece, rosewood 'board, dot inlays, chrome parts, natural, sunburst or walnut.

1977-1979		$2,200	$2,900

RD Standard Reissue
2007, 2009, 2011. 400 Silverburst made in '07. Black or Trans Amber Red versions offered as limited run in '09 in Japan and in U.S. in '11.

2007-2011	Various colors	$1,800	$2,400

Roy Smeck Radio Grande Hawaiian
1934-1939. Dreadnought acoustic flat-top, rosewood back and sides, bound body and neck, natural.

1934-1939	Brazilian, Spanish converted	$17,000	$22,300
1934-1939	Brazilian, unconverted	$13,500	$17,500

Roy Smeck Radio Grande Hawaiian Limited
1994. Centennial Guitar of the Month in '94, 100 made, Indian rosewood.

1994		$2,400	$3,100

Roy Smeck Radio Grande Hawaiian Reissue
1996. Part of SmartWood Series, Grenadillo back and sides.

1996		$2,400	$3,100

Roy Smeck Stage Deluxe Hawaiian
1934-1942. Dreadnought acoustic flat-top, mahogany back and sides, bound body, natural.

1934-1942	Spanish converted	$10,000	$13,000
1934-1942	Unconverted	$6,900	$9,000

S-1
1976-1980. Single-cut solidbody, pointed headstock, 3 single-coil pickups, similar to the Marauder, various colors.

1976-1980		$1,250	$1,625

SG
Following are models, listed alphabetically, bearing the SG name.

SG I
1972-1978. Double-cut, mahogany body, 1 mini-humbucker (some with SG Jr. P-90), wraparound bridge/tailpiece, cherry or walnut.

1972-1978		$1,125	$1,475

SG II
1972-1979. SG I with 2 mini-humbuckers (some in '75 had regular humbuckers), 2 slide switches, cherry or walnut.

1972-1979		$1,300	$1,675

SG III
1972-1977. SG II with sunburst and tune-o-matic.

1972-1977		$1,124	$1,475

SG-3
2007-2008. SG styling, SG Standard appointments, 3 gold humbuckers or 3 single coils, 1 rotor switch, 2 knobs, stop tail.

2007-2008	3 humbuckers	$1,000	$1,300
2007-2008	3 single coils	$775	$1,000

SG '61 Reissue
2003-2015. Renamed from Les Paul SG '61 Reissue, no Les Paul script on truss rod, small 'guard, stop bar tailpiece (no Deluxe Maestro vibrato), '60 slim-taper neck profile.

2003-2015		$1,600	$2,050

SG '62 Reissue/SG Reissue
1986-1991. Trapezoid markers, stop bar, 2 humbuckers, called SG Reissue '86-'87, SG '62 Reissue '88-'91. Reintroduced as Les Paul SG '61 Reissue for '93-'03 and SG '61 Reissue '03-present, cherry.

1986-1991		$1,600	$2,050

SG '62 Reissue Showcase Edition
1988. Guitar of the Month, bright blue opaque finish, 200 made.

1988		$1,700	$2,150

Les Paul '63 Corvette Sting Ray
1995-1997. Custom Shop SG-style body carved to simulate split rear window on '63 Corvette, Sting Ray inlay, 150 made, offered in black, white, silver or red.

1995-1997		$4,600	$6,000

MODEL YEAR	FEATURES	EXC. COND. LOW	HIGH

SG-90 Double
1988-1990. SG body, updated electronics, graphite reinforced neck, 2 pickups, cherry, turquoise or white.

1988-1990		$850	$1,100

SG-90 Single
1988-1990. SG body, updated electronics, graphite reinforced neck, 1 humbucker pickup, cherry, turquoise or white.

1988-1990		$775	$1,025

SG-100
1971-1972. Double-cut solidbody, 1 pickup, cherry or walnut.

1971-1972	Melody Maker pu	$1,125	$1,475
1971-1972	P-90 pu option	$1,125	$1,475
1971-1972	Sam Ash model	$1,125	$1,475

SG-200
1971-1972. Two pickup version of SG-100 in black, cherry or walnut finish, replaced by SG II.

1971-1972	2 Melody Makers	$1,300	$1,675

SG-250
1971-1972. Two-pickup version of SG-100 in cherry sunburst, replaced by SG III.

1971-1972	2 Melody Makers	$1,125	$1,475

SG-400/SG Special 400
1985-1987. SG body with 3 toggles, 2 knobs (master volume, master tone), single-single-humbucker pickups, available with uncommon opaque finishes.

1985-1987		$1,100	$1,425

SG Angus Young
2010-2016. Like Angus Signature but with small guard, stop tailpiece and tune-o-matic, Aged Cherry.

2010-2016		$1,775	$2,300

SG Angus Young Signature
2000-2009. Late-'60s Std specs with large 'guard, Deluxe Maestro lyre vibrato with Angus logo, aged cherry finish.

2000-2009		$1,775	$2,300

SG Baritone
2013-2016. Longer 27" scale, 2 exposed humbuckers, ebony 'board, Alpine White finish.

2013-2016		$1,200	$1,600

SG Carved Top - Autumn Burst
2009. Limited run of 350, highly flamed carved maple top, rosewood 'board, certificate of authenticity.

2009		$1,775	$2,300

SG Classic/SG Classic Faded
1999-2001, 2003-2013. Late '60s SG Special style, Classic on truss rod cover, large 'guard, black soapbar single-coil P-90s, dot markers, stop bar tailpiece, cherry or ebony stain.

1999-2013		$875	$1,150

SG Custom
1963-1980. Renamed from Les Paul Custom, 3 humbuckers, vibrato, made with Les Paul Custom plate from '61-'63 (see Les Paul Custom), white finish until '68, walnut and others after.

1963-1964	White, pat #, Maestro	$17,000	$22,500
1965	Early '65, white, large neck	$14,500	$19,000
1965	Late '65, white, small neck	$13,500	$17,000
1966-1968	White, large 'guard	$10,000	$12,500
1969	Walnut, lyre, 1-piece neck	$6,300	$8,300
1969	Walnut, lyre, 3-piece neck	$4,700	$6,100
1969	White, lyre, 1 piece neck	$6,300	$8,300
1969	White, lyre, 3 piece neck	$5,000	$6,500
1970	Walnut, lyre	$3,900	$5,100
1970	White, lyre	$3,900	$5,100
1970-1973	Walnut, Bigsby	$3,000	$4,000
1970-1973	White option, Bigsby	$3,800	$5,000
1974-1975	Brown, dark cherry	$2,700	$3,550
1974-1975	White option	$3,200	$4,150
1976-1979	Brown, dark cherry	$2,300	$3,000
1976-1979	White option	$3,000	$4,000
1980	Various colors	$2,100	$2,800

SG Custom '67 Reissue/Les Paul SG '67 Custom
1991-1993. The SG Custom '67 Reissue has a wine red finish, the Les Paul SG '67 Custom ('92-'93) has a wine red or white finish.

1991-1993		$2,650	$3,450

SG Custom Elliot Easton Signature
2006-2007. Custom Shop, SG Custom specs, Maestro deluxe vibrola, Pelham Blue or white, includes Certificate of Authenticity.

2006-2007		$3,275	$4,250

SG Deluxe
1971-1972, 1981-1985, 1998-1999, 2013-2018. The '70s models were offered in cherry, natural or walnut finishes, reintroduced in '98 with 3 Firebird mini-humbucker-style pickups in black, red or Ice Blue finishes, in 2013 with 3 '57 Classic humbuckers in Cobalt Fade, Lime Burst, Orange Burst or Red Fade.

1971-1972	Cherry	$1,925	$2,500
1971-1972	Natural, walnut	$1,925	$2,500
1981-1985	Various colors	$1,625	$2,150
1998-1999	Various colors	$1,225	$1,600
2013-2018	New specs, all colors	$1,775	$2,300

SG Diablo
2008. Guitar of the Month for Dec. '08, 1,000 made, '61 specs, metallic silver finish with matching headstock, 1 volume, 1 tone knob, 3-way toggle, 24 frets.

2008		$1,375	$1,775

SG Diablo Premium Plus
2012-2013. AAA maple top.

2012-2013		$1,375	$1,775

SG Diablo Tremolo
2012-2013. Diablo with Floyd Rose.

2012-2013		$1,375	$1,775

1970 Gibson SG Custom
Garrett Park

1972 Gibson SG Custom
Tom Allen

GUITARS

*2014 Gibson SG
Government Series*

*2012 Gibson SG Jeff
Tweedy Signature*

Matt Carleson

MODEL YEAR	FEATURES	EXC. COND. LOW	HIGH

SG Dickey Betts

2012. Custom Shop, 75 hand-aged include a leather certificate of authenticity signed by Betts, 250 VOS include unsigned COA, Vintage Red finish.

| 2012 | Aged, signed | $5,400 | $7,100 |
| 2012 | VOS, unsigned | $3,275 | $4,250 |

SG Elegant

2004-2013. Custom Shop, quilt maple top, gold hardware, Blue Burst, Firemist and Iguana Burst finishes.

| 2004-2013 | | $2,700 | $3,600 |

SG Elite

1987-1989. SG Custom specs, 3 humbuckers, gold hardware, ebony 'board, various colors.

| 1987-1989 | | $2,100 | $2,725 |

SG Exclusive

1979. SG with humbuckers, coil-tap and rotary control knob, block inlay, pearl logo (not decal), black/ebony finish.

| 1979 | | $1,925 | $2,500 |

SG Firebrand

1980-1982. Double-cut mahogany solidbody, rough natural finish, Gibson branded in headstock, 2 exposed humbuckers, Firebrand logo on The SG (Standard) model.

| 1980-1982 | | $900 | $1,175 |

SG Frank Zappa "Roxy"

2013. 400 offered, Maestro vibrola, 2 exposed-coil humbuckers.

| 2013 | | $2,200 | $2,900 |

SG Futura

2013-2014. Mahogany body, maple neck, rosewood 'board, 2 pickups, various colors.

| 2013-2014 | | $775 | $1,025 |

SG Goddess

2007. SG Goddess logo on truss rod cover, only 2 control knobs versus standard 4, exposed humbuckers.

| 2007 | | $900 | $1,175 |

SG Gothic

2000-2003. SG Special with satin black finish, moon and star marker on 12th fret, black hardware.

| 2000-2003 | | $875 | $1,175 |

SG Gothic Morte

2011-2012. Solid mahogany body, African Obeche 'board, 2 pickups, satin ebony finish

| 2011-2012 | | $600 | $775 |

SG Government Series

2013-2016. Made from guitar bodies, necks and 'boards returned from Federal Government after '11 raid on Gibson, with Certificate of Authenticity.

| 2013-2016 | | $1,150 | $1,500 |

SG GT

2006-2007. '61 specs with racing stripes paint job and removable tailpiece hood scoop, locking tuners, Candy Apple Red, Daytona Blue, or Phantom Black.

| 2006-2007 | | $2,450 | $3,200 |

SG Jeff Tweedy Signature

2012. SG Standard with Maestro vibrola, mahogany body and neck, rosewood 'board, Blue Mist.

| 2012 | | $2,550 | $3,300 |

SG Judas Priest Signature

2003. Custom Shop, 30 made, dot markers, exposed

MODEL YEAR	FEATURES	EXC. COND. LOW	HIGH

'57 classic humbucker and EMG58 pickups, black, large chrome metal 'guard, also sold as a set with Flying V Judas Priest, includes certificate of authenticity.

| 2003 | | $2,200 | $2,900 |

SG Judas Priest Signature Set With Flying V

2003. Custom Shop, 30 sets made.

| 2003 | | $4,800 | $6,300 |

SG Junior

1963-1971, 1991-1994. One pickup, solidbody. Prices are for an unfaded finish, cherry finish faded to brown reduces the value by 30%.

1963-1964	Cherry	$4,200	$5,400
1964	White	$4,800	$6,300
1965	Early-'65, cherry	$3,900	$5,100
1965	Late-'65, cherry	$3,100	$4,000
1965	Pelham Blue	$6,000	$7,800
1965	White	$4,100	$5,300
1966-1969	Cherry	$2,800	$3,600
1966-1969	White	$3,900	$5,000
1970-1971	Cherry or walnut	$2,500	$3,300
1991-1994	Various colors	$1,000	$1,300

SG Junior (Reintroduced)

2018-present. Gibson Original series, '60s design, mahogany body, P-90 single-coil pickup, Vintage Cherry gloss nitro finish.

| 2018-2021 | | $1,000 | $1,300 |

SG Junior Limited

2018. Double-cut, mahogany body and neck, rosewood 'board, 1 single-coil pickup, Vintage Cherry.

| 2018 | | $1,000 | $1,300 |

SG Junior P-90

2006-2007. Single P-90 pickup, large 'guard, stop tail, cherry finish.

| 2006-2007 | | $850 | $1,125 |

SG Kirk Douglas Signature

2019-present. Mother-of-pearl headstock logo, 3 BurstBucker pickups, ebony or Inverness Green.

| 2019-2021 | | $1,775 | $2,300 |

SG Les Paul '61 Custom

1997-2005. 1961 specs, SG body style, 3 humbuckers, Deluxe Maestro vibrato or stud with tune-o-matic bridge, white or silver option.

| 1997-2005 | | $2,250 | $2,925 |

SG Les Paul '62 Custom

2003. Custom Shop, Maestro vibrato, small 'guard, white.

| 1986-1990 | | $2,250 | $2,925 |

SG Les Paul '62 Custom (Custom Shop)

2003. Custom Shop, Maestro vibrato, small 'guard, white.

| 2003 | | $2,250 | $2,925 |

SG Les Paul '90 Custom

1990-1992. 1962 specs, 3 humbuckers.

| 1990-1992 | | $2,250 | $2,925 |

SG Les Paul Custom 30th Anniversary

1991. SG body, 3 humbuckers, gold hardware, TV Yellow finish, 30th Anniversary on peghead.

| 1991 | | $2,700 | $3,500 |

SG Menace

2006-2007. Carved mahogany body, 2 exposed humbuckers, flat black finish, black hardware, single brass knuckle position marker, gig bag.

| 2006-2007 | | $875 | $1,150 |

MODEL YEAR	FEATURES	EXC. COND. LOW	HIGH

SG Music Machine Stinger

2003. Custom run for dealer Music Machine, special serial number series, SG Custom with 2 pickups and SG Standard models available, black stinger paint job on neck/headstock, various colors.

| 2003 | SG Custom | $2,850 | $3,700 |
| 2003 | SG Standard | $2,850 | $3,700 |

SG Original

2013-2019. Mahogany body, slim '60s neck profile, Lyre vibrato, '57 classic pickups, Vintage Cherry. Replaced by SG Standard '61 Maestro Vibrola in '19.

| 2013-2019 | | $1,550 | $2,000 |

SG Pete Townshend Signature

2001. Signature on back of headstock.

| 2001 | | $1,600 | $2,125 |

SG Pete Townshend Signature (Custom Shop)

2000. Custom Shop Limited Edition, 250 made, SG Special with '69 specs, large 'guard, 2 cases, cherry red, COA.

| 2000 | | $1,600 | $2,125 |

SG Platinum

2005. A mix of SG Special and SG Standard specs, platinum paint on the body, back of neck, and headstock, no crown inlay, Gibson stencil logo, exposed humbucker pickups, large plantium-finish 'guard, special plantinum colored Gibson logo guitar case.

| 2005 | | $1,100 | $1,425 |

SG Pro

1971-1974. Tune-o-matic bridge, vibrato, 2 P-90 pickups, cherry, mahogany or walnut.

| 1971-1974 | | $1,575 | $2,050 |

SG R1/SG Artist

1980-1982. Active RD-era electronics. SG style but thicker body, no 'guard, ebony 'board, black finish, dot markers, renamed SG Artist in '81.

| 1980 | SG-R1 | $1,375 | $1,775 |
| 1981-1982 | SG Artist | $1,375 | $1,775 |

SG Raw Power

2009-2012. All maple body, neck and 'board, 2 exposed-coil humbuckers, offered in 9 satin finishes, including natural.

| 2009-2012 | | $1,050 | $1,350 |

SG Select

2007. Made in Nashville, TN, carved solid bookmatched AAA flame maple, 3-piece flamed maple neck, described as the most exquisite SG offered to date, 2 humbuckers, gold hardware.

| 2007 | | $2,700 | $3,500 |

SG Special

1959-1978. Rounded double-cut for '59-'60, switched to SG body early-'61, 2 P-90s '59-'71, 2 mini-humbuckers '72-'78, 2 regular humbuckers on current version, redesigned in '85. Prices are for an unfaded finish, cherry finish faded to brown reduces the value by 20%-30%. Instruments with stop tailpieces vs. Maestro tailpiece have the same value.

| 1959 | Cherry, slab, high neck pu | $8,500 | $11,000 |
| 1960 | Cherry, slab, low neck pu | $8,500 | $11,000 |

1961-1962	Cherry, SG body	$6,200	$8,100
1962	White, SG body	$7,000	$9,200
1963-1964	Cherry, Maestro or stop	$6,200	$8,100
1963-1964	White	$7,000	$9,200
1965	Cherry, Maestro or stop	$4,000	$5,200
1965	White	$5,400	$7,000
1966	Cherry, large 'guard	$3,500	$4,500
1966	Cherry, small 'guard	$3,500	$4,500
1966	White, large 'guard	$4,500	$5,800
1966	White, small 'guard	$4,900	$6,400
1967	Cherry, large 'guard	$3,500	$4,500
1967	White, large 'guard	$4,500	$5,800
1968-1969	Cherry, large 'guard	$3,500	$4,500
1970-1971	Cherry	$3,000	$3,900
1972-1978	Mini-hums	$1,450	$1,900

SG Special (redesigned)

1985-1996. In mid-'85 Gibson introduced a redesigned SG Special model with 2 control knobs (1 pickup) or 3 control knobs (2 pickups) versus the previously used 4-knob layout.

1985-1986	1 pu, 2 knobs	$700	$925
1985-1989	2 pus, 3 knobs	$800	$1,050
1990-1996	2 pus, 3 knobs	$725	$950

SG Special (reintroduced)

1996-present. In '96 Gibson reintroduced the original 4-knob layout, 2 humbucker pickups, dot markers.

| 1996-2021 | | $700 | $925 |

SG Special 3/4

1961. Only 61 shipped.

| 1961 | | $2,900 | $3,900 |

SG Special '60s Tribute

2011-2018. '60s specs including small guard, dot markers, dual P-90s, Slim Taper '60s neck profile, 4 worn-finish options.

| 2011-2018 | | $675 | $875 |

1963 SG Special Ultra Light Aged

2021. Custom Shop Murphy Lab Collection, Classic White finish.

| 2021 | | $3,000 | $4,000 |

SG Special Faded (3 pickups)

2007. Made in Nashville, TN, 3 exposed 490 humbuckers, dot markers, stop tail, SG initials on truss rod cover, 2 knobs and 6-position selector switch, hand-worn satin finish.

| 2007 | | $725 | $950 |

SG Special Faded/Faded SG Special

2002-2018. Aged worn cherry finish.

| 2002-2005 | Half moon markers | $700 | $925 |
| 2003-2018 | Dot markers | $700 | $925 |

SG Special I

1983-1985. Dot markers, 1 exposed-coil humbucker pickup with 2 knobs, called by various names including Gibson Special ('83), Special I, and SG Special I.

| 1983-1985 | | $700 | $925 |

SG Special II

1983-1985. Dot markers, 2 exposed-coil humbucker pickups with 3 knobs, called by various names including Gibson Special ('83), Special II, SG Special II.

| 1983-1985 | | $775 | $1,025 |

Gibson SG Special

1963 Gibson SG Special

Dave's Guitar Shop

1969 Gibson SG Standard

W. H. Stephens

1972 Gibson SG Standard

Paul Thomason

MODEL YEAR	FEATURES	EXC. COND. LOW	HIGH

SG Special II EMG

2007. EMG humbucker pickups, no position markers, standard 4-knob and 3-way toggle switch SG format, black satin finish over entire guitar, black hardware.

| 2007 | | $825 | $1,075 |

SG Special New Century

2006-2008. Full-body mirror 'guard, 2 exposed humbuckers, SG body, mirror truss rod cover.

| 2006-2008 | | $1,050 | $1,350 |

SG Special Robot

2008-2012. Dot markers, robot tuning.

| 2008-2012 | | $950 | $1,250 |

SG Special Robot Limited

2008. Limited run with trapezoid markers, robot tuning.

| 2008 | | $1,050 | $1,375 |

SG Special Robot Limited Silverburst

2008. Limited run of 400.

| 2008 | | $1,275 | $1,650 |

SG Special VOS Reissue

2006-2013. Custom Shop, mahogany body and neck, bound rosewood 'board, dot inlays, 2 P-90s, certificate, white, TV yellow, or faded cherry finish.

| 2006-2013 | | $2,350 | $3,050 |

SG Standard

1963-1981, 1983-present. Les Paul Standard changes to SG body, 2 humbuckers, some very early models have optional factory Bigsby. Prices are for an unfaded finish, a cherry finish faded to brown reduces the value by 30% or more.

1963-1964	Cherry, sm 'guard, dlx vibr or Bigsby	$15,700	$20,600
1964	Pelham Blue, sm 'guard, dlx vibr	$22,000	$29,000
1965	Cherry, sm 'guard, dlx vibr, lg neck	$13,500	$17,500
1965	Cherry, sm 'guard, dlx vibr, sm neck	$12,500	$16,500
1965	Pelham Blue, sm 'guard, dlx vibr	$21,000	$27,000
1966	Early '66, cherry, vibr, sm 'guard, dlx vibrato	$9,000	$11,700
1966	Late '66, cherry, lg 'guard	$6,700	$8,700
1967	Burgundy Metallic	$7,200	$9,300
1967	Cherry	$6,700	$8,700
1967	White	$8,000	$10,500
1968	Cherry, engraved lyre	$5,700	$7,500
1969	Engraved lyre, 1-piece neck	$5,700	$7,500
1969	Engraved lyre, 3-piece neck	$4,700	$6,100
1970	Engraved lyre, 3-piece neck	$3,800	$5,000
1970	Walnut, non-lyre tailpiece	$2,600	$3,400
1970-1971	Cherry, non-lyre tailpiece	$2,700	$3,600
1971	Engraved lyre, 3-piece neck	$3,500	$4,600
1972-1979	Blocks, mini 'guard, top mount	$2,100	$2,700
1980-1986	New colors, sm blocks	$1,900	$2,500
1992-1999	New specs	$1,200	$1,600
2000-2021	Standard colors	$1,200	$1,600
2006-2012	Silverburst	$1,450	$1,875

SG Standard '61 Reissue

2004-2008. Small 'guard, stop tail, Nashville tune-o-matic bridge, Gibson Deluxe Keystone tuners, standard Gibson logo and crown inlay, no Les Paul logo, Vintage Original Spec aging optional from '06. Reintroduced in '19.

| 2004-2008 | | $1,675 | $2,175 |

SG Standard '61

2019-present. Classic '61 design, 3 models offered - Maestro vibrola, Sideways or Stop Bar, mahogany body and neck, rosewood 'board, vintage cherry finish.

2019-2021	Maestro vibrola	$1,775	$2,300
2019-2021	Sideways vibrola	$1,600	$2,100
2019-2021	Stop Bar vibrola	$1,600	$2,100

1964 SG Standard (Maestro Vibrola) Murphy Lab Aged

2021-present. Custom Shop Murphy Lab Collection, heavy aged (Faded Cherry), light aged (Pelham Blue) and ultra light (Cherry Red or Pelham Blue).

2021-2022	Heavy aged	$4,800	$6,300
2021-2022	Light aged	$4,800	$6,300
2021-2022	Ultra Light aged	$3,500	$4,600

SG Standard 24 50th Anniversary

2011. Limited run, mother-of-pearl Gibson logo with gold 50th Anniversary silkscreen, 2 '57 classic pickups, antique ebony finish.

| 2011 | | $1,275 | $1,650 |

SG Standard (Etune)

2014-2018. Min-Etune robot tuners, Etune logo on truss rod.

| 2014-2018 | | $1,075 | $1,400 |

SG Standard Brian Ray '63 (Custom Shop)

2015. Silver Fox finish, Bigsby, certificate of authenticity.

| 2015 | | $3,500 | $4,500 |

SG Standard Celebrity Series

1991-1992. SG Standard with large 'guard, gold hardware, black finish.

| 1991-1992 | | $1,850 | $2,400 |

SG Standard Gary Rossington Signature

2004. '63-'64 SG Standard specs with Deluxe Maestro vibrola, '60 slim taper neck, limited edition, faded cherry aged by Tom Murphy.

| 2004 | | $5,200 | $6,800 |

SG Standard HP (High Performance)

2016-2019. Solid mahogany body and neck, AA figured maple top, 2 pickups, different colors offered each year.

| 2016-2019 | | $1,450 | $1,900 |

GUITARS

MODEL YEAR	FEATURES	EXC. COND. LOW	HIGH

SG Standard Korina (Custom Shop)
2008-2009. Custom Shop limited reissue of '60s SG Standard, 2 BurstBucker pickups, black.

2008-2009		$2,550	$3,350

SG Standard Korina Limited Edition
1993-1994. Korina version of SG Standard, limited run, natural.

1993-1994		$3,300	$4,300

SG Standard Korina/SG Standard K (Custom Shop)
2001-2008. Custom Shop serial number, large 'guard, no SG logo on truss rod, CS logo back of headstock, natural finish.

2001-2008		$4,000	$5,300

SG Standard Limited Edition
2000. Limited Edition logo back of headstock, 2 humbuckers, large pearloid guard, gold hardware, dark opaque finish.

2000		$1,150	$1,500

SG Standard Limited Edition (3 pickups)
2007. Guitar of the Week, 400 made, 3 single-coil blade pickups, 6-position rotator switch with chickenhead knob, SG logo on truss rod cover, large 'guard, satin finish.

2007		$1,075	$1,400

SG Standard Reissue
2004-2018. Reissue of near '63-'64 specs with Deluxe Maestro lyre vibrato and small 'guard, also offered with stop bar tailpiece, cherry finish, '60 slim taper neck, smooth neck heel joint, trapezoid markers, unmarked truss rod cover without Les Paul designation, formerly called Les Paul SG Standard Reissue, by 2005 part of Gibson's 'Vintage Original Spec' Custom Shop series, certificate of authenticity.

2004-2007	VOS, Maestro	$2,400	$3,100
2007-2018	VOS, stoptail	$2,400	$3,100
2008-2009	Maestro, LP logo	$2,400	$3,100

SG Standard VOS Historic
2003-2014. Custom Shop, Vintage Original Specs.

2003-2014		$2,400	$3,100

SG Standard Robby Krieger
2009. Custom Shop model, Inspired By series, based on Krieger's '67 SG, limited run of 150 with 50 aged and signed, 100 with V.O.S. finish treatment, certificate of authenticity.

2009	Aged, signed	$4,400	$5,800
2009	VOS	$3,600	$4,700

SG Standard Robby Krieger 50th Anniversary
2012. Mahogany body and neck, rosewood 'board, 2 '57 classic Alnico II pickups, Maestro tailpiece, Heritage Cherry finish.

2012		$1,850	$2,400

SG Supreme
2004-2007. '57 humbuckers, flamed maple top, split-diamond markers, various colors.

2004-2007		$2,075	$2,700

SG Tony Iommi Signature (Historic/ Custom Shop)
2001-2003. Custom Shop Historic Collection, higher-end, signature humbuckers without poles, cross inlays, ebony or Wine Red.

2001-2003		$5,000	$6,500

SG Tony Iommi Signature (Production)
2002-2003. Standard production model.

2002-2008		$2,300	$3,000

SG TV
1961-1963. Name changed from Les Paul TV, SG body, 1 pickup, white finish. In '64 called SG Junior White.

1961-1963		$5,000	$6,600

SG Voodoo/Voodoo SG
2002-2004. Carved top, black hardware, voodoo doll inlay at 5th fret, Juju finish (black with red wood filler).

2002-2004		$1,200	$1,600

SG-X
1998-2000. Previously part of the All American series, SG body with single bridge humbucker, various colors.

1998-2000		$650	$850

SG-X Tommy Hilfiger
1998. Hilfiger logo on front, dot markers, plain headstock like a SG Special, dark blue finish, 100 made.

1998		$600	$800

SG Zoot Suit
2007-2010. Body of individual dyed strips of birch.

2007-2010		$1,675	$2,175

SG-Z
1998. Z-shaped string-thru tailpiece, 2 humbuckers, split diamond markers.

1998		$1,550	$2,025

The SG
1979-1983. Offered as The SG Standard (walnut body) and The SG Deluxe (mahogany), ebony 'board, 2 humbuckers, 'The SG' truss rod logo.

1979-1983	Walnut or mahogany	$875	$1,150

Sheryl Crow Country Western Supreme
2019-present. Artist series, aged sitka spruce top, mahogany back and sides, Antique Cherry finish.

2019-2021		$3,000	$3,900

Sheryl Crow Signature
2001-2018. Artist Series, based on Sheryl Crow's 1962 Country and Western with Hummingbird influences.

2001-2018		$2,400	$3,100

Sheryl Crow Southern Jumbo Special Edition
2013-2018. Adirondack red spruce top, mahogany back and sides, rosewood 'board, with signed certificate of authenticity, Montana Sunsetburst finish. Limited production in '13.

2013-2018		$3,000	$3,900

SJ (Southern Jumbo)
1942-1969,1991-1996. Flat-top, sunburst standard, natural optional starting in '54 (natural finish version called Country-Western starting in '56), round shoulders (changed to square in '62), catalog name changed to SJ Deluxe in '70, refer to that listing.

1942-1944	Banner, Adirondack	$15,000	$20,000
1942-1944	Banner, mahogany	$11,600	$15,400
1945	Script, Sitka	$12,500	$16,500

Gibson SG Standard '61

Gibson Sheryl Crow Country Western Supreme

1960 Gibson SJ

David Stone

2017 Gibson SJ-200 Bob Dylan Player's Edition

MODEL YEAR	FEATURES	EXC. COND. LOW	HIGH
1946	Script, Sitka	$11,000	$14,500
1947	Script, Sitka	$10,000	$13,200
1948-1949	Script, Sitka	$9,000	$12,000
1950-1953		$6,400	$8,400
1954-1956	Natural option	$6,400	$8,400
1954-1959	Sunburst	$6,400	$8,400
1960-1962	Round shoulder (ends)	$5,800	$7,600
1962-1964	Square shoulder (begins)	$5,300	$7,000
1965	Cherry Sunburst	$3,800	$6,000
1965	Tobacco Sunburst	$4,300	$5,700
1966	Tobacco Sunburst	$4,200	$5,600
1966-1968	Cherry Sunburst	$3,500	$4,600
1969	Below belly bridge	$2,800	$3,700

SJ Deluxe (Southern Jumbo)
1970-1978. SJ name changed to SJ Deluxe in catalog, along with a series of engineering changes.

1970-1971	Non-adj saddle	$2,050	$2,700
1972-1973	Unbound 'board	$2,050	$2,700
1974-1978	4-ply to binding	$2,050	$2,700

SJN (Country-Western)
1956-1969. Flat-top, natural finish version of SJ, round shoulders '56-'62, square shoulders after, called the SJN in '60 and '61, the SJN Country Western after that, catalog name changed to SJN Deluxe in '70, refer to that listing.

1956-1959		$6,400	$8,400
1960-1962	Round shoulder (ends)	$5,800	$7,600
1962-1964	Square shoulder (begins)	$5,300	$7,000
1965		$3,800	$5,000
1966-1968		$3,450	$4,550
1969	Below belly bridge	$2,650	$3,500

SJN Deluxe (Country-Western Jumbo)
1970-1978. SJN name changed to SJN Deluxe in catalog, along with a series of engineering changes.

1970-1971	Non-adj saddle	$2,050	$2,700
1972-1973	Unbound 'board	$2,050	$2,700
1974-1978	4-ply to binding	$2,050	$2,700

SJ 1942 Reissue (Southern Jumbo)
2000. Custom Shop, mahogany back and sides, '42 SJ appointments, 'Only A Gibson is Good Enough' banner logo.

2000		$2,900	$3,800

SJ Reissue (Southern Jumbo)
2003-2007. Sunburst.

2003-2007		$2,200	$2,850

SJ Hank Williams Jr. Hall of Fame
1997. Custom Shop, mahogany back and sides, SJ appointments.

1997		$2,800	$3,600

SJ Hank Williams Sr.
1993. Custom Shop, 25 offered.

1993		$4,400	$5,800

SJ Kristofferson
2009-2012. Limited run of 300, AAA Sitka top, mahogany back and sides, Indian rosewood 'board, aged vintage sunburst.

2009-2012		$2,400	$3,100

MODEL YEAR	FEATURES	EXC. COND. LOW	HIGH

SJ True Vintage
2007-2008. "Only A Gibson Is Good Enough" headstock banner, sitka spruce top, dark mahogany back and sides, dual parallelogram markers.

2007-2008		$2,500	$3,300

SJ Woody Guthrie
2003-2018. Single-bound round shoulder body, mahogany back and sides, parallelogram inlays.

2003-2018		$2,200	$2,900

SJ-100
2008. Jumbo body, dot markers, crown headstock inlay, inlaid Gibson logo, natural.

2008		$1,350	$1,750

1939 SJ-100 Centennial
1994. Acoustic flat-top, limited edition, sunburst.

1994		$2,300	$3,000

1941 SJ-100
2013-2018. Sitka spruce top, mahogany back, sides and neck, rosewood 'board, Vintage Sunburst or Antique Natural.

2013-2018		$2,200	$2,900

SJ-150
Listed with J-150.

SJ-200
Listed with J-200.

1957 SJ-200 (Custom Shop)
2020-present. Aged sitka spruce top, flamed maple back and sides, 4 bar moustach bridge, VOS finish, Antique Natural or Vintage Sunburst.

2020-2021		$4,100	$5,400

SJ-200 Bob Dylan Autographed Collector's Edition
2015-2018. Exact replica of Dylan's personal highly-customized SJ-200, Indian rosewood, Sitka spruce, Dylan eye logo inlaid on headstock, abalone inlay on 'guard, label signed by Bob Dylan, 175 made, case with embroidered eye logo.

2015-2018		$11,000	$14,500

SJ-200 Bob Dylan Player's Edition
2015-2018. Adirondack red spruce, flamed maple, eye logo headstock inlay, LR Baggs Anthem pickup.

2015-2018		$5,000	$6,600

SJ-200 Centennial Limited Edition
1994. Made in Bozeman, Montana, 100 made, 'guard specs based on '38 design, inside label "Gibson 100 Years 1894-1994", includes certificate of authenticity.

1994		$3,500	$4,600

SJ-200 Custom Rosewood
2007. Custom shop, certificate of authenticity.

2007		$4,000	$5,200

SJ-200 Deluxe
2020-present. Sitka spruce top, rosewood back and sides, mother-of-pearl crown inlays, Rosewood Burst finish.

2020-2021		$4,500	$5,900

SJ-200 Elite
1998-2007. Gibson Custom Shop Bozeman, maple sides and back.

1998-2007		$3,700	$4,800

MODEL YEAR	FEATURES	EXC. COND. LOW	HIGH

SJ-200 Elite Custom Koa
2004. Figured koa, ebony board with abalone crown inlays, Antique Natural.

| 2004 | | $4,100 | $5,400 |

SJ-200 Elvis Presley
2007. Custom Shop, 250 made, kings crown logo and facsimile signature of Presley on truss rod cover, certificate of authenticity, black finish.

| 2007 | | $4,200 | $5,500 |

SJ-200 Pete Townshend Limited
2004-2012. Gibson Custom Shop Bozeman, maple sides and back.

| 2004 | Signed, 1st 50 made | $5,800 | $7,600 |
| 2004-2012 | | $3,500 | $4,600 |

SJ-200 Ray Whitley/J-200 Custom Club
1994-1995. Based on Ray Whitley's late-1930s J-200, including engraved inlays and initials on the truss rod cover, only 37 made, one of the limited edition models the Montana division released to celebrate Gibson's 100th anniversary.

| 1994-1995 | | $16,000 | $21,000 |

SJ-200 Ron Wood
Listed with J-200 Ron Wood.

SJ-200 Sea Green Limited Edition
2016. Bozeman Custom Shop, 40 made, Sitka spruce top, AAA flamed maple back and sides, mother-of-pearl crown inlays.

| 2016 | | $4,000 | $5,200 |

SJ-200 Standard
2015-present. AAA flamed maple body, on-board electronics, Wine Red or Autumnburst.

| 2015-2021 | | $3,500 | $4,500 |

SJ-200 Summer Jam Koa
2006. Custom Shop, only 6 made, offered to attendees of Gibson Guitar Summer Jam, highly figured koa back/sides.

| 2006 | | $5,300 | $7,000 |

SJ-200 True Vintage/SJ-200 Vintage
2007-2019. AAA Adirondack red spruce top, AAA Eastern curly maple back and sides, rosewood 'board, tortoise 'guard, nitro finish. True dropped from name in '19.

| 2007-2019 | | $4,300 | $5,600 |

SJ-200 Vine
2002-2018. Custom Shop, Sitka spruce top, Eastern curly maple back/sides, abalone vine inlay in 'board, abalone body trim. Limited Edition in '15, 30 made.

| 2002-2018 | | $6,500 | $8,500 |

SJ-250 Monarch
Listed with J-250 Monarch.

SJ-300
2007-2010. Super Jumbo with Indian rosewood back and sides, ebony 'board, abalone crown inlays and rosette, gold imperial tuners, active transducer.

| 2007-2010 | | $3,400 | $4,400 |

SJ-1000
Listed with J-1000.

Sonex Artist
1981-1985. Active electronics, 3 mini switches, 2 humbuckers.

| 1981-1985 | | $800 | $1,050 |

Sonex-180 Custom
1980-1982. Two Super humbuckers, coil-tap, maple neck, ebony 'board, single-cut, body of Multi-Phonic synthetic material, black or white.

| 1980-1982 | | $775 | $1,025 |

Sonex-180 Deluxe
1980-1984. Hardwood neck, rosewood 'board, single-cut, body of Multi-Phonic synthetic material, 2 pickups, no coil-tap, various colors.

| 1980-1984 | Various colors | $775 | $1,025 |
| 1982-1984 | Silverburst | $850 | $1,125 |

Sonex-180 Standard
1980. Dirty-fingers pickups, rosewood 'board, ebony finish.

| 1980 | | $775 | $1,025 |

Songbird Deluxe
1999-2002. Solid rosewood back, sides and 'board, on-board electronics. Renamed Songwriter Deluxe.

| 1999-2002 | | $1,425 | $1,850 |

Songwriter
2003-2020. Sitka spruce top, rosewood back, sides and 'board, mahogany neck, Antique Natural or Rosewood Burst. Becomes Songwriter Standard in '20.

| 2003-2020 | | $2,025 | $2,625 |

Songwriter 12-String Rosewood
2019-2020. Sitka spruce top, rosewood back and sides, Antique Natural or Rosewood Burst.

| 2019-2020 | | $2,200 | $2,900 |

Songwriter Deluxe
2003-2011. Solid rosewood back and sides, trapezoid inlays, cutaway or non-cutaway, on-board electronics.

| 2003-2011 | | $1,625 | $2,125 |

Songwriter Deluxe 12-String
2006-present. 12-string version, non-cut.

| 2006-2021 | | $1,625 | $2,125 |

Songwriter Deluxe Koa
2009. Custom Shop, all koa, cutaway.

| 2009 | | $2,625 | $3,425 |

Songwriter Deluxe Standard
2009-2012. Solid rosewood back and sides, bound ebony 'board, diamond and arrows inlays, cutaway or non-cutaway.

| 2009-2012 | | $2,075 | $2,675 |

Songwriter Deluxe Studio
2009-2018. Like Standard, but with bound rosewood 'board and double parallelogram inlays, cutaway or non-cutaway.

| 2009-2018 | | $1,600 | $2,100 |

Songwriter Modern EC Mahogany
2020-2021. Cutaway, sitka spruce top, mahogany back, sides and neck, Light Cherry Burst with nitro finish.

| 2020-2021 | | $1,700 | $2,225 |

Songwriter Modern EC Rosewood
2020-2021. Cutaway, sitka spruce top, rosewood back and sides, mahogany neck, Rosewood Burst with nitro finish.

| 2020-2021 | | $1,850 | $2,425 |

Songwriter Special
2007. Mahogany sides and back, dark opaque finish.

| 2007 | | $1,550 | $2,000 |

2011 Gibson SJ-200 True Vintage

Johnny Zapp

1982 Gibson Sonex-180 Deluxe

Imaged by Heritage Auctions, HA.com

GUITARS

2019 Gibson Songwriter

1940 Gibson Super 400N

Kevin

MODEL YEAR	FEATURES	EXC. COND. LOW	HIGH
Songwriter Special Deluxe			
2003. Custom Shop, Brazilian rosewood.			
2003		$2,300	$3,000
Songwriter Standard EC Rosewood			
2020-present. Cutaway, sitka spruce top, rosewood back and sides, Antique Natural or Rosewood Burst finish.			
2020-2021		$2,175	$2,825
Songwriter Standard Rosewood			
2020-present. Non-cut, sitka spruce top, rosewood back and sides, Antique Natural or Rosewood Burst finish.			
2020-2021		$2,100	$2,725
Songwriter Studio			
2003-2019. Non-cutaway or cutaway.			
2003-2019		$1,800	$2,350
Special 400			
1985-1986. Double-cut SG body, exposed humbucker and 2 single-coils, Kahler locking tremolo, coil tap.			
1985-1986		$750	$975
Spirit I			
1982-1987. Double rounded cutaway, 1 pickup, chrome hardware, various colors.			
1982-1987		$1,375	$1,800
Spirit I XPL			
1985-1986. Spirit I with 6-on-a-side Explorer-style headstock.			
1985-1986		$1,450	$1,875
Spirit II			
1982-1987. Spirit I with 2 pickups, bound top.			
1982-1987		$1,575	$2,050
Spirit II XPL			
1985-1987. 2 pickup version.			
1985-1987		$1,575	$2,050
SR-71			
1987-1989. Floyd Rose tremolo, 1 humbucker, 2 single-coil pickups, various colors, Wayne Charvel designed.			
1987-1989		$1,575	$2,050
Star			
1992. Star logo on headstock, star position markers, single sharp cutaway flat-top, sunburst.			
1991-1992		$1,600	$2,075
Starburst Standard/Flame			
1992-1994. Single-cut acoustic/electric, star inlays, figured maple back and sides.			
1992-1994		$1,600	$2,075
Style O			
1902-1925. Acoustic archtop, oval soundhole, bound top, neck and headstock, various colors.			
1902-1906	Paddle headstock	$5,700	$7,500
1902-1906	Paddle headstock, fancy	$7,300	$9,500
1906-1908	Slotted headstock	$6,800	$8,900
1908-1913	Solid headstock	$6,800	$8,900
1914-1921	Scroll variation	$6,800	$8,900
1922-1924	Loar era	$7,300	$9,500
1925	Scroll, truss rod	$7,300	$9,500
Style O-1			
1902. Acoustic archtop, celluloid binding.			
1902		$8,300	$10,800

MODEL YEAR	FEATURES	EXC. COND. LOW	HIGH
Style O-2			
1902. Acoustic archtop, pearl/ebony binding.			
1902		$8,300	$10,800
Style O-3			
1902. Acoustic archtop, green/white binding.			
1902		$8,300	$10,800
Style R Harp Guitar			
1902-1907. Acoustic 6-string, with 6 sub-bass strings, walnut back and sides, bound soundhole.			
1902-1907		$5,100	$6,700
Style R-1 Harp Guitar			
1902. Style R with fancier pearl and ivory rope pattern binding.			
1902		$5,100	$6,700
Style U Harp Guitar			
1902-1939. Acoustic 6-string, with 10 or 12 sub-bass strings, walnut (until about '07) or birch back and sides, bound soundhole, black.			
1902-1939		$5,600	$7,400
Style U-1 Harp Guitar			
1902-1907, 1915, 1917. Slightly fancier Style U.			
1902-1917		$6,000	$7,900
Super 300			
1948-1955. Acoustic archtop, non-cut, bound body, neck and headstock, sunburst.			
1948-1955		$3,800	$5,000
Super 300 C			
1954-1958. Acoustic archtop, rounded cutaway, bound body, neck and headstock, sunburst with natural option.			
1954-1958	Sunburst	$4,300	$5,700
Super 400			
1935-1941, 1947-1955. Introduced early '35 as Super L-5 Deluxe. Acoustic archtop, non-cut, maple, multi-bound, f-holes, sunburst (see Super 400 N for natural version).			
1935	Early, L-5, highly flamed	$15,800	$20,500
1935	Early, L-5, plain	$12,700	$16,600
1935	Late, 400, highly flamed	$13,000	$17,000
1935	Late, 400, plain	$9,800	$12,800
1936-1941	Highly flamed	$11,000	$14,200
1936-1941	Plain	$8,600	$11,200
1947-1949	Highly flamed	$6,800	$8,900
1947-1949	Plain	$5,400	$7,000
1950-1955		$5,000	$6,450
Super 400 N			
1940, 1948-1955. Natural finish version of Super 400, highly flamed, non-cut, acoustic archtop.			
1940		$12,800	$16,600
1948-1949		$9,500	$12,300
1950-1955		$8,100	$10,500
Super 400 P (Premier)			
1939-1941. Acoustic archtop, single rounded cutaway, '39 model 'board rests on top, sunburst finish.			
1939-1941		$19,000	$24,600
Super 400 PN (Premier Natural)			
1939-1940. Rounded cutaway, '39 'board rests on top, natural finish.			
1939-1940		$26,600	$34,500

The *Vintage Guitar Price Guide* shows low to high values for items in all-original excellent condition, and, where applicable, with original case or cover.

MODEL YEAR	FEATURES	EXC. COND. LOW	HIGH

Super 400 C
1948-1982. Introduced as Super 400 Premier, acoustic archtop, single-cut, sunburst finish (natural is called Super 400 CN).

1948-1949		$12,800	$16,600
1950-1959		$11,700	$15,300
1960-1964		$10,400	$13,500
1965		$7,800	$10,200
1966-1969		$6,800	$8,900
1970-1982		$5,000	$6,450

Super 400 CN
1950-1987. Natural finish version of Super 400 C.

1950-1959		$13,000	$17,200
1960-1964		$11,700	$15,300
1965		$10,800	$14,100
1966-1969		$9,400	$12,200

Super 400 CES
1951-2018. Electric version of Super 400 C, archtop, single-cut (round '51-'60 and '69-present, pointed '60-'69), 2 pickups (P-90s '51-'54, Alnico Vs '54-'57, humbuckers '57 on), sunburst (natural version called Super 400 CESN), now part of Gibson's Historic Collection.

1951-1953	P-90s	$15,100	$19,700
1954-1957	Alnico Vs	$15,100	$19,700
1957-1960	PAFs	$21,500	$28,000
1961-1962	PAFs, sharp cut	$19,300	$25,000
1963-1964	Pat #	$14,200	$18,400
1965		$10,300	$13,300
1966-1969		$8,700	$11,300
1970-1979		$7,500	$9,650
1980-2018		$7,500	$9,650

Super 400 CESN
1952-2016. Natural version of Super 400 CES, now part of Gibson's Historic Collection.

1952-1953	P-90s	$15,000	$19,500
1954-1956	Alnico Vs	$15,000	$19,500
1957-1960	PAFs	$21,500	$27,800
1961-1962	PAFs, sharp cut	$19,000	$24,700
1963-1964	Pat #	$14,000	$18,200
1965		$10,100	$13,100
1966-1969		$8,700	$11,300
1970-1979		$7,600	$9,900
1980-2016		$7,600	$9,900

Super 400 (Custom Shop)
2009. Non-cutaway, natural.

2009		$8,500	$11,100

'39 Super 400 Historic
1993-1997. Custom Shop Historic Collection, reissue of non-cut '39 version, various colors.

1993-1997		$7,400	$9,700

Super 4000 Chet Atkins
2000. Limited run of 25. AAA sitka spruce carved top, highly figured carved maple back, antique natural and faded cherry sunburst.

2000		$20,800	$27,000

Super Jumbo 100
1939-1943. Jumbo flat-top, mahogany back and sides, bound body and neck, sunburst, reintroduced as J-100 with different specs in '84.

1939-1941	Early '41	$31,000	$41,000
1941-1943	Late '41	$27,000	$35,000

Super Jumbo/Super Jumbo 200
1938-1942. Initially called Super Jumbo in '38 and named Super Jumbo 200 in '39. Name then changed to J-200 (see that listing) by '47 (with maple back and sides) and SJ-200 by the '50s. Named for super large jumbo 16 7/8" flat-top body, double braced with rosewood back and sides, sunburst finish.

1938-1940		$104,000	$136,000
1941-1942		$99,000	$130,000

Super V BJB
1978-1983. A Super V CES but with a single floating pickup.

1978-1983		$5,300	$6,900

Super V CES
1978-1993. Archtop, L-5 with a Super 400 neck, 2 humbucker pickups, natural or sunburst.

1978-1993		$5,300	$6,900

Tal Farlow
1962-1971, 1993-2018. Full body, single-cut archtop, 2 humbuckers, triple-bound top, reintroduced '93 as part of Gibson's Historic Collection.

1962-1964	Viceroy Brown	$7,500	$9,800
1965	Viceroy Brown	$7,100	$9,200
1966-1971	Viceroy Brown	$6,300	$8,300
1993-2018	Various colors	$3,600	$4,700

TG-0
1927-1933, 1960-1974. Acoustic tenor based on L-0, mahogany body, light amber.

1927-1933		$1,900	$2,500
1960-1964		$1,000	$1,300
1965		$750	$975
1966-1969		$700	$900
1970-1974		$625	$825

TG-00
1932-1943. Tenor flat-top based on L-00.

1932-1943		$1,900	$2,500

TG-1/L-1 Tenor/L-4 Tenor
1927-1937. Acoustic flat-top, tenor or plectrum guitar based on L-1, mahogany back and sides, bound body, sunburst.

1927-1937		$2,400	$3,100
1928-1932	Rare Lucas/ Johnson body	$3,500	$4,500

TG-2/L-2 Tenor
1929-1930. Acoustic tenor guitar.

1929-1930		$4,500	$5,900

TG-7
1934-1940. Tenor based on the L-7, sunburst.

1934-1940		$3,500	$4,500

TG-25/TG-25 N
1962-1970. Acoustic flat-top, tenor guitar based on B-25, mahogany back and sides, sunburst or natural (25 N).

1962-1964		$1,000	$1,300
1965		$850	$1,100
1966-1969		$750	$975
1970		$600	$775

TG-50
1934-1940, 1947-1961, 1963. Acoustic archtop, tenor guitar based on L-50, mahogany back and sides, sunburst.

1934-1940		$1,375	$1,800
1947-1963		$1,275	$1,700

1969 Gibson Super 400 CN
Loek Van Schooten

1962 Gibson Tal Farlow

1965 Gibson Trini Lopez Standard
Matt Carleson

Gilchrist Model 16

MODEL YEAR	FEATURES	EXC. COND. LOW	HIGH
Traveling Songwriter EC			
2005-2015. Solid spruce top, solid mahogany sides and back, soft cutaway, on-board electronics and EQ.			
2005-2015		$1,800	$2,400
Trini Lopez Standard			
1964-1970. Double rounded cutaway, thinline archtop, 2 humbuckers, tune-o-matic bridge, trapeze tailpiece, single-bound, cherry, Sparkling Burgundy and Pelham Blue finishes.			
1964	Cherry	$8,000	$10,400
1965	Cherry	$7,500	$9,700
1965	Pelham Blue	$8,200	$10,700
1965	Sparkling Burgundy	$7,500	$9,700
1966	Pelham Blue	$7,800	$10,200
1966-1970	Cherry	$7,300	$9,500
1966-1970	Sparkling Burgundy	$7,300	$9,500
Trini Lopez Standard (Custom Shop)			
2010-2011. Custom Shop reissue of thinline Trini Lopez Standard, diamond f-holes, 6-on-a-side tuners, trapeze tailpiece, Certificate of Authenticity, cherry red.			
2010-2011		$3,100	$4,100
Trini Lopez Deluxe			
1964-1970. Double pointed cutaway archtop, 2 humbuckers, triple-bound, sunburst.			
1964		$6,700	$8,700
1965		$6,500	$8,500
1966-1970		$6,300	$8,400
U-2			
1987-1989. Double-cut, 1 humbucker and 2 single-coil pickups, ebony or red, renamed Mach II in '90-'91.			
1987-1991		$1,150	$1,500
U-2 Showcase Edition			
1988. November 1988 Guitar of the Month series, 250 made.			
1988		$1,150	$1,500
US-1/US-3			
1986-1991. Double-cut maple top with mahogany back, 3 humbucker pickups (US-1), or 3 P-90s (US-3), standard production and Custom Shop.			
1986-1991		$1,150	$1,500
Vegas Standard			
2006-2007. Flat-top semi-hollowbody thinline, slim neck, 2 humbuckers, f-holes, split diamond inlays.			
2006-2007		$1,100	$1,400
Vegas High Roller			
2006-2007. Upgraded version, AAA maple top, gold hardware and frets, block inlays.			
2006-2007		$1,200	$1,500
Victory MV II (MV 2)			
1981-1984. Asymetrical double-cut with long horn, 3-way slider, maple body and neck, rosewood 'board, 2 pickups.			
1981-1984		$1,200	$1,500
Victory MV X (MV 10)			
1981-1984. 3 humbuckers, 5-way switch, various colors.			
1981-1984		$1,250	$1,550
WRC			
1987-1988. Designed for Gibson by Wayne R. Charvel (WRC), earlier models had Kahler trem, later			

MODEL YEAR	FEATURES	EXC. COND. LOW	HIGH
Floyd Rose, offered in red, black or white.			
1987-1988		$950	$1,250
XPL Custom			
1985-1986. Explorer-like shape, exposed humbuckers, locking tremolo, bound maple top, sunburst or white.			
1985-1986		$1,450	$1,900
Y2K Dwight Yoakam Signature			
2005. Limited run of 200, small body jumbo, spruce top, highly figured maple sides and back, 2-piece flamed maple neck, double 'guard, gloss natural finish.			
2005		$2,150	$2,800
Zakk Wylde ZV Buzzsaw			
2008. Custom Shop Inspired By series, limited run of 50, Flying V wings with SG horns, 2 humbuckers.			
2008		$3,300	$4,300

Gibson Baldwin

2005-ca. 2013. Entry-level electric and acoustic guitars, basses, amps and accessories made in China for discount store market and sold under the Signature, Maestro, Echelon, and Genesis brand names. Models include Les Paul and SG copies. Guitars have Music - Gibson logo on neckplate and brand logo on headstock.

Giffin

1977-1988, 1997-present. Professional and premium grade, production/custom, hollow-, semi-hollow-, and solidbody guitars built by luthier Roger Giffin in West San Fernando Valley, California. For '77-'88, Giffin's shop was in London. From '88 to '93, he worked for the Gibson Custom Shop in California as a Master Luthier. In '97, Giffin set up shop in Sweden for a year, moving back to California in the Spring of '98. He also built small numbers of instruments during '67-'76 and '94-'96 (when he had a repair business).

Gigliotti

2000-present. Premium grade, production/ custom, electric guitars with a metal plate top and tone chambers and designed by Patrick Gigliotti in Tacoma, Washington.

Gila Eban Guitars

Premium grade, custom, classical guitars built by luthier Gila Eban in Riverside, Connecticut, starting in 1979.

Gilbert Guitars

1965-present. Custom classical guitars by luthiers John Gilbert and William Gilbert in Paso Robles, California. Son William has handled all production since '91. John died early 2012.

Gilchrist

1977-present. Currently known more for his mandolins, luthier Steve Gilchrist, of Warrnambool, Australia, has also built premium and presentation grade, custom guitars.

MODEL YEAR	FEATURES	EXC. COND. LOW	HIGH

Acoustic Archtop
1990s-present. Very limited production.

1990s-2021		$21,000	$27,000

Gilet Guitars
1976-present. Luthier Gerard Gilet builds production/custom, premium grade, acoustic, classical, flamenco, and wooden bodied resonator guitars in Botany, Sydney, New South Wales, Australia. He also builds lap steels.

Girl Brand Guitars
1996-2012. Premium-grade, production/custom, guitars built by luthier Chris Larsen in Tucson, Arizona. Larsen now builds under the Larsen Guitar Mfg. name.

Gitane
2003-present. Intermediate and professional grade, production, classic Selmer-Maccaferri style jazz guitars made in China for Saga.

Gittler
1974-ca.1985. Minimalistic electric guitar designed by Allan Gittler, consisting basically of a thin rod with frets welded to it. A total of 560 were built, with Gittler making the first 60 in the U.S. from '74 to the early '80s. The remainder were made around '85 in Israel by the Astron corporation under a licensing agreement. Three Gittler basses were also built. Gittler emigrated to Israel in the early '80s and changed his name to Avraham Bar Rashi. He died in 2002. A U.S.-made Gittler is the only musical instrument in the Museum of Modern Art in New York.

Metal Skeleton

1971-1982		$2,200	$2,900
1982-1999		$2,000	$2,600

Giulietti
1962-1965. The Giulietti Accordion Company, New York, offered guitars and amps in the '60s.

GJ2
Gold Jackson Enterprises LLC, a partnership between luthier Grover Jackson and Jon Gold, established 2012, builds professional and premium grade, production/custom, solidbody electric guitars in Laguna Hills, California.

Glendale
2004-present. Professional grade, production/custom, solidbody guitars built by luthier Dale Clark in Arlington, Texas.

GLF
1991-1997. Solidbody electric guitars built by luthier Kevin Smith in Minnesota. In '97 he started building his ToneSmith line of guitars.

Glick Guitars
Premium grade, production/custom, acoustic and electric archtop, and acoustic guitars built in Santa Barbara, California by luthier Mike Glick, starting in '96.

Global
Late-1960s-1970s. Budget copy models, not unlike Teisco, imported from Asia for the student market. They also offered amps.

Electric Solidbody
Late-1960s-1970s.

1968		$150	$500

GMP
1990-2005. Professional and premium grade solidbody electric guitars built by GM Precision Products, Inc. of San Dimas, California. Original owners were Gary and Cameron Moline, Dave Pearson and Glenn Matjezel. Many guitars featured fancy tops or custom graphics. They also made basses. Overall production is estimated at 1120 guitars and basses. GMP reopened in '10 under new ownership (see following).

GMP (Genuine Musical Products)
2010-present. The GMP brand was acquired by Dan and Kim Lawrence in '08. Since '10, Dan along with fellow luthiers Glenn Matjezel and William Stempke build professional and premium grade, production/custom, electric guitars in San Dimas, California. They also build basses.

GMW
1998-present. Professional grade, production/custom, solidbody guitars from Lee Garver's GMW Guitarworks of Glendora, California.

Godin
1987-present. Intermediate and professional grade, production, solidbody electrics and nylon and steel string acoustic/electrics from luthier Robert Godin. They also build basses and mandolins. Necks and bodies are made in La Patrie, Quebec with final assembly in Berlin, New Hampshire. Godin is also involved in the Seagull, Norman, Richmond, Art & Lutherie, and Patrick & Simon brand of guitars. SA on Godin models stands for Synth Access.

5th Avenue Kingpin
2008-present. Full-size non-cut electric archtop, 1 or 2 P-90 pickups, plain or highly flamed top, premium price for highly flamed.

2008-2021		$700	$900

5th Avenue Uptown
2012-present. Archtop cutaway with Bigsby, f-holes, Canadian wild cherry top, back and sides, silver leaf maple neck, various colors.

2012-2021		$700	$900

Gitane DG-255 Professional Gypsy Jazz

2017 Godin 5th Avenue

Godin A6 Ultra (A Series)

Godin Passion RG-3

MODEL YEAR	FEATURES	EXC. COND. LOW	HIGH

A Series
1990s-present. Electric-acoustic nylon strings, single-cut, chambered body, 6-, 11-, 12-string, various wood and colors.

1990s-2021	A12, 12-string	$850	$1,100
1990s-2021	A6, 6-string	$525	$700
2000-2017	A11 Glissentar, 11-string	$775	$1,000

Acousticaster (6)
1987-2020. Thin line single-cut chambered maple body, acoustic/electric, maple neck, 6-on-a-side tuners, spruce top.

1987-2020		$450	$600

Acousticaster 6 Deluxe
1994-2008. Acousticaster 6 with mahogany body.

1994-2008		$525	$700

Artisan ST I/ST I
1992-1998. Offset double-cut solidbody, birdseye maple top, 3 pickups.

1992-1998		$600	$800

Flat Five X
2002-2004. Single-cut, semi-hollow with f-holes, 3-way pickup system (magnetic to transducer).

2002-2004		$850	$1,100

Freeway Classic/Freeway Classic SA
2004-2015. Offset double-cut solidbody, birdseye maple top on translucent finishes, hum-single-hum pickups.

2004-2015		$525	$700

G-1000/G-2000/G-3000
1993-1996. Offset double-cut solidbody, extra large bass horn, various pickup options.

1993-1996		$300	$400

Jeff Cook Signature
1994-1995. Quilted maple top, light maple back, 2 twin rail and 1 humbucker pickups.

1994-1995		$525	$700

L.R. Baggs Signature
1990s. Single-cut chambered thinline electric, spruce top, mahogany body, EQ.

1990s		$525	$700

LG/LGT
1995-2011. Single-cut carved slab mahogany body, 2 Tetrad Combo pickups ('95-'97) or 2 Duncan SP-90 pickups ('98-present), various colors, satin lacquer finish. LGT with tremolo.

1995-2011		$350	$450

LGX/LGXT/LGX-SA
1996-2018. Single-cut maple-top carved solidbody, 2 Duncan humbuckers, various quality tops offered. LGXT with tremolo.

1996-2018	Standard top	$600	$800
1997-2018	SA synth access	$775	$1,000
1998-2018	AA top	$925	$1,200
1998-2018	AAA top	$1,000	$1,300

Montreal
2004-present. Chambered body carved from solid mahogany, f-holes, 2 humbuckers, saddle transducer, stereo mixing output.

2004-2021		$775	$1,000

Multiac Series
1994-present. Single-cut, thinline electric with solid spruce top, RMC Sensor System electronics, available in either nylon string or steel string versions, built-in EQ, program up/down buttons.

1994-2021	Various models	$600	$1,400

Passion RG-3
2011-present. Double-cut, 3 single-coil pickups, swamp ash body, rosewood neck (RN) or maple (MN), Indigo Burst finish with artic white pearloid 'guard.

2011-2021		$1,300	$1,700

Radiator
1999-2013. Single-cut, dual pickup, pearloid top, dot markers.

1999-2013		$275	$365

Redline Series
2007-2015. Maple body and neck, rosewood 'board, Redline 1 has 1 pickup, 2 and 3 have 2 pickups (3 has Floyd Rose), various colors.

2007-2011	Redline 1	$400	$525
2008-2015	Redline 2 & 3	$435	$575

SD Series
1990s-2012. Performance series, figured maple veneer top, maple neck, maple or rosewood 'board, various colors.

1990-2012	SD22, SD24	$300	$400

Solidac - Two Voice
2000-2009. Single-cut, 2-voice technology for electric or acoustic sound.

2000-2009		$375	$500

TC Signature
1987-1999. Single-cut, quilted maple top, 2 Tetrad Combo pickups.

1987-1999		$600	$775

Velocity
2007-2011. Offset double-cut, hum/single/single.

2007-2011		$600	$775

Gold Tone
1993-present. Wayne and Robyn Rogers build their intermediate and professional grade, production/custom guitars and basses in Titusville, Florida. They also build lap steels, mandolins, ukuleles, banjos and banjitars.

Goldbug Guitars
1997-present. Presentation grade, production/custom, acoustic and electric guitars built by luthier Sandy Winters in Delavan, Wisconsin.

Golden Hawaiian
1920s-1930s. Private branded lap guitar most likely made by one of the many Chicago makers for a small retailer, publisher, cataloger, or teaching studio.

Guitars

1920-1930s	Various models	$400	$650

Goldentone
1960s. Guitars made by Ibanez most likely in the mid to late '60s. Often have a stylized I (for Ibanez) on the tailpiece or an Ibanez logo on the headstock.

MODEL YEAR	FEATURES	EXC. COND. LOW	HIGH

Goldon

German manufacturer of high-quality archtops and other guitars before and shortly after WW II. After the war, they were located in East Germany and by the late 1940s were only making musical toys.

Goodall

1972-present. Premium grade, custom flat-tops and nylon-strings, built by luthier James Goodall originally in California and, since '92, in Kailua-Kona, Hawaii.

Classical
1986. Brazilian and cedar.

1986	BC425	$6,100	$8,000

Concert Jumbo
1998-present. Various woods.

2007-2021	Red cedar/ Indian rw	$3,100	$4,100
2007-2021	Sitka/figured koa	$3,100	$4,100

Concert Jumbo Cutaway
2004-2018. Rosewood.

2004-2018		$3,500	$4,600

Jumbo KJ
1995-2011. Sitka, koa.

1995-2011		$3,200	$4,100

RS Rosewood Standard
1989-1997. Indian rosewood back and sides.

1989-1997		$3,200	$4,100

Standard
1980s-present. Jumbo-style with wide waist, mahogany back and sides, sitka spruce top.

1980s-2021		$3,000	$3,900

Goodman Guitars

1975-present. Premium grade, custom/production, archtop, flat-top, classical, and electric guitars built by luthier Brad Goodman in Brewster, New York. He also builds mandolins.

Goran Custom Guitars

1998-present. Luthier Goran Djuric builds his professional and premium grade, custom, electric guitars in Belgrade, Serbia. He also builds effects.

Gordon-Smith

1979-present. Intermediate and professional grade, production/custom, semi-hollow and solidbody guitars built by luthier John Smith in Partington, England.

Gower

1955-1960s. Built in Nashville by Jay Gower, later joined by his son Randy. Gower is also associated with Billy Grammer and Grammer guitars.

G-55-2 Flat-Top
1955-1968. Square shoulder-style flat-top, triple abalone rosette, abalone fretboard trim, dot markers, natural.

1955-1968		$1,150	$1,500

G-65 Flat-Top
1955-1968. Square shoulder-style flat-top, lower belly bridge with pearl dots on bridge, dot markers, sunburst.

1955-1968		$875	$1,150

G-100 Flat-Top

1955-1968	Brazilian rosewood	$1,275	$1,650

Goya

1952-1996. Brand initially used by Hershman Musical Instrument Company of New York City, New York, in mid-'50s for acoustic guitars made in Sweden by Levin, particularly known for its classicals. From '58 to '61 they imported Hagstrom- and Galanti-made electrics labeled as Goya; in '62 they offered electrics made by Valco. In '67 they again offered electrics, this time made by Zero Sette in Castelfidardo, Italy. By '63 the company had become the Goya Musical Instrument Corporation, marketing primarily Goya acoustics. In '67 they again offered electrics, this time made by Zero Sette in Castelfidardo, Italy. Goya was purchased by Avnet, Inc., prior to '66, when Avnet purchased Guild Guitars. In '69, Goya was purchased by Kustom which offered the instruments until '71. Probably some '70s guitars were made in Japan. The brand name was purchased by C.F. Martin in '76, with Japanese-made acoustic guitars, solidbody electric guitars and basses, banjos and mandolins imported in around '78 and continuing into the '90s.

Classical
1955-1960s. Various models.

1955-1960s	G Series	$200	$1,200
1970s-80s	Japan	$400	$600

Flamenco
1955-1960s. Various models.

1955-1960s	FL Series	$200	$1,200

Folk
1950s-1980s. Various models.

1955-1960s	F Series	$200	$1,200

Model 80/Model 90
1959-1962. Single-cut body, replaceable modular pickup assembly, sparkle top.

1959-1962		$950	$1,250

Panther S-3
1967-1968. Double-cut solidbody, 3 pickups, Panther S-3 Goya logo, volume and tone knobs with 6 upper bass bout switches, bolt-on neck.

1967-1968		$950	$1,250

Rangemaster
1967-1968. Wide variety of models.

1967-1968		$850	$1,200

Steel
1955-1960s. Various models.

1955-1960s	M and S Series	$125	$350

Graf

See listing under Oskar Graf Guitars.

Goodall Concert Jumbo

1960s Goya Rangemaster

Imaged by Heritage Auctions, HA.com

1966 Grammer
Bill Lawlor

Granata Resonator

MODEL YEAR	FEATURES	EXC. COND. LOW	HIGH

Grammer

1965-1971. Acoustic guitars built in Nashville. Founded by country guitarist Bill Grammer, music store owner Clyde Reid and luthier J.W. Gower (who also built his own line). Grammer sold the company to Ampeg in '68 who sold it again in '71, but it quickly ceased business. Originally the Grammer headstock logo had an upper-case G, Ampeg-made instruments have a lower-case one.

G-10

1965-1970. Solid Brazilian rosewood back and sides, solid spruce top, large crown-shaped bridge, pearl dot markers, natural.

1965-1967	Grammer era	$2,200	$2,900
1968-1970	Ampeg era	$1,750	$2,300

G-20

1965-1970. Flamed maple, natural.

1965-1967	Grammer era	$1,900	$2,500
1968-1970	Ampeg era	$1,750	$2,300

G-30

1965-1970. Ribbon mahogany, natural.

1965-1967	Grammer era	$1,900	$2,500
1968-1970	Ampeg era	$1,750	$2,300

G-50

1965-1970. Top-of-the-line Grammer, Brazilian rosewood back and sides, Adirondack spruce top.

1965-1967	Grammer era	$2,500	$3,300
1968-1970	Ampeg era	$2,300	$3,000

S-30

1965-1970. Solid spruce top, solid ribbon mahogany back and sides.

1965-1967	Grammer era	$1,700	$2,200
1968-1970	Ampeg era	$1,450	$1,900

Granada

Late 1960s-1980s. Japanese-made acoustic, electric solid, semi-hollow and hollowbody guitars, many copies of classic American models. They also offered basses.

Acoustic

1970-1979. Import from Japan, various copy models.

1970-1979		$150	$250

Electric

1970-1979. Import from Japan, various copy models.

1970-1979		$200	$300

Granata Guitars

1989-present. Luthier Peter Granata builds his professional grade, custom, flat-top and resonator guitars in Oak Ridge, New Jersey.

Graveel

Production/custom, solidbody guitars built by luthier Dean Graveel in Indianapolis, Indiana.

Grazioso

1950s. Grazioso was a brand name used by Selmer in England on instruments made in Czechoslovakia. They replaced the brand with their Futurama line of guitars.

GRD

1978-1982. High-end acoustic and electric guitars produced in Charles Fox's Guitar Research & Design Center in Vermont. GRD introduced the original thin-line acoustic-electric guitar to the world at the '78 Winter NAMM show.

Great Divide Guitars

2009-2011. Budget and intermediate grade, production, flat-top guitars imported from China, designed by luthier Tom Bedell, Dan Mills and Sophia Yang. They also offer Bedell Guitars.

Greco

1960s-present. Brand name used in Japan and owned by Kanda Shokai. Fuji Gen Gakki, maker of many Hoshino/Ibanez guitars, also made many Greco models during the '70s; thus often Greco guitars are similar to Ibanez. During the '70s the company sold many high-quality copies of American designs, though by '75 they offered many weird-shaped original designs, including the Iceman and carved people shapes. By the late-'70s they were offering neck-through-body guitars. Currently offering solidbody, hollowbody and acoustic guitars and basses, including models licensed by Zemaitis.

Green, Aaron

1990-present. Premium and presentation grade, custom, classical and flamenco guitars built by luthier Aaron Green in Waltham, Massachusetts.

Greene & Campbell

2002-2005. Luthier Dean Campbell built his intermediate and professional grade, production/custom, solidbody guitars in Westwood, Massachusetts. Founding partner Jeffrey Greene left the company in '04; Greene earlier built guitars under his own name. In '05, Campbell changed the name to Campbell American Guitars.

Greene, Jeffrey

2000-2002. Professional grade, production/custom, electric solidbody guitars built by luthier Jeffrey Greene in West Kingston, Rhode Island. He went to work with Dean Campbell building the Greene & Campbell line of guitars.

Greenfield Guitars

1996-present. Luthier Michael Greenfield builds his production/custom, presentation grade, acoustic steel string, concert classical and archtop guitars in Montreal, Quebec.

Gretsch

1883-present. Currently Gretsch offers intermediate, professional, and premium grade, production, acoustic, solidbody, hollowbody, double neck, resonator and Hawaiian guitars. They also offer basses, amps and lap steels. In 2012 they again started offering mandolins, ukuleles and banjos.

MODEL YEAR	FEATURES	EXC. COND. LOW	HIGH

Previous brands included Gretsch, Rex, 20th Century, Recording King (for Montgomery Ward), Dorado (Japanese imports). Founded by Friedrich Gretsch in Brooklyn, New York, making drums, banjos, tambourines, and toy instruments which were sold to large distributors including C. Bruno and Wurlitzer. Upon early death of Friedrich, son Fred Gretsch, Sr. took over business at age 15. By the turn of the century the company was also making mandolins. In the '20s, they were distributing Rex and 20th Century brands, some made by Gretsch, some by others such as Kay. Charles "Duke" Kramer joined Gretsch in '35. In '40 Gretsch purchased Bacon & Day banjos. Fred Gretsch, Sr. retired in '42 and was replaced by sons Fred, Jr. and Bill. Fred departs for Navy and Bill runs company until his death in '48, when Fred resumes control. After the war the decision was made to promote the Gretsch brand rather than selling to distributors, though some jobbing continues. Kramer becomes Chicago branch manager in '48.

In '67 Baldwin of Cincinnati bought Gretsch. During '70-'72 the factory relocated from Brooklyn to Booneville, Arkansas and company headquarters are moved to Cincinnati. A '72 factory fire drastically reduced production for next two years. In '78 Baldwin bought Kustom amps and sold Gretsch to Kustom's Charlie Roy, and headquarters are moved to Chanute, Kansas. Duke Kramer retired in '80. Guitar production ends '80-'81. Ca. '83 ownership reverted back to Baldwin and Kramer was asked to arrange the sale of the company. In '84 Fred Gretsch III was contacted and in '85 Gretsch guitars came back to the Gretsch family and Fred Gretsch Enterprises, Ltd (FGE). Initial Gretsch Enterprise models were imports made by Japan's Terada Company. In '95, some U.S.-made models were introduced. In 2003, Gretsch granted Fender the rights to develop, produce, market and distribute Gretsch guitars worldwide, including development of new products.

Binding rot can be a problem on 1950s models and prices shown are for fully original, unrestored bindings.

12-String Electric Archtop (6075/6076)
1967-1972. 16" double-cut, 2 Super Tron pickups, 17" body option available, sunburst (6075) or natural (6076).

1967-1972		$2,300	$3,000

12-String Flat-Top (6020)
1969-1972. 15 1/5" body, mahogany back and sides, spruce top, slotted headstock, dot markers.

1969-1972		$1,100	$1,450

Anniversary (6124/6125)
1958-1972, 1993-1999. Single-cut hollow body archtop, 1 pickup (Filtron '58-'60, Hi-Lo Tron '61 on), bound body, named for Gretsch's 75th anniversary. 6125 is 2-tone green with 2-tone tan an option, 6124 sunburst. Model numbers revived in '90s.

1958-1959	Green 2-tone	$2,900	$3,800
1958-1959	Sunburst	$2,050	$2,650

1960-1961	Green 2-tone or tan	$2,700	$3,600
1960-1961	Sunburst	$1,750	$2,325
1962-1964	Green 2-tone or tan	$2,200	$2,900
1962-1964	Sunburst	$1,600	$2,125
1965-1966	Various colors	$1,600	$2,125
1967-1969	Various colors	$1,375	$1,800
1970-1972	Various colors	$1,250	$1,625

Anniversary Tenor (6124)
1958-1971. Gretsch offered many models with the 4-string tenor option and also made small batches of tenors, with the same colors and pickups as standard models.

1958-1971		$1,550	$2,050

Anniversary Reissue (6124/6125)
1993-1999. 1 pickup Anniversary reissue, 6124 in sunburst, 6125 2-tone green.

1993-1999		$1,450	$1,875

Anniversary Reissue (6117/6118)
1993-present. 2 pickup like Double Anniversary, 6118 in 2-tone green with (T) or without Bigsby, 6117 is sunburst.

1993-2015	6117	$1,550	$2,000
1993-2021	6118	$1,550	$2,000

Astro-Jet (6126)
1965-1967. Solid body electric, double-cut, 2 pickups, vibrato, 4/2 tuner arrangement, red top with black back and sides.

1965-1967		$2,200	$2,900

Atkins Axe (7685/7686)
1976-1980. Solid body electric, pointed single-cut, 2 pickups, ebony stain (7685) or red rosewood stain (7686), called the Super Axe with added on-board effects.

1976-1980		$1,350	$1,775

Atkins Super Axe (7680/7681)
1976-1981. Pointed single-cut solid body with built-in phaser and sustain, five knobs, three switches, Red Rosewood (7680) or Ebony (7681) stains.

1976-1981		$2,050	$2,675

Bikini (6023/6024/6025)
1961-1962. Solid body electric, separate 6-string and bass neck-body units that slide into 1 of 3 body butterflies - 1 for the 6-string only (6023), 1 for bass only (6024), 1 for double neck (6 and bass - 6025). Components could be purchased separately.

1961-1962	6023/6024, single	$1,050	$1,400
1961-1962	6025, double	$2,150	$2,800

Billy-Bo Jupiter Thunderbird (6199)
2005-present. Billy Gibbons and Bo Diddley influenced, chambered mahogany body, laminate maple top, 2 pickups.

2005-2021		$2,250	$2,900

Black Falcon (6136BK/TBK/DSBK)
1992-1997, 2003-2015. Black version of Falcon, single-cut, 2.75" body, oversize f-holes, G tailpiece, DSBK with DynaSonic pickups replaces Filter'Tron BK in '06. Had the Limited Edition 1955 designation for '96-'97. Bigsby-equipped TBK offered '04-present.

1992-2015		$2,600	$3,400

Black Falcon (7594BK)
1992-1998. Black version of G7594 Falcon, double-cut, 2" thick body, Bigsby.

1992-1998		$2,600	$3,400

1961 Gretsch Bikini (6025)
Randy Barnett

Gretsch Billy-Bo Jupiter Thunderbird (6199)

GUITARS

1956 Gretsch Chet Atkins Hollow Body 6120

Jim Hilmar

1960 Gretsch Chet Atkins Hollowbody 6120

Paul Harbinson

MODEL YEAR	FEATURES	EXC. COND. LOW	HIGH

Black Falcon I (7593BK)
1993-1998, 2003-2005. G63136BK with Bigsby and standard f-holes. Came back in '03 as Black Falcon I with wire handle Gretsch Bigsby tailpiece.

1993-1998		$2,600	$3,400

Black Hawk (6100/6101)
1967-1972. Hollow body archtop, double-cut, 2 pickups, G tailpiece or Bigsby vibrato, bound body and neck, sunburst (6100) or black (6101).

1967-1972	6100, sunburst	$2,600	$3,400
1967-1972	6101, black	$2,600	$3,400

Black Penguin (6134B)
2003-2015. Jet black version.

2003-2015		$2,600	$3,400

Bo Diddley (1810/5810)
2000-2015. Korean-made version.

2000-2015		$225	$300

Bo Diddley (6138)
1999-present. Reproduction of rectangle-shaped, semi-hollow guitar originally made for Diddley by Gretsch, Firebird Red.

1999-2021		$1,325	$1,775

Broadkaster (Hollow Body)
1975-1980. Double-cut archtop, hollow body, 2 pickups, natural or sunburst. Red available '77-'80.

1975-1977	7603, Bigsby, natural	$1,000	$1,300
1975-1977	7604, Bigsby, sunburst	$1,000	$1,300
1975-1977	7607, G tailpiece, natural	$1,000	$1,300
1975-1977	7608, G tailpiece, sunburst	$1,000	$1,300
1977-1980	7609, red	$1,000	$1,300

Broadkaster (Solid Body)
1975-1979. Double-cut, maple body, 2 pickups, bolt-on neck, natural (7600) or sunburst (7601).

1975-1979	7600 and 7601	$1,000	$1,300

BST 1000 Beast
1979-1980. Single-cut solid body, bolt-on neck, mahogany body, available with 1 pickup in walnut stain (8210) or red stain (8216) or 2 pickups in walnut (7617, 8215, 8217) or red stain (8211).

1979-1980		$800	$1,050

BST 2000 Beast
1979. Symmetrical double-cut solid body of mahogany, 2 humbucking pickups, bolt-on neck, walnut stain (7620 or 8220) or red stain (8221).

1979		$800	$1,050

BST 5000 Beast
1979-1980. Asymmetrical double-cut solid body, neck-thru, walnut and maple construction, 2 humbucker pickups, stud tailpiece, natural walnut/maple (8250).

1979-1980		$875	$1,150

Burl Ives (6004)
1949-1955. Flat-top acoustic, mahogany back and sides, bound body, natural top (6004).

1949-1955		$875	$1,150

Chet Atkins Country Gentleman (6122/7670)
1957-1981. Hollow body, single-cut to late-'62 and double after, 2 pickups, painted f-holes until '72, real

---

after, mahogany finish (6122). Model number changes to 7670 in '71. Guitars made during and after '64 might have replaced body binding which reduces the value shown by about 10% or more.

1957-1959		$10,000	$13,000
1960		$6,600	$8,600
1961		$6,100	$8,000
1962-1963	George Harrison specs	$4,700	$6,100
1964		$4,000	$5,200
1965		$3,600	$4,700
1966-1970		$2,900	$3,800
1971-1981	7670	$2,650	$3,500

Chet Atkins Country Gentleman (6122-1958)
2007-2015. Single-cut reissue of '58.

2007-2015		$2,150	$2,800

Chet Atkins Country Gentleman (6122-1962)
2007-2015. Double-cut reissue of '62, double muffler (mutes) system, Filter'Trons.

2007-2015		$2,150	$2,800

Chet Atkins Hollow Body (6120)
1954-1966, 2007-2015. Archtop electric, single-cut to '61, double after, 2 pickups, vibrato, f-holes (real to '61 and fake after), cactus and cows engraved block inlays '54-early '56, G brand on top '54-'56, orange finish (6120). Renamed Chet Atkins Nashville in '67. Reissued single-cut in '07.

1954-1955	G brand, Western	$13,200	$17,300
1955-1956	Non-engraved, amber red	$11,500	$15,200
1957-1959	No G-brand	$10,000	$13,000
1960-1961	Single-cut	$7,700	$10,100
1961-1966	Double-cut	$3,600	$4,750
2007-2015	Single-cut	$1,825	$2,375

Chet Atkins Nashville (6120/7660)
1967-1980. Replaced Chet Atkins Hollow Body (6120), electric archtop, double-cut, 2 pickups, amber red (orange). Renumbered 7660 in '72, reissued in '90 as the Model 6120 Nashville.

1967-1969	6120	$2,600	$3,400
1970-1971	6120	$2,200	$2,900
1972-1980	7660	$1,975	$2,600

Chet Atkins Nashville (6120DC)
2007-2016. Double-cut hollow body based on '62 model, gold plated 'guard with Atkin's signature.

2007-2016		$2,025	$2,650

Chet Atkins Hollow Body (6120W-1957)
2007-2009. Western Maple Stain, western block inlays, Bigsby.

2007-2009		$2,150	$2,800

Brian Setzer Black Phoenix (6136-SLBP)
2005-2015. Artist Signature Series, nitro gloss black.

2005-2015		$2,400	$3,100

Brian Setzer Hot Rod (6120SHx)
1999-present. Like SSL, but with only pickup switch and 1 master volume control, various colors.

1999-2020		$1,575	$2,050

Brian Setzer Nashville (6120SSL, etc.)
1993-present. Hollow body electric, double-cut, 2 Alnico PAF Filtertron pickups, based on the classic Gretsch 6120.

1993-2021	Western Orange	$2,400	$3,100

MODEL YEAR	FEATURES	EXC. COND. LOW	HIGH

Chet Atkins Junior
1970. Archtop, single-cut, 1 pickup, vibrato, open f-holes, double-bound body, orange stain.

1970		$1,200	$1,575

Duane Eddy (6210DE)
1997-2003. 6120 style, 2 DeArmond single coils, Bigsby, orange.

1997-2003		$2,150	$2,800

Duane Eddy Signature Hollow Body (6120DE)
2011-present. Single-cut, Western Orange stain lacquer finish.

2011-2021		$2,150	$2,800

Eddie Cochran Signature Hollow Body (6120)
2011-present. Artist Signature Edition, maple body, rosewood 'board, Bigsby, Western maple stain.

2011-2021		$2,150	$2,800

Keith Scott Nashville (6120KS)
1999-2013. Hump-back inlays, gold hardware, metallic gold finish.

1999-2013		$2,025	$2,675

Nashville Double Neck 6/12 (6120)
1997-2002. Built in Japan, few made, all gold hardware, necks are maple with ebony 'boards, orange finish.

1997-2002		$2,775	$3,600

Nashville Jr. (6120-JR/JR2)
1998-2004. Orange, 2 pickups.

1998-2004		$1,200	$1,575

New Nashville (6120N)
2001-2003. Single-cut, humptop inlays, gold hardware.

2001-2003		$2,025	$2,650

Reverend Horton Heat (6120RHH)
2005-present. Cows and cactus inlays, TV jones pickups.

2005-2021		$2,150	$2,800

Chet Atkins Solid Body (6121)
1955-1963. Solid body electric, single-cut, maple or knotty pine top, 2 pickups, Bigsby vibrato, G brand until '57, multi-bound top, brown mahogany, orange finish (6121).

1955-1956		$10,700	$14,000
1957	G brand	$9,000	$11,800
1957-1959	No G brand	$8,000	$10,500
1960	Single-cut	$7,400	$9,700
1961-1963	Double-cut	$6,000	$7,900

Chet Atkins Tennessean (6119/7655)
1958-1980. Archtop electric, single-cut, 1 pickup until early-'61 and 2 after, vibrato. Renumbered as the 7655 in '71.

1958-1960	1 Filter-Tron	$2,900	$3,800
1960-1961	1 Hi-Lo	$2,700	$3,500
1961-1964	2 Hi-Lo	$3,000	$3,900
1965-1967	2 pickups	$2,900	$3,800
1968-1970	2 pickups	$2,700	$3,500
1971-1980	7655	$2,700	$3,500

Chet Atkins Tennessee Rose (6119-1959, 1962)
1995-2015. Import, 16" maple body, maple neck, dual FilterTron pickups.

1995-2015	1959 and 1962	$1,850	$2,400

Clipper (6185/6186/6187/7555)
1958-1975. Archtop electric, single-cut, sunburst, 1 pickup (6186) until '72 and 2 pickups (6185) from '72-'75, also available in 1 pickup natural (6187) from '59-'61.

1958-1961	6186	$1,200	$1,575
1959-1961	6187	$1,350	$1,725
1962-1967	6186	$1,175	$1,525
1968-1971	6186	$1,075	$1,400
1972-1975	7555	$1,325	$1,725

Committee (7628)
1977-1980. Neck-thru electric solid body, double-cut, walnut and maple body, 2 pickups, 4 knobs, natural.

1977-1980		$950	$1,250

Constellation (6030/6031)
1955-1960. Renamed from Synchromatic 6030 and 6031, archtop acoustic, single-cut, G tailpiece, humped block inlay.

1955-1960		$1,850	$2,425

Convertible (6199)
1955-1958. Archtop electric, single-cut, 1 pickup, multi-bound body, G tailpiece, renamed Sal Salvador in '58.

1955-1958		$2,450	$3,250

Corsair
1955-1960. Renamed from Synchromatic 100, archtop acoustic, bound body and headstock, G tailpiece, available in sunburst (6014), natural (6015) or burgundy (6016).

1955-1960	6014, 6015, 6016	$1,050	$1,375

Corvette (Hollow Body)
1955-1959. Renamed from Electromatic Spanish, archtop electric, 1 pickup, f-holes, bound body, Electromatic on headstock, non-cut, sunburst (6182), Jaguar Tan or natural (6184), and ivory with rounded cutaway (6187).

1955-1959	6182, sunburst	$1,200	$1,575
1955-1959	6184, Jaguar Tan	$1,575	$2,075
1955-1959	6184, natural	$1,950	$2,575
1957-1959	6187, ivory	$2,325	$3,075

Corvette (Solid Body)
1961-1972, 1976-1978. Double-cut slab solid body. Mahogany 6132 and cherry 6134 1 pickup for '61-'68. 2 pickup mahogany 6135 and cherry 7623 available by '63-'72 and '76-'78. From late-'61 through '63 a Twist option was offered featuring a red candy stripe 'guard. Platinum Gray 6133 available for '61-'63 and the Gold Duke and Silver Duke sparkle finishes were offered in '66.

1961-1962	Mahogany, cherry	$1,150	$1,500
1961-1963	Platinum Gray	$1,750	$2,300
1961-1963	Twist 'guard	$1,750	$2,300
1963-1965	Custom color, 1 pu	$1,750	$2,300
1963-1965	Custom color, 2 pu	$2,100	$2,750
1963-1965	Mahogany, cherry, 1 pu	$900	$1,200
1963-1965	Mahogany, cherry, 2 pu	$1,275	$1,675
1966	Gold Duke	$1,750	$2,300
1966	Silver Duke	$1,750	$2,300

Gretsch Brian Setzer Hot Rod

Gretsch Chet Atkins Tennessean (6119/7655)

Darien Zalefsky,

GUITARS

1961 Gretsch Country Club
Geoff Parsons

1964 Gretsch Double Anniversary Mono (6117/6118)
Guitar Maniacs

MODEL YEAR	FEATURES	EXC. COND. LOW	HIGH
1966-1968	Mahogany, cherry, 1 pu	$1,000	$1,300
1966-1968	Mahogany, cherry, 2 pu	$1,200	$1,575
1969-1972	Mahogany, cherry, 2 pu	$1,175	$1,550
1976-1978	7623, 2 pu	$975	$1,275

Corvette/CVT (5135)
2006-2018. Like double-cut solid body Corvette, 2 Mega'Tron pickups, Bigsby, becomes the CVT in '10.

2006-2018		$610	$810

Country Classic I/II (6122 Reissue)
1989-2006. Country Gentleman reissue in '58 (I) and '62 (II) specs. Also cataloged as G6122-1958 and G6122-1962 Country Classic.

1989-2006	'58, single-cut	$2,150	$2,800
1989-2006	'62, double-cut	$2,150	$2,800

Country Classic II Custom Edition (6122)
2005. Reissue of George Harrison's 2nd 6122 Country Gentleman, the Custom Edition has TV Jones Filtertron pickups.

2005		$2,150	$2,800

Country Club
1954-1981. Renamed from Electro II Cutaway, archtop electric, single-cut, 2 pickups (Filter Trons after '57), G tailpiece, multi-bound, various colors.

1954-1958	Sunburst	$4,450	$5,775
1954-1959	Cadillac Green	$5,700	$7,500
1954-1959	Natural	$5,150	$6,750
1959	Sunburst	$5,150	$6,750
1960-1964	Cadillac Green	$4,550	$6,000
1960-1964	Sunburst	$3,500	$4,500
1961-1962	Natural	$3,500	$4,500
1965-1969	Sunburst or walnut	$2,300	$3,000
1970-1981	Various colors	$2,400	$3,200

Country Club 1955 (6196-1955)(FGE)
1995-1999. U.S.-made reissue of Country Club, single-cut, 2 DeArmond pickups, hand-rubbed lacquer finish.

1995-1999		$2,150	$2,800

Country Club (6196, etc.)
2001-present. Includes Cadillac Green (G6196, '01-present), sunburst (G6192, '03-'08), amber natural (G6193,'03-'08), Bamboo Yellow (G6196TSP-BY, '09-'13), and smoky gray and violet 2-tone (G6196TSP-2G, '09-'12), G6196T-59GE Golden Era Edition ('16-present), T means Bigsby.

2001-2021	Cadillac Green	$2,150	$2,800
2009-2013	Bamboo Yellow	$2,150	$2,800

Country Roc (7620)
1974-1978. Single-cut solid body, 2 pickups, belt buckle tailpiece, western scene fretboard inlays, G brand, tooled leather side trim.

1974-1978		$2,200	$2,900

Custom (6117)
1964-1968. Limited production, smaller thinner version of Double Anniversary model, 2 pickups, cat's eye soundholes, red or black finish.

1964		$3,600	$4,700
1965-1966		$3,100	$4,100
1967-1968		$2,800	$3,700

MODEL YEAR	FEATURES	EXC. COND. LOW	HIGH

Deluxe Chet (7680/7681)
1972-1974. Electric archtop with rounded cutaway, Autumn Red (7680) or brown walnut (7681) finishes.

1972-1974		$2,200	$2,900

Deluxe Flat-Top (7535)
1972-1978. 16" redwood top, mahogany back and sides.

1972-1978		$2,000	$2,600

Double Anniversary Mono (6117/6118)
1958-1976. Archtop electric, single-cut, 2 pickups, stereo optional until '63, sunburst (6117) or green 2-tone (6118). Reissued in '93 as the Anniversary 6117 and 6118.

1958-1959	Green 2-tone	$3,600	$4,700
1958-1959	Sunburst	$2,600	$3,400
1960-1961	Green 2-tone	$2,800	$3,700
1960-1961	Sunburst	$2,350	$3,100
1962-1964	Green 2-tone or tan	$2,900	$3,800
1962-1964	Sunburst	$2,350	$3,100
1965-1966	Various colors	$1,700	$2,225
1967-1969	Various colors	$1,425	$1,875
1970-1976	Various colors	$1,275	$1,675

Double Anniversary Stereo (6111/6112)
1961-1963. One stereo channel/signal per pickup, sunburst (6111) or green (6112).

1961-1963	Green	$2,800	$3,700
1961-1963	Sunburst	$2,350	$3,100

Duo-Jet (6128)
1953-1971. Solid body electric, single-cut until '61, double after, 2 pickups, block inlays to late '56, then humptop until early '58, then thumbprint inlays, black (6128) with a few special order Cadillac Green, sparkle finishes were offered '63-'66, reissued in '90.

1953-1956	Black, single-cut	$6,500	$8,600
1956-1958	Black, humptop	$7,300	$9,600
1956-1958	Cadillac Green	$8,700	$11,400
1958-1960	Black, thumbprint	$5,200	$6,800
1961-1964	Black, double-cut	$4,325	$5,625
1963-1964	Sparkle, double-cut	$5,200	$6,800
1965-1966	Sparkle, double-cut	$4,300	$5,625
1965-1971	Black	$3,500	$4,600

Duo-Jet (6128TCG)
2005-2016. Cadillac Green, gold hardware, Bigsby.

2005-2016		$2,150	$2,800

Duo-Jet Reissue (6128/6128T)
1990-2017. Reissue of the '50s solid body, optional Bigsby (G6128T). Replaced by Vintage Select Edition series.

1990-2017		$1,750	$2,300

Duo-Jet Tenor (6127)
1954-1960. Electric tenor, 4 strings, block inlays, black.

1954-1960		$3,475	$4,550

Duo-Jet Vintage Select Edition '59 (6128T-59)
2017-present. Bigsby, TV Jones Filter 'Trons, black.

2017-2021		$2,150	$2,800

Elliot Easton Signature Duo-Jet (6128TEE)
2000-2005. Bigsby, gold hardware, Cadillac Green (TEE), red (TREE), black (TBEE).

2000-2005		$2,150	$2,800

MODEL YEAR	FEATURES	EXC. COND. LOW	HIGH

Eldorado (6040/6041)

1955-1970, 1991-1997. This is the larger 18" version, renamed from Synchromatic 400, archtop acoustic, single-cut, triple-bound fretboard and peghead, sunburst (6040) or natural (6041). Reintroduced in '91, made by Heritage in Kalamazoo, as the G410 Synchromatic Eldorado in sunburst or natural (G410M).

1955-1959	Natural	$3,000	$4,000
1955-1959	Sunburst	$2,400	$3,200
1960-1963	Natural	$2,200	$2,900
1960-1963	Sunburst	$2,000	$2,600
1964	Natural	$1,850	$2,450
1964	Sunburst	$1,750	$2,300
1965-1997	Natural, sunburst	$1,550	$2,000

Eldorado (6038/6039)

1959-1968. The smaller 17" version, named Fleetwood from '55 to '58, sunburst (6038) or natural (6039), also available as a full body non-cutaway.

1959-1964	Natural, sunburst	$1,450	$1,900
1965-1968	Natural, sunburst	$1,200	$1,600

Electro Classic (6006/6495)

1969-1973. Classical flat-top with piezo pickup.

1969-1970	6006	$725	$950
1971-1973	6495	$725	$950

Electro II Cutaway (6192/6193)

1951-1954. Archtop electric, single-cut, Melita bridge by '53, 2 pickups, f-holes, sunburst (6192) or natural (6193). Renamed Country Club in '54.

1951-1954	6192, sunburst	$3,950	$5,200
1951-1954	6193, natural	$4,300	$5,600

Electro II Non-Cutaway (6187/6188)

1951-1954. 16" electric archtop, 2 DeArmonds, large f-holes, block markers, 6187 sunburst, 6188 natural, label is Model 6187-8, vertical Electromatic logo on headstock.

1951-1954	6187, sunburst	$3,500	$4,600
1951-1954	6188, natural	$3,500	$4,600

Electromatic (5420T)

2013-present. Hollow body, single-cut, Bigsby.

2013-2021		$610	$810

Electromatic (5422-12)

2013-present. 12-string 5422.

2013-2021		$610	$810

Electromatic (5422T)

2013-present. Hollow body, double-cut, Bigsby.

2013-2021		$610	$810

Electromatic Hollow Body (5120/5125-29/5420)

2005-2020. Single-cut, 2 dual-coils, Bigsby, black, Aspen Green, sunburst or orange. With Filter'Tron pickups in '13 (5420).

2005-2020		$610	$810

Electromatic Hollow Body (5122/5422)

2009-2014. Double-cut version of G5120, 2 dual-coils, Bigsby, black, trans red or walnut. With Filter'Tron pickups in '13 (5422). Replaced with G5422T.

2009-2014		$610	$810

Tim Armstrong Signature Electromatic (5191BK-TA)

2010-2021		$750	$1,000

Electromatic Spanish (6185/6185N)

1940-1955. Hollow body, 17" wide, 1 pickup, sunburst (6185) or natural (6185N). Renamed Corvette (hollowbody) in '55.

1940-1949	Sunburst	$1,500	$2,000
1950-1955	Natural	$1,500	$2,000
1950-1955	Sunburst	$1,400	$1,850

Fleetwood (6038/6039)

1955-1958. Named Synchromatic prior to '55, single-cut, sunburst (6038) or natural (6039). Renamed Eldorado in '59, available by custom order.

1955-1958	Natural	$3,400	$4,500
1955-1958	Sunburst	$2,700	$3,550

Folk/Folk Singing (6003/7505/7506)

1963-1975. Lower-model of Gretsch flat-tops, 14 1/4", mahogany back and sides. Renamed from Jimmie Rodgers model, renamed Folk Singing in '63.

1963-1964		$800	$1,050
1965-1969		$675	$900
1970-1975		$575	$750

Golden Classic (Hauser/6000)

1961-1969. Grand Concert body size, nylon-string classical, 14 1/4" spruce top, mahogany back and sides, multiple inlaid sound hole purfling, inlaid headstock.

1961-1969		$525	$700

Grand Concert (6003)

1955-1959. Lower-model of Gretsch flat-tops, 14 1/4", mahogany back and sides. Renamed from Model 6003 and renamed Jimmie Rodgers in '59.

1955-1959		$825	$1,100

Guitar-Banjo

1920s. 6-string guitar neck on banjo body, slotted headstock, open back.

1920s		$625	$825

Jet 21

Late-1940s. 16" acoustic archtop, Jet 21 engraved logo on headstock, bound top and back, white 'guard, jet black finish.

1947-1948		$775	$1,025

Jet Firebird (6131)

1955-1971. Solid body electric, single-cut until '61, double '61-'71, 2 pickups, black body with red top, block inlays to late '56, then humptop until early '58, then thumbprint inlays.

1955-1956	Single-cut	$6,500	$8,600
1957-1958	Single-cut	$7,300	$9,600
1959-1960	Single-cut	$5,200	$6,800
1961-1964	Double-cut	$4,325	$5,625
1965-1967		$3,500	$4,600
1968-1971	Super Trons	$3,500	$4,600

Jet Firebird Reissue/Power Jet Firebird (6131/6131T)

1989-1997, 2003-2019. Single-cut '58 specs, red top, 2 FilterTrons, thumbprint markers, gold hardware for '91-'05, currently chrome. Bigsby available (T). Non-Bigsby 6131 ends in '05. DynaSonic-equipped TDS starts in '05 and TV Jones PowerTrons (TVP) in '06.

2003-2019		$1,700	$2,200

Jet/Pearl Jet/Blue Pearl Jet (6129/6129T)

1996-2011. Chambered mahogany body with maple top, unique Pearl or Blue Pearl finish.

1996-2011		$1,650	$2,200

2016 Gretsch Duo-Jet Reissue (6128T)
David Crunden

2015 Gretsch Electromatic (5422T)
David Mullins

2019 Gretsch Malcom Young
Signature Jet (6131-MY)

1967 Gretsch Rally (6104/6105)
Rivington Guitars

MODEL YEAR	FEATURES	EXC. COND. LOW	HIGH

Jimmie Rodgers (6003)
1959-1962. 14" flat-top with round hole, mahogany back and sides, renamed from Grand Concert and renamed Folk Singing in '63.

1959-1962		$825	$1,100

Jumbo Synchromatic (125F)
1947-1955. 17" flat-top, triangular soundhole, bound top and back, metal bridge anchor plate, adjustable wood bridge, natural top with sunburst back and sides or optional translucent white-blond top and sides.

1947-1955	Natural	$2,250	$2,950
1947-1955	White-blond	$2,500	$3,300

Malcom Young Signature Jet (6131-MY)
2018-present. Professional Collection series, double-cut mahogany body, maple top, aged white binding, semi-gloss natural finish.

2018-2021		$2,150	$2,800

Model 25 (Acoustic)
1933-1939. 16" archtop, no binding on top or back, dot markers, sunburst.

1933-1939		$675	$900

Model 30 (Acoustic)
1939-1949. 16" archtop, top binding, dot markers, sunburst.

1939-1949		$775	$1,025

Model 35 (Acoustic)
1933-1949. 16" archtop, single-bound top and back, dot markers, sunburst.

1933-1949		$850	$1,125

Model 40 Hawaiian (Acoustic)
1936-1949. Flat-top, bound top and neck, diamond inlays.

1936-1949		$950	$1,250

Model 50/50R (Acoustic)
1936-1949. Acoustic archtop, f-holes. Model 50R ('36-'39) has round soundhole.

1936-1939	TG-50 Tenor	$700	$925
1936-1949	50/50R	$1,075	$1,400

Model 65 (Acoustic)
1933-1939. Archtop acoustic, bound body, amber.

1933-1939		$1,175	$1,550

Model 75 Tenor (Acoustic)
1933-1949. 4-string tenor.

1933-1949		$775	$1,025

Model 6003
1951-1955. 14 1/4", mahogany back and sides, renamed Grand Concert in '55.

1951-1954		$825	$1,100

Monkees
Late 1966-1968. Hollow body electric, double-cut, 2 pickups, Monkees logo on 'guard, bound top, f-holes and neck, vibrato, red.

1966-1968		$3,700	$4,800

New Yorker
Ca.1949-1970. Archtop acoustic, f-holes, sunburst.

1949-1959		$1,000	$1,300
1960-1964		$925	$1,225
1965-1969		$800	$1,050
1970		$675	$900

New Yorker Tenor (6050)
1950s. 4-string tenor version.

1950s		$600	$775

Ozark/Ozark Soft String (6005)
1965-1968. 16" classical, rosewood back and sides.

1965-1968		$600	$775

Princess (6106)
1963. Corvette-type solid body double-cut, 1 pickup, vibrato, gold parts, colors available were white/grape, blue/white, pink/white, or white/gold, often sold with the Princess amp.

1963		$2,100	$2,800

Rally (6104/6105)
1967-1969. Archtop, double-cut, 2 pickups, vibrato, racing stripe on truss rod cover and pickguard, Rally Green (6104) or Bamboo Yellow (6105).

1967-1969	6104 or 6105	$2,300	$3,000

Rambler (6115)
1957-1961. Small body electric archtop, single-cut, 1 DeArmond pickup '57-59, then 1 Hi-Lo 'Tron '60-'61, G tailpiece, bound body and headstock.

1957-1959	DeArmond	$1,550	$2,050
1960-1961	Hi-Lo 'Tron	$1,300	$1,700

Rancher
1954-1980. Flat-top acoustic, triangle soundhole, Western theme inlay, G brand until '61 and '75 and after, Golden Red (orange), reissued in '90.

1954-1957	G brand	$5,400	$7,100
1958-1961	G brand	$4,900	$6,400
1962-1964	No G brand	$3,900	$5,100
1965-1969	No G brand	$3,100	$4,100
1970-1974	No G brand	$2,600	$3,400
1975-1980	G brand	$2,600	$3,400

Roc I/Roc II (7635/7621)
1974-1976. Electric solid body, mahogany, single-cut, Duo-Jet-style body, 1 pickup (7635) or 2 pickups (7621), bound body and neck.

1974-1976	Roc I	$1,525	$2,000
1974-1977	Roc II	$1,750	$2,300

Roc Jet
1970-1980. Electric solid body, single-cut, 2 pickups, adjustamatic bridge, black, cherry, pumpkin or walnut.

1970-1980		$2,000	$2,600

Round-Up (6130)
1954-1960. Electric solid body, single-cut, 2 pickups, G brand, belt buckle tailpiece, maple, pine, knotty pine or orange. Reissued in '90.

1954-1956	Knotty pine (2 knots)	$13,000	$17,000
1954-1956	Knotty pine (4 knots)	$14,500	$19,000
1954-1956	Mahogany (few made)	$12,000	$15,800
1954-1956	Maple	$12,000	$15,800
1954-1956	Pine	$13,000	$17,000
1957-1960	Orange	$12,000	$15,800

Round-Up Reissue (6121/6121W)
1989-1995, 2003-2006. Based on the '50s model, Bigsby, Western Orange.

1989-2006		$1,775	$2,300

MODEL YEAR	FEATURES	EXC. COND. LOW	HIGH

Round-Up Western Leather Trim (6130)
2006-2007. Higher-end reissue of '55 Round-Up, G brand, tooled leather trim around edge, cactus and cows inlays.

2006-2007		$2,200	$2,900

Round-Up Knotty Pine (6130KPW)
2008-2010. Like '06 6130 but with belt buckle tailpiece and knotty pine top.

2008-2010		$3,000	$4,000

Sal Fabraio (6117)
1964-1968. Double-cut thin electric archtop, distinctive cats-eye f-holes, 2 pickups, sunburst, ordered for resale by guitar teacher Sal Fabraio.

1964-1968		$2,100	$2,800

Sal Salvador (6199)
1958-1968. Electric archtop, single-cut, 1 pickup, triple-bound neck and headstock, sunburst.

1958-1959		$2,475	$3,250
1960-1962		$2,175	$2,850
1963-1964		$1,800	$2,350
1965-1968		$1,600	$2,100

Sho Bro (Hawaiian/Spanish)
1969-1978. Flat-top acoustic, multi-bound, resonator, lucite fretboard, Hawaiian version non-cut, square neck and Spanish version non- or single-cut, round neck.

1969-1978	Hawaiian	$875	$1,150
1969-1978	Spanish	$825	$1,100

Sierra Jumbo (3700)
1999-2005. Historic series, single-cut jumbo body, triangular soundhole, sunburst finish.

1999-2005		$425	$550

Silver Classic (Hauser/6001)
1961-1969. Grand Concert body size, nylon-string classical. Similar to Golden Classic but with less fancy appointments.

1961-1969		$450	$600

Silver Falcon (6136SL) (1955) (T)
1995-1999, 2003-2005. Black finish, silver features, single cut, G tailpiece available until '05, T for Bigsby available starting '05. Had the 1955 designation in the '90s.

1995-1999		$2,150	$2,800

Silver Falcon (7594SL)
1995-1999. Black finish and silver features, double-cut, 2" thick body.

1995-1999		$2,150	$2,800

Silver Jet (6129)
1954-1963. Solid body electric, single-cut until '61, double '61-'63, 2 pickups, Duo-Jet with silver sparkle top, reissued in '89. Optional sparkle colors were offered but were not given their own model numbers; refer to Duo-Jet listing for optional colors.

1954-1956	Single-cut	$6,500	$8,600
1957-1958	Single-cut	$7,300	$9,600
1959-1960	Single-cut	$5,200	$6,800
1961-1963	Double-cut	$4,325	$5,625

Silver Jet 1957 Reissue (6129-1957)
1989-2019. Reissue of single-cut '50s Silver Jet, silver sparkle. '1957' added to name in '94.

1989-2019		$1,450	$1,900

Silver Jet 1962 Reissue (6129-1962)
1996-2009. Reissue of '60s double-cut Silver Jet, silver sparkle.

1996-2009		$1,450	$1,900

Songbird (Sam Goody 711)
1967-1968. Standard body thinline double-cut with G soundholes, offered by Sam Goody of New York.

1967-1968		$3,000	$4,000

Southern Belle (7176)
1983. Electric archtop, walnut, parts from the late-'70s assembled in Mexico and U.S., 5 made with all original parts, several others without pickguard and case.

1983		$1,220	$1,600

Sparkle Jet (6129/6129T/6129TG)
1995-2019. Duo-Jet with sparkle finishes other than Silver, single-cut, 2 pickups. Many different colors offered over the years.

1995-2019		$1,450	$1,900

Streamliner Single Cutaway (6189/6190/6191)
1955-1959. Electric archtop, single-cut, maple top, G tailpiece, 1 pickup, multi-bound, Jaguar Tan (6189), sunburst (6190), or natural (6191). Name reintroduced as a double-cut in '68.

1955-1959	6189, Jaguar Tan	$2,400	$3,100
1955-1959	6190, Sunburst	$2,000	$2,600
1955-1959	6191, Natural	$2,750	$3,600

Streamliner Center Block Jr. (2655T)
2016-present. Double-cut, spruce center block, Bigsby, black, walnut stain or Golddust.

2016-2021		$425	$550

Streamliner Double Cutaway (6102/6103)
1968-1973. Reintroduced from single-cut model, electric archtop, double-cut, 2 pickups, G tailpiece, cherry or sunburst.

1968-1973		$1,550	$2,050

Sun Valley (6010/7515/7514)
1959-1977. Flat-top acoustic, laminated Brazilian rosewood back and sides, multi-bound top, natural or sunburst.

1959-1964	6010	$1,025	$1,350
1965-1970	6010	$825	$1,075
1971-1972	7515	$750	$1,000
1973-1977	7514	$750	$1,000

Super Chet (7690/7690-B/7691/7691-B)
1972-1980. Electric archtop, single rounded cutaway, 2 pickups, gold hardware, mini control knobs along edge of 'guard, Autumn Red or walnut.

1972-1980		$2,950	$3,900

Supreme (7545)
1972-1978. Flat-top 16", spruce top, mahogany or rosewood body options, gold hardware.

1972-1978	Mahogany	$3,500	$4,600
1972-1979	Rosewood	$3,500	$4,600

Synchromatic (6030/6031)
1951-1955. 17" acoustic archtop, becomes Constellation in '55.

1951-1955	6030 or 6031	$1,250	$1,650

1954 Gretsch Round-Up (6130)

Gretsch Streamliner Center Block Jr. (G2655T)

1988 Gretsch Traveling Wilburys (TW300T)
Ted Wulfers

1976 Gretsch White Falcon Stereo (6137/7595)
Rob Corley

Synchromatic (6038/6039)
1951-1955. 17" acoustic archtop, single-cut, G tail-piece, multi-bound, sunburst (6038) or natural (6039), renamed Fleetwood in '55.

MODEL YEAR	FEATURES	EXC. COND. LOW	HIGH
1951-1955	6038 or 6039	$1,400	$1,850

Synchromatic 75
1939-1949. Acoustic archtop, f-holes, multi-bound, large floral peghead inlay. Tenor available.

1939-1949		$900	$1,200
1939-1949	Tenor	$575	$750

Synchromatic Jr. (3900)
1990-2003. Historic Series, 15" single-cut archtop acoustic.

1990-2003		$925	$1,200

Synchromatic 100 (6014/6015)
1939-1955. Renamed from No. 100F, acoustic archtop, double-bound body, amber, sunburst (6014) or natural (6015), renamed Corsair in '55.

1939-1949	Natural	$850	$1,125
1939-1949	Sunburst	$750	$1,000
1950-1955	Natural	$775	$1,025

Synchromatic 160 (6028/6029)
1939-1943, 1947-1951. Acoustic archtop, cats-eye soundholes, maple back and sides, triple-bound, natural or sunburst.

1939-1943	Sunburst	$1,225	$1,625
1947-1951	Sunburst	$1,075	$1,425
1948-1951	Natural	$1,225	$1,625

Synchromatic 200
1939-1949. Acoustic archtop, cats-eye soundholes, maple back and sides, multi-bound, gold-plated hardware, amber or natural.

1939-1949		$1,325	$1,725

Synchromatic 300
1939-1955. Acoustic archtop, cats-eye soundholes until '51 and f-holes after, multi-bound, natural or sunburst.

1939-1949	Natural	$2,400	$3,200
1939-1949	Sunburst	$2,150	$2,800
1950-1955	Natural	$2,150	$2,800
1950-1955	Sunburst	$2,000	$2,600

Synchromatic 400
1940-1955. Acoustic archtop, cats-eye soundholes until '51 and f-holes after, multi-bound, gold hardware, natural or sunburst.

1940-1949	Natural	$4,800	$6,300
1940-1949	Sunburst	$4,400	$5,800
1950-1955	Natural	$4,400	$5,800
1950-1955	Sunburst	$5,300	$7,000

Synchromatic 400F/6042 Flat-Top
1947-1955. 18" flat-top, renamed 6042 in the late '40s.

1947-1948	400F	$4,775	$6,300
1949-1955	6042	$4,775	$6,300

Synchromatic G400/400C
1990-2008. Acoustic archtop, full-body, non-cut (400) or single-cut (C), sunburst.

1990-2008	G400	$1,050	$1,400
1990-2008	G400C	$1,050	$1,400

Synchromatic Limited (G450/G450M)
1997. Acoustic archtop, hand carved spruce (G450)

or maple (G450M) top, floating pickup, sunburst, only 50 were to be made.

MODEL YEAR	FEATURES	EXC. COND. LOW	HIGH
1997	Maple	$1,150	$1,500
1997	Spruce	$1,050	$1,400

Synchromatic Sierra
1949-1955. Renamed from Synchromatic X75F (see below), acoustic flat-top, maple back and sides, triangular soundhole, sunburst.

1949-1955		$1,450	$1,900

Synchromatic X75F
1947-1949. Acoustic flat-top, maple back and sides, triangular soundhole, sunburst, renamed Synchromatic Sierra in '49.

1947-1949		$1,450	$1,900

TK 300 (7624/7625)
1977-1981. Double-cut maple solid body, 1 humbucker, bolt-on neck, six-on-a-side tuners, hockey stick headstock, Autumn Red or natural.

1977-1981		$700	$925

Town and Country (6021)
1954-1959. Renamed from Jumbo Synchromatic 125 F, flat-top acoustic, maple back and sides, triangular soundhole, multi-bound.

1954-1959		$2,425	$3,200

Traveling Wilburys (TW300T)
1988-1990. Promotional guitar, solid body electric, single-cut, 1 and 2 pickups, 6 variations, graphics.

1988-1990		$450	$600

Van Eps 6-String (6081/6082)
1968-1971. Electric archtop, single-cut, 2 pickups, 6 strings.

1968-1971		$3,275	$4,300

Van Eps 7-String (6079/6080/7580/7581)
1968-1978. 7-string version, sunburst (6079) or walnut (6080), model numbers change to 7580 (sunburst) and 7581 (walnut) in '72.

1968-1971	6079 or 6080	$3,275	$4,300
1972-1978	7580 or 7581	$3,000	$4,000

Viking
1964-1975. Archtop, double-cut, 2 pickups, vibrato, sunburst (6187), natural (6188) or Cadillac Green (6189). Re-designated 7585 (sunburst) and 7586 (natural) in '72.

1964	Cadillac Green	$4,600	$6,000
1964	Natural	$4,075	$5,400
1964	Sunburst	$2,850	$3,750
1965-1971	Cadillac Green	$3,350	$4,400
1965-1971	Natural	$3,350	$4,400
1965-1971	Sunburst	$2,335	$3,050
1972-1975	Sunburst, natural	$2,125	$2,800

Wayfarer Jumbo (6008)
1969-1971. Flat-top acoustic dreadnought, non-cut, maple back and sides, multi-bound, Wayfarer and sailing ship logo on 'guard.

1969-1971		$1,000	$1,300

White Falcon Mono (6136/7594)
1955-1981. Includes the single-cut 6136 of '55-'61, the double-cut 6136 of '62-'70, and the double-cut 7594 of '71-'81.

1955-1961	6136, single-cut	$26,000	$34,000
1962-1964	6136, double-cut	$12,000	$15,700
1965-1969		$8,200	$10,800

MODEL YEAR	FEATURES	EXC. COND. LOW	HIGH
1970		$7,300	$9,600
1971-1972	7594	$6,000	$7,900
1973-1981	7594	$5,900	$7,700

White Falcon Stereo (6137/7595)
1958-1981. Features Project-O-Sonic Stereo, includes the single-cut 6137 of '58-'61, the double-cut 6137 of '62-'70, and the double-cut 7595 of '71-'81.

1958-1961	6137, single-cut	$28,000	$37,000
1962-1964	6137, double-cut	$13,000	$17,000
1965-1969		$9,000	$11,700
1970		$7,900	$10,400
1971-1972	7595	$6,500	$8,600
1973-1981	7595	$5,900	$7,700

White Falcon (Import)
1989-2021. Various imported models.

1989-2021	Various models	$2,800	$3,600

White Falcon Custom U.S.A. (6136-1955)
1995-1999. U.S.-made, single-cut, DynaSonic pickups, gold sparkle appointments, rhinestone embedded knobs, white. In '04, Current U.S. model called G6136CST is released. The import White Falcon has sometimes been listed with the 1955 designation and is not included here.

1995-1999		$3,550	$4,700

White Penguin (6134)
1955-1962. Electric solid body, single-cut until '61, double '61-'62, 2 pickups (DeArmond until '58 then Filter Tron), fewer than 100 made, white, gold sparkle bound, gold-plated parts. More than any other model, there seems a higher concern regarding forgery.

1956-1962		$87,000	$113,000

White Penguin (G6134)
1993, 2003-2018. White, single-cut, metalflake binding, gold hardware, jeweled knobs, Cadillac G tailpiece.

2003-2018		$2,275	$2,950

Greven
1969, 1975-present. Luthier John Greven builds his premium grade, production/custom, acoustic guitars in Portland, Oregon.

Grez
2009-present. Production/custom, professional and premium grade, electric solid body, semi-hollowbody, archtop and acoustic guitars, built by Barry Grzebik in Petaluma, California.

Griffin String Instruments
1976-present. Luthier Kim Griffin builds his professional and premium grade, production/custom, parlor, steel-string, and classical guitars in Greenwich, New York.

Grimes Guitars
1972-present. Premium and presentation grade, custom, flat-tops, nylon-strings, archtops, semi-hollow electrics made by luthier Steve Grimes originally in Port Townsend, Washington, and since '82 in Kula, Hawaii. He also made mandolins early on.

Grinnell
Late 1930s-early 1940s. Private brand made by Gibson for Grinnell Music of Detroit and Southeast Michigan, which at the time, was the largest music chain in the Detroit area.

KG-14
1940. Gibson-made L-00 flat-top style with maple sides and back, tortoise-style binding on top and back, ladder bracing.

1940		$1,900	$2,500

Groehsl
1890-1921. Chicago's Groehsl Company made guitars for Wards and other mass-marketers. In 1921 the company became Stromberg-Voisinet, which in turn became the Kay Musical Instrument Company.

Groove Tools
2002-2004. Korean-made, production, intermediate grade, 7-string guitars that were offered by Conklin Guitars of Springfield, Missouri. They also offered basses.

Grosh
1993-present. Professional and premium grade, production/custom, solid and semi-hollow body guitars and basses built by luthier Don Grosh originally in Santa Clarita, California and, since '05 in Broomfield, Colorado. He also builds basses. Grosh worked in production for Valley Arts from '84-'92. Guitars generally with bolt necks until '03 when set-necks were added to the line.

Classical Electric
1990s. Single-cut solidbody with nylon strings and piezo-style hidden pickup, highly figured top.

1990s		$1,450	$1,900

Custom S Bent Top/Bent Top Custom
2003-2019. Offset double-cut, figured maple carved top, 2 pickups.

2003-2019		$1,450	$1,900

Custom T Carve Top
2003-2012. Single-cut, figured maple carved top, 2 pickups.

2003-2012		$1,450	$1,900

ElectraJet Custom
2009-present. Modified offset double-cut, 2 P-90s, 2 hums, or single-single-hum pickups.

2009-2021		$1,450	$1,900

Retro Classic
1993-present. Offset double-cut, 3 pickups.

1993-2021		$1,450	$1,900

Retro Classic Vintage T
1993-present. Single-cut, black 'guard.

1993-2021		$1,450	$1,900

Gruen Acoustic Guitars
Luthier Paul Gruen builds professional grade, custom steel-string guitars, starting in 1999, in Chapel Hill, North Carolina.

Grez Guitars OM-1C

Grosh ElectraJet Custom

GUITARS

1967 Gruggett

1961 Guild Aristocrat M-75
Carter Vintage Guitars

MODEL YEAR	FEATURES	EXC. COND. LOW	HIGH

Gruggett

Mid 1960s-2012. In the 1960s, luthier Bill Gruggett worked with Mosrite and Hallmark guitars as well as building electric guitars under his own name in Bakersfield, California. He continued to make his Stradette model for Hallmark guitars until his death in October, 2012.

Guernsey Resophonic Guitars

Production/custom, resonator guitars built by luthier Ivan Guernsey in Marysville, Indiana, starting in 1989.

Guild

1952-present. Professional and premium grade, production/custom, acoustic and acoustic/electric guitars. They have built solid, hollow and semi-hollowbody guitars in the past. Founded in New York City by jazz guitarist Alfred Dronge, employing many ex-Epiphone workers. The company was purchased by Avnet, Inc. in '66 and the Westerly, Rhode Island factory was opened in '68. Hoboken factory closed in '71 and headquarters moved to Elizabeth, New Jersey. Company was in bankruptcy in '88 and was purchased by Faas Corporation, New Berlin, Wisconsin. The brand was purchased by Fender in '95 and production was moved from Westerly to the Fender plant in Corona, California in 2001. In '05, Fender moved Guild production to their newly-acquired Tacoma plant in Washington. In '08, production moved to the Ovation/Hamer plant in New Hartford, Connecticut. With the 2001 move to the Fender Corona plant, Bob Benedetto and Fender veteran Tim Shaw (who previously ran the Nashville-based custom shop) created a line of Guild acoustic guitars that were primarily based on vintage Guild Hoboken designs.

Designs of Tacoma-built Guild product were nothing like Tacoma guitars. The new Guilds were dovetail neck based with nitrocellulose finishes. Later, FMIC Guild introduced the Contemporary Series giving the Tacoma factory another line in addition to the vintage-based F and D model Traditional Series. In '14 Fender sold Guild to Cordoba Music Group, manufacturer of Cordoba acoustic guitars who moved production to Oxnard, California.

A-50
1994-1996. Original A-50 models can be found under the Cordoba A-50 listing, the new model drops the Cordoba name, size 000 flat-top, spruce top, Indian rosewood body.

1994-1996		$1,150	$1,450

Aragon F-30
1954-1986. Acoustic flat-top, spruce top, laminated maple arched back (mahogany back and sides by '59), reintroduced as just F-30 in '98.

1954-1959		$2,400	$3,175
1960-1969		$2,200	$2,900
1970-1986		$2,025	$2,650

MODEL YEAR	FEATURES	EXC. COND. LOW	HIGH

Aragon F-30 NT
1959-1985. Natural finish version of F-30.

1959-1969		$2,600	$3,400
1970-1985		$2,400	$3,175

Aragon F-30 R
1973-1995. Rosewood back and sides version of F-30, sunburst.

1973-1979		$2,400	$3,175

Aristocrat M-75
1954-1963. Electric archtop, routed semi-hollow single-cut body, 2 pickups, sunburst, natural (added '59) or cherry (added '61), reintroduced as Bluesbird M-75 in '67.

1954-1959		$4,200	$5,500
1960-1963		$3,900	$5,200

Aristocrat M-75 Tenor
Mid-late 1950s. Tenor version of 6-string Aristocrat electric, dual soapbar pickups, 4 knobs.

1950s		$2,900	$3,800

Artist Award
1961-1999. Renamed from Johnny Smith Award, single-cut electric archtop, floating DeArmond pickup (changed to humbucker in '80), multi-bound, gold hardware, sunburst or natural.

1961-1969		$7,100	$9,300
1970-1999		$5,700	$7,500

Bluegrass D-25/D-25M
1968-1999. Flat-top, mahogany top until '76, spruce after, mahogany back and sides, various colors, called Bluegrass D-25 M in late-'70s and '80s, listed as D-25 in '90s.

1968-1969		$775	$1,000
1970-1999		$750	$1,000

Bluegrass D-25-12
1987-1992, 1996-1998. 12-string version of D-25.

1987-1998		$700	$900

Bluegrass D-35
1966-1988. Acoustic flat-top, spruce top and mahogany back and sides, rosewood 'board and bridge, natural.

1966-1969		$1,300	$1,725
1970-1988		$1,200	$1,600

Bluegrass F-40/Valencia F-40
1954-1963, 1973-1983. Acoustic flat-top, spruce top, maple back and sides, rosewood 'board and bridge, natural or sunburst.

1954-1963	Valencia F-40	$3,600	$4,700
1973-1983	Bluegrass F-40	$1,550	$2,000

Bluegrass F-47
1963-1976. 16" narrow-waist style, mahogany sides and back, acoustic flat-top, spruce top, mahogany back and sides, bound rosewood 'board and bridge, natural.

1963-1969	Horses-art 'guard	$2,900	$3,800
1970-1976		$2,700	$3,600

Bluegrass Jubilee D-40
1963-1992. Acoustic flat-top, spruce top, mahogany back and sides, rosewood 'board and bridge, natural. Has been reissued.

1963-1969		$2,200	$2,900
1970-1992		$1,800	$2,350

MODEL YEAR	FEATURES	EXC. COND. LOW	HIGH

Bluegrass Jubilee D-40C
1975-1991. Acoustic flat-top, single Florentine cutaway, mahogany back and sides, rosewood 'board and bridge, natural.

1975-1991		$1,875	$2,450

Bluegrass Jubilee D-44
1965-1972. Acoustic flat-top, spruce top, pearwood back and sides, ebony 'board, rosewood bridge.

1965-1969		$1,925	$2,500
1970-1972		$1,800	$2,350

Bluegrass Jubilee D-44M
1971-1985. Acoustic flat-top, spruce top, maple back & sides, ebony fingerboard, rosewood bridge.

1971-1985		$1,800	$2,350

Bluegrass Special D-50
1963-1993. Acoustic flat-top, spruce top, rosewood back and sides, ebony fretboard, multi-bound. Reissued in '99.

1963-1968	Brazilian rosewood	$5,200	$6,800
1969-1979	Indian rosewood	$2,200	$2,900
1980-1993	Indian rosewood	$2,100	$2,700

Bluegrass Special D-50 (Reissue)/D-50
1999-2004. Also available with pickup system, initially listed as D-50. Reintroduced in '06.

1999-2004		$1,600	$2,100

Blues 90
2000-2002. Bluesbird single-cut, chambered body, unbound rosewood 'board, dots, 2 Duncan P-90s.

2000-2002		$1,175	$1,525

Bluesbird M-75 (Hollow Body)
1967-1970. Reintroduced from Aristocrat M-75, thinbody electric archtop of maple, spruce ('67) or mahogany, single-cut, 2 pickups, Deluxe has gold hardware, Standard chrome. A solidbody Bluesbird was also introduced in '70.

1967-1970		$2,500	$3,300

Bluesbird M-75 (Solid Body)
1970-1978. Solid body version of Bluesbird M-75, mahogany body, rounded cutaway, 2 pickups, CS with plain top and chrome hardware, GS flamed top and gold hardware.

1970-1978	CS	$2,350	$3,100
1970-1978	GS	$2,950	$3,900

Bluesbird M-75 (Solid Body) Reintroduced
1984-1988. Various pickups; 3 single-coil ('84-'85), 3 EMG ('86), 3 DiMarzio ('87-'88).

1984-1985	Single-coil	$1,325	$1,725
1986	EMG	$1,325	$1,725
1987-1988	DiMarzio	$1,325	$1,725

Bluesbird (Reintroduced)
1994-2003. Single-cut chambered solid body, 2 humbuckers, block inlays, available with AAA flamed maple top.

1994-2003		$1,450	$1,900
2001	Fender CS	$2,275	$2,950

Bluesbird
2011-2012. Single-cut solid body, Chesterfield headstock logo, flame maple top, block markers, 2 humbuckers, natural finish.

2011-2012		$1,450	$1,900

Brian May BHM-1
1984-1987. Electric solid body, double-cut, vibrato, 3 pickups, bound top and back, red or green, Brian May Pro, Special and Standard introduced in '94.

1984-1987		$3,400	$4,450

Brian May Pro
1994-1995. Electric solid body, double-cut, vibrato, 3 pickups, bound top and back, various colors.

1994-1995		$3,400	$4,450

Brian May Signature Red Special
1994. Signature initials on truss rod cover, script signature on back of headstock, BM serial number, dot markers, custom Duncan pickups, custom vibrola, red special finish.

1994		$3,400	$4,450

CA-100 Capri
1956-1973. Acoustic archtop version of CE-100, sharp Florentine cutaway, solid spruce top, laminated maple back and sides, rosewood 'board and bridge, nickel-plated metal parts, natural or sunburst.

1956-1959		$2,200	$2,800
1960-1973		$2,000	$2,600

Capri CE-100
1956-1985. Electric archtop, single Florentine cutaway, 1 pickup (2 pickups by '83), maple body, Waverly tailpiece, sunburst, in '59-'82 CE-100 D listed with 2 pickups.

1956-1959		$2,300	$3,000
1960-1985		$2,100	$2,700

Capri CE-100D
1956-1982. Electric archtop, single Florentine cutaway, 2 pickups, maple body, sunburst, Waverly tailpiece (D dropped, became the Capri CE-100 in '83).

1956-1959		$2,500	$3,200
1960-1982		$2,300	$3,000

Capri CE-100T Tenor
1950s. Electric-archtop Capri 4-string tenor guitar, sunburst.

1956		$2,000	$2,600

CO-1/CO-1C
2006-2008. Contemporary series, F-30 style, red cedar top, solid mahogany neck/back/sides, rosewood 'board, natural. CO-1C with soft cutaway.

2006-2008	CO-1	$925	$1,200
2006-2008	CO-1C	$1,000	$1,300

CO-2/CO-2C
2008. Contemporary series, as CO-1 but with red spruce top, ebony 'board, and offered in blonde, Antique Burst or Ice Tea Burst. CO-2C with soft cutaway.

2008	CO-2	$925	$1,200
2008	CO-2C	$1,000	$1,300

Cordoba A-50
1961-1972. Acoustic archtop, lowest-end in the Guild archtop line, named Granada A-50 prior to '61.

1961-1965		$1,225	$1,600
1966-1972		$1,125	$1,500

Cordoba T-50 Slim
1961-1973. Thinbody version of Cordoba X-50.

1961-1965		$1,300	$1,700
1966-1969		$1,200	$1,575
1970-1972		$1,100	$1,450

1971 Guild Bluegrass D-35
Imaged by Heritage Auctions, HA.com

1995 Guild Brian May Pro
Rivington Guitars

GUITARS

1965 Guild Cordoba X-50
Tom Pfeifer

1971 Guild D-40
Richard Potter

MODEL YEAR	FEATURES	EXC. COND. LOW	HIGH

Cordoba X-50
1961-1970. Electric archtop non-cut, laminated maple body, rosewood 'board, 1 pickup, nickel-plated parts.

1961-1965		$1,350	$1,775
1966-1970		$1,250	$1,650

CR-1 Crossroads Single E/Double E
1993-2000. Single-cut solid body acoustic, humbucker (S2 in '93) neck pickup and Piezo bridge, 97 single necks (Single E, '93-'97) and very few 6/12 double necks (Double E, '93, '98-'00) made by Guild custom shop.

1993-1997	Single neck	$1,675	$2,200
1993-2000	Double neck	$4,100	$5,300

Custom F-412 12-String
1968-1986. Special order only from '68-'74, then regular production, 17" wide body 12-string version of F-50 flat-top, spruce top, maple back and sides, arched back, 2-tone block inlays, gold hardware, natural finish.

1968-1969		$2,400	$3,100
1970-1986		$2,050	$2,700

Custom F-512 12-String
1968-1986, 1990. Indian rosewood back and sides version of F-412. See F-512 for reissue.

1968-1969		$2,900	$3,800
1970-1979		$2,625	$3,450
1980-1986		$2,425	$3,200

Custom F-612 12-String
1972-1973. Acoustic 12-string, similar to Custom F-512, but with 18" body, fancy mother-of-pearl inlays, and black/white marquee body, neck and headstock binding.

1972-1973	Brazilian rosewood	$4,200	$5,500
1972-1973	Indian rosewood	$2,725	$3,575

Custom Shop 45th Anniversary
1997. Built in Guild's Nashville Custom Shop, all solid wood, spruce top, maple back and sides, high-end appointments, gold hardware, natural.

1997		$2,700	$3,500

CV-1/CV-1C
2006-2008. Contemporary Vintage series, F-40 style, solid Indian rosewood back/sides, rosewood 'board. CV-1C with sharp cutaway.

2006-2008	CV-1	$925	$1,200
2006-2008	CV-1C	$1,000	$1,300

CV-2/CV-2C
2008. Contemporary Vintage series, as CV-1 but with flamed maple back/sides, ebony 'board. CV-2C with sharp cutaway.

2008	CV-2	$925	$1,200
2008	CV-2C	$1,000	$1,300

D-4 Series
1991-2002. Dreadnought flat-top, mahogany sides, dot markers.

1991-2002	6-String	$600	$800
1992-1999	12-String	$600	$800

D-6 (D-6E/D-6HG/D-6HE)
1992-1995. Flat-top, 15 3/4", mahogany back and sides, natural satin non-gloss finish, options available.

1992-1995		$600	$800

D-15 Mahogany Rush
1983-1988. Dreadnought flat-top, mahogany body and neck, rosewood 'board, dot inlays, stain finish.

1983-1988		$600	$800

D-15 12-String
1983-1985. 12-string version of Mahogany Rush D-15.

1983-1985		$600	$800

D-16 Mahogany Rush
1984-1986. Like D-15, but with gloss finish.

1984-1986		$750	$975

D-17 Mahogany Rush
1984-1988. Like D-15, but with gloss finish and bound body.

1984-1988		$750	$975

D-25/D-25M
2003. Solid mahogany body. Refer to Bluegrass D-25 for earlier models. Reintroduced in '06 as GAD-25.

2003		$750	$975

D-26 (Guitar Center)
1995. Made for Guitar Center, spruce top, mahogany back and sides, natural finish.

1995		$750	$975

D-30
1987-1999. Acoustic flat-top, spruce-top, laminated maple back and solid maple sides, rosewood 'board, multi-bound, various colors.

1987-1999		$1,150	$1,500

D-40
1999-2007. Solid spruce top, mahogany back and sides, rosewood 'board. See earlier models under Bluegrass Jubilee D-40.

1999-2007		$1,250	$1,625

D-40 Bluegrass Jubilee
2006-2014. Indian rosewood, red spruce top, mahogany back and sides, 3-piece neck (mahogany/walnut/mahogany).

2006-2014	No pickup	$1,250	$1,625
2006-2014	Duncan D-TAR	$1,325	$1,700

D-40 Richie Havens
2003-2014. Richie Havens signature logo on truss rod cover, mahogany sides and back, Fishman Matrix, natural.

2003-2014		$1,300	$1,700

D-40C NT
1975-1991. Pointed cutaway version.

1975-1991		$1,500	$2,000

D-46
1980-1985. Dreadnought acoustic, ash back, sides and neck, spruce top, ebony 'board, ivoroid body binding.

1980-1985		$1,000	$1,300

D-50
See Bluegrass Special Model.

D-55
See TV Model.

D-55 50th Anniversary
2003. Brazilian rosewood, 1953-2003 Anniversary logo.

2003		$4,500	$5,900

MODEL YEAR	FEATURES	EXC. COND. LOW	HIGH

D-60
1987-1990, 1998-2000. Renamed from D-66, rosewood back and sides ('87-'90), maple ('98-'00), scalloped bracing, multi-bound top, slotted diamond inlay, G shield logo.

1987-1990	Rosewood	$2,400	$3,200
1998-1999	Maple	$2,400	$3,200

D-64
1984-1986. Maple back and side, multi-bound body, notched diamond inlays, limited production.

1984-1986		$2,400	$3,200

D-66
1984-1987. Amber, rosewood back and sides, 15 3/4", scalloped bracing, renamed D-60 in '87.

1984-1987		$2,400	$3,200

D-70
1981-1985. Dreadnought acoustic, spruce top, Indian rosewood back and sides, multi-bound, ebony 'board with mother-of-pearl inlays.

1981-1985		$3,500	$4,600

D-70-12E
1981-1985. Only 2 made, 12-string version, Fishman electronics.

1981-1985		$3,500	$4,600

D-80
1983-1987. Non-carved heel.

1983-1987		$3,500	$4,600

D-100
1990-1998. Top-of-the-line dreadnought-size acoustic, spruce top, rosewood back and sides, scalloped bracing.

1990-1998		$3,500	$4,600

D-125
2011-2014. All mahogany with Indian rosewood 'board, natural or cherry red.

2011-2014		$450	$575

D-212 12-String/D-25-12/D-212
1981-1983, 1987-1992, 1996-present. 12-string version of D-25, laminated mahogany back and sides, natural, sunburst or black. Renamed D-25-12 for '87-'92, reintroduced as D-212 '96-present.

1981-1983		$675	$875

D-412 12-String
1990-1997. Dreadnought, 12 strings, mahogany sides and arched back, satin finished, natural.

1990-1997		$1,200	$1,550

DC-130
1994-1995. US-made, limited run, D-style cutaway, flamed maple top/back/sides.

1994-1995		$3,000	$3,900

DCE True American
1993-2000. Cutaway flat-top acoustic/electric, 1 with mahogany back and sides, 5 with rosewood.

1993-2000	DC-1, DCE-1	$650	$850
1994-2000	DCE-5	$725	$950

Del Rio M-30
1959-1964. Flat-top, 15", all mahogany body, satin non-gloss finish.

1959		$2,400	$3,200
1960-1964		$2,250	$3,000

Detonator
1987-1990. Electric solid body, double-cut, 3 pick-ups, bolt-on neck, Guild/Mueller tremolo system, black hardware.

1987-1990		$575	$750

DK-70 Peacock Limited Edition
1995-1996. Limited run of 50, koa, peacock 'guard.

1995-1996		$3,600	$4,700

Duane Eddy Deluxe DE-500
1962-1974, 1984-1987. Electric archtop, single rounded cutaway, 2 pickups (early years and '80s version have DeArmonds), Bigsby, master volume, spruce top with maple back and sides, available in blond (BL) or sunburst (SB).

1962-1964	Natural	$7,000	$9,200
1962-1964	Sunburst	$5,500	$7,200
1965	Natural	$5,600	$7,350
1965	Sunburst	$5,000	$6,550
1966	Natural	$5,200	$6,800
1966	Sunburst	$4,700	$6,200
1967-1969	Various colors	$4,700	$6,200
1970-1974	Various colors	$4,200	$5,500
1984-1987	Various colors	$3,500	$4,600

Duane Eddy Standard DE-400
1963-1974. Electric archtop, single rounded cutaway, 2 pickups, vibrato, natural or sunburst, less appointments than DE-500 Deluxe.

1963	Cherry (option)	$4,600	$6,000
1963	Natural	$4,600	$6,000
1963	Sunburst	$4,000	$5,200
1964	Cherry (option)	$4,300	$5,600
1964	Natural	$4,300	$5,600
1964	Sunburst	$4,000	$5,200
1965	Natural	$4,000	$5,200
1965	Sunburst	$3,300	$4,300
1966	Natural	$3,500	$4,600
1966	Sunburst	$3,000	$3,900
1967-1969	Various colors	$3,900	$3,900
1970-1974	Various colors	$2,500	$3,300

DV Series
1992-2001, 2007-2011. Acoustic flat-tops, mahogany or rosewood back and sides, ebony or rosewood 'board, satin or gloss finish.

1992-2001	DV-52S	$1,400	$1,825
1993-1994	DV-76	$3,450	$4,500
1993-1995	DV-62	$1,550	$2,025
1994-1995	DV-72	$2,900	$3,785
1994-1995	DV-73	$2,900	$3,785
1995-1996	DV-74 Pueblo	$3,450	$4,500
1995-1999	DV-6	$775	$1,025
1999-2000	DV-25	$1,025	$1,325
1999-2001	DV-4	$600	$800

Economy M-20
1958-1965, 1969-1973. Mahogany body, acoustic flat-top, natural or sunburst satin finish.

1958-1959		$2,000	$2,600
1960-1969		$1,850	$2,425
1970-1973		$1,650	$2,150

F-4CEHG
1992-2002. High Gloss finish, single-cut flat-top, acoustic/electric.

1992-2002		$625	$825

1975 Guild D-50
Daniel Malone

1963 Guild Duane Eddy DE-300
Earl Ward

GUITARS

2002 Guild F-47 RCE
Grand Auditorium

Imaged by Heritage Auctions, HA.com

1958 Guild Freshman M-65

Charlie Apicella

MODEL YEAR	FEATURES	EXC. COND. LOW	HIGH
F-5CE			
1992-2001. Acoustic/electric, single-cut, rosewood back and sides, dot inlays, chrome tuners.			
1992-2001		$625	$825
F-30			
1990-2001. Formerly the Aragon F-30, made in Westerly, Rhode Island.			
1990-2001		$1,075	$1,400
F-30R-LS			
1990s. Custom Shop, limited production, bearclaw spruce top, rosewood sides and back.			
1990s		$1,375	$1,800
F-44			
1984-1987. Acoustic flat-top, maple, designed by George Gruhn.			
1984-1987		$2,075	$2,675
F-45CE			
1983-1992. Acoustic/electric, single-cut, mahogany or maple back and sides, rosewood 'board, on-board electronics, natural. Early '87 model was named GF-45CE (flamed maple), by mid '87 it was back to F-45CE.			
1983-1984	Laminated mahogany	$850	$1,125
1985-1986	Flamed maple	$975	$1,275
1987	Early '87, GF-45CE	$975	$1,275
1987-1992	Mid '87, F-45CE	$975	$1,275
F-46			
1984. Jumbo body style flat-top, designed for Guild by George Gruhn.			
1984		$2,500	$3,300
F-47M/F-47MC			
2007-2016. Made in USA, solid flamed maple sides and back, MC with cutaway.			
2007-2016	F-47M	$1,600	$2,100
2007-2016	F-47MC	$1,700	$2,225
F-47R/F-47RC			
2008-2014. Solid rosewood sides and back, available with electronics, RC with cutaway.			
2008-2014		$1,600	$2,100
F-47RCE Grand Auditorium			
1999-2003. Cutaway acoustic/electric, rosewood back and sides, block inlays.			
1999-2003		$1,600	$2,100
F-50/F-50R			
2002-2016. Jumbo, solid spruce top, solid maple sides, arched laminated maple back, abalone rosette. See Navarre F-50/F-50R for earlier models.			
2002-2016	F-50, maple	$1,925	$2,500
2002-2016	F-50R, rosewood	$1,925	$2,500
F-65CE			
1992-2001. Acoustic/electric, single-cut, rosewood back and sides, block inlay, gold tuners.			
1992-2001		$1,925	$2,500
F-212 12-String/F-212XL			
1964-1986, 1998-2000. Acoustic flat-top jumbo, 12 strings, spruce top, mahogany back and sides, 16" body. Named F-212XL in '66, then XL dropped from name in '98.			
1964-1965	F-212	$1,500	$2,000
1966-1986	F-212XL	$1,500	$2,000
1998-2000	F-212	$1,125	$1,475

MODEL YEAR	FEATURES	EXC. COND. LOW	HIGH
F-312 Artist 12-String			
1964-1973. Flat-top, rosewood back and sides, spruce top, no board inlay (but some in '72 may have dots).			
1964-1968	Brazilian rosewood	$4,750	$6,200
1969-1973	Indian rosewood	$2,300	$3,100
F-412			
2002-2016. Solid spruce top, solid maple back and sides, block inlays, 12-string. See Custom F-412 for earlier models.			
2002-2016		$1,800	$2,350
F-512			
2002-present. Solid spruce top, rosewood back and sides, 12-string. See Custom F-512 for earlier models.			
2002-2021		$2,050	$2,650
Freshman M-65			
1958-1973. Electric archtop, single-cut, mahogany back and sides, f-holes, 1 single-coil (some with 2), sunburst or natural top.			
1958-1959		$2,100	$2,750
1960-1969		$1,700	$2,225
1970-1973		$1,650	$2,175
Freshman M-65 3/4			
1958-1973. Short-scale version of M-65, 1 pickup.			
1958-1959		$1,800	$2,375
1960-1969		$1,450	$1,900
1970-1973		$1,400	$1,850
FS-20CE			
1986-1987. Solid body acoustic, routed mahogany body.			
1986-1987		$725	$950
FS-46CE			
1983-1986. Flat-top acoustic/electric, pointed cutaway, mahogany, black, natural or sunburst.			
1983-1986		$850	$1,125
G-5P			
1988-ca.1989. Handmade in Spain, cedar top, gold-plated hardware.			
1988-1989		$1,050	$1,375
G-37			
1973-1986. Acoustic flat-top, spruce top, laminated maple back and sides, rosewood 'board and bridge, sunburst or natural top.			
1973-1986		$1,050	$1,375
G-41			
1974-1978. Acoustic flat-top, spruce top, mahogany back and sides, rosewood 'board and bridge, 20 frets.			
1975-1978		$1,050	$1,375
G-45 Hank Williams Jr.			
1982-1986, 1993-1996. Hank Williams Jr. logo on 'guard, flat-top.			
1982-1996		$1,300	$1,700
G-75			
1975-1977. Acoustic flat-top, 3/4-size version of D-50, spruce top, rosewood back and sides, mahogany neck, ebony 'board and bridge.			
1975-1977		$1,050	$1,375
G-212 12-String			
1974-1983. Acoustic flat-top 12-string version of D-40, spruce top, mahogany back and sides, natural or sunburst.			
1974-1983		$1,050	$1,375

MODEL YEAR	FEATURES	EXC. COND. LOW	HIGH

G-212XL 12-String
1974-1983. 17" version of G-212 12-String.

1974-1983		$1,050	$1,375

G-312 12-String
1974-1987. Acoustic flat-top 12-string version of the D-50, spruce top, rosewood back and sides. Renamed D-50-12 in '87.

1974-1987		$1,250	$1,650

GAD (Guild Acoustic Design) Series
2004-2014. Imported, all models begin with GAD, various woods, some with electronics (E).

2004-2014	Various models	$450	$1,000

George Barnes AcoustiLectric
1962-1972. Electric archtop, single-cut, solid spruce top, curly maple back and sides, multi-bound, 2 humbuckers, gold-plated hardware, sunburst or natural finish.

1962-1972		$5,000	$6,500

George Barnes Guitar in F
1963-1973. Smaller electric archtop at 13.5", 2 humbuckers, chrome hardware.

1963-1973		$5,000	$6,500

GF-25
1987-1992. Acoustic flat-top, mahogany back and sides.

1987-1992		$925	$1,200

GF-25C
1988-1991. Cutaway GF-25.

1988-1991		$1,075	$1,400

GF-30
1987-1991. Acoustic flat-top, maple back/sides/neck, multi-bound.

1987-1991		$1,275	$1,675

GF-40
1987-1991. Mahogany back and sides, multi-bound.

1987-1991		$1,425	$1,875

GF-50
1987-1991. Acoustic flat-top, rosewood back and sides, mahogany neck, multi-bound.

1987-1991		$1,575	$2,050

GF-55
1990-1991. Jumbo acoustic, spruce top, rosewood back and sides, natural.

1990-1991		$2,100	$2,750

GF-60
1987-1989. Jumbo size, rosewood or maple sides and back, diamond markers. Cutaway version available.

1987-1989	GF-60C, cutaway	$2,700	$3,500
1987-1989	GF-60M, maple	$2,600	$3,400
1987-1989	GF-60R, rosewood	$2,600	$3,400

Granada A-50 (Acoustic Archtop)
1956-1960. Lowest-end acoustic archtop in the Guild line, renamed Cordoba A-50 in '61.

1956-1960		$1,550	$2,025

Granada X-50
1954-1961. Electric archtop, non-cut, laminated all maple body, rosewood 'board and bridge, nickel-plated metal parts, 1 pickup, sunburst. Renamed Cordoba X-50 in '61.

1954-1959		$1,800	$2,350
1960-1961		$1,600	$2,100

GV (Guild Vintage) Series
1993-1995. Flat-top, rosewood back and sides, various enhancements.

1993-1995	GV-52, rw, gloss	$1,475	$1,925
1993-1995	GV-52, rw, satin	$1,200	$1,575
1993-1995	GV-70, abalone, gloss	$1,525	$2,000
1993-1995	GV-72, herringbone, gloss	$1,525	$2,000

Jet Star S-50
1963-1970. Electric solid body, double-cut, mahogany or alder body, 1 pickup, vibrato optional by '65, asymmetrical headstock until '65. Reintroduced as S-50 in '72-'78 with body redesign.

1963-1965	3-on-side	$2,050	$2,675
1966-1969	6-in-line	$1,550	$2,025
1970	6-in-line	$1,450	$1,900

JF-4NT
1992-1995. Jumbo flat-top, mahogany, natural.

1992-1995		$800	$1,050

JF-30
1987-2004. Jumbo 6-string acoustic, spruce top, laminated maple back, solid maple sides, multi-bound. Becomes GAD-JF30 in '04.

1987-2004		$1,225	$1,600

JF-30-12
1987-2004. 12-string version of the JF-30.

1987-2004		$1,225	$1,600

JF-30E
1994-2004. Acoustic/electric version.

1994-2004		$1,300	$1,700

JF-50R
1987-1988. Jumbo 6-string acoustic, rosewood back and sides, multi-bound.

1987-1988		$1,225	$1,600

JF-55
1989-2000. Jumbo flat-top, spruce top, rosewood body.

1989-2000		$1,900	$2,400

JF-55-12
1991-2000. 12-string JF-55.

1991-2000		$1,900	$2,400

JF-65
1987-1994. Renamed from Navarre F-50, Jumbo flat-top acoustic, spruce top, R has rosewood back and sides and M has maple.

1987-1994	JF-65M, maple	$2,200	$2,850
1987-1994	JF-65R, rosewood	$2,200	$2,850

JF-65-12
1987-2001. 12-string, version of JF-65.

1987-2001	JF-65M-12, maple	$2,200	$2,850
1987-2001	JF-65R-12, rosewood	$2,200	$2,850

JF-100
1992-2000. Jumbo, maple top, rosewood back and sides, abalone trim, natural. Carved heel available '94-'00.

1992-1995		$3,400	$4,400

JF-100-12
1992-2000. Jumbo 12-string version, non-carved or carved heel.

1994-2000	Carved heel	$3,400	$4,400

Guild George Barnes AcoustiLectric

1993 Guild JF-30

Imaged by Heritage Auctions, HA.com

To get the most from this book, be sure to read "Using **The Guide**" in the introduction.

1975 Guild Mark III
Rivington Guitars

1979 Guild S-70 D

MODEL YEAR	FEATURES	EXC. COND. LOW	HIGH
Johnny Smith Award			
1956-1961. Single-cut electric archtop, floating DeArmond pickup, multi-bound, gold hardware, sunburst or natural, renamed Artist Award in '61.			
1956-1961		$9,500	$12,500
Johnny Smith Award - Benedetto			
2004-2006. Only 18 custom made under the supervision of Bob Benedetto, signed by Johnny Smith, with certificate of authenticity signed by Smith and Benedetto.			
2004-2006	18 made	$6,100	$8,000
JV-72			
1993-1999. Jumbo acoustic, custom turquoise inlay.			
1993-1999		$2,725	$3,550
Liberator Elite			
1988. Limited Edition, set-neck, offset double-cut solid body, figured maple top, mahogany body, rising-sun inlays, 3 active pickups, last of the Guild solidbodies.			
1988		$1,200	$1,600
M-80CS/M-80			
1975-1984. Solidbody, double-cut, 2 pickups, introduced as M-80CS with bound rosewood 'board and block inlays, shortened to M-80 in '80 with unbound ebony 'board and dots.			
1975-1980		$1,600	$2,100
Manhattan X-170 (Mini-Manhattan X-170)			
1985-2002. Called Mini-Manhattan X-170 in '85-'86, electric archtop hollow body, single rounded cutaway, maple body, f-holes, 2 humbuckers, block inlays, gold hardware, natural or sunburst.			
1985-2002		$1,900	$2,500
Manhattan X-175 (Sunburst)			
1954-1985. Electric archtop, single rounded cutaway, laminated spruce top, laminated maple back and sides, 2 pickups, chrome hardware, sunburst. Reissued as X-160 Savoy.			
1954-1959		$2,600	$3,450
1960-1969		$2,300	$3,050
1970-1985		$2,200	$2,850
Manhattan X-175 B (Natural)			
1954-1976. Natural finish X-175.			
1954-1959		$2,600	$3,450
1960-1969		$2,300	$3,050
1970-1976		$2,200	$2,850
Mark I			
1961-1972. Classical, Honduras mahogany body, rosewood 'board, slotted headstock.			
1961-1969		$475	$625
1970-1973		$400	$525
Mark II			
1961-1987. Like Mark I, but with spruce top and body binding.			
1961-1969		$700	$925
1970-1979		$500	$650
1980-1987		$400	$525
Mark III			
1961-1987. Like Mark II, but with Peruvian mahogany back and sides and floral soundhole design.			
1961-1969		$725	$950
1970-1979		$625	$825
1980-1987		$500	$650

MODEL YEAR	FEATURES	EXC. COND. LOW	HIGH
Mark IV			
1961-1985. Like Mark III, but with flamed pearwood back and sides (rosewood offered in '61, maple in '62).			
1961-1969	Pearwood	$800	$1,050
1970-1979	Pearwood	$700	$925
1980-1985	Pearwood	$575	$750
Mark V			
1961-1987. Like Mark III, but with rosewood back and sides (maple available for '61-'64).			
1961-1968	Brazilian rw	$1,600	$2,100
1969-1979	Indian rw	$775	$1,025
1980-1987	Indian rw	$600	$800
Mark VI			
1962-1973. Rosewood back and sides, spruce top, wood binding.			
1962-1968	Brazilian rw	$2,100	$2,750
1969-1973	Indian rw	$1,000	$1,325
Mark VII Custom			
1968-1973. Special order only, spruce top, premium rosewood back and sides, inlaid rosewood bridge, engraved gold tuners.			
1962-1968	Brazilian rw	$2,400	$3,150
1969-1973	Indian rw	$1,125	$1,475
Navarre F-48			
1972-1975. 17", mahogany, block markers.			
1972-1975		$1,600	$2,100
Navarre F-50/F-50			
1954-1986, 1994-1995. Acoustic flat-top, spruce top, curly maple back and sides, rosewood 'board and bridge, 17" rounded lower bout, laminated arched maple back, renamed JF-65 M in '87. Reissued in '94 and again in '02 as the F-50.			
1954-1956		$5,300	$7,000
1957-1962	Pearl block markers	$5,300	$7,000
1963-1969	Ebony 'board	$4,800	$6,300
1970-1995		$2,400	$3,200
Navarre F-50R/F-50R			
1965-1987. Rosewood back and side version of F-50, renamed JF-65 R in '87. Reissued in '02 as F-50R.			
1965-1968	Brazilian rw	$6,500	$8,500
1969-1987	Indian rw	$3,000	$4,000
Nightbird			
1985-1987. Single-cut solid body, tone chambers, 2 pickups, multi-bound, black or gold hardware, renamed Nightbird II in '87.			
1985-1987		$2,500	$3,300
Nightbird I			
1987-1988. Like Nightbird but with chrome hardware, less binding and appointments.			
1987-1988		$2,500	$3,300
Nightbird II			
1987-1992. Renamed from Nightbird, with black hardware, renamed Nightbird X-2000 in '92.			
1987-1992		$2,500	$3,300
Nightbird X-2000			
1992-1996. Renamed from Nightbird II.			
1992-1996		$2,500	$3,300
Park Ave X-180			
2005. Cutaway acoustic archtop, 2 pickups, block markers.			
2005		$1,700	$2,250

MODEL YEAR	FEATURES	EXC. COND. LOW	HIGH
Peregrine			
1999-2005. Solid body acoustic, cutaway, Fishman.			
1999-2005	Custom	$1,050	$1,375
1999-2005	Flamed maple	$1,125	$1,475
1999-2005	S7CE, (CS)	$1,125	$1,475
1999-2005	S7CE, (CS), quilted	$1,125	$1,475
1999-2005	Standard	$950	$1,225
Polara S-100			
1963-1970. Double-cut mahogany or alder solid body, rosewood 'board, 2 single coils, built-in stand until '70, asymmetrical headstock, in '70 Polara dropped from title (see S-100), renamed Polara S-100 in '97.			
1963-1970	2 or 3 pickups	$1,975	$2,600
Roy Buchanan T-200			
1986. Single-cut solid body, 2 pickups, pointed six-on-a-side headstock, poplar body, bolt-on neck, gold and brass hardware.			
1986		$725	$950
S-50			
1972-1978. Double-cut solid body, 1 single-coil (switched to humbucker in '74), dot inlay.			
1972-1978		$1,200	$1,575
S-60/S-60D			
1976-1981. Double-cut solid body with long bass horn, 1 humbucker (60) or 2 single-coils (60D), mahogany body, rosewood 'board.			
1976-1981		$1,100	$1,450
S-65D			
1980-1981. S-60 but with 1 DiMarzio Super Distortion pickup.			
1980-1981		$1,100	$1,450
S-70D/S-70AD			
1979-1981. Solid body (mahogany D, ash AD), rosewood 'board, 3 single-coils.			
1979-1981	S-70AD	$1,250	$1,650
1979-1981	S-70D	$1,200	$1,575
S-90			
1972-1977. Double-cut SG-like body, 2 humbuckers, dot inlay, chrome hardware.			
1972-1977		$1,250	$1,650
S-100			
1970-1978, 1994-1996. S-100 Standard is double-cut solid body, 2 humbuckers, block inlays. Deluxe of '72-'75 had added Bigsby. Standard Carved '74-'77 has acorns and oakleaves carved in the top.			
1970-1978	Standard	$1,900	$2,500
1972-1975	Deluxe	$1,900	$2,500
1974-1977	Standard Carved	$1,900	$2,500
S-100 Reissue			
1994-1997. Renamed Polara in '97.			
1994-1997		$875	$1,150
S-250			
1981-1983. Double-cut solid body, 2 humbuckers.			
1981-1983		$550	$725
S-261			
Ca.1985. Double-cut, maple body, black Kahler tremolo, 1 humbucker and 2 single-coil pickups, rosewood 'board.			
1985		$550	$725

MODEL YEAR	FEATURES	EXC. COND. LOW	HIGH
S-270 Runaway			
1985. Offset double-cut solid body, 1 humbucker, Kahler.			
1985		$550	$725
S-271 Sprint			
1986. Replaced the S-270.			
1986		$550	$725
S-275			
1982-1983. Offset double-cut body, 2 humbuckers, bound figured maple top, sunburst or natural.			
1982-1983		$550	$725
S-280 Flyer			
1983-1984. Double-cut poplar body, 2 humbuckers or 3 single-coils, maple or rosewood neck, dot markers.			
1983-1984		$550	$725
S-281 Flyer			
1983-1988. Double-cut poplar body S-280 with locking vibrato, optional pickups available.			
1983-1988		$550	$725
S-284 Starling/Aviator			
1984-1988. Starling (early-'84) and Aviator (late-'84-'88), double-cut, 3 pickups.			
1984	Starling	$550	$725
1984-1988	Aviator	$550	$725
S-285 Aviator			
1986. Deluxe Aviator, bound 'board, fancy inlays.			
1986		$550	$725
S-300 Series			
1976-1983. Double-cut mahogany solid body with larger bass horn and rounded bottom, 2 humbuckers. S-300 A has ash body, D has exposed DiMarzio humbuckers.			
1976-1983	S-300	$925	$1,200
1977-1982	S-300D	$925	$1,200
1977-1983	S-300A	$925	$1,200
S-400/S-400A			
1980-1981. Double-cut solid body, mahogany (400) or ash (400A), 2 humbuckers.			
1980-1981		$1,075	$1,400
Savoy A-150			
1958-1973, 2013-present. Acoustic archtop version of X-150, available with floating pickup, natural or sunburst finish. Reissued in '13, part of Newark St. Collection.			
1958-1961	Natural	$2,500	$3,300
1958-1961	Sunburst	$2,300	$3,000
2013-2021		$1,375	$1,800
Savoy X-150			
1954-1965. Electric archtop, rounded single-cut, spruce top, maple back and sides, rosewood 'board and bridge, 1 single-coil pickup, sunburst, blond or sparkling gold finish. Reissued in '98 as X-150 Savoy.			
1954	Sunburst	$3,000	$3,950
1955-1959	Sunburst	$2,800	$3,700
1960-1965	Sunburst	$2,500	$3,300
Slim Jim T-100			
1958-1973. Electric archtop thinline, single-cut, laminated all-maple body, rosewood 'board and bridge, Waverly tailpiece, 1 pickup, natural or sunburst.			
1958-1959		$2,100	$2,750
1960-1964		$2,000	$2,625
1965-1969		$1,725	$2,275
1970-1973		$1,625	$2,125

1978 Guild S-300A
Tom Pfeifer

1957 Guild Savoy X-150
Carter Vintage Guitars

1962 Guild Slim Jim T-100 D

Brian Chambers

1965 Guild Starfire III

MODEL YEAR	FEATURES	EXC. COND. LOW	HIGH
Slim Jim T-100D			
1958-1973. Semi-hollow body electric, single Florentine cutaway, thinline, 2-pickup version of the T-100, natural or sunburst.			
1958-1959		$2,300	$3,000
1960-1964		$2,100	$2,750
1965-1969		$2,000	$2,650
1970-1973		$1,725	$2,275
Songbird S Series			
1984-1991. Designed by George Gruhn, flat-top, mahogany back, spruce top, single pointed cutaway, pickup with preamp, multi-bound top, black, natural or white. Renamed S-4 later in run.			
1984-1991		$1,125	$1,475
Standard (STD) Series			
2010-2014. Imported flat-top acoustics based on various classic Guild models.			
2010-2014		$1,250	$1,625
Standard F-112 12-String			
1968-1982. Acoustic flat-top, spruce top, mahogany back, sides and neck.			
1968-1969		$1,125	$1,475
1970-1982		$950	$1,250
Starfire I			
1960-1964. Electric archtop, single-cut thinline, laminated maple or mahogany body, bound body and neck, 1 pickup, Starfire Red finish.			
1960-1961		$1,425	$1,875
1962-1964		$1,325	$1,750
Starfire II			
1960-1976, 1997-2001. Electric archtop, single-cut thinline, laminated maple or mahogany body, bound body and rosewood neck, 2 pickups, various colors.			
1960-1961	Sunburst	$2,400	$3,150
1962	Emerald Green	$2,275	$3,000
1962-1966	Special color options	$2,525	$3,300
1962-1966	Sunburst, Starfire Red	$2,175	$2,850
1967-1969	Sunburst, Starfire Red	$2,100	$2,700
1970-1976	Sunburst, Starfire Red	$1,900	$2,500
1997-2001	Reissue	$1,400	$1,850
Starfire III			
1960-1974, 1997-2005, 2013-present. Electric archtop, single-cut thinline, laminated maple or mahogany body, bound body and rosewood neck, 2 pickups, Guild or Bigsby vibrato, Starfire Red. Reissued in '13, part of Newark St. Collection.			
1960-1966		$2,900	$3,800
1967-1974		$2,700	$3,550
1997-2005	Reissue	$1,400	$1,850
2013-2021	Newark St	$900	$1,175
Starfire IV			
1963-1987, 1991-2005. Thinline, double-cut semi-hollow body, laminated maple or mahogany body, f-holes, 2 humbuckers, rosewood 'board, cherry or sunburst.			
1963-1966		$2,900	$3,800
1967-1975		$2,700	$3,500
1976-1987		$2,200	$2,900

MODEL YEAR	FEATURES	EXC. COND. LOW	HIGH
1991-2005	Reissue	$1,500	$2,000
Starfire IV Special (Custom Shop)			
2001-2002. Nashville Custom Shop.			
2001-2002		$1,800	$2,350
Starfire V			
1963-1973, 1999-2001. Same as Starfire IV but with block markers, Bigsby and master volume, natural or sunburst finish, reissued in '99.			
1963-1966		$2,900	$3,800
1967-1973		$2,700	$3,500
1999-2001	Reissue	$1,575	$2,050
Starfire VI			
1964-1979. Same as Starfire IV but with higher appointments such as ebony 'board, pearl inlays, Guild/Bigsby vibrato, natural or sunburst.			
1964-1966		$2,900	$3,800
1967-1975		$2,700	$3,500
1976-1979		$2,200	$2,900
Starfire XII			
1966-1973. Electric archtop, 12-string, double-cut, maple or mahogany body, set-in neck, 2 humbuckers, harp tailpiece.			
1966-1969		$2,100	$2,750
1970-1973		$2,000	$2,650
Stratford A-350			
1956-1973. Acoustic archtop, rounded single-cut, solid spruce top with solid curly maple back and sides, rosewood 'board and bridge (changed to ebony by '60), sunburst.			
1956-1959		$2,900	$3,800
1960-1965		$2,700	$3,500
1966-1969		$2,400	$3,150
1970-1973		$2,300	$3,000
Stratford A-350B			
1956-1973. A-350 in blond/natural finish option.			
1956-1959		$3,250	$4,250
1960-1965		$3,000	$4,000
1966-1969		$2,700	$3,550
1970-1973		$2,550	$3,350
Stratford X-350			
1954-1965. Electric archtop, rounded single-cut, laminated spruce top with laminated maple back and sides, rosewood 'board, 6 push-button pickup selectors, sunburst finish (natural finish is X-375).			
1954-1959		$3,850	$5,000
1960-1965		$3,450	$4,550
Stratford X-375/X-350B			
1953-1965. Natural finish version of X-350, renamed X-350B in '58.			
1953-1958	X-375	$4,100	$5,400
1959-1965	X-350B	$3,300	$4,350
Stuart A-500			
1956-1969. Acoustic archtop single-cut, 17" body, A-500 sunburst, available with Guild logo, floating DeArmond pickup.			
1956-1959		$3,450	$4,500
1960-1965		$3,350	$4,400
1966-1969		$3,100	$4,050
Stuart A-550/A-500B			
1956-1969. Natural blond finish version of Stuart A-500, renamed A-500B in '60.			
1956-1959		$3,650	$4,800

MODEL YEAR	FEATURES	EXC. COND. LOW	HIGH
1960-1965		$3,350	$4,400
1966-1969		$3,100	$4,100

Stuart X-500

1953-1995. Electric archtop, single-cut, laminated spruce top, laminated curly maple back and sides, 2 pickups, sunburst.

1953-1959		$4,100	$5,400
1960-1965		$3,800	$5,000
1966-1969		$3,600	$4,800
1970-1995		$3,200	$4,200

Stuart X-550/X-500B

1953-1995. Natural blond finish Stuart X-550, renamed X-500B in '60.

1953-1959		$4,100	$5,400
1960-1964		$3,800	$5,000
1965-1969		$3,600	$4,800
1970-1995		$3,200	$4,200

Studio 301/ST301

1968-1970. Thinline, semi-hollow archtop Starfire-style but with sharp horns, 1 single-coil pickup, 2 humbuckers in '70, dot inlays, cherry or sunburst.

1968-1969	1 single-coil	$1,150	$1,500
1970	2 humbuckers	$1,350	$1,775

Studio 302/ST302

1968-1970. Like Studio 301, but with 2 pickups.

1968-1969	2 single-coils	$1,500	$1,775
1970	2 humbuckers	$1,500	$1,775

Studio 303/ST303

1968-1970. Like Studio 301, but with 2 pickups and Guild/Bigsby.

1968-1969	2 single-coils	$1,800	$2,400
1969-1970	2 humbuckers	$1,800	$2,400

Studio 402/ST402

1969-1970. Inch thicker body than other Studios, 2 pickups, block inlays.

1969-1970	2 humbuckers	$2,200	$2,900
1969-1970	2 single-coils	$2,200	$2,900

T-250

1986-1988. Single-cut body and pickup configuration with banana-style headstock.

1986-1988		$600	$775

Thunderbird S-200

1963-1968. Electric solid body, offset double-cut, built-in rear guitar stand, AdjustoMatic bridge and vibrato tailpiece, 2 humbucker pickups, changed to single-coils in '66.

1963-1965	Humbuckers	$4,500	$5,900
1966-1968	Single-coils	$3,900	$5,100

Troubadour F-20

1956-1987. Acoustic flat-top, spruce top with maple back and sides (mahogany '59 and after), rosewood 'board and bridge, natural or sunburst.

1956-1959		$2,300	$3,000
1960-1964		$2,200	$2,900
1965-1969		$2,100	$2,800
1970-1979		$1,700	$2,200
1980-1987		$1,500	$2,000

TV Model D-55/D-65/D-55

1968-1987, 1990-present (special order only for 1968-1973). Dreadnought acoustic, spruce top, rosewood back and sides, scalloped bracing, gold-plated tuners,

MODEL YEAR	FEATURES	EXC. COND. LOW	HIGH
renamed D-65 in '87. Reintroduced as D-55 in '90.			
1968-1969		$2,500	$3,300
1970-1987		$2,400	$3,150
1988-1989	D-65	$2,400	$3,150
1990-1999	D-55	$2,400	$3,150
2000-2021	D-55	$2,500	$3,200

Willy Porter Signature

2007-2008. AAA sitka spruce top, solid flamed maple sides and back, special appointments, Fishman Ellipse system.

2007-2008		$1,275	$1,675

X-79 Skyhawk

1981-1986. Four-point solid body, 2 pickups, coil-tap or phase switch, various colors. Custom graphics available '84-'86.

1981-1986		$1,050	$1,400

X-80 Skylark/Swan

1982-1985. Solid body with 2 deep cutaways, banana-style 6-on-a-side headstock, renamed Swan in '85.

1982-1985		$1,050	$1,400

X-82 Nova/Starfighter

1981-1986. Solid body, XR-7 humbuckerss, also available with 3 single-coil pickups, Quick Change SP-6 tailpiece, Adjusto-Matic bridge, Deluxe tuning machine.

1981-1983	Nova	$1,050	$1,400
1984-1986	Starfighter	$1,050	$1,400

X-88 Flying Star Motley Crue

1984-1986. Pointy 4-point star body, rocketship meets spearhead headstock on bolt neck, 1 pickup, optional vibrato.

1984-1986		$1,050	$1,400

X-88D Star

1984-1987. 2 humbucker version X-88.

1984-1987		$1,050	$1,400

X-92 Citron

1984. Electric solid body, detachable body section, 3 pickups.

1984		$925	$1,200

X-100/X-110

1953-1954. Guild was founded in 1952, so this is a very early model, 17" non-cut, single-coil soapbar neck pickup, X-100 sunburst, X-110 natural blond.

1953-1954	X-100	$2,050	$2,700
1953-1954	X-110	$2,350	$3,100

X-100 Bladerunner

1985-1987. 4-point body with large cutouts, 1 humbucker, Kahler, script Guild logo on body, cutout headstock.

1985-1987		$2,900	$3,800

X-150 Savoy/X-150D Savoy

1998-2013. Replaces Savoy X-150, 1 pickup, D has 2 pickups.

1998-2005	X-150	$1,200	$1,600
1998-2013	X-150D	$1,325	$1,750

X-160 Savoy

1989-1993. No Bigsby, black or sunburst.

1989-1993		$1,700	$2,250

X-161 Savoy/X-160B Savoy

1989-1994. X-160 Savoy with Bigsby, sunburst or black.

1989-1994		$1,700	$2,250

1975 Guild TV Model D-55
Peter Busch

1985 Guild X-100 Bladerunner
Rivington Guitars

1970 Gurian J-M

Imaged by Heritage Auctions, HA.com

Late-'60s Guyatone
LG-350T Sharp 5

Rivington Guitars

MODEL YEAR	FEATURES	EXC. COND. LOW	HIGH

X-200/X-220
1953-1954. Electric archtop, spruce top, laminated maple body, rosewood 'board, non-cut, 2 pickups. X-200 is sunburst and X-220 blond.

1953-1954	X-200	$2,400	$3,200
1953-1954	X-220	$2,600	$3,400

X-300/X-330
1953-1954. No model name, non-cut, 2 pickups, X-300 is sunburst and X-330 blond. Becomes Savoy X-150 in '54.

1953-1954	X-300	$2,400	$3,200
1953-1954	X-330	$2,600	$3,400

X-400/X-440
1953-1954. Electric archtop, single-cut, spruce top, laminated maple body, rosewood 'board, 2 pickups, X-400 in sunburst and X-440 in blond. Becomes Manhattan X-175 in '54.

1953-1954	X-400	$3,200	$4,200
1953-1954	X-440	$3,500	$4,600

X-600/X-660
1953. No model name, single-cut, 3 pickups, X-600 in sunburst and X-660 in blond. Becomes Stratford X-350 in '54.

1953	X-600	$4,200	$5,500
1953	X-660	$4,800	$6,300

X-700
1994-1999. Rounded cutaway, 17", solid spruce top, laminated maple back and sides, gold hardware, natural or sunburst.

1994-1999		$2,400	$3,200

Guillermo Roberto Guitars
Professional grade, solidbody electric bajo quintos made in San Fernando, California starting in the year 2000.

Guitar Company of America
1971-present. Professional grade, production, acoustic guitars built by luthier Dixie Michell. Originally built in Tennessee, then Missouri; currently being made in Tulsa, Oklahoma. She also offers mandolins.

Guitar Mill
2006-2011. Luthier Mario Martin built his production/custom, professional grade, semi-hollow and solidbody guitars and basses in Murfreesboro, Tennessee. He also built basses. In '11, he started branding his guitars as Mario Martin.

Gurian
1965-1981. Luthier Michael Gurian started making classical guitars on a special order basis, in New York City. In '69, he started building steel-string guitars as well. 1971 brought a move to Hinsdale, Vermont, and with it increased production. In February, '79 a fire destroyed his factory, stock, and tools. He reopened in West Swanzey, New Hampshire, but closed the doors in '81. Around 2,000 Gurian instruments were built. The guitars have unusual neck joint construction and can be difficult, if not impossible, to repair.

Dealers have reported that '70s models sometimes have notable wood cracks which require repair.

CL Series
1970-1981. Classical Series, mahogany (M), Indian rosewood (R), or Brazilian rosewood (B).

1970-1981	CLB, Brazilian rw	$3,100	$4,000
1970-1981	CLM, mahogany	$1,375	$1,800
1970-1981	CLR, Indian rw	$1,600	$2,100

FLC
1970-1981. Flamenco guitar, yellow cedar back and sides, friction tuning pegs.

1970-1981		$1,800	$2,300

JB3H
1970-1981	Brazilian rosewood	$3,200	$4,200

JM/JMR
1970-1981. Jumbo body, mahogany (JM) or Indian rosewood (JMR), relatively wide waist (versus D-style or SJ-style).

1970-1981	JM	$1,700	$2,200
1970-1981	JMR	$1,700	$2,200

JR3H
1970-1981. Jumbo, Indian rosewood sides and back, 3-piece back, herringbone trim.

1970-1981		$2,100	$2,700

S2B3H
1970-1981	Brazilian rosewood	$3,400	$4,400

S2M
1970-1981. Size 2 guitar with mahogany back and sides.

1970-1981		$1,600	$2,100

S2R/S2R3H
1970-1981. Size 2 with Indian rosewood sides and back, R3H has 3-piece back and herringbone trim.

1970-1981	S2R	$1,600	$2,100
1970-1981	S2R3H	$1,700	$2,200

S3B3H
1981	Brazilian rosewood	$3,400	$4,400

S3M
1970-1981	Mahogany	$1,600	$2,100

S3R/S3R3H
1970-1981. Size 3 with Indian Rosewood, S3R3H has 3-piece back and herringbone trim.

1970-1981	S3R	$1,600	$2,100
1970-1981	S3R3H	$1,700	$2,200

Guyatone
1933-present. Made in Tokyo by Matsuki Seisakujo, founded by Hawaiian guitarists Mitsuo Matsuki and Atsuo Kaneko (later of Teisco). Made Guya brand Rickenbacker lap steel copies in '30s. After a hiatus for the war ('40-'48), Seisakujo resumes production of laps and amps as Matsuki Denki Onkyo Kenkyujo. In '51 the Guyatone brand is first used on guitars and basses, and in '52 they changed the company name to Tokyo Sound Company. Guyatones are among the earliest U.S. imports, branded as Marco Polo, Winston, Kingston and Kent. Other brand names included LaFayette and Bradford. Production and exports slowed after '68.

MODEL YEAR	FEATURES	EXC. COND. LOW	HIGH

Hagenlocher, Henner

1996-present. Luthier Henner Hagenlocher builds his premium grade, custom, nylon-string guitars in Granada, Spain.

Hagstrom

1958-1983, 2004-present. Intermediate, professional, and premium grade, production/custom, solidbody, semi-hollowbody and acoustic guitars made in the U.S. and imported. Founded by Albin Hagström of Älvdalen, Sweden, who began importing accordions in 1921 and incorporated in '25. The name of the company was changed to A.B. Hagström, Inc. in '38, and an American sales office was established in '40. Electric guitar and bass production began in '58 with plastic-covered hollowbody De Luxe and Standard models. The guitars were imported into the U.S. by Hershman Music of New York as Goya 90 and 80 from '58-'61. Bass versions were imported in '61. Following a year in the U.S., Albin's son Karl-Erik Hagström took over the company as exclusive distributor of Fender in Scandinavia; he changed the U.S. importer to Merson Musical Instruments of New York (later Unicord in '65), and redesigned the line. The company closed its doors in '83. In 2004 American Music & Sound started manufacturing and distributing the Hagstrom brand under license from A.B. Albin Hagstrom. In 2009 U.S. Music became involved via its acqustion of JAM, and the 'new' Hagstrom established a Swedish office. A new line of instruments under the Vintage Series (made in China) included classic '60s models. Later the Northen series was introduced with instruments made entirely in Europe.

Corvette/Condor

1963-1967. Offset double-cut solidbody, 3 single-coils, multiple push-button switches, spring vibrato, called the Condor on U.S. imports.

1963-1967		$925	$1,200

D'Aquisto Jimmy

1969-1975, 1976-1979. Designed by James D'Aquisto, electric archtop, f-holes, 2 pickups, sunburst, natural, cherry or white. The '69 had dot inlays, the later version had blocks. From '77 to '79, another version with an oval soundhole (no f-holes) was also available.

1969-1975	1st design	$1,200	$1,600
1976-1979	2nd design	$1,200	$1,600

Deluxe Series

2004-2008. Carved single-cut mahogany body, set-neck, 2 humbuckers, sparkle tops or sunburst.

2004-2008	Various models	$275	$375

F Series

2004-2015. Made in China, offset double-cut basswood body, 2 or 3 pickups.

2004-2015	Various models	$200	$360

H-12 Electric/Viking XII

1965-1967. Double-cut, 2 pickups, 12 strings.

1965-1967		$450	$600

H-22 Folk

1965-1967. Flat-top acoustic.

1965-1967		$325	$425

Impala

1963-1967. Two-pickup version of the Corvette, sunburst.

1963-1967		$725	$950

Kent

1962-1967. Offset double-cut solidbody, 2 pickups.

1962-1967		$450	$600

Model I

1965-1971. Small double-cut solidbody, 2 single-coils, early models have plastic top.

1965-1971		$700	$900

Model II/F-200 Futura/H II

1965-1972, 1975-1976. Offset double-cut slab body with beveled edge, 2 pickups, called F-200 Futura in U.S., Model II elsewhere, '75-'76 called H II. F-200 reissued in 2004.

1965-1976		$700	$900

Model III/F-300 Futura/H III

1965-1972, 1977. Offset double-cut slab body with beveled edge, 3 pickups, called F-300 Futura in U.S., Model III elsewhere, '77 called H III.

1965-1969		$750	$975
1970-1977		$400	$525

Swede

1970-1982, 2004-present. Bolt-on neck, single-cut solidbody, black, cherry or natural, '04 version is set-neck.

1979-1982		$900	$1,175

Super Swede

1979-1983, 2004-present. Glued-in neck upgrade of Swede, '04 version is maple top upgrade of Swede.

1979-1983		$925	$1,200
1979-1983	Custom color	$1,200	$1,600
2004-2020	Reissue	$350	$450

Viking/V1

1965-1975, 1978-1979, 2004-present. Double-cut thinline, 2 f-holes, 2 pickups, chrome hardware, dot inlays, also advertised as the V-1. '60s had 6-on-side headstock, '70s was 3-and-3, latest version back to 6-on-side.

1965-1979		$950	$1,250
2004-2021	Reissue	$350	$450

Viking Deluxe/V2

1967-1968, 2004-present. Upscale version, gold hardware, block inlays, bound headstock and f-holes. Current version upgrades are blocks and flame maple.

1967-1968		$1,000	$1,300
2004-2021	Reissue	$350	$450

Hahn

2007-present. Professional and premium grade, custom electric guitars built by luthier Chihoe Hahn in Garnerville, New York.

Haight

1989-present. Premium and presentation grade, production/custom, acoustic (steel and classical) guitars built in Scottsdale, Arizona by luthier Norman Haight. He also builds mandolins.

1972 Hagstrom Swede
Rivington Guitars

1967 Hagstrom Viking Deluxe
Imaged by Heritage Auctions, HA.com

Hamer Archtop P-90
Imaged by Heritage Auctions, HA.com

Hamer Newport
Bernunzio Uptown Music

Halfling Guitars and Basses

Luthier Tom Ribbecke builds premium grade, production/custom, pin bridge, thinline and jazz guitars and basses, starting in 2003, in Healdsburg, California.

Hallmark

1965-1967, 2004-present. Imported and U.S.-made, intermediate and premium grade, production/custom, guitars and basses from luthiers Bob Shade and Bill Gruggett, and located in Greenbelt, Maryland. They also make basses. The brand was originally founded by Joe Hall in Arvin, California, in '65. Hall had worked for Semie Moseley (Mosrite) and had also designed guitars for Standel in the mid-'60s. Bill Gruggett, who also built his own line of guitars, was the company's production manager. Joe Hall estimates that less than 1000 original Hallmark guitars were built. The brand was revived by Shade in '04.

Sweptwing

1965-1967. Pointed body, sorta like a backwards Flying V.

1965-1967		$1,850	$2,400

Hamblin Guitars

Luthier Kent Hamblin built his premium grade, production/custom, flat-top acoustic guitars in Phoenix, Arizona and Telluride, Colorado, and presently builds in Colorado Springs. He began building in 1996.

Hamer

1974-2012, 2017-present. Intermediate grade, production, electric guitars. Hamer previously made basses and the Slammer line of instruments. Founded in Arlington Heights, Illinois, by Paul Hamer and Jol Dantzig. Prototype guitars built in early-'70s were on Gibson lines, with first production guitar, the Standard (Explorer shape), introduced in '75. Hamer was puchased by Kaman Corporation (Ovation) in '88. The Illinois factory was closed and the operations were moved to the Ovation factory in Connecticut in '97. On January 1, '08, Fender acquired Kaman Music Corporation and the Hamer brand. In '90, they started the Korean-import Hamer Slammer series which in '97 became Hamer Import Series (no Slammer on headstock). In '05 production was moved to China and name changed to XT Series (in '07 production moved to Indonesia). The U.S.-made ones have U.S.A. on the headstock. The less expensive import Slammer brand (not to be confused with the earlier Slammer Series) was introduced in '99 (see that listing). Fender suspended production of the Hamer brand at the end of 2012, later selling KMC (and Hamer brand) to Jam Industries, which relaunched Hamer in '17.

Archtop P-90

Solidbody double-cut, archtop sloping on top, P-90 pickups.

1993		$1,100	$1,425

Artist/Archtop Artist/Artist Custom

1995-2012. U.S.-made, similar to Sunburst Archtop with semi-solid, f-hole design, sunburst, named Archtop Artist, then renamed Artist (with stop tailpiece)/Artist Custom in '97.

1995-2012	Higher-end specs	$1,600	$2,100
1995-2012	Standard specs	$1,150	$1,500

Artist 25th Anniversary Edition

1998. Made in USA, 25th Anniversary Edition script logo on headstock.

1998		$1,150	$1,500

Artist Korina

2001-2012. Double-cut, bass f-hole, korina (limba) body and neck, 2 P-90s or 2 humbuckers (HB), natural gloss finish.

2001-2012		$1,850	$2,400

Artist Ultimate

1998-2012. Figured maple top, deluxe binding, gold hardware.

1998-2012		$2,500	$3,300

Blitz

1982-1984 (1st version), 1984-1990 (2nd version). Explorer-style body, 2 humbuckers, 3-on-a-side peghead, dot inlays, choice of tremolo or fixed bridge, second version same except has angled 6-in-line peghead and Floyd Rose tremolo.

1982-1984	3-on-a-side	$1,600	$2,100
1984-1990	6-in-line	$1,400	$1,800

Californian

1987-1997. Made in USA, solidbody double cut, bolt neck, 1 humbucker and 1 single-coil, Floyd Rose tremolo.

1987-1989		$2,100	$2,700
1990-1997		$1,850	$2,400

Californian Custom

1987-1997. Made in USA, downsized contoured body, offset double-cut, neck-thru-body, optional figured maple body, Duncan Trembucker and Trem-single pickups.

1987-1989		$2,100	$2,700
1990-1997		$1,800	$2,300

Californian Elite

1987-1997. Made in USA, downsized contoured body, offset double-cut, optional figured maple body, bolt-on neck, Duncan Trembucker and Trem-single pickups.

1987-1989		$2,100	$2,700
1990-1997		$1,800	$2,300

Centaura

1989-1995. Alder or swamp ash offset double-cut, bolt-on neck, 1 humbucker and 2 single-coils, Floyd Rose, sunburst.

1989-1995		$1,200	$1,600

Chaparral

1985-1987 (1st version), 1987-1994 (2nd version). Offset double-cut, glued neck, angled peghead, 1 humbucker and 2 single-coils, tremolo, second version has bolt neck with a modified peghead.

1985-1987	Set-neck	$1,400	$1,800
1987-1994	Bolt-on neck	$1,150	$1,500

MODEL YEAR	FEATURES	EXC. COND. LOW	HIGH

Daytona
1993-1997. Offset double-cut, bolt neck, dot inlay, 3 single-coils, Wilkinson tremolo.

1993-1997		$1,100	$1,400

Diablo/Diablo II
1992-1997. Offset double-cut, bolt neck, rosewood 'board, dot inlays, reversed peghead '92-'94, 2 pickups, tremolo. Diablo II has 3 pickups.

1992-1997		$975	$1,250

DuoTone
1993-2003. Semi-hollowbody, double-cut, bound top, glued-in neck, rosewood 'board, 2 humbuckers, EQ.

1993-2003		$700	$900

Echotone/Echotone Custom
2000-2002. Thinline semi-hollow archtop, f-holes, 2 humbuckers, trapezoid inlays, gold hardware.

2000-2002		$385	$500

Eclipse
1994-1996. Asymmetrical double-cut slab mahogany body, glued neck, rosewood 'board, 2 Duncan Mini-Humbuckers, cherry.

1994-1996		$775	$1,000

Eclipse (Import)
1997-1999. Import version.

1997-1999		$300	$400

Eclipse 12-String
1994-1996. 12-string version of Eclipse.

1995		$775	$1,000

FB I
1986-1987. Reverse Firebird-style body, glued-in neck, reverse headstock, 1 pickup, rosewood 'board with dot inlays, also available in non-reverse body.

1986-1987		$950	$1,250

FB II
1986-1987. Reverse Firebird-style, glued-in neck, ebony 'board with boomerang inlays, angled headstock, 2 humbuckers, Floyd Rose tremolo, also available as a 12-string.

1986-1987		$1,000	$1,325

Korina Standard
1995-1996. Limited run, Korina Explorer-type body, glued-in neck, angled peghead, 2 humbuckers.

1995-1996		$1,700	$2,200

Maestro
1990. Offset double-cut, 7 strings, tremolo, bolt-on maple neck, 3 Seymour Duncan rail pickups.

1990		$1,200	$1,500

Mirage
1994-1998. Double-cut carved figured koa wood top, transparent flamed top, initially with 3 single-coil pickups, dual humbucker option in '95.

1994-1998		$1,100	$1,400

Newport Series
1999-2012. USA, double-cut thinline, center block, f-holes, 2 humbuckers (Newport 90 has P-90s), wraparound bridge tailpiece.

1999-2012	Newport	$1,275	$1,650
1999-2012	Newport Pro	$1,350	$1,750

Phantom A5
1982-1884, 1985-1986 (2nd version). Offset double-cut, glued neck, 3-on-a-side peghead, 1 triple-coil and

1 single-coil pickup, second version same but with 6-in-line peghead and Kahler.

1982-1984		$1,375	$1,800

Phantom GT
1984-1986. Contoured body, offset double-cut, glued-in fixed neck, 6-in-line peghead, 1 humbucker, single volume control.

1984-1986		$1,375	$1,800

Prototype
1981-1985. Contoured mahogany body, double-cut with 1 splitable triple-coil pickup, fixed bridge, three-on-a-side peghead, Prototype II has extra pickup and tremolo.

1981-1985		$1,150	$1,500

Scarab I
1984-1986. Multiple cutaway body, 6-in-line peghead, 1 humbucker, tremolo, rosewood or ebony 'board, dot inlays.

1984-1986		$1,600	$2,100

Scarab II
1984-1986. Two humbucker version of the Scarab.

1984-1986		$1,600	$2,100

Scepter
1986-1990. Futuristic-type body, ebony 'board with boomerang inlays, angled 6-in-line peghead, Floyd Rose tremolo.

1986-1990		$1,700	$2,200

Slammer Series
1990-1997. Various models imported from Korea, not to be confused with Hamer's current Slammer budget line started in '98.

1990-1997		$250	$525

Special Series
1980-1983 (1st version), 1984-1985 (Floyd Rose version), 1992-1997 (2nd version), 2017-present. Double-cut solidbody, flame maple top, glued neck, 3-on-a-side peghead, 2 humbuckers, Rose version has mahogany body with ebony 'board, the 2nd version is all mahogany and has tune-o-matic bridge, stop tailpiece and Duncan P-90s, cherry red.

1980-1983	1st version	$1,800	$2,400
1984-1985	With Floyd Rose	$1,800	$2,400
1992-1997	2nd version	$1,475	$1,900
2017-2021	Reissue	$1,475	$1,900

Standard
1974-1985, 1995-2005. Futuristic body, maple top, bound or unbound body, glued neck, angled headstock, either unbound neck with dot inlays or bound neck with crown inlays, 2 humbuckers. Reissued in '95 with same specs but unbound mahogany body after '97. Higher dollar Standard Custom still available.

1974-1975	Pre-production, 20 made	$11,000	$14,500
1975-1977	Production, 50 made, PAFs	$10,000	$13,300
1977-1979	Dimarzio PAF-copy	$7,000	$9,200
1980-1985		$5,000	$6,600
1995-1999		$4,000	$5,300
2000-2005	USA, flamed top	$2,400	$3,200

1993 Hamer Special
Paul Johnson

1982 Hamer Standard
Bo Belaski

Hamer Vector
Imaged by Heritage Auctions, HA.com

Harden Engineering
Switchblade

MODEL YEAR	FEATURES	EXC. COND. LOW	HIGH
Standard (Import, XT)	*1998-2012. Import version, 2 humbuckers.*		
1998-2012		$290	$375
Standard Custom GSTC	*2007-2012. Made in USA, flamed maple top, mahogany neck, rosewood 'board.*		
2007-2012		$3,300	$4,300
Stellar 1	*1999-2000. Korean import, double-cut, 2 humbuckers.*		
1999-2000		$140	$210
Steve Stevens I	*1984-1992. Introduced as Prototype SS, changed to Steve Stevens I in '86, contoured double-cut, 6-in-line headstock, dot or crown inlays, 1 humbucker and 2 single-coil pickups.*		
1984-1992		$1,275	$1,700
Steve Stevens II	*1986-1987. One humbucker and 1 single-coil version.*		
1986-1987		$1,275	$1,700
Studio	*1993-2012. Double-cut, flamed maple top on mahogany body, 2 humbuckers, cherry or natural.*		
1993-2012		$1,000	$1,300
Studio Custom	*1997-2012. Carved figured maple, humbuckers, tune-o-matic bridge, stop tailpiece, sunburst.*		
1997-2012		$1,500	$2,000
Sunburst	*1977-1983, 1990-1992, 2018-present. Double-cut bound solidbody, flamed maple top, glued-in neck, bound neck and crown inlays optional, 3-on-a-side headstock, 2 humbuckers.*		
1977-1983		$3,100	$4,100
1990-1992		$2,150	$2,900
Sunburst (Import, XT)	*1997-2012. Import version of Sunburst, flat-top or archtop, 2 pickups.*		
1997-2012		$225	$300
Sunburst Archtop	*1991-1997. Sunburst model with figured maple carved top, 2 humbuckers, offered under various names: Standard - unbound neck and dot inlays, tune-o-matic and stop tailpiece '91-'93 (replaced by the Studio). Custom - bound neck and crown inlays '91-'93, which became the Archtop for '94-'97 (replaced by the Studio Custom). Archtop GT - Gold top with P-90 soapbar-style pickups '93-'97.*		
1991-1997 Various models		$1,650	$2,200
T-51	*1993-1997. Classic single-cut southern ash body, 2 single-coils.*		
1993-1997		$800	$1,050
T-62	*1991-1995. Classic offset double-cut solidbody, tremolo, pau ferro 'board, Lubritrak nut, locking tuners, 3-band active EQ, various colors.*		
1991-1995		$800	$1,050
TLE	*1986-1992. Single-cut mahogany body, maple top, glued neck, 6-in-line headstock, rosewood 'board, dot inlays, 3 pickups.*		
1986-1992		$1,350	$1,800

MODEL YEAR	FEATURES	EXC. COND. LOW	HIGH
TLE Custom	*1986-1992. Bound, single-cut solidbody with maple top, glued-in neck, angled headstock, ebony 'board with boomerang inlays, 3 pickups.*		
1986-1992		$1,350	$1,800
Vector	*1982-1985. V-style body (optional flame maple top), 3-on-a-side peghead, rosewood 'board, 2 humbuckers, Sustain Block fixed bridge (Kahler or Floyd Rose tremolos may also be used).*		
1982-1985		$2,450	$3,200
Vector Limited Edition Korina	*1997. 72 built in Hamer's Arlington Heights, Illinois shop, price includes original Hamer certificate of authenticity with matching serial number, Flying-V Vector style body, gold hardware, natural finish.*		
1997		$2,600	$3,400

Hanson

2009-present. Founders John and Bo Pirruccello import intermediate grade, electric guitars which are set up in Chicago, Illinois.

Harden Engineering

1999-present. Professional grade, custom, solidbody guitars built by luthier William Harnden in Chicago, Illinois. He also builds effects pedals.

Harmony

1892-1976, late 1970s-present. Huge, Chicago-based manufacturer of fretted instruments, mainly budget models under the Harmony name or for many other American brands and mass marketers. Harmony was at one time the largest guitar builder in the world. In its glory days, Harmony made over one-half of the guitars built in the U.S., with '65 being their peak year. But by the early-'70s, the crash of the '60s guitar boom and increasing foreign competition brought an end to the company. The Harmony brand appeared on Asian-built instruments starting in the late '70s to the '90s with sales mainly through mass-retail stores. In 2000, the Harmony brand was distributed by MBT International. In '02, former MBT marketing director Alison Gillette launched Harmony Classic Reissue Guitars and Basses and in '09 the trademark was acquired by Westheimer Corporation. Many Harmony guitars have a factory order number on the inside back of the guitar which often contains the serial number. Most older Harmony acoustics and hollowbodies have a date ink-stamped inside the body. DeArmond made most of the electronic assemblies used on older Harmony electrics, and they often have a date stamped on the underside.

Amplifying Resonator Model 27

1930s. Dobro-licensed with Dobro metal resonator, wood body.

1930s		$700	$925

Buck Owens

1969. Acoustic flat-top, red, white and blue. The price shown is for a guitar that has an unblemished

MODEL YEAR	FEATURES	EXC. COND. LOW	HIGH

finish, paint-wear will reduce the price, prices vary considerable due to the condition of the finish.

| 1969 | | $2,000 | $2,650 |

Cremona

1930s-1952. Full-size archtop line, Harmony and Cremona logo on headstock, natural. Cutaways became available in '53.

| 1940-1952 | | $275 | $375 |

D Series (Electric)

Late-1980s-Early-1990s. Classic electric copy models including offset double- and single-cut solidbody and double-cut thin hollowbody (D720), 1 to 3 pickups. All models begin with D, some models part of Harmony Electric series and others the Harmony Igniter series.

| 1980s-90s | Various models | $75 | $150 |

H/HG Series (Electric)

Late-1980s-Early-1990s. Classic electric copy models including offset double-cut, single-cut and double-cut semi-hollow, 1 to 3 pickups, with or without tremolo. All models begin with H or HG, some models part of Harmony Electric series and others the Harmony Igniter series.

| 1980s-90s | Various models | $95 | $150 |

H14/H15 Bob Kat

1968. Replaces Silhouette solidbody, H14 has single pickup and 2 knobs, H15 has 2 pickups. When vibrato is added it becomes the H16 model.

| 1968 | H14 | $325 | $425 |
| 1968 | H15 | $450 | $600 |

H14/H15/H17 Silhouette

1963-1967. Double-cut solidbody, H14 single pickup, H15 dual pickup, H17 dual with vibrato (offered until '66).

1963-1967	H14	$325	$425
1963-1967	H15	$450	$600
1963-1967	H17	$550	$725

H19 Silhouette De Luxe Double

1965-1969. Double-cut solidbody, deluxe pickups, block markers, advanced vibrato, sunburst.

| 1965-1969 | | $750 | $1,000 |

H37 Hollywood

1960-1961. Electric archtop, auditorium size 15.75" body, 1 pickup, Harmony and Hollywood logo on headstock, 2-tone gold metallic finish.

| 1960-1961 | | $550 | $725 |

H39 Hollywood

1960-1965. Like H37 but with sunburst.

| 1960-1965 | | $375 | $500 |

H41 Hollywood

1960-1965. Like H37 but with 2 pickups, sunburst.

| 1960-1965 | | $475 | $625 |

H42/1 and H42/2 Stratotone Newport

1957-1958. Brightly colored, single-cut, Newport headstock logo, 1 single-coil. 42/1 in sunshine yellow, /2 in metallic green.

| 1957-1958 | | $1,200 | $1,600 |

H44 Stratotone

1953-1957. First edition models had small bodies and rounded cutaway, 1 pickup with plain cover using 2 mounting rivets, sometimes called Hershey Bar pickup, '60s models had slightly larger bodies and

sharp cutaways, some with headstock logo Harmony Stratotone with atomic note graphic.

| 1953-1957 | | $1,200 | $1,600 |

H45/H46 Stratotone Mars Electric

1958-1968. Single-cut, tone chamber construction, sunburst finish, H45 with 1 pickup, H46 with 2 pickups.

| 1960s | H45 | $525 | $700 |
| 1960s | H46 | $700 | $925 |

H47/48 Stratotone Mercury Electric

1958-1968. Single-cut, tone chamber construction, H47 with 1 pickup, block inlay and curly maple sunburst top, H48 is the same with a blond top.

| 1960s | H47 | $575 | $750 |
| 1960s | H48 | $575 | $750 |

H49 Stratotone Deluxe Jupiter

1958-1965. Single-cut, tone chamber construction, 2 pickups, bound spruce top, curly maple back and 6 control knobs, blond finish.

| 1958-1965 | | $800 | $1,050 |

H53 Rocket I

1959-1973. Single-cut, f-holes, 1 pickup, trapeze, 2-tone brown sunburst ('59-'62) or red sunburst ('63 on).

| 1959-1969 | | $450 | $600 |
| 1970-1973 | | $365 | $475 |

H54 Rocket II

1959-1973. Same as H53 but with 2 pickups.

| 1959-1969 | | $750 | $1,000 |
| 1970-1973 | | $450 | $600 |

H59 Rocket III

1960-1973. Same as H53 but with 3 pickups.

| 1960-1969 | | $1,050 | $1,375 |
| 1970-1973 | | $950 | $1,250 |

H59 Rocket Reissue

2000s. Import, double-cut, 3 pickups, 6 knobs.

| 2000s | | $525 | $700 |

H60 Double Cutaway Hollowbody

1968-1970. Thinline double-cut, 2 pickups, trapeze tailpiece, sunburst.

| 1968-1970 | | $1,050 | $1,400 |

H62 Blond

1950s-1965. Thin body, dual pickup archtop, curly maple back and sides, spruce top, block markers, blond.

| 1950s-1965 | | $1,400 | $1,850 |

H62VS (Reissue)

2000s. H62 with sunburst finish.

| 2000s | | $850 | $1,150 |

H63 Espanada

1950s-1965. Thick body, single-cut, jazz-style double pickups, black finish with white appointments, by early '60s 'Espanada' logo on lower bass bout.

| 1950s-1965 | | $1,375 | $1,800 |

H64 Double Cutaway Electric

1968-1970. Double-cut electric, factory Bigsby, dot markers, sunburst.

| 1968-1970 | | $1,275 | $1,675 |

H65 Modern Trend

1956-1960. Short-scale electric thin body archtop, 1 single-coil, block inlays, Sherry Blond finish on curly maple grain.

| 1956-1960 | | $925 | $1,225 |

1968 Harmony Bob Kat H15
Tom Pfeifer

1960 Harmony Meteor H71
Tom Pfeifer

GUITARS

1970 Harmony Sovereign
Edward Sparks

**1960 Harmony
Stratotone Mars H45**
Larry Krauss

MODEL YEAR	FEATURES	EXC. COND. LOW	HIGH
H66 Vibra-Jet			
1962-1966. Thinline single-cut, 2 pickups, built-in tremolo circuit and control panel knobs and selection dial, sunburst.			
1962-1966		$1,375	$1,800
H68 Deep Body Electric			
1968-1971. Full-body single-cut electric archtop, 2 pickups, trapeze bridge, block markers.			
1968-1971		$1,275	$1,675
H70/H71 Meteor			
1958-1966. Single rounded cutaway 2" thin body, 2 pickups, 3-part f-holes, block inlays, bolt neck, H70 sunburst, H71 natural (ended '65), lefty offered '65-'66, reintroduced as H661 and H671 (without Meteor name) in '72-'74.			
1958-1965	H71, natural	$1,450	$1,900
1958-1966	H70, sunburst	$1,450	$1,900
H72/H72V Double Cutaway Hollowbody			
1966-1971. Multiple bindings, 2 pickups, cherry red, H72V has Bigsby.			
1966-1971		$1,275	$1,675
H73 Roy Smeck			
1963-1964. Electric hollowbody, single neck silver bar-style pickup or 2 Harmony pickups.			
1963-1964		$1,100	$1,450
H74 Neo-Cutaway			
1961-1967. Modified double-cut, 2 pickups, Bigsby, 3-part F-holes, dot inlays.			
1961-1967		$1,375	$1,800
H75 Double Cutaway Hollowbody			
1960-1970. Three pickups, multi-bound body, 3-part f-holes, block inlays, bolt neck, brown sunburst.			
1960-1970		$1,375	$1,800
H76 Double Cutaway Hollowbody			
1960-1962. H75 with Bigsby.			
1960-1962		$1,375	$1,800
H77 Double Cutaway Hollowbody			
Late-1960s. Same as H75, but in cherry sunburst.			
1960s		$1,375	$1,800
H78 Double Cutaway Hollowbody			
Late-1960s. H77 with Bigsby.			
1960s		$1,375	$1,800
H79 Double Cutaway Hollowbody 12-String			
1966-1970. Unique slotted headstock, cherry finish.			
1966-1970		$1,375	$1,800
H81 Rebel			
1968-1971. Single pickup version of Rebel, brown sunburst.			
1968-1971		$350	$465
H82/H82G Rebel			
Listed as a new model in 1971. Thin body, hollow tone chamber, double-cut, 2 pickups, H82 sunburst, H82G greenburst avacado shading (renumbered as H682 and H683 in '72).			
1970s	H82	$575	$750
1970s	H82G	$575	$750
H88 Stratotone Doublet			
1954-1957. Basically 2-pickup H44.			
1954-1957		$1,200	$1,600

MODEL YEAR	FEATURES	EXC. COND. LOW	HIGH
H150 Student			
1963-1969. Parlor-size acoustic.			
1963-1969		$165	$250
H162 Folk			
1950s-1971. Grand concert size acoustic, spruce top, mahogany body.			
1950s-1971		$425	$550
H165 Grand Concert			
1948-1957. Flat-top, all mahogany body. Body changed to square-shoulder in '58 (see Folk H165).			
1948-1957		$325	$425
H165/H6365 Folk			
1958-1974. Square-shouldered flat-top, all mahogany body. Renamed the H6365 in '72.			
1958-1974		$375	$500
H600 Roy Rogers			
1954-1958. 3/4 size, stencil, sold through Sears.			
1954-1958		$300	$400
H910 Classical			
1970s. Beginner guitar, natural.			
1970s		$65	$85
H945 Master			
1965-1966. 15" Auditorium-sized acoustic archtop, block markers, music note painted logo on headstock, sunburst.			
1965-1966		$250	$325
H950/H952/H1325/H1456/H1457/H6450			
1930s-1974. Line of Auditorium and Grand Auditorium acoustic archtop models.			
1950s	H950 Monterey	$200	$475
1950s	H952 Colorama	$300	$475
1950s-60s	Other models	$200	$475
1970s	H6450	$135	$190
H954 Broadway			
1930s-1971. 15-3/4" body, acoustic archtop, dot markers, sunburst.			
1930s-1971		$225	$300
H1057 Singing Cowboys			
1950s. Western chuck-wagon scene stencil top, Singing Cowboys stenciled on either side of upper bouts, brown background versus earlier Supertone version that had black background.			
1950s		$325	$425
H1200 Auditorium Series			
1948-1975. Moderately-priced acoustic archtop, treble-clef artwork on headstock, model 1213 & 1215 (shaded brown sunburst) and 1214 (blond ivory, ends in '64). Model 1215 was renamed H6415 in '72 and lasted until '75.			
1948-1975	Various models	$250	$325
H1203 Sovereign Western Special Jumbo			
1960s-1970s. 15" wide body, 000-style.			
1960s		$475	$625
H1215 Archtone			
1950-1960s. Lower-end archtop, 6-string, sunburst.			
1950-60s		$275	$375
H1215 Archtone Tenor			
1950-1960s. Lower-end archtop tenor, 4-string, sunburst.			
1950-60s		$250	$325

MODEL YEAR	FEATURES	EXC. COND. LOW	HIGH

H1250 Roy Smeck Vita Standard
1928-1931. Pear shaped body, seal-shaped sound holes.

1928-1931		$800	$1,050

H1252 Professional Hawaiian
1940. Hawaiian acoustic jumbo, high-end appointments, vertical Professional logo on front of headstock, figured koa or mahogany back and sides, spruce top, Brazilian rosewood fretboard, various-shaped fretboard markers.

1940		$2,350	$3,100

H1260 Sovereign Jumbo
1960s-1970s. Jumbo shape, 16" wide body, natural.

1960s		$625	$825
1970s		$425	$550

H1265 Sovereign Jumbo Deluxe
1965-1969. Jumbo D-style, 16" fancy.

1965-1969		$1,200	$1,600

H1266 Sovereign Jumbo Deluxe
Late-1960s-1970s. Jumbo nearly D-style, 16" wide body with out-sized 'guard, natural.

1960s		$1,200	$1,600
1970s		$600	$800

H1270 Flat-Top 12-String
1965. 16" deluxe acoustic 12-string flat-top, spruce top, mahogany sides and back, dot markers.

1965		$450	$600

H1310 Brilliant Cutaway
1953-1973. Grand Auditorium acoustic archtop, single rounded cutaway, block inlays, sunburst. Called H6510 in '72.

1953-1973		$575	$750

H1311 Brilliant Cutaway
1953-1962. As H1310, but in blond.

1953-1963		$800	$1,050

H1407/H1414/H1418 Patrician
1932-1973. Model line mostly with mahogany bodies and alternating single/double dot markers (later models with single dots), introduced as flat-top, changed to archtop in '34. In '37 line expanded to 9 archtops (some with blocks) and 1 flat-top. Flat-tops disappeared in the '40s, with various archtops offered up to '73.

1932-1973		$300	$475

H1442 Roy Smeck Artiste
1939-ca. 1942. Grand auditorium acoustic archtop, Roy Smeck Artiste logo on headstock, split rectangle markers, black with white guard.

1939-1942		$500	$650

H4101 Flat-Top Tenor
1950s-1970s. Mahogany body, 4-string.

1950s-70s		$300	$400

Holiday Rocket
Mid-1960s. Similar to H59 Rocket III but with push-button controls instead of rotary selector switch, 3 Goldentone pickups, pickup trim rings, Holiday logo on 'guard, higher model than standard Rocket.

1960s		$1,150	$1,500

Igniter Series (D/H/HG)
Late-1980s to early-1990s. Pointy-headstock electric copy models, offset double-cut, all models begin with D, H, or HG.

1980s-90s	Various models	$100	$200

MODEL YEAR	FEATURES	EXC. COND. LOW	HIGH

Lone Ranger
1950-1951. Lone Ranger headstock stencil, Lone Ranger and Tonto stencil on brown body. This model was first introduced in 1936 as the Supertone Lone Ranger with same stencil on a black body.

1950-1951		$300	$400

TG1201 Tenor
1950s. Spruce top, two-on-a-side tuners, Sovereign model tenor, natural.

1950s		$300	$400

Harptone
1893-ca. 1975. The Harptone Manufacturing Corporation was located in Newark, New Jersey. They made musical instrument cases and accessories and got into instrument production from 1934 to '42, making guitars, banjos, mandolins, and tiples. In '66 they got back into guitar production, making the Standel line from '67 to '69. Harptone offered flat-tops and archtops under their own brand until the mid-'70s when the name was sold to the Diamond S company, which owned Micro-Frets.

Acoustic
1966-mid-1970s. Various models.

1966-1970s	Deluxe/Custom	$1,350	$1,750
1966-1970s	Standard	$1,050	$1,350

Electric
1966-mid-1970s. Various models.

1966-1970s		$1,350	$1,750

Harrison Guitars
1992-present. Luthier Douglas Harrison builds premium grade, production/custom, archtop and semi-hollowbody jazz guitars in Toronto, Ontario.

Harwood
Harwood was a brand introduced in 1885 by Kansas City, Missouri instrument wholesalers J.W. Jenkins & Sons (though some guitars marked Harwood, New York). May have been built by Jenkins until circa 1905, but work was later contracted out to Harmony.

Parlor
1890s. Slotted headstocks, most had mahogany bodies, some with Brazilian rosewood body, considered to be well made.

1890s	Brazilian rosewood	$975	$1,250
1890s	Mahogany	$525	$700

Hascal Haile
Late 1960s-1986. Luthier Hascal Haile started building acoustic, classical and solidbody guitars in Tompkinsville, Kentucky, after retiring from furniture making. He died in '86.

Hauver Guitar
2001-present. Professional and premium grade, custom, acoustic guitars, built in Sharpsburg, Maryland by luthier Michael S. Hauver.

Harmony H72 Double Cutaway Hollowbody

Tom Pfeifer

1963 Harmony H1215 Auditorium

Douglas Morissette

GUITARS

1988 Heartfield RR9
Tom Pfeifer

1986 Heritage H-140
Carter Vintage Guitars

MODEL YEAR	FEATURES	EXC. COND. LOW	HIGH

Hayes Guitars

Professional and premium grade, production/custom, steel and nylon string guitars made by luthier Louis Hayes in Paonia, Colorado. He began building in 1993.

Hayman

1970-1973. Solid and semi-hollowbody guitars and basses developed by Jim Burns and Bob Pearson for Ivor Arbiter of the Dallas Arbiter Company and built by Shergold in England.

Haynes

1865-early 1900s. The John C. Haynes Co. of Boston also made the Bay State brand.

Heartfield

1989-1994. Founded as a joint venture between Fender Musical Instrument Corporation (U.S.A.) and Fender Japan (partnership between Fender and distributors Kanda Shokai and Yamano Music) to build and market more advanced designs (built by Fuji Gen-Gakki). First RR and EX guitar series and DR Bass series debut in '90. Talon and Elan guitar series and Prophecy bass series introduced in '91. The brand was dead by '94.

Electric Solidbody

1989-1994	Various models	$650	$850

Heiden Stringed Instruments

1974-present. Luthier Michael Heiden builds his premium grade, production/custom, flat-top guitars in Chilliwack, British Columbia. He also builds mandolins.

Heit Deluxe

Ca. 1967-1970. Imported from Japan by unidentified New York distributor. Many were made by Teisco, the most famous being the Teisco V-2 Mosrite copy. They also had basses.

Acoustic

1967-1970	Various models	$200	$260

Electric

1967-1970	Various models	$350	$450

Hembry Guitars

2002-present. Professional grade, production/custom, solidbody electric guitars built by luthier Scott Hembry in Shelton, Washington. He also builds basses.

Hemken, Michael

1993-2021. Luthier Michael Hemken built his premium grade, custom, archtops in St. Helena, California. He died January, 2021.

HenBev

Premium grade, production, solid and hollow body electric guitars and basses built by luthier Scotty Bevilacqua in Oceanside, California, starting in the year 2005.

MODEL YEAR	FEATURES	EXC. COND. LOW	HIGH

Henderson Guitars

Luthier Wayne C. Henderson builds premium and presentation grade, custom acoustic guitars in Rugby, Virginia. He produces around 20 guitars per year and has also made mandolins, banjos and fiddles.

Hendrick

1982-1985. Solidbody guitars built by luthier Kurt Hendrick in Texas, Ohio and Michigan. Less than 100 built, the most popular model was the Generator. Hendrick also worked with Schecter, Fender, Jackson and Epiphone.

Henman Guitars

2010-present. Owners Graham and Paris Henman offer premium grade, production/custom, solidbody and chambered electric guitars and basses built by luthier Rick Turner in Santa Cruz, California.

Heritage

1985-present. Professional, premium, and presentation grade, production/custom, hollow, semi-hollow, and solidbody guitars built in Kalamazoo, Michigan. They have also made banjos, mandolins, flat-tops, and basses in the past.

Founded by Jim Deurloo, Marvin Lamb, J.P. Moats, Bill Paige and Mike Korpak, all former Gibson employees who did not go to Nashville when Norlin closed the original Gibson factory in '84. In 2007, Vince Margol bought out Paige. In '16, a private group of local Kalamazoo investors bought the business with Deurloo, Lamb and Paige remaining active in the company.

Eagle

1986-2009. Single rounded cut semi-hollowbody, mahogany body and neck, bound body, 1 jazz pickup, f-holes, sunburst or natural.

1986-2009		$2,100	$2,750

Eagle Classic

1992-present. Standard Collection, Eagle with maple body and neck, bound neck and headstock, gold hardware, sunburst or natural.

1992-2021		$2,900	$3,750

Gary Moore

1989-1991. Single-cut solidbody, 2 pickups, chrome hardware, sunburst.

1989-1991		$1,850	$2,400

Golden Eagle

1985-2019. Single-cut hollowbody, back inlaid with mother-of-pearl eagle and registration number, multibound ebony 'board with mother-of-pearl cloud inlays, bound f-holes, gold-plated parts, ebony bridge inlaid with mother-of-pearl, mother-of-pearl truss rod cover engraved with owner's name, 1 Heritage jazz pickup, multi-bound curly maple 'guard.

1985-2019	Floating pickup	$2,700	$3,500
1985-2019	Mounted pickup	$2,700	$3,500

MODEL YEAR	FEATURES	EXC. COND. LOW	HIGH

Groove Master
2004-2018. 16" hollow-body, single rounded cutaway, neck pickup, sunburst.

| 2004-2018 | | $1,650 | $2,150 |

H-137
1980s-2021. Standard Collection, single-cut solidbody, 2 P-90s, sunburst, natural lime (early) or TV yellow (later).

| 1980s-2018 | Sunburst or natural lime | $1,225 | $1,575 |
| 2019-2021 | Sunburst or TV yellow | $1,275 | $1,650 |

H-137 AA
2018-2021. Artisan Aged Collection, sunburst or TV yellow with aged finish.

| 2018-2021 | | $1,275 | $1,650 |

H-140/H-140 CM
1985-2005, 2007-2016. Single pointed cutaway solidbody, bound curly maple ('85-'04) or solid gold top ('94-'05), 2 humbuckers, chrome parts.

1985-1996	Black	$1,225	$1,575
1985-2004	CM, curly maple	$1,225	$1,575
1994-2005	Goldtop	$1,225	$1,575
2001	CM, flamed maple	$1,225	$1,575
2007-2016	2nd edition, goldtop	$1,225	$1,575

H-147
1990-1991. Single-cut solidbody, 2 humbuckers, mahogany body, mother-of-pearl block inlays, black with black or gold hardware.

| 1990-1991 | | $1,125 | $1,450 |

H-150
1990s-present. Standard Collection, solid carved figured maple top, mahogany back, various colors.

1990s-2021	Cherry Sunburst	$1,750	$2,300
1990s-2021	Ebony	$1,650	$2,200
1990s-2021	Goldtop	$1,650	$2,200
1990s-2021	Sunburst	$1,750	$2,300

H-150 AA
2018-present. Artisan Aged Collection, sunburst, ebony, various colors with aged finish.

| 2018-2021 | | $1,750 | $2,300 |

H-150 C/H-150 CM
1985-2018. Single rounded cutaway solidbody, curly maple top, 2 pickups, chrome parts, cherry sunburst.

| 1985-2018 | Flamed | $1,750 | $2,300 |
| 1985-2018 | Goldtop | $1,600 | $2,100 |

H-150 Deluxe Limited Edition
1992. 300 made.

| 1992 | | $1,600 | $2,100 |

H-157
1989-2004. Mahogany body with maple top, natural, sunburst or black.

| 1989-2004 | | $1,775 | $2,300 |

H-157 Ultra
1993-1994. Single-cut solidbody, large block markers, highly figured maple top.

| 1993-1994 | | $1,775 | $2,300 |

H-160
1986, 2007. Limited production.

| 1986 | | $925 | $1,200 |
| 2007 | 2nd Edition | $1,000 | $1,300 |

H-170
1980s-1997. Double-cut solidbody, 2 humbuckers, bound carved top, was also a later curly maple top version (H-170CM).

| 1980s-1997 | | $1,200 | $1,600 |

H-204 DD
1986-1989. Single-cut solidbody of mahogany, curly maple top, 1-piece mahogany neck, 22-fret rosewood 'board.

| 1986-1989 | | $600 | $800 |

H-207 DD
1986-1989. Double-cut solidbody of mahogany, curly maple top, 1-piece mahogany neck, 22-fret rosewood 'board.

| 1986-1989 | | $600 | $800 |

H-357
1989-1994. Asymmetrical solidbody, neck-thru.

| 1989-1994 | | $2,100 | $2,700 |

H-516 Thin
1999-2015. Single-cut, thin all maple body, mahogany neck, 2 humbucking pickups, various colors.

| 1999-2015 | | $1,800 | $2,350 |

H-530
2016-present. Standard Collection, double-cut hollowbody, sunburst, trans cherry or antique natural.

| 2016-2021 | | $1,925 | $2,500 |

H-535
1987-present. Standard Collection, double-cut semi-hollowbody, curly maple top and back, 2 pickups, various colors.

| 1987-2018 | | $1,950 | $2,550 |
| 2019-2021 | | $1,950 | $2,550 |

H-535 AA
2018-2021. Artisan Aged Collection, various colors with aged finish.

| 2018-2021 | | $1,850 | $2,400 |

H-537
1990. Single-cut, thinline, dots.

| 1990 | | $1,450 | $1,900 |

H-550
1990-2018. Single-cut hollowbody, laminated maple top and back, multiple bound top, white bound 'guard, f-holes, 2 humbuckers.

| 1990-2018 | | $2,150 | $2,800 |

H-555
1989-2018. Like 535, but with maple neck, ebony 'board, pearl and abalone inlays, gold hardware.

| 1989-2018 | | $2,150 | $2,800 |

H-575
1987-present. Standard Collection, sharp single-cut hollowbody, solid maple top and back, cream bound top and back, wood 'guard, f-holes, 2 humbuckers.

| 1987-2019 | | $2,550 | $3,300 |
| 2020-2021 | | $2,400 | $3,150 |

H-575 AA
2018-2020. Artisan Aged Collection, various colors with aged finish.

| 2018-2020 | | $2,400 | $3,150 |

Heritage H-530

Heritage H-575

GUITARS

Hoffman Small Jumbo

2000 Höfner Jazzica Custom
Bernunzio Uptown Music

MODEL YEAR	FEATURES	EXC. COND. LOW	HIGH

H-576
1990-2004. Single rounded cut hollowbody, laminated maple top and back, multiple bound top, single bound back and f-holes and wood 'guard, 2 humbuckers.

1990-2004		$1,850	$2,400

Henry Johnson (HJ) Signature
2005-2018. Pointed single cut curly maple back and sides hollowbody, 2 humbuckers, block inlays, multi-bound.

2005-2018		$1,600	$2,100

HFT-445
1987-2000. Flat-top acoustic, mahogany back and sides, spruce top, maple neck, rosewood 'board.

1987-2000		$775	$1,025

Johnny Smith
1989-2001. Custom hand-carved 17" hollowbody, single-cut, f-holes, 1 pickup, various colors.

1989-2001 Various options	$2,900	$3,750

Kenny Burrell (KB) Groove Master
2004-2018. Single-cut 16" hollow body, 1 humbucker, gold hardware, block inlays.

2004-2018		$2,050	$2,650

Millennium Eagle 2000
2000-2009. Single-cut semi-solidbody, multiple bound curly maple top, single-bound curly maple back, f-holes, 2 humbuckers, block inlays.

2000-2009		$1,850	$2,400

Millennium Eagle Custom
2000-2009. Like ME 2000 but with curlier maple, multiple bound neck, split block inlays.

2000-2009		$2,550	$3,300

Millennium SAE
2000-2009. Single-cut semi-solidbody, laminated arch top, single cream bound top and back, f-holes, 2 humbuckers.

2000-2009		$1,150	$1,500

Millennium Ultra/Standard Ultra
2004-2016. Single-cut, ultra curly maple top, mahogany back and sides, 1-piece mahogany neck, f-holes, mother-of-pearl block inlays.

2004-2016		$1,675	$2,175

Parsons Street
1989-1992. Offset double-cut, curly maple top on mahogany body, single/single/hum pickups, pearl block markers, sunburst or natural.

1989-1992		$750	$975

Roy Clark
1992-2018. Thinline, single-cut semi-hollow archtop, gold hardware, 2 humbuckers, block markers, cherry sunburst.

1992-2018		$2,300	$3,000

SAE Custom
1992-2000. Single-cut maple semi-hollowbody, f-holes, 2 humbuckers and 1 bridge pickup.

1992-2000		$1,225	$1,575

Super Eagle
1988-2018. 18" body, single-cut electric archtop, 2 humbuckers.

1989-2018		$2,875	$3,725

MODEL YEAR	FEATURES	EXC. COND. LOW	HIGH

Super KB Kenny Burrell
2005-2011. Carved spruce top, tiger-flame maple back and sides, 2 pickups, natural or Antique Sunburst.

2005-2011		$5,500	$7,200

Sweet 16
1987-2018. Single-cut maple semi-hollowbody, spruce top, 2 pickups, pearl inlays.

1987-2018		$2,300	$3,000

Hermann Hauser
Born in 1882, Hauser started out building zithers and at age 23 added classical guitars and lutes, most built in his shop in Munich, Germany. He died in 1952. His son and grandson and great-granddaughter, Hermann II and III and Kathrin, continued the tradition. The Hermann Hauser's legacy is based on his innovative approach to bracing and top thickness which gave his instruments their own voice. Hermann I Era instruments are linked with Andres Segovia who used them. Hermann II Era instruments are linked with modern players like Julian Bream. Hermann III builds Segovia style and custom-made instruments. Kathrin Hauser, daughter of Hermann III, is a fourth generation builder. The original Hauser shop in Munich was destroyed by Allied bombing in 1946 and was moved to Reisbach in the Bavaria region, where the shop remains. Hauser instruments used paper labels on the inside back. The labels often stipulate the city of construction as well as the Hermann Hauser name. Labels are easily removed and changed, and an original instrument should be authenticated. Beautiful violin-like clear varnish finish ends in '52, approximately 400 instruments were made by Hermann I. Under Hermann II, nitrocellulose lacquer spray replaces varnish in '52, bracing patterns change in the '60s, which was a welcome change for modern players. Instruments should be evaluated on a case by case basis.

Hermann Hauser II
1952-1988. Born in 1911 and the son of Hermann Hauser I, he built between 500 and 600 classical guitars in Germany during his career. He died in 1988.

Hermann Hauser III
1988-present. Hermann III started build guitars in '74, and took over the family business upon the death of his father in '88. He continues to build Segovia style and custom-made classical guitars in Munich, Germany.

Hess
1872-ca. 1940. Located in Klingenthal, Germany, Hess built acoustic and harp guitars, as well as other stringed instruments and accordians.

Hewett Guitars
1994-present. Luthier James Hewett builds his professional and premium grade, custom/production, steel string, archtop jazz, solidbody and harp guitars in Panorama Village, Texas.

MODEL YEAR	FEATURES	EXC. COND. LOW	HIGH

Hill Guitar Company

1972-1980, 1990-present. Luthier Kenny Hill builds his professional and premium grade production/custom, classical and flamenco guitars in Felton, California and Michoacan, Mexico.

Hirade Classical

1968-present. Professional grade, production, solid top, classical guitars built in Japan by Takamine. The late Mass Hirade was the founder of the Takamine workshop. He learned his craft from master luthier Masare Kohno. Hirade represents Takamine's finest craftsmanship and material.

HML Guitars

Introduced in 1997, Howard Leese custom-designs, premium grade, electric guitars, built by luthier Jack Pimentel in Puyallup, Washington.

Hoffman Guitars

1971-present. Premium grade, custom flat-tops and harp guitars built by luthier Charles Hoffman in Minneapolis, Minnesota.

Höfner

1887-present. Budget, intermediate, professional and premium grade, production, solidbody, semi-hollow, archtop, acoustic, and classical guitars built in Germany and the Far East. They also produce basses and bowed-instruments. Founded by Karl Höfner in Schonbach, Germany. The company was already producing guitars when sons Josef and Walter joined the company in 1919 and '21 and expanded the market worldwide. They moved the company to Bavaria in '50 and to Hagenau in '97. The S in Hofner model names usually denotes cutaway.

Beatle Electric Model 459TZ

1966-1967. Violin-shaped 500/1 body, block-stripe position markers, transistor-powered flip-fuzz and treble boost, sunburst.

1966-1967		$1,325	$1,725

Beatle Electric Model 459VTZ

1966-1967. Same as Model 459TZ except with vibrato tailpiece, brown (standard) or blond option.

1966-1967	Blond option	$1,500	$1,950
1966-1967	Brown	$1,325	$1,725

Beatle Electric Model G459TZ Super

1966-1967. Deluxe version of Model 459TZ, flamed maple sides, narrow grain spruce top, gold hardware, elaborate inlays and binding, natural blond.

1966-1967		$1,450	$1,900

Beatle Electric Model G459VTZ Super

1966-1967. Same as G459TZ Super but with vibrato tailpiece.

1966-1967		$1,475	$1,900

Club Model 40 John Lennon Limited Edition

2008. Limited run of 120, single-cut, spruce top, maple back and sides, neck pickup, vertical Höfner logo on headstock, Lennon signature on 'guard.

2008		$1,700	$2,200

Club Model 50

1959-1962. Mid-level of the 'Club Series', single-cut, 2 pickups, sunburst.

1959-1962		$1,500	$1,950

Club Model 60

1959. Highest model of 'Club Series', single-cut, 2 black bar pickups, 2 knobs and 2 slider switches on control panel, high-end split-diamond style markers, natural blond finish.

1959-1962		$1,600	$2,100

Club Model 126

1954-1970. Mid-sized single-cut solidbody, dot markers, flamed maple back and sides, spruce top, sunburst. Listed with Höfner Professional Electric Series.

1954-1970		$1,000	$1,300

Committee Model 4680 Thin Electric

1961-1968. Thinline single-cut archtop, 2 pickups, split-arrowhead markers, no vibrato, sunburst.

1961-1968		$900	$1,175

Deluxe Model 176

1964-1983. Double-cut, 3 pickups, polyester varnished sunburst finish, vibrola tailpiece, similar to Model 175 polyester varnished red and gold version.

1964-1966		$900	$1,200
1967-1969		$650	$850
1970-1983		$525	$700

Galaxy Model 175

1963-1966. Double-cut, 3 pickups, red and gold vinyl covering, fancy red-patch 'guard, vibrola, similar to Model 176 polyester varnished sunburst version.

1963-1966		$900	$1,200

Golden Höfner

1959-1963. Single-cut archtop, blond, 2 pickups, f-holes.

1959-1963		$6,000	$7,800

Jazzica Custom

2000-2010. Full body, single soft cutaway, acoustic/electric archtop, carved German spruce top, sunburst.

2000-2010		$1,575	$2,050

Model 165

1975-1976. Offset double-cut, S-style body, 2 single-coil pickups, bolt-on neck.

1975-1976		$375	$500

Model 171

1975-1976. Copy of Tele-Thinline.

1975-1976		$325	$425

Model 172 II (R) (S) (I)

1962-1963. Double-cut body, polyester varnished wood (S) or scuff-proof red (R) or white (I) vinyl, 2 pickups, vibrato.

1962-1963		$400	$425

Model 173 II (S) (I)

1962-1963. Double-cut body, polyester varnished wood (S) or scuff-proof vinyl (I), 3 pickups, vibrato.

1962-1963		$450	$600

Model 178

1967-ca. 1969. Offset double-cut solidbody, 2 pickups with an array of switches and push button controls, fancy position markers, vibrola, sunburst. 178 used on different design in the '70s.

1967-1969		$475	$625

Höfner Club 50
Rivington Guitars

1961 Höfner 173 II S
Imaged by Heritage Auctions, HA.com

1950s Höfner Senator
Acoustic Archtop
Paul Johnson

1980s Hohner
Professional TE Prinz
Imaged by Heritage Auctions, HA.com

MODEL YEAR	FEATURES	EXC. COND. LOW	HIGH

Model 180 Shorty Standard
1982. Small-bodied travel guitar, single-cut, solid-body, 1 pickup. The Shorty Super had a built-in amp and speaker.

1982		$250	$325

Model 450S Acoustic Archtop
Mid-1960s. Economy single-cut acoustic archtop in Hofner line, dot markers, Höfner logo on 'guard, sunburst.

1960s		$425	$550

Model 455S Acoustic Archtop
1950s-1970. Archtop, single-cut, block markers.

1950s-1970		$575	$775

Model 456 Acoustic Archtop
1950s-1962. Full body acoustic archtop, f-holes, laminated maple top, sides, back, large pearloid blocks, two color pearloid headstock laminate.

1950s-1962		$550	$725

Model 457 President
1959-1972. Single-cut thinline archtop, 2 pickups, non-vibrato.

1959-1972		$675	$875

Model 457/12 12-String Electric
1969-1970. Comfort-thin cutaway archtop, shaded brown.

1969-1970		$575	$775

Model 462 Acoustic Archtop
Ca. 1952-1960s. Single-cut archtop, bound cat's-eye soundholes, 3-piece pearloid headstock overlay, 3-piece large block inlays. Also offered with fingerboard mounted pickup with no controls (EG) and by mid '50s with 1, 2, or 3 pickups with volume and tone knobs/switches (462S/E1, 2, or 3).

1952-1960s	462S	$500	$650
1952-1960s	462SEG	$750	$975

Model 463 Electric Archtop
1958-1960. Archtop electric, 2 or 3 pickups.

1958-1960		$975	$1,300

Model 470SE2 Electric Archtop
1961-1994. Large single rounded cutaway electric archtop on Höfner's higher-end they call "superbly flamed maple (back and sides), carved top of best spruce," 2 pickups, 3 control knobs, gold hardware, pearl inlay, natural finish only.

1961-1994		$750	$975

Model 471SE2 Electric Archtop
1969-1977. Large single pointed cutaway electric archtop, flamed maple back and sides, spruce top, black celluloid binding, ebony 'board, pearl inlays, sunburst version of the 470SE2.

1969-1977		$750	$975

Model 490 Acoustic Flat-Top
Late 1960s. 16" body, 12-string, spruce top, maple back and sides, dot markers, natural.

1960s		$200	$275

Model 490E Electric Flat-Top
Late 1960s. Flat-top 12-string with on-board pickup and 2 control knobs.

1960s		$300	$400

Model 491 Acoustic Flat-Top
1960s-1970s. Slope shoulder body style, spruce top, mahogany back and sides, shaded sunburst.

1970s		$300	$400

Model 492 Acoustic
Late-1960s. 16" body, 12-string, spruce top, mahogany back and sides, dot markers.

1960s		$285	$375

Model 492E Acoustic Electric
Late 1960s. Flat-top 12-string with on-board pickup and 2 control knobs.

1960s		$285	$375

Model 496 Jumbo Flat-Top
1960s. Jumbo-style body, selected spruce top, flamed maple back and sides, gold-plated hardware, vine pattern 'guard, sunburst.

1960s		$450	$600

Model 514-H Classical Concert
1960s. Concert model, lower-end of the Höfner classical line, natural.

1960s		$140	$180

Model 4500 Thin Electric
Late-1960s-early-1970s. Thinline archtop, single-cut, 3 options, laminated maple top and back, dot markers, top mounted controls, brown sunburst.

1960s-70s	E1, 1 pickup	$450	$600
1960s-70s	E2, 2 pus	$550	$725
1960s-70s	V2, 2 pus, vibrato	$575	$750

Model 4560 Thin Electric
Late-1960s-early-1970s. Thinline archtop, single-cut, 2 options, laminated maple top and back, 2-color headstock, large block markers, top mounted controls, brown sunburst.

1960s-70s	E2	$575	$750
1960s-70s	V2, vibrato	$625	$825

Model 4574VTZ Extra Thin
Late-1960s-early-1970s. Extra thinline acoustic, 2 pickups, vibrato arm, treble boost and flip-fuzz.

1960s-70s		$625	$825

Model 4575VTZ Extra Thin
Late-1960s-early-1970s. Extra-thinline acoustic, double-cut with shallow rounded horns, 3 pickups, vibrato arm, treble boost and flip-fuzz.

1960s-70s		$700	$900

Model 4578TZ President
1959-1970. Double-cut archtop. 'President' dropped from name by late-'60s and renamed Model 4578 Dual Cutaway, also added sharp horns.

1959-1965		$625	$825
1966-1970		$550	$725

Model 4600 Thin Electric
Late-1960s-early-1970s. Thinline acoustic, double-cut, 2 pickups, dot markers, sunburst, V2 with vibrato.

1960s-70s	E2	$550	$725
1960s-70s	V2, vibrato	$600	$800

Model 4680 Thin Electric
Late-1960s-early-1970s. Single-cut thinline electric, 2 pickups, 3-in-a-line control knobs, ornate inlays, spruce top, brown sunburst, V2 with vibrato.

1960s-70s	E2	$850	$1,100
1960s-70s	V2, vibrato	$925	$1,200

MODEL YEAR	FEATURES	EXC. COND. LOW	HIGH

Model 4700 Thin Electric
Late-1960s-early-1970s. Deluxe version of Model 4680, gold plated appointments and natural finish, V2 with vibrato.

1960s-70s	E2	$975	$1,275
1960s-70s	V2, vibrato	$1,050	$1,350

Senator Acoustic Archtop
1958-1960s. Full body archtop, floating pickup option available, f-holes, made for Selmer, London.

1958-1960		$400	$525

Senator E1
1961. Senator full body archtop jazz, single top mounted pickup and controls.

1961		$575	$750

Verythin Standard
2001-2008. Update of the 1960s Verythin line, 2 humbuckers, f-holes, dot inlays.

2001-2008		$700	$900

Hohner
1857-present. Budget and intermediate grade, production, acoustic and electric guitars and basses. They also have mandolins, banjos and ukuleles. Matthias Hohner, a clockmaker in Trossingen, Germany, founded Hohner in 1857, making harmonicas. Hohner has been offering guitars and basses at least since the early '70s. HSS was founded in 1986 as a distributor of guitars and other musical products. By 2000, Hohner was also offering the Crafter brands of guitars.

Alpha Standard
1987. Designed by Klaus Scholler, solidbody, stereo outputs, Flytune tremolo.

1987		$225	$300

G 2T/G 3T Series
1980s-1990s. Steinberger-style body, 6-string, neck-thru, locking tremolo.

1980s-90s		$300	$400

Jacaranda Rosewood Dreadnought
1978. Flat-top acoustic.

1978		$175	$225

Jack
1987-1990s. Mate for Jack Bass. Headless, tone circuit, tremolo, 2 single-coils and 1 humbucker.

1987-1992		$300	$400

L 59/L 75 Series
Late-1970s-1980s. Classic single-cut solidbody, 2 humbuckers, glued neck, sunburst, 59 has upgrade maple body with maple veneer top.

1970s-80s		$300	$400

Miller Beer Guitar
1985. Solidbody, shaped like Miller beer logo.

1985		$225	$300

Professional
1980s. Single-cut solidbody, maple neck, extra large 'guard, natural.

1980s		$300	$400

Professional Series - TE Custom
1980s-1990s. Single-cut solidbody, bolt neck.

1980s-90s		$700	$900

Professional Series - TE Prinz
Late 1980s-early 1990s. Based on Prince's No. 1 guitar, 2 single-coils, bolt neck, Professional The Prinz headstock logo, natural.

1989-1990		$700	$900

SE 35
1989-mid-1990s. Semi-hollow thinline, 2 humbuckers, natural.

1989		$300	$400

SG Lion
1980s-1990s. Offset double-cut, pointy headstock, glued neck.

1980s-90s		$225	$300

ST Series
1986-1990s. Includes the bolt neck ST 57, ST Special, ST Special S, Viper I, Viper II (snakeskin finish option), ST Victory, ST Metal S, and the ST Custom.

1986-1992		$275	$360

Standard Series - EX Artist
1970s-1980s. Solidbody, 2 humbuckers, gold hardware, neck-thru, solid maple body, rosewood 'board, tremolo.

1970s-80s		$275	$360

Standard Series - RR Custom
1970s-1980s. Randy Rhoads V body, 2 humbuckers, chrome hardware, glued neck, mahogany body, rosewood 'board, tremolo.

1970s-80s		$275	$360

Standard Series - SR Heavy
1970s-1980s. Hybrid body, 2 humbuckers, neck-thru, solid maple body, rosewood 'board, tremolo.

1970s-80s		$275	$360

Holiday
1960s. Electric, acoustic and bass guitars sold by Aldens, a Chicago catalog company. Most models built by Harmony. They also offered mandolins and banjos.

Silhouette Bobcat
1964-1967. Solidbody electric made by Harmony, similar to Harmony Silhouette, offset double-cut, 2 pickups, 4-in-a-row control knobs.

1964-1967		$375	$480

Hollenbeck Guitars
1970-2008. Luthier Bill Hollenbeck built his premium grade, production/custom, hollow and semi-hollow body acoustics and electric guitars in Lincoln, Illinois. Bill passed away in '08.

Hollingworth Guitars
1995-present. Luthier Graham Hollingworth builds his production/custom, premium grade, electric, acoustic and archtop guitars in Mermaid Beach, Gold Coast, Queensland, Australia. He also builds lap steels.

Holman
1966-1968. Built by the Holman-Woodell guitar factory in Neodesha, Kansas. The factory was started to build guitars for Wurlitzer, but that fell through by '67.

1965 Holiday Silhouette Bobcat
Tom Pfeifer

Hollingworth Guitars

GUITARS

Holst

Early-'80s Hondo Deluxe 748 Mark II

Jim Gleason

MODEL YEAR	FEATURES	EXC. COND. LOW	HIGH

Holst

1984-present. Premium grade, custom, archtop, flat-top, semi-hollow, and classical guitars built in Creswell, Oregon by luthier Stephen Holst. He also builds mandolins. Until '01 he was located in Eugene, Oregon.

Holzapfel (Holzapfel & Beitel)

1898-1930s. Carl C. Holzapfel and Clemence Beitel built guitars, banjos, and mandolins in Baltimore, but are best-known as early innovators of the 12-string guitar. Beitel left the company in 1905 and Holzapfel continued to build instruments up to the depression. He, and later his son, Carl M., mainly repaired instruments after that (up to 1988), but still would do custom builds.

Hondo/Hondo II

1969-1987, 1991-2005. Budget grade, production, imported acoustic, classical and electric guitars. They also offered basses, banjos and mandolins. Originally imported by International Music Corporation (IMC) of Fort Worth, Texas, founded by Jerry Freed and Tommy Moore and named after a small town near San Antonio, Texas. Early pioneers of Korean guitarmaking, primarily targeted at beginner market. Introduced their first electrics in '72. Changed brand to Hondo II in '74. Some better Hondos made in Japan '74-'82/'83. In '85 IMC purchases major interest in Jackson/Charvel, and the Hondo line was supplanted by Charvels. 1987 was the last catalog before hiatus. In '88 IMC was sold and Freed began Jerry Freed International and in '91 he revived the Hondo name. Acquired by MBT International in '95, currently part of Musicorp.

Acoustic Flat-Top
1969-1987, 1991-2005.

1969-2005		$100	$150

Electric Hollowbody
1969-1987, 1991-2005.

1969-2005		$175	$600

Electric Solidbody
1969-1987, 1991-2005.

1969-1987		$175	$600
1991-1999		$175	$600
2000-2005		$75	$200

Hondo Chiquita Travel Guitar

See Chiquita brand.

Longhorn
Ca. 1978-1980s. Copy of Danelectro Long Horn guitar, Dano Coke bottle-style headstock, brown-copper.

1978-80s		$450	$600

Longhorn 6/12 Doubleneck
Ca. 1978s-1980s. Copy of Danelectro Longhorn 6/12 Doubleneck guitar, Dano coke bottle-style headstock, white sunburst.

1978s-80s		$700	$925

MODEL YEAR	FEATURES	EXC. COND. LOW	HIGH

M 16 Rambo-Machine Gun
1970s-1980s. Machine gun body-style, matching machine gun-shaped guitar case, black or red. Price includes original case with form-fit interior; deduct as much as 40% less for non-original case.

1970s-80s		$450	$600

Hopf

1906-present. Intermediate, professional, premium, and presentation grade, production/custom, classical guitars made in Germany. They also make basses, mandolins and flutes.

The Hopf family of Germany has a tradition of instrument building going back to 1669, but the modern company was founded in 1906. Hopf started making electric guitars in the mid-'50s. Some Hopf models were made by others for the company. By the late-'70s, Hopf had discontinued making electrics, concentrating on classicals.

Explorer Standard
1960s. Double-cut semi-hollow, sharp horns, center block, 2 mini-humbuckers.

1960s		$800	$1,050

Saturn Archtop
1960s. Offset cutaway, archtop-style soundholes, 2 pickups, white, says Saturn on headstock.

1960s		$1,000	$1,325

Super Deluxe Archtop
1960s. Archtop, 16 3/4", catseye soundholes, carved spruce top, flamed maple back and sides, sunburst.

1960s		$1,075	$1,400

Hopkins

1998-present. Luthier Peter Hopkins builds his presentation grade, custom, hand-carved archtop guitars in British Columbia.

Horabe

Classical and Espana models made in Japan.

Classical

1960-1980s	Various models	$375	$775

Hottie

In 2009, amp builders Jean-Claude Escudie and Mike Bernards added production/custom, professional and premium grade, solidbody electric guitars built by luthier Saul Koll in Portland, Oregon.

House Guitars

2004-present. Luthier Joshua House builds his production/custom, premium grade, acoustic guitars and guitar-bouzoukis in Goderich, Ontario.

Howe-Orme

1897-ca. 1910. Elias Howe and George Orme's Boston-based publishing and distribution buisness offered a variety of mandolin family instruments and guitars and received many patents for their designs. Many of their guitars featured detachable necks.

MODEL		EXC. COND.	
YEAR	FEATURES	LOW	HIGH

Hoyer

1874-present. Intermediate grade, production, flat-top, classical, electric, and resonator guitars. They also build basses. Founded by Franz Hoyer, building classical guitars and other instruments. His son, Arnold, added archtops in the late-1940s, and solidbodies in the '60s. In '67, Arnold's son, Walter, took over, leaving the company in '77. The company changed hands a few times over the following years. Walter started building guitars again in '84 under the W.A. Hoyer brand, which is not associated with Hoyer.

Acoustic
1960s. Acoustic archtop or flat-top.

1960s		$450	$600

Junior
Early-1960s. Solidbody with unusual sharp horn cutaway, single neck pickup, bolt-on neck, dot markers, Arnold Hoyer logo on headstock, shaded sunburst.

1960s		$600	$775

Soloist Electric
1960-1962. Single-cut acoustic-electric archtop, 2 pickups, teardrop f-holes, sunburst.

1960-1962		$600	$775

Special 24
1950s-1960s. Single-cut acoustic archtop, Hoyer Special script logo on headstock, pickups added in '60s. SL was deluxe version.

1950s-60s		$1,800	$2,350

Huerga

Introduced in 1995, professional to presentation-grade, production/custom, archtop, flat-top, and metal-front solidbody electric guitars built by luthier Diego Huerga in Buenos Aires, Argentina.

Humming Bird

1947-ca.1975. Japanese manufacturer offering acoustics and electrics. By 1968 making pointy Mosrite inspirations. Probably not imported into the U.S.

Electric Solidbody

1950s		$175	$300

Humphrey, Thomas

1970-2008. Premium and presentation grade, custom, nylon-string guitars built by luthier Thomas Humphrey in Gardiner, New York. In 1996 Humphrey began collaborating with Martin Guitars, resulting in the Martin C-TSH and C-1R. Often the inside back label will indicate the year of manufacture. Humphrey died in April, 2008.

Classical
1976-1984. Brazilian or Indian rosewood back and sides, spruce top, traditionally-based designs evolved over time with Millenium becoming a benchmark design in 1985, values can increase with new designs. Valuations depend on each specific instrument and year and type of construction, price ranges are guidance only; each instrument should be evaluated on a case-by-case basis.

1976-1984		$5,700	$7,400

Millennium (Classical)
1985-2008. Professional performance-grade high-end classical guitar with innovative taper body design and elevated 'board, tops are generally spruce (versus cedar) with rosewood back and sides.

1995-2008		$10,300	$13,400

Steel String
1974. D-style, only 4 made.

1974		$3,300	$4,300

Huss and Dalton Guitar Company

1995-present. Luthiers Jeff Huss and Mark Dalton build their professional and premium grade flat-tops and banjos in Staunton, Virginia.

Hutchins

2006-present. Gary Hutchins in Sussex, U.K. imports intermediate and professional grade, production, acoustic and electric guitars and basses from China, Germany and Korea.

Ian A. Guitars

1991-present. In the early 1990s luthier Ian Anderson built guitars under his name, in 2005 he began using the Ian A. brand. He builds premium grade, production/custom, solidbody electric guitars in Poway, California.

Ibanez

1932-present. Budget, intermediate, and professional grade, production/custom, acoustic and electric guitars. They also make basses, amps, mandolins, and effects.

Founded in Nagoya, Japan, by Matsujiro Hoshino as book and stationary supply, started retailing musical instruments in 1909, importing them by '21. The company's factories were destroyed during World War II, but the business was revived in '50. The Ibanez name in use by 1957. Junpei Hoshino, grandson of founder, became president in '60; a new factory opened called Tama Seisakusho (Tama Industries). Brand names by '64 included Ibanez, Star, King's Stone, Jamboree and Goldentone, supplied by 85 factories serving global markets. Sold acoustic guitars to Harry Rosenblum of Elger Guitars ('59-ca.'65) in Ardmore, Pennsylvania, in early-'60s. Around '62 Hoshino purchased 50% interest in Elger Guitars, and ca. '65 changed the name to Ibanez.

Jeff Hasselberger headed the American guitar side beginning '73-'74, and the company headquarters were moved to Cornwells Heights, Pennsylvania in '74. By '75 the instruments are being distributed by Chesbro Music Company in Idaho Falls, Idaho, and Harry Rosenblum sells his interest to Hoshino shortly thereafter. Ca. '81, the Elger Company becomes Hoshino U.S.A. An U.S. Custom Shop was opened in '88.

Most glued-neck guitars from '70s are fairly rare. Dating: copy guitars begin ca. '71. Serial numbers

1980s Hondo H-790 Lazer
Imaged by Heritage Auctions, HA.com

1963 Hopf Saturn
Dudley Taft

Ibanez AM-225 Artist
Imaged by Heritage Auctions, HA.com

1982 Ibanez BL Blazer
Carter Vintage Guitars

MODEL YEAR	FEATURES	EXC. COND. LOW	HIGH

begin '75 with letter (A-L for month) followed by 6 digits, the first 2 indicating year, last 4 sequential (MYYXXXX). By '88 the month letter drops off. Dating code stops early-'90s; by '94 letter preface either F for Fuji or C for Cort (Korean) manufacturer followed by number for year and consecutive numbers (F4XXXX=Fuji, C4XXXX=Cort, 1994).

Pickups on Asian import electric guitars from the '50s-'70s are often considered to be the weakest engineering specification on the instrument. Old Ibanez pickups can become microphonic and it is not unusual to see them replaced.

AE (Acoustic Electric) Series
1983-present. Flat-top models include AE, AEF, AEG, AEL, AES, (no archtops).

1983-2021	Various models	$150	$475

AH10 Allan Holdsworth
1985-1987. Offset double-cut solidbody, bolt neck, bridge humbucker, dots, various colors.

1985-1987	1 pickup	$350	$475

AH20 Allan Holdsworth

1986	2 pickups	$385	$500

AM (Archtop) Series
1985-1991. Small body archtops, models include AM70, 75, 75T, 100, 225. Becomes Artstar in '92.

1985-1991	Various models	$635	$825

AM Stagemaster Series
1983-1984, 1989-1990. Made in Japan, small double-cut semi-hollow body, 2 humbuckers, models include AM50, 100, 205, 255. Model name used again, without Stagemaster in '89-'90.

1983-1984	Various models	$635	$825

Artcore Series
2002-present. Made in China, hollowbody electric, models include AF, AG, AK, AM, AS, AWD, FWD, and TM.

2002-2021	Various models	$200	$700

Artist AR50 (Jr. Artist)
1979-1983. Double-cut solidbody, dot markers, 2 humbuckers.

1979-1983		$475	$625

Artist AR100
1979-1984. Double-cut solidbody, set neck, maple top, 2 humbuckers.

1979-1984		$850	$1,125

Artist AR300
1979-1982. Symmetrical double-cut, carved maple top.

1979-1982		$950	$1,250

Artist AR500
1979-1982. 2 humbuckers, EQ.

1979-1982		$950	$1,250

Artist AS50
1980-1981. Made in Japan, semi-acoustic.

1980-1981		$525	$675

Artist AS100
1979-1981. Set neck, gold hardware.

1979-1981		$675	$885

Artist AS200

1979-1986. Double-cut semi-acoustic, flamed maple, block markers, gold hardware, 2 humbuckers, replaced Artist 2630. Artist dropped from name when model becomes hollowbody archtop in '82.

1979-1986		$1,100	$1,425

Artstar AS50
1998-1999. Laminated maple body, bound rosewood 'board, dot inlays, 2 humbuckers.

1998-1999		$525	$675

Artstar AS80
1994-2002. Double-cut semi-hollow body, dots, 2 humbuckers.

1994-2002		$525	$675

Artstar AS180
1997-1999. Double-cut semi-hollow body, plain top, dots, 2 humbuckers.

1997-1999		$675	$885

Artstar AS200
1992-2000. Flame maple top, gold hardware, 2 humbuckers, block inlays.

1992-2000		$925	$1,200

Artwood Series
1979-present. Electric-acoustics, various AW, AC models.

1979-2021	Various models	$200	$600

Blazer Series
1980-1982, 1997-1998. Offset double-cut, 10 similar BL models in the '80s with different body woods and electronic configurations. Series name returns on 3 models in late '90s.

1980-1998	Various BL models	$250	$725

Bob Weir (2681)
1975-1980, 1995. Double-cut ash solidbody, ebony 'board, tree-of-life inlay, gold-plated pickups, limited numbers. Reintroduced as a limited run in '95.

1975-1980		$1,825	$2,375

Bob Weir Standard (2680)
1976-1980. Standard production model of 2681.

1976-1980		$1,275	$1,650

Bob Weir Model One BWM1 (Cowboy Fancy)
2005. Limited run of 30, double-cut swamp ash solidbody, ebony 'board, pearl vine inlay down neck and part way around body.

2005		$2,725	$3,550

Challenger (2552ASH)
1977-1978. T-style ash solidbody.

1977-1978		$475	$625

CN100 Concert Standard
1978-1979. Double-cut solidbody, set neck, 2 humbuckers, chrome hardware, dot markers.

1978-1979		$475	$625

CN200 Concert Custom
1978-1979. Carved maple top, mahogany body, 7 layer black/white binding, bolt-on neck, gold hardware, block inlays, 2 Super 80 pickups.

1978-1979		$550	$725

CN250 Concert
1978-1979. Like CN200 but with vine inlay.

1978-1979		$675	$885

MODEL YEAR	FEATURES	EXC. COND. LOW	HIGH

DG350 Destroyer II
1986-1987. X Series, modified X-shaped basswood body, flame maple top, 2 humbuckers, trem.

1986-1987		$450	$600

DT50 Destroyer II
1980-1982. Modified alder Explorer body, 6-in-line headstock, bolt neck, 2 humbuckers, thick paint.

1980-1982		$675	$885

DT150 Destroyer II
1982-1984. Like DT50 but birch/basswood, 1 humbucker.

1982-1984		$675	$885

DT155 Destroyer II
1982-1984. Like DT150 but with 3 humbuckers.

1982-1984		$925	$1,200

DT350 Destroyer II
1984-1985. X Series, opaque finish, 1 humbucker, trem.

1984-1985		$550	$725

DT400 Destroyer II
1980-1982. Modified mahogany Explorer body, flame maple top, 6-in-line headstock, set-neck, 2 humbuckers, cherry sunburst. Model changed to DT500 in '82.

1980-1982		$675	$885

DT500 Destroyer II
1982-1984. Replaced the DT400, flame maple top.

1982-1984		$675	$885

DT555 Destroyer II Phil Collen
1983-1987. Bound basswood solidbody, 3 humbuckers, vibrato, black.

1983-1987		$2,400	$3,100

DTX120 Destroyer
2000-2004. X Series, known as the Millennium Destroyer, 2 humbuckers.

2000-2004		$275	$350

EX Series
1988-1993. Double-cut electric solidbodies with long thin horns.

1988-1993	Various models	$175	$375

FA/FG (Full Acoustic) Series
1973-1987. Single-cut full body jazz-style.

1973-1987	Various models	$1,125	$1,450

Flash (I, II, III)
1975. The Iceman was first introduced as the Flash at the Frankfurt Trade Show in West Germany in '75, it was renamed the Iceman prior to its introduction in the U.S. See Iceman 2663 listing.

FR1620/Prestige FR1620
2008-2014. Ash body, maple/walnut neck, rosewood 'board, 2 pickups, Prestige logo on headstock, black or red finish.

2008-2014		$675	$885

GAX Series
1998-2009. Symmetrical double-cut (Gibson SG style) with 2 humbuckers, lower cost of the AX line.

1998-2009	Various models	$100	$225

George Benson GB10
1977-present. Single-cut, laminated spruce top, flame maple back and sides, 2 humbuckers, 3-piece set-in maple neck, ebony 'board, sunburst or blond.

1977-1989		$2,000	$2,650

MODEL YEAR	FEATURES	EXC. COND. LOW	HIGH
1990-1999		$1,775	$2,300
2000-2021		$1,475	$1,925

George Benson GB15
2006-2010. Like GB10, but with 1 humbucker.

2006-2010		$2,075	$2,675

George Benson GB20
1978-1982. Larger than GB10, laminated spruce top, flame maple back and sides.

1978-1982		$2,725	$3,550

George Benson GB100 Deluxe
1993-1996. GB-10 with flamed maple top, pearl binding, sunburst finish 'guard, pearl vine inlay tailpiece, gold hardware.

1993-1996		$2,900	$3,800

GSA Series
2000-2011. Offset double-cut body.

2000-2011	GSA20/GSA60	$125	$250

Iceman 2663/2663TC/2663SL
1975-1978. The original Iceman Series models, called the Flash I, II and III respectively, I has 2 humbuckers, II (TC) and III (SL) have 1 triple-coil pickup.

1975-1978		$1,100	$1,425

Iceman PS10 Paul Stanley
1978-1981. Limited edition Paul Stanley model, abalone trim, Stanley's name engraved at 21st fret, reissued in '95 with upgraded model names.

1978-1981	Korina finish	$2,000	$2,600
1978-1981	Sunburst or black	$1,625	$2,125

Iceman PS10 II Paul Stanley
1995-1996. Reissue of original PS-10.

1995-1996	Black	$1,600	$2,100

Iceman PS10LTD Paul Stanley
1995-1996. Limited edition, gold mirror appointments, gold hardware, black pearl metalflake finish.

1995-1996		$2,550	$3,300

Iceman Series
1975-2010. Ibanez unique body styles with hooked lower treble horn body.

1978-1979	IC250	$1,050	$1,375
1978-1979	IC300 (Korina)	$1,050	$1,375
1978-1980	IC210	$1,050	$1,375
1978-1982	IC400	$1,100	$1,425
1978-1990	IC200	$850	$1,100
1979-1980	IC50	$850	$1,100
1981-1982	IC400 CS	$975	$1,250
1994	IC500	$975	$1,250
1994-2003	IC300	$360	$475
1995-1996	IC350	$360	$475

IMG-2010 Guitar Controller MIDI
1985-1987. Similar to Roland GR-707, slim triangle-wedge body with treble horn.

1985-1987	Guitar only	$600	$800

JEM7 Series
1988-2010. Basswood or alder body, various models, alder 7V offered until '10.

1988-2010	Various models	$1,850	$2,400

JEM77 Series
1988-1999, 2003-2010. Basswood body, monkey grip handle, 3 pickups, 'board with tree of life or pyramids inlay, finishes include floral pattern or multicolor swirl. Current version has dot inlays and solid finish.

1981 Ibanez DT50 Destroyer II
Imaged by Heritage Auctions, HA.com

2004 Ibanez JEM 77
Imaged by Heritage Auctions, HA.com

1979 Ibanez M340
Tom Pfeifer

1977 Ibanez 684 Concord
Imaged by Heritage Auctions, HA.com

MODEL		EXC. COND.	
YEAR	FEATURES	LOW	HIGH

The JEM 77BRMR Bad Horsie was introduced in '05 with a mirror finish.

| 1980-2010 | Various models | $2,550 | $3,300 |

JEM555

1994-2000. Basswood, dots and vine inlay, 3 pickups.

| 1994-2000 | | $575 | $750 |

JEM777 Series

1987-1996. Basswood body, monkey grip 3 pickups, pyramids or vine inlay.

| 1987-1996 | Various models | $2,725 | $3,550 |

JEM 10th Anniversary

1996. Limited Edition signature Steve Vai model, bolt neck, vine metal 'guard, vine neck inlays and headstock art.

| 1996 | | $4,600 | $6,000 |

JEM 20th Anniversary

2007. Steve Vai 20th Anniversary JEM model, green acrylic illuminating body, celebrates the 20th year (1987-2007) of the Ibanez JEM series, limited edition.

| 2007 | | $4,100 | $5,300 |

JEM 90th Anniversary

1997. Limited Edition signature Steve Vai model, textured silver finish, chrome 'guard.

| 1997 | | $1,850 | $2,400 |

JEM Y2KDNA (Limited Edition)

2000. Red Swirl marble finish using Steve Vai's blood in the paint.

| 2000 | | $2,725 | $3,550 |

Joe Pass JP20

1981-1990. Full body, single-cut, 1 pickup, abalone and pearl split block inlay, JP inlay on headstock.

| 1981-1990 | Sunburst | $1,500 | $1,950 |

Joe Satriani JS6

1993. Limited production, lightweight mahogany body, non-gloss finish, JS Series headstock logo.

| 1993 | | $1,275 | $1,650 |

Joe Satriani JS100

1994-2014. Offset double cut basswood body, 2 humbuckers, vibrato, red, black, white or custom finish.

| 1994-2014 | Custom finish | $575 | $750 |
| 1994-2014 | Standard finish | $425 | $550 |

Joe Satriani JS1000

1994-1996, 1998-2012. 2 DiMarzio humbuckers, lightweight body.

| 1994-2012 | Various colors | $925 | $1,200 |

Joe Satriani JS1200

2004-2016. Candy Apple Red.

| 2004-2016 | | $1,000 | $1,300 |

Joe Satriani JS 10th Anniversary

1998. Chrome-metal body, Satriani Anniversary script on back cover plate.

| 1998 | | $2,550 | $3,300 |

Joe Satriani JS 20th Anniversary

2008. Opaque finish with alien surfer graphic.

| 2008 | | $2,550 | $3,300 |

Joe Satriani Y2K

2000. Clear see-thru plexi-style body.

| 2000 | | $2,000 | $2,600 |

MODEL		EXC. COND.	
YEAR	FEATURES	LOW	HIGH

John Petrucci JPM100 P2

1996. Offset double-cut solidbody, 2 pickups, multi-color graphic.

| 1996 | | $2,000 | $2,600 |

John Petrucci JPM100 P3

1997. As P2 but with same graphic in black and white.

| 1997 | | $2,000 | $2,600 |

John Petrucci JPM100 P4

1998. As P2 but with same graphic in camo colors.

| 1998 | | $2,000 | $2,600 |

John Scofield JSM100

2001-present. Double-cut semi hollow body, 2 humbuckers, ebony 'board, gold hardware.

| 2001-2021 | | $2,100 | $2,700 |

Lee Ritenour LR10

1981-1987. Flame maple body, bound set neck, Quick Change tailpiece, 2 pickups, dark red sunburst, foam-filled body to limit feedback.

| 1981-1987 | | $1,925 | $2,500 |

M310

1982. D-size flat-top, maple back and sides, rosewood 'board.

| 1982 | | $190 | $250 |

M340

1978-1979. D-size flat-top, flamed maple back and sides, maple 'board. 'board.

| 1978-1979 | | $275 | $350 |

Maxxas

1987-1988. Solidbody (MX2) or with internal sound chambers (MX3, '88 only), 2 pickups, all-access neck joint system.

| 1987-1988 | MX2 | $1,100 | $1,425 |
| 1988 | MX3 | $1,200 | $1,550 |

MC Musician Series

1978-1982. Solidbodies, various models.

1978-1980	MC500, carved top	$1,425	$1,850
1978-1980	Neck-thru body	$1,050	$1,375
1978-1982	Bolt-neck	$825	$1,075

Mick Thompson MTM-1

2006. Seven logo on fretboard, MTM1 logo on back of headstock.

| 2006 | | $800 | $1,050 |

Model 600 Series

1974-1978. Copy era acoustic flat-tops with model numbers in the 600 Series, basically copies of classic American square shoulder dreadnoughts. Includes the 683, 684, 693 and the 6-in-line 647; there were 12-string copies as well.

| 1974-1978 | Various models | $675 | $885 |

Model 700 Series

1974-1977. Upgraded flat-top models such as the Brazilian Scent 750, with more original design content than 600 Series.

| 1974-1977 | Various models | $675 | $885 |

Model 900 Series

1963-1964. Offset double-cut solidbody with sharp curving horns, Burns Bison copy.

| 1963-1964 | 901, 1 pickup | $350 | $450 |
| 1963-1964 | 992, 2 pickups | $375 | $500 |

MODEL YEAR FEATURES	EXC. COND. LOW	HIGH

Model 1453

1971-1973. Copy of classic single-cut hollowbody, replaced by Model 2355 in '73.

| 1971-1973 | $1,475 | $1,900 |

Model 1800 Series

1962-1963. Offset double-cut solidbody (Jazzmaster-style), models came with bar (stud) or vibrato tailpiece, and 2, 3 or 4 pickups.

| 1962-1963 Various models | $350 | $450 |

Model 1912

1971-1973. Double-cut semi-hollow body, sunburst finish.

| 1971-1973 | $975 | $1,275 |

Model 2020

1970. Initial offering of the copy era, offset double-cut, 2 unusual rectangular pickups, block markers, raised nailed-on headstock logo, sunburst.

| 1970 | $750 | $975 |

Model 2240M

Early 1970s. Thick hollowbody electric copy, single pointed cutaway, double-parallelogram markers, 2 humbuckers, natural finish.

| 1971-1973 | $1,500 | $1,950 |

Model 2336 Les Jr.

1974-1976. Copy of classic slab solidbody, TV Lime.

| 1974-1976 | $550 | $725 |

Model 2340 Deluxe '59er

1974-1977. Copy of classic single-cut solidbody, Hi-Power humbuckers, opaque or flametop.

| 1974-1977 Flametop | $625 | $825 |
| 1974-1977 Opaque | $625 | $825 |

Model 2341 Les Custom

1974-1977. Copy of classic single-cut solidbody.

| 1974-1977 | $625 | $825 |

Model 2342 Les Moonlight/Sunlight Special

1974-1977. Copy of classic slab solidbody, black (Moonlight) or ivory (Sunlight).

| 1974-1977 | $625 | $825 |

Model 2343 FM Jr.

1974-1976. Copy of LP TV Jr.

| 1974-1976 | $625 | $825 |

Model 2343 Jr.

1974-1976. Copy of classic Jr., cherry mahogany.

| 1974-1976 | $625 | $825 |

Model 2344

1974-1976. Copy of classic double-cut solidbody.

| 1974-1976 | $425 | $550 |

Model 2345

1974-1976. Copy of classic sharp double-cut solidbody, set neck, walnut or white, vibrato, 3 pickups.

| 1974-1976 | $675 | $885 |

Model 2346

1974. Copy of classic sharp double-cut solidbody, vibrato, set neck, 2 pickups.

| 1974 | $675 | $885 |

Model 2347

1974-1976. Copy of classic sharp double-cut solidbody, set-neck, 1 pickup.

| 1974-1976 | $550 | $725 |

Model 2348 Firebrand

1974-1977. Copy of classic reverse solidbody, mahogany body, bolt neck, 2 pickups.

| 1974-1977 | $850 | $1,125 |

Model 2350 Les

1971-1977. Copy of classic single-cut solidbody, bolt neck, black, gold hardware, goldtop version (2350G Les) also available. A cherry sunburst finish (2350 Les Custom) was offered by '74.

| 1971-1977 | $675 | $885 |

Model 2351 Les

1974-1977. Copy of classic single-cut solidbody, gold top, 2 pickups.

| 1974-1977 | $675 | $885 |

Model 2351DX

1974-1977. Copy of classic single-cut solidbody, gold top, 2 mini-humbuckers.

| 1974-1977 | $675 | $885 |

Model 2351M Les

1974-1977. LP Standard style, sunburst.

| 1974-1977 | $675 | $885 |

Model 2352 Telly

1974-1978. Copy of early classic single-cut solidbody, 1 bridge pickup, white finish.

| 1974-1978 | $675 | $885 |

Model 2352CT

1974-1978. Copy of classic single-cut solidbody, single-coil bridge and humbucker neck pickup.

| 1974-1978 | $675 | $885 |

Model 2352DX Telly

1974-1978. Copy of classic single-cut solidbody, 2 humbuckers.

| 1974-1978 | $675 | $885 |

Model 2354

1974-1977. Copy of classic sharp double-cut solidbody, 2 humbuckers, vibrato.

| 1974-1977 | $675 | $885 |

Model 2354S

1972-1977. Stop tailpiece version of 2354.

| 1972-1977 | $675 | $885 |

Model 2355/2355M

1973-1977. Copy of classic single-cut hollowbody, sunburst or natural maple (M).

| 1973-1977 | $1,200 | $1,575 |

Model 2356

1973-1975. Copy of classic double pointed cutaway hollowbody, bowtie markers, sunburst. There was another Model 2356 in '74, a copy of a different hollowbody.

| 1973-1975 | $1,075 | $1,400 |

Model 2363R

1973-1974. Cherry finish copy of classic varitone double-cut semi-hollow body.

| 1973-1974 | $1,075 | $1,400 |

Model 2364 Ibanex

1971-1973. Dan Armstrong see-thru Lucite copy, 2 mounted humbuckers.

| 1971-1973 | $850 | $1,100 |

Model 2368 Telly

1973-1978. Copy of classic single-cut thinline, chambered f-hole body, single coil pickup, mahogany body.

| 1974-1978 | $675 | $885 |

1976 Ibanez 2355
Stoeffu Vogt

1975 Ibanez Model 2402
John DeSilva

Ibanez Model 2404 Double Axe
Greg Perrine

Ibanez Model 2405
Custom Agent

MODEL YEAR	FEATURES	EXC. COND. LOW	HIGH

Model 2368F
1973-1974. Classic single-cut black 'guard copy.

1973-1974		$675	$885

Model 2370
1972-1977. Sunburst version of Model 2363R.

1972-1977		$1,075	$1,400

Model 2372 Les Pro/2372DX Les Pro
1972-1977. Copy of classic single-cut solidbody, bolt neck, low impedance pickups, DX with gold hardware available for '73-'74.

1972-1977		$675	$885

Model 2374 Crest
1974-1976. Copy of classic double-cut semi-hollow body, walnut finish.

1974-1976		$1,050	$1,350

Model 2375 Strato
1971-1978. Strat copy, 3 single-coils, sunburst.

1971-1978		$675	$885

Model 2375 Strato 6/12
1974-1975. Double neck, 6 and 12 strings.

1974-1975		$1,475	$1,900

Model 2375ASH Strato
1974-1978. 2375 with ash body.

1974-1978		$675	$885

Model 2375WH/N/BK Strato
1974-1978. 2375 in white (WH), natural (N), and black (BK) finishes.

1974-1978		$825	$1,075

Model 2377
1974-1975. Copy of classic double sharp-cut solidbody, short production run, dot markers.

1974-1975		$550	$725

Model 2380
1973-1977. Copy of LP Recording, single-cut solidbody, low impedence pickups, small block markers.

1973-1977		$675	$885

Model 2383
1974-1976. Copy of classic double sharp cut solidbody, white or walnut, 3 humbuckers, gold hardware.

1974-1976		$675	$885

Model 2384 Telly
1974-1976. Copy of classic single-cut, f-holes, 2 humbuckers, ash body.

1974-1976		$675	$885

Model 2387 Rocket Roll/Rocket Roll Sr.
1975-1977. Copy of classic v-shaped solidbody, bolt-neck (2387) or set-neck (2387DX/2387CT), dot markers, gold-covered pickups.

1975-1977	All models	$1,600	$2,100

Model 2390
1974-1976. Copy of classic double-cut semi-hollow body, maple 'board, walnut finish.

1974-1976		$1,075	$1,400

Model 2394
Ca. 1974-ca. 1976. SG style, 2 humbuckers, maple 'board, black block inlays.

1974-1976		$675	$885

Model 2395
1974-1976. Natural finished 2390.

1974-1976		$1,075	$1,400

MODEL YEAR	FEATURES	EXC. COND. LOW	HIGH

Model 2397
1974-1976. Double-cut semi-hollow body, low impedance electronics, trapezoid markers, goldtop.

1974-1976		$1,075	$1,400

Model 2399DX Jazz Solid
1974-1976. Single-cut solidbody, sunburst, set-neck, gold hardware.

1974-1976		$1,075	$1,400

Model 2401 Signature
1974-1976. Double-cut semi-hollow archtop, gold top, bolt neck.

1974-1976		$1,075	$1,400

Model 2402/2402DX Double Axe
1974-1977. Double sharp cut solidbody 6/12 double-neck, cherry or walnut, DX model has gold hardware and white finish.

1974-1977	All models	$1,400	$1,825

Model 2404 Double Axe
1974-1977. Double sharp cut solidbody guitar/bass doubleneck copy, walnut, white available '75 only.

1974-1977		$1,400	$1,825

Model 2405 Custom Agent
1974-1977. Single-cut solidbody, set neck, scroll headstock, pearl body inlay, 2 humbuckers.

1974-1977		$1,000	$1,300

Model 2406 Double Axe
1974-1977. Double sharp cut solidbody doubleneck, two 6-strings, cherry or wlanut.

1974-1977		$1,000	$1,300

Model 2407 Stratojazz 4/6
1974-1975. Half Strat, half Jazz bass, all rock and roll!

1974-1975		$1,000	$1,300

Model 2451
1974-1977. Single-cut solidbody, maple 'board, black or natural, set neck.

1974-1977		$1,075	$1,400

Model 2453 Howie Roberts
1974-1977. Single-cut archtop, round soundhole, maple body, set neck, rosewood 'board, block markers, 1 pickup, gold hardware, burgundy or sunburst.

1974-1977		$1,475	$1,900

Model 2454
1974-1977. Copy of classic double-cut semi-hollow body, set-neck, small block markers, cherry finish over ash.

1974-1977		$1,075	$1,400

Model 2455
1974-1977. L-5 copy, sharp single-cut archtop, blocks, natural.

1974-1977		$2,200	$2,900

Model 2459 Destroyer
1975-1977. Korina finished mahogany body.

1975-1977		$2,200	$2,900

Model 2460
1975-1977. L-5 copy, rounded cut laminated archtop, blocks, natural.

1975-1977		$2,200	$2,900

MODEL YEAR	FEATURES	EXC. COND. LOW	HIGH

Model 2461
1975-1977. Copy of classic single-cut archtop, laminated spruce top, curly maple body, set-neck, ebony 'board, pearl blocks, 2 pickups, gold hardware, sunburst or natural.
1975-1977 $2,200 $2,900

Model 2464
1975-1977. Byrdland copy, rounded single-cut, blocks, natural.
1975-1977 $2,200 $2,900

Model 2469 Futura
1976-1977. Korina finished furturistic model copy.
1976-1977 $2,200 $2,900

Model 2601 to 2604 Artist
1976-1978. Upgrade acoustic flat-tops, higher end than 600 and 700 series, less of a copy model, original headstock decal.
1976-1978   All models $475 $625

Model 2612 Artist
1974-1975. Rounded double-cut solidbody, black finish, birch top, gold hardware, bound rosewood 'board, 2 humbuckers, fleur-de-lis inlay.
1974-1975 $1,075 $1,400

Model 2613 Artist
1974-1975. Natural version of 2612.
1974-1975 $1,075 $1,400

Model 2616 Artist Jazz
1974-1975. Single-cut curly maple hollow body, f-holes, fleur-de-lis, 2 humbuckers.
1974-1975 $2,075 $2,675

Model 2617 Artist
1976-1980. Pointed double-cut natural ash solidbody, set-neck, German carved top, spilt block inlays, bound ebony 'board, 2 humbuckers, later would evolve into the Professional model.
1976-1980 $1,700 $2,200

Model 2618 Artist
1976-1979. Like 2617, but with maple and mahogany body and dot markers. Becomes AR200 in '79.
1976-1979 $1,075 $1,400

Model 2619 Artist
1976-1979. Like 2618, but with split block markers. Becomes AR300 in '79.
1976-1979 $1,075 $1,400

Model 2622 Artist EQ
1977-1979. EQ, Steve Miller model. Becomes AR500 in '79.
1977-1979 $1,325 $1,725

Model 2630 Artist Deluxe
1976-1979. Double cut semi-hollow body, sunburst, name changed to AS200 in '79.
1976-1979 $1,600 $2,075

Model 2640 Artist/AR1200 Doubleneck
1977-1984. Double-cut solidbody, set 6/12 necks, 4 humbuckers, gold hardware. Called 2640 until '79 when changed to AR1200.
1977-1984 $1,625 $2,125

Model 2662 Super Cutaway
1974-1976. Solidbody, set neck, 2 dramatic cutaways, block inlays, 2 humbuckers.
1974-1976 $1,700 $2,225

Model 2671 Randy Scruggs
1976-1978. Single-cut solidbody, tree-of-life inlay, German-carve top.
1976-1978 $1,425 $1,850

Model 2700 Artist Custom
1977-1978. Cutaway, dot markers, gold hardware, natural, black, antique violin or dark satin finish.
1977-1978 $1,825 $2,375

Model 2710 Artist Custom
1978. Like Model 2700 with exotic wood and anvil case.
1978 $1,875 $2,425

Model 2800 Andorra Series
1974-1979. Classical nylon-string guitars, part of Ibanez Andorra Series, all with 2800-2899 model numbers.
1974-1979   Various models $375 $500

Model 2900 Andorra Professional Series
1974-1979. Steel-string dreadnought models with solid spruce tops, all with 2909-2912 model numbers.
1974-1979   Various models $375 $500

Pat Metheny PM
1996-present. Acoustic-electric archtops, single or single/half cutaway, 1 or 2 humbuckers.
1996-2010   PM100 $1,550 $2,000
1997-1999   PM20 $1,175 $1,525
2000-2015   PM120 $1,875 $2,425

Paul Gilbert PGM
1992-2011. Superstrat body style, painted f-holes, appointments vary with model numbers.
1997-2011   PGM300 WH $1,325 $1,725
1998   PGM 90th $1,525 $1,975
1998   PGM200 FB $1,525 $1,975

PF Performer Series Acoustics
1987-present. Mostly dreadnought size flat-tops.
1987-2021   Various models $100 $375

PF100 Performer Standard
1978-1979. Single-cut solidbody, plain birch top, mahogany body, bolt neck, dot inlays, 2 humbuckers.
1978-1979 $475 $625

PF200 Performer Custom
1978-1979. Maple top PF100.
1978-1979 $625 $800

PF300 Performer
1978-1980. Single-cut solidbody, maple top, mahogany body, set neck, 2 humbuckers, Tri-Sound.
1978-1980 $625 $800

PF400 Performer
1978-1979. Single cut solidbody, flame maple top, alder body, set neck, block inlays, 2 humbuckers, Tri-Sound.
1978-1979 $625 $885

PL Pro Line Series
1985-1987. Pro Line models begin with PL or PR.
1985-1987   Various models $400 $1,175

PR Pro Line Series
1985-1987. Pro Line models begin with PL or PR.
1985-1987   Various models $400 $1,175

Reb Beach Voyager RBM1
1991-1996. Unusual cutaway lower bout, extreme upper bout cutaways, RBM Series logo on headstock.
1991-1996 $1,175 $1,525

Ibanez Model 2671
Randy Scruggs
Greg Perrine

1985 Ibanez Pro Line PR1440
Imaged by Heritage Auctions, HA.com

To get the most from this book, be sure to read "Using *The Guide*" in the introduction.

Ibanez Steve Vai Universe UV7P

Bas van de Weijer

1979 Ibanez V302

Peter Busch

MODEL YEAR	FEATURES	EXC. COND. LOW	HIGH

RG/RS Roadster/Roadstar Series
1979-present. A large family of guitars whose model identification starts with prefix RS ('79-'81) or RG ('82-present), includes the Roadstar Standard, Roadstar Deluxe and Roadstar II models.

1979-2021	Higher-range	$600	$900
1979-2021	Highest-range	$900	$1,700
1979-2021	Low to mid-range	$300	$425
1979-2021	Lower-range	$200	$300
1979-2021	Mid-range	$425	$600

Rocket Roll II RR550
1982-1984. Flying V body, six-on-side headstock, pearloid blocks, cherry sunburst, maple top, set neck.

1982-1984		$1,200	$1,575

RT Series
1992-1993. Offset double-cut, bolt neck, rosewood 'board, dot markers.

1992-1993	Various models	$300	$600

RX Series
1994-1997. Offset double-cut, solidbodies.

1994-1997	Various models	$125	$300

S Models
1987-present. In '87 Ibanez introduced a new line of highly tapered, ultra-thin body, offset double-cut guitars that were grouped together as the S Models. Intially the S Models were going to be called the Sabre models but that name was trademarked by Music Man and could not be used. The S models will carry an S suffix or S prefix in the model name.

1987-2021	Various models	$350	$775

ST Studio Series
1978-1982. Double-cut solidbodies, lots of natural finishes, various models, even a doubleneck.

1979-1981	Various models	$350	$775

STW Double
1999. Double neck with 7-string and 6-string neck, limited edition.

1999		$2,150	$2,800

TC/TV Talman Series
1994-1998. Softer double-cut solidbodies.

1994-1998	Various models	$250	$650

USRG U.S.A. Custom Series
1994-1995. RG style guitars built in the U.S. by PBC Guitar Technology.

1994-1995	Various models	$1,225	$1,600

UV7/UV7P/UV77 Steve Vai Universe
1990-1997. Basswood 7-strings, hum/single/hum pickups. The '90-'93 white 7P and multi-colored 77 have pyramid inlays, the black '90-'97 7 has dots.

1990-1997	Various models	$1,500	$4,800

UV777 Steve Vai Universe
1998-2012. Basswood 7-string, pyramid inlays, maple 'board, hum/single/hum pickups.

1991-2012	Various models	$1,500	$2,300

V300 Vintage Series
1978-1991. Vintage Series acoustic dreadnought, spruce top, mahogany back and sides, sunburst or various colors.

1978-1991		$175	$275

Xiphos Series
2007-2015. Part of the X Series, various XP and XPT models, X-shaped solidbody electric, neck-thru construction. Replaced by Iron Label (XPIR) series in '15.

2007-2015	Various models	$950	$1,225

XV500
1985-1987. Sharply pointed X-body with scalloped bottom.

1985-1987		$875	$1,150

Ibanez, Salvador
1875-1920. Salvador Ibanez was a Spanish luthier who operated a small guitar-building workshop. In the early 1900s he founded Spain's largest guitar factory. In 1929 Japan's Hoshino family began importing Salvador Ibanez guitars. Demand for the Salvador Ibanez guitars became so great that the Hoshino family began building their own guitars, which ultimately became known as the Ibanez brand. Guitars from 1875-1920 were mostly classical style and often can be identified by a label on the inside back which stipulates Salvador Ibanez.

Ignacio Rozas
1987-present. Luthier Ignacio M. Rozas builds his classical and flamenco guitars in Madrid, Spain. He also offers factory-made guitars built to his specifications.

Illusion Guitars
1992-present. Luthier Jeff Scott builds his premium grade, production/custom, solidbody guitars in Fallbrook, California.

Imperial
Ca.1963-ca.1970. Imported by the Imperial Accordion Company of Chicago, Illinois. Early guitars made in Italy by accordion builder Crucianelli. By ca. '66 switched to Japanese guitars. They also made basses.

Imperial (Japan)
1957-1960. Early, budget grade, Japanese imports from the Hoshino company which was later renamed Ibanez.

Infeld
2003-2005. Solidbody guitars and basses offered by string-maker Thomastik-Infeld of Vienna.

Infinox
1980s. Infinox by JTG, of Nashville, offered a line of 'the classic shapes of yesterday and the hi tech chic of today'. Classic shapes included copies of many classic American solidbody designs with the block letter Infinox by JTG logo on headstock, special metallic grafteq paint finish, space-age faux graphite-feel neck, Gotoh tuning machines, Gotoh locking nut tremolo with fine tuners, all models with 1 or 2 humbucker pickups.

GUITARS

MODEL		EXC. COND.	
YEAR	FEATURES	LOW	HIGH

Interdonati

1920s-1930s. Guitars built by luthier Philip Interdonati, in New York City, originally professional grade. He also built mandolins.

Isana

1951-1974. Acoustic and electric archtop guitars built by luthier Josef Sandner in Nauheim, Germany. Elvis played one while in the army in Germany.

Acoustic Archtop

1951-1974	Various models	$450	$1,500

Island Instruments

2010-present. Luthier Nic Delisle builds professional and premium grade, production/custom, small-bodied acoustic and electric guitars in Montreal, Quebec. He also builds basses.

Italia

1999-present. Intermediate grade, production, solid, semi-solid, and hollow body guitars and basses designed by Trevor Wilkinson and made in Korea.

J Backlund Design

2008-present. Professional and premium grade, custom, electric guitars and basses designed by J. Backlund in Hixson, Tennessee, starting in 2008. He also imports Korean-made guitars under the Retronix brand.

J Burda Guitars

Flat-top guitars built by luthier Jan Burda in Berrien Springs, Michigan.

J. Frog Guitars

1978-present. Professional and premium grade, production/custom, solidbody guitars made by Ed Roman Guitars.

J.B. Player

1980s. Budget and intermediate grade, production, imported acoustic, acoustic/electric, and solidbody guitars and basses. They also offer banjos and mandolins. Founded in United States. Moved production of guitars to Korea but maintained a U.S. Custom Shop. MBT International/Musicorp took over manufacture and distribution in '89, then Kamen acquired MBT in 2005.

J.R. Zeidler Guitars

1977-2002. Luthier John Zeidler built premium and presentation grade, custom, flat-top, 12-string, and archtop guitars in Wallingford, Pennsylvania. He also built mandolins. He died in '02 at age 44.

J.S. Bogdanovich

1996-present. Production/custom, premium grade, classical and steel string guitars built by luthier John S. Bogdanovich in Swannanoa, North Carolina.

MODEL		EXC. COND.	
YEAR	FEATURES	LOW	HIGH

J.T. Hargreaves Basses & Guitars

1995-present. Luthier Jay Hargreaves builds his premium grade, production/custom, classical and steel string guitars and basses in Seattle, Washington.

Jack Daniel's

2004-2017. Acoustic and electric guitars and basses, some with Jack Daniel's artwork on the body and headstock, built by Peavey for the Jack Daniel's Distillery. There is also an amp model.

Jackson

1980-present. Currently Jackson offers intermediate, professional, and premium grade, production, electric guitars. They also offer basses. In '78 Grover Jackson bought out Charvel Guitars and moved it to San Dimas. Jackson made custom-built bolt-on Charvels. In '82 the pointy, tilt-back Jackson headstock became standard. The Jackson logo was born in '80 and used on a guitar designed as Randy Rhoad's first flying V. Jacksons were neck-through construction. The Charvel trademark was licensed to IMC in '85. IMC moved the Jackson factory to Ontario, California in '86.

Grover Jackson stayed with Jackson/Charvel until '89 (see Charvel). On October 25, 2002, Fender Musical Instruments Corp (FMIC) took ownership of Jackson/Charvel Manufacturing Inc.

Dinky Reverse DR2

1996-1998. US-made, reverse headstock, no inlay, 2 Duncan humbuckers, ebony 'board.

1996-1998		$775	$1,025

Dinky Reverse DR3/DR5

1992-2001. Import, reverse headstock, 2 humbuckers, dots (DR5) or sharkfin inlays (DR3), locking trem.

1992-1997	Dots	$365	$475
1995-2001	Sharkfin	$425	$550

DX Series

2000-2007. Standard offset double-cut body, reverse headstock.

2000-2007		$275	$375

Fusion Pro

Late 1980s-early 1990s. Import from Japan.

1980s-90s		$550	$725

Fusion U.S.A.

1992-1994. Jackson with Made In USA logo on headstock, graphics.

1992-1994		$925	$1,200

Jenna II RX10D Rhoads

2009. Limited production, Rhoads body style, named after performer Jenna Jameson.

2009		$550	$725

JSX94

1994-1995. Offset double-cut solidbody, single/single/hum, rosewood 'board, dot markers.

1994-1995		$310	$410

1997 Jackson Dinky Reverse DR2

1994 Jackson JSX94

Jackson Phil Collen
PC1 (U.S.A.)

1999 Jackson Randy Rhoads
Randy Schleyhahn

MODEL YEAR	FEATURES	EXC. COND. LOW	HIGH

JTX
1993-1995. Partial offset double-cut, single-coil neck pickup, humbucker bridge pickup, Jackson-Rose double lock vibrato, bolt-on neck, dot markers on maple fretboard, JTX truss rod cover logo.

1993-1995		$350	$475

Kelly Custom
1984-early 1990s. Solidbody, Kahler tremolo, 2 humbuckers, ebony 'board with shark's tooth inlays, bound neck and headstock.

1984-1993		$1,700	$2,200

Kelly Pro
1994-1995. Pointy-cut solidbody, neck-thru, 2 humbuckers, bound ebony 'board, sharkfin inlays.

1994-1995		$750	$975

Kelly Standard
1993-1995. Pointy cutaway solidbody, bolt neck, 2 humbuckers, dot markers.

1993-1995		$550	$725

Kelly U.S.A. (KE2)
1998-2021. Alder solidbody, flame maple top, neck-thru.

1998-2021		$1,375	$1,800

Kelly XL
1994-1995. Pointy cutaway solidbody, bolt neck, 2 humbuckers, bound rosewood 'board, sharkfin inlays.

1994-1995		$625	$825

King V (KV2)
2003-present. King V Pro reissue, neck-thru, sharkfin markers, Floyd Rose, U.S.-made.

2003-2021		$700	$925

King V Pro
1993-1995. Soft V-shaped neck-thru solidbody, sharkfin markers, 2 humbuckers.

1993-1995		$625	$825

King V STD
1993-1995. Bolt neck version of King V.

1993-1995		$325	$425

Phil Collen
1989-1991, 1993-1995. Offset double-cut maple neck-thru solidbody, 6-in-line tuners, 1 volume, bound ebony 'board, U.S.-made, early version has poplar body, 1 humbucker; later version with basswood body, 1 single-coil and 1 humbucker.

1989-1995		$1,375	$1,800

Phil Collen PC1 (U.S.A.)
1996-present. Quilt maple top, bolt-on maple neck, maple board, koa body '96-'00, mahogany body '01-present, 1 humbucker and 1 single coil '96-'97, humbucker, stacked humbucker, and single coil '98-present.

1996-2021		$1,600	$2,100

Phil Collen PC3 (Import)
1996-2001. Downscale version of Collen model, poplar body, bolt neck, humbucker\single\single.

1996-2001		$525	$700

PS Performers Series
1994-2003. Some with PS model number on truss rod cover.

1994-2003	Various models	$325	$425

MODEL YEAR	FEATURES	EXC. COND. LOW	HIGH

Randy Rhoads (Import)
1992-2011. Bolt neck import version.

1992-2011		$450	$575

Randy Rhoads Limited Edition
1992 only. Shark fin-style maple neck-thru body, gold hardware, white with black pinstriping, block inlays, 6-in-line tuners, U.S.-made, only 200 built.

1992		$5,500	$7,200

Randy Rhoads Pro Series RR3 and RR5
1995-2012. Made in Japan, various finishes.

1995-2012	RR3, bolt-on	$450	$600
2001-2011	RR5, neck-thru	$550	$725

Randy Rhoads Relic Tribute
2010-2011. Custom Shop limited edition to celebrate the 30th anniversary of the Randy Rhoads Concorde, 60 made, exacting dimension and design of Rhoads' original custom-made Concorde guitar, relic-treatment to mimic the original.

2010-2011		$6,400	$8,300

Randy Rhoads U.S.A./RR Series
1983-present. V-shaped (also referred to as concorde-shaped) neck-thru solidbody, 2 humbuckers, originally made at San Dimas plant, serial numbers RR 0001 to RR 1929, production moved to the Ontario plant by '87, serial numbers RR 1930 to present in sequential order.

1983	Early serial #, no trem	$4,600	$6,000
1983	Mid serial #, no trem	$3,200	$4,200
1983-1986	Late serial #, Kahler trem	$2,300	$3,000
1983-1986	Rose trem or string-thru	$2,300	$3,000
1987-1989	Early Ontario-built	$1,850	$2,400
1990-1992	Early '90s vintage	$1,700	$2,200
1993-2002		$1,700	$2,200
2003-2019	RR5	$1,025	$1,325
2003-2021	RR1	$1,700	$2,200

RX Series
2000-2011. Bolt-on, shark fin inlays.

2000-2008	RX10D Rhoads	$210	$275

San Dimas Serialized Plated
1980-1982. Various custom-built solidbody models, values vary depending on each individual instrument. The values are true for so-called "Serialized Plated" with Jackson neck plate, Jackson logo and serial number.

1980-1982		$3,800	$5,000

Soloist Custom
1993-1995. U.S.-made, double-cut, neck-thru solidbody, 1 humbucker and 2 single-coils, bound ebony 'board, shark's tooth inlays.

1993-1995		$1,700	$2,200

Soloist Pro
1990-1995. Import version of Soloist, with, shark's tooth inlays.

1990-1995		$675	$875

Soloist Shannon
1998. Shark fin inlays, single-single-hum pickups, Rose, signed by Mike Shannon.

1998		$1,700	$2,200

MODEL YEAR	FEATURES	EXC. COND. LOW	HIGH

Soloist Student J1 (U.S.A.)

1984-1999. Double-cut neck-thru solidbody, Seymour Duncan single-single-hum pickups, rosewood 'board, dot inlays, no binding.

1984-1986	San Dimas-built	$1,300	$1,700
1986-1999	Ontario-built	$1,300	$1,700

Soloist/Soloist USA/SL Series

1984-present. U.S.-made, double-cut, neck-thru, string-thru solidbody, 2 humbuckers, bound rosewood 'board, standard vibrato system on Soloist is Floyd Rose locking vibrato, a guitar with Kahler vibrato is worth less. Replaced by the Soloist USA in '90.

1984-1986	Custom order, Floyd Rose	$1,850	$2,400
1984-1986	Custom order, Kahler	$2,100	$2,700
1984-1986	San Dimas-built, Floyd Rose	$1,850	$2,400
1984-1986	San Dimas-built, Kahler	$1,850	$2,400
1986-1990	Custom order features	$1,850	$2,400
1986-1990	Ontario-built	$1,850	$2,400
1990-2021	Various models, includes SL1 & SL2	$1,700	$2,200

Stealth EX

1992-late 1990s. Offset double-cut, pointed headstock, H/S/S pickups, offset dot markers, tremolo, Jackson Professional logo.

1990s		$450	$575

Stealth HX

1992-1995. 3 humbucker version of Stealth, string-thru body.

1992-1995		$450	$575

Stealth XL

1993. Stealth XL truss rod cover logo, 1 humbucker, 2 single-coils, left edge dot markers.

1993		$450	$575

Surfcaster SC1

1998-2001. Jackson logo on headstock, Charvel Surfcaster styling.

1998-2001		$1,150	$1,500

Warrior Pro (Import)

1990-1992. Japanese version.

1990-1992		$375	$500

Warrior U.S.A.

1990-1992. Four point neck-thru solidbody, 1 humbucker and 1 single-coil, triangle markers, active electronics, U.S.-made, the Warrior Pro was Japanese version.

1990-1992	Red	$1,000	$1,300

Y2KV Dave Mustaine Signature

2000-2002. V-shaped body, shark tooth markers, neck-thru, 2 humbuckers.

2000-2002		$2,500	$3,200

Jackson-Guldan/Jay G Guitars

1920s-1960s. The Jackson-Guldan Violin Company, of Columbus, Ohio, mainly built inexpensive violins, violas, cellos, etc. but also offered acoustic guitars in the 1950s and early '60s, some of which were distributed by Wards. Their sales flyers from that era state - Made in America by Jackson-Guldan Craftsman. Very similar to small (13"-14") Stella economy flat-tops. Jay G name with quarter-note logo is sometimes on the headstock. They also offered lap steels and small tube amps early on.

Jacobacci

1930s-1994. Founded in France by Italian Vincent Jacobacci and originally building basso-guitars, banjos, and mandolins. Sons Roger and Andre joined the company and encouraged pop to add lapsteels and electric and regular acoustic guitars around '52. The guitars are sometimes labeled as Jaco and, from ca. '54 to ca. '66, as Jaco Major. In '58 the company introduced aluminum neck models, and in '59 their first solidbodies. In the '60s they also made instruments branded Royal, Texas, Ohio, Star and made instruments for Major Conn and other companies. By the mid '60s, they were producing mainly jazz style guitars.

Jamboree

1960s. Guitar brand exported by Japan's Hoshino (Ibanez).

James Einolf Guitars

1964-2017. Production/custom, professional grade, flat-top guitars built first in Denver, then Castle Rock, Colorado by luthier James Einolf.

James R. Baker Guitars

1996-present. Luthier James R. Baker builds his premium grade, custom, archtops in Shoreham, New York.

James Trussart

1980-present. Luthier James Trussart builds his premium grade, custom/production, solid and semi-hollow body electric guitars and basses in Los Angeles, California.

James Tyler

Early 1980s-present. Luthier James Tyler builds his professional and premium grade, custom/production, solidbody guitars and basses in Van Nuys, California, and also has a model built in Japan.

Janofsky Guitars

Production classical and flamenco guitars built by luthier Stephen Janofsky in Amherst, Massachusetts starting in 1978.

Jaros

Beginning 1995 these professional and premium grade, production/custom, solidbody and acoustic/electric guitars were originally built by father and son luthiers Harry and Jim Jaros in Rochester, Pennsylvania. In '01 Ed Roman in Las Vegas, bought the brand. He sold it in '04 to Dave Weiler in Nashville. Serial numbers under 1000 were made by the Jaros', numbers 1001-2000 were made by Ed Roman, over 2000 made by Dave Weiler.

2005 James Trussart Steel Deville
Rivington Guitars

James Tyler Studio Elite HD
Frank Manno

GUITARS

*Jason Z. Schroeder
The Chopper TL*

Jeff Traugott Model R

Jasmine

1994-2019. Budget and intermediate grade, production, steel and classical guitars offered by Takamine Jasmine or Jasmine by Takamine. Student level instruments.

Jason Z. Schroeder Guitars

1994-present. Luthier Jason Schroeder builds professional and premium grade, production/custom, electric guitars in Redding, California.

Jay Turser

1997-present. Budget and intermediate grade, production, imported acoustic, acoustic/electric, electric and resonator guitars and basses. They also amps. Designed and developed by Tommy Rizzi for Music Industries Corp.

JBG (Joe Bochar Guitars)

2009-present. Production/custom, professional grade, solidbody electric guitars built by luthier Joe Bochar in Santa Clarita, California.

JD Bluesville

John Schappell and luthier Davis Millard build their professional grade, custom/production, solidbody electric guitars in Allentown, Pennsylvania. They began in 2005.

Jeff Traugott Guitars

1991-present. Premium and presentation grade, custom, flat-top, nylon-string, and acoustic/electric guitars built by luthier Jeff Traugott, in Santa Cruz, California.

Jeremy Locke Guitars

Premium grade, production/custom, classical and flamenco guitars built by luthier Jeremy Locke in Coomera, South East Queensland, Australia, starting in 1985.

Jeronimo Pena Fernandez

1967-present. Luthier Jeronimo Pena Fernandez started building classical guitars in Marmolejo, Spain, in the '50s. In '67, he went full-time and soon became well-known for his fine work. He is now retired, but still builds a few guitars a year. Prices can vary depending on model specs, each instrument should be evaluated on a case-by-case basis.

Jerry Jones

1981-2011. Intermediate grade, production, semi-hollowbody electric guitars and sitars from luthier Jerry Jones, built in Nashville, Tennessee. They also built basses. Jones started building custom guitars in '81, and launched his Danelectro-inspired line in '87. He retired in 2011.
Electric
Various models include Baritone 6-string ('89-'11); Electric Sitar ('90-'11) with buzz-bar sitar bridge, individual pickup for sympathetic strings and custom

color gator finish; Longhorn Guitarlin ('89-'00, '05-'11) with large cutaway Guitarlin-style body, 24 frets in '89 and 31 after; and the Neptune 12-string ('81-'11) single-cut with 3 pickups.

MODEL YEAR	FEATURES	EXC. COND. LOW	HIGH
1981-2011	Neptune 12-string	$1,425	$1,850
1981-2011	Neptune 6/12 Double Neck	$2,550	$3,350
1989-2011	Baritone 6-string	$1,700	$2,225
1989-2011	Longhorn Guitarlin	$1,425	$1,850
1990-2011	Baby Sitar	$1,425	$1,850
1990-2011	Shorthorn	$1,375	$1,775
1990-2011	Sitar	$1,425	$1,850
1990-2011	U-3, 3 pickups	$1,375	$1,775

Jersey Girl

1991-present. Premium grade, production/custom, solidbody guitars made in Japan. They also build effects.

JET

1998-present. Premium grade, custom/production, chambered solidbody electric guitars built by luthier Jeffrey Earle Terwilliger in Raleigh, North Carolina.

Jewel

1920s. Instruments built by the Oscar Schmidt Co. and possibly others. Most likely a brand made for a distributor.

JG Guitars

1991-present. Luthier Johan Gustavsson builds his premium and presentation grade, production/custom, solidbody electric guitars in Malmö, Sweden.

Jim Dyson

1972-2015. Intermediate, professional and premium grade, production/custom electric guitars and basses built by luthier Jim Dyson in Torquay, Southern Victoria, Australia. He also built lap steels.

Jim Redgate Guitars

1992-present. Luthier Jim Redgate builds his premium grade, custom, nylon-string classical guitars in Belair, Adelaide, South Australia.

John Le Voi Guitars

1970-present. Production/custom, gypsy jazz, flat-top, and archtop guitars built by luthier John Le Voi in Lincolnshire, United Kingdom. He also builds mandolin family instruments.

John Page Guitars and John Page Classic

2006-present. Luthier John Page builds his custom, premium grade, chambered and solidbody electric guitars in Sunny Valley, Oregon.

MODEL YEAR	FEATURES	EXC. COND. LOW	HIGH

John Price Guitars

Custom classical and flamenco guitars built by luthier John Price, starting in 1984, in Australia.

Johnson

Mid-1990s-present. Budget, intermediate and professional grade, production, acoustic, classical, acoustic/electric, resonator and solidbody guitars and basses imported by The Music Link, Brisbane, California. Johnson also offers amps, mandolins, ukuleles and effects.

Jon Kammerer Guitars

1997-present. Luthier Jon Kammerer builds his professional and premium grade, custom/production, solidbody, chambered, hollowbody, and acoustic guitars and basses in Keokuk, Iowa.

Jones

See TV Jones listing.

Jordan

1981-present. Professional and premium grade, custom, flat-top and archtop guitars built by luthier John Jordan in Concord, California. He also builds electric violins and cellos.

Jose Oribe

1962-present. Presentation grade, production, classical, flamenco, and steel-string acoustic guitars built by luthier Jose Oribe in Vista, California.

Jose Ramirez

See listing under Ramirez, Jose.

Juliett

1960s. Guitars built by Zerosette (or Zero-Sette), an accordion builder near Castelfidardo, Italy.

JY Jeffrey Yong Guitars

2003-present. Professional and premium grade, production/custom, classical, acoustic and electric guitars and basses and harp guitars built by Jeffrey Yong in Kuala Lumpur, Malaysia.

K & S

1992-1998. Hawaiian-style and classical guitars distributed by George Katechis and Marc Silber and handmade in Paracho, Mexico. A few 16" wide Leadbelly Model 12-strings were made in Oakland, California by luthier Stewart Port. K & S also offered mandolins, mandolas and ukes. In '98, Silber started marketing guitars under the Marc Silber Guitar Company brand and Katechis continued to offer instruments under the Casa Montalvo brand.

Kakos, Stephen

Luthier Stephen Kakos builds his premium grade, production/custom, classical guitars in Mound, Minnesota starting in 1972.

MODEL YEAR	FEATURES	EXC. COND. LOW	HIGH

Kalamazoo

1933-1942, 1965-1970. Budget brand built by Gibson. Made flat-tops, solidbodies, mandolins, lap steels, banjos and amps. Name revived for a line of amps, solidbodies and basses in '65-'67. Playability and string tension will affect values of '60s electrics.

KG-1/KG-1A
1965-1969. Offset double-cut (initial issue) or SG-shape (second issue), 1 pickup, Model 1A with spring vibrato, red, blue or white.

1965-1969		$500	$650

KG-2/KG-2A
1965-1970. Offset double-cut (initial shape) or SG-shape, 2 pickups, Model 2A with spring vibrato, red, blue or white.

1965-1970		$525	$675

KG-11
1933-1941. Flat-top, all mahogany, 14" with no 'guard, sunburst.

1933-1941		$1,425	$1,850

KTG-11 Tenor
1936-1940. Tenor version of 11.

1936-1940		$725	$950

KG-12
1940-1941. Rare model, L-00, sunburst.

1940-1941		$2,250	$2,925

KG-14/KG-14N
1936-1940. Flat-top L-0-size, mahogany back and sides, with 'guard, sunburst or natural (N).

1936-1940		$2,250	$2,900

KTG-14 Tenor
1936-1940. Tenor version of 14.

1936-1940		$1,000	$1,300

KG-16
1939-1940. Gibson-made archtop, small body, f-hole.

1939-1940		$1,125	$1,475

KG-21
1936-1941. Early model 15" archtop (bent, not curved), dot markers, bound top, sunburst.

1936-1941		$1,125	$1,475

KTG-21 Tenor
1935-1939. Tenor version of 21.

1935-1939		$725	$950

KG-22
1940-1942. Early model 16" archtop.

1940-1942		$1,350	$1,750

KG-31
1935-1940. Archtop L-50-size, 16" body, non-carved spruce top, mahogany back and sides.

1935-1940		$1,350	$1,750

KG-32
1939-1942. Archtop, 16" body.

1939-1942		$1,425	$1,850

KG Senior
1933-1934. Senior Model logo, firestripe guard, bound top and bottom, rope rose.

1933-1934		$2,100	$2,725

KG Sport
1937-1942. Small body, ¾ size, Sport Model logo.

1937-1942		$2,100	$2,725

Jon Kammerer

1940 Kalamazoo KG-12
David Stone

1941 Kalamazoo KGN-32 Oriole
David Stone

1960s Kawai

MODEL YEAR	FEATURES	EXC. COND. LOW	HIGH

KGN-12 Oriole
1940-1941. Flat-top, same body as KG-14, but with maple back and sides, stencil Oriole picture on headstock, natural.

1940-1941		$2,250	$2,950

KGN-32 Oriole
1940-1941. Archtop, maple back and sides, stencil Oriole picture on headstock, natural.

1940-1941		$2,250	$2,950

KHG Series
1936-1941. Acoustic Hawaiian guitar (HG), some converted to Spanish set-up.

1936-1940	KHG-11	$1,425	$1,850
1936-1941	KHG-14	$2,250	$2,925

Kamico
1947-1951. Flat-top acoustic guitars. Low-end budget brand made by Kay Musical Instrument Company and sold through various distributors. They also offered lap steel and amp sets.

K Stratotone Thin Single
1950-1951. Similar to Kay Stratotone-style neck-thru solidbody, single slim-tube pickup.

1950-1951		$950	$1,225

Kapa
Ca. 1962-1970. Begun by Dutch immigrant and music store owner Koob Veneman in Hyattsville, Maryland whose father had made Amka guitars in Holland. Kapa is from K for Koob, A for son Albert, P for daughter Patricia, and A for wife Adeline. Crown shield logo from Amka guitars. The brand included some Hofner and Italian imports in '60. Ca. '66 Kapa started offering thinner bodies. Some German Pix pickups ca. '66. Thinlines and Japanese bodies in '69. Kapa closed shop in '70 and the parts and equipment were sold to Micro-Frets and Mosrite. Later Veneman was involved with Bradley copy guitars imported from Japan. Approximately 120,000 Kapa guitars and basses were made.

Electric
1962-1970. Various models include Challenger with 3-way toggle from '62-'66/'67 and 2 on/off switches after; Cobra with 1 pickup; Continental and Continental 12-string; Minstrel and Minstrel 12-string with teardrop shape, 3 pickups; and the Wildcat, mini offset double-cut, 3 pickups and mute.

1962-1970	Various models	$300	$775

Karol Guitars
2001-present. Luthier Tony Karol builds his custom, premium grade, acoustic and electric guitars in Mississauga, Ontario.

Kasha
1967-1997. Innovative classical guitars built by luthier Richard Schneider in collaboration with Dr. Michael Kasha. Schneider also consulted for Gibson and Gretsch. Schneider died in '97.

Kathy Wingert Guitars
1996-present. Luthier Kathy Wingert builds her premium grade, production/custom, flat-tops in Rancho Palos Verdes, California.

Kawai
1927-present. Kawai is a Japanese piano and guitar maker. They started offering guitars around '56 and they were imported into the U.S. carrying many different brand names, including Kimberly and Teisco. In '67 Kawai purchased Teisco. Odd-shaped guitars were offered from late-'60s through the mid-'70s. Few imports carrying the Kawai brand until the late-'70s; best known for high quality basses. By '90s they were making plexiglass replicas of Teisco Spectrum 5 and Kawai moon-shaped guitar. Kawai quit offering guitars and basses around 2002.

Acoustic
1956-2002		$325	$425

Electric
1956-2002	Common model	$350	$450
1956-2002	Rare model	$550	$725

Kay
Ca. 1931 (1890)-present. Originally founded in Chicago, Illinois as Groehsl Company (or Groehsel) in 1890, making bowl-backed mandolins. Offered Groehsl, Stromberg, Kay Kraft, Kay, Arch Kraft brand names, plus made guitars for S.S.Maxwell, Old Kraftsman (Spiegel), Recording King (Wards), Supertone (Sears), Silvertone (Sears), National, Dobro, Custom Kraft (St.Louis Music), Hollywood (Shireson Bros.), Oahu and others.

In 1921 the name was changed to Stromberg-Voisinet Company. Henry Kay "Hank" Kuhrmeyer joined the company in '23 and was secretary by '25. By the mid-'20s the company was making many better Montgomery Ward guitars, banjos and mandolins, often with lots of pearloid. First production electric guitars and amps are introduced with big fanfare in '28; perhaps only 200 or so made. Last Stromberg instruments seen in '32. Kuhrmeyer becomes president and the Kay Kraft brand was introduced in '31, probably named for Kuhrmeyer's middle name, though S-V had used Kay brand on German Kreuzinger violins '28-'36. By '34, if not earlier, the company is changed to the Kay Musical Instrument Company. A new factory was built at 1640 West Walnut Street in '35. The Kay Kraft brand ends in '37 and the Kay brand is introduced in late-'36 or '37.

Violin Style Guitars and upright acoustic basses debut in '38. In '40 the first guitars for Sears, carrying the new Silvertone brand, are offered. Kamico budget line introduced in '47 and Rex flat-tops and archtops sold through Gretsch in late-'40s. Kuhrmeyer retires in '55 dies a year later. New gigantic factory in Elk Grove Village, Illinois opens in '64. Seeburg purchased Kay in '66 and sold it to Valco in '67. Valco/Kay went out of business in '68 and its assets were auctioned in '69. The Kay name went

GUITARS

MODEL		EXC. COND.	
YEAR	FEATURES	LOW	HIGH

to Sol Weindling and Barry Hornstein of W.M.I. (Teisco Del Rey) who began putting Kay name on Teisco guitars. By '73 most Teisco guitars are called Kay. Tony Blair, president of Indianapolis-based A.R. Musical Enterprises Inc. (founded in '73) purchased the Kay nameplate in '79 and currently distributes Kay in the U.S. Currently Kay offers budget and intermediate grade, production, acoustic, semi-hollow body, solidbody, and resonator guitars. They also make amps, basses, banjos, mandolins, ukes, violins.

K11/K8911 Rhythm Special
1953-1961. Single-cut 17" acoustic archtop, "eighth note" headstock logo, large position markers, white 'guard, became K8911 in '57, sunburst or blond (B).

1953-1961	Blond	$975	$1,275
1953-1961	Sunburst	$925	$1,200

K20 Super Auditorium
1939-1942. 16" archtop, solid spruce top, maple back and sides, sunburst.

1939-1942		$300	$400

K20T
1970s. Japanese-made solidbody, 2 pickups, tremolo, model number on neck plate, circle-capital K logo on headstock.

1970s		$145	$190

K21/K21B Cutaway Professional
1952-1956. Single-cut 17" acoustic archtop, split block markers, sunburst or blond (B).

1952-1956	Blond	$1,200	$1,550
1952-1956	Sunburst	$1,100	$1,450

K22 Artist Spanish
1947-1956. Flat-top similar to Gibson J-100 17", spruce top, mahogany back and sides.

1947-1956		$600	$775

K26 Artist Spanish
1947-1951. Flat-top, block markers, natural.

1947-1951		$675	$875

K27 Jumbo
1952-1956. 17" Jumbo flat-top, fancy appointments.

1952-1956		$1,150	$1,500

K37T Spanish Tenor
1952-1956. Mahogany bodied archtop, tenor.

1952-1956		$250	$325

K39 Super Grand Auditorium
1947-1951. Full size acoustic archtop, faux rope binding on top, Kay script logo.

1947-1951		$375	$500

K44 Artist Archtop
1947-1951. Non-cut archtop, solid spruce top, 17" curly maple veneered body, block markers, sunburst.

1947-1951		$575	$750

K45 Professional Master Size Archtop
1952-1954. Non-cut archtop, 17" body, engraved tortoiseshell-celluloid headstock, large block markers, natural.

1952-1954		$575	$750

K45 Travel Guitar
1981. Made in Korea, known as the 'rifle guitar', 'travel guitar', or 'Austin-Hatchet copy', circle K logo.

1981		$375	$500

K46 Artist Master Size Archtop
1947-1951. Non-cut archtop, solid spruce top, 17" curly maple-veneered body, double-eighth note headstock inlay, sunburst.

1947-1951		$550	$700

K48 Artist Master Size Archtop
1947-1951. Non-cut archtop, 17" solid spruce top with figured maple back and sides, split block inlays, sunburst or black.

1947-1951		$850	$1,100

K48/K21 Jazz Special
Late-1960s. Slim solidbody with 3 reflective pickups, garden spade headstock, fancy position Circle K headstock logo, white.

1968		$500	$650

K100 Vanguard
1961-1966. Offset double-cut slab solidbody, genuine maple veneered top and back over hardwood body, sunburst.

1961-1966		$300	$400

K102 Vanguard
1961-1966. Double pickup version of the K100, sunburst.

1961-1966		$350	$450

K136 (aka Stratotone)
1955-1957. Small single-cut slab solidbody electric, similar to Harmony Stratotone style, set neck, 1 pickup, trapeze tailpiece, triangle paint graphic in Spring Green and White Mist, matching green headstock, attractive finish adds value to this otherwise lower-end student model.

1955-1957		$975	$1,250

K142 (aka Stratotone)
1955-1957. Small slab solidbody, introduced in '55 along with the K136, offered with 1 pickup or 2 pickups (more rare), trapeze tailpiece, copper finish.

1955-1957	1 pickup	$925	$1,200
1955-1957	2 pickups	$975	$1,250

K161 Thin Twin/Jimmy Reed
1952-1958. Single-cut semi-hollow body, 2 pickups.

1952-1958		$950	$1,250

K161V/VB Thin Twin
2009-present. Vintage Reissue series, single-cut hollowbody, 2 pickups.

2009-2021		$800	$1,050

K300 Double Cutaway Solid Electric
1962-1966. Two single-coils, block inlays, some with curly maple top and some with plain maple top, natural.

1962-1966		$475	$625

K360 Apollo/K365 Apollo II
1965-1968. Solidbody, 2 pickups, block inlays, vibrato.

1965-1968		$1,000	$1,300

K535 Double Cutaway Thinline
1961-1965. Thinline double-cut, 2 pickups, vibrato, sunburst.

1961-1965		$550	$725

K550 Dove
1970s. Square shoulder D-style, 2 Dove-style 'guards, capital K logo.

1970s		$130	$175

1965 Kay K100 Vanguard
Carter Vintage Guitars

1963 Kay K300
Richard Kregear

1961 Kay K776 Jazz II
Jim Bame

1950s Kay K8990 Upbeat
Curt Huettner

MODEL YEAR	FEATURES	EXC. COND. LOW	HIGH

K571/K572/K573 Speed Demon
1961-1965. Thinline semi-acoustic/electric, single pointed cutaway, some with Bigsby vibrato, with 1 (K571), 2 (K572) or 3 (K573) pickups. There was also a Speed Demon solidbody.

1961-1965	571, 1 pickup	$375	$500
1961-1965	572, 2 pickups	$450	$600
1961-1965	573, 3 pickups	$475	$625

K580 Galaxy
1961-1966. Thinline, single-cut, 1 pickup.

1961-1966		$500	$650

K592 Double Cutaway Thinline
1962-1966. Thinline semi-acoustic/electric, double Florentine cut, 2 or 3 pickups, Bigsby vibrato, pie-slice inlays, cherry.

1962-1966		$500	$650

K672/K673 Swingmaster
1961-1965. Single rounded cutaway semi-hollowbody, with 2 (K672) or 3 (K673) pickups.

1961-1965	672, 2 pickups	$1,050	$1,350
1961-1965	673, 3 pickups	$1,150	$1,500

K682 Galaxie II
1966-1968. Hollowbody, 2 pickups, vibrato tailpiece.

1966-1968		$525	$700

K775/K776 Jazz II
1961-1966. Electric thinline archtop, double-cut, standard Bigsby vibrato, 2 Gold K pickups, 4 knobs with toggle controls. Replaces Barney Kessel series as top-of-the-line model.

1961-1966	775, shaded	$1,400	$1,800
1961-1966	776, blond	$1,400	$1,800

K797 Acoustic Archtop
1930s. Full size student-intermediate acoustic archtop, 3-on-a-strip tuners, dot markers, sunburst.

1935-1937		$275	$375

K1160 Standard
1957-1964. Small 13" (standard) flat-top, laminated construction.

1957-1964		$50	$75

K1452 Aristocrat
1952. Acoustic-electric archtop, 2 pickups, sunburst.

1952		$800	$1,050

K1700/K1701 Barney Kessel Pro
1957-1960. 13" hollowbody, single-cut, Kelvinator headstock, ebony 'board with pearl inlays, white binding, 1 (K1701) or 2 (K1700) pickups, sunburst.

1957-1960	1700, 2 pickups	$1,850	$2,400
1957-1960	1701, 1 pickup	$1,675	$2,175

K1961/K1962/K1963 Value Leader
1960-1965. Part of Value Leader line, thinline single-cut, hollowbody, identified by single chrome-plated checkered, body-length guard on treble side, laminated maple body, maple neck, dot markers, sunburst, with 1 (K1961), 2 (K1962) or 3 (K1963) pickups.

1960-1965	1961, 1 pickup	$400	$525
1960-1965	1962, 2 pickups	$425	$575
1960-1965	1963, 3 pickups	$500	$650

K1982/K1983 Style Leader/Jimmy Reed
1960-1965. Part of the Style Leader mid-level Kay line. Sometimes dubbed Jimmy Reed of 1960s. Easily identified by the long brushed copper dual guardplates on either side of the strings. Brown or gleaming golden blond (natural) finish, laminated curly maple body, simple script Kay logo, with 2 (K1982) or 3 (K1983) pickups.

1960-1965	1982, 2 pickups	$575	$750
1960-1965	1983, 3 pickups	$675	$875

K3500 Studio Concert
1966-1968. 14 1/2" flat-top, solid spruce top, laminated maple back and sides.

1966-1968		$95	$125

K5113 Plains Special
1968. Flat-top, solid spruce top, laminated mahogany back and sides.

1968		$150	$200

K5160 Auditorium
1957-1965. Flat-top 15" auditorium-size, laminated construction.

1957-1965		$150	$200

K6100 Country
1950s-1960s. Jumbo flat-top, spruce x-braced top, mahogany back and sides, natural.

1957-1962		$400	$525

K6116 Super Auditorium
1957-1965. Super Auditorium-size flat-top, laminated figured maple back and sides, solid spruce top.

1957-1965		$225	$300

K6120 Western
1960s. Jumbo flat-top, laminated maple body, pinless bridge, sunburst.

1962		$200	$265

K6130 Calypso
1960-1965. 15 1/2" flat-top with narrow waist, slotted headstock, natural.

1960-1965		$275	$360

K6533/K6535 Value Leader
1961-1965. Value Leader was the budget line of Kay, full body archtop, with 1 (K6533) or 2 (K6535) pickups, sunburst.

1961-1965	6533, 1 pickup	$360	$475
1961-1965	6535, 2 pickups	$425	$550

K6700/K6701 Barney Kessel Artist
1956-1960. Single-cut, 15 1/2" body, 1 (K6701) or 2 (K6700) pickups, Kelvinator headstock, sunburst or blond.

1956-1960	6700, 2 pickups	$2,600	$3,400
1956-1960	6701, 1 pickup	$2,300	$3,000

K6878 Style Leader
1966-1968. Full size (15.75) acoustic archtop, circle K logo on 'guard, sunburst.

1966-1968		$230	$300

K7000 Artist
1960-1965. Highest-end of Kay classical series, fan bracing, spruce top, maple back and sides.

1960-1965		$335	$435

K7010 Concerto
1960-1965. Entry level of Kay classical series.

1960-1965		$100	$130

K7010 Maestro
1960-1965. Middle level of Kay classical series.

1960-1965		$200	$260

MODEL YEAR	FEATURES	EXC. COND. LOW	HIGH

K8110 Master
1957-1960. 17" master-size flat-top which was largest of the series, laminated construction.

1957-1960		$150	$200

K8127 Solo Special
1957-1965. Kay's professional grade flat-top, narrow waist jumbo, block markers.

1957-1965		$435	$575

K8700/K8701 Barney Kessel Jazz Special
1956-1960. Part of the Gold K Line, top-of-the-line model, 17" single-cut archtop, 1 (K8701) or 2 (K8700) pickups, 4 controls and toggle, Kelvinator headstock with white background, natural or shaded sunburst, Barney Kessel signature logo on acrylic scalloped 'guard, no signature logo on '60 model.

1956-1960	8700, 2 pickups	$2,600	$3,400
1956-1960	8701, 1 pickup	$2,300	$3,000

K8990/K8995 Upbeat
1956/1958-1960. Less expensive alternative to Barney Kessel Jazz Special, 2 (K8990) or 3 (K8995) pickups, Gold K Line, Kelvinator headstock, sunburst.

1956-1960	8990, 2 pickups	$1,400	$1,825
1958-1960	8995, 3 pickups	$1,550	$2,025

Wood Amplifying Guitar
1934. Engineered after Dobro/National metal resonator models except the resonator and chamber on this model are made of wood, small production.

1934		$1,700	$2,225

Kay Kraft
1927-1937. First brand name of the Kay Musical Instrument Company as it began its transition from Stromberg-Voisinet Company to Kay (see Kay for more info).

Recording King

1931-1937		$625	$825

Venetian Archtop
1930s. Unique Venetian cutaway body style, acoustic with round soundhole, flower-vine decal art on low bout.

1930s		$1,200	$1,575

KB
1989-present. Luthier Ken Bebensee builds his premium grade, custom, acoustic and electric guitars and basses in North San Juan, California. He was located in San Luis Obispo from '89-'01. He also builds mandolins.

Kel Kroydon (by Gibson)
1930-1933. Private branded budget level instruments made by Gibson. They also had mandolins and banjos. The name has been revived on a line of banjos by Tom Mirisola and made in Nashville.

KK-1
1932. 14 3/4" L-0 sytle body, colorful parrot stencils on body.

1932		$4,500	$5,900

Keller Custom Guitars
Professional grade, production/custom, solidbody guitars built by luthier Randall Keller in Mandan, North Dakota. He began in 1994.

Keller Guitars
1975-present. Premium grade, production/custom, flat-tops made by luthier Michael L. Keller in Rochester, Minnesota.

Kelly Guitars
1968-present. Luthier Rick Kelly builds professional grade, custom, solidbody electric guitars in New York, New York.

Ken Franklin
2003-present. Luthier Ken Franklin builds his premium grade, production/custom, acoustic guitars and ukuleles in Ukiah, California.

Kendrick
1989-present. Premium grade, production/custom, solidbody guitars built in Texas. Founded by Gerald Weber in Pflugerville, Texas and currently located in Kempner, Texas. Mainly known for their handmade tube amps, Kendrick added guitars in '94 and also offers speakers and effects.

Kenneth Lawrence Instruments
1986-present. Luthier Kenneth Lawrence builds his premium grade, production/custom, electric solidbody and chambered guitars and basses in Arcata, California.

Kent
1961-1969. Imported from Japan by Buegeleisen and Jacobson of New York, New York. Manufacturers unknown but many early guitars and basses were made by Guyatone and Teisco.

Acoustic Flat-Top
1962-1969. Various models.

1962-1969		$175	$350

Acoustic/Electric
1962-1969. Various models.

1962-1969		$225	$300

Electric 12-String
1965-1969. Thinline electric, double pointy cutaways, 12 strings, slanted dual pickup, sunburst.

1965-1969		$400	$525

Semi-Hollow Electric
1962-1969. Thinline electric, offset double pointy cutaways, slanted dual pickups, various colors.

1962-1969		$400	$525

Solidbody Electric
1962-1969. Models include Polaris I, II and III, Lido, Copa and Videocaster.

1962-1969	Common model	$225	$400
1962-1969	Rare model	$400	$700

Kelly Guitar

1969 Kent Model 741
Greg Perrine

GUITARS

Kiesel Jason Becker Yin Yang

*1967 Kingston Flying
Wedge Rocket*

Tom Pfeifer

MODEL		EXC. COND.	
YEAR	FEATURES	LOW	HIGH

Kevin Ryan Guitars
1989-present. Premium grade, custom, flat-tops built by luthier Kevin Ryan in Westminster, California.

KeyKord
Ca. 1929-mid 1930s.. Keykord offered guitars, ukes and banjos that had a push-button mechanism mounted over the fingerboard that "fingered" a different chord for each button. The guitars were built by Chicago's Stromberg-Voisinet (Kay).

Tenor
1920s-1930s. Venetian mahogany body, 4-string, pearloid headstock overlay.

1920s-30s		$525	$675

Kiesel
1946-present. Founded by Lowell C. Kiesel in '46. Refer to Carvin listing for more info regarding the early years. Prior to his death in 2009, L.C. had turned the business over to his sons and it was located in several different California cities over the years.

In 2015, son Mark and grandson Jeff Kiesel began the new independent Kiesel Custom Guitars. They build professional and premium grade, acoustic and electric guitars and basses in Escondido, California.

Kimbara
1970s-1980s. Japanese line of guitars and basses mainly imported into the U.K. Models were the same as the Fresher brand.

Kimberly
Late-1960s-early-1970s. Private branded import made in the same Japanese factory as Teisco. They also made basses.

Longhorn
1960s. S-style, deep double-cut, 2 pickups.

1960s		$450	$600

May Queen
1960s. Same as Teisco May Queen with Kimberly script logo on headstock and May Queen Teisco on the 'guard.

1960s		$525	$700

Kinal
1969-present. Production/custom, professional and premium grade, solid body electric and archtop guitars and basses built and imported by luthier Michael Kinal in Vancouver, British Columbia.

King's Stone
1960s. Guitar brand exported by Japan's Hoshino (Ibanez).

Kingsley
1960s. Early Japanese imports, Teisco-made.

Soldibody Electric
1960s. Four pickups with tremolo.

1960s		$350	$450

Kingslight Guitars
1980-2015. Luthier John Kingslight built his premium grade, custom/production, steel string guitars and basses in Portage, Michigan (in Taos, New Mexico for '80-'83).

Kingston
Ca. 1958-1967. Guitars and basses imported from Japan by Jack Westheimer and Westheimer Importing Corporation of Chicago, Illinois. Early examples made by Guyatone and Teisco. They also offered mandolins and banjos.

Electric
1958-1967. Various models include: B-1, soldibody, 1 pickup; B-2T/B-3T/B-4T, solidbodies, 2/3/4 pickups and tremolo; SA-27, thin hollowbody, 2 pickups, tremolo.

1958-1967	Common model	$300	$400
1958-1967	Rare model	$600	$775

Kinscherff Guitars
1990-present. Luthier Jamie Kinscherff builds his premium grade, production/custom, flat-top guitars in Austin, Texas.

Kleartone
1930s. Private brand made by Regal and/or Gibson.

Small Flat-Top

1930s		$550	$725

Klein Acoustic Guitars
First produced in 1972, luthiers Steve Klein and Steven Kauffman build their production/custom, premium and presentation grade flat-tops and basses outside Sonoma, California.

Klein Electric Guitars
1988-2007. Steve Klein added electrics to his line in '88. In '95, he sold the electric part of his business to Lorenzo German, who continued to produce professional grade, production/custom, solidbody guitars and basses in Linden, California.

K-Line Guitars
2005-present. Professional grade, production/custom, T-style and S-style guitars and basses built by luthier Chris Kroenlein in St. Louis, Missouri. He also builds basses.

Klira
1887-1980s. Founded by Johannes Klira in Schoenbach, Germany, mainly made violins, but added guitars in the 1950s. The guitars of the '50s and '60s were original designs, but by the '70s most models were similar to popular American models. The guitars of the '50s and '60s were aimed at the budget market, but workmanship improved with the '70s models. They also made basses.

Electric

1950s-60s	Common model	$400	$800
1950s-60s	Rare model	$800	$1,500

MODEL		EXC. COND.	
YEAR	FEATURES	LOW	HIGH

Knaggs

2010-present. Luthiers Joseph Knaggs and Peter Wolf build premium and presentation grade, production/custom, acoustic and electric guitars and basses in Greensboro, Maryland.

Knox

Early-mid-1960s. Budget grade guitars imported from Japan, script Knox logo on headstock.

Electric Solidbody

1960s. Student models, 2 pickups, push buttons.

1960s	Various models	$375	$500

Knutsen

1890s-1920s. Luthier Chris J. Knutsen of Tacoma and Seattle, Washington, experimented with and perfected Hawaiian and harp guitar models. He moved to Los Angeles, California around 1916. He also made steels, mandolins and ukes. Dealers state the glue used on Knutsen instruments is prone to fail and instruments may need repair.

Convertible

1909-1914. Flat-top model with adjustable neck angle that allowed for a convertible Hawaiian or Spanish setup.

1909-1914		$4,200	$5,500

Harp Guitar

1900s. Normally 11 strings with fancy purfling and trim.

1900-1910		$3,800	$5,000

Knutson Luthiery

1981-present. Professional and premium grade, custom, archtop and flat-top guitars built by luthier John Knutson in Forestville, California. He also builds basses, lap steels and mandolins.

Kohno

1960-present. Luthier Masaru Kohno built his classical guitars in Tokyo, Japan. When he died in '98, production was taken over by his nephew, Masaki Sakurai.

Koll

1990-present. Professional and premium grade, custom/production, solidbody, chambered, and archtop guitars and basses built by luthier Saul Koll, originally in Long Beach, California, and since '93, in Portland, Oregon.

Kona

1910s-1920s. Acoustic Hawaiian guitars sold by C.S. Delano and others, with later models made by the Herman Weissenborn Co. Weissenborn appointments are in line with style number, with thicker body and solid neck construction. Kona name currently used on an import line offered by M&M Merchandisers.

Style 2

1927-1928		$2,700	$3,500

MODEL		EXC. COND.	
YEAR	FEATURES	LOW	HIGH

Style 3

1920s	Koa	$3,600	$4,700

Style 4

1920s	Hawaiian	$3,600	$4,700
1920s	Spanish	$3,600	$4,700

Kona Guitar Company

2000-present. Located in Fort Worth, Texas, Kona imports budget and intermediate grade, production, nylon and steel string acoustic and solid and semi-hollow body electric guitars and basses. They also offer amps, mandolins and ukes.

Koontz

1970-late 1980s. Luthier Sam Koontz started building custom guitars in the late '50s. Starting in '66 Koontz, who was associated with Harptone guitars, built guitars for Standel. In '70, he opened his own shop in Linden, New Jersey, building a variety of custom guitars. Koontz died in the late '80s. His guitars varied greatly and should be valued on a case-by-case basis.

Kopp String Instruments

Located in Republic, Ohio from 2000-2004, luthier Denny Kopp presently builds his professional and premium grade, production/custom, semi-hollow archtop electric and hand-carved archtop jazz guitars in Catawba Island, Ohio. He started in 2000.

Kopy Kat

1970s. Budget copy-era solidbody, semi-hollow body and acoustic guitars imported from Japan. They also made basses and mandolins.

Acoustic

1970s	J-200 copy	$200	$300

Kragenbrink

Premium grade, production/custom, steel string acoustic guitars built by luthier Lance Kragenbrink in Vandercook Lake, Michigan, starting in the year 2001.

Kramer

1976-1990, 1995-present. Currently Kramer offers budget and intermediate grade, production, imported acoustic, acoustic/electric, semi-hollow and solidbody guitars. They also offer basses, amps and effects.

Founded by New York music retailer Dennis Berardi, ex-Travis Bean partner Gary Kramer and ex-Norlin executive Peter LaPlaca. Initial financing provided by real estate developer Henry Vaccaro. Parent company named BKL Corporation (Berardi, Kramer, LaPlaca), located in Neptune City, New Jersey. The first guitars were designed by Berardi and luthier Phil Petillo and featured aluminum necks with wooden inserts on back to give them a wooden feel. Guitar production commenced in late-'76. Control passed to Guitar Center of Los

Knaggs Chena Tier 2

Knutson Luthiery Classic

GUITARS

1978 Kramer 450-G Deluxe
Carter Vintage Guitars

1979 Kramer DMZ-3000

Angeles for '79-'82, which recommended a switch to more economical wood necks. Most wooden necks from Kramer's Golden Era (1981-1986) we made in Japan by ESP and shipped to the U.S.A. for final guitar assembly. Aluminum necks were phased out during the early-'80s, and were last produced in '85. In '84 they added their first import models, the Japanese-made Focus line, followed by the Korean-made Striker line. By 1986 Kramer was the top American electric guitarmaker. In '89, a new investment group was brought in with James Liati as president, hoping for access to Russian market, but the company went of business in late-'90. In '95 Henry Vaccaro and new partners revived the company and designed a number of new guitars in conjunction with Phil Petillo. However, in '97 the Kramer brand was sold to Gibson. In '98, Henry Vaccaro released his new line of aluminum-core neck, split headstock guitars under the Vacarro brand. From 1997 to 2009, sales of Kramer instruments was only through Gibson's MusicYo website. In 2010, Gibson began to distribute the brand through traditional music retail channels with new issues and 1980s legacy models. Non-U.S.-made models include the following lines: Aerostar, Ferrington, Focus, Hundred (post-'85 made with 3 digits in the 100-900), Showster, Striker, Thousand (post-'85 made with 4 digits in the 1000-9000), XL (except XL-5 made in '80s).

Serial numbers for import models include:

Two alpha followed by 4 numbers: for example AA2341 with any assortment of letters and numbers.

One alpha followed by 5 numbers: for example B23412.

Five numbers: for example 23412.

Model number preceding numbers: for example XL1-03205.

The notation "Kramer, Neptune, NJ" does indicate U.S.A.-made production.

Most post-'85 Kramers were ESP Japanese-made guitars. American Series were ESP Japanese components that were assembled in the U.S.

The vintage/used market makes value distinctions between U.S.-made and import models.

Headstock and logo shape can help identify U.S. versus imports as follows:

Traditional or Classic headstock with capital K as Kramer: U.S.A. '81-'84.

Banana (soft edges) headstock with all caps KRAMER: U.S.A. American Series '84-'86.

Pointy (sharp cut) headstock with all caps KRAMER: U.S.A. American Series '86-'87.

Pointy (sharp cut) headstock with downsized letters Kramer plus American decal: U.S.A. American Series '87-'94.

Pointy (sharp cut) headstock with downsized letters Kramer but without American decal, is an import.

MODEL YEAR	FEATURES	EXC. COND. LOW	HIGH
1984 Reissue			
2003-2007. Made in the U.S., based on EVH's Kramer, single Gibson humbucker, Rose tremolo, various colors.			
2003-2007		$625	$825
The 84 (Original Collection)			
2019-present. Alder body, maple neck, Seymour Duncan pickup, Floyd Rose trem, various colors with gloss finish.			
2019-2021		$525	$700
250-G Special			
1977-1979. Offset double-cut, tropical woods, aluminum neck, dot markers, 2 pickups.			
1977-1979		$775	$1,025
350-G Standard			
1976-1979. Offset double-cut, tropical woods, aluminum neck, tuning fork headstock, ebonol 'board, zero fret, 2 single coils, dot inlays. The 350 and 450 were Kramer's first models.			
1976-1979		$1,200	$1,550
450-G Deluxe			
1976-1980. Like 350-G, but with block inlays, 2 humbuckers. Became the 450G Deluxe in late '77 with dot inlays.			
1976-1980		$1,200	$1,550
650-G Artist			
1977-1980. Aluminum neck, ebonol 'board, double-cut solidbody, 2 humbuckers.			
1977-1980		$1,550	$2,000
Assault 220FR/Assault 220 (Modern Collection)			
2010-present. Mahogany body, 2 humbucker pickups, Floyd Rose trem, white or black gloss finish. FR dropped from name in '20.			
2010-2019	FR	$375	$500
2020-2021		$250	$325
Assault Plus (Modern Collection)			
2020-present. Mahogany body with flame maple veneer top, reverse headstock, 2 Seymour Duncan pickups, Floyd Rose trem, Bengal Burst or Trans Purple Burst.			
2020		$550	$725
Baretta			
1984-1990. Offset double-cut, banana six-on-a-side headstock, 1 pickup, Floyd Rose tremolo, black hardware, U.S.A.-made.			
1984-1985		$1,300	$2,700
1986-1987		$1,200	$1,575
1988-1990	Standard opaque	$750	$975
1988-1990	With graphics	$925	$1,200
1990	Baretta III hybrid	$675	$875
Baretta '85 Reissue			
2006. Made in the U.S., based on 1985 banana headstock model, Rose tremolo.			
2006		$750	$975
Baretta II/Soloist			
1986-1990. Soloist sleek body with pointed cutaway horns.			
1986-1990		$750	$975
Baretta (Original Collection)			
2020-present. Maple body and neck, Seymour Duncan pickup, Floyd Rose trem, Pewter Gray or Ruby Red.			
2020-2021		$450	$600

MODEL YEAR	FEATURES	EXC. COND. LOW	HIGH

Baretta Special (Original Collection)
2020-present. Mahogany body, maple neck, Alnico humbucker pickup, traditional trem, gloss finish in Candy Blue, Ruby Red or Purple.

| 2020-2021 | | $120 | $155 |

Classic Series
1986-1987. Solidbody copies of the famous Southern California builder, including offset contoured double-cut (Classic I) and slab body single-cut designs (Classic II and Classic III).

1986-1987	Classic I	$525	$675
1986-1987	Classic II	$775	$1,025
1986-1987	Classic III	$775	$1,025

Condor
1985-1986. Futuristic 4-point body with large upper bass horn and lower treble horn.

| 1985-1986 | | $750 | $975 |

DMZ Custom Series
1978-1981. Solidbody double-cut with larger upper horn, bolt-on aluminum T-neck, slot headstock, models include the 1000 (super distortion humbuckers), 2000 (dual-sound humbuckers), 3000 (3 SDS single-coils), 6000 (dual-sound humbuckers, active DBL).

1978-1981	DMZ-1000	$1,200	$1,575
1978-1981	DMZ-2000	$1,200	$1,575
1978-1981	DMZ-3000	$1,450	$1,900
1978-1981	DMZ-6000	$1,625	$2,125

Duke Custom/Standard
1981-1982. Headless aluminum neck, 22-fret neck, 1 pickup, Floyd Rose tremolo.

| 1981-1982 | | $450 | $575 |

Duke Special
1982-1985. Headless aluminum neck, two pickups, tuners on body.

| 1982-1985 | | $475 | $625 |

Elliot Easton Pro I
1987-1988. Designed by Elliot Easton, offset double-cut, six-on-a-side headstock, Floyd Rose tremolo, 2 single-coils and 1 humbucker.

| 1987-1988 | | $825 | $1,075 |

Elliot Easton Pro II
1987-1988. Same as Pro I, but with fixed-bridge tailpiece, 2 single-coils.

| 1987-1988 | | $725 | $950 |

Ferrington
1985-1990. Acoustic-electric, offered in single- and double-cut, bolt-on electric-style neck, transducers, made in Korea.

| 1985-1990 | | $400 | $525 |

Floyd Rose Signature Edition
1983-1984. Four pointed-bout body with deep cutawaybelow tremolo assembly, Floyd Rose vibrato system.

| 1983-1984 | | $825 | $1,075 |

Focus/F Series (Import)
1983-1989. Kramer introduced the Focus series as import copies of their American-made models like the Pacer, Baretta, Vanguard (Rhoads-V), and Voyager (star body). Model numbers were 1000-6000, plus the Focus Classic I, II, and III. Most models were offset, double-cut solidbodies. In '87 the Focus line was renamed the F-

Series. In '88 a neck-through body design, which is noted as NT, was introduced for a short time. The Classic series was offered with over a dozen color options.

| 1983-1989 | Various models | $250 | $525 |

Gene Simmons Axe
1980-1981. Axe-shaped guitar, aluminum neck, 1 humbucker, slot headstock, stop tailpiece, 25 were made.

| 1980-1981 | | $6,500 | $8,450 |

Gorky Park (Import)
1986-1989. Triangular balalaika, bolt-on maple neck, pointy droopy six-on-a-side headstock, 1 pickup, Floyd Rose tremolo, red with iron sickle graphics, tribute to Russian rock, reissued in late-'90s.

| 1986-1989 | | $400 | $525 |

Hundred Series
1988-1990. Import budget line, most with offset double-cut 7/8th solidbody.

| 1988-1990 | Various models | $200 | $375 |

Jersey Star
2004-2007. A reissue of the Richie Sambora model.

| 2004-2007 | | $900 | $1,175 |

Jersey Star (Original Collection)
2020-present. Alder body, maple neck, mother-of-pearl Jersey Star logo, 3 pickups, Floyd Rose trem, Candy Apple Red or Alpine White.

| 2020 | | $750 | $1,000 |

Liberty '86 Series
1986-1987. Offset double cut arched-top solidbody, pointy head, 2 humbuckers, black, white or flame-maple bound body.

| 1986-1987 | Black or white | $775 | $1,000 |
| 1986-1987 | Flame maple | $850 | $1,100 |

Metalist/Showster Series
1989-1990. Korean-made offset double-cut solidbody, metal trim in body design, pointy droopy six-on-a-side headstock, various pickup options, Floyd Rose.

| 1989-1990 | | $500 | $650 |

Night Rider
2000-2007. Inexpensive import double-cut semi-hollow, 2 humbuckers.

| 2000-2007 | | $95 | $125 |

Nightswan
1987-1990. Offset double-cut, six-on-a-side headstock, 2 Duncan humbuckers, Floyd Rose tremolo, blue metallic.

| 1987-1990 | | $1,325 | $1,725 |
| 1987-1990 | Custom color/finish | $1,475 | $1,900 |

Nightswan (Original Collection)
2020-present. Mahogany body, maple neck, 2 pickups, Floyd Rose trem, jet black metallic, vintage white with Aztec graphic or black with blue polka dots.

| 2020-2021 | | $650 | $850 |

Night-V (Modern Collection)
2020-present. Mahogany body, maple neck, 2 pickups, Floyd Rose trem, satin black finish.

| 2020-2021 | | $270 | $350 |

Night-V Plus (Modern Collection)
2020-present. Mahogany body, maple neck, 2 pickups, Floyd Rose trem, Alpine white.

| 2020-2021 | | $440 | $575 |

Late-'80s Kramer Ferrington
Imaged by Heritage Auctions, HA.com

1988 Kramer Nightswan
Jamie Wetsch

1982 Kramer Vanguard
Imaged by Heritage Auctions, HA.com

1980 Kramer XL5

MODEL YEAR	FEATURES	EXC. COND. LOW	HIGH
Pacer (Original Collection)			
2020-present. Double-cut offset maple body, 2 Seymour Duncan pickups, Floyd Rose trem, pearl white or orange tiger finish.			
2020-2021		$500	$650
Pacer Carrera			
1982-1986. Offset double-cut, wood neck, classic six-on-a-side headstock, ebonized 22-fret rosewood 'board, 2 pickups, 3-way switch, black Rockinger, restyled body with Floyd Rose in '83, banana headstock in '85.			
1982-1985		$850	$1,100
1986		$700	$925
Pacer Custom			
1983-1987. Offset double-cut, bolt-on maple neck with maple cap, 2 humbuckers, translucent finish, gold hardware.			
1983-1985		$1,000	$1,300
1986-1987		$800	$1,050
Pacer Custom I			
1987-1989. Custom with slanted hum and 2 single coils, various colors.			
1987-1989		$800	$1,050
Pacer Custom II			
1987-1989. Custom with hum and 2 single coils, various colors.			
1987-1989		$800	$1,050
Pacer Deluxe			
1983-1987. Offset double-cut, six-on-a-side headstock, hum/single/single pickups, bolt-on maple neck.			
1983-1985		$1,000	$1,300
1986-1987		$825	$1,100
Pacer Imperial			
1981-1989. Offset double cut, bolt-on maple neck with maple cap, 2 humbuckers.			
1981-1985		$1,000	$1,300
1986-1989		$825	$1,100
Pacer Special			
1981-1985. Various headstocks, 1 humbucker pickup, EVH trem.			
1981-1985		$1,000	$1,300
The Pacer			
1982-1985. Pacer with 3 single coil pickup.			
1982-1985		$1,000	$1,300
Paul Dean			
1986-1988. Offset double cut, neck-thru, hum/single/single pickups, droopy pointy head.			
1986-1988		$825	$1,100
ProAxe (U.S.A.)			
1989-1990. U.S.A.-made, offset double-cut, sharp pointy headstock, dot markers, 2 or 3 pickups, smaller 7/8ths size body, 3 models offered with slightly different pickup options. The model was discontinued when Kramer went out of business in 1990.			
1989-1990	Deluxe	$1,000	$1,300
1989-1990	Special	$1,000	$1,300
1989-1990	Standard	$1,000	$1,300
Richie Sambora			
1987-1989. Designed by Sambora, mahogany offset double-cut, maple neck, pointy droopy 6-on-a-side headstock, gold hardware, Floyd Rose, 3 pickups, 2 coil-taps.			
1987-1989		$1,225	$1,600

MODEL YEAR	FEATURES	EXC. COND. LOW	HIGH
Ripley RSG-1			
1984-1987. Offset double-cut, banana six-on-a-side headstock, 22 frets, hexophonic humbucking pickups, panpots, dual volume, Floyd Rose tremolo, black hardware, stereo output, pointy droopy headstock in '87.			
1984-1985		$1,000	$1,300
1986-1987		$800	$1,050
Savant/Showster Series			
1989-1990. Offset double-cut solidbody, pointy headstock, various pickup options.			
1989-1990	Various models	$800	$1,050
SM-1 (Original Collection)			
2020-present. Double-cut mahogany body, 3 pickups, Floyd Rose trem, gloss finish in Orange Crush, Candy Blue or Maximum Steel.			
2020-2021		$700	$900
Stagemaster Series			
1983-1987. Offset double-cut neck-thru solidbody models, smaller 7/8th body.			
1983-1985	Custom/Custom I	$1,000	$1,300
1983-1985	Deluxe/Deluxe I	$1,000	$1,300
1983-1985	Imperial	$1,000	$1,300
1983-1985	Special	$1,000	$1,300
1983-1985	Standard/Standard I	$1,000	$1,300
1986-1987	Custom/Custom I	$800	$1,050
1986-1987	Deluxe/Deluxe I	$800	$1,050
1986-1987	Imperial	$800	$1,050
1986-1987	Special	$800	$1,050
1986-1987	Standard/Standard I	$800	$1,050
1987	Deluxe II	$800	$1,050
Striker Series			
1984-1989. Offset double-cut, various pickup options, series included Striker 100, 200, 300, 400, 600 and 700 Bass.			
1984-1989	Various models	$200	$400
Sustainer			
1989. Offset double-cut solidbody, reverse pointy headstock, Floyd Rose tremolo.			
1989		$1,000	$1,300
Triax			
1986. Rare, odd shape, 2 humbuckers, Floyd Rose trem, Pearlescent Red.			
1986		$3,000	$4,000
Vanguard Series			
1981-1986. U.S.-made or American Series (assembled in U.S.). V shape, 1 humbucker, aluminum (Special '81-'83) or wood (Custom '81-'83) neck. Added for '83-'84 were the Imperial (wood neck, 2 humbuckers) and the Headless (alum neck, 1 humbucker). For '85-'86, the body was modified to a Jackson Randy Rhoads style V body, with a banana headstock and 2 humbuckers. In '99 this last design was revived as an import.			
1981-1983	Custom	$1,000	$1,300
1981-1983	Special	$1,000	$1,300
1983-1984	Imperial	$1,000	$1,300
1985-1986	Rhoads V-body	$800	$1,050
Vanguard (Reissue)			
1999-2014. Pointy headstock, 2 humbuckers, licensed Floyd Rose.			
1999-2014		$400	$525

MODEL YEAR	FEATURES	EXC. COND. LOW	HIGH

Voyager
1982-1985. Wood neck, classic headstock, rosewood 'board, 1 pickup (2 optional), Floyd Rose tremolo, black.

1982-1985		$1,000	$1,300

XKG-10
1980-1981. Aluminum neck, V-shaped body.

1980-1981		$900	$1,175

XKG-20
1980-1981. More traditional double-cut body with small horns.

1980-1981		$900	$1,175

XL Series
1980-1981, 1987-1990. The early-'80s U.S.-made models had aluminum necks and were completely different than the late-'80s wood neck models, which were inexpensive imports.

1980-1981	Aluminum neck	$1,000	$1,300
1987-1990	Wood neck	$275	$360

ZX Aero Star Series
1986-1989. Offset double-cut solidbodies, pointy six-on-a-side headstock. Models include the 1 humbucker ZX-10, 2 humbucker ZX-20, 3 single coil ZX-30, and hum/single/single ZX-30H.

1986-1989		$130	$260

Kramer-Harrison, William

Luthier William Kramer-Harrison began building in 1977, premium grade, custom, classical and flat-top guitars in Kingston, New York.

KSM

Luthier Kevin S. Moore, starting in 1988, premium grade, custom/production, solidbody electric guitars in Logan, Utah.

Kubicki

1973-present. Kubicki is best known for their Factor basses, but did offer a few guitar models in the early '80s. See Bass section for more company info.

Kustom

1968-present. Founded by Bud Ross in Chanute, Kansas, and best known for the tuck-and-roll amps, Kustom also offered guitars from '68 to '69. See Amp section for more company info.

Electric Hollowbody
1968-1969. Hollowed-out 2-part bodies; includes the K200A (humbucker, Bigsby), the K200B (single-coils, trapeze tailpiece), and the K200C (less fancy tuners), various colors.

1968-1969		$1,200	$1,550

Kwasnycia Guitars

1997-present. Production/custom, premium grade, acoustic guitars built by luthier Dennis Kwasnycia in Chatham, Ontario.

Kyle, Doug

Premium grade, custom, Selmer-style guitars made by luthier Doug Kyle in the U.K., starting in 1990.

MODEL YEAR	FEATURES	EXC. COND. LOW	HIGH

L Benito

Professional grade, steel and nylon string acoustics from luthier Lito Benito and built in Chile starting in 2001.

La Baye

1967. Designed by Dan Helland in Green Bay, Wisconsin and built by the Holman-Woodell factory in Neodesha, Kansas. Introduced at NAMM and folded when no orders came in. Only 45 prototypes made. A few may have been sold later as 21st Century. They also had basses.

2x4 6-String
1967. Narrow plank body, controls on top, 2 pickups, tremolo, 12-string version was also made.

1967		$1,450	$1,875

La Mancha

Professional and premium grade, production/ custom, classical guitars made in Mexico under the supervision of Kenny Hill and Gil Carnal and distributed by Jerry Roberts of Nashville, Tennessee. They began in 1996.

La Patrie

Production, classical guitars. Founded by luthier Robert Godin, who also has the Norman, Godin, Seagull, and Patrick & Simon brands of instruments.

La Scala

Ca. 1920s-1930s. La Scala was another brand of the Oscar Schmidt Company of New Jersey, and was used on guitars, banjos, and mandolins. These were often the fanciest of the Schmidt instruments. Schmidt made the guitars and mandolins; the banjos were made by Rettberg & Lang.

Lace Music Products

1979-present. Intermediate and professional, production, electric guitars from Lace Music Products of Cypress, California, a division of Actodyne General Inc. which was founded by Don Lace Sr., inventor of the Lace Sensor Pickup. In '96, Lace added amplifiers, followed by guitars in 2001 and Rat Fink guitars in '02.

Lacey Guitars

1974-present. Luthier Mark Lacey builds his premium and presentation archtops and flat-tops in Nashville, Tennessee.

Lado

1973-present. Founded by Joe Kovacic, Lado builds professional and premium grade, production/ custom, solidbody guitars and basses in Lindsay, Ontario. Some model lines are branded J. K. Lado.

Lafayette

Ca. 1963-1967. Sold through Lafayette Electronics catalogs. Early Japanese-made guitars and basses

1968 Kustom K200A
Tom Pfeifer

Lace Cybercaster Standard

GUITARS

1987 Langejans 12-string
Rivington Guitars

1990 Larrivee C-10 Deluxe
Carter Vintage Guitars

MODEL YEAR	FEATURES	EXC. COND. LOW	HIGH

from pre-copy era, generally shorter scale beginner instruments. Many made by Guyatone, some possibly by Teisco.

Electric
1963-1967. Various models.

| 1963-1967 | | $500 | $650 |

Laguna
2008-present. Guitar Center private label, budget and intermediate grade, production, imported electric and acoustic guitars price range.

Lakeside (Lyon & Healy)
Early-1900s. Mainly catalog sales of guitars and mandolins from the Chicago maker. Marketed as a less expensive alternative to the Lyon & Healy Washburn product line.

Harp Guitar
Early-1900s. Spruce top, rosewood finished birch back and sides, two 6-string necks with standard tuners, 1 neck is fretless without dot markers, rectangular bridge.

| 1900s | | $2,200 | $2,800 |

Parlor
Early-1900s. Spruce top, oak back and sides, cedar neck.

| 1900s | | $550 | $725 |

Lakewood
1986-present. Luthier Martin Seeliger builds his professional and premium grade, production/custom, steel and nylon string guitars in Giessen, Germany. He has also built mandolins.

Langdon Guitars
1997-present. Luthier Jeff Langdon builds his professional and premium grade, production/custom, flat-top, archtop, and solidbody guitars in Eureka, California.

Langejans Guitars
1971-2016. Premium grade, production/custom, flat-top, 12-string, and classical guitars built by luthier Delwyn Langejans in Holland, Michigan. He retired in '16.

Larrivee
1968-present. Professional and premium grade, production/custom, acoustic, acoustic/electric, and classical guitars built in Vancouver, British Columbia and, since '01, in Oxnard, California. They also offered several acoustic and a few electric basses over the years as well as ukes. Founded by Jean Larrivee, who apprenticed under Edgar Monch in Toronto. He built classical guitars in his home from '68-'70 and built his first steel string guitar in '71. Moved company to Victoria, BC in '77 and to Vancouver in '82. In '83, he began building solidbody electric guitars until '89, when focus again returned to acoustics.

MODEL YEAR	FEATURES	EXC. COND. LOW	HIGH

Up to 2002, Larrivee used the following model designations: 05 Mahogany Standard, 09 Rosewood Standard, 10 Deluxe, 19 Special, 50 & 60 Standard (unique inlay), 70 Deluxe, and 72 Presentation. Starting in '03 designations used are: 01 Parlor, 03 Standard, 05 Select Mahogany, 09 Rosewood Artist, 10 Rosewood Deluxe, 19 California Anniv. Special Edition Series, 50 Traditional Series, 60 Traditional Series, E = Electric, R = Rosewood.

Larrivee also offers Limited Edition, Custom Shop, and Custom variations of standard models although the model name is the same as the standard model. These Custom models are worth more than the values shown.

0-60
2005. Small fancy rosewood.

| 2005 | | $1,925 | $2,500 |

00-05
1996. 14.25", all mahogany.

| 1996 | | $1,300 | $1,700 |

00-09

| 2000s | | $1,350 | $1,750 |

00-10
2000s. 00-size 14" lower bout, spruce top, rosewood back and sides, gloss finish.

| 2000s | | $1,550 | $2,000 |

000-40R
2014-present. Legacy series, sitka spruce top, Indian rosewood back and sides, satin finish.

| 2014-2021 | | $1,150 | $1,500 |

000-50
2008-present. Mahogany back and sides.

| 2008-2021 | | $1,600 | $2,075 |

000-60
2006-present. Traditional Series, Indian rosewood.

| 2006-2021 | | $1,600 | $2,075 |

000-60K
Traditional Series, figured koa.

| 2012 | | $2,500 | $3,250 |

C-10 Deluxe
Late-1980s-1990s. Sitka spruce top, Indian rosewood back and sides, sharp cutaway, fancy binding.

| 1980s | | $1,700 | $2,200 |

C-72 Presentation
1990s. Spruce top, Indian rosewood back and sides, non-cut Style D, ultra-fancy abalone and pearl hand-engraved headstock.

| 1990s | Jester headstock | $2,800 | $3,600 |

C-72 Presentation Cutaway
1990s. Spruce top, Indian rosewood back and sides, sharp cutaway, ultra-fancy abalone and pearl hand-engraved headstock.

| 1990s | Mermaid headstock | $3,000 | $4,000 |

D-02/D-02E
1998-2013. Sitka spruce top, mahogany back and sides, satin finish, E with electronics.

| 1998-2013 | | $600 | $800 |

D-03E
2008-present. Solid mahogany back and sides, spruce top, satin finish, electronics.

| 2008-2021 | | $800 | $1,050 |

MODEL YEAR	FEATURES	EXC. COND. LOW	HIGH
D-O3R			
2002-present. Rosewood.			
2002-2021		$1,000	$1,300
D-O3RE			
2010-present. Rosewood, on-board electronics.			
2010-2021		$1,050	$1,375
DV-O3K			
Venetian cutaway, koa back and sides.			
2000s		$1,550	$2,025
D-04E			
2000-2004, 2013-2014. Mahogany, on-board electronics.			
2000-2014		$1,275	$1,650
D-05-12E			
2008-2013	12 strings	$1,275	$1,650
D-09			
2001-present. Rosewood, spruce top, gloss finish.			
2001-2012	Indian or walnut	$1,450	$1,900
2001-2021	Brazilian	$2,800	$3,700
D-10 Deluxe			
1995-present. Sitka spruce top, Indian rosewood back and sides, abalone top and soundhole trim.			
1995-2021		$1,925	$2,500
D-50			
2003-present. Traditional Series, mahogany back and sides.			
2003-2021		$1,450	$1,950
D-60			
2003-present. Brazilian or Indian rosewood back and sides.			
2000s	Brazilian	$2,900	$3,900
2003-2021	Indian	$1,450	$1,950
D-70			
1992-1995. Horsehead headstock inlay, ebony 'board, rosewood back and sides.			
1992-1995		$1,950	$2,550
D-Style Classical			
1970s. Rosewood body, unicorn inlays.			
1970s		$1,650	$2,150
J-05-12			
2000s. Jumbo acoustic-electric 12-string, spruce top, mahogany back and sides.			
2000s		$1,375	$1,825
J-09			
2002-2009. Jumbo, rosewood back and sides, sitka spruce top.			
2002-2009		$1,600	$2,075
J-09-12K			
Jumbo 12-string, rosewood back and sides.			
2000s		$2,100	$2,700
J-70			
1990s. Jumbo, sitka spruce top, solid Indian rosewood back and sides, presentation grade fancy appointments, limited production.			
1990s		$2,000	$2,600
JV-05 Mahogany Standard			
Mahogany back and sides, Venetian cutaway.			
2000s		$1,275	$1,650
L Series			
1980s-present. Various models, mahogany or rosewood (R) back and sides, some with on-board electronics (E).			
1990s	L-50	$1,700	$2,200
1990s-2021	L-72 (Presentation)	$3,100	$4,100
2000s	L-30 (Classical)	$1,300	$1,700
L-0 Standard Series			
1983-present. Various models, 6- or 12-string, mahogany, rosewood (R) or koa (K), some with on-board electronics (E), satin or gloss finish.			
1983-2021	L-03/03E	$800	$1,050
1983-2021	L-05/05E	$1,300	$1,700
1983-2021	L-09/09E	$1,300	$1,700
2000s	L-01	$675	$875
2000s	L-04	$825	$1,075
2008-2012	L-03K, koa	$1,150	$1,500
2008-2021	L-03R, rosewood	$875	$1,150
2008-2021	L-03R-12, 12-string	$825	$1,075
2008-2021	L-03RE	$925	$1,200
LS Series			
1990s-2011. Various models.			
1990s-2011	LS-05, mahogany	$1,300	$1,700
2008-2011	LS-03R, rosewood	$1,300	$1,700
LV Series			
1990s-present. Various models.			
1990s-2021	LV-05/05E	$1,450	$1,900
1990s-2021	LV-09/09E	$1,575	$2,050
2002	LV-19 Special Vine	$3,500	$4,500
2007-2021	LV-03/03E	$1,300	$1,700
2007-2021	LV-10/10E	$2,500	$3,250
OM Series			
1990s-present. Various models.			
1990-2000s	OM-02	$950	$1,250
1990-2000s	OM-09R, rosewood	$1,450	$1,900
1990s-2021	OM-03/03E	$1,075	$1,400
1990s-2021	OM-10 Deluxe	$2,200	$2,800
1999-2021	OM-05/05E	$1,450	$1,900
2000-2021	OM-03R, rosewood	$1,075	$1,400
2000-2021	OM-40/40E	$1,700	$2,200
2000-2021	OM-50/50E	$1,450	$1,900
2000s	OM-09K, koa	$1,925	$2,500
2008-2021	OM-60/60E	$1,550	$2,000
OMV Series			
1990s-present. Various models.			
2000s-2021	OMV-09/09E	$1,450	$1,900
2000s-2021	OMV-50/50E	$1,950	$2,600
2009-2021	OMV-60/60E	$2,050	$2,700
Parlor Walnut			
Early-2000s. Spruce top, solid walnut back and sides.			
2000s		$700	$925
PV Series			
2007-present. Various Parlor models.			
2007	PV-09, maple	$1,425	$1,850
2007-2021	PV-09/09E, rosewood	$2,850	$3,700
RS-2 Ventura			
2010-2015. Mahogany solidbody, rosewood 'board, 1 or 2 pickups, satin finish various colors.			
2010-2015		$925	$1,200
RS-4 CM Carved Top			
1988-1989. Carved top solidbody, curly maple top, single-single-humbucker pickups, sunburst or translucent finishes.			
1988-1989		$1,400	$1,800

Larrivee D-09

Larrivee OM-10
Tim Page

Leach VG Franconia

MODEL YEAR	FEATURES	EXC. COND. LOW	HIGH
SD Series			
2008-present. Various models.			
2008-2012	SD-03R	$1,450	$1,900
2008-2021	SD-50/50E	$1,900	$2,475
2008-2021	SD-60/60E	$1,550	$2,000

Larry Alan Guitars

2003-present. Professional and premium grade, production/custom, acoustic and electric guitars and basses, built by luthier Larry Alan Daft in Lansing, Michigan. He also builds effects pedals.

Larson Brothers

1900-1944. Chicago's Carl and August Larson bought Maurer & Company in 1900 where they built guitars and mandolin family instruments until 1944. Their house brands were Maurer, Prairie State and Euphonon and they also built for catalog companies Wm. C. Stahl and W. J. Dyer & Bro., adding brands like Stetson, a house brand of Dyer. See brand listings for more information.

Laskin

1973-present. Luthier William "Grit" Laskin builds his premium and presentation grade, custom, steel-string, classical, and flamenco guitars in Toronto, Ontario. Many of his instruments feature extensive inlay work.

Laurie Williams Guitars

1983-present. Luthier Laurie Williams builds his premium and presentation grade, custom/production, steel string, classical and archtop guitars on the North Island of New Zealand. He also builds mandolins.

Leach Guitars

1980-present. Luthier Harvey Leach builds his professional and premium grade, custom, flat-tops, archtops, and solidbody electrics, travel guitars and basses in Cedar Ridge, California.

Lehmann Stringed Instruments

1971-present. Luthier Bernard Lehmann builds his professional and premium grade, production/custom, flat-top, archtop, classical and Gypsy guitars in Rochester, New York. He also builds lutes, vielles and rebecs.

Lehtela

1993-present. Professional and premium grade, custom/production, acoustic, acoustic/electric, archtop, and solidbody guitars and basses built by luthier Ari Lehtela in Newell, North Carolina.

Lentz

1975-present. Luthier Scott Lentz builds his professional, premium, and presentation grade, custom/production, solidbody electric guitars in San Marcos, California.

Les Stansell Guitars

1980-present. Luthier Les Stansell builds his premium grade, custom, nylon-string guitars in Pistol River, Oregon.

Levin

1900-1973. Founded by Herman Carlson Levin and located in Gothenburg, Sweden, Levin was best known for their classical guitars, which they also built for other brands, most notably Goya from ca. 1955 to the mid '70s. They also built mandolins and ukes.

Levy-Page Special

1930s. Acoustic guitars likely built by Gibson, having many features of Kalamzoo guitars of the era. Possibly made for a distributor.

Lewis

1981-present. Luthier Michael Lewis builds his premium and presentation grade, custom/production, archtop guitars in Grass Valley, California. He also builds mandolins. He also built guitars under the D'Angelico name.

Linc Luthier

1991-present. Professional and premium grade, custom/production, electric and acoustic guitars, basses and double-necks built by luthier Linc Luthier in Upland, California.

Lindberg

Ca. 1950s. Line of guitars produced by Hoyer for Germany's Lindberg music store.

Lindert

1986-2002. Luthier Chuck Lindert made his intermediate and professional grade, production/custom, Art Deco-vibe electric guitars in Chelan, Washington.

Line 6

1996-present. Professional grade, production, imported solidbody and acoustic modeling guitars able to replicate the tones of a variety of instruments. Line 6 also builds effects and amps.

Lion

1960s. One of the brand names of guitars built for others by Egmond in Holland.

Lipe Guitars USA

1983-1989, 2000-2018. Luthier Michael Lipe built custom, professional grade, guitars and basses in Sun Valley, California. Lipe died Dec. '18.

Liscombe

1992-2013. Professional grade, production and limited custom, chambered electric guitars built by luthier Ken Liscombe in Burlington, Ontario.

1985 Lotus
Tom Pfeifer

MODEL YEAR	FEATURES	EXC. COND. LOW	HIGH

Loar (The)

2005-present. Professional grade, production, imported archtop acoustic guitars designed by Greg Rich for The Music Link, which also has Johnson and other brands of instruments. They also offer mandolins.

Lollar

1979-present. Luthier Jason Lollar builds his premium grade, production/custom, solidbody and archtop guitars in Vashon, Washington.

Lopez, Abel Garcia

Luthier Abel Garcia Lopez builds his premium grade, custom, classical guitars in Mexico starting in 1985.

Loprinzi

1972-present. Professional and premium grade, production/custom, classical and steel-string guitars built in Clearwater, Florida. They also build ukes. Founded by Augustino LoPrinzi and his brother Thomas in New Jersey. The guitar operations were taken over by AMF/Maark Corp. in '73. LoPrinzi left the company and again started producing his own Augustino Guitars, moving his operations to Florida in '78. AMF ceased production in '80, and a few years later, LoPrinzi got his trademarked name back.

Classical

1970s. Various models.

1970s	Brazilian rosewood	$1,875	$2,450
1970s	Indian rosewood	$1,125	$1,450
1970s	Mahogany	$1,025	$1,325

Lord

Mid-1960s. Acoustic and solidbody electric guitars imported by Halifax.

Acoustic or Electric Soldibody

1960s	Various models	$225	$400

Lotus

Late-1970s-2004. Budget grade acoustic and electric guitars and basses imported originally by Midco International, of Effingham, Illinois, and most recently by Musicorp. They also offered banjos and mandolins.

Louis Panormo

Early to mid-1800s. Spanish guitars made in London, England by luthier Louis (Luis) Panormo. He was born in Paris in 1784, and died in 1862.

Lowden

1973-present. Luthier George Lowden builds his premium and presentation grade, production/custom, steel and nylon string guitars in Downpatrick, Northern Ireland. From '80 to '85, he had some models made in Japan.

Flat-Top

1980s-present. Standard models include D, F, O, and S sizes and models 10 thru 32.

1980s-2021	Premium models	$4,500	$11,000
1980s-2021	Standard models	$2,200	$4,500

LSL Instruments

2008-present. Luthier Lance Lerman builds his production, professional grade, solidbody electric guitars and basses in Los Angeles, California.

LSR Headless Instruments

1988-present. Professional and premium grade, production/custom, solidbody headless guitars and basses made by Ed Roman Guitars.

LTD

1995-present. Intermediate grade, production, Korean-made solidbody guitars and basses offered by ESP.

Lucas Custom Instruments

1989-present. Premium and presentation grade, production/custom, flat-tops built by luthier Randy Lucas in Columbus, Indiana.

Lucas, A. J.

1990-present. Luthier A. J. Lucas builds his production/custom, classical and steel string guitars in Lincolnshire, England.

Luis Feu de Mesquita

2000-present. Professional and premium grade, custom, acoustic and flat-top guitars including Spanish, classical and flamenco built in Toronto, Ontario by luthier Luis Feu de Mesquita.

Luna Guitars

2005-present. Located in Tampa, Florida, Yvonne de Villiers imports her budget to professional grade, production, acoustic and electric guitars and basses from Japan, Korea and China. She also added ukuleles in '09 and amps in '10.

Luttrell Guitars

1993-present. Professional and premium grade, production/custom, acoustic, electric and resonator guitars built by luthier Ralph H. Luttrell in Sandy Springs, Georgia.

Lyle

Ca. 1969-1980. Imported by distributor L.D. Heater of Portland, Oregon. Generally higher quality Japanese-made copies of American designs by unknown manufacturers, but some early ones, at least, were made by Arai and Company. They also had basses and mandolins.

Lyon & Healy

1864-present. Founded by George Washburn Lyon and Patrick Joseph Healy, Lyon & Healy was an industry giant, operating a chain of music stores, and manufacturering harps (their only remaining product), pianos, Washburn guitars and a line of brass and wind instruments. See Washburn, American Conservatory, Lakeside, and College brands.

LSL Instruments Del Rey

1920 Lyon & Healy Thornward
Bernunzio Uptown Music

GUITARS

GUITARS

1953 Maccaferri Islander
Steve Bauman

1957 Magnatone Mark IV
Michael Wright

MODEL YEAR	FEATURES	EXC. COND. LOW	HIGH

Lyon by Washburn
1990s-2000s. Budget grade, production, solid-body guitars and basses sold by mass merchandisers such as Target.

Lyra
1920s. Instruments built by the Oscar Schmidt Co. and possibly others. Most likely a brand made for a distributor.

Lyric
Luthier John Southern started building his professional and premium grade, custom, semi-hollow and solidbody and basses guitars in Tulsa, Oklahoma in 1996.

M. Campellone Guitars
See listing under Campellone Guitars

M.Zaganin and N.Zaganin
1989-present. Luthier Márcio Zaganin began his career using the M.Zaganin brand, in 2004 it was changed to N. He builds professional and premium grade, production/custom, semi-hollow and solidbody electric guitars in São Paulo, Brazil. He also builds basses.

Maccaferri
1923-1990. Built by luthier and classical guitarist Mario Maccaferri (b. May 20, 1900, Cento, Italy; d. 1993, New York) in Cento, Italy; Paris, France; New York, New York; and Mount Vernon, New York. Maccaferri was a student of Luigi Mozzani from '11 to '28. His first catalog was in '23, and included a cutaway guitar. He also made mandolins. His Europe-era instruments are very rare. He designed Selmer guitars in '31. Maccaferri invented the plastic clothespin during World War II and used that technology to produce plastic ukes starting in '49 and Dow Styron plastic guitars in '53. He made several experimental plastic electrics in the '60s and plastic violins in the late-'80s.

Plastic (Dow Styron)
1950s. Plastic construction, models include Deluxe (archtop, crown logo), Islander (Islander logo), TV Pal (4-string cutaway) and Showtime (Showtime logo).

1950s	Deluxe	$190	$250
1950s	Islander	$170	$225
1950s	Romancer	$170	$225
1950s	Showtime	$170	$225
1950s	TV Pal	$135	$175

Madeira
1973-ca. 1984, ca. 1990. Imported Budget and intermediate grade acoustic and electric guitars distributed by Guild. The Japanese-made electrics were basically copies of Gibson, Fender and Guild models, the acoustics originally copies of Martin. The electrics only offered first year or so during the '70s run. Name revived again around '90 on imported acoustics and electrics. They also offered mandolins and banjos.

MODEL YEAR	FEATURES	EXC. COND. LOW	HIGH

Madrid
1996-present. Luthier Brandon Madrid builds his production/custom, professional and premium grade, acoustic and solidbody electric guitars, in San Diego, California. Prior to 2009 he built in Portland, Oregon.

Maestro
1950s-1970s, 2001-2012, 2022-present. Maestro is a brand name Gibson first used on 1950s accordion amplifiers. The first Maestro effects were introduced in the early-'60s and they used the name until the late-'70s. In 2001, Gibson revived the name for a line of effects, banjos and mandolins. Those were dropped in '09, when imported budget and intermediate, production, acoustic and electric guitars and amps were added. By '12 the brand was no longer listed but was reintroduced on a line of Gibson effects in '22. Since '04, the brand has also been used on an unrelated line of acoustic guitars and ukes built in Singapore.

Electric
2009-2012. Various student models, Maestro headstock logo, 'By Gibson' logo on truss rod cover.

2009-2012		$80	$150

Magnatone
Ca.1937-1971, 2013-present. Founded as Dickerson Brothers in Los Angeles, California and known as Magna Electronics from '47, with Art Duhamell president. Brands include Dickerson, Oahu (not all), Gourley, Natural Music Guild, Magnatone. In '59 Magna and Estey merged and in '66 the company relocated to Pennsylvania. In '71, the brand was taken over by a toy company. Between 1957 and '67, the company produced four different model lines of Spanish electrics. In 2013, Ted Kornblum revived the Magnatone name on a line of tube amps built in St. Louis, Missouri.

Cyclops
1930s. Dobro-made resonator guitar.

1930s	Round neck	$1,450	$1,875
1930s	Square neck	$1,450	$1,875

Mark Artist Series
1959-1961	More common	$1,075	$1,400
1959-1961	Rare	$1,375	$1,800

Mark Series
1955-1960. Solidbody series made by Paul Bigsby in small quantities, then taken over by Paul Barth at Magnatone in '59.

1955-1959	Mark IV	$2,500	$3,250
1955-1959	Mark V	$2,500	$3,250

Model Series
1962	Model 100	$375	$475
1962	Model 150	$375	$475
1962	Model 200, 2 pus	$375	$475

X-5 Zephyr
1965-1966. Double-cut with 2 DeArmond single-coil pickups, vibrato, metallic finish.

1965-1966		$525	$700

MODEL YEAR	FEATURES	EXC. COND. LOW	HIGH

X-15 Tornado
1965-1966. Offset double-cut body, 2 pickups, various options.

1965-1966		$800	$1,050

X-20 Typhoon
1965-1966. Double-cut solidbody, 3 pickups, various options.

1965-1966		$925	$1,200

Magno-Tone
1930s. Brand most likely used by a music studio (or distributor) on instruments made by others, including Regal-built resonator instruments.

Mai Kai
1910s. Line of Hawaiian guitars built in Los Angeles, California by the Shireson Brothers.

Mako
1985-1989. Line of budget to lower-intermediate solidbody guitars from Kaman (Ovation, Hamer). They also offered basses and amps.

Solidbody

1985-1989	Various models	$125	$425

Mal n' Sal
See listing for Alternative Guitar and Amplifier Company.

Malinoski
1986-present. Luthier Peter Malinoski builds his production/custom, professional and premium grade, solidbody electric guitars and basses in Hyattsville, Maryland.

Mann
Ca. 1971-ca. 1985. A brand name used in Canada by Japan's Hoshino company on some of the same acoustic and electric models as their Ibanez guitars.

Manne
1987-present. Professional and premium grade, production/custom, semi-acoustic and electric guitars and basses built by luthier Andrea Ballarin in Italy.

Manson Guitar Works
1979-present. Premium grade, production/custom, electric guitars built by luthiers Hugh Manson and Adrian Ashton in Exeter, Devon UK. They also offer a line of professional grade, guitars crafted in the Czech Republic and assembled in UK. They also build basses.

Manuel & Patterson
1993-present. Luthiers Joe Manuel and Phil Patterson build professional, premium and presentation grade, production/custom, flat-top, archtop and solidbody electric guitars in Abita Springs, Louisiana. They also offer mandolins.

Manuel Contreras
1962-1994. Luthier Manuel Gonzalez Contreras worked with José Ramírez III, before opening his own shop in Madrid, Spain, in '62.

Manuel Contreras II
1986-present. Professional grade, production/custom, nylon-string guitars made in Madrid, Spain, by luthier Pablo Contreras, son of Manuel.

Manuel Ramirez
See listing under Ramirez, Manuel.

Manuel Rodriguez and Sons, S.L.
1905-present. Professional, premium, and presentation grade, custom flat-top and nylon-string guitars from Madrid, Spain.

Manuel Velázquez
1933-2014. Luthier Manuel Velázquez (d. 2014) built his classical guitars in Puerto Rico ('72-'82), New York City, Virginia, and Florida. His son Alfredo continues to build guitars.

Manzanita Guitars
1993-present. Custom, steel-string, Hawaiian, and resonator guitars built by luthiers Manfred Pietrzok and Moritz Sattler in Rosdorf, Germany.

Manzer Guitars
1976-present. Luthier Linda Manzer builds her premium and presentation grade, custom, steel-string, nylon-string, and archtop guitars in Toronto, Ontario.

Maple Lake
2003-present. Intermediate grade, production, flat-top and acoustic/electric imported guitars from luthier Abe Wechter. Wechter also builds guitars under his own name.

MapleTree Guitars Canada
2011-present. Steve Maric, owner and luthier from Toronto, Canada, works with luthier Fulu Wang, Beijing, China to build production/custom, professional grade, acoustic guitars.

Mapson
1995-present. Luthier James L. Mapson builds his premium and presentation grade, production/custom, archtops in Santa Ana, California.

Marc Silber Guitar Company
1998-present. Intermediate and professional grade, production, flat-top, nylon-string, and Hawaiian guitars designed by Marc Silber and made in Mexico. These were offered under the K & S Guitars and/or Silber brands for 1992-'98. Silber also has ukuleles.

1965 Magnatone X-5 Zephyr
Rivington Guitars

Manson META Series MBM-1

Marchione 16" Archtop

1936 Martin 0-17

KC from Larryville Ga.

MODEL YEAR	FEATURES	EXC. COND. LOW	HIGH

Marchione Guitars

1993-present. Premium and presentation grade, custom, archtops and solidbodies built by Stephen Marchione originally in New York City, but currently in Houston, Texas.

Marcia

1920s. Instruments built by the Oscar Schmidt Co. and possibly others. Most likely a brand made for a distributor.

Marco Polo

1960-ca. 1964. Imported from Japan by Harry Stewart and the Marco Polo Company of Santa Ana, California. One of the first American distributors to advertise inexpensive Japanese guitars and basses. Manufacturers unknown, but some acoustics by Suzuki, some electrics by Guyatone.

Acoustic Hollowbody

1960-1964	Various models	$100	$275

Mario Martin Guitars

2011-present. Luthier Mario Martin builds his production/custom, professional grade, semi-hollow and solidbody guitars and basses in Murfreesboro, Tennessee. From 2006 to '11, he built guitars under the Guitar Mill brand name.

Mark Wescott Guitars

Premium grade, custom, flat-tops, built by luthier Mark Wescott, starting in 1980, in Somers Point, New Jersey.

Marling

Ca. 1975. Budget line guitars and basses marketed by EKO of Recanati, Italy; probably made by them, although possibly imported.

Acoustic

1975. Includes the steel-string S.110, and the dreadnoughts W.354 Western, and W.356 Western.

1975		$100	$275

Electric Soldibody

1975. Includes the E.400 (semi-acoustic/electric), E.490 (solidbody), E.480 (single-cut), and the 460 (Manta-style).

1975		$100	$275

Martelle

1934. Private brand attributed to Gibson and some to Kay.

De Luxe

1934. Gibson 12-fret round shoulder Jumbo construction, laminate maple or mahogany back and sides, sunburst, Hawaiian or Spanish option.

1934		$8,500	$11,000

Martin

1833-present. Intermediate, professional, premium, and presentation grade, production/custom, acoustic, acoustic/electric, archtop and resonator guitars. Founded in New York City by Christian

Frederick Martin, former employee of J. Staufer in Vienna, Austria. Moved to Nazareth, Pennsylvania in 1839. Early guitars were made in the European style, many made with partners John Coupa, Charles Bruno and Henry Schatz. Scalloped X-bracing was introduced in the late-1840s. The dreadnought was introduced in 1916 for the Oliver Ditson Company, Boston; and Martin introduced their own versions in 1931.

Martin model size and shape are indicated by the letter prefix (e.g., 0, 00, 000, D, etc.); materials and ornamentation are indicated by number, with the higher the number, the fancier the instrument (e.g., 18, 28, 35, etc.). Martin offered electric thinline guitars from '61-'68 and electric solidbodies from '78-'82. The Martin Shenandoah was made in Asia and assembled in U.S. Japanese Martin Sigma ('72-'73) and Korean Martin Stinger ('85 on) imported solidbodies.

Most Martin flat-top guitars, particularly Style 18 and above, came with a standard natural finish, therefore Martin guitar finish coloring is generally not mentioned because it is assumed to be see-through natural. Conversely, Gibson's standard finish for their flat-tops during their Golden Era was sunburst. Martin introduced their shaded (sunburst) finish as an option on their Style 18 in 1934 and their Style 28 in 1931. Values for a shaded finish should be considered on a case-by-case basis. Braced for steel strings specifications described under certain models are based on current consensus information and data provided by the late Martin employee-historian Mike Longworth, and is for guidance only. Variations from these specs have been found, so "bracing" should be considered on a case-by-case basis.

0-15

1935, 1940-1943, 1948-1961. Maple or birch in '35, all mahogany after, unbound rosewood 'board, slotted peghead and 12-fret neck until '34, solid peghead and 14-fret neck thereafter, natural mahogany.

1935	Maple or birch	$3,450	$4,500
1940-1949	Mahogany begins	$3,450	$4,500
1950-1959		$3,150	$4,100
1960-1961		$2,700	$3,500

0-15H

1940. Hawaiian neck, all mahogany.

1940		$3,550	$4,600

0-15M Elderly Instruments 40th Anniversary

2011-2012. Limited Edition, 10 made, solid mahogany body and neck, special appointments, inside label signed by Elderly Instruments president Stan Werbin and Martin CEO Chris Martin.

2011-2012		$1,075	$1,400

0-15T

1960-1963. Tenor with Style 15 appointments, natural mahogany.

1960-1963		$1,225	$1,600

0-16

1961 only. Six made.

1961		$2,700	$3,550

MODEL YEAR	FEATURES	EXC. COND. LOW	HIGH

0-16NY

1961-1977, 1979-1992, 1994. Mahogany back and sides, 12 frets, slotted peghead, unbound extra-wide rosewood 'board, natural.

1961-1969		$2,700	$3,550
1970-1979		$2,200	$2,900
1980-1989		$1,900	$2,475
1990-1994		$1,900	$2,475

0-17

1906-1917, 1929-1948, 1966-1968. First version has mahogany back and sides, 3 black soundhole rings, rosewood bound back, unbound ebony 'board, 12 frets, slotted peghead. Second version ('29 and on) is all mahogany, 3 white-black-white soundhole rings, top bound until '30, thin black backstripe, 12 frets and slotted peghead until '34, solid peghead and 14 frets beginning in '33, natural mahogany.

1906-1917	Gut	$2,450	$3,200
1929-1933	Steel, 12-fret	$3,375	$4,400
1933-1934	Flat natural, 14-fret	$4,300	$5,600
1934-1938	Gloss dark, 14-fret	$4,300	$5,600
1939	Early '39, 175 neck	$4,300	$5,600
1939	Late '39, 168 neck	$4,300	$5,600
1940-1946		$4,000	$5,200
1947-1948		$3,400	$4,400
1966-1968	Special order	$2,775	$3,650

0-17H

1930, 1935-1940. Hawaiian, mahogany back and sides, 12 frets clear of body, natural.

1930	12-fret	$3,600	$4,700
1935-1940	14-fret	$4,000	$5,200

0-17S

Early 1930s. Limited production style 17 with spruce top, unique 'guard.

1931		$5,500	$7,200

0-17T

1932-1960. Mahogany back and sides, tenor, natural.

1932-1933		$1,425	$1,850
1934-1939		$2,100	$2,750
1940-1947		$1,625	$2,125
1948-1949		$1,400	$1,825
1950-1960		$1,300	$1,700

0-18

1898-1994, 2017-present. Rosewood back and sides until 1917, mahogany back and sides after, Adirondack spruce top until 1946, slotted peghead and 12 frets until 1934, solid peghead and 14 frets after 1934, braced for steel strings in 1923, improved neck in late-1934, non-scalloped braces appear late-'44, natural. Reintroduced '17, sitka spruce, mahogany.

1898-1917	Brazilian	$4,200	$5,600
1918-1922	Mahogany, gut	$2,725	$3,550
1923-1934	12-fret, steel	$5,750	$7,500
1932-1938	14-fret	$6,350	$8,250
1939	Early '39, 175 neck	$6,350	$8,250
1939	Later '39, 168 neck	$5,650	$7,350
1940-1944		$5,275	$6,850
1945-1946		$4,500	$5,850
1947-1949		$4,300	$5,600
1950-1959		$3,925	$5,100

1960-1964		$3,525	$4,575
1965		$3,425	$4,450
1966-1969		$3,025	$3,925
1970-1979		$2,600	$3,425
1980-1989		$2,125	$2,800
1990-1994		$2,125	$2,800
2017-2021	Reintroduced	$1,750	$2,300

0-18G

1960s. Special order classical nylon-string model, natural.

1961		$1,800	$2,400

0-18K

1918-1935. Hawaiian, all koa wood, T-frets and steel T-bar neck in late-1934, natural.

1918-1933		$5,650	$7,350
1934-1935		$6,200	$8,000

0-18KH

1927-1928. Hawaiian, koa.

1927-1928		$5,650	$7,400

0-18T

1929-1932, 1936-1989, 1991-1992, 1994-1995. Mahogany body, spruce top, tenor, natural.

1929-1939		$2,400	$3,200
1940-1946		$2,050	$2,700
1947-1949		$1,850	$2,450
1950-1959		$1,775	$2,350
1960-1969		$1,650	$2,200
1970-1979		$1,350	$1,800
1980-1989		$1,125	$1,450
1991-1995		$1,125	$1,450

0-18T Nick Reynolds

2010-2011. Custom Artist Edition, mahogany.

2010-2011		$2,375	$3,100

0-18TE

1959, 1962. Only 2 made, tenor, 1 pickup.

1959, 1962		$5,600	$7,300

0-18VS Elderly Instruments 40th Anniversary Limited Edition

2012-2014. Mahogany body, sitka spruce top, slotted headstock, 12-fret neck, inside label signed by C. F. Martin IV and Elderly founder Stan Werbin.

2012-2014		$1,950	$2,525

0-20

1850-1859		$6,000	$7,800

0-21

1898-1931, 1934-1938, 1941, 1944, 1946-1948. Rosewood back and sides, Adirondack spruce top until 1946, 12 frets, T-frets and steel T-bar neck in late-1934, non-scalloped braces in late-1944, natural.

1898-1926	Gut	$7,200	$9,350
1927-1929	Steel	$9,100	$11,800
1930	14-fret (only year)	$9,100	$11,800
1930	Belly bridge	$9,100	$11,800
1931-1938		$9,100	$11,800
1941		$8,800	$11,400
1944	Non-scalloped	$8,000	$10,400
1946	Adirondack	$6,400	$8,325
1947-1948	Sitka	$6,200	$8,100

0-21K

1919-1929. Koa top, back and sides.

1919-1929		$8,500	$11,100

1919 Martin 0-18
David Stone

1926 Martin 0-21
Imaged by Heritage Auctions, HA.com

GUITARS

Martin 0-45 JB Joan Baez

Martin 0-X1E

MODEL YEAR	FEATURES	EXC. COND. LOW	HIGH
0-21T			
1929-1930, 1935, 1961.			
1929-1935		$4,600	$6,000
1961		$2,475	$3,225
0-26			
1895. Only 1 made, rosewood back and sides, ivory-bound top, rope-style purfling.			
1895		$7,600	$10,200
0-27			
1850s-1890s. Rosewood back and sides, ivory-bound top.			
1850s	Antique market value	$9,000	$11,700
1860s-90s		$7,600	$10,200
0-28			
1874-1931, 1937 (6 made), 1969 (1 made). Brazilian rosewood back and sides, herringbone binding until 1937, natural.			
1874-1895		$7,100	$9,300
1896-1897	Dark orange (rare)	$7,100	$9,300
1898-1923		$7,100	$9,300
1924-1927	Gut	$7,100	$9,300
1925-1927	Steel option	$10,200	$13,300
1928-1929	Steel (standard)	$10,200	$13,300
1930-1931	Belly bridge, 12-fret	$11,200	$14,500
1937	Belly bridge, 14-fret	$14,000	$18,200
1969	Brazilian	$6,400	$8,300
0-28H			
1927-1928. One made each year, Hawaiian, koa.			
1927-1928		$9,600	$12,800
0-28IA Ian Anderson			
2004. Limited Edition 87 made, adirondack spruce top, Indian rosewood sides and back, slotted headstock, can be converted from nylon to light steel strings.			
2004		$3,800	$5,000
0-28K			
1917-1931, 1935. Hawaiian, all koa wood, braced for steel strings in '23, natural.			
1917-1924		$8,600	$11,400
1925-1929		$9,600	$12,700
1930-1935		$10,400	$13,800
0-28T			
1930-1931, 1941. Tenor neck.			
1930-1931	Steel option	$5,200	$6,800
1941		$4,200	$5,500
0-28VS			
2009-2019. Rosewood back and sides, slotted head, 12 fret neck.			
2009-2019		$2,800	$3,700
0-30			
1899-1921. Brazilian rosewood back and sides, ivory-bound body, neck and headstock.			
1899-1921		$7,200	$9,350
0-34			
1885, 1898-1899, 1907. Brazilian rosewood.			
1885-1907		$7,700	$10,000
0-40			
1860s-1898, 1912-1913. Indian rosewood.			
1880-1913		$9,600	$12,500

MODEL YEAR	FEATURES	EXC. COND. LOW	HIGH
0-42			
1870s-1924, 1926-1930, 1 each in '34, '38,'42. Brazilian rosewood back and sides, 12 frets, natural.			
1890-1924		$14,000	$18,300
1926-1927	Gut	$14,000	$18,300
1928-1942	Steel	$21,700	$28,200
0-44 Soloist/Olcott-Bickford Artist			
1911-1931. Vahdah Olcott-Bickford Artist Model, run of 17 style-44 guitars made, Brazilian rosewood, ivory or faux-ivory-bound ebony 'board.			
1911-1931		$19,700	$25,600
0-45			
1904-1908, '11, '13, '15, '17-'20, '22-'24, '26-'30, '39. Brazilian rosewood back and sides, natural, special order only for '31-'39.			
1904-1927	Gut	$32,000	$41,700
1927-1939	Steel	$46,000	$60,000
0-45JB Joan Baez			
1998. Indian rosewood, 59 made.			
1998		$4,200	$5,600
0-45S Stephen Stills			
2007. Madagascar rosewood sides and back, Adirondack spruce top, 91 made.			
2007		$7,000	$9,000
0-X1E			
2020-present. Concert size, figured mahogany laminate, Fishman electronics.			
2020-2021		$425	$550
00-1			
1995-2002. Grand Concert, mahogany.			
1995-2002		$725	$950
00-1R			
1995-1999. Rosewood version.			
1995-1999		$725	$950
00-15			
1999-2010. Sapele/mahogany.			
1999-2010		$875	$1,150
00-15E Retro			
2017-2018. Solid mahogany top, back and sides, electronics.			
2017-2018		$1,375	$1,800
00-15M			
2009-present. All mahogany.			
2009-2021		$875	$1,150
00-15M Custom Elderly Instruments			
2010-2014. All mahogany, diamond and square inlays, custom-made for Elderly Instruments, about 10 offered each year.			
2010-2014		$850	$1,100
00-15M Elderly Instruments 40th Anniversary Limited Edition			
2012. Only 12 made, mahogany body and neck, label signed by Elderly's president Stan Werbin and Martin CEO Chris Martin.			
2012		$850	$1,100
00C-15AE			
2000-2002. Built-in electronics, natural finish.			
2000-2002		$1,000	$1,300

MODEL YEAR	FEATURES	EXC. COND. LOW	HIGH

00-16C

1962-1977, 1980-1981. Classical, mahogany back and sides, 5-ply bound top, satin finish, 12 frets, slotted peghead, natural.

1962-1969		$1,350	$1,775
1970-1977		$1,150	$1,500
1980-1981	2 made	$975	$1,275

00-16DBFM

2006. Women and Music series, deep body (DB), flamed maple (FM), slotted headstock.

| 2001-2003 | | $1,350 | $1,750 |

00-16DBM

2000-2005. Women and Music series, deep body (DB), mahogany (M), slotted headstock, gloss finish.

| 2000-2005 | | $1,350 | $1,750 |

00-16DBR

1998-2000. Women and Music series, deep body (DB), rosewood, 14-fret slotted headstock, gloss natural finish.

| 1998-2000 | | $1,350 | $1,750 |

00C-16DB

1999-2002. Women in Music series, cutaway, deep body (DB), mahogany, slotted headstock.

| 1999-2002 | | $1,575 | $2,050 |

00C-16DBRE

2005-2007. Women and Music series, rounded cutaway, deep body (DB), rosewood (R), electronics (E).

| 2005-2007 | | $1,625 | $2,150 |

00-17

1908-1917, 1930-1960, 1982-1988, 2001-2004. Mahogany back and sides, 12 frets and slotted headstock until '34, solid headstock and 14 frets after '34, natural mahogany, reissued in 2001 with a high gloss finish.

1908-1917	Gut strings	$3,125	$4,050
1930-1933	Steel, 12-fret	$4,550	$5,900
1934	14-fret, flat natural	$4,900	$6,400
1935-1938	14-fret, gloss dark	$4,900	$6,400
1939	Early '39, 175 neck	$4,900	$6,400
1939	Later '39, 168 neck	$4,500	$5,900
1940-1944		$4,500	$5,900
1945-1946		$4,100	$5,400
1947-1949		$3,700	$4,850
1950-1960		$3,400	$4,500
1982-1988		$1,900	$2,450
2001-2004	Reissue	$1,600	$2,100

00-17 Authentic 1931

2018-2020. Mahogany top, back and sides, Brazilian rosewood 'board, vintage gloss finish.

| 2018-2020 | | $3,350 | $4,350 |

00-17H

1934-1935. Hawaiian set-up, mahogany body, no binding.

| 1934-1935 | | $5,000 | $6,475 |

00-17S Black Smoke/Whiskey Sunset

2015-2020. Sitka spruce top, mahogany back and sides, rosewood 'board and bridge, on-board electronics (E) optional.

| 2015-2020 | No electronics | $1,150 | $1,500 |
| 2016-2020 | With electronics | $1,300 | $1,700 |

00-17SO Sing Out! 50th Anniversary

2000. Limited Edition, 50 made for 50th anniversary of Sing Out! Magazine, folk era logo inlays, SING OUT inlay on 20th fret, mahogany body.

| 2000 | | $1,500 | $2,000 |

00-18

1898-1995, 2016-present. Rosewood back and sides until 1917, mahogany after, braced for steel strings in '23, improved neck in late-'34, war-time design changes '42-'46, non-scalloped braces in late-'44, Adirondack spruce top until '46, natural. Reissued 2016 with sitka spruce top and mahogany back and sides.

1898-1917	Brazilian	$4,700	$6,150
1918-1922	Mahogany	$4,150	$5,400
1923-1929		$6,350	$8,250
1930-1932	12-fret	$9,800	$12,800
1933	14-fret, bar fret	$11,200	$14,500
1934-1937	14-fret	$11,200	$14,500
1938	175 neck	$11,200	$14,500
1939	Early '39, 175 neck	$11,200	$14,500
1939	Late '39, 168 neck	$9,800	$12,800
1940-1941		$9,800	$12,800
1942-1944	Scalloped	$9,800	$12,800
1944-1946	Non-scalloped	$7,400	$9,600
1947-1949		$6,000	$8,000
1950-1953		$4,400	$5,800
1954-1959		$4,100	$5,400
1960-1964		$3,800	$5,000
1965		$3,500	$4,600
1966-1969		$3,000	$4,000
1970-1979		$2,650	$3,450
1980-1989		$2,250	$2,950
1990-1995		$2,250	$2,950
2016-2021		$1,750	$2,300

00-18 Authentic 1931

2016-2018. Adirondack spruce top, mahogany back and sides, ebony 'board, Vintage Tone System (VTS), natural finish.

| 2016-2018 | | $4,400 | $5,750 |

00-18 Custom

2008. Custom Shop run of 75 or more made.

| 2008 | | $2,350 | $3,100 |

00-18 Gruhn Limited Edition

1995. Sitka spruce top, C-shaped neck profile, 25 made.

| 1995 | | $2,300 | $3,000 |

00-18 Tim O'Brien Signature

2008-2011. Limited Edition, 25.5" scale, label signed by O'Brien.

| 2008-2011 | | $4,200 | $5,450 |

00-18C

1962-1995. Renamed from 00-18 G in '62, mahogany back and sides, classical, 12 frets, slotted headstock, natural.

1962-1969		$1,800	$2,350
1970-1979		$1,300	$1,700
1980-1995		$1,100	$1,450

00-18CTN Elizabeth Cotton

2001. Commemorative Edition, 76 made.

| 2001 | | $2,300 | $3,000 |

00-18E

1959-1964. Flat-top Style 18, single neck pickup and 2 knobs, heavier bracing, natural.

| 1959-1964 | | $6,000 | $7,800 |

Martin 00-18 SH Steve Howe

1963 Martin 00-18E
Greg Perrine

1947 Martin 00-21
Imaged by Heritage Auctions, HA.com

1983 Martin 00-25K

MODEL YEAR	FEATURES	EXC. COND. LOW	HIGH

00-18G
1936-1962. Mahogany back and sides, classical, natural, renamed 00-18 C in '62.

1936-1939		$2,700	$3,500
1940-1949		$1,950	$2,550
1950-1959		$1,850	$2,400
1960-1962		$1,800	$2,350

00-18H
1935-1941. Hawaiian, mahogany back and sides, 12 frets clear of body, natural. The Price Guide is generally for all original instruments. The H conversion is an exception, because converting from H (Hawaiian-style) to 00-18 specs is considered by some to be a favorable improvement and something that adds value.

1935-1941		$6,300	$8,200

00-18H Geoff Muldaur
2006-2011. Solid Adirondack spruce top, solid mahogany sides and back, sunburst.

2006-2011		$3,100	$4,100

00-18K
1918-1925, 1934. All koa wood.

1918-1921		$3,900	$5,100
1922-1925		$5,600	$7,300
1934		$6,200	$8,100

00-18S John Mellencamp
2009-2010. Slotted, 12-fret.

2009-2010		$3,400	$4,400

00-18SH Steve Howe
1999-2000. Limited edition run of 250.

1999-2000		$2,300	$3,100

00-18T
1931, 1936, 1938-1940. Tenor version.

1931-1940		$3,300	$4,300

00-18V
1984, 2003-2015. Vintage Series, mahogany back and sides, spruce top.

1984	9 made	$2,000	$2,600
2003-2015		$1,900	$2,500

00-18V/VS Elderly Instruments 40th Anniversary
2012-2013. Limited Edition, solid (V) or slotted (VS) headstock, 12-fret, low profile.

2012-2013	V	$1,950	$2,600
2013	VS	$1,950	$2,600

00-21
1898-1996. Brazilian rosewood back and sides, changed to Indian rosewood in 1970, dark outer binding, unbound ebony 'board until 1947, rosewood from 1947, slotted diamond inlays until '44, dot after, natural.

1898-1926	Gut bracing	$7,300	$9,700
1927-1939	Steel bracing	$13,100	$17,500
1940-1943	Scalloped	$12,600	$16,800
1944-1947	Non-scalloped	$10,200	$13,500
1948-1949		$9,600	$12,800
1950-1959		$8,800	$11,500
1960-1964		$7,000	$9,300
1965		$5,500	$7,300
1966-1969	Brazilian	$5,100	$6,700
1970-1979	Indian	$2,900	$3,800
1980-1989	Indian	$2,900	$3,800
1990-1996	Indian	$2,900	$3,800

00-21 Custom
2005-2006. Custom order size 00 style 21, Brazilian rosewood sides and back.

2005-2006		$4,200	$5,500

00-21 Kingston Trio LTD
2007. 50th Anniversary of the Kingston Trio, inspired by Dave Guard's 00-21, 100 made, 12-fret, Indian rosewood, Kingston Trio label and notation "In Memory of Dave Guard 1934-1991".

2008-2009		$3,500	$4,650

00-21G
1937-1938. Gut string, Brazilian rosewood sides and back.

1937-1938		$3,000	$4,000

00-21GE Golden Era

1998-2000		$2,750	$3,650

00-21H
Hawaiian, special order, limited production.

1914	1 made	$7,000	$9,200
1934		$14,000	$18,300
1952, 1955	1 made each year	$9,000	$11,800

00-21LE
1987. Guitar of the Month, Limited Edition, 19 made.

1987		$2,300	$3,100

00-21NY
1961-1965. Brazilian rosewood back and sides, no inlay, natural.

1961-1964		$6,600	$8,500
1965		$5,500	$7,100

00-21S
1968. Slotted headstock, Brazilian rosewood sides and back.

1968		$4,750	$6,150

00-21T
1934. Tenor, Brazilian rosewood back and sides, only 2 made.

1934		$4,900	$6,400

00-25K
1980, 1985, 1988. Spruce top, koa back and sides.

1980-1988		$2,550	$3,300

00-25K2
1980, 1982-1984, 1987-1989. Koa top, back and sides.

1980-1989		$2,550	$3,300

00-28
Mid-1880s-1931, 1934, 1936-1941, 1958 (1 made), 1977 (1 made), 1984 (2 made), 2017-present. Brazilian rosewood back and sides, changed to Indian rosewood in 1977, herringbone purfling through 1941, white binding and unbound 'board after 1941, no inlays before 1901, diamond inlays from 1901-'41, dot after, natural. Reintroduced 2017, sitka spruce top, modified low oval neck.

1880s-1924	Gut	$10,000	$13,100
1925-1931	Steel	$18,300	$23,800
1934	Few made	$26,500	$34,500
1936-1941	Few made	$27,000	$36,000
1958	Special order	$11,500	$15,300
1977	Special order	$2,700	$3,600
1984	Special order	$2,300	$3,050
2017-2021	Reissue	$2,300	$3,050

MODEL YEAR	FEATURES	EXC. COND. LOW	HIGH

00-28C

1966-1995. Renamed from 00-28 G, Brazilian rosewood back and sides, changed to Indian rosewood in '70, classical, 12 frets, natural.

1966-1969	Brazilian	$3,700	$4,900
1970-1979	Indian	$1,800	$2,400
1980-1989		$1,550	$2,050
1990-1995		$1,550	$2,050

00-28G

1936-1962. Brazilian rosewood back and sides, classical, natural, reintroduced as 00-28 C in '66.

1936-1946		$5,700	$7,500
1947-1949		$4,700	$6,140
1950-1959		$4,000	$5,250
1960-1962		$3,800	$5,000

00-28K

1919-1921, 1926, 1928-1931, 1933. Hawaiian, koa back and sides.

1919-1921	34 made	$12,500	$16,200
1926-1933	1 made per year	$19,600	$25,600

00-28T

1931, 1940. Tenor, Brazilian rosewood back and sides, tenor 4-string neck, only 2 made.

1931, 1940		$7,100	$9,300

00-28VS

2009-2019. Rosewood back and sides.

2009-2019		$2,950	$3,850

00-28VS Custom Shop

2009-2013. Various Custom Shop options.

2009-2013		$3,200	$4,200

00-30

1890s-1921. Rosewood .

1899-1921		$14,700	$19,200

00-34

1898-1899. 6 made.

1898-1899		$15,700	$20,500

00-37K2 Steve Miller

2001. Flamed koa back and sides, solid Engelmann spruce top, limited run of 68.

2001		$5,300	$7,000

00-40

1913, 1917. 4 made.

1913	Brazilian	$26,500	$34,500
1917	Koa	$26,500	$34,500

00-40 Martin Stauffer

1997. Rosewood/spruce, 35 made.

1997		$6,300	$8,200

00-40H

1928-1939. Hawaiian, Brazilian rosewood back and sides, 12 frets clear of body, natural. H models are sometimes converted to standard Spanish setup, in higher-end models this can make the instrument more valuable to some people.

1928-1929	Pyramid bridge	$27,000	$36,000
1930-1939	Belly bridge	$27,000	$36,000

00-40K

Few were made (only 6), figured koa, natural.

1918	1 made	$27,000	$36,000
1930	5 made	$27,000	$36,000

00-41 Custom

2005. Custom Shop model, parlor size.

2005		$4,500	$5,800

00-42

1898-1943, 1973 (1 made). Brazilian rosewood back and sides, Indian rosewood in 1973, pearl top borders, 12 frets, ivory bound peghead until 1918, ivoroid binding after 1918, natural.

1898-1927	Pyramid bridge	$25,500	$33,300
1927-1943	Steel bracing	$40,000	$52,000
1973	1 made	$4,200	$5,500

00-42 Linda Ronstadt Limited Edition

2009-2010. Madagascar rosewood, slotted headstock.

2009-2010		$6,900	$9,000

00-42G

1936-1939. Gut string slotted headstock classical, only 3 made.

1936-1939	3 made	$11,000	$14,500

00-42JM-C John Mayer Crossroads

2019. Limited run of 50 for Guitar Center, designed by John Mayer to benefit Crossroads Centre in Antigua, Sitka spruce top, Cocobolo back and sides, gloss finish.

2019		$6,800	$9,000

00-42K

1919. Koa body, only 1 made.

1919	1 made	$39,000	$51,200

00-42K2 Robbie Robertson

2008-2009. Limited Edition, all koa body (K2), 00-12 fret style, high-end appointments.

2008-2009		$5,700	$7,400

00-42SC John Mayer

2012-2019. Sitka spruce top, cocobolo back, sides and headplate, ebony 'board.

2012-2019		$5,300	$7,000

00-44 Soloist/Olcott-Bickford Artist

1913-1939. Custom-made in small quantities, Brazilian rosewood, ivory or faux-ivory-bound ebony 'board.

1913-1939	6 made	$39,000	$50,600

00-44G

1938. Set up with gut strings, 1 made.

1938	1 made	$30,500	$40,000

00-45

1904-1929, 1970-1982, 1984-1987, 1989-1990, 1992-1993. Brazilian rosewood back and sides, changed to Indian rosewood in '70, 12 frets and slotted headstock until '34 and from '70 on 14 frets, and solid headstock from '34-'70, natural.

1904-1927	Gut	$41,000	$53,800
1927-1929	Steel	$83,000	$109,000
1970-1979	Reintroduced	$5,600	$7,300
1980-1993		$5,100	$6,650

00-45K

1919. Koa body, 1 made.

1919		$59,000	$76,800

00-45S

1970. Slotted headstock.

1970		$6,200	$8,100

00-45S Limited Edition

2002. 1902 vintage-pattern with fancy inlays, 00 size style 45, 50 made.

2002		$12,300	$16,000

1925 Martin 00-28
Izzy Miller

1975 Martin 00-45
Imaged by Heritage Auctions, HA.com

Martin 000-10E

Martin 000-15M Streetmaster

MODEL		EXC. COND.	
YEAR	FEATURES	LOW	HIGH

00-45SC John Mayer
2012-2013. Limited Edition, 25 made, slotted head-stock, cocobolo.

2012-2013		$10,800	$14,000

00-45ST Stauffer Commemorative
1997-1998. Limited Edition, 25 made, six-on-a-side headstock, 45-style appointments, 00 body, Sitka top, Brazilian rosewood back and sides.

1997-1998		$11,300	$14,700

00-55
1935. 12 made for Rudnick's Music of Akron, Ohio.

1935		$10,800	$14,400

00CMAE
1999-2001. Single-cut acoustic-electric flat-top, laminate back and sides, made in U.S.

1999-2001		$575	$750

00CXAE
2000-2013. Single-cut acoustic-electric flat-top, composite laminate back and sides, made in U.S.

2000-2013	Various colors	$450	$575

00L Earth
2021-present. Dedicated to climate control, 100% FSC-certified and 100% plastic-free, graphic art by Robert Goetzl, gig bag made from hemp.

2021-2022		$1,375	$1,800

00L Fly Fishing
2019-2021. Limited Edition, run of 100, artwork by William Matthews, sitka spruce top, Goncalo Alves back and sides, gloss finish.

2019-2021		$1,725	$3,550

00L-17 Black Smoke/Whiskey Sunset
2016-2019. Sitka spruce top, mahogany back and sides, on-board electronics optional.

2016-2019	17, No electronics	$1,150	$1,500
2016-2019	17E, Electronics	$1,300	$1,675

00L-X1AE

2017-2019		$375	$475

00L-X2E
2020-present. Sitka spruce top, figured mahogany laminate back and sides, Fishman electronics, natural finish.

2020-2021		$500	$650

00-DB Jeff Tweedy Signature
2011-2019. Custom Shop Signature Edition with solid FSC® Certified Mahogany and mahogany burst finish.

2011-2019		$1,850	$2,400

00-X1AE

2015-2019		$350	$475

00-X2E
2020-present. Sitka spruce top, figured mahogany laminate back and sides, Fishman electronics, natural finish.

2020		$475	$625

000-1
1994-2005. Solid spruce top with laminated mahogany back and sides.

1994-2005		$700	$925

000-1E
1994-2005. 000-1 with electronics.

1994-2005		$775	$1,000

MODEL		EXC. COND.	
YEAR	FEATURES	LOW	HIGH

000-1R
1994-2003. 000-1 with Indian rosewood back and sides.

1994-2003		$700	$925

000-10E
2019-present. Road Series, updated version of 000RS1, sapele top, back and sides, Fishman electronics, satin finish.

2019-2021		$500	$650

000-12E Koa
2019-present. Road Series, sitka spruce top, koa veneer back and sides, Fishman electronics, gloss finish.

2019-2021		$1,000	$1,300

000-13E
2017-2018. Road Series, updated version of 000RSG, sitka spruce top, siris back and sides, Fishman electronics, natural gloss.

2017-2018		$675	$875

000-15/000-15S
1999-2009. Mahogany body, headstock is solid or slotted (S, first offered in '00). Renamed 000-15M with solid headstock in '10.

1999-2009	000-15	$900	$1,175
2000-2009	000-15S	$975	$1,275

000-15M
2010-present. All mahogany, satin finish.

2010-2021		$800	$1,050

000-15M Burst
2016-2018. Solid mahogany, 14-fret, satin finish with added burst to top.

2016-2018		$900	$1,200

000-15M Elderly Instruments 40th Anniversary
2011-2012. 10 made, mahogany body and neck, label signed by Elderly Instruments president Stan Werbin and Martin CEO Chris Martin

2011-2012		$1,050	$1,375

000-15M StreetMaster
2017-present. Same specs as 000-15M but with distressed mahogany satin finish.

2017-2021		$800	$1,050

000-15SM
2011-present. Solid mahogany, slotted headstock, 12-fret neck, satin finish.

2011-2021		$1,000	$1,300

000-16 Series
1989-present. Mahogany back and sides, diamonds and squares inlay, sunburst, name changed to 000-16 T Auditorium with higher appointments in '96, in 2000-2005 slotted (000-16 S) and gloss finish (000-16 SGT) were offered. Various models continue to be added to this series.

1989	000-16M	$1,025	$1,350
1989-1995	000-16	$1,050	$1,350
1989-2021	000-16GT	$875	$1,125
1995-1998	000-16T	$950	$1,250
1996	000-16TR	$850	$1,125
1996-2002	000-16R	$1,025	$1,350
2001-2005	000-16RGT	$850	$1,125
2002-2003	000-16SRGT	$900	$1,175
2003-2004	000-16SGT	$900	$1,175
2019-2021	000-16E	$1,375	$1,775

MODEL YEAR	FEATURES	EXC. COND. LOW	EXC. COND. HIGH

000-17
1911, 1952. Mahogany back and sides, 1 made in 1911, 25 more in '52.

1911		$9,100	$11,800
1952		$4,100	$5,400

000-17 Black Smoke/Whiskey Sunset
2016-present. Sitka spruce top, mahogany back and sides, rosewood 'board and bridge, on-board electronics (000-17E) optional.

2016-2021	17, No electronics	$975	$1,275
2016-2021	17E, Electronics	$1,125	$1,450

000-17S
2002-2004. All mahogany, slotted headstock, 12 fret neck.

2002-2004		$1,200	$1,550

000-17SM
2013-2015. Sitka spruce top, mahogany back and sides, East Indian rosewood headplate, vintage slotted headstock.

2013-2015		$1,200	$1,550

000-18
1906, 1911-present (none in 1932-1933). Maple back and sides in '06, then rosewood until '17, and mahogany since, longer scale in '24-'34, 12-fret neck until '33, changed to 14 in '34. Improved neck late-'34, war-time changes '41-'46, non-scalloped braces in late-'44, switched from Adirondack spruce to Sitka spruce top in '46 (though some Adirondack tops in '50s and '60s), natural. Now a part of the Standard Series.

1906	Maple	$10,200	$13,500
1911-1917	Rosewood	$10,200	$13,500
1920-1922	Gut, mahogany	$9,100	$12,100
1923-1931	Steel	$15,000	$20,000
1934	Early '34, long scale	$17,100	$22,700
1934-1938	14-fret	$17,100	$22,700
1939	Early '39 175 neck	$16,000	$21,300
1939	Late '39, 168 neck	$13,000	$17,300
1940-1941		$12,000	$16,000
1942-1943	Scalloped braces	$12,000	$16,000
1944	Scalloped braces	$10,500	$13,700
1944-1947	Non-scalloped	$7,500	$10,000
1948-1949		$6,500	$8,650
1950-1953		$6,000	$8,000
1954-1959		$5,400	$7,250
1960-1964		$4,600	$6,200
1965		$4,500	$5,900
1966-1969		$3,700	$5,000
1970-1979		$2,650	$3,450
1980-1989		$2,200	$2,900
1990-1999		$2,200	$2,900
2000-2013		$1,900	$2,450
2014-2021	Standard Series	$1,900	$2,450

000-18 Authentic 1937
2008-2011. Natural or sunburst, high-X bracing.

2008-2011		$4,500	$5,800

000-18 Kenny Sultan Signature
2007-2009. Flamed mahogany sides, diamond and squares inlays, label signed by Sultan.

2007-2009		$2,850	$3,700

000-18 Norman Blake Signature
2006-2011. 12 fret neck on 14-fret body.

2006-2011		$2,850	$3,700

000-18E Retro
2012-2019. Sitka spruce top, mahogany back and sides.

2012-2019		$1,900	$2,450

000-18G
1955. Classical, 1 made.

1955		$4,150	$5,500

000-18GE Golden Era 1934 Special Edition
2007. Adirondack red spruce top, scalloped and forward shifted X-bracing, 14-fret V-shaped mahogany neck, 20-fret ebony 'board, old style decal logo.

2007		$2,850	$3,700

000-18GE Golden Era 1937 Special Edition
2006-2014. Natural or sunburst. 1937 dropped from name in '12.

2006-2014	Natural or sunburst	$2,850	$3,700

000-18GE Golden Era Sunburst
2006-2014. Sunburst version, adirondack.

2006-2014		$2,850	$3,700

000-18P
1930. Plectrum neck.

1930		$5,200	$6,800

000-18S
1976-1977. Slotted, 12-fret.

1976-1977		$3,000	$4,000

000-18T
1930, '34, '36, '38, '41. Tenor.

1930		$5,425	$7,050
1934-1938		$10,000	$13,000
1941		$6,000	$7,800

000-18V/VS Elderly Instruments 40th Anniversary
2012-2013. Limited Edition, solid (V) or slotted (VS) headstock, Sitka top, label signed by C.F. Martin IV and Stan Werbin, includes matching wood guitar stand.

2012-2013	V	$2,550	$3,325
2013	VS	$2,550	$3,325

000-18WG Woody Guthrie
1999. Signed label including artwork and model identification.

1999		$2,775	$3,600

000-21
1902-1923 (22 made over that time), 1931(2), 1938-1959, 1965 (1), 1979 (12). Brazilian rosewood back and sides, changed to Indian rosewood in '79, natural.

1902-1923		$14,800	$19,700
1931	12-fret	$18,000	$24,000
1938-1939	Early '39, 175 neck	$28,000	$36,500
1939	Late '39, 168 neck	$22,000	$29,000
1940-1941		$18,800	$24,500
1942-1943		$17,000	$22,000
1944-1945		$15,000	$20,000
1946		$11,200	$14,600
1947-1949		$9,500	$12,500
1950-1954		$8,800	$11,500
1955-1959		$8,800	$11,500
1965	Last Brazilian	$8,000	$10,700
1979	Indian	$3,000	$4,000

Martin 000-17 Black Smoke

1972 Martin 000-18
Rivington Guitars

To get the most from this book, be sure to read "Using *The Guide*" in the introduction.

GUITARS

1948 Martin 000-21
Carter Vintage Guitars

1936 Martin 000-28
M. Mattingly

000-21 10-String/Harp Guitar
1902. Only 2 made, 10 strings, Brazilian rosewood back and sides.

MODEL YEAR	FEATURES	EXC. COND. LOW	HIGH
1902		$5,200	$6,700

000-28
1902-present. Brazilian rosewood back and sides, changed to Indian rosewood in '70, herringbone purfling through '41, white binding and unbound 'board after '41, no inlays before '01, slotted diamond inlays from '01-'44, dot after, 12 frets until '32, 14 frets '31 on (both 12 and 14 frets were made during '31-'32), natural through '93, sunburst or natural after.

MODEL YEAR	FEATURES	EXC. COND. LOW	HIGH
1902-1927	Gut	$16,500	$21,500
1925-1927	Steel	$32,000	$41,500
1928		$32,000	$41,500
1929	Pyramid bridge	$32,000	$41,500
1930	Belly bridge	$32,000	$41,500
1931-1933		$32,000	$41,500
1934	Early '34 long scale	$54,200	$70,500
1934-1937	Not long scale	$49,500	$64,300
1938-1939	Early '39, 175 neck	$48,000	$63,000
1939	Late '39, 168 neck	$41,000	$54,000
1940-1941		$37,000	$49,000
1942-1944	Scalloped, herringbone	$35,000	$46,000
1944-1946	Non-scalloped, herringbone	$24,000	$32,000
1947-1949	Non-herringbone	$15,000	$19,500
1950-1952		$12,000	$15,600
1953-1955	Kluson	$12,000	$15,600
1956-1958	Kluson	$10,600	$13,800
1958-1959	Late '58, Grover	$10,600	$13,800
1960-1962		$8,550	$11,100
1964		$8,400	$10,900
1965		$6,700	$8,700
1966-1969	Early '66, Tortoise 'guard	$6,600	$8,600
1970-1979		$3,100	$4,100
1980-1989		$2,550	$3,325
1990-1999		$2,250	$2,950
2000-2021		$2,200	$2,900

000-28 Martin/Mandolin Brothers 25th Anniversary
1997-1998. Limited Edition, 25 made, mandolin 12th fret inlay, signed label.

MODEL YEAR	FEATURES	EXC. COND. LOW	HIGH
1997-1998		$3,200	$4,200

000-28 Modern Deluxe
2019-present. Sitka spruce top, Vintage Tone System, Indian rosewood back and sides. Electronics are optional (000-28E).

MODEL YEAR	FEATURES	EXC. COND. LOW	HIGH
2019-2021	28, No electronics	$2,450	$3,200
2019-2021	28E, Electronics	$3,850	$5,100

000-28 Norman Blake
2004-2008. Signature Edition, 12-fret neck on 14-fret body, B version is Brazilian rosewood.

MODEL YEAR	FEATURES	EXC. COND. LOW	HIGH
2004-2008	Brazilian	$7,700	$10,200
2004-2008	Indian	$3,700	$4,800

000-28 Perry Bechtel
2007. East Indian rosewood back and sides, 29 made.

MODEL YEAR	FEATURES	EXC. COND. LOW	HIGH
2007		$3,700	$4,900

000-28C
1962-1967. Classical, Brazilian rosewood back and sides, slotted peghead, natural.

MODEL YEAR	FEATURES	EXC. COND. LOW	HIGH
1962-1967		$4,700	$6,200

000-28EC
1996-present. Custom Signature Edition, Eric Clapton specs, sitka spruce top, Indian rosewood back and sides, herringbone trim, natural or sunburst.

MODEL YEAR	FEATURES	EXC. COND. LOW	HIGH
1996-2021	Natural	$2,850	$3,700
1996-2021	Sunburst	$2,500	$3,500

000-28EC Eric Clapton Crossroads Madagascar
2013. Limited to 150 in collaboration with Guitar Center, soundhole label hand-signed by Clapton and Chris Martin, Crossroads symbol inlaid (mother-of-pearl) into bridge, Clapton signature between 19th-20th frets, Clapton signature case and strap.

MODEL YEAR	FEATURES	EXC. COND. LOW	HIGH
2013		$5,100	$6,600

000-28ECB Eric Clapton
2002-2003. Limited edition, EC 000-28 with Brazilian rosewood, certificate of authenticity, label hand-signed by Eric Clapton and Chris Martin.

MODEL YEAR	FEATURES	EXC. COND. LOW	HIGH
2002-2003		$8,900	$11,800

000-28F
1964-1967. Folk, 12-fret, slotted.

MODEL YEAR	FEATURES	EXC. COND. LOW	HIGH
1964		$8,300	$10,800
1965		$6,700	$8,700
1966-1967		$6,600	$8,600

000-28G
1937, 1939-1940, 1946-1947, 1949-1950, 1955. Special order classical guitar, very limited production.

MODEL YEAR	FEATURES	EXC. COND. LOW	HIGH
1937-1940		$8,500	$11,200
1946		$7,900	$10,400
1947, 1949		$6,200	$8,100
1950, 1955		$5,600	$7,400

000-28GE Golden Era
1996 only. Sitka spruce top, rosewood back and sides, scalloped braces, herringbone trim, 12-fret model, natural.

MODEL YEAR	FEATURES	EXC. COND. LOW	HIGH
1996		$4,200	$5,400

000-28H
2000-2017. Herringbone top trim, production model for '00-'02, Custom Shop model made for Elderly Instruments after that (stamped Custom on neck block).

MODEL YEAR	FEATURES	EXC. COND. LOW	HIGH
2000-2002		$2,450	$3,200
2003-2017	Custom Shop	$2,500	$3,300

000-28HB Brazilian 1937 Reissue
1997. Pre-war specs including scalloped bracing, Brazilian rosewood.

MODEL YEAR	FEATURES	EXC. COND. LOW	HIGH
1997		$7,400	$9,800

000-28K
1921. Non-catalog special order model, only 2 known to exist, koa top, back and sides.

MODEL YEAR	FEATURES	EXC. COND. LOW	HIGH
1921	Rare model	$35,000	$46,000

000-28K Authentic 1921
2014-2015. Slotted, 12-fret, highly figured koa body.

MODEL YEAR	FEATURES	EXC. COND. LOW	HIGH
2014-2015		$4,300	$5,600

000-28LSH/LSH Custom
2008. Large sound hole (LSH), style 28 appointments, wild grain East Indian sides and back.

MODEL YEAR	FEATURES	EXC. COND. LOW	HIGH
2008		$2,600	$3,400

MODEL YEAR	FEATURES	EXC. COND. LOW	HIGH

000-28M Eric Clapton
2009. Limited Edition run of 461, Madagascar rosewood back and sides, Carpathian spruce top, signature between 19th and 20th frets, interior label hand-signed by Clapton, natural or sunburst.

2009		$5,200	$6,700

000-28NY
1962. 2 made.

1962		$8,000	$10,600

000-28S
1974-1977. Slotted headstock, 12-fret neck.

1974-1977		$3,350	$4,350

000-28SO Sing Out! 40th Anniversary
1990. Limited Edition, 40 made for 40th Anniversary of Sing Out! Magazine.

1990		$2,400	$3,150

000-28VS
1999-2019. Vintage Series, spruce top with aging toner, scalloped bracing, rosewood sides and back, slotted diamond markers, herringbone top trim.

1999-2019		$2,800	$3,700

000-30 Authentic 1919
2017-2018. Adirondack spruce top, Vintage Tone System, Madagascar rosewood back and sides.

2017-2018		$4,600	$6,100

000-38
1980. Rosewood back and sides, 3 made.

1980		$2,800	$3,600

000-40
1909. Ivoroid bound top and back, snowflake inlay, 1 made.

1909		$31,000	$41,000

000-40Q2GN Graham Nash
2003. Limited edition of 147 guitars, quilted mahagony top/back/sides, flying-heart logo on headstock, Graham Nash signature on frets 18-20.

2003		$3,900	$5,100

000-40SPR Peter Rowan "Midnight Moonlight" Signature
2001-2002. Limited run of 87, sitka spruce top, mahogany back and sides, phases of the moon inlays.

2001-2002		$3,000	$4,000

000-41
1975, 1996. Custom shop style 000-41.

1975		$4,300	$5,600
1996		$3,700	$4,900

000-42
1918, 1921-1922, 1925, 1930, 1932, 1934, 1938-1943, 2004-present. Brazilian rosewood back and sides, natural. The 1918-1934 price range is wide due to the variety of specifications.

1918-1925	Limited production	$39,000	$51,000
1930, 1932	2 made, 14 fret	$60,000	$79,000
1934	1 made	$77,000	$101,000
1938	27 made	$70,000	$91,000
1939	Early '39, 175 neck	$70,000	$91,000
1939	Late '39, 168 neck	$65,000	$85,000
1940-1943	Last pearl border	$67,000	$87,000
2004-2021		$4,200	$5,500

000-42 Authentic 1939
2017-2019. Adirondack spruce top with Vintage Tone System (VTS), Madagascar rosewood back and sides, ebony 'board and bridge.

2017-2019		$8,500	$11,100

000-42 Marquis
2007-2009. Indian rosewood.

2007-2009		$5,400	$7,100

000-42EC Eric Clapton
1995. Style 45 pearl-inlaid headplate, ivoroid bindings, Eric Clapton signature, 24.9" scale, flat-top, sunburst top price is $8320 ('95 price), only 461 made; 433 natural, 28 sunburst.

1995		$7,900	$10,300

000-42ECB Eric Clapton
2000-2001. With Brazilian rosewood, 200 made.

2000-2001		$14,200	$18,500

000-42EC-Z Eric Clapton Crossroads
2019-2021. Ziricote back and sides, 50 made to benefit Crossroads Centre.

2019-2021		$11,300	$14,700

000-42M Eric Clapton Limited Edition
2008-2009. Limited Edition, 250 made, Madagascar rosewood sides and back, Carpathian spruce top.

2008-2009		$7,300	$9,500

000-42SB
2004. 1935 style with sunburst finish, Indian rosewood back and sides.

2004		$4,200	$5,500

000-44 Soloist/Olcott-Bickford Artist
1917-1919. Style 44 guitars were made for guitarist Vahdah Olcott-Bickford, rosewood back and sides, 3 made.

1917-1919		$44,000	$58,000

000-45
1906, 1911-1914, '17-'19, '22-'29, '34-'42, '70-'94. Brazilian rosewood back and sides, changed to Indian rosewood in '70, 12-fret neck and slotted headstock until '34 (but 7 were made in '70 and 1 in '75), 14-fret neck and solid headstock after '34, natural.

1906-1919		$57,000	$74,000
1922-1927	Gut	$57,000	$74,000
1926-1929	Steel	$118,000	$154,000
1930-1931	000-45 designated	$118,000	$154,000
1934	Early '34, long scale	$167,000	$217,000
1934	Late '34, short scale	$150,000	$200,000
1935-1937	14 fret, CFM inlay	$150,000	$200,000
1938	Early '38	$150,000	$200,000
1938	Late '38	$140,000	$182,000
1940-1942		$115,000	$150,000
1970-1977		$7,300	$9,500
1980-1989		$6,300	$8,200
1990-1994		$5,700	$7,400

000-45 7-String
1911, 1929, 1931. 1 made each year.

1911-1931		$37,000	$48,000

000-45B
1985. Brazilian rosewood, 2 made.

1985		$14,000	$18,500

2009 Martin 000-28 M Eric Clapton
Carter Vintage Guitars

Martin 000-42 Authentic 1939

282

Martin 000-45EC Crossroads Braz. — 000E Black Walnut Ambertone   The Official Vintage Guitar magazine Price Guide 2023

GUITARS

*Martin 000-45 JR
Jimmie Rodgers*

Carter Vintage Guitars

Martin 000C12-16E Nylon

MODEL YEAR	FEATURES	EXC. COND. LOW	HIGH

000-45EC Eric Clapton Crossroads Brazilian
   2013. Limited to 18 in collaboration with Guitar Center, Brazilian rosewood, Crossroads symbol inlaid both ends of bridge, Crossroads case and strap.

| 2013 | | $34,000 | $45,000 |

000-45EC Eric Clapton Crossroads Madagascar
   2013. Limited to 55 in collaboration with Guitar Center, Crossroads symbol inlaid both ends of bridge, Crossroads case and strap.

| 2013 | | $10,000 | $13,000 |

000-45H
   1937. Brazilian rosewood, Hawaiian, 2 made.

| 1937 | | $163,000 | $213,000 |

000-45JR Jimmie Rodgers
   1997-1998. Adirondack spruce top, Brazilian rosewood back and sides, scalloped high X-braces, abalone trim, natural, 52 made. Sometimes referred to as Blue Yodel.

| 1997-1998 | | $12,500 | $16,500 |

000-45S
   1974-1976. 12-fret.

| 1974-1976 | | $8,000 | $10,500 |

000-45S Stephen Stills
   2005. Only 91 made, Indian rosewood.

| 2005 | | $10,800 | $14,000 |

000C David Gray Custom
   2005-2006. Custom Artist Edition, 000-size cutaway, Italian spruce top, mahogany back and sides, interior label signed by David Gray.

| 2005-2006 | | $2,575 | $3,350 |

000C Nylon
   2012-2018. Cutaway, 12-fret, sitka spruce top, sapele back and sides, slotted headstock, Fishman.

| 2012-2018 | | $1,225 | $1,600 |

000C Steve Miller Pegasus
   2005-2006. Cutaway, mahogany back and sides, Pegasus logo.

| 2005-2006 | | $3,000 | $3,900 |

000C12-16E Nylon
   2020-present. Gloss sitka spruce top, satin mahogany back and sides, Fishman electronics.

| 2020-2021 | | $1,250 | $1,625 |

000C-15E
   1999-2002. Cutaway, mahogany back and sides, Fishman.

| 1999-2002 | | $975 | $1,275 |

000C-16 (T Auditorium)
   1990-1998. Cutaway acoustic, mahogany back and sides, diamonds and squares inlay, name changed to 000-C16T Auditorium in '96.

| 1990-1998 | | $1,200 | $1,550 |

000C-16GTE
   1999-2003. Cutaway, mahogany.

| 1999-2003 | | $1,250 | $1,650 |

000C-16GTE Premium
   2003-2009. Mahogany back and sides.

| 2003-2009 | | $1,325 | $1,725 |

MODEL YEAR	FEATURES	EXC. COND. LOW	HIGH

000C-16RB (Baby Face)
   2000-2002. Cutaway acoustic, East Indian rosewood back and sides.

| 2000-2002 | | $1,700 | $2,200 |

000C-16RGTE
   2000-2010. Cutaway, rosewood back and sides.

| 2000-2010 | | $1,100 | $1,450 |

000C-16SGTNE
   2003-2006. Classical electric, nylon string, cutaway, mahogany body, 12-fret cedar neck, slotted headstock.

| 2003-2006 | | $1,150 | $1,500 |

000C-16SRNE
   2003-2005. Classical cutaway, rosewood body, 12-fret cedar neck, slotted headstock.

| 2003-2005 | | $1,150 | $1,500 |

000C-16T
   1996-1997. Sitka spruce top, mahogany back, sides and neck, rosewood 'board.

| 1996-1997 | | $1,000 | $1,300 |

000C-1E Auditorium
   1997-1999. Cutaway, mahogany back and sides, transducer pickup.

| 1997-1999 | | $850 | $1,125 |

000C-28 Andy Summers
   2006. Cutaway, rosewood back and sides, Buddhist Mudra inlays.

| 2006 | | $3,850 | $5,000 |

000C-28SMH Merle Haggard
   2001-2002. Cutaway, 12-fret neck, Blue Yodel No. 13 inlay.

| 2001-2002 | | $4,200 | $5,500 |

000CDB Dion The Wanderer
   2002. Cutaway acoustic/electric, 57 made, scalloped bracing, mahogany sides and back, slotted diamond and square markers, Dion logo on headstock, gloss black finish.

| 2002 | | $4,600 | $6,000 |

000CDG Doug Greth Commemorative Edition
   2011. Nylon string cutaway, slotted headstock, mahogany back and sides, 48 made.

| 2011 | | $1,625 | $2,100 |

000CJR-10E
   2019-present. Junior Series, 000JR-10 model with Fishman electronics.

| 2019-2021 | | $475 | $625 |

000CME
   1999-2002. Laminate back and sides, on-board electronics, satin finish.

| 1999-2002 | | $725 | $950 |

000CXE Black
   2003-2013. Acoustic-electric, cutaway, laminated body, black finish.

| 2003-2013 | | $500 | $650 |

000E Black Walnut Ambertone
   2020. Limited Edition, run of 125, sitka spruce top with gloss amber burst finish, satin black walnut back and sides, Fishman electronics.

| 2020 | | $1,550 | $2,000 |

GUITARS

MODEL YEAR	FEATURES	EXC. COND. LOW	HIGH

000-ECHF Bellezza Bianca
2005-2006. Eric Clapton and Hiroshi Fujiwara White Beauty model, Engleman spruce top, flamed Pacific big-leaf maple back and sides, model name logo on 20th fret, white finish, all-white case, 410 made. This and the Nera are examples of a 'collectible guitar' that is often found in near mint condition. High-end of price range shown is for near mint, nearly unplayed condition.

| 2005-2006 | | $3,000 | $4,000 |

000-ECHF Bellezza Nera
2004-2005. Eric Clapton and Hiroshi Fujiwara Black Beauty Model, 476 made, Italian Alpine spruce top, Indian rosewood back and sides, black finish.

| 2004-2005 | | $4,100 | $5,400 |

000-JBP Jimmy Buffett Pollywog
2003. Model name and number on label inside back, 168 made.

| 2003 | | $3,450 | $4,475 |

000JR-10
2019-present. Junior Series, sitka spruce top, sapele back and sides, satin finish.

| 2019-2021 | | $450 | $575 |

000-M
1997-2009. Road Series, mahogany or sapele back and sides.

| 1997-2009 | | $600 | $775 |

000-MMV Custom
2005-2018. Guitar Center model, spruce, rosewood, gloss finish.

| 2005-2018 | | $1,375 | $1,800 |

000RS1
2014-2018. Road Series, made in Mexico, sapele top, back and sides, Fishman Sonitone electronics. Replaced by 000-10E in '19.

| 2014-2018 | | $500 | $650 |

000RS2
2014-2015. Road Series as above with spruce top.

| 2014-2015 | | $500 | $650 |

000RS25 Navojoa 25th Anniversary
2014-2016. Made in Mexico, celebrates 25th Anniversary of Martin's Navojoa facility, headstock Anniversary logo, sitka spruce top, sapele back and sides, East Indian rosewood 'board.

| 2014-2016 | | $525 | $700 |

000X Hippie
2007. Limited Edition of 200, celebrates the 40th Anniversary of the 'Summer of Love'.

| 2007 | | $1,400 | $1,900 |

000X1
2000-2010. Mahogany grained HPL (high pressure laminate) back and sides, solid spruce top.

| 2000-2010 | | $350 | $450 |

000X1AE
2010-2019. 000X1 with electronics. Replaced by 000-X2E in '20.

| 2010-2019 | | $375 | $500 |

000-X2E
2020-present. X Series, sitka spruce top, figured mahogany laminate back and sides, Fishman electronics.

| 2020-2021 | | $500 | $650 |

000XE Black
2002-2005. Black satin finish.

| 2002-2005 | | $365 | $475 |

000XM Auditorium
1999-2002. Spruce top, Indian rosewood back and sides, natural finish.

| 1999-2002 | | $365 | $475 |

0000-1
1997-2001. 0000-size, mahogany.

| 1997-2001 | | $700 | $925 |

0000-18 Custom/Custom 0000-18 (Gruhn 35th Anniversary)
2005-2009. Commissioned for Gruhn Guitars 35th Anniversary, 1st year models have signed Anniversary labels, 16" lower bout, high X-brace, mahogany back and sides.

| 2005-2009 | | $2,400 | $3,100 |

0000-21S Custom (Gruhn 45th Anniversary)
2015. Commissioned for Gruhn Guitars 45th Anniversary, label signed by CF Martin IV and George Gruhn, Adirondack spruce top, Cocobolo or Guatemalan rosewood back and sides.

| 2015 | | $5,300 | $7,000 |

0000-28 Series
1997-2011. Several models, jumbo-size 0000 cutaway body, models include; H (herringbone trim, sitka spruce top), Custom (Indian rosewood, sitka), H-AG (Arlo Guthrie 30th anniversary, Indian rosewood, only 30 made), HA (herringbone trim, Adirondack).

1997-2000	0000-28H	$2,250	$2,950
1998-2006	0000-28 Custom	$2,250	$2,950
1999	0000-28H-AG	$2,250	$2,950
2011	0000-28HA	$2,250	$2,950

0000-38 (M-38)
1997-1998. Called M-38 in '77-'97 and '07-present (see that listing), 0000-size, Indian rosewood back and sides, multi-bound.

| 1997-1998 | | $2,800 | $3,600 |

1-17
1906-1917 (1st version), 1931-1934 (2nd version). First version has spruce top, mahogany back and sides, second version has all mahogany with flat natural finish.

| 1906-1934 | | $2,450 | $3,200 |

1-17P
1928-1931, 1939. Mahogany back and sides, plectrum neck, 272 made.

| 1928-1939 | | $1,450 | $1,900 |

1-18
1899-1903, 1906-1907, 1909-1921, 1923-1927. Brazilian rosewood or mahogany back and sides.

| 1899-1917 | Brazilian | $3,600 | $4,700 |
| 1918-1927 | Mahogany | $2,500 | $3,300 |

1-18H
1918. Hawaiian, only 3 made.

| 1918 | | $2,500 | $3,300 |

1-18K
1917-1919. Koa.

| 1917-1919 | | $4,400 | $5,700 |

1-18P
1929. 5-string plectrum, 1 made.

| 1929 | | $2,400 | $3,200 |

Martin 000-X2E

1890s Martin 1-21

Imaged by Heritage Auctions, HA.com

1930 Martin 2-17
Imaged by Heritage Auctions, HA.com

1890s Martin 2-24
Cody Lindsey

MODEL YEAR	FEATURES	EXC. COND. LOW	HIGH
1-18T			
	1927. Tenor 5-string, only 3 made.		
1927		$2,400	$3,200
1-20			
	1860s. Parlor guitar, rosewood back and sides.		
1867		$5,000	$6,500
1-21			
	1860s-1907, 1911, 1913-1921, 1925-1926. Initially offered in size 1 in the 1860s, ornate soundhole rings. A beautiful crack-free instrument is worth twice as much as a worn model with repaired cracks.		
1860s-1926		$5,000	$6,500
1-21P			
	1930. Plectrum.		
1930		$2,600	$3,400
1-22			
	1850s. Antique market value.		
1850s		$7,000	$9,200
1-26			
	1855, 1874, 1890, 1903. Rosewood back and sides, ivory-bound top, rope-style purfling, antique market value.		
1855-1903		$7,000	$9,200
1-27			
	1880s-1907, 1911, 1913-1921, 1925-1926. Antique market value.		
1880-1926		$7,000	$9,200
1-28			
	1880s-1904, 1906-1907, 1909, 1911-1920, 1923. Style 28 appointments including Brazilian rosewood back and sides, antique market value.		
1880s-1923		$7,000	$9,200
1-28P			
	1928-1930. Plectrum.		
1928-1930		$3,300	$4,300
1-30			
	1860s-1904, 1906-1907, 1911-1914, 1916-1917, 1919. Size 1 Style 30 with pearl soundhole trim, cedar neck, antique market value.		
1860s-1919		$7,200	$9,350
1-42			
	1858-1919. Rosewood back and sides, ivory-bound top and 'board.		
1858-1919		$9,700	$12,900
1-45			
	1904-1905, 1911-1913, 1919. Only 6 made, slotted headstock and Style 45 appointments.		
1904-1919		$20,800	$27,000
1/4 - 28			
	1973, 1979. 14 made.		
1973, 1979		$6,000	$7,800
2-15			
	1939-1964. All mahogany body, dot markers.		
1939-1964		$2,400	$3,100
2-17			
	1910, 1922-1934, 1936-1938. 1910 version has spruce top, mahogany back and sides. '22 on, all mahogany body, no body binding after '30.		
1867		$2,600	$3,400
1910		$2,450	$3,200
1922-1938		$2,450	$3,200

MODEL YEAR	FEATURES	EXC. COND. LOW	HIGH
2-17H			
	1927-1929, 1931. Hawaiian, all mahogany, 12 frets clear of body.		
1927-1931		$2,450	$3,200
2-17T			
	1927-1928. Tenor, 45 made.		
1927-1928		$1,450	$1,900
2-18			
	1857-1900, 1902-1903, 1907, 1925, 1929, 1934, 1938. Rosewood back and sides, changed to mahogany from 1917, dark outer binding, black back stripe, no dot inlay until 1902.		
1857-1938		$3,600	$4,700
2-18T			
	1928-1930. Tenor.		
1928-1930		$2,400	$3,200
2-20			
	1855-1897. Rare style only offered in size 2.		
1855-1897		$4,200	$5,500
2-21			
	1850s-1900, 1903-1904, 1909, 1925, 1928-1929. Rosewood back and sides, herringbone soundhole ring.		
1885-1929		$3,500	$4,600
2-21T			
	1928. Tenor.		
1928		$1,750	$2,300
2-24			
	1857-1898. Antique market value.		
1857-1898		$5,700	$7,500
2-27			
	1857-1880s, 1898-1900, 1907. Brazilian rosewood back and sides, pearl ring, zigzag back stripe, ivory bound ebony 'board and peghead.		
1857-1907		$6,800	$9,000
2-28			
	Brazilian rosewood back and sides, slot head.		
1880		$6,800	$9,000
2-28T			
	1928-1929. Tenor neck, Brazilian rosewood back and sides, herringbone top purfling.		
1928-1929		$4,000	$5,300
2-30			
	1874, 1902-1904, 1909-1910, 1921. Similar to 2-27, only 7 made.		
1874-1921		$7,000	$9,100
2-34			
	1850s-1898. Similar to 2-30.		
1850s-1898		$7,400	$9,700
2-40			
	1850s-1898, 1909.		
1850s-1898		$7,900	$10,300
2-42			
	1858-1900.		
1874		$9,200	$12,000
2-44			
	1930. Style 44, Olcott-Bickford Soloist custom order, only 4 made.		
1930		$15,700	$20,900
2-45T			
	1927-1928. Tenor style 45, 2 made.		
1927-1928		$8,300	$11,000

The *Vintage Guitar Price Guide* shows low to high values for items in all-original excellent condition, and, where applicable, with original case or cover.

MODEL YEAR	FEATURES	EXC. COND. LOW	HIGH

2 1/2-17
1856-1897, 1909, 1911-1914. The first Style 17s were small size 2 1/2 and 3, these early models use Brazilian rosewood.

1856-1914		$2,575	$3,375

2 1/2-18
1865-1898, 1901, 1909-1914, 1916-1923. Parlor-size body with Style 18 appointments.

1865-1917	Brazilian	$3,200	$4,200
1918-1923	Mahogany	$2,600	$3,500

2 1/2-21
1880s, 1909, 1911-1913, 1917-1921. Brazilian rosewood back and sides.

1880s-1921		$3,400	$4,500

2 1/2-42
1880s, 1911. Style 42 size 2 1/2 with Brazilian rosewood. Only 1 made 1911.

1880s-1911		$9,200	$12,000

3-17
1856-1897, 1908 (1 made). The first Style 17s were small size 2 1/2 and 3. The early models use Brazilian rosewood, spruce top, bound back, unbound ebony 'board.

1856-1870s	Brazilian	$2,600	$3,400
1880s-1908	Mahogany	$2,300	$3,000

3-21
1885. Brazilian rosewood.

1885		$3,400	$4,500

3-24
1860. Brazilian rosewood.

1860		$5,600	$7,300

3-34
1860. Brazilian rosewood.

1860		$7,200	$9,500

5-15
2003-2007. Sapele or mahogany body, shorter scale.

2003-2007		$1,050	$1,400

5-15T
1949-1963. Tenor neck, all mahogany, non-gloss finish.

1927-1930		$1,500	$1,950
1949-1963		$1,175	$1,525

5-16
1962-1963. Mahogany back and sides, unbound rosewood 'board.

1962-1963		$2,100	$2,700

5-17
1912-1914, 1916, 1927-1928, 1930-1931, 1933-1943. Special order 1912-'36, standard production '37-'43.

1912-1916		$2,100	$2,800
1927-1928		$3,200	$4,200
1930-1939		$2,450	$3,200
1940-1943		$2,325	$3,050

5-17T
1949-1958. Tenor neck, all mahogany.

1949-1958		$1,450	$1,900

5-18
1898-1899, 1912-1914, 1917, 1919-1921, 1923-1924, 1926-1932, 1934-1937, 1940-1941, 1943-1962, 1965, 1968-1977, 1979-1981, 1983-1989. Rosewood back and sides (changed to mahogany from 1917 on), 12 frets, slotted headstock.

1898-1917		$3,300	$4,300
1919-1921		$2,300	$3,100
1923-1937		$4,000	$5,300
1940-1946		$3,900	$5,100
1948-1949		$3,800	$5,000
1950-1959		$3,700	$4,900
1960-1962		$3,000	$4,000
1965		$2,700	$3,600
1966-1969		$2,300	$3,000
1970-1979		$1,900	$2,500
1980-1989		$1,725	$2,300

5-18 Marty Robbins
2009-2011. Custom Edition, 12-fret, Adirondack top, mahogany back and sides.

2009-2011		$2,050	$2,700

5-18T
1940, 1954, 1960-1961. Tenor, only 1 made each year.

1940		$1,650	$2,200
1954		$1,375	$1,800
1960-1961		$1,175	$1,550

5-21
1890s, 1902, 1912-1914, 1916-1920, 1927, 1977. Rosewood back and sides.

1890s-1977		$3,500	$4,600

5-21T
1927-1928. Tenor guitar with 21-styling.

1927-1928		$1,700	$2,300

5-28
1901-1902, 1904, 1918, 1920-1921, 1923, 1935, 1939, 1969-1970, 1977, 1980-1981, 1988, 2001-2002. Special edition, 1/2-size parlor guitar, rosewood back and sides.

1901-1923		$3,500	$4,600
1935-1939		$6,100	$7,900
1969-1988		$4,900	$6,400
2001-2002		$2,400	$3,200

7-28
1980-1995, 1997-2002. 7/8-body-size of a D-model, Style 28 appointments.

1980-1989		$2,400	$3,200
1990-2002		$2,100	$2,800

7-37K
1980-1987. 7/8-size baby dreadnought acoustic, koa back and sides, spruce top, oval soundhole.

1980-1987		$2,300	$3,000

Alternative II Resophonic
2004-2007. Textured aluminum top, matching headstock overlay, high pressure laminate sides and back, spun aluminum cone resonator, Fishman pickup.

2004-2007		$600	$800

Alternative X
2001-2013. OO-Grand Concert body shape, textured aluminum top, matching headstock overlay, spun aluminum cone resonator, Fishman pickup.

2001-2013		$600	$800

Alternative X Midi
2003-2004. Roland GK Midi pickup with 13-pin output, additional Fishman Prefix Pro pickup and preamp system, requires Roland GA-20 interface.

2003-2004		$650	$850

Alternative XT
2002-2005. Alternative with DiMarzio humbucker, volume & tone controls, coil tap, Bigsby.

2003-2005		$600	$800

1880s Martin 2 1/2-21
Imaged by Heritage Auctions, HA.com

1950 Martin 5-18
David Stone

Martin CEO-7

America's Guitar 175th Anniversary

2008. D-style, 14-fret, Adirondack spruce top, Madagascar rosewood sides and back, 175 made, 'America's Guitar' headstock inlay, '175th Anniversary 1833-2008'.

2008	$4,700	$6,200

ASD-41 Australian Series

2005. Tasmanian Blackwood sides and back, Sitka spruce top, Australian theme appointments and label.

2005	$3,900	$5,100

Backpacker

1992-present. Small-bodied travel guitar, nylon called Classical Backpacker.

1992-2022	Steel strings	$125	$225
1994-2021	Nylon strings	$120	$155

Backpacker 25th Anniversary

2017 only. Sapele.

2017	$200	$275

Bentley Snowflake First Edition

2021-present. Custom Shop Limited Edition, sitka spruce top, Madagascar rosewood back and sides, exclusive Wilson A. Bentley (photomicrography) snowflake images for neck and pickguard inlays.

2021-2022	$10,000	$13,000

Bigsby/Martin D-28 Bigsby

2018-2019. Martin partnered with Gretsch to build, Merle Travis inspired, sitka spruce top, East Indian rosewood back and sides, Bigsby headstock, natural finish.

2018-2019	$2,700	$3,600

C-1

1931-1942. Acoustic archtop, mahogany back and sides, spruce top, round hole until '33 (449 made), f-holes appear in '32 (786 made), bound body, sunburst.

1931-1933	Round hole	$2,700	$3,600
1932-1942	F-hole	$2,700	$3,500

C-1-12

1932. Only 1 made, 12-string version.

1932	$2,700	$3,500

C-1P

1931-1933, 1939. Archtop, plectrum.

1931-1933	Round hole	$1,900	$2,500
1939	F-hole	$1,900	$2,500

C-1R Humphrey

1997-2000. Solid cedar top, laminated rosewood back and sides, satin finish.

1997-2000	$1,000	$1,300

C-1T

1931-1934, 1936-1938. Archtop, tenor, round hole (71 made) or f-hole (83 made).

1931-1933	Round hole	$1,900	$2,500
1933-1938	F-hole	$1,900	$2,500

C-2

1931-1942. Acoustic archtop, Brazilian rosewood back and sides, carved spruce top, round hole until '33 (269 made), f-holes appear in '32 (439 made), zig-zag back stripe, multi-bound body, slotted-diamond inlay, sunburst.

1931-1933	Round hole	$3,900	$5,100
1932-1942	F-hole	$3,000	$4,000

C-2-12

1932. Only 1 made, 12-string version.

1932	$3,000	$4,000

Martin CS-Bluegrass-16

C-2P

1931. Archtop, plectrum, round hole, 2 made.

1931	$2,800	$3,700

C-2T

1931-1936. Archtop, tenor, round or f-hole.

1931-1934	Round hole	$2,700	$3,600
1934-1936	F-hole	$2,000	$2,600

C-3

1931-1934. Archtop, Brazilian rosewood back and sides, round soundhole until early '33 (53 made), f-holes after (58 made).

1931-1933	Round hole	$5,800	$7,600
1933-1934	F-hole	$4,600	$6,000

C-3T

1933. Archtop, tenor, 1 made.

1933	$3,800	$5,000

Car Talk Special Edition

2008-2010. D-size, East Indian rosewood back and sides, car parts and tools inlay, Car Talk credits on 'guard.

2008-2010	$3,700	$4,900

CEO Series

1997-present. Chief Executive Officer (C.F. Martin IV), Special Edition (CEO-1 through CEO-6) and Custom Signature Edition (CEO-7 through CEO-9), various woods and specs. CEO-1/1R ('97-'98), 2 ('98), 3 ('99-'00), 4 ('01-'04), 4R ('02-'10), 5 ('01-'04), 6 ('11-'13), 7 ('15-present), 8 ('15-'17), 8.2/E ('17-'18), 9 ('19-present).

1997-2016	CEO-1 to CEO-6	$1,800	$2,400
2014-2022	CEO-7	$1,800	$2,400
2015-2017	CEO-8	$2,800	$3,700
2017-2018	CEO-82	$3,800	$4,900
2017-2018	CEO-82E	$2,600	$3,400

CF-1 American Archtop

2004-2009. 17", solid maple sides, laminated maple back, ebony 'board, dot markers, 1 pickup, sunburst, natural or black.

2004-2009	$2,300	$3,100

CF-2 American Archtop

2004-2009. CF-1 with 2 humbuckers, sunburst, natural or black.

2004-2009	$2,450	$3,200

Claire's Guitar

2005-2006. Made to celebrate the birth of Claire Frances Martin, limited to 100, small parlor size, sitka spruce top, Brazilian rosewood back and sides, fancy appointments, comes with pink-lined hard case.

2005-2006	$4,600	$6,000

Concept III

2003. U.S.-made, solid spruce top, solid mahogany back and sides, cutaway, on-board electronics, sparkle-mist finish.

2003	$1,725	$2,250

Cowboy 2015 Limited Edition/LE Cowboy 2015

2015. Limited to number sold in '15, 000, 12-fret, sitka spruce top, solid Goncalo Alves back and sides, cowboy on horse artwork by William Matthews.

2015	$3,100	$4,100

MODEL YEAR FEATURES	EXC. COND. LOW	HIGH

Cowboy 2016 Limited Edition/LE Cowboy 2016

2016. Limited to number sold in '16, auditorium, 12-fret, sitka spruce top, mahogany back and sides, cowboy on bucking bronco artwork by William Matthews.

2016	$3,100	$4,100

Cowboy Series

2000-2009. Models include Cowboy X (2000, 250 made), Cowboy II ('01, 500 made), Cowboy III ('03, 750 made), and Cowboy IV ('05-'06, 250 made), Cowboy V ('06-'09, 500 made).

2001-2009 Various models	$700	$1,300

CS-21-11

2011. Limited Edition, 171 made, Madagascar rosewood.

2011	$3,900	$5,100

CS-Bluegrass-16

2016-2020. Limited to 100, Adirondack spruce top, Guatemalan rosewood back and sides, vintage gloss finish.

2016-2020	$4,400	$5,700

CS-CF Martin Outlaw-17

2017-2020. Limited to 100 made, Adirondack spruce top, mahogany back and sides, natural gloss finish.

2017-2020	$4,000	$5,300

CSN (Gerry Tolman Tribute)

2007-2009. Crosby, Stills & Nash, CSN logo on headstock, D-style, high-end appointments, East Indian rosewood back and sides. Tolman was CSN's longtime manager and was killed in car wreck in '06.

2007-2009	$2,125	$2,775

C-TSH (Humphrey/Martin)

1997-2002. Designed by classical guitar luthier Thomas Humphrey, based on his Millenium model, arched Englemann spruce top, rosewood back and sides.

1997-2002	$2,300	$3,100

Custom 15

1991-1994. Renamed HD-28V Custom 15 in ca. 2001.

1991-1994	$2,700	$3,500

Custom D Classic Mahogany

2006-2014. D body, spruce top, mahogany back and sides.

2006-2014	$725	$950

Custom D Classic Rosewood

2006-2011. D body, spruce top, rosewood back and sides.

2006-2011	$725	$950

Custom Shop 18 Style 0000

2019-2020. Adirondack, Sinker mahogany back and sides, Sinker is old growth from 1900-1920, specs can vary.

2019-2020	$2,600	$3,500

Custom Shop 18 Style Dreadnought

2019-2020. Adirondack, Sinker mahogany back and sides, specs can vary.

2019-2020	$2,600	$3,500

Custom Shop 18 Style OM

2020. Adirondack, Sinker mahogany back and sides, 14-fret, specs can vary.

2020	$2,500	$3,300

Custom Shop 28 Style Dreadnought

2020. Adirondack, Indian rosewood back and sides.

2020	$3,100	$4,100

Custom Shop 28 Style OM

2020. Adirondack, Indian rosewood back and sides, sunburst or natural.

2020	$2,900	$3,800

D-1 (D-18)

1931. Name first used for the prototype of the D-18, made in 1931.

1931	$83,000	$109,000

D-1

1992-2005, 2009. Current model with mahogany body, A-frame bracing, available as an acoustic/electric.

1992-2005	$725	$950
2009 Reintroduced	$725	$950

D12-1

1996-2001. Mahogany, satin finish, 12-string.

1996-2001	$700	$900

D-1 Authentic 1931

2016-2019. Adirondack spruce top, dark mahogany back and sides, Vintage Gloss finish.

2016-2019	$4,500	$5,900

D-1E

1994-1998, 2009. Acoustic/electric version, current model solid sitka with sapele.

1994-1998	$775	$1,025
2009	$775	$1,025

D-1GT

2011-2014. Double bound body, gloss finish top, satin back and sides.

2011-2014	$700	$925

D-1R

1994-2003, 2012. D-1 with laminated rosewood back and sides.

1994-2003	$700	$925
2012 Reintroduced	$700	$925

D-1RE

1994-1995, 1998. D-1R with various electronics.

1994-1998	$775	$1,000

D-2

1931-1932, 1934. Earliest version of the D-28, Brazilian rosewood.

1931-1934	$250,000	$328,000

D-2R

1996-2002. Style 28 appointments, laminated rosewood back and sides, natural satin finish.

1996-2002	$700	$900

D-3-18

1991. Limited Edition, run of 80, sitka spruce top, 3-piece mahogany back.

1991	$1,600	$2,100

D-3R

1996-2002. Style 35 appointments, laminated rosewood back and sides, natural satin finish.

1996-2002	$775	$1,000

D-10E

2019-present. Road Series, updated version of DSR1/DSR2, sitka spruce or sapele top, sapele back and sides, Fishman electronics, satin finish.

2019-2021	$450	$600

1993 Martin D-1

Imaged by Heritage Auctions, HA.com

Martin D-10E

Martin D-13E

1988 Martin D-16
Bernunzio Uptown Music

MODEL YEAR	FEATURES	EXC. COND. LOW	HIGH

D-11E
2019. Road Series, sitka spruce top, solid sapele back and sides, Fishman.

| 2019 | | $600 | $800 |

D-12E
2019-present. Sitka spruce top, sapele back and sides, Fishman.

| 2019-2021 | | $800 | $1,050 |

D-12E Koa
2020. Sitka spruce top, koa veneer back and sides, gloss finish.

| 2020 | | $1,050 | $1,350 |

D12 David Crosby
2009-2011. D-size 12-string, quilted mahogany body, Carpathian spruce top.

| 2009-2011 | | $3,700 | $4,800 |

D-13E
2019-present. Updated version of DRSG, sitka spruce top, siris back and sides, Fishman.

| 2019-2021 | | $800 | $1,050 |

D-15/D-15M
1997-present. Body is all mahogany up to 2002, mahogany or sapele (which is like mahogany) up to '10. Becomes the all-mahogany D-15M in '11.

| 1997-2010 | | $925 | $1,200 |
| 2011-2021 | M | $925 | $1,200 |

D-15M Burst
2015-2018. Shaded mahogany top, back and sides, satin finish.

| 2015-2018 | | $950 | $1,250 |

D-15M Elderly Instruments 40th Anniversary
2012. Only 10 made, solid mahogany body, special appointments, label signed by Elderly president Stan Werbin and Chris Martin.

| 2012 | | $1,000 | $1,300 |

D-15M StreetMaster
2017-present. Distressed mahogany satin finish.

| 2017-2021 | | $925 | $1,200 |

D-15S
2001-2009. Slotted headstock D-15, body is solid sapele or mahogany.

| 2001-2009 | | $925 | $1,200 |

D-16 Adirondack
2009-2013. Adirondack spruce top, mahogany back and sides.

| 2009-2013 | | $1,500 | $1,950 |

D-16 Lyptus
2003-2005. Lyptus back and sides.

| 2003-2005 | | $1,000 | $1,300 |

D-16A
1987-1990. North American ash back and sides, scalloped bracing.

| 1987-1990 | | $1,200 | $1,600 |

D-16E Burst
2019-2021. Mahogany burst ovangkol gloss top, satin ovangkol back and sides, Fishman electronics.

| 2019-2021 | | $1,500 | $1,950 |

D-16E Rock The Vote
2019-2021. Special Edition, designed by David Crosby, custom artwork by Robert F. Goetzl, sitka spruce gloss top, satin sycamore back and sides, Fishman electronics.

| 2019-2021 | | $1,725 | $2,250 |

D-16E Rosewood
2019-2021. Gloss sitka spruce top, satin East Indian rosewood back and sides, Fishman electronics.

| 2019-2021 | | $1,375 | $1,800 |

D-16E/D-16E Mahogany
2017-present. Gloss sitka spruce top, satin sycamore back and sides, Fishman electronics. Mahogany in '20.

| 2017-2021 | | $1,275 | $1,675 |
| 2020 | Mahogany | $1,275 | $1,675 |

D-16GT
1999-2019. D-16 with gloss top.

| 1999-2019 | | $875 | $1,125 |

D-16GTE
1999-2015. D-16GT with Fishman electronics.

| 1999-2015 | | $1,000 | $1,300 |

D-16H (1991, 1992, 1993)
1990-1994. D-16 with herringbone soundhole ring, replaced by D-16T in '94.

| 1990-1994 | | $1,150 | $1,500 |

D-16K Koa
1986. Koa back and sides.

| 1986 | | $1,525 | $1,975 |

D-16M Mahogany
1986-1990. Mahogany back and sides.

| 1986-1990 | | $1,000 | $1,300 |

D-16O Oak
1999. Red oak or white oak, 4 made.

| 1999 | | $1,000 | $1,300 |

D-16R 50th Anniversary
2010. Adirondack spruce top, rosewood back and sides, natural.

| 2010 | | $1,775 | $2,300 |

D-16R/D-16TR/D-16TRG
1995-2009. Spruce top, Indian rosewood back and sides, satin finish (R), gloss (TR) or full gloss (TRG).

| 1995-2009 | | $875 | $1,125 |

D-16RGT
1999-2019. D-16 T specs with rosewood back and sides, gloss finish.

| 1999-2019 | | $875 | $1,125 |

D-16RGT Ryman Auditorium
2007. Custom designed by George Gruhn, oak 'guard, headplate and fret markers made from original Ryman Auditorium pews, laser-etched image of Ryman on headplate, spruce top, Indian rosewood back and sides, special Ryman label.

| 2007 | | $2,775 | $3,600 |

D-16T/D-16TG
1994-1998. Mahogany back and sides, satin finish (T) or gloss (TG).

| 1994-1998 | T | $950 | $1,250 |
| 1995-1997 | TG | $875 | $1,125 |

D-16W Walnut
1987, 1990. Walnut back and sides.

| 1987, 1990 | | $875 | $1,125 |

MODEL YEAR	FEATURES	EXC. COND. LOW	HIGH

D-17

2001-2005. All solid mahogany back, sides and top, natural brown mahogany finish.

2001-2005		$875	$1,125

D-17E

2002-2003. With on-board electronics.

2002-2003		$950	$1,250

D-17M

2013-2016. Shaded spruce top, solid mahogany back and sides.

2013-2016		$875	$1,125

D-18

1931-present. Standard Series, mahogany back and sides, spruce top, black back stripe, 12-fret neck, changed to 14 frets in '34.

1931-1934	12-fret	$67,000	$90,000
1934	14-fret, dark top	$60,000	$80,000
1934-1937	14-fret	$60,000	$80,000
1938	Early '38, Advanced X	$53,000	$70,000
1938	Late '38, Rear X	$41,000	$54,500
1939	Early '39, 175 neck	$35,500	$47,500
1939	Late '39, 168 neck	$33,700	$44,800
1940-1941		$27,000	$36,000
1942-1944	Scalloped	$24,500	$32,500
1944-1946	Non-scalloped	$17,800	$23,600
1947-1949		$9,200	$12,200
1950-1959		$6,550	$8,700
1960-1964		$4,900	$6,550
1965		$4,550	$5,900
1966-1969		$3,700	$5,000
1970-1979		$2,650	$3,450
1980-1989		$2,200	$2,900
1983	50th Ann 1833-1983	$2,200	$2,900
1990-1999		$2,200	$2,900
2000-2021		$1,900	$2,450

D12-18

1973-1995. Mahogany back and sides, 12 strings, 14 frets clear of body, solid headstock.

1973-1979		$1,875	$2,450
1980-1989		$1,575	$2,050
1990-1995		$1,575	$2,050

CS-D18-12

2012-2014. Custom Shop, based on 1929 Ditson 111 (12-string), 75 made, 12-fret mahogany neck, Adirondack spruce top, Madagascar rosewood binding.

2012-2014		$3,600	$4,700

D-18 1955 CFM IV

2010. Celebrates C. F. Martin IV birthday, 55 made.

2010		$3,075	$3,975

D-18 75th Anniversary Edition

2009. '75th Anniversary Edition 1934-2009' noted on label and headstock stencil.

2009		$3,000	$4,000

D-18 Andy Griffith

2003. Bear claw spruce top, Andy's script signature on 18th fret.

2003		$2,650	$3,450

D-18 Authentic 1937

2006-2012. Authentic pre-war specs, Adirondack spruce, forward X-brace and scalloped Adirondack bracing, 14-fret neck.

2006-2012		$4,600	$6,000

D-18 Authentic 1939

2013-present. Adirondack spruce top, mahogany back, sides and neck, ebony 'board, vintage gloss finish.

2013-2019		$4,600	$6,000
2019-2021	VTS	$4,600	$6,000

D-18 Authentic 1939 Aged

2020-present. New design, Torrefied Adirondack.

2020-2021		$3,800	$4,900

D-18 Custom Adirondack

2016. Adirondack spruce top, mahogany back and sides.

2016		$2,600	$3,500

D-18 Del McCourey 50th Anniversary

2008. Adirondack spruce top, mahogany sides and back, interior label signed by Del McCourey, 50 made.

2008		$3,500	$4,600

D-18 Modern Deluxe

2019-present. Sitka spruce top with Vintage Tone System (VTS), mahogany back and sides, gloss finish.

2019-2021		$2,100	$2,700

D-18 Special

1989. Guitar of the Month, 28 made, first Martin to use rosewood for binding, heel cap and endpiece since 1932, scalloped top, mahogany back and sides, slotted-diamond markers.

1989		$2,450	$3,200

D-18CW Clarence White Commemorative Edition

2001. Rare Appalachian spruce top, 2-piece quilted mahogany back and sides, Clarence White's signature between 19th - 20th frets, aged gloss lacquer finish.

2001		$3,000	$4,000

D-18D

1975. Frap pickup.

1975		$2,200	$2,900

D-18DC David Crosby

2002. David Crosby signature at 20th fret, Englemann spruce top, quilted mahogany back and sides, 250 made.

2002		$2,900	$3,900

D-18E

1958-1959. D-18 factory built with DeArmond pickups which required ladder bracing (reducing acoustic volume and quality).

1958-1959		$7,000	$9,200

D-18E 2020

2020. Limited Edition, 2,020 offered, sitka spruce top, mahogany back and sides, electronics, gloss finish.

2020		$2,200	$2,900

D-18E Modern Deluxe

2020-2021. Torrified sitka spruce top, Fishman electronics.

2020-2021		$2,500	$3,250

D-18E Retro

2012-2019. Sitka spruce top, mahogany back and sides.

2012-2019		$1,900	$2,450

1947 Martin D-18
Folkway Music

1952 Martin D-18
Ian Gilmour

GUITARS

1968 Martin D-12-20
W. H. Stephens

1956 Martin D-21
David Stone

MODEL YEAR	FEATURES	EXC. COND. LOW	HIGH
D-18GE Golden Era			
1995, 2000-2016. 1995 version is a copy of a '37 D-18, 272 made. The current model is based on '34 model, natural or sunburst.			
1995		$2,850	$3,700
2000-2016		$2,850	$3,700
D-18GE Golden Era 1934 Special Edition			
1999-2012. Specs from '34 D-18, red Adirondack spruce top, mahogany back and sides, aged finish.			
1999-2012		$2,850	$3,700
D-18H			
1934-1935. Hawaiian.			
1934-1935		$60,000	$78,300
D-18H Huda			
1966. Huda wood, Hawaiian, 2 made.			
1966		$3,700	$4,800
D-18LE			
1986-1987. Limited Edition, quilted or flamed mahogany back and sides, scalloped braces, gold tuners with ebony buttons.			
1986-1987		$2,850	$3,700
D-18MB			
1990. Limited Edition Guitar of the Month, flame maple binding, Engelmann spruce top signed by shop foremen, X-brace, total of 99 sold.			
1990		$2,300	$3,000
D-18P			
2010-2011. Fishman electronics.			
2010-2011		$2,000	$2,600
D-18S			
1967-1994. Mahogany back and sides, 12-fret neck, slotted headstock, majority of production before '77, infrequent after that.			
1967-1969		$4,200	$5,500
1970-1979		$3,000	$3,900
1980-1989		$2,500	$3,300
1990-1994		$2,500	$3,300
D-18SS			
2009-2012. 24.9" short scale.			
2009		$2,000	$2,600
D-18V/D-18 Vintage			
1985 (V), 1992 (Vintage). Low-profile neck, scalloped braces, bound, total of 218 sold, Guitar of the Month in '85, Vintage Series in '92.			
1985	V	$2,350	$3,100
1992	Vintage	$2,350	$3,100
D-18VE			
2004-2007. D-18 V with Fishman Ellipse.			
2004-2007		$2,500	$3,250
D-18VM/D-18V/D-18VO			
1995-2011. Vintage Series, 14-fret, mahogany (M) back and sides, tortoise binding, V-neck. M dropped from name in '99. Natural finish. 48 sunburst (D-18VO) made in '95.			
1995	VO	$2,400	$3,100
1995-1998	VM	$2,400	$3,100
1999-2011	V	$2,400	$3,100
D-18VMS/D-18VS			
1996-2011. Vintage Series, 12-fret version of D-18 VM/V, M dropped from name in '99.			
1996-1999	VMS	$2,400	$3,100

MODEL YEAR	FEATURES	EXC. COND. LOW	HIGH
2000-2011	VS	$2,400	$3,100
D-19			
1977-1988. Deluxe mahogany dreadnought, optional mahogany top, multi-bound but unbound rosewood 'board.			
1977-1979		$2,650	$3,450
1980-1988		$2,200	$2,900
D12-20			
1964-1991. Mahogany back and sides, 12 strings, 12 frets clear of body, slotted headstock.			
1964-1969		$2,125	$2,750
1970-1979		$1,775	$2,325
1980-1991		$1,550	$2,000
D-21			
1955-1969. Brazilian rosewood back and sides, rosewood 'board, chrome tuners.			
1955-1959		$10,000	$13,300
1960-1964		$8,600	$11,400
1965		$7,300	$9,700
1966-1969		$6,800	$9,000
D-21 Special/D-21S			
2008-2020. Sitka spruce top, Indian rosewood back and sides, herringbone soundhole.			
2008-2020		$2,150	$2,850
D-21JC Jim Croce Signature			
1999-2000. Jim Croce signature and 1973 dime inlaid on neck, Indian rosewood back and sides, 73 made.			
1999-2000		$4,400	$5,800
D-21JCB Jim Croce Limited Edition			
1999-2001. Same as above but with Brazilian rosewood back and sides.			
1999-2001		$8,800	$11,500
D-21LE			
1985. Limited Edition, 75 made.			
1985		$2,200	$2,900
D-25K			
1980-1989. Dreadnought-size, koa back and sides, spruce top.			
1980-1989		$2,450	$3,200
D-25K2			
1980-1989. Same as D-25K, but with koa top and black 'guard.			
1980-1989		$2,450	$3,200
D-28			
1931-present. Brazilian rosewood back and sides (changed to Indian rosewood in '70), '36 was the last year for the 12-fret model, '44 was the last year for scalloped bracing, '47 was the last year herringbone trim was offered, natural. Ultra high-end D-28 Martin guitar (pre-'47) valuations are very sensitive to structural and cosmetic condition. Finish wear and body cracks for ultra high-end Martin flat-tops should be evaluated on a case-by-case basis. Small variances within the 'excellent condition' category can lead to notable valuation differences.			
1931-1936	12-fret	$217,000	$289,000
1934-1937	14-fret	$132,000	$175,000
1938	Early '38, Advanced X	$131,000	$174,000
1938	Late '38, Rear X	$126,000	$167,000
1939	Early '39, 175 neck	$124,000	$165,000

MODEL YEAR	FEATURES	EXC. COND. LOW	HIGH
1939	Late '39, 168 neck	$112,000	$149,000
1940-1941		$81,000	$106,000
1942	Scalloped	$81,000	$106,000
1943	Scalloped	$73,000	$95,000
1944	Scalloped, herringbone	$64,000	$85,000
1944-1945	Herringbone, non-scalloped	$33,000	$44,000
1946-1947	Early '47, herring-bone, non-scalloped	$31,000	$40,000
1947-1949	Late '47, non-herringbone	$15,000	$20,000
1950-1952		$12,000	$16,000
1953-1957	Kluson	$12,000	$16,000
1958-1959	Grover	$12,000	$16,000
1960-1962		$8,700	$11,500
1963-1964		$8,500	$11,100
1965		$7,500	$10,000
1966-1969	Brazilian	$7,000	$9,300
1970-1979	Indian	$3,150	$4,100
1980-1989		$2,350	$3,050
1990-1999		$2,300	$3,000
2000-2009		$2,000	$2,600
2010-2017	Standard X	$2,000	$2,600
2018-2021	Forward-shifted X	$2,050	$2,650

D12-28
1970-2018. Indian rosewood back and sides, 12 strings, 14 frets clear of body, solid headstock.

1970-1979		$2,350	$3,100
1980-1989		$2,000	$2,600
1990-1999		$2,000	$2,600
2000-2018		$2,000	$2,600

D-28 1935 Special
1993. Guitar of the Month, 1935 features, Indian rosewood back and sides, peghead with Brazilian rosewood veneer.

1993		$3,000	$4,000

D-28 1955 CFM IV
2009-2010. Limited Edition, 55 made celebrating Chris Martin IV birthyear 1955, Madagascar rosewood.

2009-2010		$3,900	$5,000

D-28 50th Anniversary
1983. Stamped inside '1833-1983 150th Anniversary', Indian rosewood back and sides.

1983		$2,375	$3,100

D-28 75th Anniversary
2009 only. Limited production celebrating 1934 to 2009, Madagascar rosewood back and sides, Adirondack spruce top.

2009		$5,100	$6,700

D-28 75th Anniversary Brazilian
1983. Brazilian rosewood back and sides.

1983		$9,000	$12,000

D-28 150th Anniversary
1983-1985. Limited production of 268, only '83 vintage have the anniversary stamp, Brazilian rosewood sides and back.

1983	150th stamp	$9,000	$12,000
1984-1985	No stamp	$9,000	$12,000

D-28 Authentic 1931
2013-2015. Adirondack spruce top, Madagascar rosewood back and sides, authentic '31 appointments, vintage gloss finish.

2013-2015		$5,500	$7,200

D-28 Authentic 1937
2007-2009, 2014-present. '37 specs, 50 made of first Brazilian rosewood batch. Reintroduced '14 with Madagascar rosewood and Vintage Tone System (VTS).

2007-2009	Brazilian	$16,700	$21,700
2014-2021	Madagascar	$5,700	$7,400
2020-2021	VTS aged	$5,000	$6,600

D-28 Authentic 1941
2013-2016. Adirondack, Madagascar rosewood.

2013-2016		$5,700	$7,400

D-28 Custom
1984. Guitar of the Month Nov. '84, double bound D-body, multi-ring rosette, rosewood back/sides, spruce top, 43 made.

1984		$3,200	$4,200

D-28 Dan Tyminski
2010-2013. Custom Artist limited edition, Indian rosewood back and sides, Adirondack spruce top, other bracing specs.

2010-2013		$3,100	$4,100

D-28CW/CWB Clarence White
2003-2014. CW has Indian rosewood back and sides, the CWB Brazilian, only 150 CWBs were to be built.

2003-2004	CWB	$7,300	$9,500
2003-2014	CW	$3,600	$4,700

D-28D
1975. Frap pickup.

1975		$3,150	$4,100

D-28DM Del McCourey Signature
2003. Limited edition of 115, natural.

2003		$3,100	$4,100

D-28E
1959-1964. Electronics, Brazilian rosewood back and sides, 2 DeArmond pickups, natural.

1959-1964		$7,700	$10,000

D-28E Modern Deluxe
2020-2021. Sitka spruce VTS aged top, East Indian rosewood back and sides, Fishman electronics, gloss finish.

2020-2021		$3,600	$4,700

D-28 Elvis Presley
2008-2010. Carpathian spruce top, East Indian rosewood back and sides.

2008-2010		$4,200	$5,400

D-28 Elvis Presley CVR
2008-2010. Carpathian spruce top, East Indian rosewood back and sides, tooled leather cover.

2008-2010		$5,200	$6,800

D-28 John Lennon
2017-2018. Custom Signature Edition, sitka spruce top with Vintage Tone System, East Indian rosewood back and sides, back inlaid with a peace sign, Lennon's self-portrait illustration beneath Martin logo on headstock.

2017-2018		$2,850	$3,800

1937 Martin D-28
Ranger Doug

1952 Martin D-28
Bernunzio Uptown Music

Martin D-28 LF Lester Flatt

1965 Martin D-35

Greg Perrine

D-28 John Lennon 75th Anniversary

2016. Limited Edition to commemorate Lennon's 75th birthday (10/9/2015), 75 made, Adirondack spruce top, Madagascar rosewood back and sides, headplate includes Lennon's famous self-portrait illustration.

2016	$8,600	$11,000

D-28 John Prine

2017-2020. Custom Signature Edition, only 70 offered, Engelmann spruce top, Madagascar rosewood back and sides, inlaid pearl angel wings on headstock.

2017-2020	$4,000	$5,200

D-28 Louvin Brothers

2015-2020. Limited run of 50, sitka spruce top, East Indian rosewood back and sides, printed Louvin Brothers artwork from "Satan is Real" album.

2015-2020	$2,450	$3,200

D-28 Marquis

2004-2017. Golden Era appointments, Adirondack top, Indian rosewood, natural or sunburst.

2004-2017	Natural	$3,200	$4,200
2004-2017	Sunburst	$3,200	$4,200
2007-2009	Madagascar option	$3,200	$4,200

D-28 Modern Deluxe

2019-present. Sitka spruce top with Vintage Tone System (VTS), East Indian rosewood back and sides, gloss finish.

2019-2021	$2,500	$3,300

D-28 Museum Edition 1941

2009-2012. Based on '41 model located in Martin's PA museum, Adirondack spruce top, Madagascar rosewood back and sides, natural finish.

2009-2012	$5,000	$6,500

D-28 Rich Robinson

2022. Custom Signature Edition, styled from Robinson's '54 D-28, sitka spruce top, East Indian rosewood back and sides, aged vintage gloss finish.

2022	$5,000	$6,600

D-28GE Golden Era

1999-2005. GE Golden Era, Brazilian rosewood, herringbone trim.

1999-2005	$8,000	$10,500

D-28HW Hank Williams

1998. Limited Edition, 150 made, replica of Hank Williams' 1944 D-28, Brazilian rosewood sides and back, scalloped braces, herringbone.

1998	$7,500	$10,000

D-28KTBS Bob Shane

2003. Bob Shane of the Kingston Trio, Signature Edition with 51 offered, sitka spruce top, East Indian rosewood back and sides, The Kingston Trio logo between 11th-13th frets, Shane's pearl signature 19th-20th frets.

2003	$3,800	$5,000

D-28LF Lester Flatt

1998. Limited Edition, 50 made, Brazilian rosewood.

1998	$7,500	$10,000

D-28LSH

1991. Guitar of the Month, Indian rosewood back and sides, herringbone trim, snowflake inlay, zigzag back stripe.

1991	$2,700	$3,500

D-28LSV

1999-2005. Large soundhole model.

1999-2005	$2,300	$3,000

D-28M Elvis Presley

2008-2010. Limited Edition, 175 made, Madagascar rosewood back and sides, Adirondack top, tooled leather cover.

2008-2010	$6,700	$8,800

D-28M Merle Travis

2008-2010. 100 made, Adirondack top, Madagascar rosewood back and sides, curly maple neck, 6-on-a-side Bigsby-style headstock, heart-diamond-spade-club inlays.

2008-2010	$4,900	$6,400

D-28M The Mamas and The Papas

2012-2014. Custom Artist, 100 made, Madagascar rosewood back and sides.

2012-2014	$2,800	$3,600

D-28P

1988-1990, 2011-2012. P indicates low-profile neck, Indian rosewood back and sides. Reintroduced 2011 with high performance neck.

1988-1990	$2,200	$2,900
2011-2012	$2,200	$2,900

D-28S

1954-1994. Rosewood back and sides, 12-fret neck.

1954-1959	Special order	$14,000	$18,200
1960-1965	Special order	$9,800	$12,800
1966-1969	Brazilian	$9,800	$12,800
1970-1979	Indian	$3,500	$4,600
1980-1989		$2,700	$3,500
1990-1994		$2,650	$3,450

D-28SW Wurlitzer

1962-1965, 1968. Made for the Wurlitzer Co.

1962-1965	$9,000	$12,000
1968	$9,000	$12,000

D-28V

1983-1985. Limited Edition, Brazilian rosewood back and sides, herringbone trim, slotted diamond inlay.

1983-1985	$6,700	$8,800

D-35

1965-present. Brazilian rosewood sides and 3-piece back, changed to Brazilian wings and Indian center in '70, then all Indian rosewood in '71, natural with sunburst option. For a brief time, on the back side, the center panel was Brazilian and the two side panels were Indian.

1965	Brazilian	$7,500	$10,000
1966-1970	Brazilian	$7,000	$9,300
1970	Center panel only	$3,500	$4,600
1970-1979	Indian	$3,200	$4,200
1980-1989		$2,450	$3,200
1983	150th center strip	$2,450	$3,200
1990-1999		$2,350	$3,100
2000-2021		$2,100	$2,700
2015	50th Anniv Label	$2,100	$2,700

D12-35

1965-1995. Brazilian rosewood back and sides, changed to Indian rosewood in '70, 12 strings, 12 frets clear of body, slotted headstock.

1965-1969	Brazilian	$5,100	$6,700

The Official Vintage Guitar magazine Price Guide 2023   **Martin** D12-35 50th Ann. L.E. — D-41A Turbo Mandolin Brothers   **293**

GUITARS

MODEL YEAR	FEATURES	EXC. COND. LOW	HIGH
1970-1979	Indian	$2,400	$3,200
1980-1989		$2,100	$2,750
1990-1995		$2,100	$2,750

D12-35 50th Anniversary Limited Edition

2015-2016. Limited to 183 (the quantity of 1st production run in '65), European spruce top, 3-piece East Indian rosewood back and sides, natural gloss finish.

2015-2016		$4,400	$5,800

D-35 30th Anniversary

1995. Limited Edition, 207 made, D-35 with '1965-1995' inlay on 20th fret, gold hardware.

1995		$3,800	$5,000

D-35 Bicentennial

1975-1976. Limited Edition, 197 made, sitka spruce top, 3-piece Indian rosewood back, eagle inlay on headstock, 13 star inlay on 'board.

1975-1976		$3,600	$4,800

D-35 Ernest Tubb

2003. Indian rosewood back and sides, special inlays, 90 built.

2003		$3,100	$4,100

D-35 Seth Avett

2013-2019. Swiss spruce top, East Indian rosewood/ flamed koa back, copper snowflake inlay.

2013-2019		$2,600	$3,400

D-35E Retro

2012-2019. Sitka spruce top, East Indian rosewood back and sides.

2012-2019		$2,200	$2,900

D-35JC Johnny Cash

2006-present. Rosewood back and sides.

2006-2021		$3,700	$4,800

D-35MP

2011-2012. Madagascar rosewood back and sides, high performance neck.

2011-2012		$2,100	$2,700

D-35P

1986-1990. P indicates low-profile neck.

1986-1990		$2,300	$3,000

D-35S

1966-1993. Brazilian rosewood back and sides, changed to Indian rosewood in '70, 12-fret neck, slotted peghead.

1966-1969	Brazilian	$10,000	$13,000
1970-1979	Indian	$3,700	$4,800
1980-1989		$2,900	$3,700
1990-1993		$2,550	$3,600

D-35SW Wurlitzer

1966, 1968. Made for the Wurlitzer Co., Brazilian rosewood.

1966, 1968		$10,000	$13,000

D-35V

1984. Limited Edition, 10 made, Brazilian rosewood back and sides.

1984		$7,000	$9,200

D-37K

1980-1994. Dreadnought-size, koa back and sides, spruce top.

1980-1994		$2,900	$3,800

D-37K2

1980-1994. Same as D-37 K, but has a koa top and black 'guard.

1980-1994		$2,900	$3,800

D-37W Lucinda Williams

2003. Only 4 made, never put into production, Aztec pearl inlay favored by Lucinda Williams, quilted mahogany sides and back.

2003		$4,000	$5,200

D-40

1997-2005. Indian rosewood back and sides, hexagon inlays.

1997-2005		$2,400	$3,200

D-40BLE

1990 Limited Edition Guitar of the Month, Brazilian rosewood back and sides, pearl top border except around 'board

1990		$7,800	$10,200

D-40DM Don McLean

1998. Only 50 made, Englemann spruce top.

1998		$6,000	$8,000

D-40FMG

1995-1996. Figured mahogany back and sides, 150 made.

1995-1996		$4,400	$5,800

D-40FW Limited Edition

1996. Figured claro walnut sides and back, 'Limited Edition D-40FW' label, 148 made.

1996		$3,000	$3,900

D-40QM Limited Edition

1996. Limited Edition, 200 made, quilted maple body.

1996		$2,800	$3,700

D-41

1969-present. Brazilian rosewood back and sides for the first ones in '69 then Indian rosewood, bound body, scalloped braces, natural.

1969	Brazilian	$20,700	$27,000
1970-1979	Indian	$3,900	$5,100
1980-1989		$3,400	$4,400
1990-1999		$3,400	$4,400
2000-2009		$3,400	$4,400
2010-2021		$3,400	$4,400

D12-41

1970-1994. Very few made, special order after '93, 12-string, 14-fret.

1970-1994		$3,500	$4,600

D-41 Porter Wagoner

2008-2011. Custom Artist series, Indian rosewood back and sides.

2008-2011		$2,900	$3,800

D-41 Special

2004-2011. D-41 with snowflake inlays.

2004-2011		$3,400	$4,400

D-41A Turbo Mandolin Brothers

2011, 2013. Two Custom Shop models made for Mandolin Bros., Adirondack top. Similar except 10 40th Anniversary models which have abalone and pearl mandolin 12th-fret inlay and label signed by Stan Jay and Chris Martin.

2011		$3,400	$4,400

1974 Martin D12-35
Peter Van Wagner

1968 Martin D-35S
David Stone

2000 Martin D-42
Rivington Guitars

*Martin D-42 Purple
Martin Flamed Myrtle*

MODEL YEAR	FEATURES	EXC. COND. LOW	HIGH

D-41BLE
1989. Limited Edition Guitar of the Month, Brazilian rosewood back and sides, pearl top border except around 'board.

1989		$7,300	$9,600

D-41DF Dan Fogelberg
2001. 141 made, East Indian rosewood back and sides, hexagon 'board inlays, pearl snowflakes inlaid on bridge.

2001		$5,400	$7,100

D-41E
1971. Indian rosewood.

1971		$4,100	$5,300

D-41GJ George Jones
2001. Style 41 appointments, limited edition of 100, label signed by the Opossum.

2001		$3,900	$5,100

D-41K Purple Martin
2013-2020. Limited to 50 with labels signed by C.F. Martin IV, highly flamed koa back and sides, purple martin-inspired inlay on 'board, bridge, and 'guard.

2013-2020		$8,700	$11,300

D-41S/SD-41S
1970-1994. Sunburst, Indian rosewood, 12-fret neck, slotted peghead.

1970-1979		$4,600	$6,000
1980-1994		$3,900	$5,200

D-42
1973-1988, 1995-present. Limited production '73-'88, Indian rosewood back and sides, spruce top, pearl rosette and inlays, snowflake 'board inlays, gold tuners, gloss finish.

1973-1988		$4,600	$6,000
1995-2021		$4,200	$5,400

D-42E
1996-2008. With Fishman Ellipse VT pickup system.

1996-2008		$4,350	$5,650

D-42 Amazon Rosewood Limited Edition
2007. Limited to 35, Amazon rosewood is similar to Brazilian rosewood but a different species.

2007		$4,500	$5,900

D-42 Flamed Mahogany
2006. Adirondack, figured mahogany, 30 made with tree-of-life inlay.

2006		$7,000	$9,100

D-42 Peter Frampton
2006-2007. Indian rosewood back and sides, Style 45 features.

2006-2007		$5,500	$7,200

D-42 Purple Martin Flamed Myrtle
2018-2021. Flamed myrtle back and sides, limited to 100 made.

2018-2021		$10,600	$13,800

D-42AR (Amazon Rosewood)
2002-2003. Limited to 30 made, Amazon rosewood is similar to Brazilian rosewood but a different species.

2002-2003		$4,500	$5,900

D-42JC Johnny Cash
1997. Rosewood back and sides, gloss black lacquer on body and neck, Cash signature inlaid at 19th fret, have label signed by Cash and C.F. Martin IV, 80 sold.

1997		$5,500	$7,200

MODEL YEAR	FEATURES	EXC. COND. LOW	HIGH

D-42K Limited Edition
1998. Limited production, highly flamed koa back and sides, sitka top with aging toner, high X-brace design, 45-style abalone snowflake inlays.

1998		$4,200	$5,400

D-42K/D-42K2
1998-2006. K has koa back and sides, the all koa body K2 was discontinued in '05.

1998-2006	D-42K	$4,200	$5,400
2000-2005	D-42K2	$4,200	$5,400

D-42LE
1988 only. Limited Edition (75 sold), D-42-style, scalloped braces, low profile neck.

1988		$4,200	$5,400

D-42SB
2006-2007. Sunburst finish, sitka spruce top, 45-style appointments.

2006-2007		$4,300	$5,600

D-42V
1985. Vintage Series, 12 made, Brazilian rosewood, scalloped braces.

1985		$7,900	$10,300

D-45
1933-1942 (96 made), 1968-present. Brazilian rosewood back and sides, changed to Indian rosewood during '69. The pre-WW II D-45 is one of the holy grails. A pre-war D-45 should be evaluated on a case-by-case basis. The price ranges are for all-original guitars in excellent condition and are guidance pricing only. These ranges are for a crack-free guitar. Unfortunately, many older acoustics have a crack or two and this can make ultra-expensive acoustics more difficult to evaluate than ultra-expensive solidbody electrics. Technically, a repaired body crack makes a guitar non-original, but the vintage market generally considers a professionally repaired crack to be original. Crack width, length and depth can vary, therefore extra attention is suggested.

1936-1938		$440,000	$570,000
1939	Early, wide neck	$440,000	$570,000
1939	Late, thin neck	$380,000	$495,000
1940-1942		$344,000	$448,000
1968		$39,000	$52,000
1969	Brazilian	$39,000	$52,000
1970-1979		$7,200	$9,500
1980-1989		$7,100	$9,300
1990-1999		$6,500	$8,500
2000-2017		$6,500	$8,500
2018-2021	New specs	$6,500	$8,500

D12-45
1970s-1987. Special order instrument, not a standard catalog item, with D-45 appointments, Indian rosewood.

1970-1979		$5,500	$7,300
1980-1987		$5,200	$6,800

D-45 100th Anniversary Limited Edition
1996. Label reads '1896-1996 C.F. Martin Commemorative Anniversary Model'.

1996		$6,500	$8,500

D-45 150th Anniversary
1983. Brazilian rosewood back and sides, sitka spruce top, '150th' logo stamp.

1983		$13,000	$17,000

MODEL YEAR	FEATURES	EXC. COND. LOW	HIGH

D-45CFMB CMR Sr. (200th Anniversary, Brazilian)

1996. Commemorating the 200th Anniversary of C.F. Martin Sr. birthday, Brazilian rosewood back and sides, style 45 Deluxe pearl bordering, fossilized ivory nut and saddle, 14-fret neck, gold hardware.

1996		$13,000	$17,000

D-45CFM CMR Sr. (200th Anniversary, East Indian)

1996. Commemorating the 200th Anniversary of C.F. Martin Sr. birthday, East Indian rosewood back and sides, style 45 pearl bordering, bone nut and saddle, 14-fret neck, gold hardware.

1996		$6,500	$8,500

D-45 (1939 Reissue Mandolin Brothers)

1990. Commissioned by Mandolin Brothers, 5 made, figured Brazilian rosewood. Original name "The Reissue 1939 Martin D-45." Said to be the first reissue of the era and the seed for the '90s Martin Custom Shop.

1990		$13,000	$17,000

D-45 (1939 Reissue)

1992. High-grade spruce top, figured Brazilian rosewood back and sides, high X and scalloped braces, abalone trim, natural, gold tuners.

1992		$13,000	$17,000

D-45 Celtic Knot

2004-2005. Brazilian rosewood, Celtic knot 'board inlays, 30 built.

2004-2005		$21,000	$27,000

D-45 Custom Shop

1984, 1991-1992. Various options and models, Indian rosewood back and sides in '84, then Brazilian rosewood.

1984	Indian	$6,600	$8,600
1991-1992	Brazilian	$14,200	$18,500

D-45 Deluxe

1993 only. Guitar of the Month, Brazilian rosewood back and sides, figured spruce top, inlay in bridge and 'guard, tree-of-life inlay on 'board, pearl borders and back stripe, gold tuners with large gold buttons, total of 60 sold.

1993		$16,800	$21,900

D-45 Deluxe CFM Sr. (200th Anniversary, Brazilian)

1996. Commemorating the 200th Anniversary of C.F. Martin Sr. birthday, 91 made, Brazilian rosewood back and sides, style 45 Deluxe pearl bordering, fossilized-ivory nut and saddle, 14-fret neck, gold hardware.

1996		$13,200	$17,200

D-45 Gene Autry

1994 only. Gene Autry inlay (2 options available), natural.

1994	Gene Autry 'board	$20,000	$26,000
1994	Snowflake 'board option	$20,000	$26,000

D-45 Marquis

2006-2008. Rosewood back and sides.

2006-2008		$7,600	$9,900

D-45 Mike Longworth Commemorative Edition

2004-2006. East Indian rosewood back and sides, Adirondack spruce top, 91 made, label signed by Mike's wife Sue and C.F. Martin IV.

2004-2006		$8,100	$10,600

D-45 Woodstock 50th Anniversary

2019-2020. Limited Edition, run of 50, East Indian rosewood back and sides, abalone inlay, Woodstock dove on headstock, '1969-2019' on 'board, peace sign on heelcap.

2019-2020		$9,500	$12,500

D-45B Brazilian

1994. Brazilian rosewood.

1994		$13,000	$17,000

D-45E Aura

2010. With Fishman Electronics Ellipse Aura technology.

2010		$6,600	$8,600

D-45E Retro

2013-2019. East Indian rosewood, Fishman.

2013-2019		$7,400	$9,600

D-45GE Golden Era

2001-2004. 167 made, '37 specs, Brazilian rosewood.

2001-2004		$21,700	$28,300

D-45K

2006-2008. Flamed koa back and sides.

2006-2008		$6,600	$8,600

D-45KLE

1991. Limited Edition koa, Engelmann, bear claw, 54 made.

1991		$6,600	$8,600

D-45LE

1987. Limited Edition, 44 made, Guitar of the Month, September '87.

1987		$14,700	$19,100

D-45S Authentic 1936

2013-present. Adirondack spruce top, Vintage Tone System, Brazilian rosewood back and sides, '36 style appointments and specs.

2013-2021		$41,000	$53,800

D-45S Deluxe

1992. Limited Edition, 50 made, Indian rosewood, spruce top, high-end appointments.

1992		$8,000	$10,500

D-45S/SD-45S

1969-1994. Brazilian rosewood back and sides in '69, Indian rosewood after, 12-fret neck, S means slotted peghead, only 50 made.

1969	Brazilian	$43,000	$56,000
1970-1979	Indian	$9,000	$11,700
1980-1994	Indian	$8,000	$10,500

D-45SS Steven Stills

1998. Brazilian rosewood back and sides, 91 made.

1998		$27,000	$35,000

D-45V Brazilian

1983. Brazilian rosewood back and sides, scalloped braces, snowflake inlay, natural.

1983		$13,200	$17,200

1968 Martin D-45
Wayne Stephens

Martin D-45S Authentic 1936

2002 Martin D-50 Deluxe
Imaged by Heritage Auctions, HA.com

2017 Martin D-200 Deluxe

MODEL YEAR	FEATURES	EXC. COND. LOW	HIGH

D-45VR/D-45V

1997-2020. Vintage specs, Indian rosewood back and sides, vintage aging toner, snowflake inlay. Name changed to D-45V in '99 (not to be confused with Brazilian rosewood D-45V of the '80s).

1997-1998	VR	$7,100	$9,300
1999-2020	V	$7,100	$9,300

D-50 Deluxe/D-50DX

2001-2003. Deluxe limited edition, 50 made, one of the most ornate Martin models ever made, Brazilian rosewood back and sides, highly ornate pearl inlay.

2001-2003		$36,000	$46,700

D-50K Deluxe/D-50K2 Deluxe

2003-2006. As D-50 Deluxe with ornate pearl inlay and highly flamed koa back and sides (K, 45 made) or highly flamed koa top, back and sides (K2, 5 made).

2003-2006	K Deluxe	$29,700	$38,500
2003-2006	K2 Deluxe	$29,700	$38,500

D-60

1989-1995. Birdseye maple back and sides, snowflake inlays, tortoiseshell binding and 'guard.

1989-1995		$2,300	$3,000

D-62

1987-1995. Flamed maple back and sides, chrome-plated enclosed Schaller tuners.

1987-1995		$2,300	$3,000

D-62LE

1986. Limited Edition, Guitar of the Month October '86, flamed maple back and sides, spruce top, snowflake inlays, natural.

1986		$2,300	$3,000

D-64

1985-1995. Flamed maple top, low profile neck.

1985-1995		$2,300	$3,000

D-76 Bicentennial Limited Edition

1975-1976. Limited to 200 made in '75 and 1,976 made in '76, Indian rosewood back and sides, 3-piece back, herringbone back stripe, pearl stars on 'board, eagle on peghead.

1975-1976		$3,600	$4,800

D-93

1993. Mahogany, spruce, 93 pertains to the year, not a style number.

1993		$2,300	$3,000

D-100 Deluxe

2004. Limited Edition, guitars have the first 50 sequential serial numbers following the millionth Martin guitar (1,000,001 to 1,000,050), fancy pearl inlay on back, 'guard, headstock, 'board and bridge. Herringbone top and rosette inlay, Adirondack spruce top, Brazilian rosewood back and sides.

2004		$36,000	$48,000

D-200 Deluxe

2017-present. Celebration of Martin's two-millionth serial number, limited to 50 offered, watch-themed highly decorative, comes with renowned watchmaker Roland G Murphy watch with matching serial no., premium case has built-in hygrometer.

2017-2021		$93,000	$121,000

D-222 100th Anniversary

2016. Commemorates 100th anniversary of the dreadnought, limited to 100, sitka spruce top, mahogany back and sides, ivoroid binding, slotted headstock.

2016		$3,000	$4,000

D-420

2017-2019. Top with custom legal weed illustration by artist Robert Goetzl, mahogany back and sides.

2017-2019		$1,700	$2,200

DJr / DJrE

2015-2018. Dreadnought Junior, sitka spruce top, sapele back and sides. DJrE with Fishman electronics.

2015-2018	No electronics	$300	$390
2015-2018	With electronics	$360	$470

DJr-10 / DJr-10E

2020-present. Dreadnought Junior, thinner 000-sized body, sitka spruce or sapele top, satin sapele back and sides. Fishman electronics available (DJr-10E).

2020-2022	No electronics	$330	$425
2020-2022	With electronics	$375	$500

DJr-10E StreetMaster

2021-present. Dreadnought Junior with thinner body and tapered neck, Fishman electronics, dark mahogany finish.

2021-2022		$450	$575

DC Series

1980s-2021. Dreadnought cutaway versions, E models have electronics, GT is gloss top, R indicates rosewood back and sides. Replaced by DC-X Series starting in '20.

1981-1997	DC-28	$2,400	$3,100
1996-2000	DC-1	$600	$800
1996-2010	DC-1E	$675	$875
1997-2000	DCM	$575	$750
1997-2005	DC-1M	$575	$750
1997-2006	DCME	$625	$800
1998	DCXM	$450	$575
1998-2001	DCXME	$450	$575
1998-2010	DC-15E	$675	$875
1999-2000	DC-1R	$600	$800
2000	DCRE	$625	$800
2000-2013	DCX1E	$450	$575
2001-2005	DCXE Black	$450	$575
2002-2003	DC-16RE	$725	$950
2003-2005	DC-16GTE Premium	$1,100	$1,450
2003-2016	DC-16GTE	$925	$1,200
2003-2019	DC-16E	$925	$1,200
2004-2013	DCX1KE	$450	$575
2004-2013	DCX1RE	$450	$575
2005	DC Trey Anastasio	$4,600	$6,000
2005	DC-16RE Aura	$750	$975
2005	DC-16RGTE Aura	$1,050	$1,350
2005-2007	DC-16E Koa	$950	$1,250
2005-2008	DC-16RGTE	$1,000	$1,300
2005-2010	DC-Aura	$2,200	$2,800
2006-2019	DC-28E	$2,100	$2,700
2009-2016	DCPA1/ DCPA1 Plus	$1,925	$2,500
2011	DCPA2/DCPA3	$1,050	$1,375

MODEL YEAR	FEATURES	EXC. COND. LOW	HIGH
2011-2016	DCPA4 Shaded	$975	$1,275
2011-2017	DCPA4 Rosewood	$1,125	$1,450
2013-2016	DCPA5	$450	$575
2013-2016	DCPA5 Black	$450	$575
2013-2016	DCPA5K Koa	$450	$575
2016-2019	DC-15ME	$675	$875
2016-2019	DC-35E	$2,200	$2,800
2017-2018	DCRSG	$775	$1,025
2017-2019	DC-18E	$2,000	$2,550
2017-2019	DCPA4	$975	$1,275
2017-2019	DCX1AE/ DCX1AE Macassar	$425	$550
2017-2019	DCX1RAE	$450	$575
2019-2021	DC-13E	$575	$750

DC-X Series
2020-present. Replaces the DC Series, dreadnought models with various woods, some with electronics.

2020-2022	DC-X2E	$550	$725

Ditson Dreadnaught 111
2007-2009. Based on 1929 Ditson 111, 12-fret neck, slot head, mahogany back and sides, Brazilian rosewood binding.

2007-2009		$4,100	$5,300

DM
1996-2009. Solid sitka spruce top, laminated mahogany back and sides, dot markers, natural satin.

1996-2009		$525	$675

DM-12
1996-2009. 12-string DM.

1996-2009		$525	$675

DM3MD Dave Matthews
Three-piece back of Indian rosewood, African padauk center wedge, Englemann spruce top, high-end appointments.

1999-2001		$5,000	$6,600

Doobie-42 Tom Johnston
2007. Signature Edition, D-42 style, 35 made, solid Indian rosewood back and sides, abalone and catseye markers, other special appointments.

2007		$4,700	$6,100

DR
1997-2008. Road Series Dreadnought, rosewood back and sides.

1997-2008		$575	$750

DR Centennial LE
2016-2020. Limited Edition celebrates '100 Years of the Dreadnought', Adirondack, East Indian rosewood, antique white binding, satin finish.

2016-2020		$1,925	$2,500

DRS1 (Road/1 Series)
2011-2019. D-size, sapele top, back and sides, satin finish, Fishman. Replaced by D-10E in '19.

2011-2019		$500	$650

DRS2 (Road/1 Series)
2012-2018. DRS1 with spruce top. Replaced by D-10E in '19.

2012-2018		$550	$700

DRSG
2017-2018. Sitka spruce top, siris back and sides, Fishman Sonitone. Replaced by D-13E in '19.

2017-2018		$725	$950

DRSGT
2014-2015. Sitka spruce top, sapele back and sides, Fishman with USB port.

2014-2015		$575	$750

DSR Sugar Ray
2003. Limited Edition of 57 made, D-17 style, all mahogany, signed by C.F. Martin IV and all members of Sugar Ray band.

2003		$4,100	$5,300

DSS-17
2018-present. Slope-shoulder dreadnought, sitka spruce top, mahogany back and sides with antique white binding, satin Black Smoke or Whiskey Sunset Burst.

2018-2019	Black Smoke	$1,050	$1,400
2019-2021	Whiskey Sunset	$1,050	$1,400

DVM Veterans
2002-2008. D-style, spruce top, rosewood back and sides, special veterans ornamentation.

2002-2008		$2,115	$2,750

Dwight Yoakam DD28
2017-2018. Custom Signature Edition, sitka spruce top, East Indian rosewood back and sides, inlaid mother-of-pearl and recon stone playing cards.

2017-2018		$3,350	$4,350

DX 175th Anniversary
2008. Rosewood HPL back and sides, founder's picture on top.

2008		$400	$525

DX Johnny Cash
2019-present. D-sized, Jett black HPL top, back and sides, custom 'board inlaid with stars and CASH logo, Cash's signature on rosette and label, Fishman electronics.

2019-2021		$475	$625

DX Series
1996-2020. D-size, high pressure wood laminate (HPL) backs and sides, exterior wood-grain image with gloss finish. M is for mahogany wood-grain, R rosewood and K koa. A 1 indicates a solid spruce top with Series 1 bracing, otherwise top is wood-patterned HPL. C indicates cutaway and E Fishman Presys Plus and AE Fishman Sonitone. Replaced by D-X Series starting in '20.

1996-2009	DXM / DMX	$375	$475
1998-2012	DXME	$375	$475
1999-2000	D12XM 12-String	$375	$475
1999-2019	DXMAE	$375	$475
2000-2014	DX1 / DX1E	$350	$450
2000-2019	DX1AE	$375	$475
2001-2009	DX1R	$375	$475
2002-2009	DXK2	$375	$475
2004-2009	DX1K	$375	$475
2008-2010	D12X1 12-String	$375	$475
2010-2020	DX1KAE	$375	$475
2011-2019	D12X1AE 12-String	$400	$525
2014-2019	DXAE Black	$375	$475
2014-2020	DXK2AE	$375	$475
2015-2019	DX1RAE	$375	$475
2017	DX420	$850	$1,125
2017-2019	DX2AE Macassar	$375	$475

Martin DC-X2E

2002 Martin DX121
Johnny Zapp

Martin GPC-13E

Martin F-65

Bill Ruxton

MODEL		EXC. COND.	
YEAR	FEATURES	LOW	HIGH

D-X Series
2020-present. New spec dreadnought models to replace the DX Series. Various options, woods and finishes.
2020-2022	D-X1E	$400	$525
2020-2022	D-X2E	$475	$625
2020-2022	D-X2E 12-String	$475	$625

E-18
1979-1983. Offset double-cut, maple and rosewood laminate solidbody, 2 DiMarzio pickups, phase switch, natural.
| 1979-1983 | | $1,700 | $2,200 |

E-28
1980-1983. Double-cut electric solidbody, carved top, ebony 'board, 2 humbuckers.
| 1980-1983 | | $1,800 | $2,300 |

EM-18
1979-1983. Offset double-cut, maple and rosewood laminate solidbody, 2 exposed-coil humbucking pickups, coil split switch.
| 1979-1983 | | $1,700 | $2,200 |

EMP-1
1998-1999. Employee series designed by Martin employee team, cutaway solid spruce top, ovangkol wood back and sides with rosewood middle insert (D-35-style insert), on-board pickup.
| 1998-1999 | | $1,950 | $2,525 |

EMP-2 Limited Edition
1999. D size, tzalam body, flying saucer inlays.
| 1999 | | $1,950 | $2,525 |

F-1
1940-1942. Archtop, mahogany back and sides, carved spruce top, multi-bound, f-holes, sunburst, 91 made.
| 1940-1942 | | $2,375 | $3,075 |

F-1-12
1941. F-1 12 string.
| 1941 | | $2,550 | $3,325 |

F-2
1940-1942. Carved spruce top, maple or rosewood back and sides, multi-bound, f-holes, 46 made.
| 1940-1942 | | $2,700 | $3,500 |

F-5
1940. 2 made.
| 1940 | | $5,000 | $6,400 |

F-7
1935-1939, 1941-1942. Brazilian rosewood back and sides, f-holes, carved top, back arched by braces, multi-bound, sunburst top finish.
| 1935-1938 | | $7,000 | $9,300 |
| 1941-1942 | | $6,500 | $8,650 |

F-9
1935-1942. Highest-end archtop, Brazilian rosewood, Martin inlaid vertically on headstock, 7-ply top binding, 45-style back strip, sunburst.
| 1935-1942 | | $14,800 | $19,700 |

F-50
1961-1965. Single-cut thinline archtop with laminated maple body, 1 pickup.
| 1961-1965 | | $1,575 | $2,050 |

F-55
1961-1965. Single-cut thinline archtop with laminated maple body, 2 pickups.
| 1961-1965 | | $2,900 | $3,800 |

F-65
1961-1965. Electric archtop, double-cut, f-holes, 2 pickups, square-cornered peghead, Bigsby, sunburst.
| 1961-1965 | | $2,900 | $3,800 |

Felix The Cat
2004-2010. Felix the Cat logo art, Don Oriolo logo, red body, Felix gig bag.
2004	Felix I, 756 made	$475	$625
2005-2006	Felix II, 625 made	$475	$625
2007-2010	Felix III, 1000 made	$475	$625

GCD-16CP (Guitar Center)
1998. 15 5/8" Style D.
| 1998 | | $1,700 | $2,200 |

GPC Series
2010-present. Standard Series (GPC-), Performing Artist (GPCPA) and X Series (GPCX), Grand Performance size, cutaway, acoustic/electric, various woods.
2010-2016	GPCPA1/Plus	$2,000	$2,575
2011	GPCPA2	$1,250	$1,625
2011-2012	GPCPA3	$1,250	$1,625
2012-2016	GPCPA5K Koa	$450	$575
2013-2016	GPCPA4	$975	$1,275
2013-2016	GPCPA5	$450	$575
2013-2016	GPCPA5 Black	$450	$575
2013-2019	GPC12PA4 12-string	$1,025	$1,350
2013-2019	GPCPA4 Rosewood	$1,100	$1,425
2013-2019	GPCPA4 Sapele	$1,250	$1,625
2016-2018	GPC-35E	$2,400	$3,100
2016-2020	GPC-18E	$2,150	$2,800
2016-2020	GPC-28E	$2,300	$3,000
2017-2018	GPC-15ME	$1,100	$1,425
2017-2018	GPCRSG	$775	$1,025
2017-2018	GPCRSGT	$625	$825
2017-2018	GPCXAE Black	$400	$525
2017-2019	GPCX1RAE	$425	$550
2017-2021	GPCX1AE	$425	$550
2017-2021	GPCX2AE Macassar	$425	$550
2017-2022	GPC-X2E	$550	$725
2019-2022	GPC-11E	$725	$950
2019-2022	GPC-13E	$850	$1,125
2020-2021	GPC-16E Rosewood	$1,450	$1,875
2020-2022	GPC-16E	$1,375	$1,800

Grand J12-40E Special
2009-2011. J12-40 with D-TAR Multi-source electronics.
| 2009-2011 | | $2,850 | $3,700 |

Grand J-28LSE
2011-2014. Baritone.
| 2011-2014 | | $2,300 | $3,000 |

Grand J-35E
2009-2011. Grand jumbo size, rosewood back and sides.
| 2009-2011 | | $2,300 | $3,000 |

Grand Ole Opry/HDO Grand Ole Opry
1999-2007. Custom Shop Limited Edition, 650 made, 'Grand Ole Opry 75th Anniversary' on neck block, WSM microphone headstock logo, off-white

MODEL YEAR	FEATURES	EXC. COND. LOW	HIGH

Micarta fingerboard, sitka spruce top, East Indian rosewood back and sides.

| 1999-2007 | | $2,900 | $3,800 |

Gruhn 50th Anniversary 0000 (Custom Shop)

2020. Celebrates Gruhn Guitar 50 years in business, interior label signed by George Gruhn, 12- or 14-fret, limited to 50 each in natural or sunburst.

| 2020 | | $5,500 | $7,200 |

GT-70

1965-1966. Electric archtop, bound body, f-holes, single-cut, 2 pickups, tremolo, burgundy or black finish.

| 1965-1966 | | $2,450 | $3,200 |

GT-75

1965-1967. Electric archtop, bound body, f-holes, double-cut, 2 pickups, tremolo, burgundy or black finish. There is also a 12-string version.

| 1965-1967 | | $2,775 | $3,600 |

Hawaiian X

2002-2004. Hawaiian scene painted on top, similar to the Cowboy guitar model, limited edition of 500.

| 2002-2004 | | $625 | $825 |

HD-7 Roger McGuinn

2005-2008. Rosewood back and sides, herringbone top trim, 7-string with double G.

| 2005-2008 | | $3,100 | $4,100 |

HD12-28

2018-present. Sitka spruce top, East Indian rosewood back and sides, natural.

| 2018-2021 | | $1,825 | $2,900 |

HD-16R Adirondack

2008-2016. Rosewood back and sides, Adirondack top.

| 2010-2016 | | $1,600 | $2,075 |

HD-16R LSH

2007-2013. Indian rosewood (R), large sound hole (LSH).

| 2007-2013 | | $1,600 | $2,075 |

HD-18JB Jimmy Buffett

1998. 424 made, solid mahogany back and sides, herringbone trim, palm tree headstock logo, Style 42 markers, Buffett pearl signature.

| 1998 | | $5,300 | $6,900 |

HD-18LE

1987. Indian rosewood.

| 1987 | | $2,150 | $2,800 |

HD-28

1976-present. Standard Series, Indian rosewood back and sides, scalloped bracing, herringbone purfling.

1976-1979		$3,300	$4,300
1980-1989		$2,550	$3,250
1990-1999		$2,400	$3,200
2000-2017	Last Standard X	$2,400	$3,200
2018-2021	Forward X	$2,400	$3,200

HD-28 1935 Special

1993. 'HD-28 1935 Special' model name on label.

| 1993 | | $2,700 | $3,500 |

HD-28 2R

1991, 1993-1997. 2R specification for 2 herringbone soundhole rings, larger soundhole.

| 1991-1997 | | $2,400 | $3,200 |

HD-28 Custom 150th Anniversary

1983. 150th Anniversary, Martin Custom Shop, Indian rosewood sides and back, '1833-1983 150th Year' stamped on inside backstrip.

| 1983 | | $2,700 | $3,500 |

HD-28 Custom/Custom HD-28

1994. Custom Shop model.

| 1994-1995 | | $2,500 | $3,300 |

HD-28AWB Custom

2008-2013. Elderly Instruments Custom model, Adirondack spruce top, rosewood back and sides, white-bound body, gloss natural finish.

| 2008-2013 | | $2,850 | $3,700 |

HD-28BLE

1990. Guitar of the Month, 100 made, Brazilian rosewood back and sides, herringbone soundhole ring, low profile neck (LE), chrome tuners, aging toner finish.

| 1990 | | $6,300 | $8,300 |

HD-28BSE

1987-1999. Brazilian rosewood, 93 made.

| 1987-1999 | | $6,300 | $8,300 |

HD-28CTB

1992. Guitar of the Month, herringbone top trim/ back stripe, fancy peghead inlay, tortoise binding, gold hardware, label signed by CF Martin IV.

| 1992 | | $2,500 | $3,300 |

HD-28E Retro

2013-2019. Solid sitka spruce top, East Indian rosewood back and sides.

| 2013-2019 | | $2,000 | $2,900 |

HD-28GM

1989. Grand Marquis, Guitar of the Month, scalloped braced Sitka spruce top with 1930s-era bracing pattern that replaced the X-brace below the soundhole, herringbone top purfling, soundhole ring and back stripe, gold tuners.

| 1989 | | $3,400 | $4,500 |

HD-28GM LSH

1994. Grand Marquis, Guitar of the Month, rosewood back and sides, large soundhole with double herringbone rings, snowflake inlay in bridge, natural (115 made) or sunburst (36 made).

| 1994 | | $2,700 | $3,500 |

HD-28KM Keb Mo

2001-2002. Signature Edition, Hawaiian koa back and sides, 252 made.

| 2001-2002 | | $2,800 | $3,700 |

HD-28LE

1985. Limited Edition, Guitar of the Month, rosewood back and sides, scalloped bracing, herringbone top purfling, diamonds and squares 'board inlay, V-neck.

| 1985 | | $3,200 | $4,200 |

HD-28LSV

1997-2005. Vintage Series, large soundhole, patterned after Clarence White's modified '35 D-28.

| 1997-2005 | | $2,500 | $3,200 |

1967 Martin GT-75
Greg Perrine

Martin HD12-28

GUITARS

Martin HD-28 VR

1981 Martin HD-35

Imaged by Heritage Auctions, HA.com

MODEL YEAR	FEATURES	EXC. COND. LOW	HIGH
HD-28M			
1988. Standard profile.			
1988		$2,300	$3,000
HD-28MP			
1990-1991, 2011-2012. Bolivian rosewood back and sides, herringbone top trim, low profile neck. Reissued in 2011 with Madagascar rosewood and modern-style neck.			
1990-1991		$2,000	$2,600
2011-2012		$2,000	$2,600
HD-28P			
1987-1989. Rosewood back and sides, scalloped braces, herringbone, low profile neck (P), zigzag back stripe.			
1987-1989		$2,000	$2,600
HD-28PSE			
1988. Signature Edition, Guitar of the Month, rosewood back and sides, signed by C.F. Martin IV and foremen, scalloped braces, herringbone top purfling, low profile neck, squared peghead, ebony tuner buttons.			
1988		$2,400	$3,200
HD-28S Custom			
1995. Slotted headstock.			
1995		$2,700	$3,500
HD-28SB/HD-28 Ambertone/HD-28SB-AMB			
2016-present. Sitka, East Indian rosewood, natural, sunburst or ambertone.			
2016-2022		$2,400	$3,200
HD-28SE			
1986-1987. Signature Edition, rosewood back and sides, signed by C. F. Martin and foremen/supervisors, '87 model was a Guitar of the Month with Brazilian rosewood.			
1986		$2,700	$3,500
1987	Brazilian	$6,000	$7,900
HD-28SO Sing Out!			
1996. Limited edition, 45 made, Indian rosewood back and sides.			
1996		$2,900	$3,800
HD-28V Custom			
2007-2012. Indian rosewood back and sides, Adirondack top, wide nut, Elderly Instruments special issue.			
2007-2012		$3,200	$4,200
HD-28V/HD-28VR			
1996-2019. 14-fret, Indian rosewood body, R dropped from name in '99.			
1996-1999	HD-28VR	$2,700	$3,600
2000-2019	HD-28V	$2,700	$3,600
HD-28VE			
2004-2006. HD-28 V with Fishman Ellipse Blend system.			
2004-2006		$2,900	$3,750
HD-28VS			
1996-2016. Slotted headstock, 12-fret, spruce top with aging toner, Indian rosewood sides and back.			
1996-2016		$3,000	$4,000

MODEL YEAR	FEATURES	EXC. COND. LOW	HIGH
HD-35			
1978-present. Indian rosewood back and sides, herringbone top trim, zipper back stripe.			
1978-1979		$3,300	$4,300
1980-1999		$2,550	$3,300
2000-2021		$2,200	$2,900
HD-35 CFM IV 60th			
2016-2020. Celebrates C.F. Martin IV's 60th birthday, limited to 60, European spruce top, 3-piece back of siris wings and East Indian rosewood wedge, personally signed label.			
2016-2020		$6,200	$8,200
HD-35 Custom			
2009. Custom Designed on neck block, Adirondack spruce top, East Indian rosewood sides and back.			
2009		$2,700	$3,500
HD-35 Nancy Wilson			
2006-2007. Englemann spruce top, 3-piece back with bubinga center wedge, 101 made.			
2006-2007		$3,400	$4,400
HD-35P			
1987-1989. HD-35 with low profile neck.			
1987-1989		$2,450	$3,200
HD-35SJC Judy Collins			
2002. 50 made, Collins signature headstock logo, wildflower headstock inlay, East Indian rosewood, 3-piece back with figured maple center.			
2002		$3,200	$4,200
HD-40 Tom Petty Signature Edition			
2004-2006. Limited run of 274, Indian rosewood sides and back, high-end appointments, inside label with signature.			
2004-2006		$5,500	$7,200
HD-40MK Mark Knopfler			
2001-2002. Limited Edition of 251 made, Mark Knopfler signature inlay 20th fret, herringbone trim, fancy marquetry soundhole rings.			
2001-2002		$4,100	$5,400
HD-40MS Marty Stuart			
1996. Indian rosewood, 250 made, pearl/abalone inlay.			
1996		$4,100	$5,400
HD-282R			
1992-1996. Large soundhole with 2 herringbone rings, zigzag backstripe.			
1992-1996		$2,300	$3,100
HD Dierks Bentley			
2013-2014. Rosewood.			
2013-2014		$3,700	$4,800
HD Elliot Easton Custom Edition			
2006-2008. Limited Edition, Adirondack spruce top with aging tone, Fishman Ellipse Aura pickup available on HDE.			
2006-2008		$3,000	$4,000
HDN Negative Limited Edition			
2003. Limited to 135 made, unusual appointments include pearloid headstock and black finish, HDN Negative Limited Edition notation on the inside label.			
2003		$3,300	$4,300

*The **Vintage Guitar Price Guide** shows low to high values for items in all-original excellent condition, and, where applicable, with original case or cover.*

MODEL YEAR	FEATURES	EXC. COND. LOW	HIGH

HJ-28
1992, 1996-2000. Limited Edition Guitar of the Month in '92, regular production started in '96. Jumbo, non-cut, spruce top, Indian rosewood sides and back, herringbone top purfling, with or without on-board electronics.

1992	Limited Edition	$2,500	$3,300
1996-2000		$2,400	$3,200

HJ-28M
1994. Mahogany/spruce, herringbone top purfling, Guitar of the Month, 72 made.

1994		$2,500	$3,300

HJ-38 Stefan Grossman
2008-2011. Custom Edition, Madagascar rosewood back and sides.

2008-2011		$3,500	$4,650

HM Ben Harper
2008-2009. Special Edition, M-style width, 000-style depth, solid Adirondack spruce top, solid East Indian rosewood sides and back, onboard Fishman Ellipse Matrix Blend.

2008-2009		$3,500	$4,650

HOM-35
1989. Herringbone Orchestra Model, Guitar of the Month, scalloped braces, 3-piece Brazilian rosewood back, bookmatched sides, 14-fret neck, only 60 built.

1989		$5,000	$6,500

HPD-41
1999-2001. Like D-41, but with herringbone rosette, binding.

1999-2001		$3,600	$4,700

HTA Kitty Wells 'Honky Tonk Angel'
2002. D-size with 000-size depth, Indian rosewood back and sides, Queen of Country Music inlay logo on headstock (no Martin headstock logo).

2002		$2,450	$3,200

J-1 Jumbo
1997-2001. Jumbo body with mahogany back and sides.

1997-2001		$850	$1,050

J12-15
2000-2008. 12-string version of J-15.

2000-2008		$850	$1,050

J12-16GT
2000-2013. 16" jumbo 12-string, satin solid mahogany back and sides, gloss solid spruce top.

2000-2013		$950	$1,250

J12-16GTE
2014-2015. Jumbo 12-string, Fishman.

2014-2015		$1,000	$1,300

J12-40/J12-40M
1985-1996. Called J12-40M from '85-'90, rosewood back and sides, 12 strings, 16" jumbo size, 14-fret neck, solid peghead, gold tuners.

1985-1990	J12-40M	$2,300	$3,000
1991-1996	J12-40	$2,300	$3,000

J12-65
1985-1995. Called J12-65M for '84-'90, 12-string, figured maple back and sides.

1985-1995		$1,925	$2,500

J-15
1999-2010. Jumbo 16" narrow-waist body, solid mahogany top, sides, and back, satin finish.

1999-2010		$950	$1,250

J-15E
2000-2001. Acoustic/electric J-15.

2000-2001		$1,000	$1,300

J-16E 12-String
2021-present. Grand 14-fret, sitka spruce top, rosewood back and sides.

2021		$1,400	$1,800

J-18/J-18M
1987-1996. Called J-18M for '87-'89, J-size body with Style 18 appointments, natural.

1987-1989	J-18M	$2,000	$2,650
1990-1996	J-18	$2,000	$2,650

J-21/J-21M
1985-1996. Called J-21M prior to '90, Indian rosewood back and sides, black binding, rosewood 'board, chrome tuners.

1985-1989	J-21M	$1,775	$2,350
1990-1996	J-21	$1,775	$2,350

J-21MC
1986. J cutaway, oval soundhole, Guitar of the Month.

1986		$1,875	$2,450

J-40
1990-present. Called J-40M from '85-'89, Jumbo, Indian rosewood back and sides, triple-bound 'board, hexagonal inlays.

1990-2021		$2,200	$3,000

J-40 Custom
1993-1996. J-40 with upgrades including abalone top trim and rosette.

1993-1996		$2,200	$3,000

J-40BK
1990-1997. Black finish and 'guard, gold hardware.

1990-1997		$2,200	$3,000

J-40M/J-40MBK
1985-1989. Jumbo, Indian rosewood back and sides, triple-bound 'board, hexagonal inlays, MBK ('88-'89) indicates black, name changed to J-40 in '90.

1985-1989	J-40M	$2,200	$3,000
1988-1989	J-40MBK	$2,200	$3,000

J-40MBLE
1987. Brazilian rosewood, Style 45 snowflakes, 17 made.

1987		$4,600	$6,000

J-40MC
1987-1989. Rounded Venetian cutaway version of J-40 M, oval soundhole, gold-plated enclosed tuners. Becomes JC-40 in '90.

1987-1989		$2,300	$3,075

J-41 Special
2004-2007. East Indian rosewood back and sides, Style 45 snowflake inlays.

2004-2007		$3,000	$4,000

J-45M Deluxe
1986. Guitar of the Month, East Indian rosewood back and sides, tortoise-colored binding, mother-of-pearl and abalone, gold tuners with ebony buttons.

1986		$3,800	$5,000

Martin HD-40 MS Marty Stuart
Imaged by Heritage Auctions, HA.com

Martin J-40

Martin JC-16 RGTE Aura
Imaged by Heritage Auctions, HA.com

2019 Martin LX1RE
Gil Hembree

MODEL YEAR	FEATURES	EXC. COND. LOW	HIGH

J-65 Custom/J-65FM
1993-1996. White binding, herringbone. Available with MEQ electronics.

1993-1996		$2,200	$2,850
1993-1996	With MEQ	$2,200	$2,850

J-65/J-65E/J-65M
1985-1995. Jumbo, maple back and sides, gold-plated tuners, scalloped bracing, ebony 'board, tortoise shell-style binding.

1985-1995		$2,100	$2,700

JC Buddy Guy Signature
2006-2007. Only 36 made, rosewood back and sides.

2006-2007		$3,000	$3,900

JC-1E
1999-2002. Jumbo, mahogany, cutaway, pickup.

1999-2002		$900	$1,175

JC-16GTE
2000-2003. Jumbo, cutaway, mahogany back and sides, gloss top, Fishman.

2000-2003		$975	$1,275

JC-16GTE Premium
2003-2005. Fishman Prefix Stereo Blender pickup system.

2003-2005		$1,075	$1,400

JC-16KWS Kenny Wayne Shepherd Signature
2001-2002. Cutaway, blue lacquer top, back and sides in gloss black, on-board electronics, 198 made.

2001-2002	198 made	$1,300	$1,675

JC-16ME Aura
2006-2009. JC-16 with maple back and sides, Fishman Aura.

2006-2009		$1,600	$2,100

JC-16RE Aura
2006-2011. Like ME, but with rosewood back and sides.

2006-2011		$1,600	$2,100

JC-16RGTE Aura
2000-2003. Like RE Aura, but with gloss top.

2000-2003		$1,200	$1,600

JC-16WE
2002-2003		$1,050	$1,375

JC-40
1990-1997. Renamed from J-40 MC, cutaway flat-top, oval sound hole.

1990-1997		$2,300	$3,050

JSO Sing Out! 60th Pete Seeger
2011. Triangular soundhole, Sitka top, East Indian rosewood back and sides, 2 'guards, 120 made. There was also a 12-string model (J12SO!).

2011		$3,000	$4,000

LE-HMSD 2015 (HMS Dreadnought Battleship)
2015. Limited Edition, HMS Dreadnought Battleship (British Royal Navy) illustrated by artist Robert Goetzl is printed on the sitka spruce top, dark mahogany back and sides, ebony 'board.

2015		$2,500	$3,300

LX Series
2003-present. The LX series is the Little Martin models, featuring small bodies with high pressure wood laminate (HPL) backs and sides with an exterior wood-grain image with a gloss finish. M is for mahogany wood-grain, R for rosewood and K for koa. They are also offered in all solid-colors. A 1 indicates a HPL spruce top, 2 is HPL koa top. E indicates electronics.

2003-2019	LXM	$200	$260
2004-2022	LX1	$210	$275
2004-2022	LXK2	$200	$260
2009	LX Elvis Presley	$350	$460
2009-2021	LX1E	$270	$350
2013-2014	LX1E Ed Sheeran	$340	$440
2013-2019	LXME	$255	$335
2017-2022	LX Black	$200	$260
2019-2021	LX1RE	$340	$440
2019-2022	LX1R	$300	$390

M2C-28
1988. Double-cut, Guitar of the Month, 22 made.

1988		$2,000	$2,600

M-3H Cathy Fink
2005. M 0000-size body, gloss finish, rosewood sides, 3-piece back with flamed koa center panel, torch headstock inlay, herringbone top trim, no Martin logo on headstock.

2005		$2,500	$3,300

M-3M George Martin
2005-2006. M Model, Style 40 appointments with Style 42 snowflake inlays, 127 made.

2005-2006		$4,100	$5,300

M-3SC Shawn Colvin
2002-2003. M 0000-size body, 120 made, mahogany sides, 3-piece mahogany/rosewood back, Fishman, Shawn Colvin & C.F.M. III signed label.

2002-2003		$2,300	$3,000

M-16GT
2001-2003 M-size single cut, gloss top, mahogany sides and back

2001-2003		$950	$1,250

M-18
1984-1988. M size, mahogany.

1984-1988		$2,200	$2,900

M-21
December 1984. Guitar of the Month, low profile neck M-Series, Indian rosewood back and sides, special ornamentation.

1984		$2,150	$2,850

M-21 Steve Earle
2008-2011. Custom Edition, East Indian rosewood back and sides, Italian Alpine spruce top.

2008-2011		$2,800	$3,700

M-30 Jorma Kaukonen
2010-2013. Custom Artist Edition, M 0000-size body, Style 30 appointments, East Indian rosewood back and sides, Maltese diamond/square inlays, optional electronics.

2010-2013		$4,500	$5,900

M-35/M-36
1978-1997, 2007-present. First 26 labeled as M-35, Indian rosewood back and sides, bound 'board, low profile neck, multi-bound, white-black-white back stripes.

1978	M-35, 26 made	$2,900	$3,900
1978-1979		$2,700	$3,600

MODEL YEAR	FEATURES	EXC. COND. LOW	HIGH
1980-1989		$2,200	$2,900
1990-2022		$2,100	$2,800
2008	175th Anniv	$2,100	$2,800

M-36B
1985. Brazilian rosewood.

1985		$4,400	$5,900

M-38 (0000-38)
1977-1997, 2007-2011. Called 0000-38 (see that listing) in '97-'98, 0000-size, Indian rosewood back and sides, multi-bound.

1977-1979		$3,000	$3,950
1980-1997		$2,800	$3,600
2007-2011		$2,800	$3,600

M-38 Koa Special
2009-2010. Sitka spruce top, highly flamed koa back and sides.

2009-2010		$2,900	$3,800

M-38B
1985. Brazilian rosewood.

1985		$5,600	$7,200

M-42 David Bromberg
2005-2006. 0000-14 body, rosewood back and sides, snowflakes, 83 made.

2005-2006		$4,100	$5,400

M-64
1985-1996. Flamed maple back and sides, tortoise-shell-style 'guard and binding. The 11 made in '85 were labeled M-64R.

1985-1996		$2,200	$2,900

MC12-41 Richie Sambora
2006. 12-string version of OMC-41 Richie Sambora, planned 200 combined models made.

2006		$4,100	$5,400

MC-16GTE
2002-2004. M-16 GT with single-cut and Fishman.

2002-2004		$925	$1,200

MC-16GTE Premium
2003-2005. Fishman Prefix Stereo Blender pickup system.

2003-2005		$1,100	$1,450

MC-28
1981-1996. Rosewood back and sides, single-cut, oval soundhole, scalloped braces.

1981-1996		$2,400	$3,100

MC-37K
1981-1982, 1987-1994. Cutaway, koa back and sides.

1981-1994		$2,550	$3,300

MC-38 Steve Howe
2009-2011. Indian rosewood back and sides, cutaway, slot headstock.

2009-2011		$5,000	$6,600

MC-68/MC-68R/MC-68+
1985-1996. Auditorium-size, single-cut, maple back and sides, scalloped bracing, verticle logo, natural or sunburst. In '85 called the MC-68 R (for adjustable truss-rod), 7 with sunburst shaded top option called MC-68+.

1985	MC-68R	$2,900	$3,700
1986-1996	MC-68	$2,900	$3,700
1986-1996	MC-68+	$3,000	$3,800

MC-DSM
2007-2010. Limited Edition of 100, cutaway, designed by District Sales Manager (DSM), spruce top, figured koa back and sides.

2007-2010		$3,000	$3,900

Mini-Martin Limited Edition
1999-2009. Size 5 Terz body, solid sitka spruce top, rosewood sides and back, vintage style Martin Geib case with green interior.

1999-2009		$1,775	$2,300

MMV
2008-2012. D-style, rosewood sides and back, nitro finish.

2008-2012		$1,125	$1,475

Model American 1
2018. Limited Edition D-body, United States sourced woods, Adirondack spruce top, sycamore back and sides, cherry neck, black walnut 'board, gloss finish.

2018		$2,300	$3,000

MTV-1 Unplugged
1996. Body is 1/2 rosewood and 1/2 mahogany, scalloped bracing, MTV logo on headstock, gloss (588 sold) or satin (73 sold) finish.

1996	Gloss finish	$1,725	$2,250
1996	Satin finish	$1,575	$2,050

MTV-2 Unplugged
2003-2004. Body is 1/2 rosewood and 1/2 maple, scalloped bracing, MTV logo on headstock.

2003-2004		$1,575	$2,050

N-10
1968-1993. Classical, mahogany back and sides, fan bracing, wood marquetry soundhole ring, unbound rosewood 'board, 12-fret neck and slotted peghead from '70.

1968-1970	Short-scale	$2,100	$2,800
1970-1979	Long-scale	$1,950	$2,600
1980-1993	Long-scale	$1,675	$2,200

N-20
1968-1992. Classical, Brazilian rosewood back and sides (changed to Indian rosewood in '69), multi-bound, 12-fret neck, solid headstock (changed to slotted in '70), natural.

1968-1969	Brazilian, short-scale	$7,100	$9,200
1969	Prismatone pu & Baldwin C-1 Amp	$8,700	$11,500
1970	Indian, short-scale	$3,600	$4,800
1970-1979	Indian, long-scale	$3,600	$4,800
1980-1992	Long-scale	$3,600	$4,800

N-20B
1985-1986. Brazilian rosewood N-20.

1985-1986		$7,200	$9,500

N-20WNB 'Trigger'
1998-1999. Designed after Willie Nelson's famous N-20 he named Trigger, 100 made, Brazilian rosewood (30) or Indian (70).

1998-1999	Brazilian	$8,800	$11,500
1998-1999	Indian	$4,300	$5,700

OM-1
1999-2002, 2009-2010. Sitka spruce top, sapele back and sides, East Indian rosewood 'board, natural satin finish.

1999-2010		$700	$925

Martin M-36

1979 Martin M-38
Gantt Kushner

2015 Martin OM-21
Rivington Guitars

1930 Martin OM-28
Jet City Guitars

MODEL YEAR	FEATURES	EXC. COND. LOW	HIGH
OM-1GT			
2011-2014. OM-1 with gloss top.			
2011-2014		$700	$925
CS-OM-13			
2013. Custom Shop Limited Edition, 80 made, Swiss spruce top, Madagascar rosewood back and sides, gloss natural finish.			
2013		$3,000	$4,000
OM-15			
2001-2003. Mahogany body, cutaway.			
2001-2003		$1,000	$1,300
OM-15M			
2015. All mahogany, natural satin finish.			
2015		$1,000	$1,300
OM-16GT			
2001-2005. Spruce top, mahogany back, sides and neck, natural gloss finish.			
2001-2005		$1,000	$1,300
OM-18			
1930-1934. Orchestra Model, mahogany back and sides, 14-fret neck, solid peghead, banjo tuners (changed to right-angle in '31).			
1930-1931	Banjo tuners, small 'guard	$32,000	$43,000
1931	Standard tuners, small 'guard	$26,000	$35,000
1932-1933	Standard tuners, large 'guard	$19,700	$26,000
OM-18 Authentic 1933			
2013-2019. Period-correct (1933) appointments, Vintage Tone System, vintage gloss finish.			
2013-2019		$4,200	$5,600
OM-18 Special			
2012. Custom Shop model.			
2012		$2,575	$3,400
OM-18GE Golden Era			
2003-2009. Mahogany back and sides, Brazilian rosewood purfling and binding.			
2003-2009		$2,850	$3,700
OM-18P			
1930-1931. Plectrum.			
1930-1931		$7,000	$9,000
OM-18V			
1999-2009. Vintage features.			
1999-2009		$2,350	$3,100
OM-18VLJ Laurence Juber			
2002, 2008-2009. Cutaway, Adirondack spruce top.			
2002-2009		$3,600	$4,800
OM-21			
1994-present. Indian rosewood back and sides, herringbone back stripe and soundhole ring, 14-fret neck, chrome tuners, natural or sunburst.			
1994-1999		$2,050	$2,650
2000-2021		$2,000	$2,600
OM-21 Special			
1991, 2007-2011. Upgrade to ebony 'board, rosewood bindings.			
1992-2011		$2,450	$3,200
OM-21 Special Limited Edition			
1991. Custom Shop, prototype to '92 production.			
1991	36 made	$2,450	$3,200

MODEL YEAR	FEATURES	EXC. COND. LOW	HIGH
OM-28			
1929-1933, 1990-1997, 2015-present. Brazilian rosewood back and sides, 14-fret neck, solid peghead, banjo tuners (changed to right-angle in '31), reintroduced with Indian rosewood for '90-'97 and again in 2015.			
1929	Banjo pegs, small 'guard, pyramid end bridge	$97,000	$129,000
1930	Early '30, banjo tuners, small 'guard, pyramid bridge	$84,000	$110,000
1930	Late '30, banjo tuners, small 'guard, belly bridge	$76,000	$100,000
1931	Early '31, banjo tuners, small 'guard, belly bridge	$76,000	$100,000
1931	Late '31, standard tuners, large 'guard	$63,000	$83,000
1931	Mid '31, banjo tuners, large 'guard	$72,000	$96,000
1932-1933	Standard tuners, full-size 'guard	$63,000	$83,000
1990-1997		$2,250	$2,950
2015-2021		$2,200	$2,900
OM-28 Authentic 1931			
2015-2019. Adirondack spruce top, Madagascar rosewood back and sides, Vintage Tone System (VTS).			
2015-2019		$5,500	$7,200
OM-28 Marquis			
2005-2015. Pre-war appointments, Adirondack top, East Indian rosewood back, sides and headplate.			
2005-2015		$3,200	$4,200
OM-28 Marquis Adirondack			
2011-2013. Adirondack spruce top.			
2011-2013		$3,200	$4,200
OM-28 Marquis Madagascar			
2007-2008. Madagascar rosewood.			
2007-2008		$3,200	$4,200
OM-28 Modern Deluxe			
2019-present. Sitka spruce top with Vintage Tone System (VTS), East Indian rosewood back and sides, '30s style script logo on headstock, gloss finish. Electronics available (OM-28E).			
2019-2021		$2,500	$3,300
2019-2021	OM-28E	$4,100	$5,400
OM-28E Retro			
2012-2019. Sitka top, Indian rosewood back and sides, herringbone binding, Fishman.			
2012-2019		$2,550	$3,400
OM-28GE Golden Era			
2003-2004. Brazilian rosewood back and sides, Adirondack spruce top.			
2003-2004		$8,000	$10,500
OM-28GE Golden Era Guatemalan Rosewood			
2015. Custom Shop model, Guatemalan rosewood back and sides.			
2015		$4,200	$5,500

The *Vintage Guitar Price Guide* shows low to high values for items in all-original excellent condition, and, where applicable, with original case or cover.

MODEL YEAR	FEATURES	EXC. COND. LOW	HIGH
OM-28JM John Mayer			
2003. Limited Edition, 404 made.			
2003		$7,900	$10,300
OM-28LE			
1985. Limited Edition only 40 made, Guitar of the Month, Indian rosewood back and sides, herringbone top binding, V-neck.			
1985		$3,300	$4,300
OM-28M Roseanne Cash			
2008. Signature Edition, Madagascar rosewood back and sides, 100 made.			
2008		$4,700	$6,100
OM-28PB Perry Bechtel			
1993. Guitar of the Month, signed by Perry Bechtel's widow Ina, Indian rosewood back and sides, zigzag back stripe, chrome tuners, V-neck, 50 made.			
1993		$4,500	$5,900
OM-28SO Sing Out! 35th Anniversary			
1985. For Sing Out! Magazine's 35th anniversary, label signed by Pete Seeger.			
1985		$3,100	$4,000
OM-28V Custom Shop (Brazilian/ Adirondack)			
2000-2001. Brazilian rosewood back and sides, Adirondack "red" spruce top, ca. 1933 prewar features including Martin gold headstock decal logo.			
2000-2001		$7,400	$9,700
OM-28VR/OM-28V			
1984-1990, 1999-2014. VR suffix until '99, then just V (Vintage Series), rosewood back and sides.			
1984-1999	OM-28VR	$3,000	$4,000
1999-2014	OM-28V	$3,000	$4,000
OM-35			
2003-2007. 000-size body, Indian rosewood sides and 3-piece back, spruce top, gloss natural finish.			
2003-2007		$2,100	$2,700
OM-40 Rory Block			
2004. Limited Edition, 38 made, 000-size, Indian rosewood back and sides, Englemann spruce top, 'the road' inlay markers, vintage-auto inlay on headstock.			
2004		$3,300	$4,400
OM-40BLE			
1990. Limited Edition, 50 made, Brazilian rosewood back and sides.			
1990		$8,200	$10,900
OM-40LE			
1994. Limited Edition, Guitar of the Month, Indian rosewood back and sides, double pearl borders, snowflake inlay on 'board, gold tuners, natural (57 sold) or sunburst (29 sold).			
1994		$4,000	$5,300
OM-41 Special			
2005-2006. Rosewood back and sides, Style 45 snowflake inlays.			
2005-2006		$3,400	$4,400
OM-42			
1930, 1999-present. Indian rosewood back and sides, Style 45 snowflake inlays, there were 2 guitars labeled OM-42 built in 1930.			
1930	2 made	$102,000	$135,000
1999-2021		$3,900	$5,100

MODEL YEAR	FEATURES	EXC. COND. LOW	HIGH
OM-42 Flamed Mahogany			
2006. Limited Edition, 30 made, flamed mahogany back and sides, vines.			
2006		$6,900	$9,200
OM-42 Koa			
2005-2008. Koa sides and back.			
2006-2008		$4,200	$5,500
OM-42PS Paul Simon			
1997. Bookmatched sitka spruce top, Indian rosewood back and sides, 42- and 45-style features, low profile PS neck, 500 planned but only 223 made.			
1997		$4,200	$5,500
OM-45			
1930-1933. OM-style, 45 level appointments. Condition is critically important on this or any ultra high-end instrument, minor flaws are critical to value.			
1930	Banjo pegs	$340,000	$450,000
1931	Right-angle tuners	$250,000	$330,000
1932-1933		$250,000	$330,000
OM-45/SOM-45/Special OM-45			
1977-1994. First batch labeled SOM-45, 2 labeled OM-45N in '94 that had square tube bar in neck and without scalloped braces.			
1977-1979		$7,200	$9,500
1980-1989		$7,100	$9,300
1990-1994		$6,500	$8,500
1994	OM-45 N option	$6,500	$8,500
OM-45 Custom Deluxe			
1998-1999. Limited custom shop run of 14, Adirondack spruce and typical Style 45 appointments.			
1998-1999		$16,800	$21,900
OM-45 Deluxe			
1930. Only 14 made, Brazilian rosewood back and sides, zipper pattern back stripe, pearl inlay in 'guard and bridge. Condition is critically important on this or any ultra high-end instrument, minor flaws are critical to value.			
1930		$340,000	$450,000
OM-45 Deluxe (Special)			
1999. 4 made on special order, highly figured Brazilian rosewood.			
1999		$21,700	$28,300
OM-45 Deluxe Golden Era			
1998. Brazilian, few made.			
1998		$21,700	$28,300
OM-45 Tasmanian Blackwood			
2005. Limited Edition, 29 made, Tasmanian Blackwood (koa-family) back and sides with curly grain, 000-size, OM and 45 style appointments.			
2005		$7,500	$9,800
OM-45/OM-45B Roy Rogers			
2006. Limited Edition, based on Roy's 1930 OM-45 Deluxe, Indian rosewood (84 made) or Brazilian rosewood (45B, 14 made).			
2006	OM-45, Indian	$9,600	$12,800
2006	OM-45B, Brazilian	$22,000	$29,000
OM-45GE Golden Era			
1999, 2001-2005. Red spruce top, Brazilian rosewood.			
1999-2005		$21,700	$28,300

2002 Martin OM-45 GE Golden Era

Carter Vintage Guitars

Martin OM True North-16

GUITARS

Martin OMC-16 E Burst

Martin OMJM John Mayer

MODEL YEAR	FEATURES	EXC. COND. LOW	HIGH

OM 1833 Custom Shop Limited Edition
2006. Italian alpine spruce top, flamed claro walnut back and sides, 000-size, low profile 14-fret neck, fancy inlay and appointments, natural gloss finish.

2006		$3,800	$5,000

OM Chris Hillman
2009-2010. Adirondack top, Indian rosewood back and sides, sunburst.

2009-2010		$3,000	$4,000

OM Jeff Daniels
2012-2013. Based on Daniels 1934 C-2 archtop conversion, Adirondack, Madagascar rosewood back and sides, sunburst.

2012-2013		$2,400	$3,100

OM Negative
2007-2008. Limited Edition, 60 made, black body and white 'board, black inside label signed Dick Boak, gloss finish.

2007-2008		$3,500	$4,600

OM True North-16/CS-OM True North-16
2016. Custom Shop Limited Edition, 50 made, Adirondack spruce top, figured koa back and sides, back features a compass design inlaid with flamed jarrah, Claro walnut, waterfall bubinga and Paua pearl, ebony headplate has True North design inlaid with mother of pearl.

2016		$10,000	$13,300

OMC Aura
2004-2011. OM size, cutaway, rosewood back and sides, Fishman Aura.

2004-2011		$2,250	$3,000

OMC Cherry
2008-2013. Sustainable wood program, solid cherry back and sides, solid rescued spruce top, 000 body, cutaway, Fishman electronics.

2008-2013		$2,250	$3,000

OMC Fingerstyle 1
2005-2008. Cutaway, Spanish cedar back and sides, no inlays.

2005-2008		$2,250	$3,000

OMC Red Birch
2005-2009. Sustainable Series, rescued spruce top, solid red birch back and sides, Fishman electronics.

2005-2009		$2,000	$2,575

OMC-1E
2009-2010. Style 28 appointments, cutaway, on-board Fishman.

2009-2010		$800	$1,025

OMC-15E
2001-2007. All solid mahogany body.

2001-2007		$1,100	$1,450

OMC-15ME
2016-present. Mahogany top, back and sides, East Indian rosewood 'board, Fishman electronics.

2016-2021		$1,100	$1,450

OMC-16E Burst
2019-present. Mahogany burst ovangkol gloss top, satin ovangkol back and sides, Fishman electronics.

2019-2021		$1,350	$1,800

OMC-16E Koa
2005-2009. Koa back and sides, on-board electronics.

2005-2009		$1,300	$1,700

MODEL YEAR	FEATURES	EXC. COND. LOW	HIGH

OMC-16E Maple
2005-2009. Maple, on-board electronics.

2005		$1,300	$1,700

OMC-16E/E Premium
2003-2007, 2017-2019. Sitka spruce top, sapele back and sides, on-board electronics. Premium model with Prefix Premium Blend electronics. Reintroduced '17 with cherry back and sides and Fishman Matrix VT.

2003-2007		$1,300	$1,700
2017-2019	16E, Reintroduced	$1,300	$1,700

OMC-16GTE
2010-2013. Gloss top, satin sapele back and sides.

2010-2013		$1,125	$1,475

OMC-16RE Aura
2005-2009. East Indian rosewood back and sides, gloss body.

2005-2009		$1,450	$1,900

OMC-16RE/RE Premium
2003-2005. Solid rosewood back and sides, on-board electronics.

2003-2005		$1,300	$1,700

OMC-16WE
2002-2003. Walnut back and sides.

2002-2003		$1,300	$1,700

OMC-18E
2017-2019. Sitka spruce top, mahogany back and sides, ebony 'board, Fishman electronics.

2017-2019		$1,300	$1,700

OMC-18LJ Laurence Juber
2008-2010. Cutaway 000, Adirondack spruce top.

2008-2010		$3,000	$4,000

OMC-28
1990. Guitar of the Month, 81 made, Indian rosewood, low profile neck, label signed by C.F. Martin IV.

1990		$2,225	$2,900

OMC-28 Laurence Juber
2004-2005. OM size, cutaway, Indian rosewood.

2004-2005		$3,700	$4,800

OMC-28BLJ Laurence Juber
2004. Brazilian rosewood, 50 made.

2004		$7,600	$9,900

OMC-28E
2006-2009, 2017-2019. OMC-28 with Fishman Ellipse. Reintroduced '17 with Fishman Aura.

2006-2009		$2,250	$2,950
2017-2019		$2,250	$2,950

OMC-28M Laurence Juber
2006-2011. Madagascar rosewood.

2006-2011		$3,700	$4,800

OMC-35E
2016-2017. Sitka spruce top, East Indian rosewood back & sides, ebony 'board and 'guard, Fishman electronics.

2016-2017		$2,300	$3,000

OMC-41 Richie Sambora
2006-2009. Madagascar rosewood sides and back, combination Style 45 and 41 appointments, 12-string is MC12-41 Richie Sambora, planned 200 made combined models.

2006-2009		$4,700	$6,100

MODEL YEAR	FEATURES	EXC. COND. LOW	HIGH

OMC-LJ Pro Laurence Juber
2013. Custom Shop Artist Edition, Adirondack spruce top, flamed maple back and sides.

2013		$3,100	$4,100

OMCPA Series
2010-2019. Performing Artist Series, OM size, cutaway, acoustic/electric, various woods.

2010-2016	OMCPA1/1 Plus	$2,000	$2,575
2011	OMCPA2	$1,250	$1,625
2011-2013	OMCPA3	$1,250	$1,625
2011-2019	OMCPA4 Sapele	$1,250	$1,625
2012-2019	OMCPA4		
	Rosewood	$1,100	$1,425

OMCRE
2008-2009. Carpathian spruce top, East Indian rosewood sides and back, Babicz adjustable neck joint, Fishman, gloss finish.

2008-2009		$2,000	$2,575

OMC-X1E Black
2020-present. Replaces OMCXAE Black. Jett black HPL top, back and sides, Fishman electronics.

2020-2021		$450	$600

OMCXK2E
2006-2009. Hawaiian Koa HPL (high pressure laminate) textured finish.

2006-2009		$525	$700

OMJM John Mayer
2003-present. Indian rosewood sides and back.

2003-2021		$2,375	$3,100

OMM
2000-2003. Solid spruce top, mahogany back and sides.

2000-2003		$700	$925

OMM John Renbourne
2011-2013. Madagascar rosewood sides and back.

2011-2013		$3,400	$4,400

OMXAE Black
2014-2019. Black HPL back and sides, black Richlite 'board.

2014-2019		$350	$475

Philadelphia Folk Festival 40th Anniversary
2002. Commemorating 40th Anniversary of Martin Philly Folk Festival, 85 made, 0000-14 fret, Englemann spruce top, Indian rosewood back and sides, PFF logo inlays, one label signed by CF Martin IV and David Baskin, one signed by festival participants, blue denium-covered hard case.

2002		$2,500	$3,300

POW MIA
2006-2010. POW MIA logo position marker lettering on fretboard, D-style body, dark finish.

2006-2010		$2,350	$3,100

PS2 Paul Simon Signature
2003. Paul Simon signature logo at bottom of fretboard, 200 made.

2003		$2,850	$3,700

R-15
1934. Archtop, sunburst.

1934	2 made	$1,550	$2,000

R-17
1934-1942. All mahogany, arched top and back, 3-segment f-holes (changed to 1-segment in '37).

1934-1942		$1,550	$2,000

R-18P
1934-1936. Only 4 made, plectrum neck.

1934-1936		$1,600	$2,100

R-18S/R-18
1932-1942. Spruce arched top (carved top by 1937), mahogany back and sides, bound top, sunburst.

1932-1942		$2,200	$2,800

R-18T
1934-1941. Tenor archtop, 14 3/8" lower bout, 2 f-holes, dot markers, sunburst.

1934-1941		$1,600	$2,100

R-21
1938. 000 body archtop, 1 made.

1938		$4,300	$5,600

SC Series
2020-present. Road Series, patented Sure Align® neck system, sitka spruce top with various wood back and sides, 10E/13E (koa), 13E Special (ziricote), CS-SC-2022 (Custom Shop, rosewood).

2020-2022	SC-13E	$1,150	$1,500
2022	CS-SC-2022	$6,000	$8,000
2022	SC-10E	$925	$1,200
2022	SC-13E Special	$1,300	$1,700
2022	SC-13E		
	Special Burst	$1,450	$1,900

Schoenberg Soloist by C.F. Martin
1987-1994. Designed by Eric Schoenberg with help from luthier Dana Bourgeois, OM body, Brazilian rosewood back and sides.

1987-1994		$6,100	$8,000

Shenandoah Series
1983-1993. Bodies and necks were built in Japan with final assembly and finishing in Nazareth and a Thinline piezo added, styled after U.S. models with a 32 added to the model name.

1983-1993	Various models	$800	$1,500

SP000 Series
1996-2002. Special Edition 000-size, spruce top with aging toner, scalloped bracing, rosewood or mahogany body.

1996-1997	SP000C-16TR	$1,250	$1,600
1996-2002	SP000-16	$1,200	$1,550
1996-2002	SP000-16R	$1,200	$1,550
1996-2002	SP000-16T	$1,200	$1,550
1996-2002	SP000-16TR	$1,200	$1,550
1997-2002	SP000C-16R	$1,250	$1,600
1999-2002	SP000C-16	$1,250	$1,600
1999-2002	SP000C-16E	$1,300	$1,675
2003	SP000C-16R (CS)	$2,100	$2,750

SP00-16RST Stauffer
2000-2002. Stauffer 6-on-a-side headstock, 12-fret neck, rosewood back and sides.

2000-2002		$1,325	$1,725

SPD12-16R
1997-2004. 12-string, solid rosewood body, abalone soundhole ring, Style-45 backstripe.

1999-2000		$1,250	$1,600

1937 Martin R-18
Frank Manno

Martin SC-10E

Martin SS-OMVine-16

1962 Maton EG240SE

MODEL YEAR	FEATURES	EXC. COND. LOW	HIGH
SPD-16 Series			
1997-2004. D-16 Series Special models.			
1996-1999	SPD-16TR	$1,325	$1,750
1997-2004	SPD-16	$1,250	$1,600
1997-2004	SPD-16T	$1,250	$1,600
1999-2001	SPD-16B Black	$1,250	$1,600
1999-2002	SPD-16M Maple	$1,200	$1,550
1999-2002	SPD-16W Walnut	$1,200	$1,550
2000	SPD-16E	$1,300	$1,650
2000-2002	SPD-16R	$1,325	$1,750
2000-2005	SPD-16K	$1,650	$2,150
2000-2005	SPD-16K2	$1,650	$2,150
SPDC-16 Series			
1997-2001. Cutaway version of SPD-16.			
1997-1999	SPDC-16TR	$1,325	$1,750
1997-2001	SPDC-16RE Rosewood	$1,375	$1,800
2000-2002	SPDC-16R	$1,325	$1,750

SPJC-16RE
2000-2003. Single-cut, East Indian rosewood body, 000-size, on-board electronics.

2000-2003		$1,375	$1,800

SPOM-16
1999-2001. Mahogany.

1999-2001		$1,375	$1,800

SS-0041GB-17
2017-2020. Limited Edition of 50, Grand Concert 12-fret, European spruce top with Vintage Tone System (VTS), Guatemalan rosewood back and sides, gloss finish.

2017-2020		$5,900	$7,600

SS-00L41-16
2016-2020. Limited Edition, Adirondack spruce top with Vintage Tone System (VTS), moabi back and sides, mahogany neck, hand-rubbed finish.

2016-2020		$3,500	$4,500

SS-OMVine-16
2016. Limited Edition of 35, NAMM show special, figured English walnut, aluminum vine inlay on ebony 'board.

2016		$8,500	$11,000

Stauffer
1830s-ca.1850s. One of C.F. Martin's earliest models, distinguished by the scrolled, six-on-a-side headstock, ornamentation varies. Each instrument should be evaluated on a case-by-case basis, those in truly original excellent condition may be worth more than the values shown.

1835	Fancy (2nd highest)	$36,000	$47,000
1835	Fancy (highest)	$120,000	$158,000
1835	Mid-level	$24,000	$32,000
1835	Plain (2nd lowest)	$17,400	$23,000
1835	Plain (lowest)	$12,700	$16,700

Sting Mini
2006. 100 made, Size 5, Western red cedar top, Solomon padauk body.

2005-2006		$2,300	$3,000

Stinger
1980s-1990s. Import copy offset S-style electric solidbody.

1980s-90s		$225	$300

MODEL YEAR	FEATURES	EXC. COND. LOW	HIGH

SW00-D8 Machiche
2006-2007. Smartwood Limited Edition, 125 made, rescued solid spruce top, sustainable machiche sides and back.

2006-2007		$1,275	$1,650

SWC
1998. Smartwood 'The Sting Signature Classical Model', machiche wood body.

1998		$1,275	$1,650

SWD
1998-2001. Smartwood D-size, built from wood material certified by the Forest Stewardship Council, sitka top, cherry back and sides, natural satin finish.

1998-2001		$1,050	$1,375

SWD Red Birch
2003-2005. Red Birch.

2003-2005		$1,050	$1,375

SWDGT
2001-2016. Gloss top SWD.

2001-2016		$1,050	$1,375

SWDTG
2000-2007. Cherry back and sides, gloss finish.

2000-2007		$1,050	$1,375

SWMGT
2002-2003. M size, cherry back and sides, gloss finish.

2002-2003		$1,050	$1,375

SWOM
2000-2001. Sustainable Woods Series.

2000-2001		$1,050	$1,375

SWOMGT
2001-2018. Smartwood OM, rescued solid sitka spruce top, sustainable cherry sides and back, gloss finish.

2001-2018		$1,075	$1,400

Yuengling 180th Anniversary Custom
2008. Celebrating 180th company anniversary, limited production, large company logo on top of body, fancy D-41 style appointments, certificate.

2008		$3,400	$4,400

Maruha

1960s-1970s. Japanese-made acoustic, classical, archtop and solidbody guitars, often copies of American brands. Probably not imported into the U.S.

Marvel

1950s-mid-1960s. Brand name used for budget guitars and basses marketed by Peter Sorkin Company in New York, New York. Sorkin manufactured and distributed Premier guitars and amplifiers made by its Multivox subsidiary. Marvel instruments were primarily beginner-grade. Brand disappears by mid-'60s. The name was also used on archtop guitars made by Regal and marketed by the Slingerland drum company in the 1930s to early 1940s.

Electric

1950s-60s	Various models	$225	$525

MODEL YEAR	FEATURES	EXC. COND. LOW	HIGH

Marveltone by Regal

1925-1930. Private branded by Regal, Marveltone pearl style logo on headstock.

Guitar

1925-1930. 14" Brazilian rosewood.

1925-1930		$2,300	$3,000

Masaki Sakurai

See Kohno brand.

Mason

1936-1939. Henry L. Mason on headstock, wholesale distribution, similar to Gibson/Cromwell, pressed wood back and sides.

Student/Intermediate Student

1936-1939. Various flat-top and archtop student/ budget models.

1936-1939		$500	$900

Mason Bernard

1990-1991. Founded by Bernie Rico (BC Rich founder). During this period BC Rich guitars were licensed and controlled by Randy Waltuch and Class Axe. Most Mason models were designs similar to the BC Rich Assassin, according to Bernie Rico only the very best materials were used, large MB logo on headstock. Around 225 guitars were built bearing this brand.

Maton

1946-present. Intermediate and professional grade, production/custom, acoustic, acoustic/electric, hollowbody and solidbody guitars built in Box Hill, Victoria, Australia. Founded by Bill May and his brother Reg and still run by the family. Only available in USA since '82.

Matsuda Guitars

See listing for Michihiro Matsuda.

Matsuoka

1970s. Ryoji Matsuoka from Japan built intermediate grade M series classical guitars that often featured solid tops and laminated sides and back.

Matt Pulcinella Guitars

1998-present. Production/custom, professional grade, electric guitars and basses built in Chadds Ford, Pennsylvania by luthier Matt Pulcinella.

Mauel Guitars

Luthier Hank Mauel builds his premium grade, custom, flat-tops in Auburn, California. He began in 1995.

Maurer

Late 1880s-1944. Robert Maurer built guitars and mandolins in the late 1880s under the Maurer and Champion brands in his Chicago shop. Carl and August Larson bought the company in 1900 and retained the Maurer name. The Larsons also built under the Prairie State, Euphonon, W. J. Dyer and Wm. C. Stahl brands.

Max B

2000-present. Luthier Sebastien Sulser builds professional grade, production/custom, electric guitars and basses in Kirby, Vermont.

May Bell

1923-1940s. Brand of flat-top guitars, some with fake resonators, marketed by the Slingerland Company. Most were made by Regal.

Maya

See El Maya.

McAlister Guitars

1997-present. Premium grade, custom, flat-tops built by luthier Roy McAlister in Watsonville, California.

McCollum Guitars

1994-2009. Luthier Lance McCollum builds his premium grade, custom, flat-top and harp guitars in Colfax, California. McCollum died in 2009.

McCurdy Guitars

1983-present. Premium grade, production/ custom, archtops built by luthier Ric McCurdy originally in Santa Barbara, California and, since '91, New York, New York.

McElroy

1995-present. Premium grade, custom, classical and flat-top steel string acoustic guitars built by luthier Brent McElroy in Seattle, Washington.

McGill Guitars

1976-present. Luthier Paul McGill builds his premium grade, production/custom, classical, resonator, and acoustic/electric guitars in Nashville, Tennessee.

McGlincy

Ca. 1974-ca. 1978. Custom flat-tops built by luthier Edward McGlincy in Toms River, New Jersey. Only 12 instruments made and owners included Gordon Lightfoot and David Bromberg. He later offered uke and guitar kits. He also operated Ed's Musical Instruments. McGlincy died in '97.

McGlynn Guitars

2005-2007. Luthier Michael J. McGlynn built his premium and presentation grade, custom, solidbody guitars in Henderson, Nevada. McGlynn died in '07.

McGowan Guitars

Luthier Brian McGowan builds his production/ custom, premium grade, steel-string acoustic guitars in Hampton, Virginia. He began in 2004.

1930s May Bell
Imaged by Heritage Auctions, HA.com

McCurdy The Moderna

GUITARS

Late-'70s MCI B-35 Guitorgan
Tom Pfeifer

Messenger
Jamsy

MODEL		EXC. COND.	
YEAR	FEATURES	LOW	HIGH

MCI, Inc

1967-1988. MusiConics International (MCI), of Waco, Texas, introduced the world to the Guitorgan, invented by Bob Murrell. Later, they also offered effects and a steel guitar. In the '80s, a MIDI version was offered. MCI was also involved with the Daion line of guitars in the late '70s and early '80s. MCI also built a double-neck lap steel.

GuitOrgan B-35

1970s (ca. 1976-1978?). Duplicated the sounds of an organ and more. MCI bought double-cut semi-hollow body guitars from others and outfitted them with lots of switches and buttons. Each fret has 6 segments that correspond to an organ tone. There was also a B-300 and B-30 version, and the earlier M-300 and 340.

1970s	Fully functional	$1,225	$1,575

McInturff

1996-present. Professional and premium grade, production/custom, solidbody guitars built by luthier Terry C. McInturff originally in Holly Springs, North Carolina, and since '04, in Moncure, North Carolina. McInturff spent 17 years doing guitar repair and custom work before starting his own guitar line.

McKnight Guitars

1992-present. Luthier Tim McKnight builds his custom, premium grade, acoustic steel string guitars in Morral, Ohio.

McPherson Guitars

1981-present. Premium grade, production, flat-tops built by luthier Mander McPherson in Sparta, Wisconsin.

Mean Gene

1988-1990. Heavy metal style solidbodies made by Gene Baker, who started Baker U.S.A. guitars in '97, and Eric Zoellner in Santa Maria, California. They built around 30 custom guitars. Baker currently builds b3 guitars.

Megas Guitars

1989-present. Luthier Ted Megas builds his premium grade, custom, archtop and solidbody guitars, originally in San Franciso, and currently in Portland, Oregon.

Melancon

Professional and premium grade, custom/production, solid and semi-hollow body guitars and basses built by luthier Gerard Melancon, beginning in 1995, in Thibodaux, Louisiana.

Mello, John F.

1973-present. Premium grade, production/custom, classical and flat-top guitars built by luthier John Mello in Kensington, California.

MODEL		EXC. COND.	
YEAR	FEATURES	LOW	HIGH

Melophonic

1960s. Brand built by the Valco Company of Chicago, Illinois.

Resonator

1965		$875	$1,150

Melville Guitars

1988-present. Luthier Christopher Melville builds his premium grade, custom, flat-tops in Milton, Queensland, Australia.

Memphis

One of the many guitar brands built by Japan's Matsumoku company.

Mercurio

2002-2005. Luthier Peter Mercurio built his custom/production solidbody guitars, featuring his interchangeable PickupPak system to swap pickups, in Chanhassen, Minnesota.

Mermer Guitars

Luthier Richard Mermer, started building in 1983, premium grade, production/custom, steel-string, nylon-string, and Hawaiian guitars in Sebastian, Florida.

Merrill Brothers

Premium grade, production/custom, steel-string and harp guitars built by luthiers Jim and Dave Merrill in Williamsburg, Virginia, starting in 1998.

Mesrobian

1995-present. Luthier Carl Mesrobian builds his professional and premium grade, custom, archtop guitars in Salem, Massachusetts.

Messenger

1967-1968. Built by Musicraft, Inc., originally of 156 Montgomery Street, San Francisco, California. The distinguishing feature of the Messengers is a metal alloy neck which extended through the body to the tailblock, plus mono or stereo outputs. Sometime before March '68 the company relocated to Astoria, Oregon. Press touted "improved" magnesium neck, though it's not clear if this constituted a change from '67. Brand disappears after '68. They also made basses.

Electric Hollowbody Archtop

1967-1968. Symmetrical double-cut body shape, metal neck with rosewood 'boards, stereo.

1967-1968		$2,100	$2,700

Metropolitan

1995-2008. Professional and premium grade, production/custom, retro-styled solidbodies designed by David Wintz reminiscent of the '50s National Res-o-glas and wood body guitars. They featured full-scale set-neck construction and a wood body instead of Res-o-glas. Wintz also made Robin and Alamo brand instruments.

Electric Solidbody

1995-2008	Various models	$1,850	$2,400

MODEL		EXC. COND.	
YEAR	FEATURES	LOW	HIGH

Meyers Custom Guitars

Professional grade, custom, solidbody electric guitars built by luthier Donald Meyers in Houma, Louisiana, beginning 2005.

Miami

1920s. Instruments built by the Oscar Schmidt Co. and possibly others. Most likely a brand made for a distributor.

Michael Collins Custom Guitars

Premium grade, custom/production, classical, flamenco and steel string guitars built in Argyle, New York, by luthier Michael Collins, starting in 1975.

Michael Collins Guitars

Luthier Michael Collins builds his professional and premium grade, custom, Selmer style, archtop and flat-top guitars, starting in 2002, in Keswick, Ontario. He also builds mandolins.

Michael Cone

1968-present. Presentation grade, production/custom, classical guitars built previously in California and currently in Kihei Maui, Hawaii by luthier Michael Cone. He also builds ukuleles.

Michael Dunn Guitars

Luthier Michael Dunn begins in 1968, builds production/custom Maccaferri-style guitars in New Westminster, British Columbia. He also offers a harp uke and a Weissenborn- or Knutsen-style Hawaiian guitar, and has built archtops.

Michael Kelly

1999-present. Founded by Tracy Hoeft and offering intermediate and professional grade, production, acoustic, solidbody and archtop guitars. The brand was owned by the Hanser Music Group from 2004-'15. They also offer mandolins and basses.

Michael Lewis Instruments

1992-present. Luthier Michael Lewis builds his premium and presentation grade, custom, archtop guitars in Grass Valley, California. He also builds mandolins.

Michael Menkevich

Luthier Michael Menkevich builds his professional and premium grade, production/custom, flamenco and classical guitars in Elkins Park, Pennsylvania, starting in 1970.

Michael Silvey Custom Guitars

2003-ca. 2007. Solidbody electric guitars built by Michael Silvey in North Canton, Ohio.

MODEL		EXC. COND.	
YEAR	FEATURES	LOW	HIGH

Michael Thames

1972-present. Luthier Michael Thames builds his premium grade, custom/production, classical guitars in Taos, New Mexico.

Michael Tuttle

2003-present. Professional and premium grade, custom, solid and hollowbody guitars and basses built by luthier Michael Tuttle in Saugus, California.

Michihiro Matsuda

1997-present. Presentation grade, production/custom, steel and nylon string acoustic guitars built by luthier Michihiro Matsuda in Oakland, California. He also builds harp guitars.

Microfrets

1967-1975, 2004-2005. Professional grade, production, electric guitars built in Myersville, Maryland. They also built basses. Founded by Ralph S. Jones, Sr. in Frederick, Microfrets offered over 20 models of guitars that sported innovative designs and features, with pickups designed by Bill Lawrence. The brand was revived, again in Frederick, by Will Meadors and Paul Rose in '04.

Serial numbers run from about 1000 to about 3800. Not all instruments have serial numbers, particularly ones produced in '75. Serial numbers do not appear to be correlated to a model type, but are sequential by the general date of production.

Instruments can be identified by body styles as follows; Styles 1, 1.5, 2, and 3. An instrument may be described as a Model Name and Style Number (for example, Covington Style 1). Style 1 has a wavey-shaped pickguard with control knobs mounted below the guard and the 2-piece guitar body has a particle board side gasket. Style 1.5 has the same guard and knobs, but no side body gasket. Style 2 has an oblong pickguard with top mounted control knobs and a pancake style seam between the top and lower part of the body. Style 3 has a seamless 2-piece body and a Speedline neck.

Baritone Signature
1971. Baritone version of Signature Guitar, sharply pointed double-cut, with or without f-holes, single- or double-dot inlays.

1971		$1,300	$1,675

Baritone Stage II
1971-ca. 1975. Double-cut, 2 pickups.

1971-1975		$1,300	$1,675

Calibra I
1969-1975. Double-cut, 2 pickups, f-hole.

1969-1975		$1,150	$1,500

Covington
1967-1969. Offset double-cut, 2 pickups, f-hole.

1967-1969		$1,725	$2,250

Golden Comet
1969. Double-cut, 2 pickups, f-hole, name changed to Wanderer.

1969		$1,500	$1,950

1997 Metropolitan Glendale
Imaged by Heritage Auctions, HA.com

Michihiro Matsuda OM

GUITARS

Microfrets Plainsman
Michael Kellum

Microfrets Spacetone
Michael Kellum

MODEL YEAR	FEATURES	EXC. COND. LOW	HIGH
Golden Melody			
1969, 2004-2005. Offset double-cut, 2 pickups, f-hole, name changed to Stage II in '69.			
1969-1971		$1,600	$2,100
Huntington			
1969-1975. Double-cut, 2 pickups.			
1969-1975		$1,725	$2,250
Orbiter			
1967-1969. Odd triple cutaway body, thumbwheel controls on bottom edge of 'guard.			
1967-1969		$1,725	$2,250
Plainsman			
1967-1969. Offset double-cut, 2 pickups, f-hole, thumbwheel controls on bottom edge of 'guard.			
1967-1969		$1,850	$2,400
Signature			
1967-1969. Double-cut, 2 pickups.			
1967-1969		$1,725	$2,250
Spacetone			
1969-1971, 2004-2005. Double-cut semi-hollow body, 2 pickups.			
1969-1971		$1,725	$2,250
Stage II			
1969-1975. Renamed from Golden Melody, offset double-cut, 2 pickups.			
1969-1975		$1,600	$2,100
Swinger			
1971-1975. Offset double-cut, 2 pickups.			
1971-1975		$1,725	$2,250
Voyager/The Voyager			
1967-1968. Early model, less than a dozen made, Voyager headstock logo (no Microfrets logo), 2 DeArmond-style single-coils, offset double-cut body, FM transmitter on upper bass bout facilitates wireless transmission to Microfrets receiver or FM radio.			
1967-1968		$3,100	$4,000
Wanderer			
1969-1971. Renamed from Golden Comet, double-cut, 2 pickups.			
1969-1971		$1,475	$1,925

Mike Lull Custom Guitars

1995-present. Professional and premium grade, production/custom, guitars and basses built by luthier Mike Lull in Bellevue, Washington.

Milburn Guitars

1990-present. Luthiers Orville and Robert Milburn build their premium grade, custom, classical guitars in Sweet Home, Oregon.

Miller

1960s. One of the brand names of guitars built for others by Egmond in Holland.

Minarik

Luthier M.E. Minarik builds his professional and premium grade, custom/production, solid and chambered body guitars in Van Nuys, California.

MODEL YEAR	FEATURES	EXC. COND. LOW	HIGH

Minerva

1930s. Resonator and archtop guitars sold through catalog stores, likely made by one of the big Chicago builders of the era.

Mirabella

1997-present. Professional and premium grade, custom archtops, flat-tops, hollowbody, and solidbody guitars and basses built by luthier Cristian Mirabella in Babylon, New York. He also builds mandolins and ukes.

Miranda Guitars

2002-present. Owner Phil Green uses components made by various shops in California to assemble and set-up, professional grade, full-size travel/silent-practice guitars in Palo Alto, California.

Mitre

1983-1985. Bolt neck, solidbody guitars and basses made in Aldenville (or East Longmeadow), Massachusetts, featuring pointy body shapes, 2 humbuckers, active or passive electronics.

MJ Guitar Engineering

1993-present. Professional and premium grade, production/custom, hollowbody, chambered and solidbody guitars and basses built by luthier Mark Johnson in Rohnert Park, California.

Mobius Megatar

2000-2019. Professional grade, production, hybrid guitars designed for two-handed tapping, built in Mount Shasta, California. Founded by Reg Thompson, Henri Dupont, and Traktor Topaz in '97, they released their first guitars in '00.

Modulus

1978-2013. Founded by Geoff Gould in the San Francisco area, and later built in Novato, California. Modulus built professional grade, production/custom, solidbody electric guitars up to '05.

Genesis 2/2T
1996-2005. Double-cut, extended bass horn alder body, bolt-on carbon fiber/red cedar neck, hum-single-single pickups, locking vibrato (2T model).

1996-2005	$1,475	$1,925

Moll Custom Instruments

1996-present. Luthier Bill Moll builds his professional and premium grade, archtops in Springfield, Missouri. He has also built violins, violas and cellos.

Monrad, Eric

1993-present. Premium, custom, flamenco and classical guitars built by luthier Eric Monrad in Healdsburg, California.

Monroe Guitars

Luthier Matt Handley builds his custom, professional grade, solidbody electric guitars and basses in State Center, Iowa. He started in 2004.

MODEL YEAR	FEATURES	EXC. COND. LOW	HIGH

Montalvo
See listing under Casa Montalvo.

Montaya
Late 1970s-1980s. Montaya Hyosung 'America' Inc., Korean acoustic and electric import copies.

Monteleone
1976-present. Presentation grade, production/custom, archtop guitars built by Luthier John Monteleone in Islip, New York. He also builds mandolins. Instruments should be evaluated on a case-by-case basis.

Montgomery Ward
The mail-order and retail giant offered a variety of instruments and amps from several different U.S. and overseas manufacturers.

Model 8379/H44 Stratotone
Mid-1950s. Private branded Harmony Stratotone, some without logo but with crown-style stencil/painted logo on headstock, many with gold-copper finish, 1 pickup.

1950s	Various models	$800	$1,050

Monty
1980-present. Luthier Brian Monty builds his professional, premium and presentation grade, production/custom, archtop, semi-hollow, solid-body, and chambered electric guitars originally in Lennoxville, Quebec, and currently in Anne de Prescott, Ontario.

Moog
1964-present. Moog introduced its premium grade, production, Harmonic Control System solid-body guitar in 2008. They also offer guitar effects.

Moon (Japan)
1979-present. Professional and premium grade, production/custom, guitars and basses made in Japan.

Moon (Scotland)
1979-present. Intermediate, professional and premium grade, production/custom, acoustic and electric guitars built by luthier Jimmy Moon in Glasgow, Scotland. They also build mandolin family instruments.

Moonstone
1972-2020. Professional, premium, and presentation grade production/custom flat-top, solid and semi-hollow electric guitars, built by luthier Steve Helgeson in Eureka, California. He also built basses. Higher unit sales in the early-'80s. Some models have an optional graphite composite neck built by Modulus. Steve passed away in June, 2020.

MODEL YEAR	FEATURES	EXC. COND. LOW	HIGH

Eclipse Standard
1979-1983. Figured wood body, offset double-cut, neck-thru, standard maple neck, dot markers, natural finish, 12-string (XII) available.

1979-1983		$1,425	$1,850
1979-1983	XII	$1,425	$1,850

Exploder
1980-1983. Figured wood solidbody, neck-thru, standard maple neck, natural finish.

1980-1983		$1,600	$2,100

Flaming V
1980-1984. Figured wood body, V-shaped, neck-thru, standard maple neck, natural finish.

1980-1984		$1,600	$2,100
M-80			

1980-1984. Figured wood double-cut semi-hollow body, standard maple or optional graphite neck, natural finish.

1980s	Maple or graphite	$2,450	$3,150

Vulcan Deluxe
1979-1983. Figured maple carved-top body, offset double-cut, diamond markers, standard maple or optional graphite neck, natural finish.

1979-1983	Maple or graphite	$2,350	$3,100

Vulcan Standard
1979-1983. Mahogany carved-top body, offset double-cutaway, dot markers, standard maple or optional graphite neck, natural finish.

1979-1983	Maple or graphite	$2,100	$2,750

Morales
Ca.1967-1968. Guitars and basses made in Japan by Zen-On, not heavily imported into the U.S., if at all.

Solidbody Electric

1967-1968	Various models	$150	$350

More Harmony
1930s. Private branded by Dobro for Dailey's More Harmony Music Studio. Private branding for catalog companies, teaching studios, publishers, and music stores was common for the Chicago makers. More Harmony silk-screen logo on the headstock.

Dobro
1930s. 14" wood body with upper bout f-holes and metal resonator, sunburst.

1930s		$1,000	$1,300

Morgaine Guitars
Luthier Jorg Tandler builds his professional and premium grade, production/custom electrics in Germany, starting in 1994.

Morgan Monroe
1999-present. Intermediate grade, production, acoustic, acoustic/electric and resonator guitars and basses made in Korea and distributed by SHS International of Indianapolis, Indiana. They also offer mandolins and banjos.

Moll Custom Instruments

1980 Moonstone Vulcan Deluxe

1968 Mosrite Joe Maphis Mark XVIII

Mathew A. Dirjish

1965 Mosrite Ventures Model

Vic Hines

MODEL YEAR	FEATURES	EXC. COND. LOW	HIGH

Morris

1967-present. Intermediate, professional and premium grade, production, acoustic guitars imported by Moridaira of Japan. Morris guitars were first imported into the U.S. from the early '70s to around '90. They are again being imported into the U.S. starting in 2001. They also offered mandolins in the '70s.

000 Copy
1970s. Brazilian rosewood laminate body.

1970s		$525	$700

Acoustic-Electric Archtop

1970s	Various models	$675	$875

D-45 Copy
1970s. Brazilian rosewood laminate body.

1970s		$600	$800

Mortoro Guitars

1992-present. Luthier Gary Mortoro builds his premium grade, custom, archtop guitars in Miami, Florida.

Mosrite

The history of Mosrite has more ups and downs than just about any other guitar company. Founder Semie Moseley had several innovative designs and had his first success in 1954, at age 19, building doubleneck guitars for super picker Joe Maphis and protégé Larry Collins. Next came the Ventures, who launched the brand nationally by playing Mosrites and featuring them on album covers. At its '60s peak, the company was turning out around 1,000 guitars a month. The company ceased production in '69, and Moseley went back to playing gospel concerts and built a few custom instruments during the '70s.

In the early-'80s, Mosrite again set up shop in Jonas Ridge, North Carolina, but the plant burned down in November '83, taking about 300 guitars with it. In early-'92, Mosrite relocated to Booneville, Arkansas, producing a new line of Mosrites, of which 96% were exported to Japan, where the Ventures and Mosrite have always been popular. Semie Moseley died, at age 57, on August 7, '92 and the business carried on until finally closing its doors in '93. The Mosrite line has again been revived, offering intermediate and premium grade, production, reissues.

Throughout much of the history of Mosrite, production numbers were small and model features often changed. As a result, exact production dates are difficult to determine.

Balladeer
1964-1965. Mid-size flat-top, slope shoulder, natural or sunburst.

1964-1965		$1,300	$1,500

Brass Rail
1970s. Double-cut solidbody, has a brass plate running the length of the 'board.

1970s		$1,200	$1,350

MODEL YEAR	FEATURES	EXC. COND. LOW	HIGH

Celebrity 1
Late-1960s-1970s. Thick hollowbody, 2 pickups, sunburst.

1960s-70s		$1,200	$1,350

Celebrity 2 Standard
Late-1960s-1970s. Thin hollowbody, 2 pickups, in the '70s, it came in a Standard and a Deluxe version.

1960s-70s		$1,200	$1,350

Celebrity 3
Late-1960s-1970s. Thin hollowbody, double-cut, 2 pickups, f-holes.

1960s-70s		$1,200	$1,350

Combo Mark 1
1966-1968. Bound body, 1 f-hole.

1966-1968		$1,850	$2,400

Custom-Built
1952-1962. Pre-production custom instruments hand-built by Semie Moseley, guidance pricing only, each instrument will vary. A wide variety of instruments were made during this period. Some were outstanding, but others, especially those made around '60, could be very basic and of much lower quality. Logos would vary widely and some '60 logos looked especially homemade.

1952-1959	Rare, high-end	$12,000	$16,000
1960-1962	Common, low-end	$1,900	$2,500

D-40 Resonator
1960s. Symmetrical double-cut thinline archtop-style body with metal resonator in center of body, 2 pickups, 2 control knobs and toggle switch.

1960s		$1,350	$1,750

D-100 Californian
1960s. Double-cut, resonator guitar with 2 pickups.

1967		$1,350	$1,750

Gospel
1967. Thinline double-cut, f-hole, 2 pickups, vibrato, Gospel logo on headstock.

1967	Sunburst	$1,725	$2,250
1967	White	$2,400	$3,100

Joe Maphis Doubleneck
1963-1968. Limited Edition reissue of the guitar Semie Moseley made for Maphis, with the smaller octave neck, sunburst.

1963-1968	Octave 6/standard 6	$4,450	$5,800
1963-1968	Standard 6/12	$4,450	$5,800

Joe Maphis Mark 1
1959-1972. Semi-hollow double-cut, 2 single-coils, spruce top, walnut back, rosewood 'board, natural.

1959-1972		$2,100	$2,700

Joe Maphis Mark XVIII
1960s. 6/12 doubleneck, double-cut, 2 pickups on each neck, Moseley tremolo on 6-string.

1960s		$3,300	$4,300

Mosrite 1988
1988-early-1990s. Has traditional Mosrite body styling, Mosrite pickups and bridge.

1988		$675	$875

Octave Guitar
1963-1965. 14" scale, 1 pickup, Ventures Mosrite body style, single neck pickup, very few made.

1963-1965		$5,000	$6,500

MODEL YEAR	FEATURES	EXC. COND. LOW	HIGH

Stereo 350
1974-1975. Single-cut solidbody, 2 outputs, 2 pick-ups, 4 knobs, slider and toggle, black.

1974-1975		$1,400	$1,800

Ventures Model
1963-1968. Double-cut solidbody, triple-bound body '63, no binding after, Vibramute for '63-'64, Moseley tailpiece '65-'68.

1963	Blue or red, bound	$7,000	$9,000
1963	Sunburst, bound	$5,600	$7,400
1964	Blue or red, Vibramute	$4,100	$6,600
1964	Sunburst, Vibramute	$5,600	$7,400
1965	Moseley (2 screws)	$3,700	$4,800
1965	Vibramute, (3 screws)	$4,500	$5,800
1966-1968	Moseley	$3,200	$4,100

Ventures (Jonas Ridge/Boonville)
1982-1993. Made in Jonas Ridge, NC or Booneville, AR, classic Ventures styling.

1982-1993		$1,950	$2,550

Ventures Mark V
1963-1967. Double-cut solidbody.

1963-1967		$1,650	$2,150

Ventures Mark XII
1966-1967. Double-cut solidbody, 12 strings.

1966-1967		$2,850	$3,700

Mossman

Professional and premium grade, production/custom, flat-top guitars built in Sulphur Springs, Texas, starting in 1965. They have also built acoustic basses. Founded by Stuart L. Mossman in Winfield, Kansas. In '75, fire destroyed one company building, including the complete supply of Brazilian rosewood. They entered into an agreement with C.G. Conn Co. to distribute guitars by '77. 1200 Mossman guitars in a Conn warehouse in Nevada were ruined by being heated during the day and frozen during the night. A disagreement about who was responsible resulted in cash flow problems for Mossman. Production fell to a few guitars per month until the company was sold in '86 to Scott Baxendale. Baxendale sold the company to John Kinsey and Bob Casey in Sulphur Springs in '89.

Flint Hills
1970-1979. Flat-top acoustic, East Indian rosewood back and sides.

1970-1979	Indian rosewood	$1,700	$2,200

Flint Hills Custom

1970-1979	Indian rosewood	$2,400	$3,100

Golden Era
1970-1977. D-style, vine inlay and other high-end appointments, Brazilian rosewood back and sides until '76, then Indian rosewood.

1970-1975	Brazilian rosewood	$3,850	$5,000
1976-1977	Indian rosewood	$2,500	$3,250

Golden Era Custom

1970-1975	Brazilian rosewood	$5,300	$6,900

Great Plains
1970-1979. Flat-top, Brazilian rosewood until '75 then Indian rosewood, herringbone trim.

1970-1975	Brazilian rosewood	$2,900	$3,750
1976-1979	Indian rosewood	$1,925	$2,500

Great Plains Custom

1970-1975	Brazilian rosewood	$4,000	$5,250

Southwind
1976-ca. 1986, mid-1990s-2002. Flat-top, abalone trim top.

1976-1979	Indian rosewood	$2,200	$2,900

Tennessee
1972-1979. D-style, spruce top, mahogany back and sides, rope marquetry purfling, rope binding.

1972-1979		$1,275	$1,650

Tennessee 12-String

1975-1979	Mahogany	$1,275	$1,650

Timber Creek
1976-1979. D-style, Indian rosewood back and sides, spruce top.

1976-1979	Indian rosewood	$2,000	$2,650

Winter Wheat
1976-1979, mid-1990s-2000s. Flat-top, Indian rosewood back and sides, abalone trim, natural finish.

1976-1979	Indian rosewood	$2,200	$2,850

Winter Wheat 12-String
1976-1979. 12-string version of Winter Wheat, natural.

1976-1979	Indian rosewood	$2,200	$2,850

MotorAve Guitars

2002-present. Luthier Mark Fuqua builds his professional and premium grade, production, electric guitars originally in Los Angeles, California, and currently in Durham, North Carolina.

Mouradian

1983-present. Luthiers Jim and Jon Mouradian build their professional and premium grade, production/custom, electric guitars and basses in Winchester, Massachusetts. Jim died in 2017.

Mozart

1930s. Private brand made by Kay.

Hawaiian (Square Neck)
1930s. Spruce top, solid mahogany sides and back, pealoid overlay on peghead with large Mozart inscribed logo, small jumbo 15 1/2" body.

1935-1939		$1,000	$1,300

Mozzani

Built in shops of Luigi Mozzani (b. March 9, 1869, Faenza, Italy; d. 1943) who opened lutherie schools in Bologna, Cento and Rovereto in 1890s. By 1926 No. 1 and 2 Original Mozzani Model Mandolin (flat back), No. 3 Mandola (flat back), No. 4 6-String Guitar, No. 5 7-, 8-, and 9-String Guitars, No. 6 Lyre-Guitar.

1975 Mossman Great Plains
David Stone

1976 Mossman Southwind

Musicman Sabre II
Tom Pfeifer

*Music Man Steve
Morse Signature*

MODEL		EXC. COND.	
YEAR	FEATURES	LOW	HIGH

M-Tone Guitars

2009-present. Professional and premium grade, production/custom, solidbody electric guitars built in Portland, Oregon by luthier Matt Proctor.

Muiderman Guitars

1997-present. Custom, premium grade, steel string and classical guitars built by luthier Kevin Muiderman currently in Grand Forks, North Dakota, and previously in Beverly Hills, Michigan, 1997-2001, and Neenah, Wisconsin, '01-'07. He also builds mandolins.

Murph

1965-1967. Mid-level electric semi-hollow and solidbody guitars built by Pat Murphy in San Fernado, California. Murph logo on headstock. They also offered basses and amps.

Electric Solidbody

1965-1967		$1,100	$1,450

Electric XII

1965-1967		$1,100	$1,450

Music Man

1972-present. Professional grade, production, solidbody guitars built in San Luis Obispo, California. They also build basses. Founded by ex-Fender executives Forrest White and Tom Walker in Orange County, California. Music Man originally produced guitar and bass amps based on early Fender ideas using many former Fender employees. They contracted with Leo Fender's CLF Research to design and produce a line of solidbody guitars and basses. Leo Fender began G & L Guitars with George Fullerton in '80. In '84, Music Man was purchased by Ernie Ball and production was moved to San Luis Obispo.

Albert Lee Signature

1993-present. Swamp ash body, figured maple neck, 3 pickups, white pearloid 'guard, Pinkburst.

1993-1996	Pinkburst	$1,200	$1,575
1996-2019	Tremolo option	$1,125	$1,450

Axis

1996-present. Offset double-cut solidbody, figured maple top, basswood body, 2 humbucker pickups, Floyd Rose.

1996-2021		$1,125	$1,450

Axis Sport

1996-2002. Two P-90s.

1996-2002		$1,125	$1,450

Axis Super Sport

2003-present. Figured top.

2003-2021		$1,125	$1,450

Edward Van Halen

1991-1995. Basswood solidbody, figured maple top, bolt-on maple neck, maple 'board, binding, 2 humbuckers, named changed to Axis.

1991-1995		$2,900	$3,850

John Petrucci 6/JP-6

2008-2021. Standard model, basswood body, maple neck, rosewood 'board, various colors with high gloss finish.

2008-2021		$1,575	$2,050

MODEL		EXC. COND.	
YEAR	FEATURES	LOW	HIGH

John Petrucci BFR

2011-2020. Ball Family Reserve (BFR).

2011-2020		$1,850	$2,400

Reflex

2011-2017. Referred to as The Game Changer, patent-pending pickup switching system, maple or rosewood neck with matching headstock, black finish.

2011-2017		$1,375	$1,800

S.U.B 1

2004-2006. Offset double-cut solidbody.

2004-2005		$500	$650

Sabre I

1978-1982. Offset double-cut solidbody, maple neck, 2 pickups, Sabre I comes with a flat 'board with jumbo frets.

1978-1982		$1,125	$1,450

Sabre II

1978-1982. Same as Sabre I, but with an oval 7 1/2" radius 'board.

1978-1982		$1,125	$1,450

Silhouette

1986-present. Offset double-cut, contoured beveled solidbody, various pickup configurations.

1986-2021		$1,125	$1,450
2006	20th Anniversary	$1,125	$1,450

Silhouette 6/12 Double Neck

2009-2014. Alder body, maple or rosewood 'boards, 4 humbuckers.

2009-2014		$1,775	$2,300

Silhouette Special

1995-present. Silhouette with Silent Circuit.

1995-2021		$1,125	$1,450

Steve Morse Signature

1987-present. Solidbody, 4 pickups, humbuckers in the neck and bridge positions, 2 single-coils in the middle, special pickup switching, 6-bolt neck mounting, maple neck.

1987-2021		$1,550	$2,000

Stingray I

1976-1982. Offset double-cut solidbody, flat 'board radius.

1976-1982		$1,125	$1,450

Stingray II

1976-1982. Offset double-cut solidbody, rounder 'board radius.

1976-1982		$1,125	$1,450

Musicvox

1996-2001, 2011-present. Intermediate grade, production, imported retro-vibe guitars and basses from Matt Eichen of Cherry Hill, New Jersey.

Myka

2003-present. Luthier David Myka builds his professional and premium grade, custom/production, solidbody, semi-hollowbody, hollowbody, archtop, and flat-top guitars in Seattle, Washington. Until '07 he was located in Orchard Park, New York.

MODEL YEAR	FEATURES	EXC. COND. LOW	HIGH

Nady

1976-present. Wireless sound company Nady Systems offered guitars and basses with built-in wireless systems for 1985-'87. Made by Fernandes in Japan until '86, then by Cort in Korea.

Lightning/Lightning II

1985-1987. Double-cut, neck-thru, solidbody, 24 frets, built-in wireless, labeled as just Lightning until cheaper second version (bolt-neck) came out in '86.

1985-1987		$360	$475

Napolitano Guitars

Luthier Arthur Napolitano began in 1993 to build professional and premium grade, custom, archtop guitars in Allentown, New Jersey.

NashGuitars

2001-present. Luthier Bill Nash builds his professional grade, production/custom, aged solidbody electric guitars and basses in Olympia, Washington.

Nashville Guitar Company

1985-present. Professional and premium grade, custom, flat-top guitars built by luthier Marty Lanham in Nashville, Tennessee. He has also built banjos.

National

Ca. 1927-present. Founded in Los Angeles, California as the National String Instrument Corporation by John Dopyera, George Beauchamp, Ted Kleinmeyer and Paul Barth. In '29 Dopyera left to start the Dobro Manufacturing Company with Rudy and Ed Dopyera and Vic Smith. The Dobro company competed with National until the companies reunited. Beauchamp and Barth then left National to found Ro-Pat-In with Adolph Rickenbacker and C.L. Farr (later becoming Electro String Instrument Corporation, then Rickenbacher). In '32 Dopyera returns to National and National and Dobro start their merger in late-'33, finalizing it by mid-'34. Throughout the '30s, National and Dobro maintained separate production, sales and distribution. National Dobro moved to Chicago, Illinois in '36. In Chicago, archtop and flat-top bodies are built primarily by Regal and Kay; after '37 all National resonator guitar bodies made by Kay. L.A. production is maintained until around '37, although some assembly of Dobros continued in L.A. (primarily for export) until '39 when the L.A. offices are finally closed. By ca. '39 the Dobro brand disappears.

In '42, the company's resonator production ceased and Victor Smith, Al Frost and Louis Dopyera buy the company and change name to Valco Manufacturing Company. Post-war production resumes in '46. Valco is purchased by treasurer Robert Engelhardt in '64. In '67, Valco bought Kay, but in '68 the new Valco/Kay company went out of business. In the Summer of '69 the assets, including brand names, were auctioned off and the National and Supro names were purchased by Chicago-

area distributor/importer Strum 'N Drum (Noble, Norma brands). The National brand is used on copies in early- to mid-'70s, and the brand went into hiatus by the '80s.

In '88 National Resophonic Guitars is founded in San Luis Obispo, California, by Don Young, with production of National-style resonator guitars beginning in '89 (see following). In the '90s, the National brand also resurfaces on inexpensive Asian imports.

National Resonator guitars are categorized by materials and decoration (from plain to fancy): Duolian, Triolian, Style 0, Style 1, Style 2, Style 3, Style 4, Don #1, Style 97, Don #2, Don #3, Style 35.

National guitars all have serial numbers which provide clues to date of production. This is a complex issue. This list combines information included in George Gruhn and Walter Carter's Gruhn's Guide to Vintage Guitars, which was originally provided by Bob Brozman and Mike Newton, with new information provided by Mike Newton.

Pre Chicago numbers:
A101-A450 1935-1936.

Chicago numbers:
A prefix (some may not have the prefix) 1936-mid-1997. B prefix Mid-1937-1938. C prefix Late-1938-1940. G prefix up to 200 Ea. 1941-ea. 1942. G suffix under 2000 Ea. 1941-ea. 1942. G suffix 2000-3000s (probably old parts) 1943-1945. G suffix 4000s (old parts) Late 1945-mid-1947.

V100-V7500 1947. V7500-V15000 1948. V15000-V25000 1949. V25000-V35000 1950. V35000-V38000 1951. X100-X7000 1951. X7000-X17000 1952. X17000-X30000 1953. X30000-X43000 1954. X43000-X57000 1955. X57000-X71000 1956. X71000-X85000 1957. X85000-X990001958.

T100-T5000 1958. T5000-T25000 1959. T25000-T50000 1960. T50000-T75000 1961. T75000-T90000 1962. G100-G5000 1962. T90000-T99000 1963. G5000-G15000 1963. G15000-G40000 1964. 1 prefix 1965-ea. 1968. 2 prefix Mid-1968.

Aragon De Luxe

1939-1942. Archtop with resonator (the only archtop resonator offered), spruce top and maple back and sides, light brown.

1939-1942		$7,500	$9,700

Big Daddy LP-457-2

1970s. Strum & Drum import, single-cut, LP-style, 2 pickups, gold hardware, black.

1970s		$350	$450

Bluegrass 35

1963-1965. Acoustic, non-cut single-cone resonator, Res-O-Glas body in Arctic White.

1963-1965		$1,775	$2,300

Bobbie Thomas

Ca.1967-1968. Double-cut thinline hollowbody, bat-shaped f-holes, 2 pickups, Bobbie Thomas on 'guard, vibrato.

1967-1968		$775	$1,000

Nash Guitars S63
John Rutherford

National Big Daddy LP-457-2
Imaged by Heritage Auctions, HA.com

GUITARS

National Don Style 1
Imaged by Heritage Auctions, HA.com

National 1105 Glenwood
Mike Newton

MODEL YEAR	FEATURES	EXC. COND. LOW	HIGH
Cameo			
1957-1958. Renamed from Model 1140 in '57, full-body acoustic archtop with carved top.			
1957-1958		$875	$1,150
Collegian			
1942-1943. Metal body resonator similar to Duolian, 14-fret round or square neck, yellow.			
1942-1943		$1,450	$1,900
Don Style 1			
1934-1936. Plain body with engraved borders, pearl dot inlay, 14 frets, single-cone, silver (nickel-plated).			
1934-1936		$8,500	$11,200
Don Style 2			
1934-1936. Geometric Art Deco body engraving, 14 frets, single-cone, fancy square pearl inlays and pearloid headstock overlay, silver (nickel-plated).			
1934-1936		$9,600	$12,600
Don Style 3			
1934-1936. Same as Style 2 but more elaborate floral engravings, fancy pearl diamond inlays, 14 frets, single-cone, silver (nickel-plated), only a very few made.			
1934-1936		$17,000	$22,300
Duolian			
1930-1939. Acoustic steel body, frosted paint finish until '36, mahogany-grain paint finish '37-'39, round neck, square neck available in '33, 12-fret neck until '34 then 14-fret.			
1930-1934	Round neck	$4,200	$5,500
EG 685 Hollow Body Electric			
1970s. Strum & Drum distributed, double-cut hollowbody copy, 2 pickups.			
1970s		$450	$600
El Trovador			
1933 only. Wood body, 12 frets.			
1933		$2,250	$2,925
Electric Spanish			
1935-1938. 15 1/2" archtop with Pat. Appl. For bridge pickup, National crest logo, fancy N-logo 'guard, black and white art deco, sunburst, becomes New Yorker Spanish '39-'58.			
1935-1938		$2,000	$2,625
Estralita			
1934-1942. Acoustic with single-cone resonator, f-holes, multi-bound, 14-fret, mahogany top and back, shaded brown.			
1934-1942		$1,050	$1,375
Glenwood 95			
1962-1964. Glenwood 98 without third bridge-mount pickup, Vermillion Red or Flame Red.			
1962-1964		$3,565	$4,650
Glenwood 98			
1964-1965. USA map-shaped solidbody of molded Res-O-Glas, 2 regular and 1 bridge pickup, vibrato, 3 tailpiece options, Pearl White.			
1964-1965		$3,775	$4,900
Glenwood 99			
1962-1965. USA map-shaped solidbody of molded Res-O-Glas, 2 regular and 1 bridge pickups, butterfly inlay.			
1962-1963	Snow White	$3,775	$4,900
1964-1965	Green/Blue	$6,800	$8,800

MODEL YEAR	FEATURES	EXC. COND. LOW	HIGH
Glenwood Deluxe			
1959-1961. Renamed from Glenwood 1105, Les Paul-shaped solidbody, wood body, not fiberglass, multi-bound, 2 pickups, factory Bigsby, vibrato, natural.			
1959-1961		$2,150	$2,800
Havana			
1938-1942. Natural spruce top, sunburst back and sides.			
1938-1942	Round neck	$1,050	$1,375
1938-1942	Square neck	$675	$900
Model 1100 California			
1949-1955. Electric hollowbody archtop, multi-bound, f-holes, trapeze tailpiece, 1 pickup, natural.			
1949-1955		$1,075	$1,400
Model 1103 Del-Mar			
1954-1957. Electric archtop, 2 pickups, adjustable bridge, sunburst finish.			
1954-1957		$1,375	$1,800
Model 1104 Town and Country			
1954-1958. Model just below Glenwood 1105, dots, 2 or 3 pickups, plastic overlay on back, natural finish.			
1954-1958	2 pickups	$2,025	$2,625
1954-1958	3 pickups	$2,300	$2,975
Model 1105 Glenwood			
1954-1958. Les Paul-shaped solidbody, wood body, not fiberglass, single-cut, multi-bound, 2 pickups, natural, renamed Glenwood Deluxe with Bigsby in '59.			
1954-1958		$2,500	$3,275
Model 1106 Val-Trol Baron			
1959-1960. Single-cut solidbody, 2 pickups, 1 piezo, block inlays, black.			
1959-1960		$1,550	$2,025
Model 1107 Debonaire			
1953-1960. Single rounded-cutaway full-depth 16" electric archtop, single neck pickup, Debonaire logo on 'guard (for most models), large raised National script logo on headstock, sunburst.			
1953-1960		$925	$1,200
Model 1109/1198 Bel-Aire			
1953-1960. Single pointed cut archtop, 2 (1109) pickups until '57, 3 (1198) after, master tone knob and jack, bound body, sunburst.			
1953-1957	1109, 2 pickups	$1,225	$1,600
1958-1960	1198, 3 pickups	$1,375	$1,800
Model 1110/1111 Aristocrat			
1941-1954. Electric full body non-cut archtop, 1 pickup, 2 knobs, early model with triple backslash markers, later with block markers, National-crest headstock inlaid logo, natural finish only until model numbers added to name in '48, shaded sunburst finish (1110) and natural (1111).			
1941-1948	Natural	$1,000	$1,300
1948-1955	1110, sunburst	$1,225	$1,600
1948-1955	1111, natural	$1,225	$1,600
Model 1120 New Yorker			
1954-1958. Renamed from New Yorker Spanish, 16.25" electric archtop, 1 pickup on floating 'guard, dot markers, blond.			
1954-1958		$925	$1,200
Model 1122 Cosmopolitan			
1954-1957. Small wood non-cutaway solidbody, dot markers, 1 pickup, 2 knobs on mounted 'guard.			
1954-1957		$775	$1,025

MODEL YEAR	FEATURES	EXC. COND. LOW	HIGH

Model 1122 Val-Trol Junior
1959-1960. Single-cut solidbody, 1 pickup and 1piezo, dot inlays, ivory.

1959-1960		$1,200	$1,550

Model 1123 Bolero
1954-1957. Les Paul-shape, control knobs mounted on 'guard, single pickup, trapeze tailpiece, sunburst.

1954-1957		$875	$1,150

Model 1124/1124B/1134 Avalon
1954-1957. Small wood solidbody, 2 pickups, 4 control knobs and switch on top-mounted 'guard, block markers, short trapeze bridge, sunburst (1124) or blond (1124B).

1954-1957	1124, sunburst	$1,350	$1,775
1954-1957	1124B/1134, blond	$1,475	$1,925

Model 1125 Dynamic
1951-1959. Full body 15.5" acoustic-electric archtop, sunburst version of New Yorker 1120 with some appointments slightly below the New Yorker, dot markers, 1 pickup, sunburst.

1951-1959		$825	$1,075

Model 1135 Acoustic Archtop
1948-1954. 17.25" full body acoustic archtop, carved top, split pearl markers.

1948-1954		$1,025	$1,325

Model 1140 Acoustic Archtop
1948-1957. 15.5" full body acoustic archtop, carved top, dot markers.

1948-1957		$725	$950

Model 1150 Flat-Top Auditorium
1951-1958. Auditorium-size flat-top, 14.25" narrow-waist, dot markers.

1951-1958		$775	$1,025

Model 1155/1155E /N-66 Jumbo
1948-1961. Flat-top acoustic with Gibson Jumbo body, mahogany back and sides, bolt-on neck.

1947	N-66	$2,600	$3,400
1948-1961	1155/1155E	$2,600	$3,400

Model 1170 Club Combo
1952-1955, 1959-1961. Electric hollowbody archtop, 2 pickups, rounded cutaway.

1952-1961		$1,375	$1,800

N600 Series
1968. Offset double-cut solidbody, 1, 2, and 3 pickup models, with and without vibrato.

1968	N624, 1 pickup	$500	$650
1968	N634, 2 pus, vibrato	$600	$800
1968	N644, 3 pus, vibrato	$775	$1,000
1968	N654, 12-string	$600	$800

N700 Series
1968. Flat-top, 700/710 dreadnoughts, 720/730 jumbos.

1968	N700 Western	$600	$800
1968	N710	$350	$475
1968	N720 Western	$400	$525
1968	N730 Deluxe	$575	$750

N800 Series
1968. Double-cut semi-hollow body, various models with or without Bigsby.

1968	No Bigsby	$600	$775
1968	With Bigsby	$700	$900

New Yorker Spanish
1939-1953. Electric archtop, 15.5" body until '47 then 16.25", 1 neck pickup, dot-diamond markers, sunburst or natural. Renamed New Yorker 1120 in '54.

1939-1946	155"	$2,000	$2,600
1947-1949	1625"	$1,700	$2,200
1950-1953	1625"	$1,475	$1,900

Newport 82
1963-1965. Renamed from Val-Pro 82, USA map-shaped Res-O-Glas, 1 pickup, Pepper Red finish.

1963-1965		$1,825	$2,375

Newport 84
1963-1965. Renamed from Val-Pro 84, USA map-shaped Res-O-Glas, 1 regular and 1 bridge pickup, Sea Foam Green finish.

1963-1965		$3,450	$4,475

Newport 88
1963-1965. Renamed from Val-Pro 88, USA map-shaped Res-O-Glas, 2 regular and 1 bridge pickup, Raven Black finish.

1963-1965		$2,300	$2,975

Reso-phonic
1956-1964. Pearloid-covered, single-cut semi-solidbody acoustic, single resonator, maroon or white, also a non-cut, square neck version was offered, which is included in these values.

1956-1964	Round neck, common finish	$1,600	$2,100
1956-1964	Round neck, rare finish	$1,775	$2,300
1956-1964	Square neck	$1,375	$1,775

Rosita
1933-1939. Plywood body by Harmony, plain metal resonator, plain appointments.

1933-1939		$1,100	$1,450

Silvo (Electric Hawaiian)
1937-1941. Nickel-plated metal body flat-top, small upper bout, f-holes, square neck, multiple straight line body art over dark background, Roman numeral parallelogram markers, National badge headstock logo, Silvo name on coverplate.

1937-1941	Silver	$3,000	$4,000

Studio 66
1961-1964. Electric solidbody of Res-O-Glas, single-cut, 1 pickup, renamed Varsity 66 in '65.

1961-1962	Sand Buff, bridge pu	$1,300	$1,700
1963-1964	Jet Black, neck pu	$1,300	$1,700

Style 0
1930-1942. Acoustic single-cone brass body (early models had a steel body), Hawaiian scene etching, 12-fret neck '30-'34, 14-fret neck '35 on, round (all years) or square ('33 on) neck.

1930-1934	Round neck, 12-fret, common etching	$3,000	$3,900
1930-1934	Round neck, 12-fret, rare etching	$3,800	$4,900
1933-1942	Square neck, common etching	$1,400	$1,800
1933-1942	Square neck, rare etching	$2,500	$3,300

1962 National Studio 66
Imaged by Heritage Auctions, HA.com

1930 National Style 0
Bernunzio Uptown Music

National Style 2 Tenor

*National Reso-Phonic
ResoLectric*

MODEL YEAR	FEATURES	EXC. COND. LOW	HIGH
1935-1942	Round, 14-fret (Knopfler assoc)	$6,200	$8,200
1935-1942	Round, 14-fret, common etching	$2,500	$3,300
1935-1942	Round, 14-fret, rare etching	$4,100	$5,400

Style 0 Tenor
1929-1930. Tenor, 4 strings, single-cone brass body, Hawaiian scene etching.

1929-1930		$900	$1,200

Style 1 Tricone
1927-1943. German silver body tricone resonator, ebony 'board, mahogany square (Hawaiian) or round (Spanish) neck, plain body, 12-fret neck until '34, 14-fret after.

1927-1943	Round neck	$6,000	$8,000
1928-1943	Square neck	$3,900	$5,100

Style 1 Tricone Plectrum
1928-1935. 26" scale versus the 23" scale of the tenor.

1928-1935	$1,950	$2,550

Style 1 Tricone Tenor
1928-1935. Tenor, 4 strings, 23" scale, square neck is Hawaiian, round neck is Spanish.

1928-1935	$1,950	$2,550

Style 1.5 Tricone
1930s. A "1/2" style like the 1.5 represents a different engraving pattern.

1930s	Round neck	$9,000	$12,000
1930s	Square neck	$3,100	$4,100

Style 2 Tricone
1927-1942. German silver body tricone resonator, wild rose engraving, square (Hawaiian) or round (Spanish) neck, 12-fret neck until '34, 14-fret after.

1927-1942	Round neck	$13,700	$18,000
1927-1942	Square neck	$4,300	$5,700

Style 2 Tricone Plectrum
1928-1935. 26" scale versus the 23" scale of the tenor.

1928-1935	$1,750	$2,300

Style 2 Tricone Tenor
1928-1935. Tenor.

1928-1935	$1,750	$2,300

Style 2.5 Tricone
1927-1928. Collector term for Style 2 with additional rose engravings on coverplate, bound ebony fretboard.

1927-1928	$8,200	$10,800

Style 3 Tricone
1928-1941. German silver body tricone resonator, lily-of-the-valley engraving, square (Hawaiian) or round (Spanish) neck, 12-fret neck until '34, 14-fret after, reintroduced with a nickel-plated brass body in '94.

1928-1939	Round neck	$14,000	$19,000
1928-1941	Square neck	$5,000	$6,500

Style 3 Tricone Plectrum
1928-1935. 26" scale versus the 23" scale of the tenor.

1928-1935	$3,100	$4,100

Style 3 Tricone Tenor
1928-1939. Tenor version.

1928-1939	$3,100	$4,100

Style 4 Tricone
1928-1940. German silver body tricone resonator, chrysanthemum etching, 12-fret neck until '34, 14-fret

after, reissued in '95 with same specs.

1928-1940	Round neck	$18,000	$24,000
1928-1940	Square neck	$4,800	$6,300

Style 35
1936-1942. Brass body tricone resonator, sand-blasted minstrel and trees scene, 12 frets, square (Hawaiian) or round (Spanish) neck.

1936-1942	Round neck	$27,000	$36,000
1936-1942	Square neck	$9,000	$12,000

Style 97
1936-1940. Nickel-plated brass body tricone resonator, sandblasted scene of female surfrider and palm trees, 12 frets, slotted peghead.

1936	Early '36, square neck	$9,800	$13,000
1936	Late '36, square neck, different 'board	$6,800	$9,000
1936-1940	Round neck	$28,000	$37,000

Style N
1930-1931. Nickel-plated brass body single-cone resonator, plain finish, 12 frets.

1930-1931	$4,500	$5,900

Triolian
1928-1941. Single-cone resonator, wood body replaced by metal body in '29, 12-fret neck and slotted headstock '28-'34, changed to 14-fret neck in '35 and solid head-stock in '36, round or square ('33 on) neck available.

1928-1936	Various colors	$3,200	$4,200
1936-1937	Fake rose-wood grain	$3,000	$3,925

Triolian Tenor
1928-1936. Tenor, metal body.

1928-1936	$1,100	$1,425

Trojan
1934-1942. Single-cone resonator wood body, f-holes, bound top, 14-fret round neck.

1934-1942	$1,400	$1,825

Val-Pro 82
1962-1963. USA map-shaped Res-O-Glas, 1 pickup, Vermillion Red finish, renamed Newport 82 in '63.

1962-1963	$1,325	$1,725

Val-Pro 84
1962-1963. USA map-shaped Res-O-Glas, 1 regular and 1 bridge pickup, snow white finish, renamed Newport 84 in '63.

1962-1963	$1,500	$1,950

Val-Pro 88
1962-1963. USA map-shaped Res-O-Glas, 2 regular and 1 bridge pickup, black finish, renamed Newport 88 in '63.

1962-1963	$2,450	$3,200

Varsity 66
1964-1965. Renamed from Studio 66 in '64, molded Res-O-Glas, 1 pickup, 2 knobs, beige finish.

1964-1965	$1,200	$1,550

Westwood 72
1962-1964. USA map-shaped solid hardwood body (not fiberglass), 1 pickup, Cherry Red.

1962-1964	$2,025	$2,625

MODEL YEAR	FEATURES	EXC. COND. LOW	HIGH
Westwood 75			
1962-1964. USA map-shaped solid hardwood body (not fiberglass), 1 regular and 1 bridge pickup, cherry-to-black sunburst finish.			
1962-1964		$2,025	$2,625
Westwood 77			
1962-1965. USA map-shaped solid hardwood body (not fiberglass), 2 regular and 1 bridge pickup.			
1962-1965	Blond-Ivory	$2,025	$2,625

National Reso-Phonic

1989-present. Professional and premium grade, production/custom, single cone, acoustic-electric, and tricone guitars (all with resonators), built in San Luis Obispo, California. They also build basses, mandolins and ukuleles. McGregor Gaines and Don Young formed the National Reso-Phonic Guitar Company with the objective of building instruments based upon the original National designs. Replicon is the aging process to capture the appearance and sound of a vintage National.

MODEL YEAR	FEATURES	EXC. COND. LOW	HIGH
Collegian			
2010-2020. Thin gauge steel body, 9.5" cone, biscuit bridge, aged ivory finish.			
2010-2020		$1,450	$1,900
Delphi			
1993-2010. Single cone, steel body.			
1993-2010		$1,700	$2,200
Dueco			
2012-2020. Gold or Silver crystalline finish.			
2012-2020		$2,100	$2,725
El Trovador			
2010-present. Wood body Dobro-style, single cone, biscuit bridge.			
2010-2021		$2,275	$2,975
Estralita Deluxe			
2006-2021. Single cone, walnut body, figured maple top, koa offered in '03.			
2006-2021	Maple or koa	$2,400	$3,100
Estralita Harlem Slim			
2010. Laminate maple.			
2010		$1,325	$1,725
Model 97			
2002-2009. Nickel-plated tricone resonator, female surfrider and palm trees scene.			
2002-2009		$2,850	$3,700
Model D			
2003-2010. Laminate wood body, spruce top, walnut back and sides, spun cone and spider bridge. Replaced by Smith and Young Model 1 (metal body) and Model 11 (wood body).			
2003-2010		$1,550	$2,025
NRP Steel			
2009-present. Steel body with rubbed nickel finish, Honduran mahogany neck, slotted headstock.			
2009-2021		$2,200	$2,850
Resoelectric Jr./Jr. II			
2005-2010. Basic model of ResoLectric with painted body, Jr. with P-90, Jr. II with Lollar lipstick-tube. Replaced by the ResoTone.			
2005-2010		$850	$1,100

MODEL YEAR	FEATURES	EXC. COND. LOW	HIGH
ResoLectric			
1992-present. Single-cut electric resonator, maple (flamed maple since '96), single biscuit, 1 regular pickup (lipstick-tube up to '95, P-90 since) and 1 under-saddle.			
1992-1995	Lipstick pickup	$1,775	$2,300
1996-2021	P-90 pickup	$1,650	$2,150
ResoRocket			
2005-present. Single-cut steel body, Tricone style grill.			
2005-2021		$2,650	$3,450
ResoRocket N			
2009-present Highly polished nickel-plated finish			
2009-2021		$2,650	$3,450
Style M-1/M-2			
1990-1994, 2003-2010. Bound mahogany body single-cone, M-1 with ebony 'board, M-2 with bound rosewood 'board.			
1990-2010		$1,650	$2,150
Style N			
1993-2005. Nickel-plated brass body single-cone resonator, plain mirror finish, 12 fret neck.			
1993-2005		$2,600	$3,400
Style O/O Deluxe/O Replicon			
1992-present. Nickel-plated brass body, Hawaiian palm tree etched. Deluxe has upgrades like figured-maple neck and mother-of-pearl diamond inlays. Replicon is replica of Mark Knopfler model.			
1992-2021	O	$2,575	$3,350
1992-2021	O Deluxe	$3,025	$3,925
1992-2021	O Replicon	$2,850	$3,700
Tricone			
1994-present. Nickel-plated brass body, bound ebony 'board.			
1994-2021	Style 1	$2,200	$2,900
1994-2021	Style 15	$2,700	$3,500
1995-2004	Style 3, Lily of the Valley	$4,700	$6,100
Triolian			
2009-present. Steel body with f-holes, sieve-hole coverplate, maple neck, 12 or 14 fret neck, ivoroid-bound rosewood 'board, mother-of-pearl markers, hand painted walnut-burst.			
2009-2021	12 fret	$1,700	$2,200
2009-2021	14 fret	$1,700	$2,200

Navarro Custom

1986-present. Professional and premium grade, production/custom, electric guitars and basses built in San Juan, Puerto Rico by luthier Mike Navarro.

Neubauer

1966-1990s. Luthier Helmut Neubauer built his acoustic and electric archtop guitars in Bubenreuth, Germany.

New Era Guitars

See listing under ARK - New Era Guitars.

New Orleans Guitar Company

1992-present. Luthier Vincent Guidroz builds his premium grade, production/custom, solid and semi-hollow body guitars in New Orleans, Louisiana.

National Westwood 77

New Orleans Custom JB16

GUITARS

Nik Huber Dolphin II

Norma Sparkle-Top

MODEL		EXC. COND.	
YEAR	FEATURES	LOW	HIGH

Nickerson Guitars

1983-present. Luthier Brad Nickerson builds his professional and premium grade, production/custom, archtop and flat-top guitars in Northampton, Massachusetts.

Nielsen

2004-present. Premium grade, custom/production, archtop guitars built by luthier Dale Nielsen in Duluth, Minnesota.

Nik Huber Guitars

1997-present. Premium grade, production/custom, electric guitars built in Rodgau, Germany by luthier Nik Huber.

Nioma

1932-1952. NIOMA, the National Institute of Music and Arts, was founded in Seattle but soon had schools across the western U.S. and Canada. By '35 they added guitar instruction, offering their own branded Spanish, resonator and lap steel (with matching amps) guitars, made by Regal, Harmony, Dickerson.

Noble

Ca. 1950-ca. 1969. Instruments made by others and distributed by Don Noble and Company of Chicago. Plastic-covered guitars made by EKO debut in '62. Aluminum-necked Wandré guitars added to the line in early-'63. By ca. '65-'66 the brand is owned by Chicago-area importer and distributor Strum 'N Drum and used mainly on Japanese-made solidbodies. Strum 'N Drum bought the National brand name in '69 and imported Japanese copies of American designs under the National brand and Japanese original designs under Norma through the early '70s.

The Noble brand disappears at least by the advent of the Japanese National brand, if not before. They also offered amps.

NoName Guitars

1999-present. Luthier Dan Kugler builds his production/custom, professional and premium grade, acoustic and basses in Conifer, Colorado.

Nordy (Nordstrand Guitars)

2003-present. Professional and premium grade, production/custom, electric guitars and basses built by luthier Carey Nordstrand in Yucaipa, California.

Norma

Ca.1965-1970. Imported from Japan by Strum 'N Drum, Inc. of Chicago (see Noble brand info). Early examples were built by Tombo, most notably sparkle plastic covered guitars and basses.

Electric Solidbody

1965-1970. Type of finish has affect on value. Various models include; EG-350 (student double-cut, 1 pickup), EG-403 (unique pointy cutaway, 2 pickups),

MODEL		EXC. COND.	
YEAR	FEATURES	LOW	HIGH

EG-400 (double-cut, 2 pickups), EG-450 (double-cut, 2 split-coil pickups), EG-421 (double-cut, 4 pickups), EG-412-12 (double-cut, 12-string).

| 1965-1968 | Blue, red, gold sparkle | $325 | $700 |
| 1965-1970 | Non-sparkle | $225 | $325 |

Norman

1972-present. Intermediate grade, production, acoustic and acoustic/electric guitars built in LaPatrie, Quebec. Norman was the first guitar production venture luthier Robert Godin was involved with. He has since added the Seagull, Godin, and Patrick & Simon brands of instruments.

Normandy Guitars

2008-present.

Northworthy Guitars

Professional and premium grade, production/custom, flat-top and electric guitars and basses built by luthier Alan Marshall in Ashbourne, Derbyshire, U.K., starting in 1987. He also builds mandolins.

Norwood

1960s. Budget guitars imported most likely from Japan.

Electric Solidbody

1960s. Offset double-cut body, 3 soapbar-style pickups, Norwood label on headstock.

| 1960s | | $175 | $300 |

Novax Guitars

1989-present. Luthier Ralph Novak builds his fanned-fret professional and premium grade, production/custom, solidbody and acoustic guitars and basses, originally in San Leandro, California, and since May '06, in Eugene, Oregon.

Noyce

1974-present. Luthier Ian Noyce builds his production/custom, professional and premium grade, acoustic and electric guitars and basses in Ballarat, Victoria, Australia.

Nyberg Instruments

1993-present. Professional grade, custom, flat-top and Maccaferri-style guitars built by luthier Lawrence Nyberg in Hornby Island, British Columbia. He also builds mandolins, mandolas, bouzoukis and citterns.

Oahu

1926-1985, present. The Oahu Publishing Company and Honolulu Conservatory, based in Cleveland, Ohio was active in the sheet music and student instrument business in the '30s. An instrument, set of instructional sheet music, and lessons were offered as a complete package. Lessons were often given to large groups of students. Instruments, lessons, and sheet music could also be purchased by mail order. The Oahu Publishing Co. advertised

The Official Vintage Guitar magazine Price Guide 2023   **Oahu** Graphic Body – **OLP (Officially Licensed Product)**   **323**

GUITARS

MODEL YEAR	FEATURES	EXC. COND. LOW	HIGH

itself as The World's Largest Guitar Dealer. Most '30s Oahu guitars were made by Kay with smaller numbers from the Oscar Schmidt Company.

Guitar Models from the Mid-'30s include: 71K (jumbo square neck), 72K (jumbo roundneck), 68B (jumbo, vine body decoration), 68K (deluxe jumbo square neck), 69K (deluxe jumbo roundneck), 65K and 66K (mahogany, square neck), 64K and 67K (mahogany, roundneck), 65M (standard-size, checker binding, mahogany), 53K (roundneck, mahogany), 51 (black, Hawaiian scene, pearlette 'board), 51K (black, pond scene decoration), 52K (black, Hawaiian scene decoration), 50 and 50K (student guitar, brown).

The brand has been revived on a line of tube amps.

Graphic Body
1930s. 13" painted artwork bodies, includes Styles 51 and 52 Hawaiian scene.

1930s	Floral, etc	$350	$450
1930s	Hawaiian scenes	$350	$450

Round Neck 14" Flat-Top
1930s. Spruce top, figured maple back and sides, thin logo.

1932	$875	$1,150

Style 50K Student
1930s. Student-size guitar, brown finish.

1935	$125	$250

Style 52K
1930s. 13" with fancy Hawaiian stencil, slotted headstock.

1930s	$325	$425

Style 65M
1933-1935. Standard-size mahogany body, checker binding, natural brown.

1933-1935	$575	$750

Style 68K De Luxe Jumbo
1930s. Hawaiian, 15.5" wide, square neck, Brazilian back and sides, spruce top, fancy pearl vine inlay, abalone trim on top and soundhole, rosewood pyramid bridge, fancy pearl headstock inlay, butterbean tuners, ladder-braced, natural. High-end model made for Oahu by Kay.

1934-1935	$4,000	$5,200

Style 71K Hawaiian
1930s. Hawaiian, gold vine pattern on bound sunburst top, dot inlays.

1930s	$1,050	$1,375

Ochoteco Guitars
1979-present. Production/custom steel- and nylon-stringed guitars built by luthier Gabriel Ochoteco in Germany until '84 and in Brisbane, Australia since.

Odessa
1981-1990s. Budget guitars imported by Davitt & Hanser (BC Rich). Mainly acoustics in the '90s, but some electrics early on.

O'Hagan
1979-1983. Designed by clarinetist and importer Jerol O'Hagan in St. Louis Park, Minnesota. Primarily neck-thru construction, most with German-carved bodies. In '81 became Jemar Corporation and in '83 it was closed by the I.R.S., a victim of recession.

SN=YYM(M)NN (e.g., 80905, September '80, 5th guitar); or MYMNNN (e.g., A34006, April 1983, 6th guitar). Approximately 3000 total instruments were made with the majority being NightWatches (approx. 200 Twenty Twos, 100-150 Sharks, 100 Lasers; about 25 with birdseye maple

Shark
1979-1983. Explorer-looking solidbody, maple body, 2 Shaller humbucker pickups, 3-piece maple/walnut laminate neck, natural.

1979-1983	$625	$825

Ohio
1959-ca. 1965. Line of electric solidbodies and basses made by France's Jacobacci company, which also built under its own brand. Sparkle finish, bolt-on aluminum necks, strings-thru-body design.

Old Kraftsman
Ca. 1930s-ca. 1960s. Brandname used by the Spiegel catalog company for instruments made by other American manufacturers, including Regal, Kay and even Gibson. The instruments were of mixed quality, but some better grade instruments were comparable to those offered by Wards.

Archtop
1930s-1960s. Various models.

1930s-40s	$365	$475
1950s-60s	$275	$375

Flat-Top
1930s-1960s. Various models.

1950s	Prairie Ramblers (stencil)	$275	$375

Jazz II K775
1960-1963. Kay 775 with Old Kraftsman logo on large headstock, small double-cut thinline, 2 pickups, Bigsby, natural.

1960-1963	$1,025	$1,350

Sizzler K4140
1959. Single-cut, single neck pickup, Sizzler logo on body with other art images.

1959	$450	$600

Thin Twin Jimmy Reed

1952-1958	$1,300	$1,700

Value Leader
1961-1965. Electric single-cut semi-solid, 1 pickup, Kay Value Leader series.

1961-1965	$350	$475

OLP (Officially Licensed Product)
2001-2009. Intermediate grade, production, imported guitars and basses based on higher dollar guitar models officially licensed from the original manufacturer. OLP logo on headstock.

1930s Oahu
Bernunzio Uptown Music

O'Hagan Twenty-Two
Christopher Tritschler

Optek Fretlight

Orpheum President
Imaged by Heritage Auctions, HA.com

MODEL		EXC. COND.	
YEAR	FEATURES	LOW	HIGH

Olson Guitars

1977-present. Luthier James A. Olson builds his presentation grade, custom, flat-tops in Circle Pines, Minnesota.

Olympia by Tacoma

1997-2006. Import acoustic guitars and mandolins from Tacoma Guitars.

OD Series

1997-2006	Various models	$100	$325

Omega

1996-2010. Luthier Kevin Gallagher built his premium grade, custom/production acoustic guitars in East Saylorsburg, Pennsylvania. He died in '10.

Oncor Sound

1980-ca. 1981. This Salt Lake City, Utah-based company made both a guitar and a bass synthesizer.

Optek

1980s-present. Intermediate grade, production, imported Fretlight acoustic/electric and electric guitars. Located in Reno, Nevada.

Fretlight

1989-present. Double-cut, 126 LED lights in fretboard controlled by a scale/chord selector.

1989-2021		$350	$450

Opus

1972-Mid 1970s. Acoustic and classical guitars, imported from Japan by Ampeg/Selmer. In '75-'76, Harmony made a line of acoustics with the Opus model name.

Original Senn

2004-present. Luthier Jeff Senn builds his professional and premium grade, production/custom, solidbody electric guitars and basses in Nashville, Tennessee.

Ormsby Guitars

2003-present. Luthier Perry Ormsby builds his custom, professional and premium grade, solid and chambered electric guitars in Perth, Western Australia.

Orpheum

1897-1942, 1944-late 1960s, 2001-2006. Intermediate grade, production, acoustic and resonator guitars. They also offered mandolins. Orpheum originally was a brand of Rettberg and Lange, who made instruments for other companies as well. William Rettberg and William Lange bought the facilities of New York banjo maker James H. Buckbee in 1897. Lange went out on his own in '21 to start the Paramount brand. He apparently continued using the Orpheum brand as well. He went out of business in '42. In '44 the brand was acquired by New York's Maurice Lipsky Music Co. who used it primarily on beginner to medium grade instruments, which were manufactured by Regal, Kay, and United Guitar (and maybe others). In the early '60s Lipsky applied the brand to Japanese and European (by Egmond) imports. Lipsky dropped the name in the early '70s. The brand was revived for '01 to '06 by Tacoma Guitars.

Auditorium Archtop 835/837

1950s. Acoustic archtop, auditorium size, dot markers, Orpheum shell headpiece, white celluloid 'guard, model 835 with spruce top/back/sides, 837 with mahogany.

1950s		$325	$425

Orpheum Special

1930s. Made by Regal, slot head, Dobro-style wood body, metal resonator, sunburst.

1930s		$850	$1,100

President

1940s. 18" pro-level acoustic archtop, Orpheum block logo and President script logo on headstock, large split-block markers, sunburst.

1940s		$1,600	$2,100

Style B

1940s. Acoustic archtop, Style B logo on headstock, block markers, sunburst.

1940s		$625	$825

Thin Twin Jimmy Reed 865E

1950s. Model 865E is the Orpheum version of the generically named Thin Twin Jimmy Reed style electric Spanish cutaway thin solidbody, hand engraved shell celluloid Orpheum headpiece, described as #865E Cutaway Thin Electric Guitar in catalog.

1950s		$1,425	$1,875

Ultra Deluxe Professional 899

1950s. 17" cutaway, 2 pickups, 2 knobs, maple back and sides, top material varies, dot markers, finishes as follows: E-C copper, E-G gold, E-G-B gold-black sunburst, E-B blond curly maple, E-S golden orange sunburst.

1950s		$1,425	$1,875

Orville

1984-1993. Orville by Gibson and Orville guitars were made by Japan's Fuji Gen Gakki for Gibson. See following listing for details. Guitars listed here state only Orville (no By Gibson) on the headstock.

Electric

1984-1993	CE Atkins	$1,000	$1,300
1984-1993	ES-335	$1,425	$1,875
1984-1993	LP Custom	$1,200	$1,550
1984-1993	LP Standard	$1,200	$1,550

Orville by Gibson

1984-1993. Orville by Gibson and Orville guitars were made by Japan's Fuji Gen Gakki for Gibson. Basically the same models except the Orville by Gibson guitars had real Gibson USA PAF '57 Classic pickups and a true nitrocellulose lacquer finish. The Orville models used Japanese electronics and a poly finish. Prices here are for the Orville by Gibson models.

The Official Vintage Guitar magazine Price Guide 2023   **Orville** Acoustic-Electric — **Ovation** Adamas Millenium   **325**

GUITARS

MODEL YEAR	FEATURES	EXC. COND. LOW	HIGH
Acoustic-Electric			
1984-1993. On-board electronics.			
1984-1993	Dove	$1,600	$2,100
1984-1993	J-160E	$1,600	$2,100
1984-1993	J-200NE	$1,600	$2,100
Electric			
1984-1993. Various models.			
1984-1993	ES-175	$1,600	$2,100
1984-1993	ES-335	$1,600	$2,100
1984-1993	Explorer	$1,500	$1,950
1984-1993	Firebird V	$1,200	$1,550
1984-1993	Firebird VII	$1,200	$1,550
1984-1993	Flying V	$1,500	$1,950
1984-1993	Les Paul Custom	$1,500	$1,950
1984-1993	Les Paul Jr	$700	$900
1984-1993	LP Standard	$1,500	$1,950
1984-1993	LP Studio JP	$1,050	$1,350
1984-1993	MM/Les Paul Jr	$575	$750
1984-1993	SG LP Custom	$1,150	$1,500
1984-1993	SG LP Standard	$1,150	$1,500

Osborne Sound Laboratories

Late 1970s. Founded by Ralph Scaffidi and wife guitarist Mary Osborne; originally building guitar amps, they did also offer solidbody guitars.

Oscar Schmidt

1879-1938, 1979-present. Budget and intermediate grade, production, acoustic, acoustic/electric, and electric guitars and basses distributed by U.S. Music Corp. (Washburn, Randall, etc.). They also offer mandolins, banjos, ukuleles and the famous Oscar Schmidt autoharp.

The original Oscar Schmidt Company, Jersey City, New Jersey, offered banjo mandolins, tenor banjos, guitar banjos, ukuleles, mandolins and guitars under their own brand and others (including Sovereign and Stella). By the early 1900s, the company had factories in the U.S. and Europe producing instruments producing instruments under their own brand as well as other brands for mail-order and other distributors. Oscar Schmidt was also an early contributor to innovative mandolin designs and the company participated in the '00-'30 mandolin boom. The company hit hard times during the Depression and was sold to Harmony by the end of the '30s. In '79, Washburn acquired the brand and it is now part of U.S. Music.

Oskar Graf Guitars

1970-present. Premium and presentation grade, custom, archtop, acoustic and classical guitars and basses built in Clarendon, Ontario, by luthier Oskar Graf. He also builds lutes.

Otwin

1950s-1960s. A brand used on electric guitars made by the Musima company of East Germany. Musima also produced guitars under their own brand.

Outbound Instruments

1990-2002. Intermediate grade, production, travel-size acoustics from the Boulder, Colorado-based company.

Ovation

1966-present. Intermediate and professional grade, production, acoustic and acoustic/electric guitars. They also build basses and mandolins. Until 2014, they also had U.S. production.

Helicopter manufacturer Kaman Corporation, founded in 1945 by jazz guitarist and aeronautical engineer Charles Huron Kaman in Bloomfield, Connecticut, decided to use their helicopter expertise (working with synthetic materials, spruce, high tolerances) and designed, with the help of employee and violin restorer John Ringso, the first fiberglass-backed (Lyracord) acoustic guitars in '65. Production began in '66 and the music factory moved to New Hartford, Connecticut, in '67. Early input was provided by fingerstyle jazz guitarist Charlie Byrd, who gave Kaman the idea for the name Ovation. Kaman Music purchased Hamer Guitars in '88, and Trace Elliot amplifiers (U.K.) in '90. In '08, Fender acquired Kaman Music Corporation and the Ovation brand; in '14 U.S. production ceased and the brand was sold to Drum Workshop, Inc., who re-opened the Hartford, CT plant in late '15.

Adamas 1581-KK Kaki King
2011-2014. Deep bowl cutaway, rosewood 'board, 12th-fret crown inlay, OP-Pro preamp, Kaki personally signs the label on each guitar.

2011-2014		$3,000	$4,000

Adamas 1587
1979-1998. Carbon top, walnut, single-cut, bowl back, binding, mini-soundholes.

1979-1998	Black Sparkle	$1,700	$2,200

Adamas 1597
1998-2003. Carbon birch composite top, on-board electronics.

1998-2003	Black	$975	$1,275

Adamas 1598-MEII Melissa Etheridge
2001-2014. Mid-depth cutaway, ebony 'board, 'ME' maple symbol at 12th fret, OP-Pro preamp, Melissa personally signs the label on each guitar.

2001-2014	12-string	$1,500	$2,000

Adamas 1687
1977-1998. Acoustic/electric, carbon top, non-cut, bowl back, mini-soundholes.

1977-1998	Sunburst	$1,700	$2,225

Adamas CVT W591
2000. Crossweave fiber top, mid-depth body, on-board electronics.

2000		$1,100	$1,450

Adamas II 1881 NB-2
1993-1998. Acoustic/electric, single-cut, shallow bowl, brown.

1993-1998		$1,600	$2,100

Adamas Millenium
2000. Limited edition, 75 made, planet inlays, Cobalt Blue.

2000		$2,400	$3,200

1993 Orville Les Paul Standard
Stoeffu Vogt

1981 Adamas II
Rivington Guitars

1994 Ovation Collectors Series 1994-7

Ovation Custom Legend 1619

MODEL YEAR	FEATURES	EXC. COND. LOW	HIGH
Anniversary Electric 1657			
1978. Deep bowl, abalone inlays, gold-plated parts, for Ovation's 10th anniversary. They also offered an acoustic Anniversary.			
1978		$425	$575
Balladeer 1111			
1968-1983, 1993-2000. Acoustic, non-cut with deep bowl, bound body, natural top, later called the Standard Balladeer.			
1976-1983		$400	$625
Balladeer Artist 1121			
1968-1990. Acoustic, non-cut with shallow bowl, bound body.			
1968-1969	Early production	$525	$675
1970-1990		$400	$575
Balladeer Classic 1122			
1970s. Classical shallow-bowl version of Concert Classic, nylon strings, slotted headstock.			
1970s		$375	$500
Balladeer Custom 1112			
1976-1990. Acoustic, deep bowl, diamond inlays.			
1976-1990		$475	$625
Balladeer Custom Electric 12-String 1655/1755			
1982-1994. 12-string version of Balladeer Custom Electric.			
1982-1994		$425	$575
Balladeer Custom Electric 1612/1712			
1976-1990. Acoustic/electric version of Balladeer Custom, deep bowl.			
1976-1990		$525	$700
Balladeer Standard 1561/1661/1761/1861			
1982-2000. Acoustic/electric, deep bowl, rounded cutaway.			
1982-2000		$500	$650
Balladeer Standard 1771 LX			
2008-2010. Acoustic/electric, mid-depth bowl, rosewood, sitka spruce top.			
2008-2010		$575	$750
Balladeer Standard 12-String 6751 LX			
2008-2010. Acoustic/electric, 12 strings, rosewood, spruce top.			
2008-2010		$675	$875
Breadwinner 1251			
1971-1983. Axe-like shaped single-cut solidbody, 2 pickups, textured finish, black, blue, tan or white.			
1971-1983		$900	$1,200
Celebrity CC-48			
2007-2013. Acoustic/electric, super shallow, laminated spruce top, white bound rosewood 'board with abalone dot inlays.			
2007-2013		$275	$375
Celebrity CC-57			
1990-1996. Laminated spruce top, shallow bowl, mahogany neck.			
1990-1996		$275	$375
Celebrity CC-63			
1984-1996. Classical, deep bowl, piezo bridge pickup.			
1984-1996		$275	$375

MODEL YEAR	FEATURES	EXC. COND. LOW	HIGH
Celebrity CK-057			
2002-2004. Acoustic/electric rounded cutaway, shallow back.			
2002-2004		$350	$475
Celebrity CS-257			
1992-2005, 2010. Made in Korea, super shallow bowl back body, single-cut, Adamas soundholes, alternating dot and diamond markers.			
1992-2005	Celebrity	$425	$575
2010	Celebrity Deluxe	$475	$625
Classic 1613/1713			
1971-1993. Acoustic/electric, non-cut, deep bowl, no inlay, slotted headstock, gold tuners, natural.			
1971-1993		$500	$650
Classic 1663/1763			
1982-1998. Acoustic/electric, single-cut, deep bowl, cedar top, EQ, no inlay, slotted headstock, gold tuners.			
1982-1998		$600	$775
Classic 1863			
1989-1998. Acoustic/electric, single-cut, shallow bowl, no inlay, cedar top, EQ, slotted headstock, gold tuners.			
1989-1998		$600	$775
Collectors Series			
1982-2008. Limited edition, different model featured each year and production limited to that year only, the year designation is marked at the 12th fret, various colors (each year different).			
1982-2008	Common models	$500	$775
1982-2008	Rare models	$700	$1,600
Concert Classic 1116			
1974-1990. Deep-bowl nylon string classical, slotted headstock.			
1974-1990		$350	$475
Contemporary Folk Classic Electric 1616			
1974-1990. Acoustic/electric, no inlay, slotted headstock, natural or sunburst.			
1974-1990		$350	$475
Country Artist Classic Electric 6773			
1995-2011. Classic electric, soft-cut, solid spruce top, slotted headstock, Ovation pickup system.			
1995-2011		$550	$725
Country Artist Electric 1624			
1971-1990. Nylon strings, slotted headstock, standard steel-string sized neck to simulate a folk guitar, on-board electronics.			
1971-1990		$600	$775
Custom Ballader 1762			
1992. Rounded cutaway, higher-end specs.			
1992		$800	$1,050
Custom Elite Guitar Center 30th Anniversary			
1994	50 made	$1,275	$1,675
Custom Legend 1117			
1970s. Non-electrical 2nd generation Ovation, higher-end with abalone inlays and gold hardware, open V-bracing pattern. Model 1117-4, natural.			
1970s		$725	$950
Custom Legend 1569			
1980s. Rounded cutaway acoustic/electric, super shallow bowl, gloss black finish.			
1980s		$650	$850

MODEL YEAR	FEATURES	EXC. COND. LOW	HIGH

Custom Legend 1619/1719
1970s. Acoustic/electric 2nd generation Ovation, electric version of model 1117, higher-end with abalone inlays and gold hardware, open V-bracing pattern.
| 1970s | | $725 | $950 |

Custom Legend 1759
1984-2004. Single-cut acoustic/electric, 12-string.
| 1984-2004 | | $725 | $950 |

Custom Legend 1769
1982, 1993, 1996-1999. Single-cut acoustic/electric.
| 1982-1999 | | $1,100 | $1,450 |

Custom Legend 1869
1994, 2003. Acoustic/electric, cutaway, super shallow bowl.
| 1994, 2003 | | $800 | $1,050 |

Custom Legend 6759
| 2003 | | $1,650 | $2,150 |

Deacon 1252
1973-1980. Axe-shaped solidbody electric, active electronics, diamond fret markers.
| 1973-1980 | | $1,100 | $1,450 |

Deacon 12-String 1253
1975. Axe-shaped solidbody, diamond inlay, 2 pickups. only a few made.
| 1975 | | $1,100 | $1,450 |

Eclipse
1971-1973. Thinline double cut acoustic-electric archtop, 2 pickups.
| 1971-1973 | | $800 | $1,050 |

Elite 1718
1982-1997. Acoustic/electric, non-cut, deep bowl, solid spruce top, Adamas-type soundhole, volume and tone controls, stereo output.
| 1982-1997 | | $825 | $1,100 |

Elite 1758
1990-1998. Acoustic/electric, non-cut, deep bowl.
| 1990-1998 | | $825 | $1,100 |

Elite 1768
1990-1998. Acoustic/electric, cutaway, deep bowl.
| 1990-1998 | | $675 | $900 |

Elite 1858 12-String
1993-2004. 12-string acoustic/electric, ebony 'board and bridge.
| 1993-2004 | | $825 | $1,100 |

Elite 1868
1983-2004. Acoustic/electric, cutaway, shallow bowl.
| 1983-2004 | | $625 | $825 |

Elite 5858
1991. Super shallow bowl, single cutaway, Adamas-style soundhole, gold hardware, on-board factory OP24 pickup.
| 1991 | | $675 | $900 |

Elite Doubleneck
1989-1990s. Six- and 12-string necks, can be ordered with a variety of custom options.
| 1989 | | $900 | $1,200 |

Elite Standard 6868
1994-1999. Elite Standard with cutaway shallow bowl.
| 1994-1999 | | $650 | $850 |

Elite T/TX 1778
2002-2018. Acoustic/electric, cutaway, U.S. T replaced by import TX in '08.
| 2002-2008 T, original version | | $825 | $1,100 |
| 2008-2018 TX, Import | | $300 | $400 |

Folklore 1614
1972-1983. Acoustic/electric, 12-fret neck on full-size body, wide neck, on-board electronics.
| 1972-1983 | | $600 | $775 |

GCXT
2008. Acoustic-electric made for Guitar Center, single-cut, flamed paint graphic.
| 2008 | | $700 | $925 |

Glen Campbell 12-String 1118 (K-1118)
1968-1982. Acoustic, 12 strings, shallow bowl version of Legend, gold tuners, diamond inlay.
| 1968-1982 | | $650 | $850 |

Glen Campbell Artist 1627
2006. Glen Campbell 40th Anniversary model, diamond inlay, gold tuners.
| 2006 | | $1,100 | $1,450 |

Glen Campbell Artist Balladeer 1127
1968-1990. Acoustic, shallow bowl, diamond inlay, gold tuners, natural.
| 1968-1990 | | $650 | $850 |

Hurricane 12-String K-1120
1968-1969. ES-335-style electric semi-hollowbody, double-cut, 12 strings, f-holes, 2 pickups.
| 1968-1969 | | $800 | $1,050 |

Josh White 1114
1967-1970, 1972-1983. Wide 12-fret neck, dot markers, classical-style tuners.
| 1967-1970 | | $700 | $925 |
| 1972-1983 | | $600 | $800 |

Legend 1117
1972-1999. Deep bowl acoustic, 5-ply top binding, gold tuners, various colors (most natural).
| 1972-1999 | | $550 | $725 |

Legend 1567/1867
1984-2004. Acoustic/electric, shallow bowl, single-cut, gold tuners.
| 1984-2004 | | $600 | $775 |

Legend 12-String 1866
1989-2007. Acoustic/electric, cutaway, 12 strings, shallow bowl, 5-ply top binding, black.
| 1989-2007 | | $600 | $775 |

Legend 1717
1990-2008. Acoustic/electric, 5-ply top binding, various colors.
| 1990-2008 | | $575 | $750 |

Legend 1767
1990s. Acoustic/electric, deep bowl, single-cut, black.
| 1990s | | $575 | $750 |

Legend Cutaway 1667
1982-1996. Acoustic/electric, cutaway, deep bowl, abalone, gold tuners.
| 1982-1996 | | $625 | $825 |

Legend Electric 1617
1972-1998. Acoustic/electric, deep bowl, abalone, gold tuners, various colors.
| 1972-1998 | | $550 | $725 |

1980 Ovation Deacon 1252
Jon Way

Ovation Glen Campbell 1118
Imaged by Heritage Auctions, HA.com

Ovation Viper 1271
Rivington Guitars

Parker NiteFly
Imaged by Heritage Auctions, HA.com

MODEL YEAR	FEATURES	EXC. COND. LOW	HIGH
Pacemaker 12-String 1115/1615			
1968-1982. Originally called the K-1115 12-string, Renamed Pacemaker in '72.			
1968-1982		$600	$775
Patriot Bicentennial			
*1976. Limited run of 1776 guitars, Legend Custom model with drum and flag decal and 1776*1976 decal on lower bout.*			
1976		$1,100	$1,450
Pinnacle			
1990-1992. Spruce or sycamore top, broad leaf pattern rosette, mahogany neck, piezo bridge pickup, sunburst.			
1990-1992		$525	$675
Pinnacle Shallow Cutaway			
1990-1994. Pinnacle with shallow bowl body and single-cut, sunburst.			
1990-1994		$525	$675
Preacher 1281			
1975-1982. Solidbody, mahogany body, double-cut, 2 pickups.			
1975-1982		$725	$950
Preacher Deluxe 1282			
1975-1982. Double-cut solidbody, 2 pickups with series/parallel pickup switch and mid-range control.			
1975-1982		$725	$950
Preacher 12-String 1285			
1975-1983. Double-cut solidbody, 12 strings, 2 pickups.			
1975-1983		$725	$950
Thunderhead 1460			
1968-1972. Double-cut, 2 pickups, gold hardware, phase switch, master volume, separate tone controls, pickup balance/blend control, vibrato.			
1968-1972	Natural or rare color	$1,500	$1,975
1968-1972	Sunburst	$1,100	$1,450
Tornado 1260			
1968-1973. Same as Thunderhead without phase switch, with chrome hardware.			
1968-1973		$800	$1,050
UK II 1291			
1980-1982. Single-cut solidbody, 2 pickups, body made of Urelite on aluminum frame, bolt-on neck, gold hardware.			
1980-1982		$925	$1,225
Ultra GS/GP Series			
1984. Korean solidbodies and necks assembled in U.S., DiMarzio pickups, offset double-cut (GS) with 1 hum, or hum/single/single or LP style (GP) with 2 humbuckers. There was also a bass.			
1984		$425	$550
Ultra Series			
1970s-2000s. Various Ultra model acoustic/ electrics.			
1970-2000s		$300	$775
Viper 1271			
1975-1982. Single-cut, 2 single-coil pickups.			
1975-1982		$750	$1,000
Viper EA 68			
1994-2008. Thin acoustic/electric, single-cut mahogany body, spruce top over sound chamber with multiple upper bout soundholes, black.			
1994-2008		$525	$700

MODEL YEAR	FEATURES	EXC. COND. LOW	HIGH
Viper III 1273			
1975-1982. Single-cut, 3 single-coil pickups.			
1975-1982		$750	$1,000
VXT Hybrid			
2007-2009. Single-cut solidbody, 2 Seymour Duncan '59 humbuckers, Fishman Power Bridge.			
2007-2009		$800	$1,050

Overture Guitars

Luthier Justin Hoffman began building in the year 2008, professional to presentation grade, custom/production, solidbody guitars and basses in Morton, Illinois.

P. W. Crump Company

1975-present. Luthier Phil Crump builds his custom flat-top guitars in Arcata, California. He also builds mandolin-family instruments.

Palen

1998-present. Premium grade, production/custom, archtop guitars built by luthier Nelson Palen in Beloit, Kansas.

Palmer

Early 1970s-present. Budget and intermediate grade, production acoustic, acoustic/electric and classical guitars imported from Europe and Asia. They also have offered electrics.

Panache

2004-2008. Budget grade, production, solidbody electric and acoustic guitars imported from China.

PANaramic

1961-1963. Guitars and basses made in Italy by the Crucianelli accordion company and imported by PANaramic accordion. They also offered amps made by Magnatone.

Acoustic-Electric Archtop

1961-1963. Full body cutaway, 2 pickups.

1961-1963		$1,050	$1,350

Paolo Soprani

Early 1960s. Italian plastic covered guitars with pushbutton controls made by the Polverini Brothers.

Paramount

1921-1942, Late 1940s. The William L. Lange Company began selling Paramount banjos, guitar banjos and mandolin banjos in the early 1920s, and added archtop guitars in '34. The guitars were made by Martin and possibly others. Lange went out of business by '42; Gretsch picked up the Paramount name and used it on acoustics and electrics for a time in the late '40s.

GB

1920s-1930s. Guitar banjo.

1920s-30s		$1,050	$1,400

MODEL YEAR	FEATURES	EXC. COND. LOW	HIGH

Style C
1930s. 16" acoustic archtop, maple back and sides.

1930s		$500	$675

Style L
1930s. Made by Martin, limited to about 36 instruments, small body with resonator, Brazilian rosewood.

1930s	Spanish 6-string	$6,600	$8,600
1930s	Tenor 4-string	$4,800	$6,300

Parker

1992-2016. U.S.-made and imported intermediate, professional, and premium grade, production/custom, solidbody guitars featuring a thin skin of carbon and glass fibers bonded to a wooden guitar body. In '05, they added wood body acoustic/electrics. They also build basses. Originally located northwest of Boston, Parker was founded by Ken Parker and Larry Fishman (Fishman Transducers). Korg USA committed money to get the Fly Deluxe model into production in July '93. Parker added a Custom Shop in '03 to produce special build instruments and non-core higher-end models that were no longer available as a standard product offering. In early '04, Parker was acquired by U.S. Music Corp. and moved USA production from the Boston area to Chicago. U.S. Music was acquired by Jam Industries in '09 and production of Parker Guitars was ceased in '16.

Concert
1997 only. Solid sitka spruce top, only piezo system pickup, no magnetic pickups, transparent butterscotch.

1997		$1,825	$2,375

Fly
1993-1994. There are many Parker Fly models, the model simply called Fly is similar to the more common Fly Deluxe, except it does not have the Fishman piezo pickup system.

1993-1994		$1,825	$2,375

Fly Artist
1998-1999. Solid sitka spruce top, vibrato, Deluxe-style electronics, transparent blond finish.

1998-1999		$2,000	$2,600

Fly Classic
1996-1998, 2000-2011. One-piece Honduras mahogany body, basswood neck, electronics same as Fly Deluxe.

1996-2011		$1,825	$2,375

Fly Classic Maple
2000. Classic with maple body (vs. mahogany), transparent butterscotch.

2000		$1,825	$2,375

Fly Deluxe
1993-2016. Poplar body, basswood neck, 2 pickups, Fishman bridge transducer, '93-'96 models were offered with or without vibrato, then non-vibrato discontinued. The Deluxe normally came with a gig bag, but also offered with a hardshell case, which would add about $50 to the values listed.

1993-2016		$1,825	$2,375

Fly Supreme
1996-1999. One-piece flame maple body, electronics same as the Fly Deluxe, highly flamed butterscotch, includes hard molded case.

1996-1999		$2,500	$3,300

MaxxFly PDF Series
2013-2016. PDF is import line of more traditionally-shaped Maxx solidbodies, various models.

2013-2016	PDF30	$350	$450
2013-2016	PDF60	$375	$475
2013-2016	PDF70	$450	$575

Mojo
2003-2010. Fly either single-cut or double-cut.

2003-2007	Single-cut	$1,200	$1,575
2003-2010	Double-cut	$1,725	$2,250

NiteFly Series
1996-2009. Two single-coil and 1 humbucker pickup NiteFly, Fishman piezo system, bolt neck, maple body for '96-'98, ash for '99-present. Called the NiteFly in '96, NiteFly NFV2 ('97-'98), NiteFly NFV4 ('98), NiteFly NFV6 ('99), NiteFly SA ('00-present).

1996-2009	Various models	$1,000	$1,300

P Series
2000-2009. Various acoustic and solidbody electric models.

2000-2009		$350	$700

Tulipwood Limited Edition
1998. Limited build of 35, standard Deluxe features with tulipwood body.

1998		$1,750	$2,275

Parkwood

2007-present. Intermediate grade, acoustic and acoustic-electric guitars, Parkwood logo on headstock.

Patrick Eggle Guitars

1991-present. Founded by Patrick Eggle and others in Birmingham, England, building solid and semi-solidbody electric guitars and basses. In '95, Eggle left the company to build acoustics.

Patrick James Eggle

2001-present. Eggle co-founded the Patrick Eggle Guitar company in '91 building solidbodies. In '95, he left to do repairs and custom work. In '01 he opened a new workshop in Bedforshire, England, building professional and premium grade, production/custom, archtop and flatop guitars. For a short time he relocated to Hendersonville, North Carolina, but in '05 returned to England and opened a shop in Oswestry.

Paul Berger

1972-2015. Acoustic guitars built by luthier Paul Berger in St. Augustine, Florida. He died in '15.

Paul H. Jacobson

1974-present. Premium grade, production/custom, classical guitars built by luthier Paul H. Jacobson in Cleveland, Missouri.

Parkwood P810

Patrick James Eggle Macon Junior

GUITARS

PRS Angelus Cutaway

1985 PRS Custom

MODEL YEAR	FEATURES	EXC. COND. LOW	HIGH

Paul Reed Smith

1985-present. Intermediate, professional and premium grade, production/custom, solid, semi-hollow body, and acoustic guitars made in the U.S. and imported. They also build basses. Paul Reed Smith built his first guitar in '75 as an independent study project in college and refined his design over the next 10 years building custom guitars. After building two prototypes and getting several orders from East Coast guitar dealers, Smith was able to secure the support necessary to start PRS in a factory on Virginia Avenue in Annapolis, Maryland. On '95, they moved to their current location on Kent Island in Stevensville. In 2001 PRS introduced the Korean-made SE Series. Acoustics were added in '08.

10th Anniversary
1995. 200 made, mother-of-pearl inlays, abalone purfling, gold pickups, either wide-fat or wide-thin neck, 10th Anniversary logo, price includes certificate of authenticity.

1995	With certificate	$3,400	$4,400

305
2010-2013. Alder body, maple neck and 'board, birds, 3 single-coils.

2010-2013		$1,075	$1,400

305 25th Anniversary
2010. 305 made, 3 single-coils, wide-fat or wide-thin, 25th Anniversary logo.

2010		$1,125	$1,450

513 Rosewood
Dec.2003-2006. Brazilian rosewood neck, newly developed PRS pickup system with 13 sound settings, hum-single-hum pickups.

2003-2006		$2,200	$2,800

513 Swamp Ash
2010. Figured ash, natural.

2010		$1,300	$1,700

513 25th Anniversary
2010. Carved figured maple top, 25th Anniversary shadow birds inlay.

2010		$1,900	$2,500

Al Di Meola Prism
2008-2014. Curly maple 10 top, 22-fret, prism multicolor finish.

2008-2014		$1,600	$2,100

Angelus Cutaway
2009-present. Flat-top, on-board electronics, European spruce top, figured mahogany back and sides, flamed maple binding. Listed under Private Stock in '20, with select wood options.

2009-2020		$2,550	$3,325

Artist/Artist I/Artist 24
1991-1994. Carved maple top, offset double-cut, 24-fret neck, bird markers, less than 500 made. A different Custom 24 Artist package was subsequently offered in the 2000s.

1991-1994		$2,875	$3,750

Artist II/Artist 22
1993-1995. Curly maple top, maple purfling on rosewood 'board, inlaid maple bound headstock, abalone birds, 22 frets, gold hardware, short run of less than 500.

1993-1995		$1,900	$2,475

Artist III
1996-1997. Continuation of the 22-fret neck with some changes in materials and specs, figured maple tops, short run of less than 500 instruments.

1996-1997		$2,125	$2,750

Artist IV
1996. Continuation of the 22-fret neck with some upgrades in materials and specs, short run of less than 70 instruments.

1996		$3,000	$4,000

Artist Limited
1994-1995. Like the Artist II with 14-carat gold bird inlays, abalone purfling on neck, headstock and truss rod cover, Brazilian rosewood 'board, 165 made.

1994-1995		$3,000	$4,000

CE 22
1994-2000, 2005-2008. Double-cut carved alder body (1995), mahogany '96-'00 and '05-'07, back to alder in '08, bolt-on maple neck with rosewood 'board, dot inlays, 2 humbuckers, chrome hardware, translucent colors, options include vibrato and gold hardware and custom colors.

1994-1995	Alder	$1,075	$1,400
1996-2000	Mahogany	$1,075	$1,400
2005-2008	Reintroduced	$1,075	$1,400

CE 22 Maple Top
1994-2008. CE 22 with figured maple top, upgrade options included gold hardware, custom colors or 10 top.

1994-2008		$1,075	$1,400

CE 24 (Classic Electric, CE)
1988-2000, 2005-2008. Double-cut, alder body to '95, mahogany '96-'00 and '05-'07, back to alder in '08, carved top, 24-fret bolt-on maple neck, 2 humbuckers, dot inlays, upgrade options included gold hardware, custom colors or 10 top.

1988-1991	Rosewood 'board	$1,075	$1,400
1992-2008		$1,075	$1,400

CE 24 Maple Top (CE Maple Top)
1989-2008. CE 24 with figured maple top, upgrade options may include any or all the following: gold hardware, custom colors or 10 top.

1989-2008		$1,075	$1,400

Chris Henderson Signature
2007-2012. Single-cut, 3 exposed humbucker pickups, carved flame maple top on mahogany body, wide flat neck profile, 22 frets.

2007-2012		$1,075	$1,400

Corvette
2005-2006. Custom 22 with Velcity Yellow finish, Standard 22 red finish, Z06 inlays, Corvette logo on body.

2005	Custom 22, yellow	$1,075	$1,400
2006	Standard 22, red	$1,075	$1,400

Custom (Custom 24/PRS Custom)
1985-present. Double-cut solidbody, curly maple top, mahogany back and neck, pearl and abalone moon inlays, 24 frets, 2 humbuckers, tremolo, options include quilted or 10 Top, bird inlays, and gold hardware. 1985 Customs should be evaluated on a case by case basis.

1985		$4,000	$18,000
1986		$4,000	$7,000

MODEL YEAR	FEATURES	EXC. COND. LOW	HIGH
1987		$2,800	$3,650
1988		$2,400	$3,125
1989		$1,875	$2,450
1990-2020		$1,550	$2,025

Custom 22

1993-2009, 2013-present. Custom 22 with flamed or quilted maple top on mahogany body, 22-fret set-neck, upgrade option is gold hardware, normally the quilt top is higher than flamed top. Listed under Private Stock in '21, with select wood options.

1993-2021		$1,550	$2,025

Custom 22 (Brazilian)

2003-2004. Limited run of 500 with Brazilian rosewood 'board, figured 10 top, pearl bird inlays.

2003-2004		$2,475	$3,225

Custom 22 20th Anniversary

2005. Abalone 20th Anniversary birds inlay, 20th engraved on truss rod cover.

2005		$1,775	$2,300

Custom 22 Soapbar

1998-2002. 3 Seymour Duncan soapbar single-coils.

1998-2002		$1,350	$1,775

Custom 22/12

December 2003-2009. 12-string version, flame or quilt maple top, hum/single/hum pickups.

2003-2009		$1,900	$2,500

Custom 24 (Brazilian)

2003-2004. Limited run with Brazilian rosewood 'board, figured 10 top, pearl bird inlays.

2003-2004		$2,800	$3,650

Custom 24 (Walnut)

1992. Seamless matched walnut over mahogany, 3 made.

1992		$2,450	$3,200

Custom 24 20th Anniversary

2005. Abalone 20th Anniversary birds inlay, 20th engraved on truss rod cover.

2005		$1,925	$2,500

Custom 24 25th Anniversary

2010. Carved figured maple top, 25th Anniversary shadow birds inlay.

2010		$1,925	$2,500

Custom 24 30th Anniversary

2015. Figured maple top, 30th Anniversary on headstock, birds in flight neck inlay.

2015		$1,925	$2,500

Dave Navarro Signature

2005-2014. Carved maple top, bird inlays, tremolo, white.

2005-2014		$1,475	$1,925

DC3

2010-2013. Double-cut contoured body, bolt-on neck, 3 special single-coils.

2010-2013		$1,000	$1,325

DGT David Grissom Trem

2007-present. Based on the McCarty Tremolo model with an added volume control, a nitro topcoat, vintage colors, large frets designed for .011 gauge strings.

2007-2021		$1,875	$2,425

Dragon I

1992. Fingerboard inlay of a dragon made of 201 pieces of abalone, turquoise and mother-of-pearl, gold hardware, 50 made. The Dragon model collector requires an instru-

-ment to be truly mint and pristine with no play wear. The values shown here are for pristine instruments. Any issue whatsoever may dramatically reduce the high-side price shown. Price includes the certificate of authenticity.

1992	Amber quilt, amber flame	$14,700	$19,000
1992	Teal black	$13,000	$17,000

Dragon II

1993. Fingerboard inlay of a dragon made of 218 pieces of gold, coral, abalone, malachite, onyx and mother-of-pearl, 100 made.

1993		$8,500	$11,000

Dragon III

1994. Fingerboard inlay of a dragon made of 438 pieces of gold, red and green abalone, mother-of-pearl, mammoth ivory, and stone, 100 made.

1994		$8,500	$11,000

Dragon 2002

2002. Limited edition of 100 guitars, ultra-inlay work depicting dragon head on the guitar body.

2002		$7,000	$9,000

Dragon 25th Anniversary

2009-2010. Multi-material dragon fingerboard inlay, green ripple abalone Modern Eagle headstock, body shape and electronics are modeled after an early company PRS guitar, 60 made.

2009-2010		$8,500	$11,000

Dragon Doubleneck

2005. Limited edition 20th Anniversary model, about 50 made.

2005		$16,000	$21,000

Dragon Millenium/Dragon 2000

1999-2000. Three-D dragon inlay in body versus neck inlay of previous models, limited production of 50 guitars.

1999-2000	Black cherry	$10,000	$13,000
1999-2000	Rare color	$12,000	$15,500

EG II

1991-1995. Double-cut solidbody, bolt-on neck, 3 single-coils, single-single-hum, or hum-single-hum pickup options, opaque finish.

1991-1995		$800	$1,050

EG II Maple Top

1991-1995. EG II with flamed maple top, chrome hardware.

1991-1995		$1,050	$1,350

EG 3

1990-1991. Double-cut solidbody, bolt-on 22-fret neck, 3 single-coil pickups.

1990-1991	Flamed 10 top	$1,000	$1,300
1990-1991	Opaque finish	$800	$1,050
1990-1991	Plain top, sunburst	$800	$1,050

EG 4

1990-1991. Similar to EG 3 with single-single-hum pickup configuration, opaque finish.

1990-1991		$800	$1,050

Golden Eagle

1997-1998. Very limited production, eagle head and shoulders carved into lower bouts, varied high-end appointments.

1997-1998		$11,500	$15,000

PRS Custom 22
Bernunzio Uptown Music

1986 PRS Custom 24
Gantt Kushner

GUITARS

PRS McCarty 594

PRS Metal
Ian Gilmour

MODEL YEAR	FEATURES	EXC. COND. LOW	HIGH

John Mayer Silver Sky
2018-present. Alder body, maple neck, rosewood or maple 'board, 3 single-coil pickups, various colors available.
| 2018-2021 | | $1,325 | $1,725 |

John Mayer Silver Sky Limited Edition
2020-2021. Lunar Ice color with unique polychromatic finish.
| 2020-2021 | | $4,800 | $6,300 |

Johnny Hiland
2006-2009. Maple fretboard.
| 2006-2009 | | $1,375 | $1,775 |

KL-33 Korina
2008. Double-cut solid korina body, rosewood 'board, PRS Mira pickups, limited run of 100.
| 2008 | | $1,450 | $1,875 |

KQ-24 Custom 24 (Killer Quilt)
2009. Limited Edition of 120, quilted maple top over korina body, 24 frets.
| 2009 | | $1,600 | $2,100 |

Limited Edition
1989-1991, 2000. Double-cut, semi-hollow mahogany body, figured cedar top, gold hardware, less than 300 made. In '00, single-cut, short run of 5 antique white and 5 black offered via Garrett Park Guitars.
| 1989-1991 | | $3,000 | $4,000 |
| 2000 | | $3,000 | $4,000 |

Limited Edition Howard Leese Golden Eagle
2009. Private Stock, curly maple top, old style mother of pearl birds, 100 made.
| 2009 | | $3,700 | $4,900 |

LTD Experience (Limited Experience)
2007. 200 built to commemorate PRS 2007 Experience Open House, 24 frets, matching headstock, maple top with mahogany body.
| 2007 | | $1,550 | $2,000 |

Mark Tremonti Model
2001-2007. Single-cut, 2 humbuckers, black or platinum finish.
| 2001-2007 | | $1,350 | $1,750 |

Mark Tremonti Signature
2007-present. Single-cut, 2 humbuckers, figured maple top (10 top upgrade offered), various finishes.
| 2007-2021 | 10 top upgrade | $1,775 | $2,300 |
| 2007-2021 | Figured maple top | $1,550 | $2,025 |

Mark Tremonti Tribal
2004-2006. With Tribal artwork, 100 made.
| 2004-2006 | | $1,700 | $2,200 |

McCarty Model
1994-2007. Mahogany body with figured maple top, upgrade options may include a 10 top, gold hardware, bird inlays. Replaced by McCarty II.
| 1994-2007 | | $1,550 | $2,000 |

McCarty II
2008-2009. Replaced the McCarty, featured new MVC (Mastering Voice Control) circuitry for switching between a single-coil voice to a heavy-metal voice, opaque finish.
| 2008-2009 | | $1,600 | $2,100 |

McCarty 1957/2008 Limited
2008. "1957/2008" logo on truss rod cover, 08 serial number series, 150 made.
| 2008 | | $2,000 | $2,600 |

McCarty 58/MC-58
2009-2011. "MC-58" logo on truss rod cover, similar to other McCarty models except for new neck shape, 57/08 humbucker pickups and V12 finish.
| 2009-2011 | | $2,125 | $2,750 |

Mcarty 594
2016-present. Figured maple top, mahogany back, bird inlays, various colors.
| 2016-2021 | | $2,550 | $3,325 |

McCarty Archtop (Spruce)
1998-2000. Deep mahogany body, archtop, spruce top, 22-fret set-neck.
| 1998-2000 | | $1,800 | $2,350 |

McCarty Archtop Artist
1998-2002. Highest grade figured maple top and highest appointments, gold hardware.
| 1998-2002 | | $3,000 | $4,000 |

McCarty Archtop II (Maple)
1998-2000. Like Archtop but with figured maple top.
| 1998-2000 | Flamed or quilt | $2,200 | $2,875 |

McCarty Hollowbody I/Hollowbody I
1998-2009. Medium deep mahogany hollowbody, maple top, 22-fret set-neck, chrome hardware. McCarty dropped from name in '06.
| 1998-2009 | | $2,075 | $2,700 |

McCarty Hollowbody II/Hollowbody II
1998-2017. Like Hollowbody I but with figured maple top and back. McCarty dropped from name in '06.
| 1998-2017 | | $2,075 | $2,700 |

McCarty Hollowbody/Hollowbody Spruce
2000-2009. Similar to Hollowbody I with less appointmentsm spruce top. McCarty dropped from name in '06.
| 2000-2009 | | $1,650 | $2,150 |

McCarty Model/McCarty Brazilian
2003-2004. Limited run of 250, Brazilian rosewood 'board, Brazilian is printed on headstock just below the PRS script logo.
| 1999 | | $2,800 | $3,650 |
| 2003-2004 | | $2,475 | $3,225 |

McCarty Rosewood
2004-2005. PRS-22 fret with Indian rosewood neck.
| 2004-2005 | | $1,775 | $2,300 |

McCarty Soapbar (Korina)
2008-2009. Korina body, 2 Duncan soapbar pickups.
| 2008-2009 | | $1,450 | $1,900 |

McCarty Soapbar (Maple)
1998-2007. Soapbar with figured maple top option, nickel hardware.
| 1998-2007 | | $1,500 | $1,950 |

McCarty Soapbar Standard
1998-2009. Solid mahogany body, P-90-style soapbar pickups, 22-fret set-neck, nickel-plated hardware, upgrade options may include gold hardware and bird inlays.
| 1998-2009 | | $1,375 | $1,800 |

McCarty Standard
1994-2006. McCarty Model with carved mahogany body but without maple top, nickel-plated hardware, upgrade options may include gold hardware and bird inlays.
| 1994-2006 | | $1,375 | $1,800 |

MODEL YEAR	FEATURES	EXC. COND. LOW	HIGH
Metal			
1985-1986. Solid mahogany body with custom 2-color striped body finish and graphics, 24-fret set-neck, nickel hardware, 2 humbuckers.			
1985-1986		$8,000	$10,500
Metal '85 Reissue (Private Stock)			
2008. With certificate of authenticity.			
2008		$3,200	$4,200
Mira			
2007-2013. 2 exposed-coil humbuckers, abalone moon inlays, various opaque finishes. Replaced by S2 Mira in '14.			
2007-2013		$750	$975
Mira 25th Anniversary			
2010. 2 soapbar single-coils, shadow bird inlays.			
2010		$750	$975
Mira Korina			
2007-2009. Korina body and neck version, natural.			
2007-2009		$875	$1,125
Mira Maple Top (MT)			
2008-2009. Figured maple, moon or bird inlays.			
2008-2009		$975	$1,250
Modern Eagle			
2004-2007. Higher-end model based on Private Stock innovations, satin nitrocellulose finish, Brazilian rosewood neck.			
2004-2007		$4,500	$6,000
Modern Eagle II/MEII			
2008-2009. Curly maple top, black rosewood neck and 'board.			
2008-2009		$3,500	$4,500
Modern Eagle Quatro/ME Quatro			
2010-2012. Updated version of Modern Eagle, 53/10 humbucker pickups, select upgraded woods.			
2010-2012		$2,500	$3,200
NF3			
2010-2013. 3 Narrowfield pickups on top-mounted 1-piece assembly, double-cut contoured body, bolt-on neck.			
2010-2013		$1,150	$1,500
P22			
2012-2016. Carved figured maple top, birds, rosewood 'board, 10-top flame optional.			
2012-2016		$2,600	$3,400
P245			
2015. Semi-hollow electric, single-cut, 2 humbuckers and a piezo.			
2015		$2,275	$2,950
Paul's Dirty 100			
2010. Private Stock run of 100, highly figured curly maple top, moon inlays, 'Paul's Dirty 100' logo on back of headstock, black gold finish, paisley hard case.			
2010		$3,200	$4,200
Paul's Guitar			
2013-present. Carved figured maple top, mahogany back and neck, Hondouran rosewood 'board with brushstroke birds, various colors. Artist package and other options offered.			
2013-2021		$2,400	$3,100
Private Stock Program			
April 1996-present. Custom instruments based around existing PRS models. Values may be somewhat			

near regular production equivalent models or higher. The Private Stock option was reintroduced by 2003. That year a standard production offering might retail at about $7,500, but a '03 Santana I Private Stock might retail at over $15,000, so each guitar should be evaluated on a case-by-case basis.

MODEL YEAR	FEATURES	EXC. COND. LOW	HIGH
1996-2021	Various models	$4,000	$8,000
PRS Guitar			

1975-1985. About 75 to 100 guitars were built by Paul Smith himself or with a team of others, from '75 to '85, before he formed the current PRS company. Each guitar from this era should be evaluated on a case-by-case basis and the values shown are for guidance only. Authentication is highly recommended; these guitars do not have a PRS serial number. Some of these went to celebrity players and, as such, may command values higher than shown here because of that connection.

MODEL YEAR	FEATURES	EXC. COND. LOW	HIGH
1975-1983	Mahogany	$6,000	$26,000
1975-1983	Maple	$10,000	$46,000
1984-1985	Preproduction with provenance	$7,000	$26,000
1985-1986	Team-built	$4,000	$8,500
Rosewood Limited			
1996. Mahogany body with figured maple top, 1-piece rosewood neck with ultra-deluxe tree-of-life neck inlay, gold hardware.			
1996		$7,000	$9,000
Santana			
1995-1998, 2011-present. Limited production special order, figured maple top, 24-fret, symmetric Santana headstock, unique body purfling, chrome and nickel-plated hardware, yellow is most popular color, followed by orange, quality of top will affect price.			
1995	1st 100 signed	$4,600	$5,950
1995-1998		$3,500	$4,600
Santana II			
1998-2007. Three-way toggle replaces former dual mini-switches, special order, Brazilian 'board.			
1998-2007		$5,000	$6,300
Santana III			
2001-2006. Less ornate version of Santana II.			
2001-2006		$1,600	$2,100
Santana (Brazilian)			
2003. Quilted or flamed maple top, Brazilian rosewood neck and fretboard, eagle inlay on headstock, Santana Brazilian logo on back cover plate, 200 made.			
2003-2004		$6,200	$8,000
Santana 25th Anniversary Santana II			
2010. Figured maple top, rosewood 'board, eagle inlay on headstock, 25th Anniversary shadow birds.			
2010		$2,000	$2,600
SC 58 Artist			
2011-2012. Artist grade figured maple top, rosewood 'board, MOP/Paua birds.			
2011-2012		$2,150	$2,775
SC 245			
2007-2010. Single-cut 22-fret, 2 humbuckers, bird markers, SC 245 logo on truss rod cover.			
2007	Flamed top, Brazilian 'board	$2,300	$3,000
2007-2010	Solid color top	$1,775	$2,300

PRS SE Custom 24
Martin Secrest

PRS Paul's Guitar

PRS SE Standard 24
Michael Mitchell

PRS Swamp Ash Special
Imaged by Heritage Auctions, HA.com

MODEL YEAR	FEATURES	EXC. COND. LOW	HIGH

SC 250
2007-2010. Figured maple top, 2 humbuckers, 25" scale and locking tuners.

| 2007-2010 | | $1,425 | $1,850 |

SC-J Thinline
2008. Large full-scale single-cut hollowbody, originally part of Private Stock program until made in limited run of 300, select grade maple top and back over a mahogany middle body section, SC-J logo on truss rod cover.

| 2008 | | $3,600 | $4,800 |

SE Series
2001-present. PRS import line, solidbody and semi-hollow.

| 2001-2021 | Higher-end models | $500 | $900 |
| 2001-2021 | Most models | $300 | $500 |

Signature/PRS Signature
1987-1991. 1,000 made, solid mahogany body, figured maple top, hand-signed signature on headstock, Vintage Yellow is most valuable color and will fetch more, orange is second, quilt top is more valuable than flametop. Each guitar should be evaluated on a case-by-case basis.

| 1987 | Various colors | $3,300 | $8,300 |
| 1988-1991 | Various colors | $2,800 | $6,300 |

Signature (Private Stock)
2011. Limited run by Private Stock, 100 made, 408 humbucker pickups (8 tonal configurations), special signature headstock and fretboard inlays.

| 2011 | | $4,800 | $6,300 |

Singlecut
2000-2004, 2005-early 2008. Single-cut mahogany body, maple top, 22-fret 'board, upgrade options include 10 top flamed maple, gold hardware, bird inlays. Replaced by SC 245 and SC 250.

2000-2007	Various specs	$1,450	$1,850
2001	Brazilian neck/'board	$2,000	$2,600
2006-2007	Artist 20th Anniv, Brazilian	$2,000	$2,600
2006-2007	Standard 20th Anniv, Indian	$1,250	$1,625
2007-2008	Ltd Ed, Indian	$1,350	$1,750

Singlecut Hollowbody II CB 25th Anniversary
2010. Semi-hollow (CB means center block), f-holes, 10 maple top, bird inlays.

| 2010 | | $1,800 | $2,350 |

Singlecut Hollowbody Standard
2008-2009. Mahogany body.

| 2008-2009 | | $1,800 | $2,350 |

Singlecut Standard Satin
2006-2007. Thinner solid mahogany body, thin nitro cellulose finish, humbuckers or soapbars.

| 2006-2007 | | $1,000 | $1,325 |

Special
1987-1990, 1991-1993. Similar to Standard with upgrades, wide-thin neck, 2 HFS humbuckers. From '91-'93, a special option package was offered featuring a wide-thin neck and high output humbuckers.

| 1987-1990 | Solid color finish | $2,300 | $3,000 |
| 1991-1993 | Special order only | $2,600 | $3,400 |

MODEL YEAR	FEATURES	EXC. COND. LOW	HIGH

Standard
1987-1998. Set-neck, solid mahogany body, 24-fret 'board, 2 humbuckers, chrome hardware. Originally called the PRS Guitar from '85-'86 (see that listing), renamed Standard 24 from '98.

1987-1989	Sunburst & optional colors	$5,200	$6,800
1990-1991	Last Brazilian 'board	$2,700	$3,600
1992-1995		$1,400	$1,850
1995-1998	Stevensville	$1,400	$1,850

Standard 22
1994-2009. 22-fret Standard.

1994-1995		$1,400	$1,850
1995-1999	Stevensville	$1,400	$1,850
2000-2009		$1,400	$1,850

Standard 24
1998-2009. Renamed from Standard, solid mahogany body, 24-fret set-neck.

| 1998-2009 | | $1,400 | $1,850 |

Starla
2008-2013. Single-cut solidbody with retro-vibe, glued neck, 2 chrome humbuckers. Replaced by S2 Starla in '14.

| 2008-2013 | | $850 | $1,100 |

Studio
1988-1991, 2011-2013. Standard model variant, 24-fret set-neck, chrome and nickel hardware, single-single-hum pickups. The Studio package of pickups was offered until '96 on other models. Reissued in '11 with 22 frets, flamed maple top.

| 1988-1991 | | $1,600 | $2,100 |
| 2011-2013 | Reintroduced | $1,600 | $2,100 |

Studio Maple Top
1990-1991. Mahogany solidbody, bird inlays, 2 single-coils and 1 humbucker, tremolo, transparent finish.

| 1990-1991 | | $1,600 | $2,100 |

Swamp Ash Special
1996-2009. Solid swamp ash body, 22-fret bolt-on maple neck, 3 pickups, upgrade options available.

| 1996-2009 | | $1,175 | $1,525 |

Swamp Ash Special 25th Anniversary
2010. Swamp ash body, bolt-on neck, 25th Anniversary shadow bird inlays.

| 2010 | | $1,175 | $1,525 |

Tonare Grand
2009-2016. Full-body flat-top, European/German spruce top, rosewood back and sides, optional Adirondack red spruce top or AAAA grade top, onboard Acoustic Pickup System.

| 2009-2016 | | $2,550 | $3,400 |

West Street/1980 West Street Limited
2008. 180 made for US market, 120 made for export market, faithful replica of the model made in the original West Street shop, Sapele top.

| 2008 | | $2,075 | $2,700 |

Pawar
1999-2010. Founded by Jay Pawar, Jeff Johnston and Kevin Johnston in Willoughby Hills, Ohio, Pawar built professional and premium grade, production/custom, solidbody guitars.

MODEL YEAR	FEATURES	EXC. COND. LOW	HIGH

PBC Guitar Technology

See Bunker Guitars for more info.

Pearl

1971-ca.1974. Acoustic and electric guitars sold by Pearl Musical Instrument Co. (Pearl drums), and built by other Japanese builders.

Peavey

1965-present. Headquartered in Meridan, Mississippi, Peavey builds budget, intermediate, professional, and premium grade, production/custom, acoustic and electric guitars. They also build basses, amps, PA gear, effects and drums. Hartley Peavey's first products were guitar amps. He added guitars to the mix in '78.

Axcelerator/AX

1994-1998. Offset double-cut swamp ash or poplar body, bolt-on maple neck, dot markers, AX with locking vibrato, various colors.

1994-1998		$400	$525

Cropper Classic

1995-2005. Single-cut solidbody, 1 humbucker and 1 single coil, figured maple top over thin mahogany body, transparent Onion Green.

1995-2005		$400	$525

Defender

1994-1995. Double-cut, solid poplar body, 2 humbuckers and 1 single-coil pickup, locking Floyd Rose tremolo, metallic or pearl finish.

1994-1995		$185	$250

Destiny

1989-1992. Double-cut, mahogany body, maple top, neck-thru-bridge, maple neck, 3 integrated pickups, double locking tremolo.

1989-1992		$300	$400

Destiny Custom

1989-1992. Destiny with figured wood and higher-end appointments, various colors.

1989-1992		$425	$575

Detonator AX

1995-1998. Double-cut, maple neck, rosewood 'board, dot markers, hum/single/hum pickups, black.

1995-1998		$210	$275

EVH Wolfgang

1996-2004. Offset double-cut, arched top, bolt neck, stop tailpiece or Floyd Rose vibrato, quilted or flamed maple top upgrade option.

1996	Pat pending		
	early production	$2,500	$3,300
1997-1998	Pat pending	$1,900	$2,500
1999-2004	Flamed maple top	$1,700	$2,250
1999-2004	Standard top	$1,250	$1,650

EVH Wolfgang Special

1997-2004. Offset double-cut lower-end Wolfgang model, various opaque finishes, flamed top optional.

1996-2004	Standard top, D-Tuna	$725	$950
1997-2004	Flamed maple top	$800	$1,050
1997-2004	Standard basswood	$675	$900

Falcon/Falcon Active/Falcon Custom

1987-1992. Double-cut, 3 pickups, passive or active

electronics, Kahler locking vibrato.

1987-1992	Custom color	$350	$475
1987-1992	Standard color	$250	$325

Firenza

1994-1999. Offset double-cut, bolt-on neck, single-coil pickups.

1994-1999		$325	$425

Firenza AX

1994-1999. Upscale Firenza Impact with humbucking pickups.

1994-1999		$375	$500

Generation Custom EX

2006-2008. Single-cut solidbody, 2 humbuckers, 5-way switch.

2006-2008		$225	$300

Generation S-1/S-2/S-3

1988-1994. Single-cut, maple cap on mahogany body, bolt-on maple neck, six-on-a-side tuners, active single/hum pickups, S-2 with locking vibrato system.

1988-1994		$400	$525

Horizon/Horizon II

1983-1985. Extended pointy horns, angled lower bout, maple body, rear routing for electronics, 2 humbucking pickups. Horizon II has added blade pickup.

1983-1985		$275	$360

HP Special USA

2008-2011. Offset cutaway, 2 humbuckers.

2008-2011		$625	$825

Hydra Doubleneck

1985-1989. Available as a custom order, 6/12-string necks each with 2 humbuckers, 3-way pickup select.

1985-1989		$675	$900

Impact 1/Impact 2

1985-1987. Offset double-cut, Impact 1 has higher-end synthetic 'board, Impact 2 with conventional rosewood 'board.

1985-1987		$275	$360

Mantis

1984-1989. Hybrid X-shaped solidbody, 1 humbucking pickup, tremolo, laminated maple neck.

1984-1989		$275	$360

Milestone 12-String

1985-1986. Offset double-cut, 12 strings.

1985-1986		$160	$210

Milestone/Milestone Custom

1983-1986. Offset double-cut solidbody.

1983-1986		$125	$175

Mystic

1983-1989. Double-cut, 2 pickups, stop tailpiece initially, later Power Bend vibrato, maple body and neck.

1983-1989		$350	$450

Nitro I Active

1988-1990. Active electronics.

1988-1990		$250	$325

Nitro I/II/III

1986-1989. Offset double-cut, banana-style headstock, 1 humbucker (I), 2 humbuckers (II), or single/single/hum pickups (III).

1986-1989	Nitro I	$160	$215
1986-1989	Nitro II	$200	$265
1986-1989	Nitro III	$250	$325

2000 Peavey EVH Wolfgang Special

Willie Moseley

Peavey Hydra Doubleneck

Peavey T-60

1988 Peavey Vandenberg

MODEL YEAR	FEATURES	EXC. COND. LOW	HIGH

Odyssey

1990-1994. Single-cut, figured carved maple top on mahogany body, humbuckers.

1990-1994		$475	$625

Odyssey 25th Anniversary

1990. Single-cut body, limited production.

1990		$625	$825

Omniac JD USA

2005-2010. Designed by Jerry Donahue, single-cut solidbody, 2 single-coils.

2005-2010		$775	$1,025

Patriot

1983-1987. Double-cut, single bridge humbucker.

1983-1987		$225	$300

Patriot Plus

1983-1987. Double-cut, 2 humbucker pickups, bi-laminated maple neck.

1983-1987		$300	$400

Patriot Tremolo

1986-1990. Double-cut, single bridge humbucker, tremolo, replaced the standard Patriot.

1986-1990		$300	$400

Predator Plus 7ST

2008-2010. 7-string.

2008-2010		$300	$400

Predator Series

1985-1988, 1990-2016. Double-cut poplar body, 2 pickups until '87, 3 after, vibrato.

1985-2016		$175	$225

Raptor Series

1997-present. Offset double-cut solidbody, 3 pickups.

1997-2021		$85	$125

Razer

1983-1989. Double-cut with arrowhead point for lower bout, 2 pickups, 1 volume and 2 tone controls, stop tailpiece or vibrato.

1983-1989		$375	$500

Reactor

1993-1999. Classic single-cut style, 2 single-coils.

1993-1999		$325	$425

Rockmaster II Stage Pack

2000s. Student solidbody Rockmaster electric guitar and GT-5 amp pack.

2000		$50	$75

Rotor Series

2004-2010. Classic futuristic body, elongated upper treble bout/lower bass bout, 2 humbuckers.

2004-2008	Rotor EXP	$275	$350
2004-2010	Rotor EX	$250	$325

T-15

1981-1983. Offset double-cut, bolt-on neck, dual ferrite blade single-coil pickups, natural. Amp-in-case available.

1981-1983	Amp-in-case	$250	$325
1981-1983	Guitar only	$185	$250

T-25

1979-1985. Synthetic polymer body, 2 pickups, cream 'guard, sunburst finish.

1979-1985		$350	$450

T-25 Special

1979-1985. Same as T-25, but with super high output pickups, phenolic 'board, black/white/black 'guard, ebony black finish.

1979-1985		$350	$450

T-26

1982-1986. Same as T-25, but with 3 single-coil pickups and 5-way switch.

1982-1986		$350	$450

T-27

1981-1983. Offset double-cut, bolt-on neck, dual ferrite blade single-coil pickups.

1981-1983		$400	$525

T-30

1982-1985. Short-scale, 3 single-coil pickups, 5-way select, by '83 amp-in-case available.

1982-1985	Guitar only	$325	$425
1983-1985	Amp-in-case	$425	$575

T-60

1978-1988. Contoured offset double-cut, ash body, six-in-line tuners, 2 humbuckers, thru-body strings, by '87 maple bodies, various finishes.

1978-1988		$550	$725

T-1000 LT

1992-1994. Double-cut, 2 single-coils and humbucker with coil-tap.

1992-1994		$275	$375

Tracer Custom

1989-1990. Tracer with 2 single humbuckers and extras.

1989-1990		$225	$300

Tracer/Tracer II

1987-1994. Offset scooped double-cut with extended pointy horns, poplar body, 1 pickup, Floyd Rose.

1987-1994		$225	$300

Vandenberg Quilt Top

1989-1992. Vandenberg Custom with quilted maple top, 2 humbuckers, glued-in neck, mahogany body and neck.

1989-1992		$1,150	$1,525

Vandenberg Signature

1988-1992. Double-cut, reverse headstock, bolt-on neck, locking vibrato, various colors.

1988-1992		$650	$850

Vortex I/Vortex II

1986. Streamlined Mantis with 2 pickups, 3-way, Kahler locking vibrato. Vortex II has Randy Rhoads Sharkfin V.

1986		$350	$450

V-Type Series

2004-2007. Offset double-cut solidbody, pointed reverse 6-on-a-side headstock, 2 humbuckers.

2004-2007		$325	$425

Wolfgang Special

1996-1997. Peavy logo on headstock (not EVH), curly maple quilt top, various colors.

1996-1997		$1,300	$1,700

Pederson Custom Guitars

2009-present. Luthier Kevin Pederson builds his premium grade, production/custom, hollowbody and solidbody guitars in Forest City, Iowa. From 1997-2009 he produced guitars under the Abyss brand name.

MODEL YEAR	FEATURES	EXC. COND. LOW	HIGH

Pedro de Miguel

1991-present. Luthiers Pedro Pérez and Miguel Rodriguez build their professional and premium grade, custom/production, classical guitars in Madrid, Spain. They also offer factory-made instruments built to their specifications.

Pedulla

1975-2019. Known for basses, Pedulla did offer a few solidbody guitar models into the early 1980s.

MVP

1981-1984. Double-cut solidbody, 2 humbuckers, dot markers, 4 knobs with main toggle and 3 mini-toggle switches, stencil Pedulla logo, MVP serial number series.

1981-1984		$1,500	$1,950

Peekamoose

1983-present. Production/custom, premium grade, solidbody, chambered, and archtop electric guitars built in New York City, New York by luthier Paul Schwartz.

Pegasus Guitars and Ukuleles

1977-present. Premium grade, custom steel-string guitars built by luthier Bob Gleason in Kurtistown, Hawaii, who also builds ukulele family instruments.

Penco

Ca. 1974-1978. Generally high quality Japanese-made copies of classic American acoustic, electric and bass guitars. Imported by Philadelphia Music Company of Limerick, Pennsylvania during the copy era. Includes dreadnought acoustics with laminated woods, bolt-neck solidbody electric guitars and basses, mandolins and banjos.

Acoustic Flat-Top

1974-1978	Various models	$125	$350

Electric

1974-1978	Solidbody	$275	$550
1974-1978	Thinline Archtop	$275	$550
1977	E-72 Howard Roberts	$800	$1,325

Penn

1950s. Archtop and acoustic guitars built by made by United Guitar Corporation in Jersey City, New Jersey, which also made Premier acoustics. Penn was located in L.A.

Pensa (Pensa-Suhr)

1982-present. Premium grade, production/custom, solidbody guitars and basses built in the U.S. Rudy Pensa, of Rudy's Music Stop, New York City, New York, started building Pensa guitars in '82. In '85 he teamed up with John Suhr to build Pensa-Suhr instruments. Name changed back to Pensa in '96.

Classic

1992-Ca. 1998. Offset double-cut, 3 single-coils, gold hardware.

1992-1998	Various models	$2,000	$2,600

MK 1 (Mark Knopfler)

1985-2018. Offset double-cut solidbody, carved flamed maple bound top, 3 pickups, gold hardware, dot markers, bolt-on neck.

1985-2018		$2,000	$2,600

Suhr Custom

1985-1989. Two-piece maple body, bolt-on maple neck with rosewood 'board, custom order basis with a variety of woods and options available.

1985-1989	Various options	$2,000	$2,600

Suhr Standard

1985-1991. Double-cut, single/single/hum pickup configuration, opaque solid finish normally, dot markers.

1985-1991		$1,800	$2,350

Perlman Guitars

1976-present. Luthier Alan Perlman builds his premium grade, custom, steel-string and classical guitars in San Francisco, California.

Perri Ink.

Custom, professional grade, solidbody electric guitars built by luthier Nick Perri in Los Angeles, California, starting in 2009.

Perry Guitars

1982-present. Premium grade, production/custom, classical guitars built by luthier Daryl Perry in Winnipeg, Manitoba. He also builds lutes.

Petillo Masterpiece Guitars

1965-present. Intermediate, professional and premium grade, custom, steel-string, nylon-string, 12-string, resonator, archtop, and Hawaiian guitars in Ocean, New Jersey, originally by father and son luthiers Phillip J. "Doc" and David Petillo. Doc died in August, 2010.

Petros Guitars

1992-present. Premium grade, production/custom, flat-top, 12-string, and nylon-string guitars built by father and son luthiers Bruce and Matthew Petros in Kaukauna, Wisconsin.

PH Guitars

2006-present. Luthier Paul A. Hartmann builds professional and premium grade, custom, acoustic archtop and electric guitars in Hyde Park, New York.

Phantom Guitar Works

1992-present. Intermediate grade, production/custom, classic Phantom, and Teardrop shaped solid and hollowbody guitars and basses assembled in Clatskanie, Oregon. They also offer the Mando-Guitar. Phantom was established by Jack Charles, former lead guitarist of the band Quarterflash. Some earlier guitars were built overseas.

1976 Penco
Reese Shellman

Phantom Guitar Works Phantom

1959 Premier A-300
Rivington Guitars

Prestige Heritage
Elite Spalt Maple

MODEL YEAR	FEATURES	EXC. COND. LOW	HIGH

Pheo

Luthier Phil Sylvester, began building in 1996, unique premium grade, production/custom, electric and acoustic guitars in Portland, Oregon.

Phoenix Guitar Company

1994-present. Luthiers George Leach and Diana Huber build their premium grade, production/custom, archtop and classical guitars in Scottsdale, Arizona.

Pieper

Premium grade, custom, solidbody guitars and basses built by luthier Robert Pieper in New Haven, Connecticut starting in 2005.

Pignose

1972-present. The original portable amp company also offers intermediate grade, production, dreadnaught and amplified electric guitars. They also offer effects. Refer to Amps section for more company info.

Pilgrim

1970's-late-1980s, 2010-present. Built in the U.K., luthier Paul Tebbutt introduced the brand back in the '70s and his guitars were available until late '80s. His designs are now used on intermediate grade, production, electric acoustic guitars, built in the Far East and distributed by John Hornby Skewes & Co. Ltd. They also offer mandolins, ukuleles and banjos.

Pimentel and Sons

1951-present. Luthiers Lorenzo Pimentel and sons build their professional, premium and presentation grade, flat-top, jazz, cutaway electric, and classical guitars in Albuquerque, New Mexico.

Player

1984-1985. Player guitars featured interchangable pickup modules that mounted through the back of the guitar. They offered a double-cut solidbody with various options and the pickup modules were sold separately. The company was located in Scarsdale, New York.

Pleasant

Late 1940s-ca.1966. Solidbody electric guitars, obviously others, Japanese manufacturer, probably not imported into the U.S.

Electric Solidbody

1940s-1966. Various models.

1940s-1966		$200	$300

Potvin

2003-present. Production/custom, professional and premium grade, chambered, hollowbody and solidbody electric guitars built by luthier Mike Potvin in Ontario.

Prairie State

1927-ca. 1940. A Larson Brothers brand, basically a derivative of Maurer & Company. The Prairie State models were slightly more expensive than the equivalent Maurer models. They featured a patented steel rod mechanism to strengthen the body, which ran from the end block to the neck block. The model usually had Brazilian rosewood back and sides, laminated necks and X-bracing. Some later models were built with figured maple.

Prairiewood

Luthier Robert Dixon of Fargo, North Dakota, began in 2005, builds professional grade, production/custom, hollowbody archtop and solidbody guitars.

Premier

Ca.1938-ca.1975, 1990s-2010. Brands originally offered by Premier include Premier, Multivox, Marvel, Belltone and Strad-O-Lin. Produced by Peter Sorkin Music Company in Manhattan, New York City, New York, who began in Philadelphia, relocating to NYC in '35. First radio-sized amplifiers and stick-on pickups for acoustic archtops were introduced by '38. After WWII, they set up the Multivox subsidiary to manufacture amplifiers ca. '46. First flat-top with pickup appeared in '46.

Most acoustic instruments made by United Guitar Corporation in Jersey City, New Jersey. Ca. '57 Multivox acquires Strad-O-Lin. Ca.'64-'65 their Custom line guitars are assembled with probably Italian bodies and hardware, Japanese electronics, possibly Egmond necks from Holland. By ca. '74-'75, there were a few Japanese-made guitars, then Premier brand goes into hiatus. The brand reappears on Asian-made budget and intermediate grade, production, solidbody guitars and basses beginning in the '90s.

Bantam Custom

1950s-1960s. Single-cut archtop, dots, earlier with white potted pickups, then metal-covered pickups, and finally Japanese-made pickups (least valued).

1950s-60s		$825	$1,100

Bantam Deluxe

1950s-1960s. Single-cut archtop, fully bound, sparkle knobs, earlier with white potted pickups, then metal-covered pickups, and finally Japanese-made pickups (least valued), block markers, 1 or 2 pickups (deduct $100 for 1 pickup).

1950s-60s	Blond, sunburst	$1,650	$2,150

Bantam Special

1950s-1960s. Single-cut archtop, dots, early models with white potted pickups, then metal-covered pickups, and finally Japanese-made pickups (least valued), 1 or 2 pickups (deduct $100 for 1 pickup).

1950s-60s		$775	$1,000

Custom Solidbody

1958-1970. Notable solidbody bass scroll cutaway, various models with various components used, finally import components only.

1958-1970	1 pickup	$500	$650
1958-1970	2 pickups	$575	$750
1958-1970	3 pickups	$775	$1,025

MODEL YEAR	FEATURES	EXC. COND. LOW	HIGH
Deluxe Archtop			
1950s-1960s. Full body 17 1/4" archtop, square block markers, single-cut, early models with white potted pickups, later '60s models with metal pickups.			
1950s-60s		$1,325	$1,725
E-727			
1958-1962. E-scroll style solidbody with scroll bass bout, 3 single-coil pickups, Premier headstock logo, made by the Multivox factory in New York.			
1958-1962		$700	$900
Semi-Pro 16" Archtop			
1950s-early-1960s. Thinline electric 16" archtop with 2 1/4" deep body, acoustic or electric.			
1950s-60s	Acoustic	$700	$900
1950s-60s	Electric	$775	$1,025
Semi-Pro Bantam Series			
1960s. Thinline electric archtop with 2 3/4" deep body, offered in cutaway and non-cut models.			
1960s		$325	$425
Special Archtop			
1950s-1960s. Full body 17 1/4" archtop, less fancy than Deluxe, single-cut, early models with white potted pickups, '60s models with metal pickups.			
1950s-60s		$875	$1,150
Studio Six Archtop			
1950s-early-1960s. 16" wide archtop, single pickup, early pickups white potted, changed later to metal top.			
1950s-60s		$525	$700

Prenkert Guitars

1980-present. Premium and presentation grade, production/custom, classical and flamenco guitars built in Sebastopol, California by luthier Richard Prenkert.

Prestige

2003-present. Intermediate, professional, and premium grade, production/custom, acoustic, solidbody and hollowbody guitars and basses from Vancouver, British Columbia.

PST Guitars

Ca. 2000-present. Professional and premium grade, custom, electric guitars and basses, built by luthier P. Scott Tucker, in King George, Virginia. He has also built acoustic guitars.

Queen Shoals Stringed Instruments

1972-ca. 2010. Luthier Larry Cadle builds his production/custom, flat-top, 12-string, and nylon-string guitars in Clendenin, West Virginia.

Queguiner, Alain

1982-present. Custom flat-tops, 12 strings, and nylon strings built by luthier Alain Queguiner in Paris, France.

Quest

1982-ca. 1986. Originally labeled Quest by Vantage, these solidbody guitars and basses were built in Japan, mostly by Chushin Gakki.

MODEL YEAR	FEATURES	EXC. COND. LOW	HIGH

R.C. Allen

1951-2014. Luthier R. C. "Dick" Allen built professional and premium grade, custom hollowbody and semi-hollowbody guitars in El Monte, California. He has also built solidbody guitars. He passed away in '14.

Rahan

1999-present. Professional grade, production/custom, solidbody guitars built by luthiers Mike Curd and Rick Cantu in Houston, Texas.

Rahbek Guitars

2000-present. Professional and premium grade, production/custom, solidbody electrics built by luthier Peter Rahbek in Copenhagen, Denmark.

Raimundo

1970s-present. Intermediate, professional and premium grade flamenco and classical guitars made in Valencia, Spain, by luthiers Antonio Aparicio and Manual Raimundo.

RainSong

1991-present. Professional grade, production, all-graphite and graphite and wood acoustic guitars built originally in Maui, and currently in Woodinville, Washington. Developed by luthier engineer John Decker with help from luthier Lorenzo Pimentel, engineer Chris Halford, and sailboard builder George Clayton.

RAM Guitars

2007-present. Luthier Ron Mielzynski builds his professional grade, production/custom, solidbody, chambered and archtop electric guitars in Fox River Grove, Illinois.

Rambler

See Strobel Guitars listing.

Ramirez, Jose

1882-present. Professional, premium, and presentation grade, custom/production, classical guitars built in Madrid, Spain. Founded by Jose Ramirez (1858-1923) who was an apprentice at the shop of Francisco Gonzales. Jose opened his own workshop in 1882 working with his younger brother, Manuel. Manuel split with Jose and opened his own, competing workshop. Jose's business was continued by Jose's son Jose Ramirez II (1885-1957), grandson Jose III (1922-1995), and great grandchildren Jose IV (1953-2000) and Amalia Ramirez. In the 1930's a larger body instrument with improved fan bracing was developed to meet the needs for more power and volume. Other refinements were developed and the Ramirez 1A Tradicional was soon introduced which found favor with Andres Segovia. The Ramirez company has produced both student and professional instruments, but in the classical guitar field, like the old-master violin business, a student model

1996 R.C. Allen Leader
Imaged by Heritage Auctions, HA.com

1966 Jose Ramirez 1A
Carter Vintage Guitars

Randy Wood Custom

1939 Recording King Carson Robinson/Model 1052

Jet City Guitars

MODEL YEAR	FEATURES	EXC. COND. LOW	HIGH

is often a very fine instrument that is now valued at $2,000 or more. In the 1980s Ramirez offered the E Series student guitar line that was built for, but not by, Ramirez. In 1991 the company offered the even more affordable R Series which was offered for about $1,300. As is typically the case, Ramirez classical guitars do not have a name-logo on the headstock. The brand is identified by a Ramirez label on the inside back which also may have the model number listed.

A/1A
1960s-2000s. Classical, Brazilian or Indian rosewood.

MODEL YEAR	FEATURES	LOW	HIGH
1960s-70s	Brazilian, cedar	$6,500	$8,400
1970s-80s	Indian	$2,900	$3,800
1980s	Brazilian	$5,300	$6,900
1990-2000s	Indian	$2,700	$3,500

A/2A

1970s-80s	Indian	$2,900	$3,750

AE Estudio

2004		$1,775	$2,300

De Camera
1980s. Classical, cedar top, Brazilian rosewood back and sides.

1980s		$2,800	$3,600

E/1E/Estudio
1988-1990s. Intermediate level.

1988-1990s		$1,300	$1,700

E/2E
1990s-2000s. Red cedar top, Indian rosewood back and sides, Spanish cedar neck, ebony 'board.

1990-2000s		$1,450	$1,900

E/3E/Estudio
1990s. Cedar, rosewood.

1990s		$1,700	$2,200

E/4E/Estudio
1980s-2000s. Top of the E Series line, solid red cedar top, solid Indian rosewood back and sides.

1980-2000s		$2,100	$2,700

Flamenco
1920s-1979. European spruce top, cyprus back and sides.

1920s-50s		$4,400	$5,700
1960-1969		$3,100	$4,000
1970-1979		$3,000	$3,900

R1
1991-2014. Red cedar top, mahogany sides and back, Spanish cedar neck, ebony 'board. Replaced by RA series in '14.

1991-2014		$575	$750

R2
1991-2014. Red cedar top, Indian rosewood back and sides, cedar neck, ebony 'board. Replaced by RA series in '14.

1991-2014		$950	$1,225

R3
1998. Cedar, rosewood.

1998		$950	$1,225

R4 Classical
1995-2014. All solid wood, Western red cedar top, rosewood back and sides. Replaced by RB series in '14.

1995-2014		$1,200	$1,575

MODEL YEAR	FEATURES	EXC. COND. LOW	HIGH

S/S1
2005-2007. Solid German spruce top, African mahogany sides and back, most affordable in Estudio line.

2005-2007		$700	$900

Segovia
Cedar, Indian rosewood.

1966		$7,100	$9,200
1974-1978		$5,000	$6,500

SP Series
2002-2018. Semi-professional level designed to be between the company's 'concert/professional' series and 'student' series.

2002-2018		$4,850	$6,300

Ramirez, Manuel

1890-1916. Brother of Jose Ramirez, and a respected professional classical guitar builder from Madrid, Spain. His small shop left no heirs so the business was not continued after Manuel's death in 1916. Manuel was generally considered to be more famous during his lifetime than his brother Jose, and while his business did not continue, Manuel trained many well known Spanish classical guitar luthiers who prospered with their own businesses. During Manuel's era his shop produced at least 48 different models, with prices ranging from 10 to 1,000 pesetas, therefore vintage prices can vary widely. Guitars made prior to 1912 have a label with a street address of Arlaban 10, in 1912 the shop moved to Arlaban 11.

Randy Reynolds Guitars

1996-2018. Luthier Randy Reynolds builds his premium grade, production/custom classical and flamenco guitars in Colorado Springs, Colorado. Reynolds announced his retirement January 1, 2019.

Randy Wood Guitars

1968-present. Premium grade, custom/production, archtop, flat-top, and resonator guitars built by luthier Randy Wood in Bloomingdale, Georgia. He also builds mandolins.

Rarebird Guitars

1978-present. Luthier Bruce Clay builds his professional and premium grade, production/custom, guitars and basses, originally in Arvada, Colorado, and currently in Hoehne, Colorado.

Rat Fink

2002-2005. Lace Music Products, the makers of the Lace Sensor pickup, offered the intermediate grade, production, guitars and basses, featuring the artwork of Ed "Big Daddy" Roth until '05.

Rayco

2002-present. Professional and premium grade, custom, resonator and Hawaiian-style acoustic guitars built in British Columbia, by luthiers Mark Thibeault and Jason Friesen.

MODEL YEAR	FEATURES	EXC. COND. LOW	HIGH

Recco

1960s. Electric guitar imports made by Teisco, pricing similar to Teisco models, Recco logo on headstock, upscale solidbodies can have four pickups with several knobs and four switches.

Electric Solidbody

1960s	4 pickups	$500	$650

Recording King

1929-1943. Brand name used by Montgomery Ward for instruments made by various American manufacturers, including Kay, Gibson and Gretsch. Generally mid-grade instruments. M Series are Gibson-made archtops.

Carson Robison/Model 1052

1938-1939. Made by Gibson, flat-top, 16", sunburst.

1938-1939		$2,400	$3,100

Kay 17" Flat-Top

1940-1941		$925	$1,200

M-2

1936-1941. Gibson-made archtop with carved top and f-holes, maple back and sides.

1936-1941		$675	$875

M-3

1936-1941. Gibson-made archtop, f-holes, maple back and sides, carved top.

1936-1941		$850	$1,100

M-4

1937-1940. Gibson-made archtop, f-holes, maple back and sides, rope-checkered binding, flying bat wing markers.

1937-1940		$1,000	$1,300

M-5

1936-1941. Gibson-made archtop with f-holes, maple back and sides, trapeze tailpiece, checkered top binding.

1936-1938	16" body	$1,300	$1,700
1939-1941	17" body	$1,400	$1,800

M-6

1938-1939. M-5 with upgraded gold hardware.

1938-1939		$1,450	$1,900

Model 681

Mid-1930s. Small flat top by Gibson, ladder-braced.

1930s		$1,400	$1,800

Model 1124

1937. 16" acoustic archtop, body by Gibson, attractive higher-end appointments, block-dot markers, sunburst.

1937		$1,800	$2,300

Ray Whitley

1939-1940. High-quality model made by Gibson, round shoulder flat-top, mahogany (Model 1028) or Brazilian rosewood (Model 1027) back and sides, 5-piece maple neck, Ray Whitley stencil script peghead logo, pearl crown inlay on peghead, fancy inlaid markers.

1939-1940	Brazilian	$24,500	$32,000
1939-1940	Mahogany	$12,300	$16,000

Roy Smeck

1938-1940. 16.25" electric archtop, large Recording King badge logo, Roy Smeck stencil logo, bar pickup, 2 control knobs on upper bass bout, dot markers.

1938-1940		$1,400	$1,800

Recording King (TML)

2005-present. Budget grade, production, acoustic cowboy stenciled guitars designed by Greg Rich for The Music Link, which also offers Johnson and other brand instruments. They also have banjos and ukes.

Redentore

2007-present. Luthier Mark Piper builds professional and premium grade, production/custom, archtop jazz, acoustic flat-top, carve-top and semi-hollow electric guitars in Columbia, Tennessee.

RedLine Acoustics and RedLine Resophonics

2007-present. Professional and premium grade, production, acoustic and resophonic guitars built in Hendersonville, Tennessee by luthiers Steve Smith, Jason Denton, Christian McAdams and Ryan Futch. They also build mandolins and plan to add lap steels.

Regal

Ca. 1895-1966, 1987-present. Intermediate and professional grade, production, acoustic and wood and metal body resonator guitars and basses. Originally a mass manufacturer founded in Indianapolis, Indiana, the Regal brand was first used by Emil Wulschner & Son. After 1900, new owners changed the company name to The Regal Manufacturing Company. The company was moved to Chicago in '08 and renamed the Regal Musical Instrument Company. Regal made brands for distributors and mass merchandisers as well as marketing its own Regal brand. Regal purchased the Lyon & Healy factory in '28. Regal was licensed to co-manufacture Dobros in '32 and became the sole manufacturer of them in '37 (see Dobro for those instruments). Most Regal instruments were beginner-grade; however, some very fancy archtops were made during the '30s. The company was purchased by Harmony in '54 and absorbed. From '59 to '66, Harmony made acoustics under the Regal name for Fender. In '87 the Regal name was revived on a line of resonator instruments by Saga.

Acoustic Hawaiian

1930s. Student model, small 13" body, square neck, glued or trapeze bridge.

1930s	Faux grain painted finish	$425	$550
1930s	Plain sunburst, birch, trapeze	$255	$335

Concert Folk H6382

1960s. Regal by Harmony, solid spruce top, mahogany back and sides, dot markers, natural.

1960s		$275	$375

Deluxe Dreadnought H6600

1960s. Regal by Harmony, solid spruce top, mahogany back and sides, bound top and back, rosewood 'board, dot markers, natural.

1960s		$275	$375

Recording King RO-T16

Redentore Psalmist

1930s Regal Model 27
Imaged by Heritage Auctions, HA.com

1978 Renaissance SPG
Rivington Guitars

MODEL YEAR	FEATURES	EXC. COND. LOW	HIGH

Dreadnought 12-String H1269
1960s. Regal by Harmony, solid spruce top, 12-string version of Deluxe, natural.

1960s		$275	$375

Esquire
1940s. 15 1/2" acoustic archtop, higher-end appointments, fancy logo art and script pearl Esquire headstock logo and Regal logo, natural.

1940s		$1,150	$1,500

Meteor
1960s. Single-cut acoustic-electric archtop, 2 pickups.

1960s		$1,350	$1,750

Model 27
1933-1942. Birch wood body, mahogany or maple, 2-tone walnut finish, single-bound top, round or square neck.

1933-1942		$1,050	$1,375

Model 45
1933-1937. Spruce top and mahogany back and sides, bound body, square neck.

1933-1937		$1,725	$2,250

Model 46
1933-1937. Round neck.

1933-1937		$1,725	$2,250

Model 55 Standard
1933-1934. Regal's version of Dobro Model 55 which was discontinued in '33.

1933-1934		$1,075	$1,400

Model 75
1939-1940. Metal body, square neck.

1939-1940		$1,925	$2,500

Model TG 60 Resonator Tenor
1930s. Wood body, large single cone biscuit bridge resonator, 2 upper bout metal ports, 4-string tenor.

1930s		$1,500	$1,950

Parlor
1920s. Small body, slotted headstock, birch sides and back, spruce top.

1920s		$300	$400

Prince
1930s. High-end 18" acoustic archtop, fancy appointments, Prince name inlaid in headstock along with Regal script logo and strolling guitarist art.

1930s		$1,925	$2,500

Spirit Of '76
1976. Red-white-blue, flat-top.

1976		$450	$600

Reliance
1920s. Instruments built by the Oscar Schmidt Co. and possibly others. Most likely a brand made for a distributor.

Relixx
2001-2013. Intermediate and professional grade, production/custom, aged vintage-style solidbody guitars built in Sanborn, New York by luthier Nick Hazlett. He discontinued complete guitars in '13 and now offers only vintage parts.

Renaissance
1978-1980. Plexiglass solidbody electric guitars and basses. Founded in Malvern, Pennsylvania, by John Marshall (designer), Phil Goldberg and Daniel Lamb. Original partners gradually leave and John Dragonetti takes over by late-'79. The line is redesigned with passive electronics on guitars, exotic shapes, but when deal with Sunn amplifiers falls through, company closes. Brandname currently used on a line of guitars and basses made by Rick Turner in Santa Cruz, California.

Fewer than 300 of first series made, plus a few prototypes and several wooden versions; six or so prototypes of second series made. SN=M(M) YYXXXX: month, year, consecutive number.

Electric Plexiglas Solidbody
1978-1980. Models include the SPG ('78-'79, DiMarzio pickups, active electronics), T-200G ('80, Bich-style with 2 passive DiMarzio pickups), and the S-200G ('80, double-cut, 2 DiMarzio pickups, passive electronics).

1978-1980		$850	$1,100

Renaissance Guitars
1994-present. Professional grade, custom, semi-acoustic flat-top, nylon-string and solidbody guitars and basses built by luthier Rick Turner in Santa Cruz, California. He also builds ukes.

Republic Guitars
2006-present. Intermediate grade, production, reso-phonic and Weissenborn-style guitars imported by American Folklore, Inc. of Austin, Texas. They also offer mandolins and ukes.

Retronix
2013-present. Korean-made solidbody guitars designed and imported by J. Backlund. They also build J. Backlund guitars.

Reuter Guitars
1984-present. Professional and premium grade, custom, flat-top, 12-string, resonator, and Hawaiian guitars built by luthier John Reuter, the Director of Training at the Roberto-Venn School of Luthiery, in Tempe, Arizona.

Reverend
1996-present. Intermediate grade, production, guitars and basses, designed by luthier and founder Joe Naylor, manufactured in South Korea, and setup by Reverend originally in Warren, Livonia, Michigan, and currently in Toledo, Ohio. There were also earlier U.S. production guitars built in Warren. Reverend has built amps and effects in the past. In 2010, Ken and Penny Haas purchased the company with Naylor continuing with design. Naylor also founded Naylor Amps, Armor Gold Cables, Stringdog, and Railhammer Pickups.

Electric
1996-present. Solid and semi-solid bodies, bolt or set-neck, various pickups.

1996-2021	Various models	$400	$1,800

MODEL YEAR	FEATURES	EXC. COND. LOW	HIGH

Rex

1920s-1940s, 1950s-1960s. Generally, beginner-grade guitars made by Kay and sold through Fred Gretsch distributors. In the '50s and '60s, the Lamberti Brothers Company in Melbourne, Australia built electrics bearing the Rex brand that were not distributed by Gretsch. They also had built amps.

Ribbecke Guitars

Premium and presentation grade, custom thinline, flat-top, and archtop guitars built by luthier Tom Ribbecke, starting in 1973, in Healdsburg, California.

Rice Custom Guitars

1998-present. Father and son luthiers, Richard Rice and Christopher Rice, build professional and premium grade, custom, solidbody, semi-hollow and hollowbody electric guitars and basses in Arlington Heights, Illinois.

Rich and Taylor

1993-1996. Custom acoustic and electric guitars, mandolins and banjos from luthiers Greg Rich and Mark Taylor (Crafters of Tennessee).

Richard Schneider

1960s-1997. Luthier Richard Schneider built his acoustic guitars in Washington state. Over the years, he collaborated with Dr. Michael A. Kasha on many guitar designs and innovations. Originally from Michigan, he also was involved in designing guitars for Gretsch and Gibson. He died in early '97.

Richie's Guitar Shop

1983-present. Intermediate and professional grade, custom, electric guitars and basses, built by luthier Richard 'Richie' Baxt, in New York City, New York.

Richmond

Luthiers Robert Godin (Godin Guitars) and Daniel Fiocco build intermediate and professional grade, production, chambered and solidbody electric guitars in Richmond, Quebec. Richmond is one of several brands used by Godin.

Richter Mfg.

1930s. One of many Chicago makers of the era, the company allegedly bought already-made guitars from other manufacturers, painted and decorated them to their liking and resold them.

Rick Hayes Instruments

2006-present. Owned by Rick and Lyn Hayes and offering professional and premium grade, production/custom, dreadnought acoustic and electric guitars, and mandolins built by Rick and Steve Hogsed in Goshen, Ohio.

MODEL YEAR	FEATURES	EXC. COND. LOW	HIGH

Rick Turner

1979-1981, 1990-present. Rick Turner has a long career as a luthier, electronics designer and innovator. He also makes the Renaissance line of guitars in his shop in Santa Cruz, California. The guitars and basses built in 1979-'81 were numbered sequentially in the order they were completed and shipped with the second part of the serial number indicating the year the instrument was built. Turner estimates that approximately 200 instruments were made during that period.

Rickenbacker

1931-present. Professional and premium grade, production/custom, acoustic and electric guitars built in California. They also build basses. Founded in Los Angeles as Ro-Pat-In by ex-National executives George Beauchamp, Paul Barth and National's resonator cone supplier Adolph Rickenbacher. Rickenbacher was born in Basel, Switzerland in 1886, emigrated to the U.S. and moved to Los Angeles in 1918, opening a tool and die business in '20.

In the mid-'20s, Rickenbacher began providing resonator cones and other metal parts to George Beauchamp and Louis Dopyera of National String Instrument Corporation and became a shareholder in National. Beauchamp, Barth and Harry Watson came up with wooden "frying pan" electric Hawaiian lap steel for National in '31; National was not interested, so Beauchamp and Barth joined with Rickenbacher as Ro-Pat-In (probably for ElectRO-PATent-INstruments) to produce Electro guitars. Cast aluminum frying pans were introduced in '32. Some Spanish guitars (flat-top, F-holes) with Electro pickups were produced beginning in '32. Ro-Pat-In changes their name to Electro String Instrument Corporation in '34, and brand becomes Rickenbacher Electro, soon changed to Rickenbacker, with a "k." Beauchamp retires in '40. There was a production hiatus during World War II.

In '53, Electro was purchased by Francis Cary Hall (born 1908), owner of Radio and Television Equipment Company (Radio-Tel) in Santa Ana, California (founded in '20s as Hall's Radio Service, which began distributing Fender instruments in '46). The factory was relocated to Santa Ana in '62 and the sales/distribution company's name is changed from Radio-Tel to Rickenbacker Inc. in '65.

1950s serial numbers have from 4 to 7 letters and numbers, with the number following the letter indicating the '50s year (e.g., NNL8NN would be from '58). From '61 to '86 serial numbers indicate month and year of production with initial letter A-Z for the year A=1961, Z=1986) followed by letter for the month A-M (A=January) plus numbers as before followed by a number 0-9 for the year (0=1987; 9=1996). To avoid confusion, we have listed all instruments by model number. For example, the Combo 400 is listed as Model 400/Combo 400. OS and NS stands for Old Style and New Style. On the 360, for example, Ric changed the design in 1964

Reverend Rick Vito Soulshaker
Rick Vito

Richie's Guitar Shop

GUITARS

1986 Rickenbacker 320
Jeff DiPaola

1990 Rickenbacker 325
Carter Vintage Guitars

to their New Style with more rounded body horns and rounded top edges and other changes. But they still offered the Old Style with more pointed horns and top binding until the late 1960s. Ric still sometimes uses the two designations on some of their vintage reissues.

Electro ES-16
1964-1971. Double-cut, set neck, solidbody, 3/4 size, 1 pickup. The Electro line was manufactured by Rickenbacker and distributed by Radio-Tel. The Electro logo appears on the headstock.

MODEL YEAR	FEATURES	LOW	HIGH
1964-1971		$1,000	$1,300

Electro ES-17
1964-1975. Cutaway, set neck, solidbody, 1 pickup.

MODEL YEAR	FEATURES	LOW	HIGH
1964-1975		$1,100	$1,400

Electro Spanish (Model B Spanish)
1935-1943. Small guitar with a lap steel appearance played Spanish-style, hollow black bakelite body augmented with 5 chrome plates (white enamel in '40), 1 octagon knob (2 round-ridged in '38), called the Model B ca. '40.

MODEL YEAR	FEATURES	LOW	HIGH
1935-1937	Chrome, 1 knob	$3,400	$4,400
1935-1937	Tenor 4-string, 1 knob	$3,400	$4,400
1938-1939	Chrome, 2 knobs	$3,400	$4,400
1940-1943	White, 2 knobs	$2,900	$3,800

Electro-Spanish Ken Roberts
1935-1939. Mahogany body, f-holes in lower bout, horseshoe pickup, Kauffman vibrato.

MODEL YEAR	FEATURES	LOW	HIGH
1935-1939		$4,200	$5,400

Model 220 Hamburg
1992-1997. Solidbody.

MODEL YEAR	FEATURES	LOW	HIGH
1992-1997		$1,000	$1,300

Model 230 GF Glenn Frey
1992-1997. Glenn Frey Limited Edition, solidbody, 2 high output humbuckers, black hardware, chrome 'guard.

MODEL YEAR	FEATURES	LOW	HIGH
1992-1997		$1,900	$2,500

Model 230 Hamburg
1983-1991. Solidbody, offset double-cut, 2 pickups, dot inlay, rosewood 'board, chrome-plated hardware.

MODEL YEAR	FEATURES	LOW	HIGH
1983-1991		$1,150	$1,500

Model 250 El Dorado
1983-1991. Deluxe version of Hamburg, gold hardware, white binding.

MODEL YEAR	FEATURES	LOW	HIGH
1983-1991		$1,050	$1,375

Model 260 El Dorado
1992-1997. Replaces 250.

MODEL YEAR	FEATURES	LOW	HIGH
1992-1997		$1,050	$1,375

Model 310
1958-1970, 1981-1985. Two-pickup version of Model 320.

MODEL YEAR	FEATURES	LOW	HIGH
1958-1960	Capri, thick body	$10,000	$13,000
1961-1969	Thinner body	$6,100	$8,000
1981-1985	Reintroduced	$1,850	$2,400

Model 315
1958-1974. Two-pickup version of Model 325.

MODEL YEAR	FEATURES	LOW	HIGH
1958-1960	Capri, thick body	$10,000	$13,000
1960-1969	Thinner body	$6,100	$8,000
1970-1973		$3,700	$4,800
1974		$3,200	$4,200

Model 320
1958-1992. Short-scale hollowbody, 3 pickups, f-holes optional in '61 and standard in '64 and optional again in '79.

MODEL YEAR	FEATURES	LOW	HIGH
1958-1960	Capri, thick body	$13,800	$17,900
1960-1969		$9,000	$11,700
1970-1973		$3,700	$4,800
1974-1979		$2,900	$3,800
1980-1992		$2,300	$3,000

Model 320/12V63
1986. Short run for Japanese market.

MODEL YEAR	FEATURES	LOW	HIGH
1986		$3,300	$4,300

Model 325
1958-1975, 1985-1992. This was a low production model, with some years having no production. In the mid-'60s, the 325 was unofficially known as the John Lennon Model due to his guitar's high exposure on the Ed Sullivan Show and in the Saturday Evening Post.

MODEL YEAR	FEATURES	LOW	HIGH
1958	John Lennon specs, 8 made	$44,900	$58,300
1959-1960		$20,200	$26,200
1961-1963		$16,500	$21,500
1964-1966	Fireglo or black	$7,800	$10,150
1966	Mapleglo	$7,800	$10,150
1967-1969		$7,800	$10,150
1970-1975		$4,000	$5,200

Model 325/12
1985-1986, 1999. Based on John Lennon's one-of-a-kind '64 325/12.

MODEL YEAR	FEATURES	LOW	HIGH
1985-1986		$2,650	$3,450
1999		$2,650	$3,450

Model 325B
1983-1984. Reissue of early '60s model.

MODEL YEAR	FEATURES	LOW	HIGH
1983-1984		$2,250	$2,950

Model 325C58
2002-2014. Copy of the '58 model that John Lennon saw in Germany.

MODEL YEAR	FEATURES	LOW	HIGH
2002-2014		$2,250	$2,950

Model 325C64
2002-present. Copy of the famous '64 model.

MODEL YEAR	FEATURES	LOW	HIGH
2002-2019		$2,250	$2,950

Model 325JL (John Lennon)
1989-1993. John Lennon Limited Edition, 3 vintage Ric pickups, vintage vibrato, maple body; 3/4-size rosewood neck, a 12-string and a full-scale version are also available.

MODEL YEAR	FEATURES	LOW	HIGH
1989-1993		$2,700	$3,600

Model 325S
1964-1967. F-holes.

MODEL YEAR	FEATURES	LOW	HIGH
1964-1967		$10,000	$13,000

Model 325V59
1984-2001. Reissue of John Lennon's modified '59 325, 3 pickups, short-scale.

MODEL YEAR	FEATURES	LOW	HIGH
1984-2001		$2,800	$3,700

Model 325V63
1984-2001. Reissue of John Lennon's '63 325.

MODEL YEAR	FEATURES	LOW	HIGH
1984-2001		$2,800	$3,700

Model 330
1958-present. Thinline hollowbody, 2 pickups, slash soundhole, natural or sunburst.

MODEL YEAR	FEATURES	LOW	HIGH
1958-1960	Capri, thick body	$9,000	$12,000

MODEL YEAR	FEATURES	EXC. COND. LOW	HIGH
1961-1969	Thinner body	$4,800	$6,200
1970-1979		$3,400	$4,400
1980-2021		$1,700	$2,200

Model 330/12

1965-present. Thinline, 2 pickups, 12-string version of Model 300.

1964	Only 1 made	$5,500	$7,300
1965-1969	330-style body	$5,500	$7,300
1970-1979		$3,400	$4,400
1980-1989		$2,000	$2,600
1990-1999		$1,800	$2,400
2000-2021		$1,700	$2,250

Model 330F

1958-1969. F-style.

1958-1960	Thick version	$9,000	$12,000
1961-1969	Thin version	$4,400	$5,800

Model 330S/12

1964 (1 made)-1965 (2 made).

1964-1965		$6,700	$8,800

Model 331 Light Show

1970-1975. Model 330 with translucent top with lights in body that lit up when played, needed external transformer. The first offering's design, noted as Type 1, had heat problems and a fully original one is difficult to find. The 2nd offering's design, noted as Type 2, was a more stable design and is more highly valued in the market.

1970-1971	Type 1 1st edition	$12,200	$15,900
1971-1975	Type 2 2nd edition	$14,500	$19,000

Model 335

1958-1977. Thinline, 330-style body, 2 pickups, vibrato, Fireglo. Called the 330VB from '85-'97.

1958-1960	Capri, thick body	$8,800	$11,500
1961-1969	Thinner body	$3,800	$4,900
1970-1973		$3,500	$4,550
1974-1977		$3,300	$4,300

Model 335F

1958-1969. F-style.

1958-1961	Thick version	$8,800	$11,500
1961-1969	Thin version	$4,400	$5,800

Model 336/12

1966-1974. Like 300-12, but with 6-12 converter comb, 330-style body.

1966-1969		$3,500	$4,650
1970-1974		$3,500	$4,650

Model 340

1958-2014. Thin semi-hollowbody, thru-body maple neck, 2 single-coil pickups, sharp point horns, very limited production '58-'65, with first notable volume of 45 units starting in '66.

1958-1960	Capri, thick body	$9,000	$12,000
1961-1969	Thinner body	$3,700	$4,800
1970-1973		$3,500	$4,500
1974-1979		$3,300	$4,300
1980-2014		$2,125	$2,750

Model 340/12

1980-2014. 12-string version, 330-style body.

1980-2014		$2,050	$2,650

Model 340F

1958-1969. F-style.

1958-1960	Thick version	$9,000	$12,000
1961-1969	Thin version	$4,400	$5,800

Model 345

1961-1974. Thinline 330-345 series, version with 3 pickups and vibrato tailpiece.

1958-1960	Capri, thick body	$9,000	$12,000
1961-1969	Thinner body	$4,200	$5,400
1970-1973		$3,500	$4,500
1974		$3,300	$4,300

Model 345 Reissue

2002. Low production, 3 pickups.

2002		$2,600	$3,400

Model 345F

1958-1969. F-style.

1958-1960	Thick version	$9,000	$12,000
1961-1969	Thin version	$4,400	$5,800

Model 350 Liverpool

1983-1997. Thinline, 3 pickups, vibrato, no soundhole.

1983-1997		$2,300	$3,000

Model 350/12V63 Liverpool

1994-2014. Vintage Series, 12-string 350V63.

1994-2014		$2,600	$3,400

Model 350SH (Susanna Hoffs)

1988-1990. Susanna Hoffs Limited Edition.

1988-1990		$4,000	$5,200

Model 350V59

1988. Very low production.

1988		$2,300	$3,000

Model 350V63 Liverpool

1994-present. Vintage Series, like 355 JL, but without signature.

1994-2021		$2,300	$3,000

Model 355/12JL (John Lennon)

1989-1993. 12-string 355 JL, limited production.

1989-1993		$3,400	$4,400

Model 355JL (John Lennon)

1989-1993. John Lennon model, signature and drawing on 'guard.

1989-1993		$3,400	$4,400

Model 360 Tuxedo

1987 only. Tuxedo option included white body, white painted fretboard, and black hardware.

1987		$2,200	$2,850

Model 360/12

1964-present. Deluxe double-cut thinline, 2 pickups, triangle inlays. The 360/12 was offered in both the Old Style (OS) body with double-bound body and pointed horns, and the New Style (NS) body with rounded top edges and rounder horns. George Harrison's original 360/12 had the OS body in a Fireglo finish. Production of the OS and NS bodies overlapped.

1964	OS, Fireglo, pointed horns, Harrison	$37,000	$49,000
1964-1969	NS, Fireglo, rounded horns	$4,900	$6,400
1964-1969	NS, Mapleglo, rounded horns	$5,000	$6,650
1964-1969	OS, Mapleglo, pointed horns	$20,500	$27,000
1965-1969	OS, Fireglo, pointed horns	$24,200	$31,700

1958 Rickenbacker Model 335 Capri

Imaged by Heritage Auctions, HA.com

1960 Rickenbacker 360F

1979 Rickenbacker 360/12WB
Ted Wulfers

2020 Rickenbacker 360
Charlie Brown

MODEL YEAR	FEATURES	EXC. COND. LOW	EXC. COND. HIGH
1970-1973		$4,700	$6,200
1974-1979		$3,100	$4,100
1980-2009		$2,400	$3,150
2010-2021		$2,250	$2,950

Model 360/12 RCA

1992. Limited edition made for RCA Nashville as gifts for their artists, has RCA dog-and-gramophone logo on pickguard.

1992		$3,300	$4,300

Model 360/12 Tuxedo

1987 only. 12-string version of 360 Tuxedo.

1987		$3,300	$4,300

Model 360/12C63

2004-present. More exact replica of the Harrison model.

2004-2021		$3,300	$4,300

Model 360/12CW (Carl Wilson)

2000. Carl Wilson, 12-string version of 360 CW.

2000		$4,200	$5,500

Model 360/12V64

1985-2003. Deluxe thinline with '64 features, 2 pickups, 12 strings, slanted plate tailpiece.

1985-2003		$3,300	$4,300

Model 360/12VP

2004. VP is vintage pickup.

2004		$3,300	$4,300

Model 360/12WB

1984-1998. 12-string version of 360WB.

1984-1998		$3,300	$4,300

Model 360/360VB

1958-1991, 2000-present. Deluxe thinline, 2 pickups, slash soundhole, bound body until '64.

1958-1960	Capri, thick body	$9,000	$12,000
1961-1967		$4,700	$6,100
1968-1969		$4,400	$5,700
1970-1973	360, no vibrato	$3,550	$4,650
1974-1989	360VB, vibrato	$2,100	$2,750
1990-2021		$1,850	$2,400

Model 360CW (Carl Wilson)

2000. Carl Wilson Limited Edition, 6-string, includes certificate, 500 made.

2000		$3,000	$3,950

Model 360DCM 75th Anniversary

2006. 360 with 75th Anniversary dark cherry metallic finish, 75 made.

2006		$3,300	$4,300

Model 360F

1959-1972. F-style.

1959-1960	Thick version	$9,000	$12,000
1961-1969	Thin version	$4,200	$5,500
1970-1972	Thin version	$3,550	$4,650

Model 360SF

1968-ca. 1972. Slanted frets (SF), standard on some models, an option on others.

1968-1972		$5,500	$7,200

Model 360V64

1991-2003. Reissue of '64 Model 360 old style body without vibrola, has binding with full length inlays.

1991-2003		$2,900	$3,750

MODEL YEAR	FEATURES	EXC. COND. LOW	EXC. COND. HIGH

Model 360WB

1984-1998. Double bound body, 2 pickups, vibrato optional (VB).

1984-1990		$2,425	$3,150
1991-1998	WB no vibrato	$2,200	$2,850
1991-1998	WBVB, vibrato	$2,425	$3,150

Model 362/12

1975-1992. Doubleneck 6 & 12, 360 features.

1975-1992		$3,150	$4,100

Model 365

1958-1974. Deluxe thinline, 2 pickups, vibrato, called Model 360 WBVB from '84-'98.

1958-1960	Capri, thick body	$9,000	$12,000
1961-1969		$4,200	$5,500
1970-1973		$4,000	$5,200
1974		$3,900	$5,000

Model 365F

1959-1972. Thin full-body (F designation), 2 pickups, Deluxe features.

1959-1960	Capri, thick body	$9,000	$12,000
1961-1969	Thin version	$4,200	$5,500
1970-1972		$4,000	$5,200

Model 366/12 Convertible

1966-1974. Two pickups, 12 strings, comb-like device that converts it to a 6-string, production only noted in '68, perhaps available on custom order basis.

1966-1968	OS	$6,000	$7,900

Model 370

1958-1990, 1994-2007. Deluxe thinline, 3 pickups. Could be considered to be a dealer special order item from '58-'67 with limited production.

1958-1960	Capri, thick body	$9,000	$12,000
1961-1969	Thin version	$4,200	$5,500
1970-1973		$4,000	$5,200
1974-1979		$3,800	$4,900
1980-1999		$2,200	$2,900
2000-2007		$2,200	$2,900

Model 370/12

1966-1990, 1994-present. Not regular production until '80, deluxe thinline, 3 pickups, 12 strings. Could be considered to be a dealer special order item in the '60s and '70s with limited production.

1966		$11,000	$14,500
1967-2021		$2,475	$3,225

Model 370/12RM (Roger McGuinn)

1988-1990. Limited Edition Roger McGuinn, 1000 made, higher-quality appointments.

1988-1990		$4,700	$6,100

Model 370F

1959-1972. F-style, 3 pickups, Deluxe features.

1959-1961	Thick version	$9,000	$12,000
1961-1969	Thin version	$4,200	$5,500
1970-1972		$4,000	$5,250

Model 370VP

2006-2007. Limited run with special specs including vintage toaster pickups (VP).

2006-2007		$3,475	$4,525

Model 370WB

1984-1998. Double bound body, 3 pickups, vibrato optional (VB).

1984-1998		$2,100	$2,700

MODEL YEAR	FEATURES	EXC. COND. LOW	HIGH

Model 375
1958-1974. Deluxe thinline, 3 pickups, vibrato, called Model 370 WBVB from '84-'98.

1958-1960	Capri, thick body	$9,000	$12,000
1961-1969	Thin version	$4,500	$5,900
1970-1974		$4,000	$5,200

Model 375F
1959-1972. F-style, 2 pickups.

1959-1960	Thick version	$9,000	$12,000
1961-1969	Thin version	$4,500	$5,900
1970-1972		$4,000	$5,200

Model 380L Laguna
1996-2005. Semi-hollow, oil-finished walnut body, Maple neck and 'board, 2 humbuckers, PZ saddle pickups optional.

1996-2005		$2,200	$2,900
1996-2005	PZ option	$2,200	$2,900

Model 381
1958-1963, 1969-1974. Double-cut archtop, 2 pickups, slash soundhole, solid 'guard, reintroduced in '69 with double split-level 'guard.

1958-1963	Low production	$9,000	$12,000
1969	Various colors, some rare	$4,500	$5,900
1970-1975		$4,000	$5,200

Model 381/12V69
1987-present. Reissue of 381/12, deep double-cut body, sound body cavity, catseye soundhole, triangle inlays, bridge with 12 individual saddles. Finishes include Fireglo, Mapleglo and Jetglo.

1987-2021	Figured top	$2,850	$3,750

Model 381JK (John Kay)
1988-1997. Limited Edition, 250 made, 2 humbucking pickups, active electronics, stereo and mono outputs, Jetglo black.

1988-1997		$2,900	$3,800

Model 381V69
1991-present. Reissue of vintage 381.

1987-2021		$2,850	$3,750

Model 382
1958-1963, 1969-1974. 381 with vibrato unit. Very light production.

1958-1963	Low production	$9,000	$12,000
1969-1974	Various colors, some rare	$4,500	$5,900

Model 383
1958-1963, 1969-1974. 381 with 3 pickups. Very light production.

1958-1963	Low production	$9,000	$12,000
1969-1974	Various colors, some rare	$4,500	$5,900

Model 384
1958-1963, 1969-1974. 381 with 3 pickups and vibrato unit. Very light production.

1958-1963	Low production	$9,000	$12,000
1969-1974	Various colors, some rare	$4,500	$5,900

Model 400/Combo 400
1956-1958. Double-cut tulip body, neck-thru, 1 pickup, gold anodized 'guard, 21 frets, replaced by Model 425 in '58. Available in black (216 made), blue turquoise (53), Cloverfield Green (53), Montezuma Brown (41), and 4 in other custom colors.

1956-1958		$4,500	$5,900

Model 420
1965-1983. Non-vibrato version of Model 425, single pickup.

1965-1968		$1,750	$2,275
1969-1983		$1,525	$1,975

Model 425/Combo 425
1958-1973. Double-cut solidbody, 1 pickup, sunburst.

1958-1959	425 Cresting Wave	$3,400	$4,400
1960		$2,500	$3,200
1961-1964		$2,000	$2,600
1965-1968		$1,750	$2,275
1969-1973		$1,450	$1,875

Model 425/12V63
1999-2000. 136 made.

1999-2000		$1,875	$2,450

Model 425V63
1999-2000. Beatles associated model, 145 JG black made, 116 BG burgundy transparent made, originally custom ordered by Rickenbacker collectors and they were not part of Rickenbacker's sales literature in the late '90s.

1999-2000		$1,725	$2,250

Model 430
1971-1982. Style 200 body, natural.

1971-1982		$950	$1,225

Model 450/Combo 450
1957-1984. Replaces Combo 450, 2 pickups (3 optional '62-'77), tulip body shape '57-'59, cresting wave body shape after.

1957-1958	450 Tulip body (Combo)	$4,500	$5,900
1958-1959	450 Cresting Wave	$3,400	$4,400
1960	Cresting Wave, flat body	$2,500	$3,300
1961-1966	Cresting Wave, super slim	$2,200	$2,900
1970-1979	Includes rare color	$1,800	$2,325
1980-1984		$1,275	$1,675

Model 450/12
1964-1985. Double-cut solidbody, 12-string version of Model 450, 2 pickups.

1964-1966		$2,400	$3,200
1967-1969		$2,300	$3,000
1970-1979	Includes rare color	$2,050	$2,700
1980-1985		$1,525	$2,000

Model 450V63
1999-2001. Reissue of '63 450.

1999-2001		$1,425	$1,850

Model 456/12 Convertible
1968-1978. Double-cut solidbody, 2 pickups, comb-like device to convert it to 6-string.

1968-1969		$3,000	$3,950
1970-1978		$2,500	$3,300

Model 460
1961-1985. Double-cut solidbody, 2 pickups, neck-thru-body, deluxe trim.

1961-1965		$3,000	$3,900
1966-1969		$2,600	$3,400
1970-1979	Includes rare color	$2,200	$2,900
1980-1985		$1,550	$2,025

1992 Rickenbacker 370
Carter Vintage Guitars

Rickenbacker 450V63
Ron O'Keefe

GUITARS

*1954 Rickenbacker Model
600/Combo 600*

Imaged by Heritage Auctions, HA.com

1983 Rickenbacker 620

Jeff DiPaola

MODEL YEAR	FEATURES	EXC. COND. LOW	HIGH

Model 480
1973-1984. Double-cut solidbody with long thin bass horn in 4001 bass series style, 2 pickups, cresting wave body and headstock, bolt-on neck.

1973-1979		$2,600	$3,400
1980-1984		$2,450	$3,200

Model 481
1973-1983. Cresting wave body with longer bass horn, 2 humbuckers (3 optional), angled frets.

1973-1979		$2,600	$3,400
1980-1983		$2,400	$3,100

Model 483
1973-1983. Cresting wave body with longer bass horn, 3 humbuckers.

1973-1979		$2,850	$3,700
1980-1983		$2,500	$3,200

Model 600/Combo 600
1954-1958. Modified double-cut, horseshoe pickup.

1954-1957	Blond/white	$4,500	$5,900
1956-1958	OT/Blue Turquoise	$4,500	$5,900

Model 610
1985-1991. Cresting-wave cutaway solidbody, 2 pickups, trapeze R-tailpiece, Jetglo.

1985-1991		$950	$1,225

Model 610/12
1988-1997. 12-string version of Model 610.

1988-1997		$1,150	$1,500

Model 615
1962-1966, 1969-1977. Double-cut solidbody, 2 pickups, vibrato.

1962-1965		$2,150	$2,775
1966-1977		$1,875	$2,450

Model 620
1974-present. Double-cut solidbody, deluxe binding, 2 pickups, neck-thru-body.

1974-1979		$1,875	$2,450
1980-2021		$1,700	$2,100

Model 620/12
1981-present. Double-cut solidbody, 2 pickups, 12 strings, standard trim.

1981-2021		$1,800	$2,200

Model 625
1962-1977. Double-cut solidbody, deluxe trim, 2 pickups, vibrato.

1962-1965		$6,500	$8,400
1966-1969		$4,000	$5,200
1970-1977		$3,100	$4,100

Model 650/Combo 650
1957-1959. Standard color, 1 pickup.

1957-1959		$4,500	$5,900

Model 650A Atlantis
1992-2003. Double cut cresting wave solidbody, maple body wings, neck-thru, 2 pickups, chrome hardware, turquoise.

1992-2003		$1,400	$1,850

Model 650C Colorado
1993-2017. Like Atlantis but with balck finish.

1993-2017		$1,400	$1,850

Model 650D Dakota
1993-2017. Like Atlantis but with walnut body wings and oil-satin finish.

1993-2017		$1,400	$1,850

Model 650E Excalibur/F Frisco
1991-2003. Like Atlantis but with brown vermilion body wings and gold hardware. Name changed to Frisco in '95.

1991-2003		$1,400	$1,850

Model 650S Sierra
1993-2017. Like Dakota but with gold hardware.

1993-2017		$1,400	$1,850

Model 660
1998-present. Cresting wave maple body, triangle inlays, 2 pickups.

1998-2021		$2,300	$3,000

Model 660/12
1998-present. 12-string 660.

1998-2021		$2,850	$3,750

Model 660/12TP (Tom Petty)
1991-1998. Tom Petty model, 12 strings, cresting wave body, 2 pickups, deluxe trim, limited run of 1000, certificate of authenticity.

1991-1998	With certificate	$5,300	$6,900

Model 660DCM 75th Anniversary
2006-2007. 75th 1931-2006 Anniversary pickguard logo.

2006-2007		$2,450	$3,200

Model 800/Combo 800
1954-1959. Offset double-cut, 1 horseshoe pickup until late-'57, second bar type after.

1954-1957	Blond/white, 1 pickup	$6,125	$8,000
1954-1957	Blue or green, 1 pickup	$6,125	$8,000
1957-1959	Blond/white, 2 pickups	$6,125	$8,000
1957-1959	Blue or green, 2 pickups	$6,125	$8,000

Model 850/Combo 850
1957-1959. Extreme double-cut, 1 pickup until '58, 2 after, various colors, called Model 850 in the '60s.

1957-1959	Various colors	$6,100	$8,000

Model 900/Combo 900
1957-1980. Double-cut tulip body shape, 3/4 size, 1 pickup. Body changes to cresting wave shape in '69.

1957-1966		$1,900	$2,500

Model 950/Combo 950
1957-1980. Like Model 900, but with 2 pickups, 21 frets. Body changes to cresting wave shape in '69.

1957-1964		$2,100	$2,800
1965-1980		$1,850	$2,425

Model 1000
1957-1970. Like Model 900, but with 18 frets. Body does not change to cresting wave shape.

1956-1966		$1,650	$2,150
1967-1970		$1,550	$2,050

Model 1993/12RM (Rose-Morris)
1964-1967. Export 'slim-line' 12-string model made for English distributor Rose-Morris of London, built along the lines of the U.S. Model 360/12 but with

MODEL YEAR	FEATURES	EXC. COND. LOW	HIGH

small differences that are considered important in the vintage guitar market.

| 1964 | Flat tailpiece | $5,800 | $7,600 |
| 1965-1967 | R tailpiece | $5,800 | $7,600 |

Model 1996RM (Rose-Morris)

1964-1967. Rose-Morris import, 3/4 size built similarly to the U.S. Model 325.

| 1964-1967 | | $9,500 | $12,300 |

Model 1996RM Reissue

2006. Reissue of the Rose-Morris version of Model 325, this reissue available on special order in 2006.

| 2006 | | $3,550 | $4,650 |

Model 1997PT (Pete Townshend)

1987-1988. Pete Townshend Signature Model, semi-hollowbody, single f-hole, maple neck, 21-fret rosewood 'board, 3 pickups, Firemist finish, limited to 250 total production.

| 1987-1988 | | $3,550 | $4,650 |

Model 1997RM (Rose-Morris)

1964-1967. Export 'slim-line' model made for English distributor Rose-Morris of London, built along the lines of the U.S. Model 335, but with small differences that are considered important in the vintage guitar market, 2 pickups, vibrola tailpiece. Rose-Morris export models sent to the USA generally had a red-lined guitar case vs. the USA domestic blue-lined guitar case.

| 1964-1967 | | $4,200 | $5,400 |

Model 1997RM Reissue

1987-1995. Reissue of '60s Rose-Morris model, but with vibrola (VB) or without.

| 1987-1995 | | $2,450 | $3,200 |

Model 1997SPC

1993-2002. 3 pickup version of reissue.

| 1993-2002 | | $1,875 | $2,450 |

Model 1998RM (Rose-Morris)

1964-1967. Export 'slim-line' model made for English distributor Rose-Morris of London, built along the lines of a U.S. Model 345 but with small differences that are considered important in the vintage guitar market, 3 pickups, vibrola tailpiece.

| 1964-1967 | | $4,100 | $5,400 |

Rickenbacker Spanish/Spanish/SP

1946-1949. Block markers.

| 1946-1949 | | $1,975 | $2,575 |

S-59

1940-1942. Arch top body built by Kay, horseshoe magnet pickup.

| 1940-1942 | | $1,825 | $2,400 |

Rigaud Guitars

1978-present. Luthier Robert Rigaud builds his premium grade, custom, parlor to jumbo acoustic guitars in Greensboro, North Carolina. He also builds ukuleles under the New Moon brand.

Ritz

1989. Solidbody electric guitars and basses produced in Calimesa, California, by Wayne Charvel, Eric Galletta and Brad Becnel, many of which featured cracked shell mosiac finishes.

MODEL YEAR	FEATURES	EXC. COND. LOW	HIGH

RKS

Professional and premium grade, production/custom, electric hollowbody and solidbody guitars and basses designed by Ravi Sawhney and guitarist Dave Mason and built in Thousand Oaks, California. They began in 2003.

Robert Cefalu

Luthier Robert Cefalu built his professional grade, production/custom, acoustic guitars in Buffalo, New York. The guitars have an RC on the headstock.

Robert Guitars

1981-present. Luthier Mikhail Robert builds his premium grade, production/custom, classical guitars in Summerland, British Columbia.

Robertson Guitars

1995-present. Luthier Jeff Robertson builds his premium grade, production/custom flat-top guitars in South New Berlin, New York.

Robin

1982-2010. Professional and premium grade, production/custom, guitars from luthier David Wintz and built in Houston, Texas. Most guitars were Japanese-made until '87; American production began in '88. Most Japanese Robins were pretty consistent in features, but the American ones were often custom-made, so many variations in models exist. They also made Metropolitan ('96-'08) and Alamo ('00-'08) brand guitars.

Avalon Classic

1994-2010. Single-cut, figured maple top, 2 humbuckers.

| 1994-2010 | Various options | $1,500 | $2,000 |

Medley Pro

1990s. Solidbody with 2 extreme cutaway horns, hum-single-single.

| 1990s | US-made | $925 | $1,200 |

Medley Special

1992-1995. Ash body, maple neck, rosewood 'board, 24 frets, various pickup options.

| 1992-1995 | | $575 | $750 |

Medley Standard

1985-2010. Offset double-cut swamp ash solidbody, bolt neck, originally with hum-single-single pickups, but now also available with 2 humbuckers.

| 1985-1987 | Japan-made | $500 | $650 |
| 1988-2010 | US-made | $1,000 | $1,300 |

Octave

1982-1990s. Tuned an octave above standard tuning, full body size with 15 1/2" short-scale bolt maple neck. Japanese-made production model until '87, U.S.-made custom shop after.

| 1990s | With original case | $725 | $950 |

Raider I/Raider II/Raider III

1985-1991. Double-cut solidbody, 1 humbucker pickup (Raider I), 2 humbuckers (Raider II), or 3 single-coils (Raider III), maple neck, either maple or rosewood 'board, sunburst.

| 1985-1991 | 1 pickup | $425 | $550 |

Rickenbacker 660
Ron O'Keefe

Rickenbacker 660/12
Ron O'Keefe

Robin Octave
Allen Eagles

Robinson Small Jumbo

MODEL YEAR	FEATURES	EXC. COND. LOW	HIGH
1985-1991	2 pickups	$450	$600
1985-1991	3 pickups	$500	$650

Ranger
1982. First production model with 2 single-coil pickups in middle and neck position, reverse headstock, dot markers.

1982		$950	$1,250

Ranger Custom
1982-1986, 1988-2010. Swamp ash bound body, bolton maple neck, rosewood or maple 'board, 2 single coils and 1 humbucker, orange, made in Japan until '86, U.S.-made after.

1982-1986	Japan-made	$500	$650
1988-2010	US-made	$950	$1,250

RDN-Doubleneck Octave/Six
1982-1985. Six-string standard neck with 3 pickups, 6-string octave neck with 1 pickup, double-cut solidbody.

1982-1985	With original case	$1,125	$1,475

Savoy Deluxe/Standard
1995-2010. Semi-hollow thinline single cut archtop, 2 pickups, set neck.

1996-2010		$1,500	$1,950

Soloist/Artisan
1982-1986. Mahogany double-cut solidbody, carved bound maple top, set neck, 2 humbuckers. Renamed Artisan in '85. Only about 125 made in Japan.

1982-1986		$725	$950

Wedge
1985-ca. 1988. Triangle-shaped body, 2 humbuckers, Custom with set neck and triangle inlays, Standard with bolt neck and dots, about 200 made.

1980s		$950	$1,225

Wrangler
1995-2002. Classic '50s single-cut slab body, 3 Rio Grande pickups, opaque finish.

1995-2002		$725	$950

Robinson Guitars
2002-present. Premium and presentation grade, custom/production, steel string guitars built by luthier Jake Robinson first in Kalamazoo, and since '08 in Hoxeyville, Michigan.

RockBeach Guitars
2005-present. Luthier Greg Bogoshian builds his custom, professional grade, chambered electric guitars and basses in Rochester, New York.

Rockinbetter
2011-2014. Intermediate grade, production electric guitars and basses, copies of Rickenbacker models, made in China.

Rocking F
See listing under Fox.

Rockit Guitar
Luthier Rod MacKenzie builds his premium grade, custom, electric guitars and basses in Everett, Washington, starting in 2006.

Rogands
Late 1960s. Produced by France's Jacobacci company and named after brothers Roger and Andre. Short-lived brand; the brothers made instruments under several other brands as well.

Roger
Guitars built in Germany by luthier Wenzel Rossmeisl and named for his son Roger. Roger Rossmeisl would go on to work at Rickenbacker and Fender.

Rogue
2001-present. Budget and intermediate grade, production, acoustic, resonator, electric and sitar guitars and basses. They also offer mandolins, banjos, ukuleles, and lap steels. They previously offered effects and amps. Fender offered instruments branded Rogue by Squire for a short period starting in '99.

Roland
Best known for keyboards, effects, and amps, Roland offered synthesizer-based guitars and basses from 1977 to '97.

Rolando
1916-ca. 1919. Private branded instruments made for the Southern California Music Company of Los Angeles, by Martin. There were three models.

00-28K/1500

1916-1919		$9,500	$12,300

Rolf Spuler
1981-2014. Presentation grade, custom, hybrid electric-acoustic guitars, built by luthier Rolf Spuler in Gebenstorf, Switzerland. He also built basses. He passed away in '14.

Roman & Lipman Guitars
1989-2000. Production/custom, solidbody guitars and basses made in Danbury, Connecticut by Ed Roman Guitars.

Roman Abstract Guitars
1989-present. Professional and premium grade, production/custom, solidbody guitars made by Ed Roman Guitars.

Roman Centurion Guitars
2001-present. Premium and presentation grade, custom guitars made by Ed Roman Guitars.

Roman Pearlcaster Guitars
1999-present. Professional and premium grade, production/custom, solidbody guitars made Ed Roman Guitars.

Roman Quicksilver Guitars
1997-present. Professional and premium grade, production/custom, solid and hollow-body guitars made by Ed Roman Guitars.

MODEL		EXC. COND.	
YEAR	FEATURES	LOW	HIGH

Roman RVC Guitars

1999-present. Professional and premium grade, production/custom, solidbody guitars made by Ed Roman Guitars.

Roman Vampire Guitars

2004-2020. Professional and premium grade, production/custom, solidbody guitars made by Ed Roman Guitars. Special orders only about '13-'20.

Rono

In 1967 luthier Ron Oates began building professional and premium grade, production/custom, flat-top, jazz, Wiesenborn-style, and resonator guitars and basses in Boulder, Colorado. He also built mandolins.

Ro-Pat-In

See Rickenbacker.

Rosetti

1950s-1960s. Guitars imported into England by distributor Rosetti, made by Holland's Egmond, maybe others.

Solid 7

1960s. Symmetrical cutaway electric semi-hollow, large 'guard with top-mounted dual pickups, 4 control knobs, value is associated with Paul McCartney's use in '60, value dependent on completely original McCartney specs.

1960s	McCartney model	$2,100	$2,800
1960s	Various other	$600	$800

Roudhloff

1810s-1840s. Luthier Francois Roudhloff built his instruments in France. Labels could state F. Roudhloff-Mauchand or Roudhloff Brothers. Valuation depends strongly on condition and repair. His sons built guitars under the D & A Roudhloff label.

Rowan

Professional and premium grade, production/custom, solidbody and acoustic/electric guitars built by luthier Michael Rowan in Garland, Texas.

Royal

Ca. 1954-ca. 1965. Line of jazz style guitars made by France's Jacobacci company, which also built under its own brand.

Royal (Japan)

1957-1960s. Early budget level instruments made by Tokyo Sound Company and Gakki and exported by Japan's Hoshino (Ibanez).

Royden Guitars

Professional grade, production/custom, flat-tops and solidbody electrics built by luthier Royden Moran in Peterborough, Ontario, starting in 1996.

RS Guitarworks

1994-present. Professional grade, production/custom, solid and hollowbody guitars built by luthier Roy Bowen in Winchester, Kentucky.

Rubio, German Vasquez

1993-present. Luthier German Vasquez Rubio builds his professional and premium grade, production/custom classical and flamenco guitars in Los Angeles, California.

Ruck, Robert

1966-2018. Premium grade, custom classical and flamenco guitars built by luthier Robert Ruck originally in Kalaheo, Hawaii, then in Eugene, Oregon. Ruck died in '18.

Running Dog Guitars

1994-present. Luthier Rick Davis builds his professional and premium grade, custom flat-tops in Seattle, Washington. He was originally located in Richmond, Vermont.

Ruokangas

1995-present. Luthier Juha Ruokangas builds his premium and presentation grade, production/custom, solidbody and semi-acoustic electric guitars in Hyvinkaa, Finland.

Rustler

1993-ca. 1998. Solidbody electrics with hand-tooled leather bound and studded sides and R branded into the top, built by luthier Charles Caponi in Mason City, Iowa.

RWK

1991-present. Luthier Bob Karger builds his intermediate grade, production/custom, solidbody electrics and travel guitars in Highland Park, Illinois.

Ryder

1963. Made by Rickenbacker, the one model with this brand was the same as their solidbody Model 425.

S. Walker Custom Guitars

2002-present. Luthier Scott Walker builds his premium grade, production/custom, solid and semi hollow body electric guitars in Santa Cruz, California.

S. Yairi

Ca. 1960-1980s. Steel string folk guitars and classical nylon string guitars by master Japanese luthier Sadao Yairi, imported by Philadelphia Music Company of Limerick, Pennsylvania. Early sales literature called the brand Syairi. Most steel string models have dreadnought bodies and nylon-string classical guitars are mostly standard grand concert size. All models are handmade. Steel string Jumbos and dreadnoughts have Syairi logo on the headstock, nylon-classical models have no logo. The Model 900 has a solid wood body, others assumed to have laminate bodies.

1960s Roger Super Cutaway
Alf Tengs-Pedersen

S. Walker Custom The Revelator

S.D. Curlee Standard

Saga Blueridge

MODEL YEAR	FEATURES	EXC. COND. LOW	HIGH

S.B. Brown Guitars

Custom flat-tops made by luthier Steve Brown in Fullerton, California.

S.B. MacDonald Custom Instruments

1988-present. Professional and premium grade, custom/production, flat-top, resonator, and solidbody guitars built by luthier Scott B. MacDonald in Huntington, New York.

S.D. Curlee

1975-1982. Founded in Matteson, Illinois by music store owner Randy Curlee, after an unsuccessful attempt to recruit builder Dan Armstrong. S.D. Curlee guitars were made in Illinois, while S.D. Curlee International instruments were made by Matsumoku in Japan. The guitars featured mostly Watco oil finishes, often with exotic hardwoods, and unique neck-thru-bridge construction on American and Japanese instruments. These were the first production guitars to use a single-coil pickup at the bridge with a humbucker at the neck, and a square brass nut. DiMarzio pickups. Offered in a variety of shapes, later some copies. Approximately 12,000 American-made basses and 3,000 guitars were made, most of which were sold overseas. Two hundred were made in '75-'76; first production guitar numbered 518.

Electric Solidbody

1975-1982. Models include the '75-'81 Standard I, II and III, '76-'81 International C-10 and C-11, '80-'81 Yankee, Liberty, Butcher, Curbeck, Summit, Special, and the '81-'82 Destroyer, Flying V.

1975-1982		$425	$550

S.L. Smith Guitars

Professional grade, production/custom, acoustic guitars built by Steven Smith in Brant Lake, New York beginning in 2007.

S.S. Stewart

The original S.S. Stewart Company (1878-1904), of Philadelphia, Pennsylvania is considered to be one of the most important banjo manufacturers of the late 19th century. Samuel Swaim Stewart died in 1988 and his family was out of the company by the early 1900s, and the brand was soon acquired by Bugellsein & Jacobsen of New York. The brand name was used on guitars into the 1960s.

Flat-Top

1930s. Gibson L-2 style body.

1932		$9,100	$11,800

S101

Budget and intermediate grade, production, classical, acoustic, resonator, solid and semi-hollow body guitars and basses imported from China by America Sejung Corp. They also offer mandolins, and banjos.

Sadowsky

1980-present. Professional and premium grade, production/custom, solidbody, semi-hollowbody, archtop, and electric nylon-string guitars built by luthier Roger Sadowsky in Brooklyn, New York. He also builds basses and amps. In '96, luthier Yoshi Kikuchi started building Sadowsky Tokyo instruments in Japan.

Saga

Saga Musical Instruments, of San Francisco, California distributes a wide variety of instruments and brands, occasionally including their own line of solidbody guitars called the Saga Gladiator Series (1987-'88, '94-'95). In the 2000s, Saga also offered component kits ($90-$130) that allowed for complete assembly in white wood.

Sahlin Guitars

Luthier Eric Sahlin hs built his premium grade, custom, classical and flamenco guitars in Spokane, Washington since 1975.

Samick

1958-2001, 2002-present. Budget, intermediate and professional grade, production, imported acoustic and electric guitars and basses. They also offer mandolins, ukes and banjos and distribute Abilene and Silvertone brand instruments.

Samick started out producing pianos, adding guitars in '65 under other brands. In '88 Samick greatly increased their guitar production. The Samick line of 350 models was totally closed out in 2001. A totally new line of 250 models was introduced January 2002 at NAMM. All 2002 models have the new compact smaller headstock and highly styled S logo.

Sammo

1920s. Labels in these instruments state they were made by the Osborne Mfg. Co. with an address of Masonic Temple, Chicago, Illinois. High quality and often with a high degree of ornamentation. They also made ukes and mandolins.

Sand Guitars

Luthier Kirk Sand opened the Guitar Shoppe in Laguna Beach, California in 1972 with James Matthews. By '79, he started producing his own line of premium grade, production/custom-made flat-tops.

Sandoval Engineering

1979-present. Luthier Karl Sandoval builds his premium grade, custom, solidbody guitars in Santa Fe Springs, California.

Sano

1944-ca. 1970. Sano was a New Jersey-based accordion company that imported Italian-made solid and semi-hollow body guitars for a few years, starting in 1966; some, if not all, made by Zero Sette. They also built their own amps and reverb units.

MODEL YEAR	FEATURES	EXC. COND. LOW	HIGH

Santa Cruz

1976-present. Professional, premium and presentation-grade, production/custom, flat-top, 12-string, and archtop guitars from luthier Richard Hoover in Santa Cruz, California. They also build a mandocello and ukuleles. Founded by Hoover, Bruce Ross and William Davis. Hoover became sole owner in '89. Custom ordered instruments with special upgrades may have higher values than the ranges listed here. Other models offer "build-your-own" options on woods and features and this means larger value ranges on those instruments.

00 12-Fret
1997-present. Indian rosewood.

1997-2021		$3,000	$3,900

000 12-Fret
1994-present. 000 size, 12-fret body, Indian rosewood back and sides, ebony 'board, ivoroid binding.

1994-2021	Indian rosewood	$3,000	$3,900
2011	Brazilian rosewood	$6,000	$7,800

Archtop
Early 1980s-2010. Originally the FJZ, by mid-'90s, called the Archtop, offering 16", 17" and 18" cutaway acoustic/electric models, often special order. Curly maple body, ebony 'board, floating pickup, f-holes, sunburst or natural. Many custom options available.

1980s-90s		$3,725	$4,900

Bob Brozman Baritone
1998-2019. Flat-top acoustic, mahogany body, spruce top.

1998-2019		$3,650	$4,800

D 12-Fret
1994-present. 12-fret neck, slotted headstock, round shoulders, mahogany back and sides, notch diamond markers, herringbone trim. Special orders vary in value and could exceed the posted range.

1994-2021		$3,200	$4,200

D Koa
1980s-1990s. Style D with koa back and sides.

1980s-90s		$3,200	$4,200

D/HR
Style D with Indian rosewood back and sides, Brazilian rosewood headstock overlay.

2000		$3,200	$4,200

D/PW Pre-War
2001-present. Pre-war D-style. "Build-your-own" options cause a wide value range.

2001-2021	Various models	$3,000	$5,800

Eric Skye 00
Signature model, Cocobolo/Adirondack.

2020		$5,000	$6,500

F
1979-present. 15 7/8" scale with narrow waist, sitka spruce top, Indian rosewood back and sides, natural.

1979-2021		$3,500	$4,600

F46R
1980s. Brazilian rosewood, single-cut.

1980s		$4,000	$5,300

Firefly
2009-present. Premium quality travel/parlor guitar, cedar top, flamed maple sides and back.

2009-2021		$3,000	$4,000

FS (Finger Style)
1988-present. Single-cut, cedar top, Indian rosewood back and sides, mahogany neck, modified X-bracing.

1988-2021		$3,200	$4,200

H
1977-present. Parlor size, originally a 13-fret neck, but soon changed to 14, Indian rosewood back and sides. The H A/E ('92-'04) added electronics and cutaway.

1977-2021	Indian rosewood	$3,200	$4,200
1994	Flamed koa	$4,300	$5,600
2005	Brazilian rosewood	$6,000	$7,800

H/13
2004-present. Like H, but with 13-fret neck, mahogany back and sides and slotted headstock.

2004-2021	Mahogany	$3,500	$4,600
2005	Flamed koa	$4,300	$5,600

H91
1990s. 14 5/8", flamed koa.

1990s		$4,300	$5,600

Model 1929 00
2010-present. 00-size, all mahogany, 12-fret neck.

2010-2021		$3,000	$4,000

OM (Orchestra Model)
1987-present. Orchestra model acoustic, sitka spruce top, Indian rosewood (Brazilian optional) back and sides, herringbone rosette, scalloped braces.

1987-2021	Brazilian rosewood	$5,900	$7,700
1987-2021	Indian rosewood	$3,200	$4,200
1995	Koa	$4,100	$5,400
2002	German spruce	$4,500	$6,000
2010	Italian spruce	$5,200	$6,800
2012	Figured mahogany	$5,800	$7,600

OM/PW Pre-War
1999-present. Indian rosewood, advanced X and scalloped top bracing.

1999-2021		$3,150	$4,100

PJ
1990s-present. Palor-size, Indian rosewood back and sides, 24" scale, 12-fret neck.

1990s-2021		$3,150	$4,100

Style 1
Indian rosewood standard, various other woods optional.

2014	Brazilian, Adirondack	$8,000	$10,500

Tony Rice
1976-present. Dreadnought, Indian rosewood body (Brazilian optional until Tony Rice Professional model available), sitka spruce top, solid peghead, zigzag back stripe, pickup optional.

1976-2021		$3,600	$4,700

Tony Rice Professional
1997-present. Brazilian rosewood back and sides, carved German spruce top, zigzag back stripe, solid peghead.

1997-2021		$6,500	$8,500

Vintage Artist (VA)
1992-present. Mahogany body, sitka spruce top, zigzag back stripe, solid peghead, scalloped X-bracing, pickup optional.

1992-2021		$3,200	$4,200

Santa Cruz D 12-Fret
Bernunzio Uptown Music

1992 Santa Cruz OM
Marshall Fleisher

GUITARS

Schechter Blackjack SLS Avenger
Michael Mitchell

Schoenberg The Quartet

MODEL YEAR	FEATURES	EXC. COND. LOW	HIGH

Vintage Artist Custom
1992-2004. Martin D-42 style, mahogany body, Indian rosewood back and sides, sitka spruce top, zigzag back stripe, solid peghead, scalloped X-bracing, pickup optional.

1992-2004		$3,150	$4,100

Vintage Jumbo (VJ)
2000-present. 16" scale, round shouldered body, sitka spruce, figured mahogany back and sides, natural.

2000-2021		$3,100	$4,000

Vintage Southerner (VS)
2007-present. Sitka spruce top standard, various other woods optional.

2007-2021		$4,900	$6,400

Santos Martinez
Ca. 1997-present. Intermediate grade, production, acoustic and electro-acoustic classical guitars, imported from China by John Hornby Skewes & Co. in the U.K.

Sardonyx
1978-1979. Guitars and basses built by luthier Jeff Levin in the back of Matt Umanov's New York City guitar shop, industrial looking design with 2 aluminum outrigger-style tubes extended from the rectangle body. Very limited production.

Saturn
1960s-1970s. Imported, most likely from Japan, solid and semi-hollow body electric guitars and basses. Large S logo with Saturn name inside the S. Many sold through Eaton's in Canada.

Saturn
1960s-1970s. Solidbody, 4 pickups.

1960s		$500	$650
1970s		$450	$600

Sawchyn Guitars
1972-present. Professional and premium grade, production/custom, flat-top and flamenco guitars and mandolins built by luthier Peter Sawchyn in Regina, Saskatchewan.

Schaefer
1997-2014. Premium grade, production/custom, flat-top acoustic guitars built by luthier Edward A. Schaefer in Austin, Texas. He previously built archtops, basses and mandolins. He retired in '14.

Schecter
1976-present. Intermediate, professional and premium grade, production/custom, acoustic and electric guitars and basses. Guitar component manufacturer founded in California by four partners (David Schecter's name sounded the best), started offering complete instruments in '79. The company was bought out and moved to Dallas, Texas in the early '80s. By '88 the company was back in California and in '89 was purchased by Hisatake Shibuya. Schecter Custom Shop guitars are made in Burbank, California and their intermediate grade Diamond Series is made in South Korea.

MODEL YEAR	FEATURES	EXC. COND. LOW	HIGH

Scheerhorn
1989-present. Professional and premium grade, custom, resonator and Hawaiian guitars built by luthier Tim Scheerhorn in Kentwood, Michigan. Around 2010, Scheerhorn becomes a division of National Reso-Phonic.

Schoenberg
1986-present. Premium grade, production/custom, flat-tops offered by Eric Schoenberg of Tiburon, California. From '86-'94 guitars made to Schoenberg's specifications by Martin. From '86-'90 constructed by Schoenberg's luthier and from '90-'94 assembled by Martin but voiced and inlaid in the Schoenberg shop. Current models made to Schoenberg specs by various smaller shops.

Schon
1986-1991. Designed by guitarist Neal Schon, early production by Charvel/Jackson building about 200 in the San Dimas factory. The final 500 were built by Larrivee in Canada. Leo Knapp also built custom Schon guitars from '85-'87, and '90s custom-made Schon guitars were also available.

Standard (Canada)
1987-1991. Made in Canada on headstock.

1987-1991		$650	$850

Standard (U.S.A.)
1986 only. Made in U.S.A. on headstock, San Dimas/Jackson model, single-cut, pointy headstock shape.

1986		$1,550	$2,000

Schramm Guitars
1990-present. Premium grade, production/custom, classical and flamenco guitars built by luthier David Schramm in Clovis, California.

Schroder Guitars
Luthier Timothy Schroeder (he drops the first e in his name on the guitars) builds premium grade, production/custom, archtops in Northbrook, Illinois. He began in 1993.

Schulte
1950s-2000. Luthier C. Eric Schulte made solidbody, semi-hollow body, hollow body and acoustic guitars, both original designs and copies, covering a range of prices, in the Philadelphia area.

Custom Copy
1982. Single-cut solidbody, figured maple top.

1982		$775	$1,025

Schulz
Ca. 1903-1917. Luthier August Schulz built harp guitars and lute-guitars in Nuremberg, Germany.

Harp Guitar
1906		$1,000	$1,300

MODEL YEAR	FEATURES	EXC. COND. LOW	HIGH

Schwartz Guitars

1992-present. Premium grade, custom, flat-top guitars built by luthier Sheldon Schwartz in Concord, Ontario.

ScoGo

Professional and premium grade, production/custom, solidbody guitars built by luthier Scott Gordon in Parkesburg, Pennsylvania starting in 2001.

Scorpion Guitars

1998-2014. Professional and premium grade, custom, solidbody guitars made by Ed Roman Guitars.

Scott French

2004-present. Professional grade, production/custom, electric guitars and basses built by luthier Scott French in Auburn, California. In '12 he discontinued offering custom built.

Scott Walker Custom Guitars

Refer to S. Walker Custom Guitars.

SeaGlass Guitars USA

2011-present. Professional grade, production/custom, electric guitars, built by luthier Roger Mello in Groton, Massachusetts.

Seagull

1982-present. Intermediate grade, production, acoustic and acoustic/electric guitars built in Canada. Seagull was founded by luthier Robert Godin, who also has the Norman, Godin, and Patrick & Simon brands of instruments.

Sebring

1980s-mid-1990s. Entry level Korean imports distributed by V.M.I. Industries.

Seiwa

Early 1980s. Entry-level to mid-level Japanese electric guitars and basses, logo may indicate Since 1956.

Sekova

Mid-1960s-mid-1970s. Entry level instruments imported by the U.S. Musical Merchandise Corporation of New York.

Selmer

1932-1952. France-based Selmer & Cie was primarily a maker of wind instruments when they asked Mario Maccaferri to design a line of guitars for them. The guitars, with an internal sound chamber for increased volume, were built in Mantes-la-Ville. Both gut and steel string models were offered. Maccaferri left Selmer in '33, but guitar production continued, and the original models are gradually phased out. In '36, only the 14 fret oval model is built. Production is stopped for WWII and resumes in '46, finally stopping in '52. Less than 900 guitars are built in total.

MODEL YEAR	FEATURES	EXC. COND. LOW	HIGH

Classique

1942. Solid Rosewood back and sides, no cutaway, solid spruce top, round soundhole, classical guitar size, possibly only 2 built.

1942		$5,000	$6,500

Concert

1932-1933. For gut strings, cutaway, laminated Indian rosewood back and sides, internal resonator, spruce top with D hole, wide walnut neck, ebony 'board, only a few dozen built.

1932		$11,500	$15,000
1933		$16,000	$21,000

Eddie Freeman Special

1933. For steel strings, 4 strings, laminated Indian rosewood back and sides, cutaway, no internal resonator, solid spruce top, D hole, black and white rosette inlays, walnut 12 fret neck, ebony 'board, 640mm scale, approx. 100 made.

1933		$5,500	$7,200

Espagnol

1932. For gut strings, laminated Indian rosewood back and sides, no cutaway, internal resonator, solid spruce top, round soundhole, wide walnut neck, ebony 'board, only a few made.

1932		$7,800	$10,200

Grand Modele 4 Cordes

1932-1933. For steel strings, 4 string model, laminated back and sides, cutaway, internal resonator, solid spruce top, D hole, walnut neck, ebony 'board, 12 fret, 640mm scale, 2 or 3 dozen made.

1932-1933		$11,500	$15,000

Harp Guitar

1933. For gut strings, solid mahogany body, extended horn holding 3 sub bass strings, 3 screw adjustable neck, wide walnut neck, ebony 'board, only about 12 built.

1933		$11,500	$15,000

Hawaienne

1932-1934. For steel strings, 6 or 7 strings, laminated back and sides, no cutaway, internal resonator, solid spruce top, D hole, wide walnut neck, ebony 'board, 2 or 3 dozen built.

1932-1934		$24,500	$32,000

Modele Jazz

1936-1942, 1946-1952. For steel strings, laminated Indian rosewood back and sides (some laminated or solid mahogany), cutaway, solid spruce top, small oval soundhole, walnut neck, ebony 'board (latest ones with rosewood necks), 14 fret to the body, 670mm scale. Production interrupted for WWII.

1936-1952		$31,000	$41,000

Modeles de Transition

1934-1936. Transition models appearing before 14 fret oval hole model, some in solid maple with solid headstock, some with round soundhole and cutaway, some 12 fret models with oval hole.

1934-1936		$18,500	$24,000

Orchestre

1932-1934. For steel strings, laminated back and sides, cutaway, internal resonator, solid spruce top, D hole, walnut neck, ebony 'board, about 100 made.

1932-1934		$33,000	$43,000

Seagull Maritime SWS Concert Hall SG

Sekova Single Cut

MODEL		EXC. COND.	
YEAR	FEATURES	LOW	HIGH

Tenor

1932-1933. For steel strings, 4 strings, laminated back and sides, internal resonator, solid spruce top, D hole, walnut neck, ebony 'board, 12 fret, 570mm scale, 2 or 3 dozen built.

1932-1933		$4,600	$6,000

Serenghetti

2007-present. Luthier Ray Patterson builds professional and premium grade, production/custom, 1-piece and neck-thru guitars and basses in Ocala, Florida.

Serge Guitars

1995-present. Luthier Serge Michaud builds his production/custom, classical, steel-string, resophonic and archtop guitars in Breakeyville, Quebec.

Series 10

1980s. Budget grade electric guitars, Series 10 by Bently on headstock.

Sexauer Guitars

1967-present. Premium and presentation grade, custom, steel-string, 12-string, nylon-string, and archtop guitars built by luthier Bruce Sexauer in Petaluma, California.

Shadow

1990s. Made in Europe, copy models such as the classic offset double cutaway solidbody, large Shadow logo on headstock, Shadow logo on pickup cover, student to intermediate grade.

Shanti Guitars

1985-present. Premium and presentation grade, custom, steel-string, 12-string, nylon-string and archtop guitars built by luthier Michael Hornick in Avery, California.

Shelley D. Park Guitars

1991-present. Luthier Shelley D. Park builds her professional grade, custom, nylon- and steel-string guitars in Vancouver, British Columbia.

Shelton-Farretta

1967-present. Premium grade, production/custom, flamenco and classical guitars built by luthiers John Shelton and Susan Farretta originally in Portland, Oregon, and since '05 in Alsea, Oregon.

Sheppard Guitars

1993-present. Luthier Gerald Sheppard builds his premium grade, production/custom, steel-string guitars in Kingsport, Tennessee.

Shergold

1968-1992. Founded by Jack Golder and Norman Houlder, Shergold originally made guitars for other brands like Hayman and Barnes and Mullins. In '75, they started building guitars and basses under

MODEL		EXC. COND.	
YEAR	FEATURES	LOW	HIGH

their own name. By '82, general guitar production was halted but custom orders were filled through '90. In '91, general production was again started but ended in '92 when Golder died.

Sherwood

Late 1940s-early 1950s. Archtop and lap steel guitars made for Montgomery Ward made by Chicago manufacturers such as Kay. There were also Sherwood amps made by Danelectro. Value ranges are about the same as Kay model equivalent.

Shifflett

1990-present. Luthier Charles Shifflett builds his premium grade, production/custom, flat-top, classical, flamenco, resophonic, and harp guitars and basses in High River, Alberta. He also builds banjos.

Sho-Bro

1969-1978. Spanish and Hawaiian style resonator guitars made by Sho-Bud in Nashville, Tennessee and distributed by Gretsch. Designed by Shot Jackson and Buddy Emmons.

7-String Dobro

1972-1978		$1,475	$1,925

Grand Slam

1978. Acoustic, spruce top, mahogany neck, jacaranda sides and back, and mother-of-pearl inlays, abalone soundhole purfling.

1970s		$650	$850

Resonator

1972-1978. Flat-top style guitar with metal resonator with 2 small circular grilled soundholes.

1972-1978		$1,075	$1,400

Siegmund Guitars & Amplifiers

1993-present. Luthier Chris Siegmund builds his professional, premium, and presentation grade, custom/production, archtop, solidbody, and resonator guitars in Los Angeles, California. He founded the company in Seattle, moving it to Austin, Texas for '95-'97. He also builds amps and effects pedals.

Sierra

Budget level imports by Musicorp, starting in 2006. There is an unrelated brand of Sierra steels and lap steels.

Sigma

1970-2007. Budget and intermediate grade, production, import acoustic and electric guitars and basses distributed by C.F. Martin Company. They also offered mandolins and banjos. Japanese-made for 1970-'72; lower-end model production moved to Korea in '73; most of remaining Japanese production moved to Korea in '83; most production moved to Taiwan and Indonesia in '96.

Acoustic/Acoustic Electric/Electric

1970-2007	Various models	$250	$750

Sherwood Deluxe
Donald DiLoreto

Silver Street Taxi
Allen McBroom

MODEL YEAR	FEATURES	EXC. COND. LOW	HIGH

Signature

2005-ca. 2013. See listing under Gibson Baldwin.

Signature Guitar Company (Canada)

1987-1990. Intermediate/professional grade, electric guitars and basses built in Ontario, Canada. Mother of pearl inlaid on 21st fret with model name and, as an option, you could custom order any model with your name inlaid on the 12th fret.

Odyssey

1987-1990. Flat-top, figured maple top, 3 pickups.

1987-1990		$1,800	$2,400

Oracle

1987-1990. Flat-top, figured maple top, 3 pickups.

1987-1990		$1,800	$2,400

Signet

1972-Mid 1970s. Acoustic flat-top guitars, imported from Japan by Ampeg/Selmer.

Silber

1992-1998. Solid wood, steel-string guitars designed by Marc Silber, made in Paracho, Mexico, and distributed by K & S Music. Silber continues to offer the same models under the Marc Silber Music brand.

Silver Street

1979-1986. Founded by brothers Bruce and Craig Hardy, production of solidbody electric guitars built in Elkhart, Indiana and later in Shelby, Michigan. Original TAXI model prototypes built by luthier Richard Schneider. Later models included Spitfire, Cobra, MX, Nightwing, Tommy Shaw and Elite, all offered with various pickups, custom paint and optional hardware. Total production estimate 550 units. See the March 2018 issue of Vintage Guitar for more info.

Various Models

1979-1986	Early small models	$600	$800
1979-1986	Larger models	$925	$1,200

Silvertone

1941-ca. 1970, present. Brand of Sears instruments which replaced their Supertone brand in '41. The Silvertone name was used on Sears phonographs, records and radios as early as the 'teens, and on occasional guitar models. When Sears divested itself of the Harmony guitar subsidiary in '40 it turned to other suppliers including Kay. In '40 Kay-made archtops and Hawaiian electric lap steels appeared in the catalog bearing the Silvertone brand, and after '41-'42, all guitars, regardless of manufacturer, were called Silvertone.

Sears offered Danelectro-made solidbodies in the fall of '54. Danelectro hollowbodies appeared in '56. By '65, the Silvertones were Teisco-made guitars from W.M.I., but never sold through the catalog. First imports shown in catalog were in '69. By '70, most guitars sold by Sears were imports and did not carry the Silvertone name.

Currently, Samick offers a line of acoustic and electric guitars, basses and amps under the Silvertone name.

Amp-In-Case

1962-1968. The black, sharp double cutaway, 1-pickup 1448, introduced in '62, came with a smaller wattage amp without tremolo. The black, 2-pickup 1449, introduced in '63, came with a higher-watt amp with tremolo and better quality Jensen speaker and was replaced by the red burst 1457 in '64. Gray tolex covered the guitar-amp case. In '66 they were replaced with the black 1451 and 1452 with soft, rounded cutaway horns.

1962-1966	1448, 1 pu, black	$625	$850
1963-1966	1449, 2 pus, black	$800	$1,050
1964-1966	1457, 2 pus, red burst	$800	$1,050
1966-1968	1451, 1 pu, round cut	$625	$825
1966-1968	1452, 2 pus, round cut	$800	$1,050

Belmont

1958. Single-cut solidbody, 2 pickups, black.

1958		$850	$1,100

Black Beauty 1384L

1956-1958. Called 'The Black Beauty' in Sears catalog, large body acoustic-electric archtop, cutaway, 2 pickups, block markers, white binding, spruce top, mahogany sides and back, black lacquer finish.

1956-1958		$1,250	$1,625

Black Beauty 1385

1957. Basically the same as model 1384L.

1957		$1,250	$1,625

Espanada

1960s. Bigsby, 2 pickups, black.

1960s		$1,250	$1,625

Estrelita

1960s. Semi-hollowbody archtop, 2 pickups, black, Harmony-made.

1960s		$1,100	$1,450

F-66

1964. Similar to Harmony Rocket III, single-cut, thinline electric, 3 pickups, Bigsby.

1964		$1,000	$1,300

Gene Autry Melody Ranch

1941-1955. 13" Harmony-made acoustic, Gene Autry signature on belly, cowboy roundup stencil, same as earlier Supertone Gene Autry Roundup.

1941-1955		$350	$500

H1214

1951. Full-size acoustic archtop, script Silvertone headstock logo, dot markers, blond with simulated grain finish.

1951		$525	$700

H1260 Sovereign Jumbo

1968. Silvertone's version of Harmony's Sovereign jumbo flat-top, dot markers, sunburst.

1968		$650	$850

H1434 Rocket

1965. Similar to Harmony Rocket H59, sold by Sears, 3 pickups, Bigsby vibrato.

1965		$1,000	$1,300

1966 Silvertone 1457 Amp-In-Case
Ted Barham

Silvertone Espanada
Mercedes Girard

Silvertone H1446

Tom Pfeifer

Silvertone H1454

Tom Pfeifer

MODEL		EXC. COND.	
YEAR	FEATURES	LOW	HIGH

Meteor
1955. Single-cut, 1 pickup, sunburst.

1955		$450	$600

Model 623
Late-1950s. Large-body acoustic archtop, dot markers, white 'guard, black finish, painted white binding to give a black and white attractive appearance.

1950s		$225	$300

Model 1300/Model 1302
1958-1959. Single-cut, 1 lipstick pickup, dot markers, 3-on-a-side symmetric headstock, bronze (1300) or black (1302).

1958-1959	1300	$650	$850
1958-1959	1302	$650	$850

Model 1301/Model 1303
1958-1959. 1300 with 2 lipstick pickups, bronze (1301) or black (1303).

1958-1959	1301	$875	$1,150
1958-1959	1303	$875	$1,150

Model 1305
1958-1959. Single-cut, 3 lipstick pickups, dot markers, 3-on-a-side symmetric headstock, white and black finish.

1958-1959		$1,300	$1,700

Model 1317
1957. Single-cut solidbody, 1 lipstick pickup, dot markers, 3-on-a-side symmetric headstock, bronze finish.

1957		$525	$675

Model 1381/Model 1382
1954-1957. Kay-made (many '50s Silvertones were made by Danelectro), slim-style electric similar to Thin Twin/Jimmy Reed, 2 lipstick pickups, 4 knobs, crown-crest logo on 'guard under strings, bolt neck, block markers, sunburst, sold without (Model 1381) and with a case (1382).

1954-1957	1381	$550	$725
1954-1957	1382	$925	$1,200

Model 1413
1962-1964. Double-cut slab body, single pickup, 2 control knobs, dot markers.

1962-1964		$225	$300

Model 1415/Model 1417
1960-1962. Single-cut, 1 lipstick pickup, 6-on-a-side dolphin headstock, dot markers, bronze (1415) or black (1417).

1960	1417	$525	$700
1961-1962	1415	$525	$700

Model 1420
1959-1963. Single-cut extra thin solidbody, bolt neck, 2 pickups, natural shaded or black finish.

1959-1963		$525	$675

Model 1423L
1960. Single-cut solidbody, 2 pickups, 5 control knobs with rotator switch, block markers, gleaming gold-color splatter-effect over black finish.

1960		$550	$725

Model 1429L
1962-1963. Harmony-made and similar to Harmony's H-75, single-cut thinline electric, 3 pickups, trapeze tailpiece, 3 toggles, 6 knobs, block marker, sunburst.

1962-1963		$925	$1,200

MODEL		EXC. COND.	
YEAR	FEATURES	LOW	HIGH

Model 1445L
1960s. Teisco-made solidbody, 3 pickups.

1960s		$700	$900

Model 1446
1962-1966. Single-cut thin acoustic archtop, 2 pickups, original factory Bigsby tailpiece, black lacquer finish with white 'guard.

1962-1966		$1,275	$1,675

Model 1454
1962-1966. Single-cut thin acoustic archtop, 3 pickups, original factory Bigsby tailpiece, red lacquer finish.

1962-1966		$1,275	$1,675

Model 1476/Model 1477
1964-1966. Offset double-cut solidbody, 2 pickups, dot markers. 4 control knobs, tremolo, black (1476) or sunburst (1477).

1964-1966	1476	$525	$700
1964-1966	1477	$525	$700

Model 1478/Model 1488 Silhouette
1964-1967. Offset double-cut, rectangular pickups, tremolo, bound 'board, block markers.

1964-1967	1478, 1 pickup	$250	$400
1964-1967	1478, 2 pickups	$300	$450
1964-1967	1488, 3 pickups	$450	$600

Model S1352

1955		$650	$850

Model S1453 Rebel
1968. Two sharp cutaway, single f-hole, 2 pickups, vibrato.

1968		$525	$700

Student-level 13" Flat-Top
1960s. Harmony-made, 13" lower bout.

1960s		$30	$60

Student-level 15.5" Flat-Top
1960s. Harmony-made, 15.5" lower bout.

1960s	Model S621	$150	$250

Simon & Patrick

1985-present. Intermediate and professional grade, production, acoustic and acoustic/electric guitars built in Canada. Founded by luthier Robert Godin and named after his sons. He also produces the Seagull, Godin, and Norman brands of instruments.

Sims Custom Shop

2007-present. Custom, professional and premium grade, electric guitars built in Chattanooga, Tennessee by luthier Patrick Sims.

Singletouch

Luthier Mark Singleton builds his professional and premium grade, custom/production, solid and semi-hollow body guitars and basses in Phillips Ranch, California.

Skylark

1981. Solidbody guitars made in Japan and distributed by JC Penney. Two set-neck models and one bolt-neck model were offered. Most likely a one-time deal as brand quickly disappeared.

MODEL YEAR	FEATURES	EXC. COND. LOW	HIGH

Slammer

1998-2009. Budget and intermediate grade, production, guitars and basses imported from Indonesia by Hamer. Not to be confused with Hamer's Korean-made series of guitars from 1990-'97 called Hamer Slammer.

Slammer Series (Import)

1998-2009	Various models	$190	$250

Slingerland

Ca. 1914-2019. Henry Slingerland opened a music school in Chicago, Illinois, in 1914 where he supplied instruments made by others to students who took his course. That grew into the Slingerland Manufacturing Company, then Slingerland Banjo and Drum Company in '28, selling banjos, guitars and ukes, built by them and others into the '40s. They also marketed the May Bell brand. Many of the guitars were made by other companies, including Regal. Slingerland ownership changed multiple times in the 1970s-80s until it was acquired by Gibson (from Gretsch) in 1994. The current owner, Drum Workshop (DW), acquired Slingerland in 2019.

Nitehawk

1930s. 16" archtop, Nitehawk logo on headstock, fancy position neck markers.

1930s		$850	$1,100

Songster Archtop/Flat-Top

1930s	Archtop	$700	$900
1930s	Flat-Top	$1,175	$1,550

Songster Tenor

1930s. Archtop.

1930s		$500	$650

Smart Fine Instruments

1986-present. Luthier A. Lawrence Smart builds his professional and premium grade, custom, flat-top guitars first in McCall and now Hailey, Idaho. He also builds mandolin-family instruments.

Smith, George

1959-2020. Custom classical and flamenco guitars built by luthier George Smith in Portland, Oregon.

Smith, Lawrence K.

1989-present. Luthier Lawrence Smith builds his professional and premium grade, production/custom, flat-top, nylon-string, and archtop guitars in Thirrow, New South Wales, Australia. He also builds mandolins.

SMK Music Works

2002-present. Luthier Scott Kenerson builds production/custom, professional grade, solidbody electric guitars and basses in Waterford, Michigan.

Smooth Stone Guitar

2007-present. Luthier R. Dale Humphries builds his professional and premium grade, production/custom, acoustic and electric guitars and basses in Pocatello, Idaho.

Solomon Guitars

1995-present. Luthier Erich Solomon builds his premium and presentation grade, production/custom, archtop, flat-top, classical and electric guitars in Epping, New Hampshire. Prior to '99 he was located in Anchorage, Alaska.

Somervell

Luthier Douglas P. Somervell built premium and presentation grade, production/custom, classical and flamenco guitars in Brasstown, North Carolina.

Somogyi, Ervin

1971-present. Luthier Ervin Somogyi builds his presentation grade, production/custom, flat-top, flamenco, and classical guitars in Oakland, California.

Sonata

1960s. Private brand Harmony-made, Sonata brand logo on headstock and pickguard.

Superior

1965. Grand Auditorium acoustic archtop, block markers, celluloid bound edges, similar to Harmony 1456, Superior logo on headstock.

1965		$475	$600

SonFather Guitars

1994-present. Luthier David A. Cassotta builds his production/custom, flat-top, 12-string, nylon-string and electric guitars in Rocklin, California.

Sorrentino

1930s. Private brand made by Epiphone and distributed by C.M.I. Quality close to similar Epiphone models.

Arcadia

1930s. Lower-end f-hole acoustic archtop similar to Epiphone Blackstone.

1930s		$575	$750

Sorrento

1960s. Electric guitar imports made by Teisco, pricing similar to Teisco models, Sorrento logo on headstock, upscale solidbodies can have four pickups with five knobs and four switches.

Electric Solidbody

1960s	4 pickups	$350	$450

Southwell Guitars

1983-present. Premium grade, custom, nylon-string guitars built by luthier Gary Southwell in Nottingham, U.K.

Sovereign

Ca. 1899-1938. Sovereign was originally a brand of The Oscar Schmidt Company of Jersey City, New Jersey, and used on guitars, banjos and mandolins starting in the very late 1800s. In the late '30s, Harmony purchased several trade names from the Schmidt Company, including Sovereign and Stella. Sovereign then ceased as a brand, but Harmony continued using it on a model line of Harmony guitars.

Silvertone flat-top
Tom Pfeifer

Smooth Stone BC Series

*Spalt Instruments
Purpleheart Special*

Starcaster
Bernunzio Uptown Music

MODEL YEAR	FEATURES	EXC. COND. LOW	HIGH

Spalt Instruments

2002-present. Professional and premium grade, production/custom, electric solidbody and hollowbody guitars and basses built by luthier Michael Spalt, originally in Los Angeles, California and since '11 in Vienna, Austria.

Sparrow Guitars

Guitars manufactured in China are dismantled and "overhauled" in Vancouver, British Columbia, starting in '04. From these imports, luthier Billy Bones builds his intermediate and professional grade, production/custom solidbody and hollowbody electric guitars.

Specht Guitars

1991-present. Premium grade, production/custom, acoustic, baritone, parlor, jazz and classical guitars and basses built by luthier Oliver Specht in Vancouver, British Columbia.

Specimen Products

1984-present. Luthier Ian Schneller builds his professional and premium grade, production/custom, aluminum and wood body guitars and basses in Chicago, Illinois. He also builds ukes and amps.

Spector/Stuart Spector Design

1975-1990 (Spector), 1991-1998 (SSD), 1998-present (Spector SSD). Known mainly for basses, Spector offered U.S.-made guitars during '75-'90 and '96-'99, and imports for '87-'90 and '96-'99. Since 2003, they again offer U.S.-professional grade, production, solidbody guitars. See Bass Section for more company info.

SPG

2006-2009. Originally professional grade, custom, solidbody and chambered guitars built by luthier Rick Welch in Farmingdale, Maine and Hanson, Massachusetts. He also built lapsteels. Currently brand is used on imported line.

Squier

See models listed under Squier in Fender section.

St. Blues

1980-1989, 2005-present. Intermediate and professional grade, production/custom, solidbody guitars and basses imported and built in Memphis, Tennessee. The original '80s line was designed by Tom Keckler and Charles Lawing at Memphis' Strings & Things.

St. George

Mid to late 1960s. Early Japanese brand imported possibly by Buegeleisen & Jacobson of New York, New York.

Electric Solidbody

1960s. Early Japanese import duplicate of Zim Gar model, top mounted controls, 3 pickups, bolt-on neck.

1960s	Sunburst	$575	$750

St. Moritz

1960s. Guitars and basses imported from Japan by the Manhattan Novelty Corp. Manufacturer unknown, but some appear to be Fuji Gen Gakki products. Generally shorter scale beginner guitars, some with interesting pickup configurations.

Stahl

1900-1941. William C. Stahl, of Milwaukee, Wisconsin, ran a publishing company, taught stringed instrument classes and sold instruments to his students as well as by mail order across America. His label claimed that he was the maker but most of his products were built by the Larson brothers of Maurer & Co. of Chicago, with the balance mostly from Washburn. The most commonly found Larson-built models are the Style 6 and 7 as seen in the ca. 1912 Stahl catalog. Jimi Hendrix was the proud owner of a Style 8. The Style 6 is a moderately trimmed 15" Brazilian rosewood beauty that is much like the highly sought Maurer Style 551. The Style 7 and 8 are pearl trimmed 13 ½" concert size Brazilians comparable to the Maurer Style 562 ½. The 1912 Stahl catalog Styles 4, 5 and 9 were built by Washburn.

Stambaugh

1995-present. Luthier Chris Stambaugh builds his professional grade, custom/production, solidbody guitars basses in Stratham, New Hampshire.

Standel

1952-1974, 1997-present. Amp builder Bob Crooks offered instruments under his Standel brand 3 different times during the '60s. In '61 Semie Moseley, later of Mosrite fame, made 2 guitar models and 1 bass for Standel, in limited numbers. Also in '61, Standel began distributing Sierra steels and Dobro resonators, sometimes under the Standel name. In '65 and '66 Standel offered a guitar and a bass made by Joe Hall, who also made the Hallmark guitars. In '66 Standel connected with Sam Koontz, who designed and produced the most numerous Standel models (but still in relatively small numbers) in Newark, New Jersey. These models hit the market in '67 and were handled by Harptone, which was associated with Koontz. By '70 Standel was out of the guitar biz. See Amp section for more company info.

Custom Deluxe 101/101X

1967-1968. Custom solidbody with better electronics, 101X has no vibrato, sunburst, black, pearl white and metallic red.

1967-1968		$1,375	$1,800

Custom Deluxe 102/102X

1967-1968. Custom thin body with better electronics, 102X has no vibrato, offered in sunburst and 5 solid color options.

1967-1968		$1,375	$1,800

Custom 201/201X

1967-1968. Solidbody, 2 pickups, vibrola, 2 pointed cutaways, headstock similar to that on Fender XII, 201X has no vibrato, sunburst, black, pearl white and metallic red.

1967-1968		$1,100	$1,500

MODEL YEAR	FEATURES	EXC. COND. LOW	HIGH
Custom 202/202X			
1967-1968. Thin body, headstock similar to that on Fender XII, 202X has no vibrato, offered in sunburst and 5 solid color options.			
1967-1968		$1,100	$1,500
Custom 420S			
1967-1968. Custom thin body with 2 pickups.			
1967-1968		$1,375	$1,800

Star

1957-1960s. Early budget level instruments made by Tokyo Sound Company and Gakki and exported by Japan's Hoshino (translates to Star) company which also has Ibanez.

Starcaster

2000s. Budget brand from Fender that has been used on acoustic, electric and bass guitars, effects, amps and drums and sold through mass retailers such as Costco, Target and others. See Fender listing for guitar values.

Starfield

1992-1993. Solidbody guitars from Hoshino (Ibanez) made in the U.S. and Japan. U.S. guitars are identified as American models; Japanese ones as SJ models. Hoshino also used the Star Field name on a line of Japanese guitars in the late '70s. These Star Fields had nothing to do with the '90s versions and were not sold in the U.S.

Starforce

Ca. 1989. Import copies from Starforce Music/ Starforce USA.

Stars

Intermediate grade, production, solidbody guitars made in Korea.

Status Graphite

Professional grade, production/custom, solidbody guitars and basses built in Colchester, Essex, U.K. Status was the first English company to produce a carbon fiber instrument.

Stauffer

1800s. Old World violin and guitar maker, Georg Stauffer. Valid attributions include signed or labeled by the maker indicating the guitar was actually made by Stauffer, as opposed to attributed to Stauffer or one of his contemporaries. See Martin for listing.

Stefan Sobell Musical Instruments

1982-present. Premium grade, production/custom, flat-top, 12-string, and archtop guitars built by luthier Stefan Sobell in Hetham, Northumberland, England. He also builds mandolins, citterns and bouzoukis.

MODEL YEAR	FEATURES	EXC. COND. LOW	HIGH

Steinberger

1979-present. Currently Steinberger offers budget, intermediate, and professional grade, production, electric guitars. They also offer basses. Founded by Ned Steinberger, who started designing NS Models for Stuart Spector in '76. In '79, he designed the L-2 headless bass. In '80, the Steinberger Sound Corp. was founded. Steinberger Sound was purchased by the Gibson Guitar Corp. in '87, and in '92, Steinberger relocated to Nashville, Tennessee.

Headless model codes for '85-'93 are: First letter is X for bass or G for guitar.

Second letter is for body shape: M is regular offset double-cut guitar body; L is rectangle body; P is mini V shaped body.

Number is pickup designation: 2 = 2 humbuckers, 3 = 3 single coils, 4 = single/single/ humbucker.

Last letter is type of tremolo: S = S-Trem tremolo; T = Trans-Trem which cost more on original retail.

GL			
1979-1984. Headless, rectangle body, 2 pickups.			
1979-1984		$2,800	$3,600

Steinegger

1976-2021. Premium grade, custom steel-string flat-top guitars built by luthier Robert Steinegger in Portland, Oregon. He retired March, 2021.

Stella

Ca. 1899-1974, 2000s. Stella was a brand of the Oscar Schmidt Company which started using the brand on low-mid to mid-level instruments in the very late 1800s. Oscar Schmidt produced all types of stringed instruments and was very successful in the 1920s. Company salesmen reached many rural areas and Stella instruments were available in general stores, furniture stores, and dry goods stores, ending up in the hands of musicians such as Leadbelly and Charlie Patton. Harmony acquired the Stella brand in '39 and built thousands of instruments with that name in the '50s and '60s. Harmony dissolved in '74. The Stella brand was reintroduced in the 2000s by MBT International.

00 Style			
1900-1930. Oak body flat-top.			
1900-1930		$525	$675
Flat-Top 15" 12-String			
1920s-1930s. Associated with early blues and folk musicians, top of the line for Stella.			
1920s-30s		$7,900	$10,300
Flat-Top by Harmony			
1950s-1960s. The low end of the Harmony-built models, US-made until the end of the '60s, student level, Stella logo on headstock, playing action can often be very high which makes them difficult to play.			
1950s-60s	13", student	$70	$210
1950s-60s	14", 12-string	$95	$240
1950s-60s	Sundale (colors)	$375	$575
1950s-60s	Tenor 4-string	$70	$210

Steinegger D-45
Carter Vintage Guitars

1968 Stella
Edward Sparks

1950 Stromberg DeLuxe
Ranger Doug

Stromberg G-3
Carter Vintage Guitars

Harp Guitar
Early-1900s.

MODEL YEAR	FEATURES	EXC. COND. LOW	HIGH
1900s		$2,100	$2,700

Singing Cowboy
2000s. Copy of Supertone (black background)/ Silvertone/Harmony Singing Cowboy, import with laminated wood construction and ladder bracing.

2000s	Stencil over black	$50	$65

Stetson
1884-ca. 1924. Stetson was a house brand of William John Dyer's St. Paul, Minnesota, music store. They started advertising this brand as early as 1894, but those built by the Larson brothers of Maurer & Co. date from ca. 1904-c. 1924. Most Stetsons were made by the Larsons. Others were built by Harmony (early ones), Washburn and three are credited to the Martin Co.

Stevenson
1999-present. Professional grade, production/ custom, solidbody electric guitars and basses built by luthier Ted Stevenson in Lachine, Quebec. He also builds amps.

Stiehler
Production/custom, professional and premium grade, acoustic electric and electric solidbody guitars and basses, built by luthier Bob Stiehler, first in Wellington and since '11 in Carson City, Nevada. He started in 2005.

Stonebridge
1981-present. Czech Republic luthier Frantisek Furch builds professional and premium grade, production/ custom, acoustic guitars. He also builds mandolins.

Stonetree Custom Guitars
1996-present. Luthier Scott Platts builds his professional and premium grade, custom/production, solidbody and chambered electric guitars and basses in Saratoga, Wyoming.

Strad-O-Lin/Stradolin
Ca.1920s-ca.1960s. The Strad-O-Lin company was operated by the Hominic brothers in New York, primarily making mandolins for wholesalers. Around '57 Multivox/Premier bought the company and also used the name on electric and acoustic guitars, basses and amps. Premier also marketed student level guitars under the U.S. Strad brand.

Electric
1960s	Various models	$375	$500

Stratosphere
1954-1958. Solidbody electrics made in Springfield, Missouri by brothers Claude and Russ Deaver, some featuring fanned frets. They also made an odd double neck called the Stratosphere Twin with a regular 6-string neck and a 12-string tuned in minor and major thirds. The brothers likely made less than 200 instruments.

MODEL YEAR	FEATURES	EXC. COND. LOW	HIGH
Electric			
1954-1958		$925	$1,200

Strobel Guitars
2003-present. Luthier Russ Strobel builds custom, professional grade, electric travel guitars and basses in Boca Raton, Florida. He also offers a production, intermediate grade, travel guitar built first in Korea and since '13 in Asia.

Stromberg
1906-1955, 2001-present. Intermediate and professional grade, production, archtop guitars imported by Larry Davis.

Founded in Boston by master luthier Charles Stromberg, a Swedish immigrant, building banjos and drums. Son Harry joined the company in 1907 and stayed until '27. Son Elmer started in 1910 at age 15. The shop was well known for tenor banjos, but when the banjo's popularity declined, they began building archtop orchestra model guitars. The shop moved to Hanover Street in Boston in '27 and began producing custom order archtop guitars, and in particular the 16" G-series and the Deluxe. As styles changed the G-series was increased to 17 3/8" and the 19" Master 400 model was introduced in '37. Stromberg designs radically changed around '40, most likely when Elmer took over guitar production. Both Charles and Elmer died within a few months of each other in '55. Most of the interest in vintage Strombergs comes out of the Boston area.

Larry Davis of WD Music Products revived the Stromberg name and introduced a series of moderately priced jazz guitars in June, 2001. The models are crafted by a small Korean shop with component parts supplied by WD.

Deluxe
1927-1955. Non-cut, 16" body to '34, 17 3/8" body after '35, also sometimes labeled Delux.

1927-1939	2 parallel 3 ladder	$4,200	$8,400
1940-1947	2 braces	$4,200	$8,400
1948-1955	1 brace	$16,000	$21,000

G-1
1927-1955. Non-cut, 16" body to '35, 17 3/8" body after '35, sunburst.

1927-1935	2 parallel 3 ladder	$4,200	$8,400
1936-1947	2 braces	$4,200	$8,400
1948-1955	1 brace	$16,000	$21,000

G-3
Early 1930s. Archtop, 16 3/8", 3 segment F-holes, ladder bracing, gold hardware, engraved tailpiece, 8-ply 'guard, 5-ply body binding, laminate maple back, fancy engraved headstock with Stromberg name, less total refinement than higher-end Stromberg models.

1927-1935	2 parallel 3 ladder	$4,200	$8,400

G-5
1952-1955. 17" cutaway.

1952-1955	1 brace	$19,000	$30,000

Master 300
1937-1955. 19" non-cut.

1937-1947	2 braces, natural	$5,250	$10,500
1937-1947	2 braces, sunburst	$6,000	$11,000

MODEL YEAR	FEATURES	EXC. COND. LOW	HIGH
1948-1955	1 brace, natural	$11,000	$21,000
1948-1955	1 brace, sunburst	$11,000	$21,000

Master 400
1937-1955. 19" top-of-the-line non-cut, the most common of Stromberg's models.

1937-1947	2 braces, natural	$11,000	$21,000
1937-1947	2 braces, sunburst	$11,000	$21,000
1948-1955	1 brace, natural	$21,000	$42,000
1948-1955	1 brace, sunburst	$21,000	$42,000

Master 400 Cutaway
1949, 1953. Only 7 cutaway Strombergs are known to exist.

1949, 1953	1 brace, natural	$48,000	$69,000

Stromberg-Voisinet
1921-ca.1932. Marketed Stromberg (not to be confused with Charles Stromberg of Boston) and Kay Kraft brands, plus guitars of other distributors and retailers. Stromberg was the successor to the Groehsl Company (or Groehsel) founded in Chicago, Illinois in 1890; and the predecessor to the Kay Musical Instrument Company. In 1921, the name was changed to Stromberg-Voisinet Company. Henry Kay "Hank" Kuhrmeyer joined the company in '23 and was secretary by '25. By the mid-'20s, the company was making many better Montgomery Ward guitars, banjos and mandolins, often with lots of pearloid.

Joseph Zorzi, Philip Gabriel and John Abbott left Lyon & Healy for S-V in '26 or '27, developing 2-point Venetian shape, which was offered in '27. The first production of electric guitars and amps was introduced with big fanfare in '28; perhaps only 200 or so made. The last Stromberg acoustic instruments were seen in '32. The Kay Kraft brand was introduced by Kuhrmeyer in '31 as the company made its transition to Kay (see Kay).

Acoustic
1921-1932. Various art and colors.

1921-1932	Various models	$300	$1,350

Stroup
Luthier Gary D. Stroup builds his intermediate and professional grade, production/custom, archtop and flat-top guitars in Eckley, Colorado, starting in 2003.

Stuart Custom Guitars
Professional and premium grade, production/custom, solid and semi-hollow body guitars built by luthier Fred Stuart, starting the year 2004, in Riverside, California. Stuart was a Senior Master Builder at Fender. He also builds pickups.

Suhr Guitars
1997-present. Luthier John Suhr builds his professional and premium grade, production/custom, solidbody electrics guitars and basses in Lake Elsinore, California. He also builds amps. He previously built Pensa-Suhr guitars with Rudy Pensa in New York.

Electric Solidbody

1997-2021	Various models	$2,500	$3,250

Sunset
2010-present. Luthier Leon White builds professional and premium grade, production/custom, electric solidbody, chambered and hollowbody guitars in Los Angeles, California.

Superior Guitars
1987-present. Intermediate grade, production/custom Hawaiian, flamenco and classical guitars made in Mexico for George Katechis Montalvo of Berkeley Musical Instrument Exchange. They also offer lap steels and mandolin-family instruments.

Supersound
1952-1974. Founded by England's Alan Wootton, building custom amps and radios. In 1958-'59 he worked with Jim Burns to produce about 20 short scale, single-cut solidbodies bearing this name. They also built a bass model. The firm continued to build amps and effects into the early '60s.

Supertone
1914-1941. Brand used by Sears, Roebuck and Company for instruments made by various American manufacturers, including especially its own subsidiary Harmony (which it purchased in 1916). When Sears divested itself of Harmony in '40, instruments began making a transition to the Silvertone brand. By '41 the Supertone name was gone.

Acoustic Flat-Top (High-End Appointments)

1920s	Pearl trim 00-42 likeness	$1,600	$2,100
1920s	Pearl trim, Lindbergh model	$1,600	$2,100

Acoustic Flat-Top 13"

1920s-30s	Non-stencil, plain top	$200	$300
1920s-30s	Stencil top	$300	$400

Gene Autry Roundup
1932-1939. Harmony made acoustic, Gene Autry signature on belly, cowboy roundup stencil, 13" body until '35, then 14".

1932-1939		$375	$500

Lone Ranger
1936-1941. Black with red and silver Lone Ranger and Tonto stencil, silver-painted fretboard, 13 1/2" wide. "Hi-Yo Silver" added in '37, changed to "Hi-Ho Silver" in '38.

1936-1941		$375	$500

Robin Hood
1930s. 13" flat-top similar to Singing Cowboys, but with green and white art showing Robin Hood and his men against a black background.

1933		$375	$500

Singing Cowboys
1938-1943. Stencil of guitar strumming cowboys around chuck wagon and campfire, branded Silvertone after '41.

1938-1943		$375	$500

Stromberg-Voisinet Hawaiian Parlor
David Stone

Suhr Pete Thorn Signature

1960 Supro Dual Tone
Imaged by Heritage Auctions, HA.com

1964 Supro Coronado II
Imaged by Heritage Auctions, HA.com

MODEL YEAR	FEATURES	EXC. COND. LOW	HIGH

Supertone Wedge
1930s. Triangle-shaped wedge body, laminate construction, blue-silver Supertone label inside sound chamber, art decals on body.

1930s		$300	$400

Supro
1935-1968, 2004-present. Budget brand of National Dobro Company and Valco. Some Supro models also sold under the Airline brand for Montgomery Ward. In '42 Victor Smith, Al Frost and Louis Dopyera bought National and changed the name to Valco Manufacturing Company. Valco Manufacturing Company name changed to Valco Guitars, Inc., in '62. Company treasurer Robert Engelhardt bought Valco in '64. In '67 Valco bought Kay and in '68 Valco/Kay went out of business. In the summer of '69, Valco/Kay brands and assets were sold at auction and the Supro and National names purchased by Chicago-area importer and distributor Strum N' Drum (Norma, Noble). In the early-'80s, ownership of the Supro name was transferred to Archer's Music, Fresno, California. Some Supros assembled from new-old-stock parts.

Amp builder Bruce Zinky revived the Supro name for a line of guitars built in the U.S. by luthier John Bolin and others. He also offers amps. In 2013, Absara Audio, LLC acquired the Supro trademark and started releasing amps and guitars in July 2014.

Arlington
1967-1967. Jazzmaster-style, wood body, 6 buttons, 4 knobs, vibrato, 2 pickups.

1966-1967	Various colors	$1,200	$1,600

Atlas
1958. Rare model, Atlas logo, semi-single cutaway, 2 pickups plus bridge-tailpiece pickup, blond finish.

1958		$1,500	$2,000

Belmont
1955-1964. For '55-'60, 12" wide, single-cut, 1 neck pickup, 2 knobs treble side in 'guard, reverse-stairs tailpiece, No-Mar plastic maroon-colored covering. For '60, size increased to 13 1/2" wide. For '62-'64, Res-o-glas fiberglass was used for the body, a slight cutaway on bass side, 1 bridge pickup, 2 knobs on opposite sides, Polar White.

1955-1962	Black or white		
	No-Mar	$1,025	$1,350
1961-1964	Polar White		
	Res-o-glas	$1,100	$1,450

Bermuda
1962 only. Slab body (not beveled), double pickups, dot markers, cherry glass-fiber finish.

1962		$1,400	$1,850

Collegian Spanish
1939-1942. Metal body, 12 frets. Moved to National line in '42.

1939-1942		$1,200	$1,550

Coronado/Coronado II
1961-1967, 2017-2021. Listed as II in '62 15 1/2" scale, single-cut thinline, 2 pickups, natural blond spruce top. Changed to slight cutaway on bass side in '62 when

MODEL YEAR	FEATURES	EXC. COND. LOW	HIGH

renamed II. Reintroduced 2017, Americana series.

1961-1962	Blond, spruce top	$1,600	$2,100
1963-1967	Black fiberglass	$1,850	$2,400
2017-2021	II, Americana Series	$575	$750

Dual-Tone
1954-1966, 2004-2014. The Dual Tone had several body style changes, all instruments had dual pickups. '54, 11 1/4" body, No Mar Arctic White plastic body ('54-'62). '55, 12" body. '58, 13" body. '60, 13 1/2" body. '62, Res-o-glas Ermine White body, light cutaway on bass side.

1954-1961	Arctic White		
	No-Mar	$1,250	$1,650
1962-1964	Ermine White		
	Res-o-glas	$1,350	$1,750

El Capitan
1948-1955. Archtop, 1 single-coil pickup.

1948-1955		$650	$850

Folk Star/Vagabond
1964-1967. Molded Res-o-glas body, single-cone resonator, dot inlays, Fire Engine Red. Name changed to Vagabond in '66.

1964-1967		$1,000	$1,300

Jamesport
2017-2021. Island Series, electric solidbody, '60s-era design, alder body, maple neck, rosewood 'board, Gold Foil pickup, antique white or jet black.

2017-2021		$400	$525

Kingston
1962-1963. Double-cut slab body, bridge pickup, glass-fiber sand finish, similar to same vintage Ozark.

1962-1963		$1,000	$1,300

Lexington
1967. Double-cut, wood body.

1967		$475	$625

Martinique (Val-Trol)
1962-1967. Single-cut, 13 1/2" wide, 2 standard and 1 bridge pickups, block markers, Val-Trol script on 'guard, Bigsby, blue or Ermine White Polyester Glas. Collectors sometimes call this Val-Trol, referring to the 6 mini tone and volume controls. Not to be confused with Silverwood model which also has 6 mini-knobs.

1962-1967		$2,250	$3,000

N800 Thinline Electric
1967-1968. Thin body, symmetrical double-cut, 2 pickups, copy model, similar to National N800 series models.

1967-1968		$625	$825

Ozark
1952-1954, 1958-1967, 2004-2013. Non-cut, 1 pickup, dot inlay, white pearloid body, name reintroduced in '58 as a continuation of model Sixty with single-cut, Dobro tailpiece.

1952-1954	White pearloid	$1,100	$1,450
1958-1961	Red	$1,100	$1,450
1962-1967	Jet Black or		
	Fire Bronze	$1,100	$1,450

Ranchero
1948-1960. Full body electric archtop, neck pickup, dot markers, bound body, sunburst.

1948-1960		$750	$1,000

MODEL YEAR	FEATURES	EXC. COND. LOW	HIGH

Rhythm Master (Val-Trol)
1959. Val-Trol 'guard.

1959		$1,875	$2,500

S710 Flat-Top
1967-1968. Jumbo-style 15.5" flat-top, block markers, asymmetrical headstock, natural.

1967-1968		$400	$525

Sahara/Sahara 70
1960-1967. 13 1/2" body-style similar to Dual-Tone, single pickup, 2 knobs, Sand-Buff or Wedgewood Blue, Sahara until '63, Sahara 70 after.

1960-1967		$1,125	$1,500

Silverwood (Val-Trol)
1960-1962, 2019-2021. Single-cut, 13 1/2" wide, 2 standard and 1 bridge pickups, block markers, natural blond, Val-Trol script on 'guard, renamed Martinique in '62. Collectors sometimes call this Val-Trol, referring to the guitar's 6 mini tone and volume controls. The Martinique also has the Val-Trol system but the knobs are not in a straight line like on the Silverwood. Reintroduced 2019, mahogany or ash body, maple neck, 2 Gold Foil pickups, Daphne Blue, Ash Natural, British Racing Green and Transparent Red.

1960-1962		$2,075	$2,700
2019-2021		$800	$1,050

Sixty
1955-1958. Single-cut, single pickup, white No-Mar, becomes Ozark in '58.

1955-1958		$775	$1,025

Special 12
1958-1960. Single-cut, replaces Supro Sixty, neck pickup 'guard mounted.

1958-1960		$775	$1,025

Stratford
1968. ES-335-style double-cut, 3 pickups, 3 switches, 6 knobs, vibrato.

1968		$675	$900

Strum 'N Drum Solidbody
1970s. Student-level import, 1 pickup, large Supro logo on headstock.

1970s	Higher-end	$450	$600
1970s	Lower-end	$350	$475

Super
1958-1964. 12" wide single-cut body style like mid-'50s models, single bridge pickup, short-scale, ivory.

1958-1964		$575	$750

Super Seven
1965-1967. Offset double-cut solidbody, short scale, middle pickup, Calypso Blue.

1965-1967		$575	$750

Suprosonic 30
1963-1967. Introduced as Suprosonic, renamed Suprosonic 30 in '64, double-cut, single neck pickup, vibrato tailpiece, more of a student model, Holly Red.

1963-1967		$625	$825

Tremo-Lectric
1965. Fiberglas hollowbody, 2 pickups, unique built-in electric tremolo (not mechanical), Wedgewood Blue finish, multiple controls associated with electric tremolo.

1965		$1,500	$1,950

MODEL YEAR	FEATURES	EXC. COND. LOW	HIGH

Tri Tone
Reintroduced 2019-2021. Single-cut mahogany body, maple neck, 3 pickups, black.

2019-2021		$875	$1,150

Westbury
Reintroduced 2017-2021. Island Series, alder body, maple neck, 2 Gold Foil pickups, black, white, turquoise, or tobacco burst.

2017-2021		$400	$525

Westwood 1580A
1955-1958. Single-cut archtop solidbody, 1 pickup.

1955-1958		$1,000	$1,300

White Holiday/Holiday
1963-1967, 2018-2021. Introduced as Holiday, renamed White Holiday in '64, fiberglas double-cut, vibrato tailpiece, single bridge pickup, Dawn White. Reintroduced 2018, Americana Series, mahogany body and neck, 2 pickups.

1963-1967		$1,175	$1,550
2018-2021		$575	$750

Suzuki Takeharu
See listing for Takeharu.

SX
See listing for Essex.

Szlag
2000-present. Luthier John J. Slog builds his professional and premium grade, custom carved, guitars and basses in Bethlehem, Pennsylvania.

T.D. Hibbs
Production/custom, professional grade, steel string and classical guitars built in Cambridge, Ontario by luthier Trevor Hibbs.

T.H. Davis
1976-2008. Professional and premium grade, custom, steel string and classical guitars built by luthier Ted Davis in Loudon, Tennessee. He also built mandolins. Davis died in '08.

T.J. Thompson
Luthier T.J. Thompson began in the 1980's building presentation grade, custom, steel string guitars in West Concord, Massachusetts.

Tacoma
1995-2009. Intermediate, and professional grade, production, acoustic guitars produced in Tacoma, Washington and New Hartford, Connecticut. They also built acoustic basses and mandolins. In October, '04, Fender acquired Tacoma and in '09 ceased production.

BM6C Thunderhawk Baritone
2004-2009. Single-cut acoustic baritone.

2004-2009		$1,050	$1,350

Supro Lexington
Rivington Guitars

Supro Super
Michael L. Waters

Tacoma DM-10
Imaged by Heritage Auctions, HA.com

Takamine PSF-94

MODEL YEAR	FEATURES	EXC. COND. LOW	HIGH

C-1C/C-1CE Chief
1997-2009. Cutaway flat-top with upper bass bout soundhole, solid cedar top, mahogany back and sides, rosewood 'board. Sides laminated until 2000, solid after, CE is acoustic/electric.

1997-2009		$450	$600
1997-2009	Fishman electronics	$500	$700

DM Series
1997-2006. Dreadnought, solid spruce top, mahogany back and sides, satin finish, natural, C suffix indicates cutaway.

1997-2006	Various models	$300	$1,100

DR Series
1997-2006. Dreadnought, solid sitka spruce top, rosewood back and sides, natural. Models include DR-20 (non-cut, herringbone trim, abalone rosette), DR-20E (with on-board electronics), DR-8C (cutaway), and DR-38.

1997-2006	Various models	$300	$1,100

EM Series
1999-2008. Little Jumbo series, spruce top, mahogany back and sides, C suffix indicates cutaway.

1999-2008	Various models	$550	$725

JM Series
1997-2006. Jumbo series, spruce top, mahogany back and sides.

1997-2006		$850	$1,100

JR-14C Jumbo Rosewood
Late-1990s. Jumbo cutaway, 16 5/8" lower bout, gloss spruce top, satin rosewood body.

1990s		$950	$1,250

JR-50CE4 Jumbo Koa
1997-2003. Jumbo cutaway, 17" lower bout, sitka spruce top, figured koa back and sides.

1997-2003		$950	$1,250

P-1/P-2 Papoose
1995-2009. Travel-size mini-flat-top, all solid wood, mahogany back and sides (P-1), with on-board electronics (P-1E) or solid rosewood (P-2), cedar top, natural satin finish.

1995-2000	P-2	$375	$475
1995-2009	P-1	$275	$375
1995-2009	P-1E	$375	$475

Parlor Series
1997-2003. Smaller 14 3/4" body, solid spruce top, various woods for back and sides.

1997-2003	PK-30 Koa	$725	$950
1997-2003	PK-40 Rosewood	$725	$950

PM Series
1997-2003. Full-size, standard soundhole.

1997-2003	Various models	$375	$975

Takamine
1962-present. Intermediate and professional grade, production, steel- and nylon-string, acoustic and acoustic/electric guitars and basses. Takamine is named after a mountain near its factory in Sakashita, Japan. Mass Hirade joined Takamine in '68 and revamped the brand's designs and improved quality. In '75, Takamine began exporting to other countries, including U.S. distribution by Kaman Music (Ovation). In '78, Takamine introduced acoustic/electric guitars. They offered solidbody electrics and some archtops for '83-'84.

Takeharu (by Suzuki)
Mid-1970s. Classical guitars offered by Suzuki as part of their internationally known teaching method (e.g. Violin Suzuki method), various sized instruments designed to eliminate the confusion of size that has been a problem for classroom guitar programs.

Taku Sakashta Guitars
1994-2010. Premium and presentation grade, production/custom, archtop, flat-top, 12-sting, and nylon-string guitars, built by luthier Taku Sakashta in Sebastopol, California. He died in February, 2010.

Tama
Ca. 1959-1967, 1974-1979. Hoshino's (Ibanez) brand of higher-end acoutic flat-tops made in Japan. Many of the brand's features would be transferred to Ibanez's Artwood acoustics.

Tamura
1970s. Made in Japan by Mitsura Tamura, the line includes intermediate grade solid wood classical guitars.

Tanglewood Guitar Company UK
1991-present. Owners Dirk Kommer and Tony Flatt in Biggin Hill, U.K. import intermediate and professional grade, production, acoustic, classical, resonator and electric guitars and basses from China. They also offer mandolins, banjos, ukuleles and amps.

Taylor
1974-present. Intermediate, professional, premium, and presentation grade, production/custom, steel- and nylon-string, acoustic, acoustic/electric, semi-hollow, and solidbody guitars built in El Cajon, California and Tecate, Mexico. They have also built basses. Founded by Bob Taylor, Steve Schemmer and Kurt Listug in Lemon Grove, California, the company was originally named the Westland Music Company, but was soon changed to Taylor (Bob designed the guitars and it fit on the logo). Taylor and Listug bought out Schemmer in '83. Bob Taylor was the first commercially successful guitar maker to harness CAD/CAM CNC technology for acoustic guitars and in '91 introduced the 410 Model, the first all-solid wood American-made guitar with a list price under $1,000. The plain-appointment model using CNC technology wsas a major innovation combining quality and price. They added semi-hollowbodies in '05 and solidbodies in '07. In '08, they added the Build To Order custom shop. In '18, they added their new V-Class bracing to most every steel-string

MODEL YEAR	FEATURES	EXC. COND. LOW	HIGH

model in the 300 Series and above. V-Class braced Taylors have a black graphite nut vs the white one on standard braced models.

Understanding Taylor's Model Numbering System:

The first digit or letter identifies the series (100 Series to 900 Series, PS-Presentation and K-Koa Series) and most models within each series share the same back and side woods and appointment package.

The second digit: 1=6-string with softwood (spruce) top; 2=6-string with hardwood top; 5=12-string with softwood top; 2=12-string with hardwood top.

The third digit is body shape: 0=Dreadnought; 2=Grand Concert; 4=Grand Auditorium; 6=Grand Symphony; 7=Grand Pacific; 8=Grand Orchestra.

A "c" at the end of the number indicates cutaway, an "e" onboard electronics, and a "N" nylon-string.

110 Series

2003-present. Dreadnought, sapele back and sides, sitka spruce top, e and ce begin '08.

2003-2016	110	$475	$625
2008-2019	110ce	$575	$725
2008-2021	110e	$525	$675

114 Series

2007-present. Grand Auditorium, sapele back and sides, sitka spruce top.

2007-2016	114	$475	$625
2008-2021	114ce	$575	$725
2008-2021	114e	$525	$675

150 Series

2016-present. Dreadnought 12-string, sitka spruce top, walnut back and sides.

2016-2021	150e	$575	$725

210 Series

2005-present. Dreadnought, sapele or Indian rosewood back and sides, sitka spruce top.

2005-2016	210	$575	$725
2005-2016	210e	$625	$800
2008-2021	210ce	$675	$850

214 Series

2004-present. Grand Auditorium, sapele or Indian rosewood back and sides, sitka spruce top.

2004-2016	214	$525	$675
2004-2016	214c	$575	$725
2005-2016	214e	$575	$725
2008-2021	214ce	$625	$775
2012-2017	214ce-N Classic	$675	$850
2014-2021	214ce-K DLX (Koa)	$725	$950
2020	214ce DLX	$900	$1,175
2020	214ce-SB DLX	$975	$1,275

224ce-K DLX

2016-present. Grand Auditorium, solid koa top, laminated koa back and sides.

2016-2021		$1,050	$1,350

254ce

2018-present. Venetian cutaway, sitka spruce top, rosewood back and sides.

2018-2021		$625	$825

310 Series

1998-2018. Dreadnought, mahogany or sapele back and sides, sitka spruce top. The non-cut 310 discontinued '07-'12, then reappeared in '13 along with 310e version.

1998-2006	310	$750	$975
1998-2018	310ce	$850	$1,075

310ce-L30

2004. Limited Edition 30th Anniversary, myrtlewood leaf inlays, koa rosette, 30th Anniversary headstock logo.

2004		$975	$1,275

312 Series

1998-present. Grand Concert, Venetian cutaway, mahogany or sapele back and sides, sitka spruce top. Non-cut 312 and 312e versions were offered in 2013. V-Class introduced '20.

1998-2019	312ce	$1,200	$1,550
2019-2021	312ce V-Class	$1,375	$1,775

314 Series

1998-2006, 2013-present. Mid-size Grand Auditorium, mahogany or sapele back and sides, sitka spruce top. Non-cut offered again in '13 along with 314e version. V-Class introduced '20.

1998-2006	314	$1,125	$1,450
1998-2019	314ce	$1,225	$1,550
2000	314ce-K (Koa)	$1,275	$1,650
2019-2021	314ce V-Class	$1,375	$1,775

314ce-LTD

2012-2018. Hawaiian Koa back and sides, Indian rosewood headstock. Also offered with nylon strings (N).

2012-2018		$1,275	$1,650

315 Series

1998-2011. Jumbo, mahogany or sapele back and sides, sitka spruce top.

1998-2011	315ce	$900	$1,175

316 Series

2012-2019. Grand Symphony, sitka spruce top, sapele back and sides.

2012-2019	316ce	$1,025	$1,300
2013-2016	316	$925	$1,200
2013-2016	316e	$975	$1,250
2018	316e Baritone-8 LTD	$1,575	$2,050

320e Baritone SLTD

2014. Limited Edition Dreadnought, mahogany top and body, Expression electronics.

2014		$1,275	$1,650

322 Series

2019-present. Grand Concert, non-cut, blackwood/mahogany top.

2019-2021	322ce V-Class	$1,475	$1,900
2020	322e	$1,425	$1,850

324 Series

2015-present. Grand Auditorium, mahogany top, African sapele back and sides.

2015-2020	324e	$1,150	$1,475
2019-2021	324ce V-Class	$1,425	$1,850
2020-2021	324	$1,100	$1,425

Taylor 214ce-SB DLX

Taylor 324e

Taylor 352ce

Taylor 414ce

MODEL YEAR	FEATURES	EXC. COND. LOW	HIGH
326e Baritone			
2015-present. Grand Symphony, special edition, 6- or 8-string, mahogany top.			
2015-2021		$1,275	$1,650
352 Series			
2019-present. Grand Concert 12-string, sitka spruce top, sapele back and sides, natural.			
2019-2021	352ce V-Class	$1,325	$1,725
354ce			
2004-2011. Grand Auditorium 12-string, cutaway, mahogany back and sides, Expression system.			
2004-2011		$1,325	$1,725
355 Series			
1998-2011. Jumbo 12-string, mahogany or sapele back and sides, sitka spruce top.			
1998-2006	355	$1,000	$1,300
1998-2011	355ce	$1,100	$1,400
356 Series			
2014-2019. Grand Symphony 12-string, sitka spruce top, sapele back and sides , non-cut, cutaway, or ce cutaway electric.			
2014-2019	356ce	$1,100	$1,400
362 Series			
2019-present. Grand Concert 12-string, mahogany top, blackwood back and sides.			
2019-2021	362ce V-Class	$1,450	$1,875
363 Series			
2020	363ce V-Class	$1,450	$1,875
410 Series			
1991-2018. Dreadnought, mahogany back and sides until '98, ovangkol after '98, sitka spruce top. Non-cut offered again in '13 along with 410e version.			
1991-2006	410	$900	$1,175
1991-2018	410ce	$1,000	$1,275
2000	410-MA, maple	$1,200	$1,575
412 Series			
1991-present. Grand Concert, mahogany back and sides until '98, ovangkol after, sitka spruce top. Cutaway electric version replaced the 412 in '98. Non-cut offered again in '13 along with 412e version.			
1991-1998	412	$1,325	$1,725
1996	412-K (Koa)	$1,550	$2,000
1998-2020	412ce	$1,550	$2,000
1998-2021	412ce-R	$1,600	$2,100
414 Series			
1998-present. Grand Auditorium, ovangkol back and sides, sitka spruce top. Non-cut offered again in '13 along with 414e version.			
1998	414-K (Koa)	$1,550	$2,000
1998-2006	414	$1,325	$1,725
1998-2021	414ce	$1,550	$2,000
2019-2021	414ce-R V-Class	$1,550	$2,000
414ce-LTD			
2013. Limited Edition, sitka spruce top, tropical mahogany neck.			
2013		$1,100	$1,425
414-L10			
2005. Limited Edition, rosewood sides and back, gloss spruce top, satin finish.			
2005		$1,100	$1,425

MODEL YEAR	FEATURES	EXC. COND. LOW	HIGH
414-L30			
2004. Limited Edition 30th Anniversary, Hawaiian koa back and sides, Engelmann spruce top, pearl and gold 30th Anniversary inlay.			
2004		$1,225	$1,575
415 Series			
1998-2006. Jumbo, ovangkol back and sides, sitka spruce top.			
1998-2006	415ce	$1,100	$1,425
416 Series			
2011-2019. Grand Symphony, ovangkol back and sides, sitka spruce top.			
2011-2019	416ce	$1,175	$1,525
418 Series			
2015-2019. Grand Orchestra, ovangkol back and sides, sitka spruce top.			
2015-2019	418e	$1,175	$1,525
420			
1990-1997. Dreadnought, Indian rosewood back and sides, sitka spruce top.			
1990-1997		$1,025	$1,325
422 Series			
1991-1998. Grand Concert, solid maple construction.			
1991-1998	422-K (Koa)	$1,300	$1,700
1997	422-R (Rosewood)	$1,300	$1,700
426ce-LTD			
2008. Limited Edition, Tasmanian blackwood top, back and sides.			
2008		$1,500	$1,950
450			
1996-1997. Dreadnought 12-string, mahogany back and sides, spruce top.			
1996-1997		$1,050	$1,350
454ce			
2004-2011. Grand Auditorium 12-string, Ovangkol back and sides, sitka spruce top.			
2004-2011		$1,125	$1,475
455 Series			
2001-2011. Jumbo 12-string, Ovangkol back and sides, sitka spruce top.			
2001-2006	455	$1,125	$1,450
2001-2011	455ce	$1,175	$1,550
455ce-LTD			
2001-2003. Limited Edition, imbuia back and sides.			
2001-2003		$1,300	$1,700
456 Series			
2012-2016. Grand Symphony 12-string.			
2012-2016	456e and 456ce	$1,600	$2,100
458e			
2016-2019. Grand Orchestra 12-string.			
2016-2019		$1,600	$2,100
510 Series			
1978-2017. Dreadnought, mahogany back and sides, spruce top. Non-cut offered again in '13 along with 510e version.			
1978-2006	510	$1,150	$1,500
1978-2017	510ce	$1,250	$1,600
510ce-AB 25th Anniversary			
1999. Limited Edition, 25th Anniversary on headstock, spruce top, mahogany back, sides and neck.			
1999		$1,900	$2,450

MODEL YEAR	FEATURES	EXC. COND. LOW	HIGH

510-LTD
2002. Limited Edition, mahogany back and sides, sitka spruce top.

2002		$1,275	$1,650

512 Series
1978-present. Grand Concert, mahogany back and sides, red cedar top. Non-cut offered again in '13-'16 along with 512e version.

1978-2000	512	$1,200	$1,550
1978-2000	512c	$1,250	$1,600
1978-2021	512ce	$1,300	$1,650
2012-2016	512ce-N	$1,300	$1,650

512ce-L10
2005. Limited Edition, American mahogany body and neck, abalone soundhole rosette, pearl diamond inlays, gold tuners.

2005		$1,300	$1,650

512-NG Nanci Griffith
1996-1997. 512ce with sunburst finish.

1996-1997		$1,700	$2,200

514 Series
1990-present. Grand Auditorium, mahogany back and sides, Engelmann or sitka spruce top. Western red cedar top on 514c and ce. Non-cut offered again in '13-'16 along with 514e version. V-Class introduced '20.

1990-1998	514	$1,550	$2,000
1996-1998	514c	$1,600	$2,050
1998-2021	514ce	$1,650	$2,100

515-LTD
1981. Limited Edition, mahogany back and sides, black binding, tortoise 'guard.

1981		$1,575	$2,050

516 Series
2008-2019. Grand Symphony, mahogany back and sides, Engelmann spruce top. Non-cut 516 offered in '13 along with 516e version.

2008-2019	516ce	$1,575	$2,050

516ce-LTD
2010. Spring Limited Editions, Tasmanian blackwood back and sides, sitka spruce top.

2010		$2,150	$2,800

518 Series
2012-2014. Grand Orchestra, tropical mahogany back and sides, sitka spruce top, tortoise 'guard.

2012-2014	518/518e	$1,575	$2,050

522 Series
2013-present. Grand Concert, all tropical mahogany. V-Class introduced '20.

2013-2018	522	$1,500	$1,950
2013-2019	522e	$1,550	$2,000
2013-2021	522ce	$1,600	$2,050

524ce-LTD
2018. Grand Auditorium, all walnut.

2018		$2,150	$2,800

554 Series
2004-2005. Grand Auditorium 12-string, mahogany.

2004-2005	554	$1,775	$2,300

555 Series
1978-2006. Jumbo 12-string, mahogany back and sides, sitka spruce top, higher-end appointments.

1994-2006	555	$1,550	$2,000
1994-2006	555ce	$1,650	$2,100

562 Series
2019-present. Grand Concert 12-strings, V-Class bracing, mahogany top.

2019-2021	562ce	$1,650	$2,100

610 Series
1978-2017. Dreadnought, big leaf maple back and sides, sitka spruce top. Non-cut offered again in '13 along with 610e version.

1978-1998	610	$1,775	$2,300
1998-2017	610ce	$1,875	$2,400
2013-2017	610e	$1,825	$2,350

612 Series
1984-present. Grand Concert, big leaf maple back and sides, sitka spruce top. Non-cut offered again in '13 along with 612e version. V-Class introduced '20.

1984-1998	612	$1,775	$2,300
1998-2021	612ce	$1,875	$2,400
2013-2016	612e	$1,825	$2,350

614 Series
1978-present. Grand Auditorium, big leaf maple back and sides, sitka spruce top. Non-cut offered again in '13 along with 614e version. V-Class introduced '20.

1978-1998	614	$1,775	$2,300
1998-2021	614ce	$1,875	$2,400
2013-2016	614e	$1,825	$2,350

615 Series
1981-2011. Jumbo, big leaf maple back and sides, sitka spruce top.

1981-1998	615	$1,775	$2,300
1981-1998	615e	$1,825	$2,350
1998-2011	615ce	$1,875	$2,400

616 Series
2008-2019. Grand Symphony, big leaf maple back and sides, sitka spruce top. Non-cut 616 offered in '13-'16 along with 616e version.

2008-2019	616ce	$2,200	$2,900
2013-2016	616e	$1,800	$2,350

618 Series
2013-present. Grand Orchestra, sitka spruce top, big leaf maple back and sides.

2013-2021	618e	$1,800	$2,350

654 Series
2004-2011. Grand Suditorium 12-string, big leaf maple back and sides, sitka spruce top.

2004-2011	654ce	$1,775	$2,300

655 Series
1978-1991, 1996-2011. Jumbo 12-string, big leaf maple back and sides, sitka spruce top.

1978-2006	655	$1,675	$2,200
1998-2011	655ce	$1,775	$2,300

656 Series
2008-2019. Grand Symphony 12-string, big leaf maple back and sides.

2018-2019	656ce	$1,775	$2,300

710 Series
1977-2017. Dreadnought, Indian rosewood back and sides, Englemann or sitka spruce top. Non-cut offered again in '13 along with 710e version.

1977-2006	710 (Spruce)	$1,550	$2,000
1990s	710-BR (Brazilian)	$2,500	$3,300

Taylor 612ce

Taylor 618e

GUITARS

2001 Taylor 710ce
Jeff Mangan

Taylor 914ce

MODEL YEAR	FEATURES	EXC. COND. LOW	HIGH
1998-2006	710 (Cedar)	$1,550	$2,000
1998-2017	710ce (Cedar)	$1,800	$2,350

710-B 25th Anniversary
1999. Limited Edition, 25th Anniversary on head-stock, spruce top, abalone rosette, Brazilian rosewood sides and back, mahogany neck.

1999		$2,500	$3,300

710ce-L30
2004. Limited Edition 30th Anniversary, Englemann top, Indian rosewood body, 30th Anniversary inlay.

2004		$1,450	$1,875

712 Series
1984-present. Grand Concert, Indian rosewood back and sides, Englemann or sitka spruce top. Non-cut offered again in '13 along with 712e version. V-Class introduced '20.

1984-2006	712	$1,775	$2,300
2000-2021	712ce	$1,875	$2,400
2013-2019	712e	$1,825	$2,350

714 Series
1996-present. Grand Auditorium, Indian rosewood back and sides, red cedar top. Non-cut offered again in '13-'16 along with 714e version. V-Class introduced '20.

1996-2006	714	$1,775	$2,300
1998-2019	714ce	$1,875	$2,400
2020-2021	714ce, V-Class	$2,000	$2,600

714-BRZ
1997. Brazilian rosewood, cedar, fancy.

1997		$3,800	$4,900

714ce-L1
2003-2004. Limited Edition, Western red cedar top, grafted walnut sides and back, pearl inlay, Hawaiian koa rosette.

2003-2004		$2,000	$2,600

714ce-S-LTD
2015. Limited Edition Grand Auditorium, sitka spruce top, blackheart sassafras back and sides.

2015		$2,000	$2,600

716ce
2007-2019. Grand Symphony, lutz spruce, Indian rosewood.

2007-2019		$2,000	$2,600

716ce-LTD
2009. Limited Edition, sitka spruce top, Madagascar rosewood back and sides.

2009		$2,000	$2,600

750
1990-2000s. Dreadnought 12-string, spruce top.

1990-2000s		$1,800	$2,325

755
1990-1998. Jumbo 12-string, rosewood back and sides.

1990-1998		$1,800	$2,325

810 Series
1975-2017. Classic Dreadnought, Indian rosewood back and sides, sitka spruce top. Non-cut offered again in '13 along with 810e version.

1975-2006	810	$1,800	$2,350
1975-2006	810e	$1,850	$2,400
1993-1998	810c	$1,850	$2,400
1996-2016	810ce-BR (Brazilian)	$2,900	$3,800
1996-2017	810ce	$1,900	$2,450

810-L30
2004. Limited Edition 30th Anniversary, maple leaf inlays, soundhole rosette, 30th Anniversary logo.

2004		$2,150	$2,800

810ce-LTD
2010. Limited Edition, Venetian cutaway, Madagascar rosewood back and sides, solid sitka spruce top.

2010		$2,250	$2,925

812 Series
1985, 1993-present. Grand Concert, Indian rosewood back and sides, sitka spruce top. Non-cut offered again in '13-'16 along with 812e version. V-Class introduced '20.

1985	812	$1,800	$2,350
1993-1998	812c	$1,850	$2,400
1998-2019	812ce	$1,900	$2,450
2013-2016	812e	$1,850	$2,400
2019-2021	812ce V-Class	$2,400	$3,200

814 Series
1993-present. Grand Auditorium, Indian rosewood back and sides, sitka spruce top. Non-cut offered again in '13 along with 814e version. V-Class introduced '20.

1993-1998	814	$2,300	$3,000
1996-1998	814c	$2,350	$3,050
1998-2019	814ce	$2,400	$3,100
2000	814-BE (Brazilian/ Englemann)	$2,900	$3,800
2020-2021	814ce V-Class	$2,400	$3,100

814ce-LTD
2012. Spring Limited Edition, cocobolo back and sides, sitka spruce top.

2012		$2,300	$3,000

815 Series
1970s-2011. Jumbo, Indian rosewood back and sides, sitka spruce top.

1970s-2006	815	$2,150	$2,800
1993-1998	815c	$2,200	$2,850
1997	815c-BR (Brazilian)	$2,900	$3,800
1998-2011	815ce	$2,250	$2,900

816 Series
2008-2019. Grand Symphony, sitka spruce top, Indian rosewood back and sides.

2008-2014	816e	$2,200	$2,850
2008-2019	816ce	$2,250	$2,900
2013-2016	816	$2,150	$2,800

818 Series
2014-present. Grand Orchestra, sitka spruce, Indian rosewood. V-Class introduced '20.

2014-2019	818e	$2,200	$2,850

854ce-LTD
2002. Grand Auditorium 12-string, Indian rosewood back and sides, sitka spruce top.

2002		$2,300	$3,000

855 Series
1981-2011. Jumbo 12-string, Indian rosewood back and sides, sitka spruce top.

1981-2011	855	$1,875	$2,450
2004-2011	855ce	$1,925	$2,500

MODEL YEAR	FEATURES	EXC. COND. LOW	HIGH

856 Series
2012-2019. Grand Symphony 12-string, sitka spruce, Indian rosewood.

2012-2018	856e	$1,900	$2,450
2013-2019	856ce	$1,950	$2,500

910 Series
1977-2017. Dreadnought, maple back and sides, changed to Brazilian rosewood in '86, wide abalone-style rosette. Non-cut offered again in '13 along with 910e version, Indian rosewood back and sides, sitka spruce top.

1977-1985	910 Maple	$2,700	$3,500
1986-2006	910 Brazilian	$4,600	$6,000
1998-2016	910ce	$2,800	$3,600

912 Series
1993-present. Grand Concert, Indian rosewood back and sides, Engelmann spruce top, abalone. Non-cut offered in '13 along with 912e version. V-Class introduced '20.

1993-2002	912c	$2,850	$3,700
1993-2019	912ce	$2,900	$3,750
2020-2021	912ce V-Class	$3,100	$3,900

914 Series
1990s-present. Grand Concert, Indian rosewood back and sides, Engelmann spruce top. Non-cut offered in '13 along with 914e version. V-Class introduced '20.

2002-2019	914ce	$2,900	$3,750
2020-2021	914ce V-Class	$3,100	$3,900

914ce-L1
2003. Fall Limited Edition, Indian rosewood back and sides, Engelmann spruce top, abalone leaf and vine inlays.

2003		$2,900	$3,750

914ce-L7
2004. Sitka spruce top, Brazilian rosewood back and sides, abalone rosette.

2004		$4,500	$5,900

916 Series
2010-2019. Grand Symphony, Florentine cutaway, Indian rosewood back and sides.

2010-2019	916ce	$2,900	$3,750

918 Series
2013-2014. Grand Orchestra, sitka spruce top, Indian rosewood back and sides.

2013-2014	918e	$2,900	$3,750

955
1996-2000. Jumbo 12 string, rosewood back and sides, spruce top.

1996-2000		$2,900	$3,750

Academy Series
2017-present. Designed for beginner guitar players, 10 is D-size and 12 is 000-size, e indicates on-board electronics.

2017-2021	10	$385	$500
2017-2021	10e	$440	$575
2017-2021	12e	$440	$575
2017-2021	12e-N	$440	$575

American Dream Series (AD)
2020-present. Grand Pacific body style, wood pairings include sapele/mahogany and ovangkol/spruce, V-Class bracing, e indicates on-board electronics.

2020-2021	AD17	$875	$1,150
2020-2021	AD17e	$1,000	$1,300
2020-2021	AD27e	$1,000	$1,300
2020-2021	AD28e	$1,000	$1,300

Baby Taylor
1996-present. 3/4-size Dreadnought, mahogany laminated back and sides until '99, sapele laminate after, various tops.

1996-2021	BT1, sitka spruce	$220	$285
1998-2021	BT2, mahogany	$220	$285
2000-2003	BT3, maple	$220	$285
2010-2021	TSBT Taylor Swift	$220	$285
2016-2021	BTe-Koa	$290	$380

Baby Rosewood
2000-2003. Laminated Indian rosewood back and sides Baby.

2000-2003		$220	$285

Baritone 6
2010-2013. Grand Symphony 6-string baritone, Indian rosewood or mahogany back and sides.

2010-2013		$2,100	$2,700

Baritone 8/GT-8 Baritone
2010-2013. Grand Symphony 8-string baritone, Indian rosewood or mahogany back and sides.

2010-2013		$2,540	$3,300

Big Baby BBT
2000-present. 15/16-size Dreadnought, sapele laminate back and sides, sitka spruce top.

2000-2021		$300	$400

Builder's Edition
2018-present. New designs from master builders, premium features. All models have 'Builder's Edition' in the model name.

2019-2021	517	$2,000	$2,600
2019-2021	717	$2,000	$2,600
2020-2021	324ce	$1,900	$2,500
2020-2021	614ce	$2,600	$3,400
2020-2021	652ce	$2,600	$3,400
2020-2021	816ce	$2,550	$3,300
2020-2021	K-14ce Koa, vine inlay	$3,400	$4,400
2020-2021	K-24ce Koa	$3,400	$4,400

Builder's Reserve (BR)
A series of special limited guitars built using Taylor's private wood reserves accumulated 30-plus years.

2008	BR VII	$2,100	$2,700

CPSM Chris Proctor Signature
2000-2001. Limited edition, 100 made, Indian rosewood body, Engelmann spruce top.

2000-2001		$1,925	$2,500

CUJO-10/CUJO-14
1997. Dreadnought (CUJO-10) or Grand Auditorium (CUJO-14), made from 100+ year old black walnut tree appearing in famous Stephen King movie "Cujo" (1983). Robert Taylor purchased the tree when it was dying of old age. The DN has spruce top, GA has cedar, both have elaborate appointments and are signed by Taylor and King. Only 125 made of each.

1997		$1,700	$2,200

Taylor American Dream AD27e

Taylor Builder's Edition 652ce

Taylor GT K21e

Taylor PS14ce

MODEL YEAR	FEATURES	EXC. COND. LOW	HIGH
Custom Dreadnought/Custom DN			
2008-2017	AA+ Indian/ Adirondack	$2,400	$3,100
Custom Grand Auditorium			
2008-2017	Adirondack/ mahogany	$2,900	$3,800
2008-2021	Figured koa	$3,600	$4,800
2008-2021	Spruce/maple	$2,900	$3,800
Custom Grand Concert			
2008-2017	Various woods	$2,900	$3,800

Custom TF

2011. Acoustic-electric, slotted headstock, rosewood, Taylor Build To Order program.

2011		$2,100	$2,700

DCSM Dan Crary Signature

1986-2000. Dreadnought, Venetian cutaway, thin spruce top, Indian rosewood back and sides, Crary signature on headstock.

1986-2000		$1,800	$2,300

DDAD Doyle Dykes Signature Anniversary

2005. Indian rosewood back and sides, soft cutaway, on-board transducer.

2005		$2,850	$3,700

DDSM Doyle Dykes Signature

2000-2012. Grand auditorium cutaway acoustic/electric, figured maple body.

2000-2012		$2,850	$3,700

DDSM-LTD Doyle Dykes Desert Rose Edition

2000-2003. Grand Auditorium, Limited Edition, 72 offered, sitka spruce, flamed maple, on-board electronics.

2000-2003		$3,000	$3,900

DMSM Dave Matthews Signature

2010-2012. Limited Edition based on 914ce, Taylor Expression pickup system.

2010-2012		$4,100	$5,400

DN Series

2007-2012. Dreadnought Series, various woods.

2007-2011	DNK (koa)	$1,900	$2,500
2007-2012	DN3	$850	$1,125
2007-2012	DN5	$1,275	$1,650
2007-2012	DN8	$1,350	$1,750

E14ce Limited Edition

2018-2019. Grand Auditorium, Venetian cutaway, V-Class bracing, spruce top, African ebony back and sides, natural finish.

2018-2019		$2,100	$2,700

GA Limited Editions

1995. Grand Auditorium Limited Editions. GA-BE has Brazilian rosewood back and sides with Engelmann spruce top, KC has koa/cedar, KS koa/spruce, MC mahogany/cedar, RS Indian rosewood/spruce, and WS walnut/spruce.

1995	GABE (Brazilian)	$4,300	$5,600
1995	GAKC (Koa)	$2,700	$3,500
1995	GAMC (Cedar)	$2,400	$3,100
1995	GARS (Indian)	$2,400	$3,100
1995	GAWS (Walnut)	$2,550	$3,300

MODEL YEAR	FEATURES	EXC. COND. LOW	HIGH
GA Series			

2007-2012. Grand Auditorium Series, various woods.

2007-2012	GA3, sitka/sapele	$850	$1,125
2007-2012	GA3-12	$850	$1,125
2007-2012	GA4, sitka/ovangkol	$950	$1,225
2007-2012	GA5, cedar/ mahogany	$1,275	$1,650
2007-2012	GA6, sitka/ flamed maple	$1,425	$1,850
2007-2012	GA6-12	$1,475	$1,900
2007-2012	GA7, cedar/ rosewood	$1,425	$1,850
2007-2012	GA8, sitka/ rosewood	$1,350	$1,750
2008-2012	GA-K-12, cedar/koa	$2,100	$2,700
2012	GACE (Fall LE)	$2,000	$2,575
2013	GAMC (Fall LE)	$2,000	$2,575

GC Series

2007-2012. Grand Concert Series, various woods.

2007-2012	GC3, sitka/sapele	$850	$1,125
2007-2012	GC4, sitka/ovangkol	$950	$1,225
2007-2012	GC5, cedar/ mahogany	$1,275	$1,650
2007-2012	GC6, sitka/fmaple	$1,425	$1,850
2007-2012	GC7, cedar/rosewood	$1,425	$1,850
2007-2012	GC8, sitka/ rosewood	$1,350	$1,750
2011	GC-LTD, all mahogany	$1,350	$1,750

GS Series

2006-present. Grand Symphony Series, various woods.

2007	GS4E-LTD	$1,275	$1,650
2007-2012	GS3, sitka/sapele	$850	$1,125
2007-2012	GS5, cedar/ mahogany	$1,275	$1,650
2007-2012	GS5-12, cedar/ mahogany	$1,350	$1,750
2007-2012	GS6, sitka/fmaple	$1,425	$1,850
2007-2012	GS7, cedar/rosewood	$1,425	$1,850
2007-2012	GS8, sitka/rosewood	$1,350	$1,750
2007-2012	GS8-12, sitka/ rosewood	$1,450	$1,875
2011-2021	GS Mini	$325	$425
2019-2021	GS Mini-e Koa	$525	$675
2019-2021	GS Mini-e Mahogany	$450	$575
2019-2021	GS Mini-e Plus	$625	$825

GT Series

2020-present. Grand Theater Series, various woods, e indicates on-board electronics.

2020-2021	GT, sitka/ash	$900	$1,175
2020-2021	GT811e, sitka/Indian	$1,950	$2,525
2020-2021	GTe, sitka/ash	$1,050	$1,350
2020-2021	GTK21e, all koa	$3,100	$4,000

Hot Rod Limited Edition HR14-LTD/HR15-LTD

2003. Grand Auditorium (HR14) or Jumbo (HR15), 32 of each made, natural finish with red-stained back and sides or gloss black with transparent black.

2003		$2,275	$2,950

The *Vintage Guitar Price Guide* shows low to high values for items in all-original excellent condition, and, where applicable, with original case or cover.

MODEL YEAR	FEATURES	EXC. COND. LOW	HIGH

K Series
1983-present. Koa Series, various models with Hawaiian koa. V-Class introduced '20.

1983-1992	K20	$2,050	$2,650
1983-2006	K10	$1,700	$2,225
1992-2002	K20c	$2,100	$2,700
1995-1998	K65, 12-string	$2,700	$3,500
1998-2000	K22	$2,150	$2,750
1998-2002	K14c	$1,800	$2,350
1998-2012	K14ce	$1,950	$2,525
2001-2006	K55, 12-string	$2,250	$2,900
2001-2016	K20ce	$2,150	$2,750
2003-2021	K22ce	$2,250	$2,900
2007-2011	K54ce	$2,800	$3,650
2007-2012	K10ce	$1,800	$2,350
2007-2021	K24ce	$2,600	$3,400
2008-2021	K26ce	$2,600	$3,400
2020-2021	K24ce V-Class	$2,600	$3,400

LKSM-6/12 Leo Kottke Signature
1981-2012. Jumbo 17" body, 6- or 12-string, rounded cutaway, sitka spruce top, mahogany back and sides, gloss finish, Leo Kottke signature.

1981-2012	12-string	$2,300	$3,000
1981-2012	6-string	$2,200	$2,900

LTG Liberty Tree L.E.
2002. Limited Edition includes DVD and certificate which are important to instrument's value, solid wood grand concert body, high-end art and appointments. Around 400 made.

2002		$5,300	$6,900

NS Series
2002-2011. Nylon Strung series, various models and woods, models include NS24e/NS24ce (Indian rosewood/spruce), NS32ce/NS34ce (mahogany/spruce), NS42ce/NS44ce (ovangkol), NS52ce/NS54ce (mahogany), NS62ce/NS64ce (maple/Engelmann) and NS72ce/NS74ce (Indian rosewood/cedar). All models were cutaway electric (ce) by '04, until '10 when NS24e was offered.

2002-2006	NS42ce	$875	$1,150
2002-2006	NS44/NS44ce	$1,000	$1,300
2002-2006	NS52ce	$1,025	$1,325
2002-2006	NS54ce	$1,175	$1,525
2002-2011	NS32ce	$850	$1,100
2002-2011	NS62ce	$1,500	$1,950
2002-2011	NS64ce	$1,525	$1,975
2002-2011	NS72ce	$1,700	$2,225
2002-2011	NS74/NS74ce	$1,987	$2,575
2004-2011	NS34ce	$875	$1,125
2010-2011	NS24e/NS24ce	$600	$775

PS Series
1996-present. Presentation Series, various models, Hawaiian koa with Engelmann spruce used early on, followed by Brazilian rosewood, by '07 a variety of woods were offered, values vary depending on specs and appointments.

1996-2021	Various options	$4,500	$7,600

Solidbody Classic
2008-2014. Single- or double-cut, ash body, 2 humbuckers or single-coils, pearl 'guard.

2008-2014		$875	$1,125

Solidbody Custom
2008-2010. Single- or double-cut, koa top with Tasmanian blackwood body in '08 and mahogany after or walnut top with sapele body, 2 humbuckers, diamond inlays, ivoroid binding.

2008-2010		$1,350	$1,750

Solidbody Standard
2008-2014. Single- or double-cut, Tamo ash top ('08-'09) and maple after, sapele body (08-'10) and mahogany after, 2 exposed coil humbuckers, ivoroid binding.

2008-2014		$775	$1,000

T3 Series
2009-2020. Semi-hollow thinline, single-cut, figured maple. T3/B with Bigsby.

2009-2020	T3, T3/B	$1,675	$2,175

T5/T5z Series
2005-2020. T5 '05-'19 and T5z introduced '20, semi-hollow thinline body, sapele back and sides, spruce, maple, or koa tops, Custom models have gold hardware and Artist inlays, Standard is chrome with micro-dots. Prices will vary depending on type of figured-wood used, figured maple and koa will be more than plain tops.

2005-2021	12-string	$1,850	$2,400
2005-2021	6-string	$1,850	$2,400

Walnut/W Series
1998-2006. Highly figured claro walnut backs and sides with spruce, cedar or walnut tops. Ivoroid, ebony, gold and abalone accents.

1998-2000	W12c	$1,925	$2,500
1998-2006	W10	$1,775	$2,300
2000-2006	W14ce	$1,975	$2,550

WHCM Windham Hill
2003. Commemorative Model, D-size, spruce top, rosewood sides and back, fancy appointments with Windham Hill logo inlay.

2003		$1,650	$2,150

XX 20th Anniversary Series
1994. Limited Edition, grand auditorium, "XX" solid 18 karat gold inlay, mother-of-pearl inlay, abalone rosette, available either mahogany back and sides with cedar top (XX-MC) or Indian rosewood with spruce (XX-RS).

1994	XX-MC	$2,500	$3,200
1994	XX-RS	$2,500	$3,200

XXV 25th Anniversary
1999-2000. Dreadnought (XXV-DR) and grand auditorium (XXV-GA) models, various woods.

1999-2000	Both models	$1,850	$2,400

XXX 30th Anniversary Series
2004-2005 Limited Edition, grand concert, "XXX" solid 18 karat gold inlay, fancy appointments, XXX-BE has Brazilian rosewood back and sides with Engelmann spruce top, KE has koa/Engelmann spruce, MS maple/spruce and RS Indian rosewood/spruce.

2004-2005	XXX-BE	$4,100	$5,300
2004-2005	XXX-KE	$2,500	$3,300
2004-2005	XXX-MS	$2,400	$3,200
2004-2005	XXX-RS	$2,400	$3,200

Taylor T-5
Charlie Brown

Taylor XXV-GA 25th Anniversary

Teisco Del Rey ET-230
Tom Pfeifer

Teisco May Queen
Rivington Guitars

MODEL YEAR	FEATURES	EXC. COND. LOW	HIGH

XXXV 35th Anniversary Series
2009. Limited Edition, various models and woods, "35" between the 11th and 12th frets. Models include DN (Dreadnought), GC (Grand Concert), GS (Grand Symphony), P (Parlor), TF (12-Fret), 9-string, plus more.

2009	All models	$2,400	$3,200

Taylor/R. Taylor Guitars
2006-2011. Bob Taylor set up the R. Taylor studio with a small group of elite luthiers to handcraft a limited amount of guitars each year, using higher grade materials and offered in a few body styles - essentially custom made models. Each style has a number of options.

Style 1

2006-2009	Various options	$2,850	$3,700

Teisco
Founded in 1946 in Tokyo, Japan by Hawaiian and Spanish guitarist Atswo Kaneko and electrical engineer Doryu Matsuda, the original company name was Aoi Onpa Kenkyujo; Teisco was the instrument name. Most imported into U.S. by Jack Westheimer beginning ca. '60 and Chicago's W.M.I. Corporation beginning around '64, some early ones for New York's Bugeleisen and Jacobson. Brands made by the company include Teisco, Teisco Del Rey, Kingston, World Teisco, Silvertone, Kent, Kimberly and Heit Deluxe.

In '56, the company's name was changed to Nippon Onpa Kogyo Co., Ltd., and in '64 the name changed again to Teisco Co., Ltd. In January '67, the company was purchased by Kawai. After '73, the brand was converted to Kay in U.S.; Teisco went into hiatus in Japan until being beifly revived in the early-'90s with plexiglas reproductions of the Spectrum 5 (not available in U.S.). Some older Teisco Del Rey stock continued to be sold in U.S. through the '70s.

Electric

1966-1969	1 pickup	$200	$300
1966-1969	2 pickups	$300	$400
1966-1969	3 pickups	$400	$500
1966-1969	4 pus or sparkle	$600	$850
1966-1969	Spectrum V	$750	$975
1968-1969	May Queen, black	$750	$975
1968-1969	May Queen, red	$750	$975
1968-1969	Phantom	$750	$975

Tele-Star
1965-ca.1972. Imported from Japan by Tele-Star Musical Instrument Corporation of New York, New York. Primarily made by Kawai, many inspired by Burns designs, some in cool sparkle finishes. They also built basses.

Electric

1966-1969	1, 2, 3 pickups	$400	$525
1966-1969	4 pus or sparkle	$450	$575
1966-1969	Amp-in-case	$350	$450
1969-1970	Double neck 6/4	$700	$925

Tempo
1950s-1970s. Solid and semi-hollow body electric and acoustic guitars, most likely imported by Merson Musical Products from Japan. They also offered basses and amps.

Terada
Japanese guitar manufacturer began producing semi-acoustic and acoustic guitars in the year 1912. They have made guitars for Ibanez, Orville by Gibson, Epiphone Japan, Gretsch, and other well-known brands. At their peak (late '70s to early '90s), they were producing around 10,000 guitars a month using 3 factories. Terada's output is presently about 1/8 of what it was at their peak.

Teuffel
1988-present. Luthier Ulrich Teuffel builds his production/custom, premium and presentation grade electric solidbody guitars in Neu-Ulm, Bavaria, Germany.

Texas
1959-ca. 1965. Line of aluminum neck electric solidbodies and basses made by France's Jacobacci company, which also built under its own brand. One, two, or three pickups.

Teye
2006-present. Luthier Teye Wijterp builds his premium and presentation grade, production/custom, solid and chambered body guitars in Austin, Texas. Some instruments are branded as Electric Gypsy guitars.

Thomas
1960s-1970s. Single, double and triple-neck electrics made by luthier Harvey Thomas in Midway, Washington. Best known for his Maltese cross shaped models, he also offered several other unique shaped designs and one-offs.

Thomas Rein
1972-present. Luthier Thomas Rein builds his premium grade, production/custom, classical guitars in St. Louis, Missouri.

Thompson Guitars
1980-present. Luthier Ted Thompson builds his professional and premium grade, production/custom, flat-top, 12-string, and nylon-string guitars in Vernon, British Columbia.

Thorell Fine Guitars
1994-present. Premium grade, custom/production, archtop, flattop and classical guitars built by luthier Ryan Thorell in Logan, Utah.

Thorn Custom Guitars
2000-present. Professional and premium grade, custom/production, solid and hollowbody electrics built

MODEL		EXC. COND.	
YEAR	FEATURES	LOW	HIGH

by luthiers Bill Thorn and his sons Bill, Jr. and Ron in Glendale, California. They started Thorn Custom Inlay in the early '90s to do custom inlay work for other builders. In '00, they added their own line of guitars.

Thornward

Ca. 1901-ca. 1910. Line of guitars sold by the Montgomery Ward company and built by others including Lyon & Healy. The name is from a combination of last names of company founder Aaron Montgomery Ward and company manager George Thorne.

Threet Guitars

1990-present. Premium grade, production/custom, flat-tops built by luthier Judy Threet in Calgary, Alberta.

Tilton

1850s-late 1800s. Built by William B. Tilton, of New York City, New York. He was quite an innovator and held several guitar-related patents. He also built banjos.

Parlor

1850s-1890s. Parlor guitar with various woods.

1850s-80s	Brazilian, fancy binding	$1,900	$2,500
1890s	Diagonal grain spruce, Brazilian	$1,525	$2,000
1890s	Pearl trim, Brazilian	$2,850	$3,700
1890s	Standard grain spruce, Brazilian	$800	$1,050

Tim Reede Custom Guitars

2004-present. Luthier Tim Reede builds his professional and premium grade, production/custom, archtop, flat-top and electric guitars in Minneapolis, Minnesota.

Timeless Instruments

1980-present. Luthier David Freeman builds his professional, premium and presentation grade, custom, flattop, 12-string, nylon-string, and resonator guitars in Tugaske, Saskatchewan. He also builds mandolins and dulcimers.

Timm Guitars

Professional grade, custom, flat-top, resonator and travel guitars built by luthier Jerry Timm in Auburn, Washington. He started in 1997.

Timtone Custom Guitars

1993-2006. Luthier Tim Diebert built his premium grade, custom, solidbody, chambered-body and acoustic guitars and basses in Grand Forks, British Columbia. He also built lap steels.

Tippin Guitar Co.

1978-present. Professional, premium and presentation grade, production/custom, flat-top guitars built by luthier Bill Tippin in Marblehead, Massachusetts.

MODEL		EXC. COND.	
YEAR	FEATURES	LOW	HIGH

Tobias

1977-2019. Known mainly for basses, Tobias did offer guitar models in the '80s. See Bass Section for more company info.

TogaMan GuitarViol

2003-present. Premium grade, production/custom, bow-playable solidbody guitars built by luthier Jonathan Wilson in Sylmar, California.

Tokai

1947-present. Japan's Tokai Company started out making a keyboard harmonica that was widely used in Japanese schools. In '65, they started producing acoustic guitars, followed shortly by electrics. In the late '60s, Tokai hooked up with Tommy Moore, a successful instrument merchandiser from Fort Worth, Texas, and by '70 they were producing private label and OEM guitars, sold in the U.S. under the brands of various importers. By the '70s, the Tokai name was being used on the instruments. Today Tokai continues to offer electrics, acoustics, and electric basses made in Japan and Korea.

ASD-403 Custom Edition

1980s. Strat copy, single-single-hum pickups, locking tremolo.

1980s		$625	$825

AST Series

Early 1980s. Strat copies, maple board (AST-56) or slab rosewood (AST-62), 3 single-coils.

1980s	AST-56	$725	$975
1980s	AST-62	$725	$975

ATE Series

Early 1980s. Tele copies, blond (ATE-52) and pink paisley (ATE-67), 2 single-coils.

1980s	ATE-52	$750	$975
1980s	ATE-67	$750	$975

Blazing Fire

1982-1984. Hybrid-shaped solidbody with 2 medium-short pointy horns, cast aluminum body.

1982-1984		$625	$825

Breezy Sound

1977-1984. Copy of '60s rosewood board Tele.

1977-1984		$625	$825

CE-180W Cat's Eyes

Late-1970s-Early-1980s. D-style flat-top, made by Tokai Gakki, Nyatoh sides and back.

1979-1980s		$300	$400

CE-250 Cat's Eyes

Late-1970s-Early-1980s. D-style flat-top.

1979-1980s		$300	$400

CE-300 Cat's Eyes

Late-1970s-Early-1980s. D-style flat-top, made by Tokai Gakki, rosewood sides and back.

1979-1980s		$450	$575

CE-400 Cat's Eyes

Late-1970s-Early-1980s. D-style flat-top, made by Tokai Gakki, rosewood sides and back.

1979-1980s		$625	$825

Tele-Star
Imaged by Heritage Auctions, HA.com

Late-'90s Tobias
Greg Perrine

GUITARS

Tom Anderson Hollow T
Curtis Hill

Tony Nobles Baritone

MODEL YEAR	FEATURES	EXC. COND. LOW	HIGH
CE-600 Cat's Eyes			
1979-1980. D-style flat-top, rosewood sides and back.			
1979-1980		$625	$825
FV48			
1980s. Flying V copy.			
1980s		$725	$950
Goldstar Sound			
1984. Replica that replaced the Springy Sound, new less pointy headstock shape.			
1984		$625	$825
J-200N			
1979-1980. Gibson J-200 natural copy.			
1979-1980		$625	$825
Les Paul Reborn			
1976-1985. LP copy with Gibson-style Tokai headstock logo and Les Paul Reborn script logo instead of Les Paul Model, renamed Reborn Old in '82, becomes Love Rock in mid-'80s.			
1976-1982	Les Paul Reborn	$875	$1,150
1982-1985	Reborn Old	$875	$1,150
Love Rock/LS Series			
1980s-2000s. Various LP Std copy models (LC are LP Custom copies), 2 humbuckers, sunburst, gold top, black, figured tops at the high end, Love Rock in script logo on headstock.			
1980s		$875	$1,150
2003	LS 75 Love Rock	$875	$1,150
2003	LS 80 Love Rock	$875	$1,150
SC Series			
Tele copies.			
2000s	SC-1	$450	$575
Silver Star			
1977-1984. Copy of post-CBS large headstock Strat.			
1977-1984		$525	$700
Springy Sound/ST-60			
1977-1984. Strat copy, original high-end nitro-finish.			
1977-1979	With skunk stripe	$975	$1,275
1979-1984	No skunk stripe	$975	$1,275
Vintage Series EX-55			
1980s. Vintage Series, Explorer copies, bolt neck, 1 or 2 humbuckers.			
1980s	1 pickup	$625	$825
1980s	2 pickups	$700	$900
Vintage Series TST			
Early-1980s. Copy of maple neck (TST-56) and rosewood slab board (TST-62) Strats, 4-bolt neck plate with serial number.			
1980s	TST-56	$750	$975
1980s	TST-62	$750	$975

Tom Anderson Guitarworks

1984-present. Professional and premium grade, production/custom, solidbody, semi-solidbody and acoustic guitars built by luthier Tom Anderson in Newbury Park, California.

Solidbody Electric

1984-present. Various models.

1984-2021	Most models	$2,000	$3,000

TommyHawk

1993-2005. Acoustic travel guitars built by luthier Tom Barth in Succasunna, New Jersey. They also offered a full-scale acoustic/electric model. Barth died in '05.

Toneline

1950s. Student-level private brand built by Chicago builders (Kay, Harmony). Typical '50s Stella brand specs like birch body with painted binding and rosette, pointed Toneline script logo on headstock.

Tonemaster

1960s. Guitars and basses, made in Italy by the Crucianelli Company, with typical '60s Italian sparkle plastic finish and push-button controls, bolt-on neck. Imported into the U.S. by The Imperial Accordion Company. They also offered guitar amps.

Rhythm Tone

1960-1963. Tonemaster headstock logo, Rhythm Tone logo on 'guard, single neck pickup, 3-in-line control knobs, bolt-on neck, black finish.

1960-1963		$875	$1,150

ToneSmith

1997-present. Luthier Kevin Smith builds his professional and premium grade, production/custom, semi-hollow body guitars and basses in Rogers, Minnesota. He previously built GLF brand guitars and built the line of Vox USA guitars from '98-'01.

Tony Nobles

Professional and premium grade, custom, acoustic and electric guitars built by luthier Tony Nobles in Wimberley, Texas starting in 1990.

Tony Vines Guitars

1989-present. Luthier Tony Vines builds his premium and presentation grade, custom/production, steel string guitars in Kingsport, Tennessee.

Torres (Antonio de Torres Jurado)

19th Century luthier most often associated with the initial development of the Classical Spanish guitar.

Tosca

1950s. Private economy brand made by Valco, possibly for a jobber, mail-order catalog or local department store.

Bolero 1123

1954-1957. Small three-quarter size electric similar to National (Valco) model 1123, single-cut, 1 neck pickup, guard mounted controls.

1954-1957		$825	$1,100

Toyota

1972-1970s. Imported from Japan by Hershman of New York, New York. At least 1 high-end acoustic designed by T. Kurosawa was ambitiously priced at $650.

MODEL		EXC. COND.	
YEAR	FEATURES	LOW	HIGH

Traphagen, Dake

1972-present. Luthier Dake Traphagen builds his premium grade, custom, classical and steel-string guitars in Bellingham, Washington.

Traugott Guitars

1991-present. Premium grade, production/custom, flat-top and acoustic/electric guitars built by luthier Jeff Traugott in Santa Cruz, California.

Traveler Guitar

1992-present. Intermediate grade, production, travel size electric, acoustic, classical and acoustic/electric guitars and basses made in Redlands, California.

Travis Bean

1974-1979, 1999. Aluminum-necked solidbody electric guitars and basses. The company was founded by motorcycle and metal-sculpture enthusiast Travis Bean and guitar repairman Marc McElwee in Southern California; soon joined by Gary Kramer (see Kramer guitars). Kramer left Travis Bean in '75 and founded Kramer guitars with other partners. Guitar production began in mid-'76. The guitars featured carved aluminum necks with three-and-three heads with a T cutout in the center and wooden 'boards. Some necks had bare aluminum backs, some were painted black. A total of about 3,650 instruments were produced. Travis Bean guitar production was stopped in the summer of '79.

Serial numbers were stamped on headstock and were more-or-less consecutive. Original retail prices were $895 to $1195.

The company announced renewed production in '99 with updated versions of original designs and new models, but it evidently never got going.

TB-500

1975-1976. Aluminum neck, T-slotted headstock, double-cut, 2 single coils mounted in 'guard, 2 controls, dot markers, white.

1975-1976		$4,800	$6,300

TB-1000 Artist

1974-1979. Aluminum neck, T-slotted headstock, double-cut archtop, 2 humbuckers, 4 controls, block inlays.

1974-1979		$4,800	$6,300
1974-1979	Rare colors	$5,500	$7,200

TB-1000 Standard

1974-1979. Similar to TB-1000 Artist, but with dot inlays.

1974-1979		$4,400	$5,800

TB-3000 Wedge

1976-1979. Aluminum neck with T-slotted headstock, triangle-shaped body, 2 humbucking pickups, 4 controls, block markers on 'board.

1976-1979		$5,200	$6,700

Tregan Guitars

2007-present. Solidbody electrics including Bison-style sharp curved horns body style, plus other less traditional styles, student and intermediate grade.

Tremblett Archtops

Luthier Mark Tremblett started in the year 2006, he builds professional grade, custom, archtop guitars in Pouch Cove, Newfoundland.

Tremcaster

2008-present. Luthier John Mosconi, along with Robert Gelley and Jeff Russell, builds professional grade, production/custom, electric and acoustic guitars in Akron, Ohio.

Trenier

1998-present. Premium grade, production/custom, archtop guitars built by luthier Bryant Trenier in Seattle, Washington. From '02 to '04 he was located in Prague, Czech Republic.

Triggs

1992-present. Luthiers Jim Triggs and his son Ryan build their professional and premium grade, production/custom, archtop, flat-top, and solidbody guitars originally in Nashville Tennessee, and, since '98, in Kansas City, Kansas. They also build mandolins.

Acoustic/Electric Archtop

1992-present. Various archtop cutaway models.

1992-2009	Byrdland 17"	$2,000	$2,700
1992-2009	Excel 17"	$3,000	$4,000
1992-2009	Jazzmaster	$1,650	$2,200
1992-2009	New Yorker 18"	$4,400	$5,800
1992-2010	Stromberg		
	Master 400	$4,400	$5,800
1997	Trinity 18"	$4,400	$5,800
2006	San Salvador	$2,700	$3,500

Trinity River

Located in Fort Worth, Texas, luthiers Marcus Lawyer and Ross McLeod import their production/custom, budget and intermediate grade, acoustic and resonator guitars and basses from Asia. They also import mandolins and banjos.

True North Guitars

1994-present. Luthier Dennis Scannell builds his premium grade, custom, flat-tops in Waterbury, Vermont.

True Tone

1960s. Guitars, basses and amps retailed by Western Auto, manufactured by Chicago guitar makers like Kay. The brand was most likely gone by '68.

Double Cutaway (K300 Kay)

1962-1966. Made by Kay and similar to their K300, double-cut solidbody, dual pickups and vibrola arm, red.

1962-1966		$450	$600

Tony Vines CX

Traveler Acoustic AG-105

GUITARS

Truetone Speed Master
Tom Pfeifer

Univox Hi Flier
Charlie Brown

MODEL YEAR FEATURES	EXC. COND. LOW	HIGH

Double Cutaway Electric Archtop (K592 Kay)
1960s. Made by Kay and similar to their K592 double-cut thinline acoustic, 2 pickups, Bigsby tailpiece, burgundy red.

1960s	$500	$650

Fun Time
Early- to mid-1960s. Student 13" flat-top, painted 5-point 'guard, red sunburst finish.

1960s	$75	$100

Imperial Deluxe
Mid-1960s. Harmony-made (Rocket), 3 pickups, trapeze tailpiece, 6 control knobs, block markers, sunburst.

1960s	$625	$825

Jazz King (K573 Kay)
1960s. Kay's K573 Speed Demon, 3 pickups, thinline archtop electric with f-hole, eighth note art on 'guard, sunburst.

1960s	$450	$600

Rock 'n Roll Electric (K100 Kay)
1960s. Kay's K100, slab body, single pickup, but with a bright red multiple lacquer finish.

1960s	$350	$450

Speed Master (K6533 Kay)
1960s. Made by Kay and similar to their K6533 full-body electric archtop Value Leader line, eighth note art 'guard, sunburst.

1960s	$375	$500

Western Spanish Auditorium
Early- to mid-1960s. 15" flat-top, laminate construction, celluloid 'guard, sunburst.

1960s	$150	$200

Tsunami
Custom, intermediate grade, one-off solidbody electric guitars built by luthier Paul Brzozowski, starting in 2009, in Cleveland, Tennessee.

Tucker
Founded by John N. "Jack" Tucker, John Morrall, and David Killingsworth in 2000, Tucker builds professional and premium grade, production/custom, albizzia wood solidbody guitars and basses in Hanalei, Hawaii.

Tuscany Guitars
2008-2013. Intermediate grade, production, classic model electric guitars imported from Asia and finished by luthier Galeazzo Frudua in San Lazzaro di Savena, Italy.

Tut Taylor
Line of professional and premium grade, production/custom, resophonic guitars built by luthier Mark Taylor of Crafters of Tennessee in Old Hickory, Tennessee. Brand named for his father, dobro artist Tut Taylor. Taylor also builds the Tennessee line of guitars, mandolins and banjos and was part of Rich and Taylor guitars for '93-'96.

MODEL YEAR FEATURES	EXC. COND. LOW	HIGH

TV Jones
1993-present. Professional and premium grade, production/custom, hollow, chambered, and solid body guitars built by luthier Thomas Vincent Jones originally in California, now in Poulsbo, Washington. The instruments have either Jones or TV Jones inlaid on the headstock. He also builds pickups.

U. A. C.
1920s. Instruments built by the Oscar Schmidt Co. and possibly others. Most likely a brand made for a distributor.

Unique Guitars
2003-ca. 2007. Professional and premium grade, production/custom, solidbody guitars and basses built by luthier Joey Rico in California. Joey is the son of Bernie Rico, the founder of BC Rich guitars.

Univox
1964-1978. Univox started out as an amp line and added guitars around '68. Guitars were imported from Japan by the Merson Musical Supply Company, later Unicord, Westbury, New York. Many if not all supplied by Arai and Company (Aria, Aria Pro II), some made by Matsumoku. Univox Lucy ('69) first copy of lucite Ampeg Dan Armstrong. Generally mid-level copies of American designs.

Acoustic Flat-Top
1969-1978. Various models.

1970s	$200	$600

Bicentennial
1976. Offset double-cut, heavily carved body, brown stain, 3 humbucker-style pickups.

1976	$850	$1,100

Deep Body Electric

1960s-70s	ES-175 style	$525	$675

Guitorgan FSB C-3000
1970s. Double-cut semi-hollow body, multiple controls, Guitorgan logo on headstock, footpedal.

1970s	Fully functional	$1,250	$1,625

Solid Body Electric
1960s-1970s. Includes Flying V, Mosrite and Hofner violin-guitar copies.

1960s-70s	Hi Flier	$650	$850
1960s-70s	Various models	$600	$800
1970s	Effector	$600	$800

Thin Line (Coily)

1960s-70s	12-string	$525	$675
1960s-70s	6-string	$525	$675

USA Custom Guitars
1999-2020. Professional and premium grade, custom/production, solidbody electric guitars built in Tacoma, Washington. They also did work for other luthiers. In late '20, USA was acquired by MJT Aged Guitar Finishes in Carthage, Missouri.

Vaccaro
1997-2002. Founded by Henry Vaccaro, Sr., one of the founders of Kramer Guitars. They offered

MODEL YEAR	FEATURES	EXC. COND. LOW	HIGH

intermediate and professional grade, production/custom, aluminum-necked guitars and basses designed by Vaccaro, former Kramer designer Phil Petillo, and Henry Vaccaro, Jr., which were made in Asbury Park, New Jersey.

Val Dez

Early-1960s-early-1970s. Less expensive guitars built by Landola in Sweden or Finland; they also made the Espana brand.

Valco

1942-1968. Valco, of Chicago, was a big player in the guitar and amplifier business. Their products were private branded for other companies like National, Supro, Airline, Oahu, and Gretsch. In '42, National Dobro ceased operations and Victor Smith, Al Frost and Louis Dopyera bought the company and changed the name to Valco Manufacturing Company. Post-war production resumed in '46. Valco was purchased by treasurer Robert Engelhardt in '64. In '67, Valco bought Kay, but in '68 the new Valco/Kay company went out of business.

Valencia

1985-present. Budget grade, production, classical guitars imported first by Rondo Music of Union, New Jersey and presently distributed by others.

Valley Arts

Ca. 1977-2010. Professional and premium grade, production/custom, semi-hollow and solidbody guitars and basses built in Nashville, Tennessee. Valley Arts originally was a Southern California music store owned by partners Al Carness and Mike McGuire where McGuire taught and did most of the repairs. Around '77, McGuire and Valley Arts started making custom instruments on a large scale. By '83, they opened a separate manufacturing facility to build the guitars. In '92 Samick acquired half of the company with McGuire staying on for a year as a consultant. Samick offered made-in-the-U.S. production and custom models under the Valley Arts name. In '02, Valley Arts became a division of Gibson Guitar Corp., which builds the guitars in Nashville. Founders Carness and McGuire were once again involved with the company. They reintroduced the line in January, '03. The brand has been inactive since '10.

Vantage

1977-1998. Budget and intermediate grade, production, acoustic and electric guitars and basses from Japan '77-'90 and from Korea '90-'98.

Vega

1889-1980s, 1989-present. Founded in Boston by the Nelson family, Vega was big in the banjo market into the 1930s, before adding guitars to their line. The company was purchased by C.F. Martin

MODEL YEAR	FEATURES	EXC. COND. LOW	HIGH

in '70 who built Vega banjos and starting in '76 they also used the brand on imported guitars, first from the Netherlands and later from Japan, with the Japanese Vegas being of higher quality. In '79, Martin sold the Vega trademark to Korea's Galaxy Trading Company. The Deering Banjo Company, in Spring Valley, California acquired the brand in '89 and uses it (and the star logo) on a line of banjos.

C Series (Archtop)

1933-1950s. Carved-top archtops, '30's models are the 14 5/8" mahogany body C-20 and C-40, 16 1/8" maple body C-60, and the C-70/C75 Vehaphone with rosewood body and gold parts, and the figured-maple body C-80 with deluxe appointments. By '40 the line was the 14-16" C-19, -26, -46, and -56, and the 17" Professional Series C-66 Professional, C-71 Soloist, C-76 Artist, and C-86 Deluxe. Optional blond finish available by '40.

MODEL YEAR	FEATURES	EXC. COND. LOW	HIGH
1933-1939	C-20	$975	$1,275
1933-1939	C-40	$975	$1,275
1933-1939	C-60	$1,475	$1,925
1933-1939	C-70	$1,675	$2,175
1933-1939	C-80	$1,875	$2,450
1938	C-75	$2,875	$3,725
1940-1949	C-19, C-26, C-46	$850	$1,100
1940-1949	C-56	$1,550	$2,000
1940-1949	C-66 Professional	$1,625	$2,100
1940-1949	C-71 Soloist	$1,700	$2,200
1940-1949	C-76 Artist	$1,850	$2,400
1940-1949	C-86 Deluxe	$1,950	$2,500

Duo-Tron Series (Electric Archtop)

1947-late 1950s. Various mid-level large body cutaway and non-cut carved-top archtops, 1, 2 or 3 (rare) floating pickups, dot or block markers, natural or sunburst.

MODEL YEAR	FEATURES	EXC. COND. LOW	HIGH
1947-50s	High-end models	$2,400	$3,150
1947-50s	Low-end models	$725	$950
1947-50s	Mid-range models	$1,075	$1,400

E-201 Electric Archtop

1959. One pickup, sunburst.

MODEL YEAR	FEATURES	EXC. COND. LOW	HIGH
1959		$1,725	$2,250

FT-90 Flat-Top

1960s. 15" body with narrow waist, dot markers, Vega logo, natural.

MODEL YEAR	FEATURES	EXC. COND. LOW	HIGH
1960s		$400	$525

G-30

1968-ca. 1970. D-style with solid spruce top and solid mahogany sides and back, Vega logo with star on headstock, dot markers, natural finish.

MODEL YEAR	FEATURES	EXC. COND. LOW	HIGH
1968-1970		$325	$425

O'Dell

1950s. Full body, single cut, acoustic-electric, 1 pickup, tailpiece controls.

MODEL YEAR	FEATURES	EXC. COND. LOW	HIGH
1950s	Sunburst	$1,050	$1,350

Parlor

Early-1900s-1920s. Small parlor-sized instrument, styles and appointment levels, including binding, purfling and inlays, vary.

MODEL YEAR	FEATURES	EXC. COND. LOW	HIGH
1900s	Mahogany	$425	$550
1910s	Brazilian	$925	$1,275
1910s-20s	Brazilian, fancy	$3,600	$4,700

Vega C-26
Imaged by Heritage Auctions, HA.com

1938 Vega C-75 Vegaphone
Michael J. Scanlon

To get the most from this book, be sure to read "Using *The Guide*" in the introduction.

GUITARS

Ventura Bruno VS III
W. H. Stephens

Versoul Henry
Kari Nieminen

MODEL YEAR	FEATURES	EXC. COND. LOW	EXC. COND. HIGH

Profundo Flat-Top
1930s-1950s. Flat-top D-style body, spruce top, mahogany or rosewood back and sides.

1930s-50s	Mahogany	$1,500	$1,950
1940s-50s	Rosewood	$2,300	$3,000

Solidbody Electric (Import)
1970s-1980s. Solidbody copies of classic designs, Vega script logo on headstock, bolt-on necks.

1970s		$275	$365

Vega Electric Archtop
1939. Full-body electric archtop, figured maple, 1 pickup, 2 control knobs, trapeze bridge, diamond markers, large Vega and star headstock logo, blond.

1939		$1,200	$1,600

Vega, Charles
1993-2010. Luthier Charles Vega built his premium, production/custom, nylon-string guitars in Baltimore, Maryland.

Veillette
1991-present. Luthiers Joe Veillette (of Veillette-Citron fame) and Martin Keith build their professional grade, production/custom, acoustic, acoustic/electric, electric 6- and 12-string and baritone guitars and basses in Woodstock, New York. They also build mandolins.

Veillette-Citron
1975-1983. Founded by Joe Veillette and Harvey Citron who met at the New York College School of Architecture in the late '60s. Joe took a guitar building course from Michael Gurian and by the Summer of '76, he and Harvey started producing neck-thru solidbody guitars and basses. Veillette and Citron both are back building instruments.

Velázquez
1948-1972. Manuel Velázquez, New York, New York, gained a reputation as a fine repairman in the late 1940s. He opened his 3rd Avenue guitar building shop in the early 1950s. By the mid-1950s he was considered by some as being the finest American builder of classical guitars. Velázquez left New York in 1972 and moved to Puerto Rico. He continued building guitars for the Japanese market. He returned to the United States in 1982. By the 2000s he built instruments with this son and daughter.

Veleno
1967, 1970-1977, 2003-2018. Premium and presentation grade, production/custom, all-aluminum electric solidbody guitars built by luthier John Veleno in St. Petersburg, Florida. First prototype in '67. Later production begins in late-'70 and lasts until '75 or '76. The guitars were chrome or gold-plated, with various anodized colors. The Traveler Guitar was the idea of B.B. King; only 10 were made. Two Ankh guitars were made for Todd Rundgren in '77. Only one bass was made. Approximately 185 instruments were made up to '77 and are sequentially numbered. In 2003, John Veleno reintroduced his brand, he died in '18.

Original (Aluminum Solidbody)
1973-1976. V-headstock, chrome and aluminum.

1973-1976	Rare color	$9,200	$12,000
1973-1976	Standard	$5,500	$7,200

Traveler
1973-1976. Limited production of about a dozen instruments, drop-anchor-style metal body.

1973-1976		$9,200	$12,000

Vengeance Guitars & Graphix
2002-present. Luthier Rick Stewart builds his professional and premium grade, custom/production, solidbody guitars and basses in Arden, North Carolina.

Ventura
1970s. Acoustic and electric guitars imported by C. Bruno Company, mainly copies of classic American models. They also offered basses.

Acoustic Flat-Top

1970s		$425	$550

Guitorgan
1970s. Based on MCI Guitorgan, converts standard electric guitar into a Guitorgan through the addition of electronic organ components, multiple switches, large Barney Kessel sharp-horned acoustic-electric style body.

1970s		$1,050	$1,350

Hollowbody Electric

1970s		$650	$850

Solidbody Electric

1970s		$650	$850

Verri
Premium grade, production/custom, archtop guitars built by luthier Henry Verri in Little Falls, New York starting in 1992.

Versoul, LTD
1989-present. Premium grade, production/custom steel-string flat-top, acoustic/electric, nylon-string, resonator, solidbody, and baritone guitars, basses and sitars built by luthier Kari Nieminen in Helsinki, Finland.

VibraWood
2012-present. Luthier John J. Slog builds custom, professional and premium grade, vintage-style guitars and basses in Bethlehem, Pennsylvania.

Vicente Tatay
1894-late 1930s. Classical guitars built by luthier Vicente Tatay and his sons in Valencia, Spain.

Victor Baker Guitars
1998-present. Professional and premium grade, custom, carved archtop, flat-top and solidbody electric guitars built by luthier Victor Baker in Philadelphia, Pennsylvania. In '10 he relocated to Brooklyn, New York and is currently in Astoria.

MODEL YEAR	FEATURES	EXC. COND. LOW	HIGH

Victor Guitars

2002-2008. Luthiers Edward Victor Dick and Greg German built their premium grade, production/custom, flat-top guitars in Denver, Colorado.

Victoria

Ca. 1902-1920s. Brand name for New York distributor Buegeleisen & Jacobson. Instruments built by the Oscar Schmidt Co. and possibly others. Most likely a brand made for a distributor.

Vigier

1980-present. Luthier Patrice Vigier builds high-end electric guitars and basses near Paris, France.

Electric Solidbody

1980-present. Various models.

MODEL YEAR	FEATURES	LOW	HIGH
1980	Arpege	$2,050	$2,650
2000-2006	Expert	$2,100	$2,700
2005-2021	Excalibur Shawn Lane	$2,100	$2,700
2020-2021	Excalibur Special	$2,425	$3,150
2020-2021	Excalibur Supra 7	$2,000	$2,600
2020-2021	Excalibur Thirteen	$2,100	$2,700
2020-2021	Excalibur Ultra Blues	$2,300	$3,000
2021	Texas Blues	$2,000	$2,600

Viking Guitars

2003-present. Premium grade, solidbody guitars made by Ed Roman Guitars. Production was '03-'04, custom only since.

Vinetto

2003-present. Luthier Vince Cunetto builds his professional grade, production/custom, solid, chambered and semi-hollow body guitars in St. Louis, Missouri.

Vintage

Ca. 1993-present. Intermediate grade, production, solidbody and semi-hollow acoustic, electro-acoustic and resonator guitars and basses, imported from China, Korea and Vietnam by John Hornby Skewes & Co. in the U.K. They also offer folk instruments.

Vintique

Luthier Jay Monterose built premium grade, custom/production, electric guitars in Suffern, New York. Vintique also manufactured guitar hardware.

Vivi-Tone

1932-1938. Founded in Kalamazoo, Michigan, by former Gibson designer Lloyd Loar, Walter Moon and Lewis Williams, Vivi-Tone built acoustic archtop guitars as well as some of the earliest electric solidbodies. They also built basses and mandolins and offered amps built by Webster Electric. A Vivi-Tone instrument must be all original. Any missing part makes this instrument practically unsellable in the vintage-market.

MODEL YEAR	FEATURES	EXC. COND. LOW	HIGH

Various Models

1932-1938	Rare models	$3,200	$4,200
1932-1938	Standard models	$2,400	$3,200
1932-1938	Tenor, 4-string	$1,900	$2,500

Vox

1954-present. Name introduced by Jennings Musical Instruments (JMI) of England. First Vox products was a volume pedal, amplifiers were brought to the market in late '57 by Tom Jennings and Dick Denny. Guitars were introduced in '61, with an Echo Unit starting the Vox line of effects in '63.

Guitars and basses bearing the Vox name were offered from '61-'69 (made in England and Italy), '82-'85 (Japan), '85-'88 (Korea), '98-2001 (U.S.), and they introduced a limited edition U.S.-made teardrop guitar in '07 and the semi-hollow Virage guitars in '08. Vox products are currently distributed in the U.S. by Korg USA.

Ace/Super Ace

1963-1968. Offset double cut solidbody, 2 single-coils. Super Ace has 3 pickups.

1963-1968	Ace	$650	$850
1963-1968	Super Ace	$850	$1,100

Apache

1960s. Modified teardrop body, 3 pickups, vibrato.

1966		$850	$1,100

Apollo

1967-1968. Single sharp cutaway, 1 pickup, distortion, treble and bass booster, available in sunburst or cherry.

1967-1968		$850	$1,100

Bobcat

1963-1968. Double-cut semi-hollowbody style, block markers, 3 pickups, vibrato, 2 volume and 2 tone controls.

1963-1965	England	$1,200	$1,600
1966-1968	Italy	$850	$1,100

Bossman

1967-1968. Single rounded cutaway, 1 pickup, distortion, treble and bass booster, available in sunburst or cherry.

1967-1968		$625	$825

Bulldog

1966. Solidbody double-cut, 3 pickups.

1966		$1,200	$1,550

Delta

1967-1968. 5-sided Phantom shaped solidbody, 2 pickups, distortion, treble and bass boosters, vibrato, 1 volume and 2 tone controls, available in white only.

1967-1968		$1,500	$2,000

Folk XII

1966-1969. Dreadnought 12-string flat-top, large 3-point 'guard, block markers, natural.

1966-1969		$400	$525

Guitar-Organ

1966. Standard Phantom with oscillators from a Continental organ installed inside. Plays either organ sounds, guitar sounds, or both. Weighs over 20 pounds. Prices vary widely due to operating issues with this model.

1966	Fully functional	$2,500	$3,300
1966	Functional 'board	$1,500	$2,000
1966	Partial function	$750	$1,000

Vintage V100 M
Thomas Booth

Vox Bossman
Imaged by Heritage Auctions, HA.com

GUITARS

1998 Vox Mark III
Frank Quarracino

Vox Tornado

MODEL YEAR	FEATURES	EXC. COND. LOW	HIGH

Harlem
1965-1967. Offset double-cut solidbody, 2 extended range pickups, sunburst or color option. Values vary widely due to operating issues with this model.

1965-1967		$850	$1,100

Hurricane
1965-1967. Double-cut solidbody, 2 pickups, spring action vibrato, sunburst or color option.

1965-1967		$725	$950

Invader (V262)
1966-1967. Solidbody double-cut, 2 pickups, on-board effects, sunburst. Must have fully-functional electronics.

1966-1967		$2,150	$2,800

Mando Guitar
1966. Made in Italy, 12-string mandolin thing.

1966		$1,200	$1,550

Mark III (U.S.A)
1998-2001. Teardrop reissue, made in U.S.A., 2 single-coils, fixed bridge or Bigsby. A limited was introduced in '08.

1998-2001		$925	$1,200

Mark III 50th Anniversary
2007. Only 100 made, teardrop body, 2 pickups, white finish.

2007		$1,125	$1,450

Mark III Limited Edition
2008. Custom Shop USA model, white hardwood body, maple neck, rosewood 'board.

2008		$1,900	$2,500

Mark III/Phantom Mark III
1963-1964. Made in England, teardrop body, 2 pickups, 2 controls, Marvin Bigsby, guitar version of Mark IV bass, while it is called a Phantom Mark III it does not have a Phantom shape.

1963-1964		$3,100	$4,100

Mark IX
1965-1966. Solidbody teardrop-shaped, 9 strings, 3 pickups, vibrato, 1 volume and 2 tone controls.

1965-1966		$1,450	$1,900

Mark VI
1965-1967. Teardrop-shaped solidbody, 3 pickups, vibrato, 1 volume and 2 tone controls.

1964-1965	England, white, Brian Jones	$3,700	$4,800
1965-1967	Italy, sunburst	$2,100	$2,800

Mark VI Reissue
1998-2001. Actually, this is a reissue of the original Phantom VI (Vox couldn't use that name due to trademark reasons), made in U.S.A.

1998-2001		$850	$1,100

Mark XII
1965-1967. Teardrop-shaped solidbody, 12 strings, 3 pickups, vibrato, 1 volume and 2 tone controls, sunburst. Reissued for '98-'01.

1965-1967		$1,700	$2,200

Meteor/Super Meteor
1965-1967. Solidbody double-cut, 1 pickup, Super Meteor with vibrato.

1965-1967	Meteor	$500	$650
1965-1967	Super Meteor	$550	$700

New Orleans
1966. Thin double-cut acoustic electric similar to ES-330, 2 pickups, a scaled down version of the 3-pickup Bobcat model.

1966		$800	$1,050

Phantom VI
1962-1967. Five-sided body, 6 strings, 3 pickups, vibrato, 1 volume and 2 tone controls.

1962-1964	English-made	$3,400	$4,400
1965-1967	Italian-made	$2,200	$2,800

Phantom XII
1964-1967. 12 string version of VI.

1964	English-made	$3,400	$4,400
1965-1967	Italian-made	$2,200	$2,800

Phantom XII Stereo
1966. Phantom XII with 3 special offset stereo pickups making 6 pickup conbinations, 3 separate pickup mode selectors, color option.

1966		$2,400	$3,200

Shadow
1965. Solidbody double-cut, 3 pickups, tremolo tailpiece, sunburst.

1965	English-made	$925	$1,200

Spitfire
1965-1967. Solidbody double-cut, 3 pickups, vibrato.

1965-1967		$850	$1,100

Starstream
1967-1968. Teardrop-shaped hollowbody, 2 pickups, distortion, treble and bass boosters, wah-wah, vibrato, 1 volume and 2 tone controls, 3-way pickup selector, available in cherry or sandburst.

1967-1968		$1,850	$2,400

Starstream XII
1967-1968. 12 string version.

1967-1968		$1,850	$2,400

Stroller
1961-1966. Made in England, solidbody, single bridge pickup, Hurricane-style contoured body, dot markers, red.

1961-1966		$325	$700

Student Prince
1965-1967. Made in Italy, mahogany body thinline archtop electric, 2 knobs, dot markers.

1965-1967		$450	$575

Super Lynx
1965-1967. Similar to Bobcat but with 2 pickups and no vibrola, double-cut, 2 pickups, adjustable truss rod, 2 bass and 2 volume controls.

1965-1967		$850	$1,100

Super Lynx Deluxe
1965-1967. Super Lynx with added vibrato tailpiece.

1965-1967		$850	$1,100

Tempest XII
1965-1967. Solidbody double-cut, 12 strings, 3 pickups.

1965-1967		$850	$1,100

Thunder Jet
1960s-style with single pickup and vibrato arm.

1960s		$625	$825

MODEL YEAR	FEATURES	EXC. COND. LOW	HIGH

Tornado
1965-1967. Thinline archtop, single pickup, dot markers, sunburst.

1965-1967		$450	$600

Typhoon
1965-1967. Hollowbody single-cut, 2 pickups, 3-piece laminated neck.

1965-1967		$525	$675

Ultrasonic
1967-1968. Hollowbody double-cut, 2 pickups, distortion, treble and bass boosters, wah-wah, vibrato, 1 volume and 2 tone controls, 3-way pickup selector, available in sunburst or cherry.

1967-1968	12-string	$1,850	$2,400
1967-1968	6-string	$1,850	$2,400

Viper
1968. Double-cut, thinline archtop electric, built-in distortion.

1968		$1,300	$1,700

Virage/Virage II
2008-2014. Semi-hollowbody made in Japan, single-cut or double (II), 2 triple-coil pickups.

2008-2014		$1,900	$2,500

Wildcat
1965-1967. Single-cut acoustic-electric archtop, 1 pickup, Wildcat and Vox logos on 'guard, dot markers.

1965-1967		$500	$650

W. J. Dyer
See listing under Dyer.

Wabash
1950s. Acoustic and electric guitars distributed by the David Wexler company and made by others, most likely Kay. They also offered lap steels and amps.

Walden Guitars
Luthier Jonathan Lee of Portland, Oregon imports production, budget to professional grade, acoustic, acoustic-electric and classical guitars from Lilan, China. He began in 1996.

Walker
1994-present. Premium and presentation grade, production/custom, flat-top and archtop guitars built by luthier Kim Walker in North Stonington, Connecticut.

Walker (Kramer)
1981. Kramer came up with idea to offer this brand to produce wood-neck guitars and basses; they didn't want to dilute the Kramer aluminum-neck market they had built up. The idea didn't last long, and few, if any, of these instruments were produced, but prototypes exist.

Wandre (Davoli)
Ca. 1956/57-1969. Solidbody and thinline hollowbody electric guitars and basses created by German-descended Italian motorcycle and guitar enthusiast, artist, and sculptor from Milan, Italy, Wandre Pioli. Brands include Wandre (pronounced Vahn-dray), Davoli, Framez, JMI, Noble, Dallas, Avalon, Avanti I and others. Until '60, they were built by Pioli himself; from '60-'63 built in Milan by Framez; '63-'65 built by Davoli; '66-'69 built in Pioli's own factory.

The guitars originally used Framez pickups, but from '63 on (or earlier) they used Davoli pickups. Mostly strange shapes characterized by neck-thru-tailpiece aluminum neck with plastic back and rosewood 'board. Often multi-color and sparkle finishes, using unusual materials like linoleum, fiberglass and laminates, metal bindings. Often the instruments will have numerous identifying names but usually somewhere there is a Wandre blob logo.

Distributed early on in the U.K. by Jennings Musical Industries, Ltd. (JMI) and in the U.S. by Don Noble and Company. Model B.B. dedicated to Brigitte Bardot. Among more exotic instruments were the minimalist Krundaal Bikini guitar with a built-in amplifier and attached speaker, and the pogo stick Swedenbass. These guitars are relatively rare and highly collectible. In '05, the brand was revived on a line of imported intermediate grade, production, solidbodies from Eastwood guitars.

Electric
1956-1969	Common models	$2,900	$3,800
1956-1969	Rare models	$3,800	$9,600

Warren
2005-present. Luthier Don Warren builds his professional and premium grade, custom/production, solidbody electric guitars in Latham, New York.

Warrior
1995-present. Professional, premium, and presentation grade, production/custom, acoustic and solidbody electric guitars and basses built by luthier J.D. Lewis in Rossville, Georgia.

Washburn
1962-present. Budget, intermediate, professional, and premium grade, production/custom, acoustic and electric guitars and basses made in the U.S., Japan, and Korea. They also make amps, banjos and mandolins.

Originally a Lyon & Healy brand, the Washburn line was revived on a line of imports in '62 by Roland who sold it to Beckman Musical Instruments in '74/'75. Beckman sold the rights to the Washburn name to Fretted Instruments, Inc. in '76. Guitars originally made in Japan and Korea, but production moved back to U.S. in '91. Currently Washburn is part of U.S. Music.

Washburn (Lyon & Healy)
1880s-ca.1949. Washburn was founded in Chicago as one of the lines for Lyon & Healy to promote high quality stringed instruments, ca. 1880s. The

Vox Ultrasonic
Imaged by Heritage Auctions, HA.com

Wandre Avalon Rock Oval

Waterloo WL-14 Scissortail

Wechter
Benjamin E. Rios

rights to manufacture Washburns were sold to J.R. Stewart Co. in '28, but rights to Washburn name were sold to Tonk Brothers of Chicago. In the Great Depression (about 1930), J.R. Stewart Co. was hit hard and declared bankruptcy. Tonk Brothers bought at auction all Stewart trade names, then sold them to Regal Musical Instrument Co. Regal built Washburns by the mid-'30s. The Tonk Brothers still licensed the name. These Washburn models lasted until ca. '49. In '62 the brand resurfaced on a line of imports from Roland.

Washington

Washington was a brand manufactured by Kansas City, Missouri instrument wholesalers J.W. Jenkins & Sons. First introduced in 1895, the brand also offered mandolins.

Waterloo

2014-present. Professional grade, production, acoustic guitars based on Depression-era models, built by Bill Collings in Austin, Texas. Waterloo was the original city name of Austin.

WL-12
2014-present. Parlor size, vintage-style sunburst finish.
2014-2021 $1,575 $2,050

WL-14 Scissortail
2014-present. Solid spruce top, maple back and sides, X-bracing.
2014-2021 $1,600 $2,100

WL-14LTR
2014-present. Acoustic 14.75", solid headstock, ladder bracing (L).
2014-2021 $1,450 $1,900

WL-14MH
2014-present. Parlor size, all mahogany.
2014-2021 $1,600 $2,100

WL-14X
2014-present. Acoustic 14.75", solid headstock, X bracing (X).
2014-2021 $1,600 $2,100

WL-JK
2014-present. Nick-named 'Jumbo King', 15.75" body, X-bracing. Optional East Indian rosewood back and sides.
2014-2021 $1,450 $1,900

WL-JK Deluxe
2014-present. Ornate appointments.
2014-2021 $1,950 $2,550

WL-K
2014-present. Lightweight 14.75", '30s Kel Kroyden inspired, optional hand-painted "Southwest' scene.
2014-2021 $1,575 $2,050

WL-S
2014-present. Slotted headstock 14", '30s Stella inspired, solid cherry wood back and sides, iced tea sunburst.
2014-2021 $1,525 $2,000

WL-S Deluxe
2014-present. Ornate appointments.
2014-2021 $2,100 $2,750

Waterstone

2003-present. Intermediate and professional grade, production/custom, electric solid and semi-hollowbody and acoustic guitars and basses imported from Korea by Waterstone Musical Instruments, LLC of Nashville, Tennessee.

Watkins/WEM

1957-present. Watkins Electric Music (WEM) was founded by Charlie Watkins. Their first commercial product was the Watkins Dominator (wedge Gibson stereo amp shape) in '57. They made the Rapier line of guitars and basses from the beginning. Watkins offered guitars and basses up to '82. They currently build accordian amps.

Wayne

1998-present. Professional and premium grade, production/custom, solidbody guitars built by luthiers Wayne and Michael (son) Charvel in Paradise, California. They also build lap steels.

Webber

1988-2020. Professional grade, production/custom flat-top guitars built by luthier David Webber in North Vancouver, British Columbia. Webber retired in '20.

Weber

1996-present. Premium grade, production/custom, carved-top acoustic and resonator guitars built by luthier Bruce Weber and his Sound To Earth, Ltd. company, originally in Belgrade, Montana, in '04 moving to Logan, Montana. They also build mandolins. In '12, Two Old Hippies (Breedlove, Bedell) acquired the brand, moving production in '13 to Oregon where Bruce Weber oversees development.

Webster

1940s. Archtop and acoustic guitars, most likely built by Kay or other mass builder.

Model 16C Acoustic Archtop
1940s $600 $800

Wechter

1984-present. Intermediate, professional and premium grade, production/custom, flat-top, 12-string, resonator and nylon-string guitars and basses from luthier Abe Wechter in Paw Paw, Michigan. The Elite line is built in Paw Paw, the others in Asia. Until '94 he built guitars on a custom basis. In '95, he set up a manufacturing facility in Paw Paw to produce his new line and in '00 he added the Asian guitars. In '04, he added resonators designed by Tim Scheerhorn. Wechter was associated with Gibson Kalamazoo from the mid-'70s to '84. He also offers the Maple Lake brand of acoustics. In '08 he moved his shop to Fort Wayne, Indiana.

MODEL		EXC. COND.	
YEAR	FEATURES	LOW	HIGH

Weissenborn

1910s-1937, present. Hermann Weissenborn was well-established as a violin and piano builder in Los Angeles by the early 1910s. Around '20, he added guitars, ukes and steels to his line. Most of his production was in the '20s and '30s until his death in '37. He made tenor, plectrum, parlor, and Spanish guitars, ukuleles, and mandolins, but is best remembered for his koa Hawaiian guitars that caught the popular wave of Hawaiian music. That music captivated America after being introduced to the masses at San Francisco's Panama Pacific International Exposition which was thrown in '15 to celebrate the opening of the Panama Canal and attended by more than 13 million people. He also made instruments for Kona and other brands. The majority of his instruments were most likely sold before the late 1920s. The Weissenborn brand has been revived on a line of reissue style guitars.

Spanish Acoustic
1920s. High-end Spanish set-up, rope binding, koa top, sides and back, limited production.

1920s		$2,500	$3,300

Style #1 Hawaiian
1920-1930s. Koa, no binding, 3 wood circle soundhole inlays.

1920s-30s		$3,500	$4,500

Style #2 Hawaiian
1920-1930s. Koa, black celluloid body binding, white wood 'board binding, rope soundhole binding.

1920s-30s		$3,800	$5,000

Style #2 Spanish
1920s. Spanish set-up, Style 2 features.

1920s		$2,700	$3,600

Style #3 Hawaiian
1920-1930s. Koa, rope binding on top, 'board, and soundhole.

1920s-30s		$5,000	$6,500

Style #4 Hawaiian
1920-1930s. Koa, rope binding on body, 'board, headstock and soundhole.

1920s-30s		$6,000	$8,000

Teardrop
Late 1920s-1930s. Teardrop/spoon shaped, Style 1 features.

1930s		$850	$1,200

Tenor

1920-1927		$1,150	$1,500

Welker Custom

Professional and premium grade, production/custom, archtop and flat-top guitars built by luthier Fred Welker in Nashville, Tennessee.

Welson

1960s-1970s. Models made by Quagliardi, an accordion maker in Italy, ranging from acoustics to solidbodies, thinlines, archtops and basses. Some acoustic Welsons were sold in the U.S. by Wurlitzer. By the '70s, they had jumped on the copy-guitar bandwagon.

MODEL		EXC. COND.	
YEAR	FEATURES	LOW	HIGH

Electric

1960s	Various models	$300	$900

Wendler

1999-present. Intermediate and professional grade, production/custom, solidbody, electro-acoustic guitars and basses from luthier Dave Wendler of Ozark Instrument Building in Branson, Missouri. He also builds amps. In '91, Wendler patented a pickup system that became the Taylor ES system.

Westbury-Unicord

1978-ca. 1983. Imported from Japan by Unicord of Westbury, New York. High quality original designs, generally with 2 humbuckers, some with varitone and glued-in necks. They also had basses.

Westminster

One of the many guitar brands built by Japan's Matsumoku company.

Westone

1970s-1990, 1996-2001. Made by Matsumoku in Matsumoto, Japan and imported by St. Louis Music. Around '81, St. Louis Music purchased an interest in Matsumoku and began to make a transition from its own Electra brand to the Westone brand previously used by Matsumoku. In the beginning of '84, the brand became Electra-Westone with a phoenix bird head surrounded by circular wings and flames. By the end of '84 the Electra name was dropped, leaving only Westone and a squared-off bird with W-shaped wings logo. Electra, Electra-Westone and Westone instruments from this period are virtually identical except for the brand and logo treatment. Many of these guitars and basses were made in very limited runs and are relatively rare.

From '96 to '01, England's FCN Music offered Westone branded electric and acoustic guitars. The electrics were built in England and the acoustics came from Korea. Matsumoku-made guitars feature a serial number in which the first 1 or 2 digits represent the year of manufacture. Electra-Westone guitars should begin with either a 4 or 84.

Weymann

1864-1933. H.A. Weymann & Sons was a musical instrument distributor located in Philadelphia that marketed various stringed instruments, but mainly known for banjos. Some guitar models made by Regal and Vega, but they also built their own instruments.

Large Models

1890-1928	Most w/Brazilian	$4,000	$6,000
1928-1932	Most w/Brazilian	$5,000	$7,000

Small Models/Standard

1890-1928	Brazilian	$3,000	$5,000
1890-1928	Mahogany	$800	$1,300
1928-1932	Brazilian	$4,000	$6,000
1928-1932	Mahogany	$1,000	$1,500

Jimmie Rodgers Signature Edition

1929-1932		$7,000	$10,000

Westminster Archtop
W. H. Stephens

Weymann Style B
Bernunzio Uptown Music

Widman Koa Gigmaster

1966 Wurlitzer Gemini

Tom Pfeifer

MODEL		EXC. COND.	
YEAR	FEATURES	LOW	HIGH

White Guitars and Woodley White Luthier

1992-present. Premium grade, custom, classical, acoustic and electric guitars, built by luthier Woodley White, first in Portland, Oregon and since 2008 in Naalehu, Hawaii.

Wicked

2004-present. Production/custom, intermediate and professional grade, semi-hollow and electric solidbody guitars and basses built by luthier Nicholas Dijkman in Montreal, Quebec.

Widman Custom Electrics

2008-present. Professional and premium grade, custom, electric guitars built in Arden, North Carolina by luthier John Widman.

Wilkanowski

Early-1930s-mid-1940s. W. Wilkanowski primarily built violins. He did make a few dozen guitars which were heavily influenced by violin design concepts and in fact look very similar to a large violin with a guitar neck.

Wilkat Guitars

1998-2013. Professional grade, custom, electric guitars and basses built by luthier Bill Wilkat in Montreal, Quebec. He retired in '13.

Wilkins

1984-present. Custom guitars built by luthier Pat Wilkins in Van Nuys, California. Wilkins also does finish work for individuals and a variety of other builders.

William C. Stahl

See listing under Stahl.

William Hall and Son

William Hall and Son was a New York City based distributor offering guitars built by other luthiers in the mid to late 1800s.

William Jeffrey Jones

2006-present. Luthier William Jeffrey Jones builds his ornately carved, professional and premium grade, production/custom, solidbody and semi-hollow electric guitars in Neosho, Missouri.

Wilson

1960s-1970s. One of the brand names of guitars built in the 1960s for others by Egmond in Holland. Also a brand name used by the U.K.'s Watkins WEM in the 1960s and '70s.

Wilson Brothers Guitars

2004-present. Intermediate and professional grade, production, imported electric and acoustic guitars and basses. Founded by Ventures guitarist Don Wilson. VCM and VSP models made in Japan; VM electrics in Korea; VM acoustic in China.

MODEL		EXC. COND.	
YEAR	FEATURES	LOW	HIGH

Windsor

Ca. 1890s-ca. 1914. Brand used by Montgomery Ward for flat-top guitars and mandolins made by various American manufacturers, including Lyon & Healy and, possibly, Harmony. Generally beginner-grade instruments.

Winston

Ca. 1963-1967. Imported from Japan by Buegeleisen and Jacobson of New York. Manufacturers unknown, but some are by Guyatone. Generally shorter scale beginner guitars and basses.

Worland

1997-present. Luthier Jim Worland builds professional through presentation grade, production/custom, acoustic flat-top guitars and harp guitars in Rockford, Illinois. He also builds under the Worlatron brand.

Worlatron

2010-present. Professional grade, production/custom, hollowbody electric-acoustic guitars and basses built by luthier Jim Worland in Rockford, Illinois.

WRC Music International

1989-mid-1990s. Guitars by Wayne Richard Charvel, who was the original founder of Charvel Guitars. He now builds Wayne guitars with his son Michael.

Wright Guitar Technology

1993-present. Luthier Rossco Wright builds his unique intermediate and professional grade, production, travel/practice steel-string and nylon-string guitars in The Dalles, Oregon. Basses were added in 2009.

Wurlitzer

Wurlitzer had full-line music stores in several major cities and marketed a line of American-made guitars in the 1920s. They also offered American- and foreign-made guitars starting in '65. The American ones were built from '65-'66 by the Holman-Woodell guitar factory in Neodesha, Kansas. In '67, Wurlitzer switched to Italian-made Welson guitars.

00-18

1920s		$5,500	$7,200

Model 2077 (Martin 0-K)

1920s. Made by Martin, size 0 with koa top, back and sides, limited production of about 28 instruments.

1920s	Natural	$4,300	$5,600

Model 2090 (Martin 0-28)

1920s. Made by Martin, size 0 with appointments similar to a Martin 0-28 of that era, limited production of about 11 instruments, Wurlitzer branded on the back of the headstock and on the inside back seam, Martin name also branded on inside seam.

1920s	Natural	$6,200	$8,100

MODEL YEAR	FEATURES	EXC. COND. LOW	HIGH

Wild One Stereo
1960s. Two pickups, various colors.

1960s		$700	$900

Xaviere
Budget and intermediate grade, production, solid and semi-hollow body guitars from Guitar Fetish, which also has GFS pickups and effects.

Xotic Guitars
1996-present. Luthier Hiro Miura builds his professional grade, production/custom guitars and basses in San Fernando, California. The Xotic brand is also used on a line of guitar effects.

XOX Audio Tools
2007-present. U.S. debut in '08 of premium grade, production/custom, carbon fiber electric guitars built by luthier Peter Solomon in Europe.

Xtone
2003-2014. Semi-hollow body electric, acoustic and acoustic/electric guitars from ESP. Originally branded Xtone on headstock, in '10 the instruments were marketed as a model series under LTD (ESP's other brand) and stated as such on the headstock.

XXL Guitars
2003-present. Luthier Marc Lupien builds his production/custom, professional grade, chambered electric guitars in Montreal, Quebec.

Yamaha
1946-present. Budget, intermediate, professional, and presentation grade, production/custom, acoustic, acoustic/electric, and electric guitars. They also build basses, amps, and effects. The Japanese instrument maker was founded in 1887. Began classical guitar production around 1946. Solidbody electric production began in '66; steel string acoustics debut sometime after that. They began to export guitars into the U.S. in '69. Production shifted from Japan to Taiwan (Yamaha's special-built plant) in the '80s, though some high-end guitars still made in Japan. Some Korean production began in '90s.

Serialization patterns:
Serial numbers are coded as follows:
H = 1, I = 2, J = 3, etc., Z = 12
To use this pattern, you need to know the decade of production.
Serial numbers are ordered as follows:
Year/Month/Day/Factory Order
Example: NL 29159 represents a N=1987 year, L=5th month or May, 29=29th day (of May), 159=159th guitar made that day (the factory order). This guitar was the 159 guitar made on May 29, 1987.

AE Series (Archtop)
1966-2011. Various archtop models.

1966-2011	Higher-end	$900	$1,200
1966-2011	Lower-end	$200	$600
1966-2011	Mid-level	$600	$900

AES Series (Semi-Hollowbody)
1990-2011. Various semi-hollowbody models.

1990-2011	Higher-end	$900	$1,200
1990-2011	Lower-end	$200	$600
1990-2011	Mid-level	$600	$900

AEX-1500
1995-2011. Full-body archtop electric, set neck, humbucker and piezo, EQ, multi-bound.

1995-2011		$900	$1,200

APX Series (Acoustic-Electric)
1987-present. Acoustic-electric, various features.

1987-2021	Higher-end	$900	$1,200
1987-2021	Lower-end	$200	$600
1987-2021	Mid-level	$600	$900

CG Series (Classical)
1984-present. Various classical models.

1984-2021	Higher-end	$350	$500
1984-2021	Lower-end	$100	$200
1984-2021	Mid-level	$200	$350

DW Series (Dreadnought)
1999-2002. Dreadnought flat-top models, sunburst, solid spruce top, higher-end appointments like abalone rosette and top purfling.

1999-2002	Higher-end	$350	$500
1999-2002	Lower-end	$100	$200
1999-2002	Mid-level	$200	$350

EG Series (Electric Solidbody)
2000-2009. Various electric solidbody models.

2000-2009		$100	$350

Eterna Series (Folk Acoustic)
1983-1994. Folk-style acoustics, there were 4 models.

1983-1994		$100	$250

FG Series (Flat-Top)
1970s-present. Economy market flat-top models, laminated sides and back, a 12 suffix indicates 12-string, CE indicates on-board electronics, many models are D-style bodies.

1970-2021	Higher-end	$500	$1,000
1970-2021	Highest-end	$1,000	$1,500
1970-2021	Lower-end	$75	$250
1970-2021	Mid-level	$250	$500

G Series (Classical)
1981-2000. Various Classical models.

1981-2000		$850	$1,100

GC Series (Classical)
1970s-present. Classical models, '70s made in Japan, '80s made in Taiwan.

1970s-2021	Higher-end	$1,100	$1,800
1970s-2021	Lower-end	$200	$600
1970s-2021	Mid-level	$600	$1,100

Image Custom
1988-1992. Electric double-cut, Brazilian rosewood 'board, maple top, 2 humbuckers, active circuitry, LED position markers, script Image logo on truss rod cover. The Image was called the MSG in the U.K.

1988-1992		$1,100	$1,800

Yamaha AES-1500

Yamaha FG-180
Kris Nocula

GUITARS

1969 Yamaha SA-30T
Rhoads Music

1973 Yamaha SG-85

MODEL YEAR	FEATURES	EXC. COND. LOW	HIGH
L Series (Flat-Top)			
1984-present. Custom hand-built flat-top models, solid wood.			
1984-2021	Higher-end	$900	$1,800
1984-2021	Lower-end	$500	$700
1984-2021	Mid-level	$700	$900
PAC Pacifica Series			
1989-present. Offset double-cut with longer horns, dot markers, large script Pacifica logo and small block Yamaha logo on headstock, various models.			
1989-2021		$150	$600
RGX Series			
1988-2011. Bolt-on neck for the 600 series and neck-thru body designs for 1200 series, various models include 110 (1 hum), 211 (hum-single), 220 (2 hums), 312 (hum-single-single), 603 (3 singles), 612 (hum-single-single), 620 (2 hums), 1203S (3 singles), 1212S (hum-single-single), 1220S (2 hums).			
1988-2011	Higher-end	$350	$600
1988-2011	Lower-end	$75	$200
1988-2011	Mid-level	$200	$350
RGZ Series			
1989-1994. Double-cut solidbodies, various pickups.			
1989-1994	Higher-end	$350	$600
1989-1994	Lower-end	$75	$200
1989-1994	Mid-level	$200	$350
SA (Super Axe) Series			
1966-1994. Super Axe series, full-size and thinline archtop models.			
1966-1994	Higher-end	$1,100	$1,500
1966-1994	Highest-end	$1,500	$2,000
1966-1994	Lower-end	$450	$800
1966-1994	Mid-level	$800	$1,100
SBG Series (Solidbody)			
1983-1992. Solidbody models, set necks, model name logo on truss rod cover.			
1983-1992	Higher-end	$1,200	$1,600
1983-1992	Highest-end	$1,600	$2,300
1983-1992	Lower-end	$500	$900
1983-1992	Mid-level	$900	$1,200
SE Series (Solidbody Electric)			
1986-1992. Solidbody electric models.			
1986-1992	Higher-end	$450	$600
1986-1992	Lower-end	$200	$350
1986-1992	Mid-level	$350	$450
SF (Super Flighter) Series			
1977-early 1980s. Super Flighter series, double-cut solidbody electrics, 2 humbuckers.			
1977-80s	Various models	$650	$900
SG-3			
1965-1966. Early double-cut solidbody with sharp horns, bolt neck, 3 hum-single pickup layout, large white guard, rotor controls, tremolo.			
1965-1966		$950	$1,250
SG-5/SG-5A			
1966-1971. Asymmetrical double-cut solidbody with extended lower horn, bolt neck, 2 pickups, chrome hardware.			
1966-1971		$1,250	$1,650

MODEL YEAR	FEATURES	EXC. COND. LOW	HIGH
SG-7/SG-7A			
1966-1971. Like SG-5, but with gold hardware.			
1966-1971		$2,300	$3,000
1993-1996	7A	$1,700	$2,200
SG-7A 20th Anniversary			
1986		$2,100	$2,800
SG-20			
1972-1973. Bolt-on neck, slab body, single-cut, 1 pickup.			
1972-1973		$450	$600
SG-30/SG-30A			
1973-1976. Slab katsura wood (30) or slab maple (30A) solidbody, bolt-on neck, 2 humbuckers, dot inlays.			
1973-1976		$500	$650
SG-35/SG-35A			
1973-1976. Slab mahogany (35) or slab maple (35A) solidbody, bolt-on neck, 2 humbuckers, parallelogram inlays.			
1973-1976		$550	$700
SG-40			
1972-1973. Bolt-on neck, carved body, single-cut.			
1972-1973		$550	$700
SG-45			
1972-1976. Glued neck, single-cut, bound flat-top.			
1972-1976		$575	$750
SG-50			
1974-1976. Slab katsura wood solidbody, glued neck, 2 humbuckers, dot inlays, large 'guard.			
1974-1976		$575	$750
SG-60			
1972 only. Bolt-on neck, carved body, single-cut.			
1972		$575	$750
SG-60T			
1973 only. SG-60 with large cast vibrato system.			
1973		$575	$750
SG-65			
1972-1976. Glued neck, single-cut, bound flat-top.			
1972-1976		$700	$900
SG-70			
1974-1976. Slab maple solidbody, glued neck, 2 humbuckers, dot inlays, large 'guard.			
1974-1976		$700	$900
SG-80			
1972 only. Bolt-on neck, carved body, single-cut.			
1972		$575	$750
SG-80T			
1973. SG-60 with large cast vibrato system.			
1973		$625	$800
SG-85			
1972-1976. Glued neck, single-cut, bound flat-top.			
1972-1976		$700	$900
SG-90			
1974-1976. Carved top mahogany solidbody, glued neck, elevated 'guard, bound top, dot inlays, chrome hardware.			
1974-1976		$850	$1,100
SG-175			
1974-1976. Carved top mahogany solidbody, glued neck, elevated 'guard, abalone bound top, abalone split wing or pyramid inlays, gold hardware.			
1974-1976		$925	$1,200

MODEL YEAR	FEATURES	EXC. COND. LOW	HIGH

SG-500
1976-1978. Carved unbound maple top, double pointed cutaways, glued neck, 2 exposed humbuckers, 3-ply bound headstock, bound neck with clay split wing inlays, chrome hardware. Reissued as the SBG-500 (800S in Japan) in '81.

1976-1978		$625	$800

SG-700
1976-1978. Carved unbound maple top, double pointed cutaways, glued neck, 2 humbuckers, 3-ply bound headstock, bound neck with clay split wing inlays, chrome hardware.

1976-1978		$850	$1,100

SG-700S
1999-2001. Set neck, mahogany body, 2 humbuckers with coil tap.

1999-2001		$850	$1,100

SG-800S
1981-1984. Eastern mahogany with maple top, set neck, 2 pickups, blue, tobacco burst or cherry sunburst.

1981-1984		$850	$1,100

SG-1000/SBG-1000
1976-1983 ('84 in Japan), 2007-2013. Carved maple top, double pointed cutaways, glued neck, 2 humbuckers, 3-ply bound headstock, unbound body, bound neck with clay split wing inlays, gold hardware. Export model name changed to SBG-1000 in '80. SBG-1000 reissued in '07.

1976-1979	SG-1000	$1,150	$1,500
1980-1983	SBG-1000	$1,150	$1,500

SG-1500
1976-1979. Carved maple top, double pointed cutaways, laminated neck-thru-body neck, laminated mahogany body wings, 2 humbuckers, 5-ply bound headstock and body, bound neck with dot inlays, chrome hardware. Name used on Japan-only model in the '80s.

1976-1979		$875	$1,150

SG-2000/SG-2000S
1976-1980 (1988 in Japan). Maple top, double pointed cutaways, neck-thru-body, mahogany body wings, 2 humbuckers, 5-ply bound headstock and body, bound neck with abalone split wing inlays, gold hardware. In '80, the model was changed to the SBG-2000 in the U.S., and the SG-2000S everywhere else except Japan (where it remained the SG-2000). Export model renamed SBG-2100 in '84.

1976-1980		$1,200	$1,600

SG-2100S
1983. Similar to SG-2000 with upgrades such as the pickups.

1983		$1,375	$1,800

SG-3000/SBG-3000/Custom Professional
1982-1992. SG-2000 upgrade with higher output pickups and abalone purfling on top.

1982-1992		$1,850	$2,400

SGV-300
2000-2006. 1960s SG model features.

2000-2006		$500	$650

SHB-400
1981-1985. Solidbody electric, set-in neck, 2 pickups.

1981-1985		$500	$650

SJ-180
1983-1994. Student Jumbo, entry level Folk Series model, laminated top.

1983-1994		$200	$265

SJ-400S
1983-1994. Student Jumbo Folk Series model, solid wood top.

1983-1994		$285	$375

SL (Studio Lord) Series
1977-1981. LP-style copy models.

1977-1981	Various models	$500	$650

SR (Super Rock'n Roller) Series
1977-1981. Strat copy models.

1977-1981	Various models	$475	$625

SSC Series (Solidbody Electric)
1983-1992. Solidbody electric models.

1983-1992	SSC-400/SC-400	$425	$560
1983-1992	SSC-500	$400	$530
1983-1992	SSC-600/SC-600	$550	$725

Weddington Classic
1989-1992. Electric solidbody, redesigned set-in neck/body joint for increased access to the higher frets.

1989-1992		$725	$950

Yanuziello Stringed Instruments
1980-present. Production/custom resonator and Hawaiian guitars built by luthier Joseph Yanuziello, in Toronto, Ontario.

Yosco
1900-1930s. Lawrence L. Yosco was a New York City luthier building guitars, round back mandolins and banjos under his own brand and for others.

Zachary
1996-present. Luthier Alex Csiky builds his professional grade, production, solidbody electric guitars and basses in Windsor, Ontario.

Zanini
2007-2020. Premium grade, production, electric guitars designed by Luca Zanini of Italy and built in the U.S.

Zaukus Guitars
2011-present. Luthier Joseph Zaukus builds his premium grade, production/custom, solidbody electric guitars in Antioch, Tennessee.

Zeiler Guitars
1992-present. Custom flat-top, 12-string, and nylon-string guitars built by luthier Jamonn Zeiler in Aurora, Indiana.

1983 Yamaha SHB-400
Imaged by Heritage Auctions, HA.com

Zanini Villano

GUITARS

Zerberus Nemesis Stone-Top

Zion

Kirby Velarde

MODEL YEAR	FEATURES	EXC. COND. LOW	HIGH

Zemaitis

1960-1999, 2004-present. Professional, premium, and presentation grade, custom/production, electric and acoustic guitars. Tony Zemaitis (born Antanus Casimere Zemaitis) began selling his guitars in 1960. He emphasized simple light-weight construction and was known for hand engraved metal front guitars. The metal front designs were originally engineered to reduce hum, but they became popular as functional art. Each hand-built guitar and bass was a unique instrument. Ron Wood was an early customer and his use of a Zemaitis created a demand for the custom-built guitars. Approximately 6 to 10 instruments were built each year. Tony retired in '99, and passed away in '02 at the age of 67. In '04, Japan's Kanda Shokai Corporation, with the endorsement of Tony Zemaitis, Jr., started building the guitars again. KSC builds the higher priced ones and licenses the lower priced guitars to Greco.

Celebrity association with Zemaitis is not uncommon. Validated celebrity provenance may add 25% to 100% (or more) to a guitar's value. Tony Zemaitis also made so-called student model instruments for customers with average incomes. These had wood tops instead of metal or pearl. Some wood top instruments have been converted to non-Zemaitis metal tops, which are therefore not fully original Zemaitis instruments.

Acoustic instruments are valued more as collectibles and less so for their acoustic sound. Originality and verifiable, documented provenance is required in the Zemaitis market as fake instruments can be a problem.

Zen-On

1946-ca.1968. Japanese manufacturer. By '67 using the Morales brand name. Not heavily imported into the U.S., if at all (see Morales).

Acoustic Hollowbody

1946-1968	Various models	$200	$350

Electric Solidbody

1946-1968	Various models	$200	$600

Zerberus

2002-present. Professional and premium grade, production/custom, electric guitars built in Speyer, Germany by luthier Frank Scheucher.

MODEL YEAR	FEATURES	EXC. COND. LOW	HIGH

Zeta

1982-2010. Zeta made solid, semi-hollow and resonator guitars, many with electronic and MIDI options, and mandolins in Oakland, California over the years, but mainly offered upright basses, amps and violins.

Ziegenfuss Guitars

2006-present. Luthier Stephen Ziegenfuss builds his professional and premium grade, custom, acoustic and solidbody electric guitars and basses in Jackson, Michigan.

Zim-Gar

1960s. Imported from Japan by Gar-Zim Musical Instrument Corporation of Brooklyn, New York. Manufacturers unknown. Generally shorter scale beginner guitars.

Electric Solidbody

1960s		$200	$600

Zimnicki, Gary

1980-present. Luthier Gary Zimnicki builds his professional and premium grade, custom, flat-top, 12-string, nylon-string, and archtop guitars in Allen Park, Michigan.

Zion

1980-present. Professional and premium grade, production/custom, semi-hollow and solidbody guitars built by luthier Ken Hoover, originally in Greensboro, North Carolina, currently in Raleigh.

Zolla

Professional grade, production/custom, electric guitars and basses built by luthier Bill Zolla in San Diego, California starting in 1979.

Zon

1981-present. Currently luthier Joe Zon only offers basses, but he also built guitars from '85-'91. See Bass Section for more company info.

Zuni

1993-present. Premium grade, custom, solidbody electric guitars built by luthier Michael Blank in Alto Pass, Illinois and Amasa, Michigan.

ZZ Ryder

Solidbody electric guitars and basses from Stenzler Musical Instruments of Ft. Worth, Texas.

BASSES

1962 Airline Pocket

Robbie Keene

Alembic Stanley Clarke
Signature Standard

Bob Moreland

A Basses

1976-2002. Luthier Albey Balgochian built his professional grade, solidbody basses in Waltham, Massachusetts. Sports the A logo on headstock.

Solidbody

1976-2002	$1,050	$1,400

Acoustic

Ca. 1965-ca. 1987, 2001-2005, 2008-present. Mainly known for solidstate amps, the Acoustic Control Corp. of Los Angeles, did offer guitars and basses from around '69 to late '74. The brand was revived in '01 by Samick for a line of amps.

Black Widow

1969-1970, 1972-1974. The AC600 Black Widow Bass (fretted and fretless) featured a black double-cut body, German carve, Ebonite 'board, 2 pickups, and a protective "spider design" pad on back. The AC650 is short-scale. The '72-'74 version had a rosewood 'board and only 1 pickup. Acoustic outsourced the production of the basses, possibly to Japan, but at least part of the final production was by Semie Moseley.

1969-1970	$1,400	$1,850
1972-1974	$1,200	$1,650

Airline

1958-1968, 2004-present. Brand for Montgomery Ward. Built by Kay, Harmony and Valco. In '04, the brand was revived on a line of reissues from Eastwood guitars.

Electric Solidbody

1958-1968	Various models	$550	$725

Pocket 3/4 (Valco/National)

1962-1968. Airline brand of double-cut Pocket Bass, short-scale, 2 pickups, 1 acoustic bridge and 1 neck humbucker, sunburst and other colors.

1962-1968	$675	$875

Alamo

1947-1982. Founded by Charles Eilenberg, Milton Fink, and Southern Music, San Antonio, Texas. Distributed by Bruno & Sons.

Eldorado (Model 2600)

1965-1966. Solidbody, 1 pickup, angular offset shape, double-cut.

1965-1966	$425	$550

Titan

1963-1970. Hollowbody, 1 pickup, angular offset shape.

1963-1970	$425	$550

Alembic

1969-present. Professional, premium, and presentation grade, production/custom, 4-, 5-, and 6-string basses built in Santa Rosa, California. They also build guitars. Established in San Francisco as one of the first handmade bass builders. Alembic basses come with many options concerning woods (examples are maple, bubinga, walnut, vermilion, wenge, zebrawood), finishes, inlays, etc., all of which affect the values listed here. These dollar amounts should be used as a baseline guide to values for Alembic.

Anniversary

1989. 20th Anniversary limited edition, walnut and vermillion with a walnut core, 5-piece body, 5-piece neck-thru, only 200 built.

1989	$2,800	$3,600

Custom Shop Built

1969-present. Various one-off and/or custom built instruments. Each instrument should be evaluated individually. Prices are somewhat speculative due to the one-off custom characteristics and values can vary greatly.

1978	Dragon Doubleneck	$9,200	$12,000
2004	Dragon 4-string, 4 made	$4,600	$6,000

Distillate

1981-1991. One of Alembic's early lower-cost models, early ones with 1 pickup, 2 pickups by '82, exotic woods, active electronics.

1981-1991	Distillate 4	$2,600	$3,400
1981-1991	Distillate 5	$2,700	$3,600

Elan

1985-1996. Available in 4-, 5-, 6- and 8-string models, 3-piece thru-body laminated maple neck, solid maple body, active electronics, solid brass hardware, offered in a variety of hardwood tops and custom finishes.

1985-1996	Elan 4	$2,400	$3,200
1985-1996	Elan 5	$2,450	$3,250
1985-1996	Elan 6	$2,550	$3,400

Epic

1993-2015. Mahogany body with various tops, extra large pointed bass horn, maple/walnut veneer set-neck, available in 4-, 5-, and 6-string versions.

1993-2015	4-string	$2,300	$3,000
1993-2015	5-string	$2,400	$3,100
1993-2015	6-string	$2,500	$3,300

Essence

1991-present. Mahogany body with various tops, extra large pointed bass horn, walnut/maple laminate neck-thru.

1991-2021	Essence 4	$2,400	$3,200
1991-2021	Essence 5	$2,450	$3,250
1991-2021	Essence 6	$2,600	$3,400

Europa

1992-present. Mahogany body with various tops, ebony 'board, available as 4-, 5-, and 6-string.

1992-2021	$3,000	$4,000

Excel

1999-present. Solidbody 5-string, set neck, several wood options.

1998-2021	$3,000	$4,000

Exploiter

1980s. Figured maple solidbody 4-string, neck-thru, transparent finish.

1984-1988	$3,000	$4,000

Mark King Signature

1989-2019. Standard or Deluxe models.

1989-2008	$6,000	$8,000

MODEL YEAR	FEATURES	EXC. COND. LOW	HIGH

Orion
1996-present. Offset double cut solidbody, various figured-wood top, 4, 5, or 6 strings.

1996-2021		$2,400	$3,200

Persuader
1983-1991. Offset double-cut solidbody, 4-string, neck-thru.

1983-1991		$2,400	$3,200

Rogue
1996-present. Double-cut solidbody, extreme long pointed bass horn..

1996-2021		$2,600	$3,400

Series I
1971-present. Mahogany body with various tops, maple/purpleheart laminate neck-thru, active electronics, available in 3 scale lengths and with 4, 5 or 6 strings.

1971-1979	All scales	$5,500	$7,300
1980-1989	All scales	$5,000	$6,600
1990-2021	Highly figured	$5,000	$6,600

Series II
1971-present. Generally custom-made option, each instrument valued on a case-by-case basis, guidance pricing only.

1971-1979		$5,700	$7,500
1980-2021		$5,200	$6,900

Spoiler
1981-1999. Solid mahogany body, maple neck-thru, 4, 5 or 6 strings, active electronics, various high-end wood options.

1981-1986	6-string	$2,600	$3,400
1981-1989	5-string	$2,500	$3,300
1981-1999	4-string	$2,400	$3,200

Stanley Clarke Signature Standard
1990-present. Neck-thru-body, active electronics, 24-fret ebony 'board, mahogany body with maple, bubinga, walnut, vermilion, or zebrawood top, 4-, 5-, and 6-string versions.

1990-2021	All scales	$5,200	$6,900

Alleva-Coppolo Basses and Guitars
1995-present. Professional and premium grade, custom/production, solidbody electric basses and guitars built by luthier Jimmy Coppolo in Dallas, Texas for '95-'97, in New York City for '98-2008, and since in Upland, California.

Alvarez
1965-present. Imported by St. Louis Music, they offered electric basses from '90 to '02 and acoustic basses in the mid-'90s.

American Showster
1986-2004, 2010-2011. Established by Bill Meeker and David Haines, Bayville, New Jersey. They also made guitars.

AS-57-B Classic
1987-1997. Bass version of AS-57 with body styled like a '57 Chevy tail fin.

1987-1997		$4,000	$5,200

Ampeg
1949-present. Ampeg was founded on a vision of an amplified bass peg, which evolved into the Baby Bass. Ampeg has sold basses on and off throughout its history. In '08 they got back into basses with the reissue of the Dan Armstrong Plexi Bass.

AEB-1
1966-1967. F-holes through the body, fretted, scroll headstock, pickup in body, sunburst. Reissued as the AEB-2 for '97-'99.

1966-1967		$3,500	$4,500

ASB-1 Devil/AUSB-1 Devil
1966-1967. Long-horn body, fretted (ASB-1) or fretless (AUSB-1), triangular f-holes through the body, fireburst.

1966-1967		$5,800	$7,600

AUB-1
1966-1967. Same as AEB-1, but fretless, sunburst. Reissued as the AUB-2 for '97-'99.

1966-1967		$3,800	$4,900

BB-4 Baby (4-string)
1962-1971. Electric upright slim-looking bass that is smaller than a cello, 4-string, available in sunburst, white, red, black, and a few turquoise. Reissued as the ABB-1 Baby Bass for '97-'99.

1962-1971	Solid color	$2,700	$3,500
1962-1971	Sunburst	$2,250	$2,900

BB-5 Baby (5-string)
1964-1971. Five-string version.

1964-1971	Solid color	$2,800	$3,700
1964-1971	Sunburst	$2,300	$3,000

Dan Armstrong Lucite
1969-1971. Clear solid lucite body, did not have switchable pickups like the Lucite guitar.

1969-1971	Clear	$2,100	$2,750
1969-1971	Smoke	$2,600	$3,400

Dan Armstrong Lucite Reissue/ADA4
1998-2001, 2008-2009. Lucite body, Dan Armstrong Ampeg block lettering on 'guard. Reissue in '08 as the ADA4.

1998-2001		$750	$1,000
2008-2009	Reintroduced	$750	$1,000

EB-1 Wild Dog
1963-1964. Made by Burns of London, along with the Wild Dog Guitar, offset double cut solidbody, 3 pickups

1963-1964		$650	$875

GEB-101 Little Stud
1973-1975. Import from Japan, offset double-cut solidbody, two-on-a-side tuners, 1 pickup.

1973-1975		$424	$550

GEB-750 Big Stud
1973-1975. Import from Japan, similar to Little Stud, but with 2 pickups.

1973-1975		$424	$550

Andreas
1995-2004. Aluminium-necked, solidbody guitars and basses built by luthier Andreas Pichler in Dollach, Austria.

1968 Ampeg AEB-1
Craig Brody

Ampeg Dan Armstrong Lucite
Imaged by Heritage Auctions, HA.com

B.C. Rich ST-III
Ken Kraynak

1965 Baldwin Vibraslim
Guillermo Albino

Angelica

1967-1975. Student and entry-level basses and guitars imported from Japan.

Electric Solidbody

1970s. Japanese imports.

MODEL YEAR	FEATURES	LOW	HIGH
1970s	Various models	$175	$400

Apollo

Ca. 1967-1972. Entry-level basses imported from Japan by St. Louis Music. They also had guitars and effects.

Electric Hollowbody

1967-1972. Japanese imports.

1967-1972		$500	$700

Arbor

1983-ca. 2013. Budget grade, production, solidbody basses imported by Musicorp (MBT). They also offered guitars.

Electric

1983-2013	Various models	$175	$400

Aria/Aria Pro II

1956-present. Budget and intermediate grade, production, acoustic, acoustic/electric, solidbody, hollowbody and upright basses. They also make guitars, mandolins, and banjos. Originally branded as Aria; renamed Aria Pro II in '75; both names used over the next several year; in '01, the Pro II part of the name was dropped altogether.

Electric

1980s	Various models	$400	$675

Austin Hatchet

Mid-1970s-mid-1980s. Trademark of distributor Targ and Dinner, Chicago, Illinois.

Hatchet

1981	Travel bass	$450	$600

B.C. Rich

1966-present. Budget, intermediate, and premium grade, production/custom, import and U.S.-made basses. They also offer guitars. Many B.C. Rich models came in a variety of colors. For example, in '88 they offered black, Competition Red, metallic red, GlitteRock White, Ultra Violet, and Thunder Blue. Also in '88, other custom colors, graphic features, paint-to-match headstocks, and special inlays were offered.

Bich

1978-1998. Solidbody, neck-thru, 2 pickups.

1978-1979	USA	$2,200	$2,900
1980-1985		$1,375	$1,800
1986-1989		$950	$1,225
1989-1993	Class Axe era	$950	$1,225
1994-1998	2nd Rico-era	$950	$1,225

Bich Supreme 8-String

Late-1970s-early-1980s.

1978-1982	Painted wood	$3,700	$4,800
1978-1982	Translucent wood	$4,100	$5,400

Eagle (U.S.A.)

1977-1996. Curved double-cut, solidbody, natural.

MODEL YEAR	FEATURES	LOW	HIGH
1977-1979	Translucent wood	$2,200	$2,900
1977-1996	Painted wood	$1,925	$2,500
1980-1996	Translucent wood	$2,100	$2,800

Gunslinger

1987-1999. Inverted headstock, 1 humbucker.

1987-1989		$700	$900
1989-1993	Class Axe era	$700	$900
1994-1999		$625	$800

Ironbird

1984-1998. Kind of star-shaped, neck-thru, solidbody, 2 pickups, active electronics, diamond inlays.

1984-1989		$1,050	$1,350
1989-1993	Class Axe era	$950	$1,225
1994-1998	2nd Rico era	$875	$1,150

Mockingbird

1976-2009. US-made, short horn until '78, long horn after.

1976	Painted	$2,100	$2,800
1976	Translucent	$2,200	$2,900
1977-1978	Painted	$1,950	$2,550
1977-1978	Translucent	$2,100	$2,800
1979-1983	Painted	$2,100	$2,800
1979-1983	Translucent	$2,100	$2,800
1984-1985	End 1st Rico-era	$1,950	$2,550
1986-1989	End 1st Rico era	$1,375	$1,800
1994-2009	New Rico-era	$1,375	$1,800

Mockingbird Heritage Classic

2007-2015. 4-string, neck-thru, quilted maple top, cloud inlay.

2007-2015		$290	$375

Nighthawk

1979-ca.1980. Bolt-neck.

1978-1982		$675	$900

NJ Series

1983-2006. Various mid-level import models include Beast, Eagle, Innovator, Mockingbird, Virgin and Warlock. Replaced by NT Series.

1983-1984	Early, Japan	$425	$550
1985-1986	Japan	$325	$425
1987-2006		$225	$300

Platinum Series

1986-2006 Lower-priced import versions including Eagle, Mockingbird, Beast, Warlock.

1986-1999	Various models	$200	$300

Seagull

1973-1975. Solidbody, single cut, changed to Seagull II in '76.

1973		$2,950	$3,850
1974-1975		$2,600	$3,375

Seagull II

1976-1977. Double-cut version.

1976-1977		$2,100	$2,700

ST-III

1987-1998. Bolt or set neck, black hardware, P-Bass/J-Bass pickup configuration, ebony 'board.

1987-1989	Bolt-on	$600	$800
1987-1989	Neck-thru	$650	$850
1989-1993	Class Axe-era	$600	$800
1994-1998	New Rico-era	$650	$850

MODEL		EXC. COND.	
YEAR	FEATURES	LOW	HIGH

Warlock (U.S.A.)

1981-2015. Bolt neck, maple body, rosewood 'board, Badass II low profile bridge by '88.

1981-1985		$1,200	$1,600
1986-1989		$1,125	$1,500

Wave

Early 1980s. Double-cut, cresting wave, neck-thru, solid body, 2 pickups, active electronics.

1983		$2,200	$2,900

B.C. Rico

1978-1982. B.C. Rich's first Japan-made guitars and basses were labeled B.C. Rico.

Eagle

1978-1982		$1,850	$2,400

Baldwin

1965-1970. The giant organ company got into guitars and basses in '65 when it bought Burns Guitars of England and sold those models in the U.S. under the Baldwin name.

Baby Bison

1965-1970. Scroll head, 2 pickups, black, red or white finishes.

1965-1966		$975	$1,250
1966-1970	Model 560	$800	$1,050

Bison

1965-1970. Scroll headstock, 3 pickups, black or white finishes.

1965-1966		$1,025	$1,325
1966-1970	Model 516	$900	$1,175

G.B. 66

1965-1966. Bass equivalent of G.B. 66 guitar, covered bridge tailpiece.

1965-1966		$700	$925

Jazz Split Sound

1965-1970. Offset double-cut solidbody, 2 pickups, red sunburst.

1965-1966	Long-scale	$975	$1,250
1966-1970	Short-scale	$800	$1,050

Nu-Sonic

1965-1966. Bass version of Nu-Sonic.

1965-1966		$700	$925

Shadows/Shadows Signature

1965-1970. Named after Hank Marvin's backup band, solidbody, 3 slanted pickups, white finish.

1965-1966	Shadows	$1,450	$1,900
1966-1970	Shadows Signature	$1,375	$1,775

Vibraslim

1965-1970. Thin body, scroll head, 2 pickups, sunburst.

1965-1966		$875	$1,150
1966-1970	Model 549	$775	$1,025

Barclay

1960s. Generally shorter-scale, student-level imports from Japan. They also made guitars.

Bass Collection

1985-1992. Mid-level imports from Japan, distributed by Meisel Music of Springfield, New Jersey. Sam Ash Music, New York, sold the remaining inventory from '92 to '94.

Black Jack

1960s. Entry-level and mid-level imports from Japan. They also offered guitars.

Bradford

1960s. House brand of W.T. Grant department store, often imported. They also offered guitars.

Brian Moore

1992-present. Brian Moore added basses in '97. Currently they offer professional grade, production, solidbody basses. They also build guitars and mandolins.

i2000 Series

2000-present. Offset double-cut solidbody with extended bass horn, 2 pickups, 4- (i4) or 5-string (i5), options include piezo (p), fretless (-f), Bartolini pickups (B), and 13-pin mid (.13).

2000-2021		$775	$1,000

Brice

1985-present. Budget grade, production, electric and acoustic basses imported by Rondo Music of Union, New Jersey.

BSX Bass

1990-present. Luthier Dino Fiumara builds his professional and premium grade, production/custom, acoustic, solidbody, semi-solid upright basses in Aliquippa, Pennsylvania.

Burns

1960-1970, 1974-1983, 1992-present. Intermediate and professional grade, production, basses built in England and Korea. They also build guitars.

Baby Bison

1965-1968. Early version had "V" headstock and long Rez-O-Tube vibrato. Later short Rezo-Tube tailpiece.

1965-1968		$750	$975

Nu-Sonic

1964-1965, 2011-2020. Offset double-cut solidbody, 2 pickups.

1964-1965		$925	$1,200

Scorpion

Introduced 1979, 2003-2009. Double-cut scorpion-like solidbody.

2003-2009		$375	$485

Cameo

1960s-1970s. Japanese- and Korean-made electric basses. They also offered guitars.

Electric

1960s-70s		$300	$400

Brian Moore I2000 Series
Richard Memmel

BSX Bass

BASSES

BASSES

Custom Kraft Bone Buzzer
Rivington Guitars

Daion
Carter Vintage Guitars

MODEL YEAR	FEATURES	EXC. COND. LOW	HIGH

Charvel

1976-present. U.S.-made from '78 to '85 and a combination of imports and U.S.-made post-'85. They also build guitars.

Pre-Pro
1980-1981. Pre-mass production basses, made Nov. '80 to '81. Refer to Charvel guitar section for details.

1980-1981	All models	$2,200	$2,900

850 XL
1988-1991. Four-string, neck-thru, active.

1988-1991		$750	$975

CX-490
1991-1994. Double-cut, 4-string, bolt neck, red or white.

1991-1994		$265	$350

Eliminator
1990-1991. Offset double-cut, active electronics, bolt neck.

1990-1991		$400	$525

Fusion
1989-1991. Active circuitry, 4- and 5-string models.

1989-1991	IV	$525	$700
1989-1991	V	$575	$750

Model 1
1986-1988. Double-cut, bolt neck, 1 pickup.

1986-1988		$450	$600

Model 2
1986-1988. Double-cut, bolt neck, 2 pickups.

1986-1988		$450	$600

Model 3
1986-1988. Neck-thru, 2 single-coils, active, master volume, bass and treble knobs.

1986-1988		$525	$700

Model 4
1986-1988. Like Model 3, but with bolt neck.

1986-1988		$625	$825

Model 5
1986-1989. Double-cut, P/J pickups.

1986-1989		$625	$825

San Dimas Serialized Plated
1981-1982. Soft headstock early models.

1981-1982		$2,200	$2,900

SB-4
1990s. Offset double cut solid, long bass horn, 2 pickups.

1990s		$400	$525

Star
1980-1981. Unique 4-point solidbody, 1 pickup, considered by Charvel collectors to be Charvel's only original early design.

1980-1981		$3,100	$4,000

Surfcaster
1991-1994. Semi-hollow, lipstick tube pickups.

1991-1994		$1,150	$1,500

Cipher

1960s. Student market basses imported from Japan. They also made guitars.

Electric Solidbody
1960s. Japanese imports.

1960s		$225	$300

MODEL YEAR	FEATURES	EXC. COND. LOW	HIGH

Clevinger

1982-present. Established by Martin Clevinger, Oakland, California. Mainly specializing in electric upright basses, but has offered bass guitars as well.

College Line

One of many Lyon & Healy brands, made during the era of extreme design experimentation.

Monster (Style 2089)
Early-1900s. 22" lower bout, flat-top guitar/bass, natural.

1915		$2,800	$3,600

Conrad

Ca.1968-1978. Student and mid-level copy basses imported by David Wexler, Chicago, Illinois. They also offered guitars, mandolins and banjos.

Electric

1970s	Various models	$300	$600

Professional Bison
1970s. Solidbody, 2 pickups.

1970s		$350	$450

Coral

1967-1969. In '66 MCA bought Danelectro and in '67 introduced the Coral brand of guitars, basses and amps. The line included several solid and semi-solidbody basses.

Deluxe D2N4
1967-1969. Offset double-cut, 2 pickups.

1967-1969	Black	$1,300	$1,700
1967-1969	Sunburst	$1,200	$1,575

Fiddle FB2B4
1967-1969. Violin bass hollow body, 2 pickups.

1967-1969		$1,775	$2,300

Firefly F2B4
1968-1969. 335-style semi-hollow, 2 pickups.

1968-1969	Red	$1,000	$1,300
1968-1969	Sunburst	$950	$1,225

Long Horn
1968-1969. Standard neck (L2B4) or extended neck (L2LB4), 4 strings.

1968	L2LB4	$1,425	$1,850
1968-1969	L2B4	$1,325	$1,725

Wasp
1967-1969. 4-string (2B4) or 6-string (2B6), black, red or sunburst.

1967-1969	2B4, black or red	$1,300	$1,700
1967-1969	2B4, sunburst	$1,075	$1,400
1967-1969	2B6, black or red	$1,450	$1,900
1967-1969	2B6, sunburst	$1,300	$1,700

Crestwood

1970s. Imported by La Playa Distributing Company of Detroit. Product line includes copies of the popular classical guitars, flat-tops, electric solidbodies and basses of the era.

Electric
1970s. Includes models 2048, 2049, 2079, 2090, 2092, 2093, and 2098.

1970s		$225	$350

The ***Vintage Guitar Price Guide*** shows low to high values for items in all-original excellent condition, and, where applicable, with original case or cover.

MODEL YEAR	FEATURES	EXC. COND. LOW	HIGH

Crown

1960s. Violin-shaped hollowbody electrics, solid-body electric guitars and basses, possibly others. Imported from Japan.

Electric Solidbody

1960s	Import	$200	$300

Custom Kraft

Late-1950s-1968. A house brand of St. Louis Music Supply, instruments built by Valco and others. They also offered guitars and amps.

Bone Buzzer Model 12178

Late 1960s. Symmetrical double-cut thin hollow body, lightning bolt f-holes, 4-on-a-side tuners, 2 pickups, sunburst or emerald sunburst.

1960s		$525	$700

D'Agostino

1976-early 1990s. Import company established by Pat D'Agostino. Solidbodies imported from EKO Italy '77-'82, Japan '82-'84, and in Korea for '84 on. Overall, about 60% of guitars and basses were Japanese, 40% Korean.

Electric Solidbody

1970s	Various models	$650	$850

Daion

1978-1984. Higher quality copy basses imported from Japan. Original designs introduced in '80s. They also had guitars.

Electric

1978-1984	Higher-end	$850	$1,100
1978-1984	Lower-end	$425	$550

Danelectro

1946-1969, 1997-present. Danelectro offered basses throughout most of its early history. In '96, the Evets Corporation, of San Clemente, California, introduced a line of Danelectro effects; amps, basses and guitars, many reissues of earlier instruments, soon followed. In early '03, Evets discontinued the guitar, bass and amp lines, but revived the guitar and bass line in '05. Danelectro also built the Coral brand instruments (see Coral).

Dane A Series

1967. Solidbody, 2 pickups, 4-string.

1967		$600	$800

Dane C Series

1967. Semi-solidbody 4- or 6-string, 2 pickups.

1967	4-string	$1,050	$1,400
1967	6-string	$1,300	$1,700

Dane D Series

1967. Solidbody, 2 pickups, 4- or 6-string.

1967	4-string	$925	$1,200
1967	6-string	$1,300	$1,700

Dane E Series

1967. Solidbody, 2 pickups, 4-string.

1967		$925	$1,200

Hawk

1967. Solidbody, 4-string, 1 pickup.

1967		$1,050	$1,400

Model 1444L

Ca.1958-ca.1964. Masonite body, single-cut, 2 pickups, copper finish.

1958-1964		$700	$900

Model 3412 Standard (Shorthorn)

1959-1966. Coke bottle headstock, 4- or 6-string, 1 pickup, kidney 'guard through '60, seal 'guard after, copper finish.

1959-1960	Kidney 'guard, 4-string	$925	$1,200
1959-1960	Kidney 'guard, 6-string	$1,375	$1,800
1961-1966	Seal 'guard, 4-string	$800	$1,050
1961-1966	Seal 'guard, 6-string	$1,300	$1,700

Model 3612 Standard (Shorthorn)

1959-1966. 6-string version.

1959-1962	Kidney 'guard	$1,375	$1,800
1961-1966	Seal 'guard	$1,300	$1,700

'58 Shorthorn Reissue

1997-2003. Reissues of classic Shorthorn bass.

1997-2003		$290	$375

Model 4423 Longhorn 4-String

1959-1966. Coke bottle headstock, 4-string, 2 pickups, tweed case '59, gray tolex after.

1959	Tweed case	$1,425	$1,850
1960-1966	Gray tolex case	$1,325	$1,750

Model 4623 Longhorn 6-String

1959-1966, 1969-1970. 6-string version.

1959	Tweed case	$1,600	$2,100
1960-1966	Gray tolex case	$1,550	$2,000
1969-1970		$1,425	$1,850

'58 Longhorn Reissue/Longhorn Pro

1997-2010. Reissues of classic Longhorn bass.

1997-2010		$290	$375

UB-2 6-String

1956-1958. Single-cut, 2 pickups, black, bronze or ivory.

1956-1958		$1,650	$2,175

David J King

1987-present. Production/custom, professional and premium grade, electric basses built by luthier David King first in Amherst, Massachusetts and since '92 in Portland, Oregon.

Dean

1976-present. Intermediate and professional grade, production, solidbody, hollowbody, acoustic, and acoustic/electric, basses made overseas. They also offer guitars, banjos, mandolins, and amps.

Baby ML

1982-1986. Downsized version of ML.

1982-1986	Import	$350	$450

Mach V

1985-1986. U.S.-made pointed solidbody, 2 pickups, rosewood 'board.

1985-1986		$1,300	$1,700

ML

1977-1986, 2001-2010. Futuristic body style, fork headstock.

1977-1983	US-made	$1,600	$2,100
1984-1986	Korean import	$425	$550

1961 Danelectro 3412
Erick Warner

1964 Danelectro 4423 Longhorn

BASSES

EKO Model 995/2 Violin
Rivington Guitars

1966 Epiphone Embassy Deluxe
Carter Vintage Guitars

MODEL YEAR	FEATURES	EXC. COND. LOW	HIGH
Rhapsody Series (USA)			
2001-2004. Scroll shaped offset double-cut, various models.			
2001-2004	12-string	$360	$475
2001-2004	8-string	$325	$425
2001-2004	HFB fretless	$230	$300

DeArmond

1999-2004. Electric basses based on Guild models and imported from Korea by Fender. They also offered guitars.

Electric

MODEL YEAR	FEATURES	EXC. COND. LOW	HIGH
1999-2004. Various imported models.			
1999-2004		$450	$600

Dingwall

1988-present. Luthier Sheldon Dingwall, Saskatoon, Saskatchewan, started out producing guitar bodies and necks, eventually offering complete guitars and basses. Currently Dingwall offers professional to premium grade, production/custom 4-, 5-, and 6-string basses featuring the Novax Fanned-Fret System.

Domino

Ca. 1967-1968. Imported from Japan by Maurice Lipsky Music of New York, mainly copies, but some original designs. They also offered guitars.

Electric

MODEL YEAR	FEATURES	EXC. COND. LOW	HIGH
1967-1968. Includes the Beatle Bass and Fireball Bass, a Vox Phantom IV copy.			
1967-1968		$425	$550

Dorado

Ca. 1972-1973. Name used briefly by Baldwin/Gretsch on line of Japanese guitar and bass imports.

Electric Solidbody

MODEL YEAR	FEATURES	EXC. COND. LOW	HIGH
1970s	Import	$325	$425

Earthwood

1972-1985. Acoustic designs by Ernie Ball with input from George Fullerton and made in Newport Beach, California. One of the first to offer acoustic basses.

Acoustic

MODEL YEAR	FEATURES	EXC. COND. LOW	HIGH
1972-1985. Big bodied acoustic bass alternative between Kay double bass and solidbody Fender bass.			
1972-1985		$2,700	$3,500

EKO

1959-1985, 2000-present. Built by the Oliviero Pigini Company, Italy. Original importers included LoDuca Brothers, Milwaukee, Wisconsin. Since about 2000, production, acoustic and electric EKO basses are again available and made in Italy and China. They also make guitars and amps.

Barracuda

MODEL YEAR	FEATURES	EXC. COND. LOW	HIGH
1967-1978. Offset double-cut semi-hollow, 2 pickups.			
1967-1978		$550	$725

MODEL YEAR	FEATURES	EXC. COND. LOW	HIGH
Cobra II			
1967-ca.1969. Offset double-cut solidbody, 2 pickups.			
1967-1969		$450	$600
Kadett			
1967-1978. Red or sunburst.			
1967-1978		$550	$725
Model 995/2 Violin			
1966-ca.1969.			
1966-1969		$775	$1,000
Model 1100/2			
1961-1966. Jaguar-style plastic covered solidbody, 2 pickups, sparkle finish.			
1961-1966		$625	$825
Rocket IV/Rokes			
1967-early-1970s. Rocket-shape design, solidbody, says Rokes on the headstock, the Rokes were a popular English band that endorsed EKO guitars. Marketed as the Rocket IV in the U.S. and as the Rokes in Europe. Often called the Rok. Sunburst, 1 pickup.			
1967-1971		$750	$975

Electra

1970-1984, 2013-present. Originally basses imported from Japan by St. Louis Music. They also offered guitars. Currently U.S.-made in Tampa, Florida.

Electric Solidbody

MODEL YEAR	FEATURES	EXC. COND. LOW	HIGH
1970s. Japanese imports, various models.			
1970s		$525	$675

MPC Outlaw

MODEL YEAR	FEATURES	EXC. COND. LOW	HIGH
1970s. Symmetric solidbody with large straight horns, 2 separate plug-in modules for different effects, MPC headstock logo, bowtie markers, sunburst.			
1970s		$675	$875

Emperador

1966-1992. Student-level basses imported by Westheimer Musical Instruments. Early models appear to be made by either Teisco or Kawai; later models were made by Cort. They also had guitars.

Electric Solidbody

MODEL YEAR	FEATURES	EXC. COND. LOW	HIGH
1960s. Japanese imports, various models.			
1960s	Beatle Violin Bass	$350	$450
1960s	Various models	$150	$300

Engelhardt

Engelhardt specializes in student acoustic basses and cellos and is located in Elk Grove Village, Illinois.

Epiphone

1928-present. Epiphone didn't add basses until 1959, after Gibson acquired the brand. The Gibson Epiphones were American-made until '69, then all imports until into the '80s, when some models were again made in the U.S. Currently Epiphone offers intermediate and professional grade, production, acoustic and electric basses.

B-1 Acoustic Viol

MODEL YEAR	FEATURES	EXC. COND. LOW	HIGH
1940-1949. Maple back and sides, cherry sunburst.			
1940-1949		$1,775	$2,300

The *Vintage Guitar Price Guide* shows low to high values for items in all-original excellent condition, and, where applicable, with original case or cover.

MODEL YEAR	FEATURES	EXC. COND. LOW	HIGH

B-2 Acoustic Viol
1940-1949. Mid-level maple back and sides.

1940-1949		$1,950	$2,550

B-3 Acoustic Viol
1940-1949. Higher-level maple back and sides.

1940-1949		$2,050	$2,650

B-4 Acoustic Viol
1940-1964. Highly figured maple back and sides.

1940-1964		$2,500	$3,250

B-5 Artist Acoustic Viol
1941-1964. Highly figured maple back and sides.

1941-1964		$3,200	$4,200

EA/ET/ES Series (Japan)
1970-1979. Production of the Epiphone brand was moved to Japan in '70. Models included the EA (electric thinline) and ET (electric solidbody).

1970-1975	Various models	$500	$850

EB-0/EB-1/EB-3/EBM-4
1991-2019. EB-0 ('98-'19), EB-1 ('98-'00), EB-3 ('99-'19) and EBM-4 ('91-'98).

1991-2019	Various models	$175	$550

Elitist Series
2003-2005. Higher-end appointments such as set-necks and USA pickups.

2003-2005	Various models	$800	$1,050

Embassy Deluxe
1963-1969. Solidbody, double-cut, 2 pickups, tune-o-matic bridge, cherry finish.

1963-1964		$5,400	$7,000
1965		$5,000	$6,500
1966-1969		$4,850	$6,300

Explorer Korina
2000-2001. Made in Korea, Gibson Explorer body style, genuine korina body, set neck, gold hardware.

2000-2001		$400	$525

Genesis
1979-1980. Double-cut solidbody, 2 humbuckers, Made in Taiwan.

1979-1980		$1,025	$1,325

Jack Cassady Signature
1997-present. Maple body, mahogany neck, rosewood 'board, 1 pickup, metallic gold or ebony finish.

1997-2021		$600	$800

Les Paul Special
1997-2013. LP Jr.-style slab body, single-cut, bolt neck, 2 humbuckers.

1997-2013		$300	$400

Newport EB-6
1962-1964	6-String	$8,900	$11,500

Newport EBD
1960-1970. Double-cut solidbody, 1 pickup (2 pickups optional until '63), 2-on-a-side tuners until '63, 4-on-a-side after that, cherry.

1960-1964		$2,400	$3,100
1965		$1,750	$2,300
1966		$1,550	$2,000
1967-1970		$1,525	$2,000

Newport EB-SF
1962-1963. Newport with added built-in fuzz, cherry.

1962-1963		$3,500	$4,500

Ripper

1998-2000, 2006-2008. Offset double-cut, 1 humbucker pickup, black or natural.

1998-2000		$525	$700

Rivoli (1 Pickup)
1959-1961, 1964-1970, 1994-2000. ES-335-style semi-hollowbody bass, 2-on-a-side tuners, 1 pickup (2 in '70).

1959-1960	Banjo tuners, natural	$6,500	$8,500
1959-1960	Banjo tuners, sunburst	$5,700	$7,400
1961	Standard tuners, natural	$3,800	$5,000
1961	Standard tuners, sunburst	$3,000	$3,900
1964		$3,000	$3,900
1965		$2,600	$3,400
1966-1969		$2,450	$3,200
1967	Sparkling Burgundy	$2,450	$3,200
1970		$2,450	$3,200

Rivoli (2 Pickups)
1970 only. Double pickup Epiphone version of Gibson EB-2D.

1970		$2,550	$3,300

Rivoli II Reissue
1995-2000. Made in Korea, set neck, blond.

1995-2000		$650	$850

Thunderbird IV
1997-2019. Reverse-style mahogany body, 2 pickups, sunburst.

1997-2019		$375	$500

Thunderbird IV (Non-Reverse)
1995-1998. Non-reverse-style mahogany body, 2 pickups, 5-string optional.

1995-1998		$375	$500

Viola
1995-present. Beatle Bass 500/1 copy, sunburst.

1995-2021		$300	$400

ESP
1975-present. Intermediate, professional, and premium grade, production/custom, electric basses. Japan's ESP (Electric Sound Products) made inroads in the U.S. market with mainly copy styles in the early '80s, mixing in original designs over the years. In the '90s, ESP opened a California-based Custom Shop. They also build guitars.

Electric
1980s-1990s. Various factory production models.

1980s-90s		$750	$975

Essex (SX)
1985-present. Budget grade, production, electric basses imported by Rondo Music of Union, New Jersey. They also offer guitars.

Estrada
1960s-1970s. Line of classical, acoustic and electric guitars and basses imported from Japan.

Violin

1960s	Import	$450	$600

1966 Epiphone Newport
Imaged by Heritage Auctions, HA.com

1997 Epiphone Rivoli 1 Pickup
Angelo Guarini

BASSES

BASSES

1964 Fender Bass VI

David Swartz

1967 Fender Coronado II

Rivington Guitars

Fender

1946-present. Intermediate, professional, and premium grade, production/custom, electric and acoustic basses made in the U.S. and overseas. Leo Fender is the father of the electric bass. The introduction of his Precision Bass in late '51 changed forever how music was performed, recorded and heard. Leo followed with other popular models of basses that continue to make up a large part of Fender's production. Please note that all the variations of the Jazz and Precision Basses are grouped under those general headings.

A custom color is worth more than a standard color. The first Precision Bass standard color was blond but changed to sunburst in the late 1950s. The Jazz Bass standard color is sunburst. To understand a custom color, you need to know what the standard color is. Some custom colors are more rare than others. Below is a list of the custom colors offered in 1960 by Fender. They are sorted in ascending order with the most valuable color, Shell Pink, listed last. In the 1960 list, Black and Blond are the least valuable and Shell Pink is the most valuable. A Fiesta Red is typically worth 12% more than a Black or Blond. In the rare color group a Foam Green is normally worth 8% more than a Shoreline Gold. The two very rare colors are often worth 30% more than a Shoreline Gold. In our pricing information we will list the standard color, then the relative value of a common custom color, and then the value of a rare custom color. Remember that the amount of fade also affects the price. These prices are for factory original custom colors with slight or no fade in excellent condition. Fade implies a lighter color, but with custom colors a faded example can also be much darker in color. Blue can fade to dark green. White can fade to deep yellow.

The Price Guide lists the standard color, plus the value of a Common Color and the value of a Rare Color. The list below defines which group a color falls into for 1960, and it is in ascending order so, for example, a Daphne Blue should be considered more valuable than a Lake Placid Blue, assuming they are in equal condition.

Common Color: Black, Blond, Candy Apple Red, Olympic White, Lake Placid Blue, Dakota Red, Daphne Blue, Fiesta Red

Rare Color: Shoreline Gold, Inca Silver, Burgundy Mist, Sherwood Green, Sonic Blue, Foam Green

Rare (Very Rare) Color: Surf Green, Shell Pink

Ashbory

2003-2006. Unique-shaped travel bass, Ashbory logo on body, Fender logo on back of headstock, previously sold under Fender's DeArmond brand.

2003-2006		$265	$345

Bass V

1965-1970. Five strings, double-cut, 1 pickup, dot inlay '65-'66, block inlay '66-'70. Please refer to the beginning of the Fender Bass Section for details on Fender color options.

1965	Common color	$4,850	$6,300

MODEL		EXC. COND.	
YEAR	FEATURES	LOW	HIGH
1965	Rare color	$6,300	$8,400
1965	Sunburst	$3,800	$5,000
1966-1970	Common color	$4,400	$5,700
1966-1970	Rare color	$5,600	$7,300
1966-1970	Sunburst	$3,200	$4,200

Bass VI

1961-1975. Six strings, Jazzmaster-like body, 3 pickups, dot inlay until '66, block inlay '66-'75. Reintroduced as Japanese-made Collectable model '95-'98. Please refer to the beginning of the Fender Bass Section for details on Fender color options.

1961-1962	Common color	$14,400	$19,000
1961-1962	Rare color	$19,000	$25,000
1961-1962	Sunburst	$8,200	$10,600
1963-1964	Common color	$13,400	$17,500
1963-1964	Rare color	$17,500	$23,000
1963-1964	Sunburst	$7,100	$9,200
1965	Common color	$12,300	$16,000
1965	Rare color	$16,000	$21,000
1965	Sunburst	$6,000	$7,800
1966-1969	Common color	$8,500	$11,000
1966-1969	Rare color	$11,000	$14,300
1966-1969	Sunburst	$5,000	$6,500
1970-1971	Custom color	$7,500	$9,700
1970-1971	Sunburst	$5,000	$6,500
1972-1974	Custom color	$7,500	$9,700
1972-1974	Natural	$3,900	$5,000
1972-1974	Sunburst	$5,400	$7,200
1972-1974	Walnut	$4,000	$5,100
1975	Black, blond, white	$5,000	$6,500
1975	Natural	$3,900	$5,000
1975	Sunburst	$4,700	$6,100
1975	Walnut	$4,000	$5,100

Bass VI Reissue (CS)

2006. Custom Shop, 3-tone sunburst, certificate of authenticity.

2006		$1,925	$2,500

Bass VI Reissue (Import)

1995-1998. Import, sunburst.

1995-1998		$1,350	$1,750

Bass VI Reissue (Japan)

Japanese market only, JD serial number.

2014		$1,050	$1,400

Bass VI Pawn Shop

2013-2014. Alder body, maple neck, rosewood 'board, 3-color sunburst.

2013-2014		$525	$675

BG Series

1997-2012. Acoustic flat-top basses, single-cut, two-on-a-side tuners, Fishman on-board controls.

1997-2012	Various models	$150	$575

Bullet (B30, B34, B40)

1982-1983. Alder body, 1 pickup, offered in short- and long-scale, red or walnut. U.S.-made, replaced by Japanese-made Squire Bullet Bass.

1982-1983		$675	$875

Bullet Deluxe

1982-1983. Fender logo with Bullet Bass Deluxe on headstock, E-series serial number, small Telecaster-style headstock shape.

1982-1983		$675	$875

MODEL YEAR	FEATURES	EXC. COND. LOW	HIGH

Coronado I
1966-1970. Thinline, double-cut, 1 pickup, dot inlay, sunburst and cherry red were the standard colors, but custom colors could be ordered.

1966-1970	Various colors	$1,600	$2,100

Coronado II
1966-1972. Two pickups, block inlay, sunburst and cherry red standard colors, but custom colors could be ordered. Only Antigua finish offered from '70 on.

1966-1969	Various colors	$1,925	$2,500
1966-1969	Wildwood option	$2,575	$3,350
1970-1972	Antigua only	$1,875	$2,450

Coronado Reissue
2014-2016. Reissue of the 2 pickup (Coronado II), block inlay.

2014-2016		$500	$650

Dimension
2004-2006. Made in Mexico, 4- or 5-string, P and J pickups.

2004-2006		$450	$575

HM
1989-1991. Japanese-made, 4 strings (IV) or 5 strings (V), basswood body, no 'guard, 3 Jazz Bass pickups, 5-way switch, master volume, master TBX, sunburst.

1989-1991	IV, 4-string	$725	$950
1989-1991	V, 5-string	$800	$1,025

Jaguar
1995, 2006-2010. Crafted in Japan, Jaguar Bass logo on headstock.

1995		$1,075	$1,400
2006-2010		$925	$1,200

Jaguar (Modern Player)
2012-2016. Made in China, koto body, maple neck and 'board, black.

2012-2016		$325	$425

Jaguar Baritone Custom
2007. Fender Jaguar Baritone Custom logo on headstock, 6-string.

2007		$1,075	$1,400

Deluxe Jaguar
2012-2014. Maple neck, rosewood 'board, 2 pickups, 3-color sunburst, Candy Apple Red, Cobalt Blue.

2012-2014		$615	$800

Troy Sanders Jaguar
2014-present. Artist series, alder body, bolt-on maple neck, 2 pickups, silverburst.

2014-2021		$600	$775

Jazz Bass
The following are variations of the Jazz Bass. The first seven listings are for the main U.S.-made models. All others are listed alphabetically after that in the following order:

Jazz
Standard Jazz
American Standard Jazz
American Standard Jazz V
American Series Jazz
American Series Jazz V
American Professional/Professional II Jazz
50th Anniversary American Standard Jazz
50th Anniversary Jazz Limited Edition
'60 Custom Shop Limited Jazz
'60s Jazz (Custom Shop)
'60s Jazz (Import)
Road Worn '60s Jazz
Vintera '60s Jazz
60th Anniversary American Jazz
60th Anniversary Road Worn Jazz
'61 Journeyman Jazz
'62 Jazz (U.S.A.)
'64 Jazz (Custom Shop)
'64 Jazz (American Vintage)
'66 Jazz Special Limited Edition
'66 Journeyman Jazz
'74 Jazz (American Vintage)
'75 Jazz (American Vintage)
75th Anniversary Commemorative Jazz
75th Anniversary Jazz (Diamond Anniversary)
Aerodyne Jazz
American Deluxe Jazz/Jazz V
American Deluxe FMT Jazz
American Elite Jazz/Jazz V
American Ultra Jazz
Contemporary Jazz
Custom Classic Jazz/Jazz V
Deluxe Jazz/Jazz V (Active)
Deluxe Power Jazz
Flea Signature Jazz
Foto Flame Jazz
FSR Standard Special Edition Jazz
Geddy Lee Signature Jazz
Gold Jazz
Highway One Jazz
Jaco Pastorius Jazz
Jazz Plus IV/Jazz Plus V
Jazz Special (Import)
Marcus Miller Signature Jazz
Masterbuilt Custom Shop Jazz
Noel Redding Signature Jazz
Rarities Flame Ash Top Jazz
Reggie Hamilton Jazz
Roscoe Beck Jazz IV/Jazz V
Select Jazz
Standard Jazz (Import)
Standard Jazz Fretless (Import)
Steve Bailey Jazz VI
Ventures Limited Edition Jazz
Victor Baily Jazz

Jazz
1960-1981. Two stack knobs '60-'62, 3 regular controls '62 on. Dot markers '60-'66, block markers from '66 on. Rosewood 'board standard, but maple available from '68 on. With the introduction of vintage reissue models in '81, Fender started calling the American-made version the Standard Jazz Bass. That became the American Standard Jazz Bass in '88, the American Series Jazz Bass in '00, back to the American Standard Jazz Bass in '08, and currently the American Professional Jazz Bass. Post '71 Jazz Bass values are affected more by condition than color or neck option. The Jazz Bass was fitted with a 3-bolt neck or bullet rod in late-'74. Prices assume a 3-bolt

Fender Troy Sanders Jaguar

1966 Fender Jazz
Frank Manno

BASSES

1966 Fender Jazz
Carter Vintage Guitars

Fender 50th Anniversary Jazz
Rivington Guitars

neck starting in '75. Please refer to the beginning of the Fender Bass Section for details on Fender color options. Post '71 Jazz Bass values are affected more by condition than color or neck option. The Jazz Bass was fitted with a 3-bolt neck or bullet rod in late-'74. Prices assume a 3-bolt neck starting in '75. Please refer to the beginning of the Fender Bass Section for details on Fender color options.

MODEL YEAR	FEATURES	EXC. COND. LOW	HIGH
1960	Common color	$26,000	$34,000
1960	Rare color	$34,000	$45,000
1960	Sunburst	$23,000	$30,000
1961-1962	Common color, stack knob	$26,000	$34,000
1961-1962	Rare color, stack knob	$34,000	$44,000
1961-1962	Sunburst, stack knob	$23,000	$30,000
1962	Common color, 3 knob, curved	$18,000	$23,000
1962	Common color, 3 knob, slab	$20,000	$26,000
1962	Rare color, 3 knob, curved	$23,000	$35,000
1962	Rare color, 3 knob, slab	$26,000	$38,000
1962	Sunburst, knob, curved	$16,000	$21,000
1962	Sunburst, 3 knob, slab	$14,000	$18,000
1963	Common color	$16,000	$21,000
1963	Rare color	$21,000	$33,000
1963	Sunburst	$11,500	$15,000
1964	Common color	$14,700	$19,000
1964	Rare color	$19,000	$28,000
1964	Sunburst, early '64	$10,500	$13,500
1964	Sunburst, late '64	$10,000	$13,000
1965	Common color	$11,500	$15,000
1965	Rare color	$15,000	$22,000
1965	Sunburst	$7,300	$9,500
1966	Common color	$8,000	$10,500
1966	Rare color	$10,500	$15,000
1966	Sunburst, blocks	$6,100	$8,000
1966	Sunburst, dots	$5,600	$7,300
1967-1969	Custom color	$10,500	$15,000
1967-1969	Sunburst	$5,600	$7,300
1970	Custom color	$8,500	$11,000
1970	Sunburst	$5,000	$6,500
1971	Custom color	$6,800	$9,000
1971	Sunburst	$4,000	$5,200
1972	Custom color	$5,200	$6,800
1972	Natural, black block option	$3,200	$4,200
1972	Natural, standard markers	$3,000	$4,000
1972	Sunburst	$3,300	$4,300
1973	Custom color	$5,200	$6,800
1973	Natural	$3,000	$4,000
1973	Sunburst	$3,300	$4,300
1973	Walnut	$3,000	$4,000
1974	Black, blond, white, 3-bolt	$3,000	$3,900

MODEL YEAR	FEATURES	EXC. COND. LOW	HIGH
1974	Black, blond, white, 4-bolt	$3,300	$4,300
1974	Natural, 3-bolt	$3,000	$3,900
1974	Natural, 4-bolt	$3,300	$4,300
1974	Sunburst, 3-bolt, late-'74	$3,000	$3,900
1974	Sunburst, 4-bolt	$3,300	$4,300
1974	Walnut, 3-bolt	$3,000	$3,900
1974	Walnut, 4-bolt	$3,300	$4,300
1975-1977	All colors	$3,000	$3,900
1978-1980	All colors	$2,500	$3,300
1981	Black & Gold	$2,400	$3,100
1981	Black, white, wine	$2,400	$3,100
1981	International colors	$3,000	$3,900
1981	Sunburst	$2,400	$3,100

Standard Jazz
1981-1984. Replaced Jazz Bass ('60-'81) and replaced by the American Standard Jazz Bass in '88. Name now used on import version. Please refer to the beginning of the Fender Bass Section for details on Fender color options.

1981-1984		$1,200	$1,600

American Standard Jazz
1988-2000, 2008-2016. Replaced Standard Jazz Bass ('81-'88) and replaced by the American Series Jazz Bass in '00, back to American Standard in Jan. '08.

1988-2016		$975	$1,275

American Standard Jazz V
1998-2000, 2008-2016. 5-string version.

1998-2016		$975	$1,275

American Series Jazz
2000-2007. Replaces American Standard Jazz Bass. Renamed American Standard in '08.

2000-2007		$975	$1,275

American Series Jazz V
2000-2007. 5-string version.

2000-2007		$975	$1,275

American Professional/Professional II Jazz
2017-present. Redesign includes V-Mod pickups, narrow-tall frets, 'deep C' neck profile, various colors. Also available left-hand model. Renamed American Professional II in '20.

2017-2021		$975	$1,275

50th Anniversary American Standard Jazz
1996. Regular American Standard with gold hardware, 4- or 5-string, gold Fender's 50th Anniversary commemorative neck plate, rosewood 'board, sunburst.

1996	IV	$1,100	$1,450
1996	V	$1,150	$1,500

50th Anniversary Jazz Limited Edition
2010. 50th anniversary of the Jazz Bass, nitro Candy Apple Red with matching headstock, mix of vintage and modern specs, rosewood 'board, block markers, 50th Anniversary neck plate.

2010		$1,900	$2,500

'60 Custom Shop Limited Jazz
2020. Limited Edition, heavy relic.

2020		$2,650	$3,450

The *Vintage Guitar Price Guide* shows low to high values for items in all-original excellent condition, and, where applicable, with original case or cover.

MODEL YEAR	FEATURES	EXC. COND. LOW	HIGH

'60s Jazz (Custom Shop)
1994-1998. Early '60s specs, relic for 1996-1998. Replaced by the CS '64 Jazz Bass. Early Relic work was done outside of Fender by Vince Cunetto or his staff.

1994-1995		$2,800	$3,700
1996	Relic (Cunetto)	$2,800	$3,700
1997-1998	Relic (Cunetto staff)	$2,700	$3,600

'60s Jazz (Import)
1991-1994, 2001-2019. Classic series, '60s features, rosewood 'board, Japan-made for first years, Mexico after.

1991-1994	Japan	$700	$950
2001-2019	Mexico	$525	$675

Road Worn '60s Jazz
2009-2019. Rosewood 'board, aged finish.

2009-2019		$575	$750

Vintera '60s Jazz
2020-present. Vintage style appointments, 3-Color Sunburst, Daphne Blue or Firemist Gold.

2020-2021		$650	$850

60th Anniversary American Jazz
2006. Rosewood 'board, 3-tone sunburst.

2006		$1,200	$1,575

60th Anniversary Road Worn Jazz
2020-2021. Road Worn lacquer finish, 3-color sunburst, Firemist Silver or Olympic White.

2020-2021		$825	$1,075

'61 Journeyman Jazz
2020. Heavy relic.

2020		$2,650	$3,450

'62 Jazz (U.S.A.)
1982-1984, 1986-2012. U.S.A.-made, American Vintage series, reissue of '62 Jazz Bass. Please refer to the beginning of the Fender Bass Section for details on Fender color options.

1982-1984		$3,200	$4,200
1986-1999		$1,800	$2,350
2000-2012		$1,350	$1,750

'64 Jazz (Custom Shop)
1998-2009. Alder body, rosewood 'board, tortoise shell 'guard. From June '95 to June '99 Relic work was done outside of Fender by Vince Cunetto and included a certificate noting model and year built, a bass without the certificate is valued less than shown.

1998-1999	Relic (Cunetto)	$2,800	$3,600
2000-2009	Closet Classic option	$2,400	$3,100
2000-2009	NOS option	$2,400	$3,100
2000-2009	Relic option	$2,550	$3,300

'64 Jazz (American Vintage)
2013-2017. American Vintage series, dot inlays.

2013-2017		$1,350	$1,750

'66 Jazz Special Limited Edition
2013. Japan, made for retailer Sweetwater, aged Oly White, 132 made for North American distribution.

2013		$925	$1,200

'66 Journeyman Jazz
2020. Relic.

2020		$2,650	$3,450

'74 Jazz (American Vintage)
2013-2017. American Vintage series, block inlays.

2013-2017		$1,450	$1,875

'75 Jazz (American Vintage)
1994-2012. American Vintage series, maple neck with black block markers.

1994-2012		$1,350	$1,750

75th Anniversary Commemorative Jazz
2021. Limited Edition, gold 75th ingot back of headstock and 75th anniversary neck plate, gold hardware, 2-color Bourbon Burst.

2021		$1,375	$1,800

75th Anniversary Jazz (Diamond Anniversary)
2021. Diamond Anniversary metallic finish with matching painted headstock, 75th engraved silver neck plate.

2021		$575	$750

Aerodyne Jazz
2003-present. Bound basswood body, P/J pickups, Deluxe Series.

2003-2021		$800	$1,025

American Deluxe Jazz/Jazz V
1998-2016. U.S., 4 (IV) or 5-string (V), active electronics, alder or ash body. Alder body colors - sunburst or transparent red, ash body colors - white, blond, transparent teal green or transparent purple.

1998-2016	IV or V	$1,225	$1,600

American Deluxe FMT Jazz
2001-2006. Flame maple top version (FMT), active EQ, dual J pickups.

2001-2006		$1,350	$1,750

American Elite Jazz/Jazz V
2016-2019. Compound radius 'board, 4 (IV) or 5-string (V), Noiseless pickups, onboard preamp, various colors.

2016-2019	IV or V	$1,350	$1,750

American Ultra Jazz
2019-present. Alder or ash body, 2 Noiseless Vintage pickups, redesigned active/passive preamp, 4- (IV) or 5-string (V), various colors with satin finish.

2019-2021	IV or V	$1,200	$1,600

Contemporary Jazz
1987. Made in Japan.

1987		$575	$750

Custom Classic Jazz/Jazz V
2001-2009. Custom Shop, slightly slimmer waist, deeper cutaways, maple or rosewood 'board, block inlays, 4 (IV) or 5-string (V).

2001-2009	IV or V	$2,100	$2,700

Deluxe Jazz/Jazz V (Active)
1995-2021. Made in Mexico, active electronics, 4 (IV) or 5-string (V), various colors.

1995-2021	IV or V	$450	$575

Deluxe Power Jazz
2006. Part of Deluxe Series with Fishman piezo power bridge.

2006		$700	$900

Flea Signature Jazz
2019-present. Flea logo neck plate, Road Worn Faded Shell Pink lacquer finish.

2019-2021		$925	$1,200

Fender Deluxe Jazz V
John Hefty

Fender Flea Signature Jazz

BASSES

BASSES

1998 Fender Roscoe
Beck Jazz V
Imaged by Heritage Auctions, HA.com

1978 Fender Mustang
Justin Nortillo

MODEL YEAR	FEATURES	EXC. COND. LOW	HIGH
Foto Flame Jazz			
1994-1996. Japanese import, alder and basswood body with Foto Flame figured wood image.			
1994-1996		$750	$975
FSR Standard Special Edition Jazz			
2007-2009. Made in Mexico, Fender Special Edition logo on back of headstock, ash body with natural finish.			
2007-2009		$500	$650
Geddy Lee Signature Jazz			
1998-present. Limited run import in '98, now part of Artist Series, black.			
1998-2021		$750	$975
Gold Jazz			
1981-1984. Gold finish and gold-plated hardware.			
1981-1984		$2,150	$2,800
Highway One Jazz			
2003-2011. U.S.-made, alder body, satin lacquer finish.			
2003-2011		$700	$900
Jaco Pastorius Jazz			
1999-present. Artist Series, standard production model made in Corona, '62 3-color sunburst body without pickup covers.			
1999-2000	Fretted	$1,350	$1,750
1999-2021	Fretless	$1,350	$1,750
Jazz Plus IV/Jazz Plus V			
1990-1994. Alder body, 4-string (IV) or 5-string (V), 2 Lace Sensors, active electronics, rotary circuit selector, master volume, balance, bass boost, bass cut, treble boost, treble cut, various colors.			
1990-1994	Various colors	$875	$1,150
Jazz Special (Import)			
1984-1991. Japanese-made, Jazz/Precision hybrid, Precision-shaped basswood body, Jazz neck (fretless available), 2 P/J pickups, offered with active (Power) or passive electronics.			
1984-1991		$600	$800
Marcus Miller Signature Jazz			
1998-2014. Artist series.			
1998-2004	Import	$875	$1,150
2005-2014	US Custom Shop	$1,550	$2,000
Masterbuilt Custom Shop Jazz			
2003-present. Various models and builders.			
2003-2021		$4,000	$8,000
Noel Redding Signature Jazz			
1997. Limited Edition import, artist signature on 'guard, sunburst, rosewood 'board.			
1997		$1,125	$1,450
Rarities Flame Ash Top Jazz			
2019-2021. Two-piece alder body with flame ash top, Plasma Red Burst finish.			
2019-2021		$1,700	$2,200
Reggie Hamilton Jazz			
2002-2016. Custom Artist series, alder body, passive/active switch and pan control.			
2002-2016		$575	$750
Roscoe Beck Jazz IV/Jazz V			
1997-2009. 5-string version offered '97-'06, 4-string '04-'09.			
1997-2006	V, 5-string	$1,650	$2,150
2004-2009	IV, 4-string	$1,600	$2,100

MODEL YEAR	FEATURES	EXC. COND. LOW	HIGH
Select Jazz			
2012-2013. US-made, figured top, rear-headstock 'Fender Select' medallion.			
2012-2013		$1,950	$2,550
Standard Jazz (Import)			
1985-2018. Standard series, Japan-made into '90, Mexico after. Not to be confused with '81-'84 American-made model with the same name. Replaced by Player Series.			
1985-1990	Japan	$875	$1,150
1991-2018	Mexico	$425	$550
Standard Jazz Fretless (Import)			
1994-2018. Standard series, fretless version. Replaced by Player Series.			
1994-2018	IV or V	$425	$550
Steve Bailey Jazz VI			
2009-2011. USA, 6-string, fretless or fretted, sunburst or black.			
2009-2011		$1,700	$2,200
Ventures Limited Edition Jazz			
1996. Made in Japan, part of Ventures guitar and bass set, dark purple.			
1996		$1,225	$1,600
Victor Baily Jazz			
2002-2011. Artist series, koa, rosewood and mahogany body, fretless with white fret markers.			
2002-2011		$1,350	$1,750
JP-90			
1990-1994. Two P/J pickups, rosewood fretboard, poplar body, black or red.			
1990-1994		$500	$650
Kingman			
2011-present. Acoustic, solid spruce top, mahogany back and sides.			
2011-2021		$400	$525
MB IV/MB V			
1994-1995. Made in Japan, offset double-cut, 1 P- and 1 J-style pickup, 4-string (IV) or 5-string (V).			
1994-1995	IV or V	$425	$550
Musicmaster			
1970-1983. Shorter scale, solidbody, 1 pickup. various colors.			
1970-1983		$1,175	$1,525
Mustang			
1966-1982. Shorter scale, solidbody, 1 pickup, offered in standard colors and, for '69-'73, Competition Red, Blue and Orange with racing stripes on the body (with matching headstock for '69-'70).			
1966-1969		$1,950	$2,550
1969-1970	Competition	$1,950	$2,550
1970-1979		$1,950	$2,550
1978-1980	Antigua finish	$1,850	$2,400
1980-1982		$1,325	$1,725
Mustang (Import)			
2002-2018. First made in Japan, later Mexico (ca. 2015), alder body, '60s features.			
2002-2018		$625	$825
Parallel Universe '51 Telecaster PJ			
2018. Limited edition, authentic '51 style, mixes elements from both Jazz and Precision Basses.			
2018		$1,350	$1,750

MODEL		EXC. COND.	
YEAR	FEATURES	LOW	HIGH

Performer
1985-1986. Swinger-like body style, active electronics, various colors.

1985-1986		$1,475	$1,900

Postmodern
2015-2019. Custom Shop, P-Bass body, Jazz Bass neck, at times offered in Relic, Journeyman Relic, NOS, and Lush Closet Classic finishes.

2015-2019	Various options	$2,350	$3,050

Precision Bass

The following are variations of the Precision Bass. The first six listings are for the main U.S.-made models. All others are listed alphabetically after that in the following order:

Precision
Standard Precision
American Standard Precision
American Series Precision
American Series Precision V
American Professional/Professional II Precision
40th Anniversary Precision (Custom Shop)
50th Anniversary American Standard Precision
50th Anniversary Precision
'50s Precision
Road Worn '50s Precision
'51 Precision
'55 Precision (Custom Shop)
'57 Precision
'57 Precision (Custom Shop)
'57 Precision (Import)
'59 Precision (Custom Shop)
60th Anniversary Precision (Mexico)
60th Anniversary Precision (USA)
'61 Precision (Custom Shop)
'62 Precision
'62 Precision (Import)
'63 Precision (U.S.A.)
75th Anniversary Commemorative Precision
75th Anniversary Precision (Diamond Anniversary)
Adam Clayton Signature Precision
Aerodyne Classic Precision Special
American Deluxe Precision
American Ultra Precision
Big Block Precision
Cabronita Precision
California Precision Special
Deluxe Active Precision Special
Elite/Gold Elite Precision Series
Foto Flame Precision
Highway One Precision
Magnificent Seven LE American Standard PJ
Mark Hoppus Signature Precision
Mike Dirnt Road Worn Precision
Nate Mendel Precision
Pino Palladino Signature Precision
Precision Jr.
Precision Lyte
Precision Special (Mexico)
Precision Special (U.S.A.)

MODEL		EXC. COND.	
YEAR	FEATURES	LOW	HIGH

Precision U.S. Plus/Plus
Precision U.S. Deluxe/Plus Deluxe
Roger Waters Precision
Select Precision
Standard/Player Precision (Import)
Sting Precision
Tony Franklin Precision
Walnut Elite Precision
Walnut Precision Special

Precision
1951-1981. Slab body until '54, 1-piece maple neck standard until '59, optional after '69, rosewood 'board standard '59 on (slab until mid-'62, curved after), blond finish standard until '54, sunburst standard after that (2-tone '54-'58, 3-tone after '58). Became the Standard Precision Bass in '81-'85, the American Standard Precision for '88-'00, the American Series Precision Bass in '00-'08, and the American Standard Precision again for '08-'16. Currently called the American Professional Precision Bass. Unlike the Jazz and Telecaster Basses, the Precision was never fitted with a 3-bolt neck or bullet rod. Please refer to the beginning of the Fender Bass Section for details on Fender color options.

YEAR	FEATURES	LOW	HIGH
1951-1954	Blond, slab	$17,700	$23,000
1955	Blond, contour	$15,000	$19,400
1956	Blond, contour	$13,000	$17,000
1956	Sunburst, contour	$12,200	$15,800
1957	Blond	$13,000	$17,000
1957	Blond, anodized guard	$13,000	$17,000
1957	Sunburst, anodized guard, late '57	$11,500	$15,000
1957	Sunburst, tortoise guard	$11,500	$15,000
1958	Blond	$13,000	$17,000
1958	Sunburst, anodized guard	$11,500	$15,000
1959	Blond	$13,000	$17,000
1959	Sunburst, anodized guard	$11,500	$15,000
1959	Sunburst, tortoise guard	$11,500	$15,000
1960	Blond	$13,000	$17,000
1960	Custom color	$21,000	$44,000
1960	Sunburst	$11,000	$14,000
1961	Custom color	$14,000	$32,000
1961	Sunburst	$10,000	$13,000
1962	Custom color, curved	$11,000	$20,000
1962	Custom color, slab	$14,000	$32,000
1962	Sunburst, curved	$10,000	$13,000
1962	Sunburst, slab	$11,000	$14,000
1963	Custom color	$10,000	$19,000
1963	Sunburst	$9,000	$12,000
1964	Custom color	$10,000	$19,000
1964	Sunburst, early '64, spaghetti logo, green guard	$10,000	$13,000
1964	Sunburst, late '64	$9,000	$12,000
1965	Custom color	$11,500	$15,000
1965	Sunburst	$6,700	$8,900

1958 Fender Precision
Phil Avelli

1959 Fender Precision
Charlie Faucher

BASSES

1973 Fender Precision
KC Cormack

Fender Road Worn '50s Precision
Johnny Zapp

MODEL YEAR	FEATURES	EXC. COND. LOW	HIGH
1966	Sunburst	$5,500	$7,300
1966-1969	Custom color	$10,500	$13,600
1970	Custom color	$6,800	$9,100
1970	Sunburst	$3,700	$4,900
1971	Custom color	$6,800	$9,100
1971	Sunburst	$3,000	$4,000
1972	Custom color	$5,300	$7,100
1972	Sunburst	$2,800	$3,800
1973	Custom color	$5,300	$7,100
1973	Natural, sunburst, walnut	$2,800	$3,800
1974	All colors	$2,800	$3,800
1975-1977	All colors	$2,350	$3,100
1978-1979	All colors	$2,150	$2,850
1980	Color with matching hdstk, gold hw	$2,800	$3,600
1980	International colors	$2,700	$3,500
1980	Other colors	$2,100	$2,700
1981	Black & gold	$2,100	$2,700
1981	International colors	$2,700	$3,500
1981	Other colors	$2,100	$2,700

Standard Precision
1981-1984. Replaces Precision Bass, various colors. Replaced by American Standard Precision '88-'00. The Standard name is used on import Precision model for '88-present.

1981-1984		$1,200	$1,600

American Standard Precision
1988-2000, 2008-2016. Replaces Standard Precision Bass, replaced by American Series Precision in '00, back to American Standard in Jan. '08.

1988-1989	Blond, gold hw	$975	$1,275
1988-2016	Various colors	$975	$1,275

American Series Precision
2000-2007. Replaces American Standard Precision Bass, various colors. Renamed American Standard in '08.

2000-2007		$975	$1,275

American Series Precision V
2000-2007. 5-string version.

2000-2007		$975	$1,275

American Professional/Professional II Precision
2017-present. Redesign includes V-Mod pickups, '63 P Bass neck profile, narrow-tall frets, various colors. Also available left-hand model. Renamed American Professional II in '20.

2017-2021		$975	$1,275

40th Anniversary Precision (Custom Shop)
1991. 400 made, quilted amber maple top, gold hardware.

1991		$2,500	$3,300

50th Anniversary American Standard Precision
1996. Regular American Standard with gold hardware, 4- or 5-string, gold 50th Anniversary commemorative neck plate, rosewood 'board, sunburst.

1996		$1,100	$1,450

50th Anniversary Precision
2001. Commemorative certificate with date and serial number, butterscotch finish, ash body, maple neck, black 'guard.

2001	With certificate	$1,100	$1,450

'50s Precision
1992-1996, 2006-2019. First run made in Japan, currently in Mexico, 1 split-coil, maple neck.

1992-1996	Japan	$600	$800
2006-2019	Mexico	$525	$675

Road Worn '50s Precision
2009-2019. Mexico, 1 split-coil, maple neck, aged finish.

2009-2019		$575	$750

'51 Precision
1994-1997, 2003-2010. Import from Japan, no pickup or bridge covers, blond or sunburst. Offered in Japan in the '90s.

1994-1997	Japan only	$700	$925
2003-2010		$600	$775

'55 Precision (Custom Shop)
2003-2011. 1955 specs including oversized 'guard, 1-piece maple neck/fretboard, preproduction bridge and pickup covers, single-coil pickup. Offered in N.O.S., Closet Classic or highest-end Relic.

2003-2006	NOS	$2,400	$3,100
2003-2006	Relic	$2,550	$3,300
2003-2011	Closet Classic	$2,400	$3,100

'57 Precision
1982-1984, 1986-2012. U.S.-made reissue, American Vintage series, various colors.

1982-1984		$3,200	$4,200
1986-1999		$1,800	$2,350
2000-2012		$1,350	$1,750

'57 Precision (Custom Shop)

2013	Heavy relic	$2,650	$3,450

'57 Precision (Import)

1984-1986	Black	$1,325	$1,725

'59 Precision (Custom Shop)
2003-2010. Custom Shop built with late-'59 specs, rosewood 'board.

2003-2008	Closet Classic	$2,400	$3,100
2003-2010	NOS	$2,400	$3,100
2003-2010	Relic	$2,550	$3,300

60th Anniversary Precision (Mexico)
2011. Made in Mexico, with 60th Anniversary gig bag.

2011		$450	$575

60th Anniversary Precision (USA)
2011. 1951-2011 Anniversary date label.

2011		$1,200	$1,575

'61 Precision (Custom Shop)
2010-2013. Made for Musician's Friend and Guitar Center.

2010-2013	Closet Classic	$2,400	$3,100
2010-2013	NOS	$2,400	$3,100
2010-2013	Relic	$2,550	$3,300

'62 Precision
1982-1984, 1986-2012. American Vintage series, alder body. No production in '85. Limited run Mary Kaye Blond (gold hardware) in '90.

1982-1984		$3,200	$4,200

MODEL YEAR	FEATURES	EXC. COND. LOW	HIGH
1986-1999		$1,800	$2,350
1990	Mary Kaye Blond	$2,200	$2,900
2000-2012		$1,350	$1,750

'62 Precision (Import)
1984-1986. Foreign-made, black.

1984-1986		$1,325	$1,725

'63 Precision (U.S.A.)
2013-2017. American Vintage series.

2013-2017		$1,175	$1,525

75th Anniversary Commemorative Precision
2021. Limited Edition, gold 75th ingot back of headstock and 75th anniversary neck plate, gold hardware, 2-color Bourbon Burst.

2021		$1,275	$1,650

75th Anniversary Precision (Diamond Anniversary)
2021. Diamond Anniversary metallic finish with matching painted headstock, 75th engraved silver neck plate.

2021		$550	$725

Adam Clayton Signature Precision
2011. Custom Shop Limited Edition.

2011		$3,300	$4,300

Aerodyne Classic Precision Special
2006. Made in Japan, labeled Precision and Aerodyne P Bass, figured maple top, matching headstock, P-J pickup.

2006		$800	$1,025

American Deluxe Precision
1998-2016. U.S., active electronics, 4 (IV) or 5-string (V), alder or ash body. Alder body colors - sunburst or transparent red. Ash body colors - white blond, transparent teal green or transparent purple.

1998-2016	IV or V	$1,225	$1,600

American Ultra Precision
2019-present. Alder or ash body, 2 Noiseless Vintage pickups, 4-string, various colors with gloss finish.

2019-2021		$1,200	$1,600

Big Block Precision
2005-2009. Pearloid block markers, black finish with matching headstock, 1 double Jazz Bass humbucker, bass and treble boost and cut controls.

2005-2009		$675	$875

Cabronita Precision
2014-2015. One Fideli'Tron pickup, 2 knobs.

2014-2015		$350	$450

California Precision Special
1997. California Series, assembled and finished in Mexico and California, P/J pickup configuration.

1997		$650	$850

Deluxe Active Precision Special
1995-2021. Made in Mexico, P/J pickups, Jazz Bass neck.

1995-2021		$450	$575

Elite/Gold Elite Precision Series
1983-1985. Active electronics, noise-cancelling pickups, Elite I (ash body, 1 pickup), Elite II (2 pickups), Gold Elite I (gold-plated hardware, 1 pickup), Gold Elite II (2 pickups), various colors.

1983-1985	Various models	$2,100	$2,700

Foto Flame Precision
1994-1996. Made in Japan, simulated woodgrain finish, natural or sunburst.

1994-1996		$750	$975

Highway One Precision
2003-2011. U.S.-made, alder body, satin lacquer finish.

2003-2011		$700	$900

Magnificent Seven LE American Standard PJ
2016. U.S., Limited Edition, P-bass body with Jazz neck, 500 made.

2016		$950	$1,250

Mark Hoppus Signature Precision
2002-2016. Mark Hoppus engraved on neck plate.

2002-2016	Mexico serial no.	$550	$725

Mike Dirnt Road Worn Precision
2014-present. '51 era P-Bass style, ash body, maple or rosewood 'board.

2014-2021		$700	$900

Nate Mendel Precision
2013-present. Ash body, rosewood 'board.

2013-2021		$550	$725

Pino Palladino Signature Precision
2006-present. Custom Shop Artist series, based on '62 used by Palladino, certificate of authenticity, Fiesta Red.

2006		$2,150	$2,800

Precision Jr.
2004-2006. 3/4 size.

2004-2006		$400	$525

Precision Lyte
1992-2001. Japanese-made, smaller, lighter basswood body, 2 pickups, sunburst.

1992-2001		$600	$800

Precision Special (Mexico)
1997-1998. Chrome hardware, 1 P- and 1 J-pickup.

1997-1998		$575	$750

Precision Special (U.S.A.)
1980-1982. Gold hardware, matching headstock, active electronics, CA Red, LP Blue, Oly White or walnut (see separate listing).

1980-1982	Rare color	$2,200	$2,800
1980-1982	Standard color	$1,800	$2,300

Precision U.S. Plus/Plus
1989-1992. P-style bass with P- and J-bass pickups.

1989-1992	Rare color	$1,000	$1,300
1989-1992	Standard color	$850	$1,100

Precision U.S. Deluxe/Plus Deluxe
1991-1994. P-style bass with P- and J-bass pickups, active electronics, no 'guard models available.

1991-1994	Rare color	$1,000	$1,300
1991-1994	Standard color	$850	$1,100

Roger Waters Precision
2010-2019. Alder body, maple neck, black.

2010-2019		$600	$775

Select Precision
2012. Alder body, flamed maple top, rear headstock 'Fender Select' medallion.

2012		$1,950	$2,550

1988 Fender '62 Precision
Jonathan Bell

Fender American Ultra Precision

Fender Squier Bronco

*1983 Fender Squier
Precision Standard*

Rivington Guitars

MODEL YEAR	FEATURES	EXC. COND. LOW	HIGH
Standard/Player Precision (Import)			

1985-present. Made in Japan into '90, and Mexico after. Not to be confused with '81-'84 American-made model with the same name. Also available left-handed. Replaced by Player Series in 18.

MODEL YEAR	FEATURES	EXC. COND. LOW	HIGH
1985-1990	Japan	$875	$1,150
1991-2021	Mexico	$425	$550
2016	Mexico, Custom		
	Art Series	$425	$550
Sting Precision			

2001-2013. Made in Japan, 2-tone sunburst, 1 single-coil, Sting's signature.

2001-2013		$550	$725
Tony Franklin Precision			

2007-present. Fretless, P and J pickups, 3-way selector, lacquer finish.

2007-2021		$1,150	$1,500
Walnut Elite Precision			

1983-1985. The Elite Series feature active electronics and noise-cancelling pickups, walnut body, 1 pickup (Elite I) or 2 (Elite II), rosewood 'board, natural.

1983-1985	Elite I	$1,900	$2,500
1983-1985	Elite II	$1,900	$2,500
Walnut Precision Special			

1980-1982. Precision Bass Special with a walnut body, natural.

1980-1982		$1,800	$2,350
Prodigy Active			

1992-1995. U.S.-made, poplar body, 1 J- and 1 P-style pickup, active.

1992-1995		$1,025	$1,350
Rhodes Piano			

1962. Electric keyboard in bass register, Fender-Rhodes sticker, Piano Bass logo, various colors.

1962		$2,150	$2,800
Squier Affinity Jazz			

1997-present. Affinity is the lower priced series made in China.

1997-2021		$115	$150
Squier Bronco			

1998-present. The lowest priced Squier bass, single coil plastic cover pickup, 3/4 body.

1998-2021		$140	$185
Squier Bullet			

1983-2000. Japanese-made, Squier-branded, replaces Bullet Bass, black.

1983-2000		$270	$350
Squier Classic Vibe Series			

2009-present. Various models.

2009-2021		$270	$350
Squier HM/HM V			

1989-1993. Korean-made, 5-string also offered.

1989-1993		$275	$350
Squier Jazz Standard			

1983-2010. Jazz bass import, without cover plates, various colors.

1983-1984	1st logo	$450	$575
1985-1989	2nd logo	$400	$525
1990-1999		$190	$250

MODEL YEAR	FEATURES	EXC. COND. LOW	HIGH
2000-2010		$175	$225
Squier Katana			

1985-1986. Made in Japan, wedge-shaped, arrow headstock.

1985-1986		$650	$850
Squier Precision Special			

1998-2010. Agathis body, P/J pickups, 4-string (IV) or 5-string (V).

1998-2010	IV or V	$115	$150
Squier Precision Standard			
1983-1984	1st logo	$450	$575
1985-1989	2nd logo	$400	$525
1990-1999	Some from Mexico	$195	$250
2000-2006	Indonesia	$145	$190
Squier Vintage Modified Series			

2007-2019. Includes Jaguar, Jazz and Precision models.

2007-2019	Various models	$175	$230
Stu Hamm Urge (U.S.A.)			

1992-1999. Contoured Precision-style body with smaller wide treble cutaway, J and P pickups, 32" scale.

1992-1999		$1,400	$1,800
Stu Hamm Urge II (U.S.A.)			

1999-2009. J and P pickups, 34" scale.

1999-2009		$1,400	$1,800
Telecaster			

1968-1979. Slab solidbody, 1 pickup, fretless option '70, blond and custom colors available (Pink Paisley or Blue Floral '68-'69). Please refer to the beginning of the Fender Bass Section for details on Fender color options.

1968	Black, nitro	$3,800	$5,000
1968	Black, poly	$3,600	$4,800
1968	Blond, nitro	$2,700	$3,600
1968	Blond, poly	$2,600	$3,450
1968	Blue Floral Paisley	$7,000	$9,000
1968	Lake Placid Blue	$4,300	$5,800
1968	Pink Paisley	$6,500	$8,700
1969-1972	4-bolt, single-coil	$2,450	$3,250
1973-1974	3-bolt, hum,		
	rare color	$2,300	$3,000
1973-1974	3-bolt, humbucker	$1,800	$2,400
1975-1979	3-bolt, humbucker	$1,650	$2,200
Zone (American Deluxe)			

2001-2006. Smaller lightweight offset double-cut, active humbuckers, exotic tone woods, U.S.-made.

2001-2006		$1,250	$1,625

Fodera

1983-present. Luthiers Vinnie Fodera and Joseph Lauricella build their professional and premium grade, production/custom, solidbody basses in Brooklyn, New York.

High-level			
1983-2021	4, 5, 6 strings	$8,100	$10,500
Mid-level			
1983-2021	4, 5, 6 strings	$7,000	$9,000
Low-level			
1983-2021	4, 5, 6 strings	$4,200	$5,500

BASSES

MODEL YEAR	FEATURES	EXC. COND. LOW	HIGH

Framus

1946-1975, 1996-present. Professional and premium grade, production/custom, basses made in Germany. They also build guitars and amps.

Atlantic Model 5/140
1960s. Single-cut thinline with f-holes, 2 pickups, sunburst or blackrose.

1960s		$600	$800

Atlantic Model 5/143
1960s. Offset double-cut thinbody with f-holes, 2 pickups, 4-on-a-side keys.

1960s		$600	$800

Atlantic Model 5/144
1960s. Double-cut thinbody with f-holes, ES-335 body style, 2 pickups. Becomes Model J/144 in '70s.

1960s		$600	$800

Charavelle 4 Model 5/153
1960s. Double-cut thinline with f-holes, 335-style body, 2 pickups, sunburst, cherry red or Sunset.

1960s		$675	$875

De Luxe 4 Model 5/154
1960s. Double-cut thinline, sharp horns and f-holes, 2 pickups, mute, sunburst or natural/blond.

1960s		$675	$875

Electric Upright
1950s. Full-scale neck, triangular body, black.

1958		$1,850	$2,400

Star Series (Bill Wyman)
1959-1968. Early flyer says, Bill Wyman of the Rolling Stones prefers the Star Bass. The model name was later changed to Framus Stone Bass. Single-cut semi-hollow body, 5/149 (1 pickup) and 5/150 (2 pickups), sunburst.

1959-1965	Model 5/150	$1,025	$1,350
1960s	Model 5/149	$950	$1,250

Strato De Luxe Star Model 5/165
Ca. 1964-ca. 1972. Offset double-cut solidbody, 2 pickups, sunburst. There was also a gold hardware version (5/165 gl) and a 6-string (5/166).

1960s		$625	$800

Strato Star Series
Ca. 1963-ca. 1972. Double-cut solidbody, 5/156/50 (1 pickup) or 5/156/52 (2 pickups), beige, cherry or sunburst.

1960s	Model 5/156/50	$625	$800
1960s	Model 5/156/52	$675	$850

T.V. Star
1960s. Offset double-cut thinbody with f-holes, 2 pickups, short-scale, sunburst or cherry red. Most expensive of the '60s Framus basses, although not as popular as the Bill Wyman 5/150 model.

1960s		$600	$800

Triumph Electric Upright
1956-1960. Solidbody bean pole electric bass, small body, long neck, slotted viol peghead, gold or black.

1956-1960		$2,000	$2,600

Fresher

1973-1985. Japanese-made, mainly copies of popular brands and not imported into the U.S., but they do show up at guitar shows. They also made guitars.

MODEL YEAR	FEATURES	EXC. COND. LOW	HIGH

Solidbody Electric

1970s		$375	$500

G&L

1980-present. Intermediate and professional grade, production/custom, electric basses made in the U.S. In '03, G&L introduced the Korean-made G&L Tribute Series. A Tribute logo is clearly identified on the headstock. They also build guitars.

ASAT
1989-2020. Single-cut, solidbody, active and passive modes, 2 humbuckers, various colors.

1989-1991	About 400 made	$1,225	$1,600
1992-2020		$1,125	$1,475

ASAT Commemorative
1991-1992. About 150 made, 4-string ASAT commemorating Leo Fender's life.

1991-1992		$1,600	$2,100

ASAT Semi-Hollow
2001-2020. Semi-hollowbody style on ASAT bass.

2001-2020		$1,135	$1,475

Climax
1992-1996. Single active humbucker MFD.

1992-1996		$950	$1,225

El Toro
1983-1989. Double-cut, solidbody, 2 active, smaller, humbuckers, sunburst.

1983-1987		$1,275	$1,650
1988-1989		$1,075	$1,400

Interceptor
1984-1991. Sharp pointed double-cut, solidbody, 2 active, smaller humbuckers, sunburst.

1984-1986		$2,650	$3,425
1988-1991	Body signature	$1,350	$1,750

JB-2
2001-2018. Alder body, 2 Alnico V pickups.

2001-2018		$1,000	$1,300

Kiloton
2016-present. Single MFD humbucker pickup, custom options and finishes.

2016-2021	Standard top	$950	$1,250
2020-2021	Premium figured	$1,300	$1,700

L-1000
1980-1994, 2008. Offset double-cut, solidbody, 1 pickup, various colors. Limited run in '08.

1980-1985	Ash	$1,100	$1,400
1980-1985	Mahogany	$1,100	$1,400
1980-1985	Maple	$1,100	$1,400
1986-1991		$1,100	$1,400
1992-1999	3-bolt	$1,100	$1,400
2008	4-bolt	$1,100	$1,400

L-1500
1997-2018. Offset double-cut solidbody, 1 MFD humbucker.

1997-2018		$1,100	$1,400

L-1500 Custom

1997	Only year made	$1,125	$1,450

L-1505
1998-2018. Five-string version, single MFD humbucker.

1998-2018		$1,275	$1,500

1972 Fender Telecaster Bass
Justin Nortillo

G&L ASAT
Imaged by Heritage Auctions, HA.com

1991 G&L SB-1
KC Cormack

Gibson EB-1
Rivington Guitars

MODEL YEAR	FEATURES	EXC. COND. LOW	HIGH
L-2000			
1980-present. Offset double-cut solidbody, 2 pickups, active electronics. Originally, the L-2000 was available with active (L-2000E) or passive (L-2000) electronics.			
1980-1985	Ash	$1,375	$1,800
1986		$1,200	$1,600
1987-1991	Leo signature	$1,200	$1,600
1992-2021		$1,200	$1,600
L-2000 30th Anniversary			
2010. Pearl Frost with matching headstock.			
2010		$1,375	$1,800
L-2000 C.L.F. Centennial			
2009-2010. Swamp ash body, blonde, black hardware, planned run of 50, Certificate of Authenticity.			
2009-2010	COA, CD	$1,450	$1,900
L-2000 Custom			
1997. Ash top, wood-grain binding upgrade.			
1997		$1,100	$1,400
L-2000 Fretless			
1980-1998. Fretless version.			
1980-1982		$1,400	$1,800
L-2000E			
1980-1982. Offset double-cut, solidbody, 2 pickups, active electronics. Originally, the L-2000 was available with active (L-2000E) or passive (L-2000) electronics.			
1980-1982		$1,425	$1,850
L-2500			
1997-present. Dual MFD humbuckers, 5-string, figured tops can vary.			
1997-2021		$1,300	$1,700
L-2500 Custom			
1997. Ash top, wood-grain binding upgrade.			
1997		$1,350	$1,750
L-5000			
1988-1993. Offset double-cut, solidbody, G&L Z-shaped split-humbucker, 5 strings, approximately 400 made.			
1988-1992		$925	$1,200
L-5500			
1993-1997		$875	$1,150
L-5500 Custom			
1997. Ash top, wood-grain binding upgrade.			
1997		$875	$1,150
LB-100			
1993-present. Follow-up to earlier Legacy Bass.			
1993-2021		$975	$1,275
Legacy			
1992-1993. Offset double-cut solidbody, 1 split-coil, renamed LB-100 in '93.			
1992-1993		$975	$1,275
Lynx			
1984-1991. Offset double-cut, solidbody, 2 single-coils, black.			
1984-1991		$975	$1,275
M-2500			
2012-present. Dual MFD humbuckers, 5-string, options and finishes.			
2012-2021		$1,300	$1,700

MODEL YEAR	FEATURES	EXC. COND. LOW	HIGH
SB-1			
1982-2000, 2014-present. Solidbody, maple neck, body and 'board, split-humbucker, 1 tone and 1 volume control. Reappears in '14.			
1982-2000		$750	$975
SB-2			
1982-present. Maple neck with tilt adjustment, 1 split-coil humbucker and 1 single-coil.			
1982-2021		$850	$1,125
Tribute Series			
2003-present. Various models, options and finishes.			
2003-2021	Various models	$250	$600

Garage by Wicked

2004-2010. A line of basses imported from China by luthier Nicholas Dijkman (Wicked) of Montreal, Quebec.

Gibson

1890s (1902)-present. Professional grade, production, U.S.-made electric basses. Gibson got into the electric bass market with the introduction of their Gibson Electric Bass in '53 (that model was renamed the EB-1 in '58 and reintroduced under that name in '69). Many more bass models followed. Gibson's custom colors can greatly increase the value of older instruments. Custom colors offered from '63 to '69 are Cardinal Red, Ember Red, Frost Blue, Golden Mist Metallic, Heather Metallic, Inverness Green, Kerry Green, Pelham Blue Metallic, Polaris White, Silver Mist Metallic.

MODEL YEAR	FEATURES	EXC. COND. LOW	HIGH
20/20			
1987-1988. Designed by Ned Steinberger, slim-wedge Steinberger style solidbody, 2 humbucker pickups, 20/20 logo on headstock, Luna Silver or Ferrari Red finish.			
1987-1988		$1,300	$1,700
Electric (EB-1)			
1953-1958. Introduced as Gibson Electric Bass in '53, but was called the EB-1 by Gibson in its last year of '58, thus, the whole line is commonly called the EB-1 by collectors, reissued in '69 as the EB-1 (see EB-1 listing), brown.			
1953-1958		$4,800	$6,300
EB			
1970, 2013-2019. Renamed from Melody Maker Bass, SG body, 1 humbucker pickup. Reintroduced in '13, 4- or 5-string, 2 pickups			
1970		$1,200	$1,600
2013-2019	Reintroduced	$500	$650
EB-0			
1959-1979. Double-cut slab body with banjo-type tuners in '59 and '60, double-cut SG-type body with conventional tuners from '61 on, 1 pickup. Faded custom colors are of less value.			
1959-1960	Cherry, slab body	$4,900	$6,500
1961	Cherry, SG body	$2,600	$3,500
1962	Cherry	$2,625	$3,500
1963	Cherry	$2,350	$3,100
1964	Cherry, late '64 truss rod	$2,050	$2,700

MODEL YEAR	FEATURES	EXC. COND. LOW	HIGH
1964	Cherry, raised truss rod	$2,350	$3,100
1965-1966	Cherry	$1,950	$2,600
1965-1966	Pelham Blue	$3,450	$4,550
1967-1968	Cherry	$1,700	$2,250
1967-1968	Pelham Blue	$2,950	$3,850
1968	Black	$2,100	$2,750
1968	Burgundy Metallic	$2,100	$2,750
1969	Cherry, solid head	$1,700	$2,250
1969	Pelham Blue	$2,950	$3,850
1969-1974	Slotted head	$1,300	$1,700
1975-1979		$1,300	$1,700

EB-0 F
1962-1965. EB-0 with added built-in fuzz, cherry.

1962-1965		$4,500	$5,900

EB-0 L
1969-1979. 34.5 inch scale version of the EB-0, various colors.

1969-1979		$1,475	$1,950

EB-1
1969-1972. The Gibson Electric Bass ('53-'58) is often also called the EB-1 (see Electric Bass). Violin-shaped mahogany body, 1 pickup, standard tuners.

1969-1972		$3,800	$5,000

EB-2
1958-1961, 1964-1972. ES-335-type semi-hollowbody, double-cut, 1 pickup, banjo tuners '58-'60 and conventional tuners '60 on.

1958	Sunburst	$4,900	$6,500
1959	Natural	$5,600	$7,300
1959	Sunburst	$4,900	$6,400
1960	Natural	$5,600	$7,300
1960	Sunburst	$4,700	$6,200
1961	Sunburst, black pu	$3,400	$4,400
1961	Sunburst, brown pu	$3,500	$4,500
1964	Sunburst	$2,700	$3,500
1965	Sunburst	$2,600	$3,400
1966-1969	Cherry, sunburst	$2,500	$3,250
1967-1969	Sparkling Burgundy	$2,600	$3,400
1967-1969	Walnut	$2,300	$3,000
1970-1972	Sunburst	$2,300	$3,000

EB-2 D
1966-1972. Two-pickup version of EB-2, cherry, sunburst, or walnut.

1966-1969	Cherry, sunburst	$3,000	$3,850
1967-1969	Sparkling Burgundy	$3,100	$4,000
1967-1969	Walnut	$2,750	$3,600
1970-1972	Cherry, sunburst	$2,750	$3,600

EB-3
1961-1979. SG-style solidbody, 2 humbuckers, solid peghead '61-'68 and '72-'79, slotted peghead '69-'71, cherry to '71, various colors after.

1961-1964		$5,500	$7,200
1965	Early '65 version	$5,500	$7,200
1965	Late '65 version	$4,000	$5,200
1965	White (rare)	$7,000	$9,200
1966		$2,800	$3,600
1967-1968		$2,400	$3,200
1969	Early '69	$2,200	$2,850
1969	Late '69	$2,000	$2,600
1970		$1,850	$2,400

MODEL YEAR	FEATURES	EXC. COND. LOW	HIGH
1971		$1,700	$2,250
1972-1979		$1,600	$2,100

EB-3 L
1969-1972. 34.5" scale version of EB-3, slotted headstock, EB-3L logo on truss rod cover, cherry, natural, or walnut.

1969-1972		$1,150	$1,500

EB-4 L
1972-1979. SG-style, 1 humbucker, 34.5" scale, cherry or walnut.

1972-1979		$1,000	$1,300

EB-6
1960-1966. Introduced as semi-hollowbody 335-style 6-string with 1 humbucker, changed to SG-style with 2 pickups in '62.

1960	Natural, 335-style	$7,600	$9,900
1960-1961	Sunburst, 335-style	$5,500	$7,200
1962-1964	Cherry, SG-style	$9,700	$12,600
1965-1966	Cherry, SG-style	$7,800	$10,200

EB-650
1991-1993. Semi-acoustic single cut, maple neck, laminated maple body with center block, 2 TB Plus pickups.

1991-1993	Blond	$3,650	$4,750
1991-1993	Blue	$3,300	$4,300
1991-1993	Other colors	$2,900	$3,800

EB-750
1991-1993. Like EB-650, but with Bartolini pickups and TCT active EQ.

1991-1993	Blond	$3,650	$4,750
1991-1993	Blue	$3,300	$4,300
1991-1993	Other colors	$2,900	$3,800

ES-335
2013. Sunburst or ebony.

2013		$1,300	$1,700

ES-Les Paul
2015-2018. Semi-solid, 3-ply maple/poplar/maple top, back and sides, rosewood 'board, mother-of-pearl inlay, faded darkburst or gold top finish.

2015-2018		$1,700	$2,200

Explorer
1984-1987, 2011-2012. Alder body, ebony 'board, dot inlays, 2 humbuckers, various colors. Limited run in '11 in sunburst or silverburst.

1984-1987	Various finishes	$1,200	$1,550
1985	Designer graphics	$1,275	$1,650
2011-2012	Silverburst	$1,100	$1,450
2011-2012	Sunburst	$1,100	$1,450

Flying V
1981-1982, 2011-2012, 2020-2021. Solidbody, Flying V body. Offered again in '20 with 2 Burstbucker pickups and Antique Natural finish.

1981-1982	Blue stain, ebony	$3,100	$4,100
1981-1982	Silverburst	$3,700	$4,800
2011-2012		$1,300	$1,700
2020-2021		$1,150	$1,500

Flying V B-2
2019-2020. Dirty Fingers humbucker pickups, satin ebony finish.

2019-2020		$900	$1,175

1967 Gibson EB-2
Izzy Miller

1982 Gibson Flying V Bass
Russell Sutherland

BASSES

1970 Gibson Les Paul Bass
Jim Mathis

1972 Gibson SB-450
Richard Memmel

BASSES

MODEL YEAR	FEATURES	EXC. COND. LOW	HIGH
Grabber			
1973-1982. Double-cut solidbody, 1 pickup, bolt maple neck, maple 'board, various colors.			
1973-1982		$1,300	$1,700
Grabber II			
2009-2011. Limited Run series, 350 offered, based on '73-'75 model, certificate of authenticity, black.			
2009-2011		$1,175	$1,550
Grabber III (G-3)			
1975-1982. Double-cut solidbody, 3 pickups, bolt maple neck, maple 'board, nickel-plated hardware, various colors.			
1975-1982		$1,425	$1,900
Gibson IV			
1986-1988. Mahogany body and neck, double-cut, 2 pickups, black chrome hardware, various colors.			
1986-1988		$1,200	$1,575
Gibson V			
1986-1988. Double-cut, 5 strings, 2 pickups.			
1986-1988		$1,200	$1,575
L9-S			
1973. Natural maple or cherry, renamed Ripper Bass in '74.			
1973		$1,575	$2,100
Les Paul			
1970-1971. Single-cut solidbody, 2 pickups, walnut finish, renamed Les Paul Triumph Bass '71-'79.			
1970-1971		$2,000	$2,650
Les Paul Money			
2007-2008. Solidbody offset double-cut, 2 humbuckers, dot markers, figured maple top over mahogany body, 400 made.			
2007-2008		$1,200	$1,600
Les Paul Signature			
1973-1979. Double-cut, semi-hollowbody, 1 pickup, sunburst or gold (gold only by '76). Name also used on LPB-3 bass in '90s.			
1973-1979	Sunburst or gold	$3,300	$4,400
Les Paul Special LPB-1			
1991-1998. 2 TB-Plus pickups, ebony 'board, dots, slab mahogany body, active electronics, also available as 5-string.			
1991-1998		$1,200	$1,575
Les Paul Deluxe Plus LPB-2			
1991-1998. Upgraded LPB-1, carved maple top, trapezoid inlays, active eq and Bartolini pickups. Flame maple top Premium version offered '93-'98.			
1991-1998		$1,350	$1,750
Les Paul Smartwood			
1998. 2 TB pickups, active electronics, trapezoid inlays.			
1998		$1,350	$1,750
Les Paul Special V			
1993-1996. Single-cut slab body, 5-string, 2 pickups, dot markers, black/ebony.			
1993-1996		$850	$1,100
Les Paul Standard			
1999-2018. Maple top, chambered mahogany body, trapezoid inlays, 2 pickups.			
1999-2018	Various colors	$1,775	$2,300

MODEL YEAR	FEATURES	EXC. COND. LOW	HIGH
Les Paul Standard LPB-3			
1991-1995. Like Les Paul Deluxe LPB-2 Bass, but with TB Plus pickups. Flame maple top Premium version offered '93-'95.			
1993-1995	Flamed top	$1,150	$1,500
Les Paul Triumph			
1971-1979. Renamed from Les Paul Bass.			
1971-1979	Various colors	$1,700	$2,250
1973-1974	Optional white	$2,000	$2,600
Melody Maker			
1967-1970. SG body, 1 humbucker pickup.			
1967-1970		$1,500	$1,950
Midtown Standard			
2012-2018. Semi-hollow body, double-cut, baked maple or rosewood board, 2 pickups.			
2012-2018		$1,275	$1,650
Nikki Sixx Blackbird/Thunderbird			
2000-2003, 2009-2010. Blackbird has black hardware and finish, iron cross inlays. '09 Thunderbird was flamed maple.			
2000-2003		$1,475	$1,900
Q-80			
1986-1988. Victory Series body shape, 2 pickups, bolt neck, black chrome hardware, renamed Q-90 in '88.			
1986-1988		$975	$1,250
Q-90			
1988-1992. Renamed from Q-80, mahogany body, 2 active humbuckers, maple neck, ebony 'board.			
1988-1992		$975	$1,250
RD Artist			
1977-1982. Double-cut solid maple body, laminated neck, 2 pickups, active electronics, string-thru-body, block inlays, various colors.			
1977-1982		$2,200	$2,900
RD Artist CMT			
1982. Flamed maple top.			
1982		$3,000	$3,900
RD Artist VI			
1980. Only 6 made, 6-string.			
1980		$5,000	$6,500
RD Standard			
1977-1979. Double-cut, solid maple body, laminated neck, 2 pickups, regular electronics, string-thru-body, dot inlays, various colors.			
1977-1979		$2,200	$2,900
Ripper			
1974-1982. Introduced as L-9 S Bass in '73, double-cut solidbody, glued neck, 2 pickups, string-thru-body, sunburst or natural maple until '76, sunburst only after. Black option '78-'79 and silverburst '80.			
1974-1976	Natural maple	$1,900	$2,500
1974-1982	Sunburst	$1,900	$2,500
1978-1979	Black option	$1,900	$2,500
1980	Silverburst option	$2,100	$2,800
Ripper II			
2009-2011. Solid maple body, 34" scale, 2 pickups, natural nitro lacquer.			
2009-2011		$1,000	$1,300

MODEL YEAR	FEATURES	EXC. COND. LOW	HIGH

SB Series

1971-1978. In '71, had oval pickups, replaced mid-model with rectangular pickups. Includes 300 and 350 (30" scale, 1 and 2 pickups), 350 (30", 2 pickups), 400 (34", 1 pickup), 450 (34", 2 pickups). The 450 was special order only.

1971-1973	SB-300, 400	$650	$850
1972-1974	SB-350, 450	$650	$850
1975-1978	SB-450 special order	$650	$850

SG Reissue/SG Standard

2005-present. Similar to '60s EB-3, 2 pickups, mahogany body, cherry or white. Renamed SG Standard in '08, various colors.

2005-2021	Various colors	$1,000	$1,300

SG Standard Faded

2013-2018. Solid mahogany body, baked maple 'board, worn cherry or ebony finish.

2013-2018		$625	$825

SG Supreme

2007-2008. Made in Nashville, SG body with AAA maple top, 2 pickups.

2007-2008		$1,200	$1,600

Thunderbird II

1963-1969. Reverse solidbody until '65, non-reverse solidbody '65-'69, 1 pickup, custom colors available, reintroduced with reverse body for '83-'84.

1963	Sunburst, reverse	$11,000	$14,500
1964	Pelham Blue, reverse	$16,400	$21,800
1964	Sunburst, reverse	$9,000	$11,800
1965	Cardinal Red, non-reverse	$10,200	$13,400
1965	Inverness Green, non-reverse	$10,200	$13,400
1965	Sunburst, non-reverse	$4,900	$6,500
1965	Sunburst, reverse	$8,900	$11,700
1966	Cardinal Red, non-reverse	$8,900	$11,700
1966	Pelham Blue	$13,200	$17,300
1966	Sunburst, non-reverse	$4,900	$6,500
1967	Cardinal Red, non-reverse	$8,800	$11,600
1967	Sunburst, non-reverse	$4,700	$6,200
1968	Cardinal Red, non-reverse	$8,900	$11,700
1968-1969	Sunburst, non-reverse	$4,675	$6,125

Thunderbird III

1979-1982. Reverse body, 2 pickups, Thunderbird logo on 'guard.

1979-1982		$3,125	$4,100

Thunderbird IV

1963-1969. Reverse solidbody until '64, non-reverse solidbody '65-'69, 2 pickups, custom colors available, reintroduced with reverse body for '86-present (see Thunderbird IV Bass Reissue).

1963	Sunburst, reverse	$13,800	$18,100
1964	Frost Blue, reverse	$26,300	$34,500

1964	Pelham Blue, reverse	$26,300	$34,500
1964	Sunburst, reverse	$13,800	$18,100
1965	Cardinal Red, non-reverse	$15,800	$20,700
1965	Inverness Green, non-reverse	$15,800	$20,700
1965	Sunburst, reverse	$13,000	$17,000
1965-1966	Sunburst, non-reverse	$7,800	$10,200
1966	White, non-reverse	$14,750	$19,300
1967-1969	Sunburst, non-reverse	$7,800	$10,200

Thunderbird IV (Reissue)

1987-2016. Has reverse body and 2 pickups, various colors.

1987-2016	Various colors	$1,650	$2,200

Thunderbird IV Zebra Wood

2007. Guitar of the Week (week 11 of '07), limited run of 400, Zebrawood body.

2007		$1,625	$2,100

Thunderbird 50th Anniversary

2013-2018. Mahogany body and neck, rosewood 'board, Bullion Gold finish.

2013-2018		$1,625	$2,100

Thunderbird 76

1976 only. Reverse solidbody, 2 pickups, rosewood 'board, various colors.

1976		$3,600	$4,800

Thunderbird 79

1979 only. Reverse solidbody, 2 pickups, sunburst.

1979		$3,600	$4,700

Thunderbird Short Scale

2011-2013. 30.5" scale, 2 pickups, nitro satin ebony finish.

2011-2013		$1,000	$1,300

Thunderbird Studio/IV Studio

2005-2007. 4- or 5-string versions.

2005-2007		$1,275	$1,650

Victory Artist

1981-1985. Double-cut, solidbody, 2 humbuckers and active electronics, various colors.

1981-1985		$1,200	$1,600

Victory Custom

1982-1984. Double-cut, solidbody, 2 humbuckers, passive electronics, limited production.

1982-1984		$1,200	$1,600

Victory Standard

1981-1986. Double-cut, solidbody, 1 humbucker, active electronics, various colors.

1981-1986		$875	$1,150

Godin

1987-present. Intermediate and professional grade, production, solidbody electric and acoustic/electric basses from luthier Robert Godin. They also build guitars and mandolins.

A Series

1990s-present. Various acoustic/electric, 4- or 5-string.

1990s-2021	A-4, A-5	$450	$600

2015 Gibson SG Standard
Rivington Guitars

Gibson Thunderbird 76
Charlie Patty

Gretsch 6119-B Broadkaster
Christophe Fié

Guild M-85 II Bluesbird
Rivington Guitars

BASSES

MODEL YEAR	FEATURES	EXC. COND. LOW	HIGH

Freeway A Series
2005-2012. Double-cut solidbodies, 4- or 5-string, passive or active..

| 2005-2012 | Freeway A-4 | $450 | $600 |
| 2005-2012 | Freeway A-5 | $475 | $625 |

Godlyke
2006-present. Professional and premium grade, production, solidbody basses from effects distributor Godlyke.

Goya
1955-1996. Originally imports from Sweden, brand later used on Japanese and Korean imports. They also offered guitars, mandolins and banjos.
Electric Solidbody

| 1960s | Various models | $550 | $800 |

Gretsch
1883-present. Intermediate and professional grade, production, solidbody, hollow body, and acoustic/electric basses. Gretsch came late to the electric bass game, introducing their first models in the early '60s. They also build guitars, amps and steels. In 2012 they again offered mandolins, ukes and banjos.

Broadkaster (6119-B)
1991-2013. Single-cut hollowbody, maple top, back and sides.

| 1991-2013 | | $1,400 | $1,825 |

Broadkaster (7605/7606)
1975-1979. Double-cut solidbody, 1 pickup, bolt-on maple neck, natural (7605) or sunburst (7606).

| 1975-1979 | | $700 | $900 |

Committee (7629)
1977-1980. Double-cut walnut and maple soldibody, neck-thru, 1 pickup, natural.

| 1977-1980 | | $725 | $950 |

G2220 Electromatic Jr. Jet II
2012-present. Short scale, 2 pickups, various colors.

| 2012-2021 | | $200 | $260 |

G5440LS Electromatic Long Scale Hollow Body
2012-2020. Single-cut, 2 pickups, "G" tailpiece, various colors.

| 2012-2020 | | $650 | $850 |

G6072 Long Scale Hollow Body
1998-2006. Reissue of the '68 double-cut hollowbody, 2 pickups, sunburst, gold hardware.

| 1998-2006 | | $1,025 | $1,325 |

Model 6070/6072
1963-1971 (1972 for 6070). Originally listed as the PX6070 Cello Bass, large thinline hollowbody double-cut archtop, fake f-holes, 1 pickup (6070) or 2 (6072), gold hardware.

1963-1964	6070, with endpin	$1,875	$2,450
1965-1972	6070, no endpin	$1,375	$1,775
1968-1971	6072, 2 pickups	$1,325	$1,725

Model 6071/6073
1968-1971 (1972 for 6071). Single-cut hollowbody, fake f-holes, 1 pickup (6071) or 2 (6073), padded back, red mahogany.

| 1968-1971 | 6073, 2 pickups | $1,750 | $2,275 |
| 1968-1972 | 6071, 1 pickup | $1,575 | $2,050 |

Model 7615
1972-1975. Offset double-cut solidbody, slotted bass horn (monkey grip), large polished rosewood 'guard covering most of the body, 2 pickups, dot markers, brown mahogany finish. Only bass offered in Gretsch catalog for this era.

| 1972-1975 | | $900 | $1,175 |

TK 300 (7626/7627)
1976-1981. Double-cut solidbody, 1 pickup, Autumn Red Stain or natural.

| 1976-1981 | | $575 | $750 |

Guild
1952-present. Guild added electric basses in the mid-'60s and offered them until '02. New owner, Cordoba Music, reintroduced acoustic and electric basses to the line in '15.
Ashbory
1986-1988, 2009. 18" scale, total length 30", fretless, silicone rubber strings, active electronics, low-impedance circuitry.

| 1986-1988 | | $425 | $550 |
| 2009 | Fender Guild reissue | $200 | $275 |

B-4 E
1993-2000. Acoustic/electric single-cut flat-top, mahogany sides with arched mahogany back, multi-bound, gold hardware until '95, chrome after.

| 1993-2000 | | $575 | $750 |

B-30 E
1987-1999. Single-cut flat-top acoustic/electric, mahogany sides, arched mahogany back, multi-bound, fretless optional.

| 1987-1999 | | $1,050 | $1,350 |

B-50 Acoustic
1975-1987. Acoustic flat-top, mahogany sides with arched mahogany back, spruce top, multi-bound, renamed B-30 in '87.

| 1975-1987 | | $1,225 | $1,575 |

B-301/B-302
1976-1981. Double-cut solidbody, chrome-plated hardware. Models include B-301 (mahogany, 1 pickup), B-301A (ash, 1 pickup), B-302 (mahogany, 2 pickups), B-302A (ash, 2 pickups), and B-302AF (ash, fretless).

1976-1981	B-301, B-301A	$800	$1,050
1976-1981	B-302, B-302A	$875	$1,150
1977-1981	B-302AF	$875	$1,150

B-401/B-402
1980-1983. Model 401 with active circuit, 1 pickup. Model 402 passive and active, 2 pickups. A for ash body.

| 1980-1981 | B-401, B-401A | $800 | $1,050 |
| 1980-1983 | B-402, B402A | $800 | $1,050 |

B-500 C Acoustic
1992-1993. Acoustic/electric flat-top, round soundhole, single-cut, solid spruce top, maple back and sides, dark stain, limited production.

| 1992-1993 | | $1,250 | $1,625 |

MODEL YEAR	FEATURES	EXC. COND. LOW	HIGH

FS-46

1983. Acoustic-electric flat-top, single-cut, sharp horn fretless.

| 1983 | | $700 | $900 |

Jet Star

1964-1970 (limited production '68-'70). Offset double-cut solidbody, short treble horn, 1 pickup, 2-on-a-side tuners '64-'66 and 4 in-line tuners '66-'70.

| 1964-1966 | 2-on-side tuners | $1,300 | $1,700 |
| 1966-1970 | 4-in-line tuners | $1,300 | $1,700 |

JS I/JS II

1970-1977. Double-cut solidbody, 30" scale, 1 pickup (JS I or I) or 2 (JS II or 2), carved-top oak leaf design available for '72-'76. 34" long scale (LS) versions offered fretted and fretless for '74-'75.

1970-1977	JS I	$1,375	$1,800
1970-1977	JS II	$1,475	$1,925
1974-1976	JS I, carved	$1,475	$1,925
1974-1976	JS II, carved	$1,575	$2,050

M-85 I/M-85 II

1967-1972. Single-cut semi-hollowbody, 1 pickup (M-85 I) or 2 (M-85 II).

| 1967-1972 | M-85 I | $1,375 | $1,800 |
| 1967-1972 | M-85 II | $1,500 | $1,950 |

M-85 I/M-85 II BluesBird

1972-1976. Single-cut solidbody archtop, Chesterfield headstock inlay, cherry mahogany, 1 humbucker pickup (I) or 2 (II).

| 1972-1973 | M-85 I | $1,575 | $2,050 |
| 1972-1976 | M-85 II | $1,675 | $2,175 |

MB-801

1981-1982. Double-cut solidbody, 1 pickup, dot inlays.

| 1981-1982 | | $675 | $875 |

SB-201/SB-202/SB-203

1982-1983. Double-cut solidbody, 1 split coil pickup (201), 1 split coil and 1 single coil (202), or 1 split coil and 2 single coils (203).

1982-1983	SB-201	$775	$1,025
1982-1983	SB-202	$825	$1,075
1983	SB-203	$850	$1,125

SB-502 E

1984-1985. Double-cut solidbody, 2 pickups, active electronics.

| 1984-1985 | | $850 | $1,125 |

SB-600/Pilot Series

1983-1993. Offset double-cut solidbody, bolt-on neck, poplar body. Models include SB-601 (1 pickup), SB-602 (2 pickups or fretless), SB-602 V (2 pickups, 5-string), SB-604 (2 pickups, offset peghead) and SB-605 (5-string, hipshot low D tuner). Models 604 and 605 are replaced in '93 with Pro4 and Pro5 Pilot.

1983-1989	SB-601	$525	$700
1983-1989	SB-602	$625	$825
1983-1989	SB-602, fretless	$625	$825
1983-1989	SB-602V	$625	$825
1986-1988	SB-604 Pilot	$625	$825
1986-1993	SB-605	$625	$825

SB-608 Flying Star Motley Crue

1984-1985. Pointy 4-point star body, 2 pickups, E version had EMG pickups.

| 1984-1985 | | $1,075 | $1,400 |

Starfire

1965-1975. Double-cut semi-hollow thinbody, 1 pickup, mahogany neck, chrome-plated hardware, cherry or sunburst.

| 1965-1969 | Single-coil | $2,200 | $2,900 |
| 1970-1975 | Humbucker | $2,200 | $2,900 |

Starfire II

1967-1978. Two-pickup version of Starfire Bass. Single-coils until '69, humbuckers after, sunburst, cherry or very rare black. Starfire II Bass Special had gold hardware.

1967-1969	2 single-coils	$2,275	$2,950
1967-1969	Black	$2,500	$3,300
1970-1978	2 humbuckers	$2,275	$2,950

Starfire II Reissue

1997-present. Reissue of 2 humbucker version.

| 1997-2021 | | $975 | $1,275 |

X-100 Blade Runner

1985-1986. Poplar body and neck, ebony 'board, 1 pickup.

| 1985-1986 | | $2,900 | $3,800 |

X-701/X-702

1982-1984. Body with 4 sharp horns with extra long bass horn, 1 pickup (X-701) or 2 (X-702), various metallic finishes.

| 1982-1984 | X-701 | $1,225 | $1,600 |
| 1982-1984 | X-702 | $1,275 | $1,650 |

GW Basses & Luthiery

2004-present. Professional and premium grade, production/custom, basses built by luthier Grandon Westlund in West Lafayette, Indiana.

Hagstrom

1921-1983, 2004-present. This Swedish guitar company first offered electric basses in '61.

Concord II Deluxe

1967-1970. Bass version of V-IN guitar, 335-style body, 2 pickups, sunburst.

| 1967-1970 | | $1,550 | $2,000 |

Coronado IV

1963-1970. Offset double cut, Bi-Sonic pickups.

| 1963-1970 | | $1,075 | $1,400 |

H-8

1967-1969. Double-cut solidbody, 8 strings, 2 pickups, various colors.

| 1967-1969 | | $1,800 | $2,350 |

Kent

1963-1964. 2 single-coils, 4 sliders.

| 1962-1966 | | $625 | $800 |

Model I B/F-100 B

1965-1973. Offset double-cut solidbody, 2 single-coils, 5 sliders, 30" scale, red, black, white or blue.

| 1965-1973 | | $700 | $900 |

Model II B/F-400

1965-1970. Like Model I, but with 30.75" scale, red, black, white or blue. Called F-400 in U.S., II B elsewhere.

| 1965-1970 | | $700 | $900 |

1967 Guild Starfire
Jay Pilzer

1966 Hagstrom Model I B
McKenzie River Music

BASSES

Hamer Chaparral 12-String

Harmony H-25
Tom Pfeifer

MODEL YEAR	FEATURES	EXC. COND. LOW	HIGH
Swede 2000 (With Synth)			
1977. Circuitry on this Swede bass connected to the Ampeg Patch 2000 pedal so bass would work with various synths.			
1977		$1,050	$1,350
Swede			
1971-1976, 2004-present. Single-cut solidbody, block inlays, bolt neck, 2 humbuckers, 30.75" scale, cherry or black			
1971-1976		$900	$1,175
Super Swede			
1979-1983, 2004-present. Like Swede, but with neck-thru body, 32" scale, sunburst, mahogany or black.			
1979-1983		$925	$1,200

Hamer

1975-2012, 2017-present. Founded in Arlington Heights, Illinois, by Paul Hamer and Jol Dantzig, Hamer was purchased by Kaman in '88. They also built guitars. Fender acquired Hamer in '08 and suspended production in '12. The brand was reintroduced in '17 by Jam Industries.

MODEL YEAR	FEATURES	EXC. COND. LOW	HIGH
8-String Short-Scale			
1978-1993. Double cut solidbody, 1 or 2 pickups, 30.5" scale.			
1978-1993		$1,850	$2,400
12-String Acoustic			
1985-2010. Semi-hollow, long scale, single cut, soundhole, 2 pickups. Import XT model added in the 2000s.			
1985-2010		$2,425	$3,150
12-String Short-Scale			
1978-1996. Four sets of 3 strings - a fundamental and 2 tuned an octave higher, double cut maple and mahogany solidbody, 30.5" scale.			
1978-1996		$1,840	$2,400
Blitz			
1982-1990. Explorer-style solidbody, 2 pickups, bolt-on neck.			
1982-1990		$1,700	$2,200
Chaparral			
1986-1995, 2000-2008. Solidbody, 2 pickups, glued-in neck, later basses have bolt-on neck.			
1986-1987	Set-neck	$1,475	$1,925
1987-1995	Bolt-on neck	$1,350	$1,750
Chaparral 5-String			
1987-1995. Five strings, solidbody, 2 pickups, glued-in neck, later basses have 5-on-a-side reverse peghead.			
1987-1995		$1,450	$1,875
Chaparral 12-String			
1992-2012. Long 34" scale 12-string, offset double cut. Import XT model added in '01.			
1992-2012	USA	$1,850	$2,400
2000-2012	Import	$250	$500
Chaparral Max			
1986-1995. Chaparral Bass with figured maple body, glued-in neck and boomerang inlays.			
1986-1995		$850	$1,100

MODEL YEAR	FEATURES	EXC. COND. LOW	HIGH
Cruise			
1982-1990, 1995-1999. J-style solidbody, 2 pickups, glued neck ('82-'90) or bolt-on neck ('95-'99), also available as a 5-string.			
1982-1990	Set-neck	$925	$1,200
1995-1999	Bolt-on neck	$850	$1,100
Cruise 5			
1982-1989. Five-string version, various colors.			
1982-1989		$1,025	$1,325
FBIV			
1985-1987. Reverse Firebird shape, 1 P-Bass Slammer and 1 J-Bass Slammer pickup, mahogany body, rosewood 'board, dots.			
1985-1987		$925	$1,200
Monaco 4			
2002-2012. Flamed maple top, rosewood 'board, Tobacco Burst or '59 Burst finish.			
2002-2012		$2,200	$2,850
Standard			
1975-1984, 2001. US-made, Explorer-style headstock, 2 humbuckers. Imported in '01.			
1975-1979	Flamed top, bound	$5,400	$7,000
1975-1984	Plain top, unbound	$3,150	$4,100
1980-1984	Flamed top, bound	$4,850	$6,300
2001	Import	$250	$500
Velocity 5			
2002-2012. Offset double-cut, long bass horn, active, 1 humbucker.			
2002-2012		$250	$500

Harmony

1892-1976, late 1970s-present. Harmony once was one of the biggest instrument makers in the world, making guitars and basses under their own brand and for others.

MODEL YEAR	FEATURES	EXC. COND. LOW	HIGH
H Series			
Late-1980s-early-1990s. F-style solidbody copies, 1 or 2 pickups, all models begin H.			
1980s-90s		$125	$200
H-22			
1959-1972. Single-cut hollowbody, 2-on-a-side, 1 pickup.			
1959-1969		$1,200	$1,600
1970-1972		$1,025	$1,325
H-22 Reissue			
2000s. Imported reissue, 1 pickup.			
2000s		$325	$425
H-25/Silhouette			
1963-1967. Offset double-cut solidbody, 1 pickup (H-25) or 2 (Silhouette).			
1963-1967	H-25	$750	$975
1963-1967	Silhouette	$800	$1,025
H-27			
1968-1972. Double-cut hollowbody, 4-on-a-side, 2 pickups.			
1968-1972		$775	$1,025

Hartke

Hartke offered a line of wood and aluminum-necked basses from 2000 to '03.

BASSES

Heartfield

1989-1994. Distributed by Fender, imported from Japan. They also offered guitars.

Electric

1989-1994. Double-cut solidbody, graphite reinforced neck, 2 single-coils, available in 4-, 5- and 6-string models.

MODEL YEAR	FEATURES	EXC. COND. LOW	HIGH
1989-1994		$275	$500

Heritage

1985-present. Mainly a builder of guitars, Kalamazoo, Michigan's Heritage has offered a few basses in the past.

HB-1

1987. P-style body, limited production, single-split pickup, 4-on-a-side tuners, figured maple body, bolt-on neck.

MODEL YEAR	FEATURES	EXC. COND. LOW	HIGH
1987		$700	$900

Höfner

1887-present. Professional grade, production, basses. They also offer guitars and bowed instruments. Höfner basses, made famous in the U.S. by one Paul McCartney, are made in Germany.

G5000/1 Super Beatle (G500/1)

1968-2011. Bound ebony 'board, gold-plated hardware, natural finish, the version with active circuit is called G500/1 Super Beatle, reissued in '94.

MODEL YEAR	FEATURES	EXC. COND. LOW	HIGH
1968-1979	LH	$2,500	$3,250
1968-1979	RH	$1,700	$2,250

Icon Series

2007-2011. Chinese versions of classic Höfners, often sold without a case or gigbag.

MODEL YEAR	FEATURES	EXC. COND. LOW	HIGH
2007-2011		$200	$300

Model 172 Series

1968-1970. Offset double-cut, 6-on-a-side tuners, 2 pickups, 2 slide switches, dot markers, 172/S shaded sunburst, 172/R red vinyl covered body, 172/I vinyl covered with white top and black back.

MODEL YEAR	FEATURES	EXC. COND. LOW	HIGH
1968-1970	172/I, white	$875	$1,150
1968-1970	172/R, red	$875	$1,150
1968-1970	172/S, sunburst	$875	$1,150

Model 182 Solid

1962-1985. Offset double-cut solidbody, 2 pickups.

MODEL YEAR	FEATURES	EXC. COND. LOW	HIGH
1962-1965		$875	$1,150

Model 185 Solid

1962-ca. 1970. Classic offset double-cut solidbody, 2 double-coil pickups.

MODEL YEAR	FEATURES	EXC. COND. LOW	HIGH
1962-1970		$875	$1,150

Model 500/1 Beatle

1956-present. Semi-acoustic, bound body in violin shape, glued-in neck, 2 pickups, right- or left-handed, sunburst. Listed as 500/1 Vintage '58, '59, '62 and '63 in '90s through 2014. Currently named 500/1 Violin Bass.

MODEL YEAR	FEATURES	EXC. COND. LOW	HIGH
1956-1959	LH or RH	$6,400	$8,300
1960	LH, McCartney	$5,500	$7,200
1960	RH	$4,500	$5,800
1961	LH	$5,500	$7,200
1961	LH, McCartney	$7,100	$9,200
1961	RH	$4,500	$5,800
1962-1963	LH	$4,500	$5,800
1962-1963	RH	$3,900	$5,100
1964	LH	$4,500	$5,800
1964	LH, McCartney	$5,800	$7,500
1964	RH	$4,500	$5,800
1964	RH, McCartney	$3,900	$5,100
1965	LH	$2,850	$3,700
1965	RH	$2,600	$3,400
1966	LH	$2,700	$3,500
1966	RH	$2,500	$3,300
1967	LH	$2,500	$3,250
1967	RH	$2,150	$2,800
1968-1973	LH	$2,500	$3,250
1968-1973	RH	$1,800	$2,375
1974-1979	LH or RH	$1,675	$2,200

'58 Model 500/1 Beatle Reissue

2008-2013. Right- or left-handed.

MODEL YEAR	FEATURES	EXC. COND. LOW	HIGH
2008-2013		$1,675	$2,175

'62 Model 500/1 Beatle Reissue

1990s-2014. Right- or left-handed.

MODEL YEAR	FEATURES	EXC. COND. LOW	HIGH
1990s-2014		$1,675	$2,175

'63 Model 500/1 Beatle Reissue

1994-2010. Right- or left-handed.

MODEL YEAR	FEATURES	EXC. COND. LOW	HIGH
1994-2010		$1,675	$2,175

'64 Model 500/1 Beatle Reissue

2015-2016. Right- or left-handed.

MODEL YEAR	FEATURES	EXC. COND. LOW	HIGH
2015-2016		$1,675	$2,175

Model 500/1 1964-1984 Reissue

1984. '1964-1984' neckplate notation.

MODEL YEAR	FEATURES	EXC. COND. LOW	HIGH
1984		$1,675	$2,175

Model 500/1 40th Anniversary

1995-1996. Only 300 made.

MODEL YEAR	FEATURES	EXC. COND. LOW	HIGH
1995-1996		$2,800	$3,600

Model 500/1 50th Anniversary

2006. Pickguard logo states '50th Anniversary Höfner Violin Bass 1956-2006', large red Höfner logo also on 'guard, 150 made.

MODEL YEAR	FEATURES	EXC. COND. LOW	HIGH
2006		$2,800	$3,600

Model 500/1 Cavern

2005. Limted run of 12, includes certificate.

MODEL YEAR	FEATURES	EXC. COND. LOW	HIGH
2005		$1,700	$2,200

Model 500/1 Cavern Music Ground

1993. UK commissioned by Music Ground, said to be one of the first accurate reissues, 40 made.

MODEL YEAR	FEATURES	EXC. COND. LOW	HIGH
1993		$1,700	$2,200

Model 500/1 Contemporary

2007-2008. Contemporary Series.

MODEL YEAR	FEATURES	EXC. COND. LOW	HIGH
2007-2008		$575	$750

Model 500/2 and Club

1965-1970, 2015-present. Similar to the 500/1, but with 'club' body Höfner made for England's Selmer, sunburst. Club Bass has been reissued in various colors.

MODEL YEAR	FEATURES	EXC. COND. LOW	HIGH
1965-1970		$1,800	$2,300
2015-2021		$1,800	$2,300

Model 500/3 Senator

1962-1964. Single-cut thin body, f-holes, 1 511b pickup, sunburst.

MODEL YEAR	FEATURES	EXC. COND. LOW	HIGH
1962-1964		$1,600	$2,100

1964 Höfner 500/1 Beatle
Steve Lee

1963 Höfner 500/2 Club
Larry Wassgren

Ibanez SR-300
Rivington Guitars

Ibanez ST-980 Studio
Willie Moseley

MODEL YEAR	FEATURES	EXC. COND. LOW	HIGH

Model 500/5
1959-1963. Single-cut body with Beatle Bass-style pickups, sunburst. Becomes President Bass in '63.

1959-1963		$3,550	$4,600

Model 500/6
Late-1960s. Introduced in '67, semi-acoustic, thinline, soft double-cut, 2 pickups, 4 control knobs, dot markers, sunburst.

1967		$1,725	$2,250

Model 500/8BZ / B500/8BZ
Late-1960s. Semi-acoustic, thinline, sharp double-cut, multiple-line position markers, built in flip-fuzz and bass boost, sunburst or natural.

1967	500/8BZ, sunburst	$1,800	$2,350
1967	B500/8BZ, natural	$1,800	$2,350

President
1963-1972. Made for England's Selmer, single-cut archtop, 2 Beatle Bass-style pickups, sunburst.

1963-1965		$2,400	$3,125
1966-1969		$1,875	$2,450
1970-1972		$1,800	$2,400

Hondo
1969-1987, 1991-2005. Budget grade, production, imported acoustic and electric solidbody basses. They also offered guitars, banjos and mandolins.

Electric Solidbody
1969-1987, 1991-2005. Various models.

1969-1999	Rare models	$400	$1,100
1969-1999	Standard models	$125	$300

Hoyer
1874-present. Intermediate grade, production, electric basses. They also build guitars.

Electric

1960s	Various models	$650	$850

Ibanez
1932-present. Intermediate and professional grade, production, solidbody basses. They also have guitars, amps, and effects.

AXB Axstar Series
1986-1987. Various headless solidbody models.

1986-1987		$350	$475

BTB Series
1999-present. Various models.

1999-2021		$250	$525

Challenger
1977-1978. Offered as P-bass or J-bass style, and with ash body option.

1977-1978		$450	$575

DB Destroyer II X Series
1984-1986. Futuristic-style body, P- and J-style pickups, dot markers, bolt neck.

1984-1986	Various models	$450	$600

DT Destroyer II Series
1980-1985. Futuristic-style body.

1983-1986	Various models	$600	$775

MODEL YEAR	FEATURES	EXC. COND. LOW	HIGH

ICB Iceman
1994-1996, 2011. Iceman body, basswood (300) or mahogany (500) body. 300 reissued in '11.

1994	ICB500, black	$525	$675
1994-1996	ICB300, white	$525	$675

Jet King
2009-2010. Retro offset double-cut solidbody, bolt neck.

2009-2010		$200	$325

MC Musician Series
1978-1988. Various models, solidbody, neck-thru.

1978-1988		$900	$1,700

Model 2030
1970-1973. First copy era bass, offset double-cut, sunburst.

1970-1973		$700	$900

Model 2353
1974-1976. Copy model, offset double-cut, 1 pickup, black.

1974-1976		$625	$825

Model 2364B
1971-1973. Dan Armstrong see-thru Lucite copy with 2 mounted humbucker pickups, clear finish.

1971-1973		$825	$1,075

Model 2365
1974-1975. Copy model, Offset double-cut, rosewood 'board, pearloid block markers, sunburst.

1974-1975		$700	$900

Model 2366B/2366FLB
1974-1975. Copy model, offset double-cut, 1 split-coil pickup, sunburst, FLB fretless model.

1974-1975		$625	$825

Model 2385
1974-1975. Copy model, offset double-cut, 1 pickup, ash natural finish.

1974-1975		$625	$825

Model 2388B
1974-1976. Ric 4001 copy.

1974-1976		$625	$825

Model 2452
1975. Ripper copy.

1975		$625	$825

Model 2459B Destroyer
1974-1977. Laminated ash body, copy of Korina Explorer-style.

1974-1977		$1,900	$2,500

Model 2537 DX
1974-1975. Hofner Beatle copy.

1974-1975		$625	$825

Model 2609B Black Eagle
1974-1976. Burns-like bass, offset double-cut solidbody, sharp curving horns.

1974-1976		$1,025	$1,325

PL Pro Line Series
1986-1987. Offset double cut solidbody.

1986-1987	Various models	$450	$575

RB/RS Roadstar Series
1983-1987. Solidbody basses, various models and colors.

1983-1987		$300	$600

BASSES

MODEL YEAR	FEATURES	EXC. COND. LOW	HIGH
Rocket Roll			
1974-1976. Korina solidbody, V-shape, natural.			
1974-1976		$2,000	$2,600
S/SB Solidbody Series			
1990-1992. Various ultra slim solidbody basses.			
1990-1992		$250	$550
SR Sound Gear Series			
1987-present. Sleek, lightweight designs, active electronics, bolt necks. Model numbers higher than 1000 are usually arched-top, lower usually flat body.			
1987-2021	Various models	$225	$475
ST-980 Studio			
1979-1980. Double cut, 8-string, bolt-on neck, walnut-maple-mahogany body.			
1979-1980		$625	$825

Imperial

Ca.1963-ca.1970. Imported by the Imperial Accordion Company of Chicago, Illinois. Early guitars and basses made in Italy, but by ca. '66 Japanese-made.

MODEL YEAR	FEATURES	EXC. COND. LOW	HIGH
Electric Hollowbody			
1960s	Various models	$175	$475
Electric Solidbody			
1960s	Various models	$175	$475

Jackson

1980-present. Intermediate, professional, and premium grade, production, solidbody basses. They also offer guitars. Founded by Grover Jackson, who owned Charvel.

MODEL YEAR	FEATURES	EXC. COND. LOW	HIGH
Concert C5P 5-String (Import)			
1998-2000. Bolt neck, dot inlay, chrome hardware.			
1998-2000		$135	$200
Concert Custom (U.S.A.)			
1984-1995. Neck-thru Custom Shop bass.			
1984-1989		$1,200	$1,575
1990-1995		$775	$1,000
Concert EX 4-String (Import)			
1992-1995. Bolt neck, dot inlay, black hardware.			
1992-1995		$250	$330
Concert V 5-String (Import)			
1992-1995. Bound neck, shark tooth inlay.			
1992-1995		$375	$480
Concert XL 4-String (Import)			
1992-1995. Bound neck, shark tooth inlay.			
1992-1995		$300	$400
Kelly Pro			
1994-1995. Pointy-cut bouts, neck-thru solidbody, shark fin marker inlays, includes Standard and Custom models.			
1994-1995		$750	$975
Piezo			
1986. Piezo bridge pickup, neck-thru, shark tooth inlays. Student model has rosewood 'board, no binding. Custom Model has ebony 'board and binding.			
1986		$1,400	$1,800
Soloist			
1996. Pointy headstock, 4-string.			
1996		$750	$975

MODEL YEAR	FEATURES	EXC. COND. LOW	HIGH
Surfcaster SC1			
1998-2001. Tube and humbucker pickups.			
1998-2001		$1,125	$1,450

Jerry Jones

1981-2011. Intermediate grade, production, semi-hollow body electric basses from luthier Jerry Jones, and built in Nashville, Tennessee. They also build guitars and sitars. Jones retired in 2011.

MODEL YEAR	FEATURES	EXC. COND. LOW	HIGH
Neptune Longhorn 4			
1988-2011. Based on Danelectro longhorn models, 4-string, 2 lipstick-tube pickups, 30" scale.			
1988-2011		$1,375	$1,800
Neptune Longhorn 6			
1988-2011. 6-string version.			
1988-2011		$1,700	$2,200
Neptune Shorthorn 4			
1988-2011. Danelectro Coke bottle headstock, short horns double cut, 2 pickups.			
1988-2011		$1,375	$1,800

Juzek

Violin maker John Juzek was originally located in Prague, Czeckoslovakia, but moved to West Germany due to World War II. Prague instruments considered by most to be more valuable. Many German instruments were mass produced with laminate construction and some equate these German basses with the Kay laminate basses of the same era. Juzek still makes instruments.

Kalamazoo

1933-1942, 1965-1970. Kalamazoo was a brand Gibson used on one of their budget lines. They also used the name on electric basses, guitars and amps from '65 to '67.

MODEL YEAR	FEATURES	EXC. COND. LOW	HIGH
Electric			
1965-1970	Various models	$500	$650

Kapa

Ca. 1962-1970. Kapa was founded by Koob Veneman in Maryland and offered basses and guitars.

MODEL YEAR	FEATURES	EXC. COND. LOW	HIGH
Electric			
1962-1970	Various models	$250	$750

Kawai

1927-present. Japanese instrument manufacturer Kawai started offering guitars under other brand names around '56. There were few imports carrying the Kawai brand until the late-'70s; best known for high quality basses. Kawai quit offering guitars and basses around 2002.

MODEL YEAR	FEATURES	EXC. COND. LOW	HIGH
Electric			
1960s-80s	Various models	$300	$800

Kay

Ca. 1931-present. Currently, budget and intermediate grade, production, imported solidbody basses. They also make amps, guitars, banjos, mandolins, ukes, and violins. Kay introduced upright acoustic laminate basses and 3/4 viols in '38 and electric basses in '54.

Jackson Concert Professional
Ken Kraynak

Jerry Jones Neptune Longhorn 4
Ken Quick

BASSES

Klira Electric Solidbody
Rivington Guitars

Kramer 650-B Artist
Imaged by Heritage Auctions, HA.com

MODEL YEAR	FEATURES	EXC. COND. LOW	HIGH
C1 Concert String			
1938-1967. Standard (3/4) size student bass, laminated construction, spruce top, figured maple back and sides, shaded light brown.			
1938-1949		$2,000	$2,650
1950-1959		$1,900	$2,500
1960-1967		$1,800	$2,400
K-160 Electronic			
1955-1956. Same as K-162, but with plain white plastic trim.			
1955-1956		$875	$1,150
K-162 Electronic			
1955-1956. Bass version of K-161Thin Twin "Jimmy Reed," single-cut, 1 tube-style pickup.			
1955-1956		$875	$1,150
K-5965 Pro			
1954-1965. Single-cut, 1 pickup. named K-5965 Pro by 1961.			
1954-1965		$875	$1,150
K-5970 Jazz Special			
1960-1964. Double-cut, pickup, Kelvinator headstock, black or blond.			
1960-1964		$2,300	$3,000
M-1 (Maestro) String			
1952-late-1960s. Standard (3/4) size bass, laminated construction, spruce top and curly maple back and sides. Model M-3 is the Junior (1/4) size bass, Model M-1 B has a blond finish, other models include the S-51 B Chubby Jackson Five-String Bass and the S-9 Swingmaster.			
1952-1967		$2,400	$3,100
M-5 (Maestro) String			
1957-late-1960s. Five strings.			
1957-1967		$2,700	$3,500
Semi-hollowbody			
1954-1966. Various models, single or double cut, 1 or 2 pickups.			
1954-1966	1 pickup	$375	$500
1954-1966	2 pickups	$425	$550
Solidbody			
1965-1968. Various models, single or double cut, 1 or 2 pickups.			
1965-1968	1 pickup	$375	$500
1965-1968	2 pickups	$425	$550

Ken Smith

See listing under Smith.

Kent

1961-1969. Guitars and basses imported from Japan by Buegeleisen and Jacobson of New York, New York. Manufacturers unknown but many early instruments by Guyatone and Teisco.

MODEL YEAR	FEATURES	EXC. COND. LOW	HIGH
Electric			
1962-1969. Import models include 628 Newport, 634 Basin Street, 629, and 635.			
1961-1969	Common model	$200	$275
1961-1969	Rare model	$475	$625

Kimberly

Late-1960s-early-1970s. Private branded import made in the same Japanese factory as Teisco. They also made guitars.

MODEL YEAR	FEATURES	EXC. COND. LOW	HIGH
Violin			
1960s		$475	$625

Kingston

Ca. 1958-1967. Imported from Japan by Westheimer Importing Corp. of Chicago. Early examples made by Guyatone and Teisco. They also offered guitars, mandolins and banjos.

MODEL YEAR	FEATURES	EXC. COND. LOW	HIGH
Electric			
1960s	Common model	$150	$375
1960s	Rare model	$400	$750

Klira

Founded 1887 in Schoenbach, Germany, mainly making violins, but added guitars and basses in the 1950s. The instruments of the '50s and '60s were aimed at the budget market, but workmanship improved with the '70s models.

MODEL YEAR	FEATURES	EXC. COND. LOW	HIGH
Electric			
1960s	Common models	$400	$800
1960s	Rare models	$800	$1,500

Kramer

1976-1990, 1995-present. Budget grade, production, imported solidbody basses. They also offer guitars. Kramer's first guitars and basses featured aluminum necks with wooden inserts on back. Around '80 they started to switch to more economical wood necks and aluminum necks were last produced in '85. Gibson acquired the brand in '97.

MODEL YEAR	FEATURES	EXC. COND. LOW	HIGH
250-B Special			
1977-1979. Offset double-cut, aluminum neck, Ebonol 'board, zero fret, 1 single-coil, natural.			
1977-1979		$790	$1,025
350-B Standard			
1976-1979. Offset double-cut, aluminum neck, Ebonol 'board, tropical woods, 1 single-coil, dots. The 350 and 450 were Kramer's first basses.			
1976-1979		$975	$1,275
450-B Deluxe			
1976-1980. As 350-B, but with 2 single-coils and blocks.			
1976-1980		$1,025	$1,325
650-B Artist			
1977-1980. Double-cut, birdseye maple/burled walnut, aluminum neck, zero fret, mother-of-pearl crowns, 2 humbuckers.			
1977-1980		$1,500	$1,950
Deluxe 8			
1980. Multi-piece body, aluminum neck.			
1980		$1,500	$1,950
DMB 2000			
1979. Bolt-on aluminum neck, slot headstock.			
1979		$1,125	$1,450

MODEL YEAR	FEATURES	EXC. COND. LOW	HIGH

DMZ 4000
1978-1982. Bolt-on aluminum neck, slot headstock, double-cut solidbody, active EQ and dual-coil humbucking pickup, dot inlay.

1978-1981		$925	$1,200
1982	Bill Wyman-type	$925	$1,200

DMZ 4001
1979-1980. Aluminum neck, slot headstock, double-cut solidbody, 1 dual-coil humbucker pickup, dot inlay.

1979-1980		$1,225	$1,600

DMZ 5000
1979-1980. Double-cut solidbody, aluminum neck, slotted headstock, 2 pickups, crown inlays.

1979-1980		$1,300	$1,700

DMZ 6000B
1979-1980. Double-cut, aluminum neck, slotted headstock, 2 pickups, crown inlays.

1979-1980		$1,300	$1,700

Duke Custom/Standard
1981-1983. Headless, aluminum neck, 1 humbucker.

1981-1983		$400	$525

Duke Special
1982-1985. Headless, aluminum neck, 2 pickups, with frets or fretless.

1982-1985		$450	$575

Ferrington KFB-1/KFB-2 Acoustic
1987-1990. Acoustic/electric, bridge-mounted active pickup, tone and volume control, various colors. KFB-1 has binding and diamond dot inlays; the KFB-2 no binding and dot inlays. Danny Ferrington continued to offer the KFB-1 after Kramer closed in '90.

1987-1990		$350	$450

Focus Series
1984-1987. Made in Japan, double-cut solidbody, 1 or 2 pickups, various models.

1984-1987		$250	$475

Forum Series
1987-1990. Made in Japan, double-cut solidbody, 2 pickups, neck-thru (I & III) or bolt-neck (II & IV).

1987-1990		$350	$625

Gene Simmons Axe
1980-1981. Axe-shaped body, aluminium neck.

1980-1981		$2,900	$5,000

Hundred Series
1988-1990. Import budget line, 7/8th solidbody, various models.

1988-1990		$200	$350

Pacer Series
1982-1984. Offset double-cut solidbody, various models.

1982-1984		$600	$1,200

Pioneer Series
1981-1986. Various models, first wood neck basses, offset double-cut, JBX or PBX pickups, dots, '81-'84 models with soft headstocks, later '84 on with banana headstocks.

1981-1986		$450	$900

Ripley
1984-1987. Offset double-cut, 4 (IV) or 5 (V) strings, stereo, pan pots for each string, front and back pickups for each string, active circuitry.

1984-1987	IV and V	$700	$925

Stagemaster Custom (Import)
1982-1985, 1987-1990. First version had an aluminum neck (wood optional). Later version was neck-thru-body, bound neck, either active or passive pickups.

1982-1985	Imperial	$925	$1,200
1982-1985	Special	$925	$1,200
1982-1985	Standard	$925	$1,200

Stagemaster Deluxe (U.S.A.)
1981. Made in USA, 8-string, metal neck.

1981		$1,125	$1,450

Striker 700
1985-1989. Korean import, offset double-cut, 1 pickup until '87, 2 after. Striker name was again used on a bass in '99.

1985-1989		$200	$400

Vanguard
1981-1983. V-shaped body, Special (aluminum neck) or Standard (wood neck).

1981-1982	Special	$925	$1,200
1983-1984	Standard	$925	$1,200

Voyager
1982-1983. X-body, headless.

1982-1983		$925	$1,200

XKB-10 (Wedge)
1980-1981. Wedge-shaped body, aluminum neck.

1980-1981		$850	$1,100

XKB-20
1981. 2nd version, more traditional double cut body.

1981		$850	$1,100

XL Series
1980-1981. Odd shaped double-cut solidbody, aluminum neck, various models.

1980-1981	XL-24, 4-string	$1,200	$1,550
1980-1981	XL-8, 8-string	$1,300	$1,675
1980-1981	XL-9, 4-string	$1,125	$1,475

ZX Aero Star Series (Import)
1986-1989. Various models include ZX-70 (offset double-cut solidbody, 1 pickup).

1986-1989		$125	$300

KSD
2003-present. Intermediate grade, production, imported bass line designed by Ken Smith (see Smith listing).

Kubicki
1973-present. Professional and premium grade, production/custom, solidbody basses built by luthier Phil Kubicki in Santa Barbara, California. Kubicki began building acoustic guitars when he was 15. In '64 at age 19, he went to work with Roger Rossmeisl at Fender Musical Instrument's research and development department for acoustic guitars. Nine years later he moved to Santa Barbara, California, and established Philip Kubicki Technology, which is best known for its line of Factor basses and also builds acoustic guitars, custom electric guitars, bodies and necks, and mini-guitars and does custom work, repairs and restorations. Phil Kubicki died in '13.

Kramer DMZ 6000B
Imaged by Heritage Auctions, HA.com

Kubicki Factor

BASSES

BASSES

Lakland Skyline Deluxe
Craig Brody

Martin BCPA4
Kris Nocula

MODEL		EXC. COND.	
YEAR	FEATURES	LOW	HIGH

Kustom

1968-present. Founded by Bud Ross in Chanute, Kansas, and best known for the tuck-and-roll amps, Kustom also offered guitars and basses from '68 to '69.

Electric Hollowbody

1968-1969	Various models	$1,200	$1,600

La Baye

1967. Short-lived brand out of Green Bay, Wisconsin and built by the Holman-Woodell factory in Neodesha, Kansas. There was also a guitar model.

Model 2x4 II

1967. Very low production, dual pickups, long-scale, small rectangle solidbody, sometimes referred to as the Bass II.

1967		$1,425	$1,850

Model 2x4 Mini

1967. Short-scale, 1 pickup, small rectangle solidbody.

1967		$1,425	$1,850

Lakland

1994-present. Professional and premium grade, production/custom, solid and hollowbody basses from luthier Dan Lakin in Chicago, Illinois. Lakland basses are built in the U.S. and overseas (Skyline series).

Electric

1994-present. Various models.

1994-2002	4-63 Classic	$2,200	$2,800
1994-2002	4-63 Deluxe	$2,500	$3,300
1994-2002	4-63 Standard	$2,200	$2,800
1994-2002	4-94 / 44-94 Classic	$2,200	$2,800
1994-2021	4-94 / 44-94 Deluxe	$2,500	$3,300
1994-2021	4-94 / 44-94 Standard	$2,200	$2,800
1998-2003	Joe Osborn	$2,600	$3,400
2012-2021	Skyline 44-60	$1,050	$1,400

Lowrider Basses

2003-2018. Professional grade, production/custom, solidbody basses made by Ed Roman Guitars.

M Basses or Maghini

1998-present. Production/custom, professional and premium grade, solidbody electric basses built in Terryville, Connecticut by luthier Jon Maghini.

Magnatone

Ca. 1937-1971, 2013-present. Founded as Dickerson Brothers, known as Magna Electronics from '47. Produced instruments under own brand and for many others.

Mark VI/Artist Mark VI

1959. Designed by luthier Paul Barth for Magnatone, double-cut, 4-string, 1 pickup.

1959		$1,350	$1,750

X-10 Hurricane

1965-1966. Offset double cut solidbody, 1 single-coil, 4-on-a-side tuners, Magnatone logo on guard and headstock, Hurricane logo on headstock.

1965-1966		$950	$1,225

MODEL		EXC. COND.	
YEAR	FEATURES	LOW	HIGH

Mako

1985-1989. Line of solidbody basses from Kaman (Ovation, Hamer). They also offered guitars and amps.

Electric Solidbody

1985-1989	Various models	$150	$500

Marco Polo

1960-ca.1964. One of the first inexpensive Japanese brands to be imported into the U.S., they also offered guitars.

Solidbody

1960s	Various models	$100	$300

Marleaux

1990-present. Luthier Gerald Marleaux builds his custom, premium grade, electric basses in Clausthal-Zellerfeld, Germany.

Marling

Ca. 1975. Budget line instruments marketed by EKO of Recanati, Italy; probably made by them, although possibly imported. They also had guitars.

Electric Solidbody

Models include the E.495 (copy of LP), E.485 (copy of Tele), and the E.465 (Manta-style).

1970s	Various models	$100	$300

Martin

1833-present. Professional grade, production, acoustic basses made in the U.S. In 1978, Martin re-entered the electric market and introduced their solidbody EB-18 and EB-28 Basses. In the '80s they offered Stinger brand electric basses. By the late '80s, they started offering acoustic basses.

00C-16GTAE

2006-2011. Mahogany back and sides, Fishman electronics.

2006-2011		$1,075	$1,400

B-1/B-1E Acoustic

2002-2006. Mahogany back and sides, E has Fishman electronics.

2002-2006		$1,075	$1,400

B-40/B-40B Acoustic

1989-1996. Jumbo, rosewood back and sides, built-in pickup and volume and tone controls. The B-40B had a pickup.

1989-1996	B-40B	$1,550	$2,000
1989-1996	No pickup	$1,350	$1,750

B-65 Acoustic

1989-1993. Like B-40 but with maple back and sides, built-in pickup and volume and tone controls.

1989-1993		$1,450	$1,875

BC-15E Acoustic

2000-2006. Single-cut, all mahogany, on-board electronics.

2000-2006		$1,250	$1,625

BC-16E Acoustic-Electric

2020-present. Solid sitka spruce top, East Indian rosewood back and sides, built-in Fishman electronics.

2020-2021		$1,600	$2,075

| MODEL | | EXC. COND. | |
| YEAR | FEATURES | LOW | HIGH |

BC-16GTE Acoustic
2009-2013. Jumbo, cutaway, mahogany back and sides.

2009-2013		$1,375	$1,800

BCPA4 Acoustic-Electric
2013-2020. Performing Artist series, single-cut, sitka spruce top, sapele back and sides.

2013-2020		$1,350	$1,750

EB-18
1979-1982. Electric solidbody, neck-thru, 1 pickup, natural.

1979-1982		$1,100	$1,450

EB-28
1980-1982. Electric solidbody.

1980-1982		$1,200	$1,550

SBL-10
1980s. Stinger brand solidbody, maple neck, 1 split and 1 bar pickup.

1980s		$150	$250

Marvel
1950s-mid-1960s. Brand used for budget guitars and basses marketed by Peter Sorkin Company in New York, New York.

Electric Solidbody

1950s-60s	Various models	$200	$550

Messenger
1967-1968. Built by Musicraft, Inc., Messengers featured a neck-thru metal alloy neck. They also made guitars.

Metal Neck
1967-1968. Metal alloy neck. Messenger mainly made guitars - they offered a bass, but it is unlikely many were built.

1967-1968		$2,050	$2,650

Messenger Upright
Made by Knutson Luthiery, see that listing.

Microfrets
1967-1975, 2004-2005. Professional grade, production, electric basses built in Myersville, Maryland. They also built guitars.

Husky
1971-1974/75. Double-cut, 2 pickups, 2-on-a-side tuners.

1971-1975		$1,050	$1,350

Rendezvous
1970. One pickup, orange sunburst.

1970		$1,125	$1,450

Signature
1969-1975. Double-cut, 2 pickups, 2-on-a-side tuners.

1969-1975		$1,600	$2,100

Stage II
1969-1975. Double-cut, 2 pickups, 2-on-a-side tuners.

1969-1975		$1,600	$2,100

Thundermaster
1967-1975. Double-cut, 2 pickups, 2-on-a-side tuners.

1967-1975		$1,600	$2,100

Modulus
1978-2013. Founded by aerospace engineer Geoff Gould, Modulus offered professional and premium grade, production/custom, solidbody basses built in California. They also built guitars.

Electric
1978-2013. Various standard models.

1978-2013		$1,500	$3,500

Mollerup Basses
In 1984 luthier Laurence Mollerup began building professional grade, custom/production, electric basses and electric double basses in Vancouver, British Columbia. He has also built guitars.

Moonstone
1972-2020. Luthier Steve Helgeson built his premium grade, production/custom, acoustic and electric basses in Eureka, California. He also built guitars.

Eclipse Deluxe
1980-1984. Double-cut solidbody.

1980-1984		$1,425	$1,850

Exploder
1980-1983. Figured wood body, Explorer-style neck-thru-body.

1980-1983		$1,425	$1,850

Vulcan
1982-1984. Solidbody, flat-top (Vulcan) or carved top (Vulcan II), maple body, gold hardware.

1982-1984		$1,425	$1,850

Morales
Ca.1967-1968. Guitars and basses made in Japan by Zen-On and not heavily imported into the U.S.

Electric Solidbody

1967-1968	Various models	$150	$400

Mosrite
Semie Moseley's Mosrite offered various bass models throughout the many versions of the Mosrite company.

Brut
Late-1960s. Assymetrical body with small cutaway on upper treble bout.

1960s		$600	$800

Celebrity
1965-1969. ES-335-style semi-thick double-cut body with f-holes, 2 pickups.

1965-1966	Custom color	$725	$950
1965-1967	Sunburst	$650	$850
1968-1969	Red	$600	$775
1969	Sunburst	$600	$775

Combo
1966-1968. Hollowbody, 2 pickups.

1966-1968		$1,250	$1,625

Joe Maphis
1966-1969. Ventures-style body, hollow without f-holes, 2 pickups, natural.

1966-1969		$1,350	$1,750

1969 Microfrets Signature
Rivington Guitars

1982 Moonstone Exploder

BASSES

1982 Musicman Cutlass I
Craig Brody

1979 Musicman Sabre
Craig Brody

BASSES

MODEL YEAR	FEATURES	EXC. COND. LOW	HIGH
Ventures			
1965-1972. Various colors, 1 or 2 pickups.			
1965	1 pickup	$1,575	$2,050
1965	2 pickups	$1,775	$2,300
1966	1 pickup	$1,450	$1,875
1966	2 pickups	$1,600	$2,100
1967-1968	1 pickup	$1,250	$1,625
1967-1968	2 pickups	$1,400	$1,800
1969	1 pickup	$1,174	$1,525
1969	2 pickups	$1,350	$1,750
1970-1972	1 pickup	$1,125	$1,450
1970-1972	2 pickups	$1,250	$1,625
V-II			
1973-1974. Ventures-style, 2 humbuckers, sunburst.			
1973-1974		$1,350	$1,750

MTD

1994-present. Intermediate, professional, and premium grade, production/custom, electric basses built by luthier Michael Tobias (who founded Tobias Basses in '77) in Kingston, New York. Since '00, he also imports basses built in Korea to his specifications.

Murph

1965-1967. Mid-level electric solidbody basses built by Pat Murphy in San Fernado, California. Murph logo on headstock. They also offered guitars and amps.

MODEL YEAR	FEATURES	EXC. COND. LOW	HIGH
Solidbody			
1965-1967		$875	$1,150

Music Man

1972-present. Intermediate and professional grade, production, electric basses. They also build guitars.

MODEL YEAR	FEATURES	EXC. COND. LOW	HIGH
Bongo			
2003-present. Double cut solidbody, squared-off horns, 2 pickups, 4-, 5- and 6-string.			
2003-2021	Bongo 4	$1,125	$1,450
2003-2021	Bongo 5	$1,250	$1,625
2003-2021	Bongo 6	$1,375	$1,800
Cutlass I/Cutlass II			
1982-1987. Ash body, graphite neck, string-thru-body.			
1982-1984	I, CLF era	$2,300	$3,000
1982-1984	II, CLF era	$2,175	$2,825
1984-1987	I, Ernie Ball era	$1,575	$2,050
1984-1987	II, Ernie Ball era	$1,700	$2,225
S.U.B. Series			
2003-2007. Offset double-cut, 4- or 5-string, 1 humbucker.			
2003-2007	IV Bass	$450	$600
2003-2007	V Bass	$525	$675
Sabre			
1978-ca.1991. Double-cut solidbody bass, 3-and-1 tuning keys, 2 humbucking pickups, on-board preamp, natural.			
1978-1984	CLF era	$2,300	$3,000
1984-1991	Ernie Ball era	$1,300	$1,700

MODEL YEAR	FEATURES	EXC. COND. LOW	HIGH
Sterling			
1993-present. Rosewood, 1 pickup, EQ, pearl blue. In '05, additional pickup options available. 5-string introduced in '08.			
1993-2021	4-string	$975	$1,275
2008-2021	5-string	$1,025	$1,325
StingRay			
1976-present. Offset double-cut solidbody, 1 pickup, 3-and-1 tuners, string-thru until '80, various colors. 5-string introduced in '87. In '05, additional pickup options available.			
1976-1979	CLF era	$3,200	$4,200
1980-1984	CLF era	$2,500	$3,250
1984-1989	Ernie Ball era	$1,450	$1,875
1987-2021	5-string	$1,450	$1,875
1990-2021	4-string	$1,300	$1,700
StingRay 20th Anniversary			
1996. 1400 made, flamed maple body.			
1996		$2,000	$2,600
StingRay Classic			
2010-2019. Ash body, birds-eye or flame maple neck, 4- or 5-string.			
2010-2019		$1,375	$1,800

National

Ca. 1927-present. National offered electric basses in the '60s when Valco owned the brand.

MODEL YEAR	FEATURES	EXC. COND. LOW	HIGH
Beatle (Violin)			
1970s. Strum & Drum era import, National script logo on headstock, 2 pickups, shaded brown finish.			
1970s		$490	$650
EG 700V-2HB German Style			
1970s. Strum & Drum era import, Beatle-style violin body, 2 humbuckers, bolt neck.			
1970s		$525	$700
N-850			
1967-1968. Semi-hollow double-cut, art deco f-holes, 2 pickups, block markers, bout control knobs, sunburst.			
1967-1968		$725	$950
Val-Pro 85			
1961-1962. Res-O-Glas body shaped like the U.S. map, 2 pickups, snow white, renamed National 85 in '63.			
1961-1962		$950	$1,225

National Reso-Phonic

1988-present. Professional grade, production/custom, acoustic and acoustic/electric resonator basses built in San Luis Obispo, California. They also build guitars, mandolins and ukuleles.

New York Bass Works

1989-present. Luthier David Segal builds his professional and premium grade, production/custom, electric basses in New York.

Norma

Ca.1965-1970. Guitars and basses imported from Japan by Chicago's Strum and Drum.

MODEL YEAR	FEATURES	EXC. COND. LOW	HIGH
Electric Solidbody			
1960s	Various models	$150	$500

MODEL YEAR	FEATURES	EXC. COND. LOW	HIGH

O'Hagan

1979-1983. Designed by Jerol O'Hagan in St. Louis Park, Minnesota. He also offered guitars.

Electric Solidbody

1979-1983. Models include the Shark Bass, Night-Watch Bass, NightWatch Regular Bass, and the Twenty Two Bass.

1979-1983		$625	$825

Old Kraftsman

1930s-1960s. Brand used by the Spiegel Company. Guitars and basses made by other American manufacturers.

Electric Solidbody

1950s	Various models	$375	$500

Orville by Gibson

1984-1993. Orville by Gibson and Orville guitars were made by Japan's Fuji Gen Gakki for Gibson. Basically the same models except the Orville by Gibson guitars had real Gibson USA pickups and a true nitrocellulose lacquer finish. The Orville models used Japanese electronics and a poly finish. Prices here are for the Orville by Gibson models.

Thunderbird

1984-1993		$1,125	$1,450

Ovation

1966-present. Intermediate and professional grade, production, acoustic/electric basses. Ovation offered electric solidbody basses early on and added acoustic basses in the '90s. They also offer guitars and mandolins.

B768/Elite B768

1990. Single-cut acoustic-electric bass, Elite body style with upper bout soundholes.

1990		$875	$1,150

Celebrity Series

1990s-2013. Deep bowl back, cutaway, acoustic/electric.

1990s-2013	Various models	$350	$450

Magnum Series

1974-1980. Magnum I is odd-shaped mahogany solidbody, 2 pickups, mono/stereo, mute, sunburst, red or natural. Magnum II is with battery-powered preamp and 3-band EQ. Magnum III and IV had a new offset double-cut body.

1974-1980	Various models	$1,150	$1,500

NSB778 Elite T Nikki Sixx Limited Edition

2005-2013. Made in USA, acoustic-electric 4-string, 1 pickup, solid spruce top, ebony 'board, custom iron cross inlays, red or gray flame finish.

2005-2013		$1,450	$1,900

Typhoon II/Typhoon III

1968-1971. Ovation necks, but bodies and hardware were German imports. Semi-hollowbody, 2 pickups, red or sunburst. Typhoon II is 335-style and III is fretless.

1968-1971	Typhoon II	$850	$1,125
1968-1971	Typhoon III	$900	$1,200

MODEL YEAR	FEATURES	EXC. COND. LOW	HIGH

Ultra

1984. Korean solidbodies and necks assembled in U.S., offset double-cut with 1 pickup.

1984		$500	$650

PANaramic

1961-1963. Guitars and basses made in Italy by the Crucianelli accordion company and imported by PANaramic accordion. They also offered amps made by Magnatone.

Electric Hollowbody

1961-1963. Double-cut hollowbody, 2 pickups, dot markers, sunburst.

1961-1963		$1,050	$1,350

Parker

1992-2016. Premium grade, production/custom, solidbody electric basses. They also built guitars.

Fly

2002-2011. Offered in 4- and 5-string models.

2002-2011		$1,600	$2,100

Paul Reed Smith

1985-present. PRS added basses in '86, but by '92 had dropped the models. In 2000 PRS started again offering professional and premium grade, production, solidbody electric basses. Bird inlays can add $100 or more to the values of PRS basses listed here.

Bass-4

1987-1991, 2007. Mahogany, set neck, 3 single-coil pickups, hum-cancelling coil, active circuitry, 22-fret Brazilian rosewood 'board. Reintroduced (OEB Series) in 2000s.

1987		$2,000	$2,600
1988-1991		$1,600	$2,100
2007		$1,600	$2,100

Bass-5

1987-1991. Mahogany, 5-string, set-neck, rosewood 'board, 3 single-coil pickups, active electronics. Options include custom colors, bird inlays, fretless 'board.

1987		$2,200	$2,800
1988-1991		$1,775	$2,300

CE Bass-4

1990-1991. Solidbody, 4-string, alder or maple body, bolt-on neck, rosewood 'board.

1990-1991	Alder	$950	$1,225
1990-1991	Maple	$1,100	$1,450

CE Bass-5

1990-1991. Solidbody, 5-string, alder or maple body, bolt-on neck, rosewood 'board.

1990-1991	Alder	$1,050	$1,350
1990-1991	Maple	$1,200	$1,550

Curly Bass-4

1987-1991. Double-cut solidbody, curly maple top, set maple neck, Brazilian rosewood 'board (ebony on fretless), 3 single-coil and 1 hum-cancelling pickups, various grades of maple tops, moon inlays.

1987		$2,700	$3,700
1988-1991		$1,775	$2,300

Ovation Magnum I
Imaged by Heritage Auctions, HA.com

1969 Ovation Typhoon II
Rivington Guitars

BASSES

BASSES

Peavey T-40

1987 Peavey Patriot

MODEL YEAR	FEATURES	EXC. COND. LOW	HIGH
Curly Bass-5			
1987-1991. Five-string version of Curly Bass-4.			
1987		$2,800	$3,800
1988-1991		$1,875	$2,425
Electric			
2000-2007. Bolt neck 4-string, offered in regular and maple top versions.			
2000-2007	Maple	$1,175	$1,525
2000-2007	Plain	$1,050	$1,375
Private Stock Program			
2010-present. Custom instruments based around existing PRS models.			
2010-2021		$3,700	$8,000
SE Series			
2014-present. Various models, i.e. SE Kestrel and Kingfisher.			
2014-2021	Higher models	$475	$625
2014-2021	Most models	$350	$450

Peavey

1965-present. Intermediate and professional grade, production/custom, electric basses. They also build guitars and amps. Hartley Peavey's first products were guitar amps and he added guitars and basses to the mix in '78.

MODEL YEAR	FEATURES	EXC. COND. LOW	HIGH
Axcelerator			
1994-1998. Offset double-cut, long thin horns, 2 humbuckers, stacked control knobs, bolt neck, dot markers.			
1994-1998		$400	$525
Cirrus Series			
1998-2012. Offset double-cut, active electronics, in 4-, 5-, 6-string, and custom shop versions.			
1998-2009	Cirrus 5	$850	$1,125
1998-2012	Cirrus 4	$800	$1,050
1998-2012	Cirrus 6	$950	$1,250
Dyna-Bass			
1987-1993. Double-cut solidbody, active electronics, 3-band EQ, rosewood 'board, opaque finish.			
1987-1993		$450	$600
Dyna-Bass Limited			
1987-1990. Neck-thru-body, ebony 'board, flamed maple neck/body construction, purple heart strips, mother-of-pearl inlays.			
1987-1990		$600	$775
Forum			
1994-1995. Double-cut solidbody, rosewood 'board, dot inlays, 2 humbuckers.			
1994-1995		$275	$350
Forum Plus			
1994. Forum Bass with added active electronics.			
1994		$275	$350
Foundation			
1984-2002. Double-cut solidbody, 2 pickups, maple neck.			
1984-2002		$275	$350
Foundation S			
1986-1991. Two split-coil pickups, maple body, rosewood 'board, black hardware, black painted headstock.			
1986-1991		$275	$350

MODEL YEAR	FEATURES	EXC. COND. LOW	HIGH
Foundation S Active			
1987-1991. Similar to Foundation S Bass with added active circuitry, provides low-impedance output, 2 pickups.			
1987-1991		$275	$350
Fury			
1983-1999. Double-cut solidbody, rosewood 'board, 1 split-coil humbucker.			
1983-1999		$275	$350
Fury Custom			
1986-1993. Fury Bass with black hardware and narrow neck.			
1986-1993		$275	$350
Fury VI			
2001-2003. 6-string, active electronics, quilt top.			
2001-2003		$365	$475
G-Bass V			
1999-2002. Offset double-cut 5-string, humbucker, 3-band EQ.			
1999-2002		$825	$1,075
Grind Series			
2001-2020. Offset double-cut, neck-thru, long bass horn, 2 pickups, 4, 5, or 6 strings.			
2001-2020	Various models	$200	$325
Liberator JT-84 John Taylor			
2007. 2 humbuckers, black with graphics.			
2007		$1,125	$1,475
Milestone Series			
1994-present. Import offset double cut, Milestone I ('94) replaced by 1 P-style pickup II ('95-'01), split humbucker IV ('99-'04); 2 single-coil III ('99-present) now just called Milestone.			
1994-2021		$100	$190
Millenium Series			
2001-2020	Various models	$200	$800
Patriot			
1984-1988. General J-Bass styling with larger thinner horns, 1 single-coil, maple neck.			
1984-1988		$165	$215
Patriot Custom			
1986-1988. Patriot with rosewood neck, matching headstock.			
1986-1988		$200	$260
RJ-IV Randy Jackson			
1990-1993. Randy Jackson Signature model, neck-thru-body, 2 split-coil active pickups, ebony 'board, mother-of-pearl position markers.			
1990-1993		$400	$525
Rudy Sarzo Signature			
1989-1993. Double-cut solidbody, active EQ, ebony 'board, 2 pickups.			
1989-1993		$575	$750
T-20FL			
1980s. Fretless double-cut solidbody, 1 pickup, also available as the fretted T-20 ('82-'83).			
1980s		$265	$350
T-40/T-40FL			
1978-1987. Double-cut solidbody, 2 pickups. T-40FL is fretless.			
1978-1987	T-40	$550	$725
1978-1987	T-40FL	$550	$725

MODEL YEAR	FEATURES	EXC. COND. LOW	HIGH

T-45
1982-1986. T-40 with 1 humbucking pickup, and a mid-frequency rolloff knob.

1982-1986		$400	$525

TL Series
1988-1998. Neck-thru-body, gold hardware, active humbuckers, EQ, flamed maple neck and body, 5-string (TL-Five) or 6 (TL-Six).

1988-1998	TL-Five	$650	$850
1989-1998	TL-Six	$725	$950

Zodiac
2006-2012. Solid alder body, maple neck, 2 pickups.

2006-2012		$275	$365

Pedulla
1975-2019. Professional and premium grade, production/custom, electric basses made in Rockland, Massachusetts. Founded by Michael Pedulla, and which offered various upscale options that affect valuation, so each instrument should be evaluated on a case-by-case basis. Unless specifically noted, the following listings have standard to mid-level features. High-end options are specifically noted; if not, these options will have a relatively higher value than those shown here. Pedualla announced his retirement in '19.

Buzz-4/Buzz-5
1980-2008. Double-cut neck-thru solidbody, fretless, long-scale, maple neck and body wings, 2 pickups, preamp, some with other active electronics, various colors, 4-, 5-, 6-, 8-string versions.

1980-1999		$1,400	$1,800

Interceptor
1980s. Double-cut, maple/walnut laminated neck-thru.

1980s		$1,225	$1,600

MVP Series
1984-2019. Fretted version of Buzz Bass, standard or flame top, 4-, 5-, 6-, 8-string versions, MVP II is bolt-on neck version.

1980s	MVP-6	$1,625	$2,125
1984-1990s	MVP-4, flame top	$1,550	$2,000
1984-1990s	MVP-4, standard top	$1,375	$1,800
1984-1990s	MVP-5	$1,550	$2,000
1990s	MVP II	$1,000	$1,300

Orsini Wurlitzer 4-String
Mid-1970s. Body style similar to late-'50s Gibson double-cut slab body SG Special, neck-thru, 2 pickups, natural. Sold by Boston's Wurlitzer music store chain.

1970s		$1,300	$1,700

Quilt Limited
Neck-thru-body with curly maple centerstrip, quilted maple body wings, 2 Bartolini pickups, available in fretted or fretless 4- and 5-string models.

1987		$1,300	$1,700

Rapture Series
1995-2019. Solidbody with extra-long thin bass horn and extra short treble horn, 4- or 5-string, various colors.

1995-2019	Rapture 4	$1,175	$1,525
1995-2019	Rapture 5	$1,275	$1,650

Series II
1987-1992. Bolt neck, rosewood 'board, mother-of-pearl dot inlays, Bartolini pickups.

1987-1992		$850	$1,100

Thunderbass Series
1993-2019. Solidbody with extra-long thin bass horn and extra short treble horn, 4-, 5- or 6-string, standard features or triple A top.

1993-1999	4, AAA top	$1,600	$2,100
1993-1999	4, Standard	$1,275	$1,650
1993-1999	5, AAA top	$1,725	$2,250
1993-1999	5, Standard	$1,425	$1,850
1993-1999	6, AAA top	$1,850	$2,400
1993-1999	6, Standard	$1,500	$1,950
2000-2019	4, AAA top	$1,600	$2,100
2000-2019	5, AAA top	$1,725	$2,250
2000-2019	6, AAA top	$1,850	$2,400

Thunderbolt Series
1994-2019. Similar to Thunderbass Series but with bolt necks, 4-, 5- or 6-string, standard AA or AAA maple or optional 5A or exotic wood (ET) tops.

1994-2019	Various models	$1,125	$1,450

Penco
Ca. 1974-1978. Generally high-quality Japanese-made copies of classic American bass guitars. They also made guitars, mandolins and banjos.

Electric
1974-1978	Various models	$150	$400

Premier
Ca.1938-ca.1975, 1990s-2010. Originally American-made instruments, but by the '60s imported parts were being used. 1990s instruments were Asian imports.

Bantam
1950-1970. Small body, single-cut short-scale archtop electric, torch headstock inlay, sparkle 'guard, sunburst.

1950-1970		$525	$675

Electric Solidbody
1960s	Various models	$375	$600

Renaissance
1978-1980. Plexiglass solidbody electric guitars and basses made in Malvern, Pennsylvania.

Plexiglas
1978-1980. Plexiglas bodies and active electronics, models include the DPB bass (double-cut, 1 pickup, '78-'79), SPB (single-cut, 2 pickups, '78-'79), T-100B (Bich-style, 1 pickup, '80), S-100B (double-cut, 1 pickup, '80), and the S-200B (double-cut, 2 pickups, '80).

1978-1980	Various models	$775	$1,025

Rickenbacker
1931-present. Professional grade, production/custom, electric basses. They also build guitars. Rickenbacker introduced their first electric bass in '57 and has always been a strong player in the bass market.

1987 Pedulla Buzz-4
Imaged by Heritage Auctions, HA.com

1958 Premier Bantam
Izzy Miller

1973 Rickenbacker 4000

Craig Brody

1968 Rickenbacker 4001

Richard Memmel

Electric Upright
1936. Cast aluminum neck and body, horseshoe pickup, extension pole.

		LOW	HIGH
1936		$4,100	$5,300

Model 1999 (Rose-Morris)
1964-1967. Export made for English distributor Rose-Morris of London, built along the lines of the U.S. Model 4000 Bass but with small differences that are considered important in the vintage guitar market.

		LOW	HIGH
1964-1966		$8,900	$11,500
1967		$7,900	$10,200

Model 2030 Hamburg
1984-1997. Rounded double-cut, 2 pickups, active electronics.

		LOW	HIGH
1984-1997		$775	$1,025

Model 2030GF (Glenn Frey)
1992-1995. Limited Edition, double-cut, 2 humbuckers, Jetglo finish.

		LOW	HIGH
1992-1995		$1,475	$1,925

Model 2050 El Dorado
1984-1992. Gold hardware, 2 pickups, active.

		LOW	HIGH
1984-1992		$1,200	$1,550

Model 2060 El Dorado
1992-1997. Gold hardware, 2 pickups, active, double-bound body.

		LOW	HIGH
1992-1997		$1,300	$1,700

Model 3000
1975-1984. Rounded double-cut, 30" scale, 1 pickup, brown sunburst.

		LOW	HIGH
1975-1984		$1,400	$1,800

Model 3001
1975-1984. Same as Model 3000 but with longer 33-1/2" scale, Wine Red.

		LOW	HIGH
1975-1984		$1,400	$1,800

Model 3261 (Rose-Morris Slim-Line)
1967. Export model made for English distributor Rose-Morris, built along the lines of a U.S. equivalent Model 4005 Bass.

		LOW	HIGH
1967		$6,000	$7,900

Model 4000
1958-1985. Cresting wave body and headstock, 1 horseshoe pickup (changed to regular pickup in '64), neck-thru-body.

		LOW	HIGH
1958-1962	Plank style	$12,500	$16,200
1963-1966		$9,300	$12,000
1967-1969		$8,500	$11,000
1970-1972		$3,400	$4,400
1973-1985		$2,200	$2,900

Model 4001
1961-1986. Fancy version of 4000, 1 horseshoe magnet pickup (changed to regular pickup in '64) and 1 bar magnet pickup, triangle inlays, bound neck.

		LOW	HIGH
1961-1963	Fireglo	$8,800	$11,500
1963-1966	Mapleglo	$7,900	$10,200
1964-1966	Fireglo	$8,200	$10,600
1967-1969	Various colors	$7,000	$9,000
1970-1972	Various colors	$4,200	$5,500
1973	Early '73 features	$3,500	$4,600
1973	Late '73 features	$2,750	$3,600
1974-1979	Various colors	$2,750	$3,600
1980-1986	Various colors	$2,600	$3,400

Model 4001C64S
2001-2014. Recreation of Paul McCartney's 4001 featuring changes he made like a reshaped body and zero-fret 'board.

		LOW	HIGH
2001-2014		$2,900	$3,800

Model 4001CS (Chris Squire)
1991-1997. Chris Squire signature model, with certificate.

		LOW	HIGH
1991-1997		$3,400	$4,400

Model 4001FL
1968-1986. Fretless version of 4001 Bass, special order in '60s, various colors.

		LOW	HIGH
1968-1986		$2,900	$3,800

Model 4001S
1964-1985. Same as Model 4000, but with 2 pickups, export model.

		LOW	HIGH
1980-1985		$1,700	$2,200

Model 4001V63
1984-2000. Vintage '63 reissue of Model 4001S, horseshoe-magnet pickup, Mapleglo.

		LOW	HIGH
1984-2000	Figured top	$3,000	$3,900
1984-2000	Plain top	$2,900	$3,800

Model 4002
1967-1985. Cresting wave body and headstock, 2 humbuckers, black 'guard, checkerboard binding.

		LOW	HIGH
1980-1985		$4,500	$5,900

Model 4003
1979-present. Similar to Model 4001, split 'guard, deluxe features.

		LOW	HIGH
1979-2021		$1,700	$2,200

Model 4003FL
1979-2017. Fretless version.

		LOW	HIGH
1979-2017		$1,700	$2,200

Model 4003 Shadow
1986. About 60 made for Guitar Center, all black 'board, inlays and hardware, Jetglo finish.

		LOW	HIGH
1986		$3,100	$4,000

Model 4003S
1986-2003, 2012-present. Standard feature version of 4003, 4 strings. Reissued in '12.

		LOW	HIGH
1986-2003		$1,750	$2,300
2012-2021	Reissue	$1,450	$1,900

Model 4003S Redneck
1988. Red body, 'board and headstock, black hardware.

		LOW	HIGH
1988		$2,800	$3,600

Model 4003S Tuxedo
1987. White body with black 'guard and hardware. 100 made.

		LOW	HIGH
1987		$2,800	$3,600

Model 4003S/5
1986-2003. Model 4003S with 5 strings.

		LOW	HIGH
1986-2003		$2,200	$2,900

Model 4003S/8
1986-2003. Model 4003S with 8 strings.

		LOW	HIGH
1986-2003		$3,400	$4,500

Model 4003S/SPC Blackstar
1989. Black version, black finish, 'board, knobs, and hardware. Also offered as 5-string.

		LOW	HIGH
1989		$2,300	$3,000

MODEL		EXC. COND.	
YEAR	FEATURES	LOW	HIGH

Model 4003W
2013-present. Solid walnut body, satin natural finish.

2013-2021		$1,550	$2,000

Model 4004C Cheyenne/4004Cii Cheyenne II
1993-2019. Cresting wave, maple neck-thru-body with walnut body and head wings, gold hardware, dot inlay. Replaced by maple top 4004Cii Cheyenne II in '00.

1993-1999	Cheyenne	$1,550	$2,000
2000-2019	Cheyenne II	$1,575	$2,050

Model 4004L Laredo
1993-present. Like Cheyenne but without walnut wings.

1993-2021		$1,375	$1,800

Model 4005
1965-1984. New style double-cut semi-hollowbody, 2 pickups, R tailpiece, cresting wave headstock.

1965-1966	Fireglo	$11,200	$14,500
1965-1966	Jetglo	$9,800	$12,700
1965-1966	Mapleglo	$10,700	$14,000
1967-1969	Fireglo	$10,200	$13,200
1967-1969	Jetglo	$8,500	$11,100
1967-1969	Mapleglo	$9,800	$12,700
1970-1979	Various colors	$6,800	$8,900
1980-1984	Various colors	$6,400	$8,300

Model 4005-6
1965-1977. Model 4005 with 6 strings.

1965-1969		$10,800	$14,000
1970-1977		$7,400	$9,600

Model 4005-8
Late-1960s. Eight-string Model 4005, Fireglo or Mapleglo.

1968-1969		$10,200	$13,200

Model 4005L (Lightshow)
1970-1975. Model 4005 with translucent top with lights in body that lit up when played, needed external transformer.

1970-1971	1st edition	$9,400	$12,200
1972-1975	2nd edition	$10,200	$13,300

Model 4005WB
1966-1983. Old style Model 4005 with white-bound body, Fireglo.

1966		$10,200	$13,200
1967-1969		$9,300	$12,000
1970-1979		$5,500	$7,200
1980-1983		$5,100	$6,600

Model 4008
1975-1983. Eight-string, cresting wave body and headstock.

1975-1979		$2,100	$2,800
1980-1983		$1,925	$2,500

Model 4080 Doubleneck
1975-1992. Bolt-on 6- and 4-string necks, Jetglo or Mapleglo.

1975-1979		$6,000	$7,900
1980-1992		$6,000	$7,900

Ritter Royal Instruments
Production/custom, solidbody basses built by luthier Jens Ritter in Wachenheim, Germany.

Rob Allen
1997-present. Professional grade, production/custom, lightweight basses made by luthier Robert Allen in Santa Barbara, California.

Robin
1982-2010. Founded by David Wintz and located in Houston, Texas, Robin built basses until 1997. Most basses were Japanese-made until '87; American production began in '88. They also built guitars and also made Metropolitan ('96-'08) and Alamo ('00-'08) brand guitars.

Freedom I
1984-1986. Offset double-cut, active treble and bass EQ controls, 1 pickup.

1984-1986		$650	$850

Freedom I Passive
1986-1989. Non-active version of Freedom Bass, 1 humbucker. Passive dropped from name in '87.

1986-1989		$650	$850

Medley
1984-1997. Offset deep cutaways, 2 pickups, reverse headstock until '89, then split headstock, back to reverse by '94. Japanese-made until '87, U.S. after.

1984-1987	Japan	$525	$675
1988-1997	USA	$1,025	$1,325

Ranger
1984-1997. Vintage style body, dot markers, medium scale and 1 pickup from '84 to '88 and long scale with P-style and J-style pickup configuration from '89 to '97.

1984-1987	Japan	$500	$650
1988-1997	USA	$925	$1,200

Rock Bass
2002-2015. Chinese-made, intermediate and professional grade, production, bolt neck solidbody basses from the makers of Warwick basses.

Roland
Best known for keyboards, effects, and amps, Roland offered synthesizer-based guitars and basses from 1977 to '86.

GR-33B (G-88) Bass Guitar Synthesizer
Early-mid 1980s. Solidbody bass with synthesizer in the guitar case, G-88 deluxe bass.

1983-1985		$925	$1,200

Roman & Blake Basses
1977-2003. Professional grade, production/custom, solidbody bass guitars made by Ed Roman Guitars.

Roman USA Basses
Professional grade, production/custom, solidbody basses made by Ed Roman Guitars starting in 2000.

Roscoe Guitars
Early 1980s-present. Luthier Keith Roscoe builds his production/custom, professional and premium grade, solidbody electric basses in Greensboro, North Carolina.

1980 Rickenbacker 4003
Bernunzio Uptown Music

Robin Freedom II
Rivington Guitars

BASSES

Sadowsky NYC Custom 21-Fret

1983 Steinberger L2
Carter Vintage Guitars

MODEL YEAR	FEATURES	EXC. COND. LOW	HIGH

S.D. Curlee
1975-1982. S.D. Curlee guitars and basses were made in Illinois; S.D. Curlee International instruments were made in Japan.
Electric Solidbody

1970s	Various models	$350	$550

Sadowsky
1980-present. Professional and premium grade, production/custom, solidbody basses built by luthier Roger Sadowsky in Brooklyn, New York. He also builds guitars and amps.

Serenader
Mainly known for lap steels this Seattle, Washington brand also built a solidbody bass.

Silvertone
1941-ca.1970, present. Brand used by Sears. Instruments were U.S.-made and imported. Currently, Samick offers a line of acoustic and electric guitars, basses and amps under the Silvertone name.
Model 1373L/1376L

1956-1959		$1,475	$1,925

Model 1442 Standard
1966-1968. Solidbody 30" standard size, 1 pickup, dot markers, shaded brown.

1966-1968		$750	$975

Model 1443 Extra Long
1966-1968. Solidbody 34" size, 2 pickups, dot markers, red sunburst.

1966-1968		$925	$1,200

Model 1444 Electric
1959-1965. Bass version of 6-string electric guitar Model 1415 (bronze) and 1416 (black), 4-on-a-side replaces the prior year coke-bottle headstock, 1 pickup on single-cut U-1 style body, black finish.

1959-1965		$850	$1,100

Simmons
2002-present. Luthier David L. Simmons builds his professional grade, production/custom, 4- and 5-string basses in Hendersonville, North Carolina.

Sinister
2003. A short run of intermediate grade, solidbody basses built for Sinister Guitars by luthier Jon Kammerer.

Smith
1978-present. Professional and premium grade, production/custom, electric basses built by luthier Ken Smith in Perkasie, Pennsylvania. Earlier models had Ken Smith on the headstock, recent models have a large S logo. He also designs the imported KSD line of basses.
American-Made

1978-2021	Various models	$3,500	$4,500

Imported

1990s	Various models	$700	$900

Soundgear by Ibanez
SDGR Soundgear by Ibanez headstock logo, intermediate grade, production, solidbody electric basses, made in Japan, Korea and Indonesia, starting in 1987.

Spector/Stuart Spector Design
1975-1990 (Spector), 1991-1998 (SSD), 1998-present (Spector SSD). Imtermediate, professional, and premium grade, production/custom, basses made in the U.S., the Czech Republic, Korea, and China. Stuart Spector's first bass was the NS and the company quickly grew to the point where Kramer acquired it in '85. After Kramer went out of business in '90, Spector started building basses with the SSD logo (Stuart Spector Design). In '98 he recovered the Spector trademark.

Squier
See models listed under Squier in Fender section.

Standel
1952-1974, 1997-present. Amp builder Bob Crooks offered instruments under his Standel brand name three different times during the '60s. See Guitar section for production details. See Amp section for more company information.
Custom Deluxe Solidbody 401
1967-1968. Custom with higher appointments, various colors.

1967-1968		$1,125	$1,450

Custom Deluxe Thinbody 402
1967-1968. Custom with higher appointments, various colors.

1967-1968		$1,125	$1,450

Custom Solidbody 501
1967-1968. Solidbody, 1 pickup, various colors.

1967-1968		$875	$1,150

Custom Thinbody 502
1967-1968. Thin solidbody, 2 pickups, various colors.

1967-1968		$875	$1,150

Steinberger
1979-present. Steinberger offers budget and intermediate grade, production, electric basses. They also offer guitars.
H Series
1979-1982. Reinforced molded plastic wedge-shaped body, headless neck, 1 (H1) or 2 (H2) high impedence pickups, black, red or white.

1979-1982	H1, black	$2,700	$3,500
1979-1982	H1, red or white	$3,800	$4,925
1979-1982	H2, black	$2,700	$3,500
1979-1982	H2, red or white	$3,800	$4,925

L Series
1979-1984. Reinforced molded plastic wedge-shaped body, headless neck, 1 (L1) or 2 (L2) low impedance active pickups, black, red or white. Evolved into XL series.

1979-1984	L1, black	$2,200	$2,900

BASSES

MODEL YEAR	FEATURES	EXC. COND. LOW	HIGH
1979-1984	L1, black, fretless	$2,100	$2,800
1979-1984	L1, red or white	$3,500	$4,500
1979-1984	L2, black	$2,200	$2,900
1979-1984	L2, black, fretless	$2,100	$2,800
1979-1984	L2, red or white	$3,500	$4,500

Q-4

1990-1991. Composite neck, Double Bass system, headless with traditional-style maple body, low-impedance pickups.

1990-1991		$1,600	$2,100

Q-5

1990-1991. Five-string version of Q Bass.

1990-1991		$1,675	$2,175

XL-2

1984-1993. Rectangular composite body, 4-string, headless, 2 pickups.

1984-1989		$2,200	$2,900
1990-1993		$2,050	$2,650

XL-2GR

1985-1990. Headless, Roland GR synthesizer controller.

1985-1990		$2,200	$2,900

XM-2

1986-1992. Headless, double-cut maple body, 4-string, 2 low-impedance pickups, optional fretted, lined fretless or unlined fretless, black, red or white.

1986-1992		$2,150	$2,800

XT-2/XZ-2 Spirit

1995-present. Headless, rectangular XL body, import.

1995-2021		$300	$400

Stewart Basses

2000-ca. 2009. Luthier Fred Stewart built his premium grade, custom/production, solidbody basses in Charlton, Maryland. He has also built guitars starting in '94.

Stinger

See Martin listing.

Supro

1935-1968, 2004-present. Supro was a budget brand for the National Dobro Company. Supro offered only two bass models in the '60s. Brand name was revived in '04.

Pocket

1960-1968. Double-cut, neck pickup and bridge mounted pickup, semi-hollow, short-scale, black.

1960-1968		$750	$975

Taurus

1967-1968. Asymmetrical double-cut, neck pickup and bridge mounted pickup.

1967-1968		$600	$775

SX

See listing for Essex.

Tacoma

1995-2009. Professional grade, production, acoustic basses produced in Tacoma, Washington. They also built acoustic guitars and mandolins.

Thunderchief

1998-2009. 17 3/4 flat-top, solid spruce top, solid mahogany back, laminated mahogany sides, rounded cutaway, bolt-on neck, dot markers, natural satin finish.

1998-2009	Various models	$790	$1,025

Taylor

1974-present. Professional and premium grade, production, acoustic basses built in El Cajon, California. They presently build guitars.

AB1

1996-2003. Acoustic/electric, sitka spruce top, imbuia walnut back and sides, designed for 'loose' woody sound.

1996-2003		$1,400	$1,850

AB2

1996-2003. Acoustic/electric, all imbuia walnut body.

1996-2003		$1,700	$2,200

AB3

1998-2003. Acoustic/electric, sitka spruce top, maple back and sides.

1998-2003		$1,700	$2,200

GS Series

2006-present. Grand Symphony, the GS Mini is scaled-down version.

2006-2021	Various models	$500	$1,275

Teisco

The Japanese Teisco line started offering basses in the '60s.

Electric

1968-1969. EB-100 (1 pickup, white 'guard), EB-200 (solidbody), EB-200B (semi-hollowbody) and Violin bass.

1968-1969	EB-100	$175	$300
1968-1969	EB-200	$650	$850
1968-1969	EB-200 B	$650	$850
1968-1969	Violin	$650	$850

Tele-Star

1965-ca.1972. Guitars and basses imported from Japan by Tele-Star Musical Instrument Corporation of New York. Primarily made by Kawai, many inspired by Burns designs, some in cool sparkle finishes.

Electric Solidbody

1960s	Various models	$150	$375

Tobias

1977-2019. Founded by Mike Tobias in Orlando, Florida. Moved to San Francisco for '80-'81, then to Costa Mesa, eventually ending up in Hollywood. In '90, he sold the company to Gibson which moved it to Burbank. The first Tobias made under Gibson ownership was serial number 1094. The instruments continued to be made by the pre-Gibson crew until '92, when the company was moved to Nashville. The last LA Tobias/Gibson serial number is 2044. Mike left the company in '92 and started a new

Taylor GS Mini-e

Teisco EB-200
Carter Vintage Guitars

BASSES

BASSES

Tobias Growler GR-5
Imaged by Heritage Auctions, HA.com

1974 Univox Hi Flier
Greg Boschert

business in '94 called MTD where he continues to make electric and acoustic basses. In '99, production of Tobias basses was moved overseas. In late '03, Gibson started again offering U.S.-made Tobias instruments; they are made in Conway, Arkansas, in the former Baldwin grand piano facility. Currently Tobias offers imported and U.S.-made, intermediate and professional grade, production, acoustic and electric basses.

Basic Series
1984-1999. 30", 32", or 34" scale, neck-thru-body in alder, koa or walnut, 5-piece laminated neck.

MODEL YEAR	FEATURES	EXC. COND. LOW	HIGH
1984-1999	Basic B-4	$2,100	$2,700
1984-1999	Basic B-5	$2,100	$2,700

Classic C-4
1978-1999. One or 2 pickups, active or passive electronics, 2-octave rosewood 'board, available in short-, medium-, and long-scale models.

1978-1999		$2,175	$2,800

Classic C-5
1985-1999. 30", 32" or 34" scale, alder, koa or walnut body, bookmatched top, ebony or phenolic 'board, hardwood neck.

1985-1999		$2,225	$2,900

Classic C-6
Ca. 1986-1999. Flamed maple and padauk neck, alder body, padauk top, ebony 'board, active electronics, 32" or 34" scale.

1986-1999		$2,300	$3,000

Growler GR-5
1996-1999. 5-string, offset double-cut, bolt neck, various colors.

1996-1999		$725	$950

Growler Limited
2009. Limited run, natural finish swamp ash body, set-neck.

2009		$850	$1,100

Killer Bee
1991-1999. Offset double-cut, swamp ash or lacewood body, various colors.

1991-1999	KB-4	$1,925	$2,500
1991-1999	KB-5	$2,000	$2,600
1991-1999	KB-6	$2,100	$2,700

Model T
1989-1991. Line of 4- and 5-string basses, 3-piece maple neck-thru-body, maple body halves, active treble and bass controls. Fretless available.

1989-1991		$1,274	$1,650

Renegade
1998-2001. Offset double-cut, 1 single-coil and 1 humbucker.

1998-2001		$1,700	$2,200

Signature S-4
1978-1999. Available in 4-, 5-, and 6-string models, chrome-plated milled brass bridge.

1978-1990	Tobias-Burbank	$3,200	$4,200
1990-1992	Gibson-Burbank	$2,600	$3,400

Standard ST-4
1992-1995. Japanese-made, 5-piece maple neck-thru, swamp ash body wings.

1992-1995		$1,200	$1,600

Toby Deluxe TD-4
1994-1996. Offset double-cut, bolt neck.

MODEL YEAR	FEATURES	EXC. COND. LOW	HIGH
1994-1996		$500	$650

Toby Deluxe TD-5
1994-1996. 5-string version.

1994-1996		$575	$750

Toby Pro 5
1994-1996. Solidbody 5-string, Toby Pro logo on truss rod cover, neck-thru body.

1994-1996		$500	$650

Toby Pro 6
1994-1996. Solidbody 6-string, Toby Pro logo on truss rod cover, neck-thru body.

1994-1996		$625	$825

Tokai
1947-present. Tokai started making guitars and basses around '70 and by the end of that decade they were being imported into the U.S. Today Tokai offers electrics, acoustics, and electric basses made in Japan and Korea.

Vintage
1970s-1980s. Tokai offered near copies of classic U.S. basses.

1970s-80s	Copy models	$500	$1,000

Tonemaster
1960s. Guitars and basses, imported from Italy, with typical '60s Italian sparkle plastic finish and push-button controls, bolt-on neck.

Electric

1960s	Various models	$550	$850

Traben
Intermediate grade, production, solidbody basses imported by Elite Music Brands of Clearwater, Florida, starting in 2004.

Travis Bean
1974-1979, 1999. The unique Travis Bean line included a couple of bass models. Travis Bean announced some new instruments in '99, but general production was not resumed.

TB-2000
1974-1979. Aluminum neck, T-slotted headstock, longer horned, double-cut body, 2 pickups, 4 controls, dot markers, various colors.

1974-1979		$3,200	$4,200

TB-4000 (Wedge Vee)
1974-1979. Bass version of Bean's Wedge guitar, few made.

1974-1979		$4,400	$5,700

True Tone
1960s. Western Auto retailed this line of basses, guitars and amps which were manufactured by Chicago builders like Kay. The brand was most likely gone by '68.

Electric

1960s	Various models	$250	$500

MODEL YEAR	FEATURES	EXC. COND. LOW	HIGH

Univox

1964-1978. Univox started out as an amp line and added guitars and basses around '69. Guitars were imported from Japan by the Merson Musical Supply Company, later Unicord, Westbury, New York. Generally mid-level copies of American designs.

Badazz
1971-ca. 1975. Based on the Guild S-100.

1971-1977		$425	$550

Bicentennial
1976. Carved eagle in body, matches Bicentennial guitar (see that listing), brown stain, maple 'board.

1976		$775	$1,025

Hi Flier
1969-1977. Mosrite Ventures Bass copy, 2 pickups, rosewood 'board.

1969-1977		$525	$675

Model 1970F 'Lectra
1969-ca. 1973. Violin bass, walnut.

1969-1973		$625	$825

Model 3340 Semi-Hollow
1970-1971. Copy of Gibson EB-0 semi-hollow bass.

1970-1971		$525	$675

Precisely
1971-ca. 1975. Copy of Fender P-Bass.

1971-1975		$525	$675

Stereo
1976-1977. Rickenbacker 4001 Bass copy, model U1975B.

1976-1977		$525	$675

Thin Line
1960s. EB-2 style, f-holes, 2 pickups.

1960s		$525	$675

Ventura

1970s. Import classic bass copies distributed by C. Bruno (Kaman). They also had guitars.

Vintage Electric

1970s	Copy models	$525	$675

Vox

1954-present. Guitars and basses bearing the Vox name were offered from 1961-'69 (made in England, Italy), '82-'85 (Japan), '85-'88 (Korea), '98-2001 (U.S.), with a limited edition teardrop bass offered in late '07. Special thanks to Jim Rhoads of Rhoads Music in Elizabethtown, Pennsylvania, for help on production years of these models.

Apollo IV
1967-1969. Single-cut hollowbody, bolt maple neck, 1 pickup, on-board fuzz, booster, sunburst.

1967-1969		$775	$1,000

Astro IV
1967-1969. Violin-copy bass, 2 pickups.

1967-1969		$975	$1,250

Bassmaster
1961-1965. Offset double-cut, 2 pickups, 2 knobs.

1961-1965		$700	$900

Clubman
1961-1966. Double-cut 2-pickup solidbody, red.

1961-1966		$475	$625

Constellation IV
1967-1968. Teardrop-shaped body, 2 pickups, 1 f-hole, 1 set of controls, treble, bass and distortion boosters.

1967-1968		$1,250	$1,625

Cougar
1963-1967. Double-cut semi-hollow body, 2 f-holes, 2 pickups, 2 sets of controls, sunburst.

1963-1967		$975	$1,250

Delta IV
1967-1968. Five-sided body, 2 pickups, 1 volume and 2 tone controls, distortion, treble and bass boosters.

1967-1968		$2,700	$3,500

Guitar-Organ
1966. The 4-string bass version of the Guitar-Organ, Phantom-style body, white.

1966	Excellent cond	$2,600	$3,400
1966	Functional	$1,700	$2,200

Mark IV
1963-1969. Made in England first (white), then Italy (sunburst), teardrop-shaped body, 2 pickups, 1 set of controls.

1963-1965	England	$2,500	$3,200
1965-1969	Italy	$1,500	$1,950

Panther
1967-1968. Double-cut solidbody, 1 slanted pickup, rosewood 'board, sunburst.

1967-1968		$525	$700

Phantom IV
1963-1969. Made in England first, then Italy, 5-sided body, 2 pickups, 1 set of controls.

1963-1964	England	$2,600	$3,400
1965-1969	Italy	$1,900	$2,500

Saturn IV
1967-1968. Single-cut, 2 f-holes, 1 set of controls, 1 pickup.

1967-1968		$650	$850

Sidewinder IV (V272)
1967-1968. Double-cut semi-hollow body, 2 f-holes, 2 pickups, 1 set of controls, treble, bass, and distortion boosters.

1967-1968		$1,125	$1,475

Stinger
1968. Teardrop-shaped, boat oar headstock.

1968		$800	$1,050

Violin
1966. Electro-acoustic bass with violin shaped body, 2 extended range pickups, sunburst.

1966		$1,050	$1,350

Wyman
1966. Teardrop-shaped body, 2 pickups, 1 f-hole, 1 set of controls, sunburst.

1966		$1,400	$1,800

Wal

1976-present. Founded in England by luthier Ian Waller and his partner Peter Stevens, forming the company under the name Electric Wood in '78. Waller died in '88, Stevens enlists help of luthier Paul Herman, and in 2000s Stevens retires and Herman takes over. In the early years, the Mark

1967 Vox Apollo IV
Rivington Guitars

1965 Vox Phantom IV
Craig Brody

BASSES

Wal Pro (Mark I)

Zemaitis GZB-2500

MODEL YEAR	FEATURES	EXC. COND. LOW	HIGH

designation was used generically. Newer contemporary models are named Mk1, Mk2 and Mk3. Prices shown will increase 5% with LED option, or 10% with rare top, but no value difference between fretted and fretless. MIDI electronics does not increase the value.

Custom (IV)
1980s-1990s. 4-string, active, no guard, generally highly figured front and back.

1980s-90s	Mark I	$6,000	$8,000
1980s-90s	Mark II	$6,000	$8,000
1980s-90s	Mark III	$6,000	$8,000

Custom (V)
1980s-1990s. 5-string, active, no guard, generally highly figured front and back.

1980s-90s	Mark II	$7,500	$10,000
1980s-90s	Mark III	$7,500	$10,000

Custom (VI)
1990s. 6-string, active, no guard, generally highly figured front and back.

1990s	Mark III	$9,000	$12,000

JG
1976-1978. 4-string, passive with either tooled leather (34 made), or leather guard.

1976-1978	Non-tooled	$6,000	$8,000
1976-1978	Tooled	$7,000	$9,000

Pro
Late-1970s. Passive, black guard.

1970s	Pro I	$3,800	$5,000
1970s	Pro II	$4,300	$5,500

Wandre (Davoli)
Ca. 1956/57-1969. Italian-made guitars and basses.

Electric

1956-1969	Common models	$2,600	$3,400
1956-1969	Rare models	$7,000	$9,000

Warwick
1982-present. Professional and premium grade, production/custom, electric and acoustic basses made in Markneukirchen, Germany; founded by Hans Peter Wilfer, whose father started Framus guitars. They also build amps.

Welson
1960s. Italian-made copy model guitars and basses.

Electric

1960s	Copy models	$150	$400

Wurlitzer
Large music retailer Wurlitzer marketed a line of American-made guitars in the 1920s. They also offered American- and foreign-made guitars starting in '65. In '67, Wurlitzer switched to Italian-made Welson guitars.

Hollowbody Electric

1960s	Italian-made	$525	$700

MODEL YEAR	FEATURES	EXC. COND. LOW	HIGH

Yamaha
1946-present. Budget, intermediate, professional and premium grade, production, electric basses. They also build guitars. Yamaha began producing solidbody instruments in '66.

Electric
1960-present. Wide variety of models.

1960-2021	Various models	$200	$1,500

Zemaitis
1960-1999, 2004-present. Tony Zemaitis began selling his guitars in '60 and he retired in '99. He emphasized simple lightweight construction and his instruments are known for hand engraved metal fronts. Each hand-built custom guitar or bass was a unique instrument. Approximately 10 custom guitars were built each year. In '04, Japan's Kanda Shokai, with the endorsement of Tony Zemaitis, Jr., started building the guitars again.

Zen-On
1946-ca.1968. Japanese-made. By '67 using the Morales brandname. Not heavily imported into the U.S., if at all (see Morales).

Electric Solidbody

1950s	Various models	$150	$400

Zim-Gar
1960s. Japanese guitars and basses imported by Gar-Zim Musical Instrument Corporation of Brooklyn, New York.

Electric Solidbody

1960s	Various models	$150	$400

Zon
1981-present. Luthier Joe Zon builds his professional and premium grade, production/custom, solidbody basses in Redwood City, California. Zon started the brand in Buffalo, New York and relocated to Redwood City in '87. He has also built guitars.

Legacy Elite
1989-present. 34" scale carbon-fiber neck, Bartolini pickups, ZP-2 active electronics.

1989-2021	V, 5-string	$1,550	$2,000
1989-2021	VI, 6-string	$1,600	$2,100

Scepter
1984-1993. Offset body shape, 24 frets, 1 pickup, tremolo.

1984-1993		$1,300	$1,700

Sonus Custom
1990s-present. Offset swamp ash body, 2 pickups.

1990s-2021		$2,100	$2,700

Zorko
Late-1950s-early-1962. Original maker of the Ampeg Baby Bass (see that listing), sold to Ampeg in 1962, Zorko logo on scroll.

Baby

1950s-1962		$2,300	$3,000

AMPS

Acoustic 115
Rivington Guitars

1980 Acoustic 165

Airline Tremolo 2Reverb
Tom Pfeifer

AMPS

MODEL YEAR	FEATURES	EXC. COND. LOW	HIGH

3 Monkeys Amps
2007-present. Intermediate and professional grade, production/custom, amps and cabinets built by Greg Howard in Raleigh, North Carolina.

3rd Power
Mid-2009-present. Professional grade, production/custom, guitar amps built in Franklin, Tennessee by Jamie Scott.

65amps
2004-present. Founded by Peter Stroud and Dan Boul, 65amps builds tube guitar head and combo amps and speaker cabs in Valley Village, California.

Ace Tone
Late-1960-1970s. Made by Sakata Shokai Limited of Osaka, Japan, early importer of amps and effects pedals. Later became Roland/Boss.

B-9
Late-1960s-early-1970s. Solid-state bass amp head.

1960s-70s		$135	$175

Mighty-5
Late-1960s-early-1970s. Tubes, 50-watt head.

1960s-70s		$105	$135

Solid A-5
Late-1960s-early-1970s. Solidstate 2x12 combo with verticle cab, reverb and tremolo, black tolex, silver grille.

1960s-70s		$155	$200

Acoustic
Ca.1965-ca.1987, 2001-2005, 2008-present. The Acoustic Control Corp., of Los Angeles, California, was mostly known for solidstate amplifiers. Heads and cabinets were sold separately with their own model numbers, but were also combined (amp sets) and marketed under a different model number (for example, the 153 amp set was the 150b head with a 2x15" cabinet). The brand was revived by Samick in '01 for a line of amps. In '08 brand back again on line of amps sold through Guitar Center and Musician's Friend.

114
Ca.1977-mid-1980s. Solidstate, 50 watts, 2x10", reverb, master volume.

1977-1984		$250	$325

115
1977-1978. Solidstate, 1x12", 50 watts, reverb, master volume.

1977-1978		$250	$325

116 Bass
1978-mid-1980s. Solidstate, 75 watts, 1x15", power boost switch.

1978-1984		$250	$325

120 Head
1977-mid-1980s. Solidstate head, 125 watts.

1977-1984		$200	$260

123
1977-1984. 1x12" combo.

1977-1984		$200	$260

124
1977-mid-1980s. Solidstate, 4x10", 5-band EQ, 100 watts, master volume.

1977-1984		$275	$350

125
1977-mid-1980s. Solidstate, 2x12", 5-band EQ, 100 watts, master volume.

1977-1984		$275	$350

126 Bass
1977-mid-1980s. Solidstate, 100 watts, 1x15", 5-band EQ.

1977-1984		$275	$350

134
1972-1976. Solidstate, 100-125 watts, 4x10" combo.

1972-1976		$275	$350

135
1972-1976. Solidstate, 125 watts, 2x12" combo, reverb, tremolo.

1972-1976		$275	$350

136
1972-1976. Solidstate, 125 watts, 1x15" combo.

1972-1976		$275	$350

140 Bass Head
1972-1976. Solidstate, 125 watts, 2 channels.

1972-1976		$200	$260

150 Head
1960s-1976. Popular selling model, generally many available in the used market. Solidstate, 110 watts until '72, 125 watts after.

1968-1976		$225	$300

150b Bass Head
1960s-1971. Bass amp version of 150 head.

1968-1971		$200	$260

153 Bass Set
1960s-1971. 150b head (bass version of 150) with 2x15" 466 cabinet, 110 watts.

1968-1971		$450	$575

165
1979-mid-1980s. All tube combo, switchable to 60 or 100 watts, brown tolex.

1979-1984		$350	$450

220 Bass Head
1977-1980s. Solidstate, 5-band EQ, either 125 or 160 watts, later models 170 or 200 watts, black tolex.

1977-1984		$250	$325

230 Head
1977-1980s. Solidstate head, 125/160 watts, 5-band EQ.

1977-1984		$250	$325

260 Head
1960s-1971. Solidstate, 275 watt, stereo/mono.

1968-1971		$650	$850

261 Head and Cabinet Set
1960s-1971. 275 watts with 2x15" cab.

1969-1971		$2,700	$3,600

270 Head
1970s. 400 watts.

1970s		$400	$525

320 Bass Head
1977-1980s. Solidstate, 5-band EQ, 160/300 watts, 2 switchable channels, black tolex.

1977-1984		$400	$525

MODEL YEAR FEATURES	EXC. COND. LOW	HIGH
360 Bass Head		
1960s-1971. One of Acoustic's most popular models, 200 watts. By '72, the 360 is listed as a "preamp only."		
1968-1971	$675	$900
370 Bass Head		
1972-1977. Solidstate bass head, 365 watts early on, 275 later, Jaco Pastorius associated.		
1972-1977 275 or 365 watt	$675	$900
402 Cabinet		
1977-1980s. 2x15" bass cab, black tolex, black grille.		
1977-1984	$225	$300
404 Cabinet		
1970s. 6x10", Jaco Pastorius associated.		
1970s	$450	$575
450 Head		
1974-1976. 170 watts, 5-band EQ, normal and bright inputs.		
1974-1976	$350	$450
455 Set		
1974-1977. 170 watt 450 head with 4x12" cabinet, black.		
1974-1977	$675	$900
470 Head		
1974-1977. 170 watt, dual channel.		
1974-1977	$350	$450
AG15		
2008-2016. Small combo, 15 watts.		
2008-2016	$37	$48
B100 (MK II)		
2008-2016. Classic style bass combo, 100 watts, 1x15.		
2008-2016	$105	$135
B200 (MK II)		
2009-2019. Bass combo, 200 watts, 1x15.		
2009-2019	$200	$260
G20-110		
1981-mid-1980s. Solidstate, 20 watts, 1x10". The G series was a lower-priced combo line.		
1981-1985	$100	$125
G20-120		
1981-mid-1980s. Solidstate, 20 watts, 1x12".		
1981-1985	$100	$125
G60-112		
1981-mid-1980s. Solidstate, 60 watts, 1x12".		
1981-1985	$125	$160
G60-212		
1981-mid-1980s. Solidstate, 60 watts, 2x12".		
1981-1985	$145	$190
G60T-112		
1981-1987. Tube, 60 watts, 1x12".		
1981-1985	$250	$325
Tube 60		
1986-1987. Combo, 60 watts, 1x12", spring reverb, bright switch, master volume control, effects loop.		
1986-1987	$250	$325

ADA

1977-2002. ADA (Analog/Digital Associates) was located in Berkeley, California, and introduced its Flanger and Final Phase in '77. The company later moved to Oakland and made amplifiers, high-tech signal processors, and a reissue of its original Flanger.

Aguilar

1995-present. U.S.-made tube and solidstate amp heads, cabinets, and pre-amps from New York City, New York. They also made effect pedals.

Aiken Amplification

2000-present. Tube amps, combos, and cabinets built by Randall Aiken originally in Buford, Georgia, and since '05 in Pensacola, Florida.

Airline

Ca.1958-1968, 2004-present. Brand for Montgomery Ward, built by Danelectro, Valco and others. In '04, the brand was revived on a line of reissues from Eastwood guitars.

MODEL YEAR FEATURES	EXC. COND. LOW	HIGH
Tube Amp 1x6" Speaker		
1958-1960s	$250	$325
Tube Amp 1x8" Speaker		
1958-1960s	$325	$425
Tube Amp 1x10" Speaker		
1958-1960s	$475	$620
Tube Amp 1x12" Speaker		
1958-1960s	$650	$850
Tube Amp Higher-End		
1958-1960s	$725	$940
Tube Amp Highest-End		
1958-1960s	$950	$1,225

Alamo

1947-1982. Founded by Charles Eilenberg, Milton Fink, and Southern Music, San Antonio, Texas, and distributed by Bruno and Sons. Alamo started producing amps in '49 and the amps were all-tube until '73; solidstate preamp and tube output from '73 to ca. '80; all solidstate for ca. '80 to '82.

Bass Solidstate Preamp-Tube Output

1973-ca.1979. Solidstate preamp section with tube output section, 35 or 40 watts, 15" speakers, combo or piggyback. Models include the Paragon Bass, Paragon Bass Piggyback, Paragon Country Western Bass, Paragon Super Bass, and the Fury Bass.

1973-1979	$175	$225

Bass Tube

1960-1972. Leatherette covered, all tube, 20 to 35 watts, 15" speakers, combo or piggyback, some with Lansing speaker option. Models include the Paragon Special, Paragon Bass, Piggyback Band, Piggyback Bass, Fury Bass, and Paragon Bass (piggyback).

1960-1972	$450	$575

Birch "A" Combo

1949-1962. Birch wood cabinets with A-shaped grill cutout, 2 to 5 tubes. Models include the Embassy Amp 3, Jet Amp 4, Challenger Amp 2, Amp 5, and the Montclair.

1949-1962	$375	$475

Mid-Power Solidstate Preamp-Tube Output

1973-ca.1979. Solidstate preamp section with tube output section, 25 watts, 12" speaker, with reverb and tremolo. Models include the Montclair.

1973-1979	$175	$225

Alamo Embassy
Imaged by Heritage Auctions, HA.com

1967 Alamo Fury
Tom Pfeifer

1974 Alamo Montclair Reverb 2565
Tom Pfeifer

Alessandro 1/2AZZ

Allen Hot Blond

1965 Ampeg B-12 X Portaflex
Tom Pfeifer

MODEL YEAR	FEATURES	EXC. COND. LOW	HIGH

Mid-Power Tube
1960-1970. Leatherette covered, all tube, 15 to 30 watts, 12" or 15" speakers, some with tremolo and reverb, some with Lansing speaker option. Models include Montclair, Paragon, Paragon Band, Titan, and Futura.

1960-1970		$500	$650

Small Solidstate Preamp-Tube Output
1973-ca.1979. Solidstate preamp section with tube output section, 3 to 12 watts, 5" to 12" speaker, some with reverb. Models include the Challenger, Capri, Special, Embassy, Dart, and Jet.

1973-1979		$175	$225

Small Tube
1960-1972. Leatherette covered, all tube, 3 to 10 watts, 6" to 10" speakers, some with tremolo. Models include the Jet, Embassy, Challenger, Capri, Fiesta, Dart, and Special.

1960-1972		$300	$400

Solidstate
Ca.1980-1982. All solidstate.

1980-1982		$40	$55

Twin Speaker Combo (Tube/Hybrid)
1973-ca.1979. Solidstate preamp section with tube output section, 20 or 70 watts, 10", 12" and 15" speaker configurations, some with reverb and tremolo. Models include the 70-watt Paragon Super Reverb Piggybacks, the 45-watt Futura 2x12, and the 20-watt Twin-Ten.

1973-1979		$300	$400

Twin Speaker Tube
1962-1972. Leatherette covered, all tube, up to 45 watts, 8", 10", 12" or 15" speaker configurations, some with tremolo and reverb, some with Lansing speaker option. Models include the Electra Twin Ten, Century Twin Ten, Futuramic Twin Eight, Galaxie Twin Twelve, Galaxie Twin Twelve Piggyback, Piggyback Super Band, Alamo Pro Reverb Piggyback, Futura, Galaxie Twin Ten, Twin-Ten, and Band Piggyback.

1962-1972		$550	$725

Alden
Small budget grade solidstate guitar and bass amps from Muse, Inc. of China.

Alesis
1992-present. Alesis has a wide range of products for the music industry, including digital modeling guitar amps. They also offer guitar effects.

Alessandro
1998-present. Tube amps built by George Alessandro in Huntingdon Valley, Pennsylvania. Founded in '94 as the Hound Dog Corporation, in '98 the company name was changed to Alessandro. The Redbone ('94) and the Bloodhound ('96) were the only models bearing the Hound Dog mark. Serial numbers are consecutive regardless of model (the earliest 20-30 did not have serial numbers). In '98 the company converted to exotic/high-end components and the name changed to Alessandro High-End Products. In '01, he added the Working Dog brand line of amps.

Allen Amplification
1998-present. Tube combo amps, heads and cabinets built by David Allen in Walton, Kentucky. He also offers the amps in kit form and produces replacement and upgrade transformers and a tube overdrive pedal.

Allston Amplifiers
2005-present. Professional and premium grade, custom, amps and cabinets built by Rob Lohr in Allston, Massachusetts.

Aloha
Late-1940s. Electric lap steel and amp Hawaiian outfits made for the Dallas-based Aloha.

Ampeg
1949-present. Ampeg was originally primarily known for their bass amps. In the eastern U.S., Ampeg was Fender's greatest challenger in the '60s and '70s bass amplifier market. Currently offering tube and solidstate heads, combos and speaker cabinets. They have also built guitars.

Amp Covering Dates: Wood veneer 1946-1949, Smooth brown 1949-1952, Dot tweed 1952-1954, Tweed 1954-1955, Rough gray 1957-1958, Rough tan 1957-1958, Cream 1957-1958, Light blue 1958, Navy blue 1958-1962, Blue check 1962-1967, Black pebble 1967, Smooth black 1967-1980, Rough black 1967-1985.

AC-12
1970. 20 watts, 1x12", accordion amp that was a market failure and dropped after 1 year.

1970		$375	$500

AX-44 C
1990-1992. AX hybrid amp with solidstate power section and 1 preamp tube, 22 watts, 2x8 combo.

1990-1992		$180	$235

B-2 Bass
1994-2000. Solidstate, 200 watts, 1x15" combo or 4x8" combo, black vinyl, black grille, large A logo.

1994-2000 1x15"		$385	$520

B-2 R Bass Head
1994-2005. 200 watts, rackmount, replaced by 450 watt B2RE.

1994-2005		$260	$335

B-3
1995-2001. Solidstate head, 150 watts, 1x15".

1995-2001		$385	$510

B-4 Bass Head
1998-2008. Solidstate 1000-watt head, early models made in USA, then outsourced.

1998-2008		$310	$410

B-5 R Bass Head
2000-2005. 500 watts, 2-channel.

2000s		$310	$410

B-12 N Portaflex
1961-1965. 25 watts, 2x12", 2 6L6 power tubes.

1961-1965		$1,850	$2,400

B-12 X/B-12 XT Portaflex
1961-1969. Tube, 50 watts, 2x12", reverb, vibrato, 2x7027A power tubes.

1961-1969		$1,850	$2,400

MODEL YEAR	FEATURES	EXC. COND. LOW	HIGH

B-15 N (NB, NC, NF) Portaflex

1960-1970. Introduced as B-15 using 2 6L6 power tubes, B-15 N in '61, B-15 NB in '62, B-15 NC with rectifier tube in '64, B-15 NF with fixed-bias 2 6L6 power tubes and 30 watts in '67, 1x15".

1960-1965		$1,850	$2,400
1966-1970	1x15	$1,850	$2,400
1967-1968	2x15	$1,850	$2,400

B-15 R Portaflex (Reissue)

1997-2007. Reissue of '65 Portaflex 1x15", blue check, 60/100 watts.

1997-2007		$1,425	$1,850

B-15 S Portaflex

1971-1977. 60 watts, 2x7027A power tubes, 1x12".

1971-1977		$1,175	$1,525

B-18 N Portaflex

1964-1969. Bass, 50 watts, 1x18".

1964-1969		$1,850	$2,400

B-25

1969 only. 55 watts, 2 7027A power tubes, 2x15", no reverb, guitar amp.

1969		$1,275	$1,700

B-25 B Bass

1969-1980. Bass amp, 55 watts, 2 7027A power tubes, 2x15".

1969-1980		$1,275	$1,700

B-50 R Rocket Bass (Reissue)

1996-2005. 50 watts, 1x12" combo, vintage-style blue check cover.

1996-2005		$255	$330

B-100 R Rocket Bass (Reissue)

1996-2005. Solidstate, 100 watts, 1x15" combo bass amp, vintage-style blue check cover.

1996-2005		$255	$330

B-115

1973-1980. 120 watts, solidstate, 1x15" combo.

1973-1980		$325	$425

B-115 E Cabinet

2006-2017. Bass cab, 1x15".

2006-2017		$210	$275

B-410 Bass

1973-1980. Solidstate, 120 watts, 4x10", black vinyl, black grille.

1973-1980		$400	$525

BA Series

1999-present. Solidstate bass combo amps, model number is speaker configuration.

1999-2021	BA-112, 75w, 1x12	$125	$160
1999-2021	BA-115, 150w, 1x15	$125	$160
2008-2016	BA-210, 300w, 2x10	$200	$260
2008-2016	BA-210, 600w, 2x10	$225	$300
2011-2021	BA-108, 25w, 1x8	$25	$35

BT-15

1966-1968. Ampeg introduced solidstate amps in '66, the same year as Fender. Solidstate, 50 watts, 1x15", generally used as a bass amp. The BT-15D has 2 1x15" cabinets. The BT-15C is a 2x15" column portaflex cabinet.

1966-1968		$425	$550

BT-18

1966-1968. Solidstate, 50 watts, 1x18", generally used as a bass amp. The BT-18D has dual 1x18" cabinets. The BT-18C is a 2x18" column portaflex cabinet.

1966-1968		$425	$550

Continental I

1956-1959. Single-channel version of Duette, 30 watts, 1x15".

1956-1959		$725	$950

Dolphin

1956-1960. Smallest combo offered during this era, 15 watts, 1x12", single-channel (I) and dual-channel (II) options.

1956-1959	Dolphin I	$550	$725
1956-1960	Dolphin II	$675	$875

Duette

1956-1958. Dual-channel, 3 combo models offered; Zephyr (20w, 1x15"), Continental (30w, 1x15") and Duette 50 D-50 (50w, 2x12", tremolo).

1956-1958	Continental Duette	$725	$950
1956-1958	Zephyr Duette	$725	$950
1957-1958	Duette 50 D-50	$1,050	$1,375

ET-1 Echo Twin

1961-1964. Tube, 30 watts, 1x12", stereo reverb.

1961-1964		$1,100	$1,425

ET-2 Super Echo Twin

1962-1964. Tube, 2x12", 30 watts, stereo reverb.

1962-1964		$1,250	$1,625

G-12 Gemini I

1964-1971. Tube, 1x12", 22 watts, reverb.

1964-1971		$800	$1,050

G-15 Gemini II

1965-1968. Tube, 30 watts, 1x15", reverb.

1965-1968		$800	$1,050

G-18

1977-1980. Solidstate, 1 channel, 10 watts, 1x8", volume, treble, and bass controls.

1977-1980		$85	$110

G-20 Gemini 20

1969-1970. Tubes, 35 watts, 2x10".

1968-1969		$800	$1,050

G-110

1978-1980. Solidstate, 20 watts, 1x10", reverb, tremolo.

1978-1980		$135	$175

G-115

1979-1980. Solidstate, 175 watts, 1x15" JBL, reverb and tremolo, designed for steel guitar.

1979-1980		$165	$215

G-212

1973-1980. Solidstate, 120 watts, 2x12".

1973-1980		$200	$260

GS-12 Rocket 2

1965-1968. This name replaced the Reverberocket 2 (II), 15 watts, 1x12".

1965-1968		$775	$1,000

GS-12-R Reverberocket 2

1965-1969. Tube, 1x12", 18 watts, reverb. Called the Reverberocket II in '68 and '69, then Rocket II in '69.

1965-1969		$775	$1,000

GS-15-R Gemini VI

1966-1967. 30 watts, 1x15", single channel, considered to be "the accordion version" of the Gemini II.

1966-1967		$775	$1,000

1969 Ampeg B-15 N
Imaged by Heritage Auctions, HA.com

AMPS

Ampeg ET-2 Super Echo Twin
Imaged by Heritage Auctions, HA.com

1967 Ampeg G-12 Gemini I
Joe Alameda

1968 Ampeg GV-15 Gemini V

Ted Wulfers

Early-'60s Ampeg J-12 Jet

Ampeg J-12 R Reverbojet

Tom Pfeifer

AMPS

MODEL YEAR	FEATURES	EXC. COND. LOW	HIGH
GT-10			
1971-1980. Solidstate, 15 watts, 1x10", basic practice amp with reverb.			
1971-1980		$150	$195
GV-15 Gemini V			
1968-1971. Unimusic-era tube amp, 30 watts, 1x15" combo, reverb and tremolo.			
1968-1971		$750	$975
GV-22 Gemini 22			
Tube, 1x12", reverb, vibrato.			
1969-1972		$800	$1,050
J-12 Jet			
1958-1964, 1967-1972. 20 watts, 1x12", 6V6GT power tubes. Second addition, also known as the Jet II, was like the J-12 D Jet but with 12AX7s.			
1958	Rough tan	$675	$875
1959	Blue	$650	$850
1960-1964	Blue	$500	$650
1967-1972	Model reappears	$350	$450
J-12 A Jet			
1964. Jet Amp with 7591A power tubes.			
1964		$500	$650
J-12 D Jet			
1966. Jet Amp with new solidstate rectifier.			
1966		$450	$575
J-12 R Reverbojet			
1967-1970. Part of Golden Glo Series, nicknamed 'copper front', 18 watts, 1x12" combo, single channel, tremolo and reverb, printed circuit replaces point-to-point wiring.			
1967-1970		$500	$650
J-12 T Jet			
1965, 2006-2008. J-12 A with revised preamp.			
1965		$500	$650
J-20 Jet			
2007-2008. Tubes, 20 watts, 1x12.			
2007-2008		$375	$485
Jet II/J-12 T			
2007-2008. 15 watts, 1x12".			
2007-2008		$250	$325
Jupiter			
1956-1958. Part of Accordiamp Series, similar to Dolphin except preamp voiced for accordion, 15 watts, 1x12".			
1956-1958		$500	$650
M-12 Mercury			
1957-1965. 15 watts, 2 channels, Rocket 1x12".			
1957-1965		$650	$850
M-15 Big M			
1959-1965. 20 watts, 2x6L6 power, 1x15".			
1959-1965		$750	$975
Model 815 Bassamp			
1955. 15 watt combo, 1 channel. Ampeg Bassamp logo on control panel.			
1955		$750	$975
Model 820 Bassamp			
1956-1958. 20 watt combo, 1 channel.			
1956-1958		$800	$1,050
Model 822 Bassamp			
1957-1958. 2 channel 820.			
1957-1958		$850	$1,100

MODEL YEAR	FEATURES	EXC. COND. LOW	HIGH
Model 830 Bassamp			
1956-1958. 30 watt combo.			
1956-1958		$900	$1,175
Model 835 Bassamp			
1959-1961. 35 watt 1x15" combo, 2 channels.			
1959-1961		$900	$1,175
New Yorker			
1956-1958. Part of Accordiamp Series, similar to Continental except preamp voiced for accordion, 30 watts, 1x15".			
1956-1958		$625	$800
Portabass (PB) Series			
2002-2008. Portabass (PB) amps and speaker cabs.			
2002-2004	PB-122H Cab	$230	$305
2002-2008	PB-250 Head	$230	$305
Portaflex (PF) Series			
2011-present. Portaflex (PF) ultra-compact amp heads offered with flip-top cabs, 350 watt or 500 watt head and 115, 210 or 410 cab options.			
2011-2021	PF350 Head	$205	$265
2011-2021	PF500 Head	$205	$265
R-12 Rocket			
1957-1963. 12 watts, 1x12", 1 channel.			
1957-1963		$650	$850
R-12 B Rocket			
1964. 12 watts, 1x12", follow-up to the R-12 Rocket.			
1964		$650	$850
R-12 R Reverberocket			
1961-1963. Rocket with added on-board reverb.			
1961-1963		$800	$1,050
R-12 R Reverberocket (Reissue)			
1996-2007. 50 watts, 2xEL34 power tubes, 1x12" (R-212R is 2x12").			
1996-2007		$425	$550
R-12 R-B Reverberocket			
1964. 7591A power tubes replace R-12-R 6V6 power tubes.			
1964		$700	$900
R-12 R-T Reverberocket			
1965. 7591A or 7868 power tubes, revised preamp.			
1965		$700	$900
R-15 R Superbreverb (Supereverb)			
1963-1964. 1x15 combo, originally called Supereverb, but Fender had a problem with that name.			
1963-1964		$900	$1,175
R-50 H Reverberocket			
1997-2003. 50 watt head usually sold with a 4x12" bottom, blue check covering.			
1997-2003	Head and cab	$525	$675
R-212 R Reverberocket Combo 50 (Reissue)			
1996-2007. 50 watts, 2x12", all tube reissue, vintage-style blue check cover, vintage-style grille.			
1996-2007		$525	$675
Rhapsody			
1956-1958. Part of Accordiamp Series, similar to Zephyr except preamp voiced for accordion, 20 watts, 1x15".			
1956-1958		$650	$850
SB-12 Portaflex			
1965-1971. 22 watts, 1x12", designed for use with Ampeg's Baby Bass, black.			
1965-1971		$875	$1,125

SBT
1969-1971. 120 watts, 1x15", bass version of SST Amp.

1969-1971	$750	$975

SE-412 Cabinet
1996-1999. 4x12" speakers.

1996-1999	$265	$350

SJ-12 R/RT Super Jet
1996-2007. 50 watts, tube, 1x12", SJ-12 RT has tremolo added.

1996-2007	$355	$460

SS-35
1987-1992. Solidstate, 35 watts, 1x12", black vinyl, black grille, large A logo.

1987-1992	$155	$200

SS-70
1987-1990. Solidstate, 70 watts, 1x12".

1987-1990	$175	$230

SS-70 C
1987-1992. Solidstate, 70 watts, 2x10", chorus, black vinyl.

1987-1992	$205	$265

SS-140 C
1987-1992. Solidstate, 2x12 combo, chorus and reverb.

1987-1992	$230	$295

SS-150 Head
1987-1992. Solidstate, 150 watts.

1987-1992	$280	$360

SS-412 Cabinet
1987-1992. Matching 4x12 cab for SS series heads.

1987-1992	$270	$350

Super Combo/Model 833 Combo/Model 950C Super Combo
1956-1960. 30 watts, 3 channels. 950C is 50 watts with 2 15" speakers (very few made).

1956-1957	Super Combo	$825	$1,075
1958	Model 833	$825	$1,075
1959-1960	Model 950C	$825	$1,075

SVT Bass Cabinets
1969-1985. Two 8x10" cabs only.

1969	$1,650	$2,150
1970-1985	$1,550	$2,025

SVT Bass Head
1969-1985. 300 watt head only.

1969	Stones World-Tour Assoc	$2,300	$3,000
1970-1979		$1,900	$2,500
1980-1985		$1,700	$2,200

SVT-II Bass Head
1989-1994. Rackmount, 300 watts, tube.

1989-1994	$900	$1,175

SVT-2 Pro Bass Head
1993-2014. 300 watts, rackmount, tube preamp and power section, black metal.

1993-2014	$950	$1,250

SVT-III Bass Head
1991-1994. Mosfet, 275/450 watts.

1991-1994	$525	$675

SVT-3 Pro Bass Head
1993-present. Tube preamp and MOS-FET power section, 450 watts, rackmount, black metal.

1993-2021	$455	$590

SVT-4 Pro Bass Head
1997-present. Rackmount, all tube preamp, MOS-FET power section yielding 1600 watts.

1997-2021	$585	$760

SVT-5 Pro Bass Head
2002-2005. Rackmount, all tube preamp, MOS-FET power section yielding 1350 watts.

2002-2005	$585	$760

SVT-6 Pro Bass Head
2005-2009. Rackmount, all tube preamp, MOS-FET power section yielding 1100 watts.

2005-2009	$390	$510

SVT-15 E Bass Cabinet
1994-2017. Compact 1x15.

1994-2017	$335	$435

SVT-100 T Bass Combo
1990-1992. Solidstate, ultra-compact bass combo, 100 watts, 2x8".

1990-1992	$355	$460

SVT-200 T Head
1987 only. Solidstate, 200 watts to 8 ohms or 320 watts to 4 ohms.

1987	$335	$435

SVT-350 Head
1995-2005. Solidstate head, 350 watts, graphic EQ.

1995-2005	$430	$555

SVT-400 Head
1987-1997. Solidstate, 2 200 watt stereo amps, rack-mountable head with advanced (in '87) technology.

1987-1997	$430	$555

SVT-410 HE Bass Cabinet
1994-present. 4x10, horn/driver.

1994-2021	$430	$555

SVT-450 H Head
2007-2017. Solidstate head, 275/450 watts.

2007-2017	$430	$555

SVT-610 HLF Cabinet
2003-present. 6x10, horn/driver.

2003-2021	$430	$555

SVT-810 E Cabinet
1994-present. 8x10.

1994-2021	$430	$555

SVT-AV Anniversary Edition
300 watt head.

2001	$725	$925

SVT-CL Classic Bass Head
1994-present. Tube, 300 watts.

1994-2021	$875	$1,125

V-2 Cabinet
1971-1980. 4x12" cab, black tolex.

1971-1980	$500	$650

V-2 Head
1971-1980. 60 watt tube head.

1971-1980	Head only	$600	$775

V-3 Head
1971-1972. 55 watt tube head.

1971-1972	Head only	$625	$875

V-4 B Bass Head
1972-1980. Bass version of V-4 without reverb.

1972-1980	Head only	$900	$1,175

1955 Ampeg 815 Bassamp
Imaged by Heritage Auctions, HA.com

1968 Ampeg SB-12 Portaflex
Tom Pfeifer

2008 Ampeg SVT Micro 210AV Cab

Anderson 45 RT

Aria Pro II Revolution II

*Ashdown RM-C210T-500
EVO II Combo*

MODEL YEAR	FEATURES	EXC. COND. LOW	HIGH
V-4 Cabinet			
1970s. Single 4x12" cabinet only.			
1970-1980		$525	$675
V-7 SC			
1981-1985. Tube, 100 watts, 1x12", master volume, channel switching, reverb.			
1981-1985		$650	$850
VH-70			
1991-1992. Varying Harmonics, 70 watts, 1x12" combo with channel switching.			
1991-1992		$310	$400
VH-140 C			
1992-1995. Varying Harmonics (VH) with Chorus (C), two 70-watt channel stereo, 2x12".			
1992-1995		$385	$500
VH-150 Head			
1991-1992. 150 watts, channel-switchable, reverb.			
1991-1992		$285	$370
VL-502			
1991-1995. 50 watts, channel-switchable, all tube.			
1991-1995		$375	$485
VL-1001 Head			
1991-1993. 100 watts, non-switchable channels, all tube.			
1991-1993		$350	$450
VL-1002 Head			
1991-1995. 100 watts, channel-switchable, all tube.			
1991-1995		$375	$485
VT-22			
1970-1980. 100 watt combo version of V-4, 2x12".			
1970-1980		$600	$775
VT-40			
1971-1980. 60 watt combo, 4x10".			
1971-1980		$600	$775
VT-60 Combo			
1989-1991. Tube, 6L6 power, 60 watts, 1x12".			
1989-1991		$350	$450
VT-60 Head			
1989-1991. Tube head only, 6L6 power, 60 watts.			
1989-1991		$375	$485
VT-120 Combo			
1989-1992. Tube, 6L6 power, 120 watts, 1x12", also offered as head only.			
1989-1992		$375	$485
VT-120 Head			
1989-1992. 120 watts, 6L6 tube head.			
1989-1992		$375	$485
Zephyr I			
1956-1959. Single-channel, 20 watts, 1x15".			
1956-1959		$600	$775

Anderson Amplifiers

1993-present. Tube amps and combos built by Jack Anderson in Gig Harbor, Washington.

Andrews

2006-present. Professional grade, production/custom, amps and cabinets built by Jeff Andrews in Dunwoody, Georgia.

ARACOM Amplifiers

1997-present. Jeff Aragaki builds his tube amp heads, combos, and cabinets in Morgan Hill, California.

Area 51

2003-present. Guitar amps made in Newaygo, Michigan (made in Texas until early '06), by Dan Albrecht. They also build effects.

Aria/Aria Pro II

1956-present. The Japanese instrument builder offered a range of amps from around '79 to '89.

Ariatone

1962. Another private brand made by Magnatone, sold by private music and accordion studios.

MODEL YEAR	FEATURES	EXC. COND. LOW	HIGH
Model 810			
1962. 12 watts, 1x8, tremolo, brown cover.			
1962		$650	$850

Ark

Owners Matt Schellenberg and Bill Compeau build professional and premium grade, production/custom amps in Farmington Hills, Michigan (cabinet shop), with all wiring done in Windsor, Ontario. They started in 2005.

Ashdown Amplification

1999-present. Founded in England by Mark Gooday after he spent several years with Trace Elliot, Ashdown offers amps, combos, and cabinets.

Audio Guild

1960s-1974. Audio Guild was already making amps under such brands as Universal and Versatone and others when they launched their own brand in the '60s.

MODEL YEAR	FEATURES	EXC. COND. LOW	HIGH
Grand Prix			
1969-1974. Tube combo 1x12, reverb and tremolo, dual channel.			
1969-1974		$725	$950
Ultraflex			
1969-1974. All-tube, higher power combo, 2 speakers, reverb and tremolo.			
1969-1974		$1,025	$1,325
Universal			
1960s-1974. Universal was a brand of Audio Guild. Tube combo amp, reverb, tremolo.			
1960s-1974		$725	$950
Versatone Pan-O-Flex			
1960s-1974. Versatone was a brand of Audio Guild. Mid-power tube amp, 1x12" and 1x8" combo, high and low gain input, volume, bass, treble and pan-o-flex balance control knobs, black cover.			
1960s-1974		$1,025	$1,325

Audiovox

Ca.1935-ca.1950. Paul Tutmarc's Audiovox Manufacturing, of Seattle, Washington, was a pioneer in electric lap steels, basses, guitars and amps.

MODEL		EXC. COND.	
YEAR	FEATURES	LOW	HIGH

Auralux

2000-2011. Founded by Mitchell Omori and David Salzmann, Auralux built effects and tube amps in Highland Park, Illinois.

Austin

1999-present. Budget and intermediate grade, production, guitar and bass amps imported by St. Louis Music. They also offer guitars, basses, mandolins, ukes and banjos.

Bacino

Tube combo amps, heads and cabinets built by Mike Bacino in Arlington Heights, Illinois starting in 2002.

Backline Engineering

2004-present. Gary Lee builds his tube amp heads in Camarillo, California. He also builds guitar effects.

Bad Cat Amplifier Company

1999-present. Originally located in Corona, California, and now in Santa Ana, Bad Cat offers class A combo amps, heads, cabinets and effects.

Baer Amplification

2009-present. Professional grade, production, bass amps built in Palmdale, California by Roger Baer.

Baldwin

Piano maker Baldwin offered amplifiers from 1965 to '70. The amps were solidstate with organ-like pastel-colored pushbutton switches.

Exterminator
1965-1970. Solidstate, 100 watts, 2x15"/2x12"/2x7", 4' vertical combo cabinet, reverb and tremolo, Supersound switch and slide controls.

1965-1970		$625	$800

Model B1 Bass
1965-1970. Solidstate, 45 watts, 1x15"/1x12", 2 channels.

1965-1970		$325	$425

Model B2 Bass
1965-1970. Solidstate, 35 watts, 1x15", 2 channels.

1965-1970		$300	$400

Model C1 Custom (Professional)
1965-1970. Solidstate, 45 watts, 2x12", reverb and tremolo, Supersound switch and slide controls.

1965-1970		$450	$575

Model C2 Custom
1965-1970. Solidstate, 40 watts, 2x12", reverb and tremolo.

1965-1970		$450	$575

Model D1 Deluxe (Professional)
1965-1970. Solidstate, 30 watts, 1x12", reverb and tremolo, Supersound switch and slide controls.

1965-1970		$450	$575

Barcus-Berry

1964-present. Pickup maker Barcus-Berry offered a line of amps from '75 to '79.

Barth

1950s-1960s. Products of Paul Barth's Barth Musical Instrument Company. Barth was also a co-founder of Rickenbacker. He also produced guitars and lap steels.

Studio Deluxe 958
1950s-1960s. Small practice combo amp.

1950s-60s		$450	$575

Basson

Speaker cabinets for guitar, bass and PA made by Victor Basson in Carlsbad, California, starting in 2001.

BC Audio

2009-present. Bruce Clement builds his production/custom, professional grade, tube amps in San Francisco, California.

Bedrock

1984-1997. Tube amp company founded by Brad Jeter and Ron Pinto in Nashua, New Hampshire. They produced 50 amps carrying the brand name Fred before changing the company name to Bedrock in '86. Around '88, Jay Abend joined the company. In '90, Jeter left and, shortly after, Pinto and Abend moved the company to Framingham, Massachusetts. The company closed in '97.

Behringer

1989-present. Founded in Germany by Uli Behringer, offering a full line of professional audio products. In '98 they added tube, solidstate, and modeling amps. They also offer effects and guitars.

Beltone

1950s-1960s. Japan's Teisco made a variety of brands for others, including the Beltone line of amps. There were also guitars sold under this name made from a variety of builders.

Benson

1967-1974. Ron Benson designed and built amps in conjunction with jazz ace Howard Roberts who needed a more versatile amp for recording sessions. Some featured built-in fuzz and plug-in equalizer modules. Originally built in California, later in Seattle. Some 2,000 amps total production.

Big M

1966-1967, 1975-1976. The Marshall name in Germany was owned by a trumpet maker, so Jim Marshall marketed his amps and cabs there under the Big M Made In England brand name until the issue was resolved. A decade later, in a failed attempt to lower speaker cabinets prices in the U.S., Marshall's American distributor built cabs, with Marshall's permission, on Long Island, mainly for sales with Marshall solidstate lead and bass heads of the time, and labeled them Big M. They were loaded with cheaper Eminence speakers, instead of the usual Celestions.

Bad Cat Cub IV 15R Handwired Series

Baer Valkyrie

BC Audio Amplifier No. 9

AMPS

Blackwing Black Hawk 15

Bogner Mephisto

*Budda Superdrive 30
Series II 212 Combo*

MODEL YEAR	FEATURES	EXC. COND. LOW	HIGH
Cabinet			
1975-1976. The M2412 with 4x12 for lead and the M2212F 2x12 bass cabs.			
1975-1976	2x12	$315	$410
1975-1976	4x12	$600	$800
JTM-45 Head			
1966-1967. Branded Big M.			
1966-1967		$5,000	$6,450

BigDog Amps

2005-2007. Tube head and combo guitar and bass amps and speaker cabinets built in Galveston, Texas, by Steve Gaines.

Bird

Ca. 1959-1965. Bird built electronic organs in the U.K. and also offered tubes amps from around '59 to '65.

Blackstar Amplification

2007-present. Intermediate and professional grade guitar amps and cabinets from Joel Richardson of Northampton, U.K. He also offers effects pedals.

Blackwing

2016-2018. Professional and premium grade head and combo amps, and cabinets built in Corona, California by James Heidrich. He died in '18.

Blankenship Amplification

2005-present. Roy Blankenship builds his tube head and combo amps and cabinets in Northridge, California. He also built amps under the Point Blank brand.

Bluetone Amplifiers

2002-present. Founded by Alex Cooper in Worcestershire, England, Bluetone offers professional grade, production amps employing their virtual valve technology.

Bogen

1932-present. Founded in New York City by David Bogen, this company has made a wide range of electronic products for consumers and industry including a few small guitar combo tube amps such as the GA-5 and GA-20 and tube PA equipment. The company name (David Bogen, New York) and model number are on the lower back panel. The '50s Bogen tube amps are well respected as tone-generating workhorses. In '56 he sold the company and it was moved to New Jersey, and they continue to offer pro audio PA gear.

Bogner

1988-present. Tube combos, amp heads, and speaker cabinets from builder Reinhold Bogner of North Hollywood, California.

MODEL YEAR	FEATURES	EXC. COND. LOW	HIGH

Bolt

Professional grade, production, tube amps and cabinets built in Salt Lake City, Utah starting in 2009. They also built the Morpheus brand effects.

Brand X

2004-2007. Small solidstate combo amps from Fender Musical Instruments Corporation.

Bronson

1930s-1950s. Private brand utilized by Detroit lap steel instruction George Bronson. These amps often sold with a matching lap steel and were made by other companies.

Lap Steel			
1930s-50s	Melody King	$475	$625
1930s-50s	Pearloid	$300	$400
1947	Supreme	$550	$725

Bruno (Tony)

1995-present. Tube combos, amp heads, and speaker cabinets from builder Tony Bruno of Cairo, New York.

Budda

1995-present. Amps, combos, and cabinets originally built by Jeff Bober and Scott Sier in San Francisco, California. In '09, Budda was acquired by Peavey and they started building Budda products in their Meridian, Mississippi Custom Shop. They also produce effects pedals.

Bugera

2008-present. Uli Behringer builds his budget and intermediate grade, production, tube amps in China. He also offers the Behringer brand.

Burriss

2001-present. Bob Burriss builds custom and production guitar and bass tube amps, bass preamps and speaker cabinets in Lexington, Kentucky. He also builds effects.

Byers

2001-2010. Tube combo amps built by Trevor Byers, in Corona, California. His initial focus was on small early-Fender era and K & F era models.

Cage

1998-present. Production/custom, professional grade, amp heads and cabinets built in Damascus, Maryland by Pete Cage.

California

2004-present. Student/budget level amps and guitar/amp packs, imported by Eleca International.

Callaham

1989-present. Custom tube amp heads built by Bill Callaham in Winchester, Virginia. He also builds solidbody electric guitars.

AMPS

MODEL YEAR	FEATURES	EXC. COND. LOW	HIGH

Campbell Sound
Intermediate and professional grade, production/custom, guitar amps built by Walt Campbell in Roseville, California, starting in 1999.

Carl Martin
1993-present. In '05, the Denmark-based guitar effects company added tube combo amps.

Carlsbro
1959-present. Guitar, bass, and keyboard combo amps, heads and cabinets from Carlsbro Electronics Limited of Nottingham, U.K. They also offer PA amps and speaker cabinets.

Carol-Ann Custom Amplifiers
2003-present. Premium grade, production/custom, tube guitar amps built by Alan Phillips in North Andover, Massachusetts.

Carr Amplifiers
1998-present. Steve Carr started producing amps in his Chapel Hill, North Carolina amp repair business in '98. The company is now located in Pittsboro, North Carolina, and makes tube combo amps, heads, and cabinets.

Artemus
2010-2015. Combo 1x12", 15/30 watts.

2010-2015		$1,450	$1,900

Bloke
2012-2015. 48 watts, 1x12".

2012-2015	1x12"	$1,300	$1,700

Hammerhead MK 1/MK 2
2000-2004 (MK 1), 2004-2008 (MK 2). 25 watts (28 for MK 2), head or combo, 1x12", 2x10" or 2x12".

2000-2004	2x12" combo	$1,000	$1,300

Impala
2013-present. Combo 1x12", 44 watts - max 55 watts, reverb.

2013-2021		$1,500	$1,950

Imperial Combo
2000-2004. 60 watts, with 1x15", 2x12" or 4x10".

2000-2004	4x10"	$2,400	$3,100

Mercury Combo
2002-2014. 1x12", tube, 8 watts, reverb, built-in attenuator.

2002-2014		$1,600	$2,100

Mercury V
2017-present. Combo 1x12", 16 watts, built in attenuator.

2017-2021		$1,600	$2,100

Raleigh
2008-present. Practice/studio amp, 1x10", 3 watts.

2008-2021		$950	$1,250

Rambler
1999-present. Class A, tubes, 28 watts pentode/14 watts triode, with 1x12", 2x10", 2x12" or 1x15" speakers.

1999-2019	1x12"	$1,550	$2,050
1999-2021	2x12"	$1,800	$2,400

Skylark
2014-present. 12 watts, 1x12" with built in attenuator.

2014-2021		$1,800	$2,300

Slant 6V (Dual 6V6)
1998-present. 40 watts, 2 channel, combo amp, 2x12" or 1x15", also available as a head.

1998-2021		$1,800	$2,300

Sportsman
2011-present. Available in 1x12 and 1x10 combos and head, 16-19 watts.

2011-2021	1x12"	$1,300	$1,700

Telestar
2018-present. Combo 17-watt with built in attenuator.

2018-2021		$1,600	$2,100

Viceroy
2006-2018. Class A, tubes, 33 or 7 watts, 1x12" or 1x15".

2006-2018		$1,550	$2,050

Carvin
1946-present. Founded in Los Angeles by Lowell C. Kiesel who sold guitars and amps under the Kiesel name until late-'49, when the Carvin brand was introduced. They added small tube amps to their product line in '47 and today offer a variety of models. They also build guitars, basses and mandolins.

Caswell Amplification
2006-present. Programmable tube amp heads built by Tim Caswell in California.

Chicago Blues Box/Butler Custom Sound
Tube combo amps built by Dan Butler of Butler Custom Sound originally in Elmhurst, then Lombard, Illinois. He began in 2001.

Clark Amplification
1995-present. Tweed-era replica tube amplifiers from builder Mike Clark, of Cayce, South Carolina. He also makes effects.

Club Amplifiers
2005-present. Don Anderson builds intermediate to premium grade, custom, vacuum tube guitar amps and cabinets in Felton, California.

CMI
1976-1977. Amps made by Marshall for Cleartone Musical Instruments of Birmingham, U.K. Mainly PA amps, but two tube heads and one combo amp were offered.

CMI Electronics
Late-1960s-1970s. CMI branded amplifiers designed to replace the Gibson Kalamazoo-made amps that ceased production in '67 when Gibson moved the electronics lab to Chicago, Illinois.

Carlsbro 60TC
Alex Drinkall

AMPS

Carr Mercury V

Carvin V3MC

AMPS

Crate Vintage Club 5212
Imaged by Heritage Auctions, HA.com

Cruzer CR-15RG

Danelectro 68
Erick Warner

MODEL YEAR	FEATURES	EXC. COND. LOW	HIGH

Sabre Reverb 1
Late-1960s-early-1970s. Keyboard amp, 1x15" and side-mounted horn, utilized mid- to late-'60s cabinets and grilles, look similar to mid-late '60s Gibson black tolex and Epiphone gray amp series, black or gray tolex and silver grille.

1960s-70s		$400	$525

CMW Amps
2002-present. Chris Winsemius builds his premium grade, production/custom, guitar amps in The Netherlands.

Colby
2012-present. Professional and premium grade, production/custom, tube amp heads, combos and cabinets built by Mitch Colby in City Island, New York. He also builds Park amps.

Comins
1992-present. Archtop luthier Bill Comins, of Willow Grove, Pennsylvania, introduced a Comins combo amp, built in collaboration with George Alessandro, in '03.

Coral
1967-1969. In '66 MCA bought Danelectro and in '67 introduced the Coral brand of guitars, basses and amps. The amp line included tube, solidstate, and hybrid models ranging from small combo amps to the Kilowatt (1000 Watts of Peak Power!), a hybrid head available with two 8x12" cabinets.

Cornell/Plexi
Amps based on the '67 Marshall plexi chassis built by Denis Cornell in the U.K. Large Plexi logo on front.

Cosmosound
Italy's Cosmosound made small amps with Leslie rotating drums in the late '60s and '70s. They also made effects pedals.

Crafter USA
1986-present. Giant Korean guitar and bass manufacturer Crafter also builds an acoustic guitar amp.

Crate
Solidstate and tube amplifiers originally distributed by St. Louis Music, beginning in 1979. In '05 LOUD Technologies acquired SLM and the Crate brand. No new Crate models listed since then.

CA Series
1995-2005. Crate Acoustic series.

1995-2005		$185	$240

Solidstate
1979-1990s. Various student to mid-level amps, up to 150 watts.

1979-90s		$70	$90

MODEL YEAR	FEATURES	EXC. COND. LOW	HIGH

Vintage Club Series
1994-2001. Various tube amps.

1994-1997	5310/VC-5310	$275	$360
1994-1999	20	$225	$300
1994-1999	30/VC-2110	$300	$400
1994-1999	30/VC-3112	$325	$425
1994-1999	50/VC-50	$300	$400
1994-1999	60/VC-60	$300	$400
1994-2001	5212/VC-5212	$275	$360

Cruise Audio Systems
1999-2003. Founded by Mark Altekruse, Cruise offered amps, combos, and cabinets built in Cuyahoga Falls, Ohio. It appears the company was out of business by '03.

Cruzer
Solidstate guitar amps built by Korea's Crafter Guitars. They also build guitars, basses and effects under that brand.

Custom Kraft
Late-1950s-1968. A house brand of St. Louis Music Supply, instruments built by others. They also offered basses and guitars.

Import Student
1960s	1x6 or 1x8	$75	$100

Valco-Made
1960s	1x12 or 1x15	$450	$575

Da Vinci
Late-1950s-early-1960s. Another one of several private brands (for example, Unique, Twilighter, Titano, etc.) that Magnatone made for teaching studios and accordion companies.

D60 Custom
1965. 2x12", reverb, vibrato.

1965		$1,450	$1,875

Model 250
1958-1962. Similar to Magnatone Model 250 with about 20 watts and 1x12".

1958-1962		$1,250	$1,625

Model 440A/D40 Custom
1964-1966. 1x12", reverb, vibrato.

1964-1966		$1,350	$1,750

Danelectro
1946-1969, 1997-present. Founded in Red Bank, New Jersey, by Nathan I. "Nate" or "Nat" Daniel. His first amps were made for Montgomery Ward in '47, and in '48 he began supplying Silvertone Amps for Sears. His own amps were distributed by Targ and Dinner as Danelectro and S.S. Maxwell brands. In '96, the Evets Corporation, of San Clemente, California, reintroduced the Danelectro brand on effects, amps, basses and guitars. In early '03, Evets discontinued the amp line, but still offers guitars, basses, and effects.

MODEL		EXC. COND.	
YEAR	FEATURES	LOW	HIGH

Cadet
1955-1969. A longstanding model name, offered in different era cabinets and coverings but all using the standard 3-tube 1x6" format. Models 122 and 123 had 6 watts. 1x6", 3 tubes, 1 volume, 1 control, 2 inputs, 16x15x6" 'picture frame' cabinet with light-colored cover, dark grille.

1955-1969	Various models	$225	$300

Challenger
1950s. Compact combo amp, 5 tubes including 2x6L6, 2 channels, bass and treble control, 2 vibrato controls, golden-brown cover, tan woven cloverleaf-shaped grille.

1950s		$450	$600

DM-10
1965-1967. Combo 'large knobs' cabinet, 10 watts, 1x8", 2 control vibrato, 2 inputs, 1 volume, 1 tone, dark vinyl with light grille, DM-10 logo next to script Danelectro logo right upper front.

1965-1967		$350	$450

DM-25
1965-1967. Stow-away piggyback, 25 watts, 1x12", reverb, vibrato, 4 inputs, 9 control knobs, dark vinyl cabinet with light grille, DM-25 logo next to script Danelectro logo below control knobs.

1965-1967		$775	$1,000

DS-50
1965-1969. 75 watts, 3x10" stow-away piggyback cabinet, reverb and tremolo, suitable for bass accordion.

1965-1969		$925	$1,200

DS-100
1967-1969. 150 watts, stow-away piggyback cabinet, 6x10" Jensens, reverb, tremolo, suitable for bass accordion, 36x22x12" cabinet weighs 79 lbs.

1965-1969		$1,725	$2,250

DTR-40
1965. Solidstate combo, 40 watts, 2x10", vibrato, DTR-40 logo under control knobs.

1965		$450	$600

Model 68 Special
1954-1957. 20 watts, 1x12", light tweed-fabric cover, light grille, leather handle, script Danelectro plexiplate logo.

1954-1957		$625	$825

Model 72 Centurion
1954-1957. Series D 1x12" combo, blond tweed, rounded front D cabinet.

1954-1957		$625	$825

Model 78A
1954-1957. Artist Series D, 115 watts,

1954-1957		$625	$825

Model 88 Commando
1954-1957. Series D, 25 watts with 4x6V6 power, suitcase-style amp with 8x8" speaker, light beige cover.

1954-1957		$1,050	$1,375

Model 89
1954-1957. Series D 1x15" combo, blond tweed, rounded front D cabinet.

1954-1957		$725	$950

Model 98 Twin 12
1954-ca.1957. Rounded front Series D 2x12", blond tweed-style cover, brown control panel, vibrato speed and strength.

1954-1957		$1,050	$1,375

Model 132 Corporal
1962-1964. 2x8", 4 tubes, 3 inputs, 4 control knobs, 19x15x7" picture frame cabinet in light-colored material with dark grille.

1962-1964		$550	$725

Model 142 Viscount
Late-1950s. Combo amp, lower watts, 1x12", light cover, brown grille, vibrato.

1959		$650	$850

Model 143 Viscount
1962-1964. 12 watts, 1x12", 6 tubes, 2 control vibrato, 1 volume, 1 tone, 'picture frame' narrow panel cabinet, light-colored cover with dark grille.

1962-1964		$550	$725

Model 217 Twin-Fifteen
1962-1964. Combo amp, 60 watts, 2x15" Jensen C15P speakers, black cover, white-silver grille, 2 channels with tremolo.

1962-1964		$900	$1,175

Model 274 Centurion
1961-1962. 15 watts, 1x12", 6 tubes, 2 channels with separate volume, treble, bass controls, Vibravox electronic vibrato, 4 inputs, 20x20x9 weighing 25 lbs., 'picture frame' cabinet with black cover and light grille.

1961-1962		$525	$675

Model 275 Centurion
1963-1964. Reverb added in '63, 15 watts, 1x12", 7 tubes, Vibravox vibrato, 2 channels with separate volume, bass, treble, picture frame cabinet with black cover and light grille.

1963-1964		$675	$875

Model 291 Explorer
1961-1964. 30 watts, 1x15", 7 tubes, 2 channels each with volume, bass, and treble controls, Vibravox vibrato, square picture frame cabinet, black cover and light grille.

1961-1964		$650	$850

Model 300 Twin-Twelve
1962-1964. 30 watts, 2x12", reverb, 8 tubes, 2 channels with separate volume, bass, and treble, Vibravox vibrato, picture frame cabinet with black cover and light grille.

1962-1964		$1,050	$1,375

Model 354 Twin-Twelve
Early 1950s. Series C twin 12" combo with diagonal speaker baffle holes, brown cover with light gold grille, Twin Twelve script logo on front as well as script Danelectro logo, diagonally mounted amp chassis, leather handle.

1950s		$1,050	$1,375

Dean
1976-present. Acoustic, electric, and bass amps made overseas. They also offer guitars, banjos, mandolins, and basses.

Danelectro Cadet
Erick Warner

1961 Danelectro 142 Viscount
Rivington Guitars

Danelectro 275 Centurion
Erick Warner

DeArmond R-5T Studio
Imaged by Heritage Auctions, HA.com

Demeter TGA-2.1

Divided By Thirteen RSA 23

MODEL YEAR	FEATURES	EXC. COND. LOW	HIGH

Dean Markley

The string and pickup manufacturer added a line of amps in 1983. Distributed by Kaman, they now offer combo guitar and bass amps and PA systems.

K Series

1980s. All solidstate, various models include K-15 (10 watts, 1x6"), K-20/K-20X (10 to 20 watts, 1x8", master volume, overdrive switch), K-50 (25 watts, 1x10", master volume, reverb), K-75 (35 watts, 1x12", master volume, reverb), K-200B (compact 1x12 combo).

1980s	K-15, K20, K20X	$40	$50
1980s	K-200B	$135	$175
1980s	K-50	$45	$60
1980s	K-75	$70	$90

DeArmond

Pickup manufacturer DeArmond starting building tube guitar amps in 1950s. By '63, they were out of the amp business. They also made effects. Fender revived the name for a line of guitars in the late '90s.

R-5T Studio

1959-1960. 1x10", low power, 1-channel, brown.

1959-1960		$3,000	$4,000

R-15

1959-1961. 1x12", 15 watts, 2 channels, no tremolo, tan.

1959-1961		$3,500	$4,500

R-15T/Model 112

1959-1961. 1x12", 15 watts, 2 channels, tremolo, tan.

1959-1961		$3,600	$4,700

Decca

Mid-1960s. Small student-level amps made in Japan by Teisco and imported by Decca Records. They also offered guitars and a bass.

Demeter

1980-present. James Demeter founded the company as Innovative Audio and renamed it Demeter Amplification in '90. Originally located in Van Nuys, in '08 they moved to Templeton, California. First products were direct boxes and by '85, amps were added. Currently they build amp heads, combos, and cabinets. They also have pro audio gear and guitar effects.

Devilcat

2012-present. Professional grade, production/custom, tube amps built in Statesboro, Georgia by Chris Mitchell.

Diaz

Cesar Diaz restored amps for many of rock's biggest names, often working with them to develop desired tones. By the early '80s he was producing his own line of professional and premium grade, high-end custom amps and effects. Diaz died in '02; his widow Maggie and longtime friend Peter McMahon resumed production in '04 under Diaz Musical Products.

Dickerson

1937-1947. Dickerson was founded by the Dickerson brothers in 1937, primarily for electric lap steels and small amps. Instruments were also private branded for Cleveland's Oahu company, and for the Gourley brand. By '47, the company changed ownership and was renamed Magna Electronics (Magnatone). Amps were usually sold with a matching lap steel.

Oasis

1940s. Blue pearloid cover, 1x10", low wattage, Dickerson silk-screen logo on grille with Hawaiian background.

1940s		$300	$400

Dime Amplification

2011-ca. 2014. Solidstate combo and head amps and cabinets from Dean Guitars, designed by Gary Sunda and Grady Champion.

Dinosaur

2004-2015. Student/budget level amps and guitar/amp packs, imported by Eleca International. They also offered effects.

Divided By Thirteen

Mid-1990s-present. Fred Taccone builds his tube amp heads and cabinets in the Los Angeles, California area. He also builds effects.

Dr. Z

1988-present. Mike Zaite started producing his Dr. Z line of amps in the basement of the Music Manor in Maple Heights, Ohio. The company is now located in its own larger facility in the same city. Dr. Z offers combo amps, heads and cabinets.

Drive

Ca. 2001-ca. 2011. Budget grade, production, import solidstate amps. They also offered guitars.

DST Engineering

2002-2014. Jeff Swanson and Bob Dettorre built their tube amp combos, heads and cabinets in Beverly, Massachusetts. They also built reverb units.

Duca Tone

The Duca Tone brand was distributed by Lo Duca Brothers, Milwaukee, Wisconsin, which also distributed EKO guitars in the U.S.

Tube

1950s. 12 watts, 1x12".

1950s		$575	$750

Dumble

1963-2022. Made by Howard Alexander Dumble, an early custom-order amp maker from California. Initial efforts were a few Mosrite amps for Semie Moseley. First shop was in '68 in Santa Cruz, California. Early on, Dumble also modified other brands such as Fender and those Dumble-modified

MODEL		EXC. COND.	
YEAR	FEATURES	LOW	HIGH

amps are also valuable, based on authenticated provenance. Top dollar goes for combos or heads with the cab. A head alone would be 10-20% lower. Higher values are considered for an amp that has not been modified in any way, unless the mod is certified as being done by Dumble. The used/vintage Dumble market is a sophisticated luxury-market for those musicians and collectors that are wealthy enough to afford these amps. Each amplifier's value should be considered on a case-by-case basis. Dealers have reported that some Dumble amplifiers will sell upwards from $90,000 to $100,000. Mr. Dumble died January, 2022.

Dynamic Amps

2008-present. David Carambula builds production/custom, professional grade, combo amps, heads and cabinets in Kalamazoo, Michigan.

Dynamo

2010-present. Professional and premium grade, production/custom, amps and cabinets built by Ervin Williams in Lake Dallas, Texas.

Earth Sound Research

1970s. Earth Sound was a product of ISC Audio of Farmingdale, New York, and offered a range of amps, cabinets and PA gear starting in the '70s. They also made Plush amps.

2000 G Half-Stack
1970s. 100 watts plus cab.

1970s		$525	$685

Model G-1000 Head

1970s	Reverb	$260	$340

Original 2000 Model 340
1970s. Black Tolex, 400-watt head and matching 2x15" cab.

1970s		$525	$685

Producer Model 440
1970s. 700-watt head and matching 2x15" cab.

1970s		$525	$685

Revival
1970s. 2x12" tweed twin copy, with similar back mounted control panel, tweed covering, but with solid-state preamp section and 4x6L6 power.

1970		$525	$685

Super Bass/B-2000
1970s. Tuck & roll black cover, 2 channels - super and normal, volume, bass, mid range, and treble tone controls, no reverb or tremolo.

1970s	Cabinet	$260	$340
1970s	Head only	$260	$340

Traveler
1970s. Vertical cab solidstate combo amp, 50 watts, 2x12 offset, black tolex.

1977		$525	$685

EBS

1988-present. The EBS Sweden AB company builds professional grade, production bass amps and cabinets in Stockholm, Sweden. They also build effects.

EchoSonic

1950s. Tube combo amps with built-in tape echo built by Ray Butts in Cairo, Illinois, with the first in '53. Used by greats such as Chet Atkins, Scotty Moore and Carl Perkins, probably less than 70 were made. Butts also developed the hum bucking Filter'Tron pickup for Gretsch.

Eden

1976-2011. Founded by David Nordschow in Minnesota as a custom builder, Eden offered a full line of amps, combos, and cabinets for the bassist, built in Mundelein, Illinois. In '02, the brand became a division of U.S. Music Corp (Washburn, Randall), they also produce the Nemesis brand of amps. In '11 Eden was sold to Marshall.

Egnater

1980-present. Production/custom, intermediate and professional grade, tube amps, combos, preamps and cabinets built in Berkley, Michigan by Bruce Egnater. He also imports some models.

Rebel
2008-present. 20-watt head, 1x12" cabinet.

2008-2021		$500	$650

Renegade Head
2009-present. 65 watts, 2 channel head.

2009-2021		$500	$650

Tourmaster Series
2009-present. 100-watt, all-tube amp and combo.

2009-2021	Various models	$500	$650

Tweaker
2013-present. 15 to 88-watt, tube heads and cabinets.

2013-2021	1x12 combo	$425	$550
2013-2021	40 watt head/ 1x12 cab	$500	$650

EKO

1959-1985, 2000-present. In '67 EKO added amps to their product line, offering three piggyback and four combo amps, all with dark covering, dark grille, and the EKO logo. The amp line may have lasted into the early '70s. Since about 2000, EKO Asian-made, solidstate guitar and bass amps are again available. They also make basses and guitars.

El Grande

1951-1953. Built by Chicago's Valco Manufacturing Co. and sold together with lap steels. El Grande logo on front, Valco logo on back chasis, all have burgundy and white covering.

Valco Spectator
1951-1953. Same as Supro Spectator, 1x8", 5 watts, volume and tone.

1951-1953		$375	$500

Eleca

2004-present. Student level imported combo amps, Eleca logo on bottom of grille. They also offer guitars, effects and mandolins.

1977 Dumble Overdrive Special
Imaged by Heritage Auctions, HA.com

AMPS

Dynamo GTS

Egnater Rebel 30 MK2

AMPS

Electro-Harmonix Dirt Road Special

Elmwood Bonneville 50

Emery Sound Combo

MODEL YEAR	FEATURES	EXC. COND. LOW	HIGH

Electar

1996-2008. The Gibson owned Electar brand offered tube and solidstate amps, PA gear and wireless systems. Though branded separately, Electar amps were often marketed with other Epiphone products, so see them listed there. Epiphone also had amp models named Electar in the 1930s.

Electro-Harmonix

1968-1981, 1996-present. Electro-Harmonix has offered a few amps to go with its line of effects.

Freedom Brothers

Introduced in 1977. Small AC/DC amp with 2x5 1/2" speakers. E-H has reissued the similar Freedom amp.

1977		$250	$325

Mike Matthews Dirt Road Special

1970s. 25 watts, 1x12" Celestion, built-in Small Stone phase shifter. A 40 watt version was released in 2019.

1977		$250	$325

Electromuse

1940s-1950s. Tube amps made by others, like Valco, and usually sold as a package with a lap steel. They also offered guitars.

Various Models

Late-1940s. Vertical cabinet with metal handle, Electromuse stencil logo on front of cab.

1948-1949	Lower power	$275	$360

Electrosonic Amplifiers

2002-2009. Intermediate and professional grade, production/custom, tube amps built by Josh Corn in Boonville, Indiana. He also builds effects.

Elk

Late-1960s. Japanese-made by Elk Gakki Co., Ltd. Many were copies of American designs. They also offered guitars and effects.

Custom EL 150L

Late-1960s. Piggyback set, all-tube with head styled after very early Marshall and cab styled after large vertical Fender cab.

1968		$375	$500

Guitar Man EB 105 (Super Reverb)

Late-1960s. All-tube, reverb, copy of blackface Super Reverb.

1968		$375	$500

Twin 60/Twin 50 EB202

Late-1960s. All-tube, reverb, copy of blackface Dual Showman set (head plus horizontal cab).

1968		$375	$500

Viking 100 VK 100

Late-1960s. Piggyback set, head styled after very early Marshall and cab styled after very large vertical Fender cab.

1968		$375	$500

Elmwood Amps

1998-present. Jan Alm builds his production/custom, professional and premium grade, guitar tube amps and cabinets in Tanumshede, Sweden.

MODEL YEAR	FEATURES	EXC. COND. LOW	HIGH

Elpico

1960s. Made in Europe, PA tube amp heads sometimes used for guitar.

PA Power Tube

1960s. Tubes, 20-watt, metal case, 3 channels, treble and bass control, 2 speaker outs on front panel, Elpico logo on front, small Mexican characterization logo on front.

1960s		$400	$525

Emery Sound

1997-present. Founded by Curt Emery in El Cerrito, California, Emery Sound specializes in custom-made low wattage tube amps.

Emmons

1970s-present. Owned by Lashley, Inc. of Burlington, North Carolina. Amps sold in conjunction with their steel guitars.

Epiphone

1928-present. Epiphone offered amps into the mid-'70s and reintroduced them in '91 with the EP series. Currently they offer tube and solidstate amps.

Century

1939. Lap steel companion amp, 1x12" combo, lattice wood front with Electar insignia "E" logo.

1939		$465	$600

Cornet

1939. Lap steel companion amp, square shaped wood box, Electar insignia "E" logo.

1939		$390	$510

E-30B

1972-1975. Solidstate model offered similarly to Gibson G-Series (not GA-Series), 30 watts, 2x10", 4 knobs.

1972-1975		$175	$225

E-60

1972-1975. Solidstate, 30 watts, 1x10", volume and tone knobs.

1972-1975		$130	$170

E-60T

1972-1975. E-60 with tremolo, volume, tone, and tremolo knobs.

1972-1975		$130	$170

E-70T

1971-1975. Solidstate, tremolo, 1x10", 3 knobs.

1971-1975		$130	$170

E-1051

Ca. 1971-1974. Tube practice amp, 1x10".

1971-1974		$175	$225

EA-12 RVT Futura

1962-1967. 50 watts, originally 4x8" but 4x10" by at least '65, '60s gray tolex, light grille.

1962-1967		$550	$725

EA-14 RVT Ensign

1965-1969. Gray tolex, silver-gray grille, 50 watts, 2x10", split C logo.

1965-1969		$510	$665

MODEL		EXC. COND.	
YEAR	FEATURES	LOW	HIGH

EA-15 RVT Zephyr
1961-1965. 14 or 20 watts, 1x15", gray tolex, light grille, split C logo on panel, tremolo and reverb, script Epiphone logo lower right grille.

1961-1965		$510	$665

EA-16 RVT Regent
1965-1969. 25 watts, 1x12", gray vinyl, gray grille, tremolo, reverb. Called the Lancer in first year.

1965-1969		$450	$600

EA-22 RVT Mighty Mite
1964-1967. 1x12", mid-level power, stereo, reverb, vibrato, old style rear mounted control panel.

1964-1967		$925	$1,200

EA-26 RVT Electra
1965-1969. Gray tolex, reverb, tremolo, footswitch, 1x12".

1965-1969		$450	$600

EA-28 RVT Pathfinder
Mid-1960s. Similar to Gibson's GA-19 RVT, medium power, 1x12, reverb and tremolo.

1964-1966		$450	$600

EA-30 Triumph
1959-1961. Low-power, limited production, 1x12, light colored cover, 3 knobs.

1959-1961		$800	$1,025

EA-32 RVT Comet
1965-1967. 1x10", tremolo, reverb.

1965-1967		$400	$525

EA-33 RVT Galaxie
1963-1964. Gray tolex, gray grille, 1x10".

1963-1964		$400	$525

EA-35 Devon
1961-1963. 1x10" until '62, 1x12" with tremolo in '63.

1961-1963		$400	$525

EA-35T Devon
1963. Tremolo, 6 knobs.

1963		$400	$525

EA-50 Pacemaker
1961-1969. 1x8" until '62, 1x10" after. EA-50T with tremolo added in '63. Non-tremolo version dropped around '67.

1961-1965	1x8	$385	$500
1966-1969	1x10	$400	$525

EA-300 RVT Embassy
1965-1969. 90 watts, 2x12", gray vinyl, gray grille, tremolo, reverb.

1965-1969		$600	$775

EA-500T Panorama
1963-1967. 65 watts, head and large cabinet, tremolo, 1x15" and 1x10" until '64, 1x15" and 2x10" after.

1964-1967		$500	$650

EA-600 RVT Maxima
1966-1969. Solidstate Epiphone version of Gibson GSS-100, gray vinyl, gray grille, two 2x10" cabs and hi-fi stereo-style amp head.

1966-1969		$350	$450

Electar
1935-1939. All models have large "E" insignia logo on front, first model Electar in rectangular box with 1x8" speaker, 3 models introduced in '36 (Model C, Model M, and Super AC-DC), the Special AC-DC was introduced in '37, later models were 1x12" combos. Old

Electar amps are rarely found in excellent working condition and prices shown are for those rare examples.

1935	Electar	$490	$635
1936-1939	Model C	$700	$925
1936-1939	Model M	$700	$925
1936-1939	Super AC-DC	$800	$1,050
1937-1939	Special AC-DC	$775	$1,000

Electar Tube 10
1997-2004. These modern Electar amps were branded as Electar, not Epiphone, but since they were often marketed with other Epi products, they are included here. 10 watt combo, all tube, 8" speaker.

1997-2004		$110	$145

Electar Tube 30
1997-2004. 30 watt combo, all tube, 10" speaker, reverb added in 2002.

1997-2004		$110	$145

Model 100
1965-1967. Made in Kalamazoo, label with serial number, Model 100 logo on small 10" speaker, blue cover, 3 tubes, 3 knobs.

1965-1967		$400	$525

Zephyr
1939-1957. Maple veneer cabinet, 30 watts with 2x6L6 power, 1x12" until '54, 1x15" after, made by Danelectro using their typical designs, Dano D-style blond covering, large split "E" logo on front, brown grille cloth, large block Zephyr logo on back panel.

1939-1953	1x12	$750	$975
1953-1957	1x15	$775	$1,025

Zephyr Dreadnaught
1939. Similar to Zephyr amp but higher power and added microphone input.

1939		$750	$975

Esteban
2005-2007. Imported brand from China, student budget level compact amps.

Compact

2005-2007		$25	$45

Estey
Late-1960s. In 1959, Magnatone merged with the Estey Organ Company and in late '66/early '67 they introduced models branded Estey and based on their budget Magnatone Starlite series.

Model T12
Late-1960s. Based on Magnatone Starlite model 412.

1960s		$425	$550

Model T22
Late-1960s. Based on Magnatone Starlite model 422 but with larger 12" speaker.

1960s		$525	$675

Model T32
Late-1960s. Based on Magnatone Starlite model 432 with reverb and vibrato.

1960s		$600	$775

Model T42
Late-1960s. Based on Magnatone Starlite model 442 bass amp.

1960s		$600	$775

Epiphone EA-30 Triumph
Imaged by Heritage Auctions, HA.com

AMPS

Epiphone EA-50 Pacemaker
Imaged by Heritage Auctions, HA.com

1964 Epiphone Zephyr
Imaged by Heritage Auctions, HA.com

AMPS

Evans AE200-2019

Fargen Mini Plex MK III

Fender Acoustasonic 15

MODEL YEAR	FEATURES	EXC. COND. LOW	HIGH

Evans Custom Amplifiers

1994-present. Professional grade, production, solidstate head and combo amps built by Scot Buffington in Burlington, North Carolina.

EVH

2007-present. Eddie Van Halen's line of professional and premium grade, production, tube amp heads and cabinets built by Fender. They also build guitars.

5150 III 50-Watt

2011-present. 50 watt head with 2x12 cab.

MODEL YEAR	FEATURES	EXC. COND. LOW	HIGH
2011-2021		$1,000	$1,300

Evil Robot

2010-2014. Produced by David Brass and Fretted Americana, made in the U.S.A., initial product produced in limited quantities is based on the '59 Tonemaster (Magnatone) Troubadour amp. Production ceased in '14.

E-Wave Amplifiers

2004-present. Built by Hangzhou Shengbei Sound Co. Ltd. in China.

Excelsior

The Excelsior Company started offering accordions in 1924 and had a large factory in Italy by the late '40s. They started offering guitars and amps, uaually built by others including Valco and possibly Sano, around '62. By the early '70s they were out of the guitar business.

Americana Stereophonic High Fidelity

Late 1960s. 50 watts, 1x15", 2x8", 2x3x9" ovals, 2xEL34 power, tube rectifier, large Excelsior logo and small Excelsior The House of Music logo, guitar and accordion inputs, stereo reverb and vibrato.

MODEL YEAR	FEATURES	EXC. COND. LOW	HIGH
1968-1969		$1,250	$1,625

Citation C-15

1962. Made by Sano, mid power with 2x6V6 power tubes, single speaker combo amp, large Citation by Excelsior logo on front panel.

MODEL YEAR	FEATURES	EXC. COND. LOW	HIGH
1962		$800	$1,050

Fargen

1999-present. Benjamin Fargen builds his professional and premium grade, production/custom, guitar and bass tube amps in Sacramento, California. He also builds guitar effects.

Fender

1946-present. Leo Fender developed many ground-breaking instruments, but Leo's primary passion was amplifiers, and of all his important contributions to musicians, none exceed those he made to the electric tube amplifier.

Tweed Fender amp circuits are highly valued because they defined the tones of rock and roll. Blackface models remained basically the same until mid-'67. Some silverface circuits remained the same as the blackface circuits, while others were changed in the name of reliability. Price Guide values are for all original, excellent condition amps. Small differences in an amp's condition can generate larger differences in selling prices. Non-original speakers will significantly reduce a pre-'68 amp's value. Reconed speakers will reduce the value, but a reconed speaker is preferable to a replacement speaker. Multi-speaker amps generally have matching speaker codes. Different speaker codes require explanation. Fender leather handles are often broken and replaced. A replacement handle drops the value of an amp. Grille cloths should have no tears and a single tear can drop the value of an amp. Each Tweed amp should be evaluated on a case-by-case basis, and it is not unusual for a Tweed amp to have a wide range of values. Alnico speaker replacement is more significant than ceramic speaker replacement. Fender converted to ceramic about '62. Speaker replacement is of less concern in post-'70 Fender amps.

From 1953 to '67, Fender stamped a two-letter date code on the paper tube chart glued inside the cabinet. The first letter was the year (C='53, D='54, etc.) with the second the month (A=January, etc.).

The speaker code found on the frame of an original speaker will identify the manufacturer, and the week and year that the speaker was assembled. The speaker code is typically six (sometimes seven) digits. The first three digits represent the Electronics Industries Association (E.I.A.) source code which identifies the manufacturer. For example, a speaker code 220402 indicates a Jensen speaker (220), made in '54 (4) during the second week (02) of that year. This sample speaker also has another code stamped on the frame. ST654 P15N C4964 indicates the model of the speaker, in this case it is a P15N 15" speaker. The sample speaker also had a code stamped on the speaker cone, 4965 1, which indicates the cone number. All of these codes help identify the originality of the speaker. The value ranges provided in the Guide are for amps with the original speaker and original speaker cone.

Most Fender speakers from the '50s will be Jensens (code 220). By the late-'50s other suppliers were used. The supplier codes are: Oxford (465), C.T.S. (137), Utah (328). JBL speakers were first used in the late-'50s Vibrasonic, and then in the Showman series, but JBL did not normally have a E.I.A. source code. An amp's speaker code should be reconciled with other dating info when the amp's original status is being verified.

Piggyback amps from '68-'79 utilize rather heavy, bulky cabinets, which can be difficult and expensive to ship. Therefore a standalone amp head from this period is worth significantly more than a standalone cabinet.

General Production Eras: Diagonal tweed era, Brown tolex era, Blackface era, Silverface era with raised Fender logo with underlining tail, Silverface era with raised Fender logo without underlining tail, Silverface era with raised Fender logo with small MADE IN USA designation.

MODEL YEAR	FEATURES	EXC. COND. LOW	HIGH

Nameplate and Logo Attribution: Fender nameplate with city but without model name (tweed era), Fender nameplate without city or model name (tweed era), Fender nameplate with model name noted (tweed era), Fender flat logo (brown era), Fender script raised logo (blackface era).

30
1980-1981. Tube combo amp, 30 watts, 2x10" or 1x12".

1980-1981	1x12	$550	$725
1980-1981	2x10	$600	$775

75
1980-1982. Tube, 75 watts, offered as a 1x15" or 1x12" combo, or as head and 4x10" or 2x12" cab.

1980-1982	1x15	$600	$775
1980-1982	2x12	$625	$825
1980-1982	4x10	$675	$875

85
1988-1992. Solidstate, 85 watt 1x12" combo, black cover, silver grille.

1988-1992		$295	$385

800 Pro Bass Head
2004-2008. Rack-mount, 800 watts, 5-band EQ.

2004-2008		$375	$490

Acoustasonic 15
2013-present. Student 1x6" amp, 15 watts.

2013-2021		$60	$80

Acoustasonic 30/30 DSP
2000-2011. Small combo, brown tolex, wheat grille. Upgrade model includes DSP (Digital Signal Processor) effects.

2000-2005	30	$205	$265
2000-2011	30 DSP	$230	$300

Acoustasonic 100 Combo
2012-2013. 100 watts, 1x8", horn.

2012-2013		$300	$385

Acoustasonic 150 Combo
2012-2017. 150 (2x75 stereo) watts, 2x8", piezo horn.

2012-2017		$300	$385

Acoustasonic Junior/Junior DSP
1998-2011. 2x40 watts, 2x8", Piezo horn.

1998-2011		$230	$300

Acoustasonic SFX/SFX II
1998-2011. SFX technology, 32 stereo digital presents, 2x80 watts, SFX is taller combo with one 10", a sideways mounted 8", and a horn. SFX II is shorter cab with 8", sideways 6".

1998-2003	SFX, tall cab	$300	$385
2003-2011	SFX II, short cab	$305	$390

Acoustasonic Ultralight
2006-2009. Small 2x125-watt 2 channel head with 2x8 w/tweeters stereo cab.

2006-2009		$635	$825

Acoustic Pro
2016-2019. 200-watt digital combo, 12" and tweeter, natural blonde cab.

2016-2019		$515	$675

Acoustic SFX
2016-2019. 160-watt digital combo, 8" and 6.5" and tweeter, natural blonde cab.

2016-2019		$515	$675

AmpCan
1997-2008. Cylindrical can-shaped battery powered portable amp.

1997-2008		$150	$195

Automatic SE
1998-2000. Solidstate 25-watt, 1x10" (12" in 2000) combo, blackface cosmetics.

1998-2000		$95	$125

Bandmaster
1953-1974. Wide-panel 1x15" combo '53-'54, narrow-panel 3x10" combo '55-'60, tolex '60, brownface with 1x12" piggyback speaker cabinet '61, 2x12" '62, blackface '62-'67, silverface '68-'74.

The Fender tweed 4x10" Bassman and tweed 3x10" Bandmaster amps are highly sensitive to condition. Because there are so few that are truly excellent, the price ranges listed may be misleading. Most Bassman amps are at best very good minus (VG-) because their tweed is so damaged and stained. It is also rare to find the original speakers, and if the frames are original, they have often been reconed. 4x10" Bassman and 3x10" Bandmasters that are excellent plus plus (Exc++) may have price ranges that are much higher than the values listed. It is estimated that 90% of the vintage 4x10" Bassman are really only VG or less. Because of the extreme condition factor for these tweed amps, the prices below include amps in very good (VG) condition. Therefore the condition for these listed amps is VG to Exc. Exc+ will be more than the values listed here. As per other high-end collectible, each amp should be taken on a case by case basis.

Fender piggyback amps include a head and separate cabinet. The prices shown are for a factory-original matching set. A factory-original set is worth 25% more than the combined value of a head and cabinet that were not originally sold together when new. Heads are worth more than cabinets. The value of a separate head is 40% of the value shown here, and the value of a separate cabinet is 35% of the value shown. In summary, the math is as follows: 40% head + 35% cabinet + 25% premium = 100% value of factory-original set.

1953-1954	Tweed, 1x15	$3,800	$4,940
1955-1958	Tweed, 3x10	$8,500	$11,000
1959-1960	Old style cab, pink-brown tolex	$8,700	$11,300
1959-1960	Tweed, 3x10	$8,700	$11,300
1960	Brown tolex, 3x10	$4,400	$5,700
1960	Brown tolex, 3x10, reverse controls	$7,900	$10,300
1961	Rough white/ oxblood, 1x12	$2,900	$3,800
1961-1962	Rough white/ oxblood, 2x12	$2,350	$3,100
1963-1964	Smooth white/ gold, 2x12	$2,350	$3,100
1964-1967	Black tolex, 2x12	$1,400	$1,825
1967-1968	Black, 2x12	$1,200	$1,550
1967-1969	Silverface, 2x12	$1,000	$1,300
1970-1974	Silverface, 2x12	$875	$1,150

Fender Acoustic Pro

AMPS

1962 Fender Bandmaster
Ted Wulfers

1964 Fender Bandmaster
Tom Pfeifer

Fender Bassbreaker 45 Combo

1960 Fender Bassman
Dennis Delzer

1963 Fender Bassman
Peter Guild

Bandmaster Reverb
1968-1980. 45 watt silverface head with 2x12" cabinet.

MODEL YEAR	FEATURES	LOW	HIGH
1968-1972		$1,100	$1,425
1973-1980		$1,050	$1,350

Band-Master VM Set
2009-2012. Vintage Modified, 40 watts, piggyback, DSP reverb and effects.

2009-2012		$475	$625

Bantam Bass
1969-1971. 50 watts, large unusual 1x10" Yamaha speaker.

1969-1971	Original speaker	$675	$875

Bassbreaker 15
2015-present. Tube, 15 watts, 1x12" combo, master volume, gray tweed standard. Also offered in FSR limited editions.

2015-2021	Combo, gray tweed	$360	$465
2015-2021	Head, gray tweed	$315	$415
2017	Combo, LE Blonde Nubtex	$375	$490
2017	Combo, LE British Green	$375	$490

Bassbreaker 45
2015-present. Head (until '18) or 2x12" combo, 45 watts, gray tweed.

2015-2018	Head	$600	$775
2016-2021	Combo	$675	$875

Bassman
1952-1971. Tweed TV front combo, 1x15" in '52, wide-panel '53-'54, narrow-panel and 4x10" '54-'60, tolex brownface with 1x12" in piggyback cabinet '61, 2x12" cabinet '61-'62, blackface '63-'67, silverface '67-'71, 2x15" cabinet '68-'71. Renamed the Bassman 50 in '72.

The Fender tweed 4x10" Bassman and tweed 3x10" Bandmaster amps are highly sensitive to condition. Because there are so few that are truly excellent, the price ranges listed may be misleading. Most Bassman amps are at best very good minus (VG-) because their tweed is so damaged and stained. It is also rare to find the original speakers, and if the frames are original, they have often been reconed. 4x10" Bassmans and 3x10" Bandmasters that are excellent plus plus (Exc++) may have price ranges that are much higher than the values listed. It is estimated that 90% of the vintage 4x10" Bassman are really only VG or less. Because of the extreme condition factor for these tweed amps, the prices below include amps in very good (VG) condition. Therefore the condition for these listed amps is VG to Exc. Exc+ will be more than the values listed here. As per other high-end collectibles, each amp should be taken on a case by case basis.

Fender piggyback amps include a head and separate cabinet. The prices shown are for a factory-original matching set. A factory-original set is worth 25% more than the combined value of a head and cabinet that were not originally sold together when new. Heads are worth more than cabinets. The value of a separate head is 40% of the value shown here, and the value of a separate cabinet is 35% of the value shown. In summary, the math is as follows: 40% head + 35% cabinet + 25% premium = 100% value of factory-original set.

MODEL YEAR	FEATURES	LOW	HIGH
1952	TV front, 1x15	$2,800	$3,650
1953-1954	Wide panel, 1x15	$2,600	$3,375
1955-1957	Tweed, 4x10, 2 inputs	$6,900	$9,000
1957-1958	Tweed, 4x10, 4 inputs	$8,700	$11,300
1959-1960	Old style cab, pink-brown tolex	$8,800	$11,450
1959-1960	Tweed, 4x10, 4 inputs	$8,800	$11,450
1961	White 1x12 6G6, tube rectifier	$3,300	$4,300
1962	Late '62, white 2x12	$2,400	$3,125
1962	White 1x12, 6G6A, ss rectifier	$3,000	$3,900
1963-1964	Smooth white 2x12, 6G6A/B	$2,400	$3,125
1964	Transition, black, white knobs	$1,750	$2,275
1965-1966	AA165/AB165, black knobs	$1,450	$1,875
1967-1969	Silverface, vertical 2x15	$850	$1,100
1970-1971	Silverface, 2x15	$700	$900

'59 Bassman
1990-2003. Tube, 45 watts, 4x10", birch ply cab, solidstate rectifier.

1990-2003		$725	$950

'59 Bassman LTD
2004-present. Lacquered Tweed (LTD), tube, 45 watts, 4x10", solid pine cab, tube rectifier.

2004-2021		$1,100	$1,425

Bassman 10
1972-1982. 4x10" combo, silverface and 50 watts for '72-'80, blackface and 70 watts after.

1972-1980	50w	$625	$815
1981-1982	70w	$625	$815

Bassman 20
1982-1985. Tubes, 20 watts, 1x15".

1982-1985		$500	$650

Bassman 25
2000-2005. Wedge shape, 1x10", 25 watts, 3-band EQ.

2000-2005		$95	$125

Bassman 50
1972-1977. 50 watts, with 2x12" cab.

1972-1977		$625	$815

Bassman 60
1972-1976. 60 watts, 1x12".

1972-1976		$625	$815

Bassman 60 (later version)
2000-2005. Solidstate, 60 watts, 1x12".

2000-2005	Combo	$95	$125

Bassman 70
1977-1979. 70 watts, 2x15" cab.

1977-1979		$625	$815

Bassman 100
1972-1977, 2000-2009. Tube, 100 watts, 4x12", name reused on solidstate combo amp.

1972-1977	4x12	$625	$815
2000-2009	1x15 combo	$200	$265

AMPS

MODEL YEAR	FEATURES	EXC. COND. LOW	HIGH

Bassman 100 T
2012-2020. 100-watt head, master volume, '65 blackface cosmetics. Usually paired with Bassman NEO cabs.

2012-2020	Head only	$875	$1,125

Bassman 135
1978-1983. Tube, 135 watts, 4x10".

1978-1983		$625	$825

Bassman 150 Combo
2005-2009. Solidstate 1x12" combo, 150 watts.

2005-2009		$210	$275

Bassman 250 Combo
2005-2006. Import from Indonesia, 250 watts, 2x10".

2005-2006		$210	$275

Bassman 300 Pro Head
2002-2012. All tube, 300 watts, 6x6550, black cover, black metal grille.

2002-2012		$775	$1,000

Bassman 400
2000-2004. Solidstate, 350 watts with 2x10" plus horn, combo, black cover, black metal grille.

2000-2004	Combo	$260	$335
2000-2004	Head	$230	$300

Bassman Bassbreaker (Custom Shop)
1998-2003. Classic Bassman 4x10" configuration. Not offered by 2004 when the '59 Bassman LTD was introduced.

1998-2003	2x12	$900	$1,175
1998-2003	4x10	$925	$1,200

Bassman NEO Cabinet
2012-present. Cabinets used with Bassman 100 T head and Super Bassman head, standard '65 black-face cosmetics.

2012-2021	115	$375	$485
2012-2021	410	$470	$610
2012-2021	610	$510	$660
2012-2021	810	$600	$775

Bassman Solidstate
1968-1971. Small head, piggyback cab. The whole late 1960s Solidstate series were unreliable and prone to overheating, more of a historical novelty than a musical instrument.

1968-1971		$485	$625

B-Dec 30
2006-2009. Bass version of the G-Dec, 30 watts, 1x10.

2006-2009		$105	$135

Blues Deluxe
1993-2005. All tube, 40 watts, reverb, 1x12", tweed covering (blond tolex optional '95 only).

1993-2005	Tweed	$485	$635
1995	Blond tolex	$485	$635

Blues Deluxe Reissue
2006-present. All tube, tweed, 40 watts, reverb, 1x12".

2006-2021		$485	$635

Blues DeVille
1993-1996. All tube Tweed Series, 60 watts, 4x10" (optional 2x12" in '94), reverb, high-gain channel, tweed cover (blond tolex optional '95 only).

1993-1996	Tweed	$575	$750
1995	Blond tolex	$575	$750

Blues DeVille Reissue
2006-2015. 60 watts, 4x10, tweed.

2006-2015		$575	$750

Blues Junior (III) (IV)/LE
1995-present. Tube, 15 watts, 1x12", spring reverb, tweed in '95, black tolex with silver grille '96 on, blond '00-'09, brown '08, surf green '09. Woody Custom Shop (hardwood) in '02-'03. III update in '10, IV in '18. Limited Edition After the Gold Rush, Surf-Tone Green, Red Nova Two-Tone, Creamy Wine Two-Tone, Navy Blues, Silver Noir Two-Tone, and Chocolate Tweed offered in '12.

1995-2021	Black	$400	$525
2002-2003	Woody, Custom Shop	$675	$875
2015-2021	Lacquer tweed	$450	$600

Bronco
1967-1972, 1993-2001. 1x 8" speaker, all tube, 5 watts until '72, 6 watts for '72-'74, ('90s issue is 15 watts), solidstate, tweed covering (blond tolex was optional for '95 only).

1967-1972	Tubes, 5w	$775	$1,000
1993-2001	Solidstate, 15w	$115	$150

Bronco 40 Bass
2012-2018. 40 watts, 1x10", 12 effects.

2012-2018		$140	$180

Bullet/Bullet Reverb
1994-2005. Solidstate, 15 watts, 1x8", with or without reverb.

1994-2005		$65	$85

BXR Series Bass

1987-2000	Various models	$70	$190

Capricorn
1970-1972. Solidstate, 105 watts, 3x12".

1970-1972		$640	$835

Champ
1953-1982. Renamed from the Champion 600. Tweed until '64, black tolex after, 3 watts in '53, 4 watts '54-'64, 5 watts '65-'71, 6 watts '72-'82, 1x6" until '57, 1x8" after.

1953-1954	Wide panel, 1x6, 5C1	$1,825	$2,350
1955-1956	Narrow panel, 1x6, 5E1	$1,825	$2,350
1956-1964	Narrow panel, 1x8, 5F1	$2,500	$3,300
1964	New cab, black, AA764	$1,075	$1,400
1964	Old cab, black, 1x8, F51	$1,900	$2,475
1965-1967	New cab, black, AA764	$825	$1,075
1968-1972	Silverface, 1x8	$625	$825
1973-1980	Silverface, 1x8	$575	$750
1981-1982	Blackface	$575	$750

Champ II
1982-1985. 18 watts, 1x10".

1982-1985		$550	$710

'57 Champ/'57 Custom Champ
2009-2011, 2016-present. Custom Series reissue, tweed, leather handle, 5 watts, 1x8". Custom added to model name in '16.

2009-2021		$700	$925

1964 Fender Bassman
Michael Butler

1975 Fender Bassman 100
Johnny Zapp

AMPS

1964 Fender Champ
Ken Ypparila

1953 Fender Champion 600
Jeffrey Smith

Fender Champion 800

1962 Fender Concert
KC Cormack

AMPS

Champ 12
1986-1992. Tube, 12 watts, overdrive, reverb, 1x12".

		LOW	HIGH
1986-1992	Black	$320	$420
1986-1992	Other colors	$420	$550

Champ 25 SE
1992-1993. Hybrid solidstate and tube combo, 25 watts, 1x12".

1992-1993		$225	$300

Champion 20
2014-present. Solidstate, 20 watts, 1x8", black and silver.

2014-2021		$65	$85

Champion 30/30 DSP
1999-2003. Small solidstate combo, 30 watts, 1x8", reverb.

1999-2003		$85	$110

Champion 40
2014-present. Solidstate, 40 watts, 1x12".

2014-2021		$115	$150

Champion 100
2014-present. Solidstate, 100 watts, 2x12", 2 channels.

2014-2021		$160	$210

Champion 100XL
2019-2021. 100 watts, 2x12", 16 on-board effects, black.

2019-2021		$270	$350

Champion 110
1993-2000. Solidstate, 25 watts, 1x10", 2 channels.

1993-2000		$110	$145

Champion 300
2004-2007. 30 watt solidstate combo, Dyna-Touch Series, DSP effects.

2004-2007		$145	$190

Champion 600
1949-1953. Replaced the Champion 800, 3 watts, 1x6", 2-tone tolex, TV front. Replaced by the Champ.

1949-1953		$1,450	$1,900

Champion 600 (later version)
2007-2012. Small 5 watt combo.

2007-2012		$150	$200

Champion 800
1948. About 100 made, TV front, luggage tweed cover, 1x8, 3 tubes, becomes Champion 600 in '49.

1948		$1,525	$1,975

Concert
1960-1965. Introduced with 40 watts and 4x10", brown tolex until '63, blackface '63-'65. In '62 white tolex was ordered by Webbs Music (CA) instead of the standard brown tolex. A wide range is noted for the rare white tolex, and each amp should be valued on a case-by-case basis. In '60, the very first brown tolex had a pink tint but only on the first year amps.

1960	Brown (pink) tolex	$2,600	$3,375
1960	Brown (pink) tweed	$2,700	$3,500
1961-1963	Brown tolex	$2,400	$3,125
1962	White tolex (Webb Music)	$2,500	$3,250
1963-1965	Blackface	$2,400	$3,125

Concert (Pro Tube Series)
1993-1995. Tube combo, 60 watts, 1x12, blackface.

1993-1995		$675	$875

Concert Reverb (Pro Tube Series)
2002-2005. 4x10" combo, reverb, tremolo, overdrive.

2002-2005		$700	$925

Concert 112
1982-1985. Tube, 60 watts, 1x12", smaller Concert logo (not similar to '60s style logo).

1982-1985		$800	$1,050

Concert 210
1982-1985. Tube, 60 watts, 2x10".

1982-1985		$825	$1,075

Concert 410
1982-1985. Tube, 60 watts, 4x10".

1982-1985		$875	$1,125

Concert II Head
1982-1987. 60 watts, 2 channels.

1982-1987		$725	$950

Cyber Champ
2004-2005. 65 watts, 1x12", Cyber features, 21 presets.

2004-2005		$225	$300

Cyber Deluxe
2002-2005. 65 watts, 1x12", Cyber features, 64 presets.

2002-2005		$250	$325

Cyber-Twin (SE)
2001-2011. Hybrid tube/solidstate modeling amp, 2x65 watts, head or 2x12" combo, becomes the SE in '05.

2001-2003	Head only	$375	$490
2001-2004	Combo	$425	$550
2005-2011	SE, 2nd Edition	$425	$550

Deco-Tone (Custom Shop)
2000. Art-deco styling, 165 made, all tube, 15 watts, 1x12", round speaker baffle opening, uses 6BQ5/ES84 power tubes.

2000		$900	$1,175

Deluxe
1948-1966. Name changed from Model 26 ('46-'48). 10 watts (15 by '54 and 20 by '63), 1x12", TV front with tweed '48-'53, wide-panel '53-'55, narrow-panel '55-'60, brown tolex with brownface '61-'63, black tolex with blackface '63-'66.

1948-1952	Tweed, TV front	$3,200	$4,200
1953-1954	Wide panel	$3,200	$4,200
1955	Narrow panel, small cab	$4,850	$6,300
1956-1960	Narrow panel, large cab	$4,750	$6,175
1961-1963	Brown tolex	$2,350	$3,050
1964-1966	Black tolex	$2,350	$3,050

Deluxe Reverb
1963-1981. 1x12", 20 watts, blackface '63-'67, silverface '68-'80, blackface with silver grille option introduced in mid-'80. Replaced by Deluxe Reverb II. Reissued as Deluxe Reverb '65 Reissue.

1963-1967	Blackface	$3,100	$4,000
1967-1968	Silverface	$2,300	$3,000
1969-1970	Silverface	$1,900	$2,475
1971-1980	Silverface	$1,350	$1,750
1980-1981	Blackface	$1,350	$1,750

MODEL YEAR	FEATURES	EXC. COND. LOW	HIGH

Deluxe Reverb Solidstate
1966-1969. Part of Fender's early solidstate series.

1966-1969		$510	$665

'57 Deluxe/'57 Custom Deluxe
2007-2011, 2016-present. Custom Series reissue, hand-wired, 12 watts, 1x12" combo, tweed. Custom added to model name in '17. A '57 Deluxe head version was offered '16-'17 and Limited Editions in '18-'19.

2007-2011		$1,525	$2,000
2016-2017	Head only	$1,375	$1,800
2016-2021		$1,525	$2,000
2018	LE Blond	$1,575	$2,050

'57 Custom Deluxe Front Row
2019. Limited Edition, 5 offered, exotic wood cab made of century-old Alaskan yellow cedar, from Hollywood Bowl bench seats.

2019	LE Exotic Wood	$5,400	$7,000

'65 Deluxe Reverb
1993-present. Blackface reissue, 22 watts, 1x12".

1993-2021		$850	$1,100

'68 Custom Deluxe Reverb
2014-present. Vintage Modified silverface reissue with modified circuit, 1x12".

2014-2021		$825	$1,075

Deluxe Reverb II
1982-1986. Updated Deluxe Reverb with 2 6V6 power tubes, all tube preamp section, black tolex, blackface, 20 watts, 1x12".

1982-1986		$1,025	$1,325

Deluxe 85
1988-1993. Solidstate, 65 watts, 1x12", black tolex, silver grille, Red Knob Series.

1988-1993		$300	$390

Deluxe 90
1999-2003. Solidstate, 90 watts, 1x12" combo, DSP added in '02.

1999-2002		$200	$260
2002-2003	DSP option	$225	$295

Deluxe 112
1992-1995. Solidstate, 65 watts, 1x12", black tolex with silver grille.

1992-1995		$200	$260

Deluxe 112 Plus
1995-2000. 90 watts, 1x12", channel switching.

1995-2000		$225	$295

Deluxe 900
2004-2006. Solidstate, 90 watts, 1x12" combo, DSP effects.

2004-2006		$275	$360

Deluxe VM
2009-2013. Vintage Modified Series, 40 watts, 1x12", black.

2009-2013		$600	$780

MD20 Mini Deluxe
2007-present. One-watt, dual 2" speakers, headphone jack, 9V adapter jack.

2007-2021		$16	$21

The Edge Deluxe
2016-2019. 12-watts, 1x12" combo, tube, tweed. The Edge front panel badge.

2016-2019		$1,650	$2,150

Dual Professional
1994-2002. Custom Shop amp, all tube, point-to-point wiring, 100 watts, 2x12" Celestion Vintage 30s, fat switch, reverb, tremolo, white tolex, oxblood grille.

1994-2002		$1,400	$1,825

Dual Professional/Super
1947. V-front, early-'47 small metal name tag "Fender/Dual Professional/Fullerton California" tacked on front of cab, 2x10 Jensen PM10-C each with transformer attached to speaker frame, tube chart on inside of cab, late-'47 renamed Super and new metal badge "Fender/Fullerton"

1947		$5,800	$7,550

Dual Showman
1962-1969. Called the Double Showman for the first year. White tolex (black available from '64), 2x15", 85 watts. Reintroduced '87-'94 as solidstate, 100 watts, optional speaker cabs.

Fender piggyback amps include a head and separate cabinet. The prices shown are for a factory-original matching set. A factory-original set is worth 25% more than the combined value of a head and cabinet that were not originally sold together when new. Heads are worth more than cabinets. The value of a separate head is 40% of the value shown here, and the value of a separate cabinet is 35% of the value shown. In summary, the math is as follows: 40% head + 35% cabinet + 25% premium = 100% value of factory-original set.

1962	Rough blond/ oxblood	$3,300	$4,300
1963	Smooth blond/wheat	$2,800	$3,650
1964-1967	Black tolex, horizontal cab	$1,900	$2,475
1968	Blackface, large vertical cab	$1,200	$1,550
1968-1969	Silverface	$1,050	$1,375

Dual Showman Reverb
1968-1981. Black tolex with silver grille, silverface, 100 watts, 2x15".

1968-1972		$1,125	$1,475
1973-1981		$1,075	$1,400

Fender '57
2007. Only 300 made, limited edition combo, hand-wired, 1x12", retro styling.

2007		$1,500	$1,950

FM Series
2003-2010. Lower-priced solidstate amps, heads and combos.

2003-2006	FM-212R, 2x12	$200	$260
2003-2010	FM-100 Head/Cab	$215	$280

Frontman Series
1997-present. Student combo amps, models include 10G (10 watts, 1x6"), 15/15B/15G/15R (15 watts, 1x8"), 25R (25 watts, 1x10", reverb), 212R (100 watts, 2x12", reverb).

1997-2004	15DSP, 15 FX selections	$48	$62
1997-2004	25DSP	$60	$80
1997-2006	65DSP	$120	$155

1955 Fender Deluxe
Jerome Pinkham

AMPS

1980 Fender Deluxe Reverb
Tom Pfeifer

1967 Fender Dual Showman
Imaged by Heritage Auctions, HA.com

Fender G-DEC

2004 Fender Hot Rod Deluxe Limited

Carter Vintage Guitars

1977 Fender Musicmaster Bass

Tom Pfeifer

MODEL YEAR	FEATURES	EXC. COND. LOW	HIGH
1997-2011	15/15B/15G/15R	$40	$52
1997-2011	65R	$80	$105
1997-2013	25R	$48	$62
2007-2013	212R	$160	$205

G-Dec
2005-2012. Digital, amp and effects presets.

2005-2009	G-Dec, small cab	$70	$95
2006-2009	G-Dec 30, larger cab	$105	$135
2007-2008	G-Dec Exec, maple cab	$170	$220
2011-2012	G-Dec Jr, Champ cab	$55	$70

H.O.T.
1990-1996. Solidstate, 25 watts, 1x10", gray carpet cover (black by '92), black grille.

1990-1996		$75	$100

Harvard Solidstate
1980-1983. Reintroduced from tube model, black tolex with blackface, 20 watts, 1x10".

1980-1983		$155	$200

Harvard Tube
1956-1961. Tweed, 10 watts, 1x10", 2 knobs volume and roll-off tone, some were issued with 1x8". Reintroduced as a solidstate model in '80.

1956-1961		$3,900	$5,100

Harvard Reverb
1981-1982. Solidstate, 20 watts, 1x10", reverb, replaced by Harvard Reverb II in '83.

1981-1982		$155	$200

Harvard Reverb II
1983-1985. Solidstate, black tolex with blackface, 20 watts, 1x10", reverb.

1983-1985		$155	$200

Hot Rod Blues Junior Limited
2000s. Compact tube combo, rough blond tolex, dark tolex sides, wheat grille.

2000s		$400	$525

Hot Rod Deluxe/Deluxe III/Deluxe IV
1996-present. Updated Blues Deluxe, tube, 40 watts, 1x12", black tolex. Various covering optional by '98, also a wood cab in 2003. III added to name in '11 with various limited edition colors. Renamed Deluxe IV in '20, offered in black.

1996-2021	Various colors	$485	$635

Hot Rod DeVille 212
1996-2011. Updated Blues DeVille, tube, 60 watts, black tolex, 2x12".

1996-2011	Various colors	$575	$750

Hot Rod DeVille 410/DeVille 410 III
1996-2018. Tube, 60 watts, black tolex, 4x10". III added to name in '11.

1996-2018	Various colors	$575	$750

J.A.M.
1990-1996. Solidstate, 25 watts, 1x12", 4 preprogrammed sounds, gray carpet cover (black by '92).

1990-1996		$75	$100

Jazz King
2005-2008. 140 watt solidstate 1x15" combo.

2005-2008		$600	$775

MODEL YEAR	FEATURES	EXC. COND. LOW	HIGH

KXR Series
1995-2002. Keyboard combo amps, 50 to 200 watts, solidstate, 1x12" or 15".

1995-2002	Various models	$185	$240

Libra
1970-1972. Solidstate, 105 watts, 4x12" JBL speakers, black tolex.

1970-1972		$625	$825

London 185
1988-1992. Solidstate, 160 watts, black tolex.

1988-1992	Head only	$275	$360

London Reverb
1983-1985. Solidstate, 100 watts, 1x12" or 2x10", black tolex.

1983-1985	1x12	$375	$490
1983-1985	2x10	$400	$525
1983-1985	Head	$275	$360

M-80 Series
1989-1994. Solidstate, 90 watts, 1x12", also offered as head only, Bass (160w, 1x15"), Chorus (90w, 2x12") and Pro (90w, rackmount).

1989-1993	M-80 Pro	$185	$240
1989-1994	M-80	$185	$240
1990-1994	M-80 Bass	$185	$240
1990-1994	M-80 Chorus	$185	$240

Machette
2012-2013. 50 watts, 1x12" tube combo, inlaid white piping and gray vinyl accents on black tolex.

2012-2013		$2,200	$2,850

Model 26
1946-1947. Tube, 10 watts, 1x10", hardwood cabinet. Sometimes called Deluxe Model 26, renamed Deluxe in '48.

1946-1947		$2,300	$3,000

Montreux
1983-1985. Solidstate, 100 watts, 1x12", black tolex with silver grille.

1983-1985		$375	$490

Musicmaster Bass
1970-1983. Tube, 12 watts, 1x12", black tolex.

1970-1980	Silverface	$500	$650
1981-1983	Blackface	$500	$650

Mustang Series
2010-present. Mustang I thru V, modeling amp effects, small combo up to a half-stack. Mustang GTX and LT added in '20.

2010-2016	II, 40w, 1x12	$130	$170
2010-2019	I, 20w, 1x8	$70	$90
2011-2016	III, 100w, 1x12	$195	$255
2011-2016	IV, 150w, 2x12	$325	$425
2011-2016	V, 150w, 4x12	$375	$490

PA-100 Head
Early to mid-1970s. All tube head, 100 watts, 4 channels with standard guitar inputs, master volume.

1970s		$525	$685

PA-135 Head
Later 1970s. All tube head, 135 watts, 4 channels, master volume.

1970s		$550	$710

AMPS

MODEL YEAR	FEATURES	EXC. COND. LOW	HIGH

Pawn Shop Special Excelsior/Excelsior Pro
2012-2013. Retro late-'40s vertical combo slate-grille cab, 13-watt 1x15" combo tube amp, tremolo, brown textured vinyl covering.

2012-2013		$285	$365

Pawn Shop Special Greta
2012-2013. Mini tube tabletop amp, 2 watts, 1x4" vintage radio-style cab, red.

2012-2013		$165	$215

Pawn Shop Special Ramparte
2014. Tube amp, 9 watts, 1x12", 2-tone chocolate and copper grille cloth with wheat.

2014		$280	$365

Pawn Shop Special Vaporizer
2014. Tube amp, 12 watts, 2x10", Rocket Red, Slate Blue or Surf Green dimpled vinyl covering with silver grille cloth.

2014		$300	$400

Performer 650
1993-1995. Solidstate hybrid amp with single tube, 70 watts, 1x12".

1993-1995		$230	$300

Performer 1000
1993-1995. Solidstate hybrid amp with a single tube, 100 watts, 1x12".

1993-1995		$245	$315

Princeton
1948-1979. Tube, 4.5 watts (12 watts by '61), 1x8" (1x10" by '61), tweed '48-'61, brown '61-'63, black with blackface '63-'69, silverface '69-'79.

Year	Features	Low	High
1948	Tweed, TV front	$2,300	$3,000
1949-1953	Tweed, TV front	$1,800	$2,400
1953-1954	Wide panel	$1,800	$2,400
1955-1956	Narrow panel, small cab	$2,400	$3,125
1956-1961	Narrow panel, large cab	$2,400	$3,125
1961-1963	Brown, 6G2	$2,225	$2,900
1963-1964	Black, 6G2	$2,100	$2,725
1964-1966	Black, AA964, no grille logo	$1,775	$2,300
1966-1967	Black, AA964, raised grille logo	$1,600	$2,075
1968-1969	Silverface, alum grille trim	$1,000	$1,300
1969-1970	Silverface, no grille trim	$900	$1,175
1971-1979	Silverface, AB1270	$900	$1,175
1973-1975	Fender logo-tail	$900	$1,175
1975-1978	No Fender logo-tail	$900	$1,175
1978-1979	With boost pull-knob	$900	$1,175

Princeton Reverb
1964-1981. Tube, black tolex, blackface until '67, silverface after until blackface again in '80.

Year	Features	Low	High
1964-1967	Blackface	$2,550	$3,300
1968-1972	Silverface, Fender logo-tail	$1,075	$1,400
1973-1979	Silverface, no Fender logo-tail	$1,075	$1,400
1980-1981	Blackface	$1,075	$1,400

Princeton Reverb II
1982-1985. Tube amp, 20 watts, 1x12", black tolex, silver grille, distortion feature.

1982-1985		$975	$1,275

'65 Princeton Reverb
2009-present. Vintage Reissue series, includes various Limited Edition colors.

2009-2021	Various colors	$575	$750

'68 Custom Princeton Reverb
2014-present. 12 watts, silver-and-turquoise front panel, aluminum grille cloth trim, black.

2014-2021		$635	$825

Princeton Chorus
1988-1996. Solidstate, 2x10", 2 channels at 25 watts each, black tolex. Replaced by Princeton Stereo Chorus in '96.

1988-1996		$190	$250

Princeton 65
1999-2003. Combo 1x2", reverb, blackface, DSP added in '02.

1999-2001		$160	$210

Princeton 112/112 Plus
1993-1997. Solidstate, 40 watts (112) or 60 watts (112 Plus), 1x12", black tolex.

Year	Features	Low	High
1993-1994	40 watts	$160	$210
1995-1997	60 watts	$160	$210

Princeton 650
2004-2006. Solidstate 65 watt 1x12" combo, DSP effects, black tolex.

2004-2006		$160	$210

Princeton Recording
2007-2009. Based on classic '65 Princeton Reverb, 15 watts, 1x10" combo, 2 on-board effects (overdrive/compression), 4-button footswitch, blackface cosmetics.

2007-2009		$650	$850

Pro
1946-1965. Called Professional '46-'48. 15 watts (26 by '54 and 25 by '60), 1x15", tweed TV front '48-'53, wide-panel '53-'54, narrow-panel '55-'60, brown tolex and brownface '60-'63, black and blackface '63-'65.

Year	Features	Low	High
1946-1953	Tweed, TV front	$3,800	$4,950
1953-1954	Wide panel	$4,100	$5,300
1955	Narrow panel, old chassis	$4,500	$5,850
1955-1959	Narrow panel, new chassis	$4,600	$6,000
1960	Pink/brown, tweed	$2,600	$3,375
1961-1962	Brown tolex	$2,400	$3,125
1963-1965	Black tolex	$2,400	$3,125

'57 Custom Pro
2016-2019. Hand-wired, 26 watts, 1x15", lacquered tweed.

2016-2019		$1,700	$2,225

Pro Reverb
1965-1982. Tube, black tolex, 40 watts (45 watts by '72, 70 watts by '81), 2x12", blackface '65-'69 and '81-'83, silverface '69-'81.

Year	Features	Low	High
1965-1967	Blackface	$2,375	$3,100
1968	Silverface	$1,650	$2,150
1969-1970		$1,525	$1,975
1971-1980	Silverface	$1,026	$1,325
1981-1982	Blackface	$1,026	$1,325

1964 Fender Princeton
Scott Anderson

AMPS

1964 Fender Princeton Reverb
Vern Juran

1959 Fender Pro
Ted Wulfers

2015 Fender Pro Junior III
Rivington Guitars

Fender Rumble 100

Fender Sidekick Bass 30

MODEL YEAR	FEATURES	EXC. COND. LOW	HIGH

Pro Reverb Solidstate
1967-1969. Fender's first attempt at solidstate design, the attempt was unsuccessful and many of these models will overheat and are known to be unreliable. 50 watts, 2x12", upright vertical combo cabinet.

1967-1969		$515	$675

Pro Reverb Reissue (Pro Series)
2002-2005. 50 watts, 1x12", 2 modern designed channels - clean and high gain.

2002-2005		$850	$1,100

Pro 185
1989-1991. Solidstate, 160 watts, 2x12", black tolex.

1989-1991		$275	$360

Pro Junior (III/IV)
1994-present. All tube, 2xEL84 tubes, 15 watts, 1x10" Alnico Blue speaker, tweed '94-'96, blonde in '95, black tolex '96-'17. Lacquered Tweed '18-present. III update in '10, IV in '18.

1994-1996	Tweed	$500	$650
1995	Blonde	$375	$490
1996-2017	Black tolex	$300	$390
2018-2021	Lacquered Tweed	$375	$490

Pro Junior 60th Anniversary Woody
2006. Recreation of original Fender model (1946-2006), 15 watts, 1x10, lacquered wood cab.

2006		$700	$900

Pro Junior Masterbuilt (Custom Shop)
Late-1990s. Transparent white-blond wood finish.

1990s		$700	$900

Prosonic
1996-2001. Custom Shop 2x10" combo or head/4x12" cab, 60 watts, 2 channels, 3-way rectifier switch, tube reverb, black, red or green.

1996-2001	Cab	$400	$525
1996-2001	Combo	$850	$1,200
1996-2001	Head	$700	$925

Quad Reverb
1971-1978. Black tolex, silverface, 4x12", tube, 100 watts. Large Fender combo amps built in the '70s are not often in excellent condition. Any grille stain or tear to the grille can mean an amp is not in excellent condition and can significantly reduce the values shown.

1971-1978		$975	$1,275

R.A.D.
1990-1996. Solidstate, 20 watts, 1x8", gray carpet cover until '92, black after.

1990-1996		$75	$100

R.A.D. Bass
1992-1994. Solidstate, 25 watts, 1x10", renamed BXR 25.

1992-1994		$75	$100

Roc-Pro 1000
1997-2001. Hybrid tube combo or head, 100 watts, 1x12", spring reverb, 1000 logo on front panel.

1997-2001	Combo	$225	$300
1997-2001	Half stack, head & cab	$325	$425

Rumble Bass
1994-1998. Custom Shop tube amp, 300 watts, 4x10" cabs, blond tolex, oxblood grille. Not to be confused with later budget Rumble series.

1994-1998	Cab	$700	$900
1994-1998	Head	$1,250	$1,625
1994-1998	Head & 2 cabs	$2,800	$3,650

Rumble Series
2003-present. Solidstate bass amps, model number indicates watts (i.e. Rumble 15 = 15 watts), models include Rumble 15 (1x8"), 25 (1x10"), 30 (1x10"), 40 (1x10"), 60 (1x12"), 75 (1x12"), 100 (1x15" or 2x10"), 150 (1x15") and 350 (2x10"). Some models discontinued '09 then restarted in '14.

2003-2009	Rumble 60	$145	$190
2003-2013	Rumble 150	$170	$220
2003-2013	Rumble 150 Head	$130	$170
2003-2013	Rumble 30	$120	$155
2003-2013	Rumble 350 Combo	$270	$350
2003-2013	Rumble 350 Head	$170	$220
2003-2013	Rumble 75	$150	$195
2003-2021	Rumble 100	$170	$220
2003-2021	Rumble 15	$55	$75
2003-2021	Rumble 25	$70	$95
2003-2021	Rumble 40	$130	$170

Scorpio
1970-1972. Solidstate, 56 watts, 2x12", black tolex.

1970-1972		$625	$825

Showman 12
1960-1966. Piggyback cabinet with 1x12", 85 watts, blond tolex (changed to black in '64), maroon grille '61-'63, gold grille '63-'64, silver grille '64-'67.

1960-1962	Rough blonde/ oxblood	$3,250	$4,200
1963-1964	Smooth blonde/gold	$2,800	$3,650
1964-1966	Black	$1,800	$2,350

Showman 15
1960-1968. Piggyback cabinet with 1x15", 85 watts, blonde tolex (changed to black in '64), maroon grille '61-'63, gold grille '63-'64, silver grille '64-'67.

1960-1962	Rough blonde /oxblood	$3,050	$3,975
1963-1964	Smooth blonde/gold	$2,700	$3,500
1964-1967	Blackface	$1,700	$2,200
1967-1968	Silverface	$1,000	$1,300

Showman Solidstate
1983-1987. Solidstate, 200 watts, 2 channels, reverb, EQ, effects loop, model number indicates size, models include; 112, 115, 210 and 212.

1983-1987	Various models	$400	$525

Sidekick 10
1983-1985. Small solidstate Japanese or Mexican import, 10 watts, 1x8".

1983-1985		$55	$75

Sidekick Bass 30
1983-1985. Combo, 30 watts, 1x12".

1983-1985		$70	$90

Sidekick Reverb 15
1983-1985. Small solidstate import, reverb, 15 watts.

1983-1985		$80	$100

Sidekick Reverb 20
1983-1985. Small solidstate Japanese or Mexican import, 20 watts, reverb, 1x10".

1983-1985		$90	$115

MODEL YEAR	FEATURES	EXC. COND. LOW	HIGH
Sidekick Reverb 30			
1983-1985. Small solidstate Japanese or Mexican import, 30 watts, 1x12", reverb.			
1983-1985		$95	$125
Sidekick Reverb 65			
1986-1988. Small solidstate Japanese or Mexican import, 65 watts, 1x12".			
1986-1988		$115	$150
Sidekick 100 Bass Head			
1986-1993. 100 watt bass head.			
1986-1993		$85	$110
Squier Champ 15			
1990s-2000s. 1x8, 15 watts, solidstate.			
1990s-00s		$45	$60
Squier SKX Series			
1990-1992. Solidstate, 15 watts, 1x8", model SKX15R with reverb. Model SKX25R is 25 watts, 1x10, reverb.			
1990-1992	15, no reverb	$35	$45
1990-1992	15R, reverb	$40	$50
1990-1992	25R, reverb	$50	$65
Squier SP10			
2003-2012. 10 watt solidstate, usually sold as part of a Guitar Pack.			
2003-2012		$35	$45
Stage 100/Stage 1000			
1999-2006. Solidstate, 1x12", combo or head only options, 100 watts, blackface. Head available until 2004.			
1999-2004	Head only	$250	$325
1999-2006	Combo	$325	$425
1999-2006	Combo stack, 2 cabs	$425	$550
Stage 1600 DSP			
2004-2006. Solidstate, 160 watts, 2x12" combo, 16 digital effects (DSP).			
2004-2006		$350	$450
Stage Lead/Lead II			
1983-1985. Solidstate, 100 watts, 1x12", reverb, channel switching, black tolex. Stage Lead II has 2x12".			
1983-1985	1x12	$225	$300
1983-1985	2x12	$225	$300
Starcaster 15G by Fender			
2000s. Student economy pac amp, sold with a guitar, strap and stand, Starcaster by Fender logo. Sold in Costco and other discounters.			
2000s		$25	$35
Steel-King			
2004-2009. Designed for pedal steel, 200 watts, solidstate, 1x15".			
2004-2009		$625	$825
Studio 85			
1988. Studio 85 logo on upper right front of grille, solidstate, 1x12" combo, 65 watts, red knobs.			
1988		$225	$300
Studio Bass			
1977-1980. Uses Super Twin design, tube, 200 watt combo, 5-band eq, 1x15".			
1977-1980		$650	$850
Studio Lead			
1983-1986. Solidstate, 50 watts, 1x12", black tolex.			
1983-1986		$260	$340

MODEL YEAR	FEATURES	EXC. COND. LOW	HIGH
Super			
1947-1963, 1992-1997. Introduced as Dual Professional in 1946, renamed Super '47, 2x10" speakers, 20 watts (30 watts by '60 with 45 watts in '62), tweed TV front '47-'53, wide-panel '53-'54, narrow-panel '55-'60, brown tolex '60-'64. Reintroduced '92-'97 with 4x10", 60 watts, black tolex.			
1947-1952	V-front	$6,000	$7,800
1953-1954	Tweed, wide panel	$4,400	$5,725
1955	Tweed, narrow panel, 6L6	$6,000	$7,800
1956-1957	Tweed, narrow panel, 5E4, 6V6	$5,000	$6,500
1957-1960	Tweed, narrow panel, 6L6	$7,400	$9,600
1960	Pink, tweed-era grille	$2,900	$3,800
1960	Pink/brown, metal knobs	$2,900	$3,800
1960	Pink/brown, reverse knobs	$2,900	$3,800
1960-1962	Brown, oxblood grille, 6G4	$2,700	$3,500
1962-1963	Brown, tan/wheat grille, 6G4	$2,700	$3,500
Super 60			
1989-1993. Red Knob series, 1x12", 60 watts, earlier versions with red knobs, later models with black knobs, offered in optional covers such as red, white, gray or snakeskin.			
1989-1993	Combo	$350	$450
1989-1993	Head	$350	$450
Super 112			
1990-1993. Red Knob series, 1x12", 60 watts, earlier versions with red knobs, later models with black knobs, originally designed to replace the Super60 but the Super60 remained until '93.			
1990-1993		$425	$550
Super 210			
1990-1993. Red Knob series, 2x10", 60 watts, earlier versions with red knobs, later models with black knobs.			
1990-1993		$425	$550
Super 410			
1992-1997. 60 watts, 4x10", black tolex, silver grille, blackface control panel.			
1992-1997		$700	$900
Super Bassman Head			
2012-present. 300-watt head, 6x6550 power tubes, master volume, standard '65 blackface cosmetics.			
2012-2021		$1,150	$1,500
Super Champ			
1982-1986. Black tolex, 18 watts, blackface, 1x10".			
1982-1986		$950	$1,225
Super Champ Deluxe			
1982-1986. Solid oak cabinet, 18 watts, upgrade 10" Electro-Voice speaker, see-thru brown grille cloth.			
1982-1986		$1,200	$1,550
Super Champ XD			
2008-2011. Tube amp with extra preamp voicing, 1x10" combo, blackface cosmetics. Replaced by X2 version.			
2008-2011		$250	$325

1963 Fender Showman
Imaged by Heritage Auctions, HA.com

AMPS

Fender Showman
Carter Vintage Guitars

1956 Fender Super
Rivington Guitars

1968 Fender Super Reverb

Michael Campbell

1958 Fender Tremolux

Scott Chapin

1962 Fender Twin

Jim Sheehan

Super Reverb

1963-1982. 4x10" speakers, blackface until '67 and '80-'82, silverface '68-'80. Large Fender combo amps built in the '70s are not often in excellent condition. Any grille stain or tear to the grille can mean an amp is not in excellent condition and can significantly reduce the values shown.

MODEL YEAR	FEATURES	EXC. COND. LOW	HIGH
1963-1964	Blackface, Fender Elec	$2,350	$3,150
1965-1967	Blackface, FMI	$2,200	$2,875
1968	Silverface, AB763	$1,450	$1,875
1969-1970	Silverface	$1,350	$1,750
1970-1972	Silverface, AA270	$1,200	$1,575
1972-1975	Int Master	$1,100	$1,425
1975-1980	MV with pull	$1,000	$1,300
1981-1982	Blackface	$1,000	$1,300

Super Reverb Solidstate

1967-1970. 50 watts, 4x10".

1967-1970		$525	$685

'65 Super Reverb

2001-present. 45 watts, all tube, 4x10", blackface cosmetics.

2001-2021		$1,050	$1,375

Super Showman XFL-1000/XFL-2000

1969-1971. Solidstate Super Showman head controlled 1 or more powered speaker cabs. The XFL-1000 was a 4x12" cab with 2 70-watt power amps, the 8x10" XFL-2000 had same power amps.

1969-1971		$600	$775

Super Six Reverb

1970-1979. Large combo amp based on the Twin Reverb chassis, 100 watts, 6x10", black tolex. Large Fender combo amps built in the '70s are not often in excellent condition. Any grille stain or tear to the grille can mean an amp is not in excellent condition and can significantly reduce the values shown.

1970-1979		$1,200	$1,550

Super Twin

1975-1980. 180 watts (6 6L6 power tubes), 2x12", distinctive dark grille.

1975-1976	Non-reverb	$900	$1,175
1976-1980	Reverb	$950	$1,225

Super-Sonic/60

2006-present. All tube, 60 watts, various options, 1x12" combo or 2x12" piggyback, blonde/oxblood or blackface. Straight and slant 4x12" cab added '11.

2006-2013	1x12, blonde/oxblood	$775	$1,000
2006-2014	1x12, blackface	$700	$900
2006-2015	2x12 piggyback, blonde	$1,000	$1,300

Super-Sonic 22 Combo Limited Edition "Black Gold" FSR

2012. 150 made, 1x12, 2-tone gold and black vinyl with white piping, black grille.

2012		$775	$1,000

Taurus

1970-1972. Solidstate, 42 watts, 2x10" JBL, black tolex, silver grille, JBL badge.

1970-1972		$525	$675

Tone Master Set

1993-2002. Custom Shop, hand-wired head with Tonemaster 2x12" or 4x12" cabinet, blonde or oxblood.

1993-2002		$1,550	$2,025

Tone Master Deluxe Reverb

2019-present. 100-watt digital, reverb and tremolo, black or blonde.

2019-2021	Black	$625	$825
2019-2021	Blonde	$675	$875

Tone Master Twin Reverb

2019-present. 200-watt digital, reverb and tremolo, black or blonde.

2019-2021	Black	$700	$925
2019-2021	Blonde	$750	$950

Tremolux

1955-1966. Tube, tweed, 1x12" '55-'60, white tolex with piggyback 1x10" cabinet '61-'62, 2x10" '62-'64, black tolex '64-'66.

1955-1960	Tweed, 1x12, narrow panel	$4,700	$6,100
1961	Rough white/ oxblood, 1x10	$2,900	$3,800
1961-1962	Rough white/ oxblood, 2x10	$2,700	$3,500
1962-1963	Rough white/ wheat, 2x10	$2,400	$3,100
1963-1964	Smooth white/ gold, 2x10	$2,400	$3,100
1964-1966	Black tolex, 2x10	$2,000	$2,600

EC Tremolux

2011-2016. Eric Clapton's variation on a '57, hand-wired, 12 watts, 1x12".

2011-2016		$1,400	$1,825

Twin

1952-1963, 1996-2010. Tube, 2x12"; 15 watts, tweed wide-panel '52-'55; narrow-panel '55-'60; 50 watts '55-'57; 80 watts '58; brown tolex '60; white tolex '61-'63. Reintroduced in '96 with black tolex, spring reverb and output control for 100 watts or 25 watts.

1952-1954	Tweed, wide panel	$8,500	$11,100
1955-1957	Tweed, 50w	$12,500	$16,250
1958-1959	Tweed, 80w	$18,000	$23,500
1960	Brown tolex, 80w	$13,000	$17,000
1960-1962	Rough white/ oxblood	$7,300	$9,500
1963	Smooth white/gold	$6,000	$8,000

'57 Twin/'57 Custom Twin

2004-2011, 2016-present. Custom Series reissue, tweed, 40 watts, 2x12". Custom added to model name in '16.

2004-2011		$1,575	$2,050
2016-2021		$1,750	$2,275

Twin Reverb

1963-1982. Black tolex, 85 watts (changed to 135 watts in '81), 2x12", blackface '63-'67 and '81-'82, silverface '68-'81, blackface optional in '80-'81 and standard in '82. Large Fender combo amps built in the '70s are not often in excellent condition. Any grille stain or tear to the grille can mean an amp is not in excellent condition and can significantly reduce the values shown.

1963-1967	Blackface	$2,700	$3,500

AMPS

MODEL YEAR	FEATURES	EXC. COND. LOW	HIGH
1968	Silverface, no master vol	$1,450	$1,875
1969-1970	Silverface, no master vol	$1,350	$1,750
1971-1972	Silverface, no master vol	$900	$1,175
1973-1975	Silverface, master vol	$900	$1,175
1976-1980	Silverface, push/pull	$900	$1,175
1980-1982	Blackface	$900	$1,175

Twin Reverb Solidstate

1966-1969. 100 watts, 2x12", black tolex.

1966-1969		$525	$675

'65 Twin Reverb

1991-present. Black tolex, 2x12", 85 watts.

1991-2021		$900	$1,175

'65 Twin Custom 15

2009-2017. 85 watt Twin Reverb with 1x15".

2009-2017		$1,000	$1,300

'68 Custom Twin Reverb

2014-present. Vintage Modified silverface reissue, 1x12", 85 watts, modified all-tube circuitry.

2014-2021		$925	$1,200

Twin Reverb II

1983-1985. Black tolex, 2x12", 105 watts, channel switching, effects loop, blackface panel, silver grille.

1983-1985		$1,025	$1,325

Twin "The Twin"/"Evil Twin"

1987-1992. 100 watts, 2x12", red knobs, most black tolex, but white, red and snakeskin covers offered.

1987-1992		$700	$925

EC Twinolux

2011-2016. Eric Clapton's variation on a '57, hand-wired, 40 watts, 2x12".

2011-2016		$2,700	$3,500

Two Tone (Custom Shop)

2001-2003. Limited production, modern styling, slanted grille, 15 watts, 1x10" and 1x12", 2-tone blonde cab, based on modified Blues Deluxe circuit, Two Tone on name plate.

2001-2003		$1,075	$1,400

Ultimate Chorus DSP

1995-2001. Solidstate, 2x65 watts, 2x12", 32 built-in effect variations, blackface cosmetics.

1995-2001		$265	$350

Ultra Chorus

1992-1994. Solidstate, 2x65 watts, 2x12", standard control panel with chorus.

1992-1994		$250	$325

Vibrasonic

1959-1963. First amp to receive the new brown tolex and JBL, 1x15", 25 watts.

1959-1963		$2,500	$3,250

Vibrasonic Custom

1995-1997. Custom Shop designed for steel guitar and guitar, blackface, 1x15", 100 watts.

1995-1997		$850	$1,100

Vibrasonic Reverb

1972-1981. Black tolex, 100 watts, 1x15", silverface.

1972-1981		$850	$1,100

Vibro-Champ

1964-1982. Black tolex, 4 watts, (5 watts '69-'71, 6 watts '72-'80), 1x8", blackface '64-'68 and '82, silverface '69-'81.

MODEL YEAR	FEATURES	EXC. COND. LOW	HIGH
1964-1967	Blackface, AA764	$1,250	$1,625
1968-1972	Silverface	$750	$975
1973-1981	Silverface	$700	$925
1982	Blackface	$700	$925

EC Vibro Champ

2011-2016. Eric Clapton's variation on a '57 Champ, hand-wired, 5 watts, 1x8".

2011-2016		$875	$1,150

Vibro-Champ XD

2008-2011. Made in China, 5 watts, 1x8.

2008-2011		$145	$185

Vibro-King Custom

1993-2012. Custom Shop combo, 60 watts, 3x10", vintage reverb, tremolo, single channel, all tube, blond or black.

1993-2012		$1,725	$2,250

Vibro-King 212 Cabinet

1993-2012. Custom Shop extension cab, blond tolex, 2x12" Celestion GK80.

1993-2012		$525	$685

Vibro-King Custom Limited Edition

2012-2013. Limited Edition production of unique colors, Chocolate Crème Two-Tone, wheat grille (25 made) and Tequila Sunrise, 3-color sunburst on figured birdseye maple cab, oxblood grille.

2012	Chocolate Crème	$2,150	$2,800
2013	Tequila Sunrise	$2,700	$3,500

Vibrolux

1956-1964. Narrow-panel, 10 watts, tweed with 1x10" '56-'61, brown tolex and brownface with 1x12" and 30 watts '61-'62, black tolex and blackface '63-'64.

1956-1961	Tweed, 1x10	$3,500	$4,600
1961-1962	Brown tolex, 1x12	$3,300	$4,300
1963-1964	Black tolex, 1x12	$3,000	$3,900

Vibrolux Reverb

1964-1982. Black tolex, 2x10", blackface '64-'67 and '81-'82, silverface '70-'80. Reissued in '96 with blackface and 40 watts.

1964-1967	Blackface	$3,150	$4,100
1968	Silverface	$2,150	$2,800
1969-1970	Silverface	$1,650	$2,150
1971-1980	Silverface	$1,250	$1,625
1981-1982	Blackface	$1,250	$1,625

Vibrolux Reverb Solidstate

1967-1969. Fender CBS solidstate, 35 watts, 2x10", black tolex.

1967-1969		$525	$675

Vibrolux Custom Reverb

1995-2013. Part of Professional Series, Custom Shop designed, standard factory built, 40 watts, 2x10", tube, white knobs, blond tolex and tan grill for '95 only, black tolex, silver grille after. Does not say Custom on face plate.

1995-2013	Various colors	$900	$1,175

'68 Custom Vibrolux Reverb

2014-2020. Silverface-style, 35 watts, 2x10", black vinyl with silver-turquoise grille.

2014-2020		$900	$1,175

1969 Fender Twin Reverb
Tom Pfeifer

AMPS

1959 Fender Vibrolux
Ted Wulfers

1966 Fender Vibrolux Reverb
Steve Brandt

1964 Fender Vibroverb
David Gant

Fryette Aether

Fuchs ODS-II

MODEL YEAR	FEATURES	EXC. COND. LOW	HIGH

Vibroverb
1963-1964. Brown tolex with 35 watts, 2x10" and brownface '63, black tolex with 1x15" and blackface late '63-'64.

| 1963 | Brown tolex, 2x10 | $7,000 | $9,000 |
| 1963-1964 | Black tolex, 1x15 | $4,900 | $6,400 |

'63 Vibroverb Reissue
1990-1995. Reissue of 1963 Vibroverb, 40 watts, 2x10", reverb, vibrato, brown tolex.

| 1990-1995 | | $1,125 | $1,475 |

'64 Vibroverb (Custom Shop)
2003-2008. Reissue of 1964 Vibroverb with 1x15" blackface specs.

| 2003-2008 | | $1,400 | $1,850 |

Yale Reverb
1983-1985. Solidstate, black tolex, 50 watts, 1x12", silverface.

| 1983-1985 | | $375 | $490 |

FireBelly Amps
2008-present. Production/custom, professional and premium grade, vintage tube amps built by Steven Cohen in Santa Monica, California.

Fishman
2003-present. Larry Fishman offers professional grade, production, amps that are designed and engineered in Andover, Massachusetts and assembled in China. They also build effects.

Loudbox 100
2006-2013. 100 watts, 1x8" with dome.

| 2006-2013 | | $240 | $310 |

Loudbox Artist Pro-LBX-600
2006-present. 120 watts,

| 2006-2021 | | $255 | $330 |

Loudbox Mini Pro-LBX-500
2006-present. 60 watts.

| 2006-2021 | | $165 | $215 |

Loudbox Performer Pro-LBX-700
2006-present. 180 watts.

| 2006-2021 | | $330 | $430 |

Flot-A-Tone
Ca.1946-early 1960s. Flot-A-Tone was located in Milwaukee, Wisconsin, and made a variety of tube guitar and accordion amps. Most were distrubuted by the Lo Duca Brothers.

Large Models
1960s. Four speakers.

| 1946-60s | | $675 | $875 |

Smaller Models
1960s. 1x8" speaker.

| 1946-60s | | $375 | $500 |

Fortune
1978-1979. Created by Jim Kelley just prior to branding Jim Kelley Amplifiers in 1980, Fortune Amplifiers logo on front panel, specifications and performance similar to early Jim Kelley amplifiers, difficult to find in original condition, professional grade, designed and manufactured by Active Guitar Electronics company.

Fox Amps
Marc Vos builds professional grade, production/custom, guitar amps and cabinets, starting 2007, in Budel, Netherlands.

Framus
1946-1977, 1996-present. Tube guitar amp heads, combos and cabinets made in Markneukirchen, Germany. They also build guitars, basses, mandolins and banjos. Begun as an acoustic instrument manufacturer, Framus added electrics in the mid-'50s. In the '60s, Framus instruments were imported into the U.S. by Philadelphia Music Company. The brand was revived in '96 by Hans Peter Wilfer, the president of Warwick, with production in Warwick's factory in Germany. Distributed in the U.S. by Dana B. Goods.

Fred
1984-1986. Before settling on the name Bedrock, company founders Brad Jeter and Ron Pinto produced 50 amps carrying the brand name Fred in Nashua, New Hampshire.

Frenzel
1952-present. Jim Frenzel built his first amp in '52 and began using his brand in '01. He offers intermediate and professional grade, production/custom, hand-wired, vintage tube, guitar and bass amps built in Mabank, Texas.

Frudua Guitar Works
1988-present. Intermediate grade, production, guitar and bass amps built by guitar luthier Galeazzo Frudua in Calusco d'Adda, Italy. He also builds guitars and basses.

Fryette
2009-present. Professional and premium grade amps, combos, and cabinets built by Steven M. Fryette, who also founded VHT amps. At the beginning of '09 AXL guitars acquired the VHT name to build their own product. Fryette continues to manufacture the VHT amp models under the Fryette brand in Burbank, California.

Fuchs Audio Technology
2000-present. Andy Fuchs started the company in '99 to rebuild and modify tube amps. In 2000 he started production of his own brand of amps, offering combos and heads from 10 to 150 watts. They also custom build audiophile and studio tube electronics. Originally located in Bloomfield, New Jersey, since '07 in Clifton, New Jersey.

Fulton-Webb
Steve Fulton and Bill Webb build their tube amp heads, combos and cabinets in Austin, Texas, beginning 1997.

MODEL YEAR	FEATURES	EXC. COND. LOW	HIGH

Gabriel Sound Garage

2004-2014. Gabriel Bucataru built his tube amp heads and combos in Arlington Heights, Illinois.

Gallien-Krueger

1969-present. Gallien-Krueger has offered a variety of bass and guitar amps, combos and cabinets and is located in San Jose, California.

Garcia

Tube amp heads and speaker cabinets built by Matthew Garcia in Myrtle Beach, South Carolina, starting in 2004. He also built effects.

Garnet

Mid 1960s-1989. In the mid '60s, "Gar" Gillies started the Garnet Amplifier Company with his two sons, Russell and Garnet, after he started making PA systems in his Canadian radio and TV repair shop. The first PA from the new company was for Chad Allen & the Expressions (later known as The Guess Who). A wide variety of tube amps were offered and all were designed by Gar, Sr. The company also produced the all-tube effects The Herzog, H-zog, and two stand-alone reverb units designed by Gar in the late '60s and early '70s. The company closed in '89, due to financial reasons caused largely by a too rapid expansion. Gar repaired and designed custom amps up to his death in early 2007.

GDS Amplification

1998-present. Tube amps, combos and speaker cabinets from builder Graydon D. Stuckey of Fenton, Michigan. GDS also offers amp kits. In January, '09, GDS bought the assets of Guytron Amplification.

Genesis

Genesis was a 1980s line of student amps from Gibson.

B40
1984-late-1980s. Bass combo with 40 watts.

1984-1989		$120	$160

G Series
1984-late-1980s. Small combo amps.

1984-1989	G10, 10w	$70	$90
1984-1989	G25, 25w	$90	$120
1984-1989	G40R, 40w, reverb	$140	$185

Genz Benz

Founded by Jeff and Cathy Genzler in 1984 and located in Scottsdale, Arizona, the company offers guitar, bass, and PA amps and speaker cabinets. In late 2003, Genz Benz was acquired by Kaman (Ovation, Hamer, Takamine). On January 1, '08, Fender acquired Kaman Music Corporation and the Genz Benz brand.

George Dennis

1991-present. Founded by George Burgerstein, original products were a line of effects pedals. In

'96 they added a line of tube amps. The company is located in Prague, Czech Republic.

Gerhart

2000-present. Production/custom, intermediate and professional grade, amps and cabinets from builder Gary Gerhart of West Hills, California. He also offers an amp in kit form.

Germino

2002-present. Intermediate to professional grade tube amps, combos and cabinets built by Greg Germino in Graham, North Carolina.

Gibson

1890s (1902)-present. Gibson has offered a variety of amps since the mid-'30s to the present under the Gibson brandname and others. The price ranges listed are for excellent condition, all original amps though tubes may be replaced without affecting value. Many Gibson amps have missing or broken logos. The prices listed are for amps with fully intact logos. A broken or missing logo can diminish the value of the amp. Amps with a changed handle, power cord, and especially a broken logo should be taken on a case-by-case basis.

Vintage amplifiers are rarely found in original, excellent condition. Many vintage amps have notable wear and have a non-original speaker. The prices shown are for fully original (except tubes and caps) amplifiers that are pleasing clean, and contain no significant wear, blemishes, grille stains, or damage.

Atlas IV
1963-1967. Piggyback head and cab, introduced with trapezoid shape, changed to rectangular cabs in '65-'66 with black cover, simple circuit with 4 knobs, no reverb or tremolo, mid-power with 2 6L6, 1x15".

1963-1965	Brown	$600	$775
1966-1967	Black	$600	$775

Atlas Medalist
1964-1967. Combo version with 1x15".

1964-1967		$575	$750

B-40
1972-1975. Solidstate, 40 watts, 1x12".

1972-1975		$275	$350

BR-1
1946-1948. 15 watts, 1x12" field-coil speaker, brown leatherette cover, rectangular metal grille with large G.

1946-1948		$750	$1,000

BR-3
1946-1947. 12 watts, 1x12" Utah field-coil speaker (most BR models used Jensen speakers).

1946-1947		$750	$1,000

BR-4
1946-1948. 14 watts, 1x12" Utah field-coil speaker (most BR models used Jensen speakers).

1946-1948		$650	$850

Garnet Gnome Reverb
John Maysenhoelder

AMPS

Gerhart Gilmore

Germino Club 40

1953 Gibson BR-6

Gibson GA-5 Les Paul Junior

1964 Gibeon GA-5 T Skylark

Tom Pfeifer

MODEL YEAR	FEATURES	EXC. COND. LOW	HIGH
BR-6			
1946-1954. 10 to 12 watts, 1x10", brown leatherette, speaker opening split by cross panel with G logo, bottom mounted chassis with single on-off volume pointer knob.			
1946-1947	Verticle cab	$650	$850
1948-1954	Horizontal cab	$650	$850
BR-9			
1948-1954. Cream leatherette, 10 watts, 1x8". Originally sold with the BR-9 lap steel. Renamed GA-9 in '54.			
1948-1954		$500	$650
Duo Metalist			
1968-early 1970s. Upright vertical combo cab, tubes, faux wood grain panel, mid-power, 1x12".			
1968-1970s		$525	$675
EH-100			
1936-1942. Electric-Hawaiian companion amp, 1x10". AC/DC version called EH-110.			
1936-1942		$725	$950
EH-125			
1941-1942. 1x12", rounded shoulder cab, brown cover in '41 and dark green in '42, leather handle.			
1941-1942		$800	$1,050
EH-126			
1941. Experimental model, 6-volt variant of EH-125, about 5 made.			
1941		$1,250	$1,625
EH-135			
1941. Experimental model, alternating and direct current switchable, about 7 made.			
1941		$1,350	$1,750
EH-150			
1935-1942. Electric-Hawaiian companion amp, 1x12" ('35-'37) or 1x10" ('38-'42). AC/DC version called EH-160.			
1935	13 3/4" square cab	$1,350	$1,750
1936-1937	14 3/4" square cab	$1,350	$1,750
1937-1942	15 3/8" round cab	$1,350	$1,750
EH-185			
1939-1942. 1x12", tweed cover, black and orange vertical stripes, marketed as companion amp to the EH-185 Lap Steel. AC/DC version called EH-195.			
1939-1942		$1,700	$2,200
EH-195			
1939-1942. EH-185 variant with vibrato.			
1939-1942		$1,700	$2,200
EH-250			
1940. Upgraded natural maple cabinet using EH-185 chassis, only 2 made, evolved into EH-275.			
1940		$2,150	$2,800
EH-275			
1940-1942. Similar to EH-185 but with maple cab and celluloid binding, about 30 made.			
1940-1942		$2,075	$2,700
Epoch Series			
2000s. Solidstate student practice amps.			
2000s	Various models	$25	$35
Falcon III F-3			
Early 1970s. Solidstate, 1x12" combo, 65 watts, made in Chicago by CMI after Gibson ceased amp production in Kalamazoo ('67), black tolex, dark grille.			
1970		$300	$400

MODEL YEAR	FEATURES	EXC. COND. LOW	HIGH
Falcon Medalist (Hybrid)			
1967. Transitional tube 1x12" combo amp from GA-19 tube Falcon to the solidstate Falcon, Falcon logo and Gibson logo on front panel, brown control panel, dark cover and dark grille, vertical combo cabinet.			
1967		$350	$450
Falcon Medalist (Solidstate)			
1968-1969. Solidstate combo, 15 watts, 1x12".			
1968-1969		$350	$450
G-10			
1972-1975. Solidstate, 10 watts, 1x10", no tremolo or reverb.			
1972-1975		$115	$150
G-20			
1972-1975. Solidstate with tremolo, 1x10", 10 watts.			
1972-1975		$135	$175
G-25			
1972-1975. 25 watts, 1x10".			
1972-1975		$180	$235
G-35			
1975. Solidstate, 30 watts, 1x12".			
1975		$200	$260
G-40/G-40R			
1972-1974. Solidstate with tremolo and reverb, 40 watts, 1x12" (G-40) and 2x10" (G-40 R).			
1972-1974		$275	$360
G-50/G-50A/G-50B			
1972, 1975. Solidstate with tremolo and reverb, models G-50 and 50 A are 1x12", 40 watts, model 50 B is a bass 1x15", 50 watts.			
1972-1975		$290	$380
G-55			
1975. 50 watts, 1x12".			
1975		$290	$380
G-60			
1972-1973. Solidstate with tremolo and reverb, 1x15", 60 watts.			
1972-1973		$315	$410
G-70			
1972-1973. Solidstate with tremolo and reverb, 2x12", 60 watts.			
1972-1973		$350	$455
G-80			
1972-1973. Solidstate with tremolo and reverb, 4x10", 60 watts.			
1972-1973		$400	$525
G-100A/G-100B			
1975. 100 watts, model 100 A is 2x12" and 100 B is 2x15".			
1975		$400	$525
G-105			
1974-1975. Solidstate, 100 watts, 2x12", reverb.			
1974-1975		$400	$525
G-115			
1975. 100 watts, 4x10".			
1974-1975		$450	$575
GA-5 Les Paul Junior			
1954-1957. Tan fabric cover (Mottled Brown by '57), 7" oval speaker, 4 watts. Renamed Skylark in '58.			
1954-1957		$525	$675

The *Vintage Guitar Price Guide* shows low to high values for items in all-original excellent condition, and, where applicable, with original case or cover.

MODEL YEAR	FEATURES	EXC. COND. LOW	HIGH

GA-5 Les Paul Junior (reissue)
2004-2008. Goldtone Series, class A, 5 watts, 1x8".

2004-2008		$300	$390

GA-5 Skylark
1958-1968. Gold cover (brown by '63 and black by '66), 1x8" (1x10" from '64 on), 4.5 watts (10 watts from '64 on), tremolo. Often sold with the Skylark Lap Steel.

1958-1959	Gold, 45w, 1x8	$475	$625
1960-1962	Gold, 45w, 1x8	$450	$575
1963	Brown, 45w, 1x8	$425	$550
1964	Brown, 10w, 1x10	$375	$500
1965-1967	Black, 10w, 1x10	$350	$450
1968	Skylark, last version	$250	$325

GA-5T Skylark
1960-1968. Tremolo, 4.5 watts early, 10 later, gold covering and 1x8" until '63, brown '63-'64, black and 1x10" after.

1960-1962	Gold, 45w, 1x8	$450	$575
1963	Brown, 45w, 1x8	$425	$550
1964	Brown, 10w, 1x10	$425	$550
1965-1967	Kalamazoo, black	$350	$450
1968	Norlin, vertical cab	$350	$450

GA-5W
Late-1960s. Norlin-era, post-Kalamazoo production, 15 watts, small speaker, volume and tone controls.

1969		$95	$125

GA-6
1956-1959. Replaced the BR-6, 8 to 12 watts, 1x12", has Gibson 6 above the grille. Renamed GA-6 Lancer in '60.

1956-1959		$725	$950

GA-6 Lancer
1960-1961. Renamed from GA-6, 1x12", tweed cover, 3 knobs, 14 watts.

1960-1961		$850	$1,100

GA-7 Les Paul TV Model
1954-1956. Basic old style GA-5 with different graphics, 4 watts, small speaker.

1954-1956		$500	$650

GA-8 Discoverer
1962-1964. Renamed from GA-8 Gibsonette, gold fabric cover, 1x12", 10 watts.

1962-1964		$500	$650

GA-8 Gibsonette
1955-1962. Tan fabric cover (gold by '58), 1x10", 8 watts (9 watts by '58). See Gibsonette for 1952-'54. Name changed to GA-8 Discoverer in '62.

1955-1957	Gibsonette logo	$550	$725
1958-1959	Gibson logo	$500	$650
1960-1962	Gibson logo, tweed	$500	$650

GA-8T Discoverer
1960-1966. Tweed, 1x10", 9-watt, tremolo. Tan cover, 1x12", 15-watt '63-'64, black after.

1960-1962	Tweed, 9w, 1x10	$525	$700
1963-1964	Tan, 15w, 1x12	$450	$585
1965-1966	Black	$425	$550

GA-9
1954-1959. Renamed from BR-9, tan fabric cover, 8 watts, 1x10". Often sold with the BR-9 Lap Steel.

1954-1959	Gibson 9 logo	$650	$850

GA-14 Titan
1959-1961. About 15 watts using 2x6V6 power tubes, 1x10", tweed cover.

1959-1961		$700	$900

GA-15 RV Goldtone
1999-2004. 15 watts, Class A, 1x12", spring reverb.

1999-2004		$450	$650

GA-15 RVT Explorer
1965-1967. Tube, 1x10", tremolo, reverb, black vinyl.

1965-1967		$425	$550

GA-17 RVT Scout
1963-1967. Low power, 1x10", reverb and tremolo.

1963	Smooth brown	$550	$725
1964-1965	Textured brown	$550	$725
1966-1967	Black	$425	$550

GA-18 Explorer
1959. Tweed, tube, 14 watts, 1x10". Replaced in '60 by the GA-18 T Explorer.

1959		$900	$1,175

GA-18T Explorer
1960-1963. Tweed, 14 watts, 1x10", tremolo.

1960-1962	Tweed	$950	$1,225
1963	Brown	$650	$850

GA-19 RVT Falcon
1961-1967. One of Gibson's best selling amps. Initially tweed covered, followed by smooth brown, textured brown, and black. Each amp has a different tone. One 12" Jensen with deep-sounding reverb and tremolo.

1961-1962	Tweed	$1,250	$1,625
1962-1963	Smooth brown	$725	$950
1964	Textured brown	$650	$850
1965-1967	Black	$500	$650

GA-20
1950-1962. Brown leatherette (2-tone by '55 and tweed by '60), tube, 12 watts early, 14 watts later, 1x12". Renamed Crest in '60.

1950-1954	Brown, single G logo	$750	$975
1955-1958	2-tone salt/maroon	$1,000	$1,300
1959	2-tone blue/blond	$1,000	$1,300

GA-20 Crest
1960-1961. Tweed, tube, 14 watts, 1x12".

1960-1961		$1,050	$1,375

GA-20 RVT
2004-2007. 15 watts, 1x12", reverb, tremolo.

2004-2007		$650	$850

GA-20 RVT Minuteman
1965-1967. Black, 14 watts, 1x12", tube, reverb, tremolo.

1965-1967		$450	$600

GA-20T
1956-1959. Tube, 16 watts, tremolo, 1x12", 2-tone. Renamed Ranger in '60.

1956-1958	2-tone	$1,000	$1,300
1959	New 2-tone	$1,000	$1,300

GA-20T Ranger
1960-1961. Tube, 16 watts, tremolo, 1x12", tweed.

1960-1962		$1,100	$1,425

GA-25
1947-1948. Brown, 1x12" and 1x8", 15 watts. Replaced by GA-30 in '48.

1947-1948		$1,175	$1,525

1960 Gibson GA-8 T Discoverer
David Stuckey

AMPS

1958 Gibson GA-9
Imaged by Heritage Auctions, HA.com

Gibson GA-20 RVT

1952 Gibson GA-40 Les Paul
Ted Wulfers

1954 Gibson GA-50 T
Imaged by Heritage Auctions, HA.com

Gibson GA-55 V
Joey Abella

MODEL YEAR	FEATURES	EXC. COND. LOW	HIGH
GA-25 RVT Hawk			
1963-1968. Reverb, tremolo, 1x15".			
1963	Smooth brown	$750	$975
1964	Rough brown	$550	$725
1965-1967	Black	$525	$675
1968	Last version	$450	$575
GA-30 (Invader)			
1948-1961. Brown until '54, 2-tone after, tweed in '60, 1x12" and 1x8", 14 watts. Renamed GA-30 Invader in '60.			
1948-1954	Brown	$1,150	$1,500
1955-1959	2-tone salt/maroon	$1,150	$1,500
1960-1961	Invader, tweed	$1,150	$1,500
GA-30 RV Invader			
1961. Tweed, 1x12" and 1x8", 14-16 watts, reverb but no tremolo.			
1961		$1,300	$1,700
GA-30 RVH Goldtone Head			
1999-2004. 30 watts, Class A head, reverb.			
1999-2004		$850	$1,100
GA-30 RVS (Stereo) Goldtone			
1999-2004. 15 watts per channel, Class A stereo, 2x12", reverb.			
1999-2004		$1,100	$1,450
GA-30 RVT Invader			
1962-1967. Updated model with reverb and tremolo, 25 watts, 1x12" and 1x10" speakers, first issue in tweed.			
1962	Tweed	$1,475	$1,925
1963	Smooth brown	$850	$1,100
1964	Rough brown	$650	$850
1965-1967	Black	$575	$750
GA-35 RVT Lancer			
1966-1967. Black, 1x12", tremolo, reverb.			
1966-1967		$575	$750
GA-40 Les Paul			
1952-1960. Introduced with the Les Paul Model guitar, 1x12" Jensen speaker, 14 watts early and 16 later, recessed leather handle using spring mounting (the handle is easily broken and replacement handle is more common than not). Two-tone leatherette covering, '50s checkerboard grille ('52-early-'55), Les Paul script logo on front of the amp ('52-'55), plastic grille insert with LP monogram, gold Gibson logo above grille. Cosmetics changed dramatically in early/mid-'55. Renamed GA-40 T Les Paul in '60.			
1952-1955	Brown 2-tone, LP grille	$1,800	$2,350
1955-1957	2-tone salt/maroon	$1,750	$2,275
1958-1959	2-tone blue/blond	$1,750	$2,275
GA-40 RVT Limited Edition			
2008-2011. GA-40RVT Limited Edition logo, 200 made, 2-tone brown/tan, front control panel, 30/15 switchable watts.			
2008-2011		$625	$950
GA-40T Les Paul			
1960-1962. Renamed from GA-40 Les Paul, 1x12", 16 watts, tremolo. Renamed Mariner in '62-'67.			
1960-1961	Tweed	$2,300	$3,000
1962	Smooth brown	$625	$825
GA-40T Mariner			
1962-1967. 1x12" combo, 25 watts, tremolo.			
1962-1963	Smooth brown	$625	$825

MODEL YEAR	FEATURES	EXC. COND. LOW	HIGH
1964	Rough brown	$500	$650
1965-1967	Black	$450	$575
GA-45 RVT Saturn			
1965-1967. 2x10", mid power, tremolo, reverb.			
1965-1967		$550	$725
GA-50/GA-50T			
1948-1955. Brown leatherette, 25 watts, 1x12" and 1x8", T had tremolo.			
1948-1955	GA-50	$1,900	$2,475
1948-1955	GA-50T	$2,000	$2,600
GA-55 RVT Ranger			
1965-1967. Black cover, 4x10", tremolo, reverb.			
1965-1967		$575	$750
GA-55/GA-55V			
1954-1958. 2x12", 20 watts, GA-55V with vibrato.			
1954-1958	GA-55	$3,400	$4,400
1954-1958	GA-55 V	$3,400	$4,400
GA-60 Hercules			
1962-1963. 25 watts, 1x15, no-frills 1-channel amp, no reverb, no tremolo.			
1962-1963		$650	$850
GA-60 RV Goldtone			
1999-2004. 60 watts, A/B circuit, 2x12", spring reverb, earliest production in England.			
1999-2004		$1,100	$1,425
GA-70 Country and Western			
1955-1958. 25 watts, 1x15", 2-tone, longhorn cattle western logo on front, advertised to have extra bright sound.			
1955-1958		$3,400	$4,425
GA-75			
1950-1955. Mottled Brown leatherette, 1x15", 25 watts.			
1950-1955		$1,625	$2,100
GA-75 Recording			
1964-1967. 2x10" speakers, no reverb or tremolo, 2 channels, dark cover, gray grille.			
1964-1967		$625	$825
GA-75L Recording			
1964-1967. 1x15" Lansing speaker, no reverb or tremolo, 2 channels, dark cover, gray grille.			
1964-1967		$600	$775
GA-77			
1954-1959. 1x15" JBL, 25-30 watts, 2x6L6 power tubes, 2-tone covering, near top-of-the-line for the mid-'50s.			
1954-1958	2-tone salt/maroon, leather handle	$1,600	$2,075
1958-1959	2-tone blue/blond, metal handle	$1,600	$2,075
GA-77 RET Vanguard			
1964-1967. Mid-power, 2x10", tremolo, reverb, echo.			
1964	Rough brown	$800	$1,025
1965-1967	Black	$575	$750
GA-77 RETL Vanguard			
1964-1967. GA-77 RET with 1x15" Lansing speaker option (L).			
1964-1967		$725	$950
GA-77 RVTL Vanguard			
1962-1967		$725	$950

| MODEL | | EXC. COND. | |
YEAR	FEATURES	LOW	HIGH

GA-77 Vanguard
1960-1961. 1x15" JBL, 25-30 watts, 2 6L6 power tubes, tweed cover, first use of Vanguard model name.

1960-1961		$1,575	$2,050

GA-78 Bell Stereo
1960. Gibson-branded amp made by Bell, same as GA-79 series, Bell 30 logo on front, 30 watts, 2x10" wedge cab.

1960		$2,100	$2,725

GA-79 RV
1960-1962. Stereo-reverb, 2x10", 30 watts.

1960-1961	Tweed	$2,500	$3,250
1962	Textured brown	$2,250	$2,925

GA-79 RVT Multi-Stereo
1961-1967. Introduced as GA-79 RVT, Multi-Stereo was added to name in '61. Stereo-reverb and tremolo, 2x10", tweed (black and brown also available), 30 watts.

1961	Tweed	$2,400	$3,200
1961-1962	Gray sparkle	$2,200	$2,900
1963-1965	Textured brown	$2,200	$2,900
1965-1967	Black	$2,100	$2,725

GA-80/GA-80T/Vari-Tone
1959-1961. 25 watts, 1x15", 2 channels, described as "6-in-1 amplifier with improved tremolo," 6 Vari-Tone pushbottons which give "six distinctively separate sounds," 7 tubes, tweed cover.

1959-1961		$1,700	$2,200

GA-83S Stereo-Vibe
1959-1961. Interesting stereo amp with front baffle mounted 1x12" and 4x8" side-mounted speakers (2 on each side), 35 watts, Gibson logo on upper right corner of the grille, tweed cover, brown grille (late '50s Fender-style), 3 pointer knobs and 3 round knobs, 4 inputs.

1959-1961		$2,550	$3,325

GA-85 Bass Reflex
1957-1958. Removable head, 25 watts, 1x12", very limited production.

1957-1958		$1,275	$1,675

GA-86 Ensemble
1960. 25 watt head plus 1x12" cab, tweed.

1960		$1,700	$2,200

GA-88S Stereo Twin
1960. Control panel and 2 separate 1x12" speaker cabs, 35 watts, 8 tubes, tweed.

1960		$3,800	$4,950

GA-90 High Fidelity
1953-1960. 25 watts, 6x8", 2 channels, advertised for guitar, bass, accordion, or hi-fi.

1953-1960		$1,450	$1,875

GA-95 RVT Apollo
1965-1967. 90 watts, 2x12", black vinyl, black grille, tremolo, reverb.

1965-1967		$650	$850

GA-100 Bass
1960-1963. 35 watts, 1x12" cabinet, for '60-'61 tweed and tripod included for separate head, for '62-'63 brown covering and Crestline Tuck-A-Way head.

1960-1961	Tweed	$1,300	$1,700
1962-1963	Smooth brown	$800	$1,050

| MODEL | | EXC. COND. | |
YEAR	FEATURES	LOW	HIGH

GA-200 Rhythm King
1957-1961. Introduced as GA-200, renamed Rhythm King in '60, 2-channel version of GA-400. Bass amp, 60 watts, 2x12".

1957-1959	2-tone	$2,100	$2,725
1959-1961	Tweed	$2,100	$2,725
1961	Smooth brown	$1,900	$2,500

GA-300 RVT Super 300
1962-1963. 60 watts, 2x12" combo, reverb, tremolo, smooth brown.

1962-1963		$1,900	$2,500

GA-400 Super 400
1956-1961. 60 watts, 2x12", 3 channels, same size as GA-200 cab, 1 more tube than GA-200.

1956-1959	2-tone	$2,300	$3,000
1959-1961	Tweed	$2,300	$3,000
1961	Smooth brown	$2,300	$3,000

GA-CB Custom-Built
1949-1953. 25-30 watts, 1x15", the top model in Gibson's '51 line of amps, described as having sound quality found only in the finest public address broadcasting systems, about 47 made, this high-end amp was replaced by the GA-77 and a completely different GA-90.

1949-1953		$2,000	$2,650

Gibsonette
1952-1954. Gibsonette logo on front, round hole. See GA-8 Gibsonette for later models.

1952-1954		$550	$725

GM05
2009-2012. Small 5 watt solidstate amp usually sold with Maestro guitar pack.

2009-2012		$25	$40

GSS-50
1966-1967. Solidstate, 50 watts, 2x10" combo, reverb and tremolo, black vinyl cover, silver grille, no grille logo.

1966-1967		$400	$525

GSS-100
1966-1967, 1970. Solidstate, 100 watts, two 24"x12" 2x10" sealed cabs, black vinyl cover, silver grille, 8 black knobs and 3 red knobs, slanted raised Gibson logo. Speakers prone to distortion. Reissued in '70 in 3 variations.

1966-1967		$400	$525

Lancer
1968-1969. CMI-Chicago produced, small combo, black upright cab, dark grille, post-McCarty era Gibson logo.

1968-1969		$80	$105

LP-1/LP-2 Set
1970. Les Paul model, piggyback amp and cab set, LP-1 head and LP-2 4x12" plus 2 horns cab, large vertical speaker cabinet, rather small compact 190 watt solidstate amp head.

1970		$400	$525

Medalist 2/12
1968-1970. Vertical cabinet, 2x12", reverb and temolo.

1968-1970		$475	$625

1958 Gibson GA-70 Country and Western
RT Jackson

AMPS

1964 Gibson GA-77 RET Vanguard
Rick Buckendahl

1961 Gibson GA-79 RV

Gibson Plus-50
Imaged by Heritage Auctions, HA.com

Goodsell Super 17 MkIV

Green Electric

MODEL YEAR	FEATURES	EXC. COND. LOW	HIGH
Medalist 4/10			
1968-1970. Vertical cabinet, 4x10", reverb and tremolo.			
1968-1970		$475	$625
Mercury I			
1963-1965. Piggyback trapezoid-shaped head with 2x12" trapezoid cabinet, tremolo, brown.			
1963-1965		$550	$725
Mercury II			
1963-1967. Mercury I with 1x15" and 1x10", initially brown trapezoid cabinets, then changed to black rectangular.			
1963-1964	Trapezoid cabs	$650	$850
1965-1967	Rectangular cabs	$650	$850
Plus-50			
1966-1967. 50 watts, powered extension amplifier. Similar to GSS-100 cabinet of the same era, 2x10" cab, black vinyl cover, silver grille, slant Gibson logo.			
1966-1967		$525	$675
Super Thor Bass			
1970-1974. Solidstate, part of the new G-Series (not GA-Series), 65 watts, 2x15", black tolex, black grille, upright vertical cab with front control, single channel.			
1970-1974		$425	$550
Thor Bass			
1970-1974. Solidstate, smaller 2x10" 50 watt version of Super Thor.			
1970-1974		$375	$500
Titan I			
1963-1965. Piggyback trapezoid-shaped head and 2x12" trapezoid-shaped cabinet, tremolo.			
1963-1965		$550	$725
Titan III			
1963-1967. Piggyback trapezoid-shaped head and 1x15" + 2x10" trapezoid-shaped cabinet, tremolo.			
1963-1964	Brown	$600	$800
1965-1967	Black	$600	$800
Titan Medalist			
1964-1967. Combo version of Titan Series with 1x15" and 1x10", tremolo only, no reverb, black.			
1964-1967		$600	$800
Titan V			
1963-1967. Piggyback trapezoid-shaped tube head and 2x15" trapezoid-shaped cabinet, tremolo.			
1963-1964	Brown	$600	$800
1965-1967	Black	$600	$800
TR-1000 T/TR-1000 RVT Starfire			
1962-1967. Solidstate, 1x12" combo, 40 watts, tremolo, RVT with reverb.			
1962-1967		$350	$450

Ginelle

Rick Emery builds his tube combo amps in Ardmore, Pennsylvania starting in 1996.

Giulietti

1962-1965. The Giulietti Accordion Company, New York, offered guitars and amps in the '60s. The amps were made by Magnatone and the models and model numbers are often similar to the Magnatone model.

MODEL YEAR	FEATURES	EXC. COND. LOW	HIGH
Pearloid Lap Steel			
1962-1965. Small student level, 1x12", 2-channel, tremolo.			
1962-1965		$225	$300
S 1x12" Combo			
1962-1965. Tremolo, 2-channel.			
1962-1965		$1,050	$1,375
S-9 (Magnatone 460)			
1962-1965. 35 watts, 2x12 plus 2 tweeters, true vibrato combo, black sparkle.			
1962-1965		$1,500	$1,950

Gjika Amplification

1980-present. Premium and presentation grade tube amp heads and cabinets built by Robert Gjika in Escondido, California.

Gnome Amplifiers

Dan Munro builds professional grade, production, guitar amps and cabinets, starting in 2008, in Olympia, Washington. He also builds effects.

Gomez Amplification

2005-2015. Tube combo amps built by Dario G. Gomez in Rancho Santa Margarita, California.

Goodsell

2004-present. Tube head and combo amps built by Richard Goodsell in Atlanta, Georgia.

Gorilla

1980s-2009. Small solidstate entry-level amps, distributed by Pignose, Las Vegas, Nevada.
Compact Practice Student
1980s-2009. Solidstate, 10 to 30 watts, compact design.

MODEL YEAR	FEATURES	EXC. COND. LOW	HIGH
1980s-2009		$25	$50

Goya

1955-1996. Goya was mainly known for acoustics, but offered a few amps in the '60s. The brand was purchased by Avnet/Guild in '66 and by Martin in the late '70s.

Grammatico Amps

2009-present. Production/custom, professional and premium grade, hand-wired, guitar and bass amps built by John Grammatico in Austin, Texas.

Green

1993-present. Amp model line made in England by Matamp (see that brand for listing), bright green covering, large Green logo on the front.

Greer Amplification

1999-present. Tube guitar amps and speaker cabinets built by Nick Greer in Athens, Georgia. He also builds effects.

Gregory

1950s-1960s. Private branded amps sold via music wholesalers, by late '60s solidstate models made by

MODEL YEAR	FEATURES	EXC. COND. LOW	HIGH

Harmony including the 007, C.I.A., Mark Six, Mark Eight, Saturn 80, most models were combo amps with Gregory logo.

Solidstate

1950s-60s	Various models	$300	$400

Gretsch

1883-present. In '05, Gretsch again starting offering amps after previously selling them from the 1950s to '73. Initially private branded for them by Valco (look for the Valco oval or rectangular serialized label on the back). Early-'50s amps were covered in the requisite tweed, but evolved into the Gretsch charcoal gray covering. The mid-'50s to early-'60s amps were part of the Electromatic group of amps. The mid-'50s to '62 amps often sported wrap-around and slanted grilles. In '62, the more traditional box style was introduced. In '66, the large amps went piggyback. Baldwin-Gretsch began to phase out amps effective '65, but solidstate amps continued being offered for a period of time. The '73 Gretsch product line only offered Sonax amps, made in Canada and Sho-Bud amps made in the U.S. In '05, they introduced a line of tube combo amps made in U.S. by Victoria Amp Company.

Artist

1946. Early post-war Gretsch amp made before Valco began to make their amps. Appears to be made by Operadio Mfg. Co., St. Charles, Illinois. Low power small combo amp, Gretsch Artist script logo on grille, round speaker baffle hole.

1946		$325	$425

Broadkaster Mini Lead 50

Late-1960s. Solidstate compact verticle combo amp.

1969		$275	$360

Carousel

Early-1960s. Solidstate,1x10" and 1x3" speakers, tremolo speed and depth knobs, brown cover.

1960s		$725	$950

Electromatic (5222)

1947-1949. Valco-made with era-typical styling, 3 slat speaker baffle openings, leather handle, two-tone leatherette, 3 tubes with small speaker, single volume knob.

1947-1949		$800	$1,050

Electromatic Artist (6155)

1950s. Small amp, 2x6V6 power, 1x10", volume and tone knobs.

1950s		$675	$875

Electromatic Deluxe (6163)

1950s. 1x12", 2x6L6, brown tweed grille. Also offered in Western Finish.

1950s		$1,025	$1,325

Model 6150 Compact

Late-1950s-1960s. Early amps in tweed, '60s amps in gray covering, no tremolo, single volume knob, no treble or bass knob, 1x8".

1950s	Brown tweed	$550	$725
1960s	Gray	$550	$725

Model 6151 Electromatic Standard/Compact Tremolo

Late-1940s-late-1960s. 1x8", various covers.

1940s-60s		$550	$725

Model 6152 Compact Tremolo Reverb

Ca.1964-late-1960s. Five watts, 11"x6" elliptical speaker early on, 1x12" later.

1964-1969		$800	$1,050

Model 6153T White Princess

1962. Compact combo, 6x9" oval speaker, higher priced than the typical small amp because it is relatively rare and associated with the White Princess guitar - making it valuable in a set, condition is very important, an amp with any issues will be worth much less.

1962		$1,075	$1,400

Model 6154 Super-Bass

Early-1960s-mid-1960s. Gray covering, 2x12", 70 watts, tube.

1960s		$875	$1,150

Model 6156 Playboy

Early-1950s-1966. Tube amp, 17 watts, 1x10" until '61 when converted to 1x12", tweed, then gray, then finally black covered.

1950s-1960	Tweed, 1x10"	$775	$1,000
1961-1962	Tweed, 1x12"	$775	$1,000
1963-1966	Black or gray, 1x12"	$775	$1,000

Model 6156 Playboy (Reissue)

2005-2007. Model G6156, made by Victoria, 15 watts, 1x12" combo amp with retro Gretsch styling.

2005-2007		$1,275	$1,650

Model 6157 Super-Bass (Piggyback)

Mid-late-1960s. 35 watts, 2x15" cabinet, single channel.

1960s		$650	$850

Model 6159 Dual Bass

Mid-late-1960s. 35 watts, tube, 2x12" cabinet, dual channel, black covering. Replaced by 6163 Chet Atkins Piggyback Amp.

1960s		$850	$1,100

Model 6160 Chet Atkins Country Gentleman

Early-late-1960s. Combo tube amp, 35 watts, 2x12" cabinet, 2 channels. Replaced by 6163 Chet Atkins Piggyback amp with tremolo but no reverb.

1960s		$875	$1,150

Model 6161 Dual Twin Tremolo

Ca.1962-late-1960s. 19 watts (later 17 watts), 2x10" with 5" tweeter, tremolo.

1962-1967		$900	$1,175

Model 6161 Electromatic Twin

Ca.1953-ca.1960. Gray Silverflake covering, two 11x6" speakers, 14 watts, tremolo, wraparound grille '55 and after.

1953-1960		$1,025	$1,325

Model 6162 Dual Twin Tremolo/Reverb

Ca.1964-late-1960s. 17 watts, 2x10", reverb, tremolo. Vertical combo amp style introduced in '68.

1964-1967	Horizontal	$900	$1,175
1968-1969	Vertical	$800	$1,050

1947 Gretsch 5222 Electromatic
Imaged by Heritage Auctions, HA.com

Gretsch 6161 Electromatic Twin
Imaged by Heritage Auctions, HA.com

1969 Gretsch 6162 Dual Twin
Rivington Guitars

AMPS

Gretsch 7154 Nashville
Imaged by Heritage Auctions, HA.com

Gries 5

Guild Master
Imaged by Heritage Auctions, HA.com

MODEL YEAR	FEATURES	EXC. COND. LOW	HIGH
Model 6163 Chet Atkins (Piggyback)			
Mid-late-1960s. 70 watts, 1x12" and 1x15", black covering, tremolo, reverb.			
1960s		$775	$1,000
Model 6163 Executive			
1959. 1x15, gray cover.			
1959		$1,625	$2,100
Model 6163 Executive (Reissue)			
2005-2007. Model G6163, boutique quality made by Victoria for FMIC Gretsch, 20 watts, 1x15", cabinet Uses to the modern retro early '60s Supro Supreme modified-triangle front grille pattern, maroon baffle with white grille, tremolo and reverb.			
2005-2007		$1,275	$1,650
Model 6164 Variety			
Early-mid-1960s. 35 watts, tube, 2x12".			
1960s		$900	$1,175
Model 6165 Variety Plus			
Early-mid-1960s. Tube amp, 35 watts, 2x12", reverb and tremolo, separate controls for both channels.			
1960s		$950	$1,225
Model 6166 Fury (Combo)			
Mid-1960s. Tube combo stereo amp, 70 watts, 2x12", separate controls for both channels, large metal handle, reverb.			
1960s		$950	$1,225
Model 6169 Electromatic Twin Western			
Ca.1953-ca.1960. Western finish, 14 watts, 2-11x6" speakers, tremolo, wraparound grill '55 and after.			
1953-1960		$6,300	$8,200
Model 6169 Fury (Piggyback)			
Late-1960s. Tube amp, 70 watts, 2x12", separate controls for both channels.			
1960s		$950	$1,225
Model 6170 Pro Bass			
1966-late-1960s. 25 or 35 watts, depending on model, 1x15", vertical cabinet style (vs. box cabinet).			
1966-1969		$775	$1,000
Model 7154 Nashville			
Introduced in 1969. Solidstate combo amp, 4' tall, 75 watts, 2x15", reverb, tremolo, magic echo.			
1969-1970s		$550	$725
Model 7155 Tornado PA System			
Introduced in 1969. Solidstate piggyback head and cab, 150 watts, 2 column speaker cabs, reverb, tremolo, magic echo.			
1969-1970s 2x2x15"		$500	$650
1969-1970s 2x4x15"		$575	$750
Model 7517 Rogue			
1970s. Solidstate, 40 watts, 2x12", tall vertical cabinet, front control panel.			
1970s		$250	$325
Rex Royal Model M-197-3V			
1950s. Small student compact amp, low power, 1x8", Rex Royal logo on grille, Fred Gretsch logo on back panel, single on-off volume knob.			
1951		$450	$575

Gries

2004-present. Dave Gries builds his intermediate and professional grade, production/custom, amps and cabinets in Mattapoisett, Massachusetts.

Groove Tubes

1979-present. Started by Aspen Pittman in his garage in Sylmar, California, Groove Tubes is now located in San Fernando. GT manufactures and distributes a full line of tubes. In '86 they added amp production and in '91 tube microphones. Aspen is also the author of the Tube Amp Book. The Groove Tubes brand was purchased by Fender in June, '08.

Guild

1952-present. Guild offered amps from the '60s into the '80s. Some of the early models were built by Hagstrom.

MODEL YEAR	FEATURES	EXC. COND. LOW	HIGH
Double Twin			
1953-1955. 35 watts, 2x12" plus 2 tweeters, 2-tone leatherette covered cab.			
1953-1955		$1,050	$1,375
G-1000 Stereo			
1992-1994. Stereo acoustic combo amp with cushioned seat on top, 4x6 and 1x10 speakers.			
1992-1994		$700	$900
Master			
Ca. 1957- Ca. 1959. Combo 2x6L6 power, tremolo, 2-tone tweed and leatherette.			
1957-1959		$575	$750
Maverick			
Late-1960s-early-1970s. Dual speaker combo, 6 tubes, verticle cab, tremolo, reverb, red/pink control panel, 2-tone black and silver grille.			
1960s-70s		$500	$650
Model One			
Mid-1970s-1977. Solidstate 1x12" vertical cab combo, 30 watts, reverb and tremolo.			
1970s		$200	$260
Model Two			
Mid-1970s-1977. Solidstate 2x10" vertical cab combo, 50 watts, reverb and tremolo.			
1977-1978		$275	$360
Model Three			
Mid-1970s-1977. Solidstate 1x15" vertical cab bass combo, 60 watts, organ and guitar.			
1977-1978		$225	$290
Model Four			
Early-1980s. Solidstate, 6 watts.			
1980s		$125	$165
Model Five			
Early-1980s. Solidstate, 10 watts, 6.25" speaker.			
1980s		$200	$260
Model Six			
Early-1980s. Same as Model Five but with reverb.			
1980s		$225	$290
Model Seven			
Early-1980s. Solidstate, 12 watts, small amp for guitar, bass and keyboard.			
1980s		$225	$290
Model 50-J			
Early-1960s. 14 watts, 1x12", tremolo, blue/gray vinyl.			
1962-1963		$700	$900
Model 66			
1953-1955. 15 watts, 1x12", tremolo, 2-tone leatherette.			
1953-1955		$700	$900

MODEL YEAR	FEATURES	EXC. COND. LOW	HIGH
Model 66-J			
1962-1963. 20 watts, 1x12", tremolo, blue/gray vinyl.			
1962-1963		$700	$900
Model 98-RT			
1962-1963. The only stand-alone reverb amp from Guild in the early '60s, 30 watts, 1x12", blue/gray vinyl.			
1962-1963		$850	$1,100
Model 99			
1953-1955. 30 watts, 1x12", tremolo, 2-tone leatherette.			
1953-1955		$675	$875
Model 99-J			
Early-1960s. 30 watts, 1x12", tremolo, blue/gray vinyl.			
1962-1963		$675	$875
Model 99-U Ultra			
Early-1960s. Piggyback 30-watt head with optional 1x12" or 1x15" cab, cab and head lock together, tremolo, blue/gray vinyl.			
1962-1963		$700	$900
Model 100-J			
Early-1960s. 35 watts, 1x15", blue/gray vinyl.			
1962-1963		$700	$900
Model 200-S Stereo Combo			
Early-1960s. 25 watts per channel, total 50 watts stereo, 2x12", tremolo, blue/gray vinyl, wheat grille.			
1962-1963		$975	$1,275
Model RC-30 Reverb Converter			
Early-1960s. Similar to Gibson GA-1 converter, attaches with 2 wires clipped to originating amp's speaker, 8 watts, 1x10", blue/gray vinyl.			
1962-1963		$700	$900
Superbird			
1968. Piggyback tube amp with 2x12 cab.			
1968		$800	$1,050
SuperStar			
Ca.1972-ca.1974. 50 watts, all tubes, 1x15" Jensen speakers, vertical combo, reverb, tremolo, black vinyl cover, 2-tone black/silver grille.			
1972-1974		$575	$750
Thunder 1			
1965-1972. Combo with single speaker, no reverb, light tan cover, 2-tone tan grille.			
1965-1972	1x10"	$400	$525
1965-1972	1x12"	$425	$550
Thunder 1 (Model T1-RVT)/T1			
1965-1972. Combo with dual speakers and reverb, light tan cover, 2-tone tan grille.			
1965-1972		$700	$900
ThunderBass			
1965-1972. Piggyback combo, 2x15".			
1965-1972	100-watt	$700	$900
1965-1972	200-watt	$725	$950
ThunderBird			
1965-1972. 50 watts, tube, 2x12", reverb, tremolo, with or without TD-1 dolly, black vinyl, black/silver grille.			
1965-1972		$700	$900
ThunderStar Bass			
1965-1972. Piggyback bass tube head or combo, 50 watts.			
1965-1972	Full stack, 2x1x15"	$800	$1,050
1965-1972	Half stack, 1x1x15"	$700	$900

MODEL YEAR	FEATURES	EXC. COND. LOW	HIGH
ThunderStar Guitar			
1965-1972. Combo, 50 watts, 1x12".			
1965-1972		$700	$900

Guyatone

1933-present. Started offering amps by at least the late '40s with their Guya lap steels. In '51 the Guyatone brand is first used on guitars and most likely amps. Guyatone also made the Marco Polo, Winston, Kingston, Kent, LaFayette and Bradford brands.

Guytron

1995-present. Tube amp heads and speaker cabinets built by Guy Hedrick in Columbiaville, Michigan. In January, '09, GDS Amplification bought the assets of Guytron Amplification.

Hagstrom

1921-1983, 2004-present. The Swedish guitar maker built a variety of tube and solidstate amps from ca. 1961 into the '70s. They also supplied amps to Guild.

Hanburt

1940-ca. 1950. Harvey M. Hansen built electric Hawaiian guitars in Seattle, Washington, some sold as a set with a small amp. The wooden amps have a large HB in the speaker cutout. He also built at least one mandolin.

Harmony

1892-1976, late-1970s-present. Harmony was one of the biggest producers of guitars, and offered amps as well. MBT International offered Harmony amps for 2000-'02.

H Series

1940s-1960s. Harmony model numbers begin with H, such as H-304, all H series models shown are tube amps unless otherwise noted as solidstate.

1940s-50s	H-190/H-191	$450	$575
1940s-50s	H-200	$450	$575
1950s	H-204, 18w, 1x12	$450	$575
1960s	H-303A, 8w, 1x8	$240	$315
1960s	H-304, low power	$240	$315
1960s	H-305A, low power	$240	$315
1960s	H-306A, 1x12	$360	$470
1960s	H-306C, 2x12	$420	$550
1960s	H-400, vol	$210	$275
1960s	H-400A, vol/tone	$240	$315
1960s	H-410A, 10w, 1x10	$420	$540
1960s	H-415, 18w, 2x12	$540	$715
1960s	H-420, 20w, 1x15	$450	$575
1960s	H-430, 30w, 2x10	$550	$700
1960s	H-440, 2x12, trem/verb	$600	$775
1960s	H-512, solidstate	$630	$810
1960s	H-530, solidstate	$550	$700

Solidstate

1970s. Various models, dark covering, dark grille.

1970s	Large models	$200	$660
1970s	Small models	$30	$55

Guytron GT100 F/V

1963 Harmony H-303A
Rivington Guitars

1965 Harmony H400A
Imaged by Heritage Auctions, HA.com

AMPS

Harry Joyce Classic 30 Watt

AMPS

Headstrong Lil' King

Headstrong Santa Cruz 20

MODEL YEAR	FEATURES	EXC. COND. LOW	HIGH

Harry Joyce

1993-2011, 2015-present. Hand-wired British tube amps, combos, and cabinets from builder/designer Harry Joyce. Joyce was contracted to build Hiwatt amps in England during the '70s. Joyce died in 2002, and the brand was carried on by Charles Bertonazzi and George Scholz until 2011. Brand brought back by Kevin Wood and Scholz through Harry Joyce USA with new versions of the classic models.

Hartke

1984-present. Guitar and bass amps, combos and cabinets made in the U.S. Founded by Larry Hartke, since the mid-'80s, Hartke has been distributed by Samson Technologies. Hartke also offered basses in the past.

Haynes

Haynes guitar amps were built by the Amplifier Corporation of America (ACA) of Westbury, New York. ACA also made an early distortion device powered by batteries. Unicord purchased the company in around 1964, and used the factory to produce its Univox line of amps, most likely discontinuing the Haynes brand at the same time.

Jazz King II
1960s. Solidstate, stereo console-style, 2x12", Haynes logo upper left side.

1960s		$400	$525

Headstrong

2003-present. Tube combo amps and cabinets built by Wayne Jones in Asheville, North Carolina.

Henriksen JazzAmp

2006-present. Professional grade, production, solidstate amps voiced for jazz guitar built by Peter Henriksen in Golden, Colorado.

Heritage

Founded in 2004 by Malcolm MacDonald and Lane Zastrow who was formerly involved with Holland amps. Located in the former Holland facility in Brentwood, Tennessee, they built tube combo and piggyback amps.

Hilgen

1960s. Mid-level amplifiers from Hilgen Manufacturing, Hillside, New Jersey. Dark tolex covering and swiggle-lined light color grille cloth. Examples have been found with original Jensen speakers.

Basso B-2501
1960s. 25 watts, 1x15" combo, swirl grille, Hilgen crest logo, compact size.

1965		$450	$590

Basso B-2502
1960s. 25 watts, 1x15" combo, swirl grille, Hilgen crest logo, large cab.

1965		$500	$650

Basso Grande B-2503
1960s. Brown sparkle cover, piggyback, 2x12".

1965		$650	$850

MODEL YEAR	FEATURES	EXC. COND. LOW	HIGH

Basso Profondo B-2502
1965. Combo 1x15".

1965		$500	$650

Champion R-2523
Mid-1960s. Highest offering in their amp line, piggyback with 2x12" cab, tremolo, reverb, swirl grille cloth.

1965		$650	$850

Galaxie T-2513
1960s. 25 watts, 2x12" piggyback cab, tremolo.

1965		$650	$850

Metero T-2511
Mid-1960s. Compact 1x12" combo, tremolo.

1965		$500	$650

Pacesetter R-2521
Mid-1960s. 1x12" combo, tremolo, reverb, swirl grille cloth.

1965		$500	$650

Star T-2512
1960s. 25 watts, 1x12" combo, tremolo.

1965		$500	$650

Troubadour T-1506
Mid-1960s. Small practice amp.

1965		$350	$450

Victor R-2522
Mid-1960s. 1x12" combo, larger cab, reverb, tremolo.

1965		$650	$850

HiWatt

1963-1984, ca.1990-present. Amp builder Dave Reeves started his Hylight Electronics in a garage in England in the early 1960s, doing amp and other electronic repairs. By 1964 he had produced the first amps bearing the Hiwatt brand. By the early '70s, Hiwatt's reputation was growing and production was moved to a factory in Kingston-upon-Thames, expanding the amp line and adding PA gear. In '81, Reeves suffered a fatal fall, and ownership of Hiwatt was taken over by Biacrown Ltd, a company made up of Hiwatt employees. Biacrown struggled and closed up in '84. From ca.1990 to ca.1994, a line of American-made Hiwatts, designed by Frank Levi, were available. By the mid-'90s, amps with the Hiwatt brand were again being built in England and, separately, imported from Asia by Fernandes.

Bass 100 Head

1980s	100w, England	$1,700	$2,200

Bulldog SA112
1980s, 1994-2019. 50 watts, combo, 1x12".

1980s		$1,500	$2,000
1994-2019		$1,425	$1,900

Bulldog SA112FL
1980s-1990s. 100 watts, combo, 1x12".

1980s		$1,500	$2,000
1990s		$1,425	$1,900

Custom 100 Head

2007	100w	$1,700	$2,200

DR-103 Custom 100 Head
1970-late-1980s, 2005-present. Tube head, 100 watts, custom Hiwatt 100 logo on front.

1970-1980s		$2,700	$3,500

MODEL YEAR	FEATURES	EXC. COND. LOW	HIGH
DR-201 Hiwatt 200 Head			
1970s. 200-watt amp head, Hiwatt 200 logo on front.			
1970s		$2,700	$3,500
DR-405 Hiwatt 400 Head			
1970s. 400-watt amp head.			
1970s		$2,700	$3,500
DR-504 Custom 50 Head			
1970-late-1980s, 1995-1999. Tube head, 50 watts.			
1970-1980s		$2,700	$3,500
Lead 20 (SG-20) Head			
1980s. Tube amp head, 30 watts, black cover, rectangular HiWatt plate logo.			
1980s		$750	$975
Lead 50R Combo			
1980s. Combo tube amp, 50 watts, 1x12", reverb, dark cover, dark grille, HiWatt rectangular plate logo.			
1980s		$1,100	$1,450
OL-103 Lead 100 Head			
1982	100w, England	$1,575	$2,100
PW-50 Tube			
1989-1993. Stereo tube amp, 50 watts per channel.			
1989-1993		$1,075	$1,400
S50L Head			
1989-1993. Lead guitar head, 50 watts, gain, master volume, EQ.			
1989-1993		$900	$1,200
SA 112 Combo			
1970s	50w, 1x12"	$3,200	$4,200
SA 212 Combo			
1970s	50w, 2x12"	$3,450	$4,500
SA 412 Combo			
1970s	50w, 4x12"	$4,300	$5,600
SE 2150 Speaker Cabinet			
1970s	2x15" vertical	$2,300	$2,900
SE 4121 Speaker Cabinet			
1970s	4x12", half stack	$2,400	$3,100
SE 4122 (Lead) Speaker Cabinet			
1971- mid-1980s. 4x12", Fane speakers, 300 watts.			
1971-1980s	4x12", half stack	$2,425	$3,150
SE 4123 (Bass) Speaker Cabinet			
1970s. Bass version of SE, often used with DR103 head, straight-front cab and stackable, black tolex with gray grille, Hiwatt logo plate in center of grille.			
1970s	4x12", half stack	$2,425	$3,150
SE 4129 (Bass) Speaker Cabinet			
1970s. SE series for bass, 4x12", often used with DR 201 head.			
1970s		$2,425	$3,150
SE 4151 Speaker Cabinet			
1970s. SE series with 4x15".			
1970s		$2,425	$3,150

Hoagland

Professional grade, production, guitar amps built by Dan Hoagland in Land O Lakes, Florida starting in 2008.

Hoffman

1993-present. Tube amps, combos, reverb units, and cabinets built by Doug Hoffman from 1993 to '99, in Sarasota, Florida. Hoffman no longer builds amps, concentrating on selling tube amp building supplies, and since 2001 has been located in Pisgah Forest, North Carolina.

Hoffmann

1983-present. Tube amp heads for guitar and other musical instruments built by Kim Hoffmann in Hawthorne, California.

Hohner

1857-present. Matthias Hohner, a clockmaker in Trossingen, Germany, founded Hohner in 1857, making harmonicas. Hohner has been offering guitars and amps at least since the early '70s.

Panther Series

MODEL YEAR	FEATURES	EXC. COND. LOW	HIGH
1980s. Smaller combo amps, master volume, gain, EQ.			
1980s	P-12, 12w	$75	$95
1980s	P-20, 20w	$75	$95
1980s	P-25R, 25w	$75	$95
1980s	PBK-20, 25w	$80	$105

Sound Producer Series

MODEL YEAR	FEATURES	EXC. COND. LOW	HIGH
1980s. Master volume, normal and overdrive, reverb, headphone jack.			
1980s	BA 130 bass	$80	$105
1980s	SP 35	$80	$105
1980s	SP 55	$80	$105
1980s	SP 75	$90	$120

Holland

1992-2004. Tube combo amps from builder Mike Holland, originally in Virginia Beach, Virginia, and since 2000 in Brentwood, Tennessee. In 2000, Holland took Lane Zastrow as a partner, forming L&M Amplifiers to build the Holland line. The company closed in '04.

Holmes

1970-late 1980s. Founded by Harrison Holmes. Holmes amplifiers were manufactured in Mississippi and their product line included guitar and bass amps, PA systems, and mixing boards. In the early '80s, Harrsion Holmes sold the company to On-Site Music which called the firm The Holmes Corp. Products manufactured by Harrison have an all-caps HOLMES logo and the serial number plate says The Holmes Company.

Performer PB-115 Bass

MODEL YEAR	FEATURES	EXC. COND. LOW	HIGH
60 watts, 1x15", black tolex.			
1980s		$140	$180

Pro Compact 210S

MODEL YEAR	FEATURES	EXC. COND. LOW	HIGH
60 watts, 2x10", 2 channels, active EQ, black tolex.			
1980s		$140	$180

Pro Compact 212S

MODEL YEAR	FEATURES	EXC. COND. LOW	HIGH
2x12" version of Pro.			
1980s		$170	$220

Rebel RB-112 Bass

MODEL YEAR	FEATURES	EXC. COND. LOW	HIGH
35 watts, 1x12", black tolex.			
1980s		$140	$180

HiWatt Bulldog SA112

AMPS

1977 HiWatt DR-505 Head
Imaged by Heritage Auctions, HA.com

Hoffmann 15

Hottie Super Chef

Hughes & Kettner Duotone

Humphrey

MODEL YEAR	FEATURES	EXC. COND. LOW	HIGH

Hondo

1969-1987, 1991-2005. Hondo has offered imported amps over the years. 1990s models ranged from the H20 Practice Amp to the H160SRC with 160 watts (peak) and 2x10" speakers.

Various Models

1970s-90s	Mid-size	$70	$100
1970s-90s	Small	$35	$70

Hottie

Jean-Claude Escudie and Mike Bernards build their budget and intermediate grade, production/custom, solid state "toaster" amps in Portland, Oregon, starting in 2005. They also offered guitars in '09.

Hound Dog

1994-1998. Founded by George Alessandro as the Hound Dog Corporation. Name was changed to Alessandro in 1998 (see that brand for more information).

Hughes & Kettner

1985-present. Hughes & Kettner offers a line of solidstate and tube guitar and bass amps, combos, cabinets and effects, all made in Germany.

Humphrey

2010-present. Custom, professional and premium grade, tube amps built in Chanhassen, Minnesota by Gerry Humphrey. He also builds preamps and reverb units.

Hurricane

Tube guitar and harmonica combo amps built by Gary Drouin in Sarasota, Florida. Drouin started the company in 1998 with harp master Rock Bottom, who died in September, 2001.

Hy Lo

1960s-1970s. Budget grade, small compact amps made in Japan, Hy Lo logo on grille.

Ibanez

1932-present. Ibanez added solidstate amps to their product line in '98. They also build guitars, basses and effects.

Idol

Late-1960s. Made in Japan. Dark tolex cover, dark grille, Hobby Series with large Idol logo on front.

Hobby Series

1968	Hobby 10	$110	$145
1968	Hobby 100	$225	$300
1968	Hobby 20	$125	$165
1968	Hobby 45	$200	$260

Impact

1963-early 1970s. Based in London, England, tube amps made by Don Mackrill and Laurie Naiff for Pan Musical Instrument Company and their music stores. About a dozen different models of combos, piggyback half-stacks and PAs were offered.

Imperial

Ca.1963-ca.1970. The Imperial Accordion Company of Chicago, Illinois offered one or two imported small amps in the '60s.

Jack Daniel's

2004-2017. Tube guitar amp built by Peavey for the Jack Daniel Distillery, offered until about '10. They offered guitars until '17.

Jackson

1980-present. The Jackson-Charvel Company offered budget to intermediate grade amps and cabinets in the late '80s and the '90s.

Jackson Ampworks

2001-present. Brad Jackson builds his tube amp heads and speaker cabinets in Bedford, Texas.

Jackson-Guldan

1920s-1960s. The Jackson-Guldan Violin Company, of Columbus, Ohio, offered lap steels and small tube amps early on. They also built acoustic guitars.

Jay Turser

1997-present. Smaller, inexpensive imported solidstate guitar and bass amps. They also offer basses and guitars.

JCA Circuits

Tube guitar combo amps built by Jason C. Arthur in Pottstown, Pennsylvania, starting in 1995.

Jennings

Late 1960s. Tom Jennings formed another company after resigning from Vox. Large block letter Jennings logo on front panel, Jennings Amplifier logo on back control plate with model number and serial number.

Jet City Amplification

2009-present. Budget to professional grade, production/custom, guitar amps and cabinets designed in Seattle, Washington by Doug White, Dan Gallagher, Michael Soldano and built in Asia.

Jim Kelley

1979-1985. Channel-switching tube amps, compact combos and heads, hardwood cabinets available, made by Jim Kelley at his Active Guitar Electronics in Tustin, California. He produced about 100 amps a year. In 1978 and early '79 he produced a few amps under the Fortune brand name for Fortune Guitars.

AMPS

MODEL		EXC. COND.	
YEAR	FEATURES	LOW	HIGH

JMI (Jennings Musical Industries)

2004-present. Tom Jennings built the Vox amps of the 1960s. They are back with tube amp heads and cabinets based on some of their classic models. Large block letter Jennings logo on front panel, Jennings Amplifier logo on back control plate with model number and serial number. They also offer effects.

Johnson

Mid-1990s-present. Line of solidstate amps imported by Music Link, Brisbane, California. Johnson also offers guitars, basses, mandolins and effects.

Johnson Amplification

Starting in 1997, intermediate and professional grade, production, modeling amps and effects designed by John Johnson, of Sandy, Utah. The company is part of Harman International. In 2002, they quit building amps, but continue the effects line.

JoMama

1994-present. Tube amps and combos under the JoMama and Kelemen brands built by Joe Kelemen in Santa Fe, New Mexico.

Jordan

1966-early 1970s. Jordan Electronics, of Alhambra, California, built a range of electronics, including, starting around 1966, solid state guitar amps and effects.

Juke

1989-present. Tube guitar and harmonica amps built by G.R. Croteau in Troy, New Hampshire. He also built the Warbler line of amps.

Kafel

Jack Kafel built his tube amp heads in Chicago, Illinois, starting in 2004.

Kalamazoo

1933-1942, 1965-1970. Kalamazoo was a brand Gibson used on one of their budget lines. They used the name on amps from '65 to '67.

Bass

1965-1967. Enclosed back, 2x10", flip-out control panel, not a commonly found model as compared to numerous Model 1 and 2 student amps.

1965-1967		$650	$850

Bass 30

Late 1960s-early 1970s. Tube combo, verticle cabinet, 2x10".

1970		$500	$650

KEA

1948-1952. Small compact amp, round speaker baffle grille, slant Kalamazoo logo on front, oxblood leatherette.

1948-1952		$525	$675

Lap Steel

1940s. Kalamazoo logo on front lower right, low power with 1-6V6, round speaker grille opening, red/brown leatherette.

1940s		$450	$585

Model 1

1965-1967. No tremolo, 1x10", front control panel, black.

1965-1967		$325	$425

Model 2

1965-1967. Same as Model 1 with tremolo, black.

1965-1967	Black panel	$425	$550
1967	Silver panel	$250	$325

Model 3

Late 1960s-early 1970s. Made by CMI Electronics in Chicago, post Gibson Kalamazoo era, student compact solidstate combo, Kalamazoo 3 logo on front panel, Kalamazoo Model 3 logo on label on speaker magnet.

1960s-70s		$115	$150

Model 4

Late 1960s-early 1970s. Made by CMI Electronics in Chicago, post Gibson Kalamazoo era, student compact solidstate combo, 3 control knobs, tone, tremolo, volume, Kalamazoo 4 logo on front panel, Kalamazoo Model 4 logo on label on speaker magnet.

1960s-70s		$115	$150

Reverb 12

1965-1967. Black vinyl cover, 1x12", reverb, tremolo.

1965-1967		$650	$850

Kay

Ca.1931-present. Kay originally offered amps up to around '68 when the brand changed hands. Currently they offer a couple small solidstate imported amps. They also make basses, guitars, banjos, mandolins, ukes, and violins.

K506 Vibrato 12

1960s. 12 watts, 1x12", swirl grille, metal handle.

1960s		$500	$650

K507 Twin Ten Special

1960s. 20 watts, 2x10", swirl grille, metal handle.

1960s		$550	$725

K700 Series

Introduced in 1965. Value Leader/Vanguard/Galazie models, transistorized amps promoted as eliminates tube-changing annoyance and reliable performance, combo amps with tapered cabinets, rear slant control panel, rich brown and tan vinyl cover, brown grille cloth.

1965	K700, 1x8	$150	$200
1965	K703, 1x8	$150	$200
1965	K704, 1x8	$150	$200
1965	K705, 1x10	$175	$225
1965	K706, 1x15	$175	$225
1965	K707, 1x12	$175	$225
1965	K708, 1x12	$175	$225
1965	K720 Bass, 1x15	$175	$225
1966	K760, 1x12	$175	$225

Jackson Ampworks The McFly

Jordan Entertainer J 110
Rivington Guitars

Kalamazoo Bass 30
Rivington Guitars

AMPS

Kelemen JoMama OverDrive

Kendrick Double Trouble

Kingsley ToneBaron

MODEL YEAR	FEATURES	EXC. COND. LOW	HIGH
Model 703			
1962-1964. Tube student amp, small speaker, 3 tubes, 1 volume, 1 tone, 2-tone white front with brown back cabinet, metal handle, model number noted on back panel, Kay logo and model number badge lower front right.			
1962-1964		$275	$360
Model 803			
1962-1964. Student amp, 1x8", 3 tubes, 1 volume, 1 tone, metal handle, 14.75x11.75x6.75" cabinet with dark gray cover.			
1962-1964		$275	$360
Model 805			
1965. Solidstate, 35 watts, 1x10", 4 control knobs, 2-tone cabinet.			
1965		$150	$200
Small Tube			
1940s	Wood cabinet	$375	$500
1950s	Various models	$375	$500
1960s	Models K503, K504,		
	K505	$425	$550

Kelemen

1994-present. Tube amps and combos under the JoMama and Kelemen brands built by Joe Kelemen in Santa Fe, New Mexico.

Kendrick

1989-present. Founded by Gerald Weber in Austin, Texas and currently located in Kempner, Texas. Mainly known for their intermediate to professional grade, tube amps, Kendrick also offers guitars, speakers, and effects.

Kent

Ca.1962-1969. Imported budget line of guitars and amps.

Guitar and Bass

1960s. Various models.

1960s	1475	$75	$100
1960s	2198	$75	$100
1960s	5999	$100	$130
1960s	6104	$150	$200
1960s	6610	$50	$65

Kiesel

See Guitar section.

King Amplification

Tube combo amps, head and cabinets built by Val King in San Jose, California startin in 2005.

Kingsley

1998-present. Production/custom, professional grade, tube amps and cabinets built by Simon Jarrett in Vancouver, British Columbia.

Kingston

1958-1967. Economy solidstate amps imported by Westheimer Importing, Chicago, Illinois.

MODEL YEAR	FEATURES	EXC. COND. LOW	HIGH
Cat Series			
Mid-1960s. Solidstate Cat Series amps have dark vinyl, dark grilles.			
1960s	P-1 3w	$75	$100
1960s	P-2, 5w	$75	$100
1960s	P-3, 8w	$80	$105
1960s	P-8T, 20w	$80	$105
Cougar BA-21 Bass Piggyback			
Mid-1960s. Solidstate, 60 watts, 2x12" cab, dark vinyl, light silver grille.			
1960s		$150	$200
Cougar PB-5 Bass Combo			
Mid-1960s. Solidstate, 15 watts, 1x8".			
1960s		$85	$110
Lion 2000 Piggyback			
Mid-1960s. Solidstate, 90 watts, 2x12" cab.			
1960s		$190	$250
Lion 3000 Piggyback			
Mid-1960s. Solidstate, 250 watts, 4x12" cab.			
1960s		$225	$300
Lion AP-281 R Piggyback			
Mid-1960s. Solidstate, 30 watts, 2x8" cab, dark vinyl cover, light silver grille.			
1960s		$150	$200
Lion AP-281 R10 Piggyback			
Mid-1960s. Solidstate, 30 watts, 2x10" cab.			
1960s		$175	$225

Kinsman

2012-present. Budget and intermediate grade, production, guitar amps and cabinets built in China and distributed worldwide by John Hornby Skewes & Co. Ltd. in England. They also use the brand on a line of guitar effects.

Kitchen-Marshall

1965-1966. Private branded for Kitchen Music by Marshall, primarily PA units with block logos. Limited production.

JTM 45 MKII 45-Watt Head

1965-1966. Private branded for Kitchen Music, JTM 45 Marshall with Kitchen logo plate, 45 watts.

1965-1966		$7,200	$9,400

Slant 4x12 1960 Cabinet

1965-1966. Slant front 4x12" 1960-style cab with gray bluesbreaker grille, black on green vinyl, very limited production.

1965-1966		$4,400	$5,700

KJL

1995-present. Founded by Kenny Lannes, MSEE, a professor of Electrical Engineering at the University of New Orleans. KJL makes budget to intermediate grade, tube combo amps, heads and an ABY box.

KMD (Kaman)

1986-ca.1990. Distributed by Kaman (Ovation, Hamer, etc.) in the late '80s, KMD offered a variety of amps and effects.

Koch

All-tube combo amps, heads, effects and cabinets built in The Netherlands.

Komet

1999-present. Intermediate to professional grade, tube amp heads built in Baton Rouge, Louisanna, by Holger Notzel and Michael Kennedy with circuits designed by Ken Fischer of Trainwreck fame. They also build a power attenuator.

Kona Guitar Company

2001-present. Budget solidstate amps made in Asia. They also offer guitars, basses, mandolins, ukes and banjos.

Krank

1996-2013, 2015-2020. Founded by Tony Krank and offering tube amp heads, combos and speaker cabinets built in Tempe, Arizona. They also built effects.

Kustom

1965-present. Kustom, a division of Hanser Holdings, offers guitar and bass combo amps and PA equipment. Founded by Bud Ross in Chanute, Kansas, who offered tuck-and-roll amps as early as '58, but began using the Kustom brand name in '65. From '69 to '75 Ross gradually sold interest in the company (in the late '70s, Ross introduced the line of Ross effects stomp boxes). The brand changed hands a few times, and by the mid-'80s it was no longer in use. In '89 Kustom was in bankruptcy court and was purchased by Hanser Holdings Incorporated of Cincinnati, Ohio (Davitt & Hanser) and by '94, they had a new line of amps available.

Prices are for excellent condition amps with no tears in the tuck-and-roll cover and no grille tears. A tear in the tuck-and-roll will reduce the value, sometimes significantly.

Kustom model identification can be frustrating as they used series numbers, catalog numbers (the numbers in the catalogs and price lists), and model numbers (the number often found next to the serial number on the amp's back panel). Most of the discussion that follows is by series number (100, 200, 300, etc.) and catalog number. Unfortunately, vintage amp dealers use the serial number and model number, so the best way is to cross-check speaker and amplifier attributes. Model numbers were used primarily for repair purposes and were found in the repair manuals. In many, but not all cases, the model number is the last digit of the catalog number; for example the catalog lists a 100 series Model 1-15J-1, where the last digit 1 signifies a Model 1 amplifier chassis which is a basic amp without reverb or tremolo. A Model 1-15J-2 signifies a Model 2 amp chassis that has reverb and tremolo. In this example, Kustom uses a different model number on the back of the amp head. For the 1-15J-2, the model number on the back panel of the amp head would be K100-2, indicating a series 100 (50 watts) amp with reverb and tremolo (amp chassis Model 2).

Model numbers relate to the amplifier's schematic and electronics, while catalog numbers describe the amp's relative power rating and speaker configuration.

Amp Chasis Model Numbers ('68-'72)
Model 1 Amp (basic)
Model 2 Amp with reverb
Model 3 Amp with Harmonic Clip and Boost
Model 4 Amp with reverb, tremolo, vibrato, Harmonic Clip and Selective Boost
Model 5 PA with reverb
Model 6 Amp (basic) with Selectone
Model 7 Amp with reverb, tremolo, vibrato, boost (different parts)
Model 8 Amp with reverb, tremolo, vibrato, boost (different parts)

Naugahyde Tuck-&-Roll 200 ('65-'67)
The very first Kustoms did not have the model series on the front control panel. The early logo stipulated Kustom by Ross, Inc. The name was then updated to Kustom Electronics, Inc. 1965-'67 amp heads have a high profile/tall "forehead" area (the area on top of the controls) and these have been nicknamed "Frankenstein models" The '65-'67 catalog numbers were often 4 or 5 digits, for example J695. The first digit represents the speaker type (J = Jensen, etc.), other examples are L995, L1195, L795RV, etc. Some '67 catalog numbers changed to 2 digits followed by 3 digits, like 4-D 140f, or 3-15C (3 CTS speakers), etc. Others sported 5 characters like 4-15J-1, where 4 = 4 speakers, 15 = 15" speakers, J = Jensen, and 1 = basic amp chassis with no effects. The fifth digit indicated amp chassis model number as described above.

Naugahyde Tuck-&-Roll 100/200/400 ('68-'71)
Starting in '68, the Kustom logo also included the model series. A K100, for example, would have 100 displayed below the Kustom name. The model series generally is twice the relative output wattage, for example, the 100 Series is a 50-watt amp. Keep in mind, solidstate ratings are often higher than tube-amp ratings, so use the ratings as relative measurements. Most '68-'70 Kustom catalog numbers are x-xxx-x, for example 1-15L-1. First digit represents the number of speakers, the 2nd and 3rd represent the speaker size, the fourth represents the speaker type (A = Altec Lansing, L = J.B.L., J = Jensen, C = C.T.S. Bass), the fifth digit represents the amp chassis number. The power units were interchangeable in production, so amps could have similar front-ends but different power units (more power and different effect options) and visa versa. Some '68 bass amp catalog numbers were 4 digits, for example 2-12C, meaning two 12" CTS speakers. Again, there were several different numbers used. Kustom also introduced the 200 and 400 amp series and the logo included the series number. The catalog numbers were similar to the 100 series, but they had a higher power rating of 100 equivalent watts (200 series), or 200 equivalent watts (400 series). Kustom U.S. Naugahyde (tuck-&-roll) covers came in 7 colors: black (the most common), Cascade (blue/green), silver (white-silver), gold (light gold), red, blue, and Charcoal (gray). The market

KJL Companion

Koch Ventura

Komet Songwriter 30

Kustom Hustler
Imaged by Heritage Auctions, HA.com

1971 Kustom K100
Bob Calla

1971 Kustom K150-8
Tom Pfeifer

historically shows color options fetching more. The market has not noticeably distinguished power and features options. Condition and color seem to be the most important. Gold and Cascade may be the rarest seen colors.

Naugahyde Tuck-&-Roll 150/250/300/500/600 (c.'71-c.'75)

The amp heads changed with a slightly slanted control panel and the Kustom logo moved to the right/upper-right portion of the front panel. They continued to be tuck-&-roll offered in the same variety of colors. The sales literature indicated a 150 series had 150 watts, 250 had 250 watts, etc.

Naugahyde Tuck-&-Roll SC (Self Contained) Series

Most SC combo amps were rated at 150 watts, with the 1-12SC listed at 50 watts. They were offered in 7 colors of tuck-and-roll. Again the model numbers indicate the features as follows: 4-10 SC is a 4 x 10", 2-10 SC is a 2x10", etc.

Super Sound Tuck-and-Roll Combo Series

The last tuck-and-roll combo amps with slightly smaller tucks. Amp control panel is noticeably smaller and the Kustom logo is in the right side of the control panel.

Black Vinyl ('75-c.'78)

By '75 ownership changes were complete and the colorful tuck-and-roll was dropped in favor of more traditional black vinyl. The products had a slant Kustom logo spelled-out and placed in a position on the grille similar to a Fender blackface baffle. Models included the I, II, III, and IV Lead amps. Heads with half- and full-stacks were available. Bass amps included the Kustom 1, Bass I, II, III, IV, and IV SRO.

Black Vinyl K logo ('78-'83)

This era is easily recognized by the prominent capital K logo.

Bass V

1990s. Large Kustom Bass V logo upper right side of amp, 35 watts, 1x12", black vinyl.

MODEL YEAR	FEATURES	EXC. COND. LOW	HIGH
1990s		$85	$110

Challenger Combo

1973-1975. 1x12" speaker.

MODEL YEAR	FEATURES	EXC. COND. LOW	HIGH
1973-1975	Black	$275	$350
1973-1975	Color option	$375	$475

Hustler Combo

1973-1975. Solidstate, 4x10", tremolo, tuck-and-roll.

MODEL YEAR	FEATURES	EXC. COND. LOW	HIGH
1973-1975	Black	$300	$400
1973-1975	Color option	$400	$525

K25/K25 C-2 SC

1960s. SC (self-contained) Series, small combo tuck-and-roll, 1x12", solidstate, reverb, black control panel.

MODEL YEAR	FEATURES	EXC. COND. LOW	HIGH
1971-1973	Black	$275	$350
1971-1973	Color option	$400	$525

K50-2 SC

1971-1973. Self-contained (SC) small combo tuck-and-roll, 1x12", reverb and tremolo.

MODEL YEAR	FEATURES	EXC. COND. LOW	HIGH
1971-1973	Black	$275	$350

MODEL YEAR	FEATURES	EXC. COND. LOW	HIGH
1971-1973	Color option	$400	$525

K100-1 1-15C Bass Set

1968-1972. The K100-1 with 1-15C speaker option with matching 1x15" cab, black tuck-and-roll standard, but several sparkle colors offered, C.T.S. bass reflex speaker.

| 1968-1972 | Black | $275 | $350 |
| 1968-1972 | Color option | $400 | $525 |

K100-1 1-15L-1/1-15A-1/1-15J-1 Set

1968-1972. K100-1 with matching 1x15" cab, black tuck-and-roll standard, but several colors offered, speaker options are JBL, Altec Lansing or Jensen.

| 1968-1972 | Black | $275 | $350 |
| 1968-1972 | Color option | $400 | $525 |

K100-1 1-D140F Bass Set

1968-1972. K100-1 with matching 1x15" JBL D-140F cab, black tuck-and-roll standard, but several sparkle colors offered.

| 1968-1972 | Black | $275 | $350 |
| 1968-1972 | Color option | $400 | $525 |

K100-1 2-12C Bass Set

1968-1972. K100-1 with matching 2x12" cab, black tuck-and-roll standard, but several sparkle colors offered, C.T.S. bass reflex speakers.

| 1968-1972 | Black | $325 | $425 |
| 1968-1972 | Color option | $700 | $900 |

K100-2 1-15L-2/1-15A-2/1-15J-2 Set

1968-1972. K100-2 head and matching 1x15" cab, black tuck-and-roll standard, but several sparkle colors offered.

| 1968-1972 | Black | $275 | $350 |
| 1968-1972 | Color option | $400 | $525 |

K100-2 2-12A-2/2-12J-2 Set

1968-1972. K100-2 head with matching 2x12" cab, black tuck-and-roll standard, but several sparkle colors offered.

| 1968-1972 | Black | $325 | $425 |
| 1968-1972 | Color option | $700 | $900 |

K100-5 PA Head

1968-1972. 50 watts, 2 channels with 8 control knobs per channel, reverb.

| 1968-1972 | Black | $375 | $475 |

K100-6 SC

1970-1972. Basic combo amp with selectone, no reverb.

| 1970-1972 | Black | $225 | $300 |

K100-7 SC

1970-1972. Combo amp with reverb, tremolo, vibrato and boost.

| 1970-1972 | Black | $275 | $350 |
| 1970-1972 | Color option | $400 | $525 |

K100-8 SC

1970-1972. Combo amp with reverb, tremolo, vibrato and boost.

| 1970-1972 | Black | $275 | $350 |
| 1970-1972 | Color option | $400 | $525 |

K100C-6 Combo

1968-1970. Kustom 100 logo middle of the front control panel, 1x15" combo, selectone option.

| 1968-1970 | Black | $275 | $350 |
| 1968-1970 | Color option | $400 | $525 |

MODEL YEAR	FEATURES	EXC. COND. LOW	HIGH

K100C-8 Combo
1968-1970. Kustom 100 logo middle of the front control panel, 4x10" combo, reverb, tremolo, vibrato.

1968-1970	Black	$375	$475

K150-1 Set
1972-1975. Piggyback, 150 watts, 2x12", no reverb, logo in upper right corner of amp head, tuck-and-roll, black or color option.

1972-1975	Color option	$400	$525

K150-2 Set
1972-1975. K150 with added reverb and tremolo, piggyback, 2x12", tuck-and-roll, black or color option.

1972-1975	Color option	$400	$525

K150-5 PA Set
1972-1975. PA head plus 2 PA cabs.

1972-1975		$325	$425

K150/150C Combo
1972-1975. Combo, 2x10".

1972-1975	Black	$250	$325

K200-1/K200B Bass Set
1966-1972. K200 head with 2x15" cab.

1966-1972	Black	$400	$525
1966-1972	Color option	$600	$775

K200-2 Reverb/Tremolo Set
1966-1972. K200-2 head with 2x15" or 3x12" cab, available with JBL D-140F speakers, Altec Lansing (A) speakers, C.T.S. (C), or Jensen (J).

1966-1972	Black	$400	$525
1966-1972	Color option	$600	$775

K250 Set
1971-1975. K250 head with 2x15" cab, tuck-and-roll cover.

1971-1975	Black	$350	$450
1971-1975	Color option	$625	$800

K300 PA Amp and Speaker Set
1971-1975. Includes 302 PA, 303 PA, 304 PA, 305 PA, head and 2 cabs.

1971-1975	Color option	$600	$775

K400-2 Reverb/Tremolo Set
1968-1972. 200 relative watts, reverb, tremolo, with 6x12" or 8x12" cab, available with JBL D-140F speakers, Altec Lansing (A), C.T.S. (C), or Jensen (J). The K400 was offered with no effects (suffix 1), with reverb and tremolo (suffix 2), with Harmonic Clipper & Boost (suffix 3), and Reverb/Trem/Clipper/Boost (suffix 4). The 400 heads came with a separate chrome amp head stand.

1968-1972	Black	$325	$425
1968-1972	Color option	$700	$900

KBA-10 Combo
Late-1980s-1990s. Compact solidstate bass amp, 10 watts, 1x8".

1990s		$35	$45

KBA-20 Combo
Late-1980s-early-1990s. KBA series were compact solidstate bass amps with built-in limiter, 20 watts, 1x8".

1989-1990		$35	$45

KBA-30 Combo
Late-1980s-early-1990s. 30 watts, 1x10".

1989-1990		$35	$45

KBA-40 Combo
Late-1980s-early-1990s. 40 watts, 1x12".

1989-1990		$60	$80

KBA-80 Combo
Late-1980s-early-1990s. 80 watts, 1x15".

1989-1990		$85	$110

KBA-160 Combo
Late-1980s-early-1990s. Solidstate bass amp with built-in limiter, 160 watts, 1x15".

1989-1990		$115	$150

KGA-10 VC
1999-2006. 10 watts, 1x6.5" speaker, switchable overdrive.

1999-2006		$35	$45

KLA-15 Combo
Late-1980s-early-1990s. Solidstate, overdrive, 15 watts, 1x8".

1989-1990		$60	$80

KLA-20
Mid-1980s-late-1980s. 1x10", MOS-FET, gain, EQ, reverb, headphone jack.

1986		$60	$80

KLA-25 Combo
Late-1980s-early-1990s. Solidstate, overdrive, reverb, 25 watts, 1x10".

1989-1990		$60	$80

KLA-50 Combo
Late-1980s-early-1990s. Solidstate, overdrive, reverb, 50 watts, 1x12".

1989-1990		$90	$115

KLA-75
Mid-1980s-late-1980s. 75 watts, reverb, footswitching.

1987		$120	$155

KLA-100 Combo
Late-1980s-early-1990s. Solidstate, reverb, 100-watt dual channel, 1x12".

1989-1990		$120	$155

KLA-185 Combo
Late-1980s-early-1990s. Solidstate, reverb, 185-watt dual channel, 1x12".

1989-1990		$140	$180

KPB-200 Bass Combo
1994-1997. 200 watts, 1x15".

1994-1997		$225	$300

SC 1-12 SC
1971-1973. 50 watts, 1x12" Jensen speaker.

1971-1973	Black	$275	$350
1971-1973	Color option	$400	$525

SC 1-15 SC
1971-1973. 150 watts, 1x15" C.T.S. speaker.

1971-1973	Black	$275	$350
1971-1973	Color option	$400	$525

SC 1-15AB SC
1971-1973. 150 watts, 1x15" Altec Lansing speaker.

1971-1973	Black	$275	$350
1971-1973	Color option	$400	$525

SC 2-12A SC
1971-1973. 150 watts, 2x12" Altec Lansing speakers.

1971-1973	Black	$300	$400
1971-1973	Color option	$400	$525

1968 Kustom K200-2
Imaged by Heritage Auctions, HA.com

AMPS

Kustom K250
Tom Pfeifer

1965 Kustom K400-2
Craig Brody

Laboga AD5200 SA
Carter Vintage Guitars

1980 Legend Rock & Roll 50
Alex Xenos

1967 Leslie 330
Imaged by Heritage Auctions, HA.com

MODEL YEAR	FEATURES	EXC. COND. LOW	HIGH
SC 2-12J SC			
1971-1973. 150 watts, 2x12" Jensen speakers.			
1971-1973	Black	$300	$400
1971-1973	Color option	$400	$525
SC 4-10 SC			
1971-1973. 150 watts, 4x10" Jensen speakers.			
1971-1973	Black	$300	$400
1971-1973	Color option	$400	$525

Lab Series

1977-1980s. Five models of Lab Series amps, ranging in price from $600 to $3,700, were introduced at the '77 NAMM show by Norlin (then owner of Gibson). Two more were added later. The '80s models were Lab Series 2 amps and had a Gibson logo on the upper-left front.

B120 Bass Combo
Ca.1984. 120 watts, 2 channels, 1x15".

1984		$325	$425

G120 R-10 Combo
Ca.1984. 120 watts, 3-band EQ, channel switching, reverb, 4x10".

1984		$375	$485

G120 R-12 Combo
Ca.1984. 120 watts, 3-band EQ, channel switching, reverb, 2x12".

1984		$375	$485

L2 Head
1977-ca.1983. 100 watts, black covering.

1977-1983		$250	$325

L3 Combo
1977-ca.1983. 60-watt 1x12".

1977-1983		$325	$425

L4 Head
1977-ca.1983. Solidstate, 200 watts, black cover, dark grille, large L4 logo on front panel.

1977-1983		$250	$325

L5 Combo
1977-ca.1983. Solidstate, 100 watts, 2x12" combo.

1977-1983		$375	$485

L5 Set
1977-ca.1983. Solidstate, 100 watts, 2x12" piggyback.

1977-1983		$375	$485

L7 Set
1977-ca.1983. Solidstate, 100 watts, 4x10" piggyback.

1977-1983		$425	$550

L9 Combo
1977-ca.1983. Solidstate, 100 watts, 1x15".

1977-1983		$325	$425

L11 Set
1977-ca.1983. 200 watts, 8x12" piggyback.

1977-1983		$475	$625

Laboga

1973-present. Adam Laboga builds intermediate and professional grade, production, tube guitar amps and cabinets in Wroclaw, Poland.

Lace Music Products

1979-present. Lace Music Products, founded by pickup innovator Don Lace Sr., offered amplifiers for a while starting in '96. They also offered amps under the Rat Fink and Mooneyes brands.

Lafayette

Ca.1963-1967. Japanese-made guitars and amps sold through the Lafayette Electronics catalogs.

Tube
1960s. Japanese-made tube, gray speckle 1x12" with art deco design or black 2x12".

1960s	Larger, 2 speakers	$225	$300
1960s	Small, 1 speaker	$175	$225

Landry

2008-present. Production, professional grade, amps and cabinets built by Bill Landry in St. Louis, Missouri.

Laney

1968-present. Founded by Lyndon Laney and Bob Thomas in Birmingham, U.K. Laney offered tube amps exclusively into the '80s. Currently they offer intermediate and professional grade, tube and solidstate amp heads and combos and cabinets.

L60 60-Watt Head

1968-1969		$1,400	$1,825

L100 100-Watt Head
1968-1969. Similar to short head Plexi Marshall amp cab, 100 watts, large Laney with underlined "y" logo plate on front upper left corner, black vinyl cover, grayish grille.

1968-1969		$1,400	$1,825

Lectrolab

1950s-1960s. Budget house brand for music stores, made by Sound Projects Company of Cicero, Illinois. Similar to Valco, Oahu, and Danelectro student amps of the '50s, cabinets were generally made from inexpensive material. The Lectrolab logo can generally be found somewhere on the amp.

Tube

1950s-60s	Larger	$400	$525
1950s-60s	Small	$300	$400

Legend

1978-1984. From Legend Musical Instruments of East Syracuse, New York, these amps featured cool wood cabinets. They offered heads, combos with a 1x12" or 2x12" configuration, and cabinets with 1x12", 1x15", 2x12" or 4x12".

A-30
1978-1984. Natural wood cabinet, 30 watts, 1x12".

1978-1984		$400	$525

A-60
1978-1984. Natural wood cabinet, transtube design dual tube preamp with solidstate power section.

1978-1984		$500	$650

MODEL YEAR	FEATURES	EXC. COND. LOW	HIGH

Rock & Roll 50
1978-1983. Mesa-Boogie-style wood compact amp, head/half stack or 1x12", 1x15" or 2x12" combo, tube preamp section and solidstate power supply.

1978-1983	1x12" combo	$400	$525
1978-1983	1x15" combo	$400	$525
1978-1983	2x12" combo	$500	$650
1978-1983	Half stack set	$750	$975

Super Lead 50
1978-1983. Rock & Roll 50-watt model with added bass boost and reverb, 1x12", hybrid tube and solid-state.

1978-1983		$400	$525

Super Lead 100
1978-1983. 100-watt version, 2x12".

1978-1983		$500	$650

Lenahan
Professional grade, production/custom, vintage-style amps and cabinets built by James T. Lenahan – presently in Fort Smith, Arkansas and prior to '91 in Hollywood, California – starting in 1983. He also built guitar effects.

Leslie
Most often seen with Hammond organs, the cool Leslie rotating speakers have been adopted by many guitarists. Many guitar effects have tried to duplicate their sound. And they are still making them.

122 / 122RV
A Hammond-only model, considered the official Hammond B-3 Leslie. RV indicates reverb.

1960s		$950	$1,225

125
Late-1960s. All tube amp with 2-speed rotating 1x12" speaker, bottom rotor only, less features.

1960s		$625	$825

142
A Hammond-only model, smaller cabinet than 122 Amp.

1960s		$800	$1,050

145
Similar to 147 Amp, but smaller and easier to move.

1960s		$825	$1,075

147 / 147RV
A universal-use model, "7" denotes "universal" useage. RV has added reverb.

1960s		$825	$1,075

Lickliter Amplification
In 2009, Michael Lickliter began building professional and premium grade, custom, guitar amps in Punta Gorda, Florida.

Line 6
1996-present. Founded by Marcus Ryle and Michel Doidic and specializing in digital signal processing in both effects and amps. They also produce tube amps. Purchased by Yamaha in 2014.

Little Lanilei
1997-present. Small hand-made, intermediate grade, production/custom, amps made by Mahaffay Amplifiers (formerly Songworks Systems & Products) of Aliso Viejo, California. They also build a reverb unit and a rotary effect.

Little Walter
2008-present. Phil Bradbury builds his professional grade, production, amp heads and cabinets in West End, North Carolina.

London City
Late 1960s-early 1970s. Intermediate to professional grade amps and cabinets made in Netherlands, London City logo.

Louis Electric Amplifier Co.
1993-present. Founded by Louis Rosano in Bergenfield, New Jersey. Louis produces custom-built tweeds and various combo amps from 35 to 80 watts.

Luker
Professional grade, production/custom, guitar and bass amps and cabinets built in Eugene, Oregon by Ken Luker, starting in 2006.

Luna Guitars
2005-present. Located in Tampa, Florida, Yvonne de Villiers imports her budget to professional grade, production, acoustic and electric guitars from Japan, Korea and China. She also imports guitars, basses and ukes.

Lyric
Late 1950s-ca. 1965. One of several private brands that Magnatone made for others, these were built for Lyric Electronics, located in Lomita, California.

Model 660 Custom
Ca. 1959-ca. 1965. 2x12" combo amp, 35 watts.

1959-1965		$1,500	$1,950

Mack
2005-present. Made in Toronto, Ontario by builder Don Mackrill, the company offers intermediate and professional grade, production, tube amps.

Mad Professor
2002-present. Bjorn Juhl and Jukka Monkkonen build their premium grade, production/custom, tube amps in Tampere, Finland. They also offer effects pedals.

Maestro
Maestro amps are associated with Gibson and were included in the Gibson catalogs. For example, in the '62-'63 orange cover Gibson catalog, tweed Maestro amps were displayed in their own section. Tweed Maestro amps are very similar to Gibson tweed amps. Maestro amps were often associated with accordions

Little Walter 9H10 Hipster
Shawn Penney

Mack Atomsmasher DB-40

Mad Professor OS 21RT

AMPS

AMPS

Maestro GA-45 Maestro
Rivington Guitars

Magnatone 108 Varsity

Magnatone 195 Melodier
Tom Pfeifer

in the early-'60s but the amps featured standard guitar inputs. Gibson also used the Maestro name on effects in the '60s and '70s and in 01, Gibson revived the name for a line of effects, banjos, and mandolins and added guitars and amps in '09.

The price ranges listed are for excellent condition, all original amps though tubes may be replaced without affecting value. The prices listed are for amps with fully intact logos. A broken or missing logo may diminish the value of the amp. Amps with a changed handle, power cord, and especially a broken logo, should be taken on a case-by-case basis.

Amp models in '58 include the Super Maestro and Maestro, in '60 the Stereo Maestro Accordion GA-87, Super Maestro Accordion GA-46 T, Standard Accordion GA-45 T, Viscount Accordion GA-16 T, in '62 the Reverb-Echo GA-1 RT, Reverb-Echo GA-2 RT, 30 Stereo Accordion Amp, Stereo Accordion GA-78 RV.

GA-1 RT Reverb-Echo
1961. Tweed, 1x8".

1961		$575	$750

GA-2 RT Deluxe Reverb-Echo
1961. Deluxe more powerful version of GA-1 RT, 1x12", tweed.

1961		$950	$1,225

GA-15 RV/Bell 15 RV
1961. 15 watts, 1x12", gray sparkle.

1961		$675	$875

GA-16T Viscount
1959-1961. 14 watts, 1x10", white cab with brown grille.

1959-1961		$550	$725

GA-45 Maestro
1955-1961. 14-16 watts, 4x8", 2-tone.

1955-1961		$1,175	$1,525

GA-45 RV Standard
1961. 16 watts, 4x8", reverb.

1961		$1,300	$1,700

GA-45T Standard Accordion
1961. 16 watts, 4x8", tremolo.

1961		$1,175	$1,525

GA-46T Super Maestro Accordion and Bass
1957-1961. Based on the Gibson GA-200 and advertised to be designed especially for amplified accordions, 60 watts, 2x12", vibrato, 2-tone cover, large Maestro Super logo on top center of grille.

1957-1961		$1,900	$2,475

GA-78 Maestro Series
1960-1961. Wedge stereo cab, 2x10", reverb and tremolo.

1960-1961	GA-78 RV Maestro 30	$2,350	$3,050
1960-1961	GA-78 RVS	$2,100	$2,725
1960-1961	GA-78 RVT	$2,100	$2,725

Magnatone
Ca.1937-1971, 2013-present. Magnatone made a huge variety of amps sold under their own name and under brands like Dickerson, Oahu, Bronson, and Estey (see separate listings). They also private branded amps for several accordion companies or accordion teaching studios like Ariatone, Audio Guild, Da Vinci, Excelsior, Giulietti, Lyric, Noble, PAC-AMP, PANaramic, Titano, Tonemaster, Twilighter, and Unique (see separate listings). In 2013, Ted Kornblum revived the Magnatone name on a line of tube amps based on the earlier models and built in St. Louis, Missouri.

Model 108 Varsity/Varsity Deluxe
1948-1954. Gray pearloid cover, small student amp or lap steel companion amp.

1948-1954		$400	$525

Model 109 Melodier Deluxe
1950s. 10 watts, 2 speakers.

1950s		$765	$990

Model 110 Melodier
1953-1954. 12 watts, 1x10", brown leatherette cover, light grille.

1953-1954		$715	$925

Model 111 Student
1955-1959. 1x8", 2-3 watts, brown leatherette, brown grille.

1955-1959		$650	$850

Model 112/113 Troubadour
1955-1959. 18 watts, 1x12", brown leatherette, brown grille, slant back rear control panel.

1955-1959		$985	$1,275

Model 118
1960. Compact, tubes, low power, volume and tone knobs, brown tolex era, Model 118 logo on rear-mounted control panel.

1960		$520	$675

Model 120B Cougar Bass
1967-1968. Initial Magnatone entry into the solid-state market, superseded by Brute Series in '68, 120 watts, 2x12" solidstate bass piggyback amp, naugahyde vinyl cover with polyester rosewood side panels.

1967-1968		$420	$550

Model 120R Sting Ray Reverb Bass
1967-1968. Initial Magnatone entry into the solid-state market, superseded by Brute Series in '68, 150 watts, 4x10" solidstate combo amp, naugahyde vinyl cover with polyester rosewood side panels.

1967-1968		$500	$650

Model 130V Custom
1969-1971. Solidstate 1x12" combo amp.

1969-1971		$300	$400

Model 150R Firestar Reverb
1967-1968. Initial Magnatone entry into the solid-state market, superseded by Brute Series in '68, 120 watts, 2x12" solidstate combo amp, naugahyde vinyl cover with polyester rosewood side panels.

1967-1968		$350	$450

Model 180 Triplex
Mid-to-late-1950s. Mid-level power using 2 6L6 power tubes, 1x15" and 1x8" speakers.

1950s		$1,050	$1,375

Model 192-5-S Troubadour
Early-1950s. 18 watts, 1x12" Jensen Concert speaker, brown alligator covering, lower back control panel, 3 chicken-head knobs, Magnatone script logo

MODEL YEAR	FEATURES	EXC. COND. LOW	HIGH

on front, Troubadour script logo on back control panel.

| 1950s | | $750 | $975 |

Model 194 Lyric
1947-mid-1950s. 1x12" speaker, old-style tweed vertical cab typical of '40s.

| 1940s | | $650 | $850 |

Model 195 Melodier
1951-1954. Vertical cab with 1x10" speaker, pearloid with flowing grille slats.

| 1951-1954 | | $700 | $900 |

Model 196
1947-mid-1950s. 1x12", 5-10 watts, scroll grille design, snakeskin leatherette cover.

| 1940s | | $650 | $850 |

Model 197 V Varsity
1948-1952. Small compact student amp, 1x8", tubes, Varsity model logo and model number on back panel, old style layout with back bottom-mounted chasis, curved cross-bars on front baffle, brown lizard leatherette, leather handle.

| 1948-1952 | | $600 | $775 |

Model 198 Varsity
1948-1954. 1x8", tubes.

| 1948-1954 | | $650 | $850 |

Model 199 Student
1950s. About 6 to 10 watts, 1x8", snakeskin leatherette cover, metal handle, slant grille design.

| 1950s | | $650 | $850 |

Model 210 Deluxe Student
1958-1960. 5 watts, 1x8", vibrato, brown leatherette, V logo lower right front on grille.

| 1958-1960 | | $650 | $850 |

Model 213 Troubadour
1957-1958. 10 watts, 1x12", vibrato, brown leatherette cover, V logo lower right of grille.

| 1957-1958 | | $1,250 | $1,625 |

Model 240 SV Magna-Chordion
1967-1968. Initial Magnatone entry into the solid-state market, superseded by Brute Series in '68, 240 watts, 2x12" solidstate stereo accordion or organ amp, naugahyde vinyl cover, polyester rosewood side panels, input jacks suitable for guitar, reverb and vibrato, lateral combo cab, rear mounted controls.

| 1967-1968 | | $425 | $550 |

Model 250 Professional
1958-1960. 20 watts, 1x12", vibrato, brown leatherette with V logo lower right front of grille.

| 1958-1960 | | $1,300 | $1,700 |

Model 260
1957-1958. 35 watts, 2x12", brown leatherette, vibrato, V logo lower right front corner of grille.

| 1957-1958 | | $1,800 | $2,350 |

Model 262 Jupiter/Custom Pro
1961-1963. 35 watts, 2x12", vibrato, brown leatherette.

| 1961-1963 | | $1,350 | $1,750 |

Model 280/Custom 280
1957-1958. 50 watts, brown leatherette covering, brown-yellow tweed grille, 2x12" plus 2x5" speakers, double V logo.

| 1957-1958 | | $1,800 | $2,350 |

Model 280A
1958-1960. 50 watts, brown leatherette covering, brown-yellow tweed grille, 2x12" plus 2x5" speakers, V logo lower right front.

| 1958-1960 | | $1,800 | $2,350 |
| 1958-1960 | With matching cab | $2,400 | $3,125 |

Model 410 Diana
1961-1963. Five watts, 1x12", advertised as a 'studio' low power professional amp, brown leatherette cover, vibrato.

| 1961-1963 | | $775 | $1,000 |

Model 412
1960s. Estey era compact student amp, low power, 1x8", tubes.

| 1960s | | $325 | $425 |

Model 413 Centaur
1961-1963. 18 watts, 1x12", brown leatherette cover, vibrato.

| 1961-1963 | | $1,150 | $1,500 |

Model 415 Clio Bass
1961-1963. 25 watts, 4x8", bass or accordion amp, brown leatherette cover.

| 1961-1963 | | $1,200 | $1,550 |

Model 422
1966-1967. Low power 1x12", 3 inputs, black vinyl, light swirl grille.

| 1966-1967 | | $650 | $850 |

Model 425
1961. Tube, 55 watts, 4x12".

| 1961 | | $1,450 | $1,900 |

Model 432
Mid-1960s. Compact student model, wavey-squiggle art deco-style grille, black cover, vibrato and reverb.

| 1960s | | $750 | $975 |

Model 435 Athene Bass
1961-1963. 55 watts, 4x10", piggyback head and cab, brown leatherette.

| 1961-1963 | | $1,475 | $1,925 |

Model 440 Mercury
1961-1963. 18 watts, 1x12", vibrato, brown leatherette.

| 1961-1963 | | $1,300 | $1,700 |

Model 450 Juno/Twin Hi-Fi
1961-1963. 25 watts, 1x12" and 1 oval 5"x7" speakers, reverb, vibrato, brown leatherette.

| 1961-1963 | | $1,500 | $1,950 |
| 1961-1963 | Extension cab only | $750 | $975 |

Model 460 Victory
1961-1963. 35 watts, 2x12" and 2 oval 5"x7" speakers, early-'60s next to the top-of-the-line, reverb and vibrato, brown leatherette.

| 1961-1963 | | $1,500 | $1,950 |

Model 480 Venus
1961-1963. 50 watts, 2x12" and 2 oval 5"x7" speakers, early-'60s top-of-the-line, reverb and stereo vibrato, brown leatherette.

| 1961-1963 | | $1,500 | $1,950 |

Model M2
1963-1964. 1x8", 12-15 watts, 1 channel.

| 1963-1964 | | $450 | $575 |

Magnatone 213 Troubadour
Imaged by Heritage Auctions, HA.com

AMPS

1958 Magnatone Model 210
tednugentlives

Magnatone 480 Venus

1966 Magnatone MP-1
Imaged by Heritage Auctions, HA.com

Magnatone M15
Imaged by Heritage Auctions, HA.com

1950 Magnatone Small Pearloid

MODEL YEAR	FEATURES	EXC. COND. LOW	HIGH
Model M6			
1964 (not seen in '65 catalog). 25 watts, 1x12", black molded plastic suitcase amp.			
1964		$625	$825
Model M7 Bass			
1964-1966. 38 watts, 1x15" bass amp, black molded plastic suitcase amp.			
1964-1966		$625	$825
Model M8			
1964-1966. 27 watts, 1x12", reverb and tremolo, black molded plastic suitcase amp.			
1964-1966		$725	$950
Model M9			
1964-1966. 38 watts, 1x15", tremolo, no reverb, black molded plastic suitcase amp.			
1964-1966		$725	$950
Model M10/M10A			
1964-1966. 38 watts, 1x15", tone boost, tremolo, transistorized reverb section, black molded plastic suitcase amp.			
1964-1966		$650	$850
Model M12 Bass			
1964-1966. 80 watts, 1x15" or 2x12", mid-'60s top-of-the-line bass amp, black molded plastic suitcase amp.			
1964-1966		$725	$950
Model M13 Imperial			
Mid-1963-1964. 1x15", 45 watts, 3 channels.			
1963-1964		$725	$950
Model M14			
1964-1966. Stereo, 75 watts, 2x12" plus 2 tweeters, stereo vibrato, no reverb, black molded plastic suitcase amp.			
1964-1966		$900	$1,175
Model M15			
1964-1966. Stereo 75 watts, 2x12" plus 2 tweeters, stereo vibrato, transistorized reverb, black molded plastic suitcase amp.			
1964-1966		$925	$1,200
Model M27 Bad Boy Bass			
1968-1971. 150 watts, 2x15" (1 passive), reverb, vibrato, solidstate, vertical profile bass amp, part of Brute Series.			
1968-1971		$350	$450
Model M30 Fang			
1968-1971. 150 watts, 2x15" (1 passive), 1 exponential horn, solidstate, vibrato, reverb, vertical profile amp.			
1968-1971		$350	$450
Model M32 Big Henry Bass			
1968-1971. 300 watts, 2x15" solidstate vertical profile bass amp.			
1968-1971		$350	$450
Model M35 The Killer			
1968-1971. 300 watts, 2x15" and 2 horns, solidstate, vibrato, vertical profile amp.			
1968-1971		$350	$450
Model MP-1 (Magna Power I)			
1966-1967. 30 watts, 1x12", dark vinyl, light grille, Magnatone-Estey logo on upper right of grille.			
1966-1967		$700	$900
Model MP-3 (Magna Power 3)			
1966-1967. Mid-power, 2x12", reverb, dark vinyl,			

MODEL YEAR	FEATURES	EXC. COND. LOW	HIGH
light grille, Magnatone-Estey logo on upper right of grille.			
1966-1967		$775	$1,000
Model MP-5 (Magna Power)			
1966-1967. Mid-power, piggyback 2x12", Magnatone-Estey logo on upper right of grille.			
1966-1967		$875	$1,125
Model PS150			
1968-1971. Powered slave speaker cabinets, 150 watts, 2x15" linkable cabinets.			
1968-1971		$225	$300
Model PS300			
1968-1971. Powered slave speaker cabinets, 300 watts, 2x15" (1 passive) linkable cabinets.			
1968-1971		$225	$300
Small Pearloid			
1947-1955. Pearloid (MOTS) covered low- and mid-power amps generally associated with pearloid lap steel sets.			
1947-1955	Fancy grille	$425	$550
1947-1955	Plain grille	$300	$400
Starlet Model 107			
1951-1952. Student model, 1x8", pearloid cover early, leatherette later, low power, single on-off volume control, Starlet logo on back panel, Magnatone logo plate upper left front of grille.			
1951-1954	Pearloid	$350	$450
1955-1959	Leatherette	$350	$450
Starlite Model 401			
1964-1966. Magnatone produced the mid-'60s Starlite amplifier line for the budget minded musician. Each Starlite model prominently notes the Magnatone name. The grilles show art deco wavy circles. Magnatone 1960-'63 standard amps offer models starting with 12" speakers. Starlite models offer 10" and below. Model 401 has 15 watts, 1x8" and 3 tubes.			
1964-1966		$400	$525
Starlite Model 411			
1964-1966. 15 watts, 1x8", 5 tubes, tremolo (not advertised as vibrato), art deco wavy grille.			
1964-1966		$425	$550
Starlite Model 441A Bass			
1964-1966. Lower power with less than 25 watts, 1x15", tube amp.			
1964-1966		$600	$775
Starlite Model Custom 421			
1964-1966. Tube amp, 25 watts, 1x10".			
1964-1966		$600	$775
Starlite Model Custom 431			
1964-1966. Tube amp, 30 watts, 1x10", vibrato and reverb.			
1964-1966		$650	$850

Mahaffay Amplifiers

2009-present. See Little Lanilei.

Mako

1985-1989. Line of solidstate amps from Kaman (Ovation, Hamer). They also offered guitars and basses.

MODEL YEAR	FEATURES	EXC. COND. LOW	HIGH

Marlboro Sound Works

1970-1980s. Economy solidstate amps imported by Musical Instruments Corp., Syosset, New York. Initially, Marlboro targeted the economy compact amp market, but quickly added larger amps and PAs.

Solid State

1970-1980s	Various models	$35	$160

Marshall

1962-present. Drummer Jim Marshall (1923-2012) started building bass speaker and PA cabinets in his garage in 1960. He opened a retail drum shop for his students and others and soon added guitars and amps. When Ken Bran joined the business as service manager in '62, the two decided to build their own amps. By '63 they had expanded the shop to house a small manufacturing space and by late that year they were offering the amps to other retailers. Marshall also made amps under the Park, CMI, Narb, Big M, and Kitchen-Marshall brands.

Mark I, II, III and IVs are generally '60s and '70s and also are generally part of a larger series (for example JTM), or have a model number that is a more specific identifier. Describing an amp only as Mark II can be misleading. The most important identifier is the Model Number, which Marshall often called the Stock Number. To help avoid confusion we have added the Model number as often as possible. In addition, when appropriate, we have included the wattage, number of channels, master or no-master info in the title. This should help the reader more quickly find a specific amp. Check the model's description for such things as two inputs or four inputs, because this will help with identification. Vintage Marshall amps do not always have the Model/Stock number on the front or back panel, so the additional identifiers should help. The JMP logo on the front is common and really does not help with specific identification. For example, a JMP Mark II Super Lead 100 Watt description is less helpful than the actual model/stock number. Unfortunately, many people are not familiar with specific model/stock numbers. VG has tried to include as much information in the title as space will allow.

Marshall amps are sorted as follows:

AVT Series - Advanced Valvestate Technology

Club and Country Series (Rose-Morris)-introduced in '78

JCM 800 Series - basically the '80s

JCM 900 Series - basically the '90s

JCM 2000 Series - basically the '00s

JTM Series

Micro Stack Group

Model Number/Stock Number (no specific series, basically the '60s, '70s) - including Artist and Valvestate models (Valvestate refers to specific Model numbers in 8000 Series)

Silver Jubilee Series

Acoustic Soloist (AS) Series

1994-present. Acoustic guitar amps, models include AS50R and D (50 watts, 2 channels, 2x8"), AS80R (40-watt x2 stereo, 3 channels, 2x8"), AS100D (50-watt x2 stereo, 4 channels, 2x8").

1994-2021	Various models	$200	$400

AVT 20

2001-2011. Solidstate, 20 watts, 12AX7 preamp tube, 1x10", Advanced Valvestate Technology (AVT) models have black covering and grille, and gold panel.

2001-2011	Combo	$175	$225

AVT 50

2001-2011. Solidstate, 50 watts, 4x12".

2001-2011	Combo	$245	$315
2001-2011	Head & cab	$390	$510

AVT 100

2001-2011. Solidstate, 100 watts, tube preamp, 1x12".

2001-2011		$270	$360

AVT 150

2001-2011. Solidstate, additional features over AVT 100. Combo (100 watts, 1x12"), Half-Stack (150 watts, 4x12") and Head only (150 watts).

2001-2011	Combo	$295	$385
2001-2011	Half-stack	$375	$500

AVT 275

2001-2007. Solidstate DFX stereo, 75 watts per side, 2x12".

2001-2007	Combo	$360	$475

Capri

1966-1967. Only about 100 made, 5 watts, 1x8, 2x8 or 1x10 combo, red cover.

1966-1967		$2,300	$3,000

Class 5

2009-2014. 5 watts, 1x10" tube combo.

2009-2014	Head	$290	$385
2009-2014	Head & cab	$315	$415

Club and Country Model 4140

1978-1982. Tubes, 100 watts, 2x12" combo, Rose-Morris era, designed for the country music market, hence the name, brown vinyl cover, straw grille.

1978-1982		$725	$950

Club and Country Model 4145

1978-1982. Tubes, 100 watts, 4x10" combo, Rose-Morris era, designed for the country music market, hence the name, brown vinyl, straw grille.

1978-1982		$725	$950

Club and Country Model 4150 Bass

1978-1982. Tubes, 100 watts, 4x10" bass combo, Rose-Morris era, designed for the country music market, hence the name, brown vinyl cover, straw grille.

1978-1982		$725	$950

Code Series

2016-present. Marshall-Softube (MST) modelling, digital capabilities, series includes; CODE25, 50, 100 and 100H. Number indicates watts.

2016-2021		$120	$195

Haze (MHZ) Series

2009-2014. All tube, multi-functional amps, MHZ15 (15w, head, 2 cabs), 40C (40w, 1x12 combo) 215 (15w, 2x1x12).

2009-2014	MHZ15	$590	$775
2009-2014	MHZ40C	$340	$440

Magnatone Starlet 107
Imaged by Heritage Auctions, HA.com

Mahaffay The Little Lanilei 3350LT

Marshall AS100D

AMPS

AMPS

1984 Marshall JCM 800 2203
Craig Brody

1986 Marshall JCM 800 2204
Scott Davis

Marshall JCM 800 4010
Stephan Brown

MODEL YEAR	FEATURES	EXC. COND. LOW	HIGH
JCM 600 Series			
1997-2000. All tube, 60 watt models with modern features, includes the JCM600 head, JCM601 1x12" combo and JCM602 2x12" combo.			
1997-2000	JCM600	$355	$470
1997-2000	JCM601	$378	$495
1997-2000	JCM602	$450	$590
JCM 800 Model 1959 Head			
1981-1991. 100 watts.			
1981-1991		$1,190	$1,525
JCM 800 Model 1987 Head			
1981-1991. 50 watts.			
1981-1991		$1,190	$1,525
JCM 800 Model 1992 Bass Head			
1981-1986. Active tone circuit.			
1981-1986		$1,190	$1,525
JCM 800 Model 2000 Head			
1981-1982. 200 watts.			
1981-1982		$1,190	$1,525
JCM 800 Model 2001 Head			
1981-1982. Bass head, 300 watts.			
1981-1982		$1,190	$1,525
JCM 800 Model 2004 Head			
1981-1990. 50 watts, master.			
1981-1990		$1,190	$1,525
JCM 800 Model 2004S Head			
1986-1987. 50 watts, short head.			
1986-1987		$1,190	$1,525
JCM 800 Model 2005 Full Stack			
1983-1990. Limited Edition, 2005 head with 2 2x12 cabs.			
1983-1990		$1,750	$2,275
JCM 800 Model 2005 Head			
1983-1990. 50 watts, split channel.			
1983-1990		$1,190	$1,525
JCM 800 Model 2203 20th Anniversary Half Stack			
1982. 20th Anniversary plate in lower right corner of matching 1960A cab, matching white tolex cover.			
1982		$2,080	$2,675
JCM 800 Model 2203 Head			
1981-1990, 2002-2020. 100 watts, master volume, reissued '02 in Vintage Series.			
1981-1990		$1,350	$1,800
2002-2020	Reissue	$850	$1,100
JCM 800 Model 2203KK Kerry King Signature			
2008-2012. King Signature logo, 100 watts, 3-band EQ.			
2008-2012		$825	$1,100
JCM 800 Model 2203ZW Zack Wylde Signature			
2002. About 600 amp heads and 60 half-stacks made.			
2002	Half-stack	$2,625	$3,400
2002	Head only	$1,450	$1,900
JCM 800 Model 2204 Head			
1981-1990. 50 watts, 1 channel, 2 inputs, master volume, front panel says JCM 800 Lead Series, back panel says Master Model 50w Mk 2.			
1981-1990		$875	$1,175

MODEL YEAR	FEATURES	EXC. COND. LOW	HIGH
JCM 800 Model 2204S Head			
1986-1987. Short head, 50 watts.			
1986-1987		$875	$1,175
JCM 800 Model 2205			
1983-1990. 50 watts, split channel (1 clean and 1 distortion), switchable, both channels with reverb, 4x12" cabinet, front panel reads JCM 800 Lead Series.			
1983-1990	Cab	$500	$675
1983-1990	Head only	$875	$1,175
JCM 800 Model 2210 Head			
1983-1990. 100 watts.			
1983-1990		$875	$1,175
JCM 800 Model 4010 Combo			
1980-1990. 50 watts, 1x12", non-reverb ('80), reverb begins '81, single channel master volume.			
1980-1990		$1,025	$1,350
JCM 800 Model 4103 Combo			
1981-1990. Lead combo amp, 100 watts, 2x12".			
1981-1990		$1,175	$1,550
JCM 800 Model 4104 Combo			
1980-1990. Tube lead amp, 50 watts, 2x12".			
1980-1990	Black	$1,025	$1,350
1980-1990	Head only	$850	$1,125
1980-1990	White option	$1,025	$1,350
JCM 800 Model 4210 Combo			
1982-1990. 50 watts, 1x12" tube combo, split-channel, single input, master volume.			
1982-1990		$1,115	$1,450
JCM 800 Model 4211 Combo			
1983-1990. Lead combo amp, 100 watts, 2x12".			
1983-1990		$1,115	$1,450
JCM 800 Model 4212 Combo			
1983-1990. 50-watt, 2x12" combo.			
1983-1990		$1,115	$1,450
JCM 800 Model 5010 Combo			
1983-1991. Solidstate, 30 watts, master volume, 1x12".			
1983-1991		$290	$375
JCM 800 Model 5150 Combo			
1987-1991. Solidstate, 150 watts, 12" Celestion, 2 channels, presence and effects-mix master controls.			
1987-1991		$350	$450
JCM 800 Model 5210 Combo			
1986-1991. Solidstate, 50 watts, channel switching, 1x12".			
1986-1991		$290	$375
JCM 800 Model 5212 Combo			
1986-1991. Solidstate, 50 watts, 2x12" split channel reverb combo.			
1986-1991		$360	$475
JCM 800 Model 5213 Combo			
1986-1991. Solidstate, 2x12", channel-switching, effects loop.			
1986-1991		$290	$375
JCM 800 Model 5215 Combo			
1986-1991. Solidstate, 1x15", Accutronics reverb, effects loop.			
1986-1991		$290	$375
JCM 900 Model 2100 Mark III Head			
1990-1993. FX loop, 100/50-watt selectable lead head.			
1990-1993		$725	$950

JCM 900 Model 2100 SL-X Head
1992-1998. Hi-gain 100 watt head amp, additional 12AX7 preamp tube.

1992-1998		$725	$950

JCM 900 Model 2500 SL-X Head
1990-2000. 50 watt version of SL-X.

1992-1998		$725	$950

JCM 900 Model 4100 Dual Reverb
1990-2017. Vintage Series, 100/50 switchable head, JCM 900 on front panel, 4x10 or 2x12 matching cab, black with black front.

1990-2017	4x10 or 2x12	$450	$600
1990-2017	Head only	$650	$850

JCM 900 Model 4101 Combo
1990-2000. All tube, 100 watts, 1x12" combo.

1990-2000		$675	$900

JCM 900 Model 4102 Combo
1990-2000. Combo amp, 100/50 watts switchable, 2x12".

1990-2000		$700	$925

JCM 900 Model 4500 Head
1990-2000. All tube, 2 channels, 50/25 watts, EL34 powered, reverb, effects loop, compensated recording out, master volume, black.

1990-2000		$600	$800

JCM 900 Model 4501 Dual Reverb Combo
1990-2000. 50/25 switchable, 1x12".

1990-2000		$675	$875

JCM 900 Model 4502 Combo
1990-2000. 50/25 switchable, 2x12".

1990-2000		$700	$900

JCM 2000 DSL Series
1998-2015. DSL is Dual Super Lead, 2 independent channels labelled classic and ultra, JCM 2000 and DSL logos both on front panel.

1998-2015	Half-stacks/combos	$240	$825

JCM 2000 TSL Series
1998-2013. TSL is Triple Super Lead, 3 independent channels labelled clean, crunch and lead, 8 tubes, JCM 2000 and TSL logos both on front panel.

1998-2013	Full-stacks	$1,200	$1,825
1998-2013	Half-stacks/combos	$630	$1,225

JCM Slash Signature Model 2555SL Set
1996. Based on JCM 800 with higher gain, matching amp and cab set, JCM Slash Signature logo on front panel, single channel, Slash Signature 1960AV 4x12" slant cab, black.

1996	4x12 cab	$700	$900
1996	Head only	$1,550	$2,000

JMD Series
2010-2013. JMD is Jim Marshall Digital. Models include JMD50 & 100 heads and JMD 102 (100w, 2x12) & 501 (50w, 1x12) combos.

2010-2013	501	$490	$650

JTM 30 Series
1995-1997. Tube combo, reverb, 30 watts, effects loops, 5881 output sections, footswitchable high-gain modes. Available as 1x15", 1x12", 2x12" or 3x10" combo or as 4x10" half-stack.

1995-1997	Combo 1x12	$435	$560

MODEL		EXC. COND.	
YEAR	FEATURES	LOW	HIGH
1995-1997	Combo 2x10	$460	$600
1995-1997	Combo 2x12	$485	$630
1995-1997	Combo 3x10	$485	$630

JTM 45 Head
1962-1964. Amp head, 45 watts. The original Marshall amp. Became the Model 1987 45-watt for '65-'66.

1962		$8,300	$10,800
1963-1964		$7,300	$9,500

JTM 45 Model 1961 MK IV 4x10 Combo
1965-1966. 45 watts, 4x10", tremolo, JTM 45 MK IV on panel, Bluesbreaker association.

1965-1966		$7,000	$9,100

JTM 45 Model 1962 MK IV 2x12 Combo
1965-1966. 45 watts, 2x12", tremolo, JTM 45 MK IV on panel, Bluesbreaker association.

1965-1966		$7,200	$9,400

JTM 45 Model 1987 Head Reissue
1988-1999. Black/green tolex.

1988-1999		$1,025	$1,350

JTM 45 Model 1987 Mark II Lead Head
1965-1966. Replaced JTM 45 Amp ('62-'64), but was subsequently replaced by the Model 1987 50-watt Head during '66.

1965-1966		$4,900	$6,500

JTM 45 Offset Limited Edition Set Reissue
Introduced in 2000. Limited run of 300 units, old style cosmetics, 45-watt head and offset 2x12" cab, dark vinyl cover, light gray grille, rectangular logo plate on front of amp and cab, Limited Edition plate on rear of cab, serial number xxx of 300.

2000		$2,450	$3,250

JTM 50 Head
1966-1967. JTM 50 panel logo, EL34 power tubes.

1966-1967		$5,000	$6,550

JTM 50 Model 1961 MK IV 4x10
1965-1972. 50 watts, 4x10", Bluesbreaker association, tremolo, JTM 50 MK IV on front panel to '68, plain front panel without model description '68-'72.

1966-1967		$6,300	$8,200
1968		$5,900	$7,700
1969		$5,300	$7,000
1970		$4,500	$6,000
1971-1972		$3,800	$5,000

JTM 50 Model 1962 Bluesbreaker Reissue
1989-1999. 50 watts, 2x12", Model 1962 reissue Bluesbreaker.

1989-1999		$1,200	$1,600

JTM 50 Model 1962 MK IV 2x12
1966-1972. 50 watts, 2x12", tremolo, Bluesbreaker association, JTM 50 MK IV on front panel to '68, plain front panel without model description '68-'72.

1966-1967		$7,700	$10,000
1968		$7,100	$9,300
1969		$5,900	$7,700
1970		$5,400	$7,100
1971-1972		$4,600	$6,000

JTM 50 Model 1963 PA Head
1965-1966. MK II PA head, block logo.

1965-1966		$2,000	$2,600

2003 Marshall JCM 2000 DSL
Imaged by Heritage Auctions, HA.com

AMPS

1964 Marshall JTM 45
Eddie Daurelle

Marshall JTM 45 1961 MK IV
Pang Leo

Marshall JVM210C

Marshall Micro Stack 3005
Tim McClutchy

Marshall Model 1922

MODEL YEAR	FEATURES	EXC. COND. LOW	HIGH
JTM 60 Series			
1995-1997. Tube, 60 watts, 1x12", 1x15", 2x12" or 3x10" combo or as 4x10" half-stack.			
1995-1997	1x12 Combo	$475	$615
1995-1997	2x12 Combo	$500	$650
1995-1997	3x10 Combo	$525	$675
1995-1997	4x10 Mini half-stack	$525	$675
JTM 310			
1995-1997. JTM 30 with 2x10".			
1995-1997		$500	$650
JTM 612 Combo			
1995-1997. Tube combo amp, 60 watts, 1x12", EQ, reverb, effects loop.			
1995-1997		$475	$615
JVM Series			
2007-present. Models (H for Head, C Combo) include 205H/205C (50-watt head/combo 2x12), 210H/210C (100-watt head/combo 2x12), 215C (50-watt 1x12 combo), 410H/410C (100-watt head/combo 2x12, 4-channel).			
2007-2017	JVM410C	$975	$1,300
2008-2021	JVM205H	$775	$1,025
2008-2021	JVM210C	$1,075	$1,400
2008-2021	JVM210H	$825	$1,075
MA Series			
2009-2013. Models include 50C (50 watts, 1x12"), 50H (50-watt head), 100C (100 watts, 2x12"), 100H (100-watt head) and 412 (4x12" slant cabinet).			
2009-2013	Half-stacks/combos	$325	$500
MB Series			
2006-2012. Bass Combo Series, models include 30C (30watts, 1x10").			
2006-2012	MB30C	$115	$150
MG Series			
1999-present. Models include 10KK (10 watts, 1x6"), 15CD, 15RCD or CDR (15 watts, 1x8"), 15MS (15 watts, micro stack, 1x8" slant and straight cabs), 15MSII, (in '02, 10" speakers), 15MSZW (15 watts, 2x1x10"), 50DFX (50 watts, 1x12"), 100DFX (100 watts, combo), 100HDFX (100-watt head), 100RCD (Valvestate Series, 100-watt), 102FX (100 watts, 2x12"), 250DFX (250 watts, combo), 412A (4x12" cabinet).			
1999-2021	Various models	$45	$300
Micro Stack 3005			
1986-1991. Solidstate head, 12 watts, 2 1x10" stackable cabs (one slant, one straight). Standard model is black, but was also offered in white, green, red, or the silver Silver Jubilee version with Jubilee 25/50 logo.			
1986-1991	Black	$275	$370
1986-1991	Green or red	$365	$495
1986-1991	White	$350	$470
1987-1989	Silver Jubilee/silver	$475	$625
Mini-Stack 3210 MOS-FET Head			
1984-1991. Model 3210 MOS-FET head with 2 4x10" cabs, designed as affordable stack.			
1984-1991		$325	$430
Model 1710 Bass Cabinet			
1990s. 1x15" speaker.			
1990s		$275	$360
Model 1912 Cabinet			
1989-1998, 2013-2017. 1x12", 150 watts.			
2013-2017		$275	$360

MODEL YEAR	FEATURES	EXC. COND. LOW	HIGH
Model 1917 PA-20 Head			
1967-1973. PA head with 20 watts, but often used for guitar, matching cabinet.			
1967-1968	Matching cab	$1,100	$1,400
1967-1968	Plexi head	$2,400	$3,100
1969-1973	Aluminum head	$1,900	$2,400
1969-1973	Matching cab	$900	$1,200
Model 1922 Cabinet			
1989-present. 2x12" extension cab for JCM 800 Series amps.			
1989-2021		$225	$290
Model 1930 Popular Combo			
1969-1973. 10 watts, 1x12", tremolo.			
1969-1972		$1,900	$2,450
1973		$2,100	$2,700
Model 1933 Amp Cabinet			
1981-1991. 1x12" extension cab for JCM 800 Series amps.			
1981-1991		$275	$350
Model 1935/1935A/1935B Bass Cabinet			
1967-1990s. Models 1935, 4x12", black, A slant front, B straight front.			
1967-1970	75w	$1,900	$2,475
1971-1972	Black, weave	$1,000	$1,300
1973-1975	Black, checkerboard	$950	$1,250
1976-1979	Black	$850	$1,100
1979-1983	260w	$500	$650
1983-1986	280w	$445	$580
1990s		$350	$450
Model 1936 Cabinet			
1981-2011. Extension straight-front cab for JCM 800/900 Series amps, 2x12" speakers, black.			
1981-2011		$350	$450
Model 1937 Bass Cabinet			
1981-1986. 4x12", 140 watts.			
1981-1986		$445	$580
Model 1958 18-Watt Lead			
1965-1968. 18 watts, 2x10" combo, Bluesbreaker cosmetics.			
1965-1968		$4,700	$6,100
Model 1958 20-Watt Lead			
1968-1972. 20 watts, 2x10" combo, tremolo.			
1968		$4,200	$5,500
1969		$3,700	$4,900
1970		$3,600	$4,700
1971-1972		$3,200	$4,200
Model 1959 Super Lead			
1966-1981. Two channels, 100 watts, 4 inputs, no master volume. Plexiglas control panels until mid-'69, aluminum after. See Model T1959 for tremolo version. Early custom color versions are rare and more valuable. Becomes JCM 800 1959 in '81.			
1966-1969	Black, plexi	$3,700	$4,900
1966-1969	Custom color, plexi	$5,300	$7,000
1969-1970	Black, aluminum	$2,200	$2,900
1969-1970	Custom color, aluminum	$4,400	$5,700
1971-1972	Black, hand-wired, small box	$2,200	$2,900
1971-1972	Custom color, hand-wired	$2,600	$3,400

AMPS

MODEL YEAR	FEATURES	EXC. COND. LOW	HIGH
1973-1975	Black, printed CB, large box	$1,450	$1,925
1973-1975	Custom color, printed CB	$1,950	$2,600
1976-1979	Black	$1,250	$1,650
1976-1979	Custom color	$1,450	$1,925
1980-1981	Black	$1,175	$1,550
1980-1981	Custom color	$1,350	$1,750

Model T1959 Super Lead (Tremolo) Head

1966-1973. Head amp, 100 watts, plexi until mid-'69, aluminum after. Tremolo version of the Model 1959 Amp.

MODEL YEAR	FEATURES	EXC. COND. LOW	HIGH
1966-1969	Black, plexi	$3,900	$5,100
1966-1969	Custom color, plexi	$5,700	$7,400
1969-1970	Black, aluminum	$1,875	$2,450
1969-1970	Custom color, aluminum	$4,425	$5,800
1971-1973	Black, hand-wired, small box	$1,700	$2,200
1971-1973	Custom color, hand-wired	$2,450	$3,200

35th Anniversary Marshall Limited Edition Set

1997. Limited Edition 1997 logo, includes matching Super Lead MKII 100-watt head, PB100 power brake and MKII 1960A slant cab, all in white covering.

1997		$2,100	$2,800

Model 1959 SLP Reissue Head

1992-2017. Vintage Series, Super Lead Plexi (SLP), vinyl covering, black, purple or white.

1992-1999	Black	$1,000	$1,300
1992-1999	Purple or white	$1,200	$1,550
2000-2017	Black	$1,200	$1,550

Model 1959 SLP Reissue Set

1992-2013. Vintage Series, 100 watt Super Lead head and matching 4x12" slant cab.

1992-2013	4x12 Cab	$475	$625

Model 1959HW

2005-present. Hand-wired, 100 watts, 4x12" slant front cab.

2005-2014	Cab	$475	$625
2005-2021	Head only	$1,000	$1,300

Model 1959RR Randy Rhoads Limited Edition

2008-2013. Randy Rhoads Tribute, full stack, 100 watts.

2008-2013		$2,100	$2,800

Model 1960 4x12 Speaker Cabinet

1964-1979. Both straight and slant front. The original Marshall 4x12" cab designed for compact size with 4x12" speakers. First issue in '64/'65 is 60-watt cab, from '65-'70 75 watts, from '70-'79 100 watts. After '79, model numbers contained an alpha suffix: A for slant front, B straight.

1966-1970	Black, weave	$2,000	$2,600
1966-1970	Custom color, weave	$2,800	$3,700
1971-1972	Black, weave	$1,100	$1,450
1971-1972	Custom color, weave	$1,525	$2,000
1973-1975	Black, checkerboard	$800	$1,050
1973-1975	Custom color, checkerboard	$1,200	$1,600

MODEL YEAR	FEATURES	EXC. COND. LOW	HIGH
1976-1979	Black	$750	$1,000
1976-1979	Custom color	$1,200	$1,600

Model 1960A/1960B 4x12 Speaker Cabinet

1980-1983 (260 watts), '84-'86 (280 watts, JCM 800 era), '86-'90 (300 watts, JCM 800 era), '90-present (300 watts, JCM 900 era, stereo-mono switching). A slant or B straight front.

1980-1983	Black	$435	$575
1980-1983	Custom color	$625	$825
1984-1986	Black	$375	$500
1984-1986	Custom color	$575	$750
1984-1986	Rare color	$775	$1,000
1987-1990	Black	$350	$450
1987-1990	Custom color	$475	$625
1987-1990	Rare color	$675	$900
2000-2007	A, Black	$325	$425
2000-2007	B, Black	$350	$450

Model 1960AC/1960BC Classic Speaker Cabinet

2005-2013. 100 watts, 4x12" Celestion G-12M-25 greenback speakers, black, AC slant front, BC straight front.

2005-2013	AC	$575	$750
2005-2013	BC	$525	$700

Model 1960AHW/1960BHW 4x12 Cabinet

2005-present. Half stack cab for HW series, AHW slant or BHW straight front.

2005-2021	A or B	$575	$750

Model 1960AV/1960BV 4x12 Cabinet

1990-present. JCM 900 updated, stereo/mono switching, AV slant, BV straight front.

1990-1999	Red vinyl, tan grille	$450	$600
1990-2012	Black vinyl black grille	$435	$575
1990-2021	Various colors	$350	$450

Model 1960AX/1960BX 4x12 Cabinet

1990-present. Cab for Model 1987X and 1959X reissue heads, AX slant, BX straight.

1990-2021	AX	$435	$575
1990-2021	BX	$435	$575

Model 1960TV 4x12 Slant Cabinet

1990-2012. Extra tall for JTM 45, mono, 100 watts.

1990-2012	Various colors	$350	$450

Model 1962 Bluesbreaker Combo

1999-2017. Vintage Series, similar to JTM 45 but with 2 reissue 'Greenback' 25-watt 2x12" speakers and addition of footswitchable tremolo effect.

1999-2017		$975	$1,300

Model 1964 Lead/Bass 50-Watt Head

1973-1976. Head with 50 watts, designed for lead or bass.

1973-1976		$875	$1,150

Model 1965A/1965B Cabinet

1984-1991. 140 watt 4x10" slant front (A) or straight front (B) cab.

1984-1991		$315	$415

Model 1966 Cabinet

1985-1991. 150 watt 2x12" cab.

1985-1991		$315	$415

Marshall 1958 18-Watt Lead
Kris Blakely

AMPS

1971 Marshall 1959 Super Lead
William Bethurem

Marshall 1962 Bluesbreaker Combo

Marshall 1974X

Marshall 1987X
Ted Wulfers

1972 Marshall 2040 Artist
Mark K

MODEL YEAR	FEATURES	EXC. COND. LOW	HIGH

Model 1967 Major 200-Watt Head
1968-1974. 200 watts, the original Marshall 200 Pig was not popular and revised into the 200 'Major'. The new Major 200 was similar to the other large amps and included 2 channels, 4 inputs, but a larger amp cab.

1968	Plexi	$2,200	$2,900
1969-1970	Aluminum	$2,000	$2,600
1971-1972	Small box	$1,050	$1,400
1973-1974	Large box	$1,025	$1,350

Model 1967 Pig 200-Watt Head
1967-early-1968 only. Head with 200 watts. The control panel was short and stubby and nicknamed the Pig, the 200-watt circuit was dissimilar (and unpopular) to the 50-watt and 100-watt circuits.

1967-1968		$2,300	$3,000

Model 1968 100-Watt Super PA Head
1966-1975. PA head with 100 watts, 2 sets of 4 inputs (identifies PA configuration), often used for guitar, matching cabinet.

1966-1969	Matching cab	$1,200	$1,600
1966-1969	Plexi	$2,725	$3,575
1969-1972	Aluminum	$2,050	$2,700
1969-1975	Matching cab	$850	$1,100

Model 1973
1965-1968. Tube combo, 18 watts, 2x12".

1965		$6,500	$8,500
1966		$6,200	$8,100
1967		$5,100	$6,600
1968		$4,500	$5,900

Model 1973 JMP Lead/Bass 20
1973 only. Front panel: JMP, back panel: Lead & Bass 20, 20 watts, 1x12" straight front checkered grille cab, head and cab black vinyl.

1973		$1,875	$2,425

Model 1974
1965-1968. Tube combo, 18 watts, 1x12".

1965		$4,000	$5,300
1966		$3,800	$5,000
1967		$3,500	$4,600
1968		$3,200	$4,250

Model 1974X/1974CX
2004-present. Handwired Series, reissue of 18-watt, 1x12" combo, extension cabinet available (CX).

2004-2021	1974CX cab	$475	$625
2004-2021	Combo	$1,175	$1,550

Model 1982/1982A/1982B Cabinet
1967-1987. Bass and lead 4x12", 100 watt 1982/1982B, upped to 120 watts in '70. Becomes higher powered 320 and 400 watts Model 1982A/B in '81 and '82.

1967-1970		$2,000	$2,600
1971-1980		$750	$1,450
1981-1982		$435	$575
1983-1987		$350	$575

Model 1986 50-Watt Bass Head
1966-1981. Bass version of 1987, 50-watt.

1966-1969	Black, plexi	$3,100	$4,100
1969-1970	Black, aluminum	$2,100	$2,800
1971-1972	Black, hand-wired, small box	$1,700	$2,300
1973-1975	Black, printed CB, large box	$1,450	$1,925

MODEL YEAR	FEATURES	EXC. COND. LOW	HIGH
1976-1979	Black	$1,250	$1,650
1980-1981	Black	$1,175	$1,550

Model 1987 50-Watt Head
1966-1981. Head amp, 50 watts, plexiglas panel until mid-'69, aluminum panel after.

1966-1969	Black, plexi	$3,100	$4,100
1966-1969	Custom color, plexi	$4,800	$6,200
1969-1970	Black, aluminum	$2,100	$2,800
1969-1970	Custom color, aluminum	$3,900	$5,200
1971-1972	Black, hand-wired, small box	$1,700	$2,300
1971-1972	Custom color, hand-wired	$2,600	$3,400
1973-1975	Black, printed CB, large box	$1,450	$1,925
1973-1975	Custom color, printed CB	$1,950	$2,600
1976-1979	Black	$1,250	$1,650
1976-1979	Custom color	$1,450	$1,925
1980-1981	Black	$1,175	$1,550
1980-1981	Custom color	$1,350	$1,750

Model 1987X Head
1992-present. Vintage Series amp, all tube, 50 watts, 4 inputs, plexi.

1992-2021		$975	$1,300

Model 1992 Super Bass Head
1966-1981. 100 watts, plexi panel until mid-'69 when replaced by aluminum front panel, 2 channels, 4 inputs.

1966-1969	Black, plexi	$3,700	$4,900
1966-1969	Custom color, plexi	$5,300	$7,000
1969-1970	Black, aluminum	$2,200	$2,900
1969-1970	Custom color, aluminum	$4,400	$5,700
1971-1972	Black, hand-wired, small box	$2,200	$2,900
1971-1972	Custom color, hand-wired	$2,600	$3,400
1973-1975	Black, printed CB, large box	$1,450	$1,925
1973-1975	Custom color, printed CB	$1,950	$2,600
1976-1979	Black	$1,250	$1,650
1976-1979	Custom color	$1,450	$1,925
1980-1981	Black	$1,175	$1,550
1980-1981	Custom color	$1,350	$1,750

Model 1992LEM Lemmy Signature Super Bass
2008-2013. Lemmy Kilmister specs, matching 100-watt head with 4x12" and 4x15" stacked cabinets.

2008-2013	Full-stack	$3,200	$4,200

Model 2040 Artist 50-Watt Combo
1971-1978. 50 watts, 2x12" Artist/Artiste combo model with a different (less popular?) circuit.

1971-1978		$1,550	$2,000

Model 2041 Artist Head/Cabinet Set
1971-1978. 50 watts, 2x12" half stack Artist/Artiste cab with a different (less popular?) circuit.

1971-1978		$1,800	$2,300

AMPS

MODEL YEAR	FEATURES	EXC. COND. LOW	HIGH

Model 2046 Specialist 25-Watt Combo
1972-1973. 25 watts, 1x15" speaker, limited production due to design flaw (amp overheats).

1972-1973		$525	$700

Model 2060 Mercury Combo
1972-1973. Combo amp, 5 watts, 1x12", available in red or orange covering.

1972-1973		$550	$725

Model 2061 20-Watt Lead/Bass Head
1968-1973. Lead/bass head, 20 watts, plexi until '69, aluminum after. Reissued in '04 as the Model 2061X.

1968-1969	Black, plexi	$3,000	$4,000
1969-1970	Black, aluminum	$2,100	$2,700
1971-1972	Black, aluminum	$1,600	$2,100
1973	Black, aluminum	$1,450	$1,900

Model 2061X 20-Watt Lead/Bass Head Reissue
2004-2017. Handwired Series, reissue of 2061 amp head, 20 watts.

2004-2014	1x12 cab	$359	$475
2004-2015	2x12 cab	$375	$500
2004-2017	Head only	$875	$1,125

Model 2068 Artist (JMP) Set
1971-1978. 100-watt head with matching Artist cab, reverb, small logo.

1971-1978		$1,550	$2,000

Model 2078 Combo
1973-1978. Solidstate, 100 watts, 4x12" combo, gold front panel, dark cover, gray grille.

1973-1978		$700	$925

Model 2103 100-Watt 1-Channel Master Combo
1975-1981. One channel, 2 inputs, 100 watts, 2x12", first master volume design, combo version of 2203 head.

1975-1981		$1,100	$1,450

Model 2104 50-Watt 1-Channel Master Combo
1975-1981. One channel, 2 inputs, 50 watts, 2x12", first master volume design, combo version of 2204 head.

1975-1981		$1,100	$1,450

Model 2144 Master Reverb Combo
1978 only. Master volume similar to 2104 but with reverb and boost, 50 watts, 2x12".

1978		$1,200	$1,600

Model 2150 100-Watt 1x12 Combo
1978. Tubes.

1978		$700	$925

Model 2159 100-Watt 2-Channel Combo
1977-1981. 100 watts, 2 channels, 4 inputs, 2x12" combo version of Model 1959 Super Lead head.

1977-1981		$1,025	$1,350

Model 2199
1979. Solidstate 2x12" combo.

1979		$460	$600

Model 2200 100-Watt Lead Combo
1977-1981. 100 watts, 2x12" combo, early solidstate, includes boost section, no reverb.

1977-1981		$525	$675

Model 2203 Lead Head
1975-1981. Head amp, 100 watts, 2 inputs, first master volume model design, often seen with Mark II logo.

1975-1981	Black	$1,175	$1,550
1975-1981	Fawn Beige	$1,250	$1,650

Model 2203X JCM800 Head Reissue
2002-2010. 100 watts.

2002-2010		$1,175	$1,550

Model 2204 50-Watt Head
1975-1981. Head only, 50 watts with master volume.

1975-1981		$1,175	$1,550

Model 2266 50-Watt Combo
2007-2013. Vintage Modern series, 2x12".

2007-2013		$650	$850

Model 2466 100-Watt Head
2007-2013. Vintage Modern series.

2007-2013		$650	$850

Model 3203 Artist Head
1986-1991. Tube head version of earlier '84 Model 3210 MOS-FET, designed as affordable alternative, 30 watts, standard short cab, 2 inputs separated by 3 control knobs, Artist 3203 logo on front panel, black.

1986-1991		$390	$520

Model 3210 MOS-FET Head
1984-1991. MOS-FET solidstate head, refer Mini-Stack listing for 3210 with 4x10" stacked cabinets. Early-'80s front panel: Lead 100 MOS-FET.

1984-1991		$270	$355

Model 3310 100-Watt Lead
1988-1991. Solidstate, 100 watts, lead head with channel switching and reverb.

1988-1991		$420	$555

Model 4001 Studio 15
1985-1992. 15 watts using 6V6 (only model to do this up to this time), 1x12" Celestion Vintage 30 speakers.

1985-1992		$675	$875

Model 4104 50-Watt Combo
1981-1990. Combo version of 2204 head, 50 watts, 2x12", master volume.

1981-1990		$1,300	$1,675

Model 4203 Artist 30-Watt Combo

1986-1991		$390	$510

Model 5002 Combo
1984-1991. Solidstate combo amp, 20 watts, 1x10", master volume.

1984-1991		$170	$225

Model 5005 Lead 12
1983-1991. Solidstate student amp, 12 watts, master volume, 1x10".

1983-1991		$195	$245

Model 5205 Reverb 12
1986. Solidstate, 12 watts, 1x10", Reverb 12 logo on front panel.

1986		$195	$245

Model 5302 Keyboard
1984-1988. Solidstate, 20 watts, 1x10", marketed for keyboard application.

1984-1988		$170	$230

1971 Marshall 2060 Mercury
Steve Lee

AMPS

2007 Marshall 2466 Vintage/Modern
Joseph Bradshaw Jr.

Marshall 4001 Studio 15
Imaged by Heritage Auctions, HA.com

Marshall 6100 30th Anniversary
Imaged by Heritage Auctions, HA.com

'50s Masco MU-5
Imaged by Heritage Auctions, HA.com

Matamp GT2 MK II

MODEL YEAR	FEATURES	EXC. COND. LOW	HIGH
Model 5502 Bass			
1984-ca.1992. Solidstate bass combo amp, 20 watts, 1x10" Celestion.			
1984-1992		$170	$230
Model 6100 30th Anniversary			
1992-1998. Head with 100/50/25 switchable watts and 4x12" cabinet (matching colors), first year and into early '93 was blue tolex, black afterwards.			
1992-1998	4x12 cab	$365	$480
1992-1998	Head only	$725	$975
Model 6101 30th Anniversary Combo			
1992-1998. 1x12" combo version of 6100 amp, first year and into early '93 was blue tolex, black afterwards.			
1992-1998		$1,050	$1,350
Model 8008 Valvestate Rackmount			
1991-2001. Valvestate solidstate rack mount power amp with dual 40-watt channels.			
1991-2001		$145	$195
Model 8010 Valvestate VS15 Combo			
1991-1997. Valvestate solidstate, 10 watts, 1x8", compact size, black vinyl, black grille.			
1991-1997		$125	$170
Model 8040 Valvestate 40V Combo			
1991-1997. Valvestate solidstate with tube preamp, 40 watts, 1x12", compact size, black vinyl, black grille.			
1991-1997		$145	$195
Model 8080 Valvestate 80V Combo			
1991-1997. Valvestate solidstate with tube 12AX7 preamp, 80 watts, 1x12", compact size, black vinyl, black grille.			
1991-1997		$145	$195
Model 8100 100-Watt Valvestate VS100H Head			
1991-2001. Valvestate solidstate head, 100 watts.			
1991-2001		$170	$220
Model 8200 200-Watt Valvestate Head			
1993-1998. Valvestate solidstate reverb head, 2x100-watt channels.			
1993-1998		$195	$255
Model 8222 Valvestate Cabinet			
1993-1998. 200 watts, 2x12 extention cab, designed for 8200 head.			
1993-1998		$145	$195
Model 8240 Valvestate Stereo Chorus			
1992-1996. Valvestate, 80 watts (2x40 watts stereo), 2x12" combo, reverb, chorus.			
1992-1996		$220	$290
Model 8280 2x80-Watt Valvestate Combo			
1993-1996. Valvestate solidstate, 2x80 watts, 2x12".			
1993-1996		$245	$315
Model 8412 Valvestate Cabinet			
1991-2001. 140 watts, 4x12 extention cab, designed for 8100 head.			
1991-2001		$195	$255
MS-2/R/C			
1990-present. Microamp series, 1 watt, battery operated, miniature black half-stack amp and cab. Red MS-2R and checkered speaker grille and gold logo MS-2C added in '93.			
1990-2021		$35	$45

MODEL YEAR	FEATURES	EXC. COND. LOW	HIGH
MS-4			
1998-present. Full-stack version of MS-2, black.			
1998-2021		$40	$50
Origin (OR) Series			
2018-present. Various tube models include; ORIGIN5, 20C, 20H and 50C. Number indicates watts, C is combo, H is head only.			
2018-2021		$220	$290
Silver Jubilee Model 2550 50/25 (Tall) Head			
1987-1989. 50/25 switchable tall box head for full Jubilee stack, silver vinyl and chrome control panel.			
1987-1989		$1,800	$2,350
Silver Jubilee Model 2551 4x12 Cabinet			
1987-1989. Matching silver 4x12" cabs for Jubilee 2550 head, various models, silver vinyl.			
1987-1989	2551A, slant	$800	$1,050
1987-1989	2551AV, Vintage 30	$800	$1,050
1987-1989	2551B, straight	$800	$1,050
1987-1989	2551BV, Vintage 30	$800	$1,050
Silver Jubilee Model 2553 50/25 (Short) Head			
1987-1988. 50/25 switchable small box head for mini-short stack, silver vinyl and chrome control panel.			
1987-1988		$1,625	$2,150
Silver Jubilee Model 2554 1x12 Combo			
1987-1989. 50/25 watts, 1x12" combo using 2550 chassis, silver vinyl and chrome control panel.			
1987-1989		$1,800	$2,350
Silver Jubilee Model 2555 Head			
1987-1989. 100/50 version of 2550 head, silver vinyl and chrome control panel.			
1987-1989		$1,625	$2,150
Silver Jubilee Model 2556 2x12 Cabinet			
1987-1989. Matching silver 2x12" cabs for Jubilee heads, various models, silver vinyl.			
1987-1989	2556A, slant	$800	$1,050
1987-1989	2556AV, Vintage 30	$800	$1,050
1987-1989	2556B, straight	$800	$1,050
1987-1989	2556BV, Vintage 30	$800	$1,050
Silver Jubilee Model 2558 2x12 Combo			
1987-1989. 50/25 watts, 2x12" combo using 2550 chassis, silver vinyl and chrome control panel.			
1987-1989		$1,750	$2,250
Silver Jubilee Model 3560 600 Head			
1987. Rackmount 2x300 watts.			
1987		$425	$550
SL-5			
2013-2015. Tube combo, 5 watts, 1x12", script logo signature on front panel.			
2013-2015		$675	$900
Super 100 40th Anniversary JTM45 MK II Full Stack			
2005. 100 watts, 2 4x12 cabs, 250 made.			
2005		$3,800	$5,000

Martin

Martin has dabbled in amps a few times, under both the Martin and Stinger brand names. The first batch were amps made by other introduced with their electric acoustics in 1959.

MODEL YEAR	FEATURES	EXC. COND. LOW	HIGH

Model 112
1959-1961. Branded C.F. Martin inside label, made by Rowe-DeArmond, 1x12 combo, limited production, 2x6V6 power tubes, 2x12AX7 preamp tubes, with tube rectifier, 4 inputs, 3 control knobs.

1959-1961		$3,600	$4,650

SS140
1965-1966		$875	$1,150

Stinger FX-1
1988-1990. 10 watts, EQ, switchable solidstate tube-synth circuit, line out and footswitch jacks.

1988-1990		$150	$195

Stinger FX-1R
1988-1990. Mini-stack amp, 2x10", 15 watts, dual-stage circuitry.

1988-1990		$175	$225

Stinger FX-6B
1989-1990. Combo bass amp, 60 watts, 1x15".

1988-1990		$175	$225

Masco
1940s-1950s. The Mark Alan Sampson Company, Long Island, New York, produced a variety of electronic products including tube PA amps and small combo instrument amps. The PA heads are also popular with harp players.

Massie
1940s. Ray Massie worked in Leo Fender's repair shop in the 1940s and also built tube amps. He later worked at the Fender company.

Matamp
1966-present. Tube amps, combos and cabinets built in Huddersfield, England, bearing names like Red, Green, White, Black, and Blue. German-born Mat Mathias started building amps in England in '58 and designed his first Matamp in '66. From '69 to '73, Mathias also made Orange amps. In '89, Mathias died at age 66 and his family later sold the factory to Jeff Lewis.

1x15" Cabinet
1970s		$850	$1,100

GT-120 Green Stack
1990s. 120 watt GT head with 4x12" straight front cab.

1993-1999		$1,750	$2,275

GT-120 Head
1971		$2,300	$3,000

Matchless
1989-1999, 2001-present. Founded by Mark Sampson and Rick Perrotta in California. Circuits based on Vox AC-30 with special attention to transformers. A new Matchless company was reorganized in 2001 by Phil Jamison, former head of production for the original company.

Avalon 35 Head
2009-2010. 35 watts head, reverb.

2009-2010		$1,625	$2,100

Brave 40 112
1997-1999. 40 watts class A, 1x12", footswitchable between high and low inputs.

1997-1999		$1,575	$2,050

Brave 40 212
1997-1999. 2x12" version of Brave.

1997-1999		$1,675	$2,175

Chief Head
1995-1999. 100 watts class A, head.

1995-1999		$2,650	$3,450

Chief 212
1995-1999. 100 watts class A, 2x12", reverb.

1995-1999		$2,800	$3,650

Chief 410
1995-1999. 100 watts class A, 4x10", reverb.

1995-1999		$2,900	$3,775

Chieftan Head
1995-1999. 40 watts class A head, reverb, chicken-head knobs.

1995-1999		$1,750	$2,275

Chieftan 112
1995-1999, 2001. 40 watts class A, 1x12", reverb.

1995-1999		$2,300	$3,000
2001	Jamison era	$2,300	$3,000

Chieftan 210
1995-1999. 40 watts class A, 2x10", reverb.

1995-1999		$2,300	$3,000

Chieftan 212
1995-1999, 2001-present. 40 watts class A, 2x12", reverb.

1995-1999		$2,500	$3,250
2001-2019	Jamison era	$2,500	$3,250

Chieftan 410
1995-1999. 40 watts class A, 4x10", reverb.

1995-1999		$2,650	$3,450

Clipper 15 112
1998-1999. 15 watts, single channel, 1x12".

1998-1999		$1,100	$1,450

Clipper 15 210
1998-1999. 15 watts, single channel, 2x10".

1998-1999		$1,200	$1,575

Clubman 35 Head
1993-1999. 35 watts class A head.

1993-1999		$1,950	$2,525

DC-30 Standard Cabinet
1991-1999. 30 watts, 2x12", with or without reverb.

1991-1999		$2,900	$3,775

DC-30 Exotic Wood Cabinet
1995-1999. 30 watts, 2x12", gold plating, limited production.

1995-1999		$4,800	$6,250

ES/EB Cabinet
ES = speaker cabinets and EB = bass speaker cabinets.

1991-1999	1x12	$450	$585
1993-1999	2x10	$550	$728
1993-1999	2x10+2x12	$700	$900
1993-1999	2x12	$575	$750
1993-1999	4x12	$750	$975
1997-1999	1x15	$465	$600
1997-1999	4x10	$650	$850

1995 Matchless Chieftan 212
Imaged by Heritage Auctions, HA.com

AMPS

Matchless Clubman 35
David Nicholas

2011 Matchless DC-30
Jacques Menache Masri

Matchless Independence 35

Matchless Nighthawk

Maven Peal RG88

MODEL YEAR	FEATURES	EXC. COND. LOW	HIGH
HC-30 Head			
1991-1999, 2003. The first model offered by Matchless, 30 watts class A head.			
1991-1999		$2,150	$2,795
2003	Jamison era	$2,150	$2,795
HC-85 Head			
1992. Only 25 made, similar to HC-30 but more flexible using various tube substitutions.			
1992		$2,275	$2,950
Hurricane Head			
1997. 15 watts class A head.			
1997		$1,300	$1,700
Hurricane 112			
1994-1997. 15 watts class A, 1x12".			
1994-1997		$1,300	$1,700
Hurricane 210			
1996-1997. 15 watts class A, 2x10".			
1996-1997		$1,575	$2,050
Independence 35 Head			
2005-2017. 35 watts, with or without reverb.			
2005-2017		$1,950	$2,525
JJ-30 112 John Jorgensen			
1997-1999. 30 watts, DC-30 chasis with reverb and tremolo, 1x12" Celestion 30, offered in white, blue, gray sparkle tolex or black.			
1997-1999		$3,800	$4,950
Lightning 15 Head			
1994-1997, 2005-present. 15 watts class A head.			
1994-1997		$1,400	$1,825
Lightning 15 112			
1994-1999, 2001-present. 15 watts class A, 1x12".			
1994-1999		$2,000	$2,600
2001-2021	Jamison era	$2,000	$2,600
Lightning 15 210			
1996-1997, 2001-2006. 15 watts class A, 2x10".			
1996-1997		$2,100	$2,725
2001-2006	Jamison era	$2,100	$2,725
Lightning 15 212			
1998, 2001-present. 15 watts class A, 2x12".			
1998-2021		$2,150	$2,800
Little Monster/The Little Monster			
2007-2009. 9 watts, offered as head, and 1x12" or 2x12" combo.			
2007-2009		$1,400	$1,825
Nighthawk			
2003-present. 15 watts, offered as head, and 1x12", 2x10" or 2x12" combo.			
2003-2014	2x10	$1,300	$1,700
2003-2021	1x12	$1,200	$1,550
2003-2021	2x12	$1,350	$1,750
Phoenix 35 (PH-35) Head			
2003-present. 35-watt head, black or red.			
2003-2021		$1,950	$2,525
SC-30 Standard Cabinet			
1991-1999. 30 watts class A, 1x12".			
1991-1999		$2,875	$3,750
2001-2006	Jamison era	$2,700	$3,500
SC-30 Exotic Wood Cabinet			
1995-1999. 30 watts class A, 1x12", gold plating, limited production.			
1995-1999		$4,500	$5,900

MODEL YEAR	FEATURES	EXC. COND. LOW	HIGH
Skyliner Reverb 15 112			
1998-1999. 15 watts, 2 channels, 1x12".			
1998-1999		$975	$1,275
Skyliner Reverb 15 210			
1998-1999. 15 watts, 2 channels, 2x10".			
1998-1999		$1,075	$1,400
Spitfire 15 Head			
1997. 15 watts, head.			
1997		$1,300	$1,700
Spitfire 15 112			
1994-1997. 15 watts, 1x12".			
1994-1997		$1,450	$1,875
Spitfire 15 210			
1996-1997. 15 watts, 2x10".			
1996-1997		$1,575	$2,050
Starliner 40 212			
1999. 40 watts, 2x12".			
1999		$1,625	$2,100
Superchief 120 Head			
1994-1999. 120 watts, class A head.			
1994-1999		$2,500	$3,250
TC-30 Standard Cabinet			
1991-1999. 30 watts, 2x10" class A, low production numbers makes value approximate with DC-30.			
1991-1999		$2,750	$3,575
TC-30 Exotic Wood Cabinet			
1991-1999. 30 watts, 2x10" class A, limited production.			
1991-1999		$3,525	$4,575
Thunderchief Bass Head			
1994-1999. 200 watts, class A bass head.			
1994-1999		$2,000	$2,600
Thunderman 100 Bass Combo			
1997-1998. 100 watts, 1x15" in portaflex-style flip-top cab.			
1997-1998		$2,750	$3,575
Tornado 15 112			
1994-1995. Compact, 15 watts, 1x12", 2-tone covering, simple controls – volume, tone, tremolo speed, tremolo depth.			
1994-1995		$925	$1,200

Maven Peal

Amps, combos and cabinets built by David Zimmerman in Plainfield, Vermont, beginning in 1999. Serial number format is by amp wattage and sequential build; for example, 15-watt amp 15-001.

Mega Amplifiers

Budget and intermediate grade, production, solidstate and tube amps from Guitar Jones, Inc. of Pomona, California.

Merlin

Rack mount bass heads built in Germany by Musician Sound Design. They also offer the MSD guitar effects.

Mesa-Boogie

1971-present. Founded by Randall Smith in San Francisco, California. Circuits styled on high-gain Fender-based chassis designs, ushering in the com-

AMPS

pact high-gain amp market. Mesa was acquired by Gibson in early 2021.

The following serial number information and specs courtesy of Mesa Engineering.

.50 Caliber/.50 Caliber+ Head

Jan. 1987-Dec. 1988, 1992-1993. Serial numbers: SS3100 - SS11,499. Mesa Engineering calls it Caliber .50. Tube head amp, 50 watts, 5-band EQ, effects loop. Called the .50 Caliber Plus in '92 and '93.

MODEL YEAR	FEATURES	EXC. COND. LOW	HIGH
1987-1988	Caliber	$650	$850
1992-1993	Caliber+	$650	$850

.50 Caliber+ Combo

Dec. 1988-Oct. 1993. Serial numbers FP11,550 - FP29,080. 50 watts, 1x12" combo amp.

1988-1993		$725	$950

20/20

Jun. 1995-2010. Serial numbers: TT-01. 20-22 watts per channel.

1995-2010		$725	$950

50/50 (Fifty/Fifty)

May 1989-2001. Serial numbers: FF001-. 100 watts total power, 50 watts per channel, front panel reads Fifty/Fifty, contains 4 6L6 power tubes.

1989-2001		$725	$950

395

Feb. 1991-Apr. 1992. Serial numbers: S2572 - S3237.

1991-1992		$975	$1,275

Bass 400/Bass 400+ Head

Aug. 1989-Aug. 1990. Serial numbers: B001-B1200. About 500 watts using 12 5881 power tubes. Replaced by 400+ Aug.1990-present, serial numbers: B1200- . Update change to 7-band EQ at serial number B1677.

1989-1990	Bass 400	$1,250	$1,625
1990-1999	Bass 400+	$1,325	$1,725

Big Block Series

2004-2014. Rackmount bass amps, models 750 (750w head) and Titan V-12 (650/1200w).

2004-2014	750	$1,250	$1,625
2006-2010	Titan V-12	$1,250	$1,625

Blue Angel Series

Jun. 1994-2004. Serial numbers BA01-. Switchable between 15, 33 or 38 watts, offered as head, 1x12" combo or 4x10" combo, blue cover.

1994-2004	Combo 1x12	$925	$1,225
1994-2004	Combo 4x10	$1,050	$1,400

Buster Bass Combo

1999-2001. 200 watts, 2x10", wedge cabinet, black vinyl, metal grille.

1999-2001		$725	$950

Buster Bass Head

Dec. 1997-Jan. 2001. Serial numbers: BS-1-999. 200 watts via 6 6L6 power tubes.

1997-2001		$725	$950

Coliseum 300

Oct. 1997-2000. Serial numbers: COL-01 - COL-132. 200 watts/channel, 12 6L6 power tubes, rack mount.

1997-2000		$1,375	$1,800

D-180 Head

Jul. 1982-Dec. 1985. Serial numbers: D001-D681. All tube head amp, 200 watts, preamp, switchable.

1982-1985		$1,050	$1,375

DC-3

Sep. 1994-Jan. 1999. Serial numbers: DC3-001 - DC3-4523. 35 watts, 1x12".

MODEL YEAR	FEATURES	EXC. COND. LOW	HIGH
1994-1999	Combo 1x12	$825	$1,075
1994-1999	Head only	$650	$850

DC-5

Oct. 1993-Jan. 1999. Serial numbers: DC1024 - DC31,941. 50-watt head, 1x12" combo.

1993-1999	Combo 1x12	$825	$1,075
1993-1999	Head only	$650	$850

DC-10

May 1996-Jan. 1999. Serial numbers: DCX-001 - DCX-999. Dirty/Clean (DC), 100 watts (6L6s), 2x12".

1993-1996	Combo 2x12	$925	$1,200
1996-1999	Head only	$775	$1,025

Electra Dyne Head

2009-2013. 45/90 watts, Black Taurus/black grille or British Tan Bronco/tan grille.

2009-2013		$1,100	$1,450

Express Series

2007-2017. Compact combo tube amps with power switching.

2007-2016	5:50, 2x12, 5-50w	$1,025	$1,350
2007-2017	5:25, 1x10, 5-25w	$875	$1,150
2007-2017	5:50, 1x12, 5-50w	$950	$1,250
2008	5:25, short head, 25w	$825	$1,075

Extension Cabinet

1980s-present. Mesa-Boogie offered 'extension cabinets' which could be mixed and matched with amp heads, using different configurations with correct impedance. Other manufacturers often consider an extension cab as an extra cab, but Mesa Engineering considers it to be the main cab (not an extra). The company has generic cabs as well as cabs associated with specific models, but both generic and model-specific fall into similar price ranges. Some other variances include; vertical or horizontal, open back or closed, slant or straight front, grille could be metal or cloth, and some cabs are designated for bass guitar. Specialized cabinets may be more than values shown.

1980-2021	Various sizes	$275	$1,100

F-30

2002-Feb. 2007. Combo, 30 watts, 1x12".

2002-2007		$525	$700

F-50

2002-Feb. 2007. Combo, 50 watts, 1x12", AB 2 6L6 power.

2002-2007		$750	$1,000
2002-2007	Head only	$700	$950

F-100

2002-Feb. 2007. Combo, 100 watts, 2x12".

2002-2007	Combo 2x12	$950	$1,225
2002-2007	Head only	$825	$1,075

Fillmore 100 Combo

2019-present. 100 watts, 1x12" or 2x12", 2 footswitchable channels.

2019-2021		$1,425	$1,900

Formula Preamp

Jul. 1998-2002. Serial numbers: F-01. Used 5 12AX7 tubes, 3 channels.

1998-2002		$450	$600

Mesa-Boogie .50 Caliber+
Imaged by Heritage Auctions, HA.com

Mesa-Boogie Blue Angel

Mesa-Boogie Express 5:50

AMPS

Mesa-Boogie Lone Star 1x12

Mesa-Boogie Mark I

Mesa-Boogie Mark II C+

MODEL YEAR	FEATURES	EXC. COND. LOW	HIGH
Heartbreaker Combo			
Jun. 1996-2001. Serial numbers: HRT-01. 60 to 100 watts switchable, 2x12" combo, designed to switch-out 6L6s, EL34s or the lower powered 6V6s in the power section, switchable solidstate or tube rectifier.			
1996-2001		$1,150	$1,500
Heartbreaker Head			
1996-2001. Head only, 100 watts.			
1996-2001		$1,050	$1,350
Lone Star Series			
2004-2020. Designed by founder Randall Smith and Doug West with focus on boutique-type amp. Class A (EL84) or AB (4 6L6) circuits, long or short head, 1x12" combo, 2x12" combo, and short head 4x10" cab, and long head 4x12" cab.			
2004-2016	Combo 1x12, hardwood	$2,000	$2,650
2004-2016	Combo 4x10, blue	$1,500	$2,000
2004-2020	Combo 1x12	$1,350	$1,800
2004-2020	Combo 2x12	$1,500	$2,000
2004-2020	Head, class A or AB	$1,250	$1,650
Lone Star Special			
2005-2020. Smaller lighter version using EL84 power tubes, 5/15/30 watts, long or short head amp or 1x12", 2x12" or 4x10" combo.			
2005-2020	Combo 1x12	$1,475	$1,950
M-180			
Apr. 1982-Jan. 1986. Serial numbers: M001-M275. Rack mount tube power amp.			
1982-1986		$750	$1,000
M-190			
1980s. Rack mount tube power amp.			
1980s		$550	$725
M-2000/Bass-2000 Head			
Jun. 1995-2003. Serial numbers: B2K-01.			
1995-2003		$800	$1,050
M6 Carbine Bass Head			
2011-2017. 600-watt head, also offered in 2x12 combo.			
2011-2017		$650	$850
Mark I Combo (Model A)			
1971-1978. The original Boogie amp, not called the Mark I until the Mark II was issued, 60 or 100 watts, 1x12", Model A serial numbers: 1-2999, very early serial numbers 1-299 had 1x15".			
1971-1978	1x12 or 1x15	$1,675	$2,225
Mark I Head			
1990. 60/100 watts, tweed cover.			
1990		$1,675	$2,225
Mark I Reissue			
Nov. 1989-Sept. 2007. Serial numbers: H001-. 100 watts, 1x12", reissue features include figured maple cab and wicker grille.			
2000-2007	Hardwood cab	$1,600	$2,125
2000-2007	Standard cab	$1,225	$1,625
Mark II B Combo			
1980-1983. Effective Aug. '80 1x12" models, serial numbers 5575-110000. May '83 1x15" models, serial numbers 560-11000. The 300 series serial numbers K1-K336.			
1981-1983	1x12 or 1x15	$1,050	$1,400
1981-1983	Hardwood cab	$1,450	$1,925

MODEL YEAR	FEATURES	EXC. COND. LOW	HIGH
Mark II B Head			
1981-1983. Head only.			
1981-1983		$750	$1,000
Mark II C/Mark II C+ Combo			
May 1983-Mar. 1985. Serial numbers 11001-14999 for 60 watts, 1x15", offered with optional white tolex cover. 300 series serial numbers after C+ are in the series K337-K422.			
1983-1985		$2,850	$3,800
1985	Hardwood cab	$3,450	$4,550
Mark II C+ Head			
1983-1985. 60-watt head.			
1983-1985	Hardwood cab	$3,350	$4,450
1983-1985	Standard cab	$2,750	$3,600
Mark II Combo			
1978-1980. Late-'78 1x12", serial numbers: 3000-5574. Effective Aug.'80 1x15", serial numbers: 300-559 until Mark II B replaced.			
1978-1980	1x12 or 1x15	$950	$1,250
Mark III Combo			
Mar. 1985-Feb. 1999. Serial numbers: 15000-28384. 300 series serialization K500-. Graphic equalizer only Mark III since Aug.'90, 100 watts, 1x12" combo. Custom cover or exotic hardwood cab will bring more than standard vinyl cover cab. There is also a Simul-Class Mark III which can run in 25, 60 or 85 watts.			
1985-1990	Black	$1,175	$1,525
1985-1990	Custom color	$1,450	$1,850
1985-1999	Custom hardwood	$1,950	$2,525
1990-1999	Graphic EQ, standard cab	$1,400	$1,825
Mark III Head			
1985-1999. 100 watts, black vinyl.			
1985-1990		$1,050	$1,400
1985-1990	Custom hardwood	$1,625	$2,150
1990-1999	Graphic EQ	$1,200	$1,550
Mark IV (Rack Mount) Head			
1990-May 2008. Rack mount version.			
1990-2008		$1,100	$1,450
Mark IV Head			
1990-May 2008. Clean rhythm, crunch rhythm and lead modes, 85 watts, EQ, 3-spring reverb, dual effects loops, digital footswitching. Also available in custom hardwood cab with wicker grille.			
1990-2008	Custom hardwood	$1,700	$2,250
1990-2008	Short head, tolex	$1,100	$1,450
Mark IV/Mark IV B Combo			
May 1990-May 2008. Changed to Model IV B Feb.'95, serial numbers: IV001. Clean rhythm, crunch rhythm and lead modes, 40 watts, EQ, 3-spring reverb, dual effects loops, digital footswitching.			
1991-1999		$1,275	$1,700
1991-1999	Custom hardwood	$2,050	$2,700
2000-2008		$1,275	$1,700
2000-2008	Custom hardwood	$2,100	$2,800
Mark V Private Reserve			
2011-2016. Special order, 1x12" combo.			
2011-2016		$4,300	$5,600
Mark V Private Reserve 40th Anniversary			
2009-2010. Limited production, 1x12 combo, 40th Anniversary logo.			
2009-2010		$4,400	$5,800

MODEL YEAR	FEATURES	EXC. COND. LOW	HIGH
Mark V/Mark Five			

2010-present. 3 channels, 10/45/90 watts, also in 1x12" combo.

| 2010-2021 | Combo 1x12 | $1,950 | $2,600 |
| 2010-2021 | Head | $1,800 | $2,400 |

Mark V:35/Mark Five:35

2015-present. 35/25/10 watts, also 1x12 combo, black.

| 2015-2021 | Combo 1x12 | $1,600 | $2,100 |
| 2015-2021 | Head | $1,750 | $2,300 |

Maverick Dual Rectifier Combo

1997-Feb. 2005. Dual channels, 4 EL84s, 35 watts, 1x12", 2x12" or 4x10" combo amp, 5AR4 tube rectifier, cream vinyl covering. Serial number: MAV. Also available as head.

1997-2005	1x12	$1,000	$1,300
1997-2005	2x12	$1,100	$1,450
2005	4x10	$1,150	$1,500

Maverick Dual Rectifier Head

1994-Feb. 2005. 35 watts, Dual Rectifier head, white/blond vinyl cover.

| 1994-2005 | | $900 | $1,200 |

Mini Rectifier Twenty-Five Head

2012-present. Ultra compact design, 10/25 watts, 2 channels.

| 2012-2021 | | $800 | $1,050 |

M-Pulse 360

Jul. 2001-2005. Serial numbers: MP3-01-. Rack mount, silver panel.

| 2001-2003 | | $775 | $1,025 |

M-Pulse 600

Apr. 2001-2011. Serial numbers: MP6-01- . Rack mount bass with 600 watts, tube preamp.

| 2001-2011 | | $850 | $1,125 |

Nomad 45 Combo

Jul. 1999-Feb. 2005. Serial numbers: NM45-01. 45 watts, 1x12, 2x12" or 4x10" combo, dark vinyl cover, dark grille.

1999-2005	1x12	$600	$800
1999-2005	2x12	$650	$850
1999-2005	4x10	$775	$1,000

Nomad 45 Head

1999-Feb. 2005. 45 watts, dark vinyl cover, dark grille.

| 1999-2005 | | $525 | $700 |

Nomad 55 Combo

Jul. 1999-2004. Serial numbers: NM55-01. 55 watts, 1x12", 2x12" or 4x10" combo.

| 1999-2004 | 1x12 | $600 | $800 |
| 1999-2004 | 2x12 | $650 | $850 |

Nomad 55 Head

Amp

| 1999-2004 | | $525 | $700 |

Nomad 100 Combo

Jul. 1999-Feb. 2005. 100 watts, 1x12" or 2x12" combo, black cover, black grille.

| 1999-2005 | 1x12 | $650 | $850 |
| 1999-2005 | 2x12 | $675 | $900 |

Nomad 100 Head

Jul. 1999-Feb. 2005. 100 watts, black cover, black grille.

| 1999-2005 | | $600 | $800 |

Princeton Boost Fender Conversion

1970. Fender Princeton modified by Randall Smith, Boogie badge logo instead of the Fender blackface logo on upper left corner of the grille. About 300 amps were modified and were one of the early mods that became Mesa-Boogie.

| 1970 | | $2,600 | $3,450 |

Quad Preamp

Sep. 1987-1992. Serial numbers: Q001-Q2857. Optional Quad with FU2-A footswitch Aug.'90-Jan.'92, serial numbers: Q2022-Q2857.

| 1990-1992 | With footswitch | $725 | $950 |

Recto Recording Preamp

2004-2018. Rack mount preamp.

| 2004-2018 | | $975 | $1,300 |

Rect-O-Verb Combo

Dec. 1998-2001. Serial numbers R50-. 50 watts, 1x12", black vinyl cover, black grille.

| 1998-2001 | | $1,000 | $1,325 |

Rect-O-Verb I Head

Dec. 1998-2001. Serial numbers: R50-. 50 watts, head with 2 6L6 power tubes, upgraded Apr.'01 to II Series.

| 1998-2001 | | $950 | $1,250 |

Rect-O-Verb II Combo

April 2001-2010. Upgrade R5H-750, 50 watts, AB, 2 6L6, spring reverb.

| 2001-2010 | | $1,025 | $1,350 |

Rect-O-Verb II Head

Apr. 2001-2010. Upgrade, serial number R5H-750.

| 2001-2010 | | $950 | $1,250 |

Road King Dual Rectifier Combo

2002-2015. 2x12" combo version, Series II upgrades start in '06.

| 2002-2005 | Select watts | $2,325 | $3,100 |
| 2006-2015 | Series II | $2,325 | $3,100 |

Road King Dual Rectifier Head

2002-May 2017. Tube head, various power tube selections based upon a chasis which uses 2 EL34s and 4 6L6, 2 5U4 dual rectifier tubes or silicon diode rectifiers, 50, 100 or 120 watts. Series II upgrades start in '06.

| 2002-2011 | | $2,200 | $2,900 |
| 2006-2017 | Series II | $2,200 | $2,900 |

Roadster Dual Rectifier

2006-May 2017. 50/100 watts, head only, 1x12" or 2x12" combo.

2006-2014	Combo 1x12	$1,950	$2,600
2006-2017	Combo 2x12	$2,025	$2,700
2006-2017	Head	$1,850	$2,450

Rocket 44

2011. 45 watts, 1x12" combo, spring reverb, FX loop.

| 2011 | | $550 | $725 |

Rocket 440

Mar. 1999-Aug. 2000. Serial numbers: R440-R44-1159. 45 watts, 4x10".

| 1999-2000 | | $725 | $950 |

Satellite/Satellite 60

Aug. 1990-1999. Serial numbers: ST001-ST841. Uses either 6L6s for 100 watts or EL34s for 60 watts, dark vinyl, dark grille.

| 1990-1999 | | $675 | $900 |

'80s Mesa-Boogie Mark III Combo
Imaged by Heritage Auctions, HA.com

Mesa-Boogie Rect-O-Verb I
Imaged by Heritage Auctions, HA.com

Mesa-Boogie Road King II Dual Rectifier Combo

AMPS

1984 Mesa-Boogie Son Of Boogie
Tom Pfeifer

Mesa-Boogie Stiletto
Imaged by Heritage Auctions, HA.com

Mesa-Boogie Subway Blues
Mark Aftab Sackoor

MODEL YEAR	FEATURES	EXC. COND. LOW	HIGH
Solo 50 Rectifier Series I Head			
Nov. 1998-Apr. 2001. Serial numbers: R50. 50-watt head.			
1998-2001		$775	$1,025
Solo 50 Rectifier Series II Head			
Apr. 2001-2011. Upgrade, serial numbers: S50-S1709. Upgrades preamp section, head with 50 watts.			
2001-2011		$775	$1,025
Solo Dual Rectifier Head			
1997-2011. Dual Rectifier Solo logo on front panel, 3x5U4, 150 watts.			
1997-2011		$1,425	$1,900
Solo Triple Rectifier Head			
1997-2011. Triple Rectifier Solo logo on front panel, 3x5U4, 150 watts.			
1997-2011		$1,450	$1,900
Son Of Boogie			
May 1982-Dec. 1985. Serial numbers: S100-S2390. 60 watts, 1x12", considered the first reissue of the original Mark I.			
1982-1985		$650	$850
Stereo 290 (Simul 2-Ninety)			
Jun. 1992-2021. Serial numbers: R0001-. Dual 90-watt stereo channels, rack mount.			
1992-2021		$900	$1,200
Stereo 295			
Mar. 1987-May 1991. Serial numbers: S001-S2673. Dual 95-watt class A/B stereo channels, rack mount. Selectable 30 watts Class A (EL34 power tubes) power.			
1987-1991		$600	$800
Stiletto Ace			
2007-2011. 50 watts, 2 channels, head or combo.			
2007-2011	Combo 1x12	$1,050	$1,400
2007-2011	Combo 2x12	$1,125	$1,500
2007-2011	Head only	$1,000	$1,325
Stiletto Series			
2004-2011. Series includes the Deuce (50 or 100 watts, 4 EL-34s) and Trident (50 or 150 watts, 6 EL-34s).			
2004-2011	Deuce	$1,225	$1,625
2004-2011	Trident	$1,300	$1,725
Strategy 400			
Mar. 1987-May 1991. Serial numbers: S001-S2627. 400 to 500 watts, power amplifier with 12 6L6 power tubes.			
1987-1991		$950	$1,225
Strategy 500			
Jun. 1991-Apr. 1992. S2,552- . Rack mount, 500 watts, 4 6550 power tubes.			
1991-1992		$1,150	$1,525
Studio .22/Studio .22+			
Nov. 1985-1988. Serial numbers: SS000-SS11499, black vinyl, black grille, 22 watts, 1x12". Replaced by .22+ Dec. '88-Aug. '93. Serial numbers: FP11,500-FP28,582. 22 watts.			
1985-1988	22	$650	$875
1988-1993	22+	$650	$875
Studio Caliber DC-2			
Apr. 1994-Jan. 1999. Serial numbers: DC2-01 - DC2-4247 (formerly called DC-2). 20 watts, 1x12" combo, dark vinyl, dark grille.			
1994-1999		$525	$700

MODEL YEAR	FEATURES	EXC. COND. LOW	HIGH
Studio Preamp			
Aug. 1988-Dec. 1993. Serial numbers: SP000-SP7890. Tube preamp, EQ, reverb, effects loop.			
1988-1993		$525	$700
Subway Reverb Rocket			
Jun. 1998-Aug. 2001. Serial numbers: RR1000-RR2461. 20 watts, 1x10".			
1998-2001		$675	$900
Subway Rocket (Non-Reverb)			
Jan. 1996-Jul. 1998. Serial numbers: SR001-SR2825. No reverb, 20 watts, 1x10".			
1996-1998		$675	$900
Subway/Subway Blues			
Sep. 1994-Aug. 2000. Serial numbers: SB001-SB2515. 20 watts, 1x10".			
1994-2000		$650	$850
TA-15 Head			
2010-2015. TransAtlantic series, lunchbox-sized tube head, 2 channels, 5/15/25 watts.			
2010-2015		$650	$850
TA-30 Combo			
2012-2015. TransAtlantic series, 15/30/40 watts, 1x12" or 2x12" combo, 2 channels.			
2012-2015		$1,125	$1,500
Trem-O-Verb Dual Rectifier Combo			
Jun.1993-Jan.2001. Serial numbers: R- to about R-21210. 100 watts, 2x12" Celestion Vintage 30.			
1993-2001		$1,200	$1,600
Trem-O-Verb Dual Rectifier Head			
Jun. 1993-Jan. 2001. 100-watt head version.			
1993-2001		$1,200	$1,600
1993-2001	Rackmount version	$1,200	$1,600
Triaxis Programmable Preamp			
Oct. 1991-2016. Serial numbers:T0001-. 5 12AX7 tube preamp, rack mount.			
1991-2016		$1,200	$1,600
Venture Bass (M-Pulse)			
2007-2009		$1,000	$1,300
V-Twin Rackmount			
May 1995-Jun. 1998. Serial numbers: V2R-001 to V2R-2258.			
1995-1998		$550	$725
WalkAbout M-Pulse Bass Head			
Sep. 2001-May 2017. Serial numbers: WK-01-. Lightweight 13 pounds, 2 12AX7s + 300 MOS-FET.			
2001-2017		$725	$950
WalkAbout Scout Convertible Combo			
2001-May 2017. Head and 1x12 combo.			
2001-2017		$1,025	$1,350

Meteoro

1986-present. Guitar, bass, harp and keyboard combo amps, heads, and cabinets built in Brazil. They also build effects.

Metropoulos Amplification

2004-present. George Metropoulos builds his professional and premium grade amps in Flint, Michigan.

MODEL YEAR	FEATURES	EXC. COND. LOW	HIGH

MG

2004-present. Tube combo guitar amps built by Marcelo Giangrande in São Paulo, Brazil. He also builds effects.

Mighty Moe Ampstraps

Peter Bellak built his guitar amp straps in Sacramento, California, starting in 2007. He also offered an amp strap for ukulele.

Milbert Amplifiers

2009-present. Professional and premium grade, production/custom, amps for guitars and cars, built in Gaithersburg, Maryland by Michael Milbert.

Mission Amps

1996-present. Bruce Collins' Mission Amps, located in Arvada, Colorado, produces a line of custom-made combo amps, heads, and cabinets.

Mojave Amp Works

2002-present. Tube amp heads and speaker cabinets by Victor Mason in Apple Valley, California.

Montgomery Ward

Amps for this large retailer were sometimes branded as Montgomery Ward, but usually as Airline (see that listing).

1x12" Combo

1950s. 1x12", about 2 6L6 power tubes, includes Model 8439 and brown covered Maestro C Series with cloverleaf grille.

1950s		$500	$650

Model 55 JDR 8437

1950s. 4x8" speakers in 'suitcase' amp cabinet, brown control panel.

1950s		$600	$800

Mooneyes

Budget solid state amp line from Lace Music Products. They also offered amps under the Rat Fink and Lace brands. Lace had a Mooneyes guitar model line.

Morley

Late-1960s-present. The effects company offered an amp in the late '70s. See Effects section for more company information.

Bigfoot

1979-ca.1981. Looks like Morley's '70s effects pedals, produced 25 watts and pedal controlled volume. Amp only, speakers were sold separately.

1979-1981		$210	$280

Mosrite

1968-1969. Mosrite jumped into the amp business during the last stages of the company history, the company was founded as a guitar company in 1954 and attained national fame in the '60s but by the time the company entered the amp business, the guitar boom began to fade, forcing the original Mosrite out of business in '69.

MODEL YEAR	FEATURES	EXC. COND. LOW	HIGH

Model 400 Fuzzrite Amp

1968-1969. Solidstate, 1x15 combo, black tolex with silver grille, reverb and tremolo.

1968-1969		$825	$1,100

Model SS-550 The Gospel

1968. Solidstate, 1 speaker combo, 2 channels normal and tremolo, reverb, black tolex.

1968		$750	$1,000

Mountain

Mountain builds a 9-volt amp in a wood cabinet. Originally built in California, then Nevada; currently being made in Vancouver, British Columbia.

Multivox

Ca.1946-ca.1984. Multivox was started as a subsidiary of Premier to manufacture amps, and later, effects. Generally student grade to low intermediate grade amps.

Murph

1965-1967. Amps marketed by Murph Guitars of San Fernado, California. At first they were custom-made tube amps, but most were later solidstate production models made by another manufacturer.

Music Man

1972-present. Music Man made amps from '73 to '83. The number preceding the amp model indicates the speaker configuration. The last number in model name usually referred to the watts. RD indicated Reverb Distortion. RP indicated Reverb Phase. Many models were available in head-only versions and as combos with various speaker combinations.

Sixty Five Head

1973-1981	65-watt	$425	$575

Seventy Five Reverb/75 Reverb

1973-1981. Head, 75 watts, reverb.

1973-1981		$425	$575

110 RD Fifty

1980-1983. 50 watts, 1x10", reverb, distortion.

1980-1983		$485	$625

112 B Bass

1983. 50 watts, 1x12".

1983		$485	$625

112 RD Fifty

1980-1983. 50 watts, 1x12", reverb, distortion.

1980-1983		$485	$625

112 RD Sixty Five

1978-1983. 65 watts, 1x12", reverb, distortion.

1978-1983		$485	$625

112 RD One Hundred

1978-1983. 100 watts, 1x12", reverb, distortion, EVM option for heavy duty 12" Electro-Voice speakers.

1978-1983		$575	$750
1978-1983	EVM option	$575	$750

112 RP Sixty Five

1978-1983. 65 watts, 1x12", reverb, built-in phaser.

1978-1983		$575	$750

Metropoulos Super-Plex

AMPS

1979 Music Man Seventy Five
Rivington Guitars

1982 Music Man 110 RD Fifty
Richard Potter

Music Man 112 HD130
Terry Loose

Music Man 212 HD130
Federico Garibotti

1967 National Bass 75
Tom Pfeifer

MODEL YEAR	FEATURES	EXC. COND. LOW	HIGH
112 RP One Hundred			
1978-1983. Combo amp, 100 watts, 1x12", reverb, built-in phaser.			
1978-1983		$575	$750
112 Sixty Five			
1973-1981. Combo amp, 65 watts, 1x12", reverb, tremolo.			
1973-1981		$575	$750
115 Sixty Five			
1973-1981. Combo amp, 65 watts, 1x15", reverb, tremolo.			
1973-1981		$575	$750
210 HD130			
1973-1981. 130 watts, 2x10", reverb, tremolo.			
1973-1981		$650	$850
210 Sixty Five			
1973-1981. 65 watts, 2x10", reverb, tremolo.			
1973-1981		$650	$850
212 HD130			
1973-1981. 130 watts, 2x12", reverb, tremolo.			
1973-1981		$650	$850
212 Sixty Five			
1973-1981. 65 watts, 2x12", reverb, tremolo.			
1973-1981		$650	$850
410 Sixty Five			
1973-1981. 65 watts, 4x10", reverb, tremolo.			
1973-1981		$650	$850
410 Seventy Five			
1982-1983. 75 watts, 4x10", reverb, tremolo.			
1982-1983		$650	$850
HD-130 Head			
1973-1981. 130 watts, reverb, tremolo.			
1973-1981		$425	$575
HD-150 Head			
1973-1981. 75/100 watts.			
1973-1981		$425	$575
RD Fifty Head			
1980-1983. 50 watts, reverb, distortion.			
1980-1983		$425	$575

Nady

1976-present. Wireless sound company Nady Systems started offering tube combo and amp heads in '06.

NARB

1973. Briefly made by Ken Bran and Jim Marshall, about 24 made, all were Marshall 100-watt tremolo half-stack, NARB logo on amp and cabinet.

MODEL YEAR	FEATURES	EXC. COND. LOW	HIGH
100 Watt Half-Stack			
1973. 100 watts, 4x12".			
1973		$3,700	$4,800

National

Ca.1927-present. National/Valco amps date back to the late-'30s. National introduced a modern group of amps about the same time they introduced their new Res-O-Glas space-age guitar models in '62. In '64, the amp line was partially redesigned and renamed. By '68, the Res-O-Glas models were gone and National introduced many large vertical and horizontal piggyback models which lasted until National's assets were assigned during bankruptcy in '69. The National name went to Chicago importer Strum N' Drum. Initially, Strum N' Drum had one amp, the National GA 950 P Tremolo/Reverb piggyback.

MODEL YEAR	FEATURES	EXC. COND. LOW	HIGH
Aztec			
1948-1950s. Combo, early '50s version with 3 Rola 7x11" speakers using 3 speaker baffle openings, about 20 watts using 2x6L6 power tubes, 2-tone brown leatherette and tweed cover. By '56, amp has one 15" speaker and does not have segmented grill.			
1948-1950s	3 Rola 7x11	$1,025	$1,325
1950s	1x15	$950	$1,225
Bass 70/Bass 75			
1962-1967. 35 watts (per channel), 2x12" (often Jensen) speakers, large knobs, Raven Black tolex with silver and white grille, designed for bass. New model name in '64 with nearly identical features but listed as total of 70 watts, in '62 called Bass 70 but renamed Bass 75 in '64.			
1962-1963	Bass 70	$900	$1,175
1964-1967	Bass 75 N6475B	$900	$1,175
Chicagoan Model 1220			
1940s-1950s. 17 watts, 1x10", tube, says "Valco Chicago 51" on control panel.			
1940s-50s		$850	$1,100
Dynamic 20			
1962-1963. 17 watts, 2x8" (often Jensen) speakers, 2 large knobs, Raven Black tolex with silver and white grille, compact student-intermediate amp.			
1962-1963		$900	$1,175
Glenwood 90			
1962-1967. 35 watts, 2x12" (often Jensen) speakers, large knobs, reverb, tremolo, Raven Black tolex with silver and white grille, top of the line, becomes the nearly identical N6490TR in '64.			
1962-1963		$1,375	$1,775
1964-1967	Model N6490TR	$1,250	$1,625
Glenwood Vibrato			
Two 12" speakers, reverb, tremolo.			
1964-1967	Model N6499VR	$1,375	$1,775
Model 75			
1940s. Vertical tweed combo cabinet, volume and tone knobs, 3 inputs.			
1940s		$600	$775
Model 100			
1940s. Tube amp, 40 watts, 1x12".			
1940s		$675	$875
Model 1202 Twin			
1954. 18 watts, 2x8" Jensen speaker, 2 channels (Instrument and microphone), horizontal flying bird logo on grille.			
1954		$900	$1,175
Model 1210 High Fidelity			
1954. 20 watts, 1x15" Jensen speaker, 4 input jacks, 2 channels (instrument and microphone), 20x24x10" combo, metal handle.			
1954		$900	$1,175
Model 1212			
1954. 12 watts, 1x12", 5 tubes, 3 inputs, 15x18x8" combo, diving flying bird logo on grille, plastic handle.			
1954		$850	$1,100

AMPS

MODEL		EXC. COND.	
YEAR	FEATURES	LOW	HIGH

Model 1215
1952. 1x12", 2 channels.

1952		$850	$1,100

Model 1275
1953. Combo 1x10", 12 watts, 5 tubes, light tan weave cover, deep brown grille cloth.

1953		$825	$1,075

Model GA 950-P Tremolo/Reverb Piggyback
1970s. Strum N' Drum/National model, solidstate, 50 watts, 2-channel 2x12" and 1x7" in 32" tall vertical cabinet, black.

1970s		$325	$425

Model N6800 - N6899 Piggyback
1968-1969. National introduced a new line of tube amps in '68 and most of them were piggybacks. The N6895 was sized like a Fender piggyback Tremolux, the N6875 and N6878 bass amps were sized like a '68 Fender large cab piggyback with a 26" tall vertical cab, the N6898 and N6899 were the large piggyback guitar amps. These amps feature the standard Jensen speakers or the upgrade JBL speakers, the largest model was the N6800 for PA or guitar, which sported 3x70-watt channels and 2 column speakers using a bass 2x12" + 1x3" horn cab and a voice-guitar 4x10" + 1x3" horn cab.

1968-1969		$650	$850

Model N6816 (Model 16)
1968-1969. Valco-made tube amp, 6 watts, 1x10" Jensen speaker, 17" vertical cab, tremolo, no reverb, black vinyl cover and Coppertone grille.

1968-1969		$450	$575

Model N6820 Thunderball Bass
1968-1969. Valco-made tube amp, about 35 watts, 1x15" Jensen speaker, 19" vertical cab, black vinyl cover and Coppertone grille.

1968-1969		$550	$725

Model N6822 (Model 22)
1968-1969. Valco-made, 6 watts tube (4 tubes) amp, 1x12" Jensen speaker, 19" vertical cab, tremolo and reverb, black vinyl cover and Coppertone grille.

1968-1969		$500	$650

National Dobro
1930s. Sold by the National Dobro Corp. when the company was still in Los Angeles (they later moved to Chicago). National Dobro plate on rear back panel, suitcase style case that flips open to reveal the speaker and amp, National logo on outside of suitcase. The noted price is for an all-original amp in excellent condition (this would be a rare find), there are other 1930s models included in the price range below.

1930s	Early metal baffle	$700	$900
1930s	Later standard baffle	$525	$675
1930s	Suitcase style	$650	$850

Newport 40
1964-1967. 17 watts, 2x10", tremolo only.

1964-1967	Model N6440T	$850	$1,100

Newport 50
1964-1967. 17 watts, 2x10", tremolo and reverb.

1964-1967	Model N6450TR	$850	$1,100

Newport 97
1964-1967. 35 watts, 1x15", rear mounted chasis, tremolo.

1964-1967	Model N6497T	$850	$1,100

Sportsman
1950s. Tweed combo with brown leatherette speaker surround, 1x10".

1950s		$825	$1,075

Student Practice
1970s. Strum N' Drum era, small solidstate, single control.

1970s		$45	$60

Studio 10
1962-1967. Five watts, 1x8", 3 tubes, 1 channel, 1 volume control, no tone control, no reverb or tremolo.

1962-1963		$550	$725
1964-1967	Model N6410	$550	$725

Tremo-Tone Model 1224
1956-1959. Small combo, tremolo, dual Rola oval 6x11" speakers, tweed, by Valco, flying bird pattern on lower front grille.

1956-1959		$1,225	$1,600

Val-Pro 80
1962-1963. 35 watts, 2x12" (often Jensen) speakers, 8 tubes, large control knobs, tremolo, black cover with white and silver trim, replaced by Glenwood 90 in '64 with added reverb.

1962-1963		$1,300	$1,700

Val-Trem 40
1962-1963. 17 watts, 2x10" (often Jensen) speakers, large knobs, Val-Trem logo on back panel, Clear-Wave tremolo, Raven Black tolex with silver and white grille, open back combo amp, becomes Newport 40 in '64.

1962-1963		$1,050	$1,375

Val-Verb 60
1962-1963. 17 watts, 2x10" (often Jensen) speakers, large knobs, Val-Verb logo on back panel, reverb, no tremolo, Raven Black tolex with silver and white grille, open back combo amp.

1962-1963		$1,250	$1,625

Westwood 16
1964-1967. Five watts using 1 6V6 power, 2 12AX7 preamp, 1 5Y3GT rectifier, tremolo, 2x8", dark vinyl cover, silver grille.

1964-1967	Model N6416T	$850	$1,100

Westwood 22
1964-1967. 5 watts, 2x8", reverb and tremolo, 1 channel, 6 tubes.

1964-1967	Model N6422TR	$925	$1,200

Naylor Engineering

1994-present. Joe Naylor and Kyle Kurtz founded the company in East Pointe, Michigan, in the early '90s, selling J.F. Naylor speakers. In '94 they started producing amps. In '96, Naylor sold his interest in the business to Kurtz and left to form Reverend Guitars. In '99 David King bought the company and moved it to Los Angeles, California, then to Dallas, Texas. Currently Naylor builds tube amps, combos, speakers, and cabinets.

1964 National Glenwood Vibrato
Imaged by Heritage Auctions, HA.com

1938 National Model C

National Model 100
Imaged by Heritage Auctions, HA.com

AMPS

1950 Oahu
Bill Parsons

Oliver Powerflex 500
Don Oflinden

Omega

MODEL YEAR	FEATURES	EXC. COND. LOW	EXC. COND. HIGH

Nemesis

From the makers of Eden amps, Nemesis is a line of made-in-the-U.S., FET powered bass combos and extension cabinets. The brand is a division of U.S. Music Corp.

Newcomb

1950s. Newcomb Audio Products, Hollywood, California, Newcomb script logo on back panel along with model number, they offered instrument amplifiers that could also be used as small PA.

Model G 12

1953. 1x12" (Rolla) combo amp, 2 controls (volume and tone), large metal handle, oxblood-brown leatherette.

1953		$425	$550

Nobels

1997-present. Effects manufacturer Nobels Electronics of Hamburg, Germany also offers a line of small practice and portable amps.

Noble

Ca. 1950-ca. 1969. From Don Noble and Company, of Chicago, Illinois, owned by Strum N' Drum by mid-'60s. They also offered guitars and amps.

Model 381/Custom 381

1950s. 2x12" and 2x5".

1958-1960		$1,350	$1,750

Norma

1965-1970. Economy line imported and distributed by Strum N' Drum, Wheeling (Chicago), Illinois. As noted in the National section, Strum N' Drum acquired the National brand in the '70s. Some early amps were tube, but the majority were solidstate.

Solid State

1969-1970	Various models	$75	$150

Oahu

The Oahu Publishing Company and Honolulu Conservatory, based in Cleveland, Ohio, started with acoustic Hawaiian and Spanish guitars, selling large quantities in the 1930s. As electric models became popular, Oahu responded with guitar/amp sets. The brand has been revived on a line of U.S.-made tube amps.

Mid-Size Combo

1940s-50s	1x10	$500	$700

Small Combo

1965. Small 1x10" combo, 1 6V6, 4 12AX7. 15Y3GT, white cover, light grille, Oahu script logo upper left grille.

1965		$750	$1,000

Small Guitar/Lap Steel

1940s-1950s. 1x8", various colors.

1940s-50s		$400	$525

Thunderbolt

1965. 1x12", 6 tubes.

1965		$1,700	$2,200

MODEL YEAR	FEATURES	EXC. COND. LOW	EXC. COND. HIGH

Oliver

Ca.1966-ca. 1978. The Oliver Sound Company, Westbury, New York, was founded by former Ampeg engineer, Jess Oliver, after he left Ampeg in '65. Tube amp designs were based upon Oliver's work at Ampeg. The Oliver Powerflex Amp is the best-known design, and featured an elevator platform that would lift the amp head out of the speaker cabinet.

Model B-120 Head

1970s. B-120 logo on front panel, 35 watts, all tube head.

1970s		$535	$700

Model G-150R Combo

1970s. Reverb, tremolo, 2 6L6 power tubes, 40 watts, 1x15", black tolex with black grille, silver control panel.

1970s		$625	$825

Model P-500 Combo

1960s. All tube combo with 15" motorized amp chassis that rises out of tall lateral speaker cabinet as amp warms up.

1960s		$850	$1,100

Orbital Power Projector

Late-1960s-early-1970s. Rotating speaker cabinet with horn, Leslie-like voice.

1960s-70s		$900	$1,175

Sam Ash Oliver Head

Late-1960s-early-1970s. Private branded for Sam Ash Music, about 30 watts using the extinct 7027A power tubes, Sam Ash script logo on front grille.

1960s-70s		$400	$525

Omega

2009-present. James Price builds his premium grade, production/custom, amps in Moravian Falls, North Carolina.

Orange

1968-1981, 1995-present. Orange amps and PAs were made in the U.K. by Cliff Cooper and Matthew Mathias. The Orange-colored amps were well-built and were used by many notable guitarists. Since '95, Cliff Cooper is once again making Orange amplifiers in the U.K., with the exception of the small Crush Practice Combo amps, which are made in Korea. '68-'70 amps made by Matamp in Huddersfield, classic designs started in '71 at Bexleyheath/London plant.

Model GRO-100 Graphic Overdrive Head

1969-1971. Four EL34 power, only 2 pre-amp tubes, short-style head, model number on back panel.

1969-1971		$3,200	$4,150

Model OR-80

1971-1981. Half-stack head and cab, 80 watts, 4x12" straight-front cab with Orange crest on grille, orange vinyl and light orange grille.

1971-1975		$3,100	$4,025
1976-1981		$2,700	$3,500

Model OR-80 Combo

1971-1981. About 80 watts, 2x12" combo.

1971-1975		$2,600	$3,375
1976-1981		$2,200	$2,850

AMPS

1977 Orange OR-120 head
Eric Van Gansen

Ovation 6012 The Kat
Imaged by Heritage Auctions, HA.com

Park G-25R

MODEL YEAR	FEATURES	EXC. COND. LOW	HIGH

Model OR-120 Graphic
1972-1981. Half-stack head and cab, 120 watts, 4x12" straight front cab with Orange crest on grille, orange vinyl and light orange grille.

1972-1975		$3,200	$4,150
1976-1981		$2,900	$3,775

Model OR-200 212 Twin
1970s. 120 watts, 2x12" combo, orange vinyl, dark grille, Orange crest on grille, reverb and vibrato, master volume.

1971-1975		$3,100	$4,025
1976-1981		$2,700	$3,500

Orepheus
Early 1960s. Private branded for Coast Wholesale Music Co., Orepheus logo on control panel along with model number.

Student Compact
1960s. Small student compact tube amps, some with 2 knobs, volume and tone.

1960s		$425	$550

Orpheum
Late-1950s-1960s. Student to medium level amps from New York's Maurice Lipsky Music.

Mid-Size/Small
Late-1950s-1960s. U.S.-made, 2 6V6 power tubes, Jensen P12R 12" speaker, light cover with gray swirl grille.

1950s-60s	Mid-Size	$550	$700
1950s-60s	Small	$425	$550

Osborne Sound Laboratories
Late 1970s. Guitar amps built by Ralph Scaffidi and wife guitarist Mary Osborne in Bakersfield, California. They also offered guitars.

Ovation
1966-present. Kaman made few amps under the Ovation name. They offered a variety of amps under the KMD brand from '85 to around '94.

Little Dude
1969-ca.1971. Solidstate combo, 100 watts, 1x15" and horn, matching slave unit also available.

1970s		$190	$250

The Kat (Model 6012)
1970s. Solidstate, 2x12" combo.

1970s		$190	$250

Overbuilt Amps
1999-2007. Tube amps and combos built by Richard Seccombe in West Hills, California. He nows works at Fender R&D.

PAC-AMP (Magnatone)
Late-1950s-early-1960s. Private branded by Magnatone, often for accordion studios.

Model 213 Troubadour
1957-1958. 10 watts, 1x12".

1957-1958		$1,250	$1,625

Model 280-A
1961-1963. About 50 watts, 2x12" + 2x5", brown leatherette, light brown grille, stereo vibrato, PAC-AMP nameplate logo.

1961-1963		$1,800	$2,350

Palette Amps
Robert Wakeling began building his tube amp heads and combos and speaker cabinets in Stillwater, Oklahoma in 2003.

PANaramic (Magnatone)
1961-1963. Private branded equivalent of '61-'63 Magnatone brown leatherette series, large PANaramic logo. Many Magnatone private brands were associated with accordion companies or accordian teaching studios. PANaramic was a brand name of PANaramic accordion. They also made guitars.

Model 260/262-Style
1961-1963. 35 watts, 2x12", gray vinyl and light grille, vibrato, large PANaramic logo.

1961-1963		$1,800	$2,350

Model 413-Style
1961-1963. 18 watts, 1x12", black leatherette cover, light silver grille, vibrato, large PANaramic logo.

1961-1963		$1,150	$1,500

Model 450-Style
1961-1963. 20 watts, 1x12", reverb and vibrato, reverb not generally included in an early-'60s 1x12" Magnatone amp, dark vinyl, dark cross-threaded grille, large PANaramic logo.

1961-1963		$1,500	$1,950

Model 1210 (250-Style)
1961-1963. 1x12" combo, 20 watts, 2.5 channels, true vibrato.

1961-1963		$1,300	$1,700

Paris
1960s. Brand name used on a line of solidstate amps distributed by a music wholesaler. Possibly built by Kay.

Master Series
1960s. Compact combo, 1x12", black tolex-style cover, silver grille, rear mounted slanted control panel.

1960s		$90	$120

Park
1965-1982, 1993-1998, 2013-present. Park amps were made by Marshall from '65 to '82. Park logo on front with elongated P. In the '90s, Marshall revived the name for use on small solidstate amps imported from Asia. Brand name acquired by Mitch Colby (Colby Amps) in '13 and used on tube head amps and cabs built in New York City.

G Series
1992-2000. Student compact amps, models include G-10 (10 watts, 1x8"), G-25R (25w, reverb), G-215R (15w, 2x8") and GB-25 (25w, 1x12" bass).

1990s	G-10	$55	$90
1990s	G-15R	$60	$100
1990s	G-215R	$70	$105

AMPS

PRS Archon

Peavey 5150 EVH
Imaged by Heritage Auctions, HA.com

Peavey 6505+

MODEL YEAR	FEATURES	EXC. COND. LOW	HIGH
1990s	G-25R	$65	$100
1990s	GB-25	$65	$100

Model 50 Head
1967-1969. Plexi, 50 watts.

1967-1969		$3,300	$4,300

Model 1001L Lead Head

1967-1969	Plexi	$4,700	$6,100
1969-1971	Aluminum	$2,700	$3,500

Model 1008A 4x12 Slant Cabinet
Late-1960s-early-1970s. Similar to Marshall 1960 4x12" cab.

1960s-70s		$2,100	$2,700

Model 1206 50W Master Volume Head
Late-1970s-1982. 50 watts, similar to JCM 800 50-watt made during same era.

1970s-1982		$2,100	$2,700

Model 1212 50W Reverb Combo
Late-1960s-early-1970s. 50 watts, 2x12", reverb, tube.

1960s-70s		$2,700	$3,500

Model 1213 100W Reverb Combo
Late-1960s-early-1970s. 100 watts, 2x12", reverb, tube.

1960s-70s		$2,700	$3,500

Model 1228 50W Lead Head
Late-1970s-1982. 50 watts, based upon Marshall 50-watt made during same era.

1970s-1982		$2,100	$2,700

Model 1229 100W Lead Head
Late-1970s-1982. 100 watts, tube.

1970s-1982		$2,100	$2,700

Model 1231 Vintage 20 LE Combo
Late-1970s-1982. 20 watts, 1x12".

1970s-1982		$2,300	$3,000

Model 1239 50W Master Volume Reverb Combo
Late-1970s-1982. 50 watts, 1x12".

1970s-1982		$2,300	$3,000

Paul Reed Smith

1985-present. In the late '80s, PRS offered two amp models. Only 350 amp units shipped. Includes HG-70 Head and HG-212 Combo. HG stands for Harmonic Generator, effectively a non-tube, solid-state amp. In '09, PRS introduced tube combo and head amps and cabinets designed by Doug Sewell.

Paul Ruby Amplifiers

2000-present. Professional grade, custom, tube amps built by Paul Ruby in Folsom, California.

Peavey

1965-present. Hartley Peavey's first products were guitar amps. He added guitars to the mix in '78. Headquartered in Meridan, Mississippi, Peavey continues to offer a huge variety of guitars, amps, and PAs. TransTube redesign of amps occurs in '95.

3120 Head
2009-2016. Tubes, 120 watts, 3 foot-switchable channels.

2009-2016		$365	$475

5150 212 Combo
1995-2004. Combo version of 5150 head, 60 watts, 2x12", large 5150 logo on front panel, small Peavey logo on lower right of grille.

1995-2004		$485	$625

5150 EVH Head/Cabinet Set
1995-2008. Half stack 5150 head and 4x12" cab, large 5150 logo on front of amp.

1995-2008	Half-stack	$975	$1,275

5150 II
1999-2004. Has 5051 II logo on front, look for 'II' designation.

1999-2004	Half-stack	$900	$1,175

6505 Series
2008-present. Promoted for modern "heavy" metal sound.

2008-2019	6505, combo 2x12, 60w	$500	$660
2008-2019	6505+, combo 1x12	$485	$635
2008-2021	6505+ head, 120w	$485	$635

Alphabass
1988-1990. Rack mount all tube, 160 watts, EQ, includes 2x15" Black Widow or 2x12" Scorpion cabinet.

1988-1990		$245	$325

Artist
Introduced in 1975 as 120 watts, 1x12", bright and normal channels, EQ, reverb, master volume.

1970s		$245	$325

Artist 110
1990s. TransTubes, 10 watts.

1990s		$115	$150

Artist 240
1975-1980s. 120 watt combo, 1x12".

1975-1980s		$185	$240

Artist 250
1990s. 100 watts, 1x12", solidstate preamp, 4 6L6 power tubes.

1990s		$190	$250

Artist VT
1990s. Combo amp, 120 watts, 1x12".

1990s		$255	$330

Audition 20
1980s-1990s. 20 watts, single speaker combo.

1980-90s		$45	$60

Audition 30
1980s-1990s. 30 watts, 1x12" combo amp, channel switching.

1980-90s		$45	$60

Audition 110
1990s. 25 watts, 1x10" combo, 2 channels.

1990s		$60	$80

Audition Chorus
1980s. 2x10-watt channels, 2x6", channel switching, post gain and normal gain controls.

1980s		$80	$105

Audition Plus
1980s. Solidstate, 20 watts, 1x10".

1980s		$55	$70

Backstage 30/Plus/50/110
1977-1991. 1x10 combo, Backstage 30 (15 then 18 watts) '77-'83, Backstage Plus (35w) '84-'87, Backstage

MODEL YEAR	FEATURES	EXC. COND. LOW	HIGH

50 (50w) '88-'89, Backstage 110 (65w) '89-'91. Name reused in 2000s on small 10-watt amp.

1977-1991		$60	$80

Backstage Chorus 208
1990-1996. 150 watts, 2x8", reverb, channel switching.

1990-1996		$100	$135

Bandit/65/75
1981-1989. 1x12" combo, originally 50 watts, upped to 65 watts in '85 and 75 in '87, renamed Bandit 112 in '90.

1981-1984	Bandit	$110	$145
1985-1986	Bandit 65	$110	$145
1987-1989	Bandit 75	$110	$145

Bandit 112/Bandit II 112
1990-present. 80 watts (II is 100), 1x12", active EQ circuit for lead channel, active controls. TransTube series in '95.

1990-1994		$130	$170
1995-2021	TransTube	$185	$240

Basic 40
1980s. 40 watts, 1x12".

1980s		$90	$115

Basic 60
1988-1995. Solidstate combo amp, 50-60 watts, 1x12", 4-band EQ, gain controls, black.

1988-1995		$130	$170

Basic 112 Bass
1996-2006. 75 watts, 1x12" bass combo, 2000-era red border control panel.

1996-2006		$130	$170

Blazer 158
1995-2005. 15 watts, 1x8", clean and distortion, later called the TransTube Blazer III.

1995-2005		$75	$100

Bluesman
1992. Tweed, 1x12" or 1x15".

1992		$250	$325

Bravo 112
1988-1994. All tube reverb, 25 watts, 1x12", 3-band EQ, 2 independent input channels.

1988-1994		$225	$300

Butcher Head
1985-1987, 2010-2017. All tube head, 120 watts. Current version is all tube, 100 watts with half power switch

1985-1987		$310	$410

Classic 20
1990s. Small tube amp with 2xEL84 power tubes, 1x10" narrow panel combo, tweed cover.

1990s		$310	$410

Classic 30/112
1994-present. Tweed combo, 30 watts, 1x12", EL84 tubes.

1994-2021	Narrow panel	$350	$450
2008-2014	Badge front	$350	$450
2008-2014	Head	$310	$410

Classic 50/212
1990-present. Combo, 50 watt, 2x12", 4 EL84s, 3 12AX7s, reverb, high-gain section.

1990-2021		$375	$500

Classic 50/410
1990-present. Combo amp, 4x10", EL84 power, reverb, footswitchable high-gain mode.

1990-2021		$375	$500

Classic 120 Head
1988-ca.1990. Tube, 120 watts.

1988-1990		$310	$400

Combo 300
1982-1993. 1x15" bass combo, 300 watts.

1982-1993		$165	$215

DECA/750
1989-ca.1990. Digital, 2 channels, 350 watts per channel, distortion, reverb, exciter, pitch shift, multi-EQ.

1989-1990		$210	$275

Decade
1970s. Practice amp, 10 watts, 1x8", runs on 12 volt or AC.

1970s		$80	$105

Delta Blues
1995-2014. 30 watts, tube combo, 4 EL84 tubes, 1x15" or 2x10", tremolo, large-panel-style cab, blond tweed.

1995-2014		$375	$500

Deuce
1972-1980s. 120 watts, tube amp, 2x12" or 4x10".

1972-1980s		$180	$240

Deuce Head
1972-1980s. Tube head, 120 watts.

1972-1980s		$140	$180

Ecoustic Series
1996-present. Acoustic combo amps, 110 (1x10) and 112 (1x12, offered until '10) at 100 watts, digital effects (EFX, later E) added in '03. E20 and E208 added in '11.

1996-2010	112	$130	$170
2003-2022	E110	$130	$170

Encore 65
1983. Tube combo, 65 watts.

1983		$245	$325

Envoy 110
1988-2020. Solidstate, 40 watts, 1x10", TransTubes.

1988-2021		$110	$140

Heritage VTX
1980s. 130 watts, 4 6L6s, solidstate preamp, 2x12" combo.

1980s		$165	$215

Jazz Classic
1980s. Solidstate, 210 watts, 1x15", electronic channel switching, 6-spring reverb.

1980s		$165	$215

JSX (Joe Satriani)
2004-2010. Joe Satriani signature, 120-watt tube head. Also offered were JSX 50 (50 watts, '09-'10), JSX 212 Combo ('05-'10) and 5-watt JSX Mini Colossal ('07-'10).

2004-2010	120w head	$650	$850

KB Series
1980s. Keyboard amp, models include KB-60 (60 watts, 1x12", reverb), KB-100 (100w, 1x15"), and KB-300 (300w, 1x15" with horn).

1980s	KB-100	$160	$210
1980s	KB-300	$220	$285
1980s	KB-60	$135	$175

Peavey Classic 30/112

Peavey Delta Blues
Imaged by Heritage Auctions, HA.com

Peavey KB-100
Imaged by Heritage Auctions, HA.com

AMPS

Peavey Nashville 400
Imaged by Heritage Auctions, HA.com

Peavey Rage 258
Imaged by Heritage Auctions, HA.com

Peavey TKO 80

MODEL YEAR	FEATURES	EXC. COND. LOW	HIGH
LTD			
1975-1980s. Solidstate, 200 watts, 1x12" Altec or 1x15" JBL.			
1975-1982		$165	$215
Mace Head			
1976-1980s. Tube, 180 watts.			
1976-1980s		$245	$325
Mark III Bass Head			
1978-1983. 300 watts, 2 channels, graphic EQ.			
1978-1983		$175	$225
MegaBass			
1986-ca. 1992. Rack mount preamp/power amp, 200 watts per 2 channels, solidstate, EQ, effects loop, chorus.			
1986-1992		$190	$250
Microbass			
1988-2005. 20 watts, 1x8" practice amp, made in China.			
1988-2005		$45	$55
Minx 110 Bass			
1987-2005. Solidstate, 35 watts RMS, 1x10" heavy-duty speaker.			
1987-2005		$95	$125
Musician Head			
Introduced in 1965 as 120 watt head, upped to 210 watts in '72.			
1965-1970s		$130	$170
Nashville 112 Steel Guitar			
2008-present. Compact size, 1x12", 80 watts.			
2008-2021		$415	$535
Nashville 400 Steel Guitar			
1982-2000. 210 watts, 1x15" solidstate steel guitar combo amp.			
1982-2000		$435	$565
Nashville 1000 Steel Guitar			
1998-2008. 1x15" speaker, solidstate steel guitar combo amp.			
1998-2008		$435	$565
Pacer			
1974-1985. Master volume, 45 watts, 1x12", 3-band EQ.			
1974-1985		$75	$100
Penta Head/Gary Rossington Signature Penta			
2005-2015. Tubes, 140 watts, 4x12", 5 selectable preamp settings. Becomes the Gary Rossington Signature Penta in 2009.			
2005-2015	Cab	$250	$325
2005-2015	Head	$290	$375
ProBass 1000			
1980s. Rack mount, effects loops, preamp, EQ, crossover, headphone output.			
1980s		$140	$180
Rage/Rage 158			
1988-2008. Compact practice amp, 15 watts, 1x8". 158 starts '95. Replaced by 25 watt Rage 258.			
1988-2008		$40	$50
Reno 400			
1984-late 1980s. Solidstate, 200 watts, 1x15" with horn, 4-band EQ.			
1980s		$140	$180

MODEL YEAR	FEATURES	EXC. COND. LOW	HIGH
Renown 112			
1989-1994. Crunch and lead SuperSat, 160 watts, 1x12", master volume, digital reverb, EQ.			
1989-1994		$140	$180
Renown 212			
1989-1994. Crunch and lead SuperSat, 160 watts, 2x12", master volume, digital reverb, EQ.			
1989-1994		$165	$215
Renown 400			
1981-late 1980s. Combo, 200 watts, 2x12", channel switching, Hammond reverb, pre- and post-gain controls.			
1980s		$210	$275
Revolution 112			
1992-2002. 100 watts, 1x12" combo, black vinyl, black grille.			
1992-2002		$185	$240
Session 400			
1974-ca. 1999. 200 watts, 1x15 or early on as 2x12, steel amp, available in the smaller box LTD, offered as a head in '76, available in wedge-shaped enclosure in '88.			
1974-1999		$425	$550
Session 500			
1979-1980s. 250 watts, 1x15", steel amp.			
1979-1985		$425	$550
Special 112			
1981-1994. 160 watts, 1x12". In 1988, available in wedge-shaped enclosure.			
1981-1994		$165	$215
Special 130			
1980s. 1x12", 130 watts.			
1980s		$165	$215
Special 212			
1995-2005. 160 watts, 2x12", transtube, solidstate series.			
1995-2005		$185	$240
Stereo Chorus 212			
1990s. 2x12" combo.			
1990s		$245	$325
Studio Pro 50			
1986-late 1980s. 50 watts, 1x12".			
1980s		$110	$145
Studio Pro 112			
1980s. Repackaged and revoiced in 1988. Solidstate, 65 watts, 1x12", Peavey SuperSat preamp circuitry, new power sections.			
1980s		$120	$155
TKO Series Bass			
1978-2011. Solidstate, 1x15, original TKO was 40 watts, followed by TKO 65 (65 watts) for '82-'87, TKO 75 for '88-'90, and TKO 80 for '91-'92. Renamed TKO 115 in '93 with 75, 80 or 100 watts until '09 when jumping to 400 watts.			
1982-1987	TKO 65	$110	$145
1988-1990	TKO 75	$145	$190
1991-1992	TKO 80	$185	$245
TNT Series Bass			
1974-2009. Solidstate, 1x15, original TNT was 45 watts, upped to 50 for '79-'81, followed by TNT 130 (130 watts) for '82-'87, TNT 150 for '88-'90, and TNT 160 for '91-'92. Renamed TNT 115 in '93 with 150, 160 or			

MODEL YEAR	FEATURES	EXC. COND. LOW	HIGH

200 watts until '09 when jumping to 600 watts (Tour TNT 115 - see Tour Series).

1982-1987	TNT 130	$290	$375
1988-1990	TNT 150	$290	$375
1991-1992	TNT 160	$290	$375

Tour Series
2004-2019. Imported bass heads and cabinets, various models.

| 2004-2019 | Various models | $290 | $375 |

Transchorus 210
1999-2000. 50 watts, 2x10 combo, stereo chorus, channel switching, reverb.

| 1999-2000 | | $240 | $315 |

Triple XXX Series
2001-2009. Made in USA.

| 2001-2009 | Head, 120w | $510 | $660 |
| 2001-2009 | Super 40, 40w, 1x12 | $450 | $600 |

Triumph 60 Combo
1980s. Tube head, effects loop, reverb, 60 watts, 1x12", multi-stage gain.

| 1980s | | $160 | $210 |

Triumph 120
1989-1990. Tube, 120 watts, 1x12", 3 gain blocks in preamp, low-level post-effects loop, built-in reverb.

| 1989-1990 | | $185 | $245 |

Ultra 60 Head
1991-1994. 60 watts, all tube, 2 6L6 power, black, black grille.

| 1991-1994 | | $240 | $315 |

Ultra Series
1998-2002. All tube combos and cabs.

1998-2002	Ulta 112, 60w	$235	$310
1998-2002	Ulta 212, 60w	$290	$375
1998-2002	Ulta 410, 60w	$290	$375
1998-2002	Ulta Plus, 120w	$335	$435

ValveKing Series
2005-2018. Tube head, combos and cabs.

2005-2016	VK212, 100w, 2x12	$270	$350
2005-2018	VK100, 100w head	$230	$295
2005-2018	VK112, 50w, 1x12	$235	$310

Vegas 400
1984-late 1980s. 210 watts, 1x15, some prefer as a steel guitar amp.

| 1980s | | $350 | $460 |

VTM Series
1987-1993. Vintage Tube Modified series, tube heads, 60 or 120 watts.

| 1987-1993 | VTM120, 120w | $310 | $400 |
| 1987-1993 | VTM60, 60w | $310 | $400 |

Vypyr Series
2008-2014. Modeling amp heads and combos, 60 and 120-watt tube and 15, 30, 75 and 100-watt solidstate models. Changes to Vypyr VIP in late '14.

2008-2014	15w, combo	$65	$85
2008-2014	30w, combo 1x12	$135	$175
2010	75w, combo	$185	$245

Wiggy 212
2001-2008. 100-watt head in mono (2x75-watt in stereo) with matching 2x12 cab, 2 EQ, 5-band sliders, rounded amp head.

| 2001-2008 | | $415 | $550 |

MODEL YEAR	FEATURES	EXC. COND. LOW	HIGH

Windsor Head
Introduced 2006 summer NAMM. All tube, 100- or 300-watt head.

| 2000s | 100w | $260 | $340 |
| 2000s | 300w | $270 | $350 |

Penn
Tube amps, combos, and cabinets built by Billy Penn, starting in 1994, originally in Colts Neck, then in Long Branch, New Jersey.

Pignose
1972-present. Pignose was started by people associated with the band Chicago, including guitarist Terry Kath, with help from designers Wayne Kimball and Richard Erlund. In '74, it was sold to Chicago's band accountant, who ran it until '82, when ownership passed to the company that made its sturdy, wood cabinets. They also offer guitars and effects.

7-100 Practice
1972-present. The original Pignose, 7"x5"x3" battery-powered portable amplifier, 1x5".

| 1972-2021 | | $60 | $80 |

30/60
1978-ca.1987. Solidstate, 30 watts, 1x10", master volume.

| 1978-1987 | | $80 | $105 |

60R Studio Reverb
Solidstate, 30 watts.

| 1980 | | $100 | $130 |

G40V
1997-2009. Tubes, 1x10", 40 watts.

| 1997-2009 | | $225 | $290 |

G60VR
1998-2009. Tubes, 1x12", 60 watts.

| 1998-2009 | | $245 | $315 |

Hog Rechargeable Portable
1995-present. Small rechargeable solidstate, models include Hog 20 (20W, 6.5" speaker) and Hog 30 (30W, 8").

| 1995-2021 | | $120 | $155 |

Plush
Late 1960s-early 1970s. Tuck and roll covered tube amps made by the same company that made Earth Sound Research amps in Farmingdale, New York.

Tube
Early-1970s. All tube heads and combos including the 450 Super 2x12" combo, 1000/P1000S head, and 1060S Royal Bass combo.

| 1971-1972 | Various models | $975 | $1,275 |

Point Blank
2002-2004. Tube amps built by Roy Blankenship in Orlando, Florida before he started his Blankenship brand.

Peavey Triple XXX
Imaged by Heritage Auctions, HA.com

Pignose Hog

Plush PRB 1000S
Imaged by Heritage Auctions, HA.com

AMPS

Polytone Taurus
Imaged by Heritage Auctions, HA.com

AMPS

1964 Premier B-160 Club Bass
Imaged by Heritage Auctions, HA.com

Premier Twin-8
Ängkvist

MODEL		EXC. COND.	
YEAR	FEATURES	LOW	HIGH

Polytone

Beginning in the 1960s and made in North Hollywood, California, Polytone offers compact combo amps, heads, and cabinets and a pickup system for acoustic bass.

Guitar or Bass

1980-2000s Various models		$365	$475

Port City

2005-present. Daniel Klein builds his amp heads, combos, and cabinets in Rocky Point, North Carolina.

Premier

Ca.1938-ca.1975, 1990s-2010. Produced by Peter Sorkin Music Company in Manhattan. First radio-sized amplifiers introduced by '38. After World War II, established Multivox subsidiary to manufacture amplifiers ca.'46. By mid-'50s at least, the amps featured lyre grilles. Dark brown/light tan amp covering by '60. By '64 amps covered in brown woodgrain and light tan. Multivox amps were made until around '84.

B-160 Club Bass

1963-1968. 15 to 20 watts, 1x12" Jensen speaker, '60s 2-tone brown styling, 6V6 tubes.

1963-1968		$775	$1,000

Model 50

1940s-1960s. In '62 this was their entry-level amp, 4 to 5 watts, 1x8" similar to Fender Champ circuit with more of a vertical suitcase-style cab.

1940s-60s		$475	$615

Model 71

1961-1962. Combo with 1x12" (woofer) and 2 small tweeters, 24 watts. '61 styling with circular speaker baffle protected with metal X frame, 2 tweeter ports on upper baffle, 2-tone light tan and brown, 8 tubes, tremolo. The '62 styling changed to baffle with a slight V at the top, and 2-tone cover.

1961	Round baffle	$1,050	$1,375
1962	V-baffle	$1,050	$1,375

Model 76

1950s-1960s. Suitcase latchable cabinet that opens out into 2 wedges, 2-tone brown, lyre grille, 1x12".

1950s-60s		$875	$1,150

Model 88 Multivox

1962. Multi-purpose combo amp, organ-stop control panel, 1x15" woofer with 2 tweeters, vertical suitcase cab, 2-tone cover, classic circular speaker baffle with X brace, 10 tubes, top-of-the-line in '62 catalog.

1962		$1,050	$1,375

Model 88N

1950s-1961. Rectangular suitcase cabinet, 2-tone tan and brown, Premier and lyre logo, 25 watts, 1x12".

1950s-1961		$1,050	$1,375

Model 100R

1960s. Combo amp, 1x12", reverb and tremolo.

1960s		$1,050	$1,375

Model 110

1962. 12-watt 1x10 student combo, lyre grille logo, 2-tone cab.

1962		$650	$850

MODEL		EXC. COND.	
YEAR	FEATURES	LOW	HIGH

Model 120/120R

1958-1963. 12-watt 1x12" combo, tremolo, reverb ('62), 2-tone brown cab.

1958-1963		$775	$1,000
1962	With reverb	$850	$1,100

Model 200 Rhythm Bass

1962. 1x15" combo bass amp.

1962		$800	$1,050

T-8 Twin-8

1950s, 1964-1966. 20 watts, 2x8", tremolo, reverb.

1950s		$1,525	$2,000
1964-1966		$1,425	$1,875

T-12 Twin-12

1958-1962. Early reverb amp with tremolo, 2x12", rectangular cabinet typical of twin 12 amps (Dano and Fender), brown cover.

1958-1959		$1,625	$2,150
1960-1962		$1,525	$2,000

Pritchard Amps

Professional grade, production/custom, single and two-channel amps and cabinets built beginning in 2004, by Eric Pritchard in Berkeley Springs, West Virginia.

Pyramid Car Audio

Inexpensive student models, imported.

Quantum

1980s. Economy amps distributed by DME, Indianapolis, Indiana.

Q Terminator Economy

1980s. Economy solidstate amps ranging from 12 to 25 watts and 1x6" to 1x12".

1980s	Various models	$30	$40

Quidley Guitar Amplifiers

Intermediate and professional grade, production/custom, tube guitar amp heads, combos and cabinets built by Ed Quidley in Wilmington, North Carolina, starting in 2006.

Quilter

2011-present. Patrick Quilter builds his intermediate and professional grade, production, guitar amps in Costa Mesa, California.

Quinn

Professional and premium grade, production/custom, amps and cabinets built by Shadwell J. Damron III, starting 2005, in Vancouver, Washington.

Randall

1960s-present. Randall Instruments was originally out of California and is now a division of U.S. Music Corp. They have offered a range of tube and solidstate combo amps, heads and cabinets over the years.

MODEL		EXC. COND.	
YEAR	FEATURES	LOW	HIGH

Rastop Designs

2002-present. Professional grade, custom amps built by Alexander Rastopchin in Long Island City, New York. He also builds effects.

Rat Fink

Early 2000s. Solidstate amp line from Lace Music Products. They also sold guitars and basses under this brand and offered amps under the Mooneyes and Lace brands.

Realistic

Radio Shack offered a couple made-in-the-U.S. combo tube amps in the '60s, including the Entertainer 34 with a flip down record turntable in the back! Their radio and stereo gear were also branded Realistic.

Reason

2007-2016. Professional grade, production/custom, amps and cabinets built by Obeid Khan and Anthony Bonadio in St. Louis, Missouri.

Red Bear

1994-1997. Tube amps designed by Sergei Novikov and built in St. Petersburg, Russia. Red Bear amps were distributed in the U.S. under a joint project between Gibson and Novik, Ltd. Novik stills builds amps under other brands.

MK 60 Lead Tube

1994-1997. Head with 4x12" half stack, Red Bear logo on amp and cab.

1994-1997		$700	$925

MK 100 Full Stack

1994-1997. 100 watts, 2x4x12".

1994-1997		$1,075	$1,400

Red Iron Amps

2001-present. Paul Sanchez builds his tube amp heads in Lockhart, Texas.

RedPlate Amps

2006-present. Professional and premium grade, production/custom, guitar amplifiers built in Phoenix, Arizona by Henry Heistand.

Reeves Amplification

2002-present. Started by Bill Jansen, Reeves builds tube amps, combos, and cabinets in Cincinnati, Ohio, based on the classic British designs of Dan Reeves.

Regal

Ca.1895-1966, 1987-present. The original Regal company distributed instruments built by them and others.

Gibson EH

1936. Rare private-branded Gibson EH amp, 1x10", single control, alligator tweed.

1936		$700	$925

Reinhardt

2004-2012. Bob Reinhardt builds his professional grade, production/custom, guitar and bass amps and cabinets in Lynchburg, Virginia. He also builds effects pedals.

Resonant Amplifiers

2007-present. Owners Wes Kuhnley and Peter Bregman build their professional grade, vacuum tube guitar and hi-fi amps in Minneapolis, Minnesota. They also build the Field Effects.

Retro-King Amplifier Company

2004-present. Tube combo and head amps built by Chuck Dean in Marcellus, New York.

Revenge Amps

Greg Perrine began building in 1996, intermediate grade, production/custom, guitar amplifiers and attenuators in Conway, Arkansas. He also imports a line of amps.

Reverend

1996-present. Joe Naylor started building amps under the Naylor brand in '94. In '96 he left Naylor to build guitars under the Reverend brand. From '01 to '05, Reverend offered tube amps, combos, and cabinets built in Warren, Michigan, that Naylor co-designed with Dennis Kager.

Rex

1950s-1960s. Tube amps built by the Lamberti Bros. Co. in Melbourne, Australia. They also built guitars. In the 1920s-1940s, Gretsch has an unrelated line of guitars with that brand.

Reynolds Valveart

1997-present. Professional and premium grade, production/custom, amps and cabinets built by Peter Reynolds in Windsor, Australia.

Rickenbacker

1931-present. Rickenbacker made amps from the beginning of the company up to the late '80s. Rickenbacker had many different models, from the small early models that were usually sold as a guitar/amp set, to the large, very cool, Transonic.

E-12

1963. 1x12" combo with tremolo depth and speed, volume, and on-off tone knobs.

1963		$650	$850

Electro-Student

Late-1940s. Typical late-'40s vertical combo cabinet, 1x12" speaker, lower power using 5 tubes, bottom mounted chassis, dark gray leatherette cover.

1948-1949		$625	$825

Hi Fi Model 98

1956. Tube amp, long horizontal cab with 3 speakers, Rickenbacker Hi Fi and Model 98 logo on back panel, blond cover, wheat grille cloth.

1956		$1,400	$1,850

Realistic MPA-20
Bernunzio Uptown Music

Reeves Custom 12

Retro-King Catalina Reverb Amp

Rickenbacker M-8
Imaged by Heritage Auctions, HA.com

1980 Rickenbacker TR-100GT
Imaged by Heritage Auctions, HA.com

Rivera Fandango

MODEL YEAR	FEATURES	EXC. COND. LOW	HIGH
Model B-9E			
	1960s. 1x12" combo, 4 knobs, gray.		
1960s		$800	$1,050
Model M-8			
	1950s-1960s. Gray, 1x8".		
1950s-60s		$550	$725
Model M-9			
	1960s. Green, 1x12".		
1960s		$700	$925
Model M-10			
	1930s. Silver metal, 1x10".		
1935		$575	$750
Model M-11			
	1950s. 12-15 watts, 1x12", 2x6V6 power. There was a different M-11 offered in the 1930s.		
1950s		$850	$1,100
Model M-12			
	1950s. 12-15 watts, 1x12", M-12 logo on back panel, brown leatherette. There was a different M-12 offered in the 1930s.		
1950s		$850	$1,100
Model M-14A			
	Late 1950s-early 1960s. 1x12 combo, mid-power 2x6V6, dual channel with vibrato, rough-brown tolex cover.		
1950s-60s		$850	$1,100
Model M-15			
	1950s-Early 1960s. 1x15" combo, 35 watts, 2 x 6L6 power tubes, model name on top panel.		
1950s-60s		$850	$1,100
Model M-16			
	1950s-Early 1960s. 1x15", 35 watts, model name on top panel.		
1950s-60s		$850	$1,100
Model M-30 EK-O-Sound			
	1961. Recording echo chamber and amp in 1x12 combo format, 11 tubes, gray grille and cover, very limited production.		
1961		$4,200	$5,500
Model M-59			
	1930s. Small lap steel amp.		
1935		$475	$625
Professional Model 200-A			
	1938. 15 watts, was sold with the Vibrola Spanish guitar.		
1938		$625	$825
RB and RG Series			
	1987-1989. Various bass (RB) and guitar (RG) amp models.		
1987-1989		$150	$300
Supersonic Model B-16			
	1960s. 4x10" speakers, gray cover.		
1960s		$925	$1,200
Supersonic Model B-22 Head			
	1960s. Tube head, gray cover.		
1960s		$725	$950
TR7			
	1978-1982. Solidstate, 7 watts, 1x10", tremolo.		
1978-1982		$130	$170
TR14			
	1978-ca.1982. Solidstate, 1x10", reverb, distortion.		
1978-1982		$130	$170

MODEL YEAR	FEATURES	EXC. COND. LOW	HIGH
TR25			
	1979-1982. Solidstate, 1x12" combo, reverb, tremolo, distortion.		
1979-1982		$175	$225
TR35B Bass			
	1978-ca.1982. Solidstate, mid-power, 1x15".		
1978-1982		$175	$225
TR50			
	1977-ca. 1982. Solid state with Rick-o-Sound stereo inputs.		
1977-1982		$175	$225
TR75G			
	1978-ca.1982. 75 watts, 2x12", 2 channels.		
1978-1982		$225	$300
TR75SG			
	1978-ca.1983. 1x10" and 1x15" speakers.		
1978-1982		$225	$300
TR100G			
	1978-ca.1982. Solidstate, 100 watts with 4x12", 2 channels.		
1978-1982		$225	$300
Transonic TS100/TS200			
	1967-1973. Trapezoid shaped combo, solidstate, 100-watt (2x12") or 200-watt (2x15"), Rick-O-Select.		
1967-1973	100w	$3,000	$4,000
1967-1973	200w	$3,500	$4,600

Risson

1970-1984, 2012-present. Bob Rissi builds his intermediate, professional and premium grade, production/custom, guitar and bass amplifiers in Placentia, California. From 1970-84 they were built in Santa Ana.

Rivera

1985-present. Amp designer and builder Paul Rivera modded and designed amps for other companies before starting his own line in California. He offers heads, combos, and cabinets. He also builds guitar pedals.

MODEL YEAR	FEATURES	EXC. COND. LOW	HIGH
Chubster 40			
	2000-present. 40 watts, 1x12" combo, burgundy tolex, light grille.		
2000-2021		$775	$1,000
Clubster 25			
	2005-2016. 25 watts, 1x10", 6V6.		
2005-2016		$650	$850
Clubster 45			
	2005-2015. 45 watts, 1x12" combo.		
2005-2015		$775	$1,000
Fandango 112 Combo			
	2001-present. 55 watts, 2xEL34, 1x12".		
2001-2021		$1,025	$1,325
Fandango 212 Combo			
	2001-2015. 55 or 100 watts, 2x12" tube amp.		
2001-2015		$1,100	$1,450
Jake Studio Combo			
	1997. 55 watts, 1x12", reverb and effects loop.		
1997		$775	$1,025
Knucklehead 55			
	1994-2002. 55-watt amp head, replaced by reverb model.		
1994-2002		$650	$850

MODEL YEAR	FEATURES	EXC. COND. LOW	HIGH

Knucklehead 100
1994-2002. 100-watt amp head, replaced by reverb model.

1994-2002		$700	$900

Knucklehead Reverb 112
2003-2007. 55 watts, 1x12" amp combo, reverb.

2003-2007		$975	$1,275

Los Lobottom/Sub 1
1999-2004. 1x12" cabinet with 300-watt powered 12" subwoofer.

1999-2004		$465	$600

M-60 Head
1990-2009. 60 watts.

1990-2009		$575	$750

M-60 112 Combo
1989-2009. 60 watts, 1x12".

1989-2009		$675	$875

M-100 Head
1990-2009. 100 watts.

1990-2009		$625	$825

M-100 212 Combo
1990-2009. 100 watts, 2x12" combo.

1990-2009		$750	$975

Pubster 25
2005-2017. 25 watts, 1x10".

2015-2017		$450	$575

Pubster 45
2005-2014. 45 watts, 1x12".

2005-2014		$485	$625

Quiana Combo
2000-present. Combo, 55 watts.

2000-2014	2x12	$875	$1,150
2000-2014	4x10	$1,025	$1,325
2000-2019	1x12	$785	$1,025

R-30 112 Combo
1993-2007. 30 watts, 1x12", compact cab, black tolex cover, gray-black grille.

1993-2007		$775	$1,000

R-100 212 Combo
1993-2007. 100 watts, 2x12".

1993-2007		$850	$1,100

Sedona 112
2008-2020. 55 watts, 1x12".

2008-2020		$1,050	$1,350

Sedona Lite 55
2005-present. For electric and acoustic guitars, 55 watts, 1x12".

2005-2021		$950	$1,225

Suprema R-55 112/115 Combo
2000-present. Tube amp, 55 watts, 1x12" (still available) or 1x15" ('00-'01).

2000-2021	1x12 or 1x15	$900	$1,175

TBR-1
1985-1999. First Rivera production model, rack mount, 60 watts.

1985-1999		$725	$950

Venus Series
2007-present. Series includes the 7/15-watt 3 combo (1x10 or 1x12), and the 15-watt 5 and 35-watt 6, both as combos (1x12, 2x12) and heads with cabs (1x12, 2x12).

2007-2021	Venus 6, 1x12	$924	$1,200
2007-2021	Venus 6, 2x12	$1,050	$1,350
2007-2021	Venus 6, head	$900	$1,175
2009-2017	Venus 3, 1x10	$825	$1,075
2009-2021	Venus 5, 1x12	$850	$1,125

Roccaforte Amps
1993-present. Tube amps, combos, and cabinets built by Doug Roccaforte in San Clemente, California.

Rocktron
1980s-present. Tube and solidstate amp heads, combos and cabinets. Rocktron is a division of GHS Strings and also offers stomp boxes and preamps.

Rogue
2001-present. They offered student-level solid-state import (Korea) compact amps up to around '06. They also offer guitars, basses, lap steels, mandolins, banjos, ukuleles and effects.

Small Solidstate
2001-2006. Various models.

2001-2006		$45	$100

Roland
Japan's Roland Corporation's products include amplifiers and keyboards and, under the Boss brand, effects.

Acoustic Chorus (AC) Series
1995-present. Number in model indicates wattage (i.e. AC-60 = 60 watts).

1995-2009	AC-100, 1x12, 2x5	$380	$495
1995-2020	AC-90, 2x8	$380	$495
1995-2021	AC-60, 2x6	$315	$410

Blues Cube
1996-present.

1996	BC60, 3x10	$255	$327
1996-2021	BC30, 1x12	$190	$245
1996-2021	BC60, 1x12	$210	$275

Bolt 60
Early 1980s. Solidstate/tube, 1x12".

1980s		$190	$245

Cube Series
1978-present. Number in model indicates wattage (i.e. Cube 20 = 20 watts).

1978-1982	Cube 100, 1x12	$190	$245
1978-1982	Cube 20, 1x8	$105	$135
1978-1983	Cube 40, 1x10	$190	$245
1978-1983	Cube 60, 1x12	$190	$245
1978-1983	Cube 60B, 1x12	$190	$245
2000-2009	Cube 30 Bass, 1x10	$125	$165
2000s	Cube 80GX, 1x12	$190	$245
2000s	Cube 80XL, 1x12	$190	$245
2006-2010	Cube 30X, 1x10	$125	$165
2006-2013	Cube 15X, 1x8	$105	$135
2006-2013	Cube 20X, 1x8	$105	$135
2008-2013	Cube 80X, 1x12	$190	$245

Jazz Chorus (JC) Series
1975-present. Includes the JC-50 (50 watts, 1x12"), JC-55 (50 watts, 2x8"), JC-77 (80 watts, 2x10"), JC-90 (90 watts, 2x10") and JC-120 (120 watts, 2x12" and 4x12").

1975-2014	JC-120, 2x12	$420	$545

Rivera Venus

Roland Blues Cube Artist

1979 Roland Cube 60B
Imaged by Heritage Auctions, HA.com

1978 Roland JC-160
Alf Tengs-Pedersen

Roland Micro Cube

1975 Sano Supernova
Tom Pfeifer

MODEL YEAR	FEATURES	EXC. COND. LOW	HIGH
1980s	JC-50, 1x12	$335	$435
1987-1994	JC-55, 2x8	$335	$435
1987-1994	JC-77, 2x10	$380	$490
1990s	JC-120, 4x12	$465	$600
1990s	JC-90, 2x10	$380	$490

Micro Cube
2000-present. Compact AC power or battery, 2 watts, 1x5".

2000-2021		$85	$110

Spirit Series
1982-1989. Compact, model number indicates wattage.

1982-1989	Spirit 30, 1x12	$85	$110
1982-1989	Spirit 40A, combo	$85	$110
1982-1989	Spirit 50, combo	$85	$110

Studio Bass

1979		$190	$245

VGA3 V-Guitar
2003-2009. GK digital modeling amp, 50 watts, 1x12" combo.

2003-2009		$190	$245

VGA5 V-Guitar

2001-2004		$190	$245

VGA7 V-Guitar

2000-2009		$210	$275

S.S. Maxwell
See info under Danelectro.

Sadowsky
1980-present. From '05 to '07, luthier Roger Sadowsky built a bass tube amp head in Brooklyn, New York. He also builds basses and guitars.

Sam Ash
1960s-1970s. Sam Ash Music was founded by Sam Ash (formerly Ashkynase) in Brooklyn, New York, in 1924, and by '66 there were about four Ash stores. During the '60s they private branded their own amp line, was built by Jess Oliver of Oliver Amps and based upon Oliver's Ampeg designs.

Sam Ash Mark II Pro Combo
1960s. 2x12" with reverb combo amp.

1960s		$675	$875

SamAmp
2004-present. Intermediate and professional grade, boutique amps built by Sam Timberlake in Vestavia Hills, Alabama.

Sano
1951-ca. 1980. Combos, heads and cabinets made in three factories around New Jersey. Founded by Joseph Zonfrilli, Louis Iorio, and Nick Sano, initially offering accordion pickups, amplifiers, and all-electric accordions. Sano patented his accordion pickup in '44 and also developed a highly acclaimed stereophonic pickup accordion and matching amp. By '66 the Sano Corporation augmented their all-tube accordion amps with new solidstate circuitry models. In the mid-'60s they offered a new line of amps specifically designed for the guitar and bass market. Sano amps

are generally low-gain, low power amplifiers. They also marketed reverb units and guitars.

Compact Combo

1960s	160R, 15w, 1x12	$525	$685
1960s	Sano-ette	$425	$550

Satellite Amplifiers
2004-present. Professional and premium grade, production/custom, tube amps, preamps and cabinets built by Adam Grimm in San Diego, California. He also builds effects.

Savage
1994-present. Tube combos, amp heads and cabinets built by Jeff Krumm at Savage Audio, in Savage, Minnesota.

Sceptre
1960s. Canadian-made. Sceptre script logo on upper left side of grille ('60s Fender-style and placement).

Signet
1960s. Low power, 1x10", Class-A 6V6 power.

1960s		$325	$425

Schaller
The German guitar accessory company began in 1945, main products in the late '50s were tube amps and they had solid-state amps in the '60s.

Schertler
Made in Switzerland, model logo (e.g. David model) on front, intermediate to professional grade, modern designs for modern applications.

SDG Vintage
2003-present. Intermediate and professional grade, production/custom, tube amps, combos and heads built by Steven Gupta in Bristow, Virginia.

Selmer
1930s-late 1970s. The Selmer UK distributor offered mid- to high-level amps starting as early as 1935 and by the '50s was one of the strongest European brands of amps.

Bassmaster 50
1960s. Amp and cabinet set.

1960s		$2,600	$3,400

Constellation 14
1962-1965. Single speaker combo, 14 watts, gray snakeskin tolex-type cover.

1962-1965		$2,500	$3,250

Futurama Caravelle
1960s. Mid-size 1x12" combo.

1960s		$1,200	$1,550

Futurama Corvette
1960s. Class A low power 1x8", 4 tubes, volume and tone controls, plus amplitude and speed tremolo controls, large script Futurama logo on front of amp, Futurama Corvette and Selmer logo on top panel.

1960s		$1,000	$1,300

MODEL YEAR	FEATURES	EXC. COND. LOW	HIGH

Little Giant
1960s. Small combo, red.

1963		$1,400	$1,825

Mark 2 Treble and Bass Head
1960s. About 30 watts (2xEL34s), requires power line transformer for U.S. use, large Selmer logo on grille.

1960s		$1,400	$1,825

Thunderbird Twin 30
1960s. 30 watts, 2x12".

1962-1965		$5,200	$6,700

Thunderbird Twin 50
1960s. 50 watts, 2x12".

1964		$5,200	$6,700
1968		$3,200	$4,200

Truvoice
1960s. Truvoice and Selectortone logo on top-mounted chasis, 30-watt combo, 1x15 or 2x12 Goodmans speaker, 2xEL34 power tubes, tremolo, 6 push button Selectortone Automatic.

1961	1x15 combo	$2,600	$3,400
1965	2x12 combo	$3,400	$4,400

Zodiac Twin 30
1964-1971. Combo amp, gray snakeskin tolex cover.

1964-1971		$3,800	$4,900

Sewell
1998-2008. Doug Sewell built his tube combo and head amps in Texas. He currently is the senior amp designer for Paul Reed Smith.

Seymour Duncan
Pickup maker Seymour Duncan, located in Santa Barbara, California, offered a line of amps from around 1984 to '95.

84-40/84-50
1989-1995. Tube combo, 2 switchable channels, 1x12", includes the 84-40 ('89-'91, 40 watts) and the 84-50 ('91-'95, 50 watts).

1989-1995	84-40 or 84-50	$250	$325

Bass 300 x 2
1986-1987. Solidstate, 2 channels (300 or 600 watts), EQ, contour boost switches, effects loop.

1986-1987		$250	$325

Bass 400
1986-1987. Solidstate, 400 watts, EQ, contour boost, balanced line output, effects loop.

1986-1987		$250	$325

Convertible
1986-1995. 60-watt; dual-channel; effects loop; Accutronics spring reverb; 3-band EQ.

1986-1987	Head only	$325	$425
1988-1995	Combo	$325	$425

KTG-2075 Stereo
1989-1993. Part of the King Tone Generator Series, 2 channels with 75 watts per channel.

1989-1993		$250	$325

SG Systems
1970s. A Division of the Chicago Musical Instrument Company (CMI), who also owned Gibson Guitars. Gibson outsourced amplifier production from Kalamazoo to CMI in '67 and CMI (Chicago) continued for a year or two with Gibson-branded amplifiers. In the early '70s CMI introduced the SG Systems brand of hybrid amplifiers, which had a tube power section and a solidstate preamp section. CMI was trying to stay modern with SG Systems by introducing futuristic features like the Notch Shift which would quickly switch between popular rock sounds and mellow jazz delivery. SG amps have a large SG logo on the front baffle and were built with metal corners. Amplifiers have similar power specs; for example, the models issued in '73 all were rated with 100-watt RMS with 200-watts peak music power, so models were based on different speaker configurations.

SG Series

1970s	SG115, 1x15	$400	$525
1970s	SG212, 2x12	$425	$550
1970s	SG215 Bass, 2x15	$425	$550
1970s	SG410, 4x10	$425	$550
1970s	SG610, 6x10	$450	$600
1970s	SG812 PA	$250	$325

Shaw
2008-present. Custom/production, intermediate and professional grade, guitar amp heads and cabinets built by Kevin Shaw in Lebanon, Tennessee.

Sherlock Amplifiers
1990-present. Dale Sherlock builds his intermediate to premium grade, production/custom, tube guitar amps and cabinets in Melbourne Victoria, Australia.

Sherwood
Late 1940s-early 1950s. Amps made by Danelectro for Montgomery Ward. There are also Sherwood guitars and lap steels made by Kay.

Sho-Bud
Introduced and manufactured by the Baldwin/Gretsch factory in 1970. Distributed by Kustom/Gretsch in the '80s. Models include D-15 Model 7838, S-15 Model 7836, Twin Tube Model 7834, and Twin Trans Model 7832.

Compactra 100
1960s. Hybrid tube, 45 watts, 1x12", model name logo on lower left control panel.

1960s		$600	$775

D15 Double
Introduced in 1970. Solidstate, 100 watts. 2 channels 1x15" JBL speaker.

1970s		$575	$750

S15 Single
Introduced in 1972. Like D15, but with single channel.

1970s		$400	$525

Sho-Bass
Introduced in 1972. 100 watts, 1x15", solidstate combo, black grille, black vinyl cover.

1970s		$400	$525

Satellite Amplifiers Barracuda

AMPS

Selmer Zodiac Twin 30
Ron Cascisa

Shaw Tonerod MG

AMPS

Siegmund Sound King

Silvertone 1331

Tom Pfeifer

Silvertone 1333

Imaged by Heritage Auctions, HA.com

MODEL YEAR	FEATURES	EXC. COND. LOW	HIGH

Twin Trans
Introduced in 1972. 100 watts, solidstate combo, 2x12", reverb, black vinyl cover, dark grille, Sho-Bud script logo front upper right.

| 1970s | | $550 | $725 |

Twin Tube
Introduced in 1972. 100 watt tube combo, 4 6L6s, 2x12", reverb, black vinyl cover, dark grille.

| 1970s | | $700 | $900 |

Siegmund Guitars & Amplifiers
1993-present. Chris Siegmund builds his tube amp heads, combos and cabinets in Los Angeles, California. He founded the company in Seattle, moving it to Austin, Texas for '95-'97. He also builds effects pedals and guitars.

Silvertone
1941-ca.1970, present. Brand used by Sears. All Silvertone amps were supplied by American companies up to around '66.

Model 1300
1948. Vertical combo cab, treble-clef logo on grille, 2-tone, 3 inputs, 2 controls.

| 1948 | | $500 | $650 |

Model 1304
1949-1951. 18 watts, 1x12, 2x6L6 power tubes, 2-tone leatherette cover, round speaker baffle hole, volume, treble, bass and tremolo control knobs, becomes Model 1344.

| 1949-1951 | | $500 | $650 |

Model 1330
1954-1957. Introduced in Sears Fall '54 catalog, 3 tubes (with rectifier), 1x6", wide-panel 13x13.75x7.5" cab in tan artificial leather, 9 lbs., replaced Model 1339 at the same price but with new wide-panel style, small Silvertone logo above the grille, replaced in '58 by Model 1390 Silvertone Meteor.

| 1954-1957 | | $250 | $325 |

Model 1331
1954-1957. Made by Danelectro, 14 lbs., 1x8" student combo, 3 tubes (with rectifier), 1 volume, 1 tone, 2 inputs, tan tweed-effect cover with brown alligator trim, large-thread wheat-gold grille, brown metal control panel.

| 1954-1957 | | $300 | $400 |

Model 1333
1954-1957. Made by Danelectro, 23 lbs., 1x12" combo, 2x6V6 power, 5 tubes (with rectifier), 2 volumes, 1 tone, 3 inputs, 2-control vibrato, tan tweed-effect cover with brown alligator trim, large-thread wheat-gold grille, brown metal control panel.

| 1954-1957 | | $525 | $675 |

Model 1334
1954-1957. Made by Danelectro, 29 lbs., heavy-duty 1x12" combo, 6 tubes (with rectifier), 2 volumes, 2 tones, 3 inputs, 2-control vibrato, tan tweed-effect cover with brown alligator trim, large-thread wheat-gold grille, brown metal control panel.

| 1954-1957 | | $575 | $750 |

Model 1335
1954-1957. Made by Danelectro, 99 lbs., heavy-duty 1x15" combo, 6 tubes (with rectifier), 2 volumes, 2 tones, 4 inputs, 2-control vibrato, tan tweed-effect cover with brown alligator trim, large-thread wheat-gold grille, brown metal control panel.

| 1954-1957 | | $600 | $775 |

Model 1336 (Twin Twelve)
1954-1957. Made by Danelectro, 26.75x17.5x9.25" cab, 45 lbs., 2x12" combo, 4x6L6 powe tubes, 3 volumes, 2 tones, 4 inputs, 2-control vibrato, tan tweed-effect cover with brown alligator trim, large-thread wheat-gold grille, brown metal control panel.

| 1954-1957 | | $900 | $1,175 |

Model 1337 "Wide Range Eight Speaker"
1956. Odd-looking suitcase cab that opens into 2 separate speaker baffles each containing 4x8" speakers, 2 preamps, 2 channels with separate controls for volume, bass and treble, 2-control vibrato, 42 lbs.

| 1956 | | $900 | $1,175 |

Model 1339
Ca.1952-1954. Sears lowest-priced amp, 3 tubes (with rectifier), 1x6", 1 input, 1 knob, maroon artificial leather cover over 10.5x8x5" verticle cab, script Silvertone logo on low right grille, 7 lbs.

| 1952-1954 | | $300 | $400 |

Model 1340
Ca.1952-1954. Sears second lowest-priced amp, 3 tubes (with rectifier), 1x6", 2 inputs, 1 knob, brown and white imitation leather cover over 15x12x8.5" verticle cab, script Silvertone logo on low right grille, 14 lbs.

| 1952-1954 | | $300 | $400 |

Model 1342 Streamlined
Ca.1952-1954. Sears third lowest-priced amp, 4 tubes (with rectifier), 1x12", 3 inputs, 2 knobs, green and beige imitation leather cover over 16x19x7.25" slanted-side cab, script Silvertone logo on low right grille, 23 lbs.

| 1952-1954 | | $525 | $675 |

Model 1344
1950-1954. Retro-styled vertical 22.5x15.5x9.5" cab with round speaker baffle hole, 1x12" combo, first Silvertone built-in vibrato, 6 tubes (with rectifier), 3 inputs, 3 controls (treble, bass, volume) plus vibrato control, maroon imitation leather cover with sports-stripe around the bottom, 33 lbs., script Silvertone logo low right side of cab.

| 1952-1954 | | $525 | $675 |

Model 1346 (Twin Twelve)
Ca.1952-1954. Danelectro-made, brown control panel, 2x12", 4 6L6s, vibrato, leather handle, tan smooth leatherette cover, 2 speaker baffle openings.

| 1952-1954 | | $900 | $1,175 |

Model 1390 Meteor
1958-1959. Renamed from Model 1330, Meteor logo on front panel, 1x6" practice amp, 3 tubes (with rectifier), tan simulated leather cover, in '60 renamed Model 1430 (but no longer a Meteor).

| 1958-1959 | | $300 | $400 |

Model 1391
1958-1959. Modern-style cab, 3 tubes (with rectifier), 5 watts, 1x8".

| 1958-1959 | | $300 | $400 |

The ***Vintage Guitar Price Guide*** shows low to high values for items in all-original excellent condition, and, where applicable, with original case or cover.

MODEL YEAR FEATURES	EXC. COND. LOW	HIGH

Model 1392
1958-1959. Modern-style cab, 6 tubes (with rectifier), 10 watts, 1x12", vibrato.

| 1958-1959 | $525 | $675 |

Model 1393
1958-1959. Modern-style cab, 7 tubes (with rectifier), 15 watts, heavy-duty 1x12", vibrato.

| 1958-1959 | $525 | $675 |

Model 1396 Two-Twelve
1958-1959. Script Two-Twelve logo on lower left front and Silvertone logo on lower right front, 50 watts, 2x12", 4x6L6 power tubes, 9 tubes (with rectifier), vibrato, 26.75x17.5x9.25" with gray and metallic fleck cover, white grille, 45 lbs.

| 1958-1959 | $900 | $1,175 |

Model 1420
1968. Tube-powered, 5 watts, 1x8" student combo.

| 1968 | $350 | $450 |

Model 1421
1968. Tube-powered, 10 watts, 1x8" combo, covered in dark olive vinyl.

| 1968 | $350 | $450 |

Model 1422
1968. Tube-powered, 40 watts, 1x12" combo, covered in dark olive vinyl.

| 1968 | $525 | $675 |

Model 1423
1968. Solidstate, 125 watts, 2x12" cab, 55 lbs., dark olive.

| 1968 | $425 | $550 |

Model 1425
1968. Solidstate, 200 watts, 6x10" cab, 86 lbs., dark olive.

| 1968 | $900 | $1,175 |

Model 1426
1968. Solidstate, 250 watts, 6x15" cab, slide switches instead of control knobs, automatic E-tone for tuning, casters for 149 lb. head and cab.

| 1968 | $900 | $1,175 |

Model 1428
1968. Solidstate, 60 watts, 1x15" cab, 36 lbs., dark olive.

| 1968 | $425 | $550 |

Model 1430
1959-1966. Silvertone's lowest-price model, 3 tubes, 1x6", previously called Model 1390 Meteor, and prior to that named Model 1330, retro cab basically unchanged since first introduced in '54.

| 1959-1966 | $300 | $400 |

Model 1431
1959-1961. 5 watts, 1x8", overhanging-top wrap-around grille cab, 3 tubes (with rectifier), light gray cover with white grille.

| 1959-1961 | $300 | $400 |

Model 1431 Bass
1968. Solidstate, 200 watts, 6x12" cab, 91 lbs., dark olive.

| 1968 | $900 | $1,175 |

Model 1432
1959-1961. 10 watts, 1x12", vibrato, overhanging-top wrap-around grille cab, 6 tubes (with rectifier), dark gray tweed-effect cover with white grille.

| 1959-1961 | $525 | $675 |

Model 1433
1959-1961. 15 watts, 1x15", vibrato, overhanging-top wrap-around grille cab, 7 tubes (with rectifier), gray with metallic fleck cover with white grille.

| 1959-1961 | $700 | $900 |

Model 1434 Twin Twelve
1959-1961. 50 watts using 4x6L6 power, 2x12" combo, vibrato, 2 channels each with volume, bass and treble controls, black cover with gold-colored trim.

| 1959-1961 | $900 | $1,175 |

Model 1459
1960s. Student tube amp, 3 watts, 1x8", black vinyl, square cab, 1 tone, 1 volume, 1 channel, 2 inputs.

| 1967-1968 | $350 | $450 |

Model 1463 Bass
1967-1968. Solidstate, 1x15", piggyback, 60 lbs., reverb, tremolo.

| 1967-1968 | $425 | $550 |

Model 1464
1967-1968. Solidstate, 100 watts, 2x12", piggyback, 60 lbs., reverb, tremolo, gray vinyl cover.

| 1967-1968 | $500 | $650 |

Model 1465
1966-1968. Solidstate, piggyback, 150 watts, 6x10", reverb, tremolo, gray vinyl cover, replaces Model 1485.

| 1966-1968 | $900 | $1,175 |

Model 1466 Bass
1966-1968. Solidstate, 150 watts, 6x10", gray vinyl cover.

| 1966-1968 | $725 | $950 |

Model 1471
1961-1963. 5 watts, 1x8", 3 tubes, 1 volume, 1 tone, 2 inputs, black leathette cover with white grille.

| 1961-1963 | $350 | $450 |

Model 1472
1960s. 10 watts, 2 6V6s provide mid-level power, 1x12", front controls mounted vertically on front right side, black cover with silver grille, large stationary handle, tremolo.

| 1961-1963 | $525 | $675 |

Model 1473 Bass
1961-1963. Designed for bass or accordion, 25 watts, 1x15" combo, 6 tubes (with rectifier), 2 channels, 4 inputs, 19x29x9" cab, 43 lbs., black leatherette with white grille.

| 1961-1963 | $700 | $900 |

Model 1474 Twin Twelve
1961-1963. Silvertone's first reverb amp, 50 watts, 4x6L6 power, 10 tubes (with rectifier), 2x12" combo, 2 control vibrato with dual remote footswitch, 2 channels each with bass, treble, and volume, 4 inputs, ground switch, standby switch, 19x29x9" combo cab, 54 lbs., black leatherette with silver grille.

| 1961-1963 | $900 | $1,175 |

Model 1481
1963-1968. Compact student amp, 5 watts, 1x8", 3 tubes (with rectifier), volume and tone controls, gray leatherette cover with white grille, replaces Model 1471.

| 1963-1968 | $350 | $450 |

Model 1482
1960s. 15 watts, 1x12", 6 tubes, control panel mounted on right side vertically, tremolo, gray leatherette.

| 1963-1968 | $525 | $675 |

Silvertone 1336
Imaged by Heritage Auctions, HA.com

AMPS

1961 Silvertone 1474 Twin Twelve
Imaged by Heritage Auctions, HA.com

1966 Silvertone 1482
Larry Niven

To get the most from this book, be sure to read "Using **The Guide**" in the introduction.

AMPS

Silvertone Model 1483
Imaged by Heritage Auctions, HA.com

Smokey

Soldano SLO-100
Imaged by Heritage Auctions, HA.com

MODEL		EXC. COND.	
YEAR	FEATURES	LOW	HIGH

Model 1483 Bass
1963-1966. 23 watts, 1x15" piggyback tube amp, gray tolex and gray grille.

1963-1966	$700	$900

Model 1484 Twin Twelve
1963-1966. 60 watts, 2x12" piggyback tube amp, tremolo and reverb, gray cover with light grille.

1963-1966	$900	$1,175

Model 1485
1963-1965. 120 watts, 6x10" (Jensen C-10Q) piggyback, 10 tubes with 5 silicon rectifiers, 2 channels, reverb, tremolo, charcoal-gray tolex-style cover, white grille, replaced in '66 by solidstate Model 1465.

1963-1965	$1,150	$1,500

Model 4707 Organ
1960s. Interesting '60s family room style cabinet with legs, 45-watt tube amp with vibrato, 1x12", front controls, could be used for organ, stereo, or record player turntable.

1960s	$500	$650

Simms-Watts
Late 1960s-1970s. Tube amp heads, combos, PA heads and cabinets made in London, England. Similar to Marshall and HiWatt offerings of the era.

Skip Simmons
1990-present. Custom and production tube combo amps built by Skip Simmons in Loma Rica, California.

Skrydstrup R&D
1997-present. Production/custom, premium grade, amps and cabinets built by Steen Skrydstrup in Denmark. He also builds effects.

Sligo Amps
2004-present. Intermediate and professional grade, production/custom, amps built by Steven Clark in Leesburg, Virginia.

SMF
Mid-1970s. Amp head and cabinets from Dallas Music Industries, Ltd., of Mahwah, New Jersey. Offered the Tour Series which featured a 150 watt head and 4x12" bottoms with metal speaker grilles and metal corners.

Tour MK 2 Head
Mid-1970s. 150-watt head, high- and low-gain inputs, master volume, 8xEL34 power tubes, black.

1970s	$1,100	$1,450

SMF (Sonic Machine Factory)
2002-2009. Tube amps and cabinets designed by Mark Sampson (Matchless, Bad Cat, Star) and Rick Hamel (SIB effects) and built in California.

Smicz Amplification
Tube combos and extension cabinets built by Bob Smicz in Bristol, Connecticut.

MODEL		EXC. COND.	
YEAR	FEATURES	LOW	HIGH

Smith Custom Amplifiers
All tube combo amps, heads and speaker cabinets built by Sam Smith in Montgomery, Alabama starting in 2002.

Smokey
1997-present. Mini amps often packaged in cigarette packs made by Bruce Zinky in Flagstaff, Arizona. He also builds Zinky amps and effects and has revived the Supro brand on a guitar and amp.

Snider
Jeff Snider has been building various combo tube amps in San Diego, California, since '95. In 1999 he started branding them with his last name.

Soldano
1987-present. Made in Seattle, Washington by amp builder Mike Soldano, the company offers a range of all-tube combo amps, heads and cabinets. They also offer a reverb unit.

Astroverb 16 Combo
1997-2020. Atomic with added reverb.

1997-2020	$725	$950

Atomic 16 Combo
1996-2001. Combo, 20 watts, 1x12".

1996-2001	$625	$825

Avenger Head
2004-2020. Single channel, 4 preamp tubes, 100-watt with 4 power tubes, or 50-watt with 2.

2004-2020	$1,150	$1,525

Decatone Combo
1998-2020. 2x12" 100-watt combo, rear mounted controls, still available as a head.

1998-2008 Combo 2x12	$1,750	$2,275
2009-2020 Head only	$1,375	$1,775

HR 50/Hot Rod 50/50+ Head
1992-2012. 50-watt single channel head.

1992-2012	$950	$1,250

HR 100/Hot Rod 100/100+ Head
1994-2001. 100-watt single channel head.

1994-2001	$950	$1,250

Lucky 13 Combo
2000-2020. 100 watts (50 also available), 2x12" combo.

2000-2020	$1,300	$1,700

Reverb-O-Sonic Combo
1990s-2020. 50 watts, 2 channels, 2x12" combo, reverb.

1990s-2020	$1,150	$1,500

SLO-100 Super Cabinet
1988-2019. 4x12" slant-front or straight-front cabinet, prices shown are for slant, deduct $100 for straight.

1988-1989	$700	$900
1990-2019	$625	$800

SLO-100 Super Lead Overdrive
1988-2020. First production model, 100-watt amp head, snakeskin cover, 4x12" cabinet. Replaced by SLO-100 Classic in '21.

1988-1989	$2,725	$3,550
1990-2009	$2,650	$3,450
2010-2020	$2,650	$3,450

MODEL YEAR	FEATURES	EXC. COND. LOW	HIGH

Sommatone

1998-present. Jim Somma builds his tube combo and head amps and cabinets in Somerville, New Jersey.

Sonax

Introduced in 1972. Budget line of solidstate amps offered by Gretsch/Baldwin, made by Yorkville Sound (Traynor) in Toronto. Introduced with dark grille and dark cover.

530-B Bass
1970s. Solidstate, 30 watts, 1x12".

1970s		$130	$175

550-B Bass
1970s. Solidstate, 50 watts, 1x15".

1970s		$145	$190

720-G
1970s. Solidstate student amp, 20 watts, 2x8", reverb.

1970s		$145	$190

730-G
1970s. Solidstate, 30 watts, 2x10", reverb and tremolo.

1970s		$210	$275

750-G
1970s. Solidstate, 50 watts, 2x12", reverb and tremolo.

1970s		$225	$290

770-G
1970s. Solidstate, 75 watts, 4x10", reverb and tremolo.

1970s		$240	$315

Songworks Systems

See listing under Little Lanilei.

Sonny Jr.

Harmonica amplifiers built by harmonica player Sonny Jr. in conjunction with Cotton Amps in Tolland, Connecticut. Was started in 1996.

Sonola

Tube combo amps made for the Sonola Accordian company of Chicago in the 1950s and '60s, possibly built by Guild or Ampeg. There are also Sonola tube amp heads from the '70s made by MHB Amplifiers in Adelaide, South Australia.

Sound City

Made in England from 1966-'67 to the late-'70s, the tube Sound City amps were Marshall-looking heads and separate cabinets. They were imported, for a time, into the U.S. by Gretsch.

50 PA Plus
Late-1960s-late-1970s. Similar to 50 Plus but with 4 channels.

1970s		$750	$975

50 Plus/50R Head
Late-1960s-late-1970s. Amp head, labeled 50 Plus or 50 R.

1960s-70s		$1,050	$1,325

120 Energizer Slave Unit
1970s. 120-watt power amp only, no preamp, Energizer Slave Unit logo on front panel.

1970s		$625	$815

120/120R Head
Early-late-1970s. The 120-watt head replaced the late-1960s 100-watt model.

1970s	120, no reverb	$1,050	$1,325
1970s	120R, reverb	$1,100	$1,425

200 Plus Head

1970s		$1,175	$1,525

Concord Combo
80 watts, 2x12" Fane speakers, cream, basketweave grille.

1968		$1,050	$1,375

L-80 Cabinet
1970s. 4x10" speaker cabinet.

1970s		$525	$700

L-412 Cabinet
1970s. 4x12" speaker cabinet.

1970s		$600	$800

X-60 Cabinet
1970s. 2x12" speaker cabinet.

1970s		$575	$750

Sound Electronics

Sound Electronics Corporation introduced a line of amplifiers in 1965 that were manufactured in Long Island. Six models were initially offered, with solidstate rectifiers and tube preamp and power sections. Their catalog did not list power wattages but did list features and speaker configurations. The initial models had dark vinyl-style covers and sparkling silver grille cloth. The amps were combos with the large models having vertical cabinets, silver script Sound logo on upper left of grille. The larger models used JBL D120F and D130F speakers. Stand alone extension speakers were also available.

Various Models
Mid-1960s. Made in U.S.A., models include X-101, X-101R, X-202 Bass/Organ, X-404 Bass and Organ, X-505R amps, hi-fi chassis often using 7868 power tubes.

1960s		$600	$775

Southbay Ampworks/ Scumback Amps

2002-present. Tube combo amps and speaker cabinets built by Jim Seavall in Whittier, California. He also builds Scumback Speakers. In '14, name changed to Scumback Amps.

Sovtek

1992-1996. Sovtek amps were products of Mike Matthews of Electro-Harmonix fame and his New Sensor Corporation. The guitar and bass amps and cabinets were made in Russia.

Mig Cabinet

1992-1996	2x12"	$350	$450

Mig Series Head
1992-1996. Tube amp heads, model number indicates watts, point-to-point wiring, models include; Mig 30, 50, 60, 100, 100B (bass).

1992-1996	Various models	$500	$650

Sound City 120 and L-412
Imaged by Heritage Auctions, HA.com

AMPS

Sound Electronics X-101
Tom Novak

Sovtek Mig 100

Specimen Horn

AMPS

Standel 25L15
Imaged by Heritage Auctions, HA.com

Star Gain Star

MODEL YEAR	FEATURES	EXC. COND. LOW	HIGH

Space Tone
See Swart Amplifiers.

Specimen Products
1984-present. Luthier Ian Schneller added tube amps and speaker cabinets in '93. He also builds guitars, basses and ukes in Chicago, Illinois.

Speedster
1995-2000, 2003-2007. Founded by Lynn Ellsworth, offering tube amps and combos designed by Bishop Cochran with looks inspired by dashboards of classic autos. In '03, Joe Valosay and Jevco International purchased the company and revived the brand with help from former owner Cory Wilds. Amps were originally built by Soldono, but later ones built by Speedster in Gig Harbor, Washington. They also built effects pedals.

Splawn
2004-present. Production, professional grade, tube amps and cabinets built by Scott Splawn in Dallas, North Carolina.

St. George
1960s. There were Japanese guitars bearing this brand, but these amps may have been built in California.

Mid-Size Tube
1965. Low power, 1x10" Jensen, 2 5065 and 2 12AX7 tubes.

1960s		$185	$300

Standel
1952-1974, 1997-present. Bob Crooks started custom building amps part time in '52, going into full time standard model production in '58 in Temple City, California. In '61 Standel started distributing guitars under their own brand and others. By late '63 or '64, Standel had introduced solidstate amps, two years before Fender and Ampeg introduced their solidstate models. In '67 Standel moved to a new, larger facility in El Monte, California. In '73 Chicago Musical Instruments (CMI), which owned Gibson at the time, bought the company and built amps in El Monte until '74. In '97 the Standel name was revived by Danny McKinney who, with the help of original Standel founder Bob Crooks and Frank Garlock (PR man for first Standel), set about building reissues of some of the early models in Ventura, California.

A-30 B Artist 30 Bass
1964-early-1970s. Artist Series, the original Standel solidstate series, 80 watts, 2x15".

1964-1969		$400	$525

A-30 G Artist 30 Guitar
1964-early-1970s. Solidstate, 80 watts, 2x15".

1964-1974		$425	$550

A-48 G Artist 48 Guitar
1964-early-1970s. Solidstate, 80 watts, 4x12".

1964-1974		$500	$650

MODEL YEAR	FEATURES	EXC. COND. LOW	HIGH

A-60 B Artist 60 Bass
1964-early-1970s. Solidstate, 160 watts, 4x15".

1964-1974		$500	$650

A-60 G Artist 60 Guitar
1964-early-1970s. Solidstate, 160 watts, 4x15".

1964-1974		$500	$650

A-96 G Artist 96 Guitar
1964-early-1970s. Solidstate, 160 watts, 8x12".

1964-1974		$550	$725

Artist XV
1960s. Piggyback, hybrid solidstate preamp with power tubes.

1962		$400	$525

C-24 Custom 24
Late-1960s-1970s. Custom Slim Line Series, solidstate, 100 watts, 2x12", dark vinyl, dark grille.

1960s-70s		$450	$575

I-30 B Imperial 30 Bass
1964-early-1970s. Imperial Series, the original Standel solidstate series, 100 watts, 2x15".

1964-1974		$475	$625

I-30 G Imperial 30 Guitar
1964-early-1970s. Imperial Series, the original Standel solidstate series, 100 watts, 2x15".

1964-1974		$500	$650

S-10 Studio 10
Late-1960s-1970s. Studio Slim Line Series, solidstate, 30 watts, 1x10", dark vinyl, dark grille.

1960s-70s		$290	$375

S-24 G
1970s. Solidstate, 2x12".

1970s		$375	$485

S-50 Studio 50
Early-late-1960s. Not listed in '69 Standel catalog, 60 watts, gray tolex, gray grille, piggyback.

1960s		$425	$550

SM-60 Power Magnifier
1970s. Tall, verticle combo solidstate amp, 100 watts, 6x10".

1970		$375	$485

Tube
1953-1958. Early custom made tube amps made by Bob Crooks in his garage, padded naugahyde cabinet with varying options and colors. There are a limited number of these amps, and brand knowledge is also limited, therefore there is a wide value range. Legend has it that the early Standel amps made Leo Fender re-think and introduce even more powerful amps.

1953-1958	Various models	$3,000	$5,900

Star
Tube amps, combos and speaker cabinets built by Mark Sampson in the Los Angeles, California area, starting 2004. Sampson has also been involved with Matchless, Bad Cat, and SMF amps.

Starcaster
See listing under Fender.

MODEL		EXC. COND.	
YEAR	FEATURES	LOW	HIGH

Starlite

Starlite was a budget brand made and sold by Magnatone. See Magnatone for listings.

Stella Vee

1999-2005. Jason Lockwood built his combo amps, heads, and cabinets in Lexington, Kentucky.

Stephenson

1997-present. Mark Stephenson builds his intermediate to premium grade, production/custom, tube amps and cabinets in Regina, Saskatchewan 1997-'99, in Hope, British Columbia 2000-'06, and since in Parksville, British Columbia. He also offers effects.

Stevenson

1999-present. Luthier Ted Stevenson, of Lachine, Quebec, added amps to his product line in '05. He also builds basses and guitars.

Stimer

Brothers Yves and Jean Guen started building guitar pickups in France in 1946. By the late '40s they had added their Stimer line of amps to sell with the pickups. Early amp models were the M.6, M.10 and M.12 (6, 10 and 12 watts, respectively). An early user of Guen products was Django Reinhardt.

Stinger

1980s-1990s. Stinger was a budget line of guitars and solidstate amps imported by Martin.

Strad-O-Lin/Stradolin

Ca.1920s-ca.1960s. The Strad-O-Lin company primarily made mandolins for wholesalers but around '57 Multivox/Premier bought the company and used the name on guitars and amps.

Compact Solidstate

1960s. Made in U.S.A., logo on control panel and grille, black grille and cover.

1960s		$125	$175

Stramp

1970s. Stramp, of Hamburg, Germany, offered audio mixers, amps and compact powered speaker units, all in aluminum flight cases.

Solidstate

1970s. Solidstate amp head in metal suitcase with separate Stramp logo cabinet.

1970s		$350	$450

Straub Amps

2003-present. Harry Straub builds his professional grade, production/custom, amps in St. Paul, Minnesota.

Suhr

1997-present. John Suhr builds his production/custom amps in Lake Elsinore, California. He also builds guitars and basses.

MODEL		EXC. COND.	
YEAR	FEATURES	LOW	HIGH

Sundown

1983-1988. Combo amps, heads and cabinets designed and built by Dennis Kager. By '88, he had sold his interest in the company.

Sunn

1965-2002. Started in Oregon by brothers Conrad and Norm Sundhold (Norm was the bass player for the Kingsman). Sunn introduced powerful amps and extra heavy duty bottoms and was soon popular with many major rock acts. Norm sold his interest to Conrad in '69. Conrad sold the company to the Hartzell Corporation of Minnesota around '72. Fender Musical Instruments acquired the brand in '85 shortly after parting ways with CBS and used the brand until '89. They resurrected the brand again in '98, but quit offering the name in '02.

100S Amp and Cabinet Set

1965-1970s. 60 watts, 1x15" JBL D130F and 1 LE 100S JBL Driver and Horn, piggyback, 5 tubes (with rectifier).

1965-1969		$1,500	$1,950

190L Amp and Cabinet Set

1970s. Solidstate, 80 watts, 2 speakers.

1970s		$750	$975

200S/215B Amp and Cabinet Set

1966-1970s. 60 watts, 2x6550s, large vertical cab with 1x15" or 2x15" speakers.

1966-1969	1x15	$1,500	$1,950
1966-1969	2x15	$1,500	$1,950

601-L Cabinet

1980s. 6x10" plus 2 tweeters cab.

1980s		$375	$485

2000S

1968-1970s. 4x6550 power tubes, 120 watts.

1968-1970s	Head & cab	$1,500	$1,950

Alpha 112

1980s. Solidstate, MOS-FET preamp section, 1x12" combo, reverb, overdrive, black.

1980s		$165	$215

Alpha 115

1980s. Solidstate, MOS-FET preamp section, 1x15", clean and overdrive.

1980s		$185	$240

Alpha 212 R

1980s. Solidstate, MOS-FET preamp section, 2x12", reverb.

1980s		$250	$325

Beta Bass

1978-1980s. Solidstate 100-watt head and combos, large Beta Bass logo on front panel.

1978-1980s	4x12	$675	$900
1978-1980s	6x10	$675	$900
1978-1980s	Combo 1x15	$675	$900
1978-1980s	Combo 2x12	$675	$900
1978-1980s	Combo 4x10	$675	$900

Coliseum 300 Bass

1970s. Solidstate, Coliseum-300 logo on front.

1970s	Head & cab	$900	$1,175

Stephenson B-100

Suhr Badger
Rob Bernstein

Sundown

Sunn Solo
Imaged by Heritage Auctions, HA.com

1970 Sunn Sceptre
Imaged by Heritage Auctions, HA.com

Sunn Stagemaster
Robert Curd

MODEL YEAR	FEATURES	EXC. COND. LOW	HIGH
Coliseum Lead			
1970s. Solidstate, Coliseum Lead logo on front.			
1970s	Head & cab	$900	$1,175
Coliseum Lead Full Stack			
1970s. Coliseum Lead logo on amp head, two 4x12" cabs.			
1970s		$1,350	$1,750
Concert 215S Bass Set			
1970s. Solidstate head, 200 watts, Model 215S tall vertical cabinet with 2x12" Sunn label speakers, dark vinyl cover, silver sparkle grille.			
1970s		$825	$1,075
Concert Lead 610S Set			
1970s. Solidstate, 200 watts, 6x10" piggyback, reverb and built-in distortion.			
1970s		$1,025	$1,325
Enforcer			
1980s. Tube, 60/100 watt 2x12" or 100 watt head.			
1980s	Combo	$800	$1,050
1980s	Head & cab	$865	$1,125
Fuse 200S			
1970s. Sunn Fuse logo and model number on front panel, 140 watts.			
1970s		$1,125	$1,475
Model T Head			
Early-1970s. 100 watts.			
1970s	Head only	$2,800	$3,675
Model T (Reissue)			
1998-2002. Reissue of '70s Model T, 100-watt head, with 4x12" cab.			
1998-2002	Head & cab	$1,300	$1,725
SB-160 Bass			
1985. Combo, 60 watts.			
1985		$365	$475
SB-200			
1985. 200 watts, 1x15", 4-band EQ, master volume, compressor.			
1985		$380	$500
Sceptre			
1968-1972. 60 watts, 6550 power tubes, tremolo, reverb.			
1968-1972	Head and cab	$1,375	$1,800
Sentura			
1967-1970s. Rectifier and power tubes, I and II versions.			
1967-1969	I, 1x15 set	$1,250	$1,625
1967-1969	II, 2x15 set	$1,300	$1,700
SL 250			
1980s. 60 watts, 2x12" combo, SL 250 logo.			
1980s		$500	$650
SL 260			
1982-ca.1985. 60 watts, 2x12" combo with reverb, SL 260 logo.			
1982-1985		$550	$725
Solarus			
1967-1970s. Tube amp (EL34s), reverb, tremolo, 2x12" 40 watt combo to '68; 60 watt head with 2x12" cab for '69 on.			
1967-1968	Combo	$700	$925
1969-1970s	Head and cab	$850	$1,100

MODEL YEAR	FEATURES	EXC. COND. LOW	HIGH
Solo II			
Early-1970s. Solo II logo on front panel, 120 watts, 2x12" combo, black tolex.			
1970s		$700	$900
Sonaro			
Early-1970s. Head and 1x15" cab, 60 watts.			
1970s	Head and cab	$700	$900
Sonic 1-40			
1967-1969. Tube head, 1x15" bass amp, 40 watts.			
1967-1969	Head and cab	$1,200	$1,550
Sonic I			
1967-1969. 125 watts, 1x15" JBL D130F in short cabinet, 5 tubes (with rectifier), piggyback, dark tolex.			
1967-1969	Head and cab	$1,200	$1,550
Sonic II			
1967-1969. 250 watts, 2x15" JBL D130F in folding horn large cabinet, 5 tubes (with rectifier), piggyback, dark tolex.			
1967-1969	Head and cab	$1,250	$1,625
Sorado			
1970s. 50 watts, tubes, 2x15" matching cab.			
1970s	Head and cab	$1,125	$1,475
Spectrum I			
1967-1969. 125 watts, 1x15" JBL D130F large cabinet, 5 tubes (with rectifier), piggyback, dark tolex cover.			
1967-1969	Head and cab	$1,150	$1,500
Spectrum II			
1967-1969. 250 watts, 2x12", piggyback, 5 tubes (with rectifier), Spectrum II logo on front panel.			
1967-1969	Head and cab	$1,225	$1,600
SPL 7250			
Dual channels, 250 watts per channel, forced air cooling, switch-selectable peak compressor with LEDs.			
1989	Head and cab	$515	$670
Stagemaster			
1980s. 120 watts, 2x12".			
1980s	Combo	$435	$565
1980s	Head and cab	$515	$670
T50C			
1998-2002. Fender era, combo 1x12", 50 watts.			
1998-2002		$575	$750

Supersound

1952-1974. Founded in the U.K. by Alan Wootton, building custom amps and radios, the firm continued to build amps and effects into the early '60s. They also built guitars and basses.

Supertone

1914-1941. Supertone was a brand used by Sears for their musical instruments. In the '40s Sears started using the Silvertone name on those products. Amps were made by other companies.

Various Models

1930s		$325	$450

Supro

1935-1968, 2004-present. Supro was a budget brand of the National Dobro Company, made by Valco in Chicago, Illinois. Amp builder Bruce

MODEL YEAR	FEATURES	EXC. COND. LOW	HIGH

Zinky revived the Supro name in '04 for a line of guitars and amps. In '13, Absara Audio, LLC acquired the Supro trademark and started releasing amps in July '14.

'64 Reverb/'64 Super
2020-present. 5 watts, 1x8", reverb, Jensen speaker, blue. Renamed Super in '22.

2020-2021	1605RJ	$575	$750

Accordion 1615T
1957-1959. Compact combo, 1x15", 24 watts, 2x6L6 power, 5V4, 3x12AX7, 2 channels, tremolo, 3 control knobs, Accordion (model) logo upper left corner of grille, Supro logo lower right, Rhino-Hide gray with white sides.

1957-1959		$950	$1,225

Bantam
1961-1966. Petite, 4 watts, 3 tubes, 1x 8" Jensen, gold weave Saran Wrap grille, Spanish Ivory fabric cover, red in '64, gray in '66. Also sold as matching set, for example in '64 with student-level red and white lap steel, add 65% to price for matching guitar and amp set.

1961-1963	1611S, Spanish ivory	$475	$625
1964-1965	S6411, red cover	$475	$625
1966	Gray cover	$475	$625

Bass Combo
Early 1960s. 35 watts, 2x12", 2 channels (bass and standard), 7 tubes, tremolo, woven embossed black and white tolex that appears grey. The '61 model 1688T has a narrow panel body style somewhat similar to the Fender narrow panel cab style of the late '50s, in '62 the cab panel was removed and the 'no panel' style became the 1688TA model, the new cab was less expensive to build and Supro offered a price reduction on applicable models in '62.

1961	1688T, narrow panel	$900	$1,175
1962-1963	1688TA, no panel	$900	$1,175

Big Star Reverb S6451TR
1964. 35 watts, 2x12", reverb and tremolo, 'no panel' cab.

1964		$1,200	$1,550

Black Magick
2017-present. 25 watts, 1x12", head (1695TH), tremolo combo (1695TJ), reverb and tremolo combo (1696RT). Extention cabinets also offered.

2017-2021	1695TH, head	$725	$935
2017-2021	1x12 cab	$310	$405
2017-2021	2x12 cab	$410	$535
2018-2021	1696RT	$945	$1,225
2020-2021	1695TJ	$845	$1,100

Blues King
2019-2020. 5 watts, 1x10".

2019-2020		$270	$350

Blues King 8
2020. 1 watt, 1x8".

2020	1808	$240	$310

Brentwood 1650T
Mid-1950s. Advertised as Supro's "finest amplifier", model 1650T described as the "professional twin speaker luxury amplifier", 2 channels including high-gain, tremolo with speed control.

1956		$1,200	$1,575

Combo
1961-1964. 24 watts, 6 tubes, 1x15" Jensen, Rhino-Hide covering in black and white, light grille, tremolo.

1961	1696T, narrow panel	$875	$1,150
1962-1963	1696TA, no panel	$875	$1,150

Combo Tremolo S6497T
1964. 35 watts, 1x15", standard 'no panel' cab, tremolo.

1964		$925	$1,200

Comet 1610B
1957-1959. Gray Rhino-Hide, 1x10".

1957-1959		$850	$1,100

Comet 1610E
Mid-1950s. Supro's only 1x10" amp from the mid-'50s, 3 input jacks, 2 control knobs, woven tweed and leatherette 2-tone covering.

1956		$850	$1,100

Coronado
1960-1963. 24 watts, 2x10", tremolo, 2 channels, 6 tubes, Supro logo upper right above grille, black and white mixed tolex appears gray, described as tremolo twin-speaker pro amp, '61 has 'narrow panel' body style, new body style in '62 becomes 1690TA model with grille only and no panel.

1960-1961	1690T, narrow panel	$1,100	$1,425
1962-1963	1690TA, no panel	$1,100	$1,425

Corsica
Mid-1960s. Redesigned vertical combo amp, reverb, tremolo, blue control panel, black tolex, silver grille.

1965-1967		$725	$950

Delta King 8
2020-2021. 1 watt, 1x8", tweed/black (1818TB) or black/cream (1818BC).

2020-2021		$275	$360

Delta King 10
2020-2021. 5 watts, 1x10", reverb, tweed/black (1820RTB) or black/cream (1820RBC).

2020-2021		$330	$425

Delta King 12
2020-2021. 15 watts, 1x12", reverb, tweed/black (1822RTB) or black/cream (1822RBC).

2020-2021		$390	$510

Dual-Tone
1961-1965, 2014-2020. 17 watts, 6 tubes, 1x12" Jensen, organ tone tremolo, restyled in '64, Trinidad Blue vinyl fabric cover, light color grille. Reintroduced in '14, 24 watts.

1961	1624T, narrow panel	$950	$1,225
1962-1963	1624TA, no panel	$950	$1,225
1964-1965	S6424T, no panel	$950	$1,225
2014-2020	1624T, no panel	$550	$700

Galaxy
2019-2020. 50 watts, 1x12".

2019-2020	1697R	$865	$1,125

Galaxy Tremolo S6488
1965. 35 watts, 2x12" (often Jensen), 7 tubes, tremolo, multi-purpose for guitar, bass and accordion.

1965		$975	$1,275

Galaxy Tremolo S6688
1966-1967. 35 watts, 2x12" (often Jensen), turquoise front control panel with Supro logo (not on grille), model name/number also on front control panel.

1966-1967		$975	$1,275

Supro 1688T
Carter Vintage Guitars

AMPS

Supro 1695T Black Magick

Supro Corsica
Imaged by Heritage Auctions, HA.com

Supro Model 24
Michael Wright

Supro Super 1606S
Steve Allen

1965 Supro Thunderbolt S6420(B)

Imaged by Heritage Auctions, HA.com

MODEL YEAR	FEATURES	EXC. COND. LOW	HIGH

Golden Holiday 1665T
Mid-1950s. Supro's model for the 'semi-professional', 2 oval 11x6" speakers, 14 watts, 6 tubes, tremolo, 2 control knobs, black and tweed cover.

1956		$1,000	$1,300

Keeley Custom
2020-2021. Designed with Robert Keeley (Keeley Electronics), 25 watts, 1x10" (Custom 10) or 1x12" (Custom 12).

2020-2021	Custom 10	$600	$775
2020-2021	Custom 12	$700	$925

Model 24
1965. 18 watts, 1x12 combo, 2 channels each with bass and treble inputs, tremolo, Model 24 logo on top panel, Calypso Blue vinyl cover.

1965		$875	$1,150

Reverb 1650R
1963. 17 watts, 1x10", 'no panel' grille front style cab, reverb.

1963		$950	$1,225

Royal Reverb 1650TR
1963-1965. 17 watts, 15 tubes, 2x10" Jensens, catalog says "authentic tremolo and magic-reverberation."

1963-1965		$1,300	$1,700

Royal Reverb S6650
1965-1967. Updated cabinet with turquoise-blue front control panel, 2x10" combo, 2 channels (standard and reverb-tremolo).

1965-1967		$775	$1,000

Special 1633E
Mid-1950s. Supro's entry level student amp, 1x8", 3 tubes, large Supro stencil logo on grille, 2-tone red and white fabric cover, leather handle, available with matching Special Lap Steel covered in wine-maroon plastic.

1956		$575	$750

Spectator 1614E
Mid-1950s. 1x8", 3 tubes, 2 control knobs, white front with red and black body.

1956		$650	$850

Sportsman S6689
1966. Piggyback, twin speakers.

1966		$925	$1,200

Statesman S6699
1966-1967, 2017-2020. Piggyback with blue-green control panel, 4x6L6 power, horizontal 2x12" cab, reverb, tremolo, script Statesman logo with model number on upper left front of chasis. Reintroduced in '17, 50 watts, 1x12" combo.

1966-1967	Piggyback	$875	$1,150
2017-2020	Combo	$990	$1,285

Studio 1644E
Mid-1950s. Supro's student model for teaching studios, 2 input jacks for student and instructor or guitar and lap steel guitar, 3 tubes, advertised for "true Hawaiian tone reproduction", covered in royal blue leatherette (in '56), available with a matching Studio Lap Steel covered in blue plastic.

1956-1957	Blue leatherette	$625	$800

MODEL YEAR	FEATURES	EXC. COND. LOW	HIGH

Super
1961-1963, 2017-2020. 4.5 watts, 3 tubes, 1x8", 1606S has contrasting black and white covering with old narrow panel cab, in '63 new 1606B has 'no panel' style cab with lighter (gray) covering. Reintroduced in '17, 5 watts, 1x8".

1961-1962	1606S	$600	$775
1963	1606B	$600	$775
2017-2020	1606	$450	$585

Super 1606E
Mid-1950s. Supro advertising states "with features important to women", oval 11x6" Rola speaker, 3 tubes, 1 control knob, 2 inputs, white (front) and grey sides, elliptical baffle soundhole with Supro logo, model number with E suffix common for '50s Supros.

1956	White and grey	$650	$850

Super Six S6406
1964-1965. Student practice amp, 4.5 watts, 1x8", blue vinyl cover.

1964-1965		$600	$775

Super Six S6606
1966. Updated version of student compact amp.

1966		$650	$850

Supreme
1961-1963. 17 watts, 1x10", designed for use with Model 600 Reverb Accessory Unit, value shown does not include the Model 600 (see Effects Section for reverb unit). The initial 1600R model was designed with a triangle-like shaped soundhole, in '62 the more typical Supro no panel cab was introduced which Supro called the new slope front design.

1961	1600R	$1,200	$1,550
1962-1963	1600S, no panel	$1,200	$1,550

Supreme 17 S6400
1964-1965. 17 watts, 1x10", cab larger than prior models of this type.

1964-1965		$850	$1,100

Supreme Twin Speaker 1600E
Mid-1950s. 2 oval 11x6" speakers, 5 tubes, 3 input jacks, 2 control knobs, grille logo states "Twin Speaker" but unlike most Supro amps of this era the Supro logo does not appear on the front.

1956		$850	$1,100

Thunderbolt S6420(B) Bass
1964-1967. 35 watts, 1x15" Jensen, introduced in the '64 catalog as a no frills - no fancy extra circuits amp. Sometimes referred to as the "Jimmy Page" based on his use of this amp in his early career.

1964-1967		$1,725	$2,250

Thunderbolt S6920
1967-1968. Redesign circuit replaced S6420B, 35 watts, 1x12".

1967-1968		$850	$1,100

Tremo-Verb S6422TR
1964-1965. Lower power using 4 12AX7s, 1 5Y3GT, and 1 6V6, 1x10", tremolo and reverb, Persian Red vinyl cover.

1964-1965		$1,200	$1,550

Trojan Tremolo
1961-1966. 5 watts, 4 tubes, 1 11"x6" oval (generally Rolla) speaker, '61-'64 black and white fabric cover and

AMPS

Saran Wrap grille, '64-'66 new larger cab with vinyl cover and light grille.

MODEL YEAR	FEATURES	EXC. COND. LOW	HIGH
1961	1616T, narrow panel	$575	$750
1962-1963	1616TA, no panel	$575	$750
1964-1966	S6461, blue cover	$575	$750

Vibra-Verb S6498VR
1964-1965. Billed as Supro's finest amplifier, 2x35-watt channels, 1x15" and 1x10" Jensens, vibrato and reverb.

1964-1965		$1,800	$2,350

Surreal Amplification
2007-present. Production/custom, professional grade amp heads, combos and cabinets built in Westminster, California by Jerry Dyer.

Swampdonkey
2006-present. Professional and premium grade, production/custom, guitar amp heads, combos and speaker cabinets built in Rural Rocky View, Alberta by Chris Czech.

Swanpro Amps
Robert Swanson started building tube combo and head amps and cabinets in Denver, Colorado in 2004.

Swart Amplifier Co. (Space Tone)
2003-present. Michael J. Swart builds tube combo and head amps and cabinets under the Swart and Space Tone brand names in Wilmington, North Carolina. He also builds effects.

SWR Sound
1984-2013. Founded by Steve W. Rabe in '84, with an initial product focus on bass amplifiers. Fender Musical Instruments Corp. acquired SWR in June, 2003.

Baby Blue Studio Bass System
1990-2003. Combo, all tube preamp, 150 watts solidstate power amp, 2x8", 1x5" cone tweeter, gain, master volume, EQ, effects-blend.

1990-2003		$375	$500

Basic Black
1992-1999. Solidstate, 100 watts, 1x12", basic black block logo on front, black tolex, black metal grille.

1992-1999		$310	$400

California Blonde
2000s. Vertical upright combo, 100 watts, 1x12" plus high-end tweeters, blond cover, thin black metal grille.

2003		$310	$400

Goliath III Cabinet
1996-2008. Black tolex, black metal grille, includes the Goliath III Jr. (2x10") and the Goliath III (4x10").

1996-2008	2x10"	$265	$350
1996-2008	4x10"	$310	$400

Strawberry Blonde
1998-2011. 80 watts, 1x10" acoustic instrument amp.

1998-2011		$310	$400

Strawberry Blonde II
2007-2011. 90 watts, 1x10" acoustic instrument amp.

2007-2011		$310	$400

Studio 220 Bass Head
1988-1995. 220 watt solidstate head, tube preamp

1988-1995		$185	$245

Workingman's Series
1995-2004. Includes 10 (200w, 2x10), 12 (100w, 1x12), 15 (bass, 1x15), replaced by WorkingPro in '05.

1995-2004	Various models	$210	$275

Symphony
1950s. Probably a brand from an teaching studio, large Symphony script red letter logo on front.

Small Tube
1950s. Two guitar inputs, 1x6" speaker, alligator tweed suitcase.

1950s		$300	$400

Synaptic Amplification
Intermediate to premium grade, production/custom, amps built in Brunswick, Maine by Steven O'Connor, starting in 2007.

Takt
Late-1960s. Made in Japan, tube and solidstate models.

GA Series
1968. GA-9 (2 inputs and 5 controls, 3 tubes), GA-10, GA-11, GA-12, GA-14, GA-15.

1968	GA-14/GA-15	$70	$90
1968	GA-9 thru GA-12	$45	$60

Talos
Doug Weisbrod and Bill Thalmann build their tube amp heads, combo amps, and speaker cabinets in Springfield, Virginia. They started building and testing prototypes in '01.

Tanglewood Guitar Company UK
1991-present. Intermediate and professional grade, production, acoustic amps imported from China by Dirk Kommer and Tony Flatt in the U.K. They also import guitars, basses, mandolins, banjos and ukes.

Tech 21
1989-present. Long known for their SansAmp tube amplifier emulator, Tech 21 added solidstate combo amps, heads and cabinets in '96.

Teisco
1946-1974. Japanese brand first imported into the U.S. around '63. Teisco offered both tube and solidstate amps.

Checkmate CM-10
1960s. Tubes or solidstate, 10 watts.

1960s	Solidstate	$50	$65
1960s	Tubes	$200	$265

Swampdonkey Gypsy

SWR California Blonde
Imaged by Heritage Auctions, HA.com

Talos Basic 2011

Tanglewood T3

Tone King Royalist 15
Carter Vintage Guitars

Top Hat King Royal

MODEL YEAR	FEATURES	EXC. COND. LOW	HIGH
Checkmate CM-15			
Late-1960s. Tubes, 15 watts.			
1960s		$225	$290
Checkmate CM-16			
1960s. Tubes or solidstate, 15 watts.			
1960s	Solidstate	$65	$85
1960s	Tubes	$225	$290
Checkmate CM-17			
1960s. Tubes, 1x10", reverb, tremolo.			
1960s		$350	$450
Checkmate CM-20			
Late-1960s. Tubes, 20 watts.			
1960s		$350	$450
Checkmate CM-25			
Late-1960s. Tubes, 25 watts.			
1960s		$350	$450
Checkmate CM-50			
Late-1950s-early-1960s. Tubes, 2 6L6s, 50 watts, 2x12" open back, reverb, tremolo, piggyback, gray tolex cover, light gray grille.			
1960s		$475	$624
Checkmate CM-60			
Late-1960s. Tubes, 60 watts, piggyback amp and cab with wheels.			
1960s		$280	$365
Checkmate CM-66			
Late-1960s. Solidstate, dual speaker combo, Check Mate 66 logo on front panel.			
1960s		$75	$100
Checkmate CM-88			
1960s. Solidstate, 10 watts, 2x8".			
1960s		$75	$100
Checkmate CM-100			
Late-1960s. Tubes, 4x6L6 power, 100 watts, piggyback with Vox-style trolley stand.			
1960s		$300	$400
King 1800			
Late-1960s. Tubes, 180 watts, piggyback with 2 cabinets, large Teisco logo on cabinets, King logo on lower right side of one cabinet.			
1960s		$500	$650
Teisco 8			
Late-1960s. Solidstate, 5 watts.			
1960s		$75	$100
Teisco 10			
Late-1960s. Solidstate, 5 watts.			
1960s		$75	$100
Teisco 88			
Late-1960s. Solidstate, 8 watts.			
1960s		$100	$130

Tempo

1950s-1970s. Tube (early on) and solidstate amps, most likely imported from Japan by Merson Musical Products. They also offered basses and guitars.

Model 39

1950s. Compact amp, vertical cab, tweed, 3 tubes, single control knob for on-off volume.			
1953		$325	$425

MODEL YEAR	FEATURES	EXC. COND. LOW	HIGH

Teneyck

1960s. Solidstate amp heads and speaker cabinets built by Bob Teneyck, who had previously done design work for Ampeg.

THD

1987-present. Tube amps and cabinets built in Seattle, Washington, founded by Andy Marshall.

The Valve

Guitar luthier Galeazzo Frudua also builds a line of professional grade, production/custom, amps in San Lazzaro di Savena, Italy.

ThroBak Electronics

2004-present. Jonathan Gundry builds his tube combo guitar amps in Grand Rapids, Michigan. He also builds guitar effects and pickups.

Titano (Magnatone)

1961-1963. Private branded by Magnatone, often for an accordion company or accordion studio, uses standard guitar input jacks.

Model 262 R Custom

1961-1963. 35 watts, 2x12" + 2x5", reverb and vibrato make this one of the top-of-the-line models, black vinyl, light silver grille.			
1961-1963		$1,350	$1,750
Model 313			
1961-1963. Like Magnatone 213 Troubadour, 10 watts, 1x12" combo, vibrato, brown tolex, brownish grille.			
1961-1963		$1,250	$1,625
Model 415 Bass			
1961-1963. 25 watts, 4x8", bass or accordion amp, black cover, darkish grille.			
1961-1963		$1,200	$1,550

TomasZewicZ Amplifiers

2008-present. Intermediate and professional grade, production/custom, tube guitar amp heads and combos built by John Tomaszewicz in Coral Springs, Florida. He also builds effects.

Tombo

This Japanese harmonica manufacturer introduced a solidbody electric ukulele and a Silvertone-esque case with onboard amplifier in the mid-1960s.

Tone Americana

2011-2014. David and Caroline Brass built intermediate and professional grade, production/custom, amp heads, combos and cabinets in Calabasas, California. They also offered an amp combo built in Asia.

Tone King

1993-present. Tube amps, combos, and cabinets built by Mark Bartel in Baltimore, Maryland. The company started in New York and moved to Baltimore in '94.

MODEL		EXC. COND.	
YEAR	FEATURES	LOW	HIGH

Tonemaster (Magnatone)

Late-1950s-early-1960s. Magnatone amps private branded for Imperial Accordion Company. Prominent block-style capital TONEMASTER logo on front panel, generally something nearly equal to Magnatone equivalent. This is just one of many private branded Magnatones. Covers range from brown to black leatherette and brown to light silver grilles. They also offered guitars.

Model 214
1959-1960. Ten watts, 1x12", vibrato, brown leatherette, V logo front lower right corner, large TONEMASTER logo.

1959-1960		$1,250	$1,625

Model 260
1961-1963. About 30 watts, 2x12", vibrato, brown leatherette and brown grille, large TONEMASTER logo on front.

1961-1963		$1,800	$2,350

Model 261 Custom
1961-1963. Tonemaster Custom 261 High Fidelity logo on back chasis panel, Tonemaster logo on front panel, 35 watts, 2x12" combo, 2 channels, vibrato.

1961-1963		$1,800	$2,350

Model 380
1961-1963. 50 watts, 2x12" and 2 oval 5"x7" speakers, vibrato, no reverb.

1961-1963		$1,800	$2,350

Model 381 Custom
1961-1963. Tonemaster Custom 381 High Fidelity logo on back chasis panel, Tonemaster logo on front panel, 2x12", 1x5".

1961-1963		$1,800	$2,350

Small Combo
1950s-1960s. 1x8", tremolo, light tan.

1950s-60s		$650	$850

ToneTron Amps
2006-present. Professional grade, custom, guitar and bass tube amps and cabinets built in Minneapolis, Minnesota by Jeffrey Falla.

ToneVille Amps
Matthew Lucci and Phil Jung began in 2013, building professional grade, production, amps and cabinets in Colorado Springs, Colorado.

Tonic Amps
2003-present. Darin Ellingson builds professional and premium grade, production/custom, amps and cabinets in Redwood City, California.

Top Hat Amplification
1994-present. Mostly Class A guitar amps built by Brian Gerhard, previously in La Habra, California, and Apex, North Carolina, and currently in Fuquay-Varina, North Carolina. He also makes effects.

Ambassador 100 TH-A100 Head
Jan.1999-2013. 100 watts, Class AB, 4 6L6s, reverb, dark green vinyl cover, white chicken-head knobs.

1999-2013		$1,150	$1,500

Ambassador T-35C 212
1999-2013. 35 watts, 2x12" combo, reverb, master volume, blond cover, tweed-style fabric grille.

1999-2013		$1,275	$1,650

Club Deluxe
1998-2009. 20 watts, 6V6 power tubes, 1x12".

1998-2009		$1,275	$1,650

Club Royale TC-R1
Jan.1998-2020. Class A using EL84s, 20 watts, 1x12". Replaced by Club Royal 20 in '21.

1998-2020		$800	$1,025

Club Royale TC-R2
Jan.1999-2014. Class A using EL84s, 20 watts, 2x12".

1999-2014		$1,225	$1,575

Emplexador 50 TH-E50 Head
Jan.1997-2020. 50 watts, Class AB vint/high-gain head. Replaced by Emplexador E-50 in '21.

1997-2020		$1,150	$1,500

King Royale/Royal
1996-present. 35 watts, Class A using 4 EL84s, 2x12". Name changed to King Royal in '21.

1996-2021		$1,350	$1,725

Portly Cadet TC-PC
Jan.1999-2004. Five watts, 6V6 power, 1x8", dark gray, light gray grille.

1999-2004		$550	$700

Prince Royale TC-PR
Jan.2000-2002. Five watts using EL84 power, 1x8", deep red, light grille.

2000-2002		$550	$700

Super Deluxe TC-SD2
Jan.2000-2012. 30 watts, Class A, 7591 power tubes, 2x12".

2000-2012		$1,275	$1,650

Torres Engineering
Founded by Dan Torres, the company builds tube amps, combos, cabinets and amp kits originally in San Mateo, California, then San Carlos and since '11 in Milton, Washington. Dan wrote monthly columns for Vintage Guitar magazine for many years and authored the book Inside Tube Amps.

Trace Elliot
1978-present. Founded in Essex, U.K. The U.S. distribution picked up by Kaman (Ovation) in '88 which bought Trace Elliot in '92. In '98 Gibson acquired the brand and in early '02 closed the factory and moved what production was left to the U.S. In '05 Peavey bought the brand name, hiring back many of the old key people, and currently offers professional grade, production, tube and solidstate, acoustic guitar and bass amp heads, combos, and cabinets, with product built in the U.K. and U.S.

Trainwreck
1983-2006. Limited production, custom-made, high-end tube guitar amp heads built by Ken Fischer in Colonia, New Jersey. Models include the Rocket, Liverpool and Express, plus variations.

ToneTron SE

AMPS

ToneTron Hall Rocker

Tonic Torpedo

Traynor SB110

Traynor YGM3 Guitar Mate Reverb

1969 Traynor YSR1 Custom Reverb

Scott Anderson

Instead of using serial numbers, he gave each amp a woman's name. Due to illness, Fischer didn't build many amps after the mid '90s, but he continued to design amps for other builders. His total production is estimated at less than 100. Each amp's value should be evaluated on a case-by-case basis. Ken wrote many amp articles for Vintage Guitar. He died in late 2006.

Ken Fisher Custom Built

1983-1998	$29,000	$37,500

Traynor

1963-present. Started by Pete Traynor and Jack Long in the back of Long & McQuade Music in Toronto, Canada where Traynor was a repairman. Currently offering tube and solidstate amp heads, combos and cabinets made by parent company Yorkville Sound, in Pickering, Ontario.

YBA1 Bass Master Head

1963-1979. 45 watts, called Dynabass for 1963-'64, this was Pete Traynor's first amp design.

1963-1979	$675	$875

YBA1A Mark II Bass Master Head

1968-1976. Like YBA1, but with 90 watts and cooling fan.

1968-1976	$675	$875

YBA3 Custom Special Bass Set

1967-1972. Tube head with 130 watts and 8x10" large vertical matching cab, dark vinyl cover, light grille.

1967-1972	$1,075	$1,400

YBA4 Bass Master

1967-1972. 45-watt 1x15" combo.

1967-1972	$925	$1,200

YCV80 Custom Valve

2003-2009. Tube, 80 watts, 4x10" combo.

2003-2009	$425	$550

YGA1 Head

1966-1967. 45 watts guitar amp, tremolo.

1966-1967	$625	$825

YGL3 Mark III

1971-1979. All tube, 80 watts, 2x12" combo, reverb, tremolo.

1971-1979	$800	$1,050

YGM3 Guitar Mate Reverb

1969-1979. Tubes, 25 watts, 1x12", black tolex, gray grille until '74, black after.

1969-1979	$800	$1,050

YGM3 Guitar Mate Reverb Reissue

2011-2013. 1x12" combo, 'flying wing' Traynor badge.

2011-2013	$475	$625

YRM1 Reverb Master Head

1973-1979. 45 watt tube amp, reverb, tremolo.

1973-1979	$575	$750

YRM1SC Reverb Master

1973-1979. YRM1 as a 4x10" combo.

1973-1979	$800	$1,050

YSR1 Custom Reverb Head

1968-1973. 45 watt tube amp, reverb, tremolo.

1968-1973	$575	$750

YVM Series PA Head

1967-1980. Public address heads, models include tube YVM-1 Voice Master, and solidstate YVM-2 and 3 Voice Mate and YVM-4, all with 4 inputs.

1967-1972	1, tubes	$500	$650
1969-1975	2, solidstate	$200	$260
1970-1980	3, solidstate, reverb	$275	$360
1972-1977	4, solidstate, reverb	$275	$360

Trillium Amplifier Company

2007-present. Brothers Stephen and Scott Campbell build their professional and premium grade, production/custom tube amps in Indianapolis, Indiana.

Trinity Amps

2003-present. Stephen Cohrs builds his production/custom, professional grade, tube amps and cabinets in Toronto, Ontario.

True Tone

1960s. Guitars and amps retailed by Western Auto, manufactured by Chicago guitar makers like Kay.

Hi-Fi 4 (K503 Hot-Line Special)

1960s. Similar to K503, 4 watts from 3 tubes, gray cabinet, gray grille, metal handle.

1960s	$300	$400

Model 5 (K503A)

1960s. 4 tubes, 1x8".

1960s	$300	$400

Vibrato 704

1960s. Solidstate, 10 watts, 1x8", white sides and gray back, gray grille.

1960s	$140	$180

Vibrato 706

1960s. Solidstate, 15 watts, 1x15", white sides and gray back, brown grille.

1960s	$155	$200

Tube Works

1987-2004. Founded by B.K. Butler in Denver, Tube Works became a division of Genz Benz Enclosures of Scottsdale, Arizona in 1997. Tube Works' first products were tube guitar effects and in '91 they added tube/solidstate amps, cabinets, and DI boxes to the product mix. In '04, Genz Benz dropped the brand.

Twilighter (Magnatone)

Late-1950s-early-1960s. Magnatone amps private branded for LoDuca Brothers. Prominent block-style capital TWILIGHTER logo on front panel, generally something nearly equal to Magnatone equivalent. This is just one of many private branded Magnatones. Covers range from brown to black leatherette, and brown to light silver grilles.

Model 213

1961-1963. About 20 watts, 1x12", vibrato, brown leatherette and brown grille.

1961-1963	$1,250	$1,625

AMPS

MODEL YEAR	FEATURES	EXC. COND. LOW	HIGH

Model 260R
1961-1963. About 18 to 25 watts, 1x12", vibrato, brown leatherette cover.
| 1961-1963 | | $1,500 | $1,950 |

Model 280A
Late-1950s-early-1960s. About 35 watts, 2x12", vibrato, brown leatherette cover.
| 1961-1963 | | $1,500 | $1,950 |

Two-Rock
1999-present. Tube guitar amp heads, combos and cabinets built by Joe Mloganoski and Bill Krinard (K&M Analog Designs) originally in Cotati, California, currently in Rohnert Park. They also build speakers.

Ugly Amps
2003-present. Steve O'Boyle builds his tube head and combo amps and cabinets in Burbank, California and Reading, Pennsylvania.

UltraSound
A division of UJC Electronics, UltraSound builds acoustically transparent amps, designed by Greg Farres for the acoustic guitarist, in Adel, Iowa.

Unique (Magnatone)
1961-1963. Private branded, typically for an accordion company or accordion studio, uses standard guitar input jacks.

Model 260R
1961-1963. Based on Magnatone 260 Series amp, 35 watts, 2x12" but with reverb, black vinyl-style cover with distinctive black diamond-check pattern running through the top and sides.
| 1961-1963 | | $1,800 | $2,350 |

Model 460
1961-1963. 35 watts, 2x12" and oval 5"x7" speakers, reverb and vibrato make it one of the top models, black vinyl, black grille.
| 1961-1963 | | $1,500 | $1,950 |

Universal (Audio Guild)
See Audio Guild amps.

Univox
1964-ca.1978. From '64 to early-'68, these were American-made tube amps with Jensen speakers. By '68, they were using Japanese components in American cabinets, still with Jensen speakers. Electronics were a combination of tube and transistors during this time; this type lasted until the mid-'70s. Around '71, Univox introduced a line of all solidstate amps, as well.

Lead Model Tube
1960s. Tube amp, 2x10" or 2x12".
| 1965-1969 | | $700 | $900 |

Model U45B Bass
1965-1968. 1x12" combo tube bass amp, 10 watts.
| 1965-1968 | | $350 | $450 |

Model U60A
1965-1968. 1x12" tube combo.
| 1965-1968 | | $400 | $525 |

Model U65R
1965-1968. 20 watts, 1x12" tube combo.
| 1965-1968 | | $450 | $585 |

Model U65RD Lead 65
1976-1978. Solidstate, 65 watts, reverb, 1x12" or 2x12" in a vertical cab.
| 1976-1978 | | $55 | $70 |

Model U102
1965-1968. 1x12" tube combo.
| 1965-1968 | | $450 | $585 |

Model U130B Bass
1976-1978. Solidstate, 130 watts, 1x15".
| 1976-1978 | | $145 | $185 |

Model U130L Lead
1976-1978. Solidstate, 130 watts.
| 1976-1978 | | $145 | $185 |

Model U155R
1965-1968. 20 watts, 1x12" tube combo.
| 1965-1968 | | $575 | $750 |

Model U202R
1965-1968. 1x12" tube combo.
| 1965-1968 | | $575 | $750 |

Model U305R
1965-1968. 30 watts, 1x15" tube combo.
| 1965-1968 | | $675 | $875 |

Model U1011 Lead Head
1976-1978. Solidstate, 100 watts, reverb, tremolo. Name also used on earlier tube head.
| 1976-1978 | | $215 | $280 |

Model U1061 Bass Head
1976-1978. Solidstate.
| 1976-1978 | | $215 | $280 |

Model U1220
1968-1971. Tubes or tube-hybrid, piggyback, 2x12".
| 1968-1971 | | $345 | $450 |

Model U1226 Head
1971-1972. 60-watt tube amp head.
| 1971-1972 | | $575 | $750 |

Model U1246B Bass Head
1976-1978. Solidstate, 60 watts.
| 1976-1978 | | $210 | $275 |

Model U1246L Lead Head
1976-1978. Solidstate.
| 1976-1978 | | $210 | $275 |

Valco
Valco, from Chicago, Illinois, was a big player in the guitar and amplifier business. Their products were private branded for other companies like National, Supro, Airline, Oahu, El Grande and Gretsch.

Valvetech
Production/custom, professional grade, amps built by Rob Pierce, starting in 1997, in Ossian, Indiana.

Trillium

AMPS

Ugly Lil' Ugly

1971 Univox U1226
Carter Vintage Guitars

Valvetrain Bennington Reverb

Vega Commander

Imaged by Heritage Auctions, HA.com

Victoria 35115

Carter Vintage Guitars

Valvetrain Amplification

2005-present. Tube combos, amp heads, and speaker cabinets built by Rick Gessner in Sorrento, Florida. He also builds reverb units.

Vamp

1970s. Tube and solidstate amps and speaker cabinets built at Triumph Electronics in England.

Bass Master Head

MODEL YEAR	FEATURES	EXC. COND. LOW	HIGH
1970s	100 watts	$1,200	$1,550

VanAmps

Tim Van Tassel, started in 1999, builds professional, production/custom, amps and cabinets in Golden Valley, Minnesota. He also builds effects.

Vega

The original Boston-based company (1903) was purchased by C.F. Martin in '70. In '80, the Vega trademark was sold to a Korean company.

A-49

1960s. Tubes, 6 watts, 1x8", tan cover.

1960s		$325	$425

Director Combo

1950s. Small to mid-size tube amp, 2-tone cover, 2 volume and 1 tone controls, rear mounted control chassis similar to Fender or Gibson from the '50s.

1950s		$500	$650

Lap Steel

1930s-1940s. Various models.

1930s	1x12, dark cover	$500	$650
1940s	1x10, tweed	$500	$650

Super

Early 1950s. 1 6L6, 1x10", vertical combo amp typical of the era.

1950s		$500	$650

Triumphal

Late-1940s. Vega Triumphal logo on back control pane, 6L6 power, 1x12".

1940s		$500	$650

Versatone (Audio Guild)

See Audio Guild amps.

Vesta Fire

1980s. Japanese imports by Shiino Musical Instruments Corp.; later by Midco International. Mainly known for effects pedals.

VHT

1989-present. Founded by Steven M. Fryette, VHT built amps, combos, and cabinets in Burbank, California. At the beginning of '09 AXL guitars acquired the VHT name and manufactures their own product under that brand. Fryette continues to build the VHT amp models under Fryette Amplification.

Vibe Amplification

2008-2013. Intermediate grade, production, tube amps, imported from Asia by Lorenzo Brogi in Bologna, Italy.

Victor

Late-1960s. Made in Japan.

Victoria

1994-present. Tube amps, combos, and reverb units built by Mark Baier in Naperville, Illinois. In '08, they changed the logo from the original script Victoria Amp Co. to the current stylized lightning bolt Victoria logo.

Cherry Bomb

2011-present. Tube tremolo, 40 watts, 1x15", alligator/cream tolex.

2011-2021		$1,475	$1,900

Double Deluxe

1994-present. 35 watts, 2x12".

1994-2021		$1,475	$1,900

Electro King

2008-present. 1957 GA-40 type circuit, tubes, 15 watts, 1x12".

2008-2021		$1,325	$1,725

Golden Melody

2008-present. Tubes, reverb, 50 watts, 2x12", alligator/brown tolex.

2008-2021		$1,475	$1,900

Ivy League

2010-present. Tweed Harvard specs, 14 watts, 1x10".

2011-2021		$1,050	$1,350

Model 518

1994-present. Tweed, 1x8".

1994-2021		$800	$1,025

Model 5112-T

2001-present. Tweed, 5 watts, 5F1 circuit, 1x12".

2001-2021		$850	$1,100

Model 20112

1994-present. Tweed, 20 watts, 1x12", tweed.

1994-2021		$1,075	$1,400

Model 35115

1994-present. Tweed combo, 28 watts, 1x15".

1994-2021		$1,375	$1,800

Model 35210

1994-present. Tweed, 28 watts, 2x10", tweed.

1994-2021		$1,475	$1,900

Model 35212-T

1990s. Tweed, 35 watts, 2x12".

1990s		$1,425	$1,850

Model 35310-T

1994-present. Tweed, 28 watts, 3x10".

1994-2020		$1,500	$1,950

Model 45115-T

2008-2009. Tweed, 45 watts, 1x15".

2008-2009		$1,375	$1,800

Model 45410-T

1994-present. Tweed, 45 watts, 4x10" combo, tweed.

1994-2021		$1,425	$1,850

Model 50212-T

2002-present. Tweed, 50 watts, 2x12" combo.

2002-2021		$1,425	$1,850

Model 80212

1994-present. Tweed, 80 watts, 2x12", tweed.

1994-2021		$1,500	$1,950

AMPS

MODEL YEAR	FEATURES	EXC. COND. LOW	HIGH

Regal
2004-2006. Class A with 1 x 6L6, 15 watts, 1x15", brown tolex cover, rear mount controls.

2004-2006		$1,375	$1,800

Regal II/Regal
2006-present. Class A, 35 watts, 1x15", tweed or vanilla tolex, rear mount controls.The II removed from name about '13.

2006-2021		$1,375	$1,800

Reverberato
1996-2016. Tube reverb unit with vibrato, tweed or color options.

1996-2016		$1,025	$1,350

Silver Sonic
2011-present. Tube reverb, 20 watts, 1x12", 2-tone black/cream cab with Sonic Blue or black tolex.

2011-2021		$1,425	$1,850

Trem d'La Trem
2007-present. Tweed design,14 watts, 1x15".

2007-2021		$1,375	$1,800

Victoriette
2001-present. 20 watts, 1x12" or 2x10", reverb, tremolo in '01.

2001-2021	2x10	$1,475	$1,900

Victorilux
2001-present. 45 watts, 2x12", 3x10" or 1x15", EL84s, reverb, tremolo.

2001-2021	3x10	$1,550	$2,000

Vintage47
2010-present. Founder/builder David Barnes, of California, builds retro-inspired compact amps that reflect old-school Valco values, handwired, intermediate and professional grade.

Vivi-Tone
1933-1938. Founded in Kalamazoo, Michigan, by former Gibson designer Lloyd Loar and others, Vivi-Tone sold small amps built by Webster Electric to accompany their early electric solidbody guitars.

V-M (Voice of Music) Corp.
1944-1977. Started out building record changers in Benton Harbor, Michigan. By the early '50s had added amplified phonographs, consoles, and tape recorders as well as OEM products for others. Their portable PA systems can be used for musical instruments. Products sport the VM logo.

Small Portable
1950s. Standard phono input for instrument, phono and microphone controls, wood combo cabinet, 1x10" or 1x12" Jensen.

1950s		$350	$450

Voltmaster
Trapezoid-shaped combo amps and reverb units made in Plano, Texas, in the late 1990s.

Voodoo
1998-present. Tube amp heads and speaker cabinets built in Lansing, New York by Trace Davis, Anthony Cacciotti, and Mike Foster.

Vox
1954-present. Tom Jennings and Dick Denney combined forces in '57 to produce the first Vox amp, the 15-watt AC-15. The period between '57-'68 is considered to be the Vox heyday. Vox produced tube amps in England and also the U.S. from '64 to '65. English-made tube amps were standardized between '60 and '65. U.S.-made Vox amps in '66 were solidstate. In the mid-'60s, similar model names were sometimes used for tube and solidstate amps. In '93 Korg bought the Vox name and current products are built by Marshall. Those amps that originally came with a trolley or stand are priced including the original trolley or stand, and an amp without one will be worth less than the amount shown. Smaller amps were not originally equipped with a trolley or stand (if a speaker cabinet mounts to it and it tilts, it is called a trolley; otherwise referred to as a stand).

4120 Bass
1966-1967. Hybrid solidstate and tube bass amp.

1966-1967		$450	$600

7120 Guitar
1966-1967. Hybrid solidstate and tube amp, 120 watts.

1966-1967		$450	$600

AC4
1961-1965. Made in England, early Vox tube design, 3.5 watts, 1x8", tremolo.

1961-1965		$1,250	$1,625

AC4TV
2009-2019. Tube, 4 watts, in 1x10 (AC4TV8 is 1x8) combo or amp head with 1x12 cab, EL84 power tube, 12AX7 powered preamp. AC4TVmini combo has 6.5 inch speaker.

2009-2013	1x12	$115	$150
2009-2013	1x8	$120	$155
2009-2013	Head only	$135	$175
2009-2019	1x10	$135	$175

AC10
1958-1965. Made in England, 12 watts, 1x10", tremolo, this tube version not made in U.S. ('64-'65).

1958-1965		$2,365	$3,075

AC10 Twin
1962-1965. Made in England, also made in U.S. '64-'65, 12 watts (2xEL84s), 2x10".

1962-1965		$2,750	$3,600

AC10C1
2015-present. Custom series, 10 watts, 1x10", black and maroon 2-tone.

2015-2021		$350	$450

AC15
1958-1965. 15 watts, 1x12", TV front changed to split front in fall '60.

1958	TV front	$3,850	$5,000
1958-1965	Split front	$3,150	$4,100

Victoria Silver Sonic

AMPS

1961 Vox AC4
Frank Silvestry

Vox AC10C1

2006 Vox AC15CC
Ted Wulfers

1963 Vox AC30 Twin
KC Cormack

1967 Vox Berkeley II V108
Rivington Guitars

MODEL YEAR	FEATURES	EXC. COND. LOW	HIGH
AC15 Twin			
1961-1965. Tube, 2x12", 18 watts.			
1961-1965	Standard colors	$3,550	$4,600
1962-1965	Custom colors	$3,800	$4,925
AC15 50th Anniversary			
2007. 50th Anniversary 1957-2007 plaque on lower left front of grille, hand wired, white tolex.			
2007		$745	$960
AC15C1			
2010-2020. Custom Series, made in China, 15 watts, 1x12", tube, reverb and tremolo.			
2010-2021		$390	$510
AC15CC (Custom Classic)			
2006-2012. Made in China, 15 watts, 1x12" tube combo, master volume, reverb, tremolo, 2-button footswitch.			
2006-2012		$390	$510
AC15H1TV			
2008-2009. Part of Heritage Collection, limited edition, 200 made, hand wired, oiled mahogany cabinet.			
2008-2009		$1,075	$1,400
AC15HW1			
2015-2021. Hand-wired, 15 watts, 1x12".			
2015-2021		$865	$1,125
AC15TB/TBX			
1996-2004. 15 watts, top boost, 1x12" Celestion (lower cost Eminence available).			
1996-2004	TB	$800	$1,050
1996-2004	TBX	$945	$1,225
AC30 Reissue Model			
1980s-1990s-2000s. Standard reissue and limited edition models with identification plate on back of amp. Models include the AC30 Reissue and Reissue custom color (1980s-1990s), AC30 25th Anniv. (1985-1986), AC30 30th Anniv. (1991), AC30 Collector Model (1990s, mahogany cabinet), AC30HW Hand Wired (1990s) and HW Limited (2000s).			
1980s	Rose Morris era	$1,425	$1,850
1985-1986	25th Anniv	$1,425	$1,850
1990s	Collector model	$2,000	$2,600
1990s	Custom colors	$1,525	$1,975
1990s	Hand wired	$2,175	$2,825
1990s	Reissue	$1,200	$1,575
1991	30th Anniv	$1,700	$2,200
1995	TBT, LE, tan	$1,525	$1,975
2000s	Hand wired LE	$2,175	$2,825
2000s	Reissue	$1,275	$1,650
AC30 Super Twin Set			
1960-1965. Piggyback head and 2x12" pressure cabinet with amp trolley.			
1960-1965		$4,400	$5,700
AC30 Twin/AC-30 Twin Top Boost			
1960-1973. Made in England, tube, 30-watt head, 36 watts 2x12", Top Boost includes additional treble and bass, custom colors available in '60-'63.			
1960-1963	Custom colors	$4,700	$6,100
1960-1965	Black	$4,100	$5,400
1966	Black	$2,750	$3,575
1967-1973	Black	$2,275	$2,950

MODEL YEAR	FEATURES	EXC. COND. LOW	HIGH
AC30BM Brian May Limited Edition			
2006-2007. Limited run of 500, 30 watts, 2x12" combo.			
2006-2007		$1,275	$1,650
AC30C2X Custom			
2004-2018. 30 watts, 2x12" Celestion Alnico Blue speakers.			
2004-2018		$575	$750
AC30CC (Custom Classic)			
2004-2012. 30 watts, 2x12", tubes, 2-button footswitch.			
2004-2012		$575	$750
AC30VR Valve Reactor			
2010-2019. 2x12" combo, digital reverb, 30 watts.			
2010-2019		$325	$425
AC50 Cabinet			
1963-1975	Black	$790	$1,025
AC50 Head			
1963-1975. Made in England, 50-watt head, U.S. production '64-'65 tube version is Westminster Bass, U.S. post-'66 is solidstate.			
1963-1975		$2,575	$3,325
AC100 MK I			
1963-1965. All tube 100-watt with 4x12 cab, due to reliability concerns it was transitioned to AC100 Super De Luxe MK II in '65.			
1963-1965		$3,950	$5,100
AC100 Super De Luxe/MK II			
1965. Solidstate 100-watt head with 4x12 cab on speaker trolley.			
1965		$2,350	$3,100
AD Series			
2004-2008. Import small to large modeling amps with single 12AXT preamp tube, chrome grills, includes applicable footswitch, some available with amp trolley (i.e. AD60VT).			
2004-2006	AD120VT	$370	$480
2004-2006	AD60VT	$220	$285
2004-2008	AD100VTH	$180	$235
2004-2008	AD15VT	$100	$130
2004-2008	AD30VT	$105	$135
2004-2008	AD50VT	$150	$200
2006-2008	AD100VT	$260	$340
Berkeley II V108 (Tube)			
1964-1966. U.S.-made tube amp, revised '66-'69 to U.S.-made solidstate model V1081, 18 watts, 2x10" piggyback.			
1964-1966		$1,150	$1,500
Berkeley II V1081 (Solidstate)			
1966-1967. U.S.-made solidstate, 35 watts, 2x10" piggyback, includes trolley stand.			
1966-1969		$700	$900
Berkeley III (Solidstate)			
1968. Berkeley III logo on top panel of amp.			
1968-1969		$900	$1,150
Buckingham			
1966-1968. Solidstate, 35 watts, 2x12" piggyback, includes trolley stand.			
1966-1968		$775	$1,025
Cambridge 15			
1999-2001. 15 watts, 1x8", tremolo.			
1999-2001		$150	$195

MODEL YEAR	FEATURES	EXC. COND. LOW	HIGH
Cambridge 30 Reverb			
1999-2002. 30 watts, 1x10", tremolo and reverb.			
1999-2002		$160	$210
Cambridge 30 Reverb Twin 210			
1999-2002. 30 watts hybrid circuit, 2x10", reverb.			
1999-2002		$205	$270
Cambridge Reverb V1031/V1032 (Solidstate)			
1966-1968. Solidstate, 35 watts, 1x10", model V1031 replaced tube version V103.			
1966-1968		$750	$1,000
Cambridge Reverb V3/V103 (Tube)			
1965-1966. U.S-made tube version, 18 watts, 1x10", a Pacemaker with reverb, superceded by solidstate Model V1031 by '67.			
1965-1966		$1,100	$1,400
Churchill PAV119 Head and V1091 Cabinet Set			
Late-1960s. PA head with multiple inputs and 2 column speakers.			
1960s	PA head only	$450	$575
1960s	Set	$800	$1,050
Climax V125/VO125 Lead Combo			
1970-1991. Solidstate, 125 watts, 2x12" combo, 5-band EQ, master volume.			
1970-1991	Combo	$650	$850
1970-1991	Half-Stack	$875	$1,125
DA Series			
2006-2013. Small digital modeling amps, AC/DC power, solidstate.			
2006-2013	DA5, 5w, 1x65	$90	$115
2007-2009	DA10, 10w, 2x6	$110	$140
2007-2009	DA20, 20w, 2x8	$115	$150
2010	DA15, 15w, 1x8	$100	$130
Defiant			
1966-1970. Made in England, 50 watts, 2x12" + Midax horn cabinet.			
1966-1970		$1,575	$2,050
Escort			
Late 1960s-1983. 2.5 watt battery-powered portable amp.			
1968-1986		$325	$425
Essex V1042 Bass			
1966-1968. U.S.-made solidstate, 35 watts, 2x12". Also called Essex Bass Deluxe.			
1966-1968		$525	$675
Foundation Bass			
1966-1970. Tube in '66, solidstate after, 50 watts, 1x18", made in England only.			
1966	Tubes	$1,525	$2,000
1967-1970	Solidstate	$650	$850
Kensington V1241 Bass			
1966-1968. U.S.-made solidstate bass amp, 22 watts, 1x15", G-tuner, called Kensington Bass Deluxe in '67.			
1966-1968		$650	$850
Night Train Series			
2009-2016. Small tube head and combo, 2 channels, Celestion speaker, models available; NT15C1 (15w, 1x12 combo), NT15H-G2 (15w, 1x12 head/cab), NT50H-G2 (50w, 2x12 head/cab).			
2009-2016	NT, 2x12 cab	$220	$285

MODEL YEAR	FEATURES	EXC. COND. LOW	HIGH
2009-2016	NT15H-G2, cab	$185	$240
2009-2016	NT15H-G2, head	$310	$400
2015-2016	NT15C1, combo	$450	$590
Pacemaker V1021 (Solidstate)			
1966-1968. U.S.-made solidstate amp, 35 watts, 1x10", replaced Pacemaker model V102.			
1966-1968		$450	$575
Pacemaker V2/V102 (Tube)			
1965-1966. U.S.-made tube amp, 18 watts, 1x10", replaced by solidstate Pacemaker model V1021.			
1965-1966		$875	$1,125
Pathfinder (Import)			
1998-present. Compact amps with 1960s cosmetics.			
1998-2013	15, 15w, 1x8	$75	$95
2002-2021	10, 10w, 1x65	$60	$80
Pathfinder V1/V101 (Tube)			
1965-1966. U.S.-made tube amp, 4 watts, 1x8", '66-'69 became U.S.-made solidstate V1011.			
1965-1966		$885	$1,150
Pathfinder V1011 (Solidstate)			
1966-1968. U.S.-made solidstate, 25 watts peak power, 1x8".			
1966-1968		$425	$550
Royal Guardsman V1131/V1132			
1966-1968. U.S.-made solidstate, 50 watts piggyback, 2x12" + 1 horn, the model below the Super Beatle V1141/V1142.			
1966-1968		$1,300	$1,700
Scorpion (Solidstate)			
1968. Solidstate, 120 watts, 4x10" Vox Oxford speaker.			
1968		$525	$700
Super Beatle Reissue Cabinet			
2011-2012. 2x15" cab only.			
2011-2012		$350	$450
Super Beatle V1141/V1142			
1965-1966. U.S.-made 120 watt solidstate, 4x12" + 2 horns, with distortion pedal (V1141), or without (V1142).			
1965-1966		$3,150	$4,100
T60			
1962-1966. Solidstate bass head, around 40 watts, sold with 2x15" or 1x12" and 1x15" cabinet.			
1962-1966		$700	$925
VBM1 Brian May Special			
2010. Compact 10-watt, 1x6" speaker, also called VBM1 Brian May Recording Amp, white cover, includes headphone/recording line out, Brian May logo on lower right grille.			
2010		$130	$170
Viscount V1151/V1152			
1966-1968. U.S.-made solidstate, 70 watts, 2x12" combo, 1151, 1153, and 1154 with distortion.			
1966-1968		$775	$1,025
VT Valvetronix/Valvetronix + Series			
2008-present. Line of digital modeling combo amps, ranging from the 15-watt, 1x8" VT15 ('08-'11) to the Valvetronix+ 120-watt, 2x12" VT120+.			
2008-2011	VT15	$100	$130
2012-2021	VT20+	$100	$130
2015-2016	VT80	$165	$215
2015-2021	VT40+	$150	$200

1967 Vox Royal Guardsman
Imaged by Heritage Auctions, HA.com

AMPS

1966 Vox Super Beatle V1141
Imaged by Heritage Auctions, HA.com

Vox VT20+

AMPS

Wallace Amplification Sophia

1963 Watkins Control ER15
Nicholas Kennett

West Laboratories Mini I
Mark Harvey

MODEL YEAR	FEATURES	EXC. COND. LOW	HIGH

Westminster V118 Bass
1966-1969. Solidstate, 120 watts, 1x18".

1966-1969		$600	$800

V-Series
See Crate.

Wabash
1950s. Private branded amps, made by others, distributed by the David Wexler company. They also offered lap steels and guitars.

Model 1158
1950s. Danelectro-made, 1x15", 2x6L6 power tubes, tweed.

1950s		$600	$775

Small Tube
1950s	3 tubes	$225	$300

Wallace Amplification
2000-present. Production/custom, professional grade, amps built by Brian Wallace in Livonia, Michigan. (Not affiliated with a 1970's amp company from the United Kingdom also called Wallace that has since gone out of business.)

Warbler
See listing under Juke amps.

Warwick
1982-present. Combos, amp heads and cabinets from Warwick Basses of Markneukirchen, Germany.

Washburn
1962-present. Imported guitar and bass amps. Washburn also offers guitars, banjos, mandolins, and basses.

Watkins
1957-present. England's Watkins Electric Music (WEM) was founded by Charlie Watkins. Their first commercial product was the Watkins Dominator (wedge Gibson stereo amp shape) in '57, followed by the Copicat Echo in '58. They currently build accordion amps.

Clubman
1960s. Small combo amp with typical Watkins styling, blue cover, white grille.

1960s		$1,050	$1,375

Dominator MK Series
1970s. Similar circuit to '50s tube amps except solidstate rectifier, 25 watts, different speaker used for different applications.

1970s	MK I, bass, 1x15	$525	$675
1970s	MK II, organ, 1x12	$525	$675
1970s	MK III, guitar, 1x12	$525	$675

Dominator V-Front
Late-1950s-1960s, 2004. 18 watts, 2x10", wedge cabinet similar to Gibson GA-79 stereo amp, tortoise and light beige cab, light grille, requires 220V step-up transformer. Was again offered in '04.

1959-1962		$2,650	$3,450

Scout
1960s. Watkins and Scout logo on top control panel, 17 watts, 1x10 combo, 6 tubes.

1960s		$1,050	$1,375

Westminster Tremolo
1959-1962. 10-watt 1x10" combo, Westminster Tremolo logo on top panel, 3 control knobs, blue and white cover.

1959-1962		$1,050	$1,375

Webcor
1940s-1950s. The Webster-Chicago Company built recording and audio equipment including portable amplifiers suitable for record turntables, PAs, or general utility. Low power with one or two small speakers.

Small
1950s	1 or 2 speakers	$265	$350

West Laboratories
1965-1970s, 2005-2015. Founded by David W. West in Flint, Michigan, moved to Lansing in '68. The '71 catalog included three tube and two solidstate amps, speaker cabinets, as well as Vocal Units and Mini Series combo amps. Amps were available as heads, piggyback half-stacks and full-stacks, with the exception of the combo Mini Series. The Fillmore tube amp head was the most popular model. West equipment has a West logo on the front and the cabinets also have a model number logo on the grille. David West reestablished his company in 2005, located in Okemos, Michigan, with models offered on a custom order basis, concentrating on lower power EL84 designs. West died November, '15.

Avalon Head
1965-1970s. 50 watts, 2 6CA7 output tubes.

1965-1970s		$700	$900

Fillmore Head
1970s. 200 watts, 4 KT88 output tubes.

1965-1970s		$2,500	$3,300

Grande Head
1970s. 100 watts, 2 KT88 output tubes.

1965-1970s		$825	$1,075

Mini IR
1970s. 50 watts, 1x12 tube combo with reverb, black tolex, large West logo and model name Mini IR on front panel.

1965-1970s		$925	$1,200

White
1955-1960. The White brand, named after plant manager Forrest White, was established by Fender to provide steel and small amp sets to teaching studios that were not Fender-authorized dealers. The amps were sold with the matching steel guitar. See Steel section for pricing.

White (Matamp)
See Matamp listing.

MODEL YEAR	FEATURES	EXC. COND. LOW	HIGH

Winfield Amplification

2001-present. Intermediate and professional grade, production, vacuum tube amps built by Winfield N. Thomas first in Greensboro, Vermont and presently in Cochise, Arizona.

Wizard

1988-present. Professional and premium grade, production/custom, guitar and bass, amps and cabinets built by Rick St Pierre in Cornwall, Ontario.

Woodson

Early 1970s. Obscure builder from Bolivar, Missouri. Woodson logo on front panel and Woodson Model and Serial Number plate on back panel, solidstate circuit, student level pricing.

Working Dog

2001-2014. Lower cost tube amps and combos built by Alessandro High-End Products (Alessandro, Hound Dog) in Huntingdon Valley, Pennsylvania.

Wright Amplification

Aaron C. Wright builds his professional grade, production/custom, amps and cabinets in Lincoln, Nebraska starting in 2004.

Yamaha

1946-present. Yamaha started building amps in the '60s and offered a variety of guitar and bass amps over the years. The current models are solidstate bass amps. They also build guitars, basses, effects, sound gear and other instruments.

Budokan HY-10G II
1987-1992. Portable, 10 watts, distortion control, EQ.

1987-1992		$50	$65

G30-112
1983-1992. Solidstate combo, 30 watts, 1x12".

1983-1992		$125	$160

G50-112
1983-1992. 50 watts, 1x12".

1983-1992		$145	$190

G100-112
1983-1992. 100 watts, 1x12" combo, black cover, striped grille.

1983-1992		$150	$200

G100-212
1983-1992. 100, 2x12" combo, black cover, striped grille.

1983-1992		$175	$225

JX30B
1983-1992. Bass amp, 30 watts.

1983-1992		$100	$135

TA-20
1968-1972. Upright wedge shape with controls facing upwards, solidstate.

1968-1972		$95	$125

TA-25
1968-1972. Upright wedge shape with controls facing upwards, 40 watts, 1x12", solidstate, black or red cover.

1968-1972		$110	$145

TA-30
1968-1972. Upright wedge shape, solidstate.

1968-1972		$125	$160

TA-50
1971-1972. Solidstate combo, 80 watts, 2x12", includes built-in cart with wheels, black cover.

1971-1972		$145	$190

TA-60
1968-1972. Upright wedge shape, solidstate, most expensive of wedge-shape amps.

1968-1972		$185	$240

VR3000
1988-1992. Combo 1x12", 2 channels, identical control sections for each channel, settings are completely independent.

1988-1992		$110	$146

VR4000
1988-1992. 50-watt stereo, 2 channels, EQ, stereo chorus, reverb and dual effects loops.

1988-1992		$175	$225

VR6000
1988-1992. 100-watt stereo, 2 channels which can also be combined, EQ, chorus, reverb and dual effects loops.

1988-1992		$230	$300

VX-15
1988-1992. 15 watts.

1988-1992		$80	$105

VX-65D Bass
1984-1992. 80 watts, 2 speakers.

1984-1992		$110	$145

YBA-65 Bass
1972-1976. Solidstate combo, 60 watts, 1x15".

1972-1976		$110	$145

YTA-25
1972-1976. Solidstate combo, 25 watts, 1x12".

1972-1976		$110	$145

YTA-45
1972-1976. Solidstate combo, 45 watts, 1x12".

1972-1976		$110	$145

YTA-95
1972-1976. Solidstate combo, 90 watts, 2x12".

1972-1976		$110	$145

YTA-100
1972-1976. Solidstate piggyback, 100 watts, 2x12".

1972-1976		$145	$190

YTA-110
1972-1976. Solidstate piggyback, 100 watts, 2x12" in extra large cab.

1972-1976		$145	$190

YTA-200
1972-1976. Solidstate piggyback, 200 watts, 4x12".

1972-1976		$165	$215

YTA-300
1972-1976. Solidstate piggyback, 200 watts, dual cabs with 2x12" and 4x12".

1972-1976		$250	$325

Winfield

Wizard Modern Classic Combo

1968 Yamaha TA-60
Tom Pfeifer

AMPS

Z.Vex Nano Head

*Zeppelin Design Labs
Percolator*

ZT Jazz Club

MODEL YEAR	FEATURES	EXC. COND. LOW	HIGH

YTA-400
1972-1976. Solidstate piggyback, 200 watts, dual 4x12".

1972-1976		$250	$325

Z.Vex Amps
2002-present. Intermediate grade, production amps built by Zachary Vex in Minneapolis, Minnesota with some subassembly work done in Michigan. He also builds effects.

Zapp
Ca.1978-early-1980s. Zapp amps were distributed by Red Tree Music, Inc., of Mamaroneck, New York.

Z-10
1978-1980s. Small student amp, 8 watts.

1979-1982		$25	$35

Z-50
1978-1980s. Small student amp, 10 watts, reverb, tremelo.

1978-1982		$30	$40

Zeppelin Design Labs
2014-present. Brach Siemens and Glen van Alkemade build budget and intermediate grade amps and cabinets in Chicago, Illinois. They also offer their products as DIY kits.

MODEL YEAR	FEATURES	EXC. COND. LOW	HIGH

Zeta
1982-2010. Solid state amps with MIDI options, made in Oakland, California. They also made upright basses and violins.

Zinky
Tube head and combo amps and cabinets built by Bruce Zinky, starting in 1999, in Flagstaff, Arizona. He also builds the mini Smokey amps (since '97), effects, and has revived the Supro brand on a guitar and amp.

ZT Amplifiers
2009-present. Ken Kantor of Berkeley, California imports intermediate grade, production, solid state compact amps from China. He also offers effects.

EFFECTS

Rocker Wah PW-1

OUTPUT   INPUT

RANGE   WIDTH

EFFECT ON/OFF

BOSS

INSTRUMENT   AMPLIFIER

WAU WAU FUZZ

ADA MP-1

Akai E2 Headrush

Ampeg Scrambler Fuzz

MODEL YEAR	FEATURES	EXC. COND. LOW	HIGH

Able Electronics

1990s. Started by John Rogers and based in Pwllheli, Wales.

Bassmaker

1990s. Octave pedal.

1990s		$100	$200

Ace Tone

1968-1972. Effects from Ace Electronic Industry, which was a part of Sakata Shokai Limited of Osaka, Japan, which also made organs, amps, pioneering Rhythm Ace FR-1 and FR-2 drum machines, etc. Their Ace Tone effects line was the predecessor to Roland and Boss.

Echo Chamber EC-10

1968-1972. Solidstate tape echo.

1968-1972		$300	$600

Expander EXP-4

1968-1972. "Expander" effect.

1968-1972		$175	$200

Fuzz Master FM-1

1968-1972. Distortion and overdrive.

1968-1972		$300	$460

Fuzz Master FM-2

1968-1972. Fuzz. Black housing. 2 Control knobs.

1968-1972		$175	$420

Fuzz Master FM-3

1968-1972. Distortion and clean boost.

1968-1972		$450	$660

Stereo Phasor LH-100

1968-1972. Phaser.

1968-1972		$275	$340

Wah Master WM-1

1968-1972. Filter wah.

1968-1972		$75	$150

Acoustyx

1977-1982. Made by the Highland Corporation of North Springfield, Vermont.

Image Synthesizer IS-1

1977-ca.1982. Synthesizer effects.

1977-1982		$50	$60

Phase Five

1977-ca.1982. Used 6 C cell batteries!

1977-1982		$50	$60

ADA

1975-2002. Analog/Digital Associates was located in Berkeley, California, and introduced its Flanger and Final Phase in '77. The company later moved to Oakland and made amplifiers, high-tech signal processors, and a reissue of its original Flanger.

Final Phase

1977-1979. Reissued in '97.

1977-1979		$375	$450

Flanger

1977-1983, 1996-2002. Reissued in '96.

1977-1979	No control pedal	$325	$400
1977-1979	With control pedal	$375	$475
1980-1983		$225	$300
1996-2002		$75	$100

MP-1

1987-1995. Tube preamp with chorus and effects loop, MIDI.

1987-1995	No foot controller	$150	$200
1987-1995	With optional foot controller	$200	$260

MP-2

Ca.1988-1995. Tube preamp with chorus, 9-band EQ and effects loop, MIDI.

1988-1995		$225	$275

Pitchtraq

1987. Programmable pitch transposer including octave shifts.

1987		$150	$200

Stereo Tapped Delay STD-1

Introduced in 1981.

1980s		$150	$200

TFX4 Time Effects

Introduced in 1982, includes flanger, chorus, doubler, echo.

1980s		$150	$200

Aguilar

1995-present. The New York, New York amp builder also offers a line of tube and solidstate pre-amps.

Akai (Akai Electric Company Ltd.)

1984-present. In '99, Akai added guitar effects to their line of electronic samplers and sequencers for musicians.

UniBass UB1

2000s. Bass octave pedal.

2000s		$50	$100

Alamo

1947-1982. Founded by Charles Eilenberg, Milton Fink, and Southern Music, San Antonio, Texas. Distributed by Bruno & Sons. Mainly known for guitars and amps, Alamo did offer a reverb unit.

Reverb Unit

1965-ca.1979. Has a Hammond reverb system, balance and intensity controls. By '73 the unit had 3 controls - mixer, contour, and intensity.

1965-1970		$300	$450

Alesis

1992-present. Alesis has a wide range of products for the music industry, including digital processors and amps for guitars.

Allen Amplification

1998-present. David Allen's company, located in Richwood, Kentucky, mainly produces amps, but they also offer a tube overdrive pedal.

Altair Corp.

1977-1980s. Company was located in Ann Arbor, Michigan.

MODEL YEAR FEATURES	EXC. COND. LOW	HIGH

Power Attenuator PW-5
1977-1980. Goes between amp and speaker to dampen volume.

1977-1980	$90	$120

Amdek

Mid-1980s. Amdek offered many electronic products over the years, including drum machines and guitar effects. Most of these were sold in kit form so quality of construction can vary.

Delay Machine DMK-200
1983. Variable delay times.

1983	$85	$115

Octaver OCK-100
1983. Produces tone 1 or 2 octaves below the note played.

1983	$75	$100

Phaser PHK-100

1983	$65	$100

Phlanger

1983	$50	$60

Ampeg

Ampeg entered the effects market in the late-1960s. Their offerings in the early-'60s were really amplifier-outboard reverb units similar to the ones offered by Gibson (GA-1). Ampeg offered a line of imported effects in '82-'83, known as the A-series (A-1 through A-9), and reintroduced effects to their product line in '05.

Analog Delay A-8
1982-1983. Made in Japan.

1982-1983	$75	$125

Chorus A-6
1982-1983. Made in Japan.

1982-1983	$50	$75

Compressor A-2
1982-1983. Made in Japan.

1982-1983	$50	$75

Distortion A-1
1982-1983. Made in Japan.

1982-1983	$50	$75

Echo Jet Reverb EJ-12
1963-1965. Outboard, alligator clip reverb unit with 12" speaker, 12 watts, technically a reverb unit. When used as a stand-alone amp, the reverb is off. Named EJ-12A in '65.

1963-1965	$550	$725

Echo Satellite ES-1
1961-1963. Outboard reverb unit with amplifier and speaker alligator clip.

1961-1963	$550	$675

Flanger A-5
1982-1983. Made in Japan.

1982-1983	$50	$75

Multi-Octaver A-7
1982-1983. Made in Japan.

1982-1983	$50	$100

Over Drive A-3
1982-1983. Made in Japan.

1982-1983	$50	$75

MODEL YEAR FEATURES	EXC. COND. LOW	HIGH

Parametric Equalizer A-9
1982-1983. Made in Japan.

1982-1983	$45	$70

Phaser A-4
1982-1983. Made in Japan.

1982-1983	$50	$75

Phazzer
1975-1979. Phase shifter, single speed knob.

1975-1979	$50	$125

Scrambler Fuzz
1969-1970. Distortion pedal, black housing. 2 Control knobs. Reissued in '05.

1969-1970	$200	$450

Sub Blaster SCP-OCT
2005-2007. Bass octave pedal.

2005-2007	$225	$380

Amplifier Corporation of America

Late '60s company that made amps for Univox and also marketed effects under their own name.

Amptweaker

2010-present. James Brown, an amp design engineer previously employed by Peavey, then for Kustom amps, now designs and builds effects in Batavia, Ohio.

amukaT Gadgets

2006-present. Guitar effects built by Takuma Kanaiwa in New York, New York.

Analog Man

1994-present. Founded by Mike Piera in '94 with full-time production by 2000. Located in Danbury, Connecticut (until '07 in Bethel), producing chorus, compressor, fuzz, and boost pedals by '03.

Astro Tone
2000s-present. Fuzz.

2000s-2021	$120	$160

Bad Bob
2000s-present. Boost.

2000s-2021	$90	$150

Beano Boost
2000s-present. Boost.

2000s-2021	$100	$160

Dual Analog Delay
2000s-present. Delay.

2000s-2021	$200	$250

Envelope Filter
2000s-present. Envelope 'auto-wah'.

2000s-2021	$140	$200

Juicer
2000s-present. Compressor.

2000s-2021	$120	$160

King of Tone
2000s-present. Overdrive pedal, 4 generations, numerous options available.

2000s-2021	$400	$720

Amptweaker Big Rock Pro II

amukaT Gadgets Tweaker

Analog Man King of Tone

EFFECTS

Analog Man Sun Bender

Analog Man Sun Face

Area 51 The Alienist

MODEL YEAR	FEATURES	EXC. COND. LOW	HIGH
Peppermint Fuzz			
2000s-present. Fuzz.			
2000s-2021		$120	$230
Prince of Tone			
2000s-present. Overdrive.			
2000s-2021		$120	$150
Sun Bender			
2000s-present. Fuzz.			
2000s-2021		$200	$240
Sun Face			
2000s-present. Fuzz.			
2000s-2021		$200	$300

Aphex Systems

1975-present. Founded in Massachusetts by Marvin Caesar and Curt Knoppel, to build their Aural Exciter and other pro sound gear. Currently located in Sun Valley, California, and building a variety of gear for the pro audio broadcast, pro music and home-recording markets.

Apollo

Ca.1967-1972. Imported from Japan by St. Louis Music, includes Fuzz Treble Boost Box, Crier Wa-Wa, Deluxe Fuzz. They also offered basses and guitars.

MODEL YEAR	FEATURES	EXC. COND. LOW	HIGH
Crier Wa-Wa			
Ca.1967-1972.			
1967-1972		$125	$200
Fuzz/Deluxe Fuzz			
Ca.1967-1972. Includes the Fuzz Treble Boost Box and the Deluxe Fuzz.			
1967-1972		$125	$240
Surf Tornado Wah Wah			
Ca.1967-1972.			
1967-1972		$180	$300

Applied

1960s. Effects brand of the Goya Music Company. Some models may have been sold under the Nomad brand.

MODEL YEAR	FEATURES	EXC. COND. LOW	HIGH
Banshee Fuzz			
1960s. Also sold as the Nomad Banshee Fuzz.			
1960s		$50	$200

Arbiter

Ivor Arbiter and Arbiter Music, London, began making the circular Fuzz Face stompbox in 1966. Other products included the Fuzz Wah and Fuzz Wah Face. In '68 the company went public as Arbiter and Western, later transitioning to Dallas-Arbiter. Refer to Dallas-Arbiter for listings.

Area 51

2003-present. Guitar effects made in Newaygo, Michigan (made in Texas until early '06), by Dan Albrecht. They also build amps.

Aria/Aria Pro II

1956-present. Aria provided a line of effects, made by Maxon, in the mid-'80s.

MODEL YEAR	FEATURES	EXC. COND. LOW	HIGH
Analog Delay AD-10			
1983-1985. Dual-stage stereo.			
1983-1985		$65	$75
Chorus ACH-1			
1986-1987. Stereo.			
1986-1987		$40	$50
Chorus CH-10			
1983-1985. Dual-stage stereo.			
1983-1985		$40	$50
Chorus CH-5			
1985-1987		$40	$50
Compressor CO-10			
1983-1985		$40	$50
Digital Delay ADD-100			
1984-1986. Delay, flanging, chorus, doubling, hold.			
1984-1986		$65	$75
Digital Delay DD-X10			
1985-1987		$65	$75
Distortion DT-10			
1983-1985. Dual-stage.			
1983-1985		$40	$50
Distortion DT-5			
1985-1987		$40	$50
Flanger AFL-1			
1986. Stereo.			
1986		$50	$60
Flanger FL-10			
1983-1985. Dual-stage stereo.			
1983-1985		$50	$60
Flanger FL-5			
1985-1987		$50	$60
Metal Pedal MP-5			
1985-1987		$40	$50
Noise Gate NG-10			
1983-1985		$30	$40
Over Drive OD-10			
1983-1985. Dual-stage.			
1983-1985		$40	$50
Parametric Equalizer EQ-10			
1983-1985		$40	$50
Phase Shifter PS-10			
1983-1984. Dual-stage.			
1983-1984		$50	$70
Programmable Effects Pedal APE-1			
1984-1986. Compression, distortion, delay, chorus.			
1984-1986		$50	$60

Arion

1984-2014. Arion offers a wide variety of budget imported effects.

MODEL YEAR	FEATURES	EXC. COND. LOW	HIGH
Guitar and Bass Effects			
1984-2014		$15	$75

Arteffect

Tom Kochawi and Dan Orr started building analog effects in 2006, in Haifa and Natanya, Israel.

Artesania Sonora Lab

2010s-present. Based in Fortaleza, Brazil.

MODEL YEAR	FEATURES	EXC. COND. LOW	HIGH
Fabrica del Fuzz			
2016-2021		$75	$150

MODEL YEAR	FEATURES	EXC. COND. LOW	HIGH

Asama

1970s-1980s. This Japanese company offered solidbody guitars with built-in effects as well as stand-alone units. They also offered basses, drum machines and other music products.

Astro Amp

Late 1960s. Universal Amplifier Corporation of New York City made and sold Astro Amps as well as Astro effects. The company also made the Sam Ash Fuzzz Boxx.

Astrotone

1966		$175	$275

ATD

Mid-1960s-early 1980s. Made by the All-Test Devices corporation of Long Beach, New York. In the mid-'60s, Richard Minz and an associate started making effects part-time, selling them through Manny's Music in New York. They formed All-Test and started making Maestro effects and transducer pickups for CMI, which owned Gibson at the time. By '75, All-Test was marketing effects under their own brand. All-Test is still making products for other industries, but by the early to mid-'80s they were no longer making products for the guitar.

PB-1 Power Booster

1976-ca.1980.

1979-1980		$50	$60

Volume Pedal EV-1

1979-ca.1980.

1979-1980		$30	$40

Wah-Wah/Volume Pedal WV-1

1979-ca.1981.

1979-1981		$50	$60

Audio Dsruption Devices

2010s. Based in Mooresville, Indiana.

Optical Ring V2

2010s. Ring modulator.

2010s		$100	$200

Audio Matrix

1979-1984. Effects built by B.K Butler in Escondido, California. He later designed the Tube Driver and founded Tube Works in 1987. He nows operates Butler Audio, making home and auto hybrid tube stereo amps.

Mini Boogee B81

1981. Four-stage, all-tube preamp, overdrive, distortion.

1981		$100	$135

Audio-Phonic

1970s. Effects built in Argentina.

Mu-Tron III

1970s. Musitronics Mu-Tron III copy.

1970s		$200	$300

Audioworks

1980s. Company was located in Niles, Illinois.

F.E.T. Distortion

1980s		$40	$55

Auralux

2000-2011. Founded by Mitchell Omori and David Salzmann, Auralux built effects and tube amps in Highland Park, Illinois.

Austone Electronics

1997-2009. Founded by Jon Bessent and Randy Larkin, Austone offered a range of stomp boxes, all made in Austin, Texas. Bessent passed away in '09.

Overdrive and Fuzz Pedals

1997-2009. Various overdrive and fuzz boxes.

1997-2009		$125	$245

Automagic

Wah pedals and distortion boxes made in Germany by Musician Sound Design, starting in 1998.

Avalanche

Late 1980s. Effects built by Brian Langer in Toronto, Ontario.

Brianizer

Late 1980s. Leslie effect, dual rotor, adjustable speed and rates.

1980s		$75	$90

Axe

1980s. Early '80s line of Japanese effects, possibly made by Maxon.

B & M

1970s. A private brand made by Sola/Colorsound for Barns and Mullens, a U.K. distributor.

Fuzz Unit

1970s. Long thin orange case, volume, sustain, tone knobs, on-off stomp switch.

1970s		$275	$325

Backline Engineering

2004-present. Guitar multi-effects built by Gary Lee in Camarillo, California. In '07, they added tube amps.

Bad Cat Amplifier Company

2000-present. Amp company Bad Cat, originally of Corona, California, also offers guitar effects. In '09 the company was moved to Anaheim.

Baldwin

1965-1970. The piano maker got into the guitar market when it acquired Burns of London in '65, and sold the guitars in the U.S. under the Baldwin name. They also marketed a couple of effects at the same time.

Banzai

2000-present. Effects built by Olaf Nobis in Berlin, Germany.

Bartolini

The pickup manufacturer offered a few effects from around 1982 to '87.

Bad Cat Double Drive

Bad Cat Siamese Drive

Banzai Cold Fusion Overdrive

EFFECTS

BBE Sonic Stomp

Beigel Sound Lab Tru-Tron 3X

EFFECTS

Blackstone Mosfet Overdrive

MODEL YEAR	FEATURES	EXC. COND. LOW	HIGH

Tube-It
1982-ca.1987. Marshall tube amplification simulator with bass, treble, sustain controls.

| 1982-1987 | Red case | $80 | $90 |

Basic Systems' Side Effects
1980s. This company was located in Tulsa, Oklahoma.

Audio Delay
1986-ca.1987. Variable delay speeds.

| 1986-1987 | | $75 | $100 |

Triple Fuzz
1986-ca.1987. Selectable distortion types.

| 1986-1987 | | $50 | $60 |

BBE
1985-present. BBE, owner of G&L Guitars and located in California, manufactures rack-mount effects and added a new line of stomp boxes in '05.

Behringer
1989-present. The German professional audio products company added modeling effects in '01 and guitar stomp boxes in '05. They also offer guitars and amps.

Beigel Sound Lab
Music product designer Mike Beigel helped form Musitronics Corp, where he made the Mu-Tron III. In 1978 he started Beigel Sound Lab to provide product design in Warwick, New York, where in '80 he made 50 rack-mount Enveloped Controlled Filters under this brand name. In 2013, Mike Beigel's Beigel Sound Lab started making a Mu-FX Tru-Tron 3X and Octave Divider.

Boostron 3
2016-2017. Combines preamp boost, compression and distortion in one pedal.

| 2016-2017 | | $225 | $325 |

Octave Divider
2015. Updated and expanded version of original Musitronics Mu-Tron Octave Divider.

| 2015 | | $325 | $400 |

Tru-Tron 3X
2015-2019. Updated and expanded version of original Musitronics Mu-Tron III envelope filter.

| 2015-2019 | | $325 | $500 |

Bell Electrolabs
1970s. This English company offered a line of effects in the '70s.

Vibrato
| 1970s | | $150 | $200 |

Bennett Music Labs
Effects built in Chatanooga, Tennessee by Bruce Bennett.

Bigsby
1948-1966. Paul Bigsby made steel guitars, pedal steels, and electric guitars and mandolins, as well as developing the Bigsby vibrato tailpiece and other components.

Foot Volume and Tone Control
1950s-1960s. Beautifully crafted pedal in a cast-aluminum housing featuring a side-to-side tone sweep.

| 1950s-60s | | $450 | $650 |

Binson
Late 1950s-1982. Binson, of Milan, Italy, made several models of the Echorec, using tubes or transistors. They also made units for Guild, Sound City and EKO.

Echorec
Ca.1960-1979. Four knob models with 12 echo selections, 1 head, complex multitap effects, settings for record level, playback and regeneration. Includes B1, B2, Echomaster1, T5 (has 6 knobs), T5E, and Baby. Used a magnetic disk instead of tape. Guild later offered the Guild Echorec by Binson which is a different stripped-down version.

| 1960s | Tube | $2,500 | $3,350 |
| 1970s | Solidstate | $700 | $800 |

Bixonic
1995-2007. The round silver distortion pedals were originally distributed by SoundBarrier Music, later by Godlyke, Inc.

Expandora EXP-2000
1995-2000. Analog distortion, round silver case, internal DIP switches.

| 1995-2000 | | $170 | $210 |

Black Arts Toneworks
2010s. Founded by Mark Wentz of Chattanooga, Tennessee.

Pharaoh
| 2010s | | $100 | $150 |

Ritual Fuzz
2010s. Inspired by the Colorsound Fuzz Box.

| 2010s | | $100 | $150 |

Black Cat Pedals
1993-2007, 2009-present. Founded by Fred Bonte and located in Texas until late 2007 when production was discontinued. In '09, using Bonte's same designs, new owner Tom Hughes restarted production in Foxon, Connecticut.

Black Cat OD-1
2010-present. Overdrive.

| 2010-2021 | | $70 | $120 |

Blackbox Music Electronics
2000-2009. Founded by Loren Stafford and located in Minneapolis, Minnesota, Blackbox offered a line of effects for guitar and bass. The Blackbox models are now made under the Ooh La La brand.

Blackout Effectors
Kyle Tompkins began building effects pedals in 2007, in Vancouver, British Columbia and now builds them in Asheville, North Carolina.

The *Vintage Guitar Price Guide* shows low to high values for items in all-original excellent condition, and, where applicable, with original case or cover.

MODEL YEAR	FEATURES	EXC. COND. LOW	HIGH

Blackstar Amplification

2007-present. Guitar effects pedals built by Joel Richardson in Northampton, U.K. He also builds amps.

Blackstone Appliances

1999-present. Distortion effects crafted by Jon Blackstone in New York City.

Mosfet Overdrive

1999-present. Though the designation doesn't appear on the housing, the original was subsequently called 2Sv1 after later versions were issued.

MODEL YEAR	FEATURES	EXC. COND. LOW	HIGH
1999	2Sv1, no controls on top	$125	$240
2000	2Sv2	$100	$200
2006-2021	2Sv3, 2Sv31, 2Sv32, 2Sv33	$95	$200
2012	Billybox Limited Edition	$150	$250

Bon, Mfg

Bon was located in Escondido, California.

Tube Driver 204

1979-ca.1981.

1979-1981		$100	$150

Boomerang

1995-present. Effects pedals built in Grapevine, Texas by Boomerang Musical Products, Ltd.

Boss

1976-present. Japan's Roland Corporation first launched effect pedals in '74. A year or two later the subsidiary company, Boss, debuted its own line. They were marketed concurrently at first but gradually Boss became reserved for effects and drum machines while the Roland name was used on amplifiers and keyboards. Boss still offers a wide line of pedals.

Acoustic Simulator AC-2

1997-2007. Four modes that emulate various acoustic tones.

1997-2007		$50	$70

Acoustic Simulator AC-3

2007-present. Four modes that emulate various acoustic tones.

2007-2021		$50	$90

Auto Wah AW-2

1991-1999. Becomes Dynamic Wah (AW-3) in 2000.

1991-1999		$40	$75

Bass Chorus CE-2B

1987-1995		$40	$50

Bass Equalizer GE-7B

1987-1995. Seven-band, name changed to GEB-7 in '95.

1987-1995		$40	$50

Bass Flanger BF-2B

1987-1994		$40	$60

Bass Limiter LM-2B

1990-1994		$35	$40

Bass Overdrive ODB-3

1994-present. Yellow case.

1994-2021		$40	$50

Blues Driver BD-2

1995-present. Blue case.

1995-2021		$45	$80
1995-2021	Keeley modded	$150	$200

Chorus Ensemble CE-1

1976-1978. Vibrato and chorus.

1976-1978		$275	$510

Chorus Ensemble CE-2

1979-1982		$140	$260

Chorus Ensemble CE-3

1982-1992		$30	$80

Chorus Ensemble CE-5

1991-present. Pale blue case.

1991-2020		$50	$95

Compressor Sustainer CS-1

1978-1982		$70	$95

Compressor Sustainer CS-2

1981-1986		$70	$110

Compressor Sustainer CS-3

1986-present. Blue case.

1986-2021		$50	$75
1986-2021	JHS modded	$90	$130

Delay DM-2

1981-1984. Analog, hot pink case.

1981-1984		$100	$245

Delay DM-3

1984-1988		$145	$195

Digital Delay DD-2

1983-1986		$60	$150

Digital Delay DD-3

1986-present. Up to 800 ms of delay, white case.

1986-1989		$70	$90
1986-2021	Keeley modded	$100	$170
1990-2021		$60	$80

Digital Delay DD-5

1995-2005. Up to 2 seconds of delay.

1995-2005		$100	$145

Digital Delay DD-6

2003-2007. Up to 5 seconds of delay.

2003-2007		$55	$100

Digital Delay DD-7

2008-present. Up to 6.4 seconds of delay, crème case.

2008-2021		$80	$110

Digital Dimension C DC-2

1985-1989. Two chorus effects and tremolo.

1985-1989		$135	$250

Digital Metalizer MZ-2

1987-1992		$80	$95

Digital Reverb RV-2

1987-1990		$95	$145

Digital Reverb RV-5

2003-2019. Dual imput and dual output, four control knobs, silver case.

2003-2019		$60	$95

Digital Reverb/Delay RV-3

1994-2004		$95	$120

Digital Sampler/Delay DSD-2

1985-1986		$100	$150

Boss Chorus Ensemble CE-2
Keith Myers

Boss Chorus Ensemble CE-3

Boss Delay DM-3
Rivington Guitars

EFFECTS

1984 Boss Distortion DS-1
Rivington Guitars

Boss Metal Zone MT-2

Boss Super Over Drive SD-1
Rivington Guitars

MODEL YEAR	FEATURES	EXC. COND. LOW	HIGH
Digital Space-D DC-3/Digital Dimension DC-3			
1988-1993. Originally called the Digital Space-D, later changed to Digital Dimension. Chorus with EQ.			
1988-1993		$130	$180
Digital Stereo Reverb RV-70			
1994-1995. Rack mount, MIDI control, reverb/ delay, 199 presets.			
1994-1995		$130	$180
Distortion DS-1			
1978-1989, 1990s-present. Orange case.			
1978-1989		$75	$150
1978-2021	Keeley modded	$100	$130
1990-1999		$30	$50
2000-2021		$20	$25
Dr. Rhythm DR-55			
1979-1989. Drum machine.			
1979-1989		$145	$195
Dual Over Drive SD-2			
1993-1998		$45	$55
Dynamic Filter FT-2			
1986-1988. Auto wah.			
1986-1988		$70	$95
Dynamic Wah AW-3			
2000-present. Auto wah with humanizer, for guitar or bass.			
2000-2021		$50	$85
Enhancer EH-2			
1990-1998		$35	$45
Flanger BF-1			
1977-1980		$55	$70
Flanger BF-2			
1980-1989		$60	$100
1990-2005		$40	$55
Foot Wah FW-3			
1992-1996		$45	$55
Graphic Equalizer GE-6			
1978-1981. Six bands.			
1978-1981		$60	$75
Graphic Equalizer GE-7			
1981-present. Seven bands, white case.			
1982-1989		$50	$90
1990-2021		$45	$70
Graphic Equalizer GE-10			
1976-1985. 10-band EQ for guitar or bass.			
1976-1985		$75	$150
Harmonist HR-2			
1994-1999. Pitch shifter.			
1994-1999		$80	$105
Heavy Metal HM-2			
1983-1991. Distortion.			
1983-1991		$60	$140
Hyper Fuzz FZ-2			
1993-1997		$45	$150
Hyper Metal HM-3			
1993-1998		$35	$45
Limiter LM-2			
1987-1992		$25	$65
Line Selector LS-2			
1991-2021. Select between 2 effects loops, white case.			
1991-2021	With adapter	$45	$85

MODEL YEAR	FEATURES	EXC. COND. LOW	HIGH
Mega Distortion MD-2			
2003-present. Red case.			
2003-2021		$45	$55
Metal Zone MT-2			
1991-present. Distortion and 3-band EQ, grey case.			
1991-2021		$30	$60
1991-2021	Keeley modded	$120	$140
Multi Effects ME-5			
1988-1991. Floor unit.			
1988-1991		$70	$140
Multi Effects ME-6			
1992-1997		$50	$100
Multi Effects ME-8			
1996-1997		$70	$120
Multi Effects ME-20			
1990-2000s		$60	$100
Multi Effects ME-25			
1990-2000s		$70	$130
Multi Effects ME-30			
1998-2002		$70	$120
Multi Effects ME-50			
2003-2009. Floor unit.			
2003-2009		$100	$165
Multi Effects ME-70			
2000s		$90	$210
Multi Effects ME-80			
2000s-present.			
2000s-2021		$125	$240
Noise Gate NF-1			
1979-1988		$40	$75
Noise Suppressor NS-2			
1987-present. White case.			
1987-2021		$40	$75
Octaver OC-2/Octave OC-2			
1982-2003. Originally called the Octaver.			
1982-2003		$75	$130
Overdrive OD-1			
1977-1979		$95	$190
1980-1985		$70	$145
Overdrive OD-2			
1990s		$20	$60
Overdrive OD-3			
1997-present. Yellow case.			
1997-2021		$45	$60
Parametric Equalizer PQ-4			
1991-1997		$45	$70
Phase Shifter PH-3			
2000-present. Added effects, light green case.			
2000-2021		$40	$70
Phaser PH-1			
1977-1981. Green box, 2 knobs.			
1977-1981		$70	$95
Phaser PH-1R			
1982-1985. Resonance control added to PH-1.			
1982-1985		$70	$120
Phaser PH-2			
1984-2001. 12 levels of phase shift, 4 knobs.			
1984-2001		$50	$85
Pitch Sifter/Delay PS-2			
1987-1993		$95	$150

The *Vintage Guitar Price Guide* shows low to high values for items in all-original excellent condition, and, where applicable, with original case or cover.

EFFECTS

MODEL YEAR FEATURES	EXC. COND. LOW	HIGH
Reverb Box RX-100		
1981-mid-1980s.		
1981-1985	$70	$95
Rocker Distortion PD-1		
1980-mid-1980s. Variable pedal using magnetic field.		
1980-1985	$45	$70
Rocker Volume PV-1		
1981-mid-1980s.		
1980-1985	$45	$55
Rocker Wah PW-1		
1980-mid-1980s. Magnetic field variable pedal.		
1980-1985	$55	$65
Slow Gear SG-1		
1979-1982. Violin swell effect, automatically adjusts volume.		
1979-1982	$300	$440
Spectrum SP-1		
1977-1981. Single-band parametric EQ.		
1977-1981	$325	$375
Super Chorus CH-1		
1989-present. Blue case.		
1989-2021	$45	$70
Super Distortion & Feedbacker DF-2		
1984-1994. Also labeled as the Super Feedbacker & Distortion.		
1984-1994	$95	$120
Super Octave OC-3		
2004-2021. Brown case.		
2004-2021	$60	$90
Super Over Drive SD-1		
1981-present. Yellow case.		
1981-1989	$50	$105
1990-2021	$30	$50
Super Phaser PH-2		
1984-1989	$45	$85
1990-2001	$30	$50
Super Shifter PS-5		
1999-2013. Pitch shifter/harmonizer, aqua case.		
1999-2013	$95	$120
Touch Wah TW-1/T Wah TW-1		
1978-1987. Auto wah, early models were labeled as Touch Wah.		
1978-1987	$95	$120
Tremolo TR-2		
1997-present. Aqua case.		
1997-2021	$65	$85
1997-2021 Keeley modded	$110	$150
Tremolo/Pan PN-2		
1990-1995	$120	$145
Turbo Distortion DS-2		
1987-present. Orange case.		
1987-2021	$70	$120
Turbo Over Drive OD-2		
1985-1994. Called OD-2R after '94, due to added remote on/off jack.		
1985-1994	$40	$100
Vibrato VB-2		
1982-1986. True pitch-changing vibrato, warm analog tone, 'rise time' control allows for slow attach, 4 knobs, aqua-blue case.		
1982-1986	$325	$460

MODEL YEAR FEATURES	EXC. COND. LOW	HIGH
Volume FV-50H		
1987-1997. High impedance, stereo volume pedal with inputs and outputs.		
1987-1997	$45	$55
Volume FV-50L		
1987-1997. Low impedance version of FV-50.		
1987-1997	$35	$45
Volume Pedal FV-100		
Late-1980s-1991. Guitar volume pedal.		
1987-1991	$35	$45

Brimstone Audio
2011-present. Shad Sundberg builds his guitar effects in California.

Browntone Electronics
2006-2012. Guitar effects built in Lincolnton, North Carolina by Tim Brown.

Bruno
Music distributor Bruno and Sons had a line of Japanese-made effects in the early '70s.

Fuzz Machine
1970s. Rebranded version of the Ibanez No. 59 Standard Fuzz.

1970s	$75	$150

Budda
1995-present. Wahs and distortion pedals originally built by Jeff Bober and Scott Sier in San Francisco, California. In '09, Budda was acquired by Peavey Electronics. They also build amps.

Bud Wah
1997-2018. Wah pedal.

1990s-2018	$90	$140

Phat Bass

2000s	$100	$145

Build Your Own Clone
2005-present. Build it yourself kits based on vintage effects produced by Keith Vonderhulls in Othello, Washington. Assembled kits are offered by their Canadian distributor.

Burriss
2001-present. Guitar effects from Bob Burriss of Lexington, Kentucky. He also builds amps.

Carl Martin
1993-present. Line of effects from Søren Jongberg and East Sound Research of Denmark. In '06 they added their Chinese-made Vintage Series. They also build amps.

Carlsbro
1959-present. English amp company Carlsbro Electronics Limited offered a line of effects from '77 to '81.

Fuzz
1970s. Tone Bender MkIII fuzz built by Sola Sound.

1970s	$300	$500

Boss Rocker Wah PW-1
Marco Antonio Rebolledo Ferrari

Boss Super Shifter PS-5
Keith Myers

Boss Tremolo TR-2

EFFECTS

Catalinbread Antichthon

Catalin Bread Sabbra Cadabra
Rivington Guitars

Chunk Systems Agent 00Funk

EFFECTS

MODEL YEAR	FEATURES	EXC. COND. LOW	HIGH
Suzz			
1970s. Built by Sola Sound.			
1970s		$300	$500
Suzz Wah Wah			
1970s. Built by Sola Sound.			
1970s		$100	$250

Carrotron
Late-1970s-mid-1980s. Carrotron was out of California and offered a line of effects.

MODEL YEAR	FEATURES	EXC. COND. LOW	HIGH
Noise Fader C900B1			
1981-ca.1982.			
1981-1982		$50	$60
Preamp C821B			
1981-ca.1982.			
1981-1982		$55	$65

Carvin
1946-present. Carvin introduced its line of Ground Effects in '02 and discontinued them in '03.

Castle Instruments
Early 1980s. Castle was located in Madison, New Jersey, and made rack-mount and floor phaser units.

MODEL YEAR	FEATURES	EXC. COND. LOW	HIGH
Phaser III			
1980-1982. Offered mode switching for various levels of phase.			
1980-1982		$100	$175

Catalinbread
2003-present. Nicholas Harris founded Catalinbread Specialized Mechanisms of Music in Seattle, Washington, in '02 to do mods and in '03 added his own line of guitar effects.

MODEL YEAR	FEATURES	EXC. COND. LOW	HIGH
Adineko			
2000s		$100	$150
Belle Epoch			
2000s		$100	$170
Callisto			
2000s		$90	$135
Echorec			
2000s		$100	$185
Formula No. 5			
2000s		$140	$230
Naga Viper			
2000s		$100	$140
Perseus			
2000s		$70	$110
Rah			
2000s		$120	$150
Sabbra Cadabra			
2000s		$100	$150
Semaphore			
2000s		$90	$120
Super Chili Picoso			
2000s		$30	$50
Topanga			
2000s		$100	$170

Cat's Eye
Dean Solorzano and Lisa Kroeker began building their analog guitar effects in Oceanside, California in 2001.

Cause & Effect Pedals
2009-present. Guitar effects pedals built in Ontario by Mark Roberts and Brian Alexson.

Celmo
The Celmo Sardine Can Compressor is made by Kezako Productions in Montcaret, France, starting in 2008.

Chandler
Located in California, Chandler Musical Instruments offers instruments, pickups, and pickguards, as well as effects.

MODEL YEAR	FEATURES	EXC. COND. LOW	HIGH
Digital Echo			
1992-2000. Rackmount, 1 second delay, stereo.			
1992-2000		$275	$425
Tube Driver			
1986-1991. Uses a 12AX7 tube. Not to be confused with the Tube Works Tube Driver.			
1980s	Large Box	$175	$330
1980s	Rackmount	$100	$215
1990s	Rackmount	$90	$150

Chapman
1970-present. From Emmett Chapman, maker of the Stick.

MODEL YEAR	FEATURES	EXC. COND. LOW	HIGH
Patch of Shades			
1981, 1989. Wah, with pressure sensitive pad instead of pedal. 2 production runs.			
1980s		$50	$75

Chicago Iron
1998-present. Faithful reproductions of classic effects built by Kurt Steir in Chicago, Illinois.

Chunk Systems
1996-present. Guitar and bass effects pedals built by Richard Cartwright in Sydney, Australia.

Clark
1960s. Built in Clark, New Jersey, same unit as the Orpheum Fuzz and the Mannys Music Fuzz.

MODEL YEAR	FEATURES	EXC. COND. LOW	HIGH
SS-600 Fuzz			
1960s. Chrome-plated, volume and tone knobs, toggle switch.			
1960s		$150	$200

Clark Amplification
1995-present. Amplifier builder Mike Clark, of Cayce, South Carolina, offers a reverb unit and started building guitar effects as well, in '98.

ClinchFX
2006-present. Hand made pedals by Peter Clinch in Brisbane, Queensland, Australia.

MODEL		EXC. COND.	
YEAR	FEATURES	LOW	HIGH

CMI
1970s. English music company.
Fuzz Unit
1970s. Built by Colorsound based on its Jumbo Tone Bender.

1970s		$150	$300

Coffin
Case manufacturer Coffin Case added U.S.-made guitar effects pedals to their product line in 2006.

Colorsound
1967-2010. Colorsound effects were produced by England's Sola Sound, beginning with fuzz pedals. In the late-'60s, wah and fuzz-wah pedals were added, and by the end of the '70s, Colorsound offered 18 different effects, an amp, and accessories. Few early Colorsound products were imported into the U.S., so today they're scarce. Except for the Wah-Wah pedal, Colorsound's production stopped by the early '80s, but in '96 most of their early line was reissued by Dick Denny of Vox fame. Denny died in 2001. Since then, Anthony and Steve Macari build Colorsound effects in London. Mutronics offered a licensed rack mount combination of 4 classic Colorsound effects for a short time in the early 2000s.
Chuck-a-Wah
1975-1977. Auto wah pedal.

1975-1977		$250	$340

Dipthonizer
1970s. "Talking" pedal with foot control.

1970s		$250	$400

Dopplatone Phase Unit
1970s. Large phase and vibrato effect with Bubble control.

1970s		$250	$340

Electro Echo
1979-1980s. Analog delay pedal.

1979-1980s		$250	$400

Flanger

1970s		$110	$210

FuzzPhaze
Introduced in 1973.

1970s		$160	$235

Jumbo Tone-Bender
1974-early 1980s. Replaced the Tone-Bender fuzz, with wider case and light blue lettering.

1974-1980s		$275	$335

Octivider
Introduced in 1973.

1970s		$160	$235

Overdriver
Introduced in 1972. Controls for drive, treble and bass.

1970s		$160	$235

Phazer
Introduced in 1973. Magenta/purple-pink case, slanted block Phazer logo on front.

1970s		$160	$235

Power Boost

1970s		$350	$625

Ring Modulator
Introduced in 1973. Purple case, Ring Modulator name with atom orbit slanted block logo on case.

1970s		$260	$285

Supa Tone Bender
1977-early 1980s. Sustain and volume knobs, tone control and toggle. Same white case as Jumbo Tone-Bender, but with new circuit.

1970s		$275	$350

Supa Wah-Swell
1970s. Supa Wah-Swell in slanted block letters on the end of the pedal, silver case.

1970s		$160	$195

Supaphase

1970s		$160	$235

Supasustain

1960s		$135	$210

Swell

1970s		$80	$90

Tremolo

1970s		$160	$210

Tremolo Reissue
1996-2009. Purple case.

1996-2009		$110	$135

Vocalizer
1979-1980s. "Talking" pedal with foot control.

1979-1980s		$200	$300

Wah Fuzz Straight
Introduced in 1973. Aqua-blue case, Wah-Fuzz-Straight in capital block letters on end of wah pedal.

1970s		$185	$300

Wah Fuzz Swell
Introduced in 1973. Yellow case, block letter Wah Fuzz Swell logo on front, three control knobs and toggle.

1970s		$260	$360

Wah Swell
1970s. Light purple case, block letter Wah-Swell logo on front.

1970s		$235	$285

Wah Wah
1970s. Dark gray case, Wah-Wah in capital block letters on end of wah pedal.

1975		$310	$350

Wah Wah Reissue
1996-2005. Red case, large Colorsound letter logo and small Wah Wah lettering on end of pedal.

1996-2005		$85	$150

Wah Wah Supremo
1970s. Silver/chrome metal case, Wah-Wah Supremo in block letters on end of wah pedal.

1975		$435	$485

Companion
1970s. Private branded by Shin-ei of Japan, which made effects for others as well.
Tape Echo

1960-1970		$400	$650

Wah Pedal

1970s		$150	$240

Clark Amplification Gainster

ClinchFX EP-PRE

EFFECTS

Colorsound Power Boost

Coopersonic Germaniac

Crazy Tube Circuits Starlight

Crowther Audio Hotcake

MODEL YEAR	FEATURES	EXC. COND. LOW	HIGH

Conn

Ca.1968-ca.1978. Band instrument manufacturer and distributor Conn/Continental Music Company, of Elkhart, Indiana, imported guitars and effects from Japan.

Strobe Tuner
Brown or later, grey, case.

MODEL YEAR	FEATURES	EXC. COND. LOW	HIGH
1960s	ST-4	$50	$100
1960s	ST-6	$75	$100
1960s	ST-8	$75	$125
1968	ST-2	$50	$100
1970s	Strobotuner ST-11	$75	$100
1970s	Strobotuner ST-12	$75	$100

Coopersonic

2006-present. Martin Cooper builds his guitar effects in Nottingham, UK.

Coron

1970s-1980s. Japanese-made effects, early ones close copies of MXR pedals.

Cosmosound

Italy's Cosmosound made small amps with Leslie drums and effects pedals in the late '60s and '70s. Cosmosound logo is on top of pedals.

Wah Fuzz CSE-3
1970s. Volume and distortion knobs, wah and distortion on-off buttons, silver case.

MODEL YEAR	FEATURES	EXC. COND. LOW	HIGH
1970s		$275	$350

Wild Sound
MODEL YEAR	FEATURES	EXC. COND. LOW	HIGH
1970s		$175	$195

Crazy Tube Circuits

2004-present. Guitar effects designed and built by Chris Ntaifotis in Athens, Greece.

Creation Audio Labs

2005-present. Guitar and bass boost pedal and re-amplifying gear built in Nashville, Tennessee.

Crowther Audio

1976-present. Guitar effects built by Paul Crowther, who was the original drummer of the band Split Enz, in Auckland, New Zealand. His first effect was the Hot Cake.

Crucial Audio

2005-present. Effects by Steve Kollander engineered and assembled in Sussex County, Delaware, with chassis manufactured by machine shops within the U.S. They also provide OEM products and design engineering services to companies including Matchless, Requisite Audio & West Coast Pedal Boards.

Apollo-18 Vacuum Tube Leslie Interface
2015-present. High-voltage vacuum tube interface module for Leslie 122 or 147 type rotary speaker systems; can be used with a tube preamp and/or two channel vacuum tube direct box.

MODEL YEAR	FEATURES	EXC. COND. LOW	HIGH
2015-2021		$960	$1,200

Das Götterdämmerung - Germanium Fuzz/Ring Modulator
2017-present. Provides full function controls combined with germanium fuzz generated from matched NOS 2N404.

MODEL YEAR	FEATURES	EXC. COND. LOW	HIGH
2017-2021		$280	$360

Echo-Nugget Vacuum Tube Analog Delay
2008-present. Tube-driven analog delay with selectable boost/tone preamp.

MODEL YEAR	FEATURES	EXC. COND. LOW	HIGH
2008-2021		$450	$550

Time Warp Vacuum Tube Analog Delay
2008-present. Tube-driven analog delay with selectable modulation/warp function.

MODEL YEAR	FEATURES	EXC. COND. LOW	HIGH
2008-2021		$450	$550

Vacuum Tube Direct Recording Interface: The DUB-5
2016-present. Interface for recording studios or live sound to sweeten the tone of instruments.

MODEL YEAR	FEATURES	EXC. COND. LOW	HIGH
2016-2021		$370	$460

Cruzer

Effects made by Korea's Crafter Guitars. They also build guitars, basses and amps under that brand.

Crybaby

See listing under Vox for early models, and Dunlop for recent versions.

CSL

1970s. Charles Summerfield Ltd., was an English music company with a line of effects made by Sola Sound.

Power Boost
MODEL YEAR	FEATURES	EXC. COND. LOW	HIGH
1970s		$100	$200

Super Fuzz
MODEL YEAR	FEATURES	EXC. COND. LOW	HIGH
1970s		$100	$200

Cusack Music

2003-present. Effects built in Holland, Michigan by Jon Cusack.

Dallas/Dallas Arbiter

Dallas Arbiter, Ltd. was based in London and it appeared in the late-1960s as a division of a Dallas group of companies headed by Ivor Arbiter. Early products identified with Dallas logo with the company noted as John E. Dallas & Sons Ltd., Dallas Building, Clifton Street, London, E.C.2. They also manufactured Sound City amplifiers and made Vox amps from '72 to '78. The Fuzz Face is still available from Jim Dunlop.

Fuzz Face
1966-1975, 1977-1981, 1986-1987. Late '70s and '80s version was built for Dallas Arbiter by Crest Audio of New Jersey. The current reissue is built by Jim Dunlop USA (see that listing).

MODEL YEAR	FEATURES	EXC. COND. LOW	HIGH
1968-1969	Red	$1,600	$2,500
1970	Red	$1,100	$2,250
1970-1975	Blue	$1,100	$2,250
1977-1980	Blue	$675	$850
1981	Grey, reissue	$450	$550

MODEL YEAR	FEATURES	EXC. COND. LOW	HIGH
Fuzz Wah Face			
1970s	Black	$550	$650
1990s	Reissue copy	$65	$80
Rangemaster Fuzzbug			
1966 Tone Bender Mk15 effect built by Sola Sound			
1966		$1,500	$2,000
Rangemaster Treble Booster			
1966. 2000s. Grey housing. 1 Control knob. On-off slider switch. Old-style round-barrel 9-volt battery powered; many converted to later rectangular battery. Various current reissues built by JMI and other firms.			
1966		$1,700	$2,850
2000s	JMI reissue	$175	$225
Sustain			
1970s		$400	$500
Treble and Bass Face			
1960s		$500	$700
Trem Face			
Ca.1970-ca.1975. Reissued in '80s, round red case, depth and speed control knobs, Dallas-Arbiter England logo plate.			
1970-1975		$500	$700
Wah Baby			
1970s. Gray speckle case, Wah Baby logo caps and small letters on end of pedal.			
1970s		$500	$600

Damage Control

2004-2009. Guitar effects pedals and digital multi-effects built in Moorpark, California. The company was founded with the release of a line of tube-driven effects pedals. In '09, it began developing products under the Strymon brand name.

MODEL YEAR	FEATURES	EXC. COND. LOW	HIGH
Demonizer			
2004-2009. Class A distortion preamp pedal powered by dual vacuum tubes.			
2004-2009		$180	$255
Liquid Blues			
2004-2009. Class A overdrive pedal powered by dual vacuum tubes.			
2004-2009		$180	$245
Solid Metal			
2004-2009. Class A distortion pedal powered by dual vacuum tubes.			
2004-2009		$180	$260
TimeLine			
2004-2009. Delay pedal powered by dual vacuum tubes.			
2004-2009		$240	$300
Womanizer			
2004-2009. Class A overdrive preamp pedal powered by dual vacuum tubes.			
2004-2009		$170	$220

Dan Armstrong

1976-1981. In '76, Musitronics, based in Rosemont, New Jersey, introduced 6 inexpensive plug-in effects designed by Dan Armstrong. Perhaps under the influence of John D. MacDonald's Travis McGee novels, each effect name incorporated a color, like Purple Peaker. Shipping box labeled Dan Armstrong by Musitronics. They disappeared a few years later but

were reissued by WD Products from '91 to '02 (See WD for those models). From '03 to '06, Vintage Tone Project offered the Dan Armstrong Orange Crusher. Since '06, a licensed line of Dan Armstrong effects that plug directly into the output of a guitar or bass (since '07 some also as stomp boxes) has been offered by Grafton Electronics of Grafton, Vermont. Dan Armstrong died in '04.

MODEL YEAR	FEATURES	EXC. COND. LOW	HIGH
Blue Clipper			
1976-1981. Fuzz, blue-green case.			
1976-1981		$100	$200
Green Ringer			
1976-1981. Ring Modulator/Fuzz, green case.			
1976-1981		$100	$280
Orange Squeezer			
1976-1981. Compressor, orange case.			
1976-1981		$125	$325
Purple Peaker			
1976-1981. Frequency Booster, light purple case.			
1976-1981		$100	$170
Red Ranger			
1976-1981. Bass/Treble Booster, light red case.			
1976-1981		$85	$100
Yellow Humper			
1976-1981. Yellow case.			
1976-1981		$85	$100

Danelectro

1946-1969, 1996-present. The Danelectro brand was revived in '96 with a line of effects pedals. They have also offered the Wasabi line of effects. Prices do not include AC adapter, add $10 for the Zero-Hum adapter.

MODEL YEAR	FEATURES	EXC. COND. LOW	HIGH
Chicken Salad Vibrato			
2000-2009. Orange case.			
2000-2009		$20	$50
Cool Cat			
1996-2018		$30	$35
Cool Cat Chorus			
1996-2018. Blue case.			
1996-2018		$20	$40
Corned Beef Reverb			
2000-2009. Blue-black case.			
2000-2009		$15	$40
Daddy-O Overdrive			
1996-2009. White case.			
1996-2009		$35	$40
Dan Echo			
1998-2009. Lavender case.			
1998-2009		$40	$45
Echo Box			
1953-ca. 1958. Reverb unit, metal housing with black endplates.			
1953-1958		$200	$450
Fab Tone Distortion			
1996-2014. Red case.			
1996-2014		$30	$40
Reverb Unit Model 9100			
1962-ca. 1967. Tube-driven spring reverb, long grey housing.			
1962-1967		$300	$475

1969 Dallas Arbiter Fuzz Face
Dean Nissen

Damage Control Solid Metal

Danelectro Daddy-O
Jim Schreck

EFFECTS

Daredevil Silver Solo

DeArmond Square Wave Distortion Generator
Jim Schreck

DeArmond Tremolo Control

MODEL YEAR	FEATURES	EXC. COND. LOW	HIGH

Daredevil

2012-present. Guitar effects pedals built in Chicago, Illinois by Johnny Wator.

Davoli

1960s-1970. Davoli was an Italian pickup and guitar builder and is often associated with Wandre guitars.

TRD
1970s. Solidstate tremolo, reverb, distortion unit.

1970s		$175	$225

DDyna Music

2008-present. Dan Simon builds his guitar effects pedals in Bothell, Washington.

Dean Markley
The string and pickup manufacturer offered a line of effects from 1976 to the early-'90s.

Overlord Classic Overdrive Model III
1990-1991. Battery-powered version of Overlord pedal. Black case with red letters.

1990-1991		$40	$70

Overlord Classic Tube Overdrive
1988-1991. Uses a 12AX7A tube, AC powered.

1988-1991		$60	$80

Voice Box 50 (Watt Model)

1976-1979		$75	$125

Voice Box 100 (Watt Model)
1976-1979, 1982-ca.1985.

1976-1979		$75	$125

Voice Box 200 (Watt Model)

1976-1979		$75	$125

DeArmond

In 1946, DeArmond may have introduced the first actual signal-processing effect pedal, the Tremolo Control. They made a variety of effects into the '70s, but only one caught on - their classic volume pedal. DeArmond is primarily noted for pickups.

Pedal Phaser Model 1900
1974-ca.1979.

1974-1979		$75	$125

Square Wave Distortion Generator
1977-ca.1979.

1977-1979		$75	$150

Thunderbolt B166
1977-ca.1979. Five octave wah.

1977-1979		$50	$100

Tone/Volume Pedal 610
1978-ca.1979.

1978-1979		$75	$125

Tornado Phase Shifter
1977-ca.1979.

1977-1979		$100	$125

Tremolo Control Model 60A/60B
The Model 60 Tremolo Control dates from ca. 1946 to the early-1950s. Model 60A dates from mid- to late-'50s. Model 60B (plastic housing), early-'60s. Also labeled as the Trem-Trol or 601.

1950s	60A	$350	$570
1960s	60B	$175	$275
1960s	800 Trem-Trol	$100	$350

MODEL YEAR	FEATURES	EXC. COND. LOW	HIGH

Twister 1930
1980. Phase shifter.

1980		$100	$125

Volume Pedal Model 602

1960s		$40	$70

Volume Pedal Model 1602
1978-ca. 1980s.

1970s		$40	$95

Volume Pedal Model 1630
1978-1980s. Optoelectric.

1970s		$35	$65

Weeper Wah Model 1802
1970s. Weeper logo on foot pedal.

1970s		$100	$125

Death By Audio

2001-present. Oliver Ackermann builds production and custom guitar effects in Brooklyn, New York.

Absolute Destruction

2000s-2021		$90	$140

Apocalyse

2000s-2021		$120	$200

Armageddon

2006		$150	$300

Crash Modulator

2005		$150	$300

Deep Animation

2000s-2021		$130	$200

Echo Dream 2

2000s-2021		$150	$230

Echo Master

2000s-2021		$150	$230

Evil Filter

2000s-2021		$100	$220

Fuzz Fuzz Fuzz

2006		$150	$300

Fuzz War

2000s-2021		$100	$160

Interstellar Overdriver

2000s-2021		$90	$140

Interstellar Overdriver 2

2000s-2021		$140	$220

Micro Dream

2000s-2021		$90	$150

Micro Harmonic Transformer

2000s-2021		$90	$160

Overdriver Deluxe

2000s-2021		$150	$235

Reverberation Machine

2000s-2021		$150	$290

Robot

2000s-2021		$120	$220

Rooms
"Stereo Reverberator" pedal.

2000s-2021		$150	$330

Soundwave Breakdown

2000s-2021		$80	$125

Space Galaxy
Prototype pedal.

2009		$250	$500

MODEL YEAR	FEATURES	EXC. COND. LOW	HIGH
Sunshine Reverberation			
Designed in collaboration with Ty Seagall, limited edition of 100 pedals.			
2013		$250	$500
Supersonic Fuzz Gun			
2000s-2021		$100	$220
Time Shadows			
Collaboration with EarthQuaker Devices, limited edition of 1,000 pedals.			
2020		$200	$330
Total Sonic Annihilation			
2000s-2021		$90	$140
Total Sonic Annihilation 2			
2000s-2021		$100	$190
Waveform Destroyer			
2000s-2021		$150	$210

DeltaLab Research

Late 1970s-early 1980s. DeltaLab, which was located in Chelmsford, Massachusetts, was an early builder of rackmount gear.

MODEL YEAR	FEATURES	EXC. COND. LOW	HIGH
DL-2 Acousticomputer			
1980s. Delay.			
1980s		$75	$125
DL-4 Time Line			
1980s. Delay.			
1980s		$75	$125
DL-5			
1980s. Various digital processing effects, blue case, rackmount.			
1980s		$175	$225
DLB-1 Delay Control Pedal			
1980s. Controls other DeltaLab pedals, chrome, Morley-looking pedal.			
1980s		$50	$75
Electron I ADM/II ADM			
1980s. Blue case, rackmount effects. Models include the Electron I ADM, and the Electron II ADM.			
1980s	Electron I ADM	$50	$75
1980s	Electron II ADM	$75	$125

Demeter

1980-present. Amp builder James Demeter and company, located in Van Nuys, California, also build guitar effects.

Denio

Line of Japanese-made Boss lookalikes sold in Asia and Australia.

Devi Ever : Fx

2009-present. Devi Ever builds his guitar effects in Portland, Oregon. Prior to '09 he built the Effector 13 effects.

Diamond Pedals

2004-present. Designed by Michael Knappe and Tim Fifield, these effects are built in Bedford, Nova Scotia.

Diaz

Early-1980s-2002, 2004-present. Line of effects from the amp doctor Cesar Diaz. Diaz died in '02; in '04, his family granted Diaz's friend Peter McMahon the license to resume production. Helping to differentiate the builder, Diaz and McMahon pedals are often signed inside.

MODEL YEAR	FEATURES	EXC. COND. LOW	HIGH
Texas Ranger			
1980s-2002, 2004-present. Treble booster. 2 control knobs. Variety of colorful housings.			
1980s-2002		$600	$800
2004-2021		$400	$600
Texas Square Face			
1980s-2002, 2004-present. Fuzz pedal. 2 control knobs. Variety of colorful housings.			
1980s-2002		$600	$1,100
2004-2021		$500	$600
Tremodillo			
1980s-2002, 2004-present. Tremolo pedal. 2 control knobs. Variety of colorful housings.			
1980s-2002		$600	$1,000
2004-2021		$500	$600

DigiTech

The DigiTech/DOD company is in Utah and the effects are made in the U.S.A. The DigiTech name started as a line under the DOD brand in the early 1980s; later spinning off into its own brand. They also produce vocal products and studio processors and are now part of Harman International Industries.

MODEL YEAR	FEATURES	EXC. COND. LOW	HIGH
Digital Delay and Sampler PDS 2000			
1985-1991. 2 second delay.			
1985-1991		$125	$175
Digital Delay PDS 1000			
1985-ca.1989. One second delay.			
1985-1989		$100	$150
Digital Delay PDS 2700 Double Play			
1989-1991. Delay and chorus			
1989-1991		$125	$175
Digital Stereo Chorus/Flanger PDS 1700			
1986-1991		$100	$150
Echo Plus 8 Second Delay PDS 8000			
1985-1991		$175	$200
Guitar Effects Processor RP 1			
1992-1996. Floor unit, 150 presets.			
1992-1996		$100	$150
Guitar Effects Processor RP 3			
1998-2003. Floor unit.			
1998-2003		$110	$150
Guitar Effects Processor RP 5			
1994-1996. Floor unit, 80 presets.			
1994-1996		$120	$175
Guitar Effects Processor RP 6			
1996-1997. Floor unit.			
1996-1997		$125	$200
Guitar Effects Processor RP 7			
1996-1997. Floor unit.			
1996-1997		$125	$175
Guitar Effects Processor RP 10			
1994-1996. Floor unit, 200 presets.			
1994-1996		$125	$175

*Death By Audio
Interstellar Overdriver*

Demeter FZO-1

EFFECTS

*Diamond Pedals
Boost-EQ BEQ1*

DigiTech Whammy Pedal WP I
Jim Schreck

DLS Effects Tremolo

1981 DOD AB Box 270
Rivington Guitars

MODEL YEAR	FEATURES	EXC. COND. LOW	HIGH
Guitar Effects Processor RP 14D			
1999. Floor unit with expression pedal, 1x12AX7 tube, 100 presets.			
1999		$300	$350
Guitar Effects Processor RP 100			
2000-2006		$100	$125
Guitar Effects Processor RP 200			
2001-2006. 140 presets, drum machine, Expression pedal.			
2001-2006		$100	$125
Hot Box PDS 2730			
1989-1991. Delay and distortion			
1989-1991		$100	$125
Modulator Pedal XP 200			
1996-2002. Floor unit, 61 presets.			
1996-2002		$100	$125
Multi Play PDS 20/20			
1987-1991. Multi-function digital delay.			
1987-1991		$125	$150
Pedalverb Digital Reverb Pedal PDS 3000			
1987-1991		$100	$125
Programmable Distortion PDS 1550			
1986-1991	Yellow case	$50	$75
Programmable Distortion PDS 1650			
1989-1991	Red case	$50	$75
Rock Box PDS 2715			
1989-1991. Chorus and distortion.			
1989-1991		$50	$75
Two Second Digital Delay PDS 1002			
1987-1991		$100	$125
Whammy Pedal Reissue			
2000-present. Reissue version of classic WP-1 with added dive bomb and MIDI features.			
2000-2020		$125	$140
Whammy Pedal WP I			
1990-1993. Original Whammy Pedal, red case, reissued as WP IV in '00.			
1990-1993		$375	$475
Whammy Pedal WP II			
1994-1997. Can switch between 2 presets, black case.			
1994-1997		$200	$275

DiMarzio
The pickup maker offered a couple of effects in the late-1980s to the mid-'90s.

MODEL YEAR	FEATURES	EXC. COND. LOW	HIGH
Metal Pedal			
1987-1989		$50	$75
Very Metal Fuzz			
Ca.1989-1995. Distortion/overdrive pedal.			
1989-1995		$50	$75

Dino's
A social co-op founded by Alessio Casati and Andy Bagnasco, in Albisola, Italy. It builds a line of boutique analog pedals as well as guitars.

Dinosaur
2004-2015. Guitar effects pedals imported by Eleca International. They also offered amps.

Divided By Thirteen
Mid-1990s-present. Fred Taccone builds his stomp box guitar effects in the Los Angeles, California area. He also builds amps.

DLS Effects
1999-present. Guitar effects pedals built by Dave Sestito in Fairport, New York.

DNA Analogic
Line of Japanese-built guitar effects distributed first by Godlyke, then Pedals Plus+ Effects Warehouse.

DOD
DOD Electronics started in Salt Lake City, Utah in 1974. Today, they're a major effects manufacturer with dozens of pedals made in the U.S. They also market effects under the name DigiTech and are now part of Harman International Industries.

MODEL YEAR	FEATURES	EXC. COND. LOW	HIGH
6 Band Equalizer EQ601			
1977-1982		$45	$65
AB Box 270			
1978-1982		$25	$30
American Metal FX56			
1985-1991		$40	$75
Analog Delay 680			
1979-ca. 1982.			
1979-1982		$120	$185
Attacker FX54			
1992-1994. Distortion and compressor.			
1992-1994		$35	$45
Bass Compressor FX82			
1987-ca.1989.			
1987-1989		$35	$45
Bass EQ FX42B			
1987-1996		$35	$45
Bass Grunge FX92			
1995-1996		$70	$170
Bass Overdrive FX91			
1998-2012. Yellow case.			
1998-2012		$35	$45
Bass Stereo Chorus Flanger FX72			
1987-1997		$45	$55
Bass Stereo Chorus FX62			
1987-1996		$45	$55
Bi-FET Preamp FX10			
1982-1996		$25	$35
Buzz Box FX33			
1994-1996. Grunge distortion.			
1994-1996		$40	$60
Chorus 690			
1980-ca.1982. Dual speed chorus.			
1980-1982		$70	$95
Classic Fuzz FX52			
1990-1997		$30	$60
Classic Tube FX53			
1990-1997		$40	$55
Compressor 280			
1978-ca.1982.			
1978-1982		$40	$65

MODEL		EXC. COND.	
YEAR	FEATURES	LOW	HIGH

Compressor FX80
| 1982-1985 | | $40 | $50 |

Compressor Sustainer FX80B
| 1986-1996 | | $40 | $50 |

Death Metal FX86
1994-2009. Distortion.
| 1994-2009 | | $50 | $80 |

Delay FX90
1984-ca.1987.
| 1984-1987 | | $70 | $110 |

Digital Delay DFX9
1989-ca.1990.
| 1989-1990 | | $55 | $90 |

Digital Delay Sampler DFX94
| 1995-1997 | | $70 | $95 |

Distortion FX55
1982-1986. Red case.
| 1982-1986 | | $30 | $50 |

Edge Pedal FX87
| 1988-1989 | | $20 | $50 |

Envelope Filter 440
| 1981-1982 | | $60 | $70 |

Envelope Filter FX25
1982-1997. Replaced by FX25B.
| 1982-1997 | | $50 | $80 |

Envelope Filter FX25B
1981-2013. Light aqua case.
| 1998-2013 | | $40 | $60 |

Equalizer FX40
| 1982-1986 | | $35 | $50 |

Equalizer FX40B
1987-2010. Eight bands for bass.
| 1987-2010 | | $35 | $50 |

Fet Preamp 210
1981-ca.1982.
| 1981-1982 | | $35 | $50 |

Flanger 670
| 1981-1982 | | $70 | $95 |

Gate Loop FX30
| 1980s | | $25 | $35 |

Gonkulator
| 1980s | | $90 | $130 |

Graphic Equalizer EQ-610
1980-ca.1982. Ten bands.
| 1980-1982 | | $45 | $60 |

Graphic Equalizer EQ-660
1980-ca.1982. Six bands.
| 1980-1982 | | $35 | $50 |

Grunge FX69
1993-2009. Distortion.
| 1993-2009 | | $35 | $65 |

Hard Rock Distortion FX57
1987-1994. With built-in delay.
| 1987-1994 | | $35 | $60 |

Harmonic Enhancer FX85
1986-ca.1989.
| 1986-1989 | | $30 | $50 |

I. T. FX100
1997. Intergrated Tube distortion, produces harmonics.
| 1997 | | $45 | $55 |

IceBox FX64
1996-2008. Chorus, high EQ.
| 1996-2008 | | $40 | $70 |

Juice Box FX51
| 1996-1997 | | $25 | $35 |

Master Switch 225
1988-ca.1989. A/B switch and loop selector.
| 1988-1989 | | $25 | $35 |

Meat Box FX32
| 1994-1996 | | $65 | $160 |

Metal Maniac FX58
| 1990-1996 | | $35 | $45 |

Metal Triple Play Guitar Effects System TR3M
| 1994 | | $35 | $45 |

Metal X FX70
| 1993-1996 | | $35 | $45 |

Milk Box FX84
1994-2012. Compressor/expander, white case.
| 1994-2012 . | | $60 | $105 |

Mini-Chorus 460
1981-ca. 1982.
| 1981-1982 | | $45 | $70 |

Mixer 240
1978-ca.1982.
| 1978-1982 | | $20 | $30 |

Momentary Footswitch
Introduced in 1987. Temporally engages other boxes.
| 1980s | | $20 | $30 |

Mystic Blues Overdrive FX102
1998-2012. Medium gain overdrive, purple case.
| 1998-2012 | | $20 | $25 |

Noise Gate 230
| 1978-1982 | | $25 | $35 |

Noise Gate FX30
1982-ca.1987.
| 1982-1987 | | $25 | $35 |

Octoplus FX35
1987-1996. Octaves.
| 1987-1996 | | $35 | $55 |

Overdrive Plus FX50B
| 1986-1997 | | $30 | $70 |

Overdrive Preamp 250
1978-1982, 1995-2020. Reissued in '95, yellow case.
| 1978-1982 | | $100 | $220 |
| 1995-2020 | | $40 | $70 |

Overdrive Preamp FX50
| 1982-1985 | | $30 | $40 |

Performer Compressor Limiter 525
| 1981-1984 | | $50 | $55 |

Performer Delay 585
| 1982-1985 | | $55 | $70 |

Performer Distortion 555
| 1981-1984 | | $35 | $45 |

Performer Flanger 575
| 1981-1985 | | $35 | $45 |

Performer Phasor 595
| 1981-1984 | | $40 | $50 |

Performer Stereo Chorus 565
1981-1985. FET switching.
| 1981-1985 | | $55 | $70 |

DOD Compressor
Sustainer FX80B

DOD Equalizer FX40B

DOD Fet Preamp 210
Keith Myers

EFFECTS

To get the most from this book, be sure to read "Using *The Guide*" in the introduction.

DOD Performer Stereo Chorus 565
Keith Myers

1981 DOD Phasor 201
Rivington Guitars

Dunlop Cry Baby EVH Wah

MODEL YEAR	FEATURES	EXC. COND. LOW	HIGH
Performer Wah Filter 545			
1981-1984		$45	$70
Phasor 201			
1981-ca.1982. Reissued in '95.			
1981-1982		$65	$95
Phasor 401			
1978-1981		$65	$95
Phasor 490			
1980-ca. 1982.			
1980-1982		$65	$95
Phasor FX20			
1982-1985		$35	$45
Psychoacoustic Processor FX87			
1988-1989		$35	$45
Punkifier FX76			
1997		$35	$45
Resistance Mixer 240			
1978-ca.1982.			
1978-1982		$25	$30
Silencer FX27			
1988-ca.1989. Noise reducer.			
1988-1989		$30	$40
Stereo Chorus FX60			
1982-1986		$35	$45
Stereo Chorus FX65			
1986-1996. Light blue case.			
1986-1996		$35	$45
Stereo Flanger FX70			
1982-ca.1985.			
1982-1985		$35	$45
Stereo Flanger FX75			
1986-1987. Silver case with blue trim.			
1986-1987		$40	$50
Stereo Flanger FX75B			
1987-1997		$40	$50
Stereo Phasor FX20B			
1986-1999		$40	$50
Stereo Turbo Chorus FX67			
1988-1991		$35	$45
Super American Metal FX56B			
1992-1996		$30	$40
Super Stereo Chorus FX68			
1992-1996		$35	$45
Supra Distortion FX55			
1986-2012. Red case.			
1986-2012		$25	$35
Thrash Master FX59			
1990-1996		$25	$45
Vibrothang FX22			
1990s		$60	$95
Votec Vocal Effects Processor and Mic Preamp			
1998-2001		$55	$60
Wah-Volume FX-17 (pedal)			
1987-2000		$40	$55

Dredge-Tone

Located in Berkeley, California, Dredge-Tone offers effects and electronic kits.

MODEL YEAR	FEATURES	EXC. COND. LOW	HIGH
DST Engineering			

2001-2014. Jeff Swanson and Bob Dettorre built reverb units in Beverly, Massachusetts. They also built amps.

Dunlop

Jim Dunlop, USA offers the Crybaby, MXR (see MXR), Rockman, High Gain, Heil Sound (see Heil), Tremolo, Jimi Hendrix, Rotovibe, Uni-Vibe and Way Huge brand effects.

MODEL YEAR	FEATURES	EXC. COND. LOW	HIGH
Cry Baby Bass			
1985-present. Bass wah.			
1985-2021		$75	$100
Cry Baby EVH Wah			
1990's-present.			
1990s-2021		$100	$170
Cry Baby Multi-Wah 535/535Q			
1995-present. Multi-range pedal with an external boost control.			
1995-2021		$70	$90
Cry Baby Wah-Wah GCB-95			
1982-present. Dunlop began manufacturing the Cry Baby in '82.			
1982-1989		$45	$75
1990-1999		$40	$70
2000-2021		$35	$50
Fuzz Face Distortion JDF2			
1993-present. Reissue of the classic Dallas Arbiter effect (see that listing for earlier versions).			
1993-2021	Red, reissue	$100	$165
High Gain Volume + Boost Pedal			
1983-1996		$35	$45
High Gain Volume Pedal GCB-80			
1983-2010		$40	$50
Jimi Hendrix Fuzz JH-2 (Round)			
1987-1993. Round face fuzz, JH-2S is the square box version.			
1987-1993		$50	$75
Rotovibe JH-4S Standard			
1989-1998. Standard is finished in bright red enamel with chrome top.			
1989-1998		$100	$160
Tremolo Volume Plus TVP-1			
1995-1998. Pedal.			
1995-1998		$125	$140
Uni-Vibe UV-1			
1995-2012. Rotating speaker effect.			
1995-1999		$250	$375
2000-2012		$200	$225

Durham Electronics

2001-present. Alan Durham builds his line of guitar effects in Austin, Texas.

Dutch Kazoo

2013-present. Guitar effects pedals built in Parker Ford, Pennsylvania by Corinne Mandell.

Dynacord

1950-present. Dynacord is a German company that makes audio and pro sound amps, as well as

MODEL YEAR	FEATURES	EXC. COND. LOW	HIGH

other electronic equipment and is now owned by TELEX/EVI Audio (an U.S. company), which also owns the Electro-Voice brand. In the '60s they offered tape echo machines and guitars. In '94 a line of multi-effects processors were introduced under the Electro-Voice/Dynacord name, but by the following year they were just listed as Electro-Voice.

EchoCord
Introduced in 1959. Tape echo unit.

1959-1960s		$275	$400

Dyno
See Dytronics.

Dytronics
Mid-1970s-early 1980s. The Japanese Dytronics company made a chorus rackmount unit for electric piano called the Dyno My Piano with flying piano keys or a lightning bolt on the front. Another version was called the Tri-Stereo Chorus and a third, called the Songbird, had a bird's head on the front.

E Bow
See Heet Sound Products.

E.W.S. (Engineering Work Store)
2007-present. Guitar effects pedals built in Tokyo, Japan for Prosound Communications in Van Nuys, California.

EarthQuaker Devices
2005-present. Jamie Stillman started building Fuzz Face and Rangemaster clones for friends and in '07, he built a modified Big Muff for Dan Auerbach of the Black Keys, who he tour-managed at the time. After extensive revisions, this became the Hoof Fuzz and he began retailing his pedals.

Acapulco Gold
2015-present. Power amp distortion. Grandma Cyclops limited-edition version was made '16 in collaboration with visual artist and Devo co-founder Mark Mothersbaugh and the Akron Art Museum.

2015-2021		$60	$90
2016	Grandma Cyclops	$75	$120

Afterneath
2014-present. Ambient reverb.

2014-2021		$100	$190

Amp Hammer II

2009		$50	$100

Arpanoid
2013-present. Polyphonic arpeggiator.

2013-2021		$140	$190

Arrows
2014-present. Preamp boost.

2014-2021		$45	$85

Avalanche Run
2016-present. Stereo reverb and delay.

2016-2021		$180	$225

Bellows
2016-2019. Fuzz driver.

2016-2019		$75	$100

Bit Commander
2011-present. Guitar synthesizer.

2011-2021		$75	$145

Black Eye

2007		$50	$100

Bows
2016-2019. Germanium preamp.

2016-2019		$75	$100

Chrysalis

2010		$50	$100

Cloven Hoof
2014-2020. Fuzz grinder.

2014-2020		$75	$115

Cloven Hoof Reaper
2015-2017. Fuzz.

2015-2017		$90	$140

Crimson Drive

2007		$50	$100

Dirt Transmitter
2008-2019. Fuzz driver.

2008-2019		$80	$100

Disaster Transport
2007. Delay pedal.

2007		$50	$150

Disaster Transport Jr.

2010		$50	$100

Disaster Transport SR
2013-2021. Advanced modulation delay and reverb.

2013-2021		$225	$275

Dispatch Master
2011-present. Hi-fi digital delay and reverb.

2011-2021		$80	$130

Dream Crusher

2009		$50	$100

Dunes
2015-2020. Mini mega overdrive.

2015-2020		$80	$120

Erupter
2017-present. Fuzz.

2017-2021		$75	$100

Fuzz Master General
2015-2019. Octave fuzz pedal.

2015-2019		$80	$130

Ghost Disaster

2010		$50	$100

Ghost Echo
2009-present. Vintage-voiced reverb.

2009-2021		$75	$140

Grand Orbiter
2009-present. Phaser/vibrato.

2009-2021		$90	$130

Gray Channel
2016-2020. Dynamic dirt doubler.

2016-2020		$90	$130

Hoof
2007-present. Germanium/silicon hybrid fuzz.

2007-2021		$90	$125

Dunlop Crybaby Multi-Wah 535Q

EarthQuaker Devices Bellows

EarthQuaker Devices Fuzz Master General

EFFECTS

EarthQuaker Devices
Interstellar Orbiter

EarthQuaker Devices Pitch Bay

EarthQuaker Devices Tone Job

EFFECTS

MODEL YEAR	FEATURES	EXC. COND. LOW	HIGH
Hoof Reaper			
	2012-present. Dual fuzz octave.		
2012-2021		$150	$200
Hummingbird			
	2007-present. Repeat percussion/tremolo.		
2007-2021		$75	$110
Interstellar Orbiter			
	2015-2020. Dual resonant filter built in collaboration with turntablist Kid Koala for his "Turntable Orchestra" tour. Features original artwork by Koala.		
2015-2020		$120	$180
Levitation			
	2008-2021. Psychedlic reverb.		
2008-2021		$80	$125
Monarch			
2010		$50	$120
Night Wire			
	2016-present. Harmonic tremolo.		
2016-2021		$90	$130
Organizer			
	2012-present. Polyphonic organ emulator.		
2012-2021		$90	$135
Palisades			
	2014-present. Mega ultimate overdrive.		
2014-2021		$120	$190
Park Fuzz Sound			
	2015-present. Reissue of the Park Amplification fuzz pedal built in cooperation with Park.		
2015-2021		$75	$120
Pitch Bay			
	2014-2017. Dirty polyphonic harmonizer.		
2014-2017		$100	$180
Pulse Machine Tremolo			
2007		$50	$100
Rainbow Machine			
	2011-present. Polyphonic pitch-shifting modulator.		
2011-2021		$120	$175
Royal Drive			
2007		$50	$100
Sea Machine			
	2010-present. Chorus.		
2010-2021		$75	$120
Sound Shank			
2009		$50	$100
Space Spiral			
	2017-2021. Modulation delay.		
2017-2021		$75	$140
Spatial Delivery			
	2016-present. Envelope filter with sample and hold functions.		
2016-2021		$75	$130
Spires			
	2016-2019. Nü-Face double fuzz.		
2016-2019		$75	$130
Stealth Fuzz			
2007		$50	$100
Talons			
	2012-2017. Hi-gain overdrive.		
2012-2017		$75	$100
Tentacle			
	2015-present. Analog octave up. Grandpa Cyclops		

MODEL YEAR	FEATURES	EXC. COND. LOW	HIGH
limited-edition version was made '16 in collaboration with visual artist and Devo co-founder Mark Mothersbaugh and the Akron Art Museum.			
2015-2021		$75	$100
2016	Grandpa Cyclops	$75	$120
Terminal			
	2014-2019. Fuzz.		
2014-2019		$75	$110
The Depths			
	2013-2017. Optical vibrato.		
2013-2017		$90	$140
The Grim Reefer			
	2014-2017. Fuzz pedal.		
2014-2017		$75	$100
The Warden			
	2013-present. Optical compression.		
2013-2021		$90	$140
Time Shadows			
	2020. Collaboration with EarthQuaker Devices, limited edition of 1,000 pedals.		
2020		$200	$330
Tone Job			
	2012-present. EQ and boost.		
2012-2021		$75	$100
Tone Reaper			
2009		$50	$100
Transmisser			
	2016-2019. Reverb.		
2016-2019		$125	$190
White Light			
2008		$150	$300
Zap Machine			
2010		$50	$100
Z-Drive			
	2015-2017. Overdrive built in collaboration with Dr. Z Amplification.		
2015-2017		$175	$220

EBS

1992-present. Bass and guitar effects built in Stockholm, Sweden by the EBS Sweden AB company. They also build bass amps.

Ecco-Fonic

1959-1968. The Ecco-Fonic was designed by Ray Stolle and sold from his radio and TV repair shop in Los Angeles. Theis first Ecco Ecco-Fonic was distributed by Fender in 1958-'59. Stolle sold the company to E.S. "Eddie" Tubin in late 1959-'60, who sold the company in 1961 to Milton Brucker. Starting in 1963, Fender offered a solidstate Ecco-Fonic designed by new-owner Bob Marks and Russ Allee and labeled as the Fender Echo.

Model 109

1959-1960. Tube-driven tape-echo unit, 2 control knobs, revised to 3 knobs, 1-piece top, gold housing.

1959	Brown case	$900	$1,500

Model 109-B

1960-1962. Tube-driven tape echo unit, 4 Control knobs, 2-piece top, gold housing.

1960-1962	Brown or black case	$400	$1,250

MODEL YEAR	FEATURES	EXC. COND. LOW	HIGH

Model 109-C
1961-1962. Tube-driven tape echo unit, multiple playback heads, black housing.

1961-1962	Black case	$400	$1,000

Echoplex
The Echoplex tape echo unit was invented around 1959 in Akron, Ohio, by Don Dixon and Mike Battle, who originally produced it in small numbers. Production was soon moved to Market Electronics in Cleveland, and those units were sold under the Maestro brand (see listings under Maestro). After Maestro dropped the Echoplex, it was marketed under the Market Electronics name from the late-'70s to the late-'80s (see listing under Market Electronics for '80s models). In '94, Gibson's Oberheim division introduced a rackmount unit called the Echoplex. In '01, it was relabeled as Gibson.

Echoplex
1959. Dixon- and Battle-built pre-Maestro production tube-driven tape echo. Black case.

1959		$900	$1,200

EchoSonic
2010s. Ray Butts of EchoSonic amp fame crafted a pioneering fuzz circuit that never went into production. Tim Masters of Florida built a limited run of stompboxes with the circuitry.

Ray-O-Fuzz
2010s. Metal housings in various colors with logo surrounded by lightning bolts. Attack and Volume controls plus footswitch.

2010s		$175	$250

Eden Analog
Guitar effects pedals built by Chris Sheppard and Robert Hafley in Pelham, Alabama, starting in 2004.

Effector 13
2002-2008. Guitar effects built by Devi Ever in Minneapolis, Minnesota. Located in Austin, Texas until mid-'04. Name changed to Devi Ever : Fx in '09.

Effectrode
1996-present. Effects pedals built in Corvallis, Oregon by Phil Taylor.

EFX
1980s. Brand name of the Los Angeles-based EFX Center; they also offered a direct box and a powered pedal box/board.

Switch Box B287
1984. Dual effects loop selector.

1984		$25	$35

EKO
1959-1985, 2000-present. In the '60s and '70s EKO offered effects made by EME and JEN Elettronica, which also made Vox effects.

Eleca
2004-present. Guitar effects pedals imported by Eleca International. They also offer guitars, mandolins and amps.

Electra
1970-1984, 2013-present. Guitar importer St. Louis Music offered Electra effects in the late '70s.

Chorus 504CH
Ca.1975-ca.1980.

1975-1980		$55	$75

Compressor 502C/602C
Ca.1975-ca.1980.

1975-1980		$45	$55

Distortion 500D
Ca.1976-ca.1980.

1976-1980		$55	$75

Flanger (stereo) 605F
Ca.1975-ca.1980.

1975-1980		$55	$75

Fuzz Wah
Ca.1975-ca.1980.

1975-1980		$75	$150

Pedal Drive 515AC
Ca.1976-ca.1980. Overdrive.

1976-1980		$40	$50

Phaser Model 501P
Ca.1976-ca.1980.

1976-1980		$50	$60

Phaser Model 875
Ca.1975-ca.1980.

1975-1980		$50	$60

Roto Phase I
1975-ca.1980. Small pocket phaser.

1975-1980		$70	$85

Roto Phase II
1975-ca.1980. Pedal phasor.

1975-1980		$80	$95

Electro-Harmonix
1968-1984, 1996-present. Founded by Mike Matthews in New York City, the company initially produced small plug-in boosters such as the LPB-1. In '71, they unveiled the awe-inspiring Big Muff Pi fuzz and dozens of innovative pedals followed. After closing in '84, Matthews again began producing reissues of many of his classic effects as well as new designs in '96.

10 Band Graphic Equalizer
1977-1981. Includes footswitch.

1977-1981		$60	$70

16-Second Digital Delay
Early-1980s, 2004-2008. An updated version was reissued in '04.

1980s	No foot controller	$500	$625
1980s	With foot controller	$675	$850
1990s		$325	$500
2004-2008		$275	$375

3 Phase Liner

1981		$50	$60

EarthQuaker Devices The Warden

EBS ValveDrive DI

Electra Phase 501

Christopher Wright

EFFECTS

E-H Attack/Decay
Jim Schreck

1974 E-H Big Muff PI
Suzie Williams

E-H Crying Tone
Jim Schreck

EFFECTS

MODEL YEAR	FEATURES	EXC. COND. LOW	HIGH
5X Junction Mixer			
1977-1981		$30	$40
Attack Equalizer			
1975-1981. Active EQ, a.k.a. "Knock Out."			
1975-1981		$150	$200
Attack/Decay			
1980-1981. Tape reverse simulator.			
1980-1981		$200	$225
Axis			
1969-1970s. Modified Mosrite Fuzzrite circuit.			
1969-1970s		$200	$500
Bad Stone Phase Shifter			
1975-1981.			
1975-1981	Three knobs	$200	$250
1975-1981	Two knobs, color switch	$175	$225
Bass Micro-Synthesizer			
1981-1984, 1999-present. Analog synthesizer sounds.			
1981-1984		$225	$300
1999-2021		$150	$175
Bassballs			
1978-1984, 1998-present. Bass envelope filter/ distortion.			
1978-1984		$200	$230
Big Muff Pi			
1971-1984. Sustain, floor unit, issued in 3 different looks, as described below.			
1970s	Black graphics, knobs in triangle pattern	$300	$490
1970s	Red/black graphics, 1/2" letters	$200	$450
1980s	Red/black graphics, 1" letters	$125	$275
Big Muff Pi (Reissue)			
1996-present. Originally made in Russia, but currently both Russian- and U.S.-made versions are available.			
1996-2021	Russian-made	$40	$65
Big Muff Sovtek			
2000s. Big Muff Pi, Electro Harmonix, and Sovtek logos on an olive green case. Sold in a wooden box.			
2000s	With wooden box	$150	$300
Black Finger Compressor Sustainer			
1977, 2003-2019. Original has 3 knobs in triangle pattern.			
1977		$125	$400
2003-2019		$75	$150
Clap Track			
1980-1984. Drum effect.			
1980-1984		$40	$60
Clone Theory			
1977-1981. Chorus effect, The Clone Theory logo.			
1977-1981		$150	$175
Crash Pad			
1980-1984. Percussion synth.			
1980-1984		$40	$60
Crying Tone Pedal			
1976-1978. Wah-wah.			
1976-1978		$175	$225
Deluxe Big Muff Pi			
1978-1981. Sustain, AC version of Big Muff Pi, includes a complete Soul Preacher unit.			
1978-1981	Red graphics	$125	$200

MODEL YEAR	FEATURES	EXC. COND. LOW	HIGH
Deluxe Electric Mistress Flanger			
1977-1983, 1996-present. AC.			
1977-1979		$150	$250
1980-1983		$125	$175
Deluxe Memory Man			
1977-1983, 1996-present. Echo and delay, featured 4 knobs '77-'78, from '79-'83 it has 5 knobs and added vibrato and chorus.			
1977-1978	4 knobs	$250	$540
1979-1983	5 knobs	$200	$360
1996-2021		$150	$165
Deluxe Octave Multiplexer			
1977-1981		$200	$250
Digital Delay/Chorus			
1981-1984. With digital chorus.			
1981-1984		$250	$300
Digital Rhythm Matrix DRM-15			
1981-1984		$225	$250
Digital Rhythm Matrix DRM-16			
1979-1983		$225	$250
Digital Rhythm Matrix DRM-32			
1981-1984		$225	$250
Doctor Q Envelope Follower			
1976-1983, 2001-2020. For bass or guitar.			
1976-1983		$100	$220
2001-2020		$30	$60
Domino Theory			
1981. Sound sensitive light tube.			
1981		$50	$100
Echo 600			
1981		$175	$225
Echoflanger			
1977-1982. Flange, slapback, chorus, filter.			
1977-1982		$200	$250
Electric Mistress Flanger			
1976-1979		$275	$475
1980-1984		$175	$240
Electronic Metronome			
1978-1980		$25	$30
Frequency Analyzer			
1977-1984, 2001-present. Ring modulator.			
1977-1984		$200	$250
Full Double Tracking Effect			
1978-1981. Doubling, slapback.			
1978-1981		$100	$150
Fuzz Wah			
Introduced around 1974.			
1970s		$175	$225
Golden Throat			
1977-1984		$500	$800
Golden Throat Deluxe			
1977-1979. Deluxe has a built-in monitor amp.			
1977-1979		$600	$800
Golden Throat II			
1978-1981		$150	$300
Guitar Synthesizer			
1981. Sold for $1,495 in May '81.			
1981		$225	$300
Hog's Foot Bass Booster			
1977-1980		$70	$90

MODEL YEAR FEATURES	EXC. COND. LOW	HIGH
Holy Grail		
2002-present. Digital reverb.		
2002-2021	$75	$90
Hot Foot		
1977-1978. Rocker pedal turns knob of other E-H effects, gold case, red graphics.		
1977-1978	$100	$200
Hot Tubes		
1978-1984, 2001-2007. Tube distortion.		
1978-1984	$125	$200
Linear Power Booster LPB-1		
1968-1983.		
1976-1979	$55	$80
1980-1983	$45	$75
Linear Power Booster LPB-2		
Ca.1968-1983.		
1968-1983	$90	$100
Little Big Muff Pi		
1976-1980, 2006-present. Sustain, 1-knob floor unit.		
1976-1980	$140	$175
2006-2021	$90	$125
Little Muff Pi		
1971-1975. Sustain, 1-knob floor unit, issued in 2 styles; blue or red graphics.		
1971-1975	$250	$360
Memory Man/Stereo Memory Man		
1976-1984, 1999-present. Analog delay, newer version in stereo.		
1976-1979	$200	$275
1980-1984	$125	$155
Micro Synthesizer		
1978-1984, 1998-present. Mini keyboard phaser.		
1978-1979	$225	$250
1978-1984	$225	$250
1998-2021	$150	$170
Mini Q-Tron/Micro Q-Tron		
2002-present. Battery-operated smaller version of Q-Tron envelope follower, changed to identical effect in smaller box Micro in '06.		
2002-2021	$40	$45
Mini-Mixer		
1978-1981. Mini mic mixer, reissued in '01.		
1978-1981	$30	$40
MiniSynthesizer		
1981-1983. Mini keyboard with phaser.		
1981-1983	$300	$400
MiniSynthesizer With Echo		
1981		
1981	$375	$500
Mole Bass Booster		
1968-1978.		
1968-1969	$60	$80
1970-1978	$40	$60
Muff Fuzz		
1976-1983. Fuzz and line boost, silver case with orange lettering.		
1976-1983	$85	$100
Muff Fuzz Crying Tone		
1977-1978. Fuzz, wah.		
1977-1978	$150	$250
Octave Multiplexer Floor Unit		
1976-1980	$175	$275

MODEL YEAR FEATURES	EXC. COND. LOW	HIGH
Octave Multiplexer Pedal		
1976-1977, 2001-present.		
1976-1977	$150	$250
2001-2021	$40	$45
Panic Button		
1981. Siren sounds for drum.		
1981	$30	$40
Poly Chorus/Stereo Polychorus		
1981, 1999-2021. Same as Echoflanger.		
1981	$175	$300
1999-2021	$125	$150
Polyphase		
1979-1981. With envelope.		
1979-1981	$175	$225
Pulsar/Stereo Pulsar		
2004-present. Variable wave form tremolo.		
2004-2021	$45	$55
Pulse Modulator		
Ca.1968 -ca.1972. Triple tremolo.		
1968-1969	$250	$325
1970-1972	$200	$250
Q-Tron		
1997-2017. Envelope controlled filter.		
1997-2017	$125	$175
Q-Tron +		
1999-present. With added effects loop and Attack Response switch.		
1999-2021	$70	$80
Queen Triggered Wah		
1976-1978. Wah/Envelope Filter.		
1976-1978	$125	$150
Random Tone Generator RTG		
1981	$40	$60
Rhythm 12 (Rhythm Machine)		
1978	$75	$125
Rolling Thunder		
1980-1981. Percussion synth.		
1980-1981	$40	$50
Screaming Bird Treble Booster		
Ca.1968-1980. In-line unit.		
1968-1980	$75	$100
Screaming Tree Treble Booster		
1977-1981. Floor unit.		
1977-1981	$100	$150
Sequencer Drum		
1981. Drum effect.		
1981	$40	$50
Slapback Echo		
1977-1978. Stereo.		
1977-1978	$150	$200
Small Clone		
1983-1984, 1999-present. Analog chorus, depth and rate controls, purple face plate, white logo.		
1983-1984	$150	$200
1999-2021	$35	$40
Small Stone Phase Shifter		
1975-1984, 1996-present. Both Russian and U.S. reissues were made.		
1975-1979	$150	$225
1980-1984	$100	$175

E-H Digital Rhythm Matrix DRM-15

Jim Schreck

1978 E-H Linear Power Booster LPB-2

Rivington Guitars

E-H Small Clone

EFFECTS

To get the most from this book, be sure to read "Using *The Guide*" in the introduction.

E-H Soul Preacher
Jim Schreck

Electro-Harmonix Switch Blade
Jim Schreck

E-H Volume Pedal
Jim Schreck

MODEL YEAR FEATURES	EXC. COND. LOW	HIGH
Solid State Reverb		
1980s. Input, output, blend and feedback controls.		
1980s	$250	$500
Soul Food		
2000s	$45	$65
2000s JHS modded	$110	$160
Soul Preacher		
1977-1983, 2007-present. Compressor sustainer. Nano version for present.		
1977-1983	$100	$150
Space Drum/Super Space Drum		
1980-1981. Percussion synthesizer.		
1980-1981	$125	$175
Switch Blade		
1977-1983. A-B Box.		
1977-1983	$45	$55
Talking Pedal		
1977-1978. Creates vowel sounds.		
1977-1978	$350	$550
The Silencer		
1976-1981. Noise elimination.		
1976-1981	$60	$80
Tube Zipper		
2001-2018. Tube (2x12AX7) envelope follower.		
2001-2018	$100	$120
Vocoder		
1978-1981. Modulates voice with instrument.		
1978-1981 Rackmount	$425	$525
Volume Pedal		
1978-1981	$45	$65
Wiggler		
2002-2019. All-tube modulator including pitch vibrato and volume tremolo.		
2002-2019	$100	$110
Worm		
2002-present. Wah/Phaser.		
2002-2021	$55	$65
Y-Triggered Filter		
1976-1977	$140	$160
Zipper Envelope Follower		
1976-1978. The Tube Zipper was introduced in '01.		
1976-1978	$200	$300

Electrosonic Amplifiers

2002-2010. Amp builder Josh Corn also offers a preamp pedal, built in Boonville, Indiana.

Elektronika

1980s-1990s. Russian effects pedals by the Soviet Ministry of Electronic Industry.

	EXC. COND. LOW	HIGH
Compressor-Sustainer		
1980s	$50	$175
Equalizer E-02		
1980s	$50	$125
Fazer-2		
1980s	$50	$125
Flanger FL-01		
1980s	$50	$90
Flanger PE-05		
1980s	$50	$125

MODEL YEAR FEATURES	EXC. COND. LOW	HIGH
Jet-Phaser		
1980s	$150	$225
Synchro-Wah		
1980s	$50	$100
Volna		
1980s. Auto wah.		
1980s	$50	$100

Elk Gakki

Late-1960s. Japanese company Elk Gakki Co., Ltd. mainly made guitars and amps, but did offer effects as well.

	EXC. COND. LOW	HIGH
Big Muff Sustainer		
1970s. Electro-Harmonix Big Muff Pi copy.		
1970s	$50	$125

Elka

In the late '60s or early '70s, Italian organ and synthesizer company Elka-Orla (later just Elka) offered a few effects, likely made by JEN Elettronica (Vox, others).

EMMA Electronic

Line of guitar effects built in Denmark and distributed by Godlyke.

	EXC. COND. LOW	HIGH
ReezaFRATzitz RF-1/ReezaFRATzitz II		
2004-present. Overdrive and distortion, red case.		
2004-2021	$80	$95

Empress Effects

2005-present. Guitar effects pedals built by Steve Bragg and Jason Fee in Ottawa, Ontario.

EMS

1969-1979. Peter Zinnovieff's English synth company (Electronic Music Studios) also offered a guitar synthesizer. The company has reopened to work on original EMS gear.

eowave

2002-present. Effects built first in Paris and now in Burgundy, France by Marc Sirguy.

Epiphone

Over the years, Epiphone offered a variety of different effect lines. Epiphone pedals which are labeled G.A.S Guitar Audio System were offered from around 1988 to '91.

Pedals

Various models with years available.

		EXC. COND. LOW	HIGH
1988-1989	Chorus EP-CH-70	$35	$45
1988-1989	Delay EP-DE-80	$45	$60
1988-1991	Compressor EP-CO-20	$35	$40
1988-1991	Distortion EP-DI-10	$35	$45
1988-1991	Flanger EP-FL-60	$40	$55
1988-1991	Overdrive EP-OD-30	$35	$45

Rocco Tonexpressor

1937. Designed by steel-guitar ace Anthony Rocco, this pedal allows steel guitarists to adjust volume and tone with their foot.

	EXC. COND. LOW	HIGH
1937	$300	$500

MODEL YEAR	FEATURES	EXC. COND. LOW	HIGH

Ernie Ball

1972-present. The Ernie Ball company also builds Music Man instruments.

Volume Pedals

1977-present. Aluminum housing.

1977-2021		$35	$75

Euthymia Electronics

Line of guitar effects built by Erik Miller in Alameda, California.

Eventide

1971-present. This New Jersey electronics manufacturer has offered studio and rackmount effects since the late '70s. In '08 they added guitar effects pedals.

EXR

The EXR Corporation was located in Brighton, Michigan.

Projector

1983-ca.1984. Psychoacoustic enhancer pedal.

1983-1984		$65	$75

Projector SP III

1983-ca.1984. Psychoacoustic enhancer pedal, volume pedal/sound boost.

1983-1984		$65	$70

Farfisa

The organ company offered effects pedals in the 1960s. Their products were manufactured in Italy by the Italian Accordion Company and distributed by Chicago Musical Instruments.

Model VIP 345 Organ

Mid-1960s. Portable organ with Syntheslalom used in the rock and roll venue.

1960s		$500	$600

Repeater

1969		$100	$150

Sferasound

1960s. Vibrato pedal for a Farfisa Organ but it works well with the guitar, gray case.

1960s		$275	$375

Wah/Volume

1969		$100	$150

Fargen

1999-present. Guitar effects built in Sacramento, California by Benjamin Fargen. He also builds amps.

Fender

1946-present. Although Fender has flirted with effects since the 1950s (the volume/volume-tone pedal and the Ecco-Fonic), the company concentrated mainly on guitars and amps. Fender effects ranged from the sublime to the ridiculous, from the tube Reverb to the Dimension IV. In 2013 Fender added a line of pedals.

'63 Tube Reverb

1994-2017. Reissue spring/tube Reverb Units with various era cosmetics as listed below. Currently offered in brown or, since '09, in lacquered tweed.

1994	White (limited run)	$400	$600
1994-1997	Black	$350	$400
1994-1997	Blond	$375	$600
1994-1997	Tweed	$375	$450
1994-2008	Brown	$350	$500
2009-2017	Lacquered Tweed	$300	$375

Blender

1968-1977, 2005-2010. Battery-operated unit with fuzz, sustain, and octave controls.

1968-1969		$290	$410
1970-1977		$275	$350
2005-2010	Reissue	$125	$175

Contempo Organ

1967-1968. Portable organ, all solidstate, 61 keys including a 17-key bass section, catalog shows with red cover material.

1967-1968		$525	$550

Dimension IV

1968-1970. Multi-effects unit using an oil-filled drum.

1968-1970		$195	$300

Echo and Electronic Echo Chamber

1963-1968. Solidstate tape echo built by Ecco-Fonic, up to 400 ms of delay, rectangle box with 2 controls '63-'67, slanted front '67-'68.

1963-1967		$300	$500
1967-1968		$225	$350

Echo-Reverb

1966-1970. Solidstate, echo-reverb effect produced by rotating metal disk, black tolex, silver grille.

1966-1970		$300	$350

Fuzz-Wah

1968-1984, 2007-2011. Has Fuzz and Wah switches on sides of pedal '68-'73, has 3 switches above the pedal '74-'84. Newer version ('07-'11) has switches on sides.

1968-1973	Switches on side	$150	$225
1974-1984	Switches above	$100	$200
2007-2011	Switches on side	$80	$90

Phaser

1975-1977, 2007-2011. AC powered, reissued in '07.

1975-1977		$95	$175
2007-2011		$50	$80

Reverb Unit

1961-1966, 1975-1978. Fender used a wide variety of tolex coverings in the early-'60s as the coverings matched those on the amps. Initially, Fender used rough blond tolex, then rough brown tolex, followed by smooth white or black tolex.

1961	Blond tolex, Oxblood grille	$1,000	$1,450
1961	Brown tolex	$1,000	$1,250
1962	Blond tolex, Oxblood grille	$1,000	$1,400
1962	Brown tolex, Wheat grille	$800	$1,200
1963	Brown tolex	$800	$1,150
1963	Rough blond tolex	$800	$1,200
1963	Smooth white tolex	$800	$1,200
1964	Black tolex	$800	$1,200

1977 E-H Zipper
Rivington Guitars

Ernie Ball 500K Stereo Volume/Pan

Fender Electronic Echo Chamber

EFFECTS

1962 Fender Reverb Unit
- *Michael Alonz*

Fishman Fission Bass Powerchord

Foxx O.D. Machine
Rich Kislia

EFFECTS

MODEL YEAR	FEATURES	EXC. COND. LOW	HIGH
1964	Brown tolex, gold grille	$800	$1,100
1964	Smooth white tolex	$800	$1,100
1965-1966	Black tolex	$775	$1,000
1966	Solidstate, flat cabinet	$150	$225
1975-1978	Tube reverb reinstated	$500	$600

Vibratone
1967-1972. Fender's parent company at the time, CBS, bought Leslie in 1965, and Fender began offering a Leslie-type rotating-speaker-emulator as the Vibratone in 1967. Based on the Leslie Model 16 cabinet and made specifically for the guitar, it featured a single fixed 4-ohm 10-inch speaker fronted by a rotating drum. Designed to be powered by an external amp. 2-speed motor. Black tolex.

MODEL YEAR	FEATURES	EXC. COND. LOW	HIGH
1967-1968	Fender cast logo in upper left corner	$600	$850
1968-1972	Fender logo plate through center	$500	$850

Volume-Tone Pedal
1954-1984, 2007-2018. Swivel foot controller.

1954-1984		$90	$100
2007-2018		$35	$40

Fernandes
1970s. Japanese guitar and effects maker.
Funky-Filter FR-3F
1970s. Built by Univox for Fernandes.

1970s		$50	$100

Field Effects by Resonant Electronic Design
Guitar effects pedals, starting in 2010, built in Minneapolis, Minnesota by Wes Kuhnley and Peter Bregman. They also build the Resonant brand amps.

Fishman
2003-present. Larry Fishman of Andover, Massachusetts offers a line of acoustic guitar effects pedals. He also builds amps.

FJA Mods
In 2002, Jerry Pinnelli began building guitar effects in Central Square, New York. He added professional grade, production, guitar amps in '07, then relocates to Charlotte, North Carolina in '18 and takes a hiatus from building.

FlexiSound
FlexiSound products were made in Lancaster, Pennsylvania.
F. S. Clipper
1975-ca.1976. Distortion, plugged directly into guitar jack.

1975-1976		$55	$65

The Beefer
1975. Power booster, plugged directly into guitar jack.

1975		$40	$50

MODEL YEAR	FEATURES	EXC. COND. LOW	HIGH

Flip
Line of tube effects by Guyatone and distributed in the U.S. by Godlyke Distributing.
Tube Echo (TD-X)
2004-2017. Hybrid tube power delay pedal.

2004-2017		$90	$100

FM Acoustics
FM Acoustics pedals were made in Switzerland.
E-1 Pedal
1975. Volume, distortion, filter pedal.

1975		$70	$80

Foxx
Foxx pedals are readily identifiable by their fur-like covering. They slunk onto the scene in 1971 and were extinct by '78. Made by Hollywood's Ridinger Associates, their most notable product was the Tone Machine fuzz. Foxx-made pedals also have appeared under various brands such as G & G, Guild, Yamaha and Sears Roebuck, generally without fur. Since 2005, reissues of some of the classic Foxx pedals are being built in Provo, Utah.

Clean Machine
1974-1978		$250	$275

Down Machine
1971-1977. Bass wah.
1971-1977	Blue case	$225	$275

Foot Phaser
1975-1977, 2006.
1975-1977		$450	$675

Fuzz and Wa and Volume
1974-1978, 2006. Currently called Fuzz Wah Volume.
1974-1978		$225	$400

Guitar Synthesizer I
1975		$300	$350

Loud Machine
1970s. Volume pedal.
1970s		$30	$45

O.D. Machine
1972-ca.1975.
1972-1975		$150	$250

Phase III
1975-1978		$100	$150

Tone Machine
1971-1978, 2005. Fuzz with Octave, blue or black housing.
1971-1978		$250	$540

Wa and Volume
1971-1978		$200	$225

Wa Machine
1971-ca.1978.
1971-1978		$150	$200

Framptone
Founded by Peter Frampton in the year 2000, Framptone offers hand-made guitar effects.
3 Banger
2000-2021. Three-way amp switch box, white housing.
2000-2021		$200	$240

MODEL YEAR FEATURES	EXC. COND. LOW	HIGH
Amp Switcher		
2000-2021. A-B switch box, white housing.		
2000-2021	$80	$100
Talk Box		
2000-2021. Talk box, white housing, no control knobs, on-off footswitch.		
2000-2021	$160	$250

Frantone
1994-present. Effects and accessories hand built in New York City.

Fulltone
1991-2022. Effects based on some of the classics of the past and built in Los Angeles, California, by Michael Fuller.

MODEL YEAR FEATURES	EXC. COND. LOW	HIGH
DejàVibe		
1991-2004. Uni-Vibe-type pedal, later models have a Vintage/Modern switch. Stereo version also available.		
1991-1993 Mono, gold housing	$175	$225
1993-2004 Mono, black housing	$150	$175
DejàVibe 2		
1997-2018. Like DejàVibe but with built-in speed control. Stereo version also available.		
1997-2018 Mono	$200	$225
Distortion Pro		
2002-2008. Red case, volume and distortion knobs with four voicing controls.		
2002-2008	$125	$150
Fat Boost		
2001-2007. Clean boost, silver-sparkle case, volume and drive knobs.		
2001-2007	$125	$135
Full-Drive 2		
1995-present. Blue case, four control knobs.		
1995-2021	$120	$145
Mini-DejàVibe		
2004-2018. Uni-Vibe-type pedal, white housing, 3 Control knobs, stereo version also available.		
2004-2018 Mono	$125	$150
OCD		
1990s-present. Obsessive compulsive drive.		
1990s-2021	$90	$110
Octafuzz		
1996-2019. Copy of the Tycobrahe Octavia.		
1996-2019	$100	$135
Soul Bender		
1994-present. Volume, tone and dirt knobs.		
1994-2021	$100	$125
Supa-Trem		
1996-2019. Black case, white Supa-Trem logo, rate and mix controls.		
1996-2019	$100	$150
Supa-Trem2		
2000s. Yellow housing, 3 control knobs.		
2000s	$150	$200
Tube Tape Echo		
2000s. Echo-Plex-style echo unit, white case.		
2000s	$675	$800

MODEL YEAR FEATURES	EXC. COND. LOW	HIGH
Tube Tape Echo TTE		
2004-present. Echoplex-style tube-powered tape unit, different colored housings.		
2004-2021	$800	$1,200

Furman Sound
1993-present. Located in Petaluma, California, Furman makes audio and video signal processors and AC power conditioning products for music and other markets.

MODEL YEAR FEATURES	EXC. COND. LOW	HIGH
LC-2 Limiter Compressor		
1990s. Rackmount unit with a black suitcase and red knobs.		
1990s	$40	$50
PQ3 Parametric EQ		
1990s. Rackmount preamp and equalizer.		
1998-1999	$110	$150
PQ6 Parametric Stereo		
1990s	$135	$175
RV1 Reverb Rackmount		
1990s	$110	$150

Fxdoctor
2003-present. Joshua Zalegowski originally built his effects in Amherst, Massachusetts, and in 2005 moved to Boston.

Fxengineering
2002-present. Production and custom guitar effects built by Montez Aldridge in Raleigh, North Carolina.

G.M. Electronics
1960s. Based in Detroit, Michigan.

MODEL YEAR FEATURES	EXC. COND. LOW	HIGH
Dual Range Fuzz Up FD3-A		
1960s. Fuzz pedal combining 2 Gibson Maestro FZ-1 Fuzz Tone circuits.		
1960s	$100	$300
Fuzz Up FM3-B		
1960s. Clone of the Gibson Maestro FZ-1 Fuzz Tone.		
1960s	$100	$250

G.S. Wyllie
2000s. Glenn Wyllie built effects in North Carolina.

MODEL YEAR FEATURES	EXC. COND. LOW	HIGH
Moonrock		
2000s. Octave fuzz.		
2000s	$200	$400
NewMoon		
2000s. Updated version of Moonrock octave fuzz.		
2000s	$200	$400
Ozo		
2000s. Ring modulator.		
2000s	$200	$400
X-Fuzz		
2000s. High-gain fuzz.		
2000s	$200	$400

G2D
1999-present. David Manning and Grant Wills build their guitar effects pedals in Auckland, New Zealand.

Fulltone Supa-Trem ST-1

Fulltone Tube Tape Echo TTE

Fxdoctor Ray Gun Phaser

EFFECTS

George Dennis Elite Wah

Gig-FX VOD

Gizmoaudio Sawmill

MODEL		EXC. COND.	
YEAR	FEATURES	LOW	HIGH

Garcia
Guitar effects built by Matthew Garcia in Myrtle Beach, South Carolina, starting in 2004. He also built amps.

Geek MacDaddy
See listing under The Original Geek.

George Dennis
1991-present. Founded by George Burgerstein, original products were a line of effects pedals. In '96 they added a line of tube amps. The company is located in Prague, Czech Republic.

Gibson
Gibson did offer a few effects bearing their own name, but most were sold under the Maestro name (see that listing).

Echoplex Digital Pro Plus
1994-2010. Rackmount unit with digital recording, sampling and digital delay. Labeled as just Echoplex until '01 when Gibson name added.

1994-2010		$425	$650

GA-3RV Reverb Unit
1964-1967. Small, compact, spring reverb unit, black tolex, gray grille.

1964-1967		$325	$400

GA-4RE Reverb-Echo Unit
1964-1967. Small, compact, lightweight accessory reverb-echo unit that produces complete reverberation and authentic echo, utilizes Gibson's "electronic memory" system for both reverb and echo, black tolex, gray grille.

1964-1967		$375	$550

Gig-FX
2004-present. Founder Jeff Purchon of Waltham, Massachusetts, imports guitar effects pedals built at his company-owned factory in Shenzhen, China.

Gizmo, Inc.
Ca.1980. Short-lived company that grew out of the ashes of Musitronics' attempt to make the Gizomotron. See Mu-Tron.

Gizmoaudio
2009-present. Guitar effects built by Charles Luke in Cumming, Georgia.

Gnome Amplifiers
Guitar effects pedals built by Dan Munro in Olympia, Washington. He started in 2008 and also builds amps.

Godbout
Godbout sold a variety of effects do-it-yourself kits in the 1970s, which are difficult to value because quality depends on skills of builder.

Effects Kits

1970s		$20	$30

MODEL		EXC. COND.	
YEAR	FEATURES	LOW	HIGH

Godley Crème
1978-1980. Kevin Godley and Lol Crème, members of the band 10cc, developed the Gizmotron, which mounted on the face of a bass or guitar and continuously strummed the strings to give a bowed-string effect. The device was built by Musitronics of New Jersey, which built the MuTron III and other effects.

Gizmotron
1978-1980. A "ultimate sustain" mechanical add-on to guitar or bass bridges with rotating plectrums.

1978-1980		$300	$500

Goodrich Sound
1970s-present. Originally located in Michigan, and currently in Dublin, Georgia, Goodrich currently offers volume pedals and a line boost.

Match Box Line Boost
Early-1980s-2011. Small rectangular line buffer/driver.

1980s-2011		$45	$55

Volume Pedal 6122
Late-1970s-1980s. Uses a potentiometer.

1970s		$45	$55

Volume Pedal 6400ST
Late-1970s-1980s. Stereo pedal, using photocells.

1970s		$45	$55

Volume Pedal 6402
Late-1970s-1980s. Uses photocell.

1970s		$45	$55

Goran Custom Guitars
1998-present. Luthier Goran Djuric from Belgrade, Serbia also offers guitar pedals.

Goya
1960s. Goya Music sold effects under the brands Goya, Applied, Nomad, Conrad and maybe more.

Fury Box

1960s		$75	$150

Greer Amplification
1999-present. Guitar stomp box effects built by Nick Greer in Athens, Georgia. He also builds amps.

Gretsch
Gretsch has offered a limited line of effects from time to time.

Controfuzz
Mid-1970s. Distortion.

1970s		$150	$225

Deluxe Reverb Unit Model 6149
1963-1969. Similar to Gibson's GA-1 introduced around the same time.

1963-1969		$475	$700

Expandafuzz
Mid-1970s. Distortion.

1970s		$200	$375

Reverb Unit Model 6144 Preamp Reverb
1963-1967. Approximately 17 watts, preamp functionality, no speaker.

1963-1967		$450	$600

MODEL		EXC. COND.	
YEAR	FEATURES	LOW	HIGH

Tremofect
Mid-1970s. Tremolo effect, 3-band EQ, speed, effect, bass, total, and treble knobs.

1970s		$225	$300

Guild
Guild marketed effects made by Binson, Electro-Harmonix, Foxx, WEM and Applied in the 1960s and '70s.

Copicat
1960s-1979. Echo.

1970s		$300	$450

DE-20 Auto-Rhythm Unit
1971-1974. 50 watt rhythm accompaniment unit. Included 20 rhythms and a separate instrument channel with its own volume control. 1x12" plus tweeter.

1971-1974		$200	$300

Echorec (by Binson)
Ca.1960-1979. Stripped-down version of the Binson Echorec.

1960s		$675	$875

Foxey Lady Fuzz
1968-1977. Distortion, sustain.

1968-1975	2 knobs, made by E-H	$200	$550
1976-1977	3 knobs in row, same as Big Muff	$250	$550

Fuzz Wah FW-3
1975-ca.1979. Distortion, volume, wah, made by Foxx.

1970s		$80	$150

HH Echo Unit
1976-ca.1979.

1970s		$200	$300

VW-1
1975-ca.1979. Volume, wah, made by Foxx.

1970s		$200	$250

Guyatone (Tokyo Sound Company)
1930s-present. Founded by Mitsuo Matsuki, maker of guitars, amps and effects. Imported stomp boxes, tape echo units and outboard reverb units distributed by Godlyke Distributing.

Bazz Box FS-1
1960s. Vox V828 Tone Bender copy.

1960s		$75	$150

Bazz Box FS-2
1960s. Univox Super-Fuzz copy.

1960s		$125	$300

Crazy-Face
1970s. Dallas-Arbiter Fuzz Face copy.

1970s		$100	$250

Sustainer FS-6
1970s. Circular Fuzz Face-like housing.

1970s		$75	$200

Wah-Fuzz FS-5

1970s		$50	$100

HAO
Line of guitar effects built in Japan by J.E.S. International, distributed in the U.S. by Godlyke.

Harden Engineering
2006-present. Distortion/boost guitar effects pedals built by William Harden in Chicago, Illinois. He also builds guitars.

Heathkit
1960s. These were sold as do-it-yourself kits and are difficult to value because quality depends on skills of builder.

TA-28 Distortion Booster
1960s. Fuzz assembly kit, heavy '60s super fuzz, case-by-case quality depending on the builder.

1960s		$140	$150

Heavy Metal Products
Mid-1970s. From Alto Loma, California, products for the heavy metal guitarist.

Raunchbox Fuzz

1975-1976		$75	$100

Switchbox
1975-1976. A/B box.

1975-1976		$25	$35

Heet Sound Products
1974-present. The E Bow concept goes back to '67, but a hand-held model wasn't available until '74. Made in Los Angeles, California.

E Bow
1974-1979, 1985-1987, 1994-present. The Energy Bow, hand-held electro-magnetic string driver.

1974-1979		$50	$60

E Bow for Pedal Steels
1979. Hand-held electro-magnetic string driver.

1979		$35	$55

Heil Sound
1960-present. Founded by Bob Heil, Marissa, Illinois. Created the talk box technology as popularized by Joe Walsh and Peter Frampton. In the '60s and '70s Heil was dedicated to innovative products for the music industry. In the late-'70s, innovative creations were more in the amateur radio market, and by the '90s Heil's focus was on the home theater market. The Heil Sound Talkbox was reissued by Jim Dunlop USA in '89.

Talk Box
1976-ca.1980, 1989-present. Reissued by Dunlop.

1976-1980		$100	$160
1989-1999		$60	$85
2000-2021		$60	$80

Henretta Engineering
2009-present. Analog guitar effects built by Kevin Henretta first in Chicago, Illinois and presently Saint Paul, Minnesota.

Hermida Audio
2003-present. Alfonso Hermida builds his guitar effects in Miramar, Florida.

Guild Tri-Oct
Mary-Anne Hammer

1970s Guyatone PS-104 Crossover Auto Wah
Rivington Guitars

Henretta Engineering The Valley Reverb

EFFECTS

EFFECTS

HomeBrew Electronics Psilocybe
Keith Myers

Ibanez Analog Delay AD9
Rivington Guitars

*1980 Ibanez Analog
Delay AD80*
Bernunzio Uptown Music

MODEL YEAR	FEATURES	EXC. COND. LOW	HIGH

High Gain
See listing under Dunlop.

Hohner
Hohner offered effects in the late-1970s.
Dirty Booster
1977-ca.1978. Distortion.

1977-1978		$55	$65

Dirty Wah Wah'er
1977-ca.1978. Adds distortion.

1977-1978		$65	$75

Fuzz Wah
1970s. Morley-like volume pedal with volume knob and fuzz knob, switch for soft or hard fuzz, gray box with black foot pedal.

1970s		$65	$75

Multi-Exciter
1977-ca.1978. Volume, wah, surf, tornado, siren.

1977-1978		$60	$70

Tape Echo/Echo Plus
1970s. Black alligator suitcase.

1970s		$200	$275

Tri-Booster
1977-ca.1978. Distortion, sustain.

1977-1978		$55	$65

Vari-Phaser
1977-ca.1978.

1977-1978		$55	$65

Vol-Kicker Volume Pedal
1977-ca.1978.

1977-1978		$30	$40

Wah-Wah'er
1977-ca.1978. Wah, volume.

1977-1978		$55	$65

HomeBrew Electronics
2001-present. Stomp box effects hand made by Joel and Andrea Weaver in Glendale, Arizona.

Honey
1967-1969. Honey Company Ltd. Was formed by ex-Teisco workers after that firm was acquired by Kawai. Honey launched several effects designed by engineer Fumio Mieda, before going bankrupt in March, '69. The company was reborn as Shin-ei and many of its designs continued production in various forms; see Shin-ei for more.
Baby Crying
1960s. Univox Super-Fuzz copy.

1960s		$125	$300

Psychedelic Machine
1967-1969. Amp head-sized effect with numerous controls.

1967-1969		$750	$1,100

Special Fuzz

1967-1970s		$500	$750

Vibra Chorus
1967-1969. Original version of the Uni-Vibe, which Shin-ei would produce after Honey went bankrupt.

1967-1969		$1,500	$3,000

MODEL YEAR	FEATURES	EXC. COND. LOW	HIGH

Hughes & Kettner
1985-present. Hughes & Kettner builds a line of tube-driven guitar effects made in Germany. They also build amps and cabinets.

Ibanez
1932-present. Ibanez effects were introduced ca. 1974, and were manufactured by Japan's Maxon Electronics. Although results were mixed at first, a more uniform and modern product line, including the now legendary Tube Screamer, built Ibanez's reputation for quality. They continue to produce a wide range of effects.
60s Fuzz FZ5 (SoundTank)
1991-1992, 1996-1998. Fuzz with level, tone and distortion controls, black plastic case, green label.

1990s		$25	$30

7th Heaven SH7 (Tone-Lok)
2000-2004. Lo, high, drive and level controls, gray-silver case, blue-green label.

2000-2004		$20	$30

Acoustic Effects PT4
1993-1998. Acoustic guitar multi-effect with compressor/limiter, tone shaper, stereo chorus, digital reverb, with power supply.

1993-1998		$75	$100

Analog Delay AD9
1982-1984. 3 control analog delay, Hot Pink metal case.

1982-1984		$200	$275

Analog Delay AD80
1980-1981. Pink case.

1980-1981		$200	$275

Analog Delay AD99
1996-1998. Reissue, 3 control knobs and on/off switch, winged-hand logo, black case.

1996-1998		$125	$150

Analog Delay AD100 (Table Unit)
1981-1983. Stand-alone table/studio unit (not rack mount) with power cord.

1981-1983		$200	$250

Analog Delay 202 (Rack Mount)
1981-1983. Rack mount with delay, doubling, flanger, stereo chorus, dual inputs with tone and level.

1981-1983		$200	$300

Auto Filter AF9
1982-1984. Replaces AF201 model.

1982-1984		$150	$200

Auto Filter AF201
1981. Two min-max sliders, 3 mode toggle switches, orange metal case.

1981		$175	$200

Auto Wah AW5 (SoundTank)
1994-1999. Plastic case SoundTank series.

1994-1999		$30	$40

Auto Wah AW7 (Tone-Lok)
2000-2010. Silver case.

2000-2010		$20	$30

Bass Compressor BP10

1986-1991		$70	$80

MODEL YEAR	FEATURES	EXC. COND. LOW	HIGH

Bi-Mode Chorus BC9
1984. Dual channel for 2 independent speed and width settings.

1984		$75	$100

Chorus CS-505
1980-1981. Speed and depth controls, gray-blue case, stereo or mono input, battery or external power option.

| 1980-1981 | | $200 | $250 |

Chorus Flanger CF7 (Tone-Lok)
1999-2010. Speed, depth, delay, regeneration controls, mode and crazy switches.

| 1999-2010 | | $35 | $55 |

Classic Flange FL99
1997-1999. Analog reissue, silver metal case, winged-hand artwork, 4 controls, 2 footswitch buttons.

| 1997-1999 | | $90 | $110 |

Classic Phase PH99
1995-1999. Analog reissue, silver metal case, winged-hand artwork, speed, depth, feedback, effect level controls, intense and bypass footswitches.

| 1995-1999 | | $90 | $110 |

Compressor CP5 (SoundTank)
| 1991-1998 | | $20 | $30 |

Compressor CP10
| 1986-1992 | | $75 | $80 |

Compressor CP830
| 1975-1979 | | $100 | $125 |

Compressor II CP835
| 1980-1981 | | $100 | $125 |

Compressor Limiter CP9
| 1982-1984 | | $100 | $125 |

Delay Champ CD10
1986-1989. Red case, 3 knobs.

| 1986-1989 | | $125 | $150 |

Delay Echo DE7 (Tone-Lok)
1999-2010. Stereo delay/echo.

| 1999-2010 | | $40 | $80 |

Delay Harmonizer DM1000
1983-1984. Rack mount, with chorus, 9 control knobs.

| 1983-1984 | | $175 | $225 |

Delay III DDL20 Digital Delay
1988-1989. Filtering, doubling, slap back, echo S, echo M, echo L, Seafoam Green coloring on pedal.

| 1988-1989 | | $100 | $125 |

Delay PDD1 (DPC Series)
1988-1989. Programmable Digital Delay (PDD) with display screen.

| 1988-1989 | | $125 | $150 |

Digital Chorus DSC10
1990-1992. 3 control knobs and slider selection toggle.

| 1990-1992 | | $75 | $100 |

Digital Delay DL5 (SoundTank)
| 1991-1998 | | $35 | $45 |

Digital Delay DL10
1989-1992. Digital Delay made in Japan, blue case, 3 green control knobs, stompbox.

| 1989-1992 | | $100 | $125 |

Distortion Charger DS10
| 1986-1989 | | $70 | $90 |

Distortion DS7 (Tone-Lok)
2000-2010. Drive, tone, and level controls.

| 2000-2010 | | $40 | $45 |

Dual Chorus CCL
| 1990s | | $60 | $100 |

Echo Machine EM5 (SoundTank)
1996-1998. Simulates tape echo.

| 1996-1998 | | $45 | $95 |

Fat Cat Distortion FC10
1987-1989. 3-knob pedal with distortion, tone, and level controls.

| 1987-1989 | | $50 | $105 |

Flanger FFL5 (Master Series)
1984-1985. Speed, regeneration, width, D-time controls, battery or adapter option.

| 1984-1985 | | $70 | $90 |

Flanger FL5 (SoundTank)
| 1991-1998 | | $25 | $35 |

Flanger FL9
1982-1984. Yellow case.

| 1982-1984 | | $100 | $150 |

Flanger FL301
1979-1982. Mini flanger, 3 knobs, called the FL-301 DX in late '81-'82.

| 1979-1982 | | $100 | $125 |

Flanger FL305
1976-1979. Five knobs.

| 1976-1979 | | $100 | $125 |

Flying Pan FP777
1976-1979. Auto pan/phase shifter, 4 control knobs, phase on/off button, pan on/off button, silver metal case with blue trim and Flying Pan winged-hand logo.

| 1976-1979 | | $575 | $725 |

Flying Pan FP777 Reissue
| 2007 | 777 made | $275 | $350 |

Fuzz FZ7 (Tone-Lok)
2000-2010. Drive, tone and level controls, gray-silver case, blue-green FZ7 label.

| 2000-2010 | | $45 | $50 |

Graphic Bass EQ BE10
1986-1992. Later labeled as the BEQ10.

| 1986-1992 | | $60 | $80 |

Graphic EQ GE9
1982-1984. Six EQ sliders, 1 overall volume slider, turquoise blue case.

| 1982-1984 | | $60 | $80 |

Graphic EQ GE10
1986-1992. Eight sliders.

| 1986-1992 | | $60 | $80 |

Graphic Equalizer GE601 (808 Series)
1980-1981. 7-slider EQ, aqua blue metal case.

| 1980-1981 | | $75 | $100 |

Guitar Multi-Processor PT5
1993-1997. Floor unit, programmable with 25 presets and 25 user presets, effects include distortion, chorus, flanger, etc, green case.

| 1993-1997 | | $100 | $125 |

Ibanez Auto Wah AW7

1983 Ibanez Compressor Limiter CP9
Mark Mondahl

1982 Ibanez Flanger FL301-DX
Bernunzio Uptown Music

EFFECTS

1975 Ibanez Overdrive OD850
Rivington Guitars

1984 Ibanez Phaser PT9
Rivington Guitars

Ibanez Stereo Chorus CS9
Keith Myers

MODEL YEAR / FEATURES	EXC. COND. LOW	HIGH
LA Metal LM7		
1988-1989. Silver case.		
1988-1989	$55	$65
LoFi LF7 (Tone-Lok)		
2000-2010. Filter, 4 knobs.		
2000-2010	$20	$30
Metal Charger MS10		
1986-1992. Distortion, level, attack, punch and edge control knobs, green case.		
1986-1992	$45	$55
Metal Screamer MSL		
1985. 3 control knobs.		
1985	$55	$65
Modern Fusion MF5 (SoundTank)		
1990-1991. Level, tone and distortion controls.		
1990-1991	$45	$50
Modulation Delay DM500		
1983-1984. Rack mount.		
1983-1984	$75	$100
Modulation Delay DM1000		
1983-1984. Rack mount with delay, reverb, modulation.		
1983-1984	$100	$125
Modulation Delay PDM1		
1988-1989. Programmable Digital Modulation pedal.		
1988-1989	$100	$125
Mostortion MT10		
1990-1992. Mos-FET circuit distortion pedal, 5 control knobs, green case.		
1990-1992	$50	$60
Multi-Effect PUE5/PUE5 Tube (Floor Unit)		
1990-1993. Yellow version has tube, blue one does not. Also available in PUE5B bass version.		
1990-1993 Tube	$350	$450
Multi-Effect UE300 (Floor Unit)		
1983-1984. Floor unit, 4 footswitches for super metal, digital delay, digital stereo chorus, and master power, 3 delay modes.		
1983-1984	$275	$350
Multi-Effect UE300B (Floor Unit)		
1983-1984. Floor unit for bass.		
1983-1984	$275	$350
Multi-Effect UE400 (Rackmount)		
1980-1984. Rack mount with foot switch.		
1980-1984	$300	$375
Multi-Effect UE405 (Rackmount)		
1981-1984. Rack mount with analog delay, parametric EQ, compressor/limiter, stereo chorus and loop.		
1981-1984	$300	$375
Noise Buster NB10		
1988-1989. Eliminates 60-cycle hum and other outside signals, metal case.		
1988-1989	$70	$75
Overdrive OD850		
1975-1979	$275	$400
Overdrive II OD855		
1977-1979. Distortion, tone, and level controls, yellow/green case, large Overdrive II logo.		
1977-1979	$300	$400

MODEL YEAR / FEATURES	EXC. COND. LOW	HIGH
Pan Delay DPL10		
1990-1992. Royal Blue case, 3 green control knobs.		
1990-1992	$95	$125
Parametric EQ PQ9		
1982-1984	$125	$175
Parametric EQ PQ401		
1981. 3 sliders, dial-in knob, light aqua blue case.		
1981	$125	$175
Phase Tone PT909		
1979-1982. Blue box, 3 knobs, early models with flat case (logo at bottom or later in the middle) or later wedge case.		
1979-1982	$140	$150
Phase Tone PT999		
1975-1979. Script logo, 1 knob, round footswitch, becomes PT-909.		
1975-1979	$125	$150
Phase Tone PT1000		
1974-1975. Morley-style pedal phase, light blue case, early model of Phase Tone.		
1974-1975	$200	$300
Phase Tone II PT707		
1976-1979. Blue box, script logo for first 2 years.		
1976-1979	$100	$130
Phaser PH5 (SoundTank)		
1991-1998	$20	$30
Phaser PH7 (Tone-Lok)		
1999-2010. Speed, depth, feedback and level controls.		
1999-2010	$35	$40
Phaser PT9		
1982-1984. Three control knobs, red case.		
1982-1984	$75	$100
Powerlead PL5 (SoundTank)		
1991-1998. Metal case '91, plastic case '91-'98.		
1991 Metal	$25	$40
1991-1998 Plastic	$15	$20
Renometer		
1976-1979. 5-band equalizer with preamp.		
1976-1979	$75	$100
Rotary Chorus RC99		
1996-1999. Black or silver cases available, requires power pack and does not use a battery.		
1996-1999 Black case	$100	$125
Session Man SS10		
1988-1989. Distortion, chorus.		
1988-1989	$70	$80
Session Man II SS20		
1988-1989. 4 controls plus toggle, light pink-purple case.		
1988-1989	$70	$80
Slam Punk SP5 (SoundTank)		
1996-1999	$35	$40
Smash Box SM7 (Tone-Lok)		
2000-2010	$30	$35
Sonic Distortion SD9		
1982-1984	$75	$100
Standard Fuzz (No. 59)		
1974-1979. Two buttons (fuzz on/off and tone change).		
1974-1979	$175	$200

MODEL YEAR	FEATURES	EXC. COND. LOW	HIGH
Stereo Box ST800			
1975-1979. One input, 2 outputs for panning, small yellow case.			
1975-1979		$175	$225
Stereo Chorus CS9			
1982-1984		$75	$100
Stereo Chorus CSL (Master Series)			
1985-1986		$70	$90
Super Chorus CS5 (SoundTank)			
1991-1998		$20	$30
Super Metal SM9			
1984. Distortion.			
1984		$75	$95
Super Stereo Chorus SC10			
1986-1992		$75	$100
Super Tube Screamer ST9			
1984-1985. 4 knobs, light green metal case.			
1984-1985		$225	$300
Super Tube STL			
1985		$75	$95
Swell Flanger SF10			
1986-1992. Speed, regeneration, width and time controls, yellow case.			
1986-1992		$55	$100
Trashmetal TM5 (SoundTank)			
1990-1998. Tone and distortion pedal, 3 editions (1st edition, 2nd edition metal case, 2nd edition plastic case).			
1990-1998		$15	$20
Tremolo Pedal TL5 (SoundTank)			
1995-1998		$45	$95
Tube King TK999			
1994-1995. Has a 12AX7 tube and 3-band equalizer.			
1994-1995	Includes power pack	$125	$200
Tube King TK999US			
1996-1998. Has a 12AX7 tube and 3-band equalizer, does not have the noise switch of original TK999. Made in the U.S.			
1996-1998	Includes power pack	$125	$200
Tube Screamer TS5 (SoundTank)			
1991-1998		$20	$25
Tube Screamer TS7 (Tone-Lok)			
1999-2010. 3 control knobs.			
1999-2010		$30	$35
Tube Screamer TS9			
1982-1984, 1993-present. Reissued in '93.			
1982-1984		$300	$700
1993-2021		$75	$125
1993-2021	AnalogMan modded	$100	$160
1993-2021	Keeley modded	$120	$200
Tube Screamer Classic TS10			
1986-1993		$175	$225
Tube Screamer TS808			
1980-1982, 2004-present. Reissued in '04.			
1980-1982	Original	$600	$1,300
2004-2021	Reissue	$75	$120
Turbo Tube Screamer TS9DX			
1998-present. Tube Screamer circuit with added 3 settings for low-end.			
1998-2021		$70	$85

MODEL YEAR	FEATURES	EXC. COND. LOW	HIGH
Twin Cam Chorus TC10			
1986-1989. Four control knobs, light blue case.			
1986-1989		$75	$100
Virtual Amp VA3 (floor unit)			
1995-1998. Digital effects processor.			
1995-1998		$55	$75
VL10			
1987-1997. Stereo volume pedal.			
1987-1997		$50	$75
Wah Fuzz Standard (Model 58)			
1974-1981. Fuzz tone change toggle, fuzz on toggle, fuzz depth control, balance control, wah volume pedal with circular friction pads on footpedal.			
1974-1981		$225	$300
Wah WH10			
1988-1997		$50	$75

Ilitch Electronics

2003-present. Ilitch Chiliachki builds his effects in Camarillo, California.

Indy Guitarist

See listing under Wampler Pedals.

InterFax Electronics

Mid-1970s-1980s. Started by Ed Giese, located in Milwaukee, Wisconsin.

HP-1 Harmonic Percolator

Mid-1970s. Distortion/fuzz unit, harmonics and balance sliders.

1970s		$175	$300

Intersound

1970s-1980s. Intersound, Inc. was located in Boulder, Colorado and was a division of Electro-Voice.

Reverb-Equalizer R100F

1977-1979. Reverb and 4-band EQ, fader.

1977-1979		$75	$100

J. Everman

Analog guitar effects built by Justin J. Everman in Richardson, Texas, starting in 2000.

Jack Deville Electronics

2008-present. Production/custom, guitar effects built in Portland, Oregon by Jack Deville.

Jacques

One-of-a-kind handmade stomp boxes and production models made in France.

JAM Pedals

2007-present. Pedals built by Jannis Anastasakis Marinos of Athens, Greece.

Black Muck

2017-2018. Fuzz distortion.

2017-2018		$190	$240

Boomster

2007-2019. Silicon clean boost.

2007-2019		$75	$100

1984 Ibanez Super Metal SM9
Mark Mondahl

Ibanez Tube Screamer TS9

EFFECTS

JAM Pedals Delay Llama

JAM Pedals LucyDreamer Supreme

JAM Pedals Ripply Fall

Jen Variophaser
Niclas Löfgren

MODEL		EXC. COND.	
YEAR	FEATURES	LOW	HIGH
Boomster Mini			
2017-present. Silicon clean boost.			
2017-2021		$50	$100
DanComp			
2007-2015. Compressor based on the Dan Armstrong Orange Squeezer compressor circuit.			
2007-2015		$200	$220
Delay Llama			
2007-present. Analog delay.			
2007-2021		$150	$200
Delay Llama Supreme			
2014-2019. Analog delay with tap tempo modulation.			
2014-2019		$275	$325
Delay Llama+			
2009-2019. Analog delay with hold function.			
2009-2019		$150	$200
Dyna-ssoR			
2007-present. Compression/sustainer.			
2007-2021		$140	$175
Fuzz Phase			
2007-2018. Germanium fuzz.			
2007-2018		$200	$240
LucyDreamer Supreme			
2017-present. Overdrive/boost.			
2017-2021		$180	$210
Rattler			
2008-present. Distortion.			
2008-2021		$140	$175
Rattler+			
2008-2018. Distortion with low-gain stage.			
2008-2018		$175	$200
Red Muck			
2008-2018. Fuzz distortion.			
2008-2018		$140	$175
Retro Vibe			
2007-present. Vibe/vibrato.			
2007-2021		$230	$275
Ripple			
2007-present. Two-stage phaser.			
2007-2021		$120	$160
Ripply Fall			
2017-present. Chorus/vibrato/phaser.			
2017-2021		$220	$280
Rooster			
2007-2018. Frequency booster.			
2007-2018		$160	$200
The Big Chill			
2011-present. Super tremolo with 2 speeds and chop effect.			
2011-2021		$175	$200
The Chill			
2007-present. Sine-wave tremolo.			
2007-2021		$120	$160
Tube Dreamer 58			
2007-present. Overdrive with selectable high-gain stage.			
2007-2021		$120	$150
Tube Dreamer 72			
2007-2018. Overdrive.			
2007-2018		$130	$160

MODEL		EXC. COND.	
YEAR	FEATURES	LOW	HIGH
Tube Dreamer 88			
2007-2018. Double overdrive.			
2007-2018		$160	$200
Tube Dreamer+			
2007-2017. Overdrive with footswitchable high-gain stage.			
2007-2017		$140	$180
Wahcko+			
2007-present. Wah-wah.			
2007-2021		$180	$220
WaterFall			
2007-present. Chorus/vibrato.			
2007-2021		$150	$200

JangleBox

2004-present. Stephen Lasko and Elizabeth Lasko build their guitar effects in Springfield, Virginia and Dracut, Massachusetts.

Jan-Mar Industries

Jan-Mar was located in Hillsdale, New Jersey.

The Talker			
1976. 30 watts.			
1976		$75	$125
The Talker Pro			
1976. 75 watts.			
1976		$100	$150

Jax

1960s-1970. Japanese imports made by Shin-ei.

Fuzz Master			
1960s		$350	$450
Fuzz Wah			
1960s		$125	$300
Vibrachorus			
1969. Rotating-speaker simulator, with control pedal. Variant of Uni-Vibe.			
1969		$750	$1,500
Wah-Wah			
1960s		$400	$500

Jen

Italy's Jen Elettronica company made a variety of guitar effects pedals in the 1960s and '70s for other brands such as Vox and Gretsch name. They also offered many of them, including the Cry Baby, under their own name.

Jennings

1960s. Dick Denny, of Vox fame, designed a short-lived line of effects for Jennings Electronic Developments of England.

Growler			
1960s. Fuzz and wah effect with a rotary foot control.			
1960s		$150	$300

Jersey Girl

1991-present. Line of guitar effects pedals made in Japan. They also build guitars.

EFFECTS

MODEL YEAR	FEATURES	EXC. COND. LOW	HIGH

Jet Sounds LTD
1977. Jet was located in Jackson, Mississippi.
Hoze Talk Box
1977. Large wood box, 30 watts.

1977		$90	$125

Jetter Gear
2005-present. Brad Jeter builds his effects pedals in Marietta, Georgia.

JHD Audio
1974-1990. Hunt Dabney founded JHD in Costa Mesa, California, to provide effects that the user installed in their amp. Dabney is still involved in electronics and builds the BiasProbe tool for tubes.
SuperCube/SuperCube II
1974-late 1980s. Plug-in sustain mod for Fender amps with reverb, second version for amps after '78.

1974-1980s		$50	$75

JHS Pedals
2007-present. Located in Mississippi 2007-08, Josh Scott presently builds his guitar and bass effects in Kansas City, Missouri.

Bonsai			
2007-2021		$190	$225
Colour Box V2			
2007-2021		$300	$395
Emperor			
2007-2021		$100	$165
Feednack Looper			
2007-2021		$90	$120
Haunting Mids			
2007-2021		$100	$130
HoneyComb			
2007-2021		$100	$135
Lime AID			
2007-2021		$120	$150
Morning Glory			
2007-2021		$125	$160
Prestige			
2007-2021		$90	$110
Pulp n Peel			
2007-2021		$100	$130
Spring Tank Reverb			
2007-2021		$100	$130
SuperBolt			
2007-2021		$90	$120

Jimi Hendrix
See listing under Dunlop.

John Hornby Skewes & Co.
Mid-1960s-present. Large English distributor of musical products, which has also self-branded products from others, over the years. The early Zonk Machines, Shatterbox and pre-amp boosts were designed and built by engineer Charlie Ramskirr of Wilsic Electronics, until his death in '68. Later effects were brought in from manufacturers in Italy and the Far East.

Bass Boost BB1			
1966-1968. Pre-amp.			
1966-1968		$250	$400
Fuzz FZIII			
1970s. Fuzz pedal, 2 control knobs, 1 footswitch.			
1970s		$150	$200
Phaser PZ111			
1970s. Phaser pedal made in Italy, 2 control knobs, 1 footswitch.			
1970s		$80	$200
Selectatone TB2			
1966-1968. Pre-amp combining treble and bass boost.			
1966-1968		$250	$650
Treble Boost TB1			
1966-1968. Pre-amp.			
1966-1968		$250	$750
Zonk Machine I			
1965-1968. Fuzz pedal, gray-blue housing, 2 control knobs, 1 footswitch, 3 germanium transistors.			
1965-1968		$1,500	$2,000
Zonk Machine II			
1966-1968. Fuzz pedal, gray-blue housing, 2 control knobs, 1 footswitch, 3 silicon transistors.			
1966-1968		$1,000	$1,500
Zonk Machine Reissue			
2000s. Reissued by JMI starting in 2013, reissues also made by the British Pedal Company, 2 control knobs, 1 footswitch.			
2000s		$150	$200
Zonk Shatterbox			
1966-1968. Combined the Zonk Machine II fuzz circuit with the Treble Boost, 2 control knobs, gold housing, 2 foot switches.			
1966-1968		$1,500	$2,000
Zonk Shatterbox Reissue			
2000s. Reissues made by the British Pedal Company, gold housing, 2 foot switches.			
2000s		$150	$200
Zoom Spring Reverb Unit			
1967-1968		$500	$700

Johnson
Mid-1990s-present. Budget line of effects imported by Music Link, Brisbane, California. Johnson also offers guitars, amps, mandolins and basses.

Johnson Amplification
Modeling amps and effects designed by John Johnson, of Sandy, Utah, starting in 1997. The company is part of Harman International. In '02, they quit building amps, but continue the effects line.

Jordan
1966-early 1970s. Jordan Electronics - originally of Alhambra, California, later in Pasadena - built a range of electronics, including, starting around 1966, solid state guitar amps and effects. Sho-Bud of Nashville, Tennessee, licensed the Boss Tone and sold it as the Sho-Sound Boss Tone. Mahoney later reissued the Boss Tone as the Buzz Tone.

JHS Pedals Sweet Tea

JHS Superbolt
Rivington Guitars

Jordan Boss Tone Fuzz

EFFECTS

Kay Rhythmer R-12

Keith Myers

Keeley Electronics Dual Fixed Filter

Keith Myers

Keeley Hooke Reverb

MODEL YEAR	FEATURES	EXC. COND. LOW	HIGH

Boss Tone Fuzz
1967-1970s. Tiny effect plugged into guitar's output jack, 2 control knobs, black plastic housing, extremely delicate wiring.

1967-70s		$150	$300

Compressor J-700
1967-1970s. Sustain and Level control knobs.

1967-70s		$75	$100

Creator Volume Sustainer Model 600
1967-1970s. Volume pedal and sustainer, side controls for Sustain and Tone.

1967-70s		$400	$540

Gig Wa-Wa Volume Pedal
1967-1970s.

1967-70s		$125	$145

Phaser
1967-1970s. Black case, yellow knobs.

1967-70s	Black case	$125	$150

Vibrasonic

1967-70s		$145	$195

Kay
1931-present. Kay was once one of the largest instrument producers in the world, offering just about everything for the guitarist, including effects.

Effects Pedals
1970s. Includes the Graphic Equalizer GE-5000, Rhythmer, and Tremolo.

1970s		$50	$75

Fuzz Tone F-1

1970s		$175	$350

Wah

1970s		$90	$120

Kazan
1970s-1980s. Effects made in Kazan, Tatarstan Republic.

Booster
1970s. Fuzz pedal with foot control.

1970s		$50	$75

Kvaker
1970s. Wah pedal.

1970s		$50	$75

Keeley
2001-present. Line of guitar effects designed and built by Robert Keeley in Edmond, Oklahoma. Keeley Electronics also offers a range of custom modifications for other effects.

Java Boost

2001-2021		$150	$210

Katana

2001-2021		$120	$180

Keio
1970s. Keio Electronic Laboratories of Japan would later become Korg in the '80s.

Synthesizer Traveler F-1
1970s. Multi-effects unit with foot pedal.

1970s		$75	$100

Kendrick
1989-present. Texas' Kendrick offers guitars, amps, and effects.

ABC Amp Switcher

1990s		$100	$140

Buffalo Pfuz

1990s		$70	$100

Model 1000 Reverb
1991-2003. Vintage style, 3 knobs: dwell, tone, and mix, brown cover, wheat grille with art deco shape.

1991-2003		$400	$450

Powerglide Attenuator
1998-present. Allows you to cut the output before it hits the amp's speakers, rack mount, metal cab.

1998-2021		$180	$200

Kent
1961-1969. This import guitar brand also offered a few effects.

Kern Engineering
Located in Kenosha, Wisconsin, Kern offers pre-amps and wah pedals.

Kinsman
2012-present. Guitar effects pedals built in China and distributed by John Hornby Skewes & Co. Ltd.

Klon
Originally located in Brookline, then in Cambridge, Massachusetts, Klon was started by Bill Finnegan, in 1994, after working with two circuit design partners on the Centaur Professional Overdrive.

Centaur
2010. Smaller overdrive unit with burnished silver case.

2010		$700	$1,000

Centaur Professional Overdrive
1994-2009. Standard size with gold case. A smaller unit was introduced in '10.

1994-2009	Gold, horse logo	$3,000	$6,000
1994-2009	Silver, no horse logo	$2,000	$4,000

KTR
2010. Smaller overdrive unit with red case.

2010		$400	$800

KMD (Kaman)
1986-ca. 1990. Distributed by Kaman (Ovation, Hamer, etc.) in the late '80s.

Effects Pedals

1986-1990	Analog Delay	$45	$60
1986-1990	Overdrive	$30	$45
1987-1990	Distortion	$30	$45
1987-1990	Flanger	$30	$50
1987-1990	Phaser	$30	$50
1987-1990	Stereo Chorus	$30	$50

Knight
1967-1972. Effects kits sold via mail-order by Chicago's Allied Radio Company.

MODEL YEAR	FEATURES	EXC. COND. LOW	HIGH

Fuzz Box KG-389

| 1967-1972 | | $50 | $200 |

Korg

Formed from Keio Electronic Laboratories of Japan. Most of the Korg effects listed below are modular effects. The PME-40X Professional Modular Effects System holds four of them and allows the user to select several variations of effects. The modular effects cannot be used alone. This system was sold for a few years starting in 1983. Korg currently offers the Toneworks line of effects.

PEQ-1 Parametric EQ

1980s. Dial-in equalizer with gain knob, band-width knob, and frequency knob, black case.

| 1980s | | $40 | $50 |

PME-40X Modular Effects

1983-1986	KAD-301 Delay	$60	$70
1983-1986	KCH-301 Chorus	$25	$35
1983-1986	KCO-101 Compressor	$45	$55
1983-1986	KDI-101 Distortion	$45	$55
1983-1986	KDL-301 Echo	$90	$110
1983-1986	KFL-401 Flanger	$40	$50
1983-1986	KGE-201 Graphic EQ	$25	$35
1983-1986	KNG-101 Noise Gate	$25	$35
1983-1986	KOD-101 Over Drive	$45	$55
1983-1986	KPH-401 Phaser	$45	$55
1983-1986	OCT-1 Octaver	$70	$80

PME-40X Professional Modular Effects System

1983-ca.1986. Board holds up to 4 of the modular effects listed below.

| 1983-1986 | | $125 | $150 |

SSD 3000 Digital Delay

1980s. Rack mount, SDD-3000 logo on top of unit.

| 1980s | | $775 | $925 |

KR Musical Products

2003-present. Kevin Randall presently builds his vintage style, guitar effects in White Marsh, Virginia.

Krank

1996-2013, 2015-2020. Tempe, Arizona, amp builder Tony Krank also built effects pedals.

Kustom

1965-present. Founded in '64 by Charles "Bud" Ross in his Chanute, Kansas, garage to build amps for his band. While Fender, Rickenbacker, and others tried and failed with solid-state amps, Ross' Kustom creations were a big hit. Kustom likely only ever made one foray into effects, producing The Bag, designed by Doug Forbes.

The Bag

1969-1971. Pioneering "talk box" effect housed in a "bota" wineskin-type bag worn over the player's shoulder. Covered in multiple styles of mod fabrics.

| 1969-1971 | | $900 | $1,500 |

Lafayette Radio Electronics

1960s-1970s. Effects that claimed to be made in the U.S., but were most likely built by Shin-ei of Japan.

Deluxe AC Super Fuzz

1969-1970s. Made by Shin-ei, AC power.

| 1969-70s | | $300 | $500 |

Echo Verb/Echo Verb II

1970s. Solid-state echo/reverb. Likely made by Shin-ei.

| 1970s | 2 instrument inputs | $175 | $300 |
| 1970s | Instrument & mic inputs | $75 | $250 |

Fuzz Sound

1970s. Likely made by Shin-ei.

| 1970s | | $150 | $250 |

Roto-Vibe

1969-1970s. Rotating-speaker simulator, with control pedal. Variant of Uni-Vibe made by Shin-ei.

| 1969-70s | | $575 | $850 |

Super Fuzz

1969-1970s. Made by Shin-ei.

| 1969-70s | | $300 | $500 |
| 1969-70s | Battery power | $300 | $500 |

Laney

1968-present. Founded by Lyndon Laney and Bob Thomas in Birmingham, U.K., this amp builder also offered a reverb unit.

Reverberation Unit

1968-1969. Sleek reverb unit, plexi-style front panel, black vinyl cover.

| 1968-1969 | | $300 | $400 |

Larry Alan Guitars

2003-present. Luthier Larry Alan Daft offers effects pedals built in Lansing, Michigan. He also builds guitars and basses.

Lectronx

1990s. Founded by Edwin C. Clothier in North Hollywood, California.

Shark

1990s. Stereo filter pedal designed to use with 2 amps.

| 1990s | | $250 | $400 |

Lehle

2001-present. Loop switches from Burkhard Georg Lehle of Lehle Gitarrentechnik in Voerde, Germany.

D.Loop Signal Router

| 2004 | | $150 | $175 |

Lenahan

Amp builder James Lenahan also offered a line of guitar pedals, built in Fort Smith, Arkansas.

Leslie

1966-1970s. In 1941, Donald Leslie began building speakers for Hammond organs to emulate pipe-

1997 Klon Centaur Overdrive
Folkway Music

KR Musical Mega Vibe
Keith Myers

Kustom The Bag
The Bag Man

EFFECTS

Line 6 DL-4 Delay Modeler

Line 6 POD X3

Mad Professor Fire Red Fuzz

organ sounds. Using a rotating baffle in front of a stationary speaker, he replicated the tremolo sound. He sold his company to CBS in 1965, and Fender launched its Vibratone based on Leslie technology in 1967. Leslie also offered its Model 16 and 18 speakers for guitarists. The Leslie 16/18 were also sold by Selmer as the Selmer-Leslie.

Model 16
1966-1970s. Rotating-speaker emulator, single fixed 4-ohm 10-inch speaker fronted by a rotating drum. Designed to be powered by an external amp. Black covering, cast Leslie badge in upper left corner.

Model/Year	Features	Low	High
1966-70s		$600	$750

Model 18
1966-1970s. Rotating-speaker emulator, single fixed 4-ohm 12-inch speaker fronted by a rotating drum. Designed to be powered by an external amp. Black covering, cast Leslie badge in upper left corner.

Model/Year	Features	Low	High
1966-70s		$500	$700

Line 6
1996-present. Founded by Marcus Ryle and Michel Doidic. Purchased by Yamaha in 2014. They also produce amps and guitars. All prices include Line 6 power pack if applicable.

DL-4 Delay Modeler
1999-present. Green case.

Year	Features	Low	High
1999-2021		$145	$175

DM-4 Distortion Modeler
1999-2018. Yellow case.

Year	Features	Low	High
1999-2018		$100	$125

FM-4 Filter Modeler
2001-2018. Purple case.

Year	Features	Low	High
2001-2018		$175	$225

MM-4 Modulation Modeler
1999-2018. Aqua blue case.

Year	Features	Low	High
1999-2018		$100	$150

POD 2.0
2001-2014. Updated version of the original Amp Modeler.

Year	Features	Low	High
2001-2014		$150	$200

Little Lanilei
1997-present. Effects made by Mahaffay Amplifiers (formerly Songworks Systems & Products) of Aliso Viejo, California. They also build amps.

Lizard Leg Effects
2007-2016. Steve Miller built a line of effects pedals in Gonzales, Louisiana.

Lock & Rock
Line of floor pedal guitar and microphone effects produced by Brannon Electronics, Inc. of Houston, Texas starting in 2003.

Loco Box
1982-1983. Loco Box was a brand of effects distributed by Aria Pro II for a short period starting in '82. It appears that Aria switched the effects to their own brand in '83.

Effects

Year	Features	Low	High
1982-1983	Analog Delay AD-01	$35	$45
1982-1983	Chorus CH-01	$55	$65
1982-1983	Compressor CM-01	$35	$45
1982-1983	Distortion DS-01	$40	$55
1982-1983	Flanger FL-01	$35	$45
1982-1983	Graphic Equalizer GE-06	$25	$35
1982-1983	Overdrive OD-01	$40	$50
1982-1983	Phaser PH-01	$45	$55

Lotus Pedal Designs
2009-ca. 2018. Guitar effects pedals built in Duluth, Minnesota by Sean Erspamer.

Loud Button Electronics
Founded in 2009 by Shawn Schoenberger in Minneapolis, Minnesota.

Morphine Dream
2010s. Analog phase shifter and distortion, based on Roland AP-7 Jet Phaser.

Year	Features	Low	High
2010s		$50	$100

Lovepedal
2000-present. Sean Michael builds his preamps and guitar stomp boxes in Detroit, Michigan.

Lovetone
Hand-made analog effects from Oxfordshire, U.K. starting in 1995.

Ludwig
For some reason, drum builder Ludwig offered a guitar synth in the 1970s.

Phase II Guitar Synth
1970-1971. Oversized synth, mushroom-shaped footswitches, vertical silver case.

Year	Features	Low	High
1970-1971		$650	$800

M.B. Electronics
Made in San Francisco, California.

Ultra-Metal UM-10
1985. Distortion.

Year	Features	Low	High
1985		$35	$40

Mad Professor
2002-present. Guitar effects pedals built by Bjorn Juhl and Jukka Monkkonen in Tampere, Finland. They also build amps.

Maestro
1950s-1970s, 2001-2012, 2022-present. Maestro was a Gibson subsidiary; the name appeared on 1950s accordion amplifiers. The first Maestro effects were the Echoplex tape echo and the FZ-1 Fuzz-Tone, introduced in the early-'60s. Maestro products were manufactured by various entities such as Market Electronics, All-Test Devices, Lowrey and Moog Electronics. In the late-'60s and early-'70s, they unleashed a plethora of pedals; some were beautiful, others had great personality. The last Maestro

MODEL YEAR	FEATURES	EXC. COND. LOW	HIGH

effects were the Silver and Black MFZ series of the late-'70s. In 2001, Gibson revived the name for a line of effects, banjos and mandolins, adding guitars and amps in '09. By '12 the brand was no longer listed but was reintroduced on a line of Gibson effects in '22.

Bass Brassmaster BB-1
1971-ca.1974. Added brass to your bass.

1971-1974		$775	$1,100

Boomerang
Ca.1969-ca.1972. Wah pedal made by All-Test Devices.

1969-1972		$175	$200

Boomerang BG-2
1972-ca.1976. Wah pedal made by All-Test Devices.

1972-1976		$200	$225

Echoplex EM-1 Groupmaster
Ca.1970-ca.1977. Two input Echoplex, solidstate.

1970-1977	Without stand	$900	$1,400

Echoplex EP-1
1959-mid-1960s. Original model, smaller green box, tube-driven tape echo, separate controls for echo volume and instrument volume, made by Market Electronics. Though not labeled as such, it is often referred to as the EP-1 by collectors.

1959-60s	Earlier small box	$800	$1,250

Echoplex EP-2
Mid-1960s-ca.1970. Larger gray or green box than original, tube-driven tape echo, single echo/instrument volume control, made by Market Electronics. Around '70, the EP-2 added a Sound-On-Sound feature. Limited-edition EP6T reissue made by Market in 1980s (see Market Electronics listing).

1960s	Larger box	$600	$1,400

Echoplex EP-3
Ca.1970-1977. Solidstate, made by Market Electronics, black box.

1970-1977		$400	$1,100

Echoplex EP-4 (IV)
1977-1978. Solidstate, last version introduced by Maestro. See Market Electronics and Echoplex brands for later models.

1977-1978		$350	$750

Echoplex Groupmaster EM-1
1970s. Large, multi-channel echo unit.

1970s		$1,400	$2,000

Echoplex Sireko ES-1
Ca.1971-mid-1970s. A budget solidstate version of the Echoplex, made by Market.

1971-1975		$250	$350

Envelope Modifier ME-1
1971-ca.1976. Tape reverse/string simulator, made by All-Test.

1971-1976		$150	$225

Filter Sample and Hold FSH-1
1975-ca.1976.

1975-1976		$500	$750

Full Range Boost FRB-1
1971-ca.1975. Frequency boost with fuzz, made by All-Test.

1971-1975		$150	$200

Fuzz MFZ-1
1976-1979. Made by Moog.

1976-1979		$150	$200

Fuzz Phazzer FP-1

1971-1974		$200	$300

Fuzztain MFZT-1
1976-1978. Fuzz, sustain, made by Moog.

1976-1978		$200	$250

Fuzz-Tone FZ-1
1962-1963. Brown housing, uses 2 AA batteries.

1962-1963		$300	$460

Fuzz-Tone FZ-1A
1965-1967, 2001-2009. Brown housing, uses 1 AA battery. Early model "Kalamazoo, Michigan" on front, later "Nashville, Tennessee".

1965-1967	Kalamazoo	$275	$470
2001-2009	Nashville	$75	$280

Fuzz-Tone FZ-1B
Late-1960s- early-1970s. Black housing, uses 9-volt battery.

1970s		$275	$325

Mini-Phase Shifter MPS-2
1976. Volume, speed, slow and fast controls.

1976		$110	$125

Octave Box OB-1
1971-ca.1975. Made by All-Test Devices.

1971-1975		$225	$300

Parametric Filter MPF-1
1976-1978. Made by Moog.

1976-1978		$350	$450

Phase Shifter PS-1
1971-1975. With or without 3-button footswitch, made by Oberheim.

1971-1975	With footswitch	$275	$325
1971-1975	Without footswitch	$175	$225

Phase Shifter PS-1A

1976		$150	$250

Phase Shifter PS-1B

1970s		$150	$250

Phaser MP-1
1976-1978. Made by Moog.

1976-1978		$250	$325

Repeat Pedal RP-1

1970s		$200	$300

Rhythm King MRK-2
1971-ca.1974. Early drum machine.

1971-1974		$400	$500

Rhythm 'n Sound G-2
Ca.1969-1970s. Multi-effect unit.

1969-1975		$600	$750

Rhythm Queen MRQ-1
Early 1970s. Early rhythm machine.

1970s		$125	$150

Ring Modulator RM-1

1971-1975	No control pedal	$550	$600
1971-1975	With MP-1 control pedal	$650	$700

Rover Rotating Speaker
1971-ca.1973. Rotating Leslie effect that mounted on a large tripod.

1971-1973	RO-1 model	$1,200	$1,600

1972 Maestro Bass Brassmaster BB-1
John Krylow

1973 Maestro Echoplex EP-3
Rivington Guitars

EFFECTS

Maestro Rover RO-1
Kyle Stevens.

EFFECTS

*1968 Maestro Sound System
for Woodwinds W-1*

Rivington Guitars

*Maestro Wha-Wha/
Volume WW-1*

Robbie Keene

Marshall Guv'nor

Keith Myers

MODEL YEAR	FEATURES	EXC. COND. LOW	HIGH

Sound System for Woodwinds W-1
1960s-1970s. Designed for clarinet or saxaphone input, gives a variety of synthesizer-type sounds with voices for various woodwinds, uses Barrel Joint and integrated microphone.

1960-1970s		$350	$400

Stage Phaser MPP-1
1976-1978. Has slow, fast and variable settings, made by Moog.

1976-1978		$175	$275

Super Fuzz-Tone FZ-1S
1971-1975		$200	$300

Sustainer SS-2
1971-ca.1975. Made by All-Test Devices.

1971-1975		$100	$160

Theremin TH-1
1971-mid-1970s. Device with 2 antennae, made horror film sound effects. A reissue Theremin is available from Theremaniacs in Milwaukee, Wisconsin.

1971-1975		$775	$975

Wah-Wah/Volume WW-1
1970s. Wah-Wah Volume logo on end of pedal, green foot pad.

1971-1975		$150	$250

Magnatone
Ca.1937-1971, 2013-present. Magnatone built very competitive amps from '57 to '66. In the early-'60s, they offered the RVB-1 Reverb Unit. The majority of Magnatone amps pre-'66 did not have on-board reverb.

Model RVB-1 Reverb Unit
1961-1966. Typical brown leatherette cover, square box-type cabinet. From '64-'66, battery operated, solidstate version of RVB-1, low flat cabinet.

1961-1963		$275	$400
1964-1966	Battery & solidstate	$200	$300

Mahoney
2000s. Reissues of the Jordan Boss Tone.

Buzz Tone
2000s. Similar black-plastic housing to the original Boss Tone. 2 Control knobs.

2000s		$40	$75

Manny's
Effects issued by New York-based retailer Manny's Music.

Fuzz
1960s. Same unit as the Orpheum Fuzz and Clark Fuzz.

1960s		$275	$490

Market Electronics
Market, from Ohio, made the famous Echoplex line. See Echoplex and Maestro sections for earlier models.

Echoplex EP-6T
1980-ca.1988. Limited-edition all-tube reissue of the Echoplex EP-2.

1980-1988		$400	$500

MODEL YEAR	FEATURES	EXC. COND. LOW	HIGH

Marshall
1962-present. The fuzz and wah boom of the '60s led many established manufacturers, like Marshall, to introduce variations on the theme. They got back into stomp boxes in '89 with the Gov'nor distortion, and currently produce several distortion/overdrive units.

Blues Breaker
1992-1999. Replaced by Blues Breaker II in 2000.

1992-1999		$130	$260

Blues Breaker II BB-2
2000-present. Overdrive pedal, 4 knobs.

2000-2021		$50	$65

Drive Master
1992-1999		$70	$140

Guv'nor
1989-1991. Distortion, Guv'nor Plus introduced in '99.

1989-1991		$125	$160

Jackhammer JH-1
1999-present. Distortion pedal.

1999-2021		$55	$60

Power Brake PB-100
1993-1995. Speaker attenuator for tube amps.

1993-1995		$190	$230

Shred Master
1992-1999		$75	$100

Supa Fuzz
Late-1960s. Made by Sola Sound (Colorsound).

1967		$550	$850

Supa Wah
Late-1960s. Made by Sola Sound (Colorsound).

1969		$300	$425

Vibratrem VT-1
1999-present. Vibrato and tremolo.

1999-2021		$50	$75

Matchless
1989-1999, 2001-present. Matchless amplifiers offered effects in the '90s.

AB Box
1990s. Split box for C-30 series amps (DC 30, SC 30, etc.).

1990s		$175	$300

Coolbox
1997-1999. Tube preamp pedal.

1997-1999		$275	$350

Dirtbox
1997-1999. Tube-driven overdrive pedal.

1997-1999		$300	$500

Echo Box
1997-1999. Limited production because of malfunctioning design which included cassette tape. Black case, 8 white chickenhead control knobs.

1990s	Original unreliable	$300	$400
1990s	Updated reliable	$700	$900

Hotbox/Hotbox II
1995-1999. Higher-end tube-driven preamp pedal.

1995-1999		$395	$565

Mix Box
1997-1999. 4-input tube mixer pedal.

1997-1999		$375	$425

MODEL YEAR	FEATURES	EXC. COND. LOW	HIGH

Reverb RV-1
1993-1999. 5 controls, tube-driven spring-reverb tank, various colors.

1993-1999		$1,400	$1,675

Reverb RV-2
2000s. 5 controls, tube-driven spring-reverb tank, various colors.

2000s		$900	$1,000

Split Box
1990s. Tube AB box.

1997	Standard AB	$275	$325

Tremolo/Vibrato TV-1
1993-1995. Tube unit.

1993-1995		$350	$480

Maxon
1970s-present. Maxon was the original manufacturer of the Ibanez line of effects. Currently offering retro '70s era stomp boxes distributed in the U.S. by Godlyke.

AD-9/AD-9 Pro Analog Delay
2001-2021. Purple case.

2001-2021		$175	$275

CS-550 Stereo Chorus
2001-2017. Light blue case.

2001-2017		$100	$130

DS-830 Distortion Master
2001-2021. Light blue-green case.

2001-2021		$100	$125

OD-820 Over Drive Pro
2001-2021. Green case.

2001-2021		$140	$175

McQuackin FX Co.
Rich McCracken II began building his analog guitar effects in 1997, first in Nashville, Tennessee, then Augusta, Georgia.

Mesa-Boogie
1971-present. Mesa added pre-amps in the mid '90s, then pedals in 2013. Mesa was acquired by Gibson in early 2021.

V-Twin Bottle Rocket

2000-2004		$100	$180

V-Twin Preamp Pedal
Dec. 1993-2004. Serial number series: V011-. 100 watts, all tube preamp, floor unit, silver case.

1993-1999		$225	$275
2000-2004	Updated tone adj	$275	$325

Metal Pedals
2006-present. Brothers Dave and Mike Pantaleone build their guitar effects in New Jersey.

Meteoro
1986-present. Guitar effects built in Brazil. They also build guitar and bass amps.

MG
2004-present. Guitar effects built by Marcelo Giangrande in São Paulo, Brazil. He also builds amps.

Mica
Early 1970s. These Japanese-made effects were also sold under the Bruno and Marlboro brand names.

Tone Fuzz
1970s. Silver case, black knobs.

1970s		$200	$250

Tone Surf Wah Siren
1970s. Wah pedal.

1970s		$150	$195

Wailer Fuzz

1970		$75	$100

Wau Wau Fuzz
1970s. Wau Wau Fuzz logo on end of pedal, black.

1970s		$150	$175

Mooer
2012-present. A line of guitar pedals built by Mooer Audio in China.

Moog/Moogerfooger
1964-present. Robert Moog, of synth fame, introduced his line of Moogerfooger analog effects in 1998. They also offer guitars.

Misc. Effects
2004-present.

2004-2010	MF-105 MuRF	$250	$400
2004-2010	Theremin	$250	$400

Moonrock
Fuzz/distortion unit built by Glenn Wyllie and distributed by Tonefrenzy starting in 2002.

Morley
Late-1960s-present. Founded by brothers Raymond and Marvin Lubow, Morley has produced a wide variety of pedals and effects over the years, changing with the trends. In '89, the brothers sold the company to Accutronics (later changed to Sound Enhancements, Inc.) of Cary, Illinois.

ABY Switch Box
1981-ca.1985. Box no pedal.

1981-1985		$25	$35

Auto Wah PWA
1976-ca.1985.

1976-1985		$25	$35

Bad Horsie Steve Vai Signature Wah
1997-present.

1997-2021		$65	$80

Black Gold Stereo Volume BSV

1985-1991		$25	$35

Black Gold Stereo Volume Pan BSP

1985-1989		$30	$40

Black Gold Volume BVO

1985-1991		$25	$35

Black Gold Wah BWA

1985-1991		$30	$40

Black Gold Wah Volume BWV

1985-1989		$30	$40

Chrystal Chorus CCB
1996-1999. Stereo output.

1996-1999		$25	$30

Meteoro Doctor Metal

Mica Wau Wau Fuzz
Marco Antonio Rebolledo Ferrari.

Morley Bad Horsie Steve Vai

EFFECTS

Morley Rotating Wah RWV
Nate Westgor

1970s Multivox Full Rotor MX-2
Keith Myers

EFFECTS

Mu-Tron Bi-Phase

MODEL YEAR FEATURES	EXC. COND. LOW	HIGH
Deluxe Distortion DDB		
1981-1991. Box, no pedal.		
1981-1991	$40	$60
Deluxe Flanger FLB		
1981-1991. Box, no pedal.		
1981-1991	$55	$65
Deluxe Phaser DFB		
1981-1991. Box, no pedal.		
1981-1991	$40	$60
Distortion One DIB		
1981-1991. Box, no pedal.		
1981-1991	$35	$45
Echo Chorus Vibrato ECV		
1982-ca.1985.		
1982-1985	$150	$225
Echo/Volume EVO-1		
1974-ca.1982.		
1974-1982	$150	$225
Electro-Pik-a-Wah PKW		
1979-ca.1982.		
1979-1982	$55	$65
Emerald Echo EEB		
1996-1999. 300 ms delay.		
1996-1999 Green case	$40	$50
Jerry Donahue JD-10		
1995-1997. Multi-effect, distortion, overdrive.		
1995-1997	$80	$90
Power Wah PWA/PWA II		
1992-2006. Wah with boost. Changed to II in '98.		
1992-2006	$40	$50
Power Wah PWO		
Ca.1969-1984, 2006-present. Reissued in '06 as 20/20 Power Wah.		
1969-1984	$60	$160
Power Wah/Boost PWB		
Introduced in 1973, doubles as a volume pedal.		
1970s	$80	$150
Power Wah/Fuzz PWF		
Ca.1969-ca.1984.		
1969-1984	$125	$250
Pro Compressor PCB		
1978-1984. Stomp box without pedal, compress-sustain knob and output knob.		
1978-1984	$45	$55
Pro Flanger PFL		
1978-1984	$100	$125
Pro Phaser PFA		
1975-1984	$100	$125
Rotating Sound Power Wah Model RWV		
1971-1982	$325	$425
Select-Effect Pedal SEL		
1980s. Lets you control up to 5 other pedals.		
1980s	$20	$30
Slimline Echo Volume 600		
1983-1985. 20 to 600 ms delay.		
1983-1985	$45	$55
Slimline Echo Volume SLEV		
1983-1985. 20 to 300 ms delay.		
1983-1985	$50	$60
Slimline Variable Taper Stereo Volume SLSV		
1982-1986	$70	$100

MODEL YEAR FEATURES	EXC. COND. LOW	HIGH
Slimline Variable Taper Volume SLVO		
1982-1986	$35	$50
Slimline Wah SLWA		
1982-1986. Battery operated electro-optical.		
1982-1986	$55	$75
Slimline Wah Volume SLWV		
1982-ca.1986. Battery operated electro-optical.		
1982-1986	$55	$75
Stereo Chorus Flanger CFL		
1980-ca. 1986. Box, no pedal.		
1980-1986	$60	$70
Stereo Chorus Vibrato SCV		
1980-1991. Box, no pedal.		
1980-1991	$80	$100
Stereo Volume CSV		
1980-ca. 1986. Box, no pedal.		
1980-1986	$30	$45
Volume Compressor VCO		
1979-1984	$30	$45
Volume Phaser PFV		
1977-1984. With volume pedal.		
1977-1984	$125	$180
Volume VOL		
1975-ca.1984.		
1975-1979	$30	$45
1980-1984	$25	$40
Volume XVO		
1985-1988	$25	$40
Volume/Boost VBO		
1974-1984	$50	$60
Wah Volume CWV		
1987-1991. Box, no pedal.		
1987-1991	$65	$80
Wah Volume XWV		
1985-ca.1989.		
1985-1989	$65	$90
Wah/Volume WVO		
1977-ca.1984.		
1977-1984	$80	$100

Morpheus

Guitar effects pedals manufactured in Salt Lake City, Utah by the same builders of the Bolt brand amps.

Mosferatu

Line of guitar effects pedals built by Hermida Audio Technology.

Mosrite

Semie Moseley's Mosrite company dipped into effects in the 1960s.

Fuzzrite

1960s-1970s, 1999. Silver housing as well as some painted housings, 2 front-mounted control knobs. Sanner reissued in '99.

1960s-70s	Mosrite logo	$275	$575
1999	Reissue, Sanner logo	$100	$225

Mu-FX

See Beigel Sound Lab.

MODEL YEAR	FEATURES	EXC. COND. LOW	HIGH

Multivox

New York-based Multivox offered a variety of effects in the 1970s and '80s.

Big Jam Effects

Multivox offered the Big Jam line of effects from 1980 to ca. '83.

MODEL YEAR	FEATURES	LOW	HIGH
1980-1983	Analog Echo/Reverb	$100	$125
1980-1983	Bi-Phase 2, Flanger, Jazz Flanger	$50	$60
1980-1983	Chorus	$45	$55
1980-1983	Compressor, Phaser, 6-Band EQ, Spit-Wah	$40	$80
1980-1983	Distortion	$70	$80
1980-1983	Octave Box	$40	$55
1981-1983	Noise Gate, Parametric EQ	$35	$45
1981-1983	Space Driver, Delay	$60	$70
1982-1983	Volume Pedal	$30	$35

Full Rotor MX-2

1978-ca.1982. Leslie effect.

1978-1982		$300	$350

Little David LD-2

1970s. Rotary sound effector in mini Leslie-type case.

1970s	With pedal	$325	$500
1970s	Without pedal	$325	$375

Multi Echo MX-201

1970s. Tape echo unit, reverb.

1970s		$200	$250

Multi Echo MX-312

1970s. Tape echo unit, reverb.

1970s		$225	$300

Rhythm Ace FR6M

1970s. 27 basic rhythms.

1970s		$60	$80

Mu-Tron

1972-ca.1980. Made by Musitronics, founded by Mike Beigel and Aaron Newman in Rosemont, New Jersey, these rugged and unique-sounding effects were a high point of the '70s. The Mu-Tron III appeared in '72 and more products followed, about 10 in all. Musitronics also made the U.S. models of the Dan Armstrong effects. In '78 ARP synthesizers bought Musitronics and sold Mutron products to around '80. In '78, Musitronics also joined with Lol Creme and Kevin Godley of 10cc to attempt production of the Gizmotron, which quickly failed (see listing under Godley Crème). A reissue of the Mu-Tron III was made available in '95 by NYC Music Products and distributed by Matthews and Ryan Musical Products. As of 2013, Mike Beigel's Beigel Sound Lab has started making a hot-rodded Tru-Tron III.

Bi-Phase

1975-ca.1980. Add $50-$75 for Opti-Pot pedal.

1971-1980	Optical pedal option	$900	$1,600
1975-1980	2-button footswitch	$900	$1,250

C-100 OptiPot Control Pedal

1975-1980	Blue case	$550	$700

C-200 Volume-Wah

1970s		$300	$350

Flanger

1977-ca.1980.

1977-1980		$800	$1,700

III Envelope Filter

1972-ca.1980. Envelope Filter.

1972-1980		$500	$1,000

Micro V

Ca.1975-ca.1977. Envelope Filter.

1970s		$200	$250

Octave Divider

1977-ca.1980.

1977-1980		$540	$780

Phasor

Ca.1974-ca.1976. Two knobs.

1974-1976		$275	$480

Phasor II

1976-ca.1980. Three knobs.

1976-1980		$200	$395

Muza

Digital guitar effects made in China, starting in 2006, by Hong Kong's Medeli Electronics Co., Ltd. They also build digital drums.

MWFX

2010s-present. Effects pedals built by Matt Warren in Somerset, England.

Glitch

2010s	Wooden case	$90	$150

MXR

1972-present. MXR Innovations launched its line of pedals in '72. Around '77, the Rochester, New York, company changed lettering on the effects from script to block, and added new models. MXR survived into the mid-'80s. In '87, production was picked up by Jim Dunlop. Reissues of block logo boxes can be differentiated from originals as they have an LED above the switch and the finish is slightly rough; the originals are smooth.

Six Band EQ

1975-1982. Equalizer.

1975-1979		$70	$85
1980-1982		$60	$70

Six Band EQ M109 (Reissue)

1987-present. Reissued by Jim Dunlop.

1987-2021		$30	$40

Ten Band EQ M108

1975-1981, 2004-present. Graphic equalizer.

1975-1981	With AC power cord	$80	$100

Analog Delay

1975-1981. Green case, power cord.

1975-1979	Earlier 2-jack model	$300	$325
1980-1981	Later 3-jack model	$150	$200

Blue Box

1972-ca.1978. Octave pedal, M-103.

1970s	Earlier script logo	$290	$400
1970s	Later block logo	$225	$250

Mu-Tron Flanger
Marco Antonio Rebolledo Ferrari

Mu-Tron III Envelope Filter

MXR Six Band EQ
Keith Myers

EFFECTS

MXR Carbon Copy M169

MXR Dyna Comp M102
Keith Myers

MXR Fullbore Metal M116
Keith Myers

MODEL YEAR	FEATURES	EXC. COND. LOW	HIGH
Blue Box M103 (Reissue)			
1995-present. Reissued by Jim Dunlop, blue case. Produces 1 octave above or 2 octaves below.			
1995-2021		$40	$45
Carbon Copy M169			
1987-present. Analog delay. 3 Control knobs. 1 Toggle switch. Green housing.			
1987-2021		$90	$110
Commande Effects			
1981-1983. The Commande series featured plastic housings and electronic switching.			
1981-1983	Overdrive	$40	$50
1981-1983	Phaser	$100	$110
1981-1983	Preamp	$40	$50
1981-1983	Stereo Chorus	$60	$70
1981-1983	Sustain	$60	$70
1981-1983	Time Delay	$70	$80
1982-1983	Stereo Flanger	$70	$80
Distortion +			
1972-1982.			
1970s	Earlier script logo	$185	$225
1970s	Later block logo	$85	$110
1980s	Block logo	$80	$95
Distortion + (Series 2000)			
1983-1985		$60	$70
Distortion + M104 (Reissue)			
1987-present. Reissued by Jim Dunlop, yellow case.			
1987-1990		$55	$65
1991-2021		$45	$55
Distortion II			
1981-1983	With AC power cord	$140	$180
Distortion III M115			
1987-present. 3 Control knobs. Red housing.			
1987-2021		$25	$60
Double Shot Distortion M151			
2003-2005. 2 channels.			
2003-2005		$65	$75
Dyna Comp			
1972-1982. Compressor.			
1970s	Block logo, battery	$90	$120
1970s	Script logo, battery	$175	$200
1980s	Block logo, battery	$65	$80
Dyna Comp (Series 2000)			
1982-1985		$65	$75
Dyna Comp M102 (Reissue)			
1987-present. Reissued by Jim Dunlop, red case.			
1987-2021		$35	$40
Envelope Filter			
1976-1983		$125	$225
Flanger			
1976-1983, 1997-present. Analog, reissued by Dunlop in '97.			
1976-1979	AC power cord, 2 inputs	$175	$225
1980-1983	AC power cord	$100	$150
1997-2021	M-117R reissue	$60	$70
Flanger/Doubler			
1979	Rack mount	$150	$175
Fullbore Metal M116			
1987-present. 6 Control knobs. Bare metal housing.			
1987-2021		$35	$100

MODEL YEAR	FEATURES	EXC. COND. LOW	HIGH
Limiter			
1980-1982. AC, 4 knobs.			
1980-1982	AC power cord	$125	$200
Loop Selector			
1980-1982. A/B switch for 2 effects loops.			
1980-1982		$50	$60
Micro Amp			
1978-1983, 1995-present. Variable booster, creme case, reissued in '95.			
1978-1983		$75	$100
1995-2021	M-133 reissue	$40	$45
Micro Chorus			
1980-1983. Yellow case.			
1980-1983		$125	$175
Micro Flanger			
1981-1982		$100	$150
Noise Gate Line Driver			
1974-1983.			
1970s	Script logo	$75	$125
1980s	Block logo	$75	$100
Omni			
1980s. Rack unit with floor controller, compressor, 3-band EQ, distortion, delay, chorus/flanger.			
1980s		$425	$475
Phase 45			
Ca.1976-1982. Battery, earlier script logo, later block.			
1970s	Script logo	$125	$200
1980s	Block logo	$100	$125
Phase 90			
1972-1982.			
1970s	Earlier script logo	$325	$425
1970s	Later block logo	$200	$275
1980s	Block logo	$150	$200
Phase 90 M101 (Reissue)			
1987-present. Reissued by Jim Dunlop, orange case.			
1987-1989	Block logo	$60	$85
1990-2021	Block or script logo	$50	$75
Phase 100			
1974-1982.			
1970s	Earlier script logo	$250	$325
1970s	Later block logo, battery	$175	$275
Phaser (Series 2000)			
1982-1985. Series 2000 introduced cost cutting die-cast cases.			
1982-1985		$60	$85
Pitch Transposer			
1980s		$400	$475
Power Converter			
1980s		$45	$60
Smart Gate M135			
2002-present. Noise-gate, single control, battery powered, gray case.			
2002-2021		$60	$80
Stereo Chorus			
1978-1985. With AC power cord.			
1978-1979		$175	$275
1980-1985		$150	$220
Stereo Chorus (Series 2000)			
1983-1985. Series 2000 introduced cost cutting die-cast cases.			
1983-1985		$55	$75

MODEL YEAR	FEATURES	EXC. COND. LOW	HIGH

Stereo Flanger (Series 2000)
1983-1985. Series 2000 introduced cost cutting die-cast cases, black with blue lettering.
| 1983-1985 | | $60 | $80 |

Super Comp M132
2002-present. 3 knobs, black case.
| 2002-2021 | | $40 | $55 |

Nobels
1997-present. Effects pedals from Nobels Electronics of Hamburg, Germany. They also make amps.

ODR-1 Natural Overdrive
1997-present. Classic overdrive, green case.
| 1997-2021 | | $30 | $40 |

TR-X Vintage Tremolo
1997-2017. Tremolo effect using modern technology, purple case.
| 1997-2017 | | $30 | $40 |

Nomad
1960s. Effects that claimed to be made in the U.S., but most likely built by Shin-ei of Japan. Models include the Verberola and the Fuzz wah, both of which were sold under other brands such as Applied, Jax USA, and Companion.

Fuzz Wah
1960s. Fuzz wah pedal similar to Morley pedals of the era with depth and volume controls and fuzz switch, silver and black.
| 1960s | | $75 | $125 |

Oberheim Electronics Inc.
1970s. Electronics company based in Santa Monica, California, which offered effects under its own name as well as building effects for Gibson/Maestro.

Voltage Controlled Filter VCF-200
1970s. Voltage-controlled filter, envelope follower and sample-and-hold circuit.
| 1970s | | $100 | $400 |

Oddfellow Effects
Jon Meleika, began in 2013, builds guitar effects pedals in Riverside, California.

Olson
Olson Electronics was based in Akron, Ohio.

Reverberation Amplifier RA-844
1967. Solidstate, battery-operated, reverb unit, depth and volume controls, made in Japan.
| 1967 | | $100 | $150 |

Ooh La La Manufacturing
2007-2014. Hand-made guitar effects built in St. Louis Park, Minnesota, including the models formerly offered under the Blackbox brand.

Option 5
2002-present. Jay Woods builds his guitar effects pedals in Mishwaka, Indiana.

Origin Effects
2012-present. Custom-built and production guitar effects made in Oxfordshire, U.K. by Simon Keats.

Ovation
Ovation ventured into the solidstate amp and effects market in the early '70s.

K-6001 Guitar Preamp
1970s. Preamp with reverb, boost, tremolo, fuzz, and a tuner, looks something like a Maestro effect from the '70s, reliability may be an issue.
| 1970s | | $100 | $125 |

PAIA
1967-present. Founded by John Paia Simonton in Edmond, Oklahama, specializing in synthesizer and effects kits. PAIA did make a few complete products but they are better known for the various electronic kit projects they sold. Values on kit projects are difficult as it depends on the skills of the person who built it.

Roctave Divider 5760
1970s. Kit to build analog octave divider.
| 1970s | | $70 | $85 |

Pandamnic
2007-2012. Guitar effects pedals made by PLH Professional Audio in West Chester, Pennsylvania.

Park
1965-1982, 1992-2000. Sola/Colorsound made a couple of effects for Marshall and their sister brand, Park. In the '90s, Marshall revived the name for use on small solidstate amps.

Pax
1970s. Imported Maestro copies.

Fuzz Tone Copy
| 1970s | | $125 | $150 |

Octave Box Copy
1970s. Dual push-buttons (normal and octave), 2 knobs (octave volume and sensitivity), green and black case.
| 1970s | | $125 | $150 |

Pearl
Pearl, located in Nashville, Tennessee, and better known for drums, offered a line of guitar effects in the 1980s.

Analog Delay AD-08
1983-1985. Four knobs.
| 1983-1985 | | $100 | $150 |

Analog Delay AD-33
1982-1984. Six knobs.
| 1982-1984 | | $175 | $225 |

Chorus CH-02
1981-1984. Four knobs.
| 1981-1984 | | $75 | $100 |

MXR Phase 90
Keith Myers

MXR Phase 100
Marco Antonio Rebolledo Ferrari

Origin Effects SlideRig

EFFECTS

Peavey Companded Chorus CMC-1

Premier Reverb Unit

Prescription Electronics Yardbox

Rivington Guitars

MODEL YEAR	FEATURES	EXC. COND. LOW	HIGH
Chorus Ensemble CE-22			
1982-1984. Stereo chorus with toggling between chorus and vibrato, 6 knobs.			
1982-1984		$125	$175
Compressor CO-04			
1981-1984		$50	$75
Distortion DS-06			
1982-1986		$40	$60
Flanger FG-01			
1981-1986. Clock pulse generator, ultra-low frequency oscillator.			
1981-1986		$75	$100
Graphic EQ GE-09			
1983-1985		$40	$55
Octaver OC-07			
1982-1986		$100	$225
Overdrive OD-05			
1981-1986		$75	$145
Parametric EQ PE-10			
1983-1984		$45	$60
Phaser PH-03			
1981-1984. Four knobs.			
1981-1984		$75	$95
Phaser PH-44			
1982-1984. Six knobs.			
1982-1984		$150	$175
Stereo Chorus CH-22			
1982-1984. Blue case.			
1982-1984		$75	$125
Thriller TH-20			
1984-1986. Exciter, 4 knobs, black case.			
1984-1986		$175	$225

Peavey

1965-present. Peavey made stomp boxes from '87 to around '90. They offered rack mount gear after that.

MODEL YEAR	FEATURES	EXC. COND. LOW	HIGH
Accelerator Overdrive AOD-2			
1980s		$30	$35
Biampable Bass Chorus BAC-2			
1980s		$30	$35
Companded Chorus CMC-1			
1980s		$25	$30
Compressor/Sustainer CSR-2			
1980s		$35	$40
Digital Delay DDL-3			
1980s		$30	$35
Digital Stereo Reverb SRP-16			
1980s		$50	$55
Dual Clock Stereo Chorus DSC-4			
1980s		$30	$35
Hotfoot Distortion HFD-2			
1980s		$25	$30

PedalDoctor FX

1996-present. Tim Creek builds his production and custom guitar effects in Nashville, Tennessee.

Pedalworx

In 2001, Bob McBroom and George Blekas began building guitar effects in Manorville, New York and Huntsville, Alabama. They also do modifications to wahs.

Pharaoh Amplifiers

1998-2010. Builder Matt Farrow builds his effects in Raleigh, North Carolina.

Pignose

1972-present. Guitar stomp boxes offered by the amp builder in Las Vegas, Nevada. They also offer guitars.

Pigtronix

2003-present. Dave Koltai builds his custom guitar effects originally in Brooklyn, and currently in Yonkers, New York and also offers models built in China.

Plum Crazy FX

Guitar effects built by Kaare Festovog in Apple Valley, Minnesota starting in 2005.

Premier

Ca.1938-ca.1975, 1990-2010. Premier offered a reverb unit in the '60s.

MODEL YEAR	FEATURES	EXC. COND. LOW	HIGH
Reverb Unit			
1961-late-1960s. Tube, footswitch, 2-tone brown.			
1960s		$250	$375

Prescription Electronics

Located in Portland, Oregon, Jack Brossart began offering a variety of hand-made effects in 1994.

MODEL YEAR	FEATURES	EXC. COND. LOW	HIGH
Dual-Tone			
1998-2009. Overdrive and distortion.			
1998-2009		$165	$175
Throb			
1996-2014. Tremolo.			
1996-2014		$165	$175
Yardbox			
1994-2014. Patterned after the original Sola Sound Tonebender.			
1994-2014		$90	$125

Pro Tone Pedals

2004-present. Guitar effects pedals built by Dennis Mollan in Dallas, Texas until early-2011, and presently in Summerville, South Carolina.

ProCo

1974-present. Located in Kalamazoo, Michigan and founded by Charlie Wicks, ProCo produces effects, cables and audio products.

MODEL YEAR	FEATURES	EXC. COND. LOW	HIGH
Rat			
1979-1987. Fuzztone, large box until '84. The second version was 1/3 smaller than original box. The small box version became the Rat 2. The current Vintage Rat is a reissue of the original large box.			
1979-1984	Large box	$250	$400
1984-1987	Compact box	$95	$170

MODEL YEAR	FEATURES	EXC. COND. LOW	HIGH

Rat 2
1987-present. Classic distortion.

1987-1999		$75	$150
2000-2021		$40	$55

Turbo Rat
1989-present. Fuzztone with higher output gain, slope-front case.

1989-2021		$40	$50

Vintage Rat
1992-2005. Reissue of early-'80s Rat.

1992-2005		$40	$50

Pro-Sound
The effects listed here date from 1987, and were, most likely, around for a short time.

Chorus CR-1
1980s		$25	$40

Delay DL-1
1980s. Analog.

1980s		$35	$55

Distortion DS-1
1980s		$20	$35

Octaver OT-1
1980s		$25	$40

Power and Master Switch PMS-1
1980s		$15	$25

Super Overdrive SD-1
1980s		$20	$35

Providence
1996-present. Guitar effects pedals built in Japan for Pacifix Ltd. and distributed in the U.S. by Godlyke Distributing, Inc.

Radial Engineering
1994-present. Radial makes a variety of products in Port Coquitlam, British Columbia, including direct boxes, snakes, cables, splitters, and, since '99, the Tonebone line of guitar effects.

Rands
1960s. Japanese music company.

Resly Machine RM-29
1960s. Copy of Maestro PS-1 Phase Shifter built by Shin-ei.

1960s		$200	$300

Rapco
The Jackson, Missouri based cable company offers a line of switch, connection and D.I. Boxes.

The Connection AB-100
1988-2017. A/B box.

1988-2017		$25	$35

Rastop Designs
2002-present. Alexander Rastopchin builds his effects in Long Island City, New York. He also builds amps.

Ray Butts Music Co.
1950s. Ray Butts ran a music store in Cairo, Illinois, where he built his famous EchoSonic amp. He experimented with building a pioneering fuzz box that never went into production and offered his NovaMatch buffer in limited production.

NovaMatch
Late-1950s. Buffer with 1Db of gain in a lipstick-tube-like unit that plugged into guitar jacks.

1950s		$200	$300

Real McCoy Custom
1993-present. Wahs and effects by Geoffrey Teese. His first wah was advertised as the Real McCoy, by Teese. He now offers his custom wah pedals under the Real McCoy Custom brand. He also used the Teese brand on a line of stomp boxes, starting in '96. The Teese stomp boxes are no longer being made. In '08 he moved to Coos Bay, Oregon.

Recycled Sound
2009-present. Greg Perrine designs attenuators in Conway, Arkansas, which are then built in China.

Red Panda
2010s-present. Based in Pittsburgh, Pennsylvania.

Bitmap
2016		$75	$125

Raster
2015		$75	$125

Red Witch
2003-present. Analog guitar effects, designed by Ben Fulton, and made in Paekakariki, New Zealand.

Reinhardt
2004-2012. Amp builder Bob Reinhardt of Lynchburg, Virginia also offers a line of effects pedals.

Retro FX Pedals
2006-ca. 2010. Guitar effects pedals built by John Jones in St. Louis, Missouri.

Retroman
2002-present. Joe Wolf builds his retro effects pedals in Janesville, Wisconsin.

Retro-Sonic
2002-present. Tim Larwill builds effects in Ottawa, Ontario.

Reverend
1996-present. Reverend offered its Drivetrain effects from '00 to '04. They also build guitars.

RGW Electronics
Guitar effects built by Robbie Wallace, starting in 2003, in Lubbock, Texas.

ProCo Rat 2

*Radial Tonebone Texas
Dual Overdrive*

Red Witch Synthotron
Rodger Reed

EFFECTS

Rocktron Banshee Talk Box
Rivington Guitars

Roger Mayer Voodoo Axe

Roland Bee Baa AF-100
Niclas Löfgren

MODEL YEAR	FEATURES	EXC. COND. LOW	HIGH

Rivera
1985-present. Amp builder Paul Rivera also offers a line of guitar pedals built in California.

Rocco
Introduced in 1937, the Rocco Tonexpressor was a volume pedal designed by New York City steel-guitarist Anthony Rocco and built and distributed by Epiphone. Generally credited with being the first guitar effect pedal.

Rockman
See listings under Scholz Research and Dunlop.

Rocktek
1986-2009. Imports formerly distributed by Matthews and Ryan of Brooklyn, New York; and later by D'Andrea USA.
Effects

MODEL YEAR	FEATURES	EXC. COND. LOW	HIGH
1986-2009	Delay, Super Delay	$30	$40
1986-2009	Distortion, 6 Band EQ, Bass EQ, Chorus,	$15	$25

Compressor

MODEL YEAR	FEATURES	EXC. COND. LOW	HIGH
1986-2009	Overdrive, Flanger, Metal Worker, Phaser, Vibrator, Tremolo	$15	$20

Rocktron
1980s-present. Rocktron is a division of GHS Strings and offers a line of amps, controllers, stomp boxes, and preamps.
Austin Gold Overdrive
1997-2011. Light overdrive.

1997-2011		$25	$35

Banshee Talk Box
1997-present. Includes power supply.

1997-2021		$65	$120

Hush Rack Mount
1980s-present.

2000-2021		$50	$100

Hush The Pedal
1996-present. Pedal version of rackmount Hush.

1996-2021		$25	$50

Rampage Distortion
1996-2013. Sustain, high-gain and distortion.

1996-2013		$25	$35

Surf Tremolo

1997-2000		$60	$80

Tsunami Chorus
1996-2009. Battery or optional AC adapter.

1996-2009	Battery power	$40	$50
1996-2009	With power supply	$50	$60

Vertigo Vibe
2003-2006. Rotating Leslie speaker effect.

2003-2006	Battery power	$50	$60
2003-2006	With power supply	$60	$70

XDC
1980s. Rack mount stereo preamp, distortion.

1980s		$100	$150

MODEL YEAR	FEATURES	EXC. COND. LOW	HIGH

Roger Linn Design
2001-present. Effects built in Berkeley, California by Roger Linn.

Roger Mayer Electronics
1964-present. Roger Mayer started making guitar effects in the U.K. in '64 for guitarists like Jimmy Page and Jeff Beck. He moved to the U.S. in '69 to start a company making studio gear and effects. Until about 1980, the effects were built one at a time in small numbers and not available to the general public. In the '80s he started producing larger quantities of pedals, introducing his rocket-shaped enclosure. He returned to the U.K. in '89.
Axis Fuzz
1987-present.

1987-2021		$125	$150

Classic Fuzz
1987-present. The Fuzz Face.

1987-2020		$175	$200

Metal Fuzz
Early 1980s-1994.

1987-1994		$125	$150

Mongoose Fuzz
1987-2017.

1987-2017		$125	$250

Octavia
1981-present. Famous rocket-shaped box.

1981-2021		$180	$400

Voodoo-1
Ca.1990-present.

1990-2021		$100	$300

Rogue
2001-present. Budget imported guitar effects. They also offer guitars, basses, lap steels, mandolins, banjos, ukuleles and amps.

Roland
Japan's Roland Corporation first launched effect pedals in 1974; a year or two later the subsidiary company, Boss, debuted its own line. They were marketed concurrently at first, but gradually Boss became reserved for compact effects while the Roland name was used on amplifiers, keyboards, synths and larger processors.
Analog Synth SPV
1970s. Multi-effect synth, rack mount.

1970s		$750	$900

Bee Baa AF-100
1975-ca.1980. Fuzz and treble boost.

1975-1980		$300	$550

Bee Gee AF-60
1975-ca.1980. Sustain, distortion.

1975-1980		$75	$125

Double Beat AD-50
1975-ca.1980. Fuzz wah.

1975-1980		$175	$200

Expression Pedal EV-5

1970s		$50	$75

MODEL YEAR	FEATURES	EXC. COND. LOW	HIGH
Expression Pedal EV-5 Reissue			
2000. Black pedal, blue foot pad.			
2000		$25	$30
Guitar Synth Pedal GR-33 and Pickup GK-2A			
2000-2005. Requires optional GK-2A pickup, blue case.			
2000-2005		$300	$550
Human Rhythm Composer R-8			
1980s. Drum machine, key pad entry.			
1980s		$175	$250
Human Rhythm Composer R-8 MK II			
2000s. Black case.			
2000s		$300	$400
Jet Phaser AP-7			
1975-ca.1978. Phase and distortion.			
1975-1978		$525	$650
Phase Five AP-5			
1975-ca.1978.			
1975-1978		$200	$225
Phase II AP-2			
1975-ca.1980. Brown case.			
1975-1980		$125	$175
Space Echo Unit			
1974-ca. 1980. Tape echo and reverb, various models.			
1970s	RE-101	$350	$500
1970s	RE-150	$350	$550
1970s	RE-200	$500	$750
1970s	RE-201	$750	$1,275
1970s	RE-301	$700	$950
1970s	RE-501	$700	$1,000
1970s	SRE-555 Chorus		
	Echo	$950	$1,100
Vocoder SVC-350			
Late-1970s-1980s. Vocal synthesis (vocoder) for voice or guitar, rack mount version of VP-330.			
1980		$550	$700
Vocoder VP-330 Plus			
Late-1970s-1980s. Analog vocal synthesis (vocoder) for voice or guitar, includes 2 1/2 octaves keyboard.			
1978-1982		$750	$900
Wah Beat AW-10			
1975-ca.1980.			
1975-1980		$70	$100

Rosac Electronics

1969-1970s. Founded by Ralph Scaffidi and former Mosrite engineer Ed Sanner with backing from Morris Rosenberg and Ben Sacco in Bakersfield, California. Made the Nu-Fuzz which was a clone of Mosrite's Fuzzrite and the Nu-Wah. Closed in mid- to late- '70s and Scaffidi went on to co-found Osborne Sound Laboratories.

Ross

Founded by Bud Ross, who also established Kustom, in Chanute, Kansas, in the 1970s. Ross produced primarily amplifiers. In about '78, they introduced a line of U.S.-made effects. Later production switched to Asia.

MODEL YEAR	FEATURES	EXC. COND. LOW	HIGH
10 Band Graphic Equalizer			
1970s		$80	$100
Compressor			
1970s. Gray or black case.			
1970s		$325	$475
Distortion			
1978-ca.1980. Brown.			
1979-1980		$50	$70
Flanger			
1977-ca.1980. Red.			
1977-1980		$100	$125
Phase Distortion R1			
1979. Purple.			
1979		$100	$125
Phaser			
1978-ca.1980. Orange.			
1978-1980		$65	$90
Stereo Delay			
1978-ca.1980.			
1978-1980		$125	$175

Rotosound

1960s. English musical company.

Fuzz Box

1967-1968. Fuzz built by Sola Sound.

1967-1968		$150	$300

Rotovibe

See listing under Dunlop.

Royal

1960s. Japanese effects company with product built by other makers, including the Thunder Electronic Co. Ltd. Of Tokyo.

Double Effect Machine RFC-1

1960s. Built by Shin-ei.

1960s		$150	$300

Fuzz Box RF-1

1960s. Expanded version of Univox Super-Fuzz with tone effects foot switch.

1960s		$150	$300

S. Hawk Ltd.

1970s. Various effect pedals, no model names on case, only company name and logo.

Hawk I Fuzz

1970s. Linear pre-amp, fuzz, headphone amp, 1 slider.

1970s		$300	$400

SAM

1970s-1980s. Effects made by the SAM Electromechanical Plant in Moscow, Russia.

Effekt-1 Fuzz-Wah-Vibrato

1970s. Fuzz pedal with foot control.

1970s		$50	$100

Sam Ash

1960s-1970s, 2013-present. Sam Ash Music was founded by Sam Ash (nee Askynase), in '24, in Brooklyn, and by '66, there were about four Ash

Roland Space Echo

1978 Ross Compressor

1978 Ross Distortion
Rivington Guitars

EFFECTS

Seymour Duncan Dirty Deed

1970s Shin-ei Fuzz Wah
Keith Myers

Siegmund DoubleDrive

EFFECTS

stores. During this time, Ash Music private branded their own amps and effects. In 2013, Sam Ash reissued the Fuzzz Boxx.

Fuzzola
1960s. Rebranded version of the Shin-ei Uni-Fuzz. There is also a Fuzzola II.

MODEL YEAR	FEATURES	EXC. COND. LOW	HIGH
1960s		$200	$400

Fuzzz Boxx
1966-1967, 2013-2019. Red, made by Astro/Universal Amplifier Company, same as Astro Amp Astrotone fuzz. Reissued in '13.

1966-1967		$400	$850
2013-2019	Reissue	$125	$150

Volume Wah
1970s. Italian-made.

1970s		$175	$200

Sangil
1960s. Ed Sanner -- designer of the Mosrite Fuzzrite -- also built and sold effects through his own company, Sangil.

Iron Butterfly
1960s. Fuzz wah pedal.

1960s		$200	$400

Sanner
1999. Reissue from Eddie Sanner, who was the engineer behind the 1960s Mosrite Fuzzrite, using the identical circuitry as the original. Issued as a limited edition.

Sano
1944-ca. 1970. Sano was a New Jersey-based accordion company that built their own amps and a reverb unit. They also imported guitars for a few years, starting in '66.

Satellite Amplifiers
2004-present. Analog effects pedals made in San Diego, California by amp builder Adam Grimm.

Schaffer-Vega
1975-1982. After Mick Jagger's wireless system for the 1975 Rolling Stones Tour of the Americas began broadcasting police calls and lottery numbers, New York recording engineer Ken Schaffer invented his Schaffer-Vega Diversity System (SVDS) as a better wireless system – although it also could be used to affect guitar tones, offering overdrive as used by AC/DC's Angus Young. SoloDallas began offering Schaffer replicas in 2015.

Diversity System
1975-1982. Wireless mic and guitar transmitter and receiver.

1975-1982		$1,250	$2,500

Schaller
The German guitar accessories company, which began in 1945, offered guitar effects off and on since the '60s and currently has reissue versions of its volume pedal and tremolo.

Scholz Research
1982-1995. Started by Tom Scholz of the band Boston. In '95, Jim Dunlop picked up the Rockman line (see Dunlop).

Equalizer

MODEL YEAR	FEATURES	EXC. COND. LOW	HIGH
1980s		$180	$300

Power Soak
| 1980s | | $150 | $270 |

Rockadapter
| 1980s | | $70 | $90 |

Rockman
| 1980s | | $120 | $200 |

Rockman X100
1980s. Professional studio processor.
| 1980s | | $125 | $300 |

Soloist
1980s. Personal guitar processor.
| 1980s | | $100 | $200 |

Stereo Chorus
| 1980s | | $120 | $280 |

Stereo Chorus Delay
| 1980s | | $120 | $280 |

Sustainer 200
| 1980s | | $300 | $550 |

Wah Volume
| 1980s | | $60 | $100 |

Seamoon
1973-1977, 1997-2002. Seamoon made effects until '77, when Dave Tarnowski bought up the remaining inventory and started Analog Digital Associates (ADA). He reissued the brand in '97.

Fresh Fuzz
1975-1977. Recently reissued by ADA.
| 1975-1977 | | $150 | $200 |

Funk Machine
1974-1977. Envelope filter. Recently reissued by ADA.
| 1974-1977 | | $200 | $345 |

Studio Phase
1975-1977. Phase shifter.
| 1975-1977 | | $75 | $125 |

Sears, Roebuck & Co.
1970s. Department-store and mail-order giant Sears sold inexpensive effects likely made in Japan by Guyatone.

Fuzz & Wa & Volume Control Pedal
| 1970s | | $50 | $100 |

Fuzz-Tone Control
1970s. Dallas-Arbiter Fuzz Face/Guyatone Crazy-Face copy.
| 1970s | | $100 | $250 |

Sekova
Mid-1960s-mid-1970s. Entry level instruments imported by the U.S. Musical Merchandise Corporation of New York.

Big Muff SE-2015
1972-1973. "Triangle" Big Muff Pi copy built by Shin-ei.
| 1972-1973 | | $150 | $225 |

MODEL YEAR	FEATURES	EXC. COND. LOW	HIGH

Selmer
1960s. English music company based in London.
Buzz-Tone

1960s		$150	$300

Seymour Duncan
In late 2003, pickup maker Seymour Duncan, located in Santa Barbara, California, added a line of stomp box guitar effects.

Shin-ei
1969-1970s. When the Honey company went bankrupt in March, '69, it was reborn as Shin-ei and many Honey designs continued in production in various forms. Their chief engineer was Fumio Mieda who later did design work for Korg. Shin-ei also made effects for Univox (including the Uni-Fuzz, Super-Fuzz and Uni-Vibe), Companion, Applied, Apollo, Jax, Nomad, Shaftsbury, Pax, Crown, Royal, Mica, Kent, Marlboro, Memphis, Bruno, Boomer, Alex, Ace Tone, Aria, Goya, Kimbara, Lord, National, Northland, Tele Star, Tempo, and probably others.

Fuzz Wah

1970s		$250	$400

FY-2 Fuzz Box
1969-1970s. 2 transistors.

1969-1970s		$250	$450

FY-6 Super Fuzz
1969-1970s. Built from fuzz circuitry of Psychedelic Machine, 6 transistors.

1969-1970s		$750	$1,100

Mica Tone Fuzz Wah

1970s		$190	$270

Octave Box OB-28
1970s. Version of the Gibson Maestro OB-1 Octave Box.

1970s		$200	$400

Phase Tone PT-18
1970s. Tremolo, vibrato and phase effects.

1970s		$400	$600

Psychedelic Machine
1969. Amp head-sized effect with numerous controls.

1969		$750	$1,100

Resly (Repeat Time) Machine
1970s. Black case, 3 speeds.

1970s		$400	$500

Sho-Bud
1956-1980. This pedal steel company offered volume pedals as well.
Sho-Sound Boss Tone
1970s-1980. Licensed version of the Jordan Boss Tone, 2 control knobs, similar black plastic housing.

1970s-80		$65	$150

Volume Pedal

1965		$90	$170

SIB
Effects pedals from Rick Hamel, who helped design SMF amps.

Siegmund Guitars & Amplifiers
1993-present. Los Angeles, California amp and guitar builder Chris Siegmund added effects to his product line in '99.

Sitori Sonics
Emanual Ellinas began building his guitar effects in Birmingham, Alabama, in 2006.

Skrydstrup R&D
1997-present. Effects pedals built by Steen Skrydstrup in Denmark. He also builds amps.

Skull Crusher
2009-2015. Partners John Kasha and Shawn Crosby of Tone Box Effects, built their guitar effects in Simi Valley, California.

Snarling Dogs
Started by Charlie Stringer of Stringer Industries, Warren, New Jersey in 1997. Stringer died in May '99. The brand is now carried by D'Andrea USA.

Sobbat
1995-present. Line of effects from Kinko Music Company of Kyoto, Japan.

Solasound/Colorsound
1962-2010. Sola was founded by London's Macari's Musical Exchange in '62, which was launched by former Vox associate Larry Macari and his brother Joe. The first product was the Tone-Bender fuzz box, designed by Gary Stewart Hurst and modeled in part on the Maestro Fuzz-Tone FZ-1. The first readily available fuzz in Britain, it was an instant success. Sola soon began making effects for Vox, Marshall, Park, and B & M and later under their own Colorsound brand. Refer to Colorsound for further listings and more company info.

Tone Bender Mk1.5

1966-1969		$1,000	$2,100

Tone Bender MkI

1965-1966		$1,500	$2,450

Tone Bender MkIII

1968-1970s		$1,500	$2,000

Tone Bender Professional MkII

1960s		$900	$2,100

Soldano
1987-present. Seattle, Washington amp builder Soldano also built a reverb unit.
Sho-Space Box
1987-2018. Tube-driven spring reverb.

1987-2018		$800	$900

SoloDallas
2015-present. Started by Filippo "SoloDallas" Olivieri to build replicas of the Schaffer-Vega Diversity System. Based in San Diego, California.

Skull Crusher Chrome

Snarling Dogs Mold Spore Psycho-Scumatic
Garrett Tung

EFFECTS

Sola/Colorsound Fuzz/Wah/Swell
Shane Richardson

Specter-3 Fuzz Wah
Ilya Shlepako

StarTouch AB Stereo

Strymon Deco

MODEL YEAR	FEATURES	EXC. COND. LOW	HIGH
Schaffer Boost Solo-X			
2015-2021		$75	$125
Schaffer Replica Classic			
2015-present. Stombox replicating the SVDS guitar effect.			
2015-2021		$140	$200
Schaffer Replica Storm			
2015-present. Stombox replicating the SVDS guitar effect.			
2015-2021		$90	$150
Schaffer Replica Tower			
2015-present. Replica of the original SVDS made by SoloDallas.			
2015-2021		$1,000	$1,300

Songbird
See Dytronics.

Sonic Edge
Guitar and bass effects pedals built by Ben Fargen in Sacramento, California starting in 2010. He also builds the Fargen amps.

Sonuus
2009-present. Guitar effects built in China and imported by owners James Clark and John McAuliffe in the U.K.

Sovtek (New Sensor Corporation)
1990s. Started by Mike Matthews, of Electro-Harmonix fame, to build EHX effects in Russia. See also Electro-Harmonix.

MODEL YEAR	FEATURES	EXC. COND. LOW	HIGH
Bass Balls			
1990s		$150	$230
Big Muff			
1990s		$150	$300
Electric Mistress			
1990s		$150	$300
Red Army Overdrive			
1990s		$150	$300
Small Stone			
1990s		$150	$250

Speedster
1995-2000, 2003-2007. Amp builder Speedster added guitar effects pedals to their product line in '04, built in Gig Harbor, Washington.

SPEKTR
1970s-1980s. Effects made in Novosibirsk, Russia.

MODEL YEAR	FEATURES	EXC. COND. LOW	HIGH
SPEKTR-1			
1970s. Analog multi-effects pedal with foot control.			
1970s		$50	$100
SPEKTR-2			
1970s. Fuzz wah.			
1970s		$50	$100
SPEKTR-3			
1970s. Volume pedal with boost, fuzz, wah and auto-wah.			
1970s		$50	$150

MODEL YEAR	FEATURES	EXC. COND. LOW	HIGH
SPEKTR-4			
1970s		$50	$100

StarTouch
2001-present. Tony Chostner builds production/custom, effects pedals in Salem, Oregon.

Stephenson
1997-present. Amp builder Mark Stephenson in Parksville, British Columbia also offers a line of guitar pedals.

Stinger
Stinger effects were distributed by the Martin Guitar Company from 1989 to '90.

MODEL YEAR	FEATURES	EXC. COND. LOW	HIGH
Effects			
1989-1990	CH-70 Stereo Chorus	$25	$55
1989-1990	CO-20 Compressor	$35	$55
1989-1990	DD-90 Digital Delay	$45	$65
1989-1990	DE-80 Analog Delay	$50	$70
1989-1990	DI-10 Distortion	$40	$65
1989-1990	FL-60 Flanger	$40	$65
1989-1990	OD-30 Overdrive	$40	$65
1989-1990	TS-5 Tube Stack	$45	$65

Strymon
2009-present. Founded in 2004 as Damage Control, the company began offering effects pedals under the Strymon name in 2009. Owners Gregg Stock, Pete Celi, and Dave Fruehling build their line of guitar pedals in Chatsworth, California.

MODEL YEAR	FEATURES	EXC. COND. LOW	HIGH
Big Sky			
2013-present. Reverberator pedal.			
2013-2021		$390	$490
BlueSky			
2010-present. Digital reverb pedal.			
2010-2021		$230	$280
Brigadier			
2010-present. dBucket delay.			
2010-2021		$175	$200
Deco			
2014-present. Tape saturation and doubletracker pedal.			
2014-2021		$245	$270
DIG			
2015-present. Dual digital delay.			
2015-2021		$220	$250
El Capistan			
2010-present. Tape echo.			
2010-2021		$210	$280
Flint			
2012-present. Tremolo and reverb.			
2012-2021		$175	$290
Lex			
2011-present. Rotary effects pedal.			
2011-2021		$230	$300
Mobius			
2012-present. Modulation pedal.			
2012-2021		$335	$405

The **Vintage Guitar Price Guide** shows low to high values for items in all-original excellent condition, and, where applicable, with original case or cover.

MODEL YEAR	FEATURES	EXC. COND. LOW	HIGH
OB.1			
2009-2020. Optical compressor and clean boost.			
2009-2020		$125	$150
Ojai			
2016-present. High current DC power supply.			
2016-2021		$125	$175
Ola			
2010-present. dBucket chorus and vibrato.			
2010-2021		$180	$235
Orbit			
2010-present. dBucket flanger.			
2010-2021		$170	$190
Riverside			
2016-present. Multistage drive.			
2016-2021		$200	$230
Sunset			
2017-present. Dual overdrive pedal.			
2017-2021		$230	$275
TimeLine			
2011-present. Delay pedal.			
2011-2021		$315	$380
Zuma			
2016-present. High current DC power supply.			
2016-2021		$160	$220

Studio Electronics
1989-present. Synth and midi developer Greg St. Regis' Studio Electronics added guitar pedal effects to their line in '03.

Subdecay Studios
2003-present. Brian Marshall builds his guitar effects in Woodinville, Washington.

Supersound
1952-1974. Founded by England's Alan Wootton, this firm built echo units in the 1960s. They also built amps, guitars and basses.

Supro
1935-1968, 2004-present. Supro offered a few reverb units in the '60s. Brand name was revived in '04.

500 R Standard Reverb Unit
1962-1963. Outboard reverb unit.

1962-1963		$250	$500

600 Reverb Power Unit
1961. Independent reverb unit amp combination to be used with Supro Model 1600R amp or other amps, 3 tubes, 1x8″ speaker.

1961		$300	$700

Swart Amplifier
2003-present. Effects pedals built by Michael J. Swart in Wilmington, North Carolina. He also builds amps.

Sweet Sound
1994-present. Line of effects from Bob Sweet, originally made in Trenton, Michigan, and then in Coral Springs, Florida. Bob died in 2008. Currently built by his brother Gerald.

Swell Pedal Company
1997-2012. Mike Olienechak builds his line of tube pedals for guitar and bass in Nashville, Tennessee.

SynapticGroove
Benjamin Harrison and Chrystal Gilles build their guitar effects in Edmond, Oklahoma, starting in 2013.

Systech (Systems & Technology in Music, Inc)
1975-1979. Started by Greg Hockman, Systech was located in Kalamazoo, Michigan.

Envelope & Repeater

1975-1979		$125	$300

Envelope Follower
1975-1979. Decay and drive controls.

1975-1979		$150	$300

Flanger
1975-1979. Sweep rate, depth and gain controls.

1975-1979		$125	$300

Harmonic Energizer
1975-1979. Filter/distortion with bandwidth, center frequency and gain controls. Silver body early, black body later.

1975-1979		$900	$1,450

Overdrive
1975-1979. EQ, distortion and gain controls. Silver body early, black body later.

1975-1979		$200	$450

Phase Shifter
1975-1979. Dual sweep rate controls plus emphasis control.

1975-1979		$150	$350

T.C. Jauernig Electronics
Tim Jauernig, of Rothschild, Wisconsin, built effects for several years before launching his T.C. Jauernig brand in 2004.

TC Electronic
1976-present. Brothers Kim and John Rishøj founded TC Electronic in Risskov, Denmark, and made guitar effects pedals for several years before moving into rack-mounted gear. Currently they offer a wide range of pro audio gear and rack and floor guitar effects.

Booster + Distortion

1980s		$325	$400

Dual Parametric Equalizer

1980s		$275	$350

Stereo Chorus/Flanger SCF
Introduced in 1982, and reissued in '91.

1980s		$175	$275

Sustain + Equalizer

1980s		$225	$300

Tech 21
1989-present. Tech 21 builds their SansAmp and other effects in New York City. They also build amps.

Strymon TimeLine

Swart FuzzyBoost

EFFECTS

TC Electronic HOF Mini

Keith Myers

Ten Bananas At Large Stereo Buffer

ThroBak Electronics Strange Master

TWA Little Dipper LD-01

MODEL YEAR	FEATURES	EXC. COND. LOW	HIGH
Sansamp			
1989-present. Offers a variety of tube amp tones.			
1989	1st year	$125	$175
1990-2021		$100	$125
XXL Pedal			
1995-2000, 2005-2012. Distortion, fuzz.			
1995-2012		$50	$75

Teese

Geoffrey Teese's first wah was advertised as the Real McCoy, by Teese. He now offers his custom wah pedals under the Real McCoy Custom brand. The Teese brand was used on his line of stomp boxes, starting in '96. The Teese stomp boxes are no longer being made.

Ten

2013-present. Guitar effects built in Spokane, Washington by Ryan Dunn and Doug Harrison. From 2001-'13 they used the ToadWorks brand.

The Original Geek

Jeff Rubin began building guitar effects pedals in Los Angeles, California under the Geek MacDaddy brand in 2004. After a breakup with his business partner in '09 he began using The Original Geek brand.

Theremaniacs

2010s-present. Started by Chuck Collins, builder of Theremins, based in Big Bend, Wisconsin.

Harmonic Percolator			
2010s-present. Replica of '70s InterFax Harmonic Percolator.			
2010s-2021		$150	$275

Thomas Organ

The Thomas Organ Company was heavily involved with Vox from 1964 to '72, importing their instruments into the U.S. and designing and assembling products, including the wah-wah pedal. Both Thomas Organ and JMI, Vox's European distributor, wanted to offer the new effect. The problem was solved by labeling the Thomas Organ wah the Crybaby. The Crybaby is now offered by Dunlop. Refer to Vox listing for Crybaby Stereo Fuzz Wah, Crybaby Wah, and Wah Wah.

ThroBak Electronics

2004-present. Jonathan Gundry builds his guitar effects in Grand Rapids, Michigan. He also builds guitar amps and pickups.

ToadWorks

See listing for Ten.

TomasZewicZ or TZZ

2008-present. Guitar effects pedals built by John Tomaszewicz in Coral Springs, Florida, which he labels TZZ. He also builds amps.

Tone Box Effects

See listing for Skull Crusher.

Tonebone

See Radial Engineering listing.

ToneCandy

2007-present. Mike Marino builds his guitar effects pedals in Santa Rosa, California.

Top Gear

1960s-1970s. Top Gear was a London music store. Their effects were made by other manufacturers.

Rotator			
1970s. Leslie effect.			
1970s		$100	$175

Top Hat Amplification

1994-present. Brian Gerhard builds his amps and effects in Fuquay-Varina, North Carolina. He previously built them in La Habra, California and Apex, North Carolina.

Traynor

1963-present. Amp and PA builder Traynor also built two spring reverb units, one tube and one solidstate, in Canada from 1966-'72 and a 7-band EQ from '73-'78.

Tremolo

See listing under Dunlop.

T-Rex

2003-present. Made in Denmark and imported by European Musical Imports.

TSVG

Mike Klein started building his guitar effects in his shop located in Philadelphia, Pennsylvania in 2011.

Tube Works

1987-2004. Founded by B.K. Butler (see Audio Matrix) in Denver, Colorado, Tube Works became a division of Genz Benz Enclosures of Scottsdale, Arizona in 1997 which dropped the brand in 2004. They also offered tube/solidstate amps, cabinets, and DI boxes.

Blue Tube			
1989-2004. Overdrive bass driver with 12AX7A tube.			
1989-2004		$100	$150
Real Tube			
Ca.1987-2004. Overdrive with 12AX7A tube.			
1987-1999		$100	$150
Tube Driver			
1987-2004. With tube.			
1987-2004		$100	$150

TWA (Totally Wycked Audio)

2009-present. Boutique analog effect pedals made in the U.S. and offered by Godlyke, Inc.

EFFECTS

MODEL YEAR	FEATURES	EXC. COND. LOW	HIGH

Tycobrahe

The Tycobrahe story was over almost before it began. Doing business in 1976-1977, they produced only three pedals and a direct box, one the fabled Octavia. The company, located in Hermosa Beach, California, made high-quality, original devices, but they didn't catch on. Now, they are very collectible. Reissues were made by Chicago Iron.

Octavia
1976-1977, 2000s. Octave doubler.

1976-1977		$1,200	$1,900
2000s	Octavia & Octavian reissue	$260	$300

Parapedal
1976-1977, 2000s. Wah.

1976-1977		$700	$1,350
2000s	Reissue, light blue	$200	$300

Pedalflanger
1976-1977. Blue pedal-controlled flanger.

1976-1977		$1,200	$1,350

UMI (United Musical Industries)

1960s. UMI was based in Farmingdale, New York.

Tone Booster
1960s. Primitive EQ unit with treble and bass boost controls.

1960s	$75	$125

Uni-Vibe

See listings under Univox and Dunlop.

Univox

Univox was a brand owned by Merson (later Unicord), of Westbury, New York. It marketed guitars and amps, and added effects in the late-'60s. Most Univox effects were made by Shin-ei, of Japan. They vanished in about '81.

Drum Machine SR-55

1970s	$175	$200

EC-80 A Echo
Early-1970s-ca.1977. Tape echo, sometimes shown as The Brat Echo Chamber.

1970s	$75	$100

EC-100 Echo
1970s. Tape, sound-on-sound.

1970s	$75	$160

Echo-Tech EM-200
1970s. Disc recording echo unit.

1970s	$130	$170

Fuzz FY-2

1970s	$185	$350

Micro 41 FCM41 4 channel mixer

1970s	$35	$50

Micro Fazer
1970s. Phase shifter.

1970s	$75	$115

Noise-Clamp EX110

1970s	$45	$55

Phaser PHZ1
1970s. AC powered.

1970s	$50	$75

Pro-Verb UR-3
1970s. Reverb (spring) unit, black tolex, slider controls for 2 inputs, 1 output plus remote output.

1970s	$85	$100

Square Wave SQ150
Introduced in 1976. Distortion, orange case.

1970s	$75	$125

Super-Fuzz
1968-1973. Made by Shin-ei and similar to the FY-6 Super Fuzz, built from fuzz circuitry of Honey/Shin-ei Psychedelic Machine, 6 transistors, battery powered.

1968-1973	Gray box, norma bypass switch	$400	$975
1968-1973	Unicord, various colors, blue bypass pedal	$350	$500

Surf Siren
1970s. Wah pedal.

1970s	$90	$150

Uni-Comp
1970s. Compression limiter.

1970s	$50	$100

Uni-Drive

1970s	$150	$200

Uni-Fuzz
1969-1973. Fuzz tone in blue case, 2 black knobs and slider switch. Made by Shin-ei, AC-powered version of Super-Fuzz, built from fuzz circuitry of Honey/Shin-ei Psychedelic Machine.

1969-1973	$350	$600

Uni-Tron 5
1975. A.k.a. Funky Filter, envelope filter.

1975	$200	$525

Uni-Vibe
Introduced ca. 1969-1970s. Rotating-speaker simulator, with control pedal. Made by Shin-ei, built from circuitry of Honey/Shin-ei Psychedelic Machine.

1960s	$1,600	$3,100
1970s	$900	$1,700

Uni-Wah Wah/Volume

1970s	$80	$125

VanAmps

Amp builder Tim Van Tassel of Golden Valley, Minnesota, also offers a line of reverb effects pedals.

Vesta Fire

Ca.1981-ca.1988. Brand of Japan's Shiino Musical Instrument Corp.

Effects

1981-1988	Chorus/Flange FLCH	$35	$50
1981-1988	Distortion DST	$35	$50
1981-1988	Flanger	$35	$50
1981-1988	Noise Gate	$25	$40
1981-1988	Stereo Chorus SCH	$35	$50

Univox Micro Fazer

Univox Super-Fuzz U-1095
Kai Hawkins

1969 Univox Uni-Vibe
Imaged by Heritage Auctions, HA.com

EFFECTS

Voodoo Lab Tremolo

1967 Vox Tone Bender
Dean Nissen

Wampler Clarksdale

MODEL YEAR	FEATURES	EXC. COND. LOW	HIGH

Vintage Tone Project
Line of guitar effects made by Robert Rush and company in Delmar, New York, starting in 2003. They also built reissues of Dan Armstong's '70s effects from '03 to '06.

VintageFX
2003-present. Effects based on vintage pedals from the '60s and '70s built by Dave Archer in Grand Island, New York.

Visual Sound
1995-2015. Effects pedals designed by Bob Weil and R.G. Keen in Spring Hill, Tennessee and built in China. They changed name to Truetone in '15.

VooDoo Lab
1994-present. Line of effects made by Digital Music Corp. in California.

Analog Chorus
1997-2012. Based on '76 CE-1.

1997-2012		$100	$120

Bosstone
1994-1999. Based on '60s Jordan Electronics Fuzz.

1994-1999		$70	$110

Micro Vibe
1996-present. Uni-Vibe rotating-speaker simulator.

1996-2021		$65	$100

Overdrive
1994-2002. Based on '70s overdrive.

1994-2002		$55	$65

Superfuzz
1999-present.

1999-2021		$75	$90

Tremolo
1995-present.

1995-2021		$55	$75

Vox
1954-present. The first Vox product was a volume pedal. Ca. '66, they released the Tone Bender, one of the classic fuzzboxes of all time. A year or so later, they delivered their greatest contribution to the effects world, the first wah-wah pedal. The American arm of Vox (then under Thomas Organ) succumbed in '72. In the U.K., the company was on-again/off-again.

Clyde McCoy Wah-Wah Pedal
Introduced in 1967, reissued in 2001-2008. Clyde's picture on bottom cover.

1967	Clyde's picture	$800	$1,050
1968	No picture	$600	$800
2001-2008	Model V-848	$150	$175

Crybaby Wah
Introduced in 1968. The Thomas Organ Company was heavily involved with Vox from '64 to '72, importing their instruments into the U.S. and designing and assembling products. One product developed in conjunction with Vox was the wah-wah pedal. Both Thomas Organ and JMI, Vox's European distributor, wanted to offer the new effect. The problem was solved

by labeling the Thomas Organ wah the Crybaby. The original wahs were built by Jen in Italy, but Thomas later made them in their Chicago, Illinois and Sepulveda, California plants. Thomas Organ retained the marketing rights to Vox until '79, but was not very active with the brand after '72. The Crybaby brand is now offered by Dunlop.

1960s	Jen-made	$200	$250
1970	Sepulveda-made	$125	$175

Double Sound
1970s. Jen-made, Double Sound model name on bottom of pedal, double sound derived from fuzz and wah ability.

1970s		$200	$250

Flanger
1970s.

1970s		$200	$250

King Wah
1970s. Chrome top, Italian-made.

1970s		$200	$250

Repeat Percussion
Late-1960s. Plug-in module with on-off switch and rate adjustment.

1968		$100	$125

Stereo Fuzz Wah
Stereo Fuzz Wah

1970s		$150	$200

Tone Bender V-828
1966-1970s. Fuzz box, reissued as the V-829 in '93.

1966-1968	Mark I, gray case	$550	$750
1969	Mark II, black case	$475	$625
1970s	Mark III	$475	$600

ToneLab Valvetronix
2003-2019. Multi-effect modeling processor (ToneLab EX or ToneLab ST), 12AX7 tube preamp.

2003-2019		$400	$425

V-807 Echo-Reverb Unit
1967. Solidstate, disc echo.

1967		$275	$375

V-837 Echo Deluxe Tape Echo
1967. Solidstate, multiple heads.

1967		$350	$450

V-846 Wah
1969-1970s. Chrome top, Italian-made.

1969	Clyde McCoy	$450	$600
1970s		$300	$425

V-847 Wah-Wah
1992-present. Reissue of the original V-846 Wah.

1992-2021		$55	$80

Volume Pedal
1954-late 1960s. Reissued as the V850.

1960s		$50	$270

Wampler Pedals
2004-present. Brian Wampler began building effects under the brand Indy Guitarist in 2004, and changed the name to Wampler Pedals in 2007. They are built in Greenwood, Indiana.

Warmenfat
2004-present. Pre-amps and guitar effects built in Sacramento, California, by Rainbow Electronics.

MODEL YEAR	FEATURES	EXC. COND. LOW	HIGH

Wasabi

2003-2008. Line of guitar effect pedals from Danelectro.

Washburn

Washburn offered a line of effects from around 1983 to ca. '89.

Effects

1980s	Analog Delay AX:9	$30	$35
1980s	Flanger FX:4	$35	$40
1980s	Phaser PX:8	$40	$45
1980s	Stack in a Box SX:3	$30	$35

Watkins/WEM

1957-present. Watkins Electric Music (WEM) was founded by Charlie Watkins. Their first commercial product was the Watkins Dominator amp in '57, followed by the Copicat Echo in '58.

Copicat Tape Echo

1958-1970s, 1985-present. The Copicat went through several detail changes, subsequently known as the Marks I, II, III, and IV versions. It has been reissued in various forms by Watkins.

1958-1970s	Solidstate	$525	$1,000
1958-1970s	Tube	$850	$1,100

Way Huge Electronics

1995-1998, 2008-present Way Huge offered a variety of stomp boxes, made in Sherman Oaks, California. Jim Dunlop revived the brand in '08.

Green Rhino Overdrive II

1990s	$100	$200

WD Music

Since 1978, WD Music has offered a wide line of aftermarket products for guitar players. From '91 to '02, they offered a line of effects that were copies of the original Dan Armstrong color series (refer to Dan Armstrong listing).

Blue Clipper

1991-2002. Fuzz.

1991-2002	$30	$45

Orange Squeezer

1991-2002. Signal compressor.

1991-2002	Light Orange case	$40	$50

Purple Peaker

1991-2002. Mini EQ.

1991-2002	$40	$50

Westbury

1978-ca.1983. Brand imported by Unicord.

Tube Overdrive

1978-1983. 12AX7.

1978-1983	$150	$200

Whirlwind

1976-present. Effects from Michael Laiacona, who helped found MXR, originally made in Rochester, New York. Currently the company offers guitar effects, DI boxes and other music devices built in Greece, New York.

Commander

1980s. Boost and effects loop selector.

1980s	$75	$100

Wilsic

1970s. Enginer Charlie Ramskirr designed effects for Hornby Skewes, but also offered DIY mail-order kits under the brand Wilsic.

Sound Vibration

1970s	$75	$100

Wilson Effects

2007-present. Guitar effects built by Kevin Wilson in Guilford, Indiana.

WMD (William Mathewson Devices)

2008-present. William Mathewson builds his instrument effects in Denver, Colorado.

Wurlitzer

Wurlitzer offered the Fuzzer Buzzer in the 1960s, which was the same as the Clark Fuzz.

Xotic Effects

2001-present. The roots of Xotic go back to a small garage in the San Fernando Valley of Southern California in 1996, producing and designing bass guitars and bass preamps, soon expanding to build boutique pedals.

AC Booster

2002-2020. Light overdrive with 20db+ of boost and 2-band EQ.

2002-2020	$75	$100

AC Plus

2007-2018. Stackable 2-channel light overdrive with 3-band EQ and compression.

2007-2018	$100	$130

AC-COMP

2010-2018. Custom Shop light overdrive with 3 compression modes. Internal DIP switches control level of compression, tonal character, and treble/presence levels.

2010-2018	$120	$130

Bass BB Preamp

2006-2021. Bass overdrive with 2 overlapping EQs and ±15dB boost/cut.

2006-2021	$130	$160

Bass RC Booster

2006-present. Bass boost with 2-band active EQ and ±15dB boost/cut.

2006-2021	$50	$80

BB Plus

2008-2020. Stackable 2-channel overdrive with 3-band EQ and compression.

2008-2020	$115	$130

BB Preamp

2005-2020. Overdrive with 30dB+ boost and 2-band EQ.

2005-2020	$80	$100

Watkins Copicat Tape Echo
Rivington Guitars

Whirlwind OC-Bass Optical Compressor

Xotic Effects Bass RC Booster

Xotic SL Drive

Xotic Effects Soul Driven

Xotic Effects X-Blender

MODEL YEAR	FEATURES	EXC. COND. LOW	HIGH
BBP-COMP			
2011-2018. Custom Shop overdrive with 3 compression modes and 2-band EQ.			
2011-2018		$140	$160
BBP-MB			
2009-2018. Custom Shop overdrive with 12dB+ mid-treble boost and 2-band EQ.			
2009-2018		$125	$140
EP Booster			
2009-present. Mini boost pedal with 20db+ of boost. Internal DIP switches control boost frequencies and EQ.			
2009-2021		$75	$90
RC Booster			
2002-2017. Clean boost with 20dB+ of transparent boost and 2-band EQ.			
2002-2017		$50	$60
RC Booster V2			
2016-present. Clean boost with 20dB+ transparent boost and 2-band EQ. Added gain channel with gain 2 control knob.			
2016-2021		$75	$90
Robotalk			
1998-2009. Envelope filter, random arpeggiator and low-pass filter. Ultra-boutique pedal, made from scratch, in limited quantities.			
1998-2009		$200	$300
Robotalk 2			
2009-present. Envelope filter with 2 separate envelope filter channels that can be combined or used individually. Internal input pad controls passive/active signals. Internal DIP switches control frequency settings.			
2009-2021		$125	$180
Robotalk-RI			
2011-2018. Custom Shop envelope filter with an enhanced arpeggiator for more wonderfully strange and mesmerizing sounds.			
2011-2018		$150	$200
SL Drive			
2013-present. Mini overdrive pedal produces tones from legendary amplifiers, the Super Lead and Super Bass. Internal DIP switches control boost frequencies and EQ settings.			
2013-2021		$65	$90
Soul Driven			
2017-present. Boost/overdrive with mid-boost and tone knobs. Internal bass boost DIP switches control up to 6dB+ of boost.			
2017-2021		$130	$140
SP Compressor			
2012-present. Mini compressor featuring a wide variety of compressor tones from vintage to subtle to modern, and more. Internal DIP switches control attack.			
2012-2021		$85	$95
Stereo X-Blender			
2011-2017. Custom Shop effects looper with 3 parallel effects loops equipped with a transparent buffer amplifier allowing feeding and mixing of effects without signal deterioration.			
2011-2017		$130	$160

MODEL YEAR	FEATURES	EXC. COND. LOW	HIGH
X-Blender			
2006-present. Series and parallel effects looper with boost switch for 6dB+ volume boost, treble and bass EQ and phase inverter switch. Dry/Wet knob in parallel mode.			
2006-2021		$85	$140
Xotic Wah			
2014-present. Wah pedal that features a 20% smaller size, bias, wah-Q, treble, and bass controls, plus internal DIP switches for even more tonal possibilities.			
2014-2021		$175	$200
Yack			
1960s. Japanese effects company.			
Fuzz Box YF-2			
1960s		$150	$400
Yamaha			
1946-present. Yamaha has offered effects since at least the early '80s. They also build guitars, basses, amps, and other musical instruments.			
Analog Delay E1005			
1980s. Free-standing, double-space rack mountsized, short to long range delays, gray case.			
1980s		$160	$180
Yubro			
Yubro, of Bellaire, Texas, offered a line of nine effects in the mid- to late-'80s.			
Analog Delay AD-800			
1980s	300 ms	$75	$125
Stereo Chorus CH-600			
1980s		$50	$75
ZVex Effects			
1995-present. Zachary Vex builds his effects in Minneapolis, Minnesota, with some subassembly work done in Michigan. Painters on staff create stock and custom versions of many pedals, which often bring higher prices. Vexter pedals are silkscreened pedals made in Taiwan. U.S. Vexters are manufactured in Taiwan, but engraved in Minnesota. California Mini models are manufactured in California. In 2000-2002, Vex built the solidbody Drip Guitar with an onboard Wah. In 2002, Vex also began building amps.			
Basstortion			
2011-present. Bass distortion, bright/dark switch.			
2011-2021		$95	$130
Box of Metal			
2007-present. High-gain distortion, switchable noise gate.			
2007-2021		$120	$150
Box of Rock			
2005-present. 2-in-1 pedal. Tube amp-type distortion pedal and clean post-gain boost.			
2005-2021		$100	$150
Channel 2			
2014-present. Mini boost pedal, master volume.			
2014-2021		$70	$90

EFFECTS

MODEL		EXC. COND.	
YEAR	FEATURES	LOW	HIGH

Distortion
2009-2020. Tube amp-style distortion, sub contour and gain switches.

2009-2021		$60	$75

Double Rock
2012-present. Dual switchable distortion/boost pedal.

2012-2021		$175	$200

Fat Fuzz Factory
2011-present. Fuzz Factory with additional 3-position mini toggle to select frequency range.

2011-2021		$175	$200

Fuzz Factory
1995-present. Powerful, tweaky, and unique germanium fuzz pedal, with idiosyncratic hand-painted housings. Also available as Vexter and US Vexter models.

1995-2014		$120	$145
1995-2021	Hand-painted	$140	$200

Fuzz Factory 7
2013-2018. Limited edition Fuzz Factory with footswitchable EQ and 9-position rotary frequency selector.

2013-2018		$300	$375

Fuzz Probe
2000-present. Theremin-controlled Fuzz Factory.

2000-2021		$100	$175

Fuzzolo
2014-present. Mini footprint 2-knob silicon fuzz for guitar and bass.

2014-2021		$80	$100

Instant Lo-Fi Junky
2011-present. Filter, compression, and wave shapeable vibrato and blend for chorus effect.

2011-2021		$150	$175

Inventobox
2010-2021. Dual pedal chassis for DIY builders or for use with Z.Vex modules.

2010-2021		$150	$200

Jonny Octave
2005-present. Octave pedal.

2005-2021		$140	$185

Lo-Fi Loop Junky
2002-present. Sampler, single 20-second sample with vibrato.

2002-2021		$150	$200

Loop Gate
2012-present. Audio looping mixer with foot switchable noise gate.

2012-2021		$100	$130

Machine
1996-present. Crossover distortion generator.

1996-2021		$150	$200

Mastrotron
2009-present. Silicon fuzz with mini toggle sub contour.

2009-2021		$70	$95

Octane I, II, and III
1995-present. Ring modulator fuzz.

1995-2021		$85	$125

Ooh Wah I and II
2003-2013. 8-step sequencer using wah filters with random sequencing.

2003-2013		$90	$115

Ringtone and Ringtone TT
2006-2013. 8-step sequencer using ring modulator.

2006-2013		$175	$190

Seek Trem I and II
2006-2013. 8-step sequencer using volume.

1999-2013		$135	$175

Seek Wah I and II
2006-2013. 8-step sequencer using wah filters.

2006-2013		$140	$180

Sonar Tremolo and Stutter
2012-present. Tremolo with wave shaping, distortion circuit, tap tempo, and auto tempo ramping.

2012-2021		$175	$190

Super Duper 2-in-1
2001-present. Dual boost with master volume on 2nd channel.

2001-2021		$120	$170

Super Hard On
1996-present. Sparkly clean boost.

1996-2021		$110	$170

Super Ringtone
2013-present. 16-step sequencer using ring modulator with MIDI sync, tap tempo, tap tempo sync, and glissando.

2013-2021		$150	$225

Super Seek Trem
2013-present. 16-step sequencer using volume with MIDI sync, tap tempo, tap tempo sync, and glissando.

2013-2021		$150	$195

Super Seek Wah
2013-present. 16-step sequencer using wah filters with MIDI sync, tap tempo, tap tempo sync, and glissando.

2013-2021		$150	$195

Tremolo Probe
2000-present. Theremin-controlled volume.

2000-2021		$100	$175

Tremorama
2004-2013. 8-step sequencer using volume with random sequencing.

2004-2013		$195	$230

Volume Probe
2000-2002. Theremin-controlled volume using coiled cable for antenna.

2000-2002		$100	$175

Wah Probe
2000-present. Theremin-controlled wah.

2000-2021		$100	$175

Woolly Mammoth
1999-present. Silicon fuzz for guitar and bass.

1999-2021		$200	$290

Zinky
Amp builder Bruce Zinky added guitar effects in late 2003, in Flagstaff, Arizona. He also builds amps and has revived the Supro brand on a guitar and amp.

ZVex Effects Double Rock

ZVex Effects Box of Rock

ZVex Fuzz Factory 7

EFFECTS

ZT Amplifiers Extortion

MODEL YEAR	FEATURES	EXC. COND. LOW	HIGH

Zoom

Effects line from Samson Technologies Corp. of Syosset, New York.

503 Amp Simulator

1998-2000		$25	$40

504 Acoustic Pedal

1997-2000. Compact multi-effects pedal, 24 effects, tuner, replaced by II version.

1997-2000		$25	$40

505 Guitar Pedal

1996-2000. Compact multi-effects pedal, 24 effects, tuner, replaced by II version.

1996-2000		$30	$40

MODEL YEAR	FEATURES	EXC. COND. LOW	HIGH

506 Bass Pedal

1997-2000. Compact multi-effects bass pedal, 24 effects, tuner, black box, orange panel. Replaced by II version.

1997-2000		$35	$45

507 Reverb

1997-2000		$25	$40

1010 Player

1996-1999. Compact multi-effects pedal board, 16 distortions, 25 effects.

1996-1999		$40	$75

ZT Amplifiers

2009-present. Effects pedals built in China and offered by Ken Kantor in Berkeley, California. He also imports amps.

EFFECTS

MANDOLINS

1900s American Conservatory Bowlback
Imaged by Heritage Auctions, HA.com

Apitius Grand Classic

MANDOLINS

MODEL YEAR	FEATURES	EXC. COND. LOW	HIGH

Airline

Ca. 1958-1968. Brand for Montgomery Ward. Instruments were built by Kay, Harmony and Valco.

Acoustic

1960s. Acoustic, plain features.

1960s		$225	$300

Electric (Kay K390)

Early-1960s. In '62 the K390 was advertised as the Kay Professional Electric Mandolin. Venetian shape with sunburst spruce top, curly maple back and sides, tube-style pickup, white 'guard, rope-style celluloid binding.

1962		$425	$550

Alvarez

1965-present. An import brand for St. Louis Music, Alvarez currently offers intermediate grade, production, mandolins. They also offer guitars, lap steels and banjos.

Model A

1970s-2000s. Classic A-style mandolin features, round soundhole or f-holes.

1970s		$450	$575

Model F

1970s-2000s. Classic F-style mandolin features, round soundhole or f-holes.

1970s		$500	$650

American Conservatory (Lyon & Healy)

Late-1800s-early-1900s. Mainly catalog sales of guitars and mandolins from the Chicago maker. Marketed as a less expensive alternative to the Lyon & Healy Washburn product line.

Arched Back

1910s. Flat back with a mild arch, standard appointments, nothing fancy.

1910s		$225	$450

Bowl Back

1917. Bowl back style, 14 ribs, Brazilian.

1917		$125	$400

Bowl Back Style G2603

Early-1900s. Bowl back-style, 28 rosewood ribs (generally more ribs and use of rosewood ribs versus mahogany indicates higher quality), color corded soundhole and edge inlay, inlaid tortoise shell celluloid guard plate underneath strings and below the soundhole, bent top, butterfly headstock inlay.

1917		$225	$600

Bowl Back Style G2604

Early-1900s. Bowl back-style, 42 rosewood ribs (generally more ribs indicated higher quality), extra fancy color corded soundhole and edge inlay around, extra fancy inlaid tortoise shell celluloid guard plate underneath strings and below the soundhole, bent top, butterfly headstock inlay.

1917		$400	$725

Anderson

1976-2019. Gerald Anderson began working with luthier Wayne Henderson in 1976, until opening his own shop in 2005. He died suddenly in '19.

F-5

1994		$5,100	$6,700

Apitius

1976-present. Luthier Oliver Apitius builds his premium and presentation grade, production/custom, mandolins in Shelburne, Ontario.

Applause

Applause offered intermediate grade, production, Ovation-styled, imported mandolins, starting in 1994. They also offer ukes.

Various Models

1990s		$125	$225

Aria/Aria Pro II

1956-present. Intermediate grade, production, acoustic and electric mandolins from Aria/Aria Pro II, which added Japanese and Korean mandolins to their line in '76.

AM200/BS Style A

1994-2012. Pear-shaped A body, plywood.

1994-2012		$185	$275

AM400/BS Style F

1994-2012. F-style, plywood.

1994-2012		$300	$425

AM600 Style F

1994-2008. F-style, solid wood.

1994-2008		$365	$475

PM750 Style F

1976-ca. 1982. F-style Loar copy, maple plywood body, sunburst.

1976-1982		$525	$700

Bacon & Day

Established in 1921 by David Day and Paul Bacon, primarily known for fine quality tenor and plectrum banjos in the '20s and '30s.

Orchestra Mando Banjo

1920s. Mandolin neck and banjo body with open back, headstock with Bacon logo.

1920s		$350	$450

Professional Mando Banjo

1920s. Figured birch back and sides, spruce top, oval sound hole, 2-point flat back, The Bacon tailpiece.

1920s		$1,450	$1,875

Senorita Mando Banjo

1930s. Mandolin neck and banjo body, 19-fret tenor.

1930s		$775	$1,000

Silverbell #1 Mando Banjo

1920s. Fancy appointments, closed-back resonator.

1920s		$850	$1,100

Bauer (George)

1894-1911. Luthier George Bauer built guitars and mandolins in Philadelphia, Pennsylvania. He also built instruments with Samuel S. Stewart (S.S. Stewart).

MODEL YEAR	FEATURES	EXC. COND. LOW	HIGH

Acme Professional Bowl Back
1894-1911. Brazilian, 29 ribs.

1894-1911	Fancy	$525	$675
1894-1911	Mid-level	$350	$450
1894-1911	Plain	$265	$340

Beltone
1920s-1930s. Acoustic and resonator mandolins and banjo-mandolins made by others for New York City distributor Perlberg & Halpin. Martin did make a small number of instruments for Beltone, but most were student-grade models most likely made by one of the big Chicago builders. They also made guitars.

Resonator
1930s. F-hole top, banjo-style resonator back.

| 1930s | | $450 | $575 |

Bohmann
1878-ca.1926. Established by Czechoslavakian-born Joseph Bohmann in Chicago, Illinois.

Bowl Back
1890-1900. Spruce top, marquetry trimmed, inlay, pearl.

1890-1900	Fancy	$700	$1,350
1890-1900	Mid-level	$525	$675
1890-1900	Plain	$350	$450

Brandt
Early 1900s. John Brandt started making mandolin-family instruments in Chicago, Illinois around 1898.

Mandola
1900s. Spruce top, rosewood body, scroll headstock, pearl and abalone fretboard binding.

| 1900s | | $700 | $1,350 |

Presentation
1900s. Spruce top, tortoise shell-bound.

| 1900s | | $450 | $1,100 |

Breedlove
1990-present. Breedlove started building professional and premium grade, mandolins in Bend, Oregon in 1997. In '15, they ceased U.S. mando production, but continued with their import line. They also produce guitars, basses, laps and ukes.

Alpine
2000s-2013. Master Class series, O-style body, spruce/maple.

| 2000s-2013 | | $1,925 | $2,500 |

K-5
1990s. Asymmetric carved top, maple body.

| 1990s | | $1,625 | $2,100 |

Olympic
1990s. Solid spruce top, teardrop-shaped, oval soundhole, highly flamed maple back, sunburst.

| 1990s | | $1,225 | $1,600 |

Quartz OF/OO
2000s. Basic A-style body with f-holes.

| 2000s | | $925 | $1,200 |

Bruno and Sons
Established in 1834 by Charles Bruno, primarily as a distributor, Bruno and Sons marketed a variety of brands, including their own. In the '60s or '70s, a Japanese-made solidbody electric mandolin was sold under the Bruno name.

Banjo Mando
1920s. Open back, 10" model.

| 1920s | | $125 | $350 |

Bowl Back
1890s-1920s. Brazilian rosewood, spruce, rosewood ribs.

| 1920s | Less fancy | $350 | $450 |
| 1920s | More fancy | $525 | $675 |

Calace
1825-present. Nicola Calace started The Calace Liuteria lute-making workshop in 1825 on the island of Procida, which is near Naples. The business is now in Naples and still in the family.

Lyre/Harp-Style
Late-1800s-early-1900s. Lyre/harp-style, 8 strings, round soundhole, slightly bent top. Condition is important for these older instruments and the price noted is for a fully functional, original or pro-restored example.

| 1900 | | $1,050 | $1,350 |

Carvin
1946-present. Carvin offered solidbody electric mandolins from around '56 to the late '60s, when they switched to a traditional pear-shaped electric/acoustic. They also offer guitars, basses and amps.

MB Models
1956-1968. Solidbody, 1 pickup, single-cut Les Paul shape until '64, double-cut Jazzmaster/Strat shape after. Models include the #1-MB and the #2-MB, with different pickups.

| 1950s | #1-MB | $1,450 | $1,875 |

Cole
1890-1919. After leaving Fairbanks & Cole in 1890, W.A. Cole started his own line. He also made guitars and banjos.

Imperial G Bowl Back
1905-1910. 27 ribs.

| 1905-1910 | | $875 | $1,125 |

Collings
1986-present. Professional and premium grade, production/custom, mandolins built in Austin, Texas. Collings added mandolins to their line in '99. They also build guitars and ukuleles.

MF
1999-present. F-style, carved top and back.

| 1999-2021 | | $3,350 | $4,350 |

MF-5 Deluxe
2005-2006. Limited production, varnish finish, hand engraved nickel tailpiece unique to each instrument.

| 2005-2006 | | $8,800 | $11,500 |

Breedlove KO

Collings MF

MANDOLINS

Collings MT

1966 Epiphone Venetian
Kerry Brown

MANDOLINS

MODEL YEAR	FEATURES	EXC. COND. LOW	HIGH

MF-5V
2007. Carved Adirondack spruce top, highly flamed maple body.

| 2007 | | $6,700 | $8,700 |

MT
1999-present. A-style, 2 f-holes, carved top and back, matte finish, tortoise-bound top.

| 1999-2021 | | $2,100 | $2,800 |

MT-2
2009-present. Like MT-2, but with oil-based varnish finish and ivoroid-bound ebony 'guard.

| 1999-2021 | | $3,200 | $4,200 |

MT-2V
| 2009-2021 | | $3,600 | $4,700 |

Crestwood
1970s. Copy models imported by La Playa Distributing Company of Detroit.

Various Models
1970s. Includes models 3039 (electric A-style), 3041 (bowl back-style, flower 'guard), 3043 (bowl back-style, plain 'guard), 71820 (A-style), and 71821 (F-style).

| 1970s | | $175 | $225 |

Cromwell
1935-1939. Private branded instruments made by Gibson at their Parsons Street factory in Kalamazoo, Michigan. Distributed by a variety of mail order companies such as Continental, Grossman, and Richter & Phillips.

GM-2
1935-1939. Spruce top, mahogony back and sides, similar to KM-11.

| 1935-1939 | | $475 | $625 |

GM-4
1935-1939. Style A, f-holes, solid wood arched top, mahogany back and sides, block capital letter Cromwell headstock logo, dot markers, elevated 'guard, sunburst.

| 1935-1939 | | $550 | $725 |

Dayton
1910-late 1930s. Mandolins built by luthier Charles B. Rauch in Dayton, Ohio. He also built banjos, violins, guitars and banjo-ukuleles.

Style B
| 1910-1930s | | $1,550 | $2,000 |

DeLucia, Vincenzo
1910s-1920s. Luthier Vincenzo DeLucia built mandolins in Philadelphia, Pennsylvania.

Various Models
Early-1900s. High quality material, rosewood body, fine ornamentation.

| 1910s | | $1,075 | $1,400 |

Ditson
Mandolins made for the Oliver Ditson Company of Boston, an instrument dealer and music publisher. Turn of the century and early-1900s models were bowl back-style with the Ditson label. The '20s

Ditson Style A flat back mandolins were made by Martin. Models were also made by Lyon & Healy of Boston, often with a Ditson Empire label.

Mandola
1920. Bowl back.

| 1920 | | $1,025 | $1,325 |

Style A
1920s. Style A flat back made by Martin, mahogany sides and back, plain ornamentation.

| 1920s | | $1,050 | $1,350 |

Style B
Style B flat back made by Martin, Adirondack top, Brazilian rosewood sides and back, herringbone soundhole trim.

| 1918 | | $1,900 | $2,500 |

Victory
1890s. Brazilian rib bowl back with fancy inlays.

| 1890s | | $700 | $900 |

Dobro
1929-1942, 1954-2019. Dobro offered mandolins throughout their early era and from the '60s to the mid-'90s.

Resonator
1930s-1960s. Resonator on wood body.

| 1930s-60s | | $975 | $1,250 |

Dudenbostel
1989-present. Luthier Lynn Dudenbostel builds his limited production, premium and presentation grade, custom, mandolins in Knoxville, Tennessee. He started with guitars and added mandolins in '96.

F-5
1996-2012. Loar-style, about 30 made.

| 1996-2012 | | $20,000 | $26,000 |

Duff Mandolins
1982-present. Premium and presentation grade, custom/production, mandolin family instruments built by luthier Paul Duff in Palmyra, Western Australia.

F-5
1990-present. Loar-style, various woods.

| 1990-2021 | Adirondack | $5,600 | $7,200 |

H-5 Mandola
2000-present. Various woods.

| 2000-2021 | Adirondack | $6,200 | $8,000 |

EKO
1961-1985, 2000-present. The Italian-made EKOs were imported by LoDuca Brothers of Milwaukee. The brand was revived around 2000, but does not currently include mandolins.

Baritone
1960s. Baritone mandolin with ornate inlays.

| 1960s | | $425 | $550 |

Octave
1960s. Octave mandolin with ornate inlays.

| 1960s | | $425 | $550 |

Epiphone

1928-present. Intermediate grade, production, acoustic mandolins. Epiphone has offered several mandolin-family models over the years. Those from the '30s to the '60s were U.S.-made, the later models imported.

Adelphi
1932-1948. A-style body, maple back and sides, f-holes, single-bound top and back.

		EXC. COND. LOW	HIGH
1932-1948		$900	$1,150

Mandobird VIII
2004-2012. Reverse Firebird-style body with mandolin neck, electric, various colors.

2004-2012		$175	$230

MM Series
1979-present. Imported A and F styles.

1979-1985	MM70, F-style	$460	$600
1979-2013	MM50, F-style	$350	$450
1980-2022	MM30, A-style	$125	$165
1998-2013	MM20, A-style	$110	$140

Strand
1932-1958. Walnut back and sides, f-holes, multi-bound, sunburst.

1944-1947		$975	$1,275

Venetian Electric
1961-1970. Gibson-made, pear-shaped body, 4 pole P-90 'dog-ear' mounted pickup, volume and tone knobs, dot markers, sunburst finish.

1961-1970		$1,425	$1,850

Windsor Special
1936-1949. Scroll body, f-holes, slot-block inlays.

1940s	Rare, high-end	$10,800	$14,000

Zephyr
1939-1958. A-style, electric, f-holes, maple body, 1 pickup, slotted block inlay.

1950s		$625	$825

Esquire

1930s. Student level instruments with painted Esquire logo and painted wood grain.

A-Style
1930s. Laminate A-style wood body, sunburst.

1930s		$275	$350

Fairbanks

1875-1922. Primarily known for banjos, Fairbanks also offered banjo mandolins when owned by Vega.

Little Wonder Banjo Mando
1920s. Banjo body, mando neck, dot inlays.

1921		$475	$625

Style K Banjo Mando
1920s. Banjo body, mando neck, dot inlays.

1920		$425	$550

Fender

1946-present. Intermediate grade, production, acoustic and acoustic/electric mandolins. Fender also offered an electric mandolin for 20 years.

Electric Solidbody

1956-1976. Often referred to as the Mandocaster by collectors.

		EXC. COND. LOW	HIGH
1956-1957	Blond	$2,950	$3,850
1958-1959	Sunburst	$2,500	$3,300
1960-1965	Sunburst	$2,200	$2,900
1966-1976	Sunburst	$2,100	$2,700

FM Series
2001-2017. Made in Korea, acoustic and acoustic-electric, models include 52E (acou-elec, A-style), 53S (acoustic, A-style), 60E (5 string, 2 pu) and 61SE (8-string, 1 pu), 62SE (acou-elec, double-cut, extended 'board), 62SCE (acou-elec, double-cut, block-end 'board), 63S (acoustic, F-style), 63SE (acou-elec, F-style), 100 (acoustic, A-style).

2001-2002	FM-60E/61SE	$360	$475
2001-2007	FM-62SE/62SCE	$360	$475
2001-2014	FM-52E	$135	$175
2001-2017	FM-53S	$160	$210
2001-2017	FM-63S	$300	$400
2011-2017	FM-63SE/63SCE	$365	$475
2013-2017	FM-100	$85	$115

Flatiron

1977-2003, 2006-2009. Gibson purchased Flatiron in 1987. Production was in Bozeman, Montana until the end of '96, when Gibson closed the Flatiron mandolin workshop and moved mandolin assembly to Nashville, Tennessee. General production tapered off after the move and Flatirons were available on a special order basis for a time. The brand was revived in '06 on an import model sold through Epiphone.

A-Style
Includes A-style Performer series (1990-'95, maple back & sides, mahogany neck, ebony board, top binding, sunburst) and Festival series (1988-'95, same, in cherry finish and with no binding).

1988-1995	Festival	$1,350	$1,750
1990-1995	Performer	$1,450	$1,925

A-2

1977-1987	Early, no truss rod	$3,300	$4,300

A-5
Teardrop shape, f-holes, figured maple body and neck, carved spruce top, X-bracing, unbound ebony 'board, nickel hardware, fleur-de-lis headstock inlay.

1987-1994	Gibson Montana	$1,625	$2,125
1996-2003		$1,625	$2,125

A-5 1
Carved top and back, bound body, dot inlays, The Flatiron headstock inlay.

1983-1985	Pre-Gibson	$3,400	$4,425

A-5 2
Carved top and back, bound body, neck, headstock and pickguard, dot inlays, modified fern headstock inlay.

1983-1985	Pre-Gibson	$4,000	$5,200

A-5 Artist
A-5 with highly figured maple body and neck, bound ebony headstock, gold hardware, fern headstock inlay.

1987-1990	Gibson Montana	$2,900	$3,800
1996-2003		$2,300	$3,000

1964 Fender Mandocaster
Reess Sutherland

1993 Flatiron A-5
Steven Squire

MANDOLINS

Ca. 1900 A. Galiano Bowl Back
William Ritter, courtesy of George Gruhn.

1924 Gibson A
David Stone

MODEL YEAR	FEATURES	EXC. COND. LOW	HIGH
A-5 Junior			
As A-5 but with tone bar bracing, mahogany neck, The Flatiron headstock inlay.			
1987-1990	Gibson Montana	$1,150	$1,500
1996-2003		$1,150	$1,500
Cadet			
Flat-top, teardrop body, spruce top, maple body, rosewood 'board, nickel hardware.			
1990-1996		$600	$800
F-Style			
Includes F-style Performer series (1990-'95, maple back & sides and neck, ebony board, fern/banner headstock inlay, top and back of body and headstock bound, sunburst top) and Festival series (1988-'95, same, but without headstock or back binding).			
1988-1995	Festival	$3,100	$4,100
1990-1995	Performer	$3,200	$4,200
2001	Festival, Gibson		
	Montana	$3,100	$4,100
F-2			
1977-1987	Early, no truss rod	$6,500	$8,500
F-5			
F-style body, f-holes, flamed maple body and neck, carved spruce top, tone bar bracing, bound ebony 'board and headstock, nickel hardware, flower pot headstock inlay, cherry finish.			
1987-1990	Gibson Montana	$4,100	$5,400
F-5 Artist			
F-5 but with X-braces, bound ebony 'board, gold hardware, fern headstock inlay, and sunburst.			
1984-1985	Pre-Gibson	$4,900	$6,400
1987-1995	Gibson Montana	$4,500	$5,900
1996-2003	Modified fern	$4,500	$5,900
Model 1			
Oval shape, spruce top, maple body, rosewood 'board, walnut headstock veneer.			
1977-1987	Pre-Gibson	$950	$1,250
1988-1995	Gibson Montana	$750	$1,000
Model 1 Mandola			
Model 1 features.			
1977-1987	Pre-Gibson	$950	$1,250
1983-1995	Gibson Montana	$750	$1,000
Model 2			
Like Model 1, but with curly maple (MC) or birdseye maple (MB) back and sides, ebony 'board, rosewood headstock veneer.			
1977-1987	Pre-Gibson	$900	$1,200
1977-1995	Flamed koa back/sides	$950	$1,250
1988-1995	Gibson Montana	$825	$1,100
Model 2 Mandola			
Model 2 features, birdseye maple (MB) or curly maple (MC) body.			
1977-1987	Pre-Gibson	$1,050	$1,400
1988-1995	Gibson Montana	$950	$1,250
Model 3 Octave			
Model 2 features, birdseye maple (MB) or curly maple (MC) body.			
1977-1987	Pre-Gibson	$1,050	$1,400
1988-1995	Gibson Montana	$950	$1,250

Framus

1946-1977, 1996-present. Founded in Erlangen, Germany by Fred Wilfer. In the '60s, Framus instruments were imported into the U.S. by Philadelphia Music Company. They offered acoustic and electric mandolins. The brand was revived in '96.

MODEL YEAR	FEATURES	EXC. COND. LOW	HIGH
12-String			
1960s		$450	$600

Freshwater

1992-2011. Luthier Dave Freshwater and family built mandolin family instruments in Beauly, Inverness, Scotland. They also built bouzoukis, dulcimers and harps.

Galiano/A. Galiano

New Yorkers Antonio Cerrito and Raphael Ciani offered instruments built by them and others under the Galiano brand during the early 1900s.

Bowl Back			
Some fancy appointments.			
1920s		$350	$450

Gaylord

1940s. Private brand made by Harmony, painted Gaylord logo on headstock.

Artistic A			
1940s	Painted logo	$190	$250

Gibson

1890s (1902)-present. Orville Gibson created the violin-based mandolin body-style that replaced the bowl back-type. Currently Gibson offers professional, premium and presentation grade, production/custom, mandolins.

Special Designations:
Snakehead headstock: 1922-1927 with production possible for a few months plus or minus.
Lloyd Loar era: Mid-1922-late 1924 with production possible for a few months plus or minus.

A-Style (Orville Gibson)			
1890s-1902. Mandolin models built during Orville Gibson era, before he sold out to others in 1902, covering a range of features and levels of appointments.			
1890s-1902	Fancy, rare	$21,000	$31,000
1890s-1902	Plain	$2,600	$7,000
A			
1902-1933. Oval soundhole, snakehead headstock '22-27, Loar era mid-'22-late-'24.			
1902-1918	Orange	$1,400	$1,800
1918-1921	Brown	$1,400	$1,800
1922-1924	Loar era	$2,550	$3,300
1925-1933		$2,350	$3,050
A-0			
1927-1933. Replaces A Jr., oval soundhole, dot inlay, brown finish.			
1927-1933		$1,400	$1,800
A-OO			
1933-1943. F-hole, dot inlay, carved bound top.			
1933-1943	Sunburst	$1,400	$1,800

MANDOLINS

A-1

1902-1918, 1922-1927, 1933-1943. Snakehead headstock '23-'27.

MODEL YEAR	FEATURES	EXC. COND. LOW	HIGH
1902-1918	Orange	$1,400	$1,800
1922-1924	Loar era	$2,800	$3,600
1925-1927	Black	$1,950	$2,550
1927	Not snaked	$2,200	$2,900
1927	Snaked	$2,200	$2,900
1929		$2,200	$2,900
1932	Re-intro, oval	$2,200	$2,900
1933-1943	Sunburst, f-holes	$1,375	$1,800

A-2/A-2Z

1902-1908, 1918-1928. A-2Z '22-'27. Renamed A-2 '27-'28. Snakehead headstock '23-'27. Lloyd Loar era mid-'22-late-'24.

MODEL YEAR	FEATURES	EXC. COND. LOW	HIGH
1902-1908	Orange	$1,600	$2,100
1918-1921	Brown	$1,600	$2,100
1922-1924	Loar era	$4,800	$6,300
1923-1924	Loar era, extra binding	$4,800	$6,300
1925-1928		$2,100	$2,800

A-3

1902-1922. Oval soundhole, single-bound body, dot inlay.

MODEL YEAR	FEATURES	EXC. COND. LOW	HIGH
1902-1917	Orange	$2,150	$2,800
1918-1922	Ivory	$2,150	$2,800

A-4

1902-1935. Oval soundhole, single-bound body, dot inlay, snakehead '23-'27.

MODEL YEAR	FEATURES	EXC. COND. LOW	HIGH
1902-1917	Various colors	$2,800	$3,600
1918-1921	Dark mahogany	$2,800	$3,600
1922-1924	Loar era	$5,500	$7,200
1925-1935	Various colors	$2,900	$3,800

A-5

1957-1979. Oval soundhole, maple back and sides, dot inlay, scroll headstock, sunburst. Name now used on extended neck version.

MODEL YEAR	FEATURES	EXC. COND. LOW	HIGH
1957-1964		$1,200	$1,575
1965-1969		$1,100	$1,450
1970-1979		$1,100	$1,400

A-5G

1988-1996. Less ornate version of the A-5 L, abalone fleur-de-lis headstock inlay.

MODEL YEAR	FEATURES	EXC. COND. LOW	HIGH
1988-1996		$1,100	$1,400

A-5L/A-5

1988-2013. Extended neck, raised 'board, flowerpot headstock inlay, curly maple and spruce, sunburst, based on custom-made 1923 Loar A-5. L has been dropped from name.

MODEL YEAR	FEATURES	EXC. COND. LOW	HIGH
1988-2013		$2,400	$3,100

A-9

2002-2013. Spruce top, maple back and sides, black bound top, satin brown finish.

MODEL YEAR	FEATURES	EXC. COND. LOW	HIGH
2002-2013		$1,200	$1,550

A-12

1970-1979. F-holes, long neck, dot inlay, fleur-de-lis inlay, sunburst.

MODEL YEAR	FEATURES	EXC. COND. LOW	HIGH
1970-1979		$1,075	$1,400

A-40

1948-1970. F-holes, bound top, dot inlay, natural or sunburst.

MODEL YEAR	FEATURES	EXC. COND. LOW	HIGH
1948-1949		$1,375	$1,775
1950-1959		$1,300	$1,675
1960-1964		$1,125	$1,450
1965-1970		$1,050	$1,350

A-50

1933-1971. A-style oval bound body, f-holes, sunburst.

MODEL YEAR	FEATURES	EXC. COND. LOW	HIGH
1933	Oval soundhole	$1,550	$2,000
1934-1941	Larger 1125" body	$1,550	$2,000
1942-1949	Smaller 10" body	$1,300	$1,700
1950-1959		$1,200	$1,600
1960-1964		$1,125	$1,500
1965-1971		$1,075	$1,400

A-75

1934-1936. F-holes, raised fingerboard, bound top and back.

MODEL YEAR	FEATURES	EXC. COND. LOW	HIGH
1934-1936		$2,100	$2,800

A-C Century

1933-1934, 1936-1937. A body, built to commemorate the 1933-1934 Century of Progress Exhibition in Chicago, pearloid 'board.

MODEL YEAR	FEATURES	EXC. COND. LOW	HIGH
1933-1937		$3,450	$4,600

A-Junior

1920-1927. The Junior was the entry level mandolin for Gibson, but like most entry level Gibsons (re: Les Paul Junior), they were an excellent product. Oval soundhole, dot markers, plain tuner buttons. Becomes A-0 in '27.

MODEL YEAR	FEATURES	EXC. COND. LOW	HIGH
1920-1927	Sheraton Brown	$1,400	$1,800

AN-Custom (Army-Navy)

Mid-1990s. Made in Bozeman, Montana, round teardrop shape, flat spruce top, flat maple back, maple rims, Gibson script logo on headstock.

MODEL YEAR	FEATURES	EXC. COND. LOW	HIGH
1995		$1,150	$1,500

Army and Navy Special Style DY/Army-Navy

1918-1922. Lower-end, flat top and back, round soundhole, no logo, round label with model name, brown stain. Reintroduced as Army-Navy (AN Custom) '88-'96.

MODEL YEAR	FEATURES	EXC. COND. LOW	HIGH
1918-1922		$700	$900

C-1

1932. Flat top, mahogany back and sides, oval soundhole, natural, painted on 'guard, a '32 version of the Army and Navy Special. This model was private branded for Kel Kroydon in the early-'30s.

MODEL YEAR	FEATURES	EXC. COND. LOW	HIGH
1932		$700	$900

CB-3 Mando-Cello (Cello Banjo)

1930s. TB-3 Mastertone rim, 4 strings.

MODEL YEAR	FEATURES	EXC. COND. LOW	HIGH
1930s		$3,700	$4,800

D "The Alrite"

1917. Round body style, round soundhole, The Alrite on inside label, colored wood on top binding and around center hole.

MODEL YEAR	FEATURES	EXC. COND. LOW	HIGH
1917		$825	$1,100

1920 Gibson A-4
Craig Brody

1950 Gibson A-50
Imaged by Heritage Auctions, HA.com

MANDOLINS

1954 Gibson EM-150
Tom Smiley

1924 Gibson F-4
Bob Moreland

MANDOLINS

MODEL YEAR	FEATURES	EXC. COND. LOW	EXC. COND. HIGH

EM-100/EM-125
1938-1943. Initially called EM-100, renamed EM-125 in '41-'43. Style A (pear-shape) archtop body, 1 blade pickup, 2 knobs on either side of bridge, dot markers, tortoise 'guard, sunburst.

| 1938-1940 | EM-100 | $1,275 | $1,650 |
| 1941-1943 | EM-125 | $1,275 | $1,650 |

EM-150
1936-1971. Electric, A-00 body, 1 Charlie Christian pickup early on, 1 P-90 later, bound body, sunburst.

1936-1940	Charlie Christian	$2,600	$3,400
1941-1949	Rectangular pu	$1,400	$1,800
1949-1964	P-90 pickup	$1,400	$1,800
1965-1971	P-90 pickup	$1,200	$1,600

EM-200/Florentine
1954-1971. Electric solidbody, 1 pickup, gold-plated hardware, 2 control knobs, dot markers, sunburst. Called the EM-200 in '60 and '61.

1954-1960	Florentine	$2,200	$2,900
1960-1961	Renamed EM-200	$2,200	$2,900
1962-1971	Renamed Florentine	$2,200	$2,900

F
1900-1903. 1900 model has O.H. Gibson Kalamazoo label, 3-point unbound body, early Gibson F-style, historically important design, inlaid star and crescent headstock. 1903 model is 3-point F-style, bound top rope-style, fancy inlay below-the-string guard, inlaid star and crescent headstock, large dot markers, black finish. Early F-style mandolin ornamentation can vary and values will vary accordingly.

1900	Signed by Orville	$6,000	$27,000
1900	Unsigned	$4,000	$22,000
1901-1902		$3,000	$14,000
1903		$2,500	$13,000

Bill Monroe Signature Model F
1991-1995. Limited run of 200, sunburst.

| 1991-1995 | Lacquer | $8,200 | $10,800 |
| 1991-1995 | Varnish | $8,200 | $10,800 |

Doyle Lawson Signature Model F
2003-2018. Artist Series, F-5 style, carved spruce top, figured maple sides and back, sunburst finish.

| 2003-2018 | | $5,800 | $7,500 |

F-2
1902-1934. Oval soundhole, pearl inlay, star and crescent inlay on peghead.

1902-1909	3-point	$3,500	$4,600
1910-1917	2-point	$3,500	$4,600
1918-1921	2-point	$3,300	$4,300
1922-1924	Loar era	$4,900	$6,300
1925-1934		$4,000	$5,200

F-3
1902-1908. Three-point body, oval soundhole, scroll peghead, pearl inlayed 'guard, limited production model, black top with red back and sides.

| 1902-1908 | | $4,000 | $5,200 |

F-4
1902-1943. Oval soundhole, rope pattern binding, various colors.

| 1902-1909 | 3-point | $5,300 | $6,900 |
| 1910-1921 | 2-point | $5,300 | $6,900 |

MODEL YEAR	FEATURES	EXC. COND. LOW	EXC. COND. HIGH
1922-1924	Loar era	$6,000	$7,800
1925-1943		$3,800	$5,000

F-5
1922-1943; 1949-1980. F-holes, triple-bound body and 'guard. The '20s Lloyd Loar era F-5s are extremely valuable. Reintroduced in '49 with single-bound body, redesigned in '70. The Loar era F-5 market is very specialized to the point that individual instrument valuations can vary based upon the actual sound of the particular instrument. Valuations should be considered on a case-by-case basis.

1922	Loar no virzi	$75,000	$97,000
1923	Loar Apr 12, 1923	$78,000	$102,000
1923	Loar Feb 8, 1923	$78,000	$102,000
1923	Loar Jul 9, 1923, side bound, Monroe date	$85,000	$110,000
1923	Loar non-side bound	$75,000	$97,000
1924	Late-1924, unsigned	$53,000	$70,000
1924	Loar Feb 18, 1924	$78,000	$102,000
1924	Loar Mar 31, 1924	$78,000	$102,000
1924	Loar no virzi	$75,000	$97,000
1924	Loar with virzi	$67,000	$87,000
1925-1929	Fern, Master Model	$45,000	$58,000
1928-1929	Fern, not Master Model	$30,000	$40,000
1930-1931	Fern peghead inlay	$30,000	$40,000
1932-1935	Fern peghead inlay	$25,000	$33,000
1936-1937	Fern peghead inlay	$18,000	$23,000
1938-1940		$18,000	$23,000
1940-1943	Fleur-de-lis peghead inlay	$15,000	$20,000
1949	Flower pot, mahogany neck	$8,000	$10,500
1950-1953	Flower pot, maple neck	$6,300	$8,200
1954	Flower pot peghead inlay	$6,300	$8,200
1955-1956	Flower pot peghead inlay	$6,000	$8,000
1957-1959	Flower pot peghead inlay	$5,000	$6,500
1960-1965		$4,500	$5,900
1966-1969	Sunburst	$3,700	$4,800
1970-1980	Sunburst	$3,300	$4,300

F-5 CMS
2016. Flamed maple back and sides, aged hand-carved spruce top.

| 2016 | | $5,700 | $7,400 |

F-5 Distressed Master Model
2004-2009. Aged finish and hardware.

| 2004-2009 | | $12,100 | $15,600 |

F-5 Fern
2003-2010. Custom Shop model.

| 2003-2010 | | $6,600 | $8,700 |

F-5 Master Model
2002-2018. F-holes, triple-bound body and guard, red spruce top, maple back and sides, flowerpot inlay.

| 2002-2018 | | $10,300 | $13,500 |

MODEL YEAR	FEATURES	EXC. COND. LOW	HIGH

F-5G/F-5G Deluxe

1997-2018. Two-point style F, Deluxe has a slightly wider neck profile.

1997-1999		$3,200	$4,200
2000-2018		$3,500	$4,500

F-5L/F-5L "The Fern"

1978-2018. Reissue of Loar F-5, gold hardware, fern headstock inlay (flowerpot inlay with silver hardware also offered for '88-'91), sunburst.

1978-1984	Kalamazoo-made	$5,000	$6,500
1984-1999		$5,000	$6,500
2000-2018		$4,100	$5,300

F-5V

1990s-2000s. Based on Lloyd Loar's original F-5s of 1922-24, varnish Cremona Brown Sunburst finish.

1990-2000s		$6,500	$8,400

F-5X

1996. F-5 Fern model, X-braced.

1996		$4,700	$6,100

Adam Steffey Signature F-5

2002-2003. Only 50 offered, signature logo on truss rod cover.

2002-2003		$5,300	$7,000

Bella Voce Signature F-5

1989. Custom Shop master-built model, high-end materials and construction, engraved tailpiece with Bella Voce F-5, sunburst.

1989		$7,400	$9,700

Bruce Weber Signature F-5

1995-1996. Label signed by Weber.

1995-1996		$5,100	$6,700

Ricky Skaggs Distressed F-5 Master Model

2007-2008. Distressed Master Model (DMM), limited to 30, hand-carved red spruce top, hand-carved Eastern flamed maple back, sides and neck.

2007-2008		$14,200	$18,700

Sam Bush Signature F-5

2000-2018. Artist Series model, carved spruce top, gold hardware, built at Opry Mill plant in Nashville.

2000-2018		$5,700	$7,400

Wayne Benson Signature F-5

2003-2006. Limited edition of 50, solid spruce top, figured maple back, sides and neck, gold hardware, vintage red satin.

2003-2006		$5,100	$6,600

F-7

1934-1940. F-holes, single-bound body, neck and 'guard, short neck, fleur-de-lis peghead inlay, sunburst.

1934-1937		$8,000	$10,500

F-9

2002-2018. F-5 style, carved spruce top, no inlays, black bound body.

2002-2018		$2,200	$2,900

F-10

1934-1936. Slight upgrade of the '34 F-7 with extended 'board and upgraded inlay, black finish.

1934-1936		$12,900	$17,000

F-12

1934-1937, 1948-1980. F-holes, bound body and neck, scroll inlay, raised 'board until '37, 'board flush with top '48-on, sunburst.

1934-1937		$9,100	$11,800
1948-1959		$3,600	$4,700
1960-1964		$3,400	$4,500
1965-1969		$2,900	$3,800
1970-1980		$2,800	$3,600

H-1 Mandola

1902-1936. Has same features as A-1 mandolin, but without snakehead headstock.

1902-1908	Orange	$1,800	$2,400
1918-1921	Brown	$2,350	$3,100
1922-1924	Loar era	$3,400	$4,400
1925-1928		$3,000	$4,000

H-1E Mandola

Late-1930s. Limited number built, electric with built-in adjustable bar pickup, sunburst.

1938		$3,900	$5,100

H-2 Mandola

1902-1922. Has same features as A-4 mandolin.

1902-1917	Various colors	$3,200	$4,200
1918-1922	Dark mahogany	$3,800	$5,000

H-4 Mandola

1910-1940. Same features as F-4 mandolin.

1910-1921		$7,800	$10,200
1922-1924	Loar era	$9,000	$11,800
1925-1940		$7,700	$10,200

H-5 Mandola

1923-1929 (available by special order 1929-1936), 1990-1991. Same features as the high-end F-5 Mandolin. This is a very specialized market and instruments should be evaluated on a case-by-case basis.

1923-1929	Loar era	$60,000	$79,000
1990-1991	Limited production	$4,600	$6,000

J Mando Bass

1912-1931. Large 24" wide A-style body, 4 strings, extension endpin for upright bass-style playing, optional colors available.

1912-1917	Sunburst	$4,800	$6,200
1918-1922	Brown	$4,800	$6,200
1923-1931	Black	$4,800	$6,200

K-1 Mandocello

1902-1943. Same features as H-1 mandola, off & on production, special order available.

1902-1908	Orange	$3,000	$4,000
1918-1921	Brown	$3,000	$4,000
1922-1924	Loar era	$3,600	$4,700
1925-1943		$3,600	$4,700

K-2 Mandocello

1902-1922. Same features as A-4, black or red mahogany.

1902-1917		$3,600	$4,700

K-4 Mandocello

1912-1929 (offered as special order post-1929). Same features as F-4 mandolin, sunburst.

1912-1921		$7,700	$10,000
1922-1924	Loar era	$13,500	$17,500
1925-1929		$7,950	$10,300

1924 Gibson F-5
Laurence Wexer

1920s Gibson K-2
Bernunzio Uptown Music

MANDOLINS

1926 Gibson MB-3
Bernunzio Uptown Music

Gilchrist Model 5

MODEL YEAR	FEATURES	EXC. COND. LOW	HIGH

M-6 (Octave Guitar)
2002-2006. A-style mandolin body, short-scale 6-string guitar neck.

2002-2006		$1,150	$1,500

MB-00 Mando Banjo
1932-1942. Banjo body, 6-string mandolin neck.

1932-1942		$760	$985

MB-1 Mando Banjo
1922-1923, 1925-1937. Banjo body, 8-string mandolin neck.

1922-1923	Trap door	$410	$530
1925-1937		$585	$760

MB-2 Mando Banjo
1920-1923, 1926-1937. Banjo body, 8-string.

1920-1923	Trap-door	$550	$710
1926-1937		$760	$985

MB-3 Mando Banjo
1923-1939. Banjo body, 8-string.

1923-1924	Trap-door	$760	$985
1925-1939		$1,635	$2,125

MB-4 Mando Banjo
1923-1932. Fleur-de-lis inlay.

1923-1924	Trap-door	$815	$1,060
1925-1932		$1,825	$2,375

MB-11 Mando Banjo
1931-1942. Pearloid headstock with fancy inlay.

1931-1942		$2,750	$3,550

MB-Jr. Mando Banjo
1924-1925. Junior, open back, budget level.

1924-1925		$390	$505

SPF-5
1938. F-style, single bar pickup with volume and tone controls, very limited production, natural.

1938		$21,000	$27,200

Gilchrist
1977-present. Premium and presentation grade, custom, mandolins made by luthier Steve Gilchrist of Camperdown, Australia. Custom ordered but were also initially distributed through Gruhn Guitars, Nashville, Tennessee and then exclusively by Carmel Music Company. Designs are based upon Gibson mandolins built between 1910 and '25.

Mandola
1999. Classical styling.

1999		$20,000	$26,000

Model 1
A-style, maple back and sides, black binding.

2000-2021		$7,000	$9,000

Model 3
A-style, sugar maple back and sides, ivoroid binding, black/white purfling.

2011-2021		$14,500	$18,700

Model 4
F-style, sugar maple back and sides, ivoroid binding.

1978-2006		$14,500	$18,700

Model 4 Junior
F-style, sugar maple back and sides, ivoroid binding.

2012-2021		$11,000	$14,200

Model 5
1978-present. Based on the Gibson '22-'24 Loar-era F-5 mandolin, Gilchrist slant logo, spruce top, flamed maple back, sides, and neck, ebony 'board, multiple binding, sunburst.

1978-2021		$19,000	$25,000
1980	G5 Model, 2 made	$28,000	$36,000

Model 5C Classical
Part of "Classical" quartet commissioned by the Nashville Mandolin Ensemble.

1993	Blond	$20,000	$26,000

Givens
1962-1992. Luthier R. L. (Bob) Givens handcrafted about 800 mandolins and another 700 in a production shop.

A
1962-1975. Early production A-style.

1962-1975		$3,300	$4,300

A-3
1975-1988. Distinguished by use of decal (the only model with Givens decal).

1975-1988		$3,300	$4,300

A-4
1988-1993. No 'board binding, simple block-like multiple-line RL Givens inlay, nicer maple.

1988-1993		$3,300	$4,300

A-5
1988-1993. Bound 'board, pearl headstock inlay.

1988-1993		$3,300	$4,300

A-6 (Torch)
1988-1992. Narrow neck, torch inlay (the only A model with this), gold hardware, snowflake markers.

1988-1992		$3,700	$4,800

A-6 Custom
1991-1992. Elaborate customized A-6 model.

1991-1992		$4,200	$5,500

A-6 Legacy
2007. Givens brand made by long time associate Steven Weill, Engelmann spruce top, Mother-of-Pearl and abalone R.L. Givens flowerpot inlay, 3-tone sunburst.

2007		$1,900	$2,500

F-5 (Fern)
1973-1985. Givens' own version with fern ornamentation.

1973-1985		$7,900	$10,300

F-5 (Loar)
1962-1972. Givens' own version based upon the Loar model F-5.

1962-1972		$7,900	$10,300

F-5 (Torch)
1988-1992. Givens F-5 with torch inlay (the only F model with this).

1988-1992		$8,800	$11,500

F-5 (Wheat Straw)
1986-1988. Givens F-5-style with wheat straw ornamentation.

1986-1988		$8,400	$10,900

MANDOLINS

MODEL		EXC. COND.	
YEAR	FEATURES	LOW	HIGH

Godin

1987-present. Intermediate grade, production, acoustic/electric mandolins from luthier Robert Godin. They also build basses and guitars.

A-8

2000-2020. Single-cut chambered body, acoustic/electric.

2000-2020		$425	$550

Goya

1955-1996. Originally made in Sweden, by the late '70s from Japan, then from Korea.

Japan/Korea-Made

1960s		$275	$350

Sweden-Made

1960s-70s		$500	$700

Gretsch

1883-present. Gretsch started offering mandolins by the early 1900s, then stopped after the late '50s. In 2012 they again offered mandolins.

New Yorker

Late 1940s-late 1950s. Teardrop shape, f-holes, arched top and back, spruce top, maple back, sides, and neck, rosewood 'board.

1940s-50s		$500	$650

G Series

2012-2017. Part of the Roots Collection, spruce top, mahogany body, rosewood 'board, includes New Yorker G9300 Standard, G9310 Supreme (antique mahogany) and G9320 Deluxe.

2012-2017	G9300 Standard	$90	$120
2012-2017	G9320 Deluxe	$110	$150

GTR

1974-1978. GTR (for George Gruhn, Tut Taylor, Randy Wood) was the original name for Gruhn Guitars in Nashville, Tennessee (it was changed in '76). GTR imported mandolins and banjos from Japan. An A-style (similar to a current Gibson A-5 L) and an F-style (similar to mid- to late-'20s F-5 with fern pattern) were offered. The instruments were made at the Moridaira factory in Matsumoto, Japan by factory foreman Sadamasa Tokaida. Quality was relatively high but quantities were limited.

A-Style

1974-1978. A5-L copy with GTR logo on headstock.

1974-1978		$1,125	$1,450

F-Style

1974-1978. F-5 Fern copy with slant GTR logo on headstock, sunburst, handmade in Japan.

1974-1978		$2,050	$2,650

Harmony

1892-1976, late 1970s-present. Founded by Wilhelm Schultz in 1892, and purchased by Sears in 1916. The company evolved into one of the largest producers of stringed instruments in the U.S. in the '30s.

Baroque H35/H835 Electric

Late 1960s-1970s. Electric version of Baroque H425 with single pickup and two controls.

1969-1970	H35	$425	$550
1971-1976	H835	$425	$550

Baroque H425/H8025

Late 1960s-1970s. F-style arched body, extreme bass bout pointy horn, close grained spruce top, sunburst.

1969-1970	H425	$425	$550
1971-1976	H8025	$425	$550

Lute H331/H8031

1960s-1970s. A-style, flat top and back, student level.

1960s	H331	$425	$550
1970s	H8031	$425	$550

M-100

1980s. A-style, sunburst.

1980s		$190	$250

Monterey H410/H417/H8017 Mandolin

1950s-1970s. A-style arched body with f-holes, sunburst.

1950s-70s	All models	$210	$275

Heritage

1985-present. Heritage offered mandolins for a number of years.

H-5

1986-1990s. F-style scroll body, f-holes.

1986-1990s		$2,600	$3,400

Höfner

1887-present. Höfner has offered a wide variety of instruments, including mandolins, over the years. They currently again offer mandolins.

Model 545/E545

1960s. Pear-shaped A-style with catseye f-holes, 545 (acoustic), E545 (acoustic-electric), block-style markers, engraved headstock, Genuine Höfner Original and Made in Germany on back of headstock, transparent brown.

1968-1969	545	$425	$550
1968-1969	E545	$525	$675

Hondo

1969-1987, 1991-2005. Budget grade, production, imported mandolins. They also offered banjos, basses and guitars. Hondo also offered mandolins from around '74 to '87.

Acoustic

1974-1987. Hondo offered A-style, F-style, and bowl back mandolin models.

1974-1987		$115	$150

Acoustic-Electric

1974-1987		$175	$225

F-Style (Loar)

1974-1987		$260	$340

Howe-Orme

1897-ca. 1910. Elias Howe patented a guitar-shaped mandolin on November 14, 1893 and later partnered with George Orme to build a variety of mandolin family instruments and guitars in Boston.

1970s Harmony Model H8025
Bernunzio Uptown Music

1960s Höfner Model 545
Imaged by Heritage Auctions, HA.com

MANDOLINS

*1900s Howe-Orme
Mandolin Style 6*

Lowell Levinger

J.L. Smith Deluxe 5-String

MODEL YEAR	FEATURES	EXC. COND. LOW	HIGH

Mandola
1897-early-1900s. Guitar body-style with narrow waist, not the common mandolin F- or S-style body, pressed (not carved) spruce top, mahogany back and sides, flat-top guitar-type trapeze bridge, decalomania near bridge.

1890s		$1,450	$1,900

Style 3
Brazilian rosewood, plain style.

1900		$1,450	$1,900

Style 4
Guitar-shaped, Brazilian rosewood, fancy style.

1900		$1,600	$2,100

Style 6
Brazilian rosewood, top-of-the-line.

1900		$3,500	$4,500

Ianuario Mandolins
1990-2009. Professional and premium grade, custom, mandolins built by luthier R. Anthony Ianuario in Jefferson, Georgia. He also built banjos and violins. Tony and his wife Ann died in an auto accident in '09.

Ibanez
1932-present. Ibanez offered mandolins from '65 to '83. In '04 they again added mandolins to the product line.

Model 511
1974-1980. A-style, f-holes, dot markers, sunburst.

1974-1980		$250	$325

Model 513
1974-1979. A-5 copy with double cutaways, oval sound hole, dot markers, sunburst.

1974-1979		$270	$350

Model 514
1974-1979. Arched back, spruce, rosewood, dot inlays, sunburst.

1974-1979		$270	$350

Model 522
1974-1978. Symmetrical double point.

1974-1978		$350	$525

Model 524 Artist
1974-1978. F-5 Loar copy, solid wood carved top and solid wood carved top and solid wood back, sunburst.

1974-1978		$775	$1,000

Model 526 (Electric)
1974-1978. A-style body, single pickup, two control knobs, sunburst.

1974-1978		$400	$600

Model 529 Artist
1982-1983. F-5 Loar era copy, solid wood carved top and solid wood spruce top and solid maple sides and back, sunburst.

1982-1983		$900	$1,150

Model M500 Series
2004-present. F-Style and A-Style bodies, acoustic and acoustic-electric option, various finishes.

2004-2021	Various models	$140	$180

Imperial
1890-1922. Imperial mandolins were made by the William A. Cole Company of Boston, Massachusetts.

Bowl Back
1890s		$250	$325

J.L. Smith
2008-present. Custom, intermediate and professional grade, mandolins built by luthier John L. Smith first in Myrtle Beach, South Carolina, and presently in Sebastian, Florida.

Johnson
Mid-1990s-present. Budget and intermediate grade, production, mandolins imported by Music Link, Brisbane, California. Johnson also offers guitars, amps, basses and effects.

MA Series A-Style
Mid-1990s-2013. Import, A-style copy. Several levels offered; range shown is for all value levels.

1990s-2013		$135	$175

MF Series F-Style
Mid-1990s-2006. Import, F-style copy. Several levels offered; range shown is for all value levels.

1990s-2006		$200	$260

Kalamazoo
1933-1942, 1946-1947, 1965-1970. Budget brand produced by Gibson in Kalamazoo, Michigan. They offered mandolins until '42.

Kalamazoo/Oriole A-Style
1930s. Kalamazoo and Oriole on the headstock, KM/A-style.

1930s		$700	$900

KK-31 Mandocello
1935-1938. Archtop, f-hole body, sunburst.

1935		$2,900	$3,800

KM-11
1935-1941. Gibson-made, A-style, flat top and back, round soundhole, dot inlay, sunburst.

1935-1941		$500	$650

KM-12N
1935-1941. A-style with f-holes, spruce top, flamed maple sides and back, bound top and bottom, natural finish.

1935-1941		$600	$800

KM-21
1936-1940. Gibson-made, A-style, f-holes, arched bound spruce top and mahogany back, sunburst.

1936-1940		$750	$975

KM-22
1939-1942. Same as KM-21 with bound top and back.

1939-1942		$850	$1,100

KMB Banjo-Mando
1930s. Banjo-mandolin with resonator.

1930s		$370	$480

MODEL YEAR	FEATURES	EXC. COND. LOW	HIGH

Kay

1931-present. Located in Chicago, Illinois, the Kay company made an incredible amount of instruments under a variety of brands, including the Kay name. From the beginning, Kay offered several types of electric and acoustic mandolins. In '69, the factory closed, marking the end of American-made Kays. The brand survives today on imported instruments.

K68/K465 Concert

1952-1968. Pear-shape, spruce top, mahogany back and sides, natural. Renamed the K465 in '66. Kay also offered a Venetian-style mandolin called the K68 in '37-'42.

1952-1968		$365	$475

K70

1939-1966. Venetian-style, bound top and back, f-holes.

1939-1959		$650	$850

K73

1939-1952. Solid spruce top, maple back and sides, A-style body, f-holes, cherry sunburst.

1939-1952		$365	$475

K390/K395 Professional Electric

1960-1968. Modified Venetian-style archtop, 1 pickup, f-hole, spruce top, curly maple back and sides, sunburst finish. Renamed K395 in '66.

1960-1968		$450	$575

K494/K495 Electric

1960-1968. A-style archtop, single metal-covered (no poles) pickup, volume and tone control knobs, sunburst. The K494 was originally about 60% of the price of the K390 model (see above) in '65. Renamed K495 in '66.

1960-1968		$360	$475

Kay Kraft

1931-1937. First brand name of the newly formed Kay Company. Brand replaced by Kay in '37.

Mandocello

1928-1935. Venetian octave mandolin.

1935		$1,000	$1,300

Mandola

1937		$650	$850

Style C Octave

1928-1935. Deluxe Venetian, rosewood back and sides.

1935		$1,400	$1,800

Venetian/Teardrop

1931-1937. Kay Kraft offered Venetian- and teardrop-shaped mandolins.

1931-1937		$375	$485

Kel Kroydon (by Gibson)

1930-1933. Private branded budget level instruments made by Gibson. They also had guitars and banjos.

KK-20 (Style C-1)

1930-1933. Flat top, near oval-shaped body, oval soundhole, natural finish, dark finish mahogany back and sides.

1930-1933		$1,025	$1,350

Kent

1961-1969. Japanese-made instruments. Kent offered teardrop, A style, and bowlback acoustic mandolins up to '68.

Acoustic

1961-1968. Kent offered teardrop, A-style, and bowl back acoustic mandolins up to '68.

1961-1968		$190	$250

Electric

1964-1969. Available '64-'66 as a solidbody electric and '67-'69 as hollowbody Venetian-style.

1964-1969		$225	$300

Kentucky (Saga M.I.)

1977-present. Brand name of Saga Musical Instruments currently offering budget, intermediate, and professional grade, production, A- and F-style mandolins. Early models made in Japan, then Korea (roughly the '90s), currently made in China.

KM Series

1980s-present. Originally made in Japan, then Korea and now China.

1980s	KM-1000 F-style	$975	$1,265
1980s	KM-180 A-style	$255	$330
1980s	KM-650 F-style	$510	$660
1980s	KM-700 F-style	$510	$660
1980s	KM-800 F-style	$720	$935
1988-2009	KM-850 F-style	$1,140	$1,485
1990-2000s	KM-250S A-style	$275	$360
1990s	KM-200S A-style	$275	$360
1990s	KM-500S A-style	$530	$690
1990s	KM-620 F-style	$525	$675
1990s	KM-675 F-style	$470	$610
1990s-2021	KM-505 A-style	$400	$525
2000-2017	KM-675 F-style	$530	$690
2000-2017	KM-700 F-style	$340	$440
2000-2021	KM-1000 F-style	$975	$1,265
2000-2021	KM-140 A-style	$110	$140
2000-2021	KM-150 A-style	$170	$220
2000-2021	KM-160 A-style	$170	$220
2000-2021	KM-750 F-style	$720	$935
2000s	KM-380S A-style	$235	$305
2000s	KM-620 F-style	$320	$415
2000s	KM-630 F-style	$360	$470
2000s	KM-800 F-style	$340	$440
2010-2021	KM-1500 Master F-5	$1,650	$2,150
2010-2021	KM-606 F-style	$550	$715
2010s	KM-615 F-style	$385	$500
2011	KM-171 A-style	$195	$255
2011-2017	KM-900 A-style	$675	$880
2020-2021	KM-670 F-style	$763	$990
2020-2021	KM-855 F-style	$915	$1,185
2021	KM-256 A-style	$350	$450

Kimble

2000-present. Luthier Will Kimble builds his premium grade, custom/production, mandolins, mandocellos, and mandolas in Cincinnati, Ohio.

1930s Kalamazoo KM-21
Imaged by Heritage Auctions, HA.com

Kentucky KM-1000
Master F-Style

MANDOLINS

Lyon & Healy Style C
Imaged by Heritage Auctions, HA.com

1953 Martin Style 2-15
Greg Perrine

MODEL YEAR	FEATURES	EXC. COND. LOW	HIGH

Kingston

Ca. 1958-1967. Mandolins imported from Japan by Jack Westheimer and Westheimer Importing Corporation of Chicago, Illinois. They also offered guitars, basses and banjos.

Acoustic

1960s	Various models	$160	$210

EM1 Electric

1964-1967. Double-cut solidbody electric, 15.75" scale, 1 pickup.

1960s		$205	$265

Knutsen

1890s-1920s. Luthier Chris J. Knutsen of Tacoma and Seattle, Washington. He moved to Los Angeles, California around 1916. He also made guitars, steels, and ukes.

Harp Mando

1910s. Harp mandolin with tunable upper bass bout with 4 drone strings, and standard mandolin neck. The mandolin version of a harp guitar.

1910s-20s		$1,800	$2,200

Lakeside (Lyon & Healy)

1890-early-1900s. Mainly catalog sales of guitars and mandolins from the Chicago maker. Marketed as a less expensive alternative to the Lyon & Healy Washburn product line.

Style G2016 12-String

1890-early-1900s. 12-string, 18 mahogany ribs with white inlay between, celluloid guard plate.

1890-1900s		$360	$475

Lyle

Ca. 1969-1980. Instruments imported by distributor L.D. Heater of Portland, Oregon. Generally Japanese-made copies of American designs. They also had basses and guitars.

TM-200

1970s	A-style	$170	$220

Lyon & Healy

1864-present. Lyon & Healy was an early large musical instrument builder and marketer, and produced instruments under many different brands.

Style A Mandocello

1910s-1920s. Scroll peghead, symmetrical 2-point body, natural.

1910s-20s		$6,400	$8,300

Style A Professional

1918-1920s. Violin scroll peghead, natural.

1918-1920s	Basic options	$6,400	$8,300
1918-1920s	Fancy options	$8,100	$10,500

Style B

1920s. Maple back and sides, 2-point body, natural.

1920s		$2,350	$3,100

Style C

1920s. Like Style A teardrop Gibson body style, oval soundhole, carved spruce top, carved maple back, natural.

1920s		$2,500	$3,300

Lyra

1920s-1930s. Private brand made by Regal, Lyra name plate on headstock.

Style A (Scroll)

1920s-1930s. Scroll on upper bass bout.

1925-1935		$465	$605

Mann Mandolins

2002-present. Luthier Jonathan Mann builds his professional grade, production/custom, acoustic and electric mandolins in Joelton, Tennessee.

Martin

1833-present. Martin got into the mandolin market in 1895 starting with the typical bowl back designs. By 1914, Gibson's hot selling, innovative, violin-based mandolin pushed Martin into a flat back, bent top hybrid design. By '29, Martin offered a carved top and carved back mandolin. Most models were discontinued in '41, partially because of World War II. Production resumed and standard models are offered up to 1993. From '94 to '02 mandolins are available on a custom order basis only. Martin offered a Backpacker mandolin up to '06.

Backpacker

1998-present. Travel guitar, bell-shaped body.

1998-2021		$125	$160

Style 0

1905-1925. Bowl back-style, 18 rosewood ribs, solid peghead.

1905-1925		$725	$950

Style 00

1908-1925. Bowl back-style, 9 rosewood ribs (14 ribs by '24), solid peghead.

1908-1925		$675	$875

Style 000

1914 only. Bowl back, solid peghead, dot inlay, 9 mahogany ribs.

1914		$675	$875

Style 1

1898-1924. Bowl back, German silver tuners, 18 ribs.

1898-1924		$800	$1,050

Style 2

1898-1924. Bowl back, 26 rosewood ribs, higher appointments than Style 1.

1898-1924		$1,150	$1,500

Style 2-15

1936-1964. Carved spruce top, maple back and sides, f-hole, single-bound back, solid headstock.

1936-1964		$1,150	$1,500

Style 2-20

1936-1942. Carved spruce triple-bound top and bound maple back and sides, f-hole, dot inlay.

1936-1942		$1,750	$2,275

Style 2-30

1937-1941. Carved spruce top and maple back and sides, multi-bound, f-holes, diamond and square inlays.

1937-1941		$2,000	$2,600

Style 3

1898-1922. Bowl back, 26 rosewood ribs, abalone and ivory-bound soundhole.

1898-1922		$1,350	$1,750

MODEL YEAR	FEATURES	EXC. COND. LOW	HIGH

Style 4
1898-1921. Bowl back, 30 rosewood ribs.

1898-1921		$1,475	$1,925

Style 5
1898-1920. Bowl back, vine inlay, abalone top trim.

1898-1920		$1,550	$2,000

Style 6
1898-1921. Bowl back, top bound with ivory and abalone, vine or snowflake inlay.

1898-1921		$1,600	$2,100

Style 20
1929-1942. Symmetrical 2-point body, carved top and back with oval soundhole, dot markers.

1929-1942		$1,800	$2,300

Style A
1914-1995. Flat back, oval soundhole, dot inlay, solid headstock.

1914-1949		$750	$975
1950-1995		$650	$850

Style AA Mandola
1915-1931, 1935, 1941. Mandola version of Style A mandolin.

1915-1941		$1,600	$2,100

Style AK
1920-1937. Koa wood version of Style A, flat back.

1920-1937		$1,300	$1,700

Style A Bitting Special
1917. Private branded, small number produced, Martin and model impressed on back of headstock.

1917		$900	$1,200

Style B
1914-1946, 1981-1987. Flat back with bent top, spruce top and rosewood back and sides, herringbone back stripe, multi-bound.

1914-1939		$1,225	$1,600
1940-1946		$1,125	$1,450
1981-1987		$850	$1,100

Style BB Mandola
1917-1921, 1932-1939. Brazilian rosewood, herringbone trim, features like Style B mandolin. This is the only Mandola offered.

1917-1939		$2,100	$2,700

Style C
1914-1934. Flat back.

1914-1916		$1,775	$2,300
1917-1934		$2,125	$2,750

Style D
1914-1916. Flat back.

1914-1916		$2,700	$3,500

Style E
1915-1937. Flat back, rosewood back and sides, bent spruce top, Style 45 snowflake fretboard inlay and other high-end appointments. Highest model cataloged.

1915-1919		$4,800	$6,200
1920-1937		$5,900	$7,700

May Flower
Ca. 1901-1910. H. J. Flower's Chicago-based May Flower Music Company offered bowl back mandolins that he may or may not have built. There were also May Flower harp guitars built by others.

Bowl Back
1901-1910. Mid-level bowl back-style with 19 rosewood ribs and mid-level appointments.

1901-1910	Fancy	$800	$1,050
1901-1910	Plain	$675	$875

Menzenhauer & Schmidt
1894-1904. Founded by Frederick Menzenhauer and Oscar Schmidt International. Menzenhauer created the guitar-zither in the U.S. He had several patents including one issued in September 1899 for a mandolin-guitar-zither. Control of operations quickly went to Oscar Schmidt.

12-String
1890s. Bowl back mandolin with 3 strings per course that were tuned in octaves, designed during an experimental era for mandolin-related instruments, 13 rosewood ribs, spruce top, inlays.

1890s		$250	$325

Mid-Missouri/The Big Muddy Mandolin Company
1995-present. Intermediate grade, production, acoustic and electric mandolins and mandolas built by luthier Michael Dulak in Columbia, Missouri. In late '06, they changed their name to The Big Muddy Mandolin Company.

M Series
1995-present. Teardrop A-style body, solid spruce top, solid maple, mahogany or rosewood back and sides.

1995-1999	M-0	$340	$440
1995-1999	M-1	$340	$440
1995-2016	M-3	$380	$495
1995-2021	M-15 Mandola	$500	$650
1995-2021	M-2	$360	$470
1995-2021	M-4	$445	$575

Mix
Carbon fiber mandolins built by Peter Mix, Will Kimball, and Matt Durham of New Millennium Acoustic Design (NewMAD) in Waterville, Vermont. They started in 2007.

Monteleone
1971-present. Primarily a guitar maker, luthier John Monteleone also builds presentation grade, custom, mandolins in West Islip, New York.

Morales
Ca.1967-1968. Japanese-made, not heavily imported into the U.S.

Electric

1967-1968		$385	$500

Mozzani
Late-1800s-early-1900s. Founder Luigi Mozzani was an Italian (Bologna) master luthier and renowned composer and musician. There are original Mozzani-built mandolins and also factory-built instruments made later at various workshops.

1916 Martin Style B
Larry Briggs

Monteleone Grand Artist
Laurence Wexer

MANDOLINS

1935 National Style 1
Bernunzio Uptown Music

Nugget Deluxe F

Original Bowl Back
Late-1800s-early-1900s. Handcrafted by Luigi Mozzani, about 24 ribs, soundhole ornamentation, snowflake-like markers.

MODEL YEAR	FEATURES	EXC. COND. LOW	HIGH
1800-1900s		$1,075	$1,400

Factory Bowl Back
1920s. Factory-built bowl back model.

1920s		$385	$500

National
Ca.1927-present. The National brand has gone through many ownership changes and offered resonator mandolins from around 1927 to '41.

Style 0
1931-early-1940s. Metal body with Hawaiian scenes, single cone resonator.

1931-1940s		$2,450	$3,150

Style 1
1928-1936. Plain metal body, single or tricone resonator.

1928-1936	Single cone	$2,100	$2,700
1928-1936	Tricone version	$2,800	$3,625

Style 2
1928-1936. Metal body with rose engraving, single or tricone resonator.

1928-1936	Single cone	$3,400	$4,400
1928-1936	Tricone version	$7,250	$9,400

Style 3
1928-1936. High-quality decorative engraving, single or tricone resonator.

1928-1936	Single cone	$4,350	$5,650
1928-1936	Tricone version	$8,200	$10,600

Style 97
1936-1940. Metal body, tricone resonator.

1936-1940		$5,200	$6,700

Triolian
1928-1940. Metal body with palm trees, single cone resonator.

1928-1940		$2,600	$3,400

Nouveau (Gibson)
1986-1989. Mandolin bodies and necks made in Japan, assembled and finished in U.S. Became Nouveau (by Epiphone) in '88 and the brand was discontinued in '89. They also made guitars.

C7
1986-1987. F-style, white wood body and neck.

1986-1987		$1,600	$2,100

Nugget
1970s-present. Luthier Mike Kemnitzer builds his premium grade mandolins in Central Lake, Michigan.

O'Dell, Doug
See listing under Old Town.

Old Hickory
2005-2010. Budget grade, production, imported F- and A-style acoustic mandolins from Musician's Wholesale America, Nashville, Tennessee. They also offer banjos.

Style A

MODEL YEAR	FEATURES	EXC. COND. LOW	HIGH
2005-2010	AC-100 mid-level	$120	$155
2005-2010	FC-100 high-level	$150	$195
2005-2010	M-1 low-level	$70	$95

Style F

2005-2010	Various models	$175	$225

Old Kraftsman
1930s-1960s. Brand name used by the Siegel Company on instruments made by Kay and others (even Gibson). Quality was mixed, but some better-grade instruments were offered.

Various Models

1950s		$300	$385

Old Town
1974-2007. Luthier Doug O'Dell built his professional and premium grade, production/custom acoustic and electric mandolins in Ohio.

EM Series Electric

1980s-2007	Various models	$1,850	$2,400

Old Wave
1990-present. Luthier Bill Bussmann builds his professional and premium grade, production/custom, mandolins and mandolas in Caballo, New Mexico. He has also built guitars and basses.

Orpheum
1897-1942, 1944-early 1970s, 2001-2006. Intermediate grade, production, mandolins. They also offered guitars. An old brand often associated with banjos, 1930s branded guitars sold by Bruno and Sons. 1950s branded guitars and mandolins sold by Maurice Lipsky Music, New York, New York. The brand was revived for '01 to '06 by Tacoma Guitars.

Mando-Banjo
1910-1930. Mandolin neck on small banjo body, fancy headstock and fretboard inlay, carved heel.

1910-1930	Model No 1	$375	$500
1910-1930	Model No 2	$475	$600
1910-1930	Model No 3	$525	$700

Model 730 E Electric
1950s. Private branded for Maurice Lipsky as a student model, A-style body, 1 bar pickup, 2 side-mounted knobs, maple back and sides, dots, sunburst.

1950s		$550	$725

Style A

1950s		$360	$475

Oscar Schmidt
1879-ca. 1939, 1979-present. Currently offering budget and intermediate grade, production, mandolins. They also offer guitars, basses, banjos, ukuleles and the famous Oscar Schmidt autoharp. The original Schmidt company offered innovative mandolin designs during the 1900-'30 mandolin boom.

Mando-Harp Style B
1890s. More zither-autoharp than mandolin, flat autoharp body with soundhole.

1890s		$190	$250

MANDOLINS

MODEL YEAR	FEATURES	EXC. COND. LOW	HIGH

Sovereign

1920s. Bowl back, bent top, rope-style binding, mahogany ribs, dot inlay, plain headstock, natural.

1920s	Basic	$300	$400
1920s	Fancy	$775	$1,000

Ovation

1966-present. Ovation added mandolins in '94 and currently offers intermediate and professional grade, production, mandolins. They also offer guitars and basses.

MCS148 (Celebrity)

1994-2017. Single-cut, small Ovation body, Ovation headstock, red sunburst.

1994-2017		$400	$525

Paris Swing

2005-2008. Intermediate grade, production, imported acoustic mandolins from The Music Link, which also offers instruments under Johnson and other brands.

Phoenix

Premium grade, production/custom, mandolins built by luthier Rolfe Gerhardt (formerly builder of Unicorn Mandolins in the '70s) in South Thomaston, Maine. Gerhardt's Phoenix company, which started in 1990, specializes in a 2-point Style A (double-cut) body style.

Ramsey

1990s. Built by luthier John Ramsey of Colorado Springs, Colorado.

Ratliff

1982-present. Professional and premium grade, production/custom, mandolin family instruments built by luthier Audey Ratliff in Church Hill, Tennessee.

R Series

1990s-present. R-5 is an F-style mando, R-4 is round-hole version of 5.

1995-2016	R-4	$1,550	$2,000
1995-2021	R-5	$2,300	$3,000

Silver Eagle

1998	A-style	$1,350	$1,750

Recording King

1929-1943. Montgomery Ward house brand. Suppliers include Gibson, Kay, Regal, and Gretsch. Brand name revived by The Music Link in '05.

Style A

1929-1943. Gibson-made, plain appointments, sunburst.

1929-1943		$450	$600

Red Diamond

Early 1980s-present. Luthier Don MacRostie builds his premium grade, production/custom, mandolins in Athens, Ohio.

Regal

Ca. 1895-1966, 1987-present. Large Chicago-based manufacturer which made their own brand name and others for distributors and mass merchandisers. Absorbed by the Harmony Company in 1954.

A-Style

1920s		$365	$475

Bicentennial 76

1976. A-style body, flat back, oval soundhole, '76 logo on 'guard, white body, red peghead, blue stars on front and back.

1976		$425	$550

Octofone

1920s-1930s. It had 8 strings, but Regal's marketing department named this the Octo because it was "eight instruments in one" as it could be tuned as a mandolin, tenor banjo, tenor guitar and other instruments.

1920s-30s		$440	$575

Resonator

1937	Model 250	$1,050	$1,375
1950s		$650	$850

Standard

1930s		$460	$600

Ultra Grand Deluxe

1930s		$650	$850

Rickenbacker

1931-present. Rickenbacker had the Electro Mandolin in the late '30s and introduced 4-, 5- and 8-string electric models in 1958 and currently offers one model.

Model 5002V58

1958-present. 8 strings, maple front, walnut back, rosewood 'board.

1958-2021		$1,375	$1,800

Rigel

1990-2006. Professional and premium grade, production/custom mandolins and mandolas built by luthier Pete Langdell in Hyde Park, Vermont.

Roberts

1980s. Built by luthier Jay Roberts of California.

Tiny Moore Jazz 5

1980s. Based on Bigsby design of the early-1950s as used by Tiny Moore, five-string electric, sunburst.

1985		$1,575	$2,050

Ryder

1992-present. Luthier Steve Ryder builds his professional and premium grade, production/custom solid and semi-hollowbody electric mandolins, mandola and octave mandolins in South Portland, Maine.

S. S. Stewart

1878-1904. S.S. Stewart of Philadelphia was primarily known for banjos. Legend has it that Stewart was one of the first to demonstrate the mass production assembly of stringed instruments.

Ratliff R-5

1930s Regal Flat Back Teardrop
Bernunzio Uptown Music

MANDOLINS

Stelling S-5

1930s Strad-O-Lin Style A
Bernunzio Uptown Music

MANDOLINS

MODEL YEAR	FEATURES	EXC. COND. LOW	HIGH

Mando-Banjo
Early-1900s. Mandolin neck and a very small open back banjo body, star inlay in headstock.

| 1900s | | $250 | $325 |

Sekova
Mid-1960s-mid-1970s. Entry level, imported by the U.S. Musical Merchandise.

Electric
1960s-1970s. Kay-Kraft-style hollowbody with f-holes, 1 pickup and Sekova logo on the headstock.

| 1960s-70s | | $375 | $490 |

Sigma
1970-2007. Budget and intermediate grade, production, import mandolins distributed by C.F. Martin Company. They also offered guitars, basses and banjos.

SM6
1970-2007. Made in Korea.

| 1970-2007 | | $250 | $325 |

Silvertone
1941-ca.1970, present. Brand name used by Sears on their musical instruments.

Arched
1941-ca.1970. Arched top and back, sunburst.

| 1940s-50s | | $300 | $390 |

Sovereign
Ca. 1899-ca. 1938. Sovereign was originally a brand of the Oscar Schmidt company of New Jersey. In the late '30s, Harmony purchased several trade names from the Schmidt Company, including Sovereign. Sovereign then ceased as a brand, but Harmony continued using it on a model line of Harmony guitars.

Bent-Top
1920s-1930s. Old-style bent top.

| 1920s-30s | | $300 | $400 |

Stanley Mandolins
Luthier Chris Stanley builds his premium grade, production/custom, A-style and F-style mandolins in Rhinelander, Wisconsin. He started in 2003.

Stathopoulo
1903-1916. Original design instruments, some patented, by Epiphone company founder A. Stathopoulo.

A-Style
1903-1916. A-style with higher-end appointments, bent-style spruce top, figured maple back and sides.

| 1903-1916 | | $775 | $1,000 |

Stella
Ca. 1899-1974, 2000s. Stella was a brand of the Oscar Schmidt Company which was an early contributor to innovative mandolin designs and participated in the 1900-'30 mandolin boom. Pre-World War II Stella instruments were low-mid to mid-level instruments. In '39, Harmony purchased the Stella name and '50s and '60s Stella instruments were student grade, low-end instruments. The Stella brand was reintroduced in the 2000s by MBT International.

Banjo-Mando
1920s. One of several innovative designs that attempted to create a new market, 8-string mandolin neck with a banjo body, Stella logo normally impressed on the banjo rim or the side of the neck.

| 1920s | | $150 | $200 |

Bowl Back
1920s. Typical bowl back, bent top-style mandolin with models decalomania, about 10 (wide) maple ribs, dot markers.

| 1920s | | $150 | $195 |

Pear-Shape
1940s-1960s. Harmony-made lower-end mandolins, pear-shaped (Style A) flat back, oval soundhole.

| 1940s-60s | | $210 | $275 |

Stelling
1974-present. Mainly known for banjos, Stelling also builds premium grade, production/custom mandolins in Afton, Virginia.

Sterling
Early-1900s. Distributed by wholesalers The Davitt & Hanser Music Co.

Stiver
1971-present. Premium grade, custom/production, mandolins built by luthier Louis Stiver in Polk, Pennsylvania.

A Model

| 1982-2021 | | $2,600 | $3,400 |

F-5

| 1982-2021 | | $3,400 | $4,400 |

Strad-O-Lin/Stradolin
Ca.1920s-ca.1960s. The Strad-O-Lin company was operated by the Hominic brothers in New York, primarily making mandolins for wholesalers. In the late '50s, Multivox/Premier bought the company and used the name on mandolins, guitars and amps.

Baldwin Electric
1950s-1960s. A-Style, single pickup, tone and volume knobs, spruce top, maple back and sides, Baldwin logo on headstock, natural.

| 1950s-60s | Various models | $300 | $400 |

Junior A
1950s-1960s. A-Style, Stradolin Jr. logo on head-stock, dot markers, sunburst.

| 1950s-60s | | $175 | $225 |

Style A
1920s-1950s. A-style body with f-holes, dot markers.

| 1940s-50s | | $435 | $565 |

Various Models

| 1920s-30s | | $435 | $565 |

MODEL YEAR	FEATURES	EXC. COND. LOW	HIGH

Summit

1990-present. Professional and premium grade, production/custom mandolins built by luthier Paul Schneider in Hartsville, Tennessee. He was originally located in Mulvane, Kansas.

Supertone

1914-1941. Brand used by Sears before they switched to Silvertone. Instruments made by other companies.

Various Models

Spruce top, mahogany back and sides, some with decalomania vine pattern on top.

1920s-30s	Basic	$275	$360
1920s-30s	Fancy	$450	$580

Supro

1935-1968, 2004-present. Budget line from the National Dobro Company. Brand name was revived in '04.

T30 Electric

1950s		$700	$900

Tacoma

1995-2009. Tacoma offered intermediate, professional and premium grade, production, electric and acoustic mandolins up to '06. They also built guitars and basses.

M Series

1999-2006. Solid spruce top, typical Tacoma bodystyle with upper bass bout soundhole, E (i.e. M-1E) indicates acoustic/electric.

1999-2004	M2/M2E, rosewood	$450	$600
1999-2006	M1/M1E, mahogany	$385	$500
1999-2006	M3/M3E, maple	$450	$600

Unicorn

1970s-late 1980s. Luthier Rolfe Gerhardt (currently luthier for Phoenix Mandolins) founded Unicorn in the mid-'70s. Gerhardt built 149 mandolins before selling Unicorn to Dave Sinko in '80. Sinko closed Unicorn in the late-'80s.

Vega

The original Boston-based company started in 1889 and was purchased by C.F. Martin in '70. The Deering Banjo Company acquired the brand in '89 and uses it on a line of banjos.

Lansing Special Bowl

1890s. Spruce top, abalone, vine inlay.

1890s		$385	$500

Little Wonder Mando-Banjo

1920s. Maple neck, resonator.

1920s		$385	$500

Mando Bass

1910s-1920s. Large upright bass-sized instrument with bass tuners, body-style similar to dual-point A-style, scroll headstock.

1910s-20s		$3,400	$4,400

Mando Cittern

1910s. Vague A-style with oval soundhole and cylinder back,10-string (five double strings tuned in 5ths), natural.

1910s		$1,850	$2,400

Mandola Lute

1915. Few made, 15" scale, 10-string.

1915		$2,075	$2,675

Style 202 Mando-Lute

Early-1900s. Basic A-style with small horns, natural spruce top, mahogany sides and cylinder back, dot markers.

1915		$1,875	$2,425

Style 205 Cylinder Back

1910s-1920s. Rounded tube cylinder shape runs the length of the back.

1910s		$1,300	$1,700
1920s		$1,150	$1,500

Style A

1910s		$510	$660

Style D 100 Electric Hollowbody

1940		$550	$715

Style F

1910s. Scroll upper bass bout, oval soundhole, Vega and torch inlay in headstock.

1910s		$775	$1,000

Style K Mando-Banjo

1910s-30s		$250	$325

Style L Mando-Banjo/Whyte Laydie

1910s-1920s. Open back banjo body and mandolin 8-string neck.

1910s-20s		$700	$900

Style S Mando-Banjo

1915		$600	$775

Super Deluxe

1910s	Sunburst	$775	$1,000

Tubaphone Style X Mando-Banjo

1922-1923		$775	$1,000

Vinaccia

Italian-made by Pasquale Vinaccia, luthier.

Bowl Back

1900-1920s. High-end appointments and 'guard, 30 rosewood ribs.

1900-1920s		$1,700	$2,200

Vivi-Tone

1933-ca. 1936. Lloyd Loar's pioneering guitar company also built early electric mandolins and mandocellos in Kalamazoo, Michigan.

Acoustic

1933-1935. Spruce top, back and sides.

1933-1935		$4,500	$5,800

Electric

1933-1935. Vivi-Tone silkscreen logo on headstock.

1933-1935		$4,500	$5,800

Electric Mandocello

1933-1935. Traditonal guitar-arch body, Vivi-Tone silkscreen logo on headstock.

1933-1935		$5,300	$6,900

Electric Mandola

1933-1935. Traditonal European teardrop/pear-shaped top, Vivi-Tone silkscreen logo on headstock.

1933-1935		$4,900	$6,300

Stiver F-5

1922 Vega Tu-Ba-Phone
Imaged by Heritage Auctions, HA.com

MANDOLINS

Ca. 1898 Washburn Model 118
Izzy Miller

1920 Washburn #1648 Bowl Back
Bernunzio Uptown Music

MODEL YEAR	FEATURES	EXC. COND. LOW	HIGH

Waldo
1891-early 1900s. Mandolin family instruments built in Saginaw, Michigan.
Bowl Back
1890s. Alternating rosewood and maple ribs, some with script Waldo logo on pickguard.

1890s	Various models	$195	$255

Washburn
1962-present. Currently offering imported intermediate and professional grade, production, mandolins.
Various Models
1974-present. Various imported models plywood to fancy carved.

1974-2021		$80	$350

Washburn (Lyon & Healy)
1880s-ca.1949. Washburn was founded in Chicago as one of the lines for Lyon & Healy to promote high quality stringed instruments, ca. 1880s. The rights to Washburn were sold to Regal which built Washburns by the mid-'30s until ca. '49. In '74 the brand resurfaced.
Bowl Back
1890s-1900s. Lyon and Healy sold a wide variety of bowl back mandolins, some Brazilian ribs with fancy inlays and bindings.

1890-1900s	Fancy	$850	$1,100
1890-1900s	Plain	$250	$330
1900s	Standard appointments	$350	$450

Style A
1920s. Professional quality.

1920s		$2,700	$3,500

Style E
1915-1923. Brazilian rosewood.

1915-1923		$575	$750

MODEL YEAR	FEATURES	EXC. COND. LOW	HIGH

Weber
1996-present. Intermediate, professional, and premium grade, production/custom, mandolins, mandolas, and mandocellos. Many former Flatiron employees, including Bruce Weber, formed Sound To Earth, Ltd., to build Weber instruments when Gibson moved Flatiron from Montana, to Nashville. Originally in Belgrade, Montana, and after '04, in Logan, Montana. They also build guitars. In '12, Two Old Hippies (Breedlove, Bedell) acquired the brand, moving production in '13 to Oregon where Bruce Weber oversees development.
Absaroka
2000s. A style body, white binding, diamond inlays.

2002		$1,975	$2,550

Alder #1 Mandola
Celtic A style body, black binding, diamond inlays.

1997		$1,200	$1,550

Alder #2 Mandola
2000-2012. Teardrop body, X-braced, spruce top, maple back and sides.

2000-2012		$1,200	$1,575

Aspen #1
1997-2011. Teardrop A-style, solid spruce top, maple sides and back, mahogany neck.

1997-2011		$875	$1,125

Aspen #2
1997-2011. Like #1, but with maple neck.

1997-2011		$900	$1,175

Beartooth
1997-2009. Teardrop A-style, solid spruce top, curly maple sides, back, and neck.

1997-2009		$1,825	$2,375

Big Sky

1999	F-style	$3,175	$4,125

Bighorn
2006-2008. A-style, oval, double Venetian.

2006-2008		$2,450	$3,200

MANDOLINS

MODEL YEAR	FEATURES	EXC. COND. LOW	HIGH
Bitterroot			
2002-present. Style A or F.			
2002-2021	A-style	$2,100	$2,750
2002-2021	F-style	$2,400	$3,200
Bridger			
2000-2015. A-Celtic style, long neck.			
2000-2015		$1,900	$2,475
Custom Vintage			
2007-present. Heritage Series.			
2007-2021	A-style	$2,825	$3,675
2007-2021	F-style	$3,925	$5,100
Fern			
1997-present. Heritage Series, top of the product line.			
1997-2021	A-style	$3,400	$4,600
1997-2021	F-style	$4,000	$5,200
Gallatin			
1999-present. Spruce top, Amber Burst finish.			
1999-2021	A-style	$1,050	$1,400
1999-2021	F-style	$1,600	$2,100
Octar			
2008. Octave mando, 15" archtop body.			
2008		$1,950	$2,550
Sage #1 Octave			
2003-2006. Octave mando, diamond inlays.			
2003-2006		$950	$1,225
Sweet Pea			
2009-2012. Travel mando.			
2009-2012		$300	$385
Y2K			
2000-2002. Celtic-style teardrop body, satin natural finish.			
2000-2002		$635	$825

MODEL YEAR	FEATURES	EXC. COND. LOW	HIGH
Yellowstone			
1997-present. A-style and F-style available, solid spruce top, curly maple sides, back, and neck, sunburst.			
1997-2021	A-style	$2,300	$3,000
1997-2021	F-style	$3,200	$4,200
2003-2021	Mandola	$3,000	$3,900
2010-2021	Octave	$2,400	$3,200

Weymann

1864-1940s. H.A. Weymann & Sons was a musical instrument distributor located in Philadelphia. They also built their own instruments.

MODEL YEAR	FEATURES	EXC. COND. LOW	HIGH
Keystone State Banjo-Mando			
1910s. Maple rim and back, ebony fretboard.			
1910s		$325	$425
Mando-Banjo			
1920s. Mandolin neck on an open banjo body.			
1920s	Various models	$310	$400
Mando-Lute			
1920s. Lute-style body, spruce top, flamed maple sides and back, rope binding, deluxe rosette, natural.			
1920s	Various models	$600	$785

Wurlitzer

The old Wurlitzer company would have been considered a mega-store by today's standards. They sold a wide variety of instruments, gave music lessons, and operated manufacturing facilities.

MODEL YEAR	FEATURES	EXC. COND. LOW	HIGH
Banjolin			
1920s. Mandolin neck on banjo body.			
1920s		$440	$575
Mando-Banjo			
1900-1910. Mandolin neck on open back banjo body, plain-style.			
1900-1910		$200	$265
Various Models			
1920s. Various woods and appointments.			
1920s		$460	$600

Weber Bitterroot A14-O
Bernunzio Uptown Music

Wurlitzer
Imaged by Heritage Auctions, HA.com

MANDOLINS

BANJOS

Bacon Blue Ribbon
Intermountain Guitar and Banjo

*1931 Bacon & Day Silver
Bell Montana Plectrum*
William Ritter/Gruhn Guitars

Banjo collectors, hobbyists, and dealers often think nothing of changing the neck on a banjo; a banjo may have a true vintage neck or a new replacement neck. So, our all original parts concept that applies to the rest of this Price Guide doesn't always apply to vintage banjos.

The banjo market operates somewhat differently than many of the other markets that are covered in the Guide. The prices shown are guidance prices only and each instrument should be evaluated on a case-by-case basis.

Acme

1893-early 1900s. Banjos made for Sears by S.S. Stewart, and later George Bauer, both of Philadelphia.

The Pearl
Open back, 5-string, pearl fretboard.

1908	$825	$1,075

The Professor
Tree-of-Life board, 5-string.

1900	$825	$1,075

Aria/Aria Pro II

1956-present. Aria offered banjos from time to time under both the Aria and Aria Pro II brand names. They also make guitars, basses, and mandolins.

Resonator 5-String
1976-1978. 5-string resonator back, Aria Pro II brand, models PB450, PB550 and PB650.

1975	$450	$600

August Pollmann

1880s-1890s. These are thought to have been made for August Pollman's New York based company, by luthier Pehr Anderberg who had a shop in Boston, Massachusetts.

Royal Professional

1890s	5-String	$350	$475

Bacon

1906-1967. Frederick Bacon was a well-known banjo player when he started selling banjos under his own name. The earliest Bacon banjos were built by other companies. By 1920, they were building their own models including the B&D (Bacon & Day) models. In 1940 Gretsch purchased the company and took over production.

FF Professional No. 3

1906-1907	5-string	$10,600	$13,800

Special

1914	5-string	$1,900	$2,450

Style C/Super Tenor

1920-1926	Tenor	$450	$575

Bacon & Day

1921-1967. B&D was not a separate company, but a line of banjos from the Bacon Banjo Company. David Day left Vega to join up with Fred Bacon in '21. Gretsch purchased Bacon in '40, and offered

Bacon and B&D banjos until '67.

MODEL YEAR	FEATURES	EXC. COND. LOW	HIGH
Blue Bell			
1922-1939	Tenor	$725	$950
Blue Ribbon 17			
1933-1939	Tenor	$575	$750
Blue Ribbon Deluxe			
1933-1939	Tenor	$1,650	$2,150
Blue Ribbon Orchestra			
1933-1939	Tenor	$1,650	$2,150
FF Professional No. 1			
1921	5-string	$1,375	$1,800
FF Professional No. 2			
1921	5-string	$1,375	$1,800
FF Professional No. 3			
1920-1922	Tenor	$650	$840
Ne Plus Ultra			
1920s	#5, Plectrum	$5,750	$7,450
1920s	#5, Tenor	$5,750	$7,450
1920s	#6, Plectrum	$6,900	$8,900
1920s	#6, Tenor	$6,500	$8,600
1920s	#7, Plectrum	$10,300	$13,500
1920s	#7, Tenor	$9,800	$13,000
1920s	#8, Plectrum	$17,000	$22,000
1920s	#8, Tenor	$16,200	$21,000
1920s	#9, Plectrum	$17,000	$22,000
1920s	#9, Tenor	$16,200	$21,000
1930s	Tenor	$6,600	$8,500
1948	Plectrum	$2,475	$3,200
1950s-60s	Tenor	$1,700	$2,200
Ne Plus Ultra Style 6			
1920s	Plectrum or Tenor	$8,150	$10,600
Roy Smeck			
1930s. Silver Bell #1, tenor.			
1930s		$1,600	$2,100
Senorita			
1930s	Plectrum	$650	$850
1950s	4-String	$475	$625
Silver Bell #1 Series			
1920-1933	#1 Plectrum	$1,700	$2,225
1920-1933	#1 Tenor	$1,700	$2,200
1920-1939	#1 5-String	$2,800	$3,650
1933-1939	#1 Montana, Plectrum	$1,700	$2,225
1933-1939	#1 Montana, Tenor	$1,575	$2,050
1933-1939	#1 Serenader, Tenor	$1,700	$2,200
1933-1939	#1 Symphonie, Tenor	$1,850	$2,400
Silver Bell #2 Series			
1920-1933	#2 Tenor	$1,675	$2,175
Silver Bell #3 Series			
1920-1933	#3 Montana, Tenor	$2,125	$2,750
1920-1933	#3 Tenor	$2,025	$2,625
1931	#3 Sultana, Tenor	$2,125	$2,750
1933-1939	#3 Montana, Plectrum	$2,300	$2,975
Silver Bell #4 Series			
1928	#4 Montana, Tenor	$3,100	$4,000
1928	#4 Tenor	$3,100	$4,000
Silver Bell #5 Series			
1920s	#5 5-String	$4,000	$5,150
Silver Bell #6 Series			
1927	#6 Montana, Tenor	$4,400	$5,700

BANJOS

The *Vintage Guitar Price Guide* shows low to high values for items in all-original excellent condition, and, where applicable, with original case or cover.

MODEL YEAR	FEATURES	EXC. COND. LOW	HIGH
Super			
1920-1925	Tenor, non-carved neck	$725	$950
1926-1927	5-String, carved neck	$2,275	$2,950
1926-1927	5-String, non-carved neck	$2,025	$2,625
1926-1927	Plectrum	$1,025	$1,325
1926-1927	Tenor, non-carved neck	$925	$1,200
Symphonie Silver Bell			

1960. By Gretsch, script Symphonie logo on headstock, fancy ornamentation, gold-plated hardware.

1960	5-String	$1,825	$2,350

Baldwin

1966-1976. Baldwin was one of the largest piano retailers in the Midwest and in 1965, they got into the guitar market. In '66 they bought the ODE Banjo company. From '66 to '71 the banjos were labeled as Baldwin; after that ODE was added below the Baldwin banner. In '76 Gretsch took over ODE production.

Ode 2R

1968	Plectrum, 4-String	$875	$1,125

Ode Style C

1968	Bluegrass, 5-String	$1,200	$1,575

Style D

1968-1969	5-String	$2,300	$2,975

Barratt

1890s. Made by George Barratt in Brooklyn, New York.

Style D 5-String

1890s	Victorian era	$300	$400

Benary and Sons

1890-1899. Manufactured by the James H. Buckbee Co. for music instrument wholesaler Robert Benary.

Celebrated Benary

1890-1899. 5-string, open back, plain appointments.

1890-1899		$400	$550

Bishline

1985-present. Professional and premium grade, production/custom, banjos built by luthier Robert Bishline in Tulsa, Oklahoma.

Boucher

1830s-1850s. William Boucher's operation in Baltimore is considered to be one of the very first banjo-shops. Boucher and the Civil War era banjos are rare. The price range listed is informational guidance pricing only. The wide range reflects conservative opinions. 150 year old banjos should be evaluated per their own merits.

Double Tack

1840s		$8,175	$10,600

Single Tack

1840s		$7,350	$9,550

Bruno and Sons

Established in 1834 by Charles Bruno, primarily as a distributor, Bruno and Sons marketed a variety of brands, including their own.

Royal Artist Tenor

1920s	Figured resonator	$525	$700

Buckbee

1863-1897. James H. Buckbee Co. of New York was the city's largest builder. The company did considerable private branding for companies such as Benery, Dobson, and Farland.

5-String

1890-1897. 5-string, open back, plain appointments.

1890-1897	High-level	$1,225	$1,600
1890-1897	Low-level	$410	$530
1890-1897	Mid-level	$650	$850

Christy

1960s. Banjos built by luthier Art Christianson in Colorado.

5-String Long Neck Folk

1965	Rare	$550	$725
1965	Standard	$400	$525

Cole

1890-1919. W.A. Cole, after leaving Fairbanks & Cole, started his own line in 1890. He died in 1909 but the company continued until 1919. He also made guitars and mandolins.

Eclipse

1890-1919	Dot diamond inlays	$1,575	$2,025
1890-1919	Flower inlays	$1,800	$2,325
1890-1919	Man-in-the-moon inlays	$2,050	$2,650

Model 4000

Fancy pearl, carved heel.

1890		$3,700	$4,800

Deering

1975-present. Greg and Janet Deering build their banjos in Spring Valley, California. In 1978 they introduced their basic and intermediate banjos. They also offer banjos under the Goodtime and Vega brands.

40th Anniversary

2015	5-String	$2,350	$3,050

B-6

1986-2002. Mahogany neck and resonator, ebony 'board, 6 strings, satin finish.

1986-2002		$875	$1,150

Basic

Resonator back, 5 strings.

1979-1982		$825	$1,075

Black Diamond

1998-2020. Black head, mahogany neck, 5 strings, ebony 'board, diamond inlays, resonator back.

2001		$1,250	$1,625

Ca. 1890 Benary and Sons Celebrated Benary

Elderly Instruments

Ca.1890s Buckbee

Kenneth Parr

BANJOS

1993 Deering Golden Era

Imaged by Heritage Auctions, HA.com

Deering Maple Blossom

MODEL YEAR	FEATURES	EXC. COND. LOW	EXC. COND. HIGH
Boston			
1982-present. Mahogany resonator and neck, 5 or 6 strings, ebony 'board, seed and vine inlays.			
1982	5-String	$800	$1,050
2012	6-String	$1,125	$1,450
Calico			
1998-present. Curly maple resonator and neck, 5 strings, ebony 'board, plectrum and tenor available.			
2007-2010		$2,800	$3,700
Calico Custom			
1997-2007.			
2007	5-String	$3,275	$4,250
Crossfire			
1998-2016. Alder body, maple neck, 5 strings, ebony 'board, diamond inlays. Available in tenor.			
2005-2016		$2,050	$2,650
D-6 Banjo-Guitar			
1995	Resonator, 6-String	$1,625	$2,100
Deluxe			
1995-2020. Mahogany resonator, mahogany or maple neck, ebony 'board, white and gold inlays on 6-string. Available 5-, 6- or 12-string, plectrum 4-string, 17- or 19-fret tenor 4-string.			
1995-2003	5- or 6-String	$1,725	$2,250
1995-2003	Plectrum 4-String	$1,325	$1,725
Eagle II			
2010-present. Resonator back, available as 5-string, 6-string, open back 5-string and 19-fret tenor.			
2010-2016	5-String	$1,425	$1,850
G.D.L. Greg Deering Limited Edition			
2001-2010. Figured walnut neck, burl walnut resonator, abalone and mother-of-pearl inlays, ebony 'board, 5 strings.			
2001		$3,500	$4,500
Golden Era			
1995-present. Deeper resonator sound chamber, curly maple, 5 strings, ebony 'board, Cremona Sunburst stain finish.			
1995-2016		$2,300	$3,000
Golden Wreath			
2006-present. Deep resonator, 5 strings, mahogany neck, ebony 'board, mother of pearl wreath inlay.			
2006		$2,300	$3,000
Goodtime 5-String			
2010-2013		$400	$525
Goodtime Special			
2001-present. Maple neck, rim and resonator, black inlays and binding. Available 4-string plectrum and 19-fret tenor, or 5-string open back.			
2010-2013	5-string	$675	$875
Grand Ole Opry			
2005. Limited Edition for Opry's 80th anniversary, hand signed by Greg and Janet Deering, only 80 produced.			
2005	5-string	$3,900	$5,100
Ivanhoe			
High-end appointments, 5-string.			
1986		$8,000	$10,350
John Hartford			
Resonator back, curly maple, 5-string, offered in 22 or 24 frets.			
2007-2015		$2,500	$3,225

MODEL YEAR	FEATURES	EXC. COND. LOW	EXC. COND. HIGH
Maple Blossom			
1983-present. Dark walnut stained maple neck, 4, 5, or 6 strings, fancy inlays, high gloss finish. Originally called the Advanced ('78-'82).			
1983-2016	5-string	$2,050	$2,650
1983-2016	Tenor	$1,400	$1,800
Saratoga Star			
2004	5-string	$3,750	$4,850
Sierra			
1998-present. Mahogany or maple neck and resonator, maple rim, ebony 'board, 4- or 5-string, electric/acoustic or openback.			
1996-2014		$1,300	$1,675
Standard			
1992	5-string	$1,300	$1,675
Tenbrooks Saratoga Star			
Curly maple neck and deep resonator, 5-string, ebony 'board.			
2010		$3,300	$4,300
Texas Calico			
1986. Limited run of 150, Texas and 1836-1986 logo on fretboard, engraved gold-plated metal hardware, 5 strings.			
1986		$8,300	$10,700

Ditson

1916-1930. The Oliver Ditson Company of Boston offered a variety of musical instruments.

Tenor			
Resonator with typical appointments, 4 strings.			
1920		$500	$650

Dobro

1929-1942, ca. 1954-2019. Guitars and mandolins were also made under the Dobro name. In '93 Gibson purchased the brand and built Dobros in Nashville, Tennessee. For more info refer to the guitar section.

Dojo			
Resonator guitar body with 5-string banjo neck.			
1988-1994		$1,475	$1,900

Dobson, C. Edgar

1880s. The Dobson brothers – Henry Clay, Charles Edgar, George Clifton, Frank Prescott, and Edward Clarendon – were banjo teachers and performers who marketed banjos in various ways over the years.

Great Echo			
1888	5-String	$900	$1,300

Dobson, George

1870-1890. Marketed by renown banjo instructor George C. Dobson of Boston, Massachusetts.

Matchless			
1880s	5-String	$800	$1,100

Dobson, H.C.

1860s-early 1900s. The oldest of the Dobson brothers, Henry C. was a successful musical instrument distributor out of New York. They were designed by Henry, but most, if not all, were made by others.

MODEL YEAR	FEATURES	EXC. COND. LOW	HIGH
Silver Chime			
1870-1890	Fancy, 5-String	$1,100	$1,700
1870-1890	Plain, 5-String	$700	$1,100

Epiphone

1873-present. Epiphone introduced banjos in the early 1920s, if not sooner, offering them up to WW II. After Gibson bought the company in '57, they re-introduced banjos to the line, which they still offer.

Black Beauty Tenor

1920		$450	$575

EB-44 Campus

1962-1970. Long neck, open back, folk-era 5-string.

1962-1970		$925	$1,200

EB-88 Minstrel

1961-1969. Flat head, standard neck, 5 strings.

1961-1969		$1,575	$2,050

EB-99

1970s. Import, higher-end, 5-string.

1970s		$600	$800

EB-188 Plantation

1962-1968. Long neck, open back, 5 strings.

1962-1968		$1,325	$1,725

Electar (Electric)

1930s	Tenor	$850	$1,100

MB-200

1998-2015. Mahogany neck and body, rosewood 'board, 5 strings.

2009		$265	$350

MB-250

1998-2013. Mahogany resonator body and neck, rosewood 'board, 5 strings.

2012		$435	$575

Peerless Plectrum

1920-1925. Has Epiphone and Peerless logo on fancy headstock.

1920-1925		$460	$600

Recording A

Ca. 1925-ca. 1935. Epiphone Recording logo on headstock, flamed maple neck and resonator, fancy pearl inlay markers.

1920s	Tenor	$1,925	$2,500

Recording B

Ca. 1925-ca. 1935.

1930s	Tenor	$2,300	$3,000

Recording Concert C Special

1930s. Tenor, maple body, fancy appointments, resonator.

1932		$3,000	$3,900

TB-100

Mid-1960s. Tenor, 11" rim.

1960s		$725	$950

White Beauty Tenor

1920. Closed-back resonator, large dot markers, White Beauty headstock logo.

1920		$450	$575

Excelsior

Ca.1885-ca. 1990. Brand name of guitars and banjos marketed by Boston's John C. Haynes & Company. Instruments were more basic without tone rings. Brand most likely faded out in very early 1890s when Haynes started their more refined line of Bay State instruments.

Model 218

1889	Open back, 5-string	$1,300	$1,700

Fairbanks/Vega Fairbanks/ A.C. Fairbanks

1875-1922. From 1875 to 1880, A. C. Fairbanks built his own designs in Boston. In 1880, W. A. Cole joined the company, starting Fairbanks & Cole, but left in 1890 to start his own line. The company went by Fairbanks Co. until it was purchased by Vega in 1904. The banjos were then branded Vega Fairbanks (see Vega listings) until 1922.

Acme (F & C)

1880-1890. 5-string, open back, fancy markers.

1880-1890		$700	$900

Electric 5-String Series

1890s	Electric	$3,425	$4,450
1890s	Imperial	$2,050	$2,650
1890s	No. 3	$3,600	$4,675
1890s	No. 5	$5,000	$6,400
1890s	No. 6	$5,500	$7,100
1901	Special	$2,375	$3,075

Electric Banjeaurine

1890s	5-string	$2,025	$2,650

Imperial Open Back

1888	5-string	$2,100	$2,750

Regent

1900-1904	5-string	$2,100	$2,750

Senator No. 1

1900-1909	5-string	$950	$1,225

Special #0

1890-1904		$650	$850

Special #2

1890-1904	5-string	$775	$1,000

Special #4

1900-1904	5-string	$975	$1,275

Tubaphone #3

1908	5-string	$2,600	$3,400

Whyte Laydie #2

1901-1904	5-string	$3,275	$4,250

Whyte Laydie #7

1901	1st year	$7,400	$9,600
1902-1908		$6,500	$8,400

Farland

Ca. 1890-1920s. Buckbee and others made instruments for New York banjo teacher and performer A. A. Farland.

Concert Grand

1900-1920	5-string	$925	$1,200

Grand Artist No. 2

1890s-1910. Ornate floral markers, open back, 5-string.

1890s-1910		$1,625	$2,125

Fender

1946-present. Fender added banjos to their product mix in the late 1960s, and continues to offer them.

1930s Epiphone Recording Concert

Imaged by Heritage Auctions, HA.com

BANJOS

Fairbanks Electric

Intermountain Guitar and Banjo

Early-1970s Fender Artist Tenor

William Ritter / Gruhn Guitars

1927 Gibson Bella Voce

William Ritter/Gruhn Guitars

BANJOS

MODEL YEAR	FEATURES	EXC. COND. LOW	HIGH
Allegro			
Late 1960s-1970s. Tenor or 5-string.			
1960s		$800	$1,050
Artist			
1960s-70s	5-string	$1,150	$1,500
FB Series			
1998-2017. Various imported 5-string models.			
2007-2012	FB-54	$225	$300
2007-2012	FB-55	$375	$500
2007-2012	FB-58	$450	$600
2007-2012	FB-59	$600	$800
Leo Deluxe			
1970s-1988. Japanese-made, fancy inlay.			
1970s		$800	$1,050

Framus

1946-1977, 1996-present. The new Framus company, located in Markneukirchen, Germany, continues to offer banjos.

MODEL YEAR	FEATURES	EXC. COND. LOW	HIGH
Various Models			
1960s		$290	$375
1970s		$200	$265

Gibson

1890s (1902)-present. Gibson started making banjos in 1918. Vega and Gibson were the only major manufacturing companies that offered banjos in their product catalog in the '50s.

RB prefix = regular banjo (5-string)

TB prefix = tenor banjo (4-string, tenor tuning)

PB prefix = plectrum banjo (4-string, plectrum tuning)

The prices shown are guidance prices only and each instrument should be evaluated on a case-by-case basis.

MODEL YEAR	FEATURES	EXC. COND. LOW	HIGH
All American			
1930-1937, 1970-1986. Tenor banjo, fancy appointments, historic art, gold hardware. Reissue offered in RB, TB, or PB.			
1930-1937	Arch top, 2-pc.		
	Flange	$10,000	$13,000
1930-1937	Flat head, 1-pc.		
	flange, rare	$43,000	$56,000
1975-1980	5-string	$6,200	$8,000
Bella Voce			
1927-1931. Tenor or plectrum, fancy appointments, flower-pattern art, gold hardware.			
1927-1931	Plectrum	$20,800	$27,000
1927-1931	Tenor	$20,800	$27,000
Christmas Limited Edition			
2008-2009. Christmas theme, 5-string, flame maple, gold parts, 12 offered.			
2008-2009		$7,000	$9,000
Earl Scruggs '49 Classic			
1992-2008. Figured maple resonator and neck, rosewood 'board, multiple bindings.			
2001-2002		$3,500	$4,500
Earl Scruggs Flint Hill Special			

2005. Commemorative Limited Edition, 20 made with first 5 signed by Earl, Flint Hill Special on headstock, figured maple resonator and neck, classic

MODEL YEAR	FEATURES	EXC. COND. LOW	HIGH
Amber Brown finish.			
2005		$4,500	$5,800
Earl Scruggs Golden Deluxe			
1991-2010. Satin gold hardware, hearts and flowers inlay.			
1997		$4,200	$5,600
Earl Scruggs Standard			
1984-2010. 5-string, high-end appointments, Standard added to model name in '92.			
1984-2010		$3,400	$4,400
ETB Electric Tenor			
1938-1941. Electric Tenor Banjo, Charlie Christian pickup.			
1934-1941		$3,000	$3,900
Flint Hill Special			
2005-2006. Earl Scruggs style, 5-string.			
2005-2006		$4,000	$5,200
Florentine Plectrum			
1927-1937. High-end appointments, gold hardware.			
1925-1930	2-piece flange	$15,800	$21,000
Florentine Tenor			
1927-1937. High-end appointments, gold hardware.			
1927-1935	40-hole	$15,500	$20,000
GB-1			
1922-1940. Guitar-banjo, style 1 appointments, 6-string neck, walnut. Trap door '22-'24, resonator diamond-flange '25-'30, 1-piece flange '31-'40.			
1922-1924		$1,275	$1,650
1925-1930		$1,775	$2,300
1931-1940		$2,550	$3,300
GB-3			
1918-1937. Guitar-banjo, style 3 appointments, mahogany. Trap door '18-'24. Mastertone, 2-piece flange, ball-bearing arch-top tone ring for '25-'26 and cast arch-top tone ring for '26-'29. Mastertone, 40-hole tone ring '28-'37. Flat head option '31-'37.			
1918-1924		$1,150	$1,500
1925-1926		$3,000	$4,000
1926-1929		$3,000	$4,000
1928-1937		$3,000	$4,000
GB-4			
1918-1931. Guitar-banjo, style 4 appointments, maple. Very early models were called GB without -4 suffix. Trap door '18-'24. Mastertone, 2-piece flange, ball-bearing arch-top tone ring for '25-'26 and cast arch-top tone ring for '26-'29. Mastertone, 40-hole tone ring '28-'31. Flat head option			
1918-1924	GB/GB-4	$2,550	$3,300
1925-1926		$3,600	$4,700
1926-1929		$3,600	$4,700
1928-1931		$3,600	$4,700
GB-5			
1924. Rare, gold plated, trap door.			
1924		$6,000	$7,700
GB-6/GB-6 Custom			
1922-1934. Guitar-banjo, style 6 appointments, special order availability. Trap door '22-'24. Mastertone, 2-piece flange, ball-bearing arch-top tone ring for '25-'26 and cast arch-top tone ring for '26-'29. Mastertone, 40-hole tone ring '28-'34. Flat head option '31-'34.			
1922-1924		$3,500	$4,500

MODEL YEAR	FEATURES	EXC. COND. LOW	HIGH
1925-1926		$5,200	$6,700
1926-1929		$5,200	$6,700
1928-1934		$5,100	$6,600

Granada PB

1929-1939. Plectrum, flat head tone ring.

1929-1939		$92,000	$120,000

Granada RB

1925-1939. 5-string banjo with either a 2-piece flange ('25-'30), or a 1-piece flange ('33-'39).

1925-1926	Ball bearing	$19,600	$25,500
1927-1930	40-hole arched	$31,000	$40,000
1929-1939	Flat head	$163,000	$212,000

Granada RB (Reissue)

1986-2010. Resonator back, hearts & flowers or flying eagle inlay, 5-string.

1986-2006	Flying eagle	$3,800	$5,000
1986-2010	Hearts & flowers	$3,800	$5,000

Granada RB Pot and Reneck

1933-1939. Original pot and replacement neck, flat head tone ring.

1933-1939		$47,000	$61,000

Granada TB

1925-1930. Tenor banjo with a 2-piece flange.

1925-1926	Ball bearing	$5,300	$6,900
1927-1930	40-hole arched	$7,100	$9,200

PB-1

1926-1930s. Plectrum Banjo (PB), bracket-shoe.

1920s		$875	$1,150

PB-2

1920s-1930s. Plectrum, bracket-shoe for '20s and 1-piece flange for '30s.

1920s	Bracket-shoe	$875	$1,150
1930s	1-piece flange	$3,500	$4,500

PB-3

1925-1927, 1929-1939. Laminated maple resonator Mastertone model, plectrum neck and tuning. Tube and plate, 2-piece flange for '25-'27. Flat head tone ring '29-'39.

1925-1927	Tube & plate	$2,200	$2,900
1929-1939	Flat head	$66,000	$86,000

PB-4

1925-1940. Plectrum with either a 2-piece flange ('25-'32), or 1-piece ('33-'40).

1925-1927	Ball bearing	$2,700	$3,500
1928-1932	Archtop	$3,500	$4,500
1933-1940	Archtop	$8,900	$11,500
1933-1940	Flat head	$54,000	$70,000

PB-7

1937-1943. Plectrum, 40-hole flat tone ring.

1940		$54,000	$70,000

PB-11

1931-1942. Plectrum, 1-piece flange, pearloid 'board, headstock and resonator cover.

1931-1942		$3,500	$4,500

PB-100

1948-1979. Plectrum with either a 1-piece flange ('48-'68), or 2-piece ('69-'79).

1969-1979		$900	$1,150

RB Jr.

1924-1925. Budget line, 5-string, open back.

1924-1925		$1,250	$1,625

RB-00

1932-1942. Maple resonator, 1-piece flange.

1933-1939		$3,800	$4,900

RB-1

1922-1940. Resonator Banjo (RB), 1-piece or diamond flange.

1922-1930	Early specs	$4,000	$5,200
1930-1932	1-piece flange	$4,000	$5,200
1933-1940	Diamond flange	$4,000	$5,200

RB-1 Reissue

1990-1993. Fleur-de-lis, brass tone ring.

1990-1993		$1,800	$2,300

RB-2

1933-1939		$6,900	$8,900

RB-3

1923-1937. Resonator, dot inlay, 5 strings, trap door or non-trap '22-'24. Mastertone, ball bearing '25-'26. Mastertone, archtop, 40-hole or no hole for '27-'29.

1922-1924		$2,450	$3,200
1925-1926		$7,100	$9,200
1927-1929		$12,300	$16,000

RB-3 Reissue

1988-2010. Called the RB-3 Wreath at end of production.

1988-2010		$3,200	$4,200

RB-4

1922-1937. Resonator 5-string, trap or non-trap door on earlier models ('22-'24), either a 2-piece flange ('25-'31), or 1-piece ('33-'37).

1922-1924		$2,900	$3,800
1925-1931	Archtop	$14,100	$18,300
1929-1937	Flat head tone ring	$85,000	$110,000
1933-1937	Archtop	$30,000	$40,000

RB-4/R-4/Retro 4

1991-2006. Resonator, flying eagle inlay, multibound.

1998-2006		$3,900	$5,000

RB-5

1995-2008. Resonator.

1995-2008		$5,800	$7,500

RB-6 New Century

1995-2008. Style 6, 5-string, figured-maple, gold sparkle binding.

2005		$6,200	$8,000

RB-7 Top Tension

1994-2008. Maple, bow-tie inlay.

2003		$3,800	$5,000

RB-11

1931-1942. Pearloid covered 'board, headstock and resonator.

1933-1939		$5,300	$6,900

RB-12

1995-2008. Carved walnut resonator, rosewood 'board, art deco inlay.

1996-2003		$4,000	$5,200

RB-75 J.D. Crowe Blackjack

1997-2006. Resonator 5-string, mahogany neck finished in vintage brown/red with aged white binding, rosewood 'board.

1997-2006		$3,500	$4,500

1924 Gibson GB-5
Intermountain Guitar and Banjo

2000 Gibson RB-4 Mastertone
Imaged by Heritage Auctions, HA.com

BANJOS

1959 Gibson RB-250

Jay Hunt

MODEL YEAR	FEATURES	EXC. COND. LOW	EXC. COND. HIGH
RB-100			
1948-1979. Maple resonator.			
1948-1965		$1,700	$2,200
1966-1979		$1,400	$1,800
RB-150			
1948-1959. Laminated mahogany resonator, bow tie inlay.			
1948-1959		$2,200	$2,900
RB-170			
1960-1973. No resonator, 5-string, dot markers, decal logo, multi-ply maple rim.			
1960-1973		$1,000	$1,300
RB-175			
1962-1973. 2000s. Open back, long neck typical of banjos of the '60s. Models include the RB-175, RB-175 Long Neck, RB-175 Folk.			
1962	RB-175	$1,200	$1,600
1962-1964	Long Neck	$1,200	$1,600
1965-1969	Folk	$1,200	$1,600
1970-1973	RB-175	$1,200	$1,600
RB-180			
1961-1967. Longneck.			
1961-1967		$1,750	$2,300
RB-250			
1954-1999, 2002-2010. Mahogany, 2-piece flange until '88, 1 after.			
1954-1959		$2,800	$3,600
1960-1965		$2,600	$3,400
1966-1969	Flat head	$1,950	$2,500
1970-1989	Mastertone	$1,850	$2,400
1990-1999		$1,850	$2,400
2002-2004	Reissue	$1,850	$2,400
RB-500			
1964-1969. Maple, 1-piece flange, gold hardware.			
1967		$3,200	$4,200
RB-800			
1964-1971, 1979-1986. Maple resonator, 1-piece flange until '69, 2 after.			
1964-1986		$3,200	$4,200
TB			
1918-1923. Renamed TB-4.			
1919		$1,100	$1,425
TB-00			
1939-1944. Maple resonator, 1-piece flange.			
1939-1944		$1,775	$2,300
TB-1			
1922-1939. Tenor banjo with a 1-piece flange.			
1922-1925		$675	$875
1926		$725	$950
1933-1939		$2,900	$3,800
TB-2			
1922-1928. Wavy flange			
1922-1928	Wavy flange	$850	$1,100
1933-1937	Pearloid board	$3,100	$4,100
TB-3			
1925-1937. Tenor banjo with either a 2-piece flange, or a 1-piece flange.			
1925-1926		$1,700	$2,200
1927-1929		$2,900	$3,750
1930-1937		$6,100	$8,100

MODEL YEAR	FEATURES	EXC. COND. LOW	EXC. COND. HIGH
TB-4			
1922-1937. Dot inlay.			
1922-1924	Trap door	$800	$1,050
1925-1926	Ball bearing	$2,925	$3,800
1927-1931	40 or no hole ring	$3,150	$4,100
1933-1937	40 or no hole ring	$5,000	$6,500
TB-5			
1922-1924	Trap door	$1,075	$1,375
1925-1926	Ball bearing	$7,000	$9,150
1927-1931	40 or no hole ring	$8,800	$11,400
TB-6			
1927-1939	Tube plate flange	$11,400	$14,800
TB-11			
1931-1942. Pearloid covered 'board, headstock and resonator.			
1931-1942		$2,250	$3,000
TB-12			
1937-1939. Produced in limited quantities, 1-piece flange, flat head tone ring, double bound walnut resonator, price levels include both original and conversion instruments, conversions with original flat head tone rings are somewhat common in the vintage banjo market.			
1937		$50,000	$65,000
TB-18			
1937. Rare model, flat head top tension.			
1937		$70,000	$90,000
TB-100			
1949-1959		$1,200	$1,575
1960-1969		$1,000	$1,300
TB-150			
1949-1959		$1,425	$1,850
TB-250			
1954-1959		$1,600	$2,100
1960-1969	Mastertone	$1,450	$1,875
1970-1996	Mastertone	$1,325	$1,725
TB-800			
1964	2 made	$3,400	$4,400
1975	Flying eagle markers	$2,900	$3,700
Trujo Plectrum			
1928-1934		$2,550	$3,300

Gold Star

1970s-present. A brand name of Saga Musical Instruments offering professional and premium grade, production banjos.

5-String

1970s-present. Various 5-string models.

1970s	G-11HF	$1,350	$1,800
1980s-2017	GF-85	$1,350	$1,800
1984	JD Crowe	$4,300	$5,700
2000-2017	GF-200	$1,350	$1,800
2006-2021	GF-100FE	$1,350	$1,800
2020	GF-100JD	$1,150	$1,500

Gold Tone

1993-present. Professional and premium grade, production/custom banjos and banjitars built by Wayne and Robyn Rogers in Titusville, Florida. They also offer guitars, basses, lap steels, mandolins and ukuleles.

Gold Star G-11HF

Elderly Instruments

The *Vintage Guitar Price Guide* shows low to high values for items in all-original excellent condition, and, where applicable, with original case or cover.

MODEL YEAR	FEATURES	EXC. COND. LOW	HIGH
5-String			
Various 5-string models.			
2009	Banjola Deluxe	$635	$825
2011	BG-250F BG Special	$540	$700
2011	CC-100 Cripple Creek	$450	$600
2011	OB-250AT	$925	$1,200
2011	OT-800	$850	$1,100
2014	TB-250 Travel	$850	$1,100
2014	WL-250 Open Back	$850	$1,100
Tenor			
Various tenor models.			
2011	IT250R Irish (China)	$475	$625

Goya

1952-1996. Martin offered Goya banjos while they owned the brand name in the '70s.

Student 5-String

1976-1996. Goya-Martin era.

1976-1996		$275	$350

Gretsch

1883-present. Gretsch offered banjos in the '20s and again in the '50s and '60s. In 2012 they again started building them.

5-String

1977		$375	$475

Broadkaster

1920s-1939. Tenor or 5-string banjo with pearloid head and board.

1920s	Tenor	$450	$575
1932-1939	5-string	$925	$1,200
1932-1939	Tenor	$325	$425

Model 6536 Folk

1960s. Open-back, 5-string, long-neck style.

1964		$540	$700

New Yorker

1930s-1960s. New Yorker logo on headstock, 5-string or tenor.

1930s-60s		$270	$350

Orchestella

1925-1929. Tenor or 5-string banjo with gold engravings.

1925-1929	5-string	$1,450	$1,900
1925-1929	Tenor	$550	$725

Tenor Short-Scale

1925-1929	Plain styling	$275	$350
1950s	Plain styling	$275	$350

GTR

1974-1978. GTR (for George Gruhn, Tut Taylor, Randy Wood) was the original name for Gruhn Guitars in Nashville, and they imported mandolins and banjos from Japan.

5-String Copy

1974-1978		$725	$950

Harmony

1892-1976, late 1970s-present. Huge, Chicago-based manufacturer of fretted instruments, mainly budget models under the Harmony name or for many other American brands and mass marketers.

MODEL YEAR	FEATURES	EXC. COND. LOW	HIGH
Bicentennial			
1976. Red, white and blue, '76 logo, 5-string.			
1976		$600	$775
Electro			
1950s. Electric banjo, 5-string, wood body, 1 pickup.			
1950s		$600	$775
Holiday Folk			
1960s. Long neck, 5-string.			
1960s		$225	$300
Reso-Tone Tenor			
1960s		$220	$285
Roy Smeck Student Tenor			
1963		$220	$285
Sovereign Tenor			
1960s		$220	$285

Howard

Howard is a brand name of Cincinnati's Wurlitzer Co. used in the 1920s on banjos built by The Fred Gretsch Manufacturing Co. The brand name was also appeared on guitars in the mid-'30s by Epiphone.

Tenor

1930s	Open back	$175	$225
1930s	Resonator	$375	$500

Huber

1999-present. Premium grade, production, 5-string banjos built by luthier Steve Huber in Hendersonville, Tennessee.

Ibanez

1932-present. Ibanez introduced their Artist line of banjos in 1978 in a deal with Earl Scruggs, but they were dropped by '84.

Model 591

1978-1984. Flat head, 5-string.

1978-1984		$975	$1,250

Model 593

1977. Vine inlay, 5-string.

1977		$1,225	$1,600

John Wesley

Introduced in 1895 by Kansas City, Missouri instrument wholesalers J.W. Jenkins & Sons, founded by cello builder John Wesley Jenkins. May have been built by Jenkins until circa 1905, but work was later contracted out to others.

Kalamazoo

1933-1942, 1965-1970. Budget brand built by Gibson. Made flat-tops, solidbodies, mandolins, lap steels, banjos and amps.

KPB Plectrum

1935-1940		$400	$525

KRB 5-String

1935-1941		$700	$925

Huber VRB-G

Kalamazoo KPB Plectrum

Imaged by Heritage Auctions, HA.com

BANJOS

1930 Ludwig Big Chief
Imaged by Heritage Auctions, HA.com

Luscomb Lion Heel
Bernunzio Uptown Music

MODEL YEAR	FEATURES	EXC. COND. LOW	HIGH

Kay

Ca. 1931 (1890)-present. Kay was a huge manufacturer and built instruments under their name and for a large number of other retailers, jobbers, and brand names.

Silva

1950s. Top of the line 5-string, Silva verticle logo along with Kay logo on headstock, block markers.

| 1950s | | $450 | $575 |

Student Tenor

| 1950s | | $175 | $225 |

Kel Kroydon

1930-1933. Private branded budget level instruments made by Gibson. They also had guitars and banjos. The name has been revived on a line of banjos by Tom Mirisola and made in Nashville.

KK-11 Tenor

| 1933-1937 | | $2,400 | $3,150 |

Kingston

Ca. 1958-1967. Imported from Japan by Westheimer Importing Corp. of Chicago. They also offered guitars, basses and mandolins.

Student Tenor

| 1965 | | $65 | $85 |

Lange

1920s-1942, Late 1940s. The William L. Lange Company began selling Paramount banjos, guitar banjos and mandolin banjos in the early 1920s. Gretsch picked up the Paramount name and used it on acoustics and electrics for a time in the late '40s. See Paramount for more listings.

Tourraine Deluxe

| 1920s | Tenor | $550 | $725 |

Leedy

1889-1930. Founded in Indianapolis by U. G. Leedy, the company started making banjos in 1924. Leedy was bought out by C. G. Conn in '30.

Arcadian

| 1925 | Plectrum | $435 | $575 |

Olympian

| 1930 | Tenor | $435 | $575 |

Solotone

1924-1930	A Tenor	$800	$1,050
1924-1930	B Tenor	$1,025	$1,325
1924-1930	C Tenor	$1,150	$1,485
1924-1930	D Tenor	$1,300	$1,700

Libby Bros.

1890s. Made in Gorham, Maine, rarity suggests limited production.

Open Back

1890-1895. Fancy position markers, 5-string.

| 1890-1895 | | $1,075 | $1,400 |

Ludwig

The Ludwig Drum Company was founded in 1909. They saw a good business opportunity and

entered the banjo market in '21. When demand for banjos tanked in the '30s, Ludwig dropped the line and concentrated on its core business.

Ambassador

| 1920s-1932 | Tenor | $825 | $1,075 |

Bellevue

1920s. Tenor, closed-back banjo with fancy appointments.

| 1920s | | $600 | $800 |

Big Chief

1930. Carved and engraved plectrum banjo.

| 1930 | | $5,300 | $6,900 |

Capitol

| 1920s | | $500 | $650 |

Columbia

| 1920s | Tenor, student-level | $325 | $425 |

Commodore

1930s. Tenor or plectrum, with gold hardware and fancy appointments.

| 1930s | Tenor | $1,025 | $1,325 |
| 1932 | Plectrum | $1,225 | $1,600 |

Deluxe

1930s. Tenor, engraved, gold hardware.

| 1930s | | $1,625 | $2,125 |

Dixie

| 1930s | Tenor | $300 | $400 |

Kenmore

1920s. Plectrum with open back or tenor resonator.

| 1920s | Plectrum | $500 | $650 |

Kingston

| 1924-1930 | Tenor | $475 | $625 |

Standard Art Tenor

1924-1930. Tenor banjo with fancy appointments.

| 1924-1930 | | $2,450 | $3,175 |

The Ace

1920s. Tenor banjo, resonator and nickel appointments.

| 1920s | | $900 | $1,175 |

Luscomb

1888-1898. John F. Luscomb was a well-known banjo player who designed a line of instruments for Thompson & Odell of Boston.

Open Back 5-String

| 1890s | | $575 | $750 |

Lyric (by Gretsch)

1930s. There are also Lyric-branded banjos made by William Schmick in the 1910s as well as current Asian-made ones.

Tenor

| 1930 | Resonator back | $475 | $625 |

Matao

1967-1983. Japanese copies of American brands, offered guitars, basses, banjos and ukes.

Bluegrass

| 1970s | 5-string | $250 | $325 |

BANJOS

Mitchell (P.J.)

1850s. Early gut 5-string banjo maker from New York City.

Gut 5-String

MODEL YEAR	FEATURES	EXC. COND. LOW	EXC. COND. HIGH
1850s		$2,450	$3,175

Morrison

Ca. 1870-ca. 1915. Marketed by New Yorker James Morrison, made by Morrison or possibly others like Buckbee. After 1875, his instruments sported the patented Morrison tone ring.

5-String

MODEL YEAR	FEATURES	EXC. COND. LOW	EXC. COND. HIGH
1885-1890		$540	$700

ODE/Muse

1961-1980. Founded by Charles Ogsbury in Boulder, Colorado, purchased by Baldwin in '66 and moved to Nashville. Until '71 the banjos were branded as Baldwin; afterwards as Baldwin ODE. Gretsch took over production in '76. Muse was a retail store brand of banjos produced by ODE from '61 to '66. In '71, Ogsbury started the OME Banjo Company in Colorado.

Model C

1976-1980. Resonator, 5-string, fancy markers.

MODEL YEAR	FEATURES	EXC. COND. LOW	EXC. COND. HIGH
1976-1980		$1,500	$1,950

Model D

1976-1980. Resonator, 5-string, gold engravings.

MODEL YEAR	FEATURES	EXC. COND. LOW	EXC. COND. HIGH
1976-1980		$2,100	$2,700

OME

1971-present. Charles Ogsbury started OME outside Boulder, Colorado after he sold his first banjo company, ODE, to Baldwin.

MODEL YEAR	FEATURES	EXC. COND. LOW	EXC. COND. HIGH
Bright Angel			
2012-2019	5-string	$2,400	$3,100
Columbine			
2012-2015	Tenor	$3,000	$4,000
Grubstake			
1972-1980	5-string	$850	$1,100
Juggernaut			
1973-1979	5-string	$1,900	$2,500
Juggernaut II			
1974	5-string	$2,400	$3,100
Juniper Megatone			
2016	5-string	$2,400	$3,100
Magician			
1997	5-string, gold	$3,100	$4,100
Mogul			
1973	5-string, silver	$2,550	$3,300
1973	Plectrum, black	$2,400	$3,100
1973	Plectrum, silver	$2,300	$2,975
1974	5-string, gold	$3,300	$4,300
Monarch			
1985-1990	5-string	$2,400	$3,100
1986	Plectrum	$2,050	$2,650
Primrose			
2013-2019	5-string	$2,600	$3,400
X 5-String			
1971		$1,050	$1,375

MODEL YEAR	FEATURES	EXC. COND. LOW	EXC. COND. HIGH
XX 5-String			
1971		$1,100	$1,450
1972	Extra long neck	$1,050	$1,375
1975		$1,050	$1,375
XX Tenor			
1973		$1,050	$1,375
XXX 5-String			
1971		$1,450	$1,900

Orpheum

1897-1922. Lange and Rettberg purchased the J.H. Buckbee banjo factory in 1897 and started making banjos under the Orpheum label. William Lange took control in 1922 and changed the name to Paramount.

MODEL YEAR	FEATURES	EXC. COND. LOW	EXC. COND. HIGH
Model #1			
1910s-20s	Tenor	$560	$725
1914-1916	5-string	$2,050	$2,650
1920-1922	Plectrum	$635	$825
Model #2			
1920-1922	5-string	$1,450	$1,900
1920-1922	Tenor	$700	$900
Model #3			
1900-1910s	5-string	$2,900	$3,750
1910s	Plectrum, fancy	$1,625	$2,100
1910s	Tenor, fancy	$850	$1,100

Paramount

1921-1935. William Lange and his Paramount company are generally accredited with commercializing the first modern flange and resonator in 1921.

MODEL YEAR	FEATURES	EXC. COND. LOW	EXC. COND. HIGH
Aristocrat			
1921-1935	Plectrum	$1,350	$1,750
1921-1935	Tenor	$1,125	$1,450
Aristocrat Special			

1921-1935. Plectrum or tenor with fancy appointments.

MODEL YEAR	FEATURES	EXC. COND. LOW	EXC. COND. HIGH
1921-1935	Plectrum	$2,050	$2,650
1921-1935	Tenor	$1,625	$2,125
Artists Supreme			

1930s. High-end appointments, 19-fret tenor, engraved gold-plated hardware.

MODEL YEAR	FEATURES	EXC. COND. LOW	EXC. COND. HIGH
1930s	Tenor	$3,500	$4,600
Banjo-Harp			

Wood resonator, all wood including spruce top, fancy.

MODEL YEAR	FEATURES	EXC. COND. LOW	EXC. COND. HIGH
1924	5-string	$1,300	$1,700
1924	Tenor, 4-string	$900	$1,175
Junior			
1921-1935	Plectrum	$650	$850
1921-1935	Tenor	$450	$575
Leader			
1921-1935	Plectrum	$775	$1,000
1921-1935	Tenor	$700	$900
Style 1			
1921-1935	Plectrum	$650	$850
1921-1935	Tenor	$525	$700
Style 2			

1921-1935. Tenor, resonator and plain appointments.

MODEL YEAR	FEATURES	EXC. COND. LOW	EXC. COND. HIGH
1921-1935		$525	$700

2003 OME Mockingbird Grand Artist SB Plectrum

William Ritter/Gruhn Guitars

1920s Orpheum Model #1

Imaged by Heritage Auctions, HA.com

BANJOS

1925 Paramount Style E Tenor
William Ritter/Gruhn Guitars

1895 S.S. Stewart Banjeaurine
William Ritter/Gruhn Guitars

MODEL YEAR	FEATURES	EXC. COND. LOW	HIGH
Style A			
1921-1935. Models include the Style A Tenor, Plectrum, and the 5-string (with resonator and fancy appointments).			
1921-1935	5-string	$1,425	$1,850
1921-1935	Plectrum	$975	$1,275
1921-1935	Tenor	$825	$1,075
Style B			
1921-1935. Models include the Style B Tenor, and the Plectrum (with resonator and fancy appointments).			
1921-1935	Plectrum	$1,425	$1,850
1921-1935	Tenor	$1,200	$1,550
Style C			
1921-1935. Models include the Style C Tenor, Plectrum, and the 5-string (with resonator and fancy appointments).			
1921-1935	5-string	$3,075	$4,000
1921-1935	Plectrum	$1,075	$1,400
1921-1935	Tenor	$975	$1,275
Style D			
1921-1935	Plectrum	$1,550	$2,025
1921-1935	Tenor	$1,375	$1,800
Style E			
1921-1935	Plectrum	$1,975	$2,550
1921-1935	Tenor	$1,800	$2,325
Style F			
1921-1935	Plectrum	$2,700	$3,500
1921-1935	Tenor	$2,550	$3,300
Super/Super Paramount			
1929-1935	Plectrum	$2,975	$3,850
1929-1935	Tenor	$2,700	$3,500
Trooper			
1921-1935	Plectrum	$525	$700
1921-1935	Tenor	$450	$575

Penco

Ca. 1974-1978. Japanese-made banjos imported into Philadelphia. They also offered guitars, basses and mandolins.

MODEL YEAR	FEATURES	EXC. COND. LOW	HIGH
Deluxe Tenor			
1970s	Japan	$210	$275

Recording King

1929-1932, 1936-1941. Brand name used by Montgomery Ward for instruments made by various American manufacturers, including Kay, Gibson and Gretsch.

MODEL YEAR	FEATURES	EXC. COND. LOW	HIGH
M-6 Tenor			
1938		$1,475	$1,900
Studio King Tenor			
1929-1932. Gibson-made, 40 hole archtop.			
1929-1932		$2,900	$3,800

Regal

Ca. 1895-1966, 1987-present. Mass manufacturer Regal made brands for others as well as marketing its own brand. In '87 the Regal name was revived by Saga.

MODEL YEAR	FEATURES	EXC. COND. LOW	HIGH
Bicentennial '76			
1976. Part of a series of Regal instruments with Bicentennial themed appointments.			
1976	5-string	$350	$450

S.S. Stewart

1878-1904. S.S. Stewart of Philadelphia is considered to be one of the most important and prolific banjo manufacturers of the late 19th century. It's estimated that approximately 25,000 banjos were made by this company. The brand name was used on guitars into the 1960s.

MODEL YEAR	FEATURES	EXC. COND. LOW	HIGH
20th Century			
1890s		$850	$1,125
American Princess			
1890s. 5-string, 10" rim.			
1890s		$775	$1,000
Banjeaurine			
1890s. Open back, 10" head, 5-string.			
1890s	Plain appointments	$875	$1,125
1890s	Style 3, fancy	$1,625	$2,125
Champion			
1895. Open back, 5-string.			
1895	Plain appointments	$875	$1,125
Concert No. 1 Pony			
Open back, 5-string, short scale.			
1891		$875	$1,125
Orchestra			
1890s. 5-string, various styles.			
1893-1894	#1, with frets	$1,125	$1,450
1893-1894	#2, fretless	$2,375	$3,075
1893-1894	#2, with frets	$1,825	$2,375
Piccolo			
1880s-1890s. 5-string, 7" rim, plain appointments.			
1880s-90s		$950	$1,250
Special Thoroughbred			
1890s-1900s. Open back, 5-string, carved heel, plain appointments.			
1890-1900s		$875	$1,125
Universal Favorite			
1892. 11" head, plain appointments.			
1892		$775	$1,000

Sekova

1960s-1970s. Imported from Japan, budget grade.

MODEL YEAR	FEATURES	EXC. COND. LOW	HIGH
5-String			
1970s		$225	$300

Silvertone

1941-ca. 1970, present. Brand of Sears instruments which replaced their Supertone brand in '41. Currently, Samick offers a line of amps under the Silvertone name.

MODEL YEAR	FEATURES	EXC. COND. LOW	HIGH
4-String			
1960s		$115	$150
5-String			
1960s		$250	$325

Slingerland

Ca. 1914-present. The parent company was Slingerland Banjo and Drums, Chicago, Illinois. The company offered other stringed instruments into the '40s. In 2019, Slingerland Drums was acquired (from Gibson) by Drum Workshop (DW).

MODEL YEAR	FEATURES	EXC. COND. LOW	HIGH
Deluxe			
1920s	Tenor, high-end	$1,200	$1,550

BANJOS

MODEL YEAR	FEATURES	EXC. COND. LOW	HIGH
May Bell			
1920s-30s	Various styles	$200	$975
Student/Economy			
1930s	Tenor	$175	$285

Stathopoulo

1917-1928. House of Stathopoulo evolved from the A. Stathopoulo brand in 1917 and in 1929 became the Epiphone Banjo Corporation, which later became Epiphone, the well known guitar brand.

Super Wonder XX Tenor			
1920s		$700	$925

Stelling

1974-present. Founded by Geoff Stelling, building premium and presentation grade, production/custom banjos in Afton, Virginia. They also build mandolins.

5-String

1974-present. Various 5-string models.

1976-1984	Staghorn	$3,850	$5,000
1977-1978	Bell Flower	$2,450	$3,175
1978-1981	Whitestar	$2,100	$2,750
1980-1985	Golden Cross	$3,100	$4,100
1983	Hartford	$2,450	$3,175
1985-1995	Master Flower	$3,100	$4,100
1985-2003	Sunflower	$2,850	$3,700
1990	Masterpiece	$4,700	$6,100
2001	Red Fox	$2,400	$3,200
2004	Crusader Deluxe	$4,200	$5,500
2006	Crusader	$3,100	$4,100
2012	Swallowtail	$3,100	$4,100

Stetson, J.F.

1880s-1900s. J. F. Stetson branded banjos were distributed by W.J. Dyer & Bros. of St. Paul, Minnesota and others.

Presentation

1890s. By Fairbanks, few made, highest-end style, open back, 5-string.

1890s		$9,600	$12,500

Studio King

1930s. Banjos made by Gibson, most likely for a mail-order house or a jobber.

TB-3 Tenor

1933-1934	2-piece flange	$3,675	$4,775
1935-1937	1-piece flange	$6,000	$7,750

Superb

1920s. Private brand made by House of Stathopoulo, Inc., the company name of Epiphone from 1917 to 1928. The brand was also used on banjo ukuleles.

Tenor

1920s		$385	$500

Supertone

1914-1941. Brand used by Sears, Roebuck and Company for instruments made by various American manufacturers, including its own Harmony subsidiary Harmony. In '40, Sears began making a transition to the Silvertone brand.

Various Models

1915-1930s		$300	$500

Thompson & Odell

1875-1898. Boston instrument importers Thompson & Odell started building banjos in the 1880s. They sold the company to Vega in 1898.

Artist

1880s	Various models	$635	$825

Tilton

1850s-late 1800s. Built by William B. Tilton, of New York City. He was quite an innovator and held several instrument-related patents. He also built guitars.

Toneking

1927. Private brand of the NY Band Instruments Company, Toneking logo on headstock.

Tenor

1927		$300	$400

Univox

1964-1978. Instruments imported from Japan by the Merson Musical Supply Company, later Unicord, Westbury, New York.

Tenor

1970s	Import	$275	$350

Van Eps

1920s. Designed by virtuoso banjo artist Fred Van Eps and sold through Lyon & Healy.

Recording

1920s	5-string	$1,075	$1,400
1920s	Tenor	$900	$1,150

Vega

1889-1980s, 1989-present. Vega of Boston got into the banjo business in 1904 when it purchased Fairbanks. Vega and Gibson were the only major manufacturing companies that offered banjos in their product catalog in the 1950s. The Deering Banjo Company acquired the brand in '89 and uses it on a line of banjos.

Artist

1927-1929	Tenor	$1,125	$1,475
1929	Plectrum, open back	$1,125	$1,475

Artist Deluxe

1931	Tenor	$1,550	$2,000

Artist Professional #9

1923-1929	Tenor	$1,950	$2,550

Earl Scruggs STII

1967-1969	5-string, resonator	$1,700	$2,200

Folk Ranger FR-5

1960s	5-string, open back	$575	$750

Folk Wonder

1960s	5-string	$675	$875

Stelling Master Flower
Elderly Instruments

1927 Vega Artist
Imaged by Heritage Auctions, HA.com

BANJOS

1924 Vega Style X No. 9 Tenor

Intermountain Guitar and Banjo

1923 Vega Whyte Laydie #7

Imaged by Heritage Auctions, HA.com

MODEL YEAR	FEATURES	EXC. COND. LOW	HIGH
Folklore SS-5			
1966. Open back, long neck folk banjo.			
1963-1966	5-string	$1,050	$1,375
FP-5 Folk Professional			
1961	5-string, rare	$1,525	$1,975
Imperial Electric			
1918-1921	5-string	$2,050	$2,650
Little Wonder			
1910s-20s	Guitar-banjo	$925	$1,200
1920s	Plectrum	$575	$750
1920s-30s	Tenor	$600	$775
1950s	5-string	$900	$1,175
Moderne Tenor			
1931	.	$1,625	$2,125
Pete Seeger			
1958-1971. 5-string, long neck banjo.			
1958-1961	Dowel-stick	$2,800	$3,700
1962-1965	PS-5	$2,800	$3,700
1966-1971	PS-5	$2,600	$3,400
Professional			
1960. 5-string banjo with a Tubaphone tone ring.			
1960	Pro II, slits	$1,300	$1,700
1960	Professional, holes	$1,425	$1,850
Ranger			
1960s. Standard appointments, 5-string, dot markers.			
1966		$525	$675
Regent			
1920s. Open back, 5-string, dot markers.			
1920s		$1,575	$2,050
Soloist			
1920s-1930s. Oettinger tailpiece.			
1927	5-string	$2,000	$3,000
1930	Tenor	$900	$1,200
Style M			
1920-1929. Tenor, with Tubaphone TR.			
1920-1929		$850	$1,100
Style N			
1910s-20s	Tenor	$425	$550
Style X No. 1			
1922-1930	Tenor	$1,550	$2,000
Style X No. 9			
1922-1930. Tenor with fancy appointments.			
1922-1930	Tenor	$1,700	$2,225
Tubaphone #3			
1908-1930	5-string	$1,800	$2,700
Tubaphone #9			
1921-1929	5-string	$5,700	$7,600
Tubaphone Deluxe			
1920s. Higher-end appointments, carved heel, Deluxe logo on tailpiece.			
1923	5-string	$8,100	$10,500

MODEL YEAR	FEATURES	EXC. COND. LOW	HIGH
V.I.P.			
1970s. Open back, 4-string, fancy engraved pearl markers, on-board electronics.			
1970	Tenor	$1,150	$1,500
1973-1974	5-string	$1,300	$1,700
V-45			
1970. Plectrum banjo, flat head tone ring, fancy appointments.			
1970s		$2,700	$3,500
Vega Lady's			
1913		$825	$1,075
Vegaphone De-Luxe			
1929	Plectrum	$3,025	$3,925
Vegaphone Professional			
1920s	Plectrum	$1,250	$1,625
1920s-30s	Tenor	$1,150	$1,525
1960s	5-string	$875	$1,125
Vegavox I 5-String			
1964		$1,550	$2,000
Vegavox I Plectrum			
1956-1959		$1,525	$1,975
Vegavox I Tenor			
1930s-1969. Vox-style deep resonator, alternating block/dot markers.			
1930s		$1,975	$2,550
1956-1959		$1,525	$1,975
1960-1969		$1,425	$1,855
Vegavox IV			
1956-1975. IV logo on truss rod cover, high-end appointments, 4-string plectrum neck.			
1956-1975	Plectrum or Tenor	$2,700	$3,500
Vegavox IV Deluxe			
1970-1973	Tenor	$3,500	$4,550
Whyte Laydie			
1975	5-string	$1,775	$2,300
Whyte Laydie #2			
1919	Vega Fairbanks	$2,850	$3,700
1923-1928	5-string	$2,850	$3,700
1923-1928	Plectrum	$1,150	$1,500
Whyte Laydie #7			
1905	5-string	$6,150	$8,000
1909	5-string	$5,700	$7,400
1920s	5-string	$5,700	$7,400
1920s	Tenor	$2,100	$2,750
Whyte Laydie Style L			
1922		$975	$1,275
Whyte Laydie Style R			
1920s-1930s. Tenor banjo with closed back.			
1920s-30s		$1,050	$1,375

The *Vintage Guitar Price Guide* shows low to high values for items in all-original excellent condition, and, where applicable, with original case or cover.

MODEL YEAR	FEATURES	EXC. COND. LOW	HIGH

Wonder
Made by C.F. Martin (brand owner in the '70s), closed back resonator style, tenor or plectrum.

1967	Plectrum	$650	$850
1973	Tenor	$650	$850

Vega/Deering
1989-present. Deering purchased the Vega brand in '89. They also make banjos under the Deering brand.

Kingston Trio
1990s-present. Folk-style banjo similar to '50s and '60s Vega Long Neck, 5-string.

1990-2000s		$2,650	$3,450

Little Wonder
Maple neck, ebony 'board, 5-string.

1999		$425	$550

Long Neck
2006	5-string	$2,650	$3,450

Old Tyme Wonder
2012-2018. Maple neck, ebony 'board, 5 strings, brown stained satin finish.

2012-2018		$975	$1,275

Senator
2009-present. Open back, 5-string.

2009-2011		$1,125	$1,450

Tubaphone #2
2005-2011. Open back, 5-string.

2005-2011		$2,300	$3,000

Washburn (Lyon & Healy)
1880s-ca.1949. Washburn was the brand name of Lyon & Healy of Chicago. They made banjos from 1880-1929.

5-String
1896	Old 1890s style	$825	$1,075

Irene
1920s	5-string	$700	$925

Model 1535
1917	5-string, open back	$1,525	$1,975

Weymann
1864-1940s. The Weymann company was founded in 1864 and got seriously into the banjo manufacturing business in 1917. They manufactured banjos until around 1930.

MODEL YEAR	FEATURES	EXC. COND. LOW	HIGH

Keystone State Style 2
1920s		$825	$1,075

Plectrum
1924-1928	Style A	$700	$925
1927	Style #1	$1,275	$1,650
1927	Style #2	$1,350	$1,750

Tenor
1922	Banjo-Harp, wood top	$1,400	$1,800
1924-1928	Style #1	$1,075	$1,400
1924-1928	Style #2	$1,200	$1,550
1924-1928	Style #4	$2,300	$3,000
1924-1928	Style #50	$475	$625
1924-1928	Style #6	$3,700	$4,800
1924-1928	Style A, low pro	$725	$950

Wildwood Banjos
1973-2018. Traditional and bluegrass banjos made originally in Arcata, California, and after '07, in Bend, Oregon.

Minstrel
1990s-2018. Maple neck, ebony 'board, tubaphone-style tone ring, 5 strings.

2013		$1,050	$1,350

Paragon
1990s-2018. Curly maple or Claro black walnut neck, ebony 'board, mother-of-pearl inlay, 5 strings.

1990s		$1,525	$1,975

Troubador
1973-2018. Curly maple neck, ebony 'board, tubaphone-style tone ring, 5 strings.

1973-2018		$1,225	$1,575

Wilson Brothers
1915-1928. Brand name, possibly made by Lyon & Healy, for the Wilson Brothers Manufacturing Company, of Chicago, which was better known as a builder of drums.

Tenor
1920s-30s	Resonator	$360	$475

Yosco
1900-1930s. Lawrence L. Yosco was a New York City luthier building guitars, round back mandolins and banjos under his own brand and for others.

Style 3
1920s	Tenor	$975	$1,275

Wildwood Troubador
Elderly Instruments

1924 Weymann #4 Tenor
William Ritter/Gruhn Guitars

BANJOS

DEALER DIRECTORY
A GEOGRAPHICAL GUIDE

Canada

Folkway Music
22 Dupont Street East
Waterloo, Ontario N2J-2G9
(855) 772-0424 (toll free)
info@folkwaymusic.com
www.folkwaymusic.com

Twelfth Fret
Grant MacNeill/Chris Bennett
2132 Danforth Avenue
Toronto, Ontario M4C 1J9
416-423-2132
416-423-1554 (Repairs)
sales@12fret.com
www.12fret.com

England

Ampaholics
Paul Goodhand-Tait
PO Box 542
Surrey, GU1-12F
001-44-1483-825102
ampaholics@aol.com
www.ampaholics.org.uk

Japan

H I Guitars
No.1 Furukawa Building
3-8-6-B1 Kanda Kajicho
Chiyoda-Ku, Tokyo 101-0045 Japan
001-81-3257-7117
higuitars@aol.com
www.hi-guitars.com

United States of America

Arizona

Guitar Pickers
2302 N Scottsdale Rd.
Scottsdale, AZ 85257
602-350-1818
www.guitarpickersaz.com

California

California World Guitar Shows
Larry Briggs
918-288-2222
www.CalShows.TV

Drew Berlin's Vintage Guitars
Drew Berlin
213-400-4244
Drew@DrewBerlin.com
www.DrewBerlin.com

Guitar's West
Gary Hernandez
41110 Sandalwood Cir STE 113
Murrieta, CA 92562
619-988-9777
www.guitarswest.net

Gryphon Strings
Richard Johnston
211 Lambert Ave
Palo Alto, CA 94306
650-493-2131
info@gryphonstrings.com
www.gryphonstrings.com

Neal's Music
Neal Shelton
Huntington Beach, CA
714-330-9428
nealmuzic@aol.com
www.nealsmusic.com

Players Vintage Instruments
Lowell Levinger
Inverness, CA
415-669-1107
info@vintageinstruments.com
www.vintageinstruments.com

Schoenberg Guitars
Eric Schoenberg
106 Main Street
Tiburon, CA 94920
415-789-0846
eric@om28.com
www.om28.com

Union Grove Music
Richard Gellis
PO Box 2635 Aptos CA 95001
831-427-0670
www.uniongrovemusic.com/

Florida

Guitar Broker
Craig & Dustin Brody
816 NW 6th Ave
Ft. Lauderdale, FL 33311
954-646-8819
vintage@guitarbroker.com
www.guitarbroker.com

Kummer's Vintage
Timm Kummer
954-752-6063
prewar99@aol.com
www.kummersvintage.com

Replay Guitar Exchange
Jim Brady
3944 Britton Plaza
Tampa, FL 33611
813-254-8800
info@replayguitar.com
www.replayguitar.com

Georgia

Atlanta Vintage Guitars
Greg Henderson
3778 Canton Road, Ste. 400
Marietta, GA 30066
770-433-1891
atlantavintageguitars@gmail.com
www.atlantavintageguitars.com

Illinois

Chicago Guitar Show
Ruth Brinkmann
817-312-7659
ruthmbrinkmann@gmail.com
www.amigoguitarshows.com

Chicago Music Exchange
Daniel Escaruiza
3316 N Lincoln Ave
Chicago, IL 60657
773-525-7773
info@chicagomusicexchange.com
www.CME6.com

SS Vintage
George Coutretsis
4422 N Clark St
Chicago,IL 60640
773-472-3333
george@ssvintage.com
www.ssvintage.com

Kansas
Mass Street Music
Jim Baggett
1347 Massachusetts St.
Lawrence, KS 66044
785-843-3535
sales@massstreetmusic.com
www.massstreetmusic.com

Maryland
Garrett Park Guitars
Rick Hogue
7 Old Solomans Island Rd
Annapolis, MD 21401
410-571-9660
info@gpguitars.com
www.gpguitars.com

Nationwide Guitars, Inc.
Bruce or Brad Rickard
P.O. Box 2334
Columbia, MD 21045
410-489-4074
nationwideguitar@gmail.com
www.nationwideguitars.com

Southworth Guitars
Gil Southworth
southworthguitar@aol.com
www.southworthguitars.com

Massachusetts
Bay State Vintage Guitars
A.J. Jones
481 Washington St
Norwood, MA 02062
617-267-6077
info@baystatevintageguitars.com
www.baystatevintageguitars.com

Michigan
Elderly Instruments
Stan Werbin
100 North Washington
Lansing,MI 48906
800-473-5810
elderly@elderly.com
www.elderly.com

Minnesota
Vintage Guitars & Parts Guitarville by Eddie Vegas
Ed Matthews
Duluth, MN 55720
218-879-3796
Ed@eddievegas.com
www.eddievegas.com

Willie's American Guitars
1382 Eustis St
St. Paul, MN 55108
651-699-1913
info@williesguitars.com
williesguitars.com

Missouri
Fly by Night Music
Dave Crocker
103 S Washington
Neosho, MO 64850-1816
417-451-5110
crocker@joplin.com
www.amigoguitarshows.com

Killer Vintage
Dave Hinson
PO Box 190561
St. Louis, MO 63119
314-647-7795
info@killervintage.com
www.killervintage.com

Nevada
A.J.'s Music
Peter Trauth
1203 Santa Ynez
Henderson, NV 89002
702-436-9300
ajsmusic@earthlink.net
www.ajsmusic.com

New Hampshire
Retromusic
Jeff Firestone
38 Washington Street
Keene, NH 03431
603-357-9732
retromusicnh@gmail.com
www.retroguitar.com

New Jersey
Kebo's Bassworkd
Kevin 'Kebo' Borden and Dr. Ben Sopranzetti
info@kebosbassworks.com
www.kebosbassworks.com

Lark Street Music
Buzz Levine
479 Cedar Ln
Teaneck, NJ 07666
201-287-1959
larkstreet@gmail.com
www.larkstreetmusic.com

New Jersey New Jersey Guitar and Bass Center
Jay Jacus
995 Amboy Ave
Edison, NJ 08837
732-225-4444 njgtrbass@aol.com
www.newjerseyguitarandbasscenter.com

New Mexico
GuitarVista
Stanley Burg
3117 Silver Ave SE
Albuquerque, NM 87106
505-268-1133
gitmaven@yahoo.com
www.guitarvistanm.com

New York
Bernunzio Uptown Music
122 East Ave
Rochester, NY 14604
585-473-6140
info@bernunzio.com
www.bernunzio.com

Imperial Guitars
Bill Imperial
2A Cherry Hill Rd
New Paltz, NY 12561
845-255-2555
IGS55@aol.com
www.imperialguitar.com

Laurence Wexer, LTD
Larry Wexer
By appointment only
NY, NY 10036
212-532-2994
lwexer@gmail.com
www.wexerguitars.com

Rivington Guitars
Howie Statland
73 E 4th St
NY, NY 10003
212-505-5313
rivingtoninfo@gmail.com
www.rivingtonguitars.com

Sam Ash
Sammy Ash
516-686-4104
sam.ash@samashmusic.com

We Buy Guitars
Richie Friedman
PO Box 60736
Staten Island, NY 10306
516-221-0563
Webuyguitars@aol.com

Well Strung Guitars
David Davidson / Paige Davidson
330 Conklin St
Farmigndale, NY 11735
516-221-0563
info@wellstrungguitars.com
www.wellstrungguitars.com

North Carolina
Coleman Music
Chip Coleman
1021 S Main St
China Grove, NC 28023-2335
704-857-5705
OR120@aol.com
www.colemanmusic.com

Midwood Guitar Studio
Douglas Armstrong
1517 Central Ave
Charlotte, NC 28205-5013
980-265-1976
sales@midwoodguitarstudio.com
www.midwoodguitarstudio.com

Ohio
Gary's Classic Guitars
Gary Dick
Cincinnati, OH
513-891-9444
garysclssc@aol.com
www.garysguitars.com

Mike's Music
Mike Reeder
2615 Vine St
Cincinnati, OH 45219

513-281-4900
www.mikesmusicohio.com

The Loft at Lay's
Dan Shinn
974 Kenmore Blvd
Akron, OH 44314
330-848-1392
info@laysguitar.com
www.theloftatlays.com

Oklahoma
Strings West
Larry Briggs
PO Box 999 - 109 N Cincinnati Ave
Sperry, OK 74073
918-288-2222
larryb@stringswest.com
www.stringswest.com

Oregon
McKenzie River Music
Artie Leider
455 West 11th
Eugene, OR 97401
541-343-9482
artie@mrmgtr.com
www.mckenzierivermusic.com

Pennsylvania
Heritage Insurance
Ed Pokrywka
826 Bustleton Pike Ste 203
Feasterville, PA 19053
800-289-8837
edp@his-pa.com
www.musicins.com

Jim's Guitars
Jim Singleton
651 Lombard Rd #119
Red Lion, PA 17356
717-417-5655
sunburst549@aol.com
www.jimsguitars.com

Vintage Instruments
Fred Oster
507 South Broad Street
Philadelphia, PA 19147
215-545-1000
vintagephiladelphia@gmail.com
www.vintage-instruments.com

Tennessee
Blues Vintage
Gabriel Hernandez

212-A McGavock Pike
Nashville, TN 37214
888-407-2717
info@bluesvintageguitars.com
www.bluesvintageguitars.com

Carter's Vintage Guitars
Christie and Walter Carter
625 8th Ave S
Nashville, TN 37203
615-915-1851
walter@cartervintage.com
www.cartervintage.com

Gruhn Guitars
George Gruhn
2120 8th Ave S
Nashville, TN 37204
615-256-2033
gruhn@gruhn.com
www.gruhn.com

Rumble Seat Music
Eliot Michael
1805 8th Ave S
Nashville, TN 37203
615-915-2510
sales@rumbleseatmusic.com
www.rumbleseatmusic.com

Texas
Boingosaurus Music LLC
Garrett Tung
Austin, TX
boingosaurusmusic@gmail.com
www.boingosaurus.com

Dallas International Guitar Festival
Jimmy Wallace
PO Box 4997186
Garland, TX 75049
972-240-2206
info@guitarshow.com
www.guitarshow.com

Heritage Auctions
Aaron Piscopo
2801 W Airport Fwy
Dallas, TX 75261
214-409-1183
AaronP@HA.com
www.HA.com

Jimmy Wallace Guitars
514 Main St
Garland, TX 75040

972-740-9925
info@JimmyWallaceGuitars.com
www.JimmyWallaceGuitars.com

Killer Vintage Specialty Guitars of Texas
Dave Hinson
3738 Haggar Way Ste 108
Dallas, TX 75209
972-707-0409
killervintagedallas@gmail.com
www.killervintagespecialtyguitars.com

Southpaw Guitars
Jim
5813 Bellaire Blvd
Houston, TX 77081
713-667-5791
info@southpawguitars.com
www.southpawguitars.com

Texas Amigos Guitar Shows
Ruth Brinkmann
800-473-6059
www.amigoguitarshows.com

Van Hoose Vintage Instruments
Thomas VanHoose
2722 Raintree Drive
Carrollton, TX 75006
972-998-8176
tv0109@yahoo.com
www.vanhoosevintage.com

Utah
Intermountain Guitar and Banjo
By appointment only
Bountiful, UT
801-322-4682/801-450-7608
guitarandbanjo@earthlink.net
www.guitarandbanjo.com

Virginia
Action Music
Matt Baker
111 Park Ave
Falls Church, VA 22046
703-534-4801
action.music@comcast.net
www.actionguitar.com

Vintage Sound
Bill Holter
PO Box 11711
Alexandria, VA
22312 703-300-2529
bhvsound@vintagesound.com
www.vintagesound.com

Wisconsin
Brian Goff's Bizarre Guitars
Brian Goff
Madison, WI
608-235-3561
Bdgoff@sbcglobal.net
www.bizarreguitars.net

Cream City Music
John Majdalani
12505 W Bluemound Rd
Brookfield, WI 53005-8026
262-860-1800
johnm@creamcitymusic.com
www.creamcitymusic.com

Dave's Guitar Shop
Dave Rogers
1227 South 3rd St
LaCrosse, WI 54601
608-785-7704
info@davesguitar.com
www.davesguitar.com

Dave's Guitar Shop
Dave Rogers
914 S 5th St
Milwaukee, WI 53204
608-790-9816
info@davesguitar.com
www.davesguitar.com

Dave's Guitar Shop
Dave Rogers
2990 Cahill Main #200
Madison, WI 53711
608-405-8770
info@davesguitar.com
www.davesguitar.com

MANUFACTURER
DIRECTORY

Alabama
Alleva Coppolo
Jimmy Coppolo
Gadsden, AL 35901
909-981-9019
jimmy@allevacoppolo.com
www.allevacoppolo.com

California
Chatsworth Guitars
www.chatsworthguitars.com

Louisiana
Bayou Guitarworks
307-699-3574
bayouguitar@gmail.com
www.bayouguitarworks.com

New York
Mirabella
Cris Mirabella
PO Box 483
St. James, NY 11780
631-842-3819
mirguitars@aol.com
www.mirabellaguitars.com

Oklahoma
Keeley Effects
Robert Keeley
www.RKFX.com

Texas
Jimmy Wallace pickups
info@JimmyWallacepickups.com
www.JimmyWallacepickups.com

Other
Bill Tuli
Ramtuli.com
collectorsdiaries.com

Earthboard
www.earthboardmusic.com

EMG Pickups
www.EMGPickups.com

J. Rockett Audio Designs
www.rockettpedals.com
support@rockettpedals.com

Lindy Fralin Pickups
www.fralinpickups.com

Gibson
www.gibson.com

TECH/REPAIR

California
National Guitar Repair
Marc Schoenberger
805-481-8532 805-471-5905
Luthier17@aol.com
www.nationalguitarrepair.com

Skip Simmons Amp Repair
Skip Simmons
4824 Bevan Rd
Loma Rica, CA 95901
530-771-7345

Delaware
Dana Sound Research
Dana Sutcliffe, Master Luthier
Wilmington, DE 19810
302-439-3677
danasoundresearchinc@gmail.com
www.danamusic.com

New York
The Guitar Specialist, Inc
Doug Proper
380 Adams Street
Bedford Hills, NY 10507
914-401-9052
Doug@guitarspecialist.com
www.guitarspecialist.com

Ohio
Lays Guitar Restoration
Dan Shinn
974 Kenmore Blvd.
Akron, OH 44314
330-848-1392
info@laysguitar.com
www.laysguitar.com

Wyoming
Anton's Musical Instrument Repair
Anton
1841 Lane 12
Powell, WY 82435
307-754-5341
luthier82435@yahoo.com
www.antonsinstrumentrepair.com

Notes

Notes

Notes

Notes